The History Of The County Palatine And Duchy Of Lancaster, Volume 1 – Primary Source Edition

Edward Baines, William Robert Whatton, James Croston, Brooke Herford, John Harland

THE HISTORY OF THE COUNTY PALATINE AND DUCHY OF LANCASTER.

Edw. Baines

THE HISTORY

OF THE

COUNTY PALATINE AND DUCHY

OF

LANCASTER.

BY THE LATE EDWARD BAINES, ESQ.

The BIOGRAPHICAL DEPARTMENT by the late W. R. WHATTON, F.R.S., F.S.A.; with the Additions of the late JOHN HARLAND, F.S.A., and the Rev. BROOKE HERFORD.

A New, Revised, and Enlarged Edition,

WITH THE FAMILY PEDIGREES (OMITTED IN THE SECOND EDITION) CORRECTED THROUGHOUT.

EDITED BY

JAMES CROSTON, F.S.A.

VICE-PRESIDENT OF THE RECORD SOCIETY.

Author of " Historic Sites of Lancashire and Cheshire," " County Families of Lancashire and Cheshire,"
" A History of the Ancient Hall of Samlesbury," &c., &c.

VOLUME I.

JOHN HEYWOOD,
DEANSGATE AND RIDGEFIELD, MANCHESTER;
AND 11, PATERNOSTER BUILDINGS,
LONDON.
1888,

PRINTED AT THE "EXCELSIOR" WORKS MANCHESTER

INTRODUCTORY NOTICE TO VOLUME I.

ALF a century has elapsed since Baines's *History of Lancashire* was first issued to the public. Its appearance was hailed with general satisfaction as the first attempt to give anything like a complete History of the Palatinate, and it has ever since been recognised as the standard topographical work on the county. In the collection and arrangement of his materials, Mr. Baines devoted many years of patient industry and scholarly research, but his production was, unfortunately, disfigured by many inaccuracies—the result of the confusing, and oftentimes contradictory, evidences of mediæval times, and the occasional acceptance, without verification, of the abstracts of other labourers in the field of antiquarian research ; but, in spite of these defects, and the huge gaps it was known to present, the original edition became exceedingly scarce, and chance copies that found their way into the market commanded correspondingly high prices.

The rarity of the work, and the frequent inquiries for it, induced the late Mr. John Harland, about twenty years ago, to undertake the preparation of a new and revised edition, pruning out what was redundant and obsolete, and bringing down the chief events in the history of important parishes and towns to his own time. More correct versions, in English, were given of the Domesday Survey, of the grants and charters to the various boroughs and towns, and of the abbreviated Latin documents contained in Mr. Baines's work. But it was always considered a defect in this edition that the family pedigrees, which formed such an important feature in the original work, were ömitted, and it has been the regret of every antiquary that Mr. Harland had not the time at his disposal to correct the many inaccuracies they undoubtedly contained, and present them to his readers in a correct and trustworthy form. Mr. Harland's death occurred just as the first volume was completed, and his literary executor, the Rev. Brooke Herford, at the request of the publishers, took up and completed with praiseworthy care the task that had fallen from his hand.

It will be obvious that a county history, and especially the history of such a county as Lancashire, could not be written fifty years ago in so complete a form as to satisfy the requirements of the student of the present day. In the period that has intervened an enormous mass of materials, which were either unknown or inaccessible when Mr. Baines wrote, have come to light. The publications of the Chetham and Record Societies, and the Transactions of the Historic Society of Lancashire and Cheshire, furnish information of the greatest possible value. The great series of calendars and state papers published under the authority of the Master of the Rolls, the ancient muniments of the Duchy of Lancaster given by the Queen to the nation in 1868, and the Records of the County Palatine transferred to the Public Record Office, London, in 1873, have thrown a flood of light on the historical and antiquarian matters connected with the Palatinate and Duchy, or indicated the sources whence original information of the greatest consequence might be obtained. These several sources have been freely laid under contribution, and, in addition, the text has been carefully revised, in some cases amplified, and every known inaccuracy set right. The return presented to Parliament by order of the House of Commons in 1879, giving the names of members of the lower house "from so remote a period as it can be obtained," has enabled the Editor to supply many omissions, and to give a more accurate and complete list of the representatives of the county than has hitherto appeared. The rearrangement of ecclesiastical districts consequent upon the creation of the new See of Liverpool, and the changes effected in the Parliamentary divisions of the county and in the representation of the boroughs under the provisions of the Reform Acts of 1884 and 1885, as well as the alterations in the old and the creation of new Courts of Law, have been duly noted; and, in addition, a record is given of the various civil changes that have occurred, with such other matters as go to make up the general history of the county since the last edition was given to the world.

A notable feature in the present edition, and one that will be more apparent when the hundreds and parishes come under review, is the reintroduction of the Family Pedigrees, to the careful revision of which special attention has been devoted, every pains having been taken to secure accuracy by excluding all matter of a doubtful or spurious character, or that cannot be proved by trustworthy evidence.

In the general arrangement of the work, the lines laid down by Mr. Baines have, as far as practicable, been adhered to, their elasticity enabling the Editor not only to bring down the record to the present time, but, where it was thought desirable or necessary, to add to the original text as a substantive part of the continuous narrative, such interesting facts as had escaped his notice, or, as is more probable, were unknown at the time he wrote, and also to bridge over the many chasms by the interpolation of such authentic evidence as more recent research has opened up. The Editor's first duty has, of course, been to verify the statements embodied in the two preceding editions, and to correct such errors, whether of fact or of inference, as came within his view. With the exception of the earlier chapters embracing the Roman and Saxon periods and the earlier ecclesiastical history, which have been in great part re-written, the text of the original work has been maintained in every essential feature, though variations and interpolations have been occasionally made where it was thought there might be a gain in lucidity without injustice being done to the Author. It may be urged that such corrections and additions should have been distinguished by brackets or otherwise from the original matter. Such a course, were it practicable, might have been a convenience to the specialist; but a very slight acquaintance with the former editions would show the extreme difficulty, not to say impossibility, Mr. Harland and Mr. Herford, in the process of condensation, and in the additions and corrections they made, having so frequently departed from the *ipsissima verba* of Mr. Baines, without such distinguishing marks, that the text of each could only have been indicated in patchwork pages, that would have been perplexing to the general reader.

Altogether the First Volume has received an accession of over one hundred pages, or more than one-third of new matter. Every care has been taken to secure accuracy of detail, and to make the History of Lancashire more interesting and trustworthy; at the same time the Editor is fully conscious of many shortcomings and imperfections, and of omissions that are, perhaps, not altogether inseparable from a work of such magnitude and so wide-reaching in its scope as that he has undertaken. Where such have occurred, he will be grateful if they are pointed out to him in order that the corrections or additions may be made in the succeeding volume.

The pleasing duty remains to the Editor of tendering his thanks for the many offers of assistance he has received in the course of his work, and for information which has greatly enhanced its value. To the Rev. Henry Parr, Vicar of Yoxford, Suffolk, he is indebted for many additional notes and corrections in the earlier lists of Sheriffs of the County; and he is under obligations of no less weight to Robert Gradwell, Esq., of Claughton-on-Brock, for communications relating to the Celtic period of Lancashire history; his thanks are also due to J. Broughton

Edge, Esq., one of Her Majesty's Coroners for the County of Lancaster, for many valuable notes concerning the Courts of the County Palatine and the changes effected by the Judicature Act of 1873. To Henry Alison, Esq., County Treasurer, and Frederic Campbell Hulton, Esq., Clerk of the Peace, he is indebted for many of the statistical tables in relation to the valuation, assessment, and rating, and also for the corrected list of Magistrates and Public Officers of the County. He desires also to acknowledge his obligations to Mrs. Arthur Tempest, of Coleby Hall, Lincoln; Mrs. Fenton Knowles, of Arncliffe, Cheetham Hill, Manchester; Miss Emma C. Abraham, of Grassendale Park, Liverpool; the Rev. W. Stuart White, of Leyland; Lieut.-Colonel Sowler, of Manchester; Colonel H. Holden, of Askham Bryam, York; John Paul Rylands, Esq., F.S.A., of Heather Lea, Claughton, Birkenhead; Thomas Helsby, Esq., of Lincolns Inn, the learned Editor of Ormerod's *History of Cheshire*; W. Thompson Watkin, Esq., of Liverpool, the Author of *Roman Lancashire* and *Roman Cheshire*; W. A. Abram, Esq., of Blackburn, the Author of the *History of Blackburn*; W. Duncombe Pink, Esq., F.R.H.S., of Leigh; W. Hewitson, Esq., Manchester; Frederick Openshaw, Esq., Hothersall Hall, Ribchester; Joseph Maghull Yates, Esq., of Manchester; R. S. Crossley, Esq., Accrington; George Porter, Esq., Fern Bank, Blackburn; and Charles E. Bowker, Esq., Fletcher Gate, Nottingham. He would be as ungracious as culpable were he to fail in acknowledging the ready assistance extended to him by the officials of the Record Office, London, and also the courteous assistance and the suggestions he has received on many occasions from Chas. W. Sutton, Esq., Chief Librarian, Free Public Libraries, Manchester, and from Mr. W. R. Credland and Mr. Lawrence Dillon, the Librarian and Sub-Librarian of the Reference Library.

Upton Hall, Prestbury, Cheshire, November, 1887.

CONTENTS OF VOLUME I.

APPENDICES.

ILLUSTRATIONS.

PEDIGREES.

₊ A full Index will be given with the concluding volume.

THE

HISTORY OF THE COUNTY PALATINE

AND DUCHY OF LANCASTER.

CHAPTER I.

Earliest Notices of Lancashire—The Roman Conquest and Rule in Britain—B.C. 55 to A.D. 448.

HE County of Lancaster, though not particularly famed for those monuments of antiquity which shed a lustre on history, local as well as national, is by no means destitute of ancient remains. Its distinguishing characteristics, however, consist in the extent of its commerce, the importance of its manufactures, the number and value of its modern institutions, and the activity and enterprise of its abundant population. In tracing the history of such a county, it becomes the duty of the historian to describe with as much brevity as is consistent with accuracy the monuments bequeathed to us by our ancestors, without exhausting the patience of his readers with prolix details and controversial disquisitions.

For nearly four thousand years of the world's existence, the history of this county and of this country is almost a blank, except so far as it may be read in its geological phenomena; and it may be confidently asserted that before the first landing of Julius Cæsar upon our shores scarcely anything is known of the people who inhabited this island, or of the government and institutions under which they lived.

According to Ptolemy, the inhabitants of the country between the lofty ridge which now separates Yorkshire from Lancashire, and the bay of Morecambe, bore the name of the *Setantii*, or *Segantii*—the dwellers in "the country of water"—which district, on the second invasion of the Romans, was included in the more extensive province of the *Brigantes*, extending on the east side of the island from the Humber to the Tyne, and on the west from the Mersey to the Solway, and comprehending the six counties of Yorkshire, Durham, Northumberland, Cumberland, Westmorland, and Lancashire. This being the most powerful and populous nation in Britain, during the Roman sway, it is the most celebrated by the best writers.[1] Dr. Henry held the opinion that the Brigantes were descended from the ancient Phrygians, who were the very first inhabitants of Europe, and that they came over to this island from the coast of Gaul before the Belgæ had arrived in that country.[2] The name doubtless originally meant the dwellers in the hill country, *brig* and *brigant* signifying in modern Welsh the top or summit, and Brigantwys the people dwelling there.

Historians are generally agreed that the aborigines of Britain, as Cæsar calls our earliest ancestors, were Gauls or Gaels, who emigrated from the Continent, and settled in this island[3] about a thousand years before the birth of Christ. The more probable conjecture is, as Cæsar intimates, that the interior parts of Britain, to the north and to the west, and consequently Lancashire, were peopled by the earliest inhabitants, and the maritime parts by those who crossed over from Belgium, in Gaul, for the purpose of invading it, almost all of whom had their names from the tribes whence they sprang, and, on the cessation of hostilities, remained here.

---

[1] Camden, vol. iii., p. 233. [2] Hist. Gt. Brit., vol. i., p. 276. [3] Rich. de Cir., b. I. cap. ii., sec. 4.

a century had now elapsed since the second invasion of Britain by the Romans, and in the course of that period there had risen up in Lancashire the stations[1] of *Mancunium* (MANCHESTER);[2] *Veratinum* (WILDERSPOOL), on the Cheshire side of the Mersey, opposite WARRINGTON ; *Brometonacum* (RIBCHESTER);[2] *Calunio* (COLNE) ; *Coccium* (WIGAN), *Ad Alaunam*—the Longovicus of the Notitia (LANCASTER); *Galacum* (OVERBOROUGH).[3]

The estuaries into which the rivers that watered these stations fell, though involved in some degree of uncertainty, from the vague and indecisive character of the Roman charts, were—THE MERSEY, called *Belisama ;* the mouth of the Wyre, called the *Portus Setantiorum*, or the *Haven of the Setantii*, and *Moricambe Estuaria*, or THE BAY OF MORECAMBE.

The Lancashire stations communicated with *Isurium* (Aldborough) and *Eboracum* (York), the Brigantine capitals, by roads constructed by the Roman soldiery, and with other towns enumerated in the Itinerary of Antoninus, and the Chorography of Ravenna.

It is conjectured that the principal part of the Roman roads in Britain was commenced by Julius Agricola to facilitate his conquests. The four grand military Roman ways bear the names of Watling Street, Hermin Street, the Fosse, and Ikening or Iknild Street ; but it is

only the first-mentioned of these roads that comes within the scope of this history. Each of the stations affords its antiquities : Ribchester abounds with remains ; and Colne, Freckleton, Lancaster, Manchester, Overborough, and Warrington, will be found, in the progress of this work, to exhibit in succession their antiquarian stores, and to proclaim their ancient alliance with the Mistress of the World. After the lapse of sixteen centuries, the county of Lancaster still presents innumerable remains of these celebrated roads. At least four great Roman roads pass through this county— two of them from north to south, and two others from west to east, and there are numerous military ways of less consequence.

The first of the Roman routes extends from Carlisle *(Luguvallium)*, in Cumberland, to Kinderton *(Condate)* in Cheshire : passing through Lancaster it advances pretty nearly due south by Galgate and Garstang, then crossing Watling Street, which extended across the country from the mouth of the Wyre to York and the east coast, the line continues by Preston, across the Ribble

[1] Whitaker's History of Manchester.
[2] The name or termination *Caster, Cester*, or *Chester*, from *Castra*, a camp, generally indicates a Roman station.
[3] Since Mr. Baines wrote, many discoveries have been made in relation to the Roman stations and roads in Lancashire, and praiseworthy efforts have been made by local antiquaries to connect the disjointed fragments. The ablest writers on the subject have been the Rev. Edmund Sibson, of Ashton-in-Makerfield ; Mr. John Just, of Bury ; Mr.

John Robson, M.D., of Warrington ; Rev. W. Thornber, M.A., Poulton-le-Fylde ; Mr. Charles Hardwick, of Manchester ; Mr. T. T. Wilkinson, F.R.A.S., of Burnley ; Mr. William Beamont, of Orford Hall, Warrington ; Mr. H. Colley March, M.D., of Manchester ; Mr. E. Kirk, of Eccles, and Mr. W. Thompson Watkin, of Liverpool. The most exhaustive account will be found in the work on "Roman Lancashire" from the pen of the last-named author.

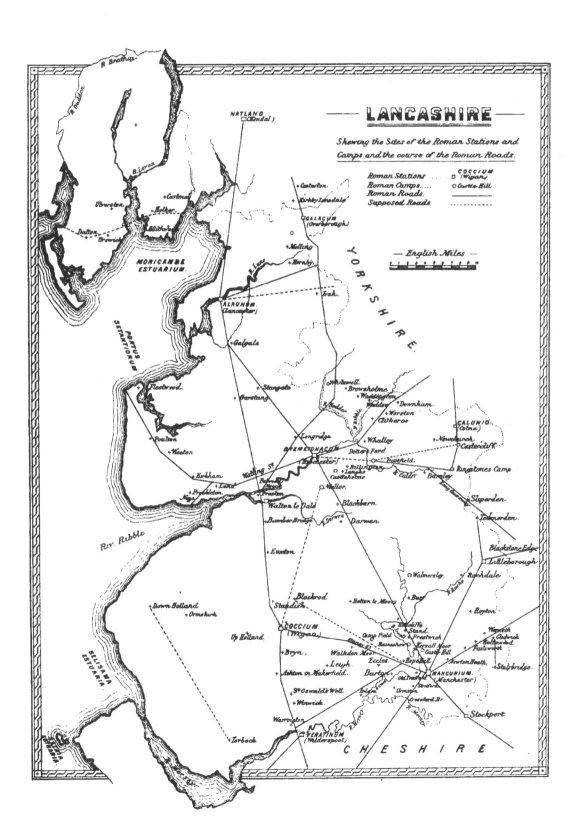

LANCASHIRE

Shewing the Sites of the Roman Stations and
Camps and the course of the Roman Roads.

Roman Stations   COCCIUM (Wigan)
Roman Camps.....   ○ Castle Hill
Roman Roads.
Supposed Roads. . . . .

— English Miles —

and the Darwen to Bamber Bridge, Euxton, and Standish, thence along the Beggar's Walk, near Gidlow, through the Mesnes, and across the ford on the Douglas, near Adam's Bridge, to Wigan *(Coccium)*. Still keeping a southerly course it leaves Bryn on the left, passes through Ashton-in Makerfield, and, running half a mile westward of St. Oswald's Well, continues to Warrington, where it crosses the pass of the Mersey at Wilderspool *(Veratinum)*; beyond, the line leads through Appleton, tends in a south-easterly direction, and, leaving the station of Northwich *(Salinæ)* on the right, is continued as Kind Street to Kinderton *(Condate)*. From this great highway a road diverges at Wigan, which runs eastward, taking the direction of Walkden Moor, where it assumes the name of Staney Street, advances by the Hope Hall Estate, crosses the highway from Manchester to Warrington, and, having passed the ford of the Irwell, at the shallow which gives denomination to Old Trafford, is continued to Castle Field. A branch from this road proceeds through the village of Stretford to the ford of the Mersey at Crossford Bridge, where there was a small station; then, pointing at Altrincham, it passes along the declivity of the hills, and enters Dunham Park. Here it takes the name of Street to Bucklow Hill; from hence it passes to Mere Town, when, leaving Northwich about half a mile to the right, it takes the name of Kind Street at Broken Cross, and proceeds to Kinderton, the *Condate* of Antoninus, now a suburb of Middlewich.

The second Roman road extends from Overborough to Slack *(Cambodunum)*, near Huddersfield, in Yorkshire. This road passes through Ribchester, across the Ribble; then, proceeding to the east of Blackburn, it crosses the Darwen and continues by the left of Cockey Moor and Blackburn Street to Spen Moor, and thence, through Radcliffe, Stand, and Prestwich; it next passes over Kersal Moor, and is carried by way of Roman Road Terrace, Bury New Road, and Strangeways to Manchester. Traversing that city obliquely, by way of Ancoats, it passes over Newton Heath to Failsworth, whence it is continued under the name of Street or Street Lane to Hollinwood, and thence by Glodwick and Hey Chapel to the summit of Austerlands, where it enters Yorkshire, passes Knoll Hill in Saddleworth, and, crossing the Manchester and Huddersfield road at Delph, leaves Marsden about a mile and a half to the south, skirts Golcar Hill, and attains the plot of *Cambodunum* (Slack), where the remains of a station exist.

The third route commences near Fleetwood, at the mouth of the Wyre—believed to have been the *Setantian (Sistuntian) Port*, or as we should express it, *The Port of Lancashire*—and continues in a southerly direction to Poulton; thence, crossing the Main Dyke from Martin Meer, it goes on by way of Staining and Weeton to Kirkham, at which point it tends eastward, and directs its course to Lund Church, near where it is joined by another road, which commences at the Neb of the Nese, near Freckleton, and, crossing the Lancaster road, leaves Preston about a mile to the right, assuming on Fulwood Moor the name of Watling Street; hence it proceeds to Ribchester, from which station it passes over Longridge Fell, and then, turning to the north, traces the Hodder to its source. From this road another branches off at Ribchester, which passes through the townships of Billington and Langho, crosses the Calder at Potter's Ford, a little above its junction with the Ribble, and continues south of Clitheroe, and by Worston and Downham into Yorkshire.

The fourth Roman road commences at the ford of the Mersey near Warrington, and passes through Barton and Eccles to Manchester. It afterwards traverses the townships of Moston, Chadderton, and Royton, and keeping about a quarter of a mile to the right of Rochdale, by the Oldham road, continues through Littleborough; afterwards, mounting the British Apennines, it sweeps over Rombold's Moor, on the north side of the Aire, and advances to Ilkley, the *Olicana* of Ptolemy, where stood the temple of Verbeia, the goddess of the Wharf.

The Roman Stations in Lancashire occur in the second and the tenth routes of the Itinerary of Antoninus, and are thus arranged :—

ITER. II.

*   *   *   *   *   *   *

EBVRACVM	(LEG. VI. vic.)	...	*York.*
CALCARIA	M.P.M. IX.	...	*Tadcaster.*
CAMBODVNO	M.P.M. XX.	...	*Slack.*
MAMUCIO	M.P.M. XVIII.	...	*Manchester.*
CONDATE	M.P.M. XVIII.	...	*Kinderton.*
DEVA	(LEG. XX. vic.) M.P.M. XX.	...	*Chester.*

ITER. X.

From Whitley Castle, near Alston, in the county of Durham, to Chesterton, in Staffordshire.[1]

A CLANOVENTA.			From *Whitley Castle.*
GALAVA	M.P.M. XVIII.	...	*Kirkby Thore.*
ALONE	M.P.M. XII.	...	*Borrowbridge in Lonsdale.*
CALACVM	M.P.M. XVIII.	...	*Overborough.*
BREMETONACI	M.P.M. XXVII.	...	*Ribchester.*
COCCIO	M.P.M. XX.	...	*Wigan.*
MANCVNIO	M.P.M. XVII.	...	*Manchester.*
CONDATE	M.P.M. XVIII.	..	*Kinderton.*
MEDIOLANO	M.P.M. XVIII.	...	*Chesterton.*[2]

Several other roads, called Vicinal-ways, are to be found in this county, but the routes described form the principal military communications. These roads generally consist of a regular pavement, formed by large boulder stones or fragments of rock imbedded in gravel, and vary in width from four to fourteen yards. It is a singular characteristic of the Roman roads that they are not carried over rivers by bridges, but by fords, except where the rivers are impassable, and then bridges are thrown over.[3]

A remarkable example of the pavement of a Roman way, and perhaps the most perfect of its kind in the kingdom, remains exposed to view on the western slope of Blackstone Edge, where the Roman road climbs the steep mountain ridge and extends in an easterly direction towards Halifax. Some interesting particulars of this ancient highway are given in the *Transactions of the Lancashire and Cheshire Antiquarian Society* (v. i., pp. 73-86); and in a paper read before the Rochdale Literary and Philosophical Society, November, 1879, Dr. H. Colley March thus describes the mode of construction:—

"The portion of the road is exactly sixteen feet in width. In some places there are distinct indications of a deep trench on each side, dug into the earth for the purpose of drainage. The roadway is transversely arched, so that the water would run from and not towards the centre. The road is paved with squared blocks. These are laid with great care, and are held by strong kerbs, which stand up some two inches above the level of the causeway. Exactly in the middle of the road is a line of massive stones, fitted together with great precision, while the other smaller stones, of which the general pavement consists, are of ordinary sandstone. These especial ones are always of the very hardest and densest grit. Along these stones has been cut, by the mason's art, a deep and wide trough. The bottom of the trough is slightly, but invariably, convex. The width of the trough at its upper and widest part is one foot four inches, its true width across the bottom is one foot one and a half inch. Its depth in the centre varies from three and a half inches to five and a half inches. To return to the road in general: As before said, its total width, outside all, is sixteen feet; but the kerbstones, being above its level, cannot be counted in. These vary in width from five and a quarter to six and three-quarter inches. We may safely consider, then, that the practicable width of the road inside the kerbstone is fifteen feet. This causeway of fifteen feet is divided by the central trough into two roads of equal width, the measurement from the inside of the kerbstone to the outside of the troughstone being six feet. Each of these two roads is grooved by longitudinal furrows, and no one entertains the least doubt that these furrows are wheel-tracks."

At the top of the hill the trough described ceases, though the square blocks are in places still preserved; but further on, where the descent begins to be steep, on the Yorkshire side of the hill, the trough recommences.

The terror of the Roman name, and the vigour of their arms, seemed scarcely able to keep in subjection the inhabitants of Britain, who sought every opportunity to shake off the foreign yoke. According to Herodian, the proprætor in Britain addressed a dispatch to the Emperor Severus, to the effect that "the insurrections and inroads of the Barbarians, and the havoc they made far and near, rendered it necessary that he should either increase the Roman force in this country or that he should come over in person." On this intimation, the Emperor, though then advanced in life, and sinking under bodily infirmities, repaired to Britain, and established his court in *Eboracum* (York), the capital of the Brigantes. Having collected his force round that city (A.D. 207), the Emperor, attended by his sons Caracalla and Geta, marched from York, at the head of a powerful army, to the North, where he drove the Caledonians within their frontier and erected or restored a stone wall within the vallum of Hadrian. This wall was the great artificial boundary of Roman England from sea to sea. It has been customary to ascribe the earthen rampart to Hadrian and the stone wall to Severus; but it has of late years been shown by Mr. Bruce, on what appears conclusive authority, that they are essential parts of one fortification, and the probability is that Severus repaired the work of Hadrian. The loss of Roman soldiers in this expedition, according to Dion Cassius, amounted to 50,000 men, partly by war and partly in cutting down the woods

---

[1] The list given above is from Mr. Watkin's *Roman Lancashire*, and it is very much more correct than either of those printed in the previous editions of this work. The Itinerary is supposed to have been compiled about A.D. 320. The letters M.P., which occur in many of the copies of this Itinerary, have been supposed to signify *mille passus*, a thousand paces, usually called Roman miles, equal 4884·28 English feet, the English mile being 5,280 feet, or 446 feet longer than the Roman mile; but, as pointed out by Mr. J. B. Davidson (*Archæological Journal*, v. xxxvii., p. 316), on the authority of MM. Parthey and Pinder, the letters preceding the numerals should be M.P.M., *milia plus minus*—miles, more or less.—C.

[2] The Itineraries of Richard of Cirencester relating to Lancashire, which have appeared in the previous editions of this work, are omitted, the MS. being of very doubtful authority, and believed by many antiquaries to be a forgery.—C.

[3] Galen ix. c. 8. methodi.

and draining the mosses, for which the north of England, and Lancashire in particular, is to the present day distinguished. To commemorate his victories, Severus coined money with the

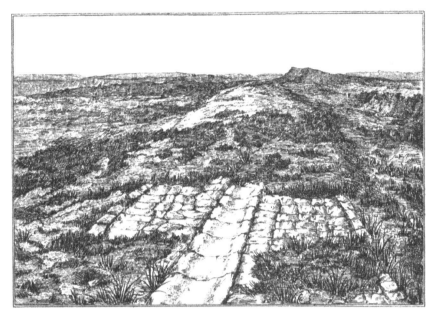

ROMAN ROAD—BLACKSTONE EDGE.

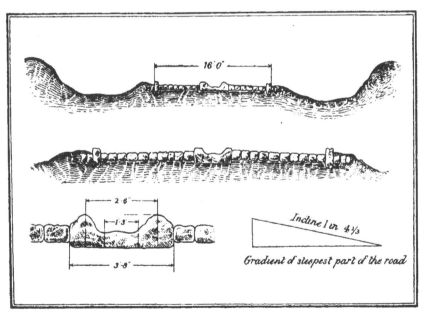

SECTIONS OF THE ROMAN ROAD—BLACKSTONE EDGE.

inscription, VICTORIÆ BRITANNICÆ. He also assumed the name of BRITANNICUS MAXIMUS, and gave to his son Geta the name of BRITANNICUS.

Mints were established by the Romans at eleven of their British stations, two of which were York and Chester; and it is probable that from these northern mints the coin was circulated over Lancashire. No fewer than fifty different Roman coins have been found at Standish, in this county, near the ancient Coccium, several of which are from dies struck by the Emperor Severus.

After the death of Severus at York (February 4, A.D. 211), and the return of Caracalla to Rome, a long and profound silence is observed by the Roman historians as to the affairs of Britain, and it is not till the reign of Diocletian—when Carausius, himself a Briton, who, being sent by the emperor with a fleet to guard the Belgic coast, embraced the opportunity to pass over into this island, and got himself proclaimed emperor at York—that any incident appertaining to the subject of this history is recorded.

The usurpation by Carausius of the sovereign power in Britain occurred A.D. 286. After six years of dominion, in which the naval strength of Britain was greatly increased, he was betrayed and assassinated by his minister Allectus, at *Eboracum*—the second emperor who had met that fate in the Brigantian territory. Diocletian and Maximianus refused to recognise the sovereignty of Allectus, and sent a powerful force under Constantius Chlorus against him; and in three more years independent Britain was again subjected to the rule of the Cæsars, by the defeat of this second usurper, and quietly remained under the imperial government of Constantius Chlorus. When (A.D. 305) the two emperors, Diocletian and Maximianus, took the singular resolution of resigning their authority, these two Cæsars, Constantius and Galerius, were declared *Augusti*. In the division of the empire, the western provinces fell to the lot of Constantius who came over to Britain, but he did not long enjoy the imperial dignity, for, falling sick at *Eboracum*, on his return

COIN OF THE EMPEROR SEVERUS.

from an expedition against the Caledonians, he died there, July 25th, A.D. 306, having in his last moments declared his son Constantine his heir and successor in the empire. He was the third emperor who had died at York, and the honour of the *apotheosis* or *deification* was conferred upon him by the Roman senate. Constantine, afterwards called the Great, began his auspicious reign at York, where he was present at his father's death, and was saluted by the troops stationed in the city as emperor, on which occasion, as is said, a golden ball was presented to him as a symbol of his sovereignty over the island. Upon his conversion to Christianity he placed a cross upon the ball, and ever since his time, the globe, surmounted by the cross, has been used as the emblem of majesty in all the kingdoms of Christendom.

The conversion of Constantine took place in A.D. 311. The coincidence, says Mr. Thompson Watkin,[1] is a singular one, that, as from Britain went forth the general (and emperor) who was destined to put an end to the Jewish dispensation (Vespasian), so in Britain the first sovereign who embraced Christianity, and was the means of its adoption by the bulk of the ancient world, assumed the purple; and this latter event took place in Brigantian territory, of which Lancashire formed a part. The civil government of Britain was remodelled by Constantine, and under his beneficent rule the country seems to have enjoyed profound peace. Christian churches were founded, and, according to Gough, there was a Bishop of York (the capital of the Brigantes) at the Council of Arles, A.D. 315. At his death, which occurred May 22, A.D. 337, the empire was divided among his three sons, Constantinus, Constantius, and Constans, Britain falling to the share of the last named. Not content with his part of the empire, Constantinus invaded the territories of his youngest brother, in which invasion he lost his life, and was succeeded in Britain by Constans, who thus became sole emperor of the west, including Britain. Constans, after a reign of thirteen years, having fallen in the village of St. Helena, at the foot of the Pyrenees (whither he had been pursued

[1] Roman Lancashire, p. 18.

by Magnentius, A.D. 350), his only surviving brother succeeded to the purple; and he was succeeded by Julian, nephew of Constantine the Great, in whose reign the statue of the Brigantine goddess found in the ruins of a temple in Annandale, in the year 1732, is supposed to have been erected.

One of the most interesting discoveries of Roman remains in Lancashire was made during the summer of 1796, at Ribchester, by a youth, the son of Joseph Walton, in a hollow, nine feet below the surface of the ground, that had been made in the waste land at the side of the road leading to the church, and near the bed of the river. It is conjectured that when these antiquities were deposited in this place the sand was thrown amongst them to preserve them in a dry state, but they are in general much defaced by the corrosive effect of sand upon copper during a period of nearly two thousand years. These antiquities were purchased by Charles Townley, Esq., of Townley Hall, in this county, from the persons who found them, and they are described by that gentleman in a letter addressed by him to the Rev. John Brand, secretary to the Society of Antiquaries, the substance of which will be found in its proper place in these volumes. It will be sufficient to say here that they consist of a helmet, a number of patera, the remains of a vase, a bust of Minerva, the remains of two basins, a number of circular plates, and various other curiosities, many of which appear to have been appropriated to religious uses.

"The helmet (says Mr. Townley) deserves the particular attention of the curious as the remains of remote ages; very few ancient ones, decorated with embossed figures, have as yet appeared. The three or four which were preserved in the Museum at Portici are esteemed to be the most richly ornamented, and the best as to style of workmanship; but when this helmet was in its proper state, it must have been equal, at least, to those in point of decoration, and in respect to its having a vizor imitating so exactly the human features, I believe it to be the only ancient example of the kind that has yet been discovered. This singularity may excite a doubt whether such a helmet was destined for real combat, or only for the enrichment of occasional trophies which were erected in the celebration of military festivals, or carried in procession amongst the Greeks and Romans. Trophies of this sort are seen on various medals, with the names of the people, whose subjugation such trophies are meant to record, inserted upon them, as for example, DE SARMATIS—DE GERMANIS, on the medals of Marcus Aurelius and Commodus. The superior style of workmanship of the mask to that of the headpiece is also remarkable. In the former, the beauty of the features, the excellent work of the figures in relief, and more particularly by the sharp edges and lines with which the eyebrows, eyelids, and lips are marked, after the manner of Grecian art preceding the Cæsars, denote it to have been executed some ages before the headpiece, the coarse and heavy work of which corresponds with that of the artists employed in the reign of Septimius Severus, and particularly with the sculpture upon the arch of that emperor, situated near the Capitol Hill at Rome. The cheek measures ten inches and a half from its junction to the skull-piece, at the top of the forehead, to its bottom under the chin. A row of small detached locks of hair surrounds the forehead a little above the eyes, reaching to the ears, which are well delineated. Upon the locks of hair rests the bottom of a diadem or tutulus, which at the centre in the front is two inches and a quarter in height, diminishing at the extremities to one inch, and it is divided horizontally into two parts, bearing the proportionate heights just mentioned.[1] The lower part projects before the higher, and represents a bastion wall, separated into seven divisions by projecting turrets with pyramidal tops, exceeding a little the height of the wall. The apertures for missile weapons of defence are marked in each of the turrets. Two arched doors appear in the middle division of this wall, and one arched door in each of the extreme divisions. The upper part of the diadem, which recedes a little, so as to clear the top of the wall and of the turrets, was ornamented with seven embossed figures, placed under the seven arches, the abutments of which are heads of genii. The central arch, and the figure that was within it, are destroyed, but the other six are filled with a repetition of the following three groups: A Venus, sitting upon a marine monster; before her a draped figure with wings, bearing a wreath and a palm branch, and behind her a triton, whose lower part terminates in tails of fishes. Two serpents are represented on each side of the face, near the ears, from whence the bodies of these reptiles surround each cheek, and are joined under the chin. The union of various characters recalls the Pantheic representations of the goddess Isis; and when the accompaniments of the work are attentively considered, I am persuaded they will be found to represent the goddess in her generating, preserving, and destroying capacities, which primitively constituted her universal dominion, and characterised her as the Dea Triformis."

In 1839, while some excavations were being made near the site of the Roman castrum at Manchester, a remarkably fine bronze statuette of Jupiter Stator was found. The figure, which measures 5¼ inches in height, had at the time of its discovery a rod in one hand and the thunderbolts of Jove in the other. It is now (with a silver coin of the Emperor Trajan, A.D. 98 to A.D. 117, found with it) in the possession of Mr. John Leigh, of the Manor House, Hale, Cheshire.

Britain was soon after this period divided into two consular provinces, Maxima Cæsariensis and Valentia, and into three præsidial districts—Britannia Prima, Britannia Secunda, and Flavia Cæsariensis.[2] This division was probably made in the reign of Valentinian, after the memorable victory obtained by Theodosius over the united power of the Picts and the Scots[3] (A.D. 308-9), and Lancashire came under the consular government of Maxima Cæsariensis, as forming part of that province. From this period the Roman power rapidly declined, and the empire was menaced with desolation by the Continental barbarians. The inhabitants and troops that were quartered in Britain, fearing lest the Vandals should pass over the sea, and subdue them with the rest, revolted from their obedience to Honorius, and set up one Marcus, whom they declared emperor; but they soon deprived him of his dignity and his life, placing Gratian in his room, who was a countryman of their own. Within four months they murdered him also, and conferred the sovereignty upon

[1] From subsequent information it is ascertained that a Sphinx was found with these remains, which the person who discovered them omitted to deliver to Mr. Townley, but which, it is judged, served to decorate the top of the helmet.

[2] Notitia Imperii.

[3] Echard, vol. iii. pp. 272, 273.

one Constantine, not so much in respect to his courage or his quality, for he was a very inconsiderable man in the army, but in regard to his name, which they looked upon as fortunate, hoping he would do as much as Constantine the Great had done, who had been advanced to the imperial dignity in the same island. This new prince, immediately after his promotion, passed over into Gaul, taking with him the very flower of the British youth. After subduing Spain and Northern Italy, he was assassinated in A.D. 411. His expeditions had so utterly exhausted the military force of the island that it was wholly broken, and the country left naked to her invaders (A.D. 448).[1] Britain, being thus deprived both of the Roman soldiers and of the most vigorous part of her own population, became an easy prey to the incursions of the northern invaders, the Picts and Scots, to whose inroads the county of Lancaster was peculiarly exposed. The wall of Hadrian, or of Severus, though it stretched across the island, and was built of solid stone, twelve feet in height and eight feet in thickness, and though it was strengthened by fortresses well supplied with munitions of war, no longer formed a barrier against the inroads of the enemy.

The country was garrisoned, and the conquest principally achieved and maintained, during the four centuries that Britain was subject to the Roman sway, by three out of the twenty-nine Roman legions, namely —Legio II.; Legio VI., Victrix, principally stationed in the Brigantian capital of Eboracum (York); and Legio XX., usually called Valens Victrix (mighty and victorious), long stationed at Chester.[2]

The manufacture of woollens was introduced into England, and probably into Lancashire, at an early period of the Roman conquest, and the luxury of dress soon succeeded the painting of the body. After-ages have increased and perfected these useful fabrics, and the ancient country of the Brigantes is still the most famous of all the districts of England for this invaluable production of the loom.

The religion of the Romans consisted, till after their final departure from Britain, of the idolatry of the Pantheon, though the

BRONZE STATUETTE—JUPITER STATOR—FOUND AT MANCHESTER.

light of Christianity began to dispel the mist of heathenism during the reign of Constantius Chlorus, the father of Constantine the Great. Constantine erected the first episcopal see in Britain, and the seat of that high dignity was at Eboracum. Constantine not only favoured the Christian doctrine, but, to display his attachment to Christianity, he stamped upon his coins the emblem of the Cross, A.D. 311. The progress of the true faith was, however, continually retarded by the wars with which this country was distracted, and it was not till a later period of British history that the great body of the nation could be called Christians. The lapse of sixteen centuries, during which time fifty generations of men have passed over the stage of time, though it has consigned to destruction numberless Roman remains, has served to bring to light a great mass of antiquities in the stations of Lancashire. Hence in Manchester, and in Lancaster, we have altars,

statues, coins, and medals. In Ribchester, a rich collection of antiquities, consisting of masks, helmets, and domestic utensils, serves to show that this retired village was once an abode of the conquerors of the world, besides numerous articles in the precious metals and in bronze that have been found at different times at Overborough, Littleborough, Walmersley, Standish, and Kirkham, but of these each in its proper place.

[1] Ammianus Marcellinus, lib. xxvii. c. 8.   [2] A Roman legion, when full, consisted of about 6,000 infantry and 400 cavalry.

FIGURE OF VICTORY FOUND AT
UPHOLLAND, NEAR WIGAN.

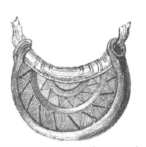

ROMAN BULLA OF GOLD (ACTUAL SIZE)
FOUND NEAR MANCHESTER, 1772.

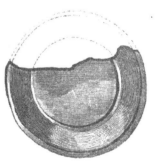

ROMAN DISHES FOUND IN CASTLEFIELD,
MANCHESTER.

ROMAN DISHES FOUND IN CASTLEFIELD,
MANCHESTER.

CHAPTER II.

The Saxon Period—Invasions, Conquests, and Short Rule of the Danes—Termination of the Saxon and Danish Dynasties of England—the Norman Conquest—A.D. 448 to 1066.

HE progress in civilisation made by the Britons during the four hundred years that this county and this country were occupied by the Romans, was almost obliterated by the six centuries which succeeded, of invasion from without and discord within the island. One redeeming event served, however, to dispel the night of heathen darkness; and the general introduction of Christianity, perverted and contaminated though it was by superstition and error, irradiated the gloom of the Saxon, the Danish, and the Norman dominion. So fair a country as Britain, suddenly abandoned by its Roman conquerors, and possessed by a people without union in the government, and without reliance upon themselves, naturally became a prize for foreign competition; and the struggles for independence were rather the transient and convulsive efforts of despair than the dauntless energies of patriotic confidence. The ships which transported the legionaries of Rome from the shores of Britain had scarcely weighed anchor when the invading hordes of Scots and Picts dislodged the British troops from their fortresses, and, forcing a passage through, or passing round, the Roman wall, penetrated into the counties of Cumberland and Lancashire, and even to the gates of York, from whence they menaced the other parts of the island. The state of the country at that time, as described by one of the earliest British historians,[1] serves to show that considerable progress had been made in the arts, in commerce, and in agriculture; and that the people no longer painted their bodies, or depended for their food on the precarious resources of the chase.

"This island of Britain (says this ecclesiastic, writing in the middle of the sixth century) is 800 miles in length and 200 in breadth, embraced by the embowed bosoms of the ocean, with whose most spacious and on every side impassable enclosure she is strongly defended, enriched with the mouths of noble floods, by which outlandish commodities have in times past been transported into the same, besides other rivers of lesser account, strengthened with eight-and-twenty cities, and some other castles, not meanly fenced with fortresses of walls, embattled towers, gates, and buildings (whose roofs, being raised aloft with threatening hugeness, were mighty in the aspiring tops compacted), adorned with her large spreading fields, pleasantly seated hills, even framed for good husbandry, which ever mastereth the ground, and mountains most convenient for the changeable pastures of cattle; watered with clear fountains and sundry brooks, beating on the snow-white sands; together with silver streams gliding forth with soft sounding noise, and leaving a pledge of sweet savours on bordering banks, and lakes gushing out abundantly in cold running rivers."[2]

This description of the wealth of Britain, and of its scenery, drawn thirteen hundred years ago, was doubtless applicable to the county of Lancaster at the time of the departure of the Romans.

"After this (continues our author) Britain being now despoiled of all armed soldiers, and of her own brave and valorous youth (who quitted the island along with the Romans, never returning to their homes), and absolutely ignorant of all practice of war, was trampled many years under the feet of two very fierce outlandish nations—the Scots and the Picts. Upon whose invasion, and most terrible oppression, she sent ambassadors, furnished with letters, to Rome, humbly beseeching, with piteous prayers, the hosts of soldiers to redress her wrongs, and vowing with the whole power of her mind her everlasting subjection to the Roman empire, if they would allow their soldiers to return, and to chase away their foes. These letters were indicted to this purpose— '*The Lamentations of the Britons unto Agitius, thrice Consul.*' 'The barbarians drive us to the sea, the sea drives us back to the barbarians. Thus, of two kinds of death, one or other must be our choice, either to be swallowed up by the waves or butchered by the sword.' In this deplorable condition, no relief could be afforded by the Romans: the Goths were at their own gates; and to aggravate the miseries of the Britons, a dreadful famine raged in the ravished country, which obliged many of them to yield their necks to the yoke of the invaders for a little food; and those who had too much constancy to submit to this humiliation were constrained to seek refuge in the mountains, or to conceal themselves in caves and thickets."[3]

Repulsed by the Roman government, and without confidence in their own strength, the Britons sought assistance from the Saxons, a nation of warriors and pirates. The military renown of these people pointed them out as the most efficient of auxiliaries, while their ambition and their avarice made them in reality the most dangerous of allies. To avert a present danger, ambassadors were sent to the heads of their government, and to this urgent invitation the chiefs of the Saxons replied: "Know ye, that the Saxons will be fast friends to the Britons, and ready at all times to assist them in their necessity, for a suitable return. With joy, therefore, embark again for your country, and make your countrymen glad with these good tidings." The Saxons were confederated tribes, consisting of the Angles (and hence Anglo-Saxons), the Jutes, and the

---

[1] Gildas.   Epist. of Gildas, cap. i.   [3] Epist. of Gildas, cap. xvii.

genuine Saxons.[1] They were settled on the shores of the German Ocean, and extended from the Eyder to the Rhine. The etymology of their name is involved in the obscurity of remote antiquity. Their leaders are supposed to have bequeathed the appellation to their followers. The first Saxon expedition to England, which consisted of 1,000 soldiers, embarked in three vessels, called *cyulæ*, or *ceols*, composed of hides,[2] under the command of Hengist and Horsa,[3] the latter serving under the former, and both being in the fourth generation from Woden, one of the principal gods of the Saxons. On their arrival in England (A.D. 449) they were directed by Vortigern, the British king, to march against the enemy, then spread over the greater part of the country of the Brigantes; and on their arrival in the neighbourhood of York a bloody engagement took place, in which the Picts and the Scots were driven out of Lancashire and Yorkshire, and compelled to take refuge within their own borders. The Saxon generals, disinclined to finish the campaign by a single battle, neglected to follow up this victory, and their troops remained in York and in Manchester, to recover from the fatigues of their journey, and to recruit their numbers with fresh levies. Vortigern, held by the double tie of gratitude to Hengist and love for the fascinating daughter of Horsa, Rowena (Rumwen), became insensible to the danger that menaced his country, and the king closed his eyes to those dangerous designs of ambition in his foreign auxiliaries which every day became more manifest to his people. Having possession of Manchester and York, the Saxons sent for a further supply of troops from Germany, which speedily arrived in seventeen *ceols*, and were encamped in the Isle of Thanet. This measure naturally increased the suspicion of the Britons, and they expressed their displeasure by refusing to provide for the fresh levies. A proclamation commanding them to quit the country immediately followed, at which Hengist took deadly offence, and the Saxons, who had come to expel invaders, now assumed themselves the character of open enemies. Further reinforcements, under the command of Octa, the son of Hengist, and Ebissa, the son of Octa, soon after arrived, and marched to the north, spreading themselves over the Brigantian districts, which were soon to assume another name. The demands of the Saxons rose with the concessions of the Britons; and it at length became clear that nothing short of the full possession of this fair island would allay the cravings of their ambition and cupidity. Digusted with the blindness and effeminacy of Vortigern, his people drove him from his throne, and Vortimer, his son, reigned in his stead. After several battles between the Britons and the Saxons, fought with various success, in one of which Vortimer fell, Vortigern again ascended the throne, and Hengist demanded a conference between the Saxon chiefs and the British nobility, to arrange terms, as was alleged, for the Saxons quitting the kingdom. This meeting took place upon the plain of Ambrij or Amesbury, now called Salisbury Plain. The unsuspecting Britons came unarmed, but the perfidious Saxons had each a short skeine concealed under his cassock. After the conference the horns of festivity went round, till the spirits of the assembly had become exhilarated, when, at the terrible exclamation of "Nemed Saxes!" out rushed the Saxon weapons. The unarmed Britons fell before the perfidious assassins, and three hundred of the bravest chiefs and the most elevated men of the country perished on the spot.[4] Hengist now possessed himself of the southern part of the island, which he erected into a principality, under the designation of the Kingdom of Kent, while Octa and Ebissa remained settled in Northumbria. The fortunes of the Britons were partially retrieved by Aurelius Ambrosius, a Briton of Roman extraction. Under his direction the military spirit of his countrymen was roused into action, and after marching from Totnes, at the head of a formidable force, accompanied by Uther, his brother, surnamed Pendragon, he arrived before the gates of York, when he summoned Octa to surrender. A council of war being called, it was determined by the Saxons to surrender at discretion, and to cast themselves upon the clemency of the Britons. Ambrosius granted a free pardon to the invaders, and, instead of shipping them out of the country, he assigned to them a district on the borders of Scotland. Ebissa, who had probably occupied Manchester while Octa was stationed in York, encouraged by the success of his kinsman's appeal to the conqueror's clemency, came and surrendered himself in the same manner, and met with a similar reception. The gratitude of the Saxons did not outlive their merciful conqueror. On the death of Ambrosius, who was succeeded by Uther the Pendragon (A.D. 449), Octa and Ebissa revolted, and issued from their northern retreat by the route of Ribchester and Wigan, both which places they took, as well as Manchester and Warrington. On their arrival before York an obstinate battle took place under the walls of that city, which ended in the defeat and capture of the two ingrates.[5]

The history of the country between the departure of the Roman legionaries and the rise of the Saxon power is so blended with legend and romance that it is almost impossible to distinguish fact from fable. The last glimmer of ancient literature is lost in the general darkness, and we

---

[1] With these, it is supposed, were some bodies of Frislans.—II.
[2] Nennius, cap. xxviii. [really from Gildas].
[3] About A.D. 428, according to Dr. D. H. Haigh's *Conquest of Britain by the Saxons.*—H.
[4] Nennius, c. xlviii.
[5] Geof. Mon. Polichron, etc.

are compelled to advance in the light of tradition, which reveals nothing distinctly. Many of the events of that period are so inextricably interwoven with the mythical legends and poetic imagery of the Monkish writers that it is difficult to separate the grains of historical truth from the mass of traditional chaff. Not that the two things are necessarily antagonistic, for the respective lines of divergence may not be altogether out of harmony with the central verity, but the accounts which have been handed down are so bewildering that it is necessary to receive them with the greatest reserve. Mr. Fiske, of the Harvard University, in his "Myths and Mythmakers," goes so far even as to affirm his belief that the story of Hengist and Horsa is unworthy of credit, though admitting that it probably embodies an historical occurrence. There is little doubt that the achievments of the little band of buccaneers who followed their lead has been greatly expanded, and the claim made of their being the immediate descendants of Woden gives colour to the suggestion of a mythical origin. We may, however, accept the main outlines of the events recorded, though the seductive graces of Rowena, the daughter of Horsa, who corrupted the king of the Britons by love and wine, is doubtless a later embellishment of the original narrative.

The son and successor of Uther, born of Lady Igerna, wife of Gorlois Duke of Cornwall, was, according to the old chroniclers, the renowned king Arthur (A.D. 467). Trained to arms by Ambrosius, under whose commission he for some time fought,[1] and animated by the wrongs of the Britons, over whom he was appointed to reign, he became himself the leader of their wars, and in all of them he came off conqueror. The first of his battles was fought at the mouth of the river called the Glem. The second, third, fourth, and fifth, upon another river called the Douglas, in the territory of Linuis. The sixth was on a stream which bears the name of Bassas. The seventh was in the wood of Caledon. The eighth was at Castle Guinnion (or Caer-wen). The ninth at the city of Legion (Chester). The tenth on the banks of the river Ribroit. The eleventh on the hill Agned Cathregonion. The twelfth at Mount Badon (Bath).

The Rev. R. W. Morgan, in his "Cambrian History," thus localises the Arthurian victories:—

"First, at Gloucester. Second at Wigan, ten miles from the Mersey. (This battle lasted through the night. In A.D. 1780, on cutting through the tunnel, three cartloads of horseshoes were found and removed). Third, at Blackrod. Fourth, at Penrith, between the Loder and Elmot (the Lowther and Eamont), on the spot still called King Arthur's Castle. Fifth, on the Douglas, in Douglas Vale. Sixth, at Lincoln. Seventh, on the edge of the Forest of Celidon (Ettrick Forest), at Melrose. Eighth, at Caer Gwynion. Ninth, between Edinburgh and Leith. Tenth, at Dumbarton. Eleventh, at Brixham, Torbay. Twelfth, at Mont Baden, above Bath."

Nennius, it will be seen, speaks of four battles having been fought on the river Douglas, but Giraldus only refers to one, which, according to his representation, occurred about the year 500, and resulted in the loss of the greater part of both armies, though victory remained with Arthur, who pursued his enemy, Colgrin, to York, and there besieged him. Mr. Daniel H. Haigh, one of the latest writers who contend for the substantial veracity of the statement embodied in the Arthurian romance, in his "Conquest of Britain by the Saxons," says,

"The river Douglas, which falls into the estuary of the Ribble, is certainly that which is indicated here (the Douglas referred to by Nennius), and although it was one of Arthur's tactics to get round his adversaries, so as to be able to attack them when least expected (which will account for the conflict being considerably to the west of the direct line from London to York), it is extremely improbable that he would have gone so far north as the Douglas in Lothian, when his object was to attack Colgrin at York. The reading which the Paris MS. and Henry of Huntington give is, I believe, correct, and represents Ince, a name which is retained to this day by a township near to this river, a little more than a mile to the south-west of Wigan, and by another about fifteen miles to the west, and which may possibly have belonged to a considerable tract of country. . . . Neither the Brut nor Boece mention more than one battle at this time, but the latter says that Arthur 'pursued the Saxons, continually slaughtering them, until they took refuge in York,' and that 'having had so frequent victories he there besieged them;' and these expressions may well imply the four victories gained in one prolonged contest on the Douglas, and another on the river Bassas, i.e., Bashall Brook, which falls into the Ribble near Clitheroe, in the direct line of Colgrin's flight to York."

That some great battles were fought on the banks of the Douglas,[2] in early times, the remains since discovered abundantly testify, and the balance of testimony seems in favour of the hypothesis that the Lancashire river was the scene of the four battles mentioned by Nennius,[3] and which Mr. Haigh believes to have been one prolonged contest.

The history of Arthur is mixed up with so much romance as to render it extremely difficult to separate truth from fiction. The ingenuity and research of Mr. Whitaker, the historian of Manchester, have placed this subject in so strong and interesting a light, in the second chapter of his Saxon History of Manchester, that it may be quoted with advantage, with the exception of those passages for which the public is indebted more to the vigorous imagination of the author than to historical evidence:—

[1] Malmesbury, f. 4. [2] In some copies the name is given as "Dubglas," and in others it is rendered "Duggles." [3] Nennius, capp. lxv. lxvi.

"The second, third, fourth, and fifth battles of Arthur are supposed to have been fought in our own county (Lancashire), and upon the banks of our little Douglas.[1] And the name of the river concurs with the tradition concerning Arthur, and three battles prove the notion true. On the traditionary scene of this engagement remained, till the year 1770, a considerable British barrow, popularly denominated Hasty-Knoll. It was originally a vast collection of small stones taken from the bed of the Douglas; and great quantities had been successively carried away by the neighbouring inhabitants. Many fragments of iron had been also occasionally discovered in it, together with remains of those military weapons which the Britons interred with their heroes at death. On finally levelling the barrow, there was found a cavity in the gravel immediately under the stones, about seven feet in length, the evident grave of the British officer, and all filled with the loose and blackish earth of his perished remains. At another place, near Wigan, was discovered, about the year 1741, a large collection of horse and human bones, and an amazing quantity of horse-shoes, scattered over a large extent of ground—an evidence of some important battle upon the spot. The very appellation of Wigan is a standing memorial of more than one battle at that place, *Wig* signifying, in Saxon, a fight, and *Wig-en* being its plural. According to tradition, the first battle fought near Blackrod was uncommonly bloody, and the Douglas was crimsoned with blood to Wigan. Tradition and remains concur to evince the fact that a second battle was fought near Wigan Lane many ages before the rencounter in the civil wars. The defeated Saxons appear to have crossed the hill of Wigan, where another engagement or engage-ments ensued; and in forming the canal there, about the year 1735, the workmen discovered evident indications of a considerable battle on the ground. All along the course of the channel from the termination of the Dock to the point of Pool Bridge, from forty to fifty roods in length, and seven or eight yards in breadth, they found the ground everywhere containing the remains of men and horses. In making the excavations, a large old spur, carrying a stem four or five inches in length, and a rowel as large as a halfcrown, was dug up; and five or six hundredweight of horseshoes were collected. The point of land on the south side of the Douglas, which lies immediately fronting the scene of the last engagement, is now denominated the Parson's Meadow; and tradition reports a battle to have been fought in it. The dispirited Saxons fell before the superior bravery and dauntless spirit of the Britons. These four battles were fought upon the river Douglas, and in the region Linuis. In this district was the whole course of the current, from its source to its conclusion, and the words '*super flumen quod vocatur Douglas, quod est in Linuis*' (upon the river called Douglas, which is in Linuis), show the stream to have been less known than the region. This was therefore considerable; one of the cantreds or great divisions of the Sistuntian kingdom, and comprised, perhaps, the western half of south Lancashire. From its appellation of Linuis, or the Lake, it seems to have assumed the denomination from the Mere of Marton, which was once the most considerable object within it, and was traversed by the Romans in canoes of a single tree.[2] Thus by four successive victories had Arthur subdued the great army of the Saxons, which had so often beaten the Britons of the north, and then held the Sistuntii in bondage. But Lancashire was not yet entirely delivered. The castles which had been previously erected there by the provincials would naturally be garrisoned by the Saxons on their conquest of the country, and the towns and their vicinities more immediately bridled by their barbarous oppressors. Tradition asserts Manchester to have been thus circumstanced in particular at this period."[3]

Here, in the Castle Field, according to this authority, stood the Roman castle, now occupied by the Saxon commander Sir Tarquin, who was not expelled till after two desperate attempts to carry the fortress, in which the Britons at length succeeded, and Tarquin fell before the victors. The traditions of Lancashire still cherish and uphold the memory of Sir Tarquin, the lord of the castle, and the knights of the Round Table, many of whom are supposed to have fallen within the tyrant's toils, till Sir Lancelot du Lake slew the sanguinary knight, and liberated his captives.[4]

Accepting without question the statements of Nennius and Giraldus, the rev. historian of Manchester had so much faith in the historic personalty of Arthur and the knights of "the noble order of the table round," that he not only fixed the sites of several of their presumed exploits in Lancashire, but, following tradition, located at Castle Field, Manchester, the legendary fortress of the giant Tarquin, who is represented as having held threescore and four of Arthur's knights in thraldom until he himself fell beneath the stalwart arm of Sir Lancelot du Lake. It is scarcely necessary to say that, notwithstanding Mr. Whitaker's ingenuity, Sir Tarquin, Sir Lancelot, and their knightly compeers, are as much the product of the imagination as are Merlin, Mordred, Sir Gawain, or any other of the personages immortalised in the heroic story which Caxton printed and Tennyson in later times wrought into verse, and we must be content to treat the traditions of their existence as we treat those which reveal to us the actions of Chronos and Rhea, of Inachus, Danaus, and Prometheus. That there was a British chieftain who resisted the invaders during some portion of the two or three centuries over which the Anglo-Saxon conquest extended, and whose deeds of prowess were the admiration of his contemporaries, is extremely probable; and it is not less likely that the chroniclers of an uncritical age gathered up the floating legends of other heroes, mythical and real, and crystallised them, so to speak, on a single personage, whose indi-viduality in a truly historic sense is lost in the fairy web of fiction that has been spun around him.

The last of Arthur's victories was achieved at the battle of Badon Mount (Bath); and Mr. Whitaker contends that these memorable engagements not only checked the progress of Cerdic, but annihilated the Saxon army, and that a long interval of repose, extending through seventy years, followed. It appears, however, from the Saxon chronicles, that Cerdic died in the year 534 [515 or 516], " and was succeeded by his son Cynic [Creoda, or his grandson Cyneric] in the government of Wessex; and that he," in the peculiar language of these chronicles, " reigned after-wards twenty-six winters." It is also shown, from the history of our Anglo-Saxon ancestors, that Ella and Ida reigned in Deira and Bernicia within thirteen years from the supposed death of Arthur, and that the Saxon conquests gradually advanced till all England was subdued, and erected into seven sovereign states, under the name of the *Heptarchy*. The propriety of this appellation has been disputed, and the term *Octarchy* adopted in its stead. The difference is capable of an

[1] Higden, p. 225.   [2] Leigh's Lancashire, b. i., p. 18.   [3] Whitaker's Manchester, vol. ii., b. ii., c. 2.
[4] The same tradition attaches to Brougham Castle, in Westmorland.—C.

easy explanation—Northumbria being considered one kingdom by the advocates for the Heptarchy, and two (that is, Deira and Bernicia) by the supporters of the Octarchical division. The seven kingdoms were—Sussex, Kent, Wessex, East Anglia, Essex, Mercia, and Northumbria. This latter kingdom, which alone concerns the subject of this history, was occasionally divided into two, under the names of Deira and Bernicia, but in its integrality it may be exhibited thus, with the succession of its Saxon sovereign princes: Northumbria consisted of the counties of Lancaster, York, Durham, Westmorland, Cumberland, Northumberland: and its kings were—(1) Ella, or Ida, (2) Adda, or Elappea, (3) Theodwald, (4) Fretnulse, (5) Theodrick, (6) Ethelrick, (7) Ethelfrid, (8) Edwin, (9) Oswald, (10) Egfrid, (11) Alkfryd, (12) Osred, (13) Kenred, (14) Oswick, (15) Ceolulph, (16) Ecgbert, (17) Oswalph, (18) Ediswald, (19) Elured, (20) Æthelred, (21) Alfwald, and (22) Osred.

This kingdom existed 379 years, dating its commencement from 547, and its desolation in 926. During the Roman period, the largest portion of this county took its name from the Brigantes; but the Saxons, from its local situation to the *North of the Humber*, changed its designation to "Northan Humber Londe," or Northumberland. The Saxon inhabitants of this kingdom were the Angles, who arrived from Anglia, now known as the Duchy of Holstein,[1] or Angloen, in Pomerania, as early as the year 449 [428], though their kingdom of Northumberland was not established till one hundred years after that date. It has been conjectured that Mercia included Deira, or that the country between the Mersey and the Ribble was within the Mercian territory. But the preponderance of evidence is in favour of the more generally recognised limits, namely, that the Humber and the Mersey to the south, and the Solway and the Tyne to the north, formed the Northumbrian boundary; and that when this kingdom was divided, the kingdom of Deira consisted of the counties of Lancaster, York, Westmorland, Cumberland, and Durham, precisely the ancient Brigantine limits, while Bernicia comprehended Northumberland and the south of Scotland between the Tweed and the Firth of Forth. Over the beginnings of Northumbria, the former territory of the Brigantes, there hangs, if possible, even greater obscurity than over any other of the kingdoms which sprang up after the Saxon colonisation. For a century and a half thick darkness overspreads the history of the country, and in regard to contemporary events we are only able to grope our way to probable conclusions through a bewildering mass of broken memories and traditions, and the obscure data of philological research. Assuming it to have consisted of the two states, Deira and Bernicia, it is difficult to reconcile the theory with actual facts, except upon the supposition that, at the outset, those kingdoms occupied only the tract of country between the Humber and the Grampian Hills on the eastern side of the great mountainous ridge known in these later days as the English Appenines. This country was colonised by innumerable petty chiefs and their clans, who, arriving, some from Scandinavia, some from Germany, settled upon the first spot that offered them a resting place.[2] Fiercely they contended with each other; the weak fell before the stronger, assassination followed assassination, and massacre succeeded to massacre. The strife waged between the eaorls and the petty chieftains in these two kingdoms of Deira and Bernicia long hindered the full conquest of Brigantium, the western side of the island—the country of the old Sistuntii—remaining for a lengthened period after the departure of the Roman legionaries, a part of the great Celtic kingdom of Strathclyde—Strathclwdd Wealas, as it was sometimes called—which, maintaining its independence, extended eastwards from the Irish Sea to the range of hills that formed the watershed, and stretched southwards from the Clyde to the river Dee, where it joined up to the smaller British states which occupied what we now call Wales, Chester forming the connecting link between the two countries. Lancashire appears to have been included in the district of Teyrulluug, which embraced the territory between Aerven (the river Dee), and Argoed Derwenwyd (the Derwent of modern times). The name implies that it was a royal demesne, and as the country was but sparsely populated, there being few inhabitants beyond those who had been induced to settle around the principal Roman stations, there is good reason to believe that the more northern parts of the county including the Furness district, were great tracts of forest country, the haunt of the wolf, the wild boar, and other animals of prey or of the chase. Eventually the new comers won their way into these western parts, though it was only after a long and stubborn resistance on the part of the native race, and when the decisive victory at Bangor-Iscoed had been gained, that the country was brought under subjection to Saxon rule. The system of government established by our Saxon ancestors had in it the germ of freedom, if it did not always exhibit the fruits. In religion they were idolaters, and when they settled in Britain, their idols, altars, and temples soon overspread the country. They had a god for every day in the week. *Thor*, or *Thur*, represented Thursday; *Woden* conferred his name on Wednesday; *Friga*, or *Fricge*, presided over Friday; *Seater* over

---

[1] Saxon Chronicle, A.D. 449.   [2] Palgrave, English Commonwealth I. 426.

Saturday; and *Tuisco*, the tutelar god of the Germans, conferred his name on Tuesday. The attributes of the first four of these deities corresponded with those of the Roman deities, Jupiter, Mars, Venus, and Saturn; *Tuisco's* parallel was Mercury; the Saxons had also their *Ermenseul*, who, like Mercury, was the bestower of wit; and *Heile*, a sort of Æsculapius, the preserver and restorer of health. Besides these gods, the Saxons worshipped the sun and the moon, who each conferred a name on one of the days of the week; *Sunnan* on Sunday, and *Monan* on Monday. The people worshipped the statues of these gods. THOR, the supreme, was seated on a throne, and on either side of him stood WODEN and FRIGA (husband and wife). Thor, according to the prevailing superstition, bore rule in the air, and governed the thunder, the lightning, and the winds; he likewise directed the weather and regulated the seasons, giving plenty or inflicting famine at his will. Woden made war, and ministered rigour against enemies; while Friga bestowed upon mortals peace and pleasure. So gross was the Saxon superstition, and so strong their incentives to war, that they believed if they obtained the favour of Woden by their valour they should be admitted after their death into his hall, and, reposing on couches, should satiate themselves with ale from the skulls of their enemies whom they had slain in battle! This beverage was in high esteem amongst them; and Eoster, to whom they sacrificed in the month of April, gave the name to Easter, by which the festival of the resurrection is designated in the Christian system. The Saxon women were not allowed to contract a second marriage, and a similar restriction applied to the men, except those in elevated stations who were childless; for, amongst such, "to be without children was to be without reputation." The most dismal feature of their superstition was the custom which they had in war, after a successful enterprise, of selecting by lot, and sacrificing, one-tenth of their captives to their sanguinary gods.[1] In this spirit they offered human sacrifices to obtain success in battle. Revolting as this heathendom was, and debasing in some essentials, there were yet manifestations of a spirit which did not walk in the world without believing in some presiding influences which governed human actions. Before the arrival of the Saxons, Christianity had taken root in England; under Constantine it prospered, and for a time spread its healing branches, recommending itself even to the Roman legionaries; but the invasion of the Saxon infidels for a lengthened period obscured, though it did not actually extinguish, the light of the Gospel in Britain; and both Gildas and Bede concur in representing the Saxons, at that period, as a nation "odious both to God and man,"[2] the subverters of altars, and the enemies of the priesthood. The sweeping away of whatever remained of Roman rites or had been created of Christian worship was a dominant principle in the life of the new comers, but at the same time their heathendom possessed some capacity of assimilation with that faith before which the classical paganism of the ancient world had retreated, and it is a pregnant fact in the history of our Anglo-Saxon progenitors, as Mr. Kemble points out, that, at the beginning of the sixth century, "Christianity met with but little resistance among them, and enjoyed an easy triumph, or, at the worst, a careless acquiescence, even among those whose pagan sympathies could not be totally overcome."[3] Before Gregory, surnamed the Great, had attained the pontifical chair, he formed the pious design of undertaking the conversion of the Saxon Britons. Observing in the market-place at Rome a number of Saxon youths exposed to sale, whom the Roman merchants in their trading voyages had bought from their British parents, being struck with their beauty, he inquired to what country they belonged, and was told they were *Angles*, from the kingdom of Deira. Moved by the same spirit that now actuates so many of the people of England towards the heathen nations, he determined himself to undertake a mission to Britain, to convert the heathen of that country. The popular favour of the monk disinclined the people to allow him to be exposed to so much danger in person; but no sooner had he assumed the purple than he resolved to fulfil his benevolent design towards the Britons, and he pitched upon the monk Augustine to preach the Gospel in that island. In the year 596, Augustine, at the head of about forty missionaries, embarked from Italy, and landed in the Isle of Thanet. His arrival was immediately announced to Ethelbert, king of Kent, who received him graciously, gave him liberty to preach and teach in all his kingdom, and eventually became himself a convert, was baptised in the lowly church of St. Martin, outside the walls of Canterbury, where the missionaries first began to meet, and a multitude of his subjects followed his example. In 604, the neighbouring East Saxons were proselytised; in 627 the East Angles adopted the Christian faith: and in the following year the example extended to Mercia. Thus the flame spread from kingdom to kingdom, till the whole heptarchy had become Christian.

Lancashire, as already shown, remained unsubdued long after other parts of England had submitted to the invader, but it was doubtless the scene of many petty invasions and sanguinary

[1] Sid. Apoll. Epist. vi., l, 8.   [2] Gildas, Brit. Epist. xxiii.; Bede l. i., 22.   [3] The Saxons in England, v. i., p. 443.

4

encounters, the details of which have become lost in the mists of time, and the sites even forgotten. In 607, as the Anglo-Saxon chronicle records, or, according to the annals of Ulster, in 612, "Ethelfrith (the powerful Northumbrian king) led his army to Chester, and there slew numberless Welshmen; and so was fulfilled the prophecy of Augustine, wherein he saith, 'If the Welsh will not be at peace with us, they shall perish at the hands of the Saxons.' There were also slain two hundred priests who came to pray for the army of the Welsh." Florence of Worcester puts the number at "twelve hundred British priests, who had joined the army, to offer prayers on their behalf," but this is, doubtless, an exaggeration. They were the monks of Bangor—the British Oxford from whence Christianity had spread far and near—who disdained subjection to Augustine, and had refused to join the Italian missionaries. Their house, which Ethelfrith subsequently destroyed, had been founded before A.D. 180, and was the ancient Bancorbury, as Bede calls it, but more generally known as Bangor-is-y-Coed (the high choir under the trees), or Bangor Monachorum, and occupied a position on an island in the river Dee, a few miles south of Chester. Mr. J. R. Green, in his "Making of England," thus describes the march of Ethelfrith's army through Lancashire to Chester and Bangor-is-y-Coed: "Though the deep indent in the Yorkshire shire-line to the west proves," he says, "how vigorously the Deirans had pushed up the river valleys into the moors, it shows that they had been arrested by the pass at the head of the Ribblesdale; while further to the south the Roman road that crossed the moors from York to Manchester was blocked by the unconquered fastnesses of Elmet, which reached away to the yet more difficult fastnesses of the Peak. But the line of defence was broken as the forces of Ethelfrith pushed over the moors along the Ribblesdale into our southern Lancashire. His march was upon Chester, the capital of Gwynedd, and probably the refuge place of Edwine."[1]

In A.D. 620, Edwin, king of Northumbria, one of the best and wisest of the Saxon sovereigns, on his expedition against the Sistuntii of the south, subdued the Brigantes of the West Riding of Yorkshire; then crossing the moorland ridge separating Yorkshire from Lancashire, he entered Manchester, and permanently reduced the town under the dominion of the Saxons. Having married Ethelburga, the daughter of Ethelbert, a Christian princess, he received Paulinus with distinguished favour; and in the year 627 that ecclesiastic was consecrated archbishop of the Northumbrians, his episcopal see being at York, where, as previously stated, there had been an ecclesiastical settlement in the time of the Emperor Constantine. Edwin himself embraced the Christian religion with his whole court; and on Easter Sunday, in the year 627, the king and his nobles were all baptised at York. The great body of the people followed the example of their sovereign and his chiefs, and in one day it is alleged 10,000 persons, besides women and children, were baptised by Paulinus in the river Swale, since designated the Northumbrian Jordan.[2] Christianity now became the prevailing religion. The people of Lancashire, like those of Yorkshire, embraced the doctrines of the Cross; the venerable Paulinus was indefatigable in the discharge of the duties of his mission; and the waters of the Ribble, as well as those of the Swale, were, it is said, resorted to for the baptism of his converts. This was not the first occasion, however, that the rays of Christian truth had illumined the pagan darkness of this part of Britain. Though cut off from the See of York, the diocese of the Northumbrian bishop, Lancashire, whilst an integral part of the kingdom of Strathclyde, must necessarily have been included in the diocese of Glasgow, where, in the time of Rydderch,[3] the King of Strathclyde (A.D. 573 to A.D. 601), the saintly Kentigern, connected through his mother, Thenew, with the royal family of the Cumbrian Britons, sat down on the banks of the Molendinar, a little stream that falls into the Clyde, hung his bell on a tree beside the clearing in the forest to summon his savage neighbours, and planted a small religious establishment on the spot where, centuries later, his successors reared the present cathedral of Glasgow, that became the centre of Christian missionary effort. The diocese presided over by Kentigern must have been co-extensive with the kingdom of Strathclyde, which, as already stated, reached southwards to the river Dee, and included the whole of Lancashire; and it is recorded that when driven by persecution from his bishopric, in 543, he took refuge in Wales with St. David, and while there founded, on the banks of the Elwy, the episcopal See of Llanelwy, subsequently named, in compliment to his follower and successor, St. Asaph. Kentigern was afterwards recalled to his home, and resumed his residence at Glasgow. Jocelyn records that when Kentigern left Carlisle, on the occasion of his banishment, he went into Wallia (Wales), and that when he was recalled from Llanelwy by Rydderch he returned from Wallia. He was

[1] The infant Prince Edwin, son of Ella.
[2] The improbability of the story is beyond question. Had Paulinus laboured from dawn to dusk—say for sixteen hours without intermission —he must have despatched his converts at the rate of more than ten a minute to complete the ten thousand, saying nothing of the additional women and children; unless, as some writers, in their desire to disarm incredulity, have explained that the apostle, having baptised ten, sent them into the stream to baptise a hundred, and so multiplied his assistants as the rite proceeded, while he prayed on the shore.—C.
[3] "Rodorchus filius Tothail, qui in Petra Cluaithe regnavit." Adamn. in V.S. Columbæ—Skene. Chron., Pref. xcv.

contemporary with Columba, the founder of the celebrated monastery of I-colm-kill, the Iona of modern times, and it is recorded that when the Scoto-Irish monk came to see Kentigern at his little church beside the Clyde, they interchanged their respective pastoral staves as a token of brotherly affection.   Thus the first faint glimmerings of Christian truth broke in upon the heathen darkness of Lancashire, the work of evangelisation being carried on by missionaries of a religious system of native growth, and devoid of the impressive aspects of Roman civilisation.

The century which saw the establishment of Christianity among the Anglo-Saxons and that which followed it was a period of incessant warfare.   The pagan princes were sometimes in the ascendant, and at others those who had been converted held dominion; while, not unfrequently, rulers who had listened to Christian teachers and had been baptised, relapsed into paganism.   In 633 Edwin, king of Northumbria, the friend and patron of Paulinus, was defeated and slain in a great battle at Heathfield—the present Hatfield, near Doncaster, in the West Riding of Yorkshire— by his rival, Cadwalla, king of the Western Britons—the Brit-Welsh—aided by Penda, king of Mercia.   The town was destroyed, when Paulinus retired, and, accompanied by the widowed queen, Ethelburga, and her children, made his way to the coast, took ship, and sailed for Kent.   A great slaughter was made of the Northumbrians by the Brit-Welsh Christians, who were jealous of their rivals, and hated them with more than ordinary sacerdotal intensity.   The victors swept over the country, and burned and destroyed in their merciless greed of conquest, and the vanquished were maddened in the anguish of a struggle for very life.   After this conflict Northumbria lapsed into its former state of paganism, and whatever glimmerings of light there might have been as the result of the teaching of Paulinus were quickly extinguished.

Having shattered the power of Northumbria, Penda returned into Mercia to develop his schemes of ambition, his design, apparently, being the reduction of all England.   Meanwhile two princes of the houses of Ella and Ida were raised to the throne; Osric becoming king of Deira, in which Lancashire was included; and Eanfrid, the son of Æthelfrith, of Bernicia.   Their reigns were brief, and their deaths inglorious; Cadwalla slew them both; the twelve months of their sway were denominated "the unhappy year," and their names were obliterated from the Fasti of Northumbria.[1]   To them succeeded Oswald, a man of great piety and valour, who had received his Christianity from Aidan, a monk of Iona, on whom he afterwards bestowed the island and bishopric of Lindisfarne, the Holy Island of the present day.   Shortly after his accession, Oswald, with his Northumbrian army, encountered the forces of Cadwalla on the plain called Heavenfield (A.D. 635), believed to be near Hexham, a little to the south of the line of the Roman wall.   In a state of indescribable enthusiasm his army advanced against Cadwalla, routed his forces, and killed the redoubted king himself, by which the waves of devastation were rolled back to the south.   After this victory Oswald established himself with great power on the Northumbrian throne, Deira and Bernicia were united, and he applied himself to the Christianising and civilising of his people.   On his invitation Aidan, with a band of Scoto-Irish monks, came from Iona and settled upon the lonely sea-washed rock, where the Abbey of Lindisfarne arose, and from whence a religious system of native growth, and unconnected with the Italian mission, gradually permeated through the northern and midland districts of Britain.   Northumbria listened to the preaching of these Celtic apostles, Teutonic heathenism was subdued, and in A.D. 652 the British bishop, Finan, the successor of Aidan, became the recognised head of the Northumbrian church.   Numerous churches arose, and Christianity, as modified by the influence of the British character, became the prevailing creed throughout Oswald's kingdom.

From that period to the present Christianity has maintained its ascendency in the northern parts of Britain; and in 678 the south Saxons, who were the last of the states to bow down to idols, discarded their superstitions, and became the worshippers of the only true God. The British churches, which the Saxons had not demolished, had fallen into decay; but they were now repaired, and the heathen temples were many of them converted into places of Christian worship, with appropriate dedications; and the Saxon churches in London, York, and Manchester were distinguished by the names of St. Paul, St. Peter, and St. Mary.   The feasts of dedication were instituted to preserve the memory of the consecration of the churches; and these annual festivals, which commenced in the evening preceding the celebration of the dedication, were called church wakes, which have gradually assumed a secular character, and are now ranked amongst the village festivals of Lancashire.   It must not, however, be supposed that this evangelising of the country, or even the baptism of so many thousands at a time, implied that the mass of the people had adopted anything like an intelligent Christian faith.   The old monastic chroniclers may disguise the truth, but up to this time heathenism beat in the very heart of the nation.   The

[1] Hist. Mont. S. Aug., p. 177.   Beda iii., 1.

mission despatched by Gregory, and the evangelists whom the Celtic church had sent out from Iona and from Lindisfarne, had each done a great work; but there was a greater still to be accomplished, which involved the labour of centuries. In only too many instances, when the petty Saxon states adopted Christianity, the people merely followed the example of their chiefs, copied their ceremonial, and adopted the Saviour and the Virgin, in some vague and distorted ideal, into their pagan demonology.

Coeval with the churches, a number of castles were also erected, or re-edified; and it is conjectured that not fewer than twelve considerable ones arose south of the Ribble—Wall-ey, Wal-ton, Child-wall, and Win-wick, Black-stone, Seph-ton, Stan-dish, and Pen-wortham,[1] Wig-an, Roch-dale, Middle-ton, and Bury. These were, probably, the seats of twelve Saxon chiefs, before the institution of parishes; and became, therefore, the seats of as many parochial churches.[2] The victories of Oswald served but to inflame the resentment of the pagan Penda, king of Mercia, who fought against him and slew him at Maserfeld, according to the Saxon Chronicles,[3] or, according to the Venerable Bede, at Maserfelth. The battle was fought on the 5th of August A.D. 642, but there is a conflict of testimony as to the locality of the battle-field—Camden, Pennant, and Sharon-Turner fix the site at Oswestry, in Shropshire; Dr. Ingram, the translator of the Saxon annals, names Mirfield, in Yorkshire; but other authorities, with greater show of reason, give the preference to Makerfield, or Macerfield, near Winwick, in Lancashire. The ancient chroniclers agree in representing Penda as the assailant, and that he led his forces from Mercia. Oswestry was forty or fifty miles within Penda's kingdom, and consequently an unlikely place in which to encounter an antagonist acting on the defensive; while Winwick, in the "Fee of Makerfield," was on the direct route of an enemy marching from Mercia into Northumbria, and answers to the expression of Bede that Oswald died "*pro patria dimicans.*" A little more than half a mile to the north of Winwick, on the rising ground to the right of the old Roman road leading from Warrington, through Winwick and Ashton-in-Makerfield to Golborne and Wigan, is an ancient well, still venerated by the inhabitants, which has been known from time immemorial as "St. Oswald's Well." Tradition still points to Bradley Hall, in the immediate locality, as occupying the site of one of Oswald's residences, and on the south wall of the church of Winwick, which is dedicated to St. Oswald, is a Latin inscription that is still decipherable—

Hic locus, Oswalde, quondā placuit tibi valde
Nortanhunbrorū fueras rex, nūc que polorum,
Regna tenes, prato passus Marcelde, vocato
Poscimus hinc a te nostri memor esto beate,

which Mr. Beamont has thus Englished:—

This place of yore did Oswald greatly love,
Northumbria's king, but now a saint above,
Who in Marcelde's field did fighting fall,
Hear us, oh, blest one, when here to thee we call.

An addition to the inscription sets forth that the wall was restored in 1530. These evidences all point to the probability that the battle in which the great Christian King of Northumbria fell was fought at Makerfield, in Winwick parish, and not at Oswestry, as Camden and some other writers have affirmed. Oswald was buried in three places. Lindisfarne received his head; his hands were deposited at Bamborough; and the monks of Burdency, in Lincolnshire, became the possessors of his bones. The superstition of the times clung with marvellous tenacity about these relics, and a blaze of miracles were believed to accompany the sacred dust.

After the battle at Maserfeld the victorious Penda advanced northwards, burning and devastating the whole country on his line of march until he reached Bamborough, where Oswy, the brother and successor of Oswald, was believed to have retired. An attempt was made to burn the place, but the wind being unfavourable and driving the flames in the faces of the assailants, they withdrew. Relieved of the presence of Penda, Oswy sought to hold the entire kingdom of Northumbria, but in A.D. 644 he was compelled to admit a partner in the sovereignty and to cede Deira to Oswin, a prince of the House of Ella, while he retained the other component part, Bernicia. Determined on uniting Northumbria, Oswy collected a force for the invasion of Deira, when Oswin, who had endeavoured to conceal himself, was betrayed and put to death by the truculent Bernician. Meanwhile another storm was preparing to burst over his kingdom: a fresh quarrel had arisen between Oswy and Penda, the old warrior king of Mercia. The implacable Mercian had held sway for nearly thirty years, and carried fire and sword wherever his power could reach; he was relentless in the pursuit of conquest; five kings had fallen under his hand, and his people, partaking of the character of their prince, "squatted like ghouls amid the ruins of

[1] Domesday Book, fo. 270.   [2] Bede, lib. iii., cap. 9. a. 3.   Saxon Chron. A.D. 642.

the old Romano-British villages and towns." But his day was drawing near its close. In the autumn of 655 he gathered his pagan hordes for a last assault upon Christian Northumbria. Oswy strove to avert the conflict, and delivered his youngest son Ecgfrith as a hostage into Penda's hands, but the sacrifice was useless. Overtures for peace having failed, the Northumbrian gathered his forces and prepared for the defence of his kingdom. The two armies met at Winwid-field, when a fierce battle ensued, in which the Mercian king was slain, and Penda and paganism fell together. The site of this battle, like that in which Oswald fell, has been disputed. Most authorities assign the neighbourhood of Leeds. Bede says " the battle was fought near the river Vinwed (now the Aire), which then, with the great rains, had not only filled its channel, but over-flowed its banks, so that many more were drowned in the flight than destroyed by the sword," but Mr. Thomas Baines, in his *Historical Notes on the Valley of the Mersey*, contends that it was on the banks of the stream which joins the Mersey below Winwick, and affirms that " Penda met his death within two or three miles of the place at which Oswald had fallen;" but this view is dis-countenanced by the further statement of Bede, that " King Oswy concluded the aforesaid war in the country of Loides (Leeds)."

After the fall of Penda, Oswy overran the whole country of the Mercians, subjecting every-thing to his dominion; upon Peada, his son-in-law, he conferred the under kingship of the pro-vinces lying south of the Trent, and under his fostering care Christianity spread through the country of the middle English. The story of the conversion of Peada is full of interest, and one that is not altogether wanting in the element of romance. Oswy had a son Alchfrid, who had married one of king Penda's daughters, so that the two royal though rival houses were linked by marriage. The young princess's brother, Peada, visited the Northumbrian court for the purpose of soliciting the hand of Oswy's daughter Alchfleda. He was received with kindness, and the princess promised to him on the condition of his renouncing paganism. Alchfrid undertook to explain the hopes and truths of the Gospel, and his persuasion won Peada over to Christianity. He and his attendants were baptised by Finan, the successor of Aidan in the see of Lindisfarne, and on his return with his bride to his own kingdom, he took with him Diuma, a Scot, who was consecrated by Finan, and three other presbyters of the same church, to instruct and baptise his people. Diuma, who was the first bishop of the Mercians or Middle Angles, came direct from Iona and took up his abode at Repton, near Derby, the then capital of Mercia, his diocese being co-extensive with that kingdom. Thus was founded the church of the Middle Angles, and thus commenced that long and unbroken episcopal line which, since the days of St. Chad, when the seat was transferred from Repton—eleven years after Diuma's death—has had its chief centre in the old city of Lichfield, and until the erection of the separate see of Chester, in the reign of Henry VIII., included within its spiritual supervision the greater portion of South Lancashire. For some years, the people of Lancashire, with the rest of their fellow-subjects of the kingdom of Deira, had been in a state of constant hostility with their ancient allies and neighbours, the people of Bernicia; but under the rule of Oswy their differences were reconciled, and they united in allegiance to one sovereign. It was not, however, until the reign of Oswy's successor, Ecgfrith, (A.D. 670-685) that the portion of Lancashire north of the Ribble which had been included in the Cumbrian portion of Strathclyde became absorbed in the Northumbrian kingdom. "The Welsh states across the western moors," says Mr. J. R. Green, "had owned, at least from Oswald's time, the Northumbrian supremacy, but little actual advance had been made by the English in this quarter since the victory of Chester (607), and northward of the Ribble the land between the moors and the sea still formed a part of the British kingdom of Cumbria. It was from this tract of what we now know as Northern Lancashire and the Lake District Ecgfrith's armies chased the Britons in the early years of his reign."[1]

A new era was now opening in the ecclesiastical history of this province, the effects of which were to be felt through a long series of ages, and to influence in no small degree the future interests of the nation. Monastic institutions began to prevail in Northumbria about the middle of the seventh century, under the fostering hand of that distinguished prelate Wilfrid, sole bishop of Northumberland; and in a few years a number of such houses sprang up in Lancashire and other parts of the province. The practice of introducing relics into the churches belongs also to this age, and innumerable were the pilgrimages made to Rome and to the venerable places which had been hallowed by the blood of the martyrs, to collect the remains of the saints. By the constitution of the western churches, the pope was invested with a patriarchal authority over them; but the Britons had never acknowledged the pontifical jurisdiction. Theodore, the archbishop of Canter-bury, having long seen the necessity for affording to the people some more extensive means of

[1] The Making of England.

religious instruction than they at that time possessed, and for dividing such of the bishoprics as were too large for the proper discharge of the episcopal duties, recommended to the king to convene a synod in 673, at which Ecgfrith and his Saxon barons were present. By this synod or assembly, which met at Hertford, it was provided, by a unanimous decision, that as the number of Christians was daily increasing, new sees should be erected; and, as if in anticipation of some formidable opposition, a declaration was appended to the decrees, to the effect that whoever presumed to violate them should be degraded of his sacerdotal office and excommunicated.[1] In virtue of these canons, the bishopric of the East Angles was divided into two, and the dominions of the Mercians which lay beyond the Severn were assigned to the new see of Hereford. Wilfrid still remained the sole bishop amongst the Northumbrians, and his diocese reached from the Firth of Forth to the Humber, on the east of the kingdom, and from the Firth of Clyde to the Mersey, on the west. No prelate in these early days had aggrandised the church so much as Wilfrid. With influence almost unbounded in all parts of the kingdom, and amongst all the upper classes, from the greatest to the humblest of the Saxon barons, he was enabled to procure manors and lordships for the erection and endowments of churches; and in his time the precedent was first established of alienating the demesnes of the crown to augment the revenues of the church. Wilfrid was munificent and ostentatious, affable and accomplished, ambitious and intractable, pious but proud. By one of the decrees of the synod, it was directed that the bishopric of this prelate should be divided into two, Deira and Bernicia, of which York was to be the capital of one, and Hexham of the other. The haughty spirit of the prelate was wounded by this partition, which he did not hesitate to designate as an unjust spoliation. After in vain attempting to induce the king and the Archbishop of Canterbury to repeal the synod's decision, Wilfrid appealed to the pope in person, and his holiness, conceiving this a fit opportunity for establishing his patriarchal power in Britain, set aside the sentence of the English archbishop, and decreed the restoration of Wilfrid to the whole of his former bishopric, but the mandate was rejected by a convocation of all the English bishops; Wilfrid was deprived, his property confiscated, and his person committed to prison. After a contest of twenty-seven years, he was reinstated in the see of Hexham, but the Saxon bishops refused to admit the authority of the Roman pontiff in any affairs relating to the British churches, though, when the angry passions excited by this controversy had subsided, the pontifical claim was again advanced. Although the Britons had lived securely in Furness, relying upon the fortifications with which nature had guarded them, nothing proved impregnable to the Saxon conquerors; for it appears that in the early part of the reign of Ecgfrith, king of Northumberland, that monarch "gave St. Cuthbert the land called Carthmell (the present Cartmel), and all the Britons in it,"[2] which, if the statement is correct, would most likely be in the year 685, when Ecgfrith caused Cuthbert to be created a bishop.[3] Bede, or Beda, a native of the kingdom of Northumbria, died in 734, after a life of unparalleled literary labour. This venerable ecclesiastic, who was born in the year 672,[4] ranks the first in the number of early British historians, though his works are marred by legendary tales, which serve to show that his mind was not free from the superstitions which for so many ages afterwards prevailed in the county of Lancaster, to an extent scarcely equalled in any other part of the kingdom. In the time of Bede, but in what exact year is not ascertained, the ecclesiastical divisions of parishes were first established, and before the middle of the seventh century, and within twenty-five years from the conversion of the Saxon inhabitants of Northumbria to the Christian faith, churches were erected in the various districts of this country, to which ministers were appointed by the respective founders to dispense the ordinances of religion.

The Saxon heptarchy was now drawing towards its termination. Ambition agitated all parts of the country by its conflicts, and the face of nature seemed to sympathise with the general disorder. Dreadful forewarnings came over Lancashire and the other parts of the land of the Northumbrians,[5] which excited general terror amongst the people. Storms were soon followed by "a great famine; and not long after, on the sixth day before the ides of January (793), the harrowing of heathen-men (the Danes) made lamentable havock in the Church of God." "In the year 799," adds the Saxon Chronicle, "a severe battle was fought in the Northumbrian territory during Lent, on the fourth day before the nones of April, at Whalley; wherein Alric, the son of Herbert, was slain, and many others with him." This is the first time in which the parish of Whalley is mentioned in civil history. Simeon of Durham writes: "A league or confederacy was made

[1] Bede, lib. iv. c. 5.
[2] Camden's Brit. vol. iii. p. 380.
[3] After this (the synod of Twiford) an assembly was holden, and Ecgfrith sat therein, and Theodores, archbishop of this island, with many other noble counsellors, and they all unanimously chose the blessed Cuthbert as bishop. Then they quickly sent a writ with a message to the blessed man, but they could not bring him from his minster (Lindisfarne). Then rowed the king himself, Ecgfridus, to the island (Farne), and Bishop Trumwine, with other pious men, and they much besought the saint, bent their knees, and begged with tears, until they drew him weeping from the solitude to the synod together with them. (Bibl. Bodl. MSS., Bodley, 340, Hom. in Nat. 8. Archb. f. 64.)
[4] At Wearmouth, in the bishopric of Durham.
[5] Saxon Chron. A.D. 793.

by the murderers of King Ethelred. Wada, leader in that league, went with his forces to fight against Eardulph, the king, in a place called by the English Billangahoh, near Whalley, and many were slain on both sides; and Wada, the leader, fled with his troops."[1]

Although we possess but little information respecting the details of this conflict, or of the political complications out of which it arose, there is little difficulty in fixing the locality of the struggle. "The site assigned to it," says Mr. Hardwick, "has never been doubted. The names recorded by the old chroniclers are still extant in the locality, with such orthographic or phonetic changes in their descent from the eighth to the nineteenth century as philologists would anticipate. The *Hwelleage* of the Anglo-Saxon Chronicle, as well as the monk of Durham's mediæval Latin *Walalega*, are identical with the present Whalley; while *Billangahoh* is represented by its descendants Billinge, Billington, and Langho. Archæological remains have likewise contributed important evidence. Three large tumuli for centuries have marked the scene of the struggle, one of which, near to Langho, has been removed, and the remains of a buried warrior exhumed. According to J. M. Kemble, and other Anglo-Saxon scholars, Billington signifies the homestead or settlement of the sept or clan of the Billings, as Birmingham is that of the Beormings. This rule likewise applies to many other localities where the local nomenclature presents similar features. Consequently, from legitimate analogy, we learn that Waddington, on the right bank of the Ribble, opposite Clitheroe, is the homestead, town, or settlement of Wadda (the chief of the conspiracy against Eardulf) and his dependents; and Waddow, in its immediate neighbourhood, the how or hill of Wadda."[2] Canon Raines mentions that in 1836 a large mound near the Ribble was removed when a kist-vaen was discovered, formed of rude stones, and containing human bones, and the rusty remains of some spear heads of iron. Mr. Abram, the historian of Blackburn, also made an examination in 1876, but with only negative results. He, however, inclines to the belief that the battle was fought on the line of the Roman road which leads from the Wyre by way of Preston to Ribchester, and crossing the Calder a little above the junction with the Ribble, continues in the direction of Clitheroe, and to the north of Pendle Hill into Yorkshire. "Eardulf," he says, "encountered the insurgent army on the extreme verge of his kingdom (for it seems certain that the south side of the Ribble was then a part, not of the Saxon kingdom of Northumbria, but of that of Mercia). Wadda and his army had probably been driven upon the neutral territory before the decisive battle could be forced upon him."

Ecgbert, the son of Alckmund, king of Wessex (A.D. 800), having mounted the throne of his ancestors, penetrated successively into Devonshire and Cornwall, and ravaged the country from east to west. After the conquest of Mercia, Ecgbert marched against Eanred, king of the Northumbrians; but this prince, feeling that resistance was hopeless, acknowledged his superiority, and the whole Anglo-Saxon heptarchy merged in the kingdom of Wessex, under the sway of Ecgbert, and thus was accomplished that consolidation of authority which justified him in taking the title of king of England, though a large portion of the country over which his authority extended was merely a kind of nominal "overlordship," which carried very little governing influence. Before Ecgbert ascended the throne, the Northmen had commenced their attacks upon Britain; and so early as 787 a small expedition, in three piratical galleys, landed in Dorsetshire. The invaders were principally, though not exclusively, from the promontory of Denmark, the *Cambrica Chersonesus* of Tacitus. In 794 a more formidable armament effected a landing in Britain, and spread devastation amongst the Northumbrians, plundering the monastery of King Everth, at the entrance to the Wear. The resistance made to the invaders was so determined that some of their leaders were slain; several of their ships were shattered by the violence of a storm; and such of them as escaped the fury of the waves fell by the sword. The following year Eardulf, the viceroy or king of Northumbria, ascended the throne, and was consecrated in the capital of York.[3] In A.D. 800 Northumbria was again subjected to a Danish visitation, and the immediate cause of this invasion is said to have been this: Osbert, the viceroy of Ethelred, having violated the wife of the Earl Bruen Bocard, the latter invited Godericke, the king of Denmark, to take possession of the country. Godericke received this invitation with great alacrity, and despatched a strong armament to Britain. On their arrival in Northumbria, on the coast of Holderness, the Danes fell upon the inhabitants with the utmost fury, and massacred all before them, without regard to age, sex, or condition. Marching on to York, they took possession of that city, and slew Osbert, the tyrant, by whose lust his country had been involved in so much ruin. Emboldened by their success in the north, they

---

[1] Dr. Whitaker supposes Billange, or Billinge, to have been at that time the name of the whole ridge, extending from the mountain near Blackburn, now bearing that appellation, to Whalley. Billangaton will, on that supposition, be the orthography of Billington, and Billangahoh, or the low hill by Billinge, will leave after cutting off the first syllable the modern village of Langho. Of this great battle there are, however, no remains, unless a large tumulus near Hacking Hall, and in the immediate vicinity of Langho, be supposed to cover the remains of Alric, or some other chieftain amongst the slain.—*History of Whalley*, book I. cap. iii. p. 50. Ed. 1872.
[2] Ancient Battlefields in Lancashire, pp. 133-4.
[3] Sax. Chron.

advanced into Norfolk, and demanded of Edmund, the king of the West Saxons, that he should surrender his throne. With this insolent summons he refused to comply; on which a bloody battle ensued, at Thetford, which ended in the overthrow of the Saxons, and in the execution of their king, who, because he would not abjure the Christian faith for the errors of paganism, was bound to a stake, and shot by the arrows of the Danish invaders.[1]

The situation of Lancashire, and of the other parts of Northumbria, must now have been most deplorable: for forty years the war raged amongst them with remorseless atrocity and varying success. Ælla, the governor, like Osbert, fell by the sword, when Inguar, the presumed son of Raynar Lodbrok, ascended the throne, and the Danes remained masters of the situation. Æthelred for a while kept the field, but at length his life and his power fell before the superior discipline of the Teutonic invaders. The Danes, in the fury of their warfare, laid waste every town and place that resisted their sway; but their especial fury was directed against religious houses. The exactions they made upon the impoverished people, advanced from £10,000 to £40,000 a year, which sum in those days was considered of enormous amount. Lancashire, and, no doubt, other parts of the island, were in A.D. 869 visited by one of the most dreadful calamities to which mankind are sub-ject—a severe famine, and its inevitable consequence, a mortality of cattle and of the human race.[2] Agriculture was but imperfectly understood, and almost every district of the same kingdom was left to depend upon its own precarious resources. The contest between the Anglo-Saxons and the Danes, in this and the neighbouring counties, had withdrawn the husbandman from his employ-ment; and, having neglected to sow, of course he had nothing to reap. The consequence was, that not only many parts of these fair regions mourned in want, but they were absolutely depopulated. Merciless and slow-consuming famine devoured its wretched victims, and the small share which might have fallen to the native inhabitants was consumed by the ruthless Danes, who, from their principal station in York, spread like swarms of locusts across the island, from sea to sea. In the year 876 Halfden, one of the sons of the mythical hero Raynar Lodbrok, according to the Saxon Chronicle, "appropriated the lands of Northumbria, and they thenceforth continued ploughing and tilling them." From which it may be assumed that the newcomers had settled down more as emigrants than roving pirates, though always ready to exchange the ploughshare for the sword in the prospect of a successful foray on the lands of their Anglo-Saxon neighbours. Both Northumbria and East Anglia had now fallen under the sanguinary sword of the Danish invaders, who began to aspire to the conquest of the whole island. Mercia next became the object of their attack, and Ethelred, king of Wessex, fell in a battle fought with the invaders at Merton. Alfred was now advanced to the throne of Wessex; but within a month of his elevation, he was attacked and defeated at Wilton (A.D. 871).[3] A new swarm of Danes soon after landed, under three of their princes, Guthrum, Oscitel, and Amund, and proceeded into Northumbria, the favourite seat of their power. The husbandmen became the slaves of the invaders, and the thanes were made subservient to their purposes of avarice and aggrandisement. The noble spirit of Alfred bent beneath the storm, and, finding no security upon the throne, he withdrew from his elevated station, and took up his residence in an obscure part of the kingdom, as guest in the family of a swineherd, where there occurred the incident of his letting the cakes burn. The hospitable rustic, notwithstanding the asperity of his wife's temper, obtained the favour of the king. By his advice he applied himself to learning; and Alfred, on his return to power, acknowledged the obligation he had received, by elevating his host from the shepherd's crook to the bishop's crozier, and afterwards made him bishop of Win-chester.[4] The humiliation of Alfred disciplined his temper, purified his heart, and served to enlighten his already profound understanding. His measures to regain his throne, and to surround it with its only impregnable bulwark, the love and confidence of the people, were judicious and exemplary. An auspicious incident at this juncture occurred to fortify his courage, for having, in the assumed character of a minstrel, observed the conduct of the Danes in their encampments, he suddenly assembled a strong force, and inflicted a signal overthrow upon the invaders, at Eddington, near Westbury (A.D. 878), where the Danes were encamped. With a generosity equal to his bravery, he gave them their lives, on the condition that they should, through their leader Guthrum, exchange paganism for Christianity. The peace of Wedmore followed—Alfred and Guthrum's peace, as it was called—when Guthrum was baptised by the name of Æthelstan, and the people became gradually one—Guthrum being permitted, with his followers, to colonise East Anglia, on his acknowledging Alfred as his over-lord, and the Northumbrians were afterwards put under his rule. The sovereignty of Mercia, on the defeat of the Danes, fell into the power of Alfred, and, without avowedly incorporating it with Wessex, he discontinued its regal honours, and constituted Ethelred

---

[1] The Danes, like the original Saxons, were idolaters; their principal god was Thor, and to him they offered human sacrifices.
[2] Asser, 20.

[3] Saxon Chron. A.D. 871.
[4] Malmsb. p. 242.

his military commander, to whom he afterwards married his daughter Ethelfleda. To fortify his kingdom against hostile attacks, he rebuilt the cities and castles which had been destroyed by the invaders; but his principal care was to construct a navy for the protection of the coast, and he has ever been considered as the founder of the English marine. In Northumbria the Danes continued to govern till towards the close of Alfred's reign, when Anarawd abandoned his power in that kingdom, and besought the friendship of Alfred. The king received him hospitably; and, to confirm the good intentions that he had formed in favour of the Christian faith, he became his sponsor in baptism, and his friend in all the relations of life. The state of learning in Lancashire, in the ninth century, may be inferred from Alfred's own declaration—"When I took the kingdom," said he, "there were very few on the south side of the Humber, the most improved part of England, who could understand their daily prayers in English, or translate a letter from the Latin. I think there were not many beyond the Humber; they were so few, that I cannot indeed recollect one single instance on the south of the Thames, when I took the kingdom."[1] The encouragement given to learning by this enlightened and benevolent monarch was highly exemplary; he instituted schools for the instruction of his nobles in reading and writing, much after the model of the Lancasterian schools of more recent times. The invasion of the Danes, and their predatory depredations, particularly in the county of Lancaster, and the other parts of the kingdom of Northumbria, had almost destroyed the ancient police of the kingdom. To remedy this disorganised state of society, Alfred changed the ancient provisional divisions of England into counties, and the distribution of these into hundreds, which were again subdivided into tenths or tithings. Under these divisions the population of the country has been ever since arranged; and every person was directed to belong to some hundred or tithing (tenth), while every hundred and tithing became pledged to the preservation of the public peace and security in their district, and were made answerable for the conduct of their several inhabitants. In consequence of this arrangement, every criminal accused was sure to be apprehended; and it may be supposed that in this part of the kingdom the number of the lawless was at first very large.

In the division of Britain into counties, the south-western portion of the Brigantine territory of the Romans, and of the Northumbrian kingdom of the Saxons, was named Loncasterscyre or *Lonceshire*, from the capital of Loncaster, the castle on the Lone or Lune. South Lancashire, then included in Cestrescire or Cheshire, was divided into six hundreds—Derby, Newton, Walton, Blackburn, Salford, and Leyland—since reduced to four by the annexation of Newton and Warrington to West Derby. The designation of each of these hundreds was derived from the principal place in the division, in the reign of Alfred; and those names now serve to indicate the mutations to which places as well as persons are exposed. Of the names of the Lancashire tithings we have no distinct remains; but the nearest approximation to them may be found in each ten of our modern townships. Hitherto the administration of justice was confided to a species of provisional prefects, but in the time of Alfred the functions of these officers were divided into those of judges and sheriffs. The institution of juries belongs to the same period; and so tenacious was Alfred of the faithful discharge of the judicial office in penal judgments, that he caused forty-four justices to be executed as murderers, because they had exceeded their duty, and condemned to death unjustly the persons they judged.[2] Alfred compiled a code of laws (the DOM-BOC), which he enlarged with his own hand. Amongst his other legal institutions, it is perfectly clear that he had none corresponding with our Court of Chancery, since it appears that he hastened the decision of causes, and allowed no delay exceeding fifteen days.[3] Death deprived the world of this great monarch in A.D. 900 at the age of fifty-two years. He was a pattern for kings in the time of extremity—a bright star in the history of mankind. Living a century after Charlemagne, he was, perhaps, a greater man, in a circle happily more limited.[4]

In the century which succeeded the death of Alfred, there is little to relieve the contests of ambition which so generally prevailed. Lancashire and the whole Northumbrian territory had, by the clemency of Alfred, become a species of Danish colony. There the resident Danes concocted their schemes of ambition and aggression against the Saxon power; and upon the shores of Yorkshire and Lancashire fresh swarms of invaders effected their landing, and found succour and support. Edward the Elder succeeded to the power of his father; but his title was disputed by Ethelwald, son of King Ethelbert, who established his head-quarters in York, and was joined by the Northumbrians in his rebellion. The insurgents, quitting their stronghold in the north, marched into Kent, where a sanguinary battle ensued, and Ethelwald fell in the action, when his followers sought their safety in flight. Unsubdued, though vanquished, the Northumbrians penetrated again into Wessex, where they were again defeated, and pursued with great slaughter into their own

[1] Alfred's Preface, p. 82.   [2] Mirroir des Justices, cap. ii. sec. 3.   [3] Mirroir, p. 245.   [4] Herder's Outlines, p. 245.
5

country. Following up his successes, Edward subdued the two next princes of Northumberland, Reginald and Sidoc, and acquired the dominion of that province. In his wars between the Mersey and the Humber the king was assisted by his sister Ethelfleda, the widow of Ethelbert, Earl of Mercia, who, after her husband's death, had retained the possession of the government of that province. This princess is extolled by the early British historians as the wisest lady in Britain, the very emblem of her illustrious father Alfred. She appears to have been a ruler of the Amazonian type, who defended her country against the Danes "with the bravery and fidelity of an experienced warrior," and earned the eulogium of Henry of Huntington—"Cæsar merited triumph, but thou art more illustrious than Cæsar." To her munificence the Mercians were indebted for the rebuilding of the city of Chester, while her royal brother built the ancient city of Thelwall, on the southern bank of the Mersey, and placed a garrison there.[1] The more effectually to maintain his dominion over the province of Northumbria the king collected an army in Mercia, which he ordered to march to Manchester, which place he repaired and garrisoned.[1]

In the excess of antiquarian disputation, a controversy has arisen, whether, in the era of the Saxon heptarchy, the country between the Mersey and the Ribble, comprehending the southern part of Lancashire, was included in the kingdom of Northumbria; and Dr. Whitaker maintains that this district, under the heptarchy, formed a portion not of Northumbria but of Mercia. To this assertion are opposed the generally-received opinion that the kingdom of Mercia was terminated on its north-western boundary by the river Mersey, and the positive fact that in the Saxon Chronicle, the highest existing authority perhaps upon this subject, Manchester is said to be in Northumbria. The passage is conclusive upon this point: "This year (A.D. 923) went King Edward with an army, late in the harvest, to Thelwall, and ordered the borough to be repaired, and inhabited, and manned. And he ordered another army also from the population of Mercia, the while he sat there, to go to Manchester, *in Northumbria*, to repair and to man it." The country now denominated Lancashire had no separate existence as a county until long after the time when the others were formed, and it was then made up by adding a portion of Yorkshire and a scrap of Westmorland to the district lying between the Ribble and the Mersey, which had previously been included in Cestrescire and it is not unlikely that the low-lying lands on the western side of the shire were during the Anglo-Saxon and Danish period governed by tributary chiefs—resembling the Lords-Marchers of Wales of later date—sometimes under Northumbria and sometimes under Mercia, as the changing fortunes of war gave one power or the other the dominancy.

The ascendency of the Danish power in Northumbria, owing to their colonisation in that kingdom by Alfred, subjected this part of Britain to a frequent recurrence of the horrors of war when all the other parts of the island were at peace. On the accession in 925 of Æthelstan, the son of Edward the Elder, and grandson of the renowned Alfred, Sihtric, the Danish ruler of Bernicia, who a few years previously had assassinated his brother Niel, the sovereign of Deira, and seizing his country had made himself king of all Northumbria, acknowledged his supremacy or overlordship and solicited the hand of his sister Eadgetha in marriage. "They came together," says the Saxon Chronicle, "at Tamworth, on the 3rd before the kalends of February, and Æthelstan gave him his sister." As a condition precedent the Dane embraced Christianity; and thus were supposed to be united the Anglo-Saxon and Scandinavian kings. But the alliance was soon dissolved. Sihtric relapsed into paganism, repudiated his wife, and while Æthelstan was preparing to avenge the wrong, died, or, as is more likely, was murdered. His sons by a former marriage, Guthfric and Anlaf fled, the one into Scotland and the other into Ireland, where the Danes had established their authority. Æthelstan led an army into their country, and quickly annexed the Northumbrian kingdom to his dominions. The Anglo-Saxon Chronicle gives a pithy summary of the events of this year (926). "And Sihtric perished; and king Æthelstan obtained the kingdom of the North-humbrians: and he ruled all the kings who were on this island:—First, Howel, king of the West Welsh (the people of Cornwall); Constantine, the king of the Scots; Uwen (Owain), king of the Gwentian people (the people of Gwent or Monmouthshire); and Ealdred, son of Ealdulf, of Bamborough; and they confirmed the peace by pledge, and by oaths, at the place called Eamot on the 4th of the Ides of July, and then renounced all idolatry, and after that submitted to him in peace." Guthfric returned the next year in arms to claim the Northumbrian kingdom, but was defeated by Æthelstan, and, making his submission, was received with kindness. The power which Æthelstan had thus won by the sword he retained in peace for about ten years, when a league was formed by the Scots, the Cumbrian Britons, and the Welsh, with the object of placing Anlaf, the son of Sihtric, on the Northumbrian throne, and in a short time the whole of the north was in revolt. In order to extinguish the spirit of rebellion, and to give security to his throne, Æthelstan marched into

Scotland, ravaged Caithness, and recrossing the border into Northumbria gained a signal victory at Brunanburh (A.D. 934), by which the confederacy against the Saxon power was completely overthrown, when he reunited Northumbria to the rest of his kingdom, and in that way acquired the title of the first English monarch, thus eclipsing the fame of Alfred, who had suffered the Danes to divide the kingdom with him by apportioning to them Northumbria and East Anglia.[1] It is somewhat remarkable that so little should be known respecting the decisive conflict at Brunanburh—the most important in its political and social results of any fought during the Anglo-Saxon period, and "the bloodiest fight that this island ever saw." The date even is uncertain, and a bewildering confusion exists as to the actual site. The Saxon song says it was at Brunanburh; Ethelweard, a contemporary, names the place Brunandune; and Simeon of Durham, Weondune. Ingulph says Brunford, and Camden names Ford, near Bromeridge, in Northumberland. Mr. Holderness argues with much show of reason that the site is at Kirkburn, a village three miles south-west of Driffield, near where the highway runs through a township with the suggestive name of Battleburn, and Mr. Hardwick, in his "Ancient Battlefields of Lancashire," believes that he has discovered the key that may unlock the mystery in the extraordinary discovery of buried treasure in Cuerdale, on the banks of the Ribble, in 1840. This "find" consisted of a leaden chest, containing ancient coins and treasure to the amount of 975 oz. of silver in ingots, rings, armlets, chains, and, besides, about 7,000 coins of various descriptions, dating from 815 to 930; and he argues that "this great chest was buried near the 'pass of the Ribble,' at Cuerdale, opposite Preston, during this troubled period, and probably on the retreat of the confederated Irish, Scotch, Welsh, Scandinavian, and Anglo-Danish armies, after their disastrous defeat by the English under Æthelstan, at the great battle of Brunanburh, in 937." Tradition, which almost invariably has a substratum of truth underlying it, has always pointed to this ford over the Ribble as the scene of an early conflict. It is very nearly where the line of the great Roman road from the north is crossed by the Watling Street from the Wyre, running by Preston to York, and would thus be equally on the line of march of the Scots coming from the north, the Irish journeying from the west, and the armies of Æthelstan advancing either from Mercia or Northumbria, whilst the date of the greater portion of the coins coincides very nearly with that of Æthelstan's victory. It is very evident that the chest was buried after some signal military disaster, to prevent its falling into the hands of the enemy, and we have no record of any great military event at this time except the battle of Brunanburh, the slaughter at which left Æthelstan at peace for some years. Æthelstan among other laws enacted (A.D. 935) that any merchant who should make three voyages over the sea with his own manufactures, should have the rank of a thane,[2] that is, should rank with the privileged orders. By this means encouragement was given to manufactures and to commerce at the same time; and that agriculture might receive its share of the royal favour, any ceorl who had five hides of his own land, a church, a kitchen, a bell-house, and a separate office in the king's hall, also became a thane.

The Anglo-Danish Northumbrians, still impatient of the Saxon rule, broke out again into rebellion, in the reign of Edmund, the successor of Æthelstan, and chose Anlaf, who had returned from Ireland, as their king.[3] Anlaf, who had been aided by Wulfstan, archbishop of York, being victorious, concluded a treaty with Edmund, by which England was partitioned, and all the country north of Watling Street abandoned to the Anglo-Danes. But shortly after, the capricious Northmen rose in revolt against their prince, when Edmund marched suddenly into the southern part of Northumbria (Lancashire and Yorkshire), and again subjected the country to his dominion, when, to appease his indignation and to conciliate his confidence, the chiefs offered to embrace the Christian religion, and abandon their idolatry.

From the middle to the end of the tenth century the Anglo-Saxon Chronicles are almost entirely occupied by the wars in Northumbria and the changes in the monastic orders, which were then taking place under the influence of the ambitious Dunstan, abbot of Glastonbury. Under the auspices of Dunstan, the Benedictine rule was introduced into nearly fifty monasteries south of the Trent; but, notwithstanding Wilfrid's endeavours in former times, and Dunstan's energies and activity in the present day, there was not before the Norman conquest a single monk in all the Northumbrian territory.[4] The tribute of Danegeld, a tax upon the people to repel the ravages of the Danes, was imposed for the first time in the year 991, and was at first of the amount of £10,000.[5] All the land in the county contributed to this impost by a rateable assessment, except the lands of the church, which were exempt on account of the efficacy of the prayers of the clergy,

[1] "The truth seems to be," says Sharon Turner, "that Alfred was the first monarch of the Anglo-Saxons, but Æthelstan was the first monarch of England. . . . After the battle of Brunanburh Æthelstan had no competitor; he was the immediate sovereign of all England. He was even nominal lord of Wales and Scotland."—C.

[2] Wilkin's Leges Anglo-Sax. p. 71.
[3] Saxon Chron. A.D. 941.
[4] Sim. Dunelm. A.D. 1074.
[5] Saxon Chron. A.D. 991.

which were supposed to form an equivalent for their contributions. "The payment of Danegeld was first ordained on account of the pirates; for in their ravages of our country they did all they could to desolate it. To check their insolence, Danegeld was levied annually, 12d. on every hide throughout the country, to hire men to oppose the pirates. From this tax every church, and every estate held in property by the church, wheresoever it lay, was exempted, contributing nothing towards this payment, because more dependence was placed on the prayers of the church than on the defence of arms."[1] The produce of this tax, which was at first employed in resisting the Danes, was afterwards used to purchase their forbearance. Their irruptions and exactions became continually more oppressive, and in the year 1010 the base expedient was resorted to of purchasing peace from them by the payment of £48,000.

It is remarkable that in the whole of the Saxon Chronicles the term "Lancashire" never once occurs, though the neighbouring counties in the kingdom of Northumbria are mentioned in those ancient annals several times. It is also remarkable that the name of Lancashire is not to be found in the Domesday Book of William the Conqueror, though the manors and lands are described in that imperishable record with the usual accuracy and precision.[2]

The long and inglorious reign of Æthelred was perpetually distracted by the invasions of the Danes, first under Sweyn and afterwards under Cnut, his son and successor; and in the reign of Edmond Ironside the king was obliged to surrender up one-half his kingdom, by awarding to Cnut, Mercia, East Anglia, and Northumbria, which he had entirely subdued. The unfortunate Edmond survived the treaty by which his kingdom was dismembered only a month, having been murdered at Oxford by two of his chamberlains (A.D. 1016); and in this way the succession of Cnut the Dane to the throne of England was secured.

In order to gratify the ambition of the chief of the English nobility, and to attach them to his interest, Cnut created Thurkill earl or viceroy of East Anglia, and Edric earl of Mercia, and having caused Uhtred, earl of Northumbria, who had been an ally of Edmond Ironside to be assassinated, he bestowed that earldom on the Norwegian Jarl, Eric, whom he afterwards employed to murder Edric, reserving to himself only the government of Wessex. But this power of the earls was of short duration; Thurkill and Eric were in 1021 expelled from the kingdom, and Cnut became sole monarch of England. Finding himself firmly seated on his throne, he restored the Saxon customs, to which the people were attached, in a general assembly of the states; justice was administered with impartiality; the lives and property of all the people were protected, and the Danes were gradually incorporated with his subjects. Cnut, though cruel, crafty, and treacherous, was the greatest sovereign of his age, and had the fame to reign over six kingdoms.[3] The impression of his character left upon the English mind is not altogether that of a barbarous conqueror. He came with a powerful will to make a foreign domination endurable by a show of impartiality, and to substitute the strength of despotism for the feebleness of anarchy. When he ceased to be an enemy to England he became a real friend. His power was too strong to be disputed, and he therefore wielded it with moderation when the contest for supremacy was over. The closest connection subsisted between Northumbria and Scotland in the reign of Cnut, and even Cumberland was subject to the Scotch king. This division of his kingdom was inconsistent with the policy of Cnut, who, after marching through Lancashire at the head of a formidable army, took possession of Cumberland, and placed Duncan, the grandson of Malcolm, in possession of that province, subject to the throne of England.

Cnut, by a treaty with Richard, duke of Normandy (A.D. 1035), had stipulated that his children by Emma, the sister of that prince, should succeed to the throne of England; but, in violation of that engagement, he appointed his illegitimate son by Elfgiva, the son of a shoemaker, as the scandal of those times assumes—Harold, surnamed Harefoot for his speed, as his successor, instead of Harthcnut, the son of that princess. A short and disturbed reign was terminated in 1030, by the succession of Hardicanute who appointed Siward, duke of Northumbria, along with Godwine, Earl of Wessex, and Leofric, Earl of Mercia, to put down the insurrection which prevailed against his government. Edward the Confessor, the son of Æthelred, of the house of Cerdic and the lineal descendant of the Saxon kings, succeeded to the throne in 1041, to the prejudice of Sweyn, king of Norway, the eldest son of Cnut. The English flattered themselves that, by the succession of Edward, they were delivered for ever from the dominion of the Danes, and their rejoicings were unbounded; but the court was soon filled with Normans, to the prejudice

[1] Camden, vol. i. p. 177.

[2] Mr. Baines quotes a MS. of Dr. Kuerden as to the division of the kingdom of Northumbria, by King Ecgbert, into shires or counties, and these again into hundreds, wapentakes, or ridings; but the statement is exceedingly inaccurate and without authority. The Lancashire, as we know it at the present day, as previously stated, had no separate existence as a county until after the time when the others were formed.

It is true there was a Lan-castre-scire in Saxon times, but the name was given to designate the tract of country that spread round the town of Lancaster, where the Saxon chiefs were seated after the Roman power had passed away, and not to the present county; the larger parishes as well as the hundreds, at the time, being not unfrequently denominated "Shires."—C

[3] Saxo, 196.

of the Anglo-Saxon nobility, and the language and the fashions of France were very generally introduced. This circumstance gave great offence to the native nobles, who, with Godwine at their head, supported by his three sons, Gurth, Sweyn, and Tostig, rose in rebellion against the king. On the death of Earl Godwine (A.D. 1035), one of the most powerful nobles of his time, his son Harold aspired to the English throne, and was joined by Macbeth, an ambitious Scotch nobleman, who had put to death his sovereign, Duncan, King of Scotland, and usurped his throne. In the wars which ensued, the men of Lancashire were deeply engaged, and Siward, Earl of Northumberland, resisted the usurper with all his force; his object being to depose the assassin and raise Duncan's son Malcolm, prince of Cumbria, who had married Siward's daughter, to the throne. To defeat the ambitious progress of Harold, the king cast his eye towards his kinsman, William, Duke of Normandy, as his successor. This prince was the natural son of Robert, Duke of Normandy, by Harlotta, daughter of a tanner in Falaise.[1] The character of the young prince qualified him for the duties of government in the age in which he lived, and to a courage the most intrepid he added a severity the most inflexible. During a visit paid by Harold to Rouen, William disclosed to him the intentions of Edward, and prevailed upon him, by an offer of one of his daughters in marriage, and by other motives of fear and reward, to promise that he would support his claims to the throne of England. Not satisfied with a promise, on which he had little reliance, William required Harold to take an oath in ratification of that engagement; and, in order to give increased solemnity to the pledge, he secretly conveyed, under the altar on which Harold agreed to swear, the relics of some of the most revered martyrs. Notwithstanding this solemn engagement, which Harold considered as extorted, and therefore not binding, on his return to England he resorted to every means in his power to strengthen his influence. Tostig, a tyrannical prince, the brother of Harold, who had succeeded to the earldom of Northumbria, in suppressing disorder in his territory, acted with so much cruelty and injustice in the counties of York and Lancaster, that the inhabitants, headed by the thanes, rose in rebellion against him, and expelled him from his government. Morcar and Edwin, the sons of Earl Leofric, who possessed great power in this part of the kingdom, concurred in the insurrection; and the former, being elected chief in the place of Tostig, advanced from York with an army collected on the north of the Mersey and of the Humber, to oppose Harold, who had, through the royal favour, been appointed governor of Wessex, and who was commissioned by the king, on the representation of Tostig, to reduce and chastise the Northumbrians. Morcar, "advancing south with all the shire, and with Nottinghamshire, and Derbyshire, and Lancashire[2]," marched to Northampton. Here they were met by Harold, at the head of the king's forces, and a desperate battle appeared inevitable; but Morcar, wishing first to appeal to Harold's generosity and sense of justice, rather than to the issue of arms, represented to him that Tostig had acted with so much injustice and oppression in his government, that the inhabitants of Yorkshire and of Lancashire, with those of Durham, Northumberland, Cumberland, and Westmorland, being accustomed to the government of the law, and being determined to support their birthright, preferred death to slavery, and had taken the field determined to perish rather than submit to the iron yoke of the tyrant. After communicating with the king, Harold abandoned the cause of his brother, and obtained a royal amnesty for the insurgents, who returned to their homes as conquerors, driving before them all the cattle they could collect, amounting to many thousands. Morcar was from this time confirmed in his government of Northumbria; and Harold, instead of consummating the family alliance contracted with the daughter of William of Normandy, married the daughter of Morcar. The death of Edward (January 5, 1066) speedily followed the suppression of the great northern insurrection, and his body was interred in the abbey of Westminster, "which he had himself erected to the honour of God and St. Peter, and all God's saints."[3] The religious zeal of this sovereign, with whom the Saxon line of English kings terminated, procured him the name of Confessor; and his love of justice induced him to complete a code of laws from the works of Æthelberht, Ina, and Alfred, though those which pass under his name were, according to Sir Henry Spelman, composed after his death. This sovereign was the first who touched for the king's evil—a superstition which maintained its hold of public credulity through six centuries, and was not discontinued till the time of the Stuarts.

Though, by the will of Edward, William of Normandy was appointed his successor, Harold, stepped into the vacant throne without hesitation, having first been crowned at York, where he was residing at the time of the king's death, by Aldred the archbishop, nor did he quit this part of the kingdom till four months afterwards, when he repaired to London,[4] having been everywhere received in his progress with the most joyous acclamation. Earl Tostig, who had taken refuge in Flanders with Earl Baldwin, his father-in-law, on his expulsion from Lancashire, collected a large

        [1] Brompton, p. 910.   [2] Saxon Chron., A.D. 1035.   [3] Saxon Chron.   [4] Saxon Chron. 1066.

fleet and endeavoured to regain his forfeited possessions by sailing up the Humber and penetrating into Northumbria. Finding his power ineffectual, he associated himself with Harold Hardrada, king of Norway, who with 300 ships assembled in the Isle of Wight, and there remained all the summer. On the approach of autumn, Hardrada appeared off the Yorkshire coast with his 300 ships, and was joined by Earl Tostig, who had replenished his force amongst the Danish Northumbrians, and, after entering the Humber, they sailed up the Ouse towards York. On receiving this intelligence, Harold, whose army was collected in the south, under the expectation of an invasion undertaken by the Normans, hastened to the north by forced marches. But before his arrival, Edwin, earl of Mercia, and Morcar, earl of Northumberland, had gathered from Lancashire, and other parts of the earldoms, a considerable force, with the intention of repelling the invaders. On their arrival at Fulford, a village south of York, a sanguinary battle ensued, in which the slaughter was so great that the Norwegians traversed the marshes on the bodies of the fallen,[1] and in which Morcar and Edwin were obliged to seek safety in flight, leaving the invaders in possession of the field. After demanding hostages and prisoners from the inhabitants of York, the "Northmen" marched to Stamford Bridge, where they were surprised by Harold (Sept. 27), at the head of the largest force ever collected in England. Before the battle commenced, a proposal was sent by Harold to his brother, offering to re-instate him in the government of Northumbria, if he would withdraw from the field. To which Tostig, in the insolence of his spirit, replied, "Last winter such a message might have spared much blood; but now what do you offer for the king, my ally?" "Seven feet of ground," said the Saxon general.[2] The die was cast. For some time the passage of the bridge was disputed by one of the Norwegians, who, owing to the narrowness of the bridge, withstood the "English folk,"[3] so that they could not pass. In vain did they aim at him their javelins; he still maintained his ground, till a soldier came under the bridge, and pierced him terribly inwards, under the coat of mail. Then Harold marched over the bridge, at the head of his army, when a dreadful slaughter ensued, both of the Norwegians and the Flemings, in which were slain Hardrada, the fair-haired king of Norway, and Tostig, the expatriated earl of Northumbria. The fleet of the Norwegians fell also into the hands of Harold, who allowed Prince Olave, the son of Hardrada, to depart the kingdom, with twenty of his vessels, taking with him the wreck of the Norwegian and Flemish army. This act of generosity, as historians are accustomed to consider it, was not unmixed with policy. A still more formidable invasion was approaching, and Harold wished to be freed from one body of his enemies before he had to encounter another. The shouts of victory were heard across the island, from the Humber to the Mersey; but scarcely had those shouts subsided, before intelligence was received that William of Normandy had landed at Pevensy, at the head of 60,000 men, supported by a fleet of 3,000 sail,[4] and was constructing a castle at the port of Hastings. Harold received the news of William's landing without any emotions of dismay, while he was at dinner in his favourite city of York. Hastening to London at the head of his army, which had been diminished by the battle of Stamford Bridge, and which was discontented by being denied a share of the spoil, he received a message from Duke William, who offered Harold his choice of three proposals—to reign in fealty under William, whom he had sworn to serve; or to decide the dispute by single combat; or to submit the cause to the arbitration of the pope: to which Harold replied, that the God of battles should be the arbitrator, and decide the differences between them. Yielding to the impetuosity of his own temper, instead of listening to the wise counsels of his brother Gurth, he marched from London without due preparation, in the vain hope of surprising the Normans in the south, as he had surprised the Norwegians in the north.

The night before the battle of Hastings was passed by the invaders in preparations and in prayer, while the English devoted their hours to festivity and joyful anticipations. The fate of England hung on the issue of the day. Before the battle commenced, on the 14th October, 1066, William joined in the solemnity of religious worship, and received the sacrament at the hands of the bishop; and to give increased effect to these solemnities he hung round his neck the relics on which Harold had sworn to support his claims to the English throne.[5] He divided his army into three bodies. In front he placed his light infantry, armed with arrows and balistæ, led by Montgomery. The second division, commanded by Martel, consisted of his heavy-armed battalions. His cavalry, at whose head he stood in person, formed the third line, and was so disposed that they stretched beyond the infantry, and flanked each wing of the army. The English army, chiefly infantry, were arranged by Harold in the form of a wedge, meant to be impenetrable. Their shields covered their bodies; their arms wielded the battle-axe. Harold, whose courage was equal to his station, quitted

[1] Snorre, p. 155; Ork. Saga, p. 95.
[2] Snorre, p. 160.
[3] Saxon Chron.

[4] The "Roman de Rou" says 696, which is more probable.
[5] Will. of Malms., p. 101.
[6] Guil. Pict., p. 201.

his horse to share the danger and glory on foot.   His brothers, Gurth and Sweyn, accompanied him, and his banner, in which the figure of a man in combat, woven sumptuously with gold and jewels, shining conspicuously, was planted near him.[1]   The English, occupying the high ground, which was flanked by a wood, not only received the discharge of the Norman weapons with patient valour, but returned the attack with their battle-axes and ancient weapons with so much effect that the foot and the cavalry of Bretagne and all the other allies of William on the left wing, gave way. The impression extended along the whole line, and was increased by a rumour that the duke had fallen.   Dismay began to unnerve his army; and a general flight seemed about to ensue.[2]   William, to arrest the progress of the panic, and to convince his soldiers of his safety, rushed amongst the fugitives, and, with his helmet thrown from his head, exclaimed, "Behold me—I live; and will conquer yet, with God's assistance.   What madness influences you to fly?   What way can be found for your escape?   They whom, if you choose, you may kill like cattle, are driving and destroying you.   You fly from victory—from deathless honour.   You run upon ruin and everlasting disgrace. If you continue to retreat every one of you will perish."[3]   The Normans rallied, and made a desperate onset; but the English, forming a wall of courageous soldiery, remained unbroken. William, finding all his efforts to penetrate their ranks fruitless, resolved to hazard a feigned retreat.   A body of a thousand horse were entrusted with this critical operation.   Having rushed upon the English with a horrible outcry, they suddenly checked themselves, as if panic-struck, and affected a hasty flight.   The English entered eagerly on the pursuit with apparent success; for the Normans, having retired upon an excavation somewhat concealed, fell into their own trap; many of them perished, and some of the English shared the same fate.   While this manœuvre was occupying their attention, the duke's main body rushed between the pursuers and the rest of their army.   The English endeavoured to regain their position: the cavalry turned upon them, and, thus enclosed, many of them fell victims to the skilful movements of their adversaries.   At length they rallied and regained their position, but, uninstructed by experience, they suffered themselves to be twice afterwards decoyed by a repetition of the same artifice.   In the heat of the struggle twenty Normans confederated to attack and carry off the English standard.   This service they effected, though not without the loss of many of their number.[3]   The battle continued through the day with frequent changes of fortune.   Harold was more distinguished for the bravery of a soldier than for the skill of a general.   William united the two characters.   He had three horses killed under him. While Harold lived his valourous countrymen seemed invincible.   Fertile in expedients, the duke directed his archers not to shoot directly at the English, but to discharge their arrows vigorously upwards towards the sky.   The random shafts descended into the English ranks like impetuous hail, and one of them pierced the gallant Harold in the eye,[4] and, penetrating the brain, terminated his life.   A furious charge of the Norman horse increased the disorder.   Panic scattered the English, and the Normans vigorously pursued them through the broken ground.   A part of the fugitives rallied, and, indignant at the prospect of surrendering their country to foreigners, they sought to renew the contest.   William, perceiving that the critical moment for sealing the victory had arrived, ordered Count Eustace and his soldiers to the attack.   The duke, with a vigour and energy peculiar to himself, joined in the final conflict, and secured the victory of Hastings and the crown of England.   The body of Harold was found by his mistress, Edith, "the Lady of the Swan Neck," near those of his two brothers, Leofwine and Gurth, who were also slain in the battle, and was sent, at the request of his mother, Githa, for interment to the monastery of Waltham, which he had founded.[5]

The battle of Hastings terminated the Saxon dynasty in England, after a continuance, with occasional interruptions, of six hundred years.   During this long period the foundations of some of the most important of our public institutions were laid, and it may be interesting, even for the illustration of local history, shortly to advert to their nature and origin.   In the Saxon period, the mechanical arts, so closely interwoven with the interests of society, met with liberal encouragement. The wisest of their monarchs invited from all quarters skilful and industrious foreigners; they encouraged manufactures of every kind, and prompted men of activity to betake themselves to navigation, and to push commerce into the most remote countries.   As an indication of an approach towards a state of free traffic, and of the increase of commerce, it is mentioned that Cnut,

[1] Will. of Malm. p. 191.
[2] Guil. Pict. 202.
[3] Brompton, p. 960.
[4] Henry of Hunt., p. 368 ; Will. of Malms. p. 101.
[5] Though the commonly-received account is that the corpse of Harold was carried from the battle-field, and buried at Waltham, the Anglo-Saxon people long refused to believe that the last of their kings had perished at Hastings.   They believed that his wounds were healed amidst friends ; that he waited in some safe seclusion ready to lead his faithful English when the opportunity for deliverance should approach;

and that the tomb shown did not mark his last resting-place.   Giraldus Cambrensis, among the older historians, and Sir Francis Palgrave, among modern writers, relate a tradition that Harold escaped alive from the field of battle, and lived in seclusion at Chester, where he ended his days as a monk or lay-brother.   The last-named authority considers that the tomb at Waltham was nothing more than a cenotaph, which is certainly at variance with the "Hic Jacet," upon the tomb, and the circumstantial account given by Fuller in his "Church History," wherein he describes the opening of the tomb towards the close of Elizabeth's reign, when a skeleton was discovered inside it.—C.

about the year 1028, established mints for the coinage of money in thirty-seven cities and towns of England. A silver penny, coined at York about the year 630, and marked with the name of Edwin, the Northumbrian monarch, is supposed to be the earliest specimen of coinage in this island after the abdication of the Romans. The king and his barons enfranchised the principal towns, to encourage the progress of manufactures, and Manchester was of the favoured number.

It must be admitted, however, that whatever progress our Anglo-Saxon ancestors had made in commerce and in manufactures since the time of the Roman sway in Britain, this country had retrograded deplorably in the practice of the fine arts. As early as the reign of Severus, the sculpture and the painting of Rome had obtained a high degree of perfection; but in the Saxon times these accomplishments were almost extinct in the island, and the coinage of Northumbria, in the reigns of Æthelstan, of Harold surnamed Harefoot, and of Edward the Confessor, as exhibited in the following specimens, serve sufficiently to prove the lamentable deterioration:—

The Anglo-Saxons were divided into four classes—men of birth, men of property, freemen, and serviles. Their money was in pounds, shillings, and pence; twenty shillings constituted a pound, and twelve pence a shilling, as at present—with this difference, however, that twenty shillings weighed a pound troy—and hence the term *pound*. Guilds, or communities of mutual protection, were formed by persons engaged in trade, which sought at once to protect the interests of those branches of business, and to provide for the members of their fraternities in sickness and old age.[1] Markets and fairs were pretty generally established; attention was paid to agriculture; and the yeoman was held in deserved estimation. Their monarchy was partly hereditary and partly elective; and the power of their sovereigns not absolute, but limited. Their Witena-Gemot of "wise men" formed the great council of the nation, and was a body, the foundation of our parliaments, that at once enacted laws and administered justice. Besides the trial by jury, they had the trial by ordeal of water and of iron: by the iron ordeal, the accused carried a piece of red-hot iron three feet, or nine feet, according to the magnitude of the offence; in the water ordeal, he plunged his hand into a vessel of boiling-hot water up to the wrist in some cases, and to the elbow in others; the hand was then bound up, and sealed for three days, at the end of which time the bandage and seal were removed; when, if the hand was found clean, he was pronounced innocent, if foul, guilty.[2] This was a trial, not a punishment, and it was performed before the priest, in the presence of two witnesses, after due preparation. Sometimes the party choosing this mode of trial *prepared* his own hand, to endure the fiery trial; and sometimes probably *prepared* the hand of the priest, and thus induced him to abate the height of the temperature. There was another ordeal by water: the culprit, having a rope tied about him, was plunged into a river two ells and a half deep; if he sank, he was acquitted; but if he floated, being considered deficient in weight of goodness, he was condemned.[3] The punishments were various, and consisted of banishment, slavery, branding, amputation of limb, mutilation of the nose, ears, and lips, plucking out the eyes, stoning, or hanging. The trial by jury was a rational and enlightened inquiry. The Saxons have the merit of having introduced this invaluable institution into England; and some authors contend that it originated in the time of Alfred, but it is certain that it was in use amongst the earliest Saxon colonists.[4] The trial by jury did not at once attain perfection, and it is probable that Alfred matured and perfected the institution. Originally a man was cleared of an accusation, if twelve persons came forward and swore that they believed him to be innocent of the alleged crime.[5] This was a jury in its earliest form. Afterwards it became necessary that twelve men, peers or equals of the litigants, should hear the evidence on both sides, and that they on their oaths should say whether the accused was guilty or innocent.

The *Feudal System* arose in England during the Saxon dynasty, and for many ages exercised an influence and control over society, not only in this country, but over the whole of the western nations of the world. Though the system was introduced into this country by the Anglo-Saxons, it was not till the Norman Conquest that it received its complete consummation. In the heat of the battle of Hastings, William had promised his followers that the lands of England should be theirs

---

[1] Eden on the Poor Laws.   [2] Wilk. Leg. Ins, p. 27.   [3] Textus Roffensis.   [4] Black. Com. cap. xxiii.   [5] Turner's Ang. Sax. iv. 337.

MAP of
LANCASHIRE.
AD MLXXVI
According to the Doomsday Survey
in the
Orthography & Character
of that
Document.

English Miles

if victory crowned their efforts; and the possessions of Earl Tostig, as well as those of the other Saxon barons, between the Mersey and the Ribble, and to the north of the latter river, speedily became the knights' fees of the houses of Lacy and Poictou. In the partition of the spoil, the most considerable share fell to the king. These lands became the subject of feudal tenures;[1] the king conferred them upon his favourites *in capite*, on the condition that they should faithfully serve him in war and in peace, and on payment of a certain annual fine; and they again granted their Lancashire manors to Goisfridus, Willielmus, Tetbaldus, and others, as their feudatories. These thanes had their socmen and villeins—in other words, their farmers and their slaves—some holding by military and others by rustic obligations; but all, from the highest to the lowest, under feudal tenures. The whole frame of society was involved in this comprehensive system.[2]

The six centuries embraced in this chapter, considered in regard to their results, constitute the most important period in the history of the county and of the kingdom. In that time the Britain of the Cæsars became the England we now know; and out of the British, Roman, Saxon, and Danish stock—the admixture of tribes and blood that then represented the courage, enterprise, energy, and self-reliance of Europe—emerged the English people. The Teutonic and Scandinavian invasion was more ruthless, more destructive, and more complete than any which had preceded it: it submerged every usage and obliterated every trace of existing institutions— the laws, the customs, the Christianity, the language of the people, and, to a large extent, the very names of places disappeared. The heathen and the stranger came from across the German Sea; wave followed wave from the inexhaustible breeding grounds of the north, sweeping away the dying civilisation of the Latin world, but depositing in its stead a fruitful soil, from which the civilisation of a later time was to spring. The piratical Viking followed in the wake of the adventurous Saxon. Pierced by barbarian hordes, torn by internal divisions, and ruled by foreign masters, the country was for a long time like a seething cauldron, and the scene of overwhelming and crushing calamity.

The history of these times is full of doubt and obscurity. We know only the general results, we know very little of the details, yet it was amid these desolating wars, these internal feuds, these fierce conflicts of races, and from these discordant elements, that gradually, and by slow and insensible development, there sprang up a perdurable nation, that has preserved its free spirit under every form of alien domination or domestic oppression, a nation that in every conflict, whether that of regal despotism or feudal or ecclesiastical assumption, has asserted the right of individual liberty, and upheld, with ever-increasing strength, the great principle of the equality of all men before the law. Under the stern discipline of these times England developed her national character, and by slow process built up the fabric of her law; for that resulted from the principle of growth rather than from that of creation. To the Saxon mind we owe much of the English Constitution. Upon their civilisation, rudely developed though it might be, were founded many of the principles of government which have retained their vitality through the long centuries that have intervened, for the Norman despotism was absorbed by the Anglo-Saxon freedom, and feudality could neither destroy the principles of self-government nor weaken the love of personal liberty. Their indomitable spirit of independence is wrought into the life-blood of our own Saxon-sprung race; from their customs we derive many of our own; and it is in the elements of their social state that we discover the origin of that of to-day. The humanising influences of the Christian religion melted down the rude Saxon, the restless Jute, and the idolatrous Angle, and took from them their fierce despotism, their barbarous rites, and their cruel customs; while their mother tongue, terse and vigorous, has gradually formed into a language that is spoken in every quarter of the world.

[1] Discussions have at various times taken place upon the question, "Was the land system of this period feudal?" It engaged the attention of the Irish Court of King's Bench in the reign of Charles I., and arose through the issuing of a "commission of defective titles" in the preceding reign. In a paper on "The History of Landholding in England" in the "Transactions" of the Royal Historic Society of Great Britain, Mr. Fisher says: "In the course of the argument the existence of feudal tenures, before the landing of William of Normandy, was discussed, and Sir Henry Spelman's views, as expressed in the Glossary, were considered. The Court unanimously decided that feudalism existed in England under the Anglo-Saxons, and it affirmed that Sir Henry Spelman was wrong. This decision led Sir Henry Spelman to write his 'Treatise on Feuds,' which was published after his death, in which he reasserted the opinion that feudalism was introduced into England at the Norman invasion. This decision must, however, be accepted with a limitation. I think there was no separate order of nobility under the Saxon rule. The king had his councillors, but there appears to have been no order between him and the *folc-gemot*. The earls and the thanes met with the people, but did not form a separate body. The thanes were country gentlemen, not senators. The outcome of the Heptarchy was the earls or caldermen.

This was the only order of nobility among the Saxons. They corresponded to the position of lieutenants of counties, and were appointed for life. In 1045 there were nine such officers; in 1065 there were but six. Harold's earldom at the former date comprised Norfolk, Suffolk, Essex, and Middlesex; and Godwin's took in the whole south coast from Sandwich to the Land's End, and included Kent, Sussex, Hampshire, Wiltshire, Devonshire, and Cornwall. Upon the death of Godwin, Harold resigned his earldom and took that of Godwin, the bounds being slightly varied. Harold retained his earldom after he became king, but on his death it was seized upon by the Conqueror, and divided among his followers. The Crown relied upon the *Liberi Homines*, or freemen. The country was not studded with castles filled with armed men. The *house* of the thane was an unfortified structure, and while the laws relating to land were, in my view, essentially *feudal*, the government was different from that to which we apply the term *feudalism*, which appears to imply baronial castles, armed men, and an oppressed people."—C.

[2] Mr. Baines gives here a very long quotation as to the feudal system from a MS. of Dr. Kuerden, in the Chetham Library, which, from its want of authority and accuracy, loose style, and strange phraseology, is not deemed worth reprinting.—H.

6

CHAPTER III.

O sooner was the Norman Conqueror seated on the throne of England than he began to exercise the power of conquest with all the rigour which the jealousy of his own mind and the insubordinate disposition of his new subjects dictated. The doctrines inculcated by Machiavel, in his instructions to conquering princes. were practised by William of Normandy in England five centuries before they were promulgated by the Italian politican. He left no art untried to root out the ancient nobility, to curb the power of the established clergy, or to reduce the commonality to the lowest state of penury and dependence. Earls Morcar and Edwin, who had so successfully resisted the tyrannical power of Earl Tostig, were among the first to revolt from the yoke of the tyrant. To give effect to their resistance, they raised forces in Lancashire and Cheshire, as well as in the other northern counties, and fixed upon the celebrated Northumbrian capital, the city of York, then amongst the first cities in the kingdom, superior even to London, as their stronghold. The inhabitants of York rising in arms, slew Robert Fitz-Richard. the governor,[1] and besieged in the castle William Mallet, on whom the command had devolved. At this juncture two of the sons of King Sweyne, with two hundred and forty ships, arrived from Denmark, under the command of Duke Osborne, brother to the king. The troops disembarked on the banks of the Humber, where they were met by Edgar Atheling, and Earls Waltheof and Gospatric, with large levies of Northumbrians from Yorkshire, Lancashire, Cumberland, and Durham, "riding and marching," says the Saxon Chronicle, "full merrily towards York." This alarming revolt the Conqueror hastened to subdue ; and such was the violence of his rage, that, on his way to the north, he swore repeatedly, by the "splendour of God," that he would not leave a soul of the insurgents alive. The strength of the Saxon barons was increased by the junction of a large force under Bethwin, king of North Wales. Preliminary to his arrival, William had suspended Morcar, and appointed Robert de Comyn, a Norman baron, to the earldom of Northumberland. The orders given to Robert were, to subdue the refractory spirit of the people, without regard to the shedding of blood ;[2] and a guard of seven hundred men was placed around his person. The intrepid Northumbrians, roused by a sense of their own wrongs, and by the indignity offered to the Earl Morcar, rose in open insurrection, and put to death the Norman, with every individual composing his guard. The first measure taken by William, on his arrival at York, was to offer mercy to the insurgents, on their submission to his authority ; and the chiefs, finding themselves unequal to contend with the power that was brought against them, accepted the proffered clemency. The Earls Morcar and Edwin, accompanied by Gospatric, and Edgar Atheling, their lawful prince, fled into Scotland under the protection of King Malcolm. Unmindful of that general amnesty which he had offered, the Conqueror directed the most severe proscription against the Saxon inhabitants of these regions, hundreds of whom fell under the cruel inflictions of the Normans. To guard against a surprise, the Conqueror caused numerous castles to be erected in the north of England ; and in the city of York two castles sprang up under the direction of the Normans. These precautions were not confined to inland fortifications ; they extended also to the coast, and the castles of Lancaster and of Liverpool, on the Lune and the Mersey, were both erected during the early part of the Conqueror's reign, by Roger de Poictou, one of the most distinguished amongst the Norman barons. Notwithstanding the severity practised by William on the suppression of the first insurrection, he allowed the Earls Morcar and Edwin to retain their estates in Lancashire, Yorkshire, and Cheshire, though he extended the rigours of confiscation over the lands of many of their followers. The forfeitures, attainders and other acts of violence, soon produced another insurrection—the flame of insurrection, lighted up amongst the brave Northumbrians, spread into other parts of the kingdom ; but the king, well aware that the most imminent danger existed in

---

[1] Order. Vital. p. 512.　　　　[2] Wal. Hemingford, Canon of Gisburgh.

the counties of York and Lancaster, determined to march once more against them, and placing himself at the head of a powerful army, he left London to take his revenge upon the insurgents. By common consent, Earl Waltheof was appointed governor of the city of York by the Saxon barons, while the Danish general took up his intrenchments between the Humber and the Trent, in order to keep the Normans in check. On the arrival of William and his army before York, he sent his summons to the governor, offering him clemency if he surrendered promptly, but threatening the most terrible vengeance if he attempted to withstand his authority. He pushed on the siege with vigour, and was not less vigorously resisted. A breach having been made in the walls by the engines of the besiegers, the governor himself, being a man of prodigious might and strength, stood single in the breach, and cut off the heads of several Normans who attempted to enter.[1] For six months the siege was sustained, and the struggle was sanguinary and exhausting; and it was not till William had reinforced the besieging army again and again that he gained possession of the city. Famine at length effected what force could not achieve; and William not only promised forgiveness to the governor, but also the most reasonable terms to his troops, on the condition of surrender. Under the influence of that admiration which bravery inspires amongst the brave, the Conqueror gave to Waltheof his niece Judith, daughter of the Countess Albemarle, in marriage, and created him also Earl of Northumberland. The reconciliation was only temporary. William, impatient of opposition, brought the gallant earl to the block, on account of another conspiracy, and this was the first nobleman whose life was terminated in England by decapitation. Earls Morcar and Edwin, no longer able to sustain their own dignity, or to preserve the public rights, quitted the seats of their earldoms in Northumbria and Mercia. Edwin, in attempting to make his escape into Scotland, was betrayed by some of his followers, and killed by a party of Normans, to the deep affliction of the men of Lancashire and Cheshire, where the ardour of his patriotism, and his personal accomplishments, had gained all hearts; while Earl Morcar was thrown into prison, and consigned to future obscurity. Lucia, the sister of the Earls Morcar and Edwin, was presented in marriage to Ivo Talbois, the first Baron of Kendal, who came over with the Conqueror. This baron was distinguished by the favour of his prince, who granted to him that part of Lancashire which adjoins Westmorland, as well as the confiscated lands of his wife's brother in Lincolnshire. William viewed the inhabitants of Northumbria as the most formidable enemies to his power; and in order to satiate his rage and to prevent further resistance, he razed the city of York to the ground; and with it fell many of the principal nobility and gentry, as well as the humbler inhabitants. Nor did his implacable vengeance rest here: he laid waste the whole of the fertile country between the Humber and the Tees, a distance of sixty miles, so that, for nine years afterwards, neither spade nor plough was put into the ground.[2] If any of the wretched inhabitants escaped, they were reserved for a more lingering fate, being forced through famine to eat dogs and cats, horses, and even human flesh. The towns, villages, hamlets, and scattered habitations throughout Northumbria were reduced to ashes; all the implements of agriculture—carts, ploughs, harrows—were piled in heaps, and consumed with fire; the corn was burnt in the granaries; horses, cattle, sheep, were slaughtered in the fields or at the stalls, in short, everything that could serve for the support of human life was utterly consumed. The tyrant gave full sway to all the ferocious passions of his nature, and gloated his eyes upon the wasted lands and the innumerable corpses of the slain. His breast was steeled against compassion, and whenever a Northumbrian appeared, he was cut down by the sword or pierced by the lances of the Normans. So unsparing was the destruction, that the inhabitants could scarcely recognise their own lands; and when the Domesday Book was compiled, though the survey was not commenced till ten years afterwards, many townships remained uncultivated, which is the reason why *Wasta* [waste] so often occurs in the Domesday Survey of Yorkshire. In that part of this ancient document which concerns Lancashire, the returns are more fully made, though not under the head of a distinct county; and a presumption naturally arises that the Conqueror's severity was practised with less rigour between the Mersey and the Duddon than between the Humber and the Tees. In the north of Lancashire, included within the ancient limits of Richmondshire, several vacancies are found; and in the south-eastern part of the district, between the Ribble and the Mersey, the scanty return of names may be accounted for by the vicinity of that part of Salford hundred to the devoted county of York.

By a charter remarkable for its comprehensive brevity,[3] William, while at York, granted the lands and towns and the rest of the inheritance of Earl Edwin to his nephew, Alan, son of Eudo, Duke of Brittany, whom he afterwards named Earl of Richmond, and in this way nearly two

[1] William of Malmsbury.
[2] Malms. p. 103, Knighton. Ingulf. p. 79. Sim. of Dur. p. 199.
[3] This charter does not create a different title, but gives the lands as held by the former possessor. The monarch assumed the function of the *folc-gemot*, but the principle remained—the feudee only became tenant for life. Each estate reverted to the crown on the death of him who held it; but, previous to acquiring possession, the new tenant had to cease to be his own "man," and became the "man" of his superior. This was called "homage" and was followed by "investiture."—C.

hundred manors and townships were transferred by a dash of the pen, and an impression of the seal, from the unfortunate Edwin to the trusty follower of the victorious William. The Conqueror soon placed all the land of the kingdom under that system of feudal tenure which had already been partially introduced under the Saxon dynasty. These possessions, with very few exceptions besides the royal demesnes, were divided into baronies, which were conferred, with the reservation of stated services and payments, on the most considerable of the Normans. The great barons, who held of the crown, shared out a large part of their lands to other foreigners, who bore the names of knights or vassals, and who paid their lord the same duty and submission in peace and in war which he himself owed to his sovereign. The whole kingdom contained about seven hundred chief tenants, and 60,215 knights' fees;[1] and as none of the English were admitted into the first rank, the few who retained their landed possessions were glad to be received under the protection of some powerful Norman baron, though at the cost of an oppressive burden on those estates which they had received as a free inheritance from their ancestors.[2]

Having broken the spirit of the laity, the Conqueror now proceeded to appropriate a large share of the enormous property of the clergy to his own use. The first step he took for the attainment of this object was to seize not only all the riches[3] and valuable effects which the English had lodged in the religious houses throughout the kingdom during the troubles, but even the charters, shrines, and treasures belonging to the monasteries themselves, resolving at the same time that none of the English monks or clergy should ever be preferred to any of the vacant sees, and that those who already possessed them should be stripped of their dignities. In consequence of this resolution, Stigand, Archbishop of Canterbury, was removed from his episcopal office on various groundless pretences, but without the colour of justice. Adding cruelty to injustice, William imprisoned the deprived prelates, and kept them in confinement all the rest of their lives. In this province, the king, during the feast of Pentecost, named Thomas, a canon of Bayeux, to the see of York. The principles he had adopted in Normandy he introduced into England, and seemed quite ready to act upon the determination he had made in the former country—namely, "that if any monk, who was his subject, should dispute his will, he would cause him to be hanged forthwith." In Saxon times, the clergy, not only in this province, but throughout the nation generally, held their lands and possessions by a different tenure from the laity, called *frank-almoigne*, subject to no secular service, to no rents or impositions, but such as they consented to lay upon themselves in their councils or synods, which privilege they had extorted, after some resistance, from the superstitious Æthelwulf. Their estates, derived from the bounty of the Saxon kings and their nobles, were so great, that they possessed more than a third part of the kingdom ; the computation being that of the 60,215 knights' fees the clergy held 28,015,[4] exclusive of their plate, jewels, and various other treasures. With such enormous riches at their disposal they became unduly powerful ; and William, jealous of that power, and suspicious of their fidelity, reduced all their lands to the common tenure of knights' service and barony. The new prelates were required to take an oath of fealty, and to do homage to the king, before they could be admitted to their temporalities ; they were also subject to an attendance upon the king in his court-baron, to follow him in his wars with their knights and quota of soldiers, to pay him their usual aids, and to perform all the other services incident to the feudal tenures. The clergy remonstrated most bitterly against this new revolution ; but William was inexorable, and consigned to prison or to banishment all who opposed his will. While the power of the clergy was thus curtailed, that of the barons, who were now chiefly Norman, was increased. In their manors they had absolute jurisdiction ; they gave laws and administered justice in their courts-baron to their vassals ; and suits between the tenants of different lords were tried in their hundred, or county courts, while the king's courts took cognisance only of those between the barons themselves.[5]

By a synod held in London (A.D. 1075) the precedency of the bishops was settled, according to the priority of their consecration, except with regard to such sees as had particular privileges annexed to them. "Hitherto the bishops had resided in small towns or villages, for the purpose, as was alleged, of sacred retirement; but at this synod it was determined that the see of Lichfield, in which diocese the greater part of Lancashire was at that time included, should be removed to Chester. It was now ordained, for the first time, that no bishop, abbot, or clergyman, should judge any person to the loss of life or limb, or give his vote or countenance to any other for that purpose ;" and to comply with this canon, the prelates have ever since withdrawn from the House of Lords in such cases, satisfying themselves with entering a protest in favour of their right, without exercising it.[6] The activity of William's mind suggested to him a great national work, which will

[1] Orderic. Vitalis, p. 523.
[2] The drenghes mentioned in the Domesday Book, "Newton Hundred," were probably of this number.—B.

[3] Sim. of Dur. Ann. of Waver. T. Sprott's Chron. p. 114.
[4] T. Sprott's Chron. p. 114.
[5] Carte's Hist. vol. I. p. 421.
[6] Brist. Monast. p. 33.

be held throughout all ages as a redeeming feature in his life, and will serve to transmit his memory with veneration to posterity.

"After the synod," says the Saxon Chronicle, "the king held a large meeting, and very deep consultation with the council, about this land; how it was occupied, and by what sort of men. Then sent he his men over all England into each shire, commissioning them to find out—'How many hundreds of hides were in the shire, what lands the king himself had, and what stock upon the land; or what dues he ought to have by the year from the shire.' Also he commissioned them to record in writing, 'How much land his archbishops had, and his diocesan bishops, and his abbots, and his earls; what or how much each man had, who was an occupier of land in England, either in land or stock, and how much money it was worth.' So very narrowly, indeed, did he commission them to trace it out, that there was not one single hide, nor a yard of land; nay, moreover (it is shameful to tell, though he thought it no shame to do it), not even an ox, nor a cow, nor a swine, was there left, that was not set down in his writ. And all the recorded particulars were afterwards brought to him." That nothing might be wanted to render this record complete, and its authority perpetual, the survey was executed by Norman commissioners, called "the king's justiciaries," consisting of nobles and bishops, acting under royal appointment, and associated, probably, with some of the principal men of each shire. The inquisitors, upon the oaths of the sheriffs, the lord of each manor, the presbyters of every church, the reeves of every hundred, the bailiffs and six villeins of every village, were to inquire into the name of the place, who held it in the time of King Edward, who was the present possessor, how many hides in the manor, how many carucates in demesne, how many homagers, how many villeins, how many cotarii, how many servi, what free-men, how many tenants in socage; what quantity of wood, how much meadow and pasture, what mills and fish-ponds; how much added or taken away, what the gross value in King Edward's time, and how much each free-man or soc-man had or has. All this was to be triply estimated: first, as the estate was held in the time of the Confessor; then, as it was bestowed by King William; and thirdly, as its value stood at the formation of the survey. The jurors were, moreover, to state whether any advance could be made in the value. The book contains, besides these details of property and tenure, many curious reports of the ancient rights and privileges of the people, and especially of the towns. The "Laws of King Edward," for which our Saxon ancestors so often and so stoutly contended in the earlier years of the Norman conquest, are nowhere to be found so clearly set forth as in this work of the very man who, not perhaps without reason, was generally accused and suspected of an intention to violate them.

The exact time occupied in taking the whole survey of the kingdom is differently stated by historians; but the probability is, that it was commenced A.D. 1080; and it is evident, from the date inserted at the end of the second volume, that it was completed in 1086. It is remarkable that in this survey the name of Lancashire does not occur; but that part of it which lies between the Ribble and the Mersey is surveyed under Cheshire, while the northern part of the county, including Amounderness and the hundred of Lonsdale, north and south of the Sands, is comprehended under Yorkshire. The devastation made by the Conqueror in the three most northern counties of England rendered it impossible to take an exact survey of that district; and the return in Amounderness, that "sixteen of the villages in this hundred have few inhabitants (how many is not known), and the rest are waste," sufficiently indicates that the hand of the spoiler had lain heavy upon that hundred. By the Domesday return the king acquired an exact knowledge of all the possessions of the crown. It furnished him with the means of ascertaining the strength of the country, pointed out the possibility of increasing the revenue in certain districts, and formed a perpetual register of appeal for those whose titles to their estates might in future be disputed. This purpose it has served ever since its completion; and even now, at the end of eight hundred years, such is the credit of this document, that if a question arises whether a manor, parish, or lands, be ancient demesne, the issue must be tried by this book, whence there is no appeal. The two volumes which contain the survey are now, by common consent, called Domesday Book, from Dome (*cenus*) and Boc (book). It has, however, borne other designations, and has been known as *Rotulus Wintoniæ, Scriptura Thesauri Regis, Liber de Wintonia,* and *Liber Regis.* Sir Henry Spelman adds, *Liber Judiciarius, Censualis Angliæ, Angliæ Notitia et Lustratio,* and *Rotula Regis.*[1]

---

[1] In the original edition, an attempt was made, by what has been called "Domesday type," to represent the numerous peculiarly abbreviated Latin words in this ancient record. All who care to read this, and the number must be very few, can now see the beautiful fac-simile of the original, taken by photo-zincography under the direction of Lieut.-Col. Sir Henry James, of the Ordnance Survey, which has been published in a separate vol. at a moderate price. We give the translation, as made from a careful examination of the fac-simile by William Beamont, Esq., of Orford Hall, Warrington, in his "Literal Extension and Translation of Domesday Book—Cheshire and Lancashire, etc."—and by his permission.

BETWEEN RIBBLE AND MERSEY.

[SOUTH LANCASHIRE.]

ROGER DE POICTOU HELD THE UNDERMENTIONED LAND BETWEEN RIBBLE AND MERSEY.

IN [WEST] DERBY HUNDRED.

Surveyed under the head of Cestre-Scire (Cheshire).

King Edward [the *Confessor*] had there one manor named *Derbei*, with six *Berewicks*.[1] There are four hides.[2] The land is fifteen carucates.[3] There is a forest two leagues[4] long and one broad ; and an aery of hawks.

Uctred held six manors, *Rabil* (ROBY), *Chelnulveslei* (KNOWSLEY), *Cherchebi* (KIRKBY), *Crosebi* (CROSBY), *Magele* (MAGHULL), and *Achetun* (AUGHTON I.) There are two hides [of land]. The woods are two leagues long and the same broad, and there are two aeries of hawks.

Dot held *Hitune* (HUYTON) and *Torboc* (TARBOCK). There is one hide quit of every custom duties but the gelt [danegeld[5]]. The land is four carucates. It was worth twenty shillings.

Bernulf held *S!ochestede* (TOXTETH I.) One virgate[6] and half a carucate of land there paid four shillings.

Stainulf held *Stochestede* (TOXTETH II.) There one virgate and half a carucate of land were worth four shillings.

Five Thanes held *Sextone* (SEFTON). There was one hide there worth sixteen shillings.

Uctred held *Chirchedele* (KIRKDALE). There is half a hide quit of every custom but the gelt. It was worth ten shillings.

Winestan held *Waletone* (WALTON-ON-THE-HILL). There were two carucates and three *bovates* [or oxgangs] of land worth eight shillings.

Elmœs held *Liderlant* (LITHERLAND). There was half a hide. It was worth eight shillings.

Three Thanes held *Hinne* (INCE BLUNDELL) for three manors. There was half a hide. It was worth eight shillings.

Ascha held *Torentun* (THORNTON). There was half a hide. It was worth eight shillings.

Three Thanes held *Mele* (MEOLS) for three manors. There is half a hide. It was worth eight shillings.

Uctred held *Ulventune* (LITTLE WOOLTON). There are two carucates of land, and half a league of wood. It was worth sixty-four pence.

Edelmund held *Esmedune* (SMITHDOWN, now LIVERPOOL). There is one carucate of land. It was worth thirty-two pence.

Three Thanes held *Alretune* (ALLERTON) for three manors. There is half a hide. It was worth eight shillings.

Uctred held *Spec* (SPEKE). There are two carucates of land. It was worth sixty-four pence.

Four Radmans [Knight Riders] held *Cildewelle* (CHILDWALL) for four manors. There is half a hide. It is worth eight shillings. There was a priest there having half a carucate of land in frank-almoin [free-alms].

Ulbert held *Wibaldeslei* (WINDLE, WINDLESHAW, WHISTON, BOLD, PARBOLD, and PRESCOT). There are two carucates of land. It was worth sixty-four pence.

Two Thanes held *Uvetone* (MUCH WOOLTON) for two manors. There is one carucate of land. It was worth thirty pence.

Leving held *Wavertreu* (WAVERTREE). There are two carucates of land. It was worth sixty-four pence.

Four Thanes held *Boltelai* (BOOTLE) for four manors. There are two carucates of land. It was worth sixty-four pence. A priest had one carucate of land to the church at *Waletone* (WALTON-ON-THE-HILL).

Uctred held *Achetun* (AUGHTON II.). There is one carucate of land. It was worth thirty-two pence.

Three Thanes held *Fornebei* (FORMBY) for three manors. There are four carucates of land. It was worth ten shillings.

Three Thanes held *Einulvesdel* (AINSDALE). There are two carucates of land. It was worth sixty-four pence.

Steinulf held *Hoiland* (DOWN HOLLAND). There are two carucates of land. It was worth sixty-four pence.

Uctred held *Daltone* (DALTON). There is one carucate of land. It was worth thirty-two pence.

The same *Uctred* [held] *Schelmeresdele* (SKELMERSDALE). There is one carucate of land. It was worth thirty-two pence.

The same *Uctred* [held] *Literland* (LITHERLAND II.) There is one carucate of land. It was worth thirty-two pence.

Wibert held *Erengermeles* (RAVEN'S MEOLS). There are two carucates of land. It was worth eight shillings. This land was quit [of every tax] except the gelt.

Five Thanes held *Otegrimele* (ORRELL in Sefton). There is half a hide. It was worth ten shillings.

Uctred held *Latune* (LATHOM) with one berewick. There is half a hide [of land]. There is a wood one league long and half a league broad. It was worth ten shillings and eightpence.

Uctred held *Hirletun* (HURLESTON, in Scarisbrick) and half of *Merretun* (MARTIN). There is half a hide. It was worth ten shillings and eightpence.

Godeve held *Melinge* (MELLING). There are two carucates of land ; [and] a wood one league long and half a league broad. It was worth ten shillings.

Uctred held *Leiate* (LYDIATE). There are six bovates of land ; [and] a wood one league long and two furlongs broad. It was worth sixty-four pence.

Two Thanes held six bovates of land for two manors in *Holand* (DOWN HOLLAND II.). It was worth two shillings.

Uctred held *Acrer* (ALTCAR). There is half a carucate of land. It was waste.

Teos held *Bartune* (BARTON in Down Holland). There is one carucate of land. It was worth thirty-two pence.

Chetel held *Heleshale* (HALSALL). There are two carucates of land. It was worth eight shillings.

All this land is rateable to the gelt ; and fifteen manors rendered nothing to *King Edward* but the gelt.

This manor of *Derbei* (WEST DERBY), with its aforesaid hides, rendered to *King Edward* in farm a rent of twenty-six pounds and two shillings. Three of these hides, the tax whereof the [king] remitted to the thanes who held them, were free: These rendered four pounds and fourteen shillings and eight pence.

---

[1] The *berewick* was a small manor belonging to a larger.

[2] The hide was an uncertain and variable quantity of land.

[3] The carucate, carve, or plough-land, was, like the hide, an uncertain and variable quantity of land. In the last line but three of the survey of Derby Hundred, are the words, "In every hide there are six carucates of land." This probably applies to all South Lancashire, within which the carucate was the sixth part of a hide, whatsoever quantity the latter implies.

[4] The *leuva*, here translated league, has often been rendered mile. It was half-way between a measure of length containing twelve furlongs, each of forty perches of five and a half yards long, or about as long as about a mile and a half of our present measure.—W. BEAMONT.

[5] Gelt or Dane-geld was a tax originating out of the practice of buying off the Danish invaders by the payment of large sums of money. The amount levied was originally one Saxon shilling (afterwards increased to two shillings) upon every hide of land in the kingdom. The tax was first imposed about the year 991, and the payment continued until the reign of Edward the Confessor, when, in consequence of the great discontent of the nation, it was remitted ; but in course of time, or in the Conqueror's reign, it seems to have been applied to the private purposes of the monarch.—C.

[6] The virgate, or yard-land, was two bovates or oxgangs, or one-fourth of a hide, and, like it, was a variable quantity.

All these thanes[1] were accustomed to render two ores[2] of pennies for each carucate of land; and by custom they, like the villeins, made the king's (manor) houses and what belonged to them; and (constructed) the fisheries, and the hays[3] and stands[4] in the wood. And whoever came not to these when he ought, was fined two shillings, and afterwards came and worked until the work was finished. Each of them sent his mowers one day in August to cut the king's corn. If he failed [herein] he was fined two shillings.

If any freeman committed theft, or forestel,[5] or broke the king's peace, he was fined forty shillings.

If any one shed blood, committed rape, or absented himself from the shiremote without reasonable excuse, he was fined ten shillings.

If he absented himself from the hundred court, or came not when there was a plea, and when he was summoned by the reeve, he made amends by five shillings.

If [the reeve] commanded anyone to go on a service [to which he was bound], and he did not go, he was fined four shillings.

If any one desired to withdraw from the king's land, he paid forty shillings, and had liberty to go where he would.

If any one desired to take up the land of his deceased father, he paid for it forty shillings as a relief.

If he was not willing to pay this, the king took both the land and all the father's cattle.

Uctred held *Crosebi* (CROSBY) and *Chirchedele* (KIRKDALE) for one hide, and was free of all customs but these six : breach of the peace, forestel, heinfare, continuing a fight after oath given [to the contrary], not paying a debt until after judgment given, and not keeping a time appointed him by the sheriff. The fine for these was forty shillings. They paid the king's gelt, however, like the rest of the country.

In *Otringemele* (ORRELL in Sefton) and *Herleshala* (HALSALL) and *Hiretun* (TARLETON), there were three hides free from the gelt of the carucates of land, and from forfeitures for blood or rape; but they rendered all other customs.

Of this manor of *Derbei* (WEST DERBY) the following men hold land by the gift of *Roger of Poictou* :—*Goisfrid* two hides and half a carucate, *Roger* one hide and a half, *William* one hide and a half, *Warin* half a hide, *Goisfrid* one hide, *Tetbald* one hide and a half, *Robert* two carucates of land, [and] *Gilebert* one carucate of land. These have four carucates in their demesne, and [there are] forty-six villeins,[6] and one radman,[7] and sixty-two bordars,[8] and two serfs,[9] and three maid-servants. They have among them twenty-four carucates. The wood is three leagues and a half long, and one league and a half and forty perches broad; and there are three aeries of hawks. The whole is worth eight pounds and twelve shillings. In every hide there are six carucates of land.

But the demesne of this manor, which *Roger* held, is worth eight pounds. In this demesne there are now three carucates and six neatherds, and one radman, and seven villeins.

IN NEWTON HUNDRED.

In *Newton* (NEWTON), in the time of *King Edward* [the *Confessor*], there were five hides. Of these one was in the demesne. The church of the same manor had one carucate of land; and *Saint Oswald* of the same vill had two carucates of land free of everything.

The other land of this manor, fifteen men called *Drenghes*[10] held for fifteen manors, which were berewicks[11] of this manor; and among them all these men rendered thirty shillings. There is wood there ten leagues long and six leagues and two furlongs broad, and there are aeries of hawks.

All the freemen of this hundred, except two, had the same custom as the men of *Derbeishire* [West Derby Hundred], but in August they mowed two days more than they on the king's tillage lands. The two [excepted men] had five carucates of land, and had the forfeitures for bloodshed, rape, and pannage [in the woods] for their men. The rest were the king's. This whole manor [of *Newton*] rendered to the king a farm of ten pounds ten shillings. Now there are six drenghes and twelve villeins, and four bordars, who have nine carucates amongst them. The demesne is worth four pounds.

IN WARRINGTON HUNDRED.

King Edward held *Walintune* (WARRINGTON) with three berewicks; there is one hide. To the same manor there belonged thirty-four drenghes, who had that number of manors; in which there were forty-two carucates of land, and one hide and a half. *Saint Elfin* held one carucate of land, free of all custom except the gelt. The whole manor with the hundred rendered to the king a farm rent of fifteen pounds less two shillings. There are now two carucates in the demesne, and eight men with one carucate.

These men hold land there : *Roger* one carucate of land, *Tetbald* one carucate and a half, *Warin* one carucate, *Radulf* five carucates, *William* two hides and four carucates of land, *Adelard* one hide and half a carucate, [and] *Osmund* one carucate of land. The whole is worth four pounds and ten shillings. The demesne is worth three pounds and ten shillings.

IN BLACKBURN HUNDRED.

King Edward held *Blacheburne* (BLACKBURN). There are two hides and two carucates of land. Of this land the church had two carucates; and the church of St. Mary in *Whalley* two carucates of land, [both of them] free of all customs. In the same manor there is a wood one league long and the same broad, and there was an aery of hawks.

To this manor or hundred were attached twenty-eight freemen, holding five hides and a half and forty carucates of land for twenty-eight manors. There is a wood there six leagues long and four broad, and [the manors] were all subject to the above customs.

In the same hundred *King Edward* had *Hunnicot* (HUNCOTE, near Dunkenhalgh), two carucates of land, and *Waletune* (WALTON-LE-DALE) two carucates, and *Peniltune* (PENDLETON) half a hide. The whole manor, with the hundred, yielded the king a farm-rent of thirty-two pounds and two shillings.

Roger de Poictou gave all this land to *Roger de Busli* and *Albert Greslet*, and there are so many men who have eleven carucates and a half; to whom they have granted freedom [from all customs] for three years, wherefore it is not now valued.

---

[1] Thanes were the nobility and gentry.

[2] The ora was not a coin, but money of computation, each ora being worth twenty pence.—W. B.

[3] Hays: railed or hedged enclosures in the forest. –C.

[4] *Stabiliture* were the stands, stalls, or stations in the forest, where the deer might be aimed at and taken with less difficulty.—W. B.

[5] *Forestel* (to steal before another) was the assaulting or obstructing of any person on the king's highway. *Heinfare* (q.d. bind-departing) was a forfeiture for flight for murder, for killing the lord's servant or hind, or for enticing or inveigling him away.

[6] Villeins or *villani*, so named from *villa*, a country farm, whereat they were dependant to do service. They were unfree, registered as of the soil, and bound to till the lord's lands, holding by the base tenure called villenage.—C.

[7] Radman: a feudal vassal, attendant on the lord as his guard: the more modern name being retainer. –C.

[8] Bordars were a class of small, unfree cottage tenants, bound to supply the lord with poultry and eggs, and other small provisions for his board or entertainment.—C.

[9] Bondmen.—C.

[10] Drenghes held their lands (manors or berewicks) by free-socage, or, in Anglo-Norman, "frank-ferme;" the services of which were not only certain but honourable. According to Spelman they were such as at the coming of the Conqueror, being put out of their estates, were afterwards restored thereunto, on their making it appear their were owners thereof, and neither in *auxilio* or *consilio* against him. ·-C.

[11] Berewicks were villages or hamlets belonging to a manor, of which mesne manors were made.- C.

IN SALFORD HUNDRED.

King Edward held *alford*. There are three hides and twelve carucates of [barren or] waste land. There is a forest three leagues long and the same broad. There are many hays and an aery of hawks there.

King Edward held *Radeclive* (RADCLIFFE) for a manor. There is one hide, and another hide there belongs to *Salford*. The church of St. Mary and the church of St. Michael held in *Mamecestre* (Manchester) one carucate of land, free from all customs but the gelt.

To this manor or hundred belonged twenty-one berewicks, which so many thanes held for so many manors, in which there were eleven hides and a half and ten carucates and a half of land. The woods there are nine leagues and a half long and five leagues and a furlong broad.

One of these thanes, *Gamel*, holding two hides of land in *Recedham* (ROCHDALE), was free of all customs but these six, viz, theft, heinfare, forestel, breach of the peace, not keeping the term set him by the reeve, and continuing a fight after an oath given to the contrary. The fine for these was forty shillings. Some of these lands were free from every custom except gelt, and some were free even from the gelt.

The whole manor of Salford with the hundred rendered thirty-seven pounds and four shillings. Of this manor there are now in the demesne two carucates and [there are] eight serfs and two villeins with one carucate. The demesne is worth one hundred shillings.

Of the land of this manor these knights hold, by the gift of *Roger de Poictou*: [i.e.] *Nigel* three hides and half a carucate of land, *Warin* two carucates of land, another *Warin* one carucate and a half, *Goisfrid* one carucate, and *Gamel* two carucates of land. In these [lands] there are three thanes and thirteen villeins, and nine bordars, and one priest, and ten serfs: they have twenty-two carucates amongst them. The whole is worth seven pounds.

IN LEYLAND HUNDRED.

King Edward held *Lailand* (LEYLAND). There is one hide and two carucates of land. There is a wood two leagues long and one broad, an aery of hawks. To this manor there belonged twelve carucates of land, which twelve freemen held as so many manors. In these there were six hides and eight carucates of land. The woods there are six leagues long and three leagues and a furlong broad. The men of this manor and of *Salford* were not bound by the custom to work at the king's hall, or to reap for him in August. They only made one hay in the wood; and they had the forfeiture for bloodshed and rape. In the other customs of the other manors above [mentioned] they bore their part. The whole manor of *Leyland*, with the hundred, rendered to the king a farm-rent of nineteen pounds and eighteen shillings and twopence. Of the land of this manor *Hirard* holds one side and a half, *Robert* holds three carucates, *Radulph* two carucates of land, *Roger* two carucates of land, [and] *Walter* one carucate of land. There are four radmans, a priest, and fourteen villeins, and six bordars and two neatherds there. They have eight carucates among them. There is a wood three leagues long and two leagues broad, and there are four aeries of hawks there. The whole is worth fifty shillings. It is in part waste.

King Edward held *Peneverdant* (PENWORTHAM). There are two carucates of land, and it rendered tenpence. There is now a castle there. In the demesne there are two carucates, and six burgesses, and three radmans and eight villeins, and four neatherds. They have four carucates among them all. There is half a fishery. There are a wood and series of hawks, as in the time of *King Edward*. It is worth three pounds.

In these six hundreds, of *Derby, Newton, Warrington, Blackburn, Salford,* and *Leyland,* there are one hundred and eighty-eight manors. In which there are eighty hides, less one, rateable to the gelt. In the time of *King Edward* the whole was worth one hundred and forty-five pounds and two shillings and twopence. When *Roger of Poictou* received it from the king it was worth one hundred and twenty pounds. The king now holds it, and has in his demesne twelve carucates, and [there are] nine knights holding a fee. Amongst them and their men there are one hundred and fifteen carucates and three oxen. The demesne which *Roger* held is valued at twenty-three pounds and ten shillings. What he bestowed on his knights, at twenty pounds and eleven shillings.

[NORTH LANCASHIRE.]

Surveyed under the head of Euruicscire (Yorkshire).

AMOUNDERNESS.

In *Prestune* (PRESTON) Earl *Tosti*[1] had six carucates rateable to the gelt, and to it these lands belong :—

Estun (ASHTON-ON-RIBBLE) two carucates ; *Lea* (LEA) one carucate ; *Salewic* (SALWICK) one carucate ; *Cliftun* (CLIFTON) two carucates ; *Neutune* (NEWTON with SCALES) two carucates ; *Frecheltun* (FRECKLETON) four carucates ; *Rigbi* (RIBBY with WRAY) six carucates.

Chicheham (KIRKHAM) four carucates ; *Treueles* (two carucates) ; *Westbi* (WESTBY) two carucates ; *Pluntun* (LITTLE PLUMPTON) two carucates ; *Widetun* (WEETON) three carucates ; *Pres* (PREESE), two carucates ; *Wartun* (WARTON), four carucates.

Lidun (LYTHAM) two carucates ; *Meretun* (MARTON in POULTON) six carucates ; *Latun* (LATTON with WARBRECK) six carucates ; *Staininghe* (STAINING) six carucates ; *Carlentun* (CARLETON) four carucates ; *Biscopham* (BISPHAM) eight carucates.

Rushale (ROSSALL), two carucates ; *Brune* (BRINING) two carucates ; *Torenton* (THORNTON) six carucates ; *Poltun* (POULTON in the FYLDE) two carucates ; *Singletun* (SINGLETON) six carucates ; *Greneholf* (GREENHALGH) three carucates.

Eglestun (ECCLESTON) four carucates ; another *Eglestun* (ECCLESTON, Great and Little) two carucates ; *Edeleswic* (ELSWICK) three carucates ; *Inscip* (INSKIP) two carucates ; *Sorbi* (SOWERBY) one carucate ; *Aschebi* (NATEBY) one carucate.

Michelesecherche (ST. MICHLE-LE-WYRE) two carucates ; *Catrehale* (CATTERALL) two carucates ; *Clactune* (CLAUGHTON) two carucates ; *Neuhuse* (NEWHOUSE or NEWSHAM) one carucate ; *Pluntun* (GREAT PLUMPTON) five carucates.

Brocton (BROUGHTON) one carucate ; *Witingheham* (WHITTINGHAM) two carucates ; *Bartun* (BARTON in PRESTON) three carucates ; *Gusansarghe* (GOOSNARGH) one carucate ; *Halctun* (HAIGHTON) one carucate.

Trelefelt (THRELFALL in the FYLDE) one carucate ; *Watelei* (WHEATLEY) one carucate ; *Chipinden* (CHIPPING)[2] three carucates ; *Actun* (ALSTON) one carucate ; *Fiscuic* (FISHWICK) one carucate ; *Grimesarge* (GRIMSARGH) two carucates.

Ribelcastre (RIBCHESTER)[3] two carucates ; *Bilevirde* (BILLBOROUGH) two [or three] carucates ; *Suenesat* (SWAINSET) one carucate ; *Fortune* (FORTON) one carucate ; *Crimeles* (CRIMBLES) one carucate ; *Cherestanc* (GARSTANG) six carucates ; *Rodecliff* (RAWCLIFFE) two carucates ; another *Rodeclif* (RAWCLIFFE) two [or three] carucates ; a third *Rodeclif* (Upper, Middle, and Out) three carucates ; *Hameltune* (HAMBLETON) two carucates.

---

[1] Tosti or Tostig was second son of Earl Godwine and brother of Harold the last of the Saxon kings; he was chief minister of state to Edward the Confessor, and succeeded Siward in the Earldom of Northumberland He was slain at the battle of Stamford Bridge, September 25th, 1066.—C

[2] Chipping and Ribchester are now in Blackburn Hundred. -C.

Stalmine (STALMINE) four carucates ; *Pressouide* (PREESALL) six carucates ; *Midehope* (MYTHORP or MYTHOP) one carucate.

All these villa belong to *Prestune* (PRESTON) ; and there are three churches. In sixteen of these vills there are but few inhabitants ; but how many there are is not known.

The rest are waste.[1] *Roger de Poictou* had [the whole].

[IN LONSDALE VALE.]

In *Haltun* (HALTON) Manor *Earl Tosti* had six carucates of land rateable to the gelt.

In *Aldeclif* (ALDCLIFF) two carucates ; *Tiernun* (THORNHAM) two carucates ; *Hillun* (HILLHAM) one carucate ; *Loncastre* (LANCASTER) six carucates ; *Chercaloncastre* (CHURCH LANCASTER) two carucates.

Hotun (HUTTON) two carucates ; *Neutun* (NEWTON) two carucates ; *Ouretun* (OVERTON) four carucates ; *Middeltun* (MIDDLETON) four carucates ; *Hietune* (HEATON) four carucates ; *Hessam* (HEYSHAM) four carucates.

Oxeneclif (OXCLIFF) two carucates ; *Poltune* (POULTON-LE-SANDS) two carucates ; *Toredholme* (TORRISHOLME) two carucates ; *Schertune* (SKERTON) six carucates ; *Bare* (BARE) two carucates ; *Sline* (SLYNE) six carucates.

Bodeltone (BOLTON) four carucates ; *Chellet* (KELLET) six carucates ; *Stopeltierne* (STAPLETON-TERNE) two carucates ; *Neuhuse* (NEWSOME) two carucates ; *Chreneforde* (CARNFORTH) two carucates.

All these villa belong to *Haltune* (HALTON).

In *Witetune* (WHITTINGTON) Manor *Earl Tosti* had six carucates of land r. teable to the gelt.

In *Neutune* (NEWTON) two carucates ; *Ergune* (ARKHOLME) six carucates ; *Ghersinctune* (GRESSINGHAM) two carucates ; *Hotun* (HUTTON) three carucates ; *Cantesfelt* (CANTSFIELD) three carucates.

Irebi (IRKBY) three carucates ; *Borch* (BURROW)[2] three carucates ; *Lech* (LECK) three carucates [all in Lancashire]. *Borctune* (BURTON-IN-LONSDALE) four carucates ; *Bennulfeswic* (BARNOLDSWICK) one carucate ; *Inglestune* (INGLETON) [in Yorkshire] six carucates.

Costretune (CASTERTON) [in Westmorland] three carucates ; *Berebrune* (BARBON) [Westmorland] three carucates ; *Sedberge* (SEDBERGH, in Yorkshire) three carucates ; *Tiernebi* (TIERNSIDE, in Westmorland) six carucates.

All these villa belong to *Witetune* (WHITTINGTON).

TWELVE MANORS.—In *Ovstevric* and *Heldetune* (AUSTWICK, in Yorkshire, and KILLINGTON, in Westmorland) [there are twelve manors—viz.], *Clapeham* (CLAPHAM, in Yorkshire), *Middelun* (MIDDLETON, Westmorland), *Manzerge* (MANSERGH, Westmorland), *Cherchebi* (KIRKBY-LONSDALE), *Lupetun* (LUPTON, Westmorland), *Prestun* (PRESTON PATRICK, Westmorland), *Holme* (HOLME, Westmorland), *Bortun* (BURTON, Westmorland), *Hotune* (HUTTON ROOF, Westmorland).

Wartun (WARTON), *Clactun* (CLAUGHTON), *Catun* (CATON). These *Torfin* held for twelve manors.

In these there are forty-three carucates rateable to the gelt.

FOUR MANORS.—In *Benetain* (BENTHAM, Yorkshire) [there are four manors—viz.] *Wininctune* (WENNINGTON), *Tathaim* (TATHAM), *Farleton* (FARLTON), *Tunestalle* (TUNSTALL).

Chetel had [these for] four manors, and there are in them eighteen carucates rateable to the gelt, and three churches.

In *Hougun Manor* (HAWCOAT in Dalton, Furness and Furness Fells) *Earl Tosti* had four carucates of land rateable to the gelt.

In *Chilvestrevic* (KILLERWICK) three carucates ; *Sourebi* (SOWERBY) three carucates ; *Hietun* (HEATON) four carucates ; *Daltune* (DALTON) two carucates ; *Warte* (SWARTH) four carucates ; *Neutun* (NEWTON) six carucates.

Walletun (WALTON) six carucates ; *Suntun* (SANTON) two carucates ; *Fordebodele* two carucates ; *Rosse* (ROOSE) six carucates ; *Hert* (HERT) two carucates ; *Lies* (LEECE) six carucates ; another *Lies* (LEECE) two carucates.[3] *Glassertun* (GLEASTON) two carucates ; *Steintun* (STAINTON) two carucates ; *Cliverton* (CLIVERTON)[4] four carucates ; *Ouregrive* (ORGRAVE, now called TITEUP) three carucates ; *Meretun* (MARTON, alias MARTIN) four carucates ; *Pennigetun* (PENNINGTON) two carucates ; *Gerleuuorde* (KIRKBY-IRELETH) two carucates ; *Borch* (BURROW) six carucates ; *Berretscige* (BARDSEY) four carucates ; *Wiingham* (WITTINGHAM) four carucates ; *Bodele* (BOOTLE, in Cumberland) four carucates.

Santacherche (KIRK-SANTON) one carucate ; *Hougenai* (WALNEY) six carucates. All these villa belong to *Hougun* (FURNESS).

NINE MANORS.—In *Stircaland* (STRICKLAND) [there are nine manors—viz.] *Mimet* (MINET), *Cherchebi* (KIRKBY-KENDAL), *Helsingetune* (HELSINGTON), *Steintun* (STAINTON), *Bodelforde* (BODELFORD), *Hotun* (OLD HUTTON), *Bortun* (BURTON-IN-KENDAL, Westmorland), *Daltun* (DALTON-IN-KENDAL, Lancashire), *Patun* (PATTON-IN-KENDAL, Westmorland).

Gilemichel had these. In them are twenty carucates of land rateable to the gelt.

MANOR.—In *Cherchebi* (KIRKBY-KENDAL) [Manor] *Duvan* has six carucates so rateable.

MANOR.—In *Aldinghame* (ALDINGHAM in Furness) [Manor] *Ernulf* had six carucates so rateable.

MANOR.—In *Ulurestun* (ULVERSTON) *Turulf* has six carucates so rateable.

In *Bodeltun* (BOLTON with URSWICK) there are six carucates ; in *Dene* (DEAN) one carucate.

THE KING'S LAND IN CRAVEN, WEST RIDING, YORKSHIRE.

In *Mellinge* (MELLING), *Hornebi* (HORNBY), and *Wenningetun* (WENINGTON) [Manor], *Ulf* had nine carucates rateable to the gelt.

In *Berewicc* (BORWICK), *Orme* had one carucate and a half so rateable.

THE LAND OF ROGER OF POICTOU.

In the two MANORS of *Lanesdale* and *Cocreham* (LONSADLE and COCKERHAM) *Ulf* and *Machel* had two carucates rateable to the gelt,

In the three MANORS of *Estun* (ASHTON), *Ellhale* (Ellel), and *Scozforde* (SCOTFORTH) *Cliber*, *Machern*, and *Ghilemichel*, had six carucates liable to the gelt ; [i.e., in *Estun* two carucates] ; in *Ellhale* (ELLEL) two carucates ; in *Scozforde* (SCOTFORTH) two carucates.

In *Biedun* Manor (BEETHAM, Westmorland), *Earl Tosti* had six carucates rateable to the gelt ; *Roger of Poictou* now has them, and *Ernuin*, a priest under him. In *Jalant* (YEALAND CONYERS) four carucates ; in *Fureltun* (FARLETON) four carucates ; in *Prestun* (PRESTON RICHARD, Westmorland) three carucates.

In *Berewicc* (BORWICK) two carucates ; in *Hennecastre* (HINCASTER, Westmorland) two carucates ; in *Euresheim* (HEVERSHAM, Westmorland) two carucates ; in *Lefuenes* (LEVENS, Westmorland) two carucates.[5]

---

[1] The following townships and hamlets are not mentioned in the above account—much land in this part lay *waste*, viz., *Barnacre with Bonds, Norbeck, Bleasdale, Brockholes, Kellamergh, Catus Clevely, Fullwood, Thistleton, Hardhorn with Newton, Holleth, Hothersall, Kirkland, Warbrick, Ingol and Cottom, Medler, Witham, Pilling, Ribbleston, Wray, Wyresdair, Larbrick, Esprech, Roseacre, Wharless, Ewes, Bartell with Cutyforth,* and other places, all in Amounderness.—C.

[2] Overborough.—C.

[3] *Fordebodule, Hert,* and one or two of the Leeces, were all on the coast, and are said to have been washed away by the sea.— W. Beamont.

[4] Chiverton, which stood on the banks at the lower end of Cartmel, has been washed away by the sea.

[5] Under the heads " Yorkshire, the Land of Gospatric West Riding," and " The King's Land in Yorkshire," Mr. Beamont has introduced the following two entries, which are not found in this part of the Domesday Survey, as photo-zincographed, but which undoubtedly relate to Ulverstone, the capital of Furness, in Lancashire : " In *Ulvestone* (ULVERSTON) manor, *Gospatric* had six carucates of land rateable to the gelt. The land is three carucates. There are now there four villeins, but they do not plough. The vill is a league long, and half as broad. In King Edward's time it was worth twenty shillings, now ten shillings." " In *Ulvestone* (ULVERSTONE) manor, *Gospatric* held six carucates rateable to the gelt. The land is two carucates."

Of the different ranks of men mentioned in the Domesday Survey, it may be stated briefly that the *barons* were of two classes—the greater, or king's barons, who held directly of the crown; and the smaller barons, or those of the county who held under the earl. *Thane* was the Saxon equivalent for the Norman baron. At the period of Domesday Survey thanes were, however, of three classes: (1) the king's thanes, holding directly from the crown; (2) those holding under nobles, lords of mesne manors, or vavasors; and (3) franklins, freeholders, or yeomen, called thanes, from their lands being hereditary and their tenure free. Again, there were two classes of thanes—the ecclesiastic, called in Saxon mass-thanes, and the temporal or secular thanes. Both of these were again divided into two classes; the greater thanes were next in rank to earls, being the king's thanes, and called Barones Regis. The inferior the Saxons called the less thanes, without any addition, as the smaller barons, such as lords of manors, the less valvasores, or vavasors, and freeholders. After the invasion of the Normans, many military men of that rank and appellation, endowed with the title of knight, were called by the name of thanes, and afterwards of *milites* or *equites*—knights. *Freemen* were all holders of land by free, as distinguished from servile, tenure. *Radmans*, or road-men, were probably riders or horsemen, not always free; *drenghes* were a sort of allodial tenants, between the freemen and the villeins, rendering services to the lord, but personally exempt from the performance of them, which was done by the villeins holding under them. *Bordars* held their small portion of land by the service of supplying the lord's *board* or table with poultry, eggs, and other small articles of food. The *neatherds (bovarii)* or hinds tended the cattle, etc., and were less servile than the *villeins*, whose tenure and service were servile, and who were either *regardant*, or attached to the land, or *in gross*—*i.e.* attached to the person of their lord, who was able to sell or dispose of them at his pleasure. The *serfs (servi)* were bond men and women employed only in and about their lord's house. The villeins appear to have corresponded to the Saxon *ceorls*, as the serfs did to the Saxon *theows* or slaves.

The great baronial proprietors, both Saxon and Norman, of the "Honor of Lancaster" were amongst the most unfortunate of their order. The Earls Morcar and Tostig had suffered the fate so common to men in exalted stations in those turbulent times; and Roger de Poictou, the third son of Roger de Montgomery, though endowed with three hundred and ninety-eight manors, as the reward of the services rendered by his family to the Conqueror, was doomed to surrender them all as the price of his rebellion. The proprietors, at the time of taking the survey, had greatly increased in number, and the manners and customs of the people, as developed in the survey of the six hundreds between the Mersey and the Ribble, form the most valuable feature of this ancient record.[1] The tenure by which the thanes held the land in the hundred of Derby was—two ores of pennies for a carucate: this must have been most indulgent as far as the rent was concerned, but the obligation to build the king's houses, to attend his fisheries, to repair his fences, and to reap his harvest, would add not a little to the pressure upon the thanes. Such was the inequality of the laws in these times that in some districts—Orrel, Halsall, and Everton, for instance—the occupiers were exempt not only from the principal tax (dane-geld), but they were exonerated from the punishment justly due to some crimes of the greatest enormity; while, in other places, the offence of rape, and of the tenant absenting himself from the shire-mote or hundred court, were to be punished with the same severity—viz., a fine of ten shillings! It appears also that there were in these six hundreds one hundred and eighty-eight manors, and that their annual value, when Roger de Poictou received them from the king, was scarcely equal to that of a small estate in our times. The contrast between the nature of landed possessions in this district, in the time when the dane-geld tax was enforced in 1086, and the time when the property-tax existed in 1814, is the most striking; in the former all the lands between Mersey and Ribble were valued at £120—in the latter at £2,569,761. Allowing for the difference in the value of money at the two periods, the statement will stand thus:—

$$
\begin{aligned}
\text{Annual value in 1086, £120} \times 110 = \quad &\text{£13,200} \\
\text{In 1814} \quad \dots \quad \dots \quad \dots \quad &2,569,761 \\
\cline{2-2}
\text{Increased value} \quad \dots \quad &\text{£2,556,561}
\end{aligned}
$$

The Saxon titles consisted of Etheling, Heretog, Ealderman, and Thane, but they all merged at the Conquest into the more general and comprehensive title of Norman Baron. At the head of the *Capitanei Regni*, or chiefs of the realm, in the earlier of these periods, stood the Ethelings. These

[1] The appellation *Christis Crofte* was anciently given to this tract, and it is celebrated as a place of security in troublesome times, in the following metrical prophecy:—

> "When all England is alofte,
> Safe are they that are in Christis Crofte :
> And where should Christis Crofte be
> But between Ribble and Mersey."

were noble persons of the first rank, as princes sprung from the blood royal, and were endowed accordingly with great fees and offices in the kingdom. Of this description was Edgar Etheling, but the Conquest deprived him of his inheritance. Amongst the Saxons were certain magistrates called aldermen. These were princes and governors of provinces, earls, presidents, senators, tribunes, and the like. They were of different ranks, as *Aldermannus totius Angliæ* (the alderman of all England), in later times imagined to be *capitalis Angliæ Justiciarus* (chief justice of England); *Aldermannus Regis* (king's alderman), so called because he was constituted by the king, or that he exercised regal authority in the province committed to his charge; *Aldermannus Comitatûs* (of a county), sometimes taken *pro Schyreman et ipso Comite* (for the shireman and the comes or earl himself). The office of alderman was to inspect the county's arms, and to raise forces within his jurisdiction; to repress the refractory, and to promote public justice. The bishops were nobles inferior in rank to earls. By the laws of Alfred and Æthelstan, the lives of the dignitaries, both in the church and state, were valued, and the rate at which their heads were estimated serves to show their relative dignity. The head of the archbishop, the earl, or satrap, was valued at 15,000 thrymses; the bishop and alderman, at 8,000; the *Belli Imperator et summus præpositus* (the commander and chief officer of war), or vice-comes (sheriff), at 4,000 thrymses. From which it appears that the alderman held the middle station between the earl and the sheriff. After the Conquest, the alderman's office grew out of use, and was superseded almost entirely by the sheriff.

Honors were hereditable before the Conquest by earls and barons, and for the most part to such as were of the blood-royal; hence the honor of Lancaster had been possessed successively by earls Tostig and Morcar. By the Norman law, honors became a feudal patrimony of any of the high barons, generally adjoined to the principal seat of the baron. The great baron of Lancashire, Roger de Poictou, so called from having married Almodis of Poictou, ranked amongst the Capitales Barones, holding immediately from the crown. The barons who held of him were called Barones Comitatûs (barons of the county), and held free courts for all pleas and complaints, except those belonging to the earl's sword. The ancient barons in their lordships or baronies took cognisance of litigation and robberies, and enjoyed and used the privileges which are called sac, soc, tol, theam, infangthef, fairs, and markets.[1] The distinction between an honor and a manor consists principally in the much greater extent for the former, and in the courts held in each. A manor was composed of demesne and services, to which belong a three weeks' court, where the free-holders, being tenants of the manor, sit covered, and give judgment in all suits that are there pleading. But an honor has either a castle, as at Lancaster, or at least the site of a castle, or some principal house of state, and consists of demesnes and services, to which a number of manors and lordships, with all their appurtenances and other regalities, are annexed. To every manor a court baron is attached. In an honor, an honorable court is kept once every year at least, and oftener if required, at which court all the freeholders of all the manors which stand united to the honor make their appearance, and in which suitors do not sit, but stand bareheaded. Over that court should be hung a cloth of state, with a chair of state, upon which chair should be laid a cushion made of cloth of gold, or what is becoming and decent for a place of honour, and upon which there ought to be embroidered the arms belonging to the honor.

The barons of the honor of Lancaster, in the time of the Conqueror, are thus set forth in Kenion's MSS. :—

"LIST OF BARONS COM. LANC. under Roger de Poictou. Godefridus, his sheriff of Derby—Yardfridus, Baron of Widnes—Paganus Villers, Baron of Warrington—Albertus Grelle, Baron of Manchester—Burun [Byron], Baron of Ratchdale and Totington—Ilbert Lacy, Baron of Clitheroe—Warinus, Baron of Newton—Warinus Bushli or Bushel, Baron of Penwortham—Roger de Montbegon, Baron of Hornby—William Marshall, Baron of Cartmel—Michael Flemingus, Baron of Glaston—William de Lancaster and Robert de Furness, Barons of Ulverston—Wil. de Lancaster, Baron of Nether Wiresdal—Theobaldus *Walter*, Baron of Weeton."—*N.B.*—Another copy says, "Theob. *Pincerna*" (*i.e.* the Butler).

Roger Montgomery, or Roger de Poictou, as he is more commonly designated, the grantee of the greater part of what afterwards became the county of Lancaster, and the richest and most powerful of all the Conqueror's feudatories, forms such an important figure in the history of Lancashire in Norman times as to render some notice of him necessary. The members of the House of Montgomery took a leading part in the affairs of France and Normandy during many generations prior to the fight at Hastings, and French as well as English chroniclers have given many, though sometimes confusing and contradictory, statements concerning them. They were descended from one of the fierce Scandinavian adventurers, who, under Rollo and previous

---

[1] *Sac* was the power of administering justice; *Soc*, of hearing and determining causes and disputes, with the power of levying forfeitures and fines; *Tol*, an acquittance from payment of duties or tolls in every part of the kingdom; *Theam*, a royalty granted over their villein tenants, as well as over their wives and children and goods, to dispose of them at pleasure. Spelman calls it a right of trying their bondmen and serfs. *Infangthef* was the privilege of trying thieves taken within their lordship; *Outfangthef*, a royalty granted by the king, with power to try and punish a thief dwelling out of the baron's liberty or fee, for a theft committed out of his jurisdiction, if he be taken within it.

invaders, settled in the province of Neustria, and gave its new name to Normandy, and appear to have derived their patronymic from their fief or estate—Mons Gommerici or Montgomery in the department of Calvados. There is a charter contained in the chartulary of Troarn which is said to have been founded by Roger Montgomery, son of Roger Magnus, or the great Roger, and the great grandfather of Roger de Poictou, in 1022, in which he somewhat arrogantly describes himself as *Rogerius ex Northmannis Northmannus Magni antem Rogerii filius*—Roger a Norseman among the Norsemen—indicating that he was a Northman rather than a Norman, and consequently of the older race of the wave which flowed from the North prior to the time of Rollo. The interests of the family were largely advanced by a fortunate marriage made by Hugh, the eldest of the five sons of Roger Montgomery, a descendant of the haughty Norseman, with Joscelini, one of the nieces, or an illegitimate daughter, as has been suggested, of Gunnor, wife of Richard I., Duke of Normandy. The eldest son of the marriage carried the fortunes of the family to still greater heights, and laid the foundation of his territorial influence by his marriage with Mabel, daughter and eventually heir of William Talvace, Earl of Belesme and Perch, an alliance by which his position was at once established—the house of Belesme being, as there is evidence to believe, a branch of the ducal house of Normandy. Through his wife, this Roger represented the greatest family in Normandy, next to that of the ducal house, and it was possibly in right of his wife that he ranked among the earls. The marriage is stated by Mr. Planché, though on what authority does not appear, to have taken place in 1048, and a dozen years later he had conferred upon him, on the forfeiture for treachery by Turstin, the viscounty of Exmes or Hiesmois, a district or county which in early times was held as an appanage by the sons of the Norman dukes. Mr. Freeman relying very much upon the testimony of Wace, affirms that this Roger was one of the companions of Duke William at Hastings, in 1066, and that he commanded one of the divisions of the army engaged in that famous conflict. Wace gives some minute particulars as to his share in the fight, but his name does not occur on the roll of Battle Abbey, and Orderic Vitalis states distinctly that at the time of the expedition he was left with Matilda, the duke's wife, as governor of Normandy. Mr. Planché has expressed a doubt as to the reliability of Wace's statement, and still more recently Mr. Howorth has endeavoured to show that it was not Roger who married the heiress of Belesme, but his younger son of the same name—Roger de Poictou, the grantee of Lancashire; but if Mr. Planché's statement is correct that the marriage with Mabel of Belesme took place in 1048, the third son of that marriage must have been too young in 1066 to have been entrusted with the command of an important division at Hastings. Whether Roger, the father, was at Hastings, or left at the head of Matilda's council in 1066, certain it is that at the end of the following year he attended the Conqueror on his return to England, and then had conferred upon him the earldoms of Chichester and Arundel, as he had subsequently those of Shrewsbury and Montgomery—the last being the only Norman name given to a county in this island. By his marriage with the rich heiress of William Talvace, Earl Roger had five sons and four daughters. Robert, the eldest, became Count of Belesme. Hugh, the second, succeeded to the earldoms of Arundel and Shrewsbury; but it is with the third son, Roger, that we are more immediately concerned. He married Almodis, Countess de la Marche, in her own right, which title was used by Roger and his descendants as Count de la Marche in Poictiers, from which circumstance he was commonly known as Roger of Poictou, and it was on this Roger was conferred the vast possessions in Lancashire, with lands in Yorkshire, Derbyshire, Nottinghamshire, and Leicestershire, in all 398 manors. Like many a proud noble, both before and since his time, Roger de Poictou had his head turned by the extent of his possessions, and rebelled against his sovereign. Having towards the close of William's reign espoused the cause of Duke Robert of Normandy, the Conqueror's eldest son, he was, for his defection, deprived of his honours and estates, which passed into the possession of the Crown. On the accession of William Rufus they were restored to him, in the hope that he would support the claim of the usurper, which he did; but on the death of the king he declared for the real heir, Robert, against the recognised successor, Henry, when he was again deprived of his possessions and banished the kingdom, his princely inheritance passing to the king.

In tracing the barony of Lancaster, we find the founder of this illustrious house to have been Ivo de Talebois, otherwise Taillebois, otherwise Talboys, of the house of Anjou, who came over with the Conqueror, and who, in virtue of his marriage with Lucy, the sister of the Saxon Earls Edwin and Morcar, seconded by the favour of his prince, obtained a large portion of the north of Lancashire, and so much of Westmorland as comes under the designation of the barony of Kendal. The Richmond Fee, the Marquis Fee, and the Lumley Fee, formed portions of this barony, and William, the great-grandson of Ivo de Talebois, first caused himself, by royal licence, to be called William de Lancaster and Baron of Kendal, before the king in Parliament.

PEDIGREE OF **ROGER DE POICTOU,** LORD OF THE HONOR OF LANCASTER.

Roger de Montgomery, son of Rogerus Magnus ; founder of Troarn (1022) ; exiled in Paris 1037 = ...

Roger.   Robert,   Hugh de Montgomery = Joceline, niece of Gunnor,   William, killed by   Gilbert, killed by
            living in 1060.   Duchess of Normandy.   Barno de Glotis,   Barno de Glotis,
                                                                                1060.   1060.

(1) Mabel, dau. and even- = Roger de Montgomery, = (2) Adeliza, dau. of   Gilbert, poisoned   Other issue.
tually heir of William   Viscount of Exmes ;   Everard de Pusay,   by his sister-in-
Talvace, Ct. of Belesme ;   created Earl of Arundel, standard bearer   law, Mabel
mar. c. 1048 ; died 1086.   Chichester, Shrews-   of Robert Curt-   Belesme, in 1065.
                            bury, and Montgomery;   hose, Duke of
                            died 1094.   Normandy.

Everard de Montgomery, chaplain to
King Henry I.

Robertde Montgomery,   Hugh, Earl of   Roger, surnamed = Almodis, dau. of   Arnold, Earl of   Philip died   1. Emma, Abbess of
Count of Belesme,   Arundel and   of Poictou,   Audebert, 2nd   Pembroke,   at the   Almeneches.
Earl of Arundel,   Shrewsbury,   Earl of Lan-   Count de la   mar. the dau.   siege of   2. Maud, wife of
Shrewsbury, &c.,   1094 ; slain in caster, Count   Marche, in   of the King of   Antioch.   Robert, Earl of
1098 ; forfeited his   battle in   de la Marche   Poictiers,   Leinster ; ban-   Mortain, half-
English earldom in   Anglesea,   in right of his   widow of . . .   ished with her   brother of
1102 ; imprisoned at   1098 ; died   wife ; banished   brothers Robt.   William the
Wareham by Henry   childless ; 2nd in 1102 ; 3rd   and Roger in   Conqueror.
I., 1113 ; married   son.   son.   1102 ; died   3. Mabel, wife of
Agnes, daughter and   childless.   Hugh de Neu-
heir of Guy, Count   chatel.
of Ponthieu ; 1st son.   4. Sybil, wife of
                                                                                                             Robert Fitz
                                                                                                             Hamon, Lord of
                                                                                                             Corboil, in Nor-
                                                                                                             mandy, and in
                                                                                                             Glamorgan, of
                                                                                                             Wales.

Audebert, 3rd Count = Oungarde.   Eudes.   Boson.   Ponce, wife of Walgrave, 2nd Count
de la Marche ; died   of Angouleme.
1145.

Audebert, 4th Count =   Bosun.   Margaret, wife of Guy, Viscount   Sybil, wife of . . .
de la Marche.   of Limoges.   de Reigni.

Audebert, 5th Count de la Marche. Sold his county to Henry II., King of England, 1177.

"SUCCESSION OF THE BARONS OF LANCASHIRE.—1. Sheriff of Derby, Godfrid, Peverel, Ferrers. 2. Castellan of Liverpool, Molineux. 3. Barony of Widness, divided between Lacy and Grelly. 4. Barony of Warington, Paganus, afterwards Butler. 5. Barony of Newton, Langton. 6. Barony of Manchester, Grelly [La Warre], West, Mosley. 7. Barony of Rochdale, Baldwin Teutonicus, afterwards Byron. 8. Barony of Cliderow, Lacy, the Crown, Monk, Montague. 9. Barony of Penwortham, Bussell, Lacy, the Priory, Fleetwood. 10. Barony of Hornby, Roger de Montbegon. 11. Barony of Furnes, Michael Fleming. 12. Barony of Wiresdale, Wm. de Lancaster. 13. Barony of Weeton and Amounderness, Theobald Walter."[1]

"STATIONS OF THE ANCIENT BARONS.[2]—Roger de Poictou, Earl of Lancaster, prudently stationed his barons in the most vulnerable places, to preserve his earldom in quiet. 1. He built a castle at Liverpool against the passage over the water from Cheshire, and there placed his trusty friend, Vivian Molineux, to be governor and castellanus in the utmost limits of his earldom ;[3] and for his greater assistance he placed near him, at Derby, his vice-comes, Godefridus ; and not far above, at or opposite Runcorn, being another passage out of Cheshire, he fixed Yardfrid, another baron, at Widness ; and a little above that, at Warrington, another passage, and near unto the church, was the seat of another barony, given to Paganus Villers, to defend the ford at Latchford, before a bridge was made at Warrington ; and a little distance, at Newton, was the seat of the Banisters, a barony in King John's time, to strengthen the former, and opposite a high ford or boat called Holyn Farc Passage, out of Cheshire, at Stratford, as well as to keep guard against another Cheshire barony, called Stockport, he placed Albertus Grelle, an eminent baron ; then approaching the hilly mountain from Yorkshire, at a different passage from Ratchdale, an ancient barony, afterwards succeeded by Lord Buryn, the present

---

[1] From Percival's MSS. The barony of Cartmel appears to be omitted.
[2] From Kenion's MSS.
[3] A castellanus is the prefect or governor of a castle, acting there in place of the lord, and sometimes called castaldus, gustaldius ; his office is called castaldia, castallanea being first the name of an office and afterwards of a dignity. These castellans were appointed by dukes and earls, who enjoyed vast territories, and in some fortified places stationed military guards or garrisons to repel enemies. They were civil judges,

to determine the disputes of the people. Having become powerful, and the sons often succeeding to the father's office, they at last obtained from the lords the right of holding office in fee ; and by little and little passing the bounds of their jurisdiction, they transformed the wand of an inferior justice into the sword of the superior, making the force of the dignity to consist more in the fulness of baronial power than in the mere name of baron. Spelman, p. 128, voce Castellanus.

baron thereof ; then ascending easterly among those hills at Clidero, he placed Ilbert Lacy, a baron, near the adjacent passage into Yorkshire ; and more northward, not far from his own castle at Lancaster, at Hornby, he placed Roger de Montbegon. Then upon the northern boundary, from the Scots in Cumberland, was placed at Gleston, Michael Flandrensis ; and shortly after the abbot of Furness (4th W. Rufus, 1090-1), placed upon the west part, possessing the Foldra and Walney, who convened with William de Lancaster ; and long afterwards the king bestowed the same upon Ingelianus de Guyas in marriage with his sister ; afterwards it was alienated, and came to the possession of the families of Kirkby and Tells. From thence returning southward to Kartmel, which in King John's time came to William de Marshall, governor to King Henry III., and proceeding southward on the river Wyre, one side guarded by William de Lancaster, lord of that part of the barony of Netherwyrsdal belonging likewise to the lords of Furness, and the other side environed with the barony of Weeton, which (temp. W. Rufus) was an appendant to the barony of Penwortham, and bestowed upon Abardus Bussell, brother of Warinus Bussell, and continued in the renowned noble family of Thobaldus Pincerna, from whom proceeded the Duke of Ormond. And lastly, on that famous estuary of Ribble at Penwortham, where remained an ancient castle from the time of the Saxons, here was placed the barony given to Warinus Bussell, who had this place bestowed upon him temp. William the Conqueror, though it had then no baron. Leyland and great part of Amounderness did anciently belong to the Bussells, for in the survey temp. Will. I., I find one Rog. de Busli and Albert Greslet, who had Blackburn hundred, and afterwards, upon division between them, Greslet had part of Leyland hundred, as Brindle, Worthington, etc. . . . and a knight's fee in Dalton, Wrightington, and P. . . .[1] which he gave in marriage with a daughter to one Orme, the son of Edward of Ashton-under-Line. Montbegon had another part of Leyland hundred, which he held as annexed to Hornby, as most part of Croston parish—viz. Croston, Madeley, Chorley, Haskenmore, Tarlton ; and Hole, formerly part of Warinus's barony, belonged to the Villers, and afterwards to Montbegon, as likewise Sherington, Welsh Whittle, and Chernoc Gogard, Adlington, and Duxbury belonged to Greslet. N.B.—The baron of Warington had divers territories in Derby hundred to be assistant to the baron of Derby, and a fee or two in the hundred of Amounderness, as the baron of Manchester held divers fees in the hundred of Leyland ; the baron of Newton a knight's fee in Blackburn hundred," etc.[2]

The more particular succession of the barons of Lancashire will be most advantageously treated in the hundreds to which the baronies belong ; but the rise of the honor into a duchy, and the achievements of the noble and royal house of Lancaster, from the Conquest to the period when they attained the consummation of their dignity, by giving a sovereign to the throne of England, belong to this portion of our history.

The castle of Lancaster, built by Roger de Poictou, not only served as a military fortress to preserve the power of his royal benefactor, but it was used also as the baronial residence. It appears from the "Baronia de Manchester," that Robert Busli held Blackburn hundred on a temporary tenure only for three years, hence it was not appropriated before Lacy was its lord ; and the probability is that he held under De Poictou. In the reign of Rufus, Roger de Poictou granted a charter to our Lady of Lancaster, to which Albert Greslet, the first baron of Manchester, was a witness.[3] In the interval between the first division of property, under the Norman dynasty and the Domesday Survey, the possessions of Roger were forfeited to the crown, by his defection from the royal cause. The honor of Lancaster was, however, restored to him in the time of William Rufus, but it was finally alienated on the banishment of Roger, in 2 Henry I. (1102). From that time it remained in the crown till it was bestowed on Ranulf de Bricasard (styled also De Meschines), the third Earl of Chester. The precise time when this grant was made, and the circumstances which called for so strong a manifestation of the royal bounty, are not ascertained ; but the following translation of an almost illegible charter in the British Museum sufficiently authenticates the fact[4] :—

"RANULF, Earl of Chester, to his constable, dapifer, justiciaries, sheriffs, and bailiff, that are betwixt Ribble and Mersey, and to all his men, French and English, greeting :—Know me to have granted and confirmed to the Abbot of Evesham, and the monks there serving God, all possessions, lands, and tenements, and all liberties given and granted by Warin and Albert Buissel in all things ; and also that they may have their courts in Hocwice of all their tenants, as truly as I have mine at Penwortham, for him and all his tenants, housebote and haybote, for building or burning, and useful for all other his necessities, without disturbance of me, or of any in my name, or of any other whatsoever. I also will and firmly command, that no man against the same monks, concerning my grant and confirmation, shall interfere upon any occasion, exaction, or confirmation. I will warrant the aforesaid abbot, convent, and their successors, without fine or demand, for fear of my forfeiture, but they shall hold the same freely and honourably in all places ; and I, Ranulf, and my heirs, the aforesaid concession and confirmation to the aforesaid abbot and their successors will warrant and without fine.—Teste meipso."

---

[1] Probable Parbold.
[2] It is right to state that these lists of baronies and barons, derived from the MSS. of Kenion and Percival, have no satisfactory authority.—H.
[3] Kuerden's MSS., folio 271.
[4] Harl. MSS., cod 7386.

CHAPTER IV.

URING the disturbed reign of Stephen, Ranulf or Randle, surnamed "De Gernons," from the place of his birth,[1] the fourth Palatine Earl of Chester, after having surprised the castle of Lincoln, and taken the king prisoner in the decisive battle fought there, February 2, 1141, possessed himself of a third part of the whole realm of England,[2] and amongst his possessions were the lands ceded to his father, Randle de Meschines, between the Ribble and the Mersey. From Ranulf or Randle, the son, they descended (1153-55) to Hugh de Kevelioc, and in 1180 to Ranulf or Randle, surnamed "De Blundeville," son of Hugh, and grandson of the second Randle. Ranulf de Blundeville, surnamed "The Good," in 13 Henry III. (1228), had a confirmation from the king of all his lands between the Ribble and the Mersey, and was made chief lord, under the king, of the whole county of Lancaster, with all its forests, hays, homages, and other appurtenances. At the same time he executed the office of sheriff by his deputies in the third, fourth, fifth, sixth, and ninth years of that king. Ranulf paid down forty marks of silver for these lands to Roger de Maresey, and afterwards two hundred marks more; and agreed further to render annually, at Easter, a pair of white gloves, or one penny, for all services whatsoever. This earl, who built the castle of Beeston, in Cheshire, and founded the abbey of Dieu-la-Cres, near Leek, in Staffordshire, after enjoying his possessions for many years, died at Wallingford, Nov., 1232, and was buried at Chester. Having no legitimate issue, his whole inheritance was shared by his four sisters and co-heiresses. Maud, the eldest, married David, Earl of Huntingdon, brother to William, King of Scots, and by him had John, surnamed "The Scot," who succeeded to the earldom of Chester;[3] Mabil, the next, married William de Albini, Earl of Arundel; Agnes, the third sister, married William, Earl Ferrers, the sixth in lineal descent from Robert de Ferrers, raised by King Stephen to the earldom of Derby, for his prowess at the Battle of the Standard, in the third year of his reign (1137). The heirs of the first Earl of Derby were usually called Earls Ferrers, though they were likewise Earls of Derby. This Agnes had the manor and castle of Chartley, in Staffordshire, and the lands in that part of Wales called Powis; and also the manor of West Derby, and all Earl Ranulf's lands between the Ribble and Mersey; with Buckbrock in Northamptonshire, and Navenby in Lincolnshire. In the eighth Henry III. (1223-4) William, Earl Ferrers, was constituted governor of the castle and honor of Lancaster;[4] and the next year he executed the sheriff's office for this county for three parts of the year, as he did likewise for the whole of the tenth and the eleventh years of the king's reign (1225-7). In addition to £50 for the relief of the lands of his wife's inheritance, he and she were bound to pay yearly a goshawk, or fifty shillings, into the king's exchequer, as had been usual for lands lying between the rivers Ribble and Mersey. In 26 Henry III. (1241) he gave a fine of £100 to the king for the livery of the three hundreds of West Derby, Leyland, and Salford, which had been seized into the king's hands for certain misdemeanours of his bailiffs. This earl died on the 20th of September, 1247, and his countess survived him only one month—they having lived together as man and wife seventy-seven years. William, Earl Ferrers, son and heir of the above earl and countess, had

---

[1] Gernon, or Vernon, in Normandy, the letters G and V in the beginning of words being indifferently used.—C.

[2] Nichols's Leicestershire, to which we have been much indebted for the historical materials relating to the illustrious house of Lancaster.—B.

[3] This John, the seventh palatine earl, married Helen, daughter of Llewellyn, Prince of North Wales. He died childless in 1237, having, as is believed, been poisoned by his wife, when his possession should by right have devolved upon his sisters, but Henry III., unwilling, as he said, "that so great an inheritance should be divided among distaffs,"

took the earldom into his own hands, and gave them other lands instead. Of these sisters, Margaret, the eldest, was grandmother of John Baliol, who became a competitor for the crown of Scotland. Isabella, the second sister, married Robert le Brus, Lord of Annandale, and was grandmother of the heroic Robert Bruce—the "Bruce of Bannockburn."—C.

[4] Dugdale's Baron. ex Pat. 8, n. 3, m. 12. There were eight Earls of Derby of this family, whose name seems to have been spelled *Ferrers*; whilst that of their descendants, of Chartley, Tamworth, and Groby, is usually spelled *Ferrers*.—H.

livery of his lands and castle in the year 1247; and the next year he obtained a mandate to the sheriff of Lancashire for the enjoyment of such lands between Ribble and Mersey as his uncle Ranulf, Earl of Chester, formerly possessed. He also obtained a charter for free warren, for himself and his heirs, in all his demesne, throughout his lordships in Lancashire and elsewhere. Three years afterwards he procured a special grant from the king of such officers, for conservation of the peace between Ribble and Mersey, as Ranulf, Earl of Chester, formerly had, which officers were maintained at the expense of the inhabitants. By Margaret, his second wife, one of the daughters and co-heiresses of Roger de Quincy, Earl of Winchester, he had two sons. Robert succeeded him in the earldom of Derby, and settled at Groby, in Leicestershire. This unfortunate earl took part with Simon de Montfort, Earl of Leicester, in the rebellion, and was in consequence deprived of his earldom and all his estates in 1265, among which were all his lands between Ribble and Mersey. These possessions Henry III. united with the honor of Lancaster, and gave to Edmund, surnamed "Crouchback,"[1] his youngest son, who, by that king's favour, was created first Earl of Lancaster in 1267; and thus terminated the connection of the great families of the Earls of Chester and Ferrers with the county.

EARLS OF LANCASTER.

Edmund Crouchback was the distinguished favourite of his father; and on St. Luke's Day (October 18), in the year 1253, the king convened many of his nobles, along with the Bishop of Romania, who came to him from Pope Innocent IV., and having brought a ring from his Holiness, used it as a symbol to invest Edmund with the dominion of Sicily and Apulia, whereupon he had the title of King of Sicily. This grant produced some of the most important events in our history; amongst others, the association of the barons against Henry III.; the appointing of conservators of the peace in this and the other counties of England; and the settling of the democratical part of our constitution on a permanent basis by Simon de Montfort, Earl of Leicester, while the king was his prisoner. Prince Edmund, about the same time that he took the title of King of Sicily, was made Earl of Chester. Upon Innocent's death, Alexander VI. confirmed Prince Edmund in the grant of the kingdom of Sicily in due form, but he never obtained possession; but Pope Urban VI., by a bull in 1263, having revoked the deed, Edmund renounced the claim to the crown of that kingdom. The prince was amply compensated for the loss of that imaginary power, for on the 4th of August, 1265, his brother Edward having defeated the Earl of Leicester and his adherents, in the battle of Evesham, the king, by his letters-patent bearing date the the 25th of October, created him Earl of Leicester, giving him therewith the honor of Hinckley and the stewardship of England. The next year he received from his royal father the honor, town, and castle of Derby, with all the effects belonging to Robert de Ferrers, Earl of Derby. In addition to other grants he received also the honor, earldom, castle, and town of Lancaster, with the forests of Wyresdale and Lonesdale.[2]

The following year (1267) the king announced to his knights, vassals, and other tenants of the honor of Lancaster, that he had given to his son Edmund that honor, with the wards, reliefs, and escheats attached to it. In the same year, during the king's residence at York, he issued a declaration, from which it appears, that although he granted the possessions in the county of Lancaster to his son Edmund, for his sustentation, that grant was not to operate to the injury of Roger de Lancaster. The royal bounty was still further extended in the following year by a grant from the king of possessions forfeited by the treason of Simon de Montfort.[3] In the year 1284

[1] Edmund Crouchback was so named, not, as is commonly supposed, from any deformity of person, but from his having worn a cross upon his back in token of a crusading vow.

[2] In a footnote on this page Mr. Baines gives the substance of various royal grants, &c., to Edmund Crouchback, in the original Latin, for which we have substituted an English translation of the essential parts of these documents:—

1. (51 Henry III. 1266-67).—The king grants to Edmund, his son, his castle of Kenilworth, and that he may have free chace and free warren in all demesne lands and woods belonging to the castle.

2. (Idem).—The king grants to the forenamed Edmund the honor, castle, and manor of Monmouth, with appurtenances.

3. (Idem).—The king grants to the forenamed Edmund the castles of Grossemunde, Skenefrith, and Blauncbastel.

4. (June 30, 51 Henry III. 1267).—Henry, king, &c., grants, &c., to our most dear son Edmund, the honor, earldom, castle, and vill of Lancaster, with the vaccaries and forests of Wiresdale and Lonsdale, and Newcastle-under-Lyne; and the manor, castle, and forest of Pickering; and our vill of Goninemecestr [Godmanchester]; and the rent of our vill of Huntingdon, with all appurtenances. To have, &c., with knights' fees, advowsons of churches, charters, liberties, customs, and all other things, to the honor, earldom, castle, villa, demesne, vaccaries, forests, and rent aforesaid, appertaining, &c. Witnesses—John de Warren, Earl

of Surrey; Humfrey de Bohun, Earl of Hereford and Essex; Philip Basset; Roger de Somery; Alan la Rusche; Stephen de Eddeworthe; Bartholomew de Bigod, and others. Given by our hand at St. Paul's, London, 30th June, in the 51st year of our reign [1267].

[3] Three more Latin documents are appended in notes to this page, of which the following is the substance:—

1. (52 Henry III. 1268).—The king, to the knights, freemen, and all other tenants of the honor of Lancaster, greeting. Whereas we have lately given to Edmund our son the aforesaid honor, with wards, reliefs, escheats, and all other things appurtenant and belonging to that honor, &c. We command that to the same Edmund and his heirs, in all things that to the same honor belong, ye may be attentive (or maintenant) and answering. Witness the king at Westminster, 8th February, 52nd year of his reign. [8th February, 1268.]

2. (52 Henry III. 1268).—The king, &c.: Whereas we formerly (or lately) committed to our beloved and faithful Roger de Lancaster our county of Lancaster, with appurtenances, that he might have its keeping while he lived, so that he rendered to us yearly one hundred marks [£66 13s. 4d.] to our exchequer; and afterwards that county, with its appurtenances, we granted to our most dear son Edmund towards his maintenance; We, willing in this respect to the same Roger, make our special promise to him in good faith, that in the premises we will preserve him free from any injury to which he may be liable at times. Witness the

Edward I., in an inspeximus, dated at Lincoln on the 18th of August, confirmed the grant of the honor of Lancaster made by Henry III. to his brother Edmund, and forbade the sheriffs of Norfolk, Suffolk, Lincoln, Nottingham, Leicester, Derby, York, Rutland, and Stafford, or their officers from entering the honor of Lancaster.[1]

These vast possessions laid the foundation of the future greatness of the house of Lancaster, the power and influence of which increased to such a magnitude as ultimately to seat the family on the throne of these realms.   In 21 Edward I. (1291) Prince Edmund procured licence to make a castle of his house in the parish of St. Clement Danes, in the county of Middlesex, called the Savoy; and he founded that house of nuns of the order of St. Clara called the Minoresses, without Aldgate, in London. He also was the chief builder of the Grey-friars house in Preston, in this county. This great earl, by Blanche, his second wife (his first wife, Aveline, daughter and heir of William de Fortibus, Earl of Albemarle, died childless in the year of her marriage, 1269), daughter of Robert, earl of Artois (third son of Lewis VIII., King of France), and widow of Henry of Navarre, had three sons—Thomas, Henry, and John—and a daughter. In 24 Edward I. (1296), being sent with the Earl of Lincoln and twenty-six bannerets into Gascony, they sat down before Bordeaux; but, seeing no likelihood of its surrender, they marched to Bayonne. Here their army began to dissolve, on account of their treasure being exhausted, and Prince Edmund became so much affected by the embarrassments of their situation that he fell sick and died, about the feast of Pentecost (May 13), 1296.

Thomas, Earl of Lancaster, the eldest son and immediate successor of Prince Edmund, did homage in 26 Edward I. (1297-8), and had livery of his lands, except the dowry of Blanche, his mother. After this ceremony, he marched into Scotland through Lancashire, the king himself being in the expedition. Being sheriff of Lancashire by inheritance, he appointed Richard de Hoghton his deputy in that office. In the next year he was summoned to Parliament by the king. In 4 Edward II. (1310) he married Alice, the sole daughter of Henry de Lacy, Earl of Lincoln, and, in virtue of that marriage, became possessed of the castles and lands belonging to that distinguished house. With this accession of property the Earl of Lancaster became the most opulent as well as the most powerful subject in England, and possessed in his own right, and that of his wife, no fewer than six earldoms, attended with all the jurisdictions and power which in that age, and under the feudal system, were annexed to landed possessions. In the following year he was the chief of those nobles who entered into a combination against Piers de Gaveston, the king's Gascon favourite, who had bestowed on him the nick-name of "The Old Hog," with the avowed intention of defending the religion of the state, and restoring the people's liberties. Being made choice of by the barons for their general, the Earl of Lancaster sent messengers to the king, requiring the delivery of Piers into their hands, or that he should be banished the realm. Such was the inveteracy of the nobles against the royal favourite that it is said that Henry de Lacy charged his son-in-law, the Earl of Lancaster, upon his deathbed, that he should maintain his quarrel against Gaveston. This injunction the earl faithfully obeyed, and, after a protracted struggle with the king, the Earls of Lancaster, Hereford, and Arundel, having seized Gaveston in the castle of Warwick, conveyed him to Blacklow Hill, a little knoll on the road near Guy's Cliff, where his head was struck off without the formality of a trial (1312). The king soon after hearkened to terms of accommodation, and granted to the Earl of Lancaster, and to the other delinquent barons, pardon of their offence, stipulating only that they should, on their knees, ask his forgiveness in public.[2] With these mild conditions they very cheerfully complied, and having made their submission they were again received into the royal favour. Gaveston was succeeded in the royal confidence by Hugh le Despenser, or Spenser, and by his father, a venerable nobleman, whose wisdom and moderation were not sufficient to check the opposite qualities in his son. No sooner was Edward's attachment declared for the Spensers, than the turbulent barons, headed

king, at York, 15th September, 52nd year of his reign. [15th September, 1268.]

3. (53 Henry III. 1269).—The king to all his bailiffs, &c.: Whereas by our charter we have given and granted to our son Edmund the honor, vill, and castle of Leicester, and all the lands and tenements of the same honor, with knights' fees, and other its appurtenances, which formerly belonged to Simon de Montfort, Earl of Leicester, our enemy, and which, according to the law and custom of our kingdom, by the war which he excited against us in our kingdom, and by the battle in which at Evesham he, our enemy, was slain, became forfeit and escheated to us—to have, &c., to the same Edmund for ever: We, willing to show our grace more fully to the same son, grant to him the stewardship of England, which the same Simon formerly had, to have, &c., for the whole of his life, with all things pertaining to the said stewardship, of our special grace. Witness the king, at Windsor, 9th May, in the 53rd year of his reign. [9th May, 1269.]

[1] This inspeximus of Edward I. recites the original grant of his father

Henry III., and confirms it: The king, &c. We have inspected the letters which our father the Lord Henry [III.], of renowned memory, made to our dearest brother Edmund, Earl of Lancaster, in these words: "Henry, &c., to the sheriffs of the counties [named in the text], and to all other sheriffs and stewards in whose bailiwicks the honor of Lancaster exists, greeting." [After reciting the grant of the honor, &c., this confirmation forbids the sheriffs enumerated either to enter themselves or to send or permit their bailiffs to enter or intermeddle with anything belonging to that honor, or to the men of the honor, unless required to do so by the bailiffs of his said son. If any of them or their bailiffs should find or discover anything of those which to that honor belong, they are without delay to render it to the bailiffs of his said son. They are not to distrain on any tenants of the honor, unless required by the bailiffs of the earl.] "Witness myself at Lincoln, the 18th day of August, in the 52nd year of our reign." [18th August, 1268.]—We accept these letters [patent] for ourselves and our heirs in the form aforesaid, &c.

[2] Ryley, p. 558.

again by the Earl of Lancaster, concerted plans for their ruin, and manifested their discontent by withdrawing from Parliament. One gross act of injustice so alarmed the Earl of Hereford that he complained to Thomas, Earl of Lancaster, who thereupon mustered a number of the barons, with their adherents, at Shireburne, and from thence marched, armed and with banners, to St. Albans, on their way plundering the manors of the elder Spenser as they previously had those of the son, and with the determination to reform the administration of the government. The barons next marched to London with all their forces, stationed themselves in the neighbourhood of that city, and exhibited before the Parliament, which was then sitting, charges against the Spensers, who were both of them at that time absent from the country. These charges the lay-barons declared to be proved, and passed a sentence of attainder and perpetual exile against the ministers as enemies of the king and his people (1321). The Commons, though now an estate in Parliament, were yet so little considered, that their assent was not required; and even the votes of the prelates were dispensed with on the present occasion. To secure themselves against consequences, the barons obtained from the king an indemnity for their illegal proceedings.[1] The following year the king raised a powerful army, with which he marched into Wales, and so far recovered confidence in his own strength as to recall the Spensers. Many of the barons, considering their cause hopeless, sent in their submission; but the Earl of Lancaster, in order to prevent the total ruin of his party, summoned together his vassals and retainers, and, having received the promise of reinforcements, advanced with his forces against the king, who had collected an army of thirty thousand men. The earl, being aware of the inferiority of his own force, despatched into Lancashire Sir Robert de Holland (whom he had advanced from the humble office of his butler to the dignity of knighthood, with a stipend of two thousand marks [£1,333] per annum), to bring up five hundred men out of that county. The required force was raised without difficulty, but the knight, it is commonly asserted, instead of bringing them to the earl, conducted them to the king. The statement is, however, unsupported by any reliable evidence. Sir Robert de Holland, after the defeat at Burton-on-Trent, surrendered to the king and escaped the penalty of death, but the whole of his vast possessions were confiscated to the crown. There was a belief that he had acted faithlessly to the Earl of Lancaster, and in consequence he incurred such hatred from the people that, being found in a wood near Henley-on-Thames (2 Edward III., 1328), he was seized and beheaded on the nones (7th) of October, and his head sent to Henry, Earl of Lancaster, then at Waltham Cross. The charge of treachery has, however, never been established, and was, in all probability, devised by the adherents of Earl Henry to secure his removal, and thereby prevent his becoming repossessed of the manors which had been conferred upon him by Earl Thomas. This is evident by the efforts made by Earl Henry to prevent the restoration of the confiscated lands. On the 17th February, 1 Edward III. (1327), the sheriffs were directed to seize into the king's hands all the confiscated estates, in order that they might be restored to their owners.[2] In the same year Robert de Holland, and Matilda, his wife, complain, by petition, that the king's writ of December 2nd has not been obeyed by the sheriffs, and they pray for an Exchequer certification of their property then in the king's hands.[3] The certificate was granted, on which Sir Robert was opposed in council by the Earl of Lancaster, who alleged that the writs directed to the sheriffs for livery of lands in their possession were contrary to form and law, and prayed that they might be revoked.[4] The proceedings in this case are at great length, but Sir Robert was finally reinstated. The Earl of Lancaster marched to his castle at Pontefract, the ancient seat of the Lacys. Having called a council of the barons by whom he was surrounded, which sat in the Black-friars in Pontefract, they advised him to march to Dunstanburgh, in Northumberland; but this advice he declined, and resolved to remain at Pontefract, whereupon Sir Roger de Clifford, one of his knights, drawing out his dagger, swore that he would plunge it into the breast of the earl if he would not submit to the counsel that had been given to him. Under the influence of these cogent arguments the earl quitted Pontefract and marched to Boroughbridge, where, finding the country-people in arms, and William, Lord Latimer, then governor of the city of York, and Sir Andrew de Harcla, warden of Carlisle and the Marches, ready to encounter him, the battle commenced without delay. The first discharge of arrows from the archers of the royal army proved so fatal to the Lancasterian force that the earl betook himself to a chapel, which he refused to yield to Harcla, though he saw his force partly dispersed and partly destroyed. Looking on the crucifix in the chapel, he said: "Good Lord, I render myself to Thee, and put myself into Thy mercy." His prayers were unavailing: the royal forces entered the chapel, and the earl was made prisoner. To add indignity to his misfortune, his

---

[1] Tottle's Collect., part ii., p. 54.   [2] Rot. Parlt. v. ii. p. 1, et seq   [3] Ibid, p. 29.   [4] Ibid, p. 18.

enemies took off his coat of armour, and putting upon him one of his men's liveries, they carried him first to York and afterwards to Pontefract, where he was pelted by the mob, and confined in the tower of the castle. "Being brought into the hall, in the presence of the king, he had sentence of death by these justices, viz., Aymer, Earl of Pembroke, Edmund, Earl of Kent, John de Bretaigne, and Sir Robert Malmethorpe. His defence was not listened to by his judges, and the earl, in the bitterness of his complaint, exclaimed, 'Shall I die without answer?' After quitting the court he was exposed to fresh insults, and being set upon a wretched horse, without bridle, he was paraded through the streets with a friar's hood upon his head. On his way to the place of execution, he cried, 'King of heaven, have mercy on me! for the king of the earth *nous ad guerthi* (hath abandoned us).' Having arrived at a hill without the town, he knelt down towards the east, until Hugin de Muston caused him to turn his face towards Scotland, when an executioner from London cut off his head (March 22, 1322)." A number of the earl's followers were afterwards condemned and executed, others fled beyond the seas, and, for a time, the public tranquillity was restored. His character is differently estimated. His partisans represented him as a saint; his enemies as a sinner, and that of no ordinary magnitude. By the former he is said to have wrought miracles after his death; by the latter he is described as a turbulent subject, an arbitrary master, and a faithless husband. The just way to estimate his character is to make due allowance for the prejudices both of his friends and his enemies, and the conclusion will then be that he was a munificent benefactor to the poor, a devoted adherent to his own order, and a man of more than ordinary mental powers; while, at the same time, he was ambitious, incontinent, and disloyal. Many miracles were reported to have been wrought at the tomb of this Earl of Lancaster; and the people flocked in great numbers to the place of his execution, till the king, at the instance of the Spensers, set guards to restrain them. So great indeed was the veneration paid to him that they worshipped his picture, which, with other things, was painted on a tablet in St. Paul's Cathedral, London, till the king, by his special letters to the bishop, dated from York, in June, 1323, inhibited them from so doing. Notwithstanding this inhibition, the memory of the deceased earl was cherished with the deepest veneration; and it was generally believed, in that age of superstition, that, in addition to other miracles, blood issued from his tomb. In the reign of Edward III. the king, in compliance with the wishes of his subjects, presented a petition to the pope, beseeching him to grant canonisation to the departed earl Thomas;[1] but it does not appear that this saint was ever added to the calendar.

Ancient slander asserts that Alice, the wife of Thomas, Earl of Lancaster, was repudiated by her husband, on account of her familiarity with Sir Ebulo le Strange, a younger son of Lord Strange, of Knockin. However this may be, after the death of her husband she was married by Sir Ebulo without the king's licence; and all the lands of her inheritance, which were held of the king *in capite*, were seized and detained. This confiscation was not relaxed till she delivered up those lands which lay in the counties of Lancaster, Chester, and York, and gave the castle and lordship of Denbigh, in Wales, and also the castle of Bullingbrook, in the county of Lincoln, and lands in other parts of the kingdom, unto Hugh le Despenser, the royal favourite. After being divested of these immense possessions, the lands which she still held amounted to no less a sum in annual value than 3,000 marks (£2,000). At the death of this lady, which occurred in 1348, all the lands of that great inheritance, which descended to her from Henry de Lacy, late Earl of Lincoln, by virtue of the grant made by her father and by the grant of King Edward I., came to Henry, Earl of Lancaster, afterwards the Duke of Lancaster, which lands lay in the Blackburn hundred, Rochdale, Tottington, and Penwortham, in the county of Lancaster; Halton in the county of Chester; Bowland and Snaith, in the county of York; and divers other parts of the kingdom.

A household book of Thomas, Earl of Lancaster, preserved in the records of Pontefract, and quoted by Stow, exhibits a curious illustration of the manners and customs of the early part of the fourteenth century. This book, kept by Henry Leicester, his cofferer, shows the amount of the disbursements of Thomas, Earl of Lancaster, in his domestic expenses, for the year 1313, which were no less than £7,359 13s. 0¾d. At that time silver was of the value of one shilling and eightpence the ounce, or 20s. the pound troy. His total expenses, therefore, in one year, amounted in our money to about twenty-two thousand pounds—an immense amount, when the great disparity in the price of provisions between that time and this is considered.

---

[1] Rot. Rom. et Franc. 1 Edw. III. [1327] n. 4 in Turr. Lond.

HOUSEHOLD BOOK OF THOMAS, EARL OF LANCASTER, IN THE YEAR 1313.

	£	s.	d.
Charge of the pantry, buttery, and kitchen	3405	0	0
To 184 tuns 1 pipe of red or claret wine, and two tuns of white wine	104	17	6
To grocery	180	17	0
To 6 barrels of sturgeon	19	0	0
To 6,800 stock-fishes, so-called, and for dried fishes of all sorts, as lings, haberdines [salted cod], &c.	41	6	7
To 1,714 pounds of wax, vermilion, and turpentine	314	7	4½
To 2,319 pounds of tallow-candles for the household, and 1870 of lights for Paris candles called perchers	31	14	3
To charge of the earl's great horses[1] and servants' wages	486	4	3½
To linen for the earl and his chaplains, and for the pantry	43	17	0
To 129 dozen [skins] of parchment, and ink	4	8	3½
To 2 cloths of scarlet for the earl's use; one of russet for the bishop of Anjou; 70 of blue for the knights; 28 for the esquires; 15 of medley for the clerks; 15 for the officers; 19 for the grooms; 5 for the archers; 4 for the minstrels and carpenters, with the sharing and carriage for the earl's liveries at Christmas	460	15	0
To 7 furs of variable miniver, or powdered ermine, 7 hoods of purple, 395 furs of budge[2] for the liveries of barons, knights, and clerks; 123 furs of lamb, bought at Christmas for the esquires	147	17	8
To 65 saffron-coloured cloths for the barons and knights in summer; 12 red cloths for the clerks; 26 ray cloths for the esquires; 1 for the officers; and 4 ray cloths[3] for carpets in the hall.	345	13	8
To 100 pieces of green silk for the knights; 14 budge furs for surcoats; 13 hoods of budge for clerks; 75 furs of lambs for liveries in summer, with canvas and cords to truss them	72	19	0
To saddles for the lord's summer liveries	51	6	8
To 1 saddle for the earl, of the prince's arms	2	0	0
To several items [the particulars in the account defaced]	241	14	1½
To horses lost in the service of the earl	8	6	8
To fees paid to earls, barons, knights, and esquires	623	15	5
To gifts to knights of France, the queen of England's nurses, to the countess of Warren, esquires, minstrels, messengers, and riders	92	14	0
To 168 yards of russet cloth, and 24 coats for poor men, with money given the poor on Maundy Thursday	8	16	7
To 24 silver dishes; 24 saucers; 24 cups; 1 pair of paternosters; 1 silver coffer; all bought this year	103	5	6
To diverse messengers about the earl's business	34	19	8
To sundry things in the earl's chamber	5	0	0
To several old debts paid this year	88	16	0½
The expenses of the countess at Pickering, in the pantry, buttery, kitchen, &c.	235	13	4½
In wine, wax, spices, cloths, furs, &c., for the countess's wardrobe	154	7	4½
Total	£7359	13	0¾

A maximum on the price of provisions was established by royal proclamation in 1314, by which the following rates were fixed:—

"The best grass-fed ox alive, 16s.; the best grain-fed ox, £1 4s.; the best cow alive and fat, 12s.; the best hog of two years old, 3s. 4d.; the best shorn mutton, 1s. 2d.; the best goose, 3d.; the best capon, 2½d.; the best hen, 1½d.; the best chickens, 2 for 1½d.; the best young pigeons, 3 for 1d.; 20 eggs, 1d. This maximum, after existing for twelve years, was repealed in the year 1326."

Henry, brother and heir of Thomas, Earl of Lancaster, obtained a grant of the custody of the castles and honors of Lancaster, Tutbury, and Pickering, 20 Edward II. (1326); and in the first year of Edward III. (1327) an Act was passed for reversing the attainder of his unfortunate brother; whereupon he became possessed of all the lands and lordships which had been seized on the death of his brother, namely, the earldoms of Lancaster and Leicester, and all the other lands of which Edmund his father and Thomas his brother were formerly possessed. This document, which is preserved in the national archives in the Tower of London, serves to shed much light upon the local history of the age.[4] The life of this earl was not remarkable for any great political event connected with the house of Lancaster. He died in 1345, leaving issue, by Maud, his wife, daughter

[1] The number of the earl's horses was generally about 1,500.
[2] Lambskin, dressed with the wool outwards.
[3] Striped cloths.

[4] ACT OF RESTITUTION.
A.D. 1327, 1st Edward III. (class. 1 Edward III. p. 1, m. 3, in Turr. Lond.)—The king to his beloved Adam de Boghier, late farmer of the manor of Berleye, in Co. York, greeting—Whereas we have taken the homage of our beloved and faithful cousin [i.e. kinsman] Henry, Earl of Lancaster and Leicester, brother and heir of Thomas, late Earl of Lancaster, deceased, for all lands and tenements which the same Thomas, his brother, held of the lord Edward, late King of England, our father, in chief, on the day on which he died, and we have restored to him those lands and tenements, and have commanded that they be delivered to him. We, willing to show special grace to the same earl in this respect, grant unto him all the issues and arrearages of the farms of the lands and tenements which were those of the aforesaid Thomas, on the day on which he died, etc. [These issues and arrears, from the time when Adam became farmer of the manor, he is to deliver in the aforesaid form, being exonerated by the king.] Witness the king at Stannford, 23d April [1327]. [Then follow the signatures or subscriptions of various functionaries, high and low, of and within the honor of Lancaster—viz.] JOHN DE LANCASTER, custodian of the honor of Lancaster.

GEOFFREY DE WERBURTON, sheriff of Lancashire.
JOHN DE KYLVYNTON, custodian of the honor of Pykeryng.
ROBERT FONCHER, custodian of Melbourne & farmer of the honor of Tuttebury.
WILLIAM DAVID the elder, ROBERT DE HILTON, & their fellows, farmers of the vill of Tuttebury.
THOMAS DE ROLLESTON, farmer of the vill of Rolleston.
PHILIP DE SOMERVILL, farmer of the manor of Barton.
RICHARD DE WYTHENHULL, NICHOLAS DE SALOPIA, & their fellows, farmers of the manor of Adgerleye.
ROBERT LE HUNTE, JOHN DE VERNEY, & their fellows, farmers of the manor of Utoxhather.
WILLIAM DAVID, farmer of the manor of Yoxhale.
JOHN DE KYNARDESEYE, farmer of the manor of Marchinton.
The PRIOR OF TUTTEBURY, farmer of the manor of Scropton.
HUGH DE MEINELL the elder, ROBERT FOUCH, & their fellows, farmers of the hundred of Appeltre.
ROBERT FOUCH, JOHN DE DENUM, & their fellows, farmers of the manors of Beaurepair, Doffeld', Heigheg', Holebrok, Suthewode, Wyneleye, Holond, Newebiggynge, Edricheshay, Alrewasseloic, & Coldebroc, with the members.

and heir of Sir Patrick Chaworth, Knight, Lord of Kidwelly, Henry, his son and heir, and six daughters: Maud, married (1) to William de Burgh, Earl of Ulster, by whom she had an only daughter, Elizabeth, who married Lionel, Duke of Clarence, second son of Edward III., and (2) Ralph, son and heir of the Earl of Suffolk; Blanche, to Thomas Lord Wake, of Lydell; Eleanor (1) to John de Beaumont, Earl of Buchan, (2) to Richard Fitz-Alan, Earl of Arundel, having the pope's dispensation for the same, on account of their affinity, and likewise because in his tender years he had contracted matrimony with Isabel, the daughter of Hugh le Despenser, his kinswoman in the second degree of consanguinity; Isabel, abbess of Amesbury; Joan, married to John, Lord Mowbray of Axholme; and Mary, to Henry, Lord Percy.

Henry, son and heir of Henry, surnamed Grismond, from the place of his birth, obtained, in 7 Edward III. (1333), a grant from his father, dated at Kenilworth, 28th December, of the castle and town of Kidwelly, with the whole territory of Carnwathland; as also of the castles of Oggemor, Grossmont, Skenefrith, and the Manor of Ebboth. In 9 Edward III. (1335) he was in the expedition to Scotland, at which time he gave such proof of his valour and military skill that he obtained from the king a grant of certain lands at Berwick-upon-Tweed, which had belonged to Peter de Kymeringham. On the 7th of April, 1336, he was made captain-general of the king's army in that realm; and in May following he received the title of banneret. Two years afterwards he was advanced to the title and dignity of the Earl of Derby; having besides the annual fee of £20 per annum (usually given in lieu of the third penny of the pleas of the county, which the earls anciently had), a pension of 1,000 marks (£666 13s. 4d.), to be received yearly during his father's life, out of the customs of London, Boston, and Kingston-upon-Hull, until the king should otherwise provide for him in lands, or rents, of that value. Shortly after this, King Edward, designing to clear the Isle of Cadsant of the garrison which the French had placed there, sent over this earl with considerable forces; where, upon the first encounter, the gallant Earl of Derby advanced so far that he was struck down, when, by the valour of the famous Sir Walter Manney, he was raised up, and placed out of danger; the gallant knight crying, "Lancaster for the Earl of Derby."[1]

In 16 Edward III. (1342) the earl was in another expedition into France, having with him of his retinue 5 bannerets, 50 knights, 144 esquires, and 200 archers on horseback; and had for his wages in that service an assignation of a hundred and eighty sacks of wool, taking for himself eight shillings *per diem*, for every banneret four shillings, every knight two shillings, every esquire one shilling, and every archer sixpence. He had also the same year an assignation of 1,000 marks for guarding the marches of Scotland. In 18 Edward III. (1344) the Earl of Lancaster was engaged in another expedition to the south of France; and, according to Walsingham, after taking the strong town of Brigerac, he subjected no less than fifty-six cities and places of note to the dominion of King Edward; and such was the terror of his name that the cry of "A Derby!" "A Derby!" carried dismay into the enemy's camp. In this year of his great exploits his father died, as already mentioned, on which the Earl of Derby succeeded to the honor, castle, and earldom of Lancaster, and was made the king's lieutenant in Aquitaine.

The famous Order of the Garter was first instituted in 1349; of which, next to the king, Prince Edward was the first knight-companion, and the Earl of Lancaster the second.[2]

After the siege of Poictiers, of which the Earl of Lancaster, Derby, and Leicester was the hero, he was appointed by the king, together with William de Clinton, Earl of Huntingdon, Renaud de Cobham, Sir Walter Manney, William Lovell, and Stephen de Consintone, to hear and determine all disputes relating to arms. At this time he had of his own retinue 800 men at arms, and 2,000 archers, with 30 banners, and kept such hospitality that he spent a hundred pounds a day. After the truce, it was found also that he had expended, in those wars of France in which the battles of Crecy and of Poictiers were fought, about seventeen thousand pounds sterling, besides the pay

JOHN DE KYNARDESEYE, WALTER WALTERSHEF, & their fellows, farmers of the wapentake of Wirkesworth & Assebourne, with the members.
LAURENCE COTERELL, & his fellows, farmers of the lead-mines of the same wapentake.
NICHOLAS DE HUNGERFORD, farmer of the quarry of Roweclif.
THOMAS DE RADECLIVE, HENRY DE BEK, farmers of the manors of Spondon.
WILLIAM COKENY, farmer of the borough of Asshebourne.
GILBERT HENRY DE YOXHALE, farmer of the hundred of Gresclole.
EDMUND DE ASSHEBY, keeper of the fees of the honor of Lancaster in the counties of Lincoln, Notyngham, Stafford', & York, & of the manors of Wadinton & Alkeborugh.
JOHN DE WYVILL, farmer of the manor of Ridelinton.
RICHARD DE WHATTON, late farmer of the courts of Bothemeshull & Crophull, in the county of Notingham.
MARY, countess of PEMBROKE, for the manor of Hegham.
WILLIAM TRUSSEL, escheator on this side [i.e. south of] Trent.
SIMON DE GRYMESBY, escheator beyond [i.e. north of] Trent.
ODO DE STOK, late keeper of the castle of Kenilworth.

[1] Sir John Froissart's Chronicles, liv. i. chap. 30.
[2] The number received into this order consists of twenty-five persons besides the sovereign; and as it has never been enlarged, except as hereafter stated, the value of this badge of honourable distinction continues unimpaired. The particular cause of its origin is unknown: but a story prevails, that the mistress of King Edward, at a court ball, dropped her garter, and the king, taking it up, observed some of the courtiers to smile significantly, as if they thought he had not obtained the favour by accident; upon which he exclaimed, "*Honi soit qui mal y pense*" (Evil be to him that evil thinks), which was adopted as the motto of the order. By a statute of January 17th, 1805, it was ordained that the order should consist of the sovereign and twenty-five knights companions, always including in their number the Prince of Wales, together also with such lineal descendants of George III. as might be elected from time to time. Special statutes have since been adopted for the admission of sovereigns and extra knights, the latter of whom have, however, always been incorporated into the number of the "Companions" on the occasion of vacancies.—C.

which he had from the king. In consideration whereof he obtained a grant, bearing date from the camp before Calais, 21 Edward III. (1347), to himself and his heirs-male, of the castle and town of Brigerac, which was one of the places he had taken by strong assault; likewise of all the lands and goods which he had taken at St. John d'Angelyn, until their ransom were satisfied; and soon after he procured another grant to himself and his heirs-male, of Horeston Castle, in the county of Derby, and the annual rent of forty pounds issuing out of the town of Derby. Soon after this he was constituted the king's lieutenant and captain-general in the parts of Poictou; he then bore the titles of Earl of Lancaster, Leicester, Lincoln, Derby, Grismond, and Ferrers; he was made by David Bruce, King of Scotland, Earl of Moray, and, to crown his dignities, and to reward his merit, the title of Duke of Lancaster was conferred upon him by special charter bearing date March 6th, 26 Edward III. (1353).

DUKES OF LANCASTER.

Henry, the first Duke of Lancaster, having received his title to the dukedom by the general consent of all the prelates and peers then sitting in Parliament at Westminster, for his life, he was invested therewith by cincture or girding of a sword, with power to have a chancery in the county of Lancaster, and to issue out writs there, under his own seal, as well touching pleas of the crown as any other relating to the common laws of this realm; as also to enjoy all other liberties and "Jura Regalia" belonging to a county palatine, in as ample a manner as the Earl of Chester was known to have within that county. Under the term "Jura Regalia," says Sir Thomas Hardy, the late Deputy-Keeper of the Public Records, "the Duke of Lancaster had the exclusive administration of justice by his Courts of Equity and Common Law in the Duchy and Palatinate of Lancaster. These courts (closely analogous in their construction and in their practice to the King's Superior Courts) consist of a Court of Chancery, a Court of Common Pleas for the decision of civil suits, and a Court of Criminal Jurisdiction. The judges of the Common Law Court are appointed by royal commission under the seal of the County Palatine, the judges selected being now the Crown Judges appointed for the northern circuit, and the practice in the court resembles, as nearly as circumstances will admit, that of the Court of Common Pleas at Westminster. By the operation, however, of the Judicature Act, 36 and 37 Vict., c. 66, s. 16, the jurisdiction of the Court of Common Pleas at Lancaster has been transferred to the High Court of Justice. The Court of Criminal Jurisdiction in no way differs from that of the Queen's ordinary court."[1]

In the Harleian MSS. in the British Museum[2] a document is preserved, containing the names of some of the principal and subordinate officers of the Duchy of Lancaster, with a list of the salaries paid for their services, of which the following is a translation :—

FEES AND WAGES OF THE OFFICERS WITHIN THE KING'S DUCHY OF LANCASTER, MADE IN THE 22ND OF THE REIGN OF EDWARD IV. (1482).

	£	s.	d.
Richard, Duke of Gloucester, head-steward there, per ann.	6	13	4
Thomas Molineux, constable of the castle of Liverpool	6	13	4
The same, head-forester of Simon's Wood, and King's parker of Croxteth	3	10	4
The same, high-steward of West Derbyshire and Salfordshire	5	0	0
Thomas, Lord Stanley, receiver of the county of Lanc. per ann.	6	13	4
Hugh Worthington, forester of Quernmore	4	11	0
Two foresters of Wiresdale, each of them per ann. 30s. 4d.	3	0	8
Richard Pilkington, keeper of the park of Hyde and Fulwood, per ann.	1	10	4
Thomas, Lord Stanley, parker of the park of Toxteth	3	0	8
Thomas Richardson, one forester of the wood of Mirescough	3	0	8
John Adamson, another forester of the same wood, per ann.	3	0	8
Two foresters in Blesedale, per ann.	1	10	4
Sir James Harrington, knt., seneschal of Lonsdale and Amounderness	4	4	0
The same Sir James, keeper of the park of Quernmore, per ann.	2	5	6
Thomas Thwayte, chancellor of the county palatine of Lanc.	40	0	0
Sir H. Fairfax, knt., chief justice of the king at Lanc. per ann.	26	13	4
Richard Pigot, another king's justice at Lanc. per ann.	23	6	8
John Hawardyn, king's attorney-general at law there, per ann.	6	13	4
John Lake, clerk of crown pleas	2	0	0
John Bradford, clerk of common pleas	2	0	0
John Lake, William Bradford, and John Bradford, clerks of the crown in co. Lanc. in time of sessions, or their wages for 40 days, each of them 2s. per day	6	0	0
Ranulphus Holcrofte, baron of the king's bench at Lancaster, per ann.	4	0	0
Thomas Bolron, crier of all sessions and courts of the king within the county of Lanc., per ann.	2	0	0
Thomas Ratcliff, Esq., constable of the king's castle of Lancaster, per ann.	13	6	8
Thomas Barowe, master-mason of the king's castles within the counties of Lancaster and Chester	12	3	4
Peter Wraton, king's carpenter at Lancaster, and clerk of the king's works there	7	3	8
Total £200	1	2	

[1] Thirty-fifth Report, p. viii.   [2] Cod. 433. fo. 317 a.

CLYDEROWE, WITH ITS MEMBERS.	£	s.	d.
Richard, Duke of Gloucester, steward of the lordship of Penwortham	1	0	0
Thomas, Lord Stanley, receiver of the lordship of Clyderowe	6	13	4
Brian Talbot, constable of the castle of Clyderowe	10	0	0
Roger Banaster, porter of the castle there, per ann.	2	0	8
John Cays, parker of the park of Musbury, per ann.	1	10	4
John Talbot, parker of the park of Ightenhull, per ann.	2	0	8
Robert Harington, parker of the park of Radam, per ann.	1	10	4
John Hunter, keeper of the chace of Trowdon, per ann.	2	0	8
Richard Shrobury, keeper of the park of Lathegryne, and paler of the same	2	5	6
Total	£29	1	6

The Duke of Lancaster, deeply imbued with the chivalrous spirit of the age in which he lived, obtained a licence from the king to proceed to Syracuse to fight against the infidels. To guard against the possible consequences of this crusade, he obtained a royal grant, providing that, in case he should depart this life before his return, his executors should retain all his estates, castles, manors, and lands in their possession, until his debts were discharged. On his journey he was taken prisoner in Germany, and constrained to give three thousand scutes of gold for his liberty.[1] This surprisal was made at the instance of the Duke of Brunswick; and learning, before he came to his destination, that the Christians and the pagans had made a truce, he returned to Cologne, where he observed "that it did not belong to a person of the Duke of Brunswick's rank to deal with a stranger in the manner that the duke had dealt with him; that he had never offended him; and that if the duke thought proper to interfere with his concerns he would find him ready to play a soldier's part." This conversation having been communicated to the Duke of Brunswick, he sent the Duke of Lancaster a letter of challenge to meet him at Calais in single combat. The Duke of Lancaster accepted this challenge with alacrity, and taking with him fifty knights and a large retinue, he proceeded towards the scene of action. A rencounter between two personages of so much distinction excited the deepest interest both in France and England; and great efforts were made, but without success, to reconcile the combatants without an appeal to arms. On the appointed day they entered the lists, and having taken the usual oaths, mounted their horses for the combat. In the moment of trial, the courage of the Duke of Brunswick failed him, and he quitted the quarrel, and submitted himself to the award of the King of France. The king and his court, who were to have witnessed the combat, now became the mediators, and at a great feast reconciled the dukes to each other.

Henry, who, for his deeds of piety, was styled "The Good Duke of Lancaster," out of his devout respect to the canons of the collegiate church at Leicester, permitted the priests to enclose their woods, and stored them with deer out of his own parks. After this time he received special command from the king to keep a strict guard upon the sea-coasts of Lancashire, and to arm all the lanciers who were raised in his territories for the public service. In 31 Edward III. (1357) John, King of France, having been taken prisoner by Edward the Black Prince, was brought into this country. The captive monarch became the guest of Henry, Duke of Lancaster, in his stately palace in the Savoy, which he had completed at the expense of fifty two thousand marks (£34,666), obtained at the taking of Brigerac. The Duke of Lancaster, having terminated his career of military renown, devoted himself to works of piety, and

"By a deed, bearing date the second of January, in the 35th of Edward III., he gave to the monks at Whalley, in this county, and to their successors, two cottages, seven acres of land, one hundred and eighty-three acres of wood, two hundred acres of wood, called Ramsgrove, all lying in the chase of Blackburn; likewise two messuages, a hundred and twenty-six acres of land, twenty-six acres of meadow, and a hundred and thirty acres of pasture called Standen, Holcroft, and Grenelache, lying within the townships of Penhulton and Clitheroe, with the fold and foldage of Standen, to support and maintain two recluses in a certain place within the churchyard of the parochial church of Whalley, and their successors recluses there; as also two women-servants to attend them there, to pray for the soul of him the said duke, his ancestors and heirs; that is to say, to find them every week throughout the year seventeen loaves of bread, such as usually were made in their convent, each of them weighing fifty shillings sterling; and seven loaves of the second sort, of the same weight; and also eight gallons of their better sort of beer; and threepence for their food. Moreover, every year, at the feast of All Saints, to provide for them ten large fishes, called stock-fish; one bushel of oatmeal for pottage; one bushel of rye; two gallons of oil for their lamps; one pound of tallow for candles; six loads of turf, and one load of faggots, for their food; likewise to repair their habitations; and to find a chaplain, with a clerk, to sing mass, in the chapel belonging to these recluses, every day; and also all vestments, and other utensils and ornaments, for the same chapel; the nomination of successors, upon deaths, to be in the duke and his heirs."

This "Good Duke of Lancaster," by his will bearing date, at the castle of Leicester, the 15th of March, 35 Edward III. (1361), wherein he styles himself Duke of Lancaster, Earl of Derby, Lincoln, and Leicester, Steward of England, and Lord of Brigerac and Beauford, bequeathed his body to be buried in the Collegiate Church of our Lady of Leicester. He only survived the making of this

---

[1] The scute was of the value of half a noble, or 3s. 4d., so that 3,000 scutes represent £500.

testament nine days. At that time a plague raged in England, which, in allusion to the great plague in 1349, Barnes calls the "second plague, nothing near," says he, "so dismal and universal as the former, but much more destructive to the nobility and prelacy." Thus died the great, valiant, and liberal prince, Henry Plantagenet, March 24th, 1361. He left issue by Isabella, his wife, daughter of Henry Bellmont or Beaumont, lord of Folkingham, two daughters, his heirs, Maud, twenty-two years old, first married to Ralph, son and heir of Ralph, Lord Stafford, and after to William of Bavaria, son of Lewis the emperor; and Blanche, nineteen years old, married to John of Gaunt, Earl of Richmond, fourth son of King Edward III. Maud, the elder, had for her moiety an assignment of the manors in the counties of Berks, Leicester, Northampton, Rutland, and Huntingdon, and also the lordship of Beauford and Nogent in France.

"And to John, Earl of Richmond, and Blanche his wife, whose homage was then taken by reason of issue between them, the castle and town of Pontefract; the manors of Bradeform, Almanbury, Altofts, Warnfeld, Rothewell, Ledes, Roundehay, Scoles, Berewyck, Kepax, Aberford, Knottingley, with the mills there; Beghale, Kamsale, Ouston, Elmesdale, Akworth, and Staincros; the bailiwick and honor of Pontefract; a certain rent called castle ferme, with the pleas and perquisites, also the manors of Kriteling and Barlay; except such lands therein as were held for life (the reversion to the said duke), the castle of Pickering, with the soke and all its members; the manors of Esyngwold and Scalby, with the members, all in the county of York; the wapentakes (or rather *hundreds*) of *Leyland, Amunderness, and Lonsdale;* the manors of Oves-[1 Ulues]-walton, Preston, Singleton, Riggeby, and Wra, Overton, Skirton; the towns of Lancaster and Slyne; the royal bailiwick of *Blackburnshire,* the office of master-forester beyond Ribbel; the vaccary of Wyresdale, likewise the manors of Penwortham, Totyngton, and Rachedale; the wapentake of Clyderhowe, with the demense lands there; the lordship of Bowland, the vaccary of Bowland and Blackburnshire; the forest of Blackburnshire and the park of Ightenhull, with the appurtenances in Blackburnshire, all in the county of Lancaster. The castle and manor of Dunstanburgh, with the manors of Shoplaye, Stamford, Burton, and Emeldon; also the fishing of Twede, in the county of Northumberland. The manor of Hinckley, with the bailiwick there, in the county of Leicester; the castle and manor of Kenilworth, with the pool and mill there; the manors of Wotton, Shrewle, Radesle, and Ashtul, with their appurtenances, in the county of Warwick; the manors of Halton, Ronkore, More, Whitelawe, Congleton, Kelershole, and Bedestan; the bailiwick of Halton; the town of Wyndenes [Widnes], sergeanty of Wyndenes, in the county of Lancaster. In addition to these great lordships and lands, there was a further assignment made unto the Earl of Richmond, and Blanche his wife, of the manors of Coggleshul, Cridelyng, Bailey, Kilbourne, Toresholme, Marthesdon, Swanyngton, Passenham; likewise certain lands in Daventre and Hinkele, with the mills of Lilleborn; also the manor of Uggele, in the county of Essex."

John of Gaunt, Duke of Lancaster, was born at Gaunt (Ghent), in Flanders, from whence he derived his surname, between the 25th and 31st of March, 1340; and on the 20th of September, 1343, he was created Earl of Richmond, having therewith a grant in tail general of all the castles, manors, and lands belonging to that earldom, and all the prerogatives and royalties which John, late Duke of Britany and Richmond, enjoyed.[1] In 1355 he attended the king, his father, on an expedition into Flanders, and in 1357 had a grant in special tail of the castle and lordship of Lydell, in the county of Northumberland. Having obtained (May 19, 1359) a dispensation from Rome, he was married at Reading, in Berkshire, to his cousin, the lady Blanche, second daughter and co-heir of Henry Plantagenet, Duke of Lancaster. In 1361 he obtained a special charter for divers privileges to himself and his heirs by Blanche, his wife—namely, return of writs, pleas of *Withernam*,[2] felons' goods, etc., in all the lordships and lands whereof he was then possessed, with freedom for himself and his heirs, and all the tenants and residents upon the lands, and fees which belonged to Henry, Earl of Lancaster, from all manner of tolls of what kind soever throughout the whole kingdom. The same year having issue by his wife, and doing his homage, he had an assignation of her property in all the lands whereof her father died possessed. And, by virtue of the king's licence, he obtained a further grant from John, Bishop of Lincoln, Richard, Earl of Arundel, and others, to himself, his wife, and their issue, of the castle of Bolingbroke, with the park, knights' fees, and advowsons of the churches thereto belonging, together with other manors in the counties of Stafford, Northumberland, and Derby. In 1362, upon the death of Maud, the widow of William, Duke of Bavaria, without issue, he had, in right of the said Blanche, the sister and heir of Maud, all the possessions appertaining to her moiety of the estate of Henry, Duke of Lancaster, deceased. Whereupon he was in Parliament declared Duke of Lancaster,[3] in right of his wife Blanche; and the king girt him with a sword, and set on his head a cap of fur, and a circlet of gold with pearls therein; and created him Duke of Lancaster, with all the liberties and regalities of an earl palatine;[4] as also Earl of Leicester, Lincoln, and Derby, with the office

---

[1] Cart. in officinâ ducatûs Lancastriæ.

[2] When a distress is removed out of the county, and the sheriff, upon a replevin, cannot make deliverance to the party distressed.

[3] By the deed of creation, dated 36 Edward III. (1362), the king, in consideration of the growing activity and praiseworthy deeds of his dearest son, John, Earl of Lancaster, gives to the earl the name and honour of duke, and appoints him to be Duke of Lancaster, and invests him with the same title and honour by girding him with a sword, and the placing of a cap of dignity on his head. To have and to hold the same title and honour of Duke of Lancaster to him and to his lawful heirs-male for ever. This grant is witnessed by Simon, Archbishop of Canterbury, William of Winchester, chancellor, S. of Ely, treasurer, bishops; Richard, Earl of Arundel, Robert of Suffolk, Thomas de Vere, our chancellor of Oxford, earls; Edward le Despenser, Ralf de Nevill, John de Nevill, John atte Lee, steward of our household, and others. Given by

our own hand in full Parliament, at Westminster, 13th November, 36th of our reign [1362].

[4] "Counties palatine," says Blackstone, "are so called *a palatio,* because the owners thereof (the Earl of Chester, the Bishop of Durham, and the Duke of Lancaster) had in those counties *jura regalia,* as fully as the king hath in his palace; *regalem potestatem,* as Bracton expresses it." Anciently palatinates took very much the character of distinct sovereignties, and not unfrequently local writers, when referring to England, spoke of it as "another country," standing much in the same position to a palatinate as, say, for example, Lancashire, that France did to Normandy, and Normandy to Brittany. It must, however, be understood that the county palatine and the duchy of Lancaster are not conterminous or identical in jurisdiction, the latter comprising much territory that lies at a vast distance from the county.—C.

of high-steward of England. In 1366, after having been empowered to vest several of his estates in feoffees, in order to make a settlement on his lady, and to discharge some pecuniary incumbrances, the Duke of Lancaster joined his brother, Prince Edward, at Bordeaux, on behalf of Don Pedro, King of Castile, who, owing to an insurrection of his subjects, fled into Gascony for aid. On breach of the truce, in 1369, he was sent with a considerable force to give battle to the French, being retained to serve the king for half a year, with 300 men-at-arms, 500 archers, 3 bannerets, 80 knights, and 216 esquires; but the King of France would not allow a battle to be risked which might terminate as other great battles had done; and so suffered Lancaster to march through the northern provinces without molestation. On his return from Calais to England, at the close of the year, he found that his wife, the lady Blanche, had been taken off by the great pestilence, and that she had been interred with great funeral pomp in St. Paul's Cathedral in the month of September previously.

In 1370 the Duke of Lancaster was again engaged in an expedition into Gascony; and Peter the Cruel, King of Castile and Leon, whom Edward, Prince of Wales, had invested in his kingdom, having left at his death two daughters, who, to avoid the usurper, their uncle, had taken refuge in Gascony, he married Constance, the elder of the sisters, and gave the hand of the other, Isabel, to his younger brother Edmund, Earl of Cambridge and Duke of York. Soon afterwards he assumed the title of King of Castile and Leon, and supported his claim by force of arms, but without success. He impaled also the arms of Castile and Leon with his ducal coat. On his return to England, in 1372, the duke was empowered to surrender to the king his father his earldom of Richmond, with all the castles, manors, &c., to the same belonging, in exchange for numerous other manors in the counties of York, Norfolk, Suffolk, Huntingdon, and Sussex. Soon afterwards he headed two formidable expeditions against France, both of which failed. In 1377 he obtained the manors of Grenested, Seford, and Leighton, with several privileges in the same, and the castle and honor of Tikhill. He had licence also to give his lordships of Gryngeleye and Wheteley to Catherine Swynford, his concubine (widow of Sir Hugh Swynford, knight, and daughter of Sir Paen Roelt, knight, a native of Hainault, and Guienne king of arms), for life.

During this year he procured the grant of a chancery in his dukedom of Lancaster, with all other royalties pertaining to a county palatine, to hold in as ample a manner as the Earl of Chester ever enjoyed the same; with an obligation of sending two knights to Parliament as representatives of the commonalty of the county of Lancaster, with two burgesses for every borough within the said county.[1] He had licence also to coin money for the space of two years, from the 12th of June (1377), in the city of Bayonne, or the castle of Guyssen, or any other place within the seneschalcy of Landere, of gold, silver, or any other metal whatsoever.

In this year (1377) John Wycliffe, the most eminent of all the Lollards at that time—the "Morning-Star of the Reformation," as he has been beautifully called—being convened before the Archbishop of Canterbury, the Bishop of London, John, Duke of Lancaster, and Lord Percy, at the Blackfriars, in London, the duke had the magnanimity to speak in favour of Wycliffe, and to make some strong observations upon the bishops. So unusual a departure from the orthodoxy of the day gave great offence to the episcopal bench, and produced so much discontent among the citizens that they rose in tumult, and determined to murder the duke, and to set fire to his house in the Savoy. This tumult Courtenay, the Bishop of London, much to his honour, succeeded in quelling; but the Duke of Lancaster was obliged to seek safety in flight, and it was not till after the death of his father that a reconciliation was effected between him and the citizens of London, under the mediation of Richard II. After the death of Edward III., consultation being had about the solemnity of the coronation of King Richard II., John, King of Castile and Leon, Duke of Lancaster, appeared before the king in council, and claimed, as Earl of Leicester, the office of seneschal of England; as Duke of Lancaster, the right of bearing the principal sword called the *curtana*, on the day of the coronation; and as Earl of Lincoln, to carve for the king sitting at table on the day of his coronation. Diligent examination being made before certain of the king's council concerning these demands, it sufficiently appeared that the duke, as holding by the law of

[1] By this grant the king, after praising the prowess in war and wisdom in council conspicuous in his son, and also the probity, activity, and excelling wisdom of his dearest son John, King of Castile and Leon, Duke of Lancaster, &c., and being desirous to reward these high merits, of his certain knowledge and cheerful heart, with the assent of his prelates and nobles now assembled in Parliament at Westminster, grants to the same John, for the whole of his life, that he may have within the county of Lancaster his chancery and his writ under his seal as record from the office of chancery, his justiciars, as well for pleas of the crown as for whatsoever other pleas may be held at common law, and recognisance thereof, the issuing of executions by his writ and his officers of the same chancery, and whatsoever other liberties and *jura regalia*, appurtenant to the county palatine, as entirely and freely as the Earls of Chester have theirs within the county of Chester. Tenths, fifteenths, and other quotas and subsidies, by the commonalty of our kingdom, and tenths and other quotas by the clergy of the same, we grant and impose, as the same are granted and imposed by the Apostolic See; and pardons for life and members, in cases where, in that county, for any offence, life or limb is forfeit. &c. Our same son, at our mandate, shall cause to be sent to our Parliaments and councils, two knights for the commonalty of the said county, and two burgesses for every borough within the said county, &c. Witness the king, at Westminster, 28th February [51 Edward III., 1377], by the king himself, with the assent of the entire Parliament. *Rymer*, tom. iii. pt. iii., p. 1073. *Ed. regent.*

England, after the death of Blanche his wife, had established his claim; and it was agreed that he should exercise the offices by himself, or proper deputies, and receive the fees thereunto belonging: Accordingly, on the Thursday before the coronation, which was on the Thursday following, by order of the king, he sat judicially, and kept his court in the Whitehall of the king's palace at Westminster, and there received the bills and petitions of all such of the nobility and others as, by reason of their tenure, or otherwise, claimed to do service at the new king's coronation, and to receive the accustomed fees and allowances.[1]   He was also, with Edmund, Earl of Cambridge, and certain bishops, appointed one of the protectors of the king during his minority.

JOHN OF GAUNT'S GATEWAY, LANCASTER CASTLE.

In 2 Richard II. (1378-9) the duke obtained authority to establish a treasury, with barons and other proper officers, within his duchy of Lancaster.[2]

[1] A portrait of John of Gaunt, Duke of Lancaster, in this capacity, is preserved in the Cottonian MSS. in the British Museum.

[2] Though it is stated in the text that this grant was made in the second regnal year of Richard II., it appears by the deed itself that it was in his thirteenth year; and therefore not in 1379 but in 1390. After reciting by inspeximus the charter of Edward III., granting to our dearest uncle John the title and honour of Duke of Lancaster, &c., Richard grants to his said uncle that he may have a chancery for life within the county, and in short confirms all that is granted by the former charter. It enlarges the grant by authorising the duke to have approved faithful and efficient men for collecting the tenths, fifteenths, subsidies, &c.   And that he may have justices itinerant, and for the pleas of the forest within the said county.   And further that he may have his exchequer in the said county, and barons and other necessary officers in the same exchequer, as well as whatever jurisdiction, executions, and customs are reasonably used in the exchequer of England.   The duke and his heirs to have and hold all and singular liberties and the appointment of justices for the pleas of the forests, excepting those pleas in which the king is a party, and all tenths, fifteenths, &c.   Witnesses: the Archbishop of Canterbury, the Bishops of London and Winchester (the chancellor); the Dukes Edward of York, Thomas of Gloucester (our uncles); the earls Richard of Arundel, William of Salisbury, Henry of Northumberland.   Richard le Scrope, John Devereux, steward of our household, and others.   Given at Westminster, by our hand, 16 February, 13th of our reign [1390.]

In this early period of our history, personal slavery prevailed to a greater extent in England than in any other country of Europe.[1] The barons had struggled for liberty, and had, to a certain extent, secured its possession from the crown by the deed of Magna Charta, extorted from King John and confirmed by Henry III. and Edward I. But this liberty was almost exclusively enjoyed by the privileged classes, who themselves exercised despotic power over their vassals. The rights of those who tilled the ground and performed the other duties of humble citizens were imperfectly understood and subject to daily violation; and so unequal was the pressure of taxation that the rich and the poor were confounded together in one indiscriminate mass, and called upon (1378) to pay a poll-tax, amounting to three groats on every individual throughout the land, male and female, above the age of fifteen years. The collection of this unequal and odious impost produced a rebellion, excited by John Ball, a popular preacher, and led by Wat Tyler, Jack Straw, and others: The Duke of Lancaster, one of the king's ministers, and who was supposed to be his principal adviser, became extremely unpopular; and the insurgents, having broken into the city of London, burnt down the Duke of Lancaster's palace of the Savoy and also the Temple, sacked the palace of the Archbishop of Canterbury, demolished Newgate, and cut off the heads of a number of gentlemen who attempted to resist their lawless outrages, amongst whom was Simon Sudbury, the primate and chancellor of England, and Sir Robert Hales, the high treasurer. This insurrection was suppressed by the determined conduct of Walworth, the lord mayor of London, who resented the insolence shown towards the king on the part of Wat Tyler, by a violent blow with his sword, which brought him to the ground, where he was soon despatched by others of the king's attendants (1381). Richard, taking advantage of the temporary panic, contrived to conciliate the people, and, by his wisdom and moderation, prevailed upon them to disperse. During this insurrection, the Duke of Lancaster fled before the popular hatred over the Border, and took refuge in Scotland, where he occupied himself in negotiating a peace, in which he happily succeeded. On this occasion, William, Earl of Douglas, with a degree of generous forbearance which seldom fails to obtain its reward, told the duke that he had been acquainted from the first with the distracted state of England, but was so far from wishing to take advantage of the critical situation in which the duke and his country were placed, either for carrying on the war or extorting more favourable terms of peace, that he might remain in Scotland, as their guest, until the insurrection should cease; or, if he chose to return, he might have an escort of five hundred horsemen. The duke expressed his acknowledgments, but declined the offer. On his return to England, being excluded from Berwick by Sir Matthew Redman, governor under the Earl of Northumberland, he accepted the earl's pledge of honour, and returned into Scotland, where he remained until the popular tumult had subsided. So extensive was the popular indignation against the measures of the king and his ministers, and so intense the feeling against the Duke of Lancaster during the rebellion of Wat Tyler, that the Lady Constance, wife of the duke, hastened from Leicester to the castle at Pontefract for refuge, expecting security there, but when she arrived, her own servants dared not permit her to enter the place, and she was constrained to go seven miles by torchlight to Knaresborough Castle, where she continued till the violence of the storm subsided and till the duke returned from Scotland. In 1384 the Duke of Lancaster was despatched, with a powerful military and naval force, to Scotland, to avenge the injuries which the English had received during the war with France,[2] and to prevent a repetition of them, by some memorable act of chastisement. The duke advanced to Edinburgh, and at the same time the fleet was despatched to ravage the coast of Fife. His soldiers strongly urged him to burn the capital, but the duke, cherishing a grateful remembrance of the hospitality which he had experienced three years before, preserved the city from destruction.[3] A little before Easter, in 1384, John Latimer, an Irish Carmelite friar, charged the Duke of Lancaster with an intention to destroy the king and to usurp the crown; but on being summoned to meet this accusation, the duke completely established his loyalty, when he demanded that the slanderer should be committed to safe custody. Sir John Holland, a Lancashire knight, and son-in-law of Lancaster, undertook the charge, and the next day Latimer was found dead, having, it is said, been strangled by his keeper. The king, being under the guidance of evil counsellors, resolved upon the death of the Duke of Lancaster; but private information having reached him from one of those that were in the plot, he retired to his castle at Pontefract, and through the mediation of the Princess Joan (the "Fair Maid of Kent"), mother of the king, a perfect reconciliation took place. The next year he desired leave of the king, and also of the lords and commons in Parliament,

[1] Froissart, liv. ii. chap. 74.
[2] In connection with the war an incident occurred that, while strongly characteristic of the age, gives to the quarrel an air of the ludicrous. There is preserved among the public records a letter from Richard, who was then a youth of seventeen years, to the Duke of Lancaster, in which he gravely proposes that the quarrel between England and France should be determined by single combat between himself and the French king, Charles VI., who was then in his fifteenth year. There is no evidence, however, that John of Gaunt gave any encouragement to this precocious heroism.—C.
[3] Buchanan: Rerum Scotiarum Historia, lib. ix. cap. 45.

to go into Spain for the recovery of his wife's inheritance; and ordained his son, Henry, Earl of Derby, his lieutenant of all he had in England, placing around him a safe and judicious council. When he took his leave, the king presented him with a coronet of gold, and the queen gave another to his wife; orders were also given that he should be addressed by the title of "King of Spain." His train consisted of no less than a thousand spears of knights and esquires, two thousand archers, and a thousand tall yeomen. Having landed in Britany, near the castle of Brest, he was resisted by two of the forts, in the assault of which he lost many of his men; but he ultimately triumphed, and, having sailed with his fleet to the Garonne, he marched to the Spanish frontier and carried the town of Bayonne. After this, the King of Castile sent to him to treat of a marriage between his daughter and the duke's son; and through the mediation of the Duke of Berry a truce was concluded. In 1388 the duke was appointed lieutenant of Aquitaine.

The disputes which had so long existed in Spain concerning the right to the kingdom of Castile and Leon were at length amicably settled, by an agreement that Henry, eldest son of John, King of Castile and Leon, and of Portugal, should marry Catherine, the duke's only daughter, by his wife Constance; and that the duke should quit his claim to Spain on condition of receiving, for his own and daughter's life, a yearly payment of 16,000 marks, and in case his wife should survive him, that she should have annually 12,000 marks (£8,000). The duke returned to England in November, 1389, with much treasure; for it is said that he had forty-seven mules laden with chests of gold for his second payment, and several great men of Spain, as guarantees for his future annuity. On his return he relieved Brest, in Britany, then besieged by the French. In the following year (1390) he was created Duke of Aquitaine by the consent of the lords and commons of England, on which occasion a splendid cap was put upon his head, and a rod of gold was given to him, to hold his new dignity of the king of England as king of the realm of France. In 13 Richard II. (1390) he obtained a further confirmation of the privileges of his duchy of Lancaster, in the appointment of a chancery court there, with the power to issue writs under his own seal; likewise an exchequer, with barons and other necessary officers, and power to make justices itinerant for the pleas of the forest, etc.[1] His attachment to his favourite Catherine Swynford remained unaltered, notwithstanding the disparity of their stations; and, after the death of his second wife, Constance, he married her at Lincoln, on the octaves of the Epiphany (1395), at which, say the Chroniclers, there was no little admiration in regard to her low birth.

"This woman was born in Henault, daughter of a knight of that country. She was brought up in her youth in the Duke of Lancaster's house, and attended on his first wife, the Duchess Blanche of Lancaster; and in the days of his second wife, the Duchess Constance, he kept the aforesaid Catharine as his concubine, who afterwards was married to a knight of England, named Swinford, that was now deceased. Before she was married the duke had by her three children, two sons and a daughter. One of the sons was named Thomas de Beaufort; and the other Henrie, who was brought up at Aken, in Almaine, proved a good lawyer, and was afterwards Bishop of Winchester. For the love that the duke had to these his children, he married their mother, the said Catharine Swinford, being now a widow, whereof men marvelled much, considering her mean estate was far unmeet to match with his highness, and nothing comparable in honour to his other two former wives. And indeed, the great ladies of England, as the Duchess of Gloucester, the Countess of Derby, Arundel, and others, descended of the blood royal, greatly disdained that she should be matched with the Duke of Lancaster, and by that means be accounted second person in the realm, and preferred in room before them, and thereof they said that they would not come in any place where she should be present, for it should be a shame to them that a woman of so base a birth, and concubine to the duke in his other wife's days, should go and have place before them. The Duke of Gloucester also, being a man of an high mind and a stout stomach, misliked his brother matching so meanly; but the Duke of York bare it well enough; and verily the lady herself was a woman of such bringing up and honourable demeanour, that envy could not in the end but give place to well deserving."[2]

In 1396 the king negotiated a marriage with Isabella, daughter of Charles VI. of France, then a child eight years old, with, as he said, the approval of his two uncles, Lancaster and York. The two kings, accompanied by hundreds of nobles and knights, with all the pomp of the gorgeous ceremonials of that age, met between Calais and Ardres, and there embraced and drank wine together out of jewelled cups. On a subsequent day they met again at the boundary of their two camps, when the child-queen arrived with a cavalcade of golden chariots and silken litters, with ladies wearing garlands of pearls and diamonds. She was presented by her uncles to Richard, who promised to cherish her as his wife. The Duchesses of Lancaster and Gloucester then received her, and she set forward to Calais, where the marriage was celebrated on the 4th of November.

Three years after the Duke of Lancaster's third marriage, in a Parliament convened at London, he procured an act for legitimising the children whom he had by Catherine Swynford, the legitimation having been preceded by a similar act of the Pope; and in another Parliament, held in September in the same year, called the Great Parliament, the Earl of Arundel was, by the Duke of Lancaster, who sat that day as high steward, condemned of treason on charges of which

---

[1] See note 2, page 58 *supra*.   [2] Holinshed, p. 485.

he had previously received the Royal pardon, and beheaded on Tower Hill, September 21st, 1397. During this Parliament the duke's eldest son, the Earl of Derby, was created Duke of Hereford. In 1396-97, the Duke of Lancaster had a renewal and amplification of the privileges of his duchy of Lancaster.[1] He also obtained the hundreds of Southgrenhow and Laundishe, in the county of Norfolk, which had come into the king's hands by the attainder of the Earl of Arundel. In 1398, after obtaining from the king an ample renunciation of all claim on any part of his inheritance, with a confirmation of the dower of the castles of Knaresborough and Tickhill to Catherine his wife, and a settlement of the manor of Bradford and Almondbury on his eldest legitimatised son, John Beaufort, Marquis of Somerset and Dorset, he was constituted lieutenant in the marches towards Scotland, from the beginning of the twenty-eight years' truce between that country and England. In October, Henry of Bolingbroke, the duke's son, received sentence of banishment; and from that period this disgrace produced the most pungent sorrow in the mind of his venerable father, who was soon afterwards seized with a fatal illness and died. His death, which occurred February 3rd, 1398-9, was much lamented by his friends; but neither the king nor the people sympathised in their sorrow. He was interred with great funeral pomp near the body of Blanche, his first wife, for whom and for himself he had erected, soon after her decease, a sumptuous monument, surmounted with the ducal arms.

An inscription was afterwards placed on a pensile tablet, which, after enumerating his various titles and honours, states that he was thrice married, first to Blanche, daughter and heir of Henry, Duke of Lancaster, by whom he received a most ample inheritance; secondly to Constance (who is buried here), daughter and heir of Peter, King of Castile and Leon, in whose right he was entitled to use the title of king, etc. She bore him one daughter, Catharine, who had children by Henry, King of Spain. His third wife was Catharine, of a knightly family, and a lady of extraordinary beauty, who bore him a numerous progeny, of which stock, by the mother's side, Henry VII., most prudent king of England, married one, whose felicitous marriage with Elizabeth, daughter of King Edward IV. of the house of York, united the royal families of Lancaster and York, and restored peace to England. This illustrious prince John, named Plantagenet, King of Castile and Leon, Duke of Lancaster, Earl of Leicester, Lincoln, and Derby, Lieutenant of the king in Aquitaine and High Steward of England, died in the 22nd year of the reign of Richard II. and A.D. 1399.

The bequests of John, Duke of Lancaster, were munificent; but the largest portion of his estates descended to his only surviving son and heir by Blanche of Lancaster. Throughout his life the Duke of Lancaster surpassed all the great men of his age in power and fortune; but he was not so universally respected as his brother the Black Prince, the good Duke of Lancaster, or his eldest son, Henry of Bolingbroke, Earl of Derby. Some defects in the moral character of John of Gaunt, his haughty carriage towards inferiors, and his public support of Wycliffe the reformer, added to his want of success in arms, contributed to lower him in the public estimation; though his readiness on all occasions to apply his ample fortune in the discharge of his public duties, and his zeal in the cause of his country, served to rank him amongst the most illustrious of her benefactors.

The ducal family of the house of Lancaster had, by its marriage alliances, become connected with many of the most powerful barons of the kingdom, and Henry of Bolingbroke, the representative of this house after the death of his father, John of Gaunt, impelled partly by his wrongs, but principally by his ambition, wrested the sceptre from the feeble hands of his royal cousin, and ascended the throne of England almost without a struggle. By this act of usurpation the seed was sown for the long and sanguinary intestine wars between the rival houses of Lancaster and York, which served for so many years to deluge the country with blood.

[1] This is an exemplification and full confirmation of preceding charters, as in 1st Richard II. And further, for the greater security of the duke, the king declares and grants to him that he may have all fines for transgressions, etc., for agreeing to grant licence, and all issues and forfeitures of all men, tenants and residents in his lands, and fees, and whatsoever fines, "year, day, and waste," in whatsoever courts of the king, and what by the hands of his officers may be levied for fines and amercements aforesaid. And that he may have, in the aforesaid lands and fees, assise of bread, wine, and ale, etc., and other things which belong to the office of clerk of the markets, and fines, etc., so that the clerk of the king's markets be not injured. And that he may have the chattels of felons and fugitives, the return of all writs, summonses, and precepts of the king, etc., and their execution, so that no officer of the king be injured thereby. And if it happen that the officers of the duke be amerced in the king's courts for negligence, etc., such fines and amercements may be to the duke. And that he may have the chattels [or cattle] called "waif and stray," doodands, treasure-trove, and the chattels called "manu opera," etc. [This last term has two meanings: (1) Stolen goods taken upon a thief, apprehended in the fact; and (2) Cattle, or any implements used to work in husbandry. Most probably it is here intended in its former sense.]—H.

DESCENT OF THE **EARLS** AND **DUKES** OF **LANCASTER**, OF THE HOUSE OF ANJOU OR PLANTAGENET,

FROM THE CONQUEST TO THE ACCESSION OF HENRY IV.

Herlweine de = Enniss, or
Contoville. *da4* Arietta. | Enma.

Robert, 6th Duke of Normandy,
5th in descent from Rollo.

WILLIAM, Illegitimate son, surnamed the Conqueror, = Maud, d. of Baldwin V., Earl of Flanders, descended King of England; born, 1027; died, September 9, from Alfred the Great and Charlemagne; mar. 1087. 1033; died, Nov. 2, 1083.

Richard, Earl of Avranches, = Emme, or
in Normandy, *da* Goe- living, 1082. | Emma.

Robert, sur- | William II., sur- = Maud, dau. of | Henry I., sur- = Adelisa, dau. of | Cicely. | Stephen, = Adela, d.
named Curt- | named Rufus, | Malcolm III. | named Beau- | Godfrey, Dk. | Constan- | Count of | Bloisand
hose, Duke of | King of Eng- | K. of Scots, | clerc, King of | of Lorraine, | tine. | Eustace, | unmar.
Normandy. | Land, b. about | descended | England, b. | and Count of | Adeliza. | Count of | d. 1137.
Richard, died | 1060; died, un- | from Alfred | 1070 ; died, | Braleul. | | Bloisand |
young. | married, Aug. | the Great; | Dec. 1, 1135. | | | Chartres |
| 2, 1100. | died May 1, | | | | |
| | 1118. | | | | |

Hugh D'Avranches, = Ermentrude, | Judith. | Rundolph (de = Isabel, mar
surnamed Lupus | d. of Hugh | Albreda. | Briensard, | Richard, Earl
1st Norman Earl | de Clare- | | Viscount of | of Corbeil, in
of Chester; died | mont, E. of | | the Bessin, | Normandy,
July 27, 1101. | Beauvais. | | in Nor- | and had Ro-
| | | mandy. | bert.

William, | Henry.
Duke of Normandy, | Maud.
perpr of Ger- | Stephen, Count = Matilda, d. and h. of
many; died, | of Boulogne | Eustace, Count of Bou-
May 22, 1125. | and Mortain, | logne; died,
s.p. | King of Eng- | May 3, 1151.
| land; d. Oct. | Baldwin.
| 25, 1154. | Eustace.
| | William.

Richard, 2nd Earl = Maud, *w/* | Ottwell | Geva Ranulph, *d/* = Lucy, d. of Yvo | William, = Em = Maud, born | Geoffrey Plan- = William, = Adelisa, dau. of | Henry. | Maud.
of Chester, b. | Lucy, d. of | Robert, | de Meschines, | de Taillbois, | peror of | 1104 ; d. | tagnet, Ct. | Theobald. | Eleanor.
1083; d. 1119; | Stephen, E. | Philip. | 3rd Earl of | widow of | Normandy, | Sept. 10, | of Anjou ; d. | Maud. | Joan.
no issue. | of Blois. | | Chester; | Roger Fitz- | mar. Matilda, | 1167. | Sept. 7, 1150. |
		hnd a grant of the	Gerald, Lord	d. of Fulke,	
		House of Lanca-	of Spalding.	Count of An-
		ter; d. 1128-9.		jou ; b. 1102;
				d. 1120.

Randle, surnamed = Matilda, dau. of | Alico. | HENRY II., succeeded his = Eleanor, Duchess of Guienne,
Gerons, 4th Earl | Robert, Earl | Agnes. | uncle Stephen as King | eldest d. and h. of William,
of Chester; d. | of Gloucester, | | of England ; b. 1133; d. | Duke of Guienne and Aqui-
1153-5. | natural son of | | July 7, 1189. | taine: m. 1151 ; d. June 26,
| King Henry I. | | | 1202.

Geoffrey, mar. Constance, = JOHN, surnamed = Isabel, d. and h.
d. and h. of Conan, Duke | youngest | of Aymer, Ct.
of Bretagne and Earl of | son of | of Angouleme;
Richmond, *jure ux*: b. | William, | mar. 1200; d
Sept. 23, 1158 ; d. Aug. | Earl of | 1246.
19, 1186. His widow re-mar. (1) Randle | Gloucester.
Blundeville, 6th Earl of Chester, and (2)
Guy, Viscount of Thouars.

Hugh, surnamed = Bertha, d. of Simon, | Richard. | RICHARD I., surnamed = Berengaria, dau. of | Cicely. | HENRY III., King = Eleanor, 2nd d. and co-h. | Richard, Earl of Cornwall | Joan, Queen of
Kyvelioc, 5th | Count of Montfort | | Cœur du Lion, King | Sancho IV., King | mar. to Sir War- | of England, b. | of Raymond Berenger, | and Count of Poictou, | Scots.
Earl of Ches- | and Evreux, in | | of England : b. Sept. 6, 1157 ; | of Navarre ; mar. | ren de Bostock, | Oct. 1, 1206. | Count of Provence : m. | King of the Romans ; d. | Eleanor, w. of
ter; d. 1180. | Normandy. | | d.s.p. April 6, 1199. | May 12, 1191. | Kt. | | Jan. 14, 1236 ; d. June | 1271. | Wm. Mares-
| | | | | | | 25, 1291. | | chal, Earl of
| | | | | | | | | Pembroke.
| | | | | | | | | Isabella, Em-
| | | | | | | | | press of Gor-
| | | | | | | | | many.

Randle, surnamed the = (1) Constance, d. and | Matilda, wife of David, | Robert, son of = Ha wisia, Countess | EDWARD I., King = Margaret, dau. of | EDMUND, = Blanche, Dowager | Margaret, mar.
Good, *ala* Blundo- | h. of Conan, Duke | Earl of Huntingdon, | Saher de | of Lincoln by | of England ; | Philip III., King | Crouchback, | Qn. Countess | Alexander
ville, 6th Earl of | of Bretagne and Earl of | and Angus, bro. to | Quincy, Earl | Margery. | born *rtine* 17, | of France ; mar. | Earl of | Palatine of | III., King of
Chester, Duke of | Richmond, widow | William, King of | of Winches- | she had also the | 1239 ; d. July | Sept. 8, 1299 ; d. | Chester, 1253 ; | Champagne and | Scotland.
Bretague, and E. of | of Geoffrey Planta- | Scotland; | ter. | castle and manor | 7, 1307. | Feb. 14, 1317. | Earl of | Brye, Count of | Beatrice, mar.
Richmond, *jure ux*.; | genet, 4th son of K. | Mabilla, w. of William | | of Bollingbroke, | | | Leicester & Steward | Robert, Count of | John, Duke
d. Oct. 26 (5 kl. Nov.), | Henry II., divorced | d'Albini, Earl of | | co. Lincoln. Re- | | | of Leicester, 1267 ; Earl | Artois, bro. to | of Brittany,
1232, s.p. | 1199. | Arundel. | | mar. to Sir War- | | | of Lancaster, 1267 : Earl | St. Louis, King | and Earl of
| (2) Clemence, sister of | Agnes, w. of William | | ren de Bostock, | | | of England, 1274 ; King | of France. | Richmond.
Geoffrey de Fulgers,	de Ferrers, Earl of		Kt.			of Sicily; b. Jan. 16,
widow of Alan de	Derby. Co-heirs of					1245 ; d. 1296.
Dinnnt.	their brother.					

(1) | | HENRY III., King, = Eleanor, d. and co-h. of = Avoline, d. and h. of = Edmund, of Wood-
Alice, d. of William = John de Lacy, eldest = Margaret de Quincy, d. | EDWARD I., King, = Eleanor, d. of Fer- | born *rtine* 17, | William de Fortibus, | stock, cr. Earl of
d.s.p. | son and h. of Roger | and co-h. Countess | of England ; | dinand III., King | 1239 ; d. Nov. 27, | Earl of Albemarle : m. | Kent, 1321 ; m. Mar-
("Peter") de Aquila. | de Lacy, surnamed | of Lincoln in right | | of Castile ; mar. | 1290. | April 1, 1269; d. the | garet, d. of John,
| Hell, Baron of Hal- | of her mother. | | 1254 ; d. Nov. 27, | | same year, s.p. | Lord Wake, of Lid-
| ton; had the Earldom | | | 1290. | | | dull; b. 1801; d.
| of Lincoln re-granted | | | | | | 1329; had issue.
| to him 1232 ; d. July | | | | | |
| 22, 1240. | | | | | |

(2) | | | Eleanor, Joan, Margaret, | Thomas, of Brotherton, Duke
Edmund de Lacy, 9th = Alice, d. of Manfred, | EDWARD II., = Isabel, dau. of | Mary, Elizabeth. | of Norfolk, Earl Marshal;
Baron of Halton, sur- | Marquis of Saluzzo, | King of England ; | Philip IV. of | | b. June 1, 1300; mar. (1)
vived his father, but | by Beatrix of Savoy; | born April 25, 1284 ; | France ; mar. | | Alice, d. of Sir Roger Hales,
having predeceased | m. 1247. | deposed Jan. 25, | Jan. 28, 1808 ; | | and (2) Mary, d. of William,
his mother, did not | | 1327 ; d. Sept. 21, | d. August 22, | | Lord Ross, widow of William,
acquire the Earldom | | 1327. | 1357. | | Lord Bruco, widow of Gower; d.
of Lincoln ; d. June | | | | |

Margaret, d. of William = Henry de Lacy, 10th Baron of = Ivan, dau. of
Longespee; m. 1256.   Halton, knighted 1272; Earl   Wm. Martin,
                       of Cornwall and Lincoln,   Lord Keinis;
                       Lord of the Honors of Clith- d. s.p.
                       eroe and Denbigh; b. 1251;
                       d Feb. 5, 1310.

Edward III, = Philippa, 3rd d.   John of Eltham, Joan, m. David
K. of England;   of William,   Earl of Corn-   II., King of
born Nov. 13,   Ct. of Holland   wall; d. un-   Scotland; d
1312; d. June   and Hainault;   mar. 1336.   s.p. 1357.
21, 1377.   mar. Jan. 24,   Eleanor, w. of
                 1328; d. Aug.   Reynold, 1st
                 17, 1369.   Duke of Gel-
                                                    dres; d. s.p
                                                    April 22, 1355.

Edward Prince—Joan, the   William, d   Lionel, Duke   Edmund of Isabel,
of Wales, "the "Maid of   young.   of Clarence.   Langley,   Joan.
Black Prince," Kent,"   Thomas, of Blanche.
Duke of Aqui-   d of Edmund,   Woodstock. Mary.
tamia; b. June Earl of   Margaret.
15, 1330; d.   Kent,
July 8, 1376.   widow of Sir
                Thos. Holland;
                d July 8, 1384.

the Sovereigns of
   ENGLAND.

John of Gaunt, Duke = Blanche, youngest
of LANCASTER; m.   d. and eventually
(1)Blanche; m.   sole heir of Henry,
and (2)Constance,   Duke of Lancaster,
and each of Peter,   and coh. of Peter,
King of Castile and   King of Castile and
Leon, and (3) Katha- Leon, and (3) Katharine, d. of Sir John rine, d. of Sir John
Payne Roet, and w.   Payne Roet, and w.
of Sir Otes Swyn-   of Sir Otes Swyn-
fort.   fort.

Edmund, d.   John, d.   Margaret.
young.   young.

Henry, Earl of Lancaster and = Isabel, d. of Henry Beaumont,
Leicester, Steward of England; or Beaumont, Lord of Folke-
cr. Earl of Derby March 16,   ingham.
1337, Earl of Lincoln, August
20, 1349, and Duke of Lancaster, March 6, 1351. K.G.
d March 24, 1360.

Maud, eldest d. and coh., m. (1)   Blanche, youngest d. and sole
Ralph, 8. and h. of Ralph,   heir to her father and sister
Stafford, and (2) William the W(?)   in May 8, 1569; d. 1369.
Count of Bavaria, Holland, and
Zealand; d s.p 1362.

Mary de Bohun, youngest d. = Henry, Duke of Lancaster,
and co-h. of Humphrey,   styled Earl of Derby in his
Earl of Hereford, Essex,   father's lifetime, cr. Duke of
and Northampton, Con-   Hereford Sept 29, 1397; on
stable of England; mar.   the deposition of Richard II,
1380; d. 1394.   1399, was crowned King of
                             England, by the title of Henry
                             IV; born at Bolingbroke about
                             1366; died March 20, 1413.

the Sovereigns of

CHAPTER V.

ENRY PLANTAGENET, surnamed of Bolingbroke from the place of his birth,
the only surviving son of John of Gaunt, by his first wife, Blanche, daughter and
sole heir of Henry, first Duke of Lancaster, was in character diametrically the
reverse of his sovereign, King Richard II. His talents were of a superior order;
his manners were popular, and even fascinating; and his ambition led him to
aspire to a higher station than that of the first subject in the realm, which his
father had so long occupied.

In the second year of the reign of Richard II. (1378-9), Henry, though only
eleven years old, was thought of age to receive knighthood, and in 1380 he was betrothed, with
the consent of the king, to Mary de Bohun, the younger daughter and coheiress of Humphrey de
Bohun, K.G., late Earl of Essex, Hereford, and Northampton, and hereditary constable of England.
In 1385 he was summoned to Parliament by the title of Henry, Earl of Derby. In the eleventh
year of the reign he was engaged with the Duke of Gloucester in the combination, professedly for
the removal of the king's favourites, but in reality to retain the control over the sovereign, who
had then just come of age, at which his majesty took great offence, but having subsequently made
full confession of his improper conduct, and sued for pardon, Richard was reconciled to him, and in
the 21st year of his reign (1397-8) we find the king on the last day of the session (September 29)
"sitting in Parliament in royal majesty, holding in his hand a rod, and making his cousin, Sir
Henry of Lancaster, Earl of Derby, a duke, by the title of Duke of Hereford." This reconciliation,
was, however, short-lived, a violent quarrel having arisen between the Duke of Hereford and the
Duke of Norfolk with reference to some alleged treasonable expressions regarding the conflict at
Radcot Bridge in 1388, which terminated in an appeal to arms. The Parliament in which the
charge was made was sitting at Shrewsbury. Hereford and Norfolk were both ordered into
custody, and the dispute was referred to the Court of Chivalry, which decreed that the quarrel
should be determined by wager of battle at Coventry on the 16th September following. On the
day appointed the combatants entered the lists, but when the heralds had made proclamation the
king, with, as was said, the advice of his council, of which the Duke of Lancaster, father of
the Duke of Hereford, was at the head, sent them both into exile: Hereford for ten years,
Norfolk for life.[1] In some of the versions relating to this memorable duel, it is represented that
Henry, Duke of Hereford, lodged the information against Thomas, Duke of Norfolk; but Sir
John Froissart, a contemporary writer, states the matter differently, and more probably, by representing that the secret of the confidential conversation between the Duke of Hereford and the
Duke of Norfolk was divulged by the latter; and this construction is supported by the more
severe sentence passed upon that duke, "because he had sowen sedicion in this realme by his
woordes, whereof he could make no profe."[2]

---

[1] A pompous description of the Lists of Coventry is given in *Ball's
Chronicle*.

[2] The following is Hereford's written account of the conversation
between himself and Norfolk as they were riding between Brentford and
London, as given in the Rolls of Parliament:—

Norfolk: "We are on the point of being undone."
Hereford: "Why so?"
Norfolk: "On account of the affair at Radcotbridge."
Hereford: "How can that be, since he has granted us pardon, and has
declared in Parliament that we behaved as good and loyal subjects."
Norfolk: "Nevertheless, our fate will be like that of others before us.
He will annul that record."

Hereford: "It will be marvellous indeed if the king, after having said
so before the people, should cause it to be annulled."
Norfolk: "It is a marvellous and false world that we live in."
Norfolk then related a plot of certain of the king's council to undo
six other lords, amongst whom were Lancaster, Hereford, and himself.
Hereford: "God forbid! It will be a wonder if the king should assent
to such designs. He appears to make me good cheer, and has promised
to be my good lord. Indeed, he has sworn by St. Edward to be a good
lord to me and the others."
Norfolk: "So has he often sworn to me by God's body, but I do not
trust him the more for that."—C.

The nation was highly incensed by the king's behaviour to the Duke of Hereford, who was the darling of the principal peers, of the city of London, and of the people.　They held that he had committed no crime, and had been condemned without trial; that by his banishment they were deprived of their best protector; and they thought themselves by that event exposed to all the malice and indignation of an incensed and vindictive tyrant.　As the duke passed through the city of London on horseback, on his leaving the kingdom, he was followed by more than 40,000 people, who cried after him, and bewailed his fate and their own in the most moving manner.　He was accompanied on this occasion by trumpets and instruments of music, and with the more melting sounds of universal lamentation.　The Mayor of London, and others of the principal citizens, followed him to Deptford; and some accompanied him as far as Dover, on his way to Calais, where he arrived October 3rd, 1398, and on landing was received by the Dukes of Orleans and Berry, of Bourbon and Burgundy.　On the duke's arrival at Paris he was very graciously received by the Court of France, where he was soon offered in marriage the widowed daughter of the Duke of Berry, uncle of Charles VI., Mary de Bohun, the mother of Henry of Monmouth, and of five other children being then dead.　To prevent this union, King Richard sent the Earl of Salisbury, his ambassador, to the Court of France, where the earl represented the Duke of Hereford as a person guilty of traitorous designs against his prince; upon which the treaty of marriage proceeded no further.　After his departure, he received letters from his father, advising him rather to go into Castile than into Hungary; but the Duke of Lancaster becoming sick, his son continued in Paris, where the news reached him of his father's death.　The king, availing himself of the exile of the Duke of Hereford, now become Duke of Lancaster, seized the possessions of his father, John of Gaunt, into his own hands, and lavished them with his usual profusion upon his favourites.[1]　Shortly after this time, the king was obliged to embark for Ireland, to suppress a rebellion which had arisen in that oppressed country.　He set sail from Milford on the 4th June, 1399, and, during his absence, England fell into great distraction.　In this exigency, the people of London sent for their favourite Henry, who had then become Duke of Lancaster, promising him their assistance, if he would accept of the government.[2]　With such encouragement, and aided by the Duke of Britany, he took ship at Le Port Blanc, and landed at Ravenspur, at the mouth of the Humber, in Yorkshire, in July, when he was met by a number of nobles in the north, and their followers.　On his arrival at Doncaster he found himself at the head of a considerable army, and the common people in all places greeting his return with enthusiasm.　The injustice practised towards him by the king, in first banishing him from the realm without proof of guilt, and then seizing upon his patrimonial inheritance, in violation of his letters-patent, excited the indignation of the nation towards the oppressor, and their sympathy and enthusiasm in favour of the oppressed.　His march through the country was a triumph; everywhere the castles yielded to his summons, and on his arrival at Bristol his forces were augmented to 60,000.　To oppose this formidable force, the Duke of York, who had been left viceroy of the kingdom during the king's absence, assembled an army of 40,000 men at St. Albans; but their attachment to the royal cause was so lukewarm that they went over to the Duke of Lancaster, on his representation that he sought not the subversion of the throne, but the recovery of his paternal possessions, which the king had seized, on the death of his illustrious father.　The intelligence of this invasion reached the king while he was leading his army among the bogs and thickets of Ireland, on which he hastened back into England, and landed in Wales, near a place called Barkloughly Castle;[3] where, finding that he was almost totally forsaken, he went on to Conway Castle, in the county of Caernarvon.[4]　The duke, on hearing of the king's arrival, marched to Chester, which city he entered on the 9th August.　From thence he despatched the Earl of Northumberland to the king at Conway, who proposed that a Parliament should be called, to remove the grievances of which the country complained, and particularly to arbitrate between the king and the Duke of Lancaster.　Richard, scarcely aware of the danger by which he was menaced, consented to an interview, at Flint Castle, with the Duke of Lancaster, who, it was represented, would there ask pardon on his knees on condition of the estates and honours of his family being restored.　While journeying to Flint, Northumberland, who had a large force concealed behind the rocks, seized the king's bridle.　In this way he became his prisoner, and was, under various pretences of friendship and loyalty, after a sojourn of three days at Chester, conducted to London, where the cavalcade was met by the mayor and principal citizens, the people shouting, as it passed,

[1] This procedure was in direct contravention of the king's pledge, for before the departure of Hereford he had promised and confirmed, by his letters patent, that in case any succession should happen in his absence, for which he ought to do homage, that he might, by his attorney, be permitted to prosecute, and have liberty of succession or heritages, and that his homage and fealty might be respected.—C.

[2] Froissart.

[3] Holinshed, 499.

[4] He went first to Harlech or Harddloch Castle, thence to Carnarvon, afterwards to Beaumaris, and finally to Conway, where he arrived at daybreak.　It is difficult to say which of these castles has been corrupted into Barkloughly.　The Monk of Evesham maintains that Harlech was the place of the king's landing, and a recent writer in the *Archæologia Cambrensis*, while affirming his belief that the king landed at Barmouth, is of opinion that Harlech is the Barkloughly named.　See *Traison et Mort Richard II.*, 189 and 232, and *Arch. Camb.*, January, 1858, p. 10.—O.

10

" Long live the Duke of Lancaster." To give an air of justice to the ultimate designs of the duke, he caused a Parliament to be convened under the authority of Richard, by which Parliament the king was, on the 29th September, declared to have forfeited his throne by extortion, rapine, and injustice. Being thus deposed by the suffrages of two estates of the realm, the throne was declared vacant, and the head of the noble house of Lancaster ascended the throne of these realms, by the style and title of Henry IV.[1] On receiving this dignity before the assembled Parliament, the new monarch crossed himself on the forehead, and, calling upon the name of Christ, said—

" In the name of Fadher, Son, and Holy Ghost, I, Henry of Lancaster, challenge this rewme of Yngland, and the croun, with all the members, and the appurtenances ; als I that am descendit by right line of the blode, coming fro the gude lorde King Henry therde, and throghe that right that God of his grace hath sent me, with help of kyn and of my frendes to recover it ; the which rewme was in poynt to be ondone by defaut of governance, and undoing of the gude lawes." [2]

A tradition had prevailed amongst the vulgar that Edmund Crouchback, Earl of Lancaster, son of Henry III., was really the eldest brother of Edward I., but that, owing to some deformity in his person, he had been supplanted in the succession by his younger brother; and as the present Duke of Lancaster inherited from Edmund by his mother, this genealogy constituted him the true heir to the throne. This was, however, a topic rather to be insinuated than declared, and the best grounds of Henry's claim were the misrule of his predecessor, and the affections of the people over whom he was himself called to govern,[3] for the posterity of Lionel, Duke of Clarence, third son of Edward III., had a prior claim to that of the heir of John of Gaunt, the fourth son. At the time of Richard's deposition the hereditary claim of the Clarence branch was vested in Edmund Mortimer, Earl of March, who was the grandson of Philippa, the daughter of Lionel, but he was then only ten years of age. When the Parliament deposed Richard and chose Henry in his stead the Archbishop of Canterbury preached a sermon, taking for his text the words, " A *man* shall reign over my people," and in the course of his address he enlarged upon · the theme that when the King of kings threatened his people He said, " I will make *children* to rule over them," his remarks being evidently aimed at the youthful Earl of March. When in 1385 Roger Mortimer was declared presumptive heir to the throne, John of Gaunt asserted that his own son Henry was the true heir, as descended from Edmund Crouchback, the eldest son, as he incorrectly affirmed, of Henry III., who, he alleged, had been set aside on account of his deformity. Henry of Lancaster's claim by blood as " coming fro the gude lorde Kyng Henry therde " would have been of little avail, had he not been at the head of a powerful army, and known to be a man of vigour and ability, supported moreover by the chief nobles. Edmund Mortimer, whose claim to the crown was set aside by the enthronement of Henry IV., died without issue in 1424. He had a sister Anne, who married the second son of Edmund Langley, Duke of York, and in her son arose the pretension to the crown of the House of York.

Henry, Duke of Lancaster, being now seated upon the throne of England, the unfortunate Richard was sent to the duke's castle at Pontefract. Here he was detained in confinement for some time; but so short is the distance between the throne and the grave of a deposed monarch, that his life was speedily terminated, either by the hand of the assassin or the more protracted misery of famine. Richard's reign being thus terminated, his successor turned his attention to the appointment of his new officers. The office of high steward, which he possessed in right of his earldom of Leicester, derived from the Lacys, he conferred upon his second son, Lord Thomas, whose incapacity, from his nonage, was supplied by the Earl of Worcester; while the office of Chancellor of the Duchy of Lancaster was given to John de Wakeringe, a divine of considerable influence with his royal master. Mr. Justice Blackstone, in his Commentaries,[4] observes, that " the county palatine, or Duchy of Lancaster, was the property of Henry Bolingbroke, the son of John of Gaunt, at the time when he wrested the crown from King Richard II. and assumed the title of King Henry IV :" and he adds, he was too prudent to suffer this to be united to the crown, lest, if he lost one, he should lose the other also. But this is a mode of expression at variance with

[1] Froissart thus describes the surrender of the crown : " On a day the Duke of Lancaster, accompanied with lords, dukes, prelates, earls, barons, and knights and of the notablest men of London, and of other good towns, rode to the Tower, and there alighted. Then King Richard was brought into the hall, apparelled like a king in his robes of estate, his sceptre in his hand, and his crown on his head. Then he stood up alone, not holden nor stayed by no man, and said aloud, ' I have been King of England, Duke of Aquitaine, and Lord of Ireland, about twenty-two years, which signiory, royalty, sceptre, crown, and heritage, I clearly resign here to my cousin, Henry of Lancaster; and I desire him here, in this open presence, in entering of the same possession, to take this sceptre ;' and so delivered it unto the duke, who took it." The Parliament met on the 30th September, in Westminster Hall ; the throne was empty ; the Duke of Lancaster sat in his place as a peer. The resignation of the king was read, and each member expressed aloud his acceptance of it. After reading the articles of impeachment, thirty-three in number, the Act of deposition was solemnly pronounced by eight commissioners. Henry then approached the throne, and having challenged his right to the crown, was led by the Archbishops of Canterbury and York to the royal chair of state, " All the people wonderfully shouting for joy."—C.

[2] Knyghton, p. 2757 ; Rot. Parl. iii., 422.

[3] It is said that John of Gaunt put forward a claim in Parliament 19 Richard II. that his son Henry should be adjudged heir to the kingdom of England, as being (through his mother) grandson of Edmund, first Earl of Lancaster, who, he pretended, was elder brother of Edward I., who had been supplanted by reason of a deformity in his back, but which, as previously explained, was the Crusaders' cross—hence the name " Crouchback." The claim appears scarcely probable, as it not only set aside the right of his brother Lionel, but reflected on the title of the king and his two predecessors.—C.

[4] Vol. i. intro. sec. 4, p. 118.

the usual accuracy of that distinguished writer's style, and would seem to imply that the county palatine of Lancaster and the duchy of Lancaster are co-extensive, and that the terms are convertible. This, however, is by no means the case—the county palatine being confined to the county, while the duchy of Lancaster, as we have already intimated, and, as we shall speedily show more specifically, comprehends not only the county of Lancaster but many other portions of the kingdom. It has been justly observed by Plowden[1] in the celebrated "Duchy of Lancaster Case," 4 Elizabeth (1562), and by Sir Edward Coke[2] in his fourth Institute, that the new monarch was well aware that " he held the Duchy of Lancaster by sure and indefeasible title, but that his title to the crown was not so assured: for that, after the decease of Richard II. the right of the crown was in the heir of Lionel, Duke of Clarence, *third* son of Edward III.; John of Gaunt

THE CHAPEL ROYAL WITHIN THE PRECINCTS OF THE DUCAL RESIDENCE OF THE SAVOY

father of Henry IV., being but the fourth son." One of his first measures after ascending the throne was, therefore, to pass an Act, sanctioned by Parliament, ordaining that his eldest son Henry should have and bear the name and title of Duke of Lancaster, in addition to his other titles (of Prince of Wales, Duke of Aquitaine and Cornwall, and Earl of Chester); and that neither the inheritance of his duchy of Lancaster, or its liberties, should be changed, transferred, or diminished, through his assumption of the royal dignity; but that they should retain their distinctive character and privileges, and be adminstered and governed in like manner, as if he had never attained the royal dignity. It was further directed that all ecclesiastical benefices in the said duchy should be conferred by himself and his heirs, so that the (lord) chancellor, treasurer, or other officers of the state, should not interfere, by reason of their respective offices,

[1] P. 215.   [2] P. 205.

with the collection or preservation, or even with the visitation, of benefices within the duchy; and that all receivers, bailiffs, and other servants of the duchy, etc., should appear before certain special auditors and ministers, and not before the treasurer and barons of the king's exchequer, and account and answer for profits and benefits of the duchy, without any interference of the treasurer and barons. (See *Rot. Parl.* III. 428.)

Steadily pursuing the principle here laid down, it was by a subsequent Act[1] ordained that the right of succession to the duchy of Lancaster after the king's death should belong to his eldest son, Henry, Prince of Wales, and his heirs; and in default of heirs to Thomas, his second son, and that the ancient rights, statutes, and customs of the duchy, should be maintained and observed inviolate. Having thus fixed the succession to the property of the duchy by all the force of legislative enactments, the next care of the king was to establish a court, called the Duchy Court of Lancaster, in which all questions of revenue and council affecting the duchy possessions might be decided. This court is now held at the duchy office, Lancaster Place, Strand, London, W.C.; thence issue all patents and commissions of office or dignities, all orders or grants affecting the limits and revenues, and all acts of authority within the duchy. It was also a court of appeal from the chancery of the county palatine of Lancaster, which court, as previously stated, was a court of equity for matters of equity arising within the county of Lancaster, until the passing of the Judicature Act, 36 and 37 Vict. c. 66, s. 16, by the operation of which the jurisdiction of the Court of Common Pleas at Lancaster has been transferred to the High Court of Justice. The Court of Criminal Jurisdiction in no way differs from that of the Queen's ordinary court. The record office of the duchy of Lancaster, where the deeds are deposited, has been frequently changed: within living memory, Gray's Inn, Somerset House, and Great George's Street, has each in succession afforded them a depository; but the office of the duchy now seems permanently fixed within the precinct of the ancient ducal residence of the Savoy, in Lancaster Place, Waterloo Bridge, London,[2] of which bridge the northern arch abuts against Her Majesty's inheritance of the duchy of Lancaster, and the southern against her inheritance of the duchy of Cornwall. The duchy chambers at Westminster being within the precincts described in old statutes as a royal residence, the proceedings are dated before Her Majesty, "at her palace at Westminster," and not, as other royal acts, at the personal residence of the monarch. In this court she is not only presumed to be present, as in others, but to be personally acting by the advice of her chancellor, and other ministers, for the affairs of her duchy.[3]

When that intolerable nuisance, the court of Star Chamber, existed, in contravention of the provisions of Magna Charta, which direct that no freeman shall be deprived of his liberty or property but by lawful judgment of his peers, the duchy of Lancaster had also its Star Chamber, and the chancellor of the duchy and council of his court punished without law, and decreed without authority; but this power was swept away by the Act 16 Car. I. (1640-1), which ordained that from the first of August, 1641, this power should be abolished in every court within the realm, and that from henceforth no court should exercise the jurisdiction of star-chamber.[4]

Two years after the succession had been settled upon Prince Henry and his heirs, the manor of Brotilby, and fee of La Haye, in the county of Lincoln, with the wardship of the castle of Lincoln formerly in the possession of Thomas, Earl of Lancaster, and which then remained in the hands of the king, through the forfeiture of Thomas, son of Thomas, Earl of Kent, was incorporated with his inheritance of Lancaster, as parcel of the duchy; and it was ordained that it should

---

[1] 8 Henry IV. 1406-7.

[2] The site of the palace of the Savoy, the ancient residence of the Dukes of Lancaster, was granted, 30 Henry III. (1245-6), by the king to Peter, Earl of Savoy and Richmond, uncle to his Queen Eleanor, who erected his palace upon it. This stately residence was given by Peter de Savoy to the fraternity of Mountjoy, of whom it was bought by Queen Eleanor for her second son, Edmund Crouchback, Earl of Lancaster. After the execution of her son, Earl Thomas, in 1322, the Savoy became the property of his brother and successor, Earl Henry, who enlarged it at an expense of 52,000 marks, making it so magnificent that, according to Knighton, there was no mansion in the realm to be compared with it in beauty and stateliness. After the decease of the earl's son, Henry, first Duke of Lancaster, John of Gaunt, who had married his younger daughter, Blanche, became, in consequence, the possessor of the Savoy. Within its walls he received and entertained the captive King John of France after the victory at Poictiers. John of Gaunt lived at the Savoy in almost regal state; and here, Geoffrey Chaucer, who had married Philippa, a lady of the Duchess Blanche's household, and the sister to Catherine Swynford, whom the duke married for his third wife, was a frequent visitor, and is said to have written several of his poems while residing within the palace. During John of Gaunt's occupancy, the Savoy was twice pillaged by a mob; the first time in 1376, when the duke had made himself obnoxious by his bold speech to the Bishop of London, in St. Paul's, at the citation of John Wycliffe; the second occasion being in 1381, when the insurgents, under Wat Tyler, reduced it to a heap of ruins, in which condition it remained until 1505, when Henry VII. had the site cleared and commenced building thereon a hospital of St. John the Baptist, "to receive and lodge nightly one hundred poor folks." After various

vicissitudes a great portion of the building was taken down in 1819 to form the road from the Strand to Waterloo Bridge. The Savoy Church, which is a "royal peculiar," and, consequently, in many respects, free from episcopal control, was formerly the chapel of the hospital; it was destroyed by fire in 1864, but rebuilt in 1866, at the cost of the Queen, in memory of the Prince Consort.—C.

[3] In 1868 Her Majesty graciously presented the whole of the ancient muniments of the Duchy of Lancaster to the nation. This munificent gift was followed, five years later, by the transfer, pursuant to a request of the Chancellor of the Duchy of Lancaster, dated 25th July, 1873, of the records of the Courts of Equity and Common Law, which until then were deposited in the record rooms of Lancaster Castle, and in the charge of three several persons: (1) The Registrar of the Court of Chancery of the County Palatine, the custodian of the Chancery Records; (2) The Protho-notary, who had the charge of the Records of the Court of Common Pleas; (3) The Clerk of the Crown, in whose custody were the criminal proceedings of the Palatinate; and the whole of these original evidences are now carefully preserved in the Public Record Office, on the Rolls Estate, at the back of the old Rolls Chapel.—C.

[4] In the Act for dissolving the Court of Star Chamber and taking away the whole of its powers, all the ancient statutes, including the Great Charter, which declare that no freeman shall be imprisoned or condemned but by the judgment of his peers, or by the law of the land, are recited, and it is affirmed that the authority of the Star Chamber, under the statute of Henry VII., has been abused, and the decrees of the Court have been found "to be an intolerable burden to the subjects, and the means to introduce an arbitrary power and government."—C.

descend to his heirs, and that all the tenants of these possessions should be governed in the same manner and by such officers as the other lordships and manors of the inheritance.[1] Henry IV., Duke of Lancaster, died on the 25th March, 1413, in his forty-seventh year, and was buried at Canterbury.

Soon after Henry V. ascended the throne (in 1414) he confirmed the acts of his royal father with regard to the Duchy of Lancaster; and it was directed, with the sanction of Parliament, that all the liberties and franchises of this duchy should in all things be maintained and exercised for ever, according to the tenor of the charters already granted, and that the seal hitherto used in the duchy, and all matters under that seal which had hitherto been given and granted, should have force, without the reclamation of the king or his officers; and that the seal of the duchy should be used for ever in transacting the business of the duchy. As several honors, castles, and manors, which were the inheritance of Mary, one of the daughters and heiresses of Humphrey de Bohun, Earl of Hereford, Essex, and Northampton, whose heir the king was, had descended to him by hereditary right, the king separated all these possessions from the crown, and incorporated them with his duchy of Lancaster, appointing that they should be administered by the officers of the duchy, as they had been accustomed to be; and that the vassals and tenants of this inheritance, and the resiants within the same, should enjoy the liberties and franchise of the duchy. He also ordained that all ecclesiastical benefices attached to the duchy inheritance should be conferred under the seal of the duchy, without the interference of the chancellor and treasurer of England. To render this ordinance complete, it was further directed that all the castles, honors, and lands which had come into possession of the king's father, Henry IV., in consequence of a grant made in the first year of his reign (1400), as to escheats, forfeitures, and recovery, should be incorporated with the duchy, and that any other honors, castles, or manors which had come by escheats, forfeitures, or recovery should also be joined to the duchy, and that they should be ruled and governed by the officers and ministers of the duchy, under the sanction of the duchy seal.[2]

In the third year of the reign of Henry V. (1415) it was directed that two of the chief seneschals (stewards) of his inheritance for the time being, besides the number of guardians limited by form of statutes, should act in all the counties of the kingdom, and that they should exercise their office of seneschal in all commissions of the peace, and that no donations, pardons, or releases, which concerned in any manner the duchy of Lancaster, or that emanated therefrom, should be valid except under the seal designed for the duchy. Two other Acts,

ARMORIAL INSIGNIA OF HENRY OF LANCASTER, AFTERWARDS KING HENRY IV, FROM HIS TOMB AT CANTERBURY.

the first passed in the ninth year of Henry V. (1421) and the second in the first of Henry VI. (1422-3), annex other possessions of the Bohun family to the duchy of Lancaster.

It was the misfortune of Henry VI. to be deeply involved in debt; and his expectation that two Lancashire knights would remove all his embarrassments, by the discovery of the philosopher's stone![3] was not sufficient to prevent his creditors from urging their demands in a tone little suited

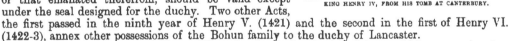

---

[1] Act of 10 Henry IV. (1409).

[2] Act 2 Henry V. (1414).

[3] The belief in alchemy was widely prevalent at this time. In 1438 the king commissioned three philosophers to make the precious metals, but, as might be expected, he received no returns from them in either gold or silver. His credulity, however, seems to have been unshaken by disappointment, for in the twenty-fourth year of his reign (1446) he issued his royal licence to Sir Edmund Trafford and Sir Thomas Ashton, two Lancashire knights, authorising them to make gold. The original patent, of which the following is a translation, was found by Fuller in the Tower of London: "The King to all whom, &c., greeting,—Know ye, that whereas our beloved and loyal Edmund de Trafford, knight, and Thomas Ashton, knight, have, by a certain petition shewn unto us, set forth that although they were willing, by the art and science of philosophy, to translate (transmute) imperfect metals from their own kind, and then to transubstantiate them by their said art or science, as they say, into

perfect gold or silver, unto all manner of proofs or trials, to be expected or endured as any gold or silver growing in any mine; notwithstanding certain persons ill-willing and maligning them, conceiving them to work by unlawful art, and so may hinder and disturb them in the trial of the said art and science: WE, considering the premises, and willing to know the conclusion of the said work or science, of our special grace have granted and given leave to the same Edmund and Thomas, and to their servants, that they may work and try the aforesaid art and science lawfully and freely, without any hindrance of ours, or of our officers, whatsoever; any statute, act, ordinance, or provision made, ordained, or provided to the contrary notwithstanding. In witness whereof, &c., the King at Westminster, the 7th day of April." When Henry granted this licence he was overriding the provisions of the Act 5, Henry IV., cap. 4, which made it felony for any of the king's subjects "to multiply gold or silver, or to use the craft of multiplication," &c.—the only Act, it is said, which has never been violated.—C.

to the refinement of a court. To satisfy these demands he was driven to the expedient of mortgaging, for five years, the revenues of the duchies of Lancaster and Cornwall, and the terms of this mortgage, as given in the 18th Henry VI. (1440) sufficiently indicate the importunity of the royal creditors, and the petulancy of the king under their demands.

The revenues of the duchy having reverted to the king, as Duke of Lancaster, an Act was passed in the 39 Henry VI. (1460-61), appointing that there should appertain to the duchy one chief steward and one auditor in the northern parts, and one other chief steward and one other auditor in the southern parts, with one chancellor, one receiver-general, and one attorney-general in and of all the duchy, with one chief-steward, and one attorney-general in the county of palatine of Lancaster. While the mortgage existed, several new offices had been created, but by this Act those offices were abolished as burdensome in fees and unnecessary for use. Hitherto the archives of the duchy had been lodged in the church and priory of St. Bartholomew, in West Smithfield, London, much to the annoyance of the prior and his convent. On a representation that the church had become much occupied and encumbered with "divers great chests containing the books" of the duchy of Lancaster, and that divine service was interrupted by the entrance of ministers, under colour of an examination of the books, and that no little disturbance was created thereby, the king directed that the prior and convent, and their successors, should be exonerated from the custody of the said books and documents; and the officers of the duchy were ordered to remove their chests, with their contents, out of the priory into the Tower of London, or into such other place as might be found convenient to deposit them (1460).[1]

Although the court of the duchy of Lancaster was instituted in the early part of the reign of Henry IV., no *post-mortem* inquisitions are registered in this court earlier than the first of Henry V. (1413). The duty of collecting and arranging the inquisitions has been performed by the direction of the Commissioners of Public Records, and a list of these inquisitions is published along with a list of the pleadings, consisting of bills, answers, depositions, and surveys, relating to the suits in that court, in two volumes, entitled *Ducatus Lancastriæ*. These volumes are thus described by the persons charged with the duty of collecting and arranging the materials:—

"According to the returns made to the select committee of the House of Commons in the year 1800, the INQUISITIONS POST MORTEM in this repository then found amounted to 2,400, beginning with the first year of King Henry V. (1413), and ending with the eighteenth year of King Charles the First (1642). A more recent investigation has shown their number to amount to 3,569; which it has also been found necessary to put in a better state of arrangement, and to clean, repair, and bind them in volumes. The PLEADINGS consist of bills, answers, and depositions and surveys, in suits exhibited in the duchy court, commencing with the first year of King Henry VII., and are continued to the present time.   (Signed)   "R. J. HARPER.
                                                                                                      JOHN CALEY.
       Dated "Office of the Duchy of Lancaster, 1823."   WM. MINCHIN."

The Inquisitions and Pleadings contain a great fund of local information; but they would, in the most condensed form, occupy an inconveniently large space in our county history; and the necessity for their insertion is materially diminished since the *Ducatus*, thanks to the liberality of Parliament, is presented to many of the public libraries in this kingdom, and is therefore easily accessible; suffice it to say, that the records, of which the *Ducatus* exhibits little more than an index, are to be found in the Record Office, in London, and their number, as far as regards the county palatine of Lancaster, stands thus: Inquisitions Post Mortem, in vol. i 2,105; in vol. ii. (*Nil*). Pleadings in vol. i. 1,594; in vol. ii. 1,589. Total 3,183.[2]

The hostility of the house of York to the house of Lancaster did not extend to the revenues of the duchy, for no sooner had Edward IV. ascended the throne than he confirmed all the charters and liberties of the duchy of Lancaster, in a manner the most ample, except that he joined the duchy inheritance to the crown.[3] Henry VII., not to be outstripped by a member of the rival

[1] 39 Henry VI. (1460).

[2] Since the removal of the muniments of the Duchy and Palatinate of Lancaster to the Public Record Office, a very comprehensive list of the various classes of documents, illustrated by numerous examples, and containing valuable lists both of persons and places, has been edited by Mr. Walford D. Selby, of the Record Office, and issued by the Record Society (vols. vii. and viii.). Volume vii. deals with (1) the Records of the Duchy of Lancaster, with special reference to the Lancashire and Cheshire manors belonging to it, (2) the Records of the Palatinate of Lancashire, and (3) those of the Superior and Abolished Courts as far as they relate to the two counties, the value of such class of records being as far as possible shown by examples of the various and important documents they contain. Volume viii. deals with the various Indices to the Records, which have from time to time been compiled, together with such special classes of documents as Special Commissions, Licences and Pardons, Royalist Composition Papers, &c., &c., all of which throw much new light on the past history of the two counties, and indicate the best sources of information to be consulted by those working at either local or family history.—C.

[3] AN ACT FOR INCORPORATING AND ALSO FOR CONFISCATING THE DUCHY OF LANCASTER TO THE CROWN OF ENGLAND FOR EVER (1 *Edward* IV.—1461).—"It is declared and adjudged by the assent and advice of the Lords Spiritual and Temporal, and of the Commons, being in this present Parliament, and by the authority of the same, that the same Henry, late called King Henry the Sixth, for the considerations of the great, heinous, and detestable matters and offences before specified by him, committed against his faith and ligeance to our said Liege Lord, King Edward the Fourth, his true, righteous, and natural liege Lord, offended and hurt unjustly and unlawfully the Royal Majesty of our said sovereign Lord, stand by the advice and assent convicted and attainted of High Treason. And that it be ordained and established by the same advice, assent, and authority, that he the same Henry forfeit unto the same our Liege Lord Edward the Fourth, and to his heirs, and to the said Crown of England, all Castles, Manors, Lordships, Towns, Townships, Honors, Lands, Tenements, Rents, Services, Fee-Farms, Knights' Fees, Advowsons, Hereditaments, and Possessions, with their appurtenances which he or any other to his use had the third day of March last past, being of the Duchy of Lancaster, or that were any parcel or member of the same Duchy, or thereunto annexed or united in the first year of the reign of Henry, late called King Henry the Fifth, or at any time since. And that it be ordained and established by the same advice, assent, and authority, that the same Manors, Castles, Lordships, Honors, Towns, Townships, Lands Tenements, Rents, Services, Fee-Farms, Knights' Fees, Advowsons

house, enacted in the first year of his reign (1485) that all the lands of the duchy of Lancaster which had been alienated from that inheritance in the reign of Edward IV. should be re-invested in the king and his heirs for ever, as amply and largely, and in like manner, form, and condition, separate from the crown of England, and possessions of the same, as the three Henrys, or Edward IV., or any of them, had and held the same. Ever since the period when Henry IV. mounted the throne of England, the duchy of Lancaster has indeed always been considered by the reigning monarch as one of the richest gems in the crown, though for state purposes it has been kept separate and distinct from the regal revenues and possessions. When the Act for regulating the order of wards and liveries was passed, a special proviso was introduced, to guard against the royalties, liberties, and jurisdictions of the county palatine and the duchy of Lancaster suffering prejudice ; and when Henry VIII. had impaired the revenues of the duchy of Lancaster by a number of gifts, grants, and sales, indemnity against the consequences of these alienations was found for the king, as Duke of Lancaster, by a grant from Parliament (in 1545) of the manor of Ripon and its dependencies in the county of York, and of the vaccary in the forest of Ashedowne, with its rents and manors in the county of Sussex, both of which were attached to the duchy, and the revenues received and accounted for as duchy lands. The example set by the father was closely and speedily imitated by his children ; and in the time of Philip and Mary the duchy possessions were restored to their former extent by an Act expressed in these very significant terms :—

"AN ACT FOR THENLARGYNG OF THE DUCHIE OF LANCASTRE.

" Forasmuch as the Kyng and Quene our sovereigne Lorde and Ladyie, considering and regarding the state of the Duchie of Lancastree, being one of the most famous Princeliest and Stateliest peeces of our said Sovereigne Ladie the Quenes auncyent Enheritance, doo pceyve and consider that the Possessions and yerely Revenues of the said Duchie arre and have been of late greatlye diminished, as well by reason of Sundry Giftes, Grant° and Sales, made by the late Kinges of famous memorye, Henry theight and Edoarde the Sixte, late Kings of Englande, Father and Brother to our said Sovereigne Ladie the Quenes Highnes, as also by reason of sundries Exchainges made wth dyvers their loving Subjectes, of Sundry Manors, Landes, Tentes, Possessions, and Hereditaments, lately belonging to the same Duchie ; and the Manors, Landes, Tentes, Possessions, and Hereditaments, being receyved and taken in recompence of the said Exchanges, bee not annexed to the said Duchie, but been in thorder svey and govern^ance of other Courtes and Places, so by theyr Highnes taken and receyved in Exchange ; And forasmuche also as theyr Maties doo mynde and intende to preserve, avaunce, mayntaine, and contynue thauucient and honourable Estate of the said Duchie ; Our said Sovereigne Lord and Ladye therefor bee pleased and contented that yt be enacted, ordeyned, and established by their Maties wth thassent of the Lordes Spuall and Temporall, and the Comõns in this pnte pliament assembled, and by thauctoritee of the same, That all Honors, Castels, Lordeshippes, Manors, Landes, Tenementes, Possessions, and Hereditaments w^thin this Realme of Englande, wch at any tyme synce the xxviij^th daye of Januarie, in the first yere of the Reigne of our saide late Sovereigne Lorde Kynge Edoarde the Sixte (1547), were pcell of the Possessions of the said Duchie of Lancastre, or wch were united and annexed to the said Duchie by aucthorite of pliament lres Patentes or otherways, and wch at any time since the sayd xxviij daye of Januarie, have been, given, granted, alyenated, bargayned, solde, exchanged, or otherwayse severed from the said Duchie, by our said late Sovereigne Lord King Edoarde the Sixte, or by our Sovereigne Lady the Quene that now ys, or by our Sovereigne Lorde and Ladie the King and Quenes Maties that now bee, to or wth any pson or psons, and wch sayd Honors, Castles, Lordshippes, Manors, Landes, Tentes, and Hereditamentes, since such Giftes, Grants, Alienacons, Bargaynes, Sales, Exchanges, or Severance thereof so made as is aforesaid been, cõmon, or returned agayn to thandes of our said late Sovereigne Lorde King Edwarde the Sixte, or to thandes of our said Sovereigne Ladie the Quene, or to thandes of our Sovereigne Lord and Ladie the King and Quene, cr to thandes of her M^tie, her heires, and successors, in Possession, Revercon, Remainder, or other ways, and wch now bee or remain in thandes of our saide Sovereigne Lord and Lady the King and Quenes Maties, of any estate of inheritance, shall from the time the same came reverted agayn to thandes of our said late Sovereygne Lorde Kinge Edward the Sixte, or to thandes of our said Sovereigne Lady the Quene, or thandes of our said Sovereyne Lord and Ladye the King and Quene, by aucthoritee and force of this Acte bee united and annexed for ever unto the sayd Duchye of Lancastree, and shalbe adjudged, demed, and taken for ever for, and as pcels and membres of the said Duchie of Lancastre," etc.

In the following reign a systematic return was made of the fees, privileges, writs, and advowsons attached to the duchy of Lancaster and its officers, a copy of which has been preserved, and is as follows :—

Hereditaments, and Possessions, with their appurtenances in England, Wales, and Calais, and the Marches thereof, make, and from the said day of March be to the said Dutchy of Lancaster corporate, and be called the Dutchy of Lancaster. And that our said sovereign Lord, King Edward the Fourth, have, seize, take, hold, enjoy, and inherit all the said Manors and Castles, and other the Premisses with their appurtenances, by the same name of Dutchy, from all other his inheritances separate, from the said fourth day of March, to him and to his heirs Kings of England perpetually, and that the County of Lancaster be a county Palatine : And that our Liege and Sovereign Lord, King Edward the Fourth, and his heirs, have, as parcel of the said Dutchy, the same County of Lancaster and County Palatine, and a Seal, Chancellor, Judges, and Officers for the same ; and all manner of Liberties, Customs, Laws Royal, and Franchises in the same County Palatine lawfully and rightfully used, and over that another Seal, called the Seal of the Dutchy of Lancaster, and a Chancellor for the keeping thereof, Officers and Counsellors for the guiding and governance of the same Dutchy, and of the particular officers, ministers, tenants, and inhabitants thereof, in as great, ample, and large form as Henry, calling himself Henry the Fifth, at any time therein had, use, and enjoy lawfully. And by the same authority the said officers and ministers, and also the said tenants and inhabitants of and in the same Dutchy, have, use, exercise, and enjoy such and all Liberties, Privileges, and Customs, as the officers, ministers, tenants, and inhabitants of the same Dutchy had, used, exercised, or enjoyed lawfully in the time of the same Henry, calling himself King Henry the Fifth ; and that also in the same Dutchy be used, had, and occupied all such Freedoms, Liberties, Franchises, Privileges, Customs, and Jurisdictions, as were used therein lawfully before the said fourth day of March. And the officers, ministers, tenants, and inhabitants of or in the said Dutchy be entreated and demeaned according to the same Freedoms, Liberties, Franchises, Customs, Privileges, and Jurisdictions, and not distrained, areted, nor compelled to the contrary in anywise."

HERE BEGINNETH THE BOOKE

WHICH IS KNOWN BY THE NAME OF AND TREATING OF THE FEES, PRIVILEGES, WRITTS, ADVOWSONS, AND OTHER OFFICERS THAT BELONG TO THE DUCHY AND COUNTY PALATINE OF LANCASTER [ABOUT 1588].

FEES OF THE DUTCHY.

The chancellor's fee of the Dutchy £238 16 4	much more as makes both their salaries amount
The attorney of the Dutchy............................. 66 5 4	to £76 : 17 : 8]
The auditor for the north partes 68 13 4	The sum of all the payments which are paid to all
The auditor for the south partes 68 13 4	the officers, or allowed as salarys in the dutchy,
[Besides to both of them murrey cloth, green cloth for their tables and for their lying in London, as	in the whole amount to £641 3 4

An ESTIMATE of the REVENUES of the DUCHY OF LANCASTER, collected by the particular Receivers of the Honors belonging to the said Duchy, and yearly paid by the Receiver-General.

REVENUES OF THE DUTCHY PER ANNUM.

The receiver of Cliderhow and Halton, payeth to the general Receiver of the dutchy £1700	The receiver of Leicester................................ £400
The receiver of Pomfrett and Knasbrough, com. 69 annis 1800	The receiver of Furness 1000
The receiver of Tickhull 500	The receiver of Bullingbroke 900
The receiver of Pickeringleigh 350	Augmentation of Lancaster 400
The receiver of Duntanborough 80	The receiver of the colledge and chantry rents in the county of Stafford and Derby................................ 40
The receiver of Tutbury, p. ann. 1500	
The receiver of Longberington 80	£8,600

SOUTH DIVISION.

The receiver of Higham Ferars £800	The receiver of Essex and Hartford £1000
The receiver of Norfolk and Suffolk 200	The receiver of the marches of Wales and Monmouth ... 100
The receiver of Sussex.. 300	The receiver of Kilwaldid 100
The receiver of the south parts 1000	£4,800

So that the whole receipts of the general receiver of the Dutchy one year with another amounteth to .... [1] £14,000 0 0

The receiver is to pay to the treasurer of his Majesties most honourable chamber £4000 0 0

And to the cofferer of his Majesties household 7000 0 0

For fees to the court officers 641 3 4

For expenses of the *mass* songs, and others, per ann. 100 0 0

                              Total disbursements 11,741 3 4

So that remains *communibus annis*, in the custody of the general receiver, to be disposed of according to his majesty's use, upon Mr. Chancellor, Sir Francis Walsingham[2] 2258 16 8

                                                  £14,000 0 0

The accounts of the duchy, as brought up to December 31, 1885, are as follows: The balance in hand at the commencement of the year was £23,566. The net rents and profits accruing to Her Majesty were £45,047; royalties, rents, &c., £14,926; dividends of stocks, £3,072; producing, with various items of minor importance, a total gross income of £99,347, but of this only £88,832 was paid. The arrears on the 31st December amounted to £10,515. On the disbursement side £45,000 was paid to Her Majesty; in various payments, £22,507, including a payment of £2,000 to the Chancellor; leaving a balance of £21,525. The revenues of the duchy have in thirty-eight years increased from £29,000 in 1847 to £65,265 in 1885, the net payments to Her Majesty at these two periods being respectively £12,000 and £45,000.

A DECLARATION of all the FORESTS, CHASES, and PARKES, belonging to the DUTCHY OF LANCASTER, out of which the Chancellor, Attorney-General, Receiver-General, and two Auditors, are to have deer, summer and winter.

In Lancashire.	*In Staffordshire.*	*In Derbyshire.*	Castle Donnington parke.
The forest of Bolland.	Yoxalward parke.	High Peak forest.	Barnes parke.
The forest of Wiersdale.	Agardesley parke.	Shattell parke.	New parke of Leicester.
The forest of Bleasdale.	Rolleston parke.	Melbure parke.	Tonley parke.
Legrame parke.	Marchington ward.	Mansfield parke.	Pekelton parke.
Mierscough parke.	Tutbury parke.	Morley parke.	
Toxteth parke.	Hockeley parke.	Posterne parke.	*In Wiltshire.*
Quernmore parke.	Rowley parke.	Ravensdale parke.	Loxley parke.
	High Levis parke.		Alborne chace.
In Cheshire.		*In Leicestershire.*	Everley parke.
Halton parke.		The forest of Leicester.	

---

[1] It may be presumed that the statement of Revenue this year is not equal to the average year, as the figures do not correspond with this amount.

[2] Sir Francis Walsingham was chancellor in 1588.—(See list). This fixes the period when this account was taken, or the rates affixed, concurring with the Entry of the Fees of the "Justices of the *Queen's* Bench."

PARKES AND CHASES.

In Hamshire, Kingsomburne parke.—The chace of Holt, and the Parke, Dorsetshire.—Kirby parke, in Lincolnshire.—Higham Ferrers, in Northamptonshire.

In Yorkshire.	Havery parke.	Weecks parke.	*In Hertfordshire.*
Poulfret parke.	Conisbrough parke.	Two other parkes there are in *Suf-*	Hartingfordbury parke.
Cridlinge parke.	Altafts parke.	*folk.* Eyste parke there also.	Two more parkes in do.
Kepax parke.	Acworth parke, and the New		Kingslaugby park, do.
Blausby parke.	parke of Wakefield.	*In Essex.*	
Pickeringly forest.		The great parke of Plashey.	
Billon parke.	*In Sus ex.*	The little parke there.	Oldney park, *Buckinghamshire.*
The old parke of Wakefield.	Hunsde parke.	Coppedhull parke.	Hungerford park, *Berkshire.*
Hay parke.	The forest of Ashdowne.	Higheater parke there.	

FEES DUE PER ANNUM TO THESE OFFICERS.

	£	s.	d.		£	s.	d.
Bailiffe of the manor of Salford	6	13	4	The under steward of Ormskirk appointed by the Earl			
Bailiffe of Derby wapontake	4	0	8	of Derby	2	0	0
Bailiffe of manᵣ of West Derby	3	0	8	Fee of the clerk of the court there	1	13	4
Mᵣ of the forest of Wiersdale	1	10	0	The fee of the auditor	28	0	0
Mᵣ of Amounderness forest	3	0	0	The fee of the receiver per annum	15	0	0
The escheator of county palatine	5	0	0	The reward of the said receiver	13	6	8
The sheriff of Lanc. hath for allowance	9	0	0	The fee for Furness	6	0	0
The constable of Liverpool castle	6	13	4	The baylives of Dalton's fee	2	0	0
The maister of Symonwood forest, and keeper of				The ditto of Hawkshead's fee	2	13	4
Toxteth parke hath for his fees, per annum	2	0	0	The ditto of Beamond and Bolton	2	10	0
Steward of the wapontake of Derby and Salford	5	0	0	Fee of all the manors pertaining to Furness			
The receiver of the co. palat.	6	13	4	monastery	26	13	4
Porter of Lancaster castle	4	11	0	Fee of the receiver there	20	0	0
Steward of Amounderness	2	0	0	Clerk of the court there	6	13	4
Steward of Lonsdale	2	0	0	Baylive of Furness liberty	4	0	0
Keeper of Quernmore parke	2	5	6	Keeper of woods in plane of Furnes	2	0	0
Mᵣ of the forest wood of Myerscough	4	11	0	Reward of the auditor	6	13	4
Maister of Wiresdale et Quernmore	3	0	8	The stipend of a clerk to serve in the chapel at			
The chancellor's fee of the county palatine, per annum	40	0	0	Farnworth	3	12	10
The justice of the *queen's* bench for his office in county				The stipend of a clerk to serve in the chapel at			
palatine	36	13	4	Litherpoole	4	17	5
And for dyett	13	6	8	The fee of a clerk and school mᵣ of Walton, per			
To another justice for his office in county palatine,				annum	5	13	4
and dyett too	40	0	0	The clerk's stipend at Blackrodes	4	4	1½
Attᵧ of County palatine	6	13	4	The clerk of Clitherow stipend	3	9	1
Clerk of yᵉ crown for county	2	0	0	The stipend of the clerk of Padiham Chappel	6	19	2
Clerk of the common pleas	2	0	0	The chaplin's fee in the chappel of Harewood, per			
Clerk of crown and pleas	6	0	0	annum	4	6	6
Barons of the exchequer there	4	0	0	The clerk in the chappel of Whalley	4	8	11
Cryer of the sessions at Lancaster	2	0	0	The stipend of a clerke to serve in the chappel of			
Master of Bolland forest	6	13	4	Rufford, per annum	3	2	2
Steward of ponds for his fee	1	0	0	The stipend of a clerke and school maister at			
Receiver of Clitheroe	15	13	4	Manchester, per annum	4	0	2
Steward of Blackburn, Tottington, and Clederhow, for				Clerke of Beckonshawe chappel	2	16	5
his fee	3	6	8	The stipend of a clerk and school-master at Leyland	3	17	10
Constable of Clitherow castle	10	0	0	The stipend of a clerk and school-master at Preston	2	18	2
The keeper and porter of the gaole in the castle of				Clerke and steward of Wigan	5	10	0
Clitherow	3	0	8	The clerke of Croston's stipend	3	19	9
Messenger of the Dutchy	2	0	0	The payment made unto seven weomen praying			
The keeper of the parkes' fees	2	5	8	within the late colledge, called Knowle's Alms			
Fee of the bailive of Ormskirk	2	0	0	house, per annum	35	15	0
Bailif of Burscough fee	2	13	4	Payd to two persons and the surveyor thereof	5	10	0

A NOTE of all the BENEFICES and SPIRITUAL LIVINGS belonging to the DUTCHY OF LANCASTER.

(r) for rectory—(v) for vikarage.

	£	s.	d.		£	s.	d.
Comit. Berks.				Dedham (v) per ann.	10	0	0
Henton Rectory	23	7	5	Essex (v) per ann.	8	0	0
				Longton (v) per ann.	18	3	8
In Comitat. Ebor.				Laugham (v or r)	17	0	0
Methley (r) clare	25	8	11	*Gloucester.*			
Darrington (v) per ann.	0	0	0				
Ackeworth (r) per ann.	22	1	0	Tiberton (r)	7	16	0
Croston (r) per ann.	10	0	1½	*Hartford.*			
Slaitborne (r) per ann.	0	0	0				
Kirkbram (with r)	12	18	4	Saint Andrews with St. Nicholas	12	1	2
Ouston (v) per ann.	7	2	1½	*In Com. Lincoln.*			
Castleford (r) per ann.	20	13	0	Hartringfordbury(r)	16	0	0
Bradford (v)	20	0	0	Ounley (r) clere	9	3	4
Berwickes of Elemitt	33	12	4	Whittingham (r)—	18	6	8
In Com. Essex.				Hantley (r) per ann.	6	4	6
Stamford rivers (r)	26	13	4	Stoopings parva (r)	9	19	4
Munden (v)	12	12	0	Norcot (r)	12	10	0

11

	£	s.	d.		£	s.	d.
South Somersetes (r)	22	6	8	Beeston (r)	16	0	0
Bennington (v)	20	0	2	Plumbstead (r)	5	3	2
Salt Thetby (r)	7	0	2				
Southreston (r)	5	10	2	*In Comit. Northamp.*			
Morningerby (r)	9	8	4	Inchester (v)	8	0	0
Thoresby (r)	6	9	6	Passenham (r)	20	0	0
In Comit. Lancastrie.				Preston (v)	15	4	0
Pennington Don clear (r)	0	0	0	Widd (v)	3	6	10
Dalton (v) and clear	17	6	8	Bethome (v) clear	13	17	4
In Com. Leicester.				Millome (v)	8	5	8
Hathurend (v)	12	0	0	Urswick (v) sunt Richmondsha.	7	17	4
St. Peter, Leicester (v)	2	5	0	*In Com. Stafford.*			
Desford (r)	2	9	7	Tudbury (v)	7	0	0
Whitwicke vic.	9	14	4	Rolston (r)	13	9	6
Viccaria de pembe valet, per ann.	6	6	8	Tatenhill (r)	26	0	0
Mandeoallocke seue [sive] Monobon (v)	9	13	4	Wolstanton (r)	32	3	9
Swafield (r)	6	8	6	*In Com. Suffolk.*			
Mamelly vic. valet, per ann.	6	13	4	Clare (v)	4	18	8
Shibden (v)	9	4	9	Eyken (v)	6	13	4
Trunche (r)	10	13	4	Holmesett (v) cleare	0	0	0
Southropes (r)	6	0	0	Stratford	18	0	0
Sydestrond (r)	5	10	0	Somersham (r)	8	0	0
Northrope (r)	0	0	0	Hunden (v)	7	13	4
Mondesley (r)	8	9	9	*In Co. Wilts.*			
In Comit. Norfolk.				Poole (r)	17	12	5
Themingham rector	6	0	0	Ashley (r)	9	16	4
Withrope (r)	5	5	2	*In Co. Westmorland.*			
Malilaske (r)	5	0	0	Orton (v)	16	17	4

"The valuation of some parsonages and vicarages within the dutchy appeareth not in the records remaining in the dutchy office, but may be found in the office of the first-fruits, where the same are best known."—*Birch's MSS.*

From the time of Queen Elizabeth to the reign of Charles II. no material change took place in the duchy court of Lancaster, with the exception of the abolition of the duchy court of Star Chamber already noticed; but in the 12th Charles II. (1660) the last remaining vestige of the feudal system, after having existed in this country for at least six hundred years, was swept away,[1] and with it the privileges of wards and liveries attached to the duchy of Lancaster, although those privileges had been thought worthy of special protection a century before. The progress of knowledge had burst the bonds of vassalage, and although the system introduced, or completed, by the Norman conquerors, had taken deep root, and identified itself with the whole frame of society, the tenures *in capite*, and *knights' service*, were now declared "more burthensome, grievous, and prejudicial to the kingdom than beneficial to the king," and they were, therefore, for ever abolished. During the interval between the year 1642, when the public treasury passed into the hands of the Parliament, and the year 1660, when Charles II. obtained the royal inheritance, the revenues of the duchy of Lancaster were applied to the exigences of the state, first under the administration of Lord Newburgh, and subsequently under the chancellorships of William Lenthall, Speaker of the House of Commons, John (President) Bradshawe, Thomas Fell, and Sir Gilbert Gerard, Bart.; the latter of whom was displaced at the Restoration by Francis Lord Seymour, who, as a mark of the royal favour, obtained this lucrative appointment for his attachment to the House of Stuart. To facilitate the proceedings in the duchy court, an Act was passed in the 16th and 17th Charles II. (1665), empowering the chancellor of the duchy to grant commissions for taking affidavits within the county palatine of Lancaster, and other places in the several counties of the kingdom within the survey of the duchy court, whereby the same validity was given to those affidavits as if they had been sworn, as hitherto, in the duchy chamber at Westminster, and to render these proceedings, in the incipient state, as little burthensome as possible, it was directed that the very moderate fee of twelve pence, and no more, should be received by the person empowered to take the affidavits.

The Chancellor of the Duchy of Lancaster is an officer of considerable eminence, changing with the Government, and frequently having a seat in the Cabinet. He holds his office by letters patent, and, if a peer, takes precedence according to his rank in the peerage; if not, he takes precedence next after the Chancellor of the Exchequer and immediately before the Lord Chief Justice of the Queen's Bench. He formerly sat as judge of the duchy court of Lancaster held at Westminster, in which all causes any way relating to the revenue of the duchy were tried, another branch of the same court being established at Preston, called the Court of the County Palatine of Lancaster, for the same purpose in that county as the other was at Westminster. The duties of

[1] Rot. Parl. 12 Car. II. p. 3. nu. 4.

the office are now nominal. The chancellor has the appointment to forty-one livings in various parts of the country, and of all the borough magistrates within the county of Lancaster. In recent years he has acted as Vice-president of the Committee of the Privy Council on Agriculture.

From the first creation of the duchy of Lancaster, in 1351, to 1886, there have been one hundred and thirteen chancellors of the duchy. The following is a complete list of those officers :—

CHANCELLORS of the DUCHY and COUNTY PALATINE of LANCASTER, from the first Creation of the Dukedom in 1351, to the present time, December, 1886.

34 Edward III.	Sir Henry de Haydok	Chancellor of Henry, first duke, 1360.
46 Edward III.	Ralph de Ergham, clerk	Bishop of Sarum, 1372.
51 Edward III.	Thomas de Thelwall, clerk	Created Chancellor of Co. Pal., 16th April, 1377.
1 Richard II.	Sir John de Yerborough, clerk	
6 Richard II.	Sir Thomas Stanley	November 10th, pro temp., 1382.
6 Richard II.	John Scarle	November 29th, 1382.
7 Richard II.	Sir William Okey	October, 1383.
1 Henry IV.	John de Wakering	1399-1400.
1 Henry IV.	William Burgoyne, Esq.	1399-1400.
6 Henry IV.	Sir Thomas Stanley	May 15th, 1405.
11 Henry IV.	John Springthorpe, clerk	March 30th, 1410.
1 Henry V.	John Woodhouse	4th April, 1413.
1 Henry VI.	John Woodhouse, contd.	20th January, 1423.
2 Henry VI.	William Troutbecke, Esq.	10th June, 1424.
9 Henry VI.	Walter Sherington, clerk	16th February, 1431.
17 Henry VI.	William Troutbeck	7th May, 1439, Chancellor for life.
20 Henry VI.	William Tresham	3d July, 1442, Chancellor in reversion.
26 Henry VI.	William Tresham	1st November, 1447.
27 Henry VI.	John Say, Esq.	10th June, 1449.
1 Edward IV.	John Say, Esq.	16th June, 1461.
11 Edward IV.	Sir Richard Fowler, Kt.	10th June, 1471, also Chan. of Excheq.
17 Edward IV.	Sir John Say, Kt.	3rd November, 1477.
18 Edward IV.	Thomas Thwaites	2nd April, 1478, also Chan. of Excheq.
1 Richard III.	Thomas Metcalfe	7th July, 1483.
1 Henry VII.	Sir Reginald Bray, Knt.	13th September, 1485.
19 Henry VII.	Sir John Mordant, Knt.	24th June, 1504.
21 Henry VII.	Sir Richard Empson, Knt.	3rd October, 1505.
1 Henry VIII.	Sir Henry Marny, Knt.	14th May, 1509.
14 Henry VIII.	Sir Richard Wingfield, Knt.	14th April, 1523.
17 Henry VIII.	Sir Thomas More, Knt.	31st December, 1525, made Chancellor of England.
21 Henry VIII.	Sir William Fitzwilliams, Knt.	3rd November, 1529 (after Earl of Southampton).
35 Henry VIII.	Sir John Gage, Knt.	10th May, 1543.
1 Edward VI.	Sir William Paget, Knt.	1st July, 1547.
6 Edward VI.	Sir John Gate, Knt.	7th July, 1552.
1 Queen Mary	Sir Robert Rochester, Knt.	1553—54.
4 & 5 Philip & Mary	Sir Edward Walgrave, Knt.	22nd June, 1558.
1 Elizabeth	Sir Ambrose Cave, Knt.	1558—59.
10 Elizabeth	Sir Ralph Sadler, Knt.	16th May, 1568.
19 Elizabeth	Sir Francis Walsingham, Knt.	15th June, 1577.
32 Elizabeth	Sir Thomas Henage, Knt.	1590.
37 Elizabeth	Sir Robert Cecil, Knt.	7th October, 1595.
43 Elizabeth	Sir John Fortescue, Knt.	16th September, 1601.
13 James I.	Sir Thomas Parry, Knt., and John Daccomb, Esq.	27th May, 1615.
14 James I.	Sir John Daccombe, Knt.	5th June, 1616.
15 James I.	Sir Humphrey May, Knt.	23rd March, 1618.
5 Charles I.	Edward, Lord Newburgh	16th April, 1629.
Feb. 10th, 1644	William, Lord Grey of Wake, and William Lenthall, Esq.	
1649	John Bradshawe	1st August, 1649.
1655	Thomas Fell	1655.
1659	Sir Gilbert Gerard, Bart.	14th May, 1659.
12 Charles II.	Charles, Lord Seymour of Trowbridge	9th July, 1660.
16 Charles II.	Sir Thomas Ingram, Knt.	21st July, 1664.
23 Charles II.	Sir Robert Carr, Knt. and Bart.	22nd February, 1671.
32 Charles II.	Sir Thomas Ingram, Knt.	Feb. 14, 1680.
34 Charles II.	Sir Thomas Chicheley, Knt.	21st November, 1682.
1 William and Mary	Robert, Lord Willoughby of Eresby	21st March, 1689.
9 William III.	Thomas, Earl of Stamford	4th May, 1697.
1 Queen Anne	Sir John Leveson Gower, Bart. (afterwards Lord Gower)	12th May, 1702.
5 Queen Anne	James, Earl of Derby	10th June, 1706.
9 Queen Anne	William, Lord Berkeley of Stratton	21st September, 1710.
1 George I.	Henage, Earl of Aylesford	6th November, 1714.
2 George I.	Richard, Earl of Scarborough	12th March, 1715.
3 George I.	Nicholas Lechemere, Esq. (afterwards Lord Lechemere for life)	19th June, 1717.
1 George II.	John, Duke of Rutland	17th July, 1727.

8 George II.	.......George, Earl of Cholmondeley	May, 1735.
16 George II.	.........Richard, Lord Edgecumbe...................	22nd December, 1742.
34 George II.	.........Thomas Hay, Viscount Dupplin (after-	
	wards Earl of Kinnoull)	27th February, 1760.
3 George III.	.........James, Lord Strange	13th December, 1762
11 George III.	.........Thomas, Lord Hyde (afterwards Earl of	
	Clarendon)	14th June, 1771.
22 George III.	.........John, Lord Ashburton	17th April, 1782.
23 George III.	.........Edward, Earl of Derby	29th August, 1783.
24 George III.	.........Thomas, Earl of Clarendon	31st December, 1783.
27 George III.	......Charles, Lord Hawkesbury (afterwards	
	Lord Liverpool)	6th September, 1787.
44 George III.	.........Thomas, Lord Pelham (afterwards Earl	
	of Chichester)	11th November, 1803.
44 George III.	........Henry, Lord Mulgrave	6th June, 1804.
45 George III.	........Robert, Earl of Buckinghamshire...........	11th January, 1805.
45 George III.	.........Dudley, Lord Harrowby (afterwards Earl	
	of Harrowby)............................	10th July, 1805.
46 George III.	.........Edward, Earl of Derby	12th February, 1806.
47 George III.	........The Right Hon. Spencer Perceval (after-	
	wards First Lord of the Treasury)[1]	30th March, 1807.
52 George III.	.........Robert, Earl of Buckinghamshire	25th May, 1812.
52 George III.	.........The Right Hon. Charles Bathurst	23rd June, 1812.
4 George IV.	.........Nicholas Vansittart (afterwards Lord	
	Bexley)	13th February, 1823.
9 George IV.	........George, Earl of Aberdeen, K.T.............	26th January, 1828.
9 George IV.	........The Right Hon. Charles Arbuthnot.........	2nd June, 1828.
1 William IV.	........Henry Richard, Lord Holland	25th November, 1830.
5 William IV.	....Charles Watkin Williams Wynn	26th December, 1834.
5 William IV.	.........Henry Richard, Lord Holland (again)	23rd April, 1835.
4 Victoria	.........Geo. William Frederick, Earl of Clarendon..	31st October, 1840.
4 Victoria	.. ..Sir George Grey, Bart.	23rd June, 1841.
5 Victoria	.............Chas. Henry Somerset, Lord Granville ...	3rd September, 1841.
10 Victoria	.............John, Lord Campbell (appointed Lord	
	Chief Justice, K.B., 1850)	6th July, 1846.
13 Victoria	... .Geo. Frederick William, Earl of Carlisle ...	6th March, 1850.
15 Victoria	... .A. Christopher...............................	27th February, 1852.
16 Victoria	... .Edward Strutt (afterwards Lord Belper)	28th December, 1852.
18 Victoria	.............Granville George, Earl Granville, K.G. ...January, 1855.	
18 Victoria	....Dudley, Earl of Harrowby, K.G. ....10th February, 1855.	
19 Victoria	.............Matthew Talbot Baines	December, 1855.
21 Victoria	.............James, Duke of Montrose, Knt. ....25th February, 1858.	
22 Victoria	.............Sir George Grey...............................	18th June, 1859.
24 Victoria	.............Edward Cardwell (afterwards Viscount	
	Cardwell)	July, 1861.
27 Victoria	... .George William Frederick, Earl of Claren-	
	don, K.G.	April, 1864.
29 Victoria	.............George Joachim Goschen	January, 1866.
30 Victoria	... ...William Reginald, Earl of Devon	July, 1866.
30 Victoria	.............John Wilson Patten (afterwards Lord	
	Winmarleigh)	June, 1867.
32 Victoria	...........Colonel Thomas Edward Taylour	September, 1868.
32 Victoria	...........Frederick Temple, Earl of Dufferin	December, 1868.
35 Victoria	.........Hugh Culling Eardley Childers	August, 1872.
36 Victoria	.........John Bright.................................	September, 1873.
36 Victoria	...........Colonel Thomas Edward Taylour...........	21st February, 1874.
42 Victoria	...........John Bright.................................	28th April, 1880.
45 Victoria	...........John, Earl of Kimberley, pro tem.	July, 1882.
46 Victoria	...........John George Dodson (afterwards Lord	
	Monk Bretton)	December, 1882.
47 Victoria	...........George Otto Trevelyan.................	October, 1884.
47 Victoria	...........Henry Chaplin	June, 1885.
48 Victoria	...........Edward Heneage.............................	7th February, 1886.
48 Victoria	...........Sir Ughtred James Kay-Shuttleworth, Bt.	March, 1886.
49 Victoria	...........Lord John James Robert Manners	August, 1886.

We have thus sketched, with a rapid hand, principally from official documents, a connected and authentic history of the duchy of Lancaster, one of "the most famous, princeliest, and stateliest of inheritances." The connection of the duchy with the ducal and royal House of Lancaster is too close to admit of separation. They serve to illustrate and to ennoble each other, and to have exhibited them apart would have derogated from the dignity of both. In each successive reign, from the period when Henry of Bolingbroke ascended the throne of this kingdom to the present time, with the exception of the interregnum of the Commonwealth, the sovereigns of England have enjoyed the title of duke and the revenues of the duchy of Lancaster, both of which are now in

---

[1] When Mr. Perceval became First Minister of the Crown in 1809, he continued to hold the office of Chancellor of the Duchy of Lancaster conjointly with the two superior offices of First Lord of the Treasury and Chancellor of the Exchequer, the only instance on record of the three offices having been united in the same individual.—O.

possession of our gracious sovereign, and will descend as an inalienable inheritance to the successors of the present monarch.

The proceedings of the duchy court, during a period of over four hundred and eighty years, are full of interest in all the counties of the kingdom to which the duchy extends, but in the county palatine of Lancaster they have a peculiar claim to that distinction; and it may tend essentially to the convenience of those who at present, or in future times, may have occasion to consult the records of that duchy, to be presented with the following authentic information, both as to their nature, and as to their places of deposit:—

THE DUCHY RECORDS.

"Return from the Deputy-Clerk of the Council, and Keeper of the Records in the Duchy of Lancaster, to the Committee on the Public Records of this Kingdom, made in virtue of an order from the select Committee, with an answer to the enquiry, Whether all the Records of the Duchy are open to public inspection?

"In obedience to your Order of the 21st February last, I herewith return answers to the several Queries put to me, with respect to the Records of this Office, under the Custody of the Clerk of the Council, and the two Auditors, to whom I, in this respect, act as deputy; but beg leave at the same Time to state, that such only are considered as public, and open for public Inspection, as in any wise relate to, or concern Judicial Proceedings, the remainder being collected for the purpose of better managing and improving the Inheritance of his Majesty's Possessions in right of his Duchy of Lancaster; and the Officers of the Duchy think themselves at liberty to withhold them from public inspection, except for the purposes before mentioned, or by command of his Majesty, as Duke of Lancaster, signified by his chancellor of the Duchy.

"The Answer to the First Question is contained in the following list of Records in the Office of the Duchy of Lancaster:—

Account of the purchase Money arising from the Sale of Rents under the several acts of Parliament,—19 Geo. III. 1779, to the present time [*i.e.* 1800].

Awards for inclosures, in which the Duchy Property has been concerned,—27 Geo. II. 1754, to the present Time.

Bills and Answers and Depositions in the Duchy Court of Lancaster, and of such as have been transmitted from the County Palatine to be heard in the Duchy Court,—1 Hen. VII. to the present Time.

Charters and Grants of various Kings under the Great Seal, as well as of private Persons (remaining in Boxes), to the King's Sons, and to Ecclesiastical Persons, of Lands within the Surveys of the Duchy,—1 King Stephen, 1135, to 10 Queen Elizabeth, 1558. (?1568)

Charters and Grants in Fee Farm, some of which are enrolled in the Office, and others remain on Parchment, with the Royal Sign Manual. The original Charters of the Duchy and County Palatine to the King's Son, and Grants of Lands to Individuals of the possessions of the Duchy,—51 Ed. III. 1377, to 1 Queen Anne, 1702.

Court Rolls of such Manors as formerly belonged to the Duchy, and have since been granted away, and of such as are at present demised by Leases under the Duchy Seal,—1283 to the present Time.[1]

Decrees of the Duchy Court inrolled in Books, and some drafts with the Attorney General's Signature,—1 Hen. VII. to the present Time.[2]

Grants of Rents under the several Acts, to enable the Chancellor and Council to dispose of the Fee Farm and other Rents, and to enfranchise Copyhold Estates,—20 Geo. III. 1780, to the present Time.

Inquisitions *Post Mortem*, consisting of 2400 of various Lands and Tenements, within all the Counties in England,—1 Hen. V. 1413, to 18 Car. 1, 1642.[3]

Leases, Drafts, and Inrolments, of such as have passed the Duchy Seal, of Land and Tenements, Parcel of the Possessions of the Duchy,—1 Hen. VIII. 1510, to the present Time.

Ministers and Receivers Accounts of the Rents and Revenues of the Duchy,—1135, to the present Time.

Patents of Offices granted under the Duchy Seal,—1 Hen. VIII. 1510, to the present Time.

Presentations to Livings under the Duchy Seal,—1 Hen. VIII. 1510, to the present Time.

Rentals and Particulars of Lands belonging to the Duchy, collected together in Bags and Presses, and consisting of various other documents, of such Descriptions, that they cannot be comprised under one Head, registered into Counties, and in the Catalogue are the Names of places alphabetically arranged,—51 Ed. III. 1377, to the present Time.

Registers of Leases, Warrants, Grants, and other Documents, under Royal Signs Manual, inrolled in Books, of John, Duke of Lancaster, in the Time of Edw. the Third, and of various Kings, relating to the Possessions of the Duchy,—51 Edw. III. 1377, to 8 Hen. VI. 1430.

Revenue Proceedings in Duchy Court inrolled in Books,—6 Car. I. 1630, to the present Time.

Special Commissions of Sewers, and to survey estates belonging to the Duchy,—23 Eliz. (1581), to the present Time.

Privy Seals and Bills, being the particulars prepared previous to the granting any Leases or Offices under the Duchy Seal,—1 James I. (1603), to the present Time.

"The Building wherein the Records are kept is situate on the East Side of Somerset Place,[4] is in good Condition and Security, with respect to the Rooms where the Records are deposited; but many of them have been obliged to be lately removed from the lower part on account of the Dry Rot, which has affected the Basement Story. As the Records yearly increase, more Room will be wanted at some future Period, for the Accommodation of them. The Office was appropriated to the use of the Duchy of Lancaster under the Act for erecting the Buildings at Somerset House, and is therefore public Property. But this office was given to the Duchy in consideration of Accommodations and Concessions made by his Majesty in right of his Duchy, from such parts of the manor of Savoy as belonged to the Duchy. The Records, except those of very ancient Date (which were, in some degree, destroyed by the vermin in the late office), are in good preservation; and such as are not contained in Books are arranged in Presses, according

---

[1] These documents, which at the present time are under arrangement, include rolls for the following places in Lancashire: Accrington Manor, Amounderness Wapentake, Beamont in Bolton, Blackburnshire, Possessions of Burscough Priory, Possessions of Cartmell Priory, Chatburne Manor, Clitheroe, Colne Manor, Colton, Possessions of Conished Priory, Great Crosby Manor, Dalton Manor, Flookborough, Possessions of Furness Monastery, Ightenhull Manor, Liverpool Lordship, Lonsdale Hundred, Ormskirk Manor, Pendleton Manor, Penwortham Manor, Rochdale Hundred, Salford Wapentake, Tottington Manor, Ulverston Barony, West Derby Hundred and Worston Manor.—C.

[2] The Decrees and Orders made in Suits originated in the Duchy Chambers, are enrolled in 47 thick volumes, beginning in the reign of Edward IV. and coming down to the present time. The reference to the Orders and Decrees enrolled is, by the ancient calendars, alphabetically arranged, under the name of Plaintiff and Defendant.—C.

[3] The *Inquisitiones post mortem* were taken either before the Escheator of the County Palatine or before special Commissioners, by virtue of Writs of *Diem clausit extremum*, or commissions emanating from the Court of Chancery of the Palatinate. They begin before Henry V., the earliest being of the reign of Edward I., and they come down to the time of Charles I., though only a very small portion are of an earlier date than the reign of Henry VII. They are all arranged and bound in volumes, the references being by means of the printed calendar.—C.

[4] The Records are now removed to the Public Record Office.—C.

to their Dates, tied up with paper and string, and numerically indorsed ; and in the course of every summer a person is employed to remove the Dust from them, and put new paper and string to such as want it. The Books are deposited in Closets, indorsed according to their dates and Subjects. There are correct general Indexes, Repertories, and Calendars, of all the Records in the Office, with reference to the particular Subjects which they contain ; and as fresh Records are transmitted to the Office, they are continued to be entered in existing Calendars ; and these additions are minutely attended to, without any Expense on that account being borne by the King as Duke of Lancaster. Several Years ago, according to what I have been informed, a Fire happened at the Duchy's Office, Gray's Inn, by which accident several Records were destroyed, and some are supposed to have been stolen. Some of these have been recovered from persons who have voluntarily surrendered them ; and some few Indexes and Catalogues, which had been made for the use of the officers who had the care of the Records ; but I know of none now existing in any place, from whence they are likely to be regained ; and such ample Repertories have since been made, and the Records arranged in such order, that they would hardly be of use if recovered. I am employed in the arrangements of the Records myself, and a clerk assists me in placing and replacing them, for which no Salary or allowance whatever is paid, but a fee of 8s. 6d. is charged for the production of each Record, which is the sole allowance, as well for the trouble and producing them, as for arranging them and keeping them in proper preservation, and for making the Indexes, Repertories, and Calendars, and the further sum of 1s. is charged per folio for Copies, or 16d. if there is any considerable difficulty arising from the Antiquity or Language of the Record. Attendance with the Records themselves is so seldom demanded, that no Fee has been regularly settled for that purpose ; but if in London, a charge is made of one guinea, besides the coach-hire ; and if in the country, two guineas a day, with the travelling charges, and all other expenses, would be expected. No account has been kept of the profits derived by searches for public records. independent of those where fees have been received for other searches, from whence any average can be taken. The answer to the Sixth Question is, I presume, contained in the answer to the foregoing questions. I am not apprised of any regulation that can be made for rendering the use of the said Records more convenient for proper Inspection.

"May 8, 1800.   "R. J. HARPER, Deputy-Clerk of the Council."

"Several Fee Farm Rolls of this Duchy have been lately transferred to this Office from the Augmentation Office."

"Return to a further Question to the Clerk of the Council and Keeper of the Records of the Duchy of Lancaster.

"Query.—Are there in your custody, as such Officer, any Calendars, or Indexes to the Inquisitions *Post Mortem* mentioned in your Return to this Committee, and upon what plan are they formed—and are they in a state sufficiently correct for publication, if it should be thought to conduce to the benefit of the Public to have the same printed ? "

"Answer.—There are, as stated in my former Return, several Inquisitions *Post Mortem*, Traverses, and other Inquisitions of divers kinds, remaining in this Office under my care, commencing in the beginning of the Reign of Henry V. and finishing 18 Charles I., amounting to nearly 2,400 in number, some of which consist of many large Skins of Parchment put on Files, in several bundles, secured from future injuries by strong covers, and to which there is a regular Alphabetical Index and Calendar, in one Volume divided into the several Reigns of the Kings before mentioned, and containing the names of Persons, and all places mentioned in each Inquisition, omitting none that are legible. The first directing immediately to the several lands each person died possessed of ; the other referring to each Inquisition, in which any particular Lands are to be found. I know of no objection to publishing the above Index, if it should be thought conducive to the public benefit ; and understand it will fill about 90 Pages when printed.

"June 27, 1810.   "R. J. HARPER, Deputy-Clerk of the Council."

Through the munificent gift of Her Majesty the Queen, the nation acquired in 1868 the whole of the valuable private muniments belonging to the duchy of Lancaster. This collection of records, commencing even before the creation of the palatinate, contains innumerable documents of extraordinary age and variety, relating not only to the county palatine as a subordinate regality, but to the government and jurisdiction of the entire dominion of the duchy, with its possessions in almost every county in the kingdom. These archives were transferred from the Duchy Office, Lancaster Place, to the Public Record Office, between the 30th November and 8th December, 1868, and are fully described in the Appendix to the Thirtieth Report of the Deputy Keeper of the Public Records, pp. 1 to 43.[1] In this report they are arranged under thirty-three divisions or classes, the contents of which are given in a condensed form in the following summary :—

SUMMARY.

1. Pleadings or proceedings by bill, and answers in the Chancery of the Duchy of Lancaster, Henry VII. to Elizabeth, arranged and bound in separate volumes .... 213 vols.
2. Bills and answers in bundles, 1603-1809...... 207 bundles.
3. Depositions, examinations, surveys, &c., Henry VIII. to Philip and Mary, arranged and bound in volumes .... 81 vols.
4. Depositions, examinations, surveys, &c., in bundles, Elizabeth to 1818 .... 198 bundles.
5. Books of orders and decrees enrolled, Edward IV. to 1825 .... 47 vols.
6. Draft decrees, Henry VIII. to George I., in bundles................................ 139 bundles.
7. Inquisitions post mortem, Edward I. to Charles I., bound in volumes .... 30 vols.
8. Draft injunctions, 12 James I. to 1748........ 23 bundles.
9. Affidavits, reports, certificates, orders, petitions, &c., 2 Elizabeth to 1800 .... 26 "
10. Several boxes containing original charters and grants under seal...........................
11. Registers, cowchers, and books of enrolment of patents, leases, &c. .... 115 vols.

12. Privy seals and bills for patents, and grants of lands and manors, Henry VII. to 1767.. 43 bundles.
13. Draft patents, Philip and Mary to 1760 ...... 47 "
14. Draft leases, Henry VIII. to 1760 .... 104 "
15. Counterparts of leases, Edward VI. to 1758... 61 "
16. Draft presentations to churches, Elizabeth to George I............................ 3 "
17. Draft warrants and commissions to survey, &c., 13 Elizabeth to 1785 .... 80 bundles.
18. Books of surveys of lands, manors, &c. .... 30 vols.
19. Books of surveys of woods.. .... 13 "
20. Judges' commissions, &c., 1675 to 1774 ...... 9 bundles.
21. Sheriffs' bills, 1684 to 1758 .—............ 5 "
22. Draft commissions of sewers, &c., 30 Elizabeth to 1800.......... .... 5 "
23. Inquisitions or extents for debt, Elizabeth to Charles II. .... 7 "
24. Security bonds, Henry VIII. to 1716 .... 9 "
25. Large collection of miscellaneous records in drawers, distinguished by letters of the alphabet, A to Z, and AA to HH...........
26. Miscellaneous records. catalogued and described .... 43 "

---

[1] The general inventory was prepared by Mr. William Hardy, the present Deputy Keeper of the Public Records, who had the custody of these documents previous to their transfer from the Duchy of Lancaster Office.—C.

27. Miscellaneous (undescribed)	11 bundles.	30. Court rolls, Edward I. to 1760	85 bundles.
28. Ministers' accounts, viz., of the wardrobe and treasurer of the household, receiver general's accounts, and valores or states of revenue, Edward III. to 1771	23 „	31. Old plans and maps contained in a large box, numbered respectively 1 to 117 .... 32. Oliver Cromwell's surveys .... 33. Calendars and indices to many of the above classes	
29. Ministers' accounts of honors and manors, Edward I. to 1760	455 „		60 vols.

The Seal of the Duchy of Lancaster is as ancient as the duchy itself; as is also the Seal of the County Palatine. The seal of the duchy remains with the chancellor of the duchy at Westminster; that of the county palatine is kept at Preston, in the office of the keeper of the seal. All grants and leases of land, tenements, and offices, in the county palatine of Lancaster, in order to render them valid, must pass under the seal of the county palatine, and no other; and all grants and leases of lands, tenements, and offices out of the county palatine, and within the survey of the duchy, must pass under the seal of the duchy, and no other seal.[1] The custom, however, is to seal all deeds of lands, &c., within the county palatine with both the duchy and the county palatine seals, and all without the county, but within the survey of the duchy of Lancaster, with the duchy seal only. These seals are essentially the same as those that have been used since the days of John of Gaunt, but new seals are engraved in each successive dukedom. Those at present in use are extremely splendid, and may rank amongst the first efforts of art in this department.

THE DUCHY SEAL.

Represents the Queen seated on her throne, in royal robes, wearing the Collar of the Most Noble Order of the Garter, and the Imperial Crown. In her right hand she holds the Royal Sceptre, and her left hand supports the Orb and Cross. On the dexter side, with the arm resting upon the throne, is an allegorical figure of Law, holding the sword by the point in one hand and a book in

THE DUCHY SEAL.

the other. Supporting the throne, on the sinister side, is the figure of Justice, holding the balance on one hand and the sword on the other. In the two outer compartments there are, on the dexter side, a Lion sejant, crowned with the Imperial Crown, and supporting between the paws a Banner of Arms of the United Kingdom of Great Britain and Ireland; and, on the sinister side, a Unicorn sejant and addorsed, gorged with a Prince's Crown, and supporting a Banner of Arms of the Duchy of Lancaster, viz., *gules*, three lions passant guardant *or*, a label of three points, each charged with three fleurs-de-lis. In the rear of the throne is a winged figure representing Fame, with two trumpets, and round the Seal is the Royal style—

VICTORIA · DEI · GRATIA · BRITANNIARVM · REGINA · FIDEI · DEFENSOR.

On the reverse is a Shield of the Arms of the Duchy, placed in pale, between two ostrich feathers erect ermine, each issuant from an escrol. Above the Shield is a ducal helmet, from

[1] Sir Edward Coke's Fourth Part of the Institutes of the Laws of England, fo. 210.

which flows the lambrequin, and on the helmet rests the crest, being upon a chapeau, turned-up ermine, a lion statant guardant, gorged with a label of three points, each charged with three fleurs-de-lis.　The Seal is circumscribed with the inscription—

Sigillum ✱ Ducatus ✱ Lancastriæ. ✱

The County Palatine Seal.

Represents the Queen on horseback, upon a mount in base, with the Royal sceptre in her right hand.　On the dexter side is a rose, ensigned by a prince's coronet.　Beneath the mount is a talbot dog courant, gorged with a collar, and the whole is circumscribed with the Royal style—

Victoria Dei Grat: Britanniarum Regina Fid: Def:

The reverse of the Seal bears a Shield of the Arms of the Duchy as above described, surmounted by a helmet with the lambrequin.　On each side of the Shield is an ostrich feather erect, ermine, issuant from an escrol.　The Seal is circumscribed—

Sigillum Comitat. Palatin. Lancastriæ.

THE COUNTY PALATINE SEAL.

Although the offices of the duchy and the county palatine, except that of the chancellor's, are little subject to political changes, the list of officers is frequently varying by the inevitable operations of time.　In December, 1886, these lists were as follows:—

Officers of the Duchy of Lancaster.

Chancellor—The Right Hon. Lord John James Robert Manners, G.C.B., M.P.
Vice-Chancellor—Henry Fox Bristowe, Esq., Q.C.
Attorney-General—Henry Wyndham West, Esq., Q.C.
Receiver-General—General the Right Hon. Sir Henry Frederick Ponsonby, K.C.B.

Auditor—Francis Alfred Hawker, Esq.
Clerk of the Council and Registrar—John Gardner Dillman Engleheart, Esq., C.B.
Coroner—Samuel Frederick Langham, Esq.
Clerk in Court and Solicitor—Francis Whitaker, Esq.

Officers of the County Palatine.[1]

Chancellor—The Right Hon. Lord John James Robert Manners, G.C.B., M.P.
Lord Lieutenant—The Right Hon. the Earl of Sefton.
High Sheriff (1886)—Sir Andrew Barclay Walker, Baronet.
Attorney-General—(In abeyance.)
Comptroller, Chancery of Lancaster—W. E. Sanger, Esq.
District Registrar of the Chancery of Lancashire—Alexander Pearce, Esq.
Clerks to the Lieutenancy—Messrs. Wilson, Deacon, Wright, and Wilsons.

Under Sheriff—W. T. Sharp, Esq.
Acting Under Sheriffs—Messrs. Wilson, Deacon, Wright, and Wilsons.
Constable of Lancaster Castle — The Right Hon. Lord Winmarleigh.
Seal Keeper and Clerk of Assize and Associate—Thomas Moss Shuttleworth, Esq.
Clerk of the Peace—Frederick Campbell Hulton, Esq.
Deputy Clerks of the Peace—Thomas Wilson and Samuel Campbell Hulton Sadler, Esqs.

---

[1] For a list of various other County Officers—as Chief and other Constables, Keepers of Gaols, Bridgemasters, Surveyors, etc.—see Appendix No. III.

CORONERS.

Laurence Holden—Lancaster.
Frederick Price—Salford.
James Broughton Edge—Bolton.
F. N. Molesworth—Rochdale.

Henry John Robinson—Blackburn.
Samuel Brighouse—Ormskirk.
Dr. Joseph B. Gilbertson—Preston.

Coroner for the Liberty and Manor of Furness, Ulverston—
    John Poole.
Coroner for the Manor of Walton-le-Dale—William Ascroft.

Coroner for the Manor of Prescot—Frederick Smith.
Coroner for the Manor of Hale.—John R. Bucton.

From the institution of the duchy of Lancaster, seals were, no doubt, in use, and the words, in the act already quoted, serves to prove that it was not now introduced for the first time.

In the British Museum[1] there is a manuscript entitled "Ducatus Lancastriæ," on the subject of the honors and dignities of the dukedom of Lancaster, written in the age of Elizabeth, and attributed to Sir William Fleetwood, recorder of London, one of the worthies of Lancashire, which supplies a hiatus in the early period of the history of the honor of Lancaster, wherein the learned civilian scrutinises the claims of Edmund Crouchback to the title of Earl of Lancaster, with as little ceremony as he was accustomed to use in scrutinising the representations of the suitors in the recorder's court.

DUCATUS LANCASTRIÆ.[2]

Lancaster is an ancient honor; its dukedom being made of a number of honors. Honors were dignities before the Conquest, as may be seen by the agreement made between King Stephen and Henry, Duke of Normandy, son to Maude the empress, for succession of the crown. Stephen was son to Adela, daughter to the Conqueror. After Stephen's death, Henry Plantagenet (son of the empress) was King of England, and had issue Henry, whom he crowned king in his lifetime; after his death, Richard Cœur de Lion, who created his brother John (Comte Sans Terre, Earl Lackland), Earl of Lancaster, and the town and territory of Bristol, and the counties of Nottingham, Devon, and Cornwall. Richard died without issue, leaving young Arthur and his sister, children of Geoffrey, his next brother [older than John] and heir. John, nevertheless, was crowned King of England, who had issue Henry and Richard and four daughters. Henry (III.), his eldest son, is crowned king, and grants to his brother (Richard) the earldom of Cornwall, with great possessions. In the 26 Henry III. (1241-2) came into England a nobleman, Piers of Savoy, who, because of his wisdom and prudence, was of the king's council in all things. To him the king gave the whole earldom of Lancaster, parcel of which earldom is the Savoy, a place without the bars of the new Temple, London, which in those days was known as a *Vanaforia*, since named "Maner Mori Templi," at this day the Savoy, parcel of the possessions of the dukedom of Lancaster. Piers of Savoy built him a house there, calling it by the name of the country whence he came, the Savoy. This Piers, Earl of Lancaster, being of great age, and his son being an alien born, and therefore not capable of inheriting the earldom, it escheated to the king, and was vested in the crown. Henry III. had six sons and two daughters—John, Richard, William, Henry (who died without issue), Edward, afterwards king by succession, and Edmund, surnamed Crouchback, of whom is descended the family and noble house of Lancaster; for the king, to the exalting of his blood, by letters patent, dated Lincoln, 8th August, in his 22d year (1237-8), granted to his dearly beloved son Edmund the honor of Lancaster, with all men, wards, reliefs, escheats, rents, and all other things pertaining to the honor, to be to him and the legitimate heirs of his body for ever. He also gave him and his heirs the honor of Leicester, etc., on 17th June, 55th year (1271). There is not any record or proof extant that this Edmund was created either Earl of Lancaster or Leicester;[3] but an earl natural is evermore a king's son, who, by his birthright, is an earl born, etc. As King John, on King Richard granting him the honor of Lancaster, was named Earl of Lancaster, not by creation but by birthright, so Edmund Crouchback had the two aforesaid honors granted him, and so was named Earl of Lancaster and Leicester. The honor of Lancaster, as by record appears, extends chiefly into Lancashire, Middlesex, Norfolk, Suffolk, Lincoln, Nottingham, Derby, York, Rutland, and Staffordshire, etc. Edmund Crouchback, second son of Henry III., being advanced to these honors and dignities, had two sons—Thomas and Henry. This Thomas was erroneously attainted in a Parliament of Edward II. by the policy of Hugh le Despencer, the father and his son, and was put to death at Pontefract; but in a Parliament 1st Edward III. (1327) this judgment was reversed, and the earl's dooms and possessions restored to the next heir, his brother Henry, who was not only Earl of Lancaster and Leicester by lineal descent, but also heritor to divers other earldoms, honors, &c. This Henry was afterwards created Duke of Lancaster by Edward III. He had issue only one daughter, Blanche, afterwards married to John of Gaunt, by means whereof the said John of Gaunt was created Duke of Lancaster, and by the assent of the Lady Blanche, his wife, all the possessions of the dukedom were lawfully conveyed to the said John the Duke, the Lady Blanche, and to the heirs of the body of John, etc. After which the said John had issue of the said Blanche, Henry of Bolinbroke, afterwards king by the name of King Henry IV., who had issue Henry V. The latter had issue Henry VI., which king had issue; after whose death the right and title to the dukedom, by force of the said entail [passed] unto John, Earl of Somerset, son of the said John, Earl of Lancaster, by Catharine Swynford, third wife of the duke; which John, Earl of Somerset, had issue Margaret, the Countess of Richmond and Derby; which Margaret had issue Henry VII., who married Elizabeth, eldest daughter of Edward IV., by whom he had issue Henry VIII., who had issue, our sovereign lady the Queen Elizabeth, in whose sacred person are contained the two houses of Lancaster and York, etc.

---

[1] Harl. Coll. No. 2077.
[2] The original document being long and verbose, and full of contracted words, we give the above as its substance.—H.

[3] Serjeant Fleetwood is in error: Prince Edmund was created Earl of Leicester by letters patent of 49 Henry III. (1264-5), and Earl of Lancaster 51 Henry III. (1266-7), both which patents are still extant.

CHAPTER VI.

CLOSELY connected with the duchy of Lancaster are the courts and privileges of the county palatine. Upon the subject of the palatinate privileges, Selden observes "that the counties of Chester and Durham are such by prescription or immemorial custom, or at least as old as the Norman Conquest; but that Lancashire, as a palatine county, is of more modern date, and was so created by Edward III., after it became a duchy, in favour of Henry Plantagenet, first Earl and then Duke of Lancaster, whose heiress being married to John of Gaunt, the king's son, the franchise was greatly enlarged and confirmed in Parliament, to honour John of Gaunt himself, whom, on the death of his father-in-law, the king had also created Duke of Lancaster.[1]

Upon this subject the authorities are conflicting: Lancashire appears to have enjoyed palatine jurisdiction under Earl Morcar, before the Norman Conquest; but after that event, which changed the whole frame of society, these privileges remained in abeyance till they were partially revived in the early part of the twelfth century, and fully confirmed in the time of the " Good Duke of Lancaster " and of John of Gaunt.

We give an extract from an original letter from Dr. "Kuerden, in his own hand," dated Preston, 20th Jan., 1664, to his brother, both in law and in pursuits, Mr. Randle Holme, in the Harleian Collection in the British Museum :—[2]

"Mr. Townly and myself are in hott pursuit of our coutryes affaires, and in retriuing the glory of our Palatinate out of monumetal ashes, and are able by this time to prove our county a Palatinate Jurisdiction under Rog. Pictavensis, before the grand survey of Doomsday's Record in yᵉ Echqʳ and forfeted before that time, restored again in Will the second's time, forfeited againe by Pictavensis at the battell of *Teuerchbuy*, [Tewkesbury] in the beginning of Henry I., bestowed then on Stephen before he was king, and continuated for his reigne in his son, W. Comes Boloniæ et Moritoniæ, till about the 5ᵗʰ of Richard the first, then given to Jᵒ Earl Moreton, afterwards to P. of Savoy, and by Henry 3ᵈ conferred on Edmund Crouchback, our first earl by charter, though some of these latter had not their Jura Regalia as at first."

Counties palatine are so called *a palatio*, because the owners thereof, the Earl of Chester,[3] the Bishop of Durham, and the Duke of Lancaster, had in those counties *jura regalia* as fully as the king had in his palace; *regalem potestatem in omnibus*.[4] The peculiar jurisdiction and form of proceedings of the courts of law in the county palatine of Lancaster are the result of those privileges which were granted to its early earls and dukes, to induce them to be more than ordinarily watchful against the predatory incursions from the Scotch border, and to prevent their tenants from leaving the territory defenceless and exposed to hostile aggressions, while seeking redress at the more distant tribunals of the realm.[5] Law was to be administered by the officers and ministers of the duke, and under his seal, and anciently all offences were said to be against his peace, his sword, and dignity, and not, as now, "against the peace of our lord the king, his crown, and dignity." The king's ordinary writs for redress of private grievances, or the punishment of offences between man and man, were not available within the county palatine—such writs then ran in the name of the duke; but in matters between the king and the subject the palatine privileges could not contravene the exercise of the sovereign power, and the prerogative writs were of force, lest injuries to the state should be remediless. Since 27 Henry VIII. (1535) all writs have run in the name of the king, and are tested before the owner of the franchise. Hence it is that all ordinary writs out of the king's court at Westminster, for service in this county, are addressed to the chancellor of the duchy, commanding him to direct the sheriff to execute them, and that all processes to that officer, out of the chancery of the county palatine, are not tested before the king or his justices at Westminster, as in other counties. The franchise and revenue of the duchy being under different

---

[1] Tit. Honour, part ii. sec. 8. p. 677.
[2] Cod. 2042.
[3] The Palatinate of Chester was abolished in 1830, when the whole of the offices of purely palatinate origin and jurisdiction were dissolved.—C.
[4] Bracton, lib. iii. c. 8. sec. 4.
[5] Upon this account there were formerly two other counties palatine—border counties as they were called: Pembrokeshire and Hexhamshire, the latter now united with Northumberland; but these were abolished by Parliament—the former, 27 Henry VIII. (1535); the latter, 14 Elizabeth (1572). By the first-mentioned of these Acts the powers of owners of counties palatine were much abridged, the reason for their continuance having in a manner ceased, though still all writs are witnessed in their names, and all forfeitures for treason by the common law accrue to them.

guiding and governance from those of the crown, all honours and immunities, and all redress within this county, with very few exceptions, must be derived from the chancellor of the duchy, as the principal minister of the king, in his capacity as Duke of Lancaster. Until the passing of the Judicature Acts justices of assize, of gaol-delivery were, and justices of the peace are still, and ever since the creation of the county palatine of Lancaster have been, made and assigned by commission, under the seal of the county palatine,[1] and the sheriffs for the county of Lancaster are appointed in the same way. The election of sheriff for this county palatine, in 1824, formed an exception to the general rule. The practice is to date the writ before his majesty, "at his palace at Westminster;" but on this occasion, when John Entwistle, Esq., of Foxholes, was appointed, that document was dated from "the palace at Brighton." Anciently, sheriffs, like coroners, were chosen by the freeholders;[2] but popular elections growing tumultuous, this practice was abolished.

The choice of the sheriffs in the palatine counties is conducted in a different manner from that of the choice of these officers in the other counties of the kingdom. The usual mode of election is for the judges, having met in the Exchequer chamber on the morrow of St. Martin (Nov. 12), to return for each of the counties, not palatine, the names of three persons, resident in each county, to the king—and for the king, with a small instrument, to prick the name of one of the three, usually the first upon the list, as sheriff. But for the county of Lancaster, the chancellor of the duchy selects the three names, which he submits to the king, as Duke of Lancaster, usually on some day between the 1st and the 20th of February in each year; and the king chooses one of the three, generally that at the head of the list. In the early periods of British history, the sheriffs continued in office for a number of years, as will be seen in the following list, and some for the whole term of their life; but since the 28th Edward III. (1354), the office can only be held legally for one year. Nor was it unusual in early times to elect to this office the most exalted peers of the realm. Before the Conquest, the county of Lancaster, with some other jurisdictions, was committed to the Earl of Northumbria, in the large sense, and sometimes to the Earl of Deira, being the more southern part of that kingdom or province. The last of these earls in the Saxon times were Earls Tosti and Morcar, whose possessions are noted in Domesday Book.

The following list is compiled from the manuscripts of Mr. Hopkinson, compared by the late Matthew Gregson, Esq., with that of the late George Kenyon, Esq., which we have collated with and corrected from a MS. (No. 259) in the British Museum, endorsed, "Nomina Vicecomitum collecta ex Rotulis Pellium recepta apud Westmonasterium. De Termino Michaelis, anno primo Regis Edwardi primi" (1273):—[3]

SHERIFFS OF LANCASHIRE FROM THE EARLIEST RECORDS TO 1886.

NORMAN LINE.

WILL. II. 1087-1100.

1087. Geoffrey was sheriff, and the only one named until 1156. Probably the person called Goisfrid in the Domesday Survey. "Inter Ripā 7 Mersham." No sheriffs are named during the reigns of Henry I. and Stephen.

PLANTAGENET OF ANJOU.

HENRY II. 1155-1189.

1156. Ralph Pigot, for four years.
1160. Robert de Montalt, for three years.
1163. Hugh de Owra.
1164. Galfr. de Valoines, Baron of Derby.
1165. Idem.
1166. William de Vesci.
1167. Idem.
1168. Rogerus de Herlebeck (William de Vesci, K.)
1170. Idem (Herlebeck, K.)
1171. Idem.
1172. Ralph Fitz-Bernard.
1173. Idem.
1174. Idem. (Rad. de Glanvill, K.)
1175. Idem.
1176. Idem. (K. Rob. H.)
1177. Robert (probably in error for Ralph) Fitz-Bernard (Ralph Fitz-Bernard, K.)

1178 to 1183. Ralph Fitz-Bernard.
1184. Gilbert Pipard.
1185. Gilbert Pipard and Peter Pipard for him.
1186. Idem.
1187. Idem.
1188. Gilbert Pipard.

RICHARD I. 1189-1199.

1189. Gilbert Pipard.
1190. Henry de Cornhill.
1191. Idem.
1192. Ralph de Cornhill.
1193. Idem.
1194. Theobald Walter, of Preston, and Wm. Radcliffe for him (Theobald Walter, K.)
1195. Theobald Walter and Benedict Garnet for him.
1196. Idem.   Idem.
1197. Theobald Walter and Robert Vavasour for him.
1198. Theobald Walter and Nicholas Pincerna or le Boteler for him.

JOHN. 1199-1216.

1199. Theobald Walter.
1200. Rob. de Tattershall.
1201. 1202. 1203. Richard Vernon.

---

[1] Coke's 4th Institute, p. 205.
[2] Coke's 2d Institute, p. 174.
[3] Kenyon dates from the year of appointment; Hopkinson from the year in which the shrievalty ends; so the apparent difference of a year runs throughout their lists (*Gregson's Fragments*, p. 225). In the list above

Kenyon's dates are followed, as comprising nearly ten months of the year's shrievalty. The authorities for various readings are marked K. for Kenyon, H. for Hopkinson, and G. for Greswell. For many additional particulars and corrections in the lists the Editor is indebted to the courtesy of the Rev. Henry Parr, Vicar of Yoxford, Suffolk.— C.

1205. Roger Lacy, of Clitheroe.
1206. Roger de Lacy and Adam de Lacy for him.
1207. Roger de Lacy and Robert Wallensis, Gilbert Fitz-Reynfride, and Adam Fitz-Roger for him.
1208. Gilbert Fitz-Reynfride and Adam Fitz-Roger for him; (Gilbert fil. Reinford, K.)
1209 }
to } Gilbert Fitz-Reynfride and Adam Fitz-Roger for him.
1216. }

HENRY III. 1216-1272.

1216. Ranulph, Earl of Chester.
1217. Ranulph, Earl of Chester, and Jordan his son for him.
1218. Idem.
1219. Idem.   Idem.
1220. Idem.   Idem.
1221. Idem.   Idem.
1222. Idem.   Idem.
1223. Idem.   Idem.
1224. William de Ferrars, Earl of Derby, William de Ferrars and Robert Montjoy for him.
1225. Idem.
1226. William de Ferrars and Gerard Etwell for him.
1227. Adam de Eland, of Rochdale.
1228. Idem.
1229. Idem.
1230. Idem.
1231. Idem.
1232. Idem.
1233. Sir John Byron.
1234. William Lancaster, of Lancaster, and Simon de Thornton for him.
1235. Idem. Idem.
1236. Robert de Lathom, of Lathom,
1237. William de Lancaster and Simon de Thornton for him.
1238. Idem.   Idem.
1239. Idem.   Idem.
1240. Idem.   Idem.
1241. Idem.   Idem.
1242. Idem.   Idem.
1243. William de Lancaster and Richard le Boteler for him.
1244. Idem.   Idem.
1245. William de Lancaster and William and Matthew Redmayne.
1246. Idem.   Idem.
1247. Idem.   Idem.
1248. { William de Lancaster and Matthew Redmayne.
       { Robert Latham (half-year).
1249. Idem.
1250. Idem for seven years further.
1256. Patrick de Ulnesby.
1257. Idem.
1258. William Pincerna (or le Boteler, as he is named in the writ), of Bewsey.
1259. Geoffrey de Chetham, of Chetham (as Fermor).
1260. Geoffrey de Chetham.
1261. Geoffrey de Chetham and Ralph de Dacre.
1262. Geoffrey de Chetham and Adam de Montalt.
1263. Adam de Montalt and Robert de Lathom, K.
1270. John de Cancefield.
1272. Ranulph de Dacre.

EDWARD I. 1172-1307.

1273. Thomas Travers.
1274. William Gentyl (Henry de Lea, H.)
1275. Ranulph de Dacre.
1276. Nicholas de Lee.
1277. Henry de Lee.
1278. Gilbert de Clifton, of Clifton.
1279. Roger de Lancaster, of Lancaster.
1280. Ralph de Montjoy.
1281. Thomas Banister.
1282. Richard de Hoghton, of Hoghton.
1283. Thomas de Lancaster.
1284. }
1285. } Henry de Lee.
1286. Robert de Latham and Gilbert de Clifton for him.
1287. Gilbert de Clifton, of Clifton.
1288. Robert de Leyborne.
1289. Gilbert de Clifton.
1290. Roger de Lancaster, of Lancaster.

1291. Ralph Mountjoy (to 1297, K.)
1292. Richard de Hoghton, of Hoghton.
1293 }
to } Ralph Montjoy.
1298. }
1299. Edmund Plantagenet, Earl of Lancaster, and Richard de Hoghton for him; Thomas, Earl of Lancaster, by inheritance; and Richard de Hoghton for him.
1300. Richard de Hoghton, of Hoghton.
1301. Idem.
1302. Thomas Travers, of Nateby.

EDWARD II. 1307-1327.

1303 }
to } Thomas Plantagenet, Earl of Lancaster.
1308. }
1309. William Gentyl.
1310. Thomas Plantagenet, Earl of Lancaster.
1311 }
to } Richard de Bickerstaffe.
1320. }
1321. Gilbert Southworth, of Southworth (Wm. le Gentyl, K.)
1323. John d'Arcy.
1326. Geoffrey de Warburton.

EDWARD III. 1327-1377.

1328. William Gentyl.
1329. John de Hambury.
1330. John de Burghton.
1331. John de Hambury and Sir Geoffrey de Warburton.
1332. John de Denam.
1333. }
1334. } Robert Foucher (others say Toucher).
1335. William Clapham.
1339. }
1340. } Robert de Radcliffe, of Ordsall.
1344. Stephen Ireton.
1345. John le Blount.
1348. John Cockayne.
1355. Richard de Radclyffe, of Radclyffe Tower.
1358. William de Radclyffe, of Radclyffe Tower.
1359. John Ipree, vice Sheriff (no Sheriff's name found).
1360. William de Radclyffe, of Radclyffe Tower.
1363. John Ipree, vice Sheriff.
1371. Geoffrey de Chetham, of Chetham.
1375. }
1376. } Richard Towneley, of Towneley.

RICHARD II. 1377-1399.

1377. Richard de Towneley, of Towneley.
1378. Thomas de Bobbeham.
1379. Nicholas Harrington, of Farlton, for six years.
1385. Ralph Radclyffe, for three years.
1389. Robert Standish.
1392. Sir Ralph Standish, of Standish.
1393. Sir John Butler, of Rawcliffe, for three years.
1397. Richard Molyneux, of Sephton.

HOUSE OF LANCASTER.

HENRY IV. 1399-1413.

1400. Thomas Gerard, of Bryn.
1401. }
1404. } John Boteler, of Rawcliffe.
1405. Sir Ralph Radclyffe.
1406. Idem.
1407 }
to } Sir John Bold, of Bold, four years.
1410. }
1411. }
1412. } Sir Ralph Stanley.

HENRY V. 1413-1422.

1413. Sir Ralph Stanley and Nicholas Longford.
1414. William Bradshaw and Robert Longford.
1415. }
1418. } Robert Urswick, of Urswick.
1419. Robert Lawrence, of Ashton.
1420. }
1421. } Richard Radclyffe, of Ordsall.

HENRY VI. 1422-1461.

1423 }
1426. } Richard Radclyffe, of Ordsall.

1427. }
1429. } Robert Lawrence, of Ashton.

1441 }
1442. } Sir John Byron, of Clayton.

1459. Nicholas Byron, of Clayton. (Idem John, H.)

HOUSE OF YORK.

EDWARD IV. 1461-1483.

1462. John Broughton, of Broughton.

1463. }
1465. } Thomas Pilkington, of Pilkington.

1466. Sir Robert Urswick, of Urswick.
1473. Thomas Pilkington, of Pilkington.
1476. Thomas Molyneux, of Sephton.
1482. Thomas Pilkington, of Pilkington.

HOUSE OF TUDOR.

(UNION OF YORK AND LANCASTER.)

HENRY VII. 1485-1509.

1501. }
1508. } Sir Edward Stanley, of Hornby.

HENRY VIII. 1509-1547.

1512. } Sir Edward Stanley, of Hornby ; afterwards Baron
1514. } Monteagle.

1520. }
1527. } Edward Stanley, Baron Monteagle, of Hornby.

1528. Sir Alexander Osbaldeston, of Osbaldeston.
1532. Sir John Towneley, of Towneley.
1542. Sir Thomas Southworth, of Samlesbury.
1546. Sir Alexander Radclyffe, of Ordsall.

EDWARD VI. 1547-1553.

1547. Sir Alexander Radclyffe.
1548. Sir Thomas Gerard, of Bryn.
1549. Sir Robert Worsley, of Worsley.
1550. Sir Peter Legh, of Haydock.
1551. Sir John Atherton, of Atherton.
1552. Sir Thomas Talbot.
1553. Sir Thomas Gerard, of Bryn.

MARY. 1553-1558.

1554. Sir Marmaduke Tunstall, of Thurland.
1555. Sir John Atherton, of Atherton.
1556. Sir Thomas Langton, of Newton.
1557. Sir Edmund Trafford, of Trafford.
1558. Sir Thomas Gerard, of Bryn.

ELIZABETH. 1558-1603.

1559. John Talbot, of Salesbury, Esq.
1560. Sir Robert Worsley, of the Boothes, Knt.
1561. Sir John Atherton, of Atherton, Knt.
1562. Sir John Southworth, of Samlesbury, Knt.
1563. Sir Thomas Hesketh, of Rufford, Knt.
1564. Thomas Hoghton, of Hoghton, Esq.
1565. Edmund Trafford, of Trafford, Esq.
1566. Sir Richard Molyneux, of Sefton, Knt.
1567. Sir Thomas Langton, Knt.
1568. Edward Holland, of Denton, Esq.
1569. John Preston, of the Manor, Esq.
1570. Thomas Boteler, of Bewsey, Esq.
1571. Edmund Trafford, of Trafford, Esq.
1572. John Byron, of Clayton, Esq. (Francis Holt, Esq., Fuller).
1573. Richard Holland, of Denton, Esq.
1574. William Booth, of Barton, Esq.
1575. Francis Holt, of Grislehurst, Esq.
1576. Richard Bold, of Bold, Esq.[1]
1577. Robert Dalton, of Thurland, Esq.
1578. John Fleetwood, of Penwortham, Esq.
1579. Ralfe Assheton, of Middleton, Esq.
1580. Sir Edmund Trafford, of Trafford, Knt.
1581. Sir John Byron, of Byron and Clayton, Knt.

1582. Richard Holland, of Denton, Esq.
1583. John Atherton, of Atherton, Esq.
1584. Edmund Trafford, of Trafford, Esq.
1585. Thomas Preston, of the Manor, Esq.
1586. Richard Assheton, Esq. (and Richard Bold, Esq.) K.
1587. John Fleetwood, of Penwortham, Esq.
1588. Thomas Talbot, of Bashall, Esq.
1589. Sir Richard Molyneux, of Sephton, Knt.
1590. Richard Bold, of Bold, Esq.
1591. James Assheton, of Chadderton, Esq.
1592. Edward Fitton, Esq.
1593. Richard Assheton, of Middleton, Esq.
1594. Ralph Assheton, of Great Lever, Esq.
1595. Thomas Talbot, of Bashall, Esq.
1596. Richard Holland, of Denton, Esq.
1597. Sir Richard Molyneux, of Sephton, Knt.
1598. Richard Asheton, of Middleton, Esq.
1599. Sir Richard Hoghton, of Hoghton, Knt.
1600. Robert Hesketh, of Rufford, Esq.
1601. Cuthbert Halsall, of Halsall, Esq.
1602. Sir Edmund Trafford, of Trafford, Knt.

HOUSE OF STUART.

JAMES I. 1603-1625.

1603. John Ireland, of Hutt, Esq.
1604. Sir Nicholas Moseley, of Aucoats, Knt.
1605. Ralph Barton, of Smithells, Esq.
1606. Edmund Fleetwood, of Rossall, Esq.[2]
1607. Sir Richard Assheton, of Middleton, Knt.
1608. Robert Hesketh, of Rufford, Esq.
1609. Sir Edmund Trafford, of Trafford, Knt.
1610. Roger Nowell, of Read, Esq.
1611. John Fleming, of Coniston, Esq.
1612. Sir Cuthbert Halsall, of Halsall, Knt.
1613. Robert Bindloss, of Borwick, Esq.
1614. Richard Sherburne, of Stonyhurst, Esq.
1615. Edmund Stanley, Esq.
1616. Rowland Mosley, of Hough End, Esq.
1617. Sir Edmund Trafford, of Trafford, Knt.
1618. Richard Shuttleworth, of Gawthorpe, Esq.
1619. John Holte, of Stubley, Esq.
1620. Leonard Ashawe, of Asshawe, Esq.
1621. Edmund More, of Bank Hall, Esq.
1622. Gilbert Ireland, of Hale, Esq.
1623. Sir George Booth, of Ashton-under-Lyne, Knt. and Bart.
1624. Sir Rafe Assheton, of Whalley, Baronet.

CHARLES I. 1625-1649.

1625. Richard Holland, of Heaton, Esq.
1626. Roger Kirkbye, of Kirkbye, Esq.
1627. Sir Edward Stanley, of Bickerstaffe, Baronet.
1628. Edmund Asheton, of Chadderton, Esq.
1629. Edward Rawsthorne, of Newhall, Esq.
1630. Thomas Hesketh, of Rufford, Esq.
1631. Richard Bold, of Bold, Esq.
1632. Nicholas Townley, of Royle, Esq.
1633. Ralph Assheton, of Middleton, Esq.
1634. Ralph Standish, of Standish, Esq.
1635. Humphrey Chetham (The Benefactor), of Manchester, Esq.
1636. William ffarington, of Worden, Esq.
1637. Richard Shuttleworth, of Gawthorpe, Esq.
1638. Roger Kirkbye, of Kirkbye, Esq.
1639. Sir Edward Stanley, of Bickerstaffe, Baronet.
1640. Robert Holte, of Stubley, Esq.
1641. Peter Egerton, of Shawe, Esq.
1642. Sir John Girlington, of Thurland, Knt.
1643. Gilbert Hoghton, of Hoghton, Esq.

1644. }
1645. } John Bradshawe, Esq. (No Sheriffs elected during the
1646. } Civil Wars—*Gregson*).
1648. }

COMMONWEALTH. 1649-1660.

1648. Sir Gilbert Ireland, of the Hutt, Knt., until May, 1649.
1649. John Hartley, of Strangeways, Esq., until December, 1649

---

[1] Fuller, in his *Worthies*, has a different order of succession for the four years 1572-75—viz. 1572 (14 Elizabeth), Francis Holt ; 1573, Richard Holland ; 1574, William Booth, and 1575, Francis Holt again ; omitting John Byron.

[2] Fuller omits John Ireland, and gives the three following Nicholas Mosley, Knt., Thomas Baker, Esq., and Edward Fleetwood, Esq.

1650. Edward Hopwood, of Hopwood, Esq.
1651. Henry Wrigley, of Chamber Hall, Esq.
1652. Alexander Barlow, of Barlow, Esq.
1652. John Parker, of Extwisle, Esq.
1654. Peter Bold, of Bold, Esq.
1655. John Atherton, of Chowbent, Esq.
1656. John Starkie, of Huntroyd, Esq.
1657. Hugh Cooper, of Chorley, Esq.
1658. Robert Bindlosse, of Borwick, Esq.
1659. Sir Richard Hoghton, of Hoghton, Baronet.

RESTORATION.

CHARLES II. 1660-1684.

1660. George Chetham, of Turton, Esq.
1661. } Sir George Middleton, of Leighton, Baronet.
1662. }
1663. John Girlington, of Thurland, Esq.
1664. Thomas Preston, of Holker, Esq.
1665. } William Spencer, Esq.
1666. }
1667. John Arden, Esq.
1668. } Thomas Greenhalgh, of Brandlesome, Esq.
1669. }
1670. Christopher Banister, of Bank, Esq.
1671. Sir Henry Sclater, of Light Oaks, Knt.
1672. } Sir Robert Bindlosse, of Borwick, Baronet.
1673. }
1674. Sir Peter Brooke, of Astley, Knt.
1675. } Alexander Butterworth, of Belfield, Esq.
1676. }
1677. } Alexander Rigby, of Layton, Esq.
1678. }
1679. Sir Roger Bradshaigh, of Haigh, Bart.
1680. William Johnson, of Rishton Grange, Esq.
1681. Lawrence Rosthorne, of Newhall, Esq.
1682. } Thomas Leigh, of Bank, Esq.
1683. }
1684. Peter Shakerley, of Shakerley, Esq.

JAMES II. 1684-1688.

1685. Peter Shakerley, of Shakerley, Esq.
1686. William Spencer, Esq., two years. (Peter Shakerley, K.)
1688. Thomas Richardson, of Rawnhead, nominated but not sworn in.

WILLIAM AND MARY. 1668-1702.

1689. James Birch, of Birch Hall, Esq.
1690. Peter Bold, of Bold, Esq.
1691. Alexander Rigby, of Layton, Esq.
1692. Francis Livesey, of Livesey, Esq.
1693. Thomas Rigby, of Gorse, Esq.
1694. Thomas Asshurst, of Asshurst, Esq.
1695. Richard Spencer, of Preston, Esq.
1696. Thomas Norreys, of Speke, Esq.
1697. Roger Manwaring, of Morley, Esq.
1698. William West, of Middleton, Esq.
1699. Robert Dukinfield, of Dukinfield, Esq.
1700. Thomas Rigby, of Middleton, Esq.
1701. William Hulme, of Davy Hulme, Esq.

ANNE. 1702-1714.

1702. Roger Nowell, of Read, Esq.
1703. Peter Egerton, of Shawe, Esq.
1704. George Birch, of Birch Hall, Esq. Succeeded by his brother, Thomas Birch.
1705. Richard Spencer, of Preston, Esq.
1706. Christopher Dauntesey, of Agecroft, Esq.
1707. Edmund Cole, of Lancaster, Esq.
1708. Miles Sandys, of Graythwaite, Esq.
1709. Roger Kirkby, of Kirkby, Esq. (died in office). Succeeded by Alexander Hesketh, Esq.
1710. Roger Parker, of Extwistle, Esq.
1711. Sir Thomas Standish, of Duxbury, Bart.
1712. William Rawsthorne, of Newhall, Esq.
1713. Richard Valantine, of Preston, Esq.
1714. William ffarington, of Werden, Esq.

HOUSE OF BRUNSWICK.

GEORGE I. 1714-1727.

1715. Jonathan Blackburne, of Orford, Esq.

1716. Thomas Crisp, Wigan, Esq.
1717. Samuel Crooke, of Crooke, Esq.
1718. Richard Norreys, of Speke, Esq.
1719. Thomas Stanley, of Clitheroe, Esq.
1720. Robert Mawdesley, of Mawdesley, Esq.
1721. Benjamin Hoghton, Esq.
1722. Benjamin Gregge, of Chamber Hall, Esq.
1723. Sir Edward Stanley, of Bickerstaffe, Bart.
1724. William Tatham, of Over Hall, Esq.
1725. Miles Sandys, of Graythwaite, Esq.
1726. Edmund Hopwood, of Hopwood, Esq.

GEORGE II. 1727-1760.

1727. Daniel Wilson, of Dalham Tower, Esq.
1728. Joseph Yates, of Peel, Esq.
1729. William Greenhalgh, of Myerscough, Esq.
1730. James Chetham, of Smedley, Esq.
1731. William Leigh, of West Houghton, Esq.
1732. John Parker, of Breightmet, Esq.
1733. John Greaves, of Culcheth, Esq.
1734. William Bushel, of Preston, Esq., M.D.
1735. Arthur Hambleton, of Liverpool, Esq.
1736. Sir Darcey Lever, of Alkrington, Knt., LL.D.
1737. Thomas Horton, of Chadderton, Esq.
1738. Samuel Chetham, of Castleton, Esq.
1739. Sir Ralph Assheton, of Middleton, Bart.
1740. Roger Hesketh, of North Meols, Esq.
1741. Robert Dukinfield, of Manchester, Esq.
1742. Robert Bankes, of Winstanley, Esq.
1743. John Blackburne, of Orford, Esq.
1744. Robert Radclyffe, of Foxdenton, Esq.
1745. Daniel Willis, of Red Hall, Esq.
1746. William Shawe, of Preston, Esq.
—1747. Samuel Birche, of Ardwick, Esq.
1748. George Clarke, of Hyde (Co. Chester), Esq.
1749. Rigby Molyneux, of Preston, Esq.
1750. Charles Stanley, of Cross Hall, Esq.
1751. James Fenton, of Lancaster, Esq.
1752. Richard Townley, jun., of Belfield, Esq
1753. John Bradshaw, of Manchester, Esq.
1754. Thomas Hesketh, of Rufford, Esq.
1755. Thomas Johnson, of Manchester, Esq.
1756. James Barton, of Penwortham, Esq.
1757. James Bailey, of Withington, Esq.
1758. Robert Gibson, of Myerscough, Esq.
1759. Edward Whitehead, of Claughton, Esq.
1760. Samuel Hilton, of Pennington, Esq.

GEORGE III. 1760-1820.

1761. Sir William ffarington, of Shaw Hall, Knt.
1762. Thomas Braddyll, of Conishead, Esq.
1763. Thomas Blackburne, of Hale, Esq.
1764. Sir William Horton, of Chadderton, Bart.
1765. John Walmesley, of Wigan, Esq
1766. Edward Gregge, of Chamber Hall, Esq.
1767. Alexander Butler, of Kirkland, Esq.
1768. Thomas Butterworth Bayley, of Hope, Esq.
1769. Dorning Rasbotham, of Birch House, Esq.
1770. Nicholas Ashton, of Liverpool, Esq.
1771. Sir Ashton Lever, of Alkrington, Knt.
1772. William Cunliffe Shawe, of Preston, Esq.
1773. Thomas Patten, of Bank Hall, Esq.
1774. Geoffrey Hornby, of Preston, Esq.
1775. Sir Watts Horton, of Chadderton, Bart.
1776. Lawrence Rawsthorne, of Newhall, Esq.
1777. Samuel Clowes, of Chorlton, Esq.
1778. Wilson Gale Braddyll, of Conishead, Esq.
1779. John Clayton, of Carr Hall, Esq.
1780. John Atherton, of Walton Hall, Esq.
1781. John Blackburne, of Orford, Esq.
1782. Sir Frank Standish, of Duxbury, Bart.
1783. James Whalley, of Clerk Hill, Esq.
1784. William Bankes, of Winstanley, Esq.
1785. John Sparling, of Liverpool, Esq.
1786. Sir John Parker Mosley, of Ancoats, Bart.
1787. William Bamford, of Bamford, Esq.
1788. Edward Falkner, of Fairfield, Esq.
1789. William Hulton, of Hulton, Esq.
1790. Charles Gibson, of Lancaster, Esq.
1791. James Starky, of Heywood, Esq

1792. William Assheton, of Cuerdale, Esq.
1793. Thomas Townley Parker, of Cuerden, Esq.
1794. Sir Henry Philip Hoghton, of Walton, Bart.
1795. Robinson Shuttleworth, of Preston, Esq.
1796. Richard Gwillym, of Bewsey, Esq.
1797. Bold Fleetwood Hesketh, of Rossall, Esq.
1798. John Entwisle, of Foxholes, Esq.
1799. Joseph Starkie, of Redvales, Esq.
1800. James Ackers, of Lark Hill, Esq.
1801. Sir Thomas Dalrymple Hesketh, of Rufford, Bart.
1802. Robert Gregge Hopwood, of Hopwood, Esq.
1803. Isaac Blackburne, of Orford, Esq.
1804. Thomas Lister Parker, of Browsholme, Esq.
1805. Meyrick Bankes, of Winstanley, Esq.
1806. Le Gendre Pierse Starkie, of Huntroyd, Esq.
1807. Richard Legh, of Shaw Hill, Esq.
1808. Thomas Clayton, of Carr Hall, Esq.
1809. Samuel Clowes, of Broughton, Esq.
1810. William Hulton, of Hulton, Esq.
1811. Samuel Chetham Hilton, of Moston Hall, Esq.
1812. Edmund Greaves, of Culcheth, Esq.
1813. William ffarington, of Shawe Hall, Esq.
1814. Lawrence Rawsthorne, of Penwortham, Esq.
1815. Le Gendre Pierse Starkie, of Huntroyd, Esq.
1816. William Townley, of Townhead, Esq.
1817. Robert Townley Parker, of Cuerden, Esq.
1818 Joseph Feilden, of Witton House, Esq.
1819. John Walmesley, of Castle Mere, Esq.

GEORGE IV. 1820-1830.

1820. Robert Hesketh, of Rossall Hall, Esq.
1821. Thomas Richard Gale Braddyll, of Conishead Priory, Esq.
1822. James Shuttleworth, of Barton Lodge, Esq.
1823. Thomas Green, of Slyne, Esq.
1824. John Entwisle, of Foxholes, Esq.
1825. John Hargreaves, of Ormerod House, Esq.
1826. James Penny Machell, of Penny Bridge, Esq.
1827. Charles Gibson, of Quernmore Park, Esq.
1828. Edmund Hornby, of Dalton Hall, Esq.
1829. Henry Bold Hoghton, of Bold, Esq.
1830. Peter Hesketh, of Rossall Hall, Esq.

WILLIAM IV. 1830-1837.

1831. Peregrine Edward Towneley, of Towneley, Esq.
1832. George Richard Marton, of Capernwray, Lancaster, Esq.
1833. Sir John Gerard, of New Hall, Bart.
1834. Thomas Joseph Trafford, of Trafford, Esq.
1835. Thomas Clifton, of Lytham, Esq.
1836. Charles Standish, of Standish, Esq.

VICTORIA. 1837.

1837. Thomas Bright Crosse, of Shaw Hill, Esq.
1838. William Blundell, of Crosby Hall, Esq.

1839. Charles Scarisbrick, of Scarisbrick, Esq.
1840. Thomas Fitzherbert Brockholes, of Brockholes, Esq.
1841. Sir Thomas Bernard Birch, of the Hazels, Liverpool, Bart
1842. Thomas Robert Wilson France, of Rawcliffe Hall, Esq.
1843. William Garnett, of Lark Hill, Salford, Esq.
1844. John Fowden Hindle, of Woodfold Park, Esq.
1845. Pudsey Dawson, of Hornby Castle, Esq.
1846. William Standish Standish, of Duxbury Park, Esq.
1847. William Gale, of Lightburne House, Ulverston, Esq.
1848. Sir Thomas George Hesketh, of Rufford Hall, Bart.
1849. John Smith Entwisle, of Foxholes, Rochdale, Esq.
1850. Clement Royds, of Mount Falinge, Rochdale, Esq.
1851. Thomas Percival Heywood, of Claremont, Pendleton, Esq.
1852. Thomas Weld-Blundell, of Ince Blundell, Esq.
1853. John Talbot Clifton, of Lytham Hall, Esq.
1854. Richard Fort, of Read Hall, Clitheroe, Esq.
1855. John Pemberton Heywood, of Norris Green, West Derby, Esq.
1856. Robert Needham Philips, of The Park, Prestwich, Esq.
1857. Charles Towneley, of Towneley, Esq.
1858. George Marton, of Capernwray, Esq.
1859. Sir Robert Tolver Gerard, of Garswood, Bart.
1860. Henry Garnett, of Wyreside, Lancaster, Esq.
1861. Sir Humphrey de Trafford, of Trafford Park, Bart.
1862. Wm. Allen Francis Saunders, of Wennington Hall, Esq.
1863. Sir William Brown, of Richmond Hill, Liverpool, Bart.
1864. Sir James Philips Kay-Shuttleworth, of Gawthorpe, Burnley, Bart.
1865. William Preston, of Ellel Grange and Liverpool, Esq.
1866. Sir Elkanah Armitage, Pendleton, Manchester, Knight.
1867. Thomas Dicconson, of Wrightington Hall, Esq.
1868. Le Gendre Nicholas Starkie, of Huntroyd, Esq.
1869. Benjamin N. Jones, of Lark Hill, Liverpool, Esq.
1870. Henry F. Rigge, of Wood Broughton, Grange-over-Sands, Esq.
1871. Sir James Watts, of Abney Hall, Cheadle, Knight.
1872. Thomas Wrigley, of Timberhurst, Bury, Esq.
1873. Sir James Ramsden, of Abbot's Wood, Furness Abbey, Knight.
1874 Richard Smethurst, of Ellerbeck, Chorley, Esq.
1875. John Pearson, of Golborne Park, Newton-le-Willows, Esq.
1876. Oliver Ormerod Walker, of Chesham, Bury, Esq.
1877. George Blucher Heneage Marton, of Capernwray, Esq.
1878. Nathaniel Eckersley, of Standish Hall, Wigan, Esq.
1879. William Garnett, of Quernmore Park, Lancaster, Esq.
1880. Ralph John Aspinall, of Standen Hall, Clitheroe Esq.
1881. William Foster, of Hornby Castle, Lancaster, Esq.
1882. George M'Corquodale, of Newton-le-Willows, Esq.
1883. Thomas Ashton, of Ford Bank, Didsbury, Esq.
1884. Thomas Brooks, of Crawshaw Hall, Rawtenstall, Esq.
1885. James Williamson, of Ryelands, Lancaster, Esq.
1886. Sir Andrew Barclay Walker, of The Grange, Gateacre, Baronet.

The county palatine of Lancaster is parcel of the duchy of Lancaster, and the sovereign has a seal, chancellor, and other officers, for the county palatine, and others for the duchy, both of which are managed separately from the possessions of the king.[1] It is one of the privileges of a county palatine that none of its inhabitants can be summoned out of their own county, except in case of treason, or error by any writ or process.[2] In the early periods of the palatine privileges in Lancashire, these distinctions of law were not so well understood as at present; hence a number of legal harpies were in the daily habit of seizing the inhabitants and their property, and conveying them away under form of law, though they had no jurisdiction whatever in the county. These violent and illegal proceedings kept those parts of the county wherein they were practised in a continual ferment. Large assemblies of the people rose to resist the intruders; and riots, and even murders, frequently ensued. So intolerable an evil called for a strong remedy, which the law had not then provided, but in the 28 Henry VI. (1449-50) an Act was passed by which it was ordained that if any "misruled" persons, under colour of law, made a distress where they had no fee, seigniory, or cause, to take such distress in the counties and seigniories in Wales, or in the duchy of Lancaster, they should be adjudged guilty of felony, and punished accordingly.[3] An ancient petition to Parliament from the inhabitants of this county has been

[1] Plow. Com. p. 219, on the Duchy of Lancaster case, so elaborately argued, by which it was decided that a lease under the duchy seal of land, parcel of the Duchy of Lancaster, made by Edward VI. in his nonage, to commence after the end of a former lease in esse, was good, and not avoidable by reason of his nonage.
[3] Coke's 4th Institute, p. 411.

preserved, wherein that protection was loudly called for, which the legislature were not slow to grant. A most extraordinary piece of legislation, relating to the county palatine of Lancaster, took place four years after this, by which an Act, made for a temporary purpose, was declared perpetual.   By this Act it was ordained that if any person should be outlawed in the county palatine of Lancaster he should forfeit such of his land and goods as were found in that county, but in no other;[1] 31 Henry VI. (1453), and that this should be the extent of his punishment, however aggravated might be his offence. The effect of such a law was to encourage crime to an alarming extent, for if any "foreigner" came into the county palatine of Lancaster, and committed any treason, murder, or robbery, or made and violated any contract, the sole redress for the injured party was against his lands and effects in the county, which generally were of no value. The pernicious consequence of this law soon became too palpable to be endured, and two years after it had been made "perpetual" it was repealed, in 33 Henry VI. (1455).[2] The defeat of this insidious measure did not prevent its repetition in the seventh year of the reign of Henry VII. (1491-2), when, in the absence of the "knights of the shire, and other noble persons of the county," an Act of Parliament was obtained, at the instance, and by the influence, of a single individual, probably one of the adherents of the deposed tyrant Richard, by which it was ordained that persons residing out of the county should neither be liable to process in the county of Lancaster nor should forfeit for their offences in the county any goods but such as were to be found within its limits. It may easily be conceived that no long time was necessary to discover this legislative error; and accordingly, we find that, in the very same Parliament, an Act was passed (1491-2) which, after reciting "that the Countie of Lancastre is and of long tyme hath byn a Countie Palantyne, made and ordeyned for grete consideracion, and within the same hath byn had and used Jurisdiccion Roiall, and all things to a Countie Palantyne belonging, in the dayes of the noble Progenitours of our soverayn Lord the King, unto the begynnyng of this present Parliament," proceeds to enact, "that the said County Palatyne, and every parte of the Jurisdiccion thereof, be in every poynt touching all Processes, Forfaiture, and other thinges, as large and of like force and effecte, as it was the day next before the first day of this present Parliament, and as if the said Acte had not bin made."

The bitter rivalry between the partisans of the houses of York and Lancaster still agitated the country. The madness of party raged with its utmost violence, and though the strength of the baronage was broken, there still remained men of fortune and influence accustomed to equip their retainers in liveries, and to furnish them with badges of distinction indicating to which house they belonged. Their power lay in the posts of disorderly dependents who swarmed round their houses, ready to furnish a force in case of revolt, while in peace they became centres of outrage and defiance to the law. The natural consequence of this condition of things was to increase the general agitation and to embarrass the general administration of the laws. The wars of the Roses showed that the power of the nobles was too great for the comfort or safety of the sovereign. Henry, therefore, to destroy their physical influences, determined on rigidly putting down retainers.   Edward had ordered the dissolution of these military households in his Statute of Liveries, and the statute was made more penal by Henry, and enforced with the utmost severity.[3] It is probable, also, that there were local feuds mixed up with these elements of general discord, which so far exceeded the corrective power of the police that a law was enacted, by which it was declared that no person should give liveries or badges, or retain, as their menial servants, officers or men learned either in civil or ecclesiastical law, by any oath or promise, under the penalty of one hundred shillings per month for every person so retained, to be recovered before the justices at their usual sessions of oyer and terminer, or before the king's justices in the counties palatine of Lancaster and Chester.[4]   The palatine privilege had, in the reign of Edward VI., been perverted to the injury of the inhabitants, by subjecting them to the consequences of outlawry without their knowledge. As the king's writ of proclamation awarded upon an exigent against any inhabitant of Lancashire, in any action involving the process of outlawry, did not run in Lancashire, it was necessarily sent to the sheriff of an adjoining county, and the consequence was that many persons were outlawed without their own knowledge. When the trade and commerce of the county began to be extended, this grievance manifested itself so frequently that an Act was passed (6 Edward VI., 1552) whereby it was enacted that whenever any writ or exigent from the Court of King's Bench or Common Pleas should issue against any person residing in Lancashire, a writ of proclamation should be awarded to the sheriff of the county palatine of Lancaster, and not to the

---

[1] Statutes of the Realm, vol. ii. p. 356.
[2] Statutes of the Realm, vol. ii. p. 365.
[3] On a visit to the Earl of Oxford, one of the most devoted adherents of the Lancastrian cause, the king found 5,000 of his host's retainers in livery drawn up to receive him. "I thank you for your good cheer, my

Lord," said Henry on his departure, "but I may not endure to have my laws broken in my sight. My attorney must speak with you," the earl, as the consequence, being fined £10,000.—C.
[4] Statutes of the Realm, vol. ii. p. 426.

sheriff of any adjoining county; and that the sheriff of Lancashire should make and return the proclamation accordingly.

During the civil wars between prerogative and privilege, when Charles I. had the nominal authority of the sovereign, but when the two houses of Parliament exercised the royal functions, the powers of the Duke of Lancaster, like those of the King of England, were assumed by the promoters of the Commonwealth; and an ordinance remains upon record (of 10th February, 1644), by which John Bradshaw was appointed to discharge the duties of sheriff of this county, which position he retained for four successive years, in contravention of the Act of 28 Edw. III. (1354), till the king was deposed, and until he, the acting sheriff of the county palatine of Lancaster, in the capacity of president of the Parliamentary tribunal, consigned his monarch to the block. In 1648, Sir Gilbert Ireland, of the Hutt and Hale—the partisan and friend of Cromwell, who was also member of Parliament for Liverpool, and governor of Chester Castle—was appointed by the Parliament, and retained the office until May, 1649, after which the appointments were made annually under the seal of the Commonwealth. With the Restoration, in 1660, the authority and the revenues of the Duke of Lancaster reverted to the king. In order to secure the ducal prerogatives and the ancient privileges of the county, a number of courts have, in the succession of ages, risen up in Lancashire, involving the jurisprudence of the county. The reason of these immunities, as assigned by Sir Edward Coke, is, "for that the county of Lancaster is a county palatine, and the duke," at its institution, "had *jura regalia*," or royal prerogatives, within the county—"to exercise all manner of jurisdiction, high, mean, and low." "This county palatine (of Lancaster)," adds Sir Edward, "was the youngest brother, and yet best beloved of all other, for it hath more honors, manors, and lands annexed unto it than any of the rest, by the house of Lancaster, and by Henry VIII. and Queen Mary, albeit they were descended also of the house of York, viz., from Elizabeth, the eldest daughter of Edward IV." The nature of the courts in the duchy and county palatine of Lancaster, ecclesiastical, civil, and criminal, may be thus stated:—

THE ECCLESIASTICAL COURTS ARE—

The Prerogative Court of York, within which province this county lies; the Courts for the Dioceses of Manchester and Liverpool; and the Court for the Archdeaconry of Richmond. Probates of wills and letters of administration, of persons dying within the county of Lancaster, have ceased to be granted by the ecclesiastical and diocesan courts of Manchester and Chester, and are now, under the Probate Act of 1847, granted by her Majesty's Courts of Probate, of which there are three in Lancashire—one at Manchester for the city of Manchester and the hundred of Salford; one at Lancaster for the county, except the hundreds of West Derby (diocese of Liverpool) and Salford, and the city of Manchester (diocese of Manchester); and one at Liverpool for the hundred of West Derby (within the diocese of Liverpool). Until the institution of the bishopric of Chester (32 Henry VIII. 1540), at the period of the Reformation Lancashire lay within the dioceses of Lichfield and Coventry, and wills proved from this county, at that time, were deposited at Lichfield, where those wills now remain, though some early wills were proved in the Prerogative Court of Canterbury, as the old diocese of Lichfield and Coventry was under the jurisdiction of the Archbishop of Canterbury. These are now preserved at Somerset House, London. After the erection of the See of Chester, wills in the northern part of Lancashire were usually proved at Richmond, in Yorkshire, and these were a few years ago removed to Somerset House. Prior to the passing of the Judicature Act, 1873 [1]

THE COURTS OF LAW WERE—

SUPERIOR COURTS.	*The High Court of Chancery. *The Exchequer. The Chancery of the Duchy. The Chancery of the County Palatine. *The Queen's Bench. *The Common Pleas at Westminster. The Common Pleas at Lancaster. The Judges' Commission of all manner of Pleas. The Commission of Oyer and Terminer.

The Courts marked thus * have a general jurisdiction, and are not peculiar to this county.

---

[1] For many of the particulars relating to the changes effected by the Judicature Act, 1873, the Editor is indebted to the courtesy of Mr. J. Broughton Edge, Esq., one of Her Majesty's Coroners for the County of Lancaster.—C.

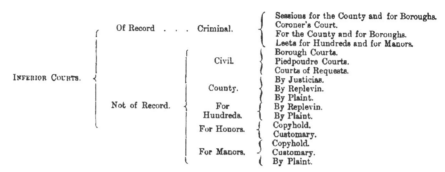

	Of Record . . .	Criminal.	Sessions for the County and for Boroughs. Coroner's Court. For the County and for Boroughs. Leets for Hundreds and for Manors.
INFERIOR COURTS.		Civil.	Borough Courts. Piedpoudre Courts. Courts of Requests.
	Not of Record.	County.	By Justicias. By Replevin. By Plaint.
		For Hundreds.	By Replevin. By Plaint.
		For Honors.	Copyhold. Customary.
		For Manors.	Copyhold. Customary. By Plaint.

THE HIGH COURT OF CHANCERY AND THE COURT OF EXCHEQUER

had concurrent jurisdiction in this county with the chanceries of the duchy, and the county palatine, in all matters requiring the interference of equity to remedy the defects, or mitigate the rigours, of law. But in affairs where the authority is derived by statute, or commission from the crown, as in bankruptcy and matters of a fiscal nature, the lord chancellor has an exclusive jurisdiction, and the barons of the exchequer paramount authority.

THE CHANCERY OF THE DUCHY OF LANCASTER

has been for many years practically obsolete, but not abolished. It used to be a court of appeal for the chancery of the county palatine; but now all appeals from the latter go to the Court of Appeal. It has a nominal jurisdiction in reference to the estates of the duchy, which lie in various counties, and are generally called "Duchy Liberties."[1]

THE CHANCERY OF THE COUNTY PALATINE OF LANCASTER

is an original and independent court, as ancient as the 50th of Edward III. (1376), and the proceedings were carried on by English bill and decree. The chief office is at Preston, and the court was formerly held four times a year—namely, once at each assize at Lancaster, and once at Preston in the interval of each assize. This court is now appointed to be held at Preston, Liverpool, and Manchester, at all of which places there are now registries. The business at Preston, however, is so light, that, by arrangement, there is seldom a court at Preston; the Preston business being taken at Liverpool or at Manchester, as more convenient to the bar, etc. The process of the court was formerly by subpoena, attachment, attachment with proclamations, commission of rebellion, sequestration, and writ of assistance, etc.; now the general practice of the court, except in some particular cases where it is governed by its own particular rules, is similar to the practice of the Chancery Division of the High Court of Justice in almost everything, except in despatch and expense. The chancery of Lancashire has concurrent jurisdiction with the High Court in all matters of equity, whether concerning lands lying within the palatine or concerning transitory suits, its cognisance of which depends on the person or lands of the defendant being amenable to the process of this court; but its jurisdiction is *exclusive* of all other courts of equity, when both the subject of the suit and the residence of the parties litigant are within the county; and in such case a defendant may insist on his right to be sued in this chancery by demurrer or plea to any other equitable process.

The court, in point of fact, exercises a concurrent jurisdiction with the Chancery Division of the High Court in all matters of equity within the county palatine, particularly in matters of account, fraud, mistake, trusts, foreclosures, tithes, infants, partition, and specific performance of contracts and agreements. It formerly interfered to restrain parties from proceeding in actions at law, and for that purpose granted the writs of injunction. And it now issues injunctions to stay waste and trespass in cases where irreparable mischief might arise, unless the parties were immediately restrained from doing the acts complained of. It was likewise auxiliary or assistant to the jurisdiction of courts of law, as by removing legal impediments to the fair decision of a question depending, either by compelling a discovery which may enable them to decide, or by perpetuating testimony when in danger of being lost, before the matter to which it relates can be made the subject of judicial investigation; but as all the branches of the High Court have now power to grant

[1] In 20 James I, (1624-5) an order was made " that noe Cause above £10 value, of either reall or personall, shalbe determined in the County Palatine of Lancaster; but to be heard before the Chancellor of the Duchy at Westminster." Booke of Orders, Division v., No. 29, 20 Jac. 1.

injunctions, and to compel discovery, in causes depending in it, these powers are no longer peculiar to courts of chancery. It also has jurisdiction, on *ex parte* applications, in appointing guardians for infants, and in allowing them a competent maintenance out of their property, and in enabling them to make conveyances of their trust and mortgaged estates for the benefit of the parties beneficially entitled. Although the bills are addressed to the chancellor of the duchy, the vice-chancellor of the county palatine is the judge of the court, and the causes and all motions and petitions are set down and heard before him. The chancellor of the duchy, assisted by the two judges in commission for the county palatine, used to sit to hear causes at Westminster, either commenced originally in the duchy chamber, or which had been transmitted there by way of appeal from the court of chancery of the county palatine, but now this jurisdiction is exercised by the Court of Appeal as hereinafter mentioned.

THE COURT OF QUEEN'S BENCH AND THE COURT OF COMMON PLEAS AT WESTMINSTER

had concurrent jurisdiction with the court of common pleas for the county palatine of Lancaster in almost all cases, and could enforce their jurisdiction over personal actions, unless *conusance* of the cause was claimed, or the palatinate jurisdiction pleaded, or error was brought, after judgment by default, with the venue laid in Lancashire, and the want of an original was assigned for error. In the two first instances, the superior courts could not refuse to allow the privilege when properly claimed; and in the last, the want of jurisdiction became apparent, from the circumstance of there being, in the chancery at Westminster, cursitors for the issuing of writs into every county but the counties palatine; and therefore, upon a cause of action arising in Lancashire, there was no proper officer from whom an original could have been obtained to warrant the subsequent proceedings in the court at Westminster. The cases where the jurisdiction of the courts above was excluded, and that of the common pleas at Lancaster adopted, were chiefly pleas of lands within the county, or actions against corporations existing in Lancashire. All writs out of the courts at Westminster (except Habeas Corpus and Mittimus) were directed to the chancellor, and not to the sheriff, in the first instance; and, where execution of them had to be done by the sheriff, the chancellor issued his mandate to that officer, and, on receiving his return, certified in his own name to the court above that the writ had been duly executed; and if the chancellor returned that he commanded the sheriff, and had received from him no answer, the court above would rule the sheriff to return the mandate. There was only one franchise in the county having the execution of writs by its own officer, viz. *the Liberty of Furness*, to the bailiff of which the sheriff directed his precepts, and received from him the requisite returns.

THE COURT OF COMMON PLEAS FOR THE COUNTY PALATINE OF LANCASTER

was an original superior Court of Record at Common Law, having jurisdiction over all real actions for lands, and in all actions against corporations within the county, as well as over all personal actions where the defendant resided in Lancashire, although the cause of action might have arisen elsewhere; but this court had no jurisdiction beyond the limits of the county. The judges of this court were appointed by commission from the king, under the seal of the duchy of Lancaster, but in the name of the king, pursuant to the statute of 27 Henry VIII. (1535). The judges, according to usage, were only two, being the judges appointed on the northern circuit, whose commission continued in force so long as the same judges continued to be appointed to that circuit. Its returns were on the first Wednesday in every month. The office of the prothonotary was at Preston, where the records for the preceding twenty years were kept, those for previous years being deposited at Lancaster, where the court sat every assize before one of the two judges of the courts at Westminster who had chosen the northern circuit, and who were half-yearly commissioned, the one as the chief justice, and the other as one of the "justices of the common pleas at Lancaster." The patent of the judges for the common pleas at Lancaster also appointed one of the judges "chief justice, and the other, one of the justices o ｀all *manner of pleas* within the county palatine," and under this the causes sent by *mittimus* from the courts at Westminster were tried at bar; but as there was no clause of *nisi prius* in the jury process by *mittimus* to Lancaster (it being out of the ordinary circuit of the judges), they could not be assisted by a serjeant on the civil side as in other counties. By the same commission were tried at bar all *pleas of the crown*, whether removed by *certiorari*, or otherwise directed so to be tried. This court was a great advantage to the commercial county of Lancaster, as well because its process for arrests to any amount reached to all parts of the county, and might be had without the delay of sending to London, as from the celerity and excellency of its practice. A great majority of the causes tried at Lancaster, as well as at Liverpool and at Manchester, were brought in the common pleas of the county palatine, and in point of importance were equal to those sent down for trial there from the courts at Westminster. In this court, actions might be brought within about three weeks from the time of holding the assizes; and execution might be had after trial, as soon as the assizes terminated, without waiting till the following term, which, at the summer assizes especially embraces a considerable period. The advantage of this promptitude in legal processes in Lancashire was so strongly felt that the principle is now extended to the general law of the country; and still further improved by an Act of Parliament passed in the early part of 1831, for the more speedy judgment and execution in actions brought in his Majesty's courts at Westminster; and the proceedings in the court of common pleas of the county palatine of Lancaster were facilitated by making all writs of inquiry or damage returnable on the first Wednesday in every month (in addition to the first and last days of each assize), in lieu of being returnable, as formerly, on any of the return days in Easter and Michaelmas terms respectively. The general official business of the court of common pleas in Lancashire was transacted by the deputy of the prothonotary. The office of prothonotary was a patent office, in the gift of the Crown, in right of the duchy of Lancaster. Henry Wyndham West, Esq., QC., is (1886) the Attorney-General.

Previous to every assize, commissions of Oyer and Terminer and General Gaol Delivery were formerly issued, under which the senior judge presided in the crown court, and delivered all the gaols within the county. The official proceedings in criminal cases within the county were conducted by the clerk of the crown, or his deputy.[1] The office of clerk of the crown was in the gift of the chancellor of the duchy for the time being, but is now in that of the lord chancellor. The office is held at Preston. At the end of the assizes, three copies are made of the calendar of the prisoners; one of which is signed by the senior judge, and delivered to the clerk of the crown, in whose custody it is kept; another copy is signed by the clerk of the crown, and kept by the judge; and a third, signed by the same officer, is left with the high sheriff or the gaoler. Under this authority, and without any special warrant, all executions take place. The judge writes the word "reprieved" or "respited," opposite to the name of each convict sentenced to die, but not left for execution; and such as have not either of these words written opposite their names are hanged. On behalf of those who are reprieved, the judge addresses a letter, called "the Circuit Letter" to the crown, recommending them to mercy on the grounds therein specified, which letter is transmitted to the office of the secretary of state, and generally, indeed invariably, produces a commutation of punishment.

The assizes were formerly held half-yearly, and at Lancaster only. But great changes and improvements have been made in this respect since 1830. After a royal commission in 1829, various reports of committees of county magistrates, and several numerously-signed petitions and memorials from populous towns in South Lancashire, it was determined to hold assizes for the criminal and civil business of the two hundreds of West Derby and Salford, at Liverpool; and accordingly assizes have been held there from the year 1835 in the Sessions House, Chapel Street, and from the 8th December, 1851 in St. George's Hall. Still the business of the assizes increased so greatly, and the inconvenience of jurors, suitors, prosecutors, witnesses, and others, having to travel thirty or forty miles to the assizes, and many of them to remain there for a number of days, at a great distance from home, led to a growing requirement that the hundred of Salford should have assizes for its business. Accordingly assizes for that hundred were held for the first time in the splendid new Assize Courts at Manchester in July, 1864; and this county now has three places of assize—at Lancaster, for the hundreds of Amounderness, Blackburn, Leyland, and Lonsdale; at Liverpool for the West Derby hundred; and at Manchester for the hundred of Salford. Besides the usual periods of spring and autumn, or Lent and Michaelmas, it has also been deemed necessary to have a winter assize, both at Liverpool and Manchester, chiefly for the delivery of the gaols of prisoners committed too late for trial at the August assizes, and who would otherwise be incarcerated before trial till the following March, and of late four assizes have been held in each year,

By section 16 of the supreme court of Judicature Act, 1873 (36 and 37 Vict., c. 66), the jurisdiction of the superior courts above-mentioned, with the exception of that of the chancery of the duchy and that of the chancery of the county palatine, were transferred to the high court of justice constituted by that Act. And by section 18 of the same Act the appellate jurisdiction of the duchy and palatine courts were transferred to the court of appeal also constituted by that Act. By section 95, however, the Act was not, except so far as is therein expressly directed, to affect the offices, position, or functions of the chancellor of the county palatine, and consequently the jurisdiction of the county palatine chancery still remains. The present vice-chancellor, H. Fox Bristowe, Esq., Q.C., by giving up the whole of his time to the duties of the office, and by

---

[1] Appendix to Evans on the Court of Common Pleas of the County Palatine of Lancaster.

appointing regular fixed sittings, has very much increased the business of that court, and the complaints of former times as to the delay arising from its procedure, cannot now be justly brought against it.

There are also registries of the high court of justice at Manchester, Liverpool, and Preston, in which proceedings can be taken in as full and ample a manner as in the Master's office in London. The present registrars are, at Manchester, Mr. H. J. Walker; at Liverpool, Messrs. T. E. Paget and Francis D. Lowndes; and at Preston, Mr. T. M. Shuttleworth.

The Courts of Inferior Jurisdiction

are either Courts, which, upon recording their judgment, can award that the party condemned shall be fined or imprisoned, or they are Courts not of record, and consequently not possessing the power to make such an award. Of the former class, some are more conversant in matters of criminal, and others of civil nature. The Criminal Courts of Record are—the General Sessions, held annually and quarterly, before the justices of the peace for the county. The Annual Sessions are held in July, at Preston, and afterwards, by various adjournments, until the numerous county affairs, placed by various statutes, under the peculiar cognisance of this court, are transacted. These are annually accumulating; and the matters of county finance have now become so much the objects of magisterial care and public interest, that its sittings bear no very distant resemblance to those of Parliament.

The General Quarter Sessions,

called the "County Sessions" to distinguish them from those of boroughs, are held, according to statute, at Lancaster, the first week after the 11th of October; the first week after the 20th of December; the first week after the 31st of March; and the first week after the 24th of June, in each year; and thence, by adjournment, at Preston, Kirkdale (Liverpool), and Salford. At these three places intermediate sessions are also held midway between the winter sessions. The multifarious matters under the cognisance of this court are too well known to require enumeration. A very considerable number of barristers attend the last adjournments; and many judicious arrangements have been made, which evince the anxious desire of the magistrates to reduce, as much as possible, the time consumed, and the enormous sums annually expended, in the prosecution of offenders. The bench have the power, and frequently exercise it, to effect a further saving of both, by dividing the sessions, and trying indictments and appeals in different courts at the same time.

Similar sessions are held in the boroughs of Manchester, Bolton, Blackburn, Wigan, and Liverpool, before the Recorders of those boroughs, agreeably to the respective charters, or to immemorial prescription, which presupposes such a charter anciently granted, and now lost or decayed.

Another court of record of criminal judicature is the coroner's court, rapidly assembled on the discovery of any dead body, and composed of the officer and a jury selected by the constables of some of the four townships next adjoining to that spot on which the corpse was first found. The name of the officer is supposed to be derived from the circumstance of his examination of the witnesses, and pronouncing of sentence, being in a ring or circle of people assembled round the deceased, or in *corona populi.* Others derive the name *coroner* from *coronator,* because he holds *placita coronæ,* or pleas of the crown, and the chief justice of the Queen's Bench is the chief coroner of England. He is elected by the freeholders, upon a writ requiring the sheriff to hold a county court for the election, and returned into chancery. In this county there are seven coroners, each of whom has full power to act throughout Lancashire; but the exercise of such power is limited by order in Council to certain districts therein named, unless during a vacancy of the office, in the absence of the coroner from one district, when any other coroner of the county may act in such district. The coroner is bound by law to discharge his office in person, or by a deputy lawfully appointed by the coroner and approved by the Lord Chancellor, to come when sent for, and to view the body in the presence of the jury; and if the corpse cannot be found, no inquest can be held. He must also inquire of every death in prison, whether naturally or by misfortune. There are other duties attached to the office, such as the execution of process where the sheriff is party, or in contempt; the taking and entering of appeals of murder, rape, and robbery, etc.; the judgment on the writs of outlawry; the inquests of wreck and treasure-trove; and others of less frequent occurrence, and less public concernment, than its ordinary painful and unpleasant task: the office is of high antiquity, and great public utility, when executed according to the spirit and for the end of its original institution. The coroner is a conservator of the peace, at common law, *virtute officii.* The remaining court of record, for the punishment of offences, is the Leet. Formerly the sheriff perambulated the county, and held his criminal court in every hundred.   This was called the *Torn*, or *Tourn;* but when the delay, inconvenience, and expense of that officer "taking a turn" through so extensive a district became manifest, this court was made stationary in every hundred, and was held, as at present, before the steward of the hundred.

A singular instance occurs, as early as the time of Edward II., of the exactions to which the inhabitants of Lancashire were subjected by the itinerant visits of some of the ostentatious sheriffs in their periodical *tourns* through the county; but to these grievances they did not tamely submit, as appears from an ancient indictment presented by the grand jury, of which the following is a translation :—[1]

"LANCASTER. { The Grand Jury of the Wapentake of West Derby present that '*Willielmus le Gentil*,' at the time when he was sheriff, and when he held his Town in the said Wapentake, ought to have remained no longer in the Wapentake than three nights with three or four horses, whereas he remained there at least nine days with eight horses, to the oppression of the people ; and that he quartered himself one night at the house of '*Dns de Turbat*,' and another night at the house of one '*Robertus de Bold*,' another at the house of '*Robertus de Grenlay*,' and elsewhere, according to his will, at the cost of the men of the Wapentake."

For this offence, and for another of a more extraordinary kind, which will be exhibited in the parliamentary history of the county, the sheriff was placed in duress; but the record adds, that "the said '*Willielmus Gentil*' is enlarged upon the manucaption of four manucaptors."

At the period when the comites or earls divested themselves of the charge of the counties, that duty devolved upon the sheriffs, as the name *shire-reeve*, or bailiff of the shire, imports; and, in like manner, when the hundredors ceased to govern the divisions styled hundreds, their office was supplied by the steward—*i.e. stede-ward*, or governor of the place.   This officer is one of those conservators of the peace who still remain such by virtue of his office.   The six hundreds in Lancashire—viz. Lonsdale, Amounderness, Blackburn, Leyland, West Derby, and Salford—were anciently styled shires.   Thus Leland, temp. Henry VIII. speaks of Manchester standing in Salford-shire; and, in common with all the hundreds north of the Trent, they bear the synonymous name of wapentakes, from the ancient custom of the heads of families assembling armed, upon the summons of the hundredor, and touching his weapon, to testify their fealty.   In many parts of this county, lands and manors are held by suit to the hundred leet, of which service this was probably the sign and symbol, and such are called hundred lands.   The leet must be held at least twice in every year, and within a month of Easter and Michaelmas respectively.   It is held before the steward of the hundred, or his deputy, and a jury impanelled by him.   The amercements are limited only by the assessment of at least two men, according to the measure of the fault, agreeably to a provision of Magna Charta.   Anterior to the statutes which have given to the sessions concurrent jurisdiction, its duties embraced every offence, from eaves-dropping and vagrancy, to high treason; but, although contrary to several very learned dicta, every statute affecting it has preserved, and none has diminished, its powers; which are seldom called into exercise, except to abate nuisances, punish deficient measures, and appoint the high and petty constables, and other municipal officers.   Its proceedings have two singular characteristics—the entire absence of fees and lawyers.   The increase of population and the influence of feudal lords gave rise to *manorial leets* (which were granted to obviate the necessity of the tenants of a particular manor being obliged to attend the torn, or general leet of the hundred), held before the stewards of the several lords of manors, or their deputies; and, by custom, the leets of several manors may be held at once in some certain place within one of the manors.

THE INFERIOR COURTS OF RECORD OF CIVIL JUDICATURE

are—(1) The Courts of Boroughs, usually held before the principal corporate officer, and the recorder or steward, and having jurisdiction, in personal actions, to an unlimited amount.   Such is the Court of Passage at Liverpool, the Court of Record at Manchester, the Borough Court of Preston, and others, as numerous and as various as the respective charters or prescriptions.   (2) The *Piedpoudre Court* is a court of record, having unlimited jurisdiction over all contracts arising within a fair, before the lord or owner, or his steward or clerk of the fair.   It was the lowest and most speedy court in the realm, except one now extinct, called the Court of Trail-baton, where the judge was bound to decide whilst the bailiff drew his staff or trailed his baton round the room. (3) The Court of Requests in Manchester, as elsewhere, has been superseded by the County Courts.

THE INFERIOR COURTS, NOT OF RECORD

are all calculated for the redress of civil, and not of criminal, injuries.   It has been seen that the sheriff had a court-leet called the torn, which was the *criminal* court of the county   he had also

[1] Rot. plac. coram R. 17 Edw. II. m. 72 (1823-4).

his court-baron or *civil* court, which formerly travelled round the county in the same manner as the torn. The same complaint of expense, delay, and inconvenience attended this rotary process; and long before the torn was localised in the hundreds, the *County Court*, or Sheriff's Court, became stationary in the county town, and its jurisdiction was limited to those suits in which the parties dwelt in several hundreds. In both hundred and county courts matters to any amount were originally determined, until the statute of Gloucester directed that no suits should be commenced without the king's writ, unless the cause of action did not exceed 40s.

THE HUNDRED COURTS

have concurrent jurisdiction with the County Court in certain personal actions under 40s. in value, and are held from three weeks to three weeks, before the steward of the hundred, or his deputy, and a jury, within the respective jurisdictions. No suit can be removed by the defendant, before judgment, without bail, to the satisfaction of the court; nor by the losing party, after judgment, without similar security in double the amount of the judgment.

There is in this county one Honor or Superior Manor, having numerous dependent manors under it. It is the *Honor of Clitheroe*, the jurisdiction of which is very extensive. It has courts in the nature of courts-leet, at which the lords of the inferior manors owe suit; and others in the nature of copyhold courts, for the admittance of tenants by copy of court-roll under the various forfeited manors within the honor.[1]

There are also numerous other manors in various parts of the county; some of which have copyhold courts, and others only courts-baron for the redress of the tenants' grievances; some have courts-leet, and some few courts for the recovery of debts and damages under 40s., held according to their various local customs.

It has been complained of as a defect of the superior courts, that their sittings and offices are at too great a distance from the centre of business and the mass of the population. The evil of the inferior judicatures of a civil nature is, that, owing to the restrictions upon the amount of the sums sought to be recovered, and the diminished value of money, the time of respectable juries and professional men is wasted upon trifling suits, when it might be advantageously applied to ease the superior courts of those matters which are too small to deserve their cognisance, and yet too great to pass remediless, save at the risk or ruin of individuals. Several unsuccessful attempts have been made to remedy both these grievances. The answer to such has been, that it is dangerous to render more easy, cheap, and speedy the administration of justice, lest the people should contract a love of litigation, which would injure them more than the delay or denial of redress.

It should be stated that although the Hundred or Wapentake Courts and the old Borough Courts are not abolished, they do not dispose of much business, with the exception of such courts as the Court of Record for Salford Hundred and the Manchester City Court of Record, which are now amalgamated by the Salford Hundred Court of Record Act, 1868. The smaller courts are virtually superseded by the County Courts, established under the County Courts Act, and which are held all over the kingdom.

RECORDS OF THE COUNTY PALATINE.

The principal public records connected with the jurisprudence of the county palatine of Lancaster may be classed under three heads :—(1) Those which were in the department of the Deputy Clerk of the Crown at Lancaster. (2) Those which were in the department of the Prothonotary of Her Majesty's Court of Common Pleas for the county of Lancaster; and (3) Those which were in the department of the Registrar of the Court of Chancery of Lancashire. The records of these Courts of Equity and Common Law are now deposited in the Public Record Office, London, pursuant to a request of the Chancellor of the Duchy of Lancaster, dated 25th July, 1873. Soon after the appointment of the Commissioners of Public Records, issued in virtue of a recommendation of the two Houses of Parliament, in the year 1800, the commissioners instituted inquiries into the nature of these records and the places of their deposit; and from the answers returned to those inquiries it appears—

---

[1] The General Courts of the Duke of Buccleuch and Queensberry, for the several manors and forests within the Honor of Clitheroe, are now usually holden as follows :—

The Halmot Court and Court Baron for the Manor of Chatburn, Worston, and Pendleton, at Clitheroe Castle.

The Halmot Court and Court Baron for the Manor of Tottington, at the National School in Ramsbottom.

The Halmot Court and Court Baron of the Manor of Ightenhill, at the Court House in Burnley.

The Halmot Court and Courts Baron for the several Manors of Accrington Old-hold and Accrington New-hold, at the Court House in Haslingden.

The Halmot Courts and Courts Baron for the Manor of Colne, and the Forest of Trawden, at the Court House in Colne.

The Halmot Court and Court Baron for the Forest of Pendle, at the Court House in Higham.

The Audit is afterwards holden at Clitheroe Castle. *History of Whalley*, v. ii. p. 292, note, ed. 1872.—C.

FIRST.—That the public records, rolls, instruments, and manuscript books and papers in the custody of the clerk of the crown for the county palatine of Lancaster, consist of instruments, and other *criminal proceedings* in the crown office for the county palatine ; the records of such instruments and proceedings, and different books of entries, though not very numerous, are supposed to be all that have been preserved. These records (except the proceedings at two or three preceding assizes, which are kept in the office of the deputy-clerk of the crown in Preston) are deposited in the new office or room that has been fitted up in Lancaster Castle for the reception of these and other records of the county ; Lancaster Castle being supposed to be the property of the crown, in right of the duchy of Lancaster. For eighty or ninety years past, the indictments, etc., are so far arranged, that any proceeding inquired for may be easily referred to ; antecedent to that period, such as have been preserved are promiscuously placed together in no regular order, but are in tolerable preservation. All the proceedings at each assizes within the period first mentioned are entered or docketed in books, by referring to which the proceedings in each prosecution may be known ; but there are no indexes or catalogues except that, upon some of the older rolls, the contents are endorsed. All searches are made by or in the presence of the deputy-clerk of the crown, or his confidential clerks, who are employed in the custody and arrangements of the records, and give attendance as occasion may require without any remuneration from the public. Office copies of records are charged after the rate of eightpence for each sheet, consisting of seventy-two words, and the usual fee upon a search is 6s. 8d., and the deputy-clerk of the crown charges for attending at Lancaster during the assizes with a record, a guinea. The searches in this office are very rare, and, of course, the fees upon them very inconsiderable.

SECOND.—The public records, rolls, instruments, and manuscript books and papers in the custody of the deputy prothonotary of the *court of common pleas*, in and for the county palatine of Lancaster, consist of fines and recoveries, records, writs, minutes, papers, and proceedings in real, personal, and mixed actions, instituted in this court, along with some few enrolments of deeds ; and they are supposed to be the whole of the records or papers relating to this court since its creation. These records and other documents, for a period of upwards of fifty years, are lodged at the office of the deputy prothonotary, which (with other principal law officers of this county palatine) is held at Preston, on account of its central situaton. All the early records and documents are now lodged in an ancient tower or chamber within the castle of Lancaster, which has been very commodiously fitted up for their reception at the expense of the county. The records and other documents are methodically arranged in separate compartments, according to their dates, and are in general in very good preservation. There are docket rolls or indexes to all the records, containing the names of the parties to the fines, recoveries, and suits recorded at each assizes. As the records of this court are kept at a distance of twenty-two miles from the office, a person is appointed at Lancaster by the deputy prothonotary, vulgarly called *custos rotulorum*, who is entrusted with the care of the records, etc., whose duty is to attend every search, and to take care that every record be duly and safely restored to its proper place, for which a fee is due.[1]

THIRD.—The public records, etc., in the custody of the registrar of the *court of chancery of the county palatine* of Lancaster, consist of bills, answers, and other pleadings, depositions, order-books, decrees, decree-books, and other books for entries in causes, and other matters instituted in that court ; and are supposed to be the whole of the records or papers that have been preserved since its creation. These documents, anterior to the year 1740, were kept in a room or chamber in the castle of Lancaster ; such as are subsequent to that period are at the office of the deputy-registrar in Preston, which is the private property of the deputy-registrar. The old records are deposited in an office fitted up in the early part of the present century in Lancaster Castle for their reception, at the expense of the county. The bills, answers, and depositions, are upon different files, with the respective years in which they are filed marked upon labels affixed to them ; but neither these, nor the other books or proceedings, appear ever to have been well arranged ; many of them are much defaced, and almost, if not wholly, unintelligible. The bills, answers, depositions, etc., have usually been indexed (or entered in a pye-book) when brought to the registrar's office to be filed : there are no indexes of the other proceedings, and many of the indexes first mentioned have been lost, and the remainder are not accurate. Various circumstances have caused these records or papers to be at different times removed. All searches in this office are made by, or in the presence of, the deputy-registrar or his confidential clerks, who are employed in the custody and arrangement of the records, and give attendance as occasion requires, without any salaries or emoluments paid by the public. There are charges for copying proceedings, etc., and fees for search, also for a journey of the deputy-registrar from Preston to Lancaster, and his expenses. Owing to the irregular state of the records, few searches are made.

The places of deposit of the records of the county palatine[2] may be summarily stated as follows :

Records and other Instruments.	Date.	Where kept.
County Palatine of Lancaster. Chancery :		
Bills, Pleadings, Depositions, Orders, and Decrees	1740 to 1800. Dates wanting before 1740 ; 1135 to 1558	Register of the County Palatine Duchy Office (now in the Record Office).
Charters and Grants of various kinds	1136 to 1558.................	
Common Pleas :—		
Fines and Recoveries, Writs, Minutes, Proceedings in Actions, and Inrolment of Deeds........................	Geo. III.	Prothonotary's Office at Preston (now in the Record Office).
The Records before his present Majesty's Reign	Dates wanting	
Pleas of the Crown :—		
Indictments and other Criminal proceedings, and Books of Entries........................	About 50 years before 1800	Castle, Lancaster (now in the Record Office).
Collectanea relating to the History and Antiquities thereof, made by the three Holmes	......	British Museum.
Collection of Names of the King's Castles, Mansions, Parks, Forests, Chases, etc., within the survey of the Duchy of Lancaster	......	University Library, Camb.
Iter Forestæ...................	8 Edward III.	Lincoln's Inn Library.
Nona Roll	15 Edward III.	King's Rememb. Office.
Ecclesiastical Survey (a copy)	26 Henry VIII.	First-Fruits Office.
Survey of Estates therein not granted in Fee-farm	1629	University Library, Camb.
Catalogue of Charters throughout England and Wales............		Ashmolean Museum.
Fee-farm, Rolls of	Temp. Interregni	Augmentation Office.

[1] Return made by William Cross, Esq., deputy prothonotary to the Commissioners of Public Records.

[2] A very comprehensive account of the Records of the Palatinate of Lancashire, and those of the Superior and Abolished Courts preserved in Her Majesty's Public Record Office, from the pen of Mr. Walford D. Selby, will be found in volumes vii. and viii. of the publications of the Record Society.—C.

The archives of the ecclesiastical courts, so far as they concern the county of Lancaster, are to be found at Lichfield, from the earliest period of their preservation up to the year 1590, in the custody of the registrar of the diocese of Lichfield and Coventry; and since that period, in the custody of the deputy-registrar of the diocese of Chester, the deputy-registrar of the consistory court of the archdeaconry of Richmond; and the deputy-registrar of the five several deaneries of Amounderness, Copeland, Lonsdale, Kendal, and Furness. These depositories may be classed under four heads:—

FIRST.—There are in the custody of the registrar of the diocese of Lichfield and Coventry, in right of the bishops' see, original manuscripts, or episcopal registers, or acts, of the bishops of Lichfield and Coventry, from the year 1296, except that there are some chasms in several of the bishops' times. These registers contain acts on institutions of rectors and vicars, and some entries of appropriations of rectories and endowments of vicarages in the diocese. There are also books of the judicial proceedings in causes in the court, from about the year 1450. Original wills, and grants of letters of administration, from 1526 to 1590, when the ecclesiastical archives belonging to the diocese of Chester ceased to be kept at Lichfield.

SECOND.—There are deposited in the public episcopal registry at Chester, in which diocese—until the creation successively of the sees of Manchester and Liverpool [1]—the county of Lancaster was situated, original wills or copies thereof proved there, from the year 1590, to the present time, and bonds given by persons administering to the effects of persons dying intestate. Sundry pleadings and proceedings exhibited in causes in the consistory court of Chester, and books of the acts in the same causes. Nine folio volumes, commencing in the year 1525, containing entries of sentences of consecrations of churches, chapels, and burial-grounds in the diocese, faculties for rebuilding and improving churches, chapels, and parsonage-houses, confirmation of seats, and other ecclesiastical commissions and faculties. Proceedings on the installations of bishops, patents of the officers of the vicar-general and official principal commissaries; rural deans, registrars, proctors, and apparitors. Three books, commencing in 1500, containing entries of presentations or institutions to ecclesiastical benefices within the diocese. Four books, commencing in 1752, containing entries of institutions, licenses to curacies, ordinations, and other episcopal acts. Several books of subscriptions to the liturgy and the articles of the church of England, by persons ordained, and clergymen admitted to benefices or cures. A volume usually called *Bridgman's Ledger*, having been chiefly collected by Dr. John Bridgman, who was appointed Bishop of Chester in 1619, containing copies of various appropriations, endowments, compositions, grants, agreements, leases, charters, orders by the crown, rentals of synodals, procurations, pensions, tenths, and subsidies; patents and statutes of grammar schools. A volume, usually called *Gastrell's Notitia*, being compiled by Dr. Francis Gastrell, elected lord bishop of Chester in 1714, containing an account of the then population of each parish, number of families, Catholics, Dissenters, families of note, patrons, wardens, schools, endowments, charities, and several other particulars of each parish and chapelry in the diocese; entries of licenses of marriage; probates of wills, and letters of administration; names of the clergy; church and chapel wardens; account of exhibits at episcopal visitations, and correction books; original presentation to benefices, and nominations to curacies and schools, and terriers and parish and chapel registers.[2] There are two other registries in the archdeaconry of Richmond, at Lancaster and Richmond. All the foregoing records are deposited in the public episcopal registry in Chester, which is a stone building, slated, and commodiously fitted up for the safe and convenient preservation of the records and papers deposited therein. The records and papers are, in general, in good preservation, except the most ancient part; from time or inevitable accident, they are in many parts imperfect before the year 1650, and for ten years following quite deficient. From that period, the wills, and most of the registries and entries, are regular and correct. There are complete indexes to the wills, registries, and entries of institutions, from their commencement, except in the parts before mentioned to be deficient. There are several manuscript volumes in the possession of the bishop of the diocese, containing a particular account of the extent and population of the diocese, number of Catholics and Dissenters, state of parsonage-houses, residence of clergy, schools, charities, and several other particulars relative to the diocese, being answers to queries addressed by different bishops to the clergy of the diocese. The number of parishes in the diocese of Chester was, in the year 1800, two hundred and sixty-two.

THIRD.—The records, instruments, and papers, in the custody of the deputy registrar of the consistory court of the archdeaconry of Richmond, formerly in the diocese of Chester, consist entirely of original wills; bonds taken upon the issuing of letters of administration, tuition, and curation; affidavits and bonds relative to marriage-licenses; proceedings in ecclesiastical suits; enrolment of faculties for pews and galleries in churches and chapels; terriers and duplicates of parish registers; and such other matters as relate to the office and jurisdiction of the commissary of the said archdeaconry of Richmond, but do not comprehend any record or instrument of any other nature or description. From the most ancient of the said records, to the year 1750, they comprise the wills, administration and tuition bonds, which have arisen from every part of the said archdeaconry of Richmond; but since that year a division took place, and the wills and other papers and records not relating to such business as is usually called contentious, arising within the five deaneries of Amounderness, Kendal, Copeland, Lonsdale, and Furness, part of the said archdeaconry, are deposited in the parish church of Lancaster, under the custody of another officer there. From the most remote period, the duplicates of parish registers, terriers, and all other records, proceedings, and papers (except those of a contentious nature, and the wills, etc., of the period first before mentioned) of the five deaneries, are also deposited at Lancaster; whilst all other wills, papers, and records, arising within this archdeaconry have continued to be deposited, and remain in the registry of the consistory court at Richmond. The registry at Richmond is part of the ancient chapel, called Trinity Chapel, in the centre of the market-place of the borough of Richmond, sufficiently large and commodious, and in most respects secure; but having several dwelling-houses and shops, wherein fires are directly underneath, as well as adjoining to it, it is in some measure exposed to danger. The state of preservation of the records, etc., at Richmond, is in general very good, though some few of the ancient wills have suffered by the access of moisture in certain places, particularly in the corners of the roof, which are now perfectly repaired, and all increase of decay is prevented as much as possible. The wills are arranged alphabetically in bundles of ten years each; the terriers and parish registers in parcels, according to their several parishes; and all the rest of the records, with sufficient regularity to answer the purposes of those who require searches to be made. There is no regular catalogue, schedule, or repertory of the records, nor any index, except of the terriers and faculties, and of such of the wills and administrations as have arisen within the present century, within the three deaneries of Richmond, Catterick, and Boroughbridge, commonly called the three Yorkshire deaneries.

FOURTH.—The original wills within the five deaneries of Amounderness, Copeland, Lonsdale, Kendal, and Furness, within the archdeaconry of Richmond, preserved and kept at Lancaster, proved and approved before the worshipful commissary (for the time being) of the said archdeaconry or his surrogates, or before the vicar-general or his surrogates respectively, since the first of November, 1748, are registered, deposited, and kept in a convenient room, called the registry of the east end, of and within the parish church of Lancaster, where are also deposited all bonds taken on granting letters of administration, curation, tuition, and marriage licenses

---

[1] In 1847, by virtue of the Act 10 and 11 Vic., c. 108, the collegiate church of Manchester was elevated to the dignity of a cathedral, and made the seat of a bishop, and in 1880 the See of Liverpool was created.- C.

[2] Bishop Gastrell's *Notitia Cestriensis* has been edited by the Rev. Canon Raines, and printed for the Chetham Society, in 4 vols. viii. xix. xxi. and xxii. of the Society's series.- H.

14

within these five deaneries. And in the same place are also deposited and kept copies of the parochial registers delivered in by the church and chapel wardens within the five deaneries at each visitation. The register or place of deposit is deemed very secure, and well accommodated for the keeping of the several instruments. The several wills and instruments are well preserved, and the wills and administration, curation, and tuition bonds belonging to each of the said deaneries, are kept separate and apart from each other; and those of each deanery arranged annually, and also decennially, in alphabetical order. The bonds on granting marriage licenses are arranged in numerical order. There are distinct alphabetical books for each of the deaneries, called "Act Books," in each of which are entered schedules containing a short entry of the probate of each will, and of every administration, curation, and tuition, granted within each of the deaneries respectively; to each of which act books is prefixed or annexed an alphabetical index of contents.

The following exhibits a condensed view of the places of deposit of the records and other instruments connected with the ecclesiastical affairs of the county of Lancaster:—

ECCLESIASTICAL.

Records and other Instruments.	Date.	Where kept.
Diocese of Chester and of Manchester—		
Installations of Bishops, Patents of Officers, etc..............	.....	
Terriers and Parish and Chapel Registers	......	
Presentation to Benefices, Nominations to Curacies and Schools	......	
Appropriations, Endowments, Compositions, Grants, Agreements, Leases, Orders, etc..............................	......	
Licenses of Marriage, Probates of Wills, and Letters of Administration	. ....	Bishop's Registry of Chester, or of Manchester or Liverpool, as the case may be.
Proceedings in causes, and Books of Acts of the Consistory Court	......	
Presentations and Institutions to Ecclesiastical Benefices ...	Commencing 1500	
Consecrations of Churches, Chapels, etc , and Faculties for rebuilding Churches	1525 \}	to the present time.
Original Wills, or Copies of [1]..................................	1590	
Population of Parishes, Account of	1714 \}	
Richmond Archdeaconry, Consistory Court—		
Wills, Original..	......	
Bonds on granting Letters of Administration, etc..............	......	
Marriage Licenses and Affidavits thereon	......	
Parochial Registers, Copies of	......	
Act Books, containing Entries of Probates....................	......	Consistory Registry, Richmond.
Proceedings in Suits	......	
Inrolment of Faculties for Pews, etc.	......	
Terriers	......	
Duplicates of Parish Registers	......	
Wills, Original..	1748 to the present time.	Commissary Registry, Lancaster.
Administration, Curation, and Tuition Bonds		
Act Books, containing Entries of Probates....................		
The earliest date—		
Chester..	1500	Registry, Chester.
Lichfield and Coventry Diocese—		
Ecclesiastical Survey	26 Hen. VIII.	First Fruits Office.
Terriers of Rectories and Vicarages.............	......	
Registers containing Institutions of Rectors and Vicars, Appropriation of Rectories, and Endowments of Vicarages	1296 to the present time, with chasms.	
Judicial Proceedings in Causes	1450 \}	Bishop's Registry, Lichfield.
Wills and Grants		
Administration, Letters of	1526 \}	to present time.
Licenses		
Registers of Parishes	1660 \}	

---

[1] As to the wills of persons resident, or having property, within the county palatine of Lancashire, much interesting information has been printed of late years. Especially deserving of notice are four vols. entitled "Lancashire and Cheshire Wills and Inventories," edited by the Rev. G. J. Piccope, and Mr. J. P. Earwaker, B.A., vols. xxxiii., li. and liv., old series, and vol. iii. new series of the Chetham Society's series; embracing the wills of persons of various ranks and grades within the period A.D. 1480-1746. Of wills relating to Lancashire, but lodged in registries in Durham and Yorkshire, much information will be found in the following works, published by the Surtees Society: Vol. ii., "Wills and Inventories illustrative of the history, manners, etc , of the Northern Counties of England, from the 11th century downwards" (chiefly from the registry at Durham); edited by Dr. Raine; vol. xxxviii., a continuation of vol. ii., "Wills from the registry at Durham." edited by the Rev. W. Greenwell; and vol. xxvi., "Wills and Inventories from the Register at Richmond," edited by Rev. J. Raine, jun. Vol. iv., "Testamenta Eboracensia: Wills illustrative, etc., of the province of York, from A.D. 1300 downwards." Vol. i. edited by Dr. Raine; vol. xxx. (vol. ii.), 1429-1462, edited by the Rev. J. Raine; vol. xlv. (vol. iii.), "Wills from the registry at York" (1395-1491). At the end of this volume are "Dispensations for Marriage, Marriage Licenses," etc., from the registers of York, Durham, and Richmond, 1374-1581. In addition to those works, Mr. J. P. Earwaker has edited for the Record Society, vols. ii. and iv.: "An Index to the Wills and Inventories now preserved in the Court of Probate, at Chester, from 1545 to 1650" together with (1) "A List of the Transcripts of Early Wills preserved in the Consistory Court, Chester." (2) "A List of the Wills printed by the Chetham Society." (3) "A List of the Wills seen and noted by the Revs. J. and G. J. Piccope and not now to be found at Chester." (4) "A List of the Wills preserved in Harl. MS. 1991 in the British Museum." (5) "A List of the Lancashire and Cheshire Wills proved in the Prerogative Court of Canterbury, 1650-1660," and (6) "A List of the Lancashire and Cheshire Administration granted in the Prerogative Court of Canterbury 1650-1660."—C.

CHAPTER VII.

The Earldom of Lancaster possessed by King John—Privileges to the Honor of Lancaster in Magna Charta—Forest-Laws, and Assize of the Forest at Lancaster—Grant of Land between Mersey and Ribble—Large Drains on Lancashire for Men and Money for the Wars—Wars of the Barons—Edward II. the Prisoner of Thomas Earl of Lancaster—Analysis of Landed Possessions in the County from Testa de Nevill.—A.D. 1164-1327.

ESUMING the chronological order of our history from the period at which it had arrived when we commenced the history of the dukes and duchy of Lancaster, it is proper to correct an error into which the learned Selden has fallen, when he says, "That Lancashire, till Henry III. created his youngest son Edmund Crookback earl of it (A.D. 1266), I think was no county; for in one of our old year books a learned judge[1] affirms that in this Henry's time was the first sheriff's turn held there."

That sheriffs were elected for this county upwards of a century before Henry III. ascended the throne of these realms is already abundantly clear. In the Domesday Survey of the date of 1086, the county of Lancaster, as we have already seen, is surveyed as portions of the adjoining counties of York and Chester, but it is not named in that survey; and after a diligent examination of the public records, the first mention we find of the county is in the Pipe Roll[2] in the Exchequer Office, seventy-eight years after that survey was completed. The Pipe Rolls commence with 5 Stephen (A.D. 1140), and contain returns from a great number of the sheriffs of other counties, but the name of Lancashire does not occur till the 11th Henry II. (1165), after which the returns for Lancashire seem to be regular under every year, at least for some time. It is thus manifest that Selden is in error in supposing that Lancashire was "no county" till the time of Henry III., and that it had no sheriff till 1266, when Edmund Crouchback was created Earl of Lancaster. The records of the duchy of Lancaster are stated by Mr. Harper to be of as early a date as the first of Stephen, but those do not of course apply to the duchy, which was not created till more than one hundred years afterwards. In the Chapter House at Westminster there is, amongst its immense circular documental storeys, a bag of Lancashire fines, marked "Lancastria," in which several ancient deeds are deposited, of the date of 7 Richard I. (1195-6), relating to ecclesiastical affairs.

In the reign of John, the men of Lancashire complained that their privileges were infringed by Roger Poer, who had deprived them of more than a hundred acres of wood and forest land, which they had been accustomed to enjoy as common of pasture.[3] The complaint of the men of Lancashire was made with peculiar propriety to King John, who, though he was surnamed Sansterre, or Lackland, possessed the earldom and honor of Lancaster, which were conferred upon him as an inheritance, while he was Earl of Morton or Mortaigne, by his brother Richard I. in the excess of his bounty. The death of Richard soon after opened the way to the throne for John, who hastened to assume the crown, and to secure his possession, as is alleged, did not hesitate to imbrue his hands in the blood of his nephew Arthur, who, as the son of Richard's brother, Geoffrey, third son of Henry II., had a better title, had the crown descended by strict hereditary succession.[4] During the reign of Richard, the spirit of crusading had been at its height; not only the flower of the

---

[1] Thorp, 17 Edward III. (1343) fol. 566.

[2] The Great Roll of the Exchequer, or *Rotulus Annalis*, called the Pipe, was the record of the account of the Court of Exchequer, formerly containing the accounts of the whole revenues of the Crown, digested under the hands of the several counties, and annually written out in order to the charging and discharging of the sheriffs and other accountants. The earliest Pipe Roll preserved is assigned to the 31 Henry I. (1130), and is the most ancient record of the Court of Exchequer with the exception of Domesday Book. In the Appendix to the Thirty-first Report of the Deputy Keeper of the Public Records (pp. 299-302) the names are given of the Lancashire accountants from the earliest period to the reign of Edward I., and at the commencement of the list is this note: "The following names are given because the title 'Vicecomes' is frequently applied to the officer who returns an account *de honore*. But Lancaster does not appear to have been always on the same footing with other counties before it became a county palatine by patent 25 Edward III. In the earlier years it seems to have been included in Northumberland. It is, however, distinctly called a county in 6 Henry III." (1221).—C.

[3] Abbrev. Placit. Rot. 1. p. 24.

[4] Over the precise circumstances of the fate of Arthur there hangs a terrible mystery, and the statements that have come down to us rest very much upon the authority of popular tradition. One writer says that Arthur vanished in a manner unknown to all, while another says the king was suspected of having killed him with his own hand. A more circumstantial account says, he took Arthur into a boat, stabbed him twice with his own hand, and threw the dead body into the river, about three miles from the castle. That he was murdered, and if not actually by the hand at least by the instigation of John, there is little doubt, for there was nothing in his nature to lead him to stop short at assassination. "Foul as it is, hell itself is defiled by the fouler presence of John." was the terrible verdict of his contemporaries, and this has passed into the sober judgment of history. There is, however, a passage on the Patent Rolls (p. 36) which throws a curious and interesting side-light on the events of this period. In a "safe-conduct," granted by the king, and dated on the 24th of August, at Chinon, he says to Alan Fitz-Count and others who were desirous of seeing him, as he had been informed by "Furmie, servant of Arthur, our nephew,"—"We command you, however, that ye do naught whereby evil may befal our nephew Arthur."—C.

most distinguished families in Lancashire, but in every part of Christendom, embarked in these holy wars with the utmost enthusiasm; and though a few splinters from the wood of the real cross were purchased by the sacrifice of more than 300,000 men, such was the excitation of the times, that a knight-templar seldom failed to rank amongst the first of public benefactors. To these wars future ages are indebted, if not for the introduction, at least for the development of the science of heraldry and coat armour, by which the incased knights were distinguished on the plains of Palestine, and since which time illustrious families have used them to adorn their pedigrees.

When the great bulwark of British freedom, Magna Charta, was wrested from King John on the field of Runnymede (1215), by the intrepid barons, special privileges were granted to the honor of Lancaster by name; and it was provided in the articles appendant to that charter, that "if any one should hold of any escheat as of the honor of Walingeford, Notingeham, Bologne, or Lankastr', or of other escheats which are in the king's hands, and are baronies, and he die, his heir shall not give any other relief, or perform any other service, to the king, than he should perform to the baron; and that the king hold it in the same manner as the baron." The Charter of Forests was scarcely less appreciated in Lancashire than Magna Charta. The number and extent of the forests in this county made the severity of the laws by which they were protected oppressive in the extreme (though the rigour of the laws had already been relaxed in their favour), and the immunities conferred on the people by these memorable charters would have immortalised the memory of the king had they flowed spontaneously from the royal bounty, instead of having been dictated by an imperious necessity over which he had no control.

The Forest-Laws are of great antiquity in this country; they are of Saxon origin; and, like the laws of Draco, they are written in blood.

A charter of forests was granted by Canute, in the year 1016, called " The Charter and Constitution of Forests," introduced by this royal declaration : "These are the Constitutions of the Forest, which I, Canute, king, with the advice of my nobles, do make and stablish, that both peace and justice may be done to all the churches of our kingdom of England, and that every offender may suffer according to his quality, and the manner of his offence." By this charter, four of the best freemen (*Pagened*, Verderors) were appointed in every province of the kingdom, to distribute justice, called "The Chief Men of the Forest." There were placed under each of these four men of middle sort (*Lespegend*, Regardors), to take upon themselves the care and charge by day " as well of the vert as of the venison."[1] Under each of these, two of the meaner sort of men (*Tinemen*, Foresters) were appointed to take care of the vert and the venison by night. These officers were supported at the cost of the state, the first class receiving a stipend of two hundred shillings a-year, the second of sixty, and the third of fifteen each, with certain equipments and immunities. "The Chief Men of the Forest" were clothed with royal powers in the administration of the laws of the forest. If any man offered violence to one of these chief men, if a freeman, he was to lose his freedom and all that he had; and if a villein, his right hand was to be cut off, for the first offence; for the second he suffered death, whether a freeman or a slave. Offences in the forest were punished according to the manner and quality of the offender : any freeman, either casually or wilfully chasing or hunting a beast of the forest, so that by swiftness of the course the beast pant for breath, was to forfeit ten shillings to the king; if not a freeman, twenty; if a bondman, to lose his skin! If the beast chased be a royal beast (a staggon), and he shall pant and be out of breath, the freeman to lose his liberty for a year, the bondman for two years, and the villein to be outlawed. A freeman or a bondman killing any beast of the forest, to pay double its value for the first offence, the same for the second, and for the third to forfeit all that he possesses. Bishops, abbots, and barons, not to be challenged for hunting in the forests, except they kill royal beasts, and then to make restitution to the king. Every freeman to be allowed to take his own vert, or venison, in the purlieus of the forest, or when hunting in his own ground, but he must refrain from the king's venery. Freemen only to keep the dogs called greyhounds, and the knees of those dogs to be cut before the chief men, unless they be removed, and kept ten miles from the bounds of the royal forest. Velterans,[2] or Langerans, small dogs, as well as Ramhundt, might be kept without cutting their knees. If a dog became mad, and bit a beast of the forest, the owner was required to make a recompense according to the price of a freeman—that is, twelve times two hundred shillings; but if a royal beast was bitten by a mad dog, then the owner was to answer as for the greatest offence in the forest— namely, with his own life! Such substantially were the forest laws of Canute the Dane.

William the Norman, another royal Nimrod, did not relax the severity of these laws; but, by afforesting large tracts of land, very much extended the field of their operation. Though the Conqueror displayed a large share of his sanguinary and rapacious character in the north, there is no reason to suppose that he deprived any man of his possessions to enlarge the forests of Lancashire. It is said of him, however, by Mapes, perhaps with some monkish exaggeration, that in afforesting the New Forest, in Hampshire, for the free enjoyment of the chase, "he took away much land from God and man, and converted it to the use of wild beasts and the sport of his dogs, for which he demolished thirty-six churches, and exterminated the inhabitants."[3] The retribution which followed was speedy and signal; three of the immediate descendants of the great spoliator lost their lives while engaged in the chase in this forest, amongst whom was William Rufus, who fell by the arrow of his bow-bearer, Sir Walter Tyrrell.

Richard I. was much addicted to the pleasures of the chase, and, as one of the highest favours he could bestow upon his brother John, Earl of Morton, he gave him, as we here learn, the honor of Lancaster, and the royal prerogatives of forest in this county. John, having received so much from his sovereign, felt disposed to allow the knights, thanes, and freeholders of the county of Lancaster to share in the royal bounty; and for this purpose he granted them a charter, whereby

[1] The rert is covert, the trees, and the herbage of the forest; and, according to Sir Edward Coke, whatever beast of the forest is for the food of man is venison.

[2] A kind of terrier. Langeran is a corruption of a Danish word, and should more likely be Langrun or Longsnout.—C.

[3] Lib. de Script. Brit. 187. c. 159.

they and their heirs, without challenge of him and his heirs, were allowed to fell, sell, and give, at their will, their forest woods, without being subject to the forest regulations, and to hunt and take hares, foxes, rabbits, and all kinds of wild beasts, except stag, hind, and roebuck, and wild hogs, in all parts within his forests beyond the demesne hays of the county.[1] This charter he confirmed to them in the first year of his reign (1199), before the celebrated "Carta de Foresta" (1224) for ameliorating the rigours of the forest laws was sketched; and his successor, Henry III., confirmed these franchises to the lieges of Lancashire four years after he had signed that charter. These grants, so ratified and confirmed, were not sufficient to protect "the lieges" against the annoyance of the royal foresters, and on the 18th of Edward II. (1324-25) we find them presenting a petition to the king, praying that they may enjoy their chartered privileges without molestation.[2] The answer to this petition was—"Let them come into the Chancery, and show their charters and confirmations;" and then—"Le Roi se avisera;" which was a form of refusal.

The parks, forests, and chases[3] of Lancashire, in the time of the Edwards, according to the records in the duchy office, were: Wyresdale, Lonsdale, Quernmore, Amounderness, Bleasdale, Derbyshire (West Derby), Fullwood, Symoneswood, Lancaster, Croxteth, Toxteth; and included in the general term of the Forest of Lancaster were the forests of Bowland, Blackburnshire, Pendle, Trawden, Accrington, and Rossendale; in a word, the high region on the eastern side of the county, the successive possessions of the houses of Lacy and of Lancaster.

Though the "Carta de Foresta,"[4] and the "Assisa et Consuetudines Forestæ," of the 6th Edward I. (1278) had so far relaxed the rigour of the forest-laws as no longer to allow the life of a man to be put on a level with the life of a stag, yet assizes of forests were stately held in this county, at which the Justices in Eyre north of the Trent presided, and where offences committed against "the vert and the venison" were visited with heavy penalties.

A record of the Forest Assize held at Lancaster, 15 Edward I. (1286),[5] discloses pretty fully the system of forest jurisprudence. We have therein the Justices in Eyre, "Justiciarii Itinerantes," north of the Trent, assisted by the Foresters of the Fee, in their ministerial capacity, for they had no judicial office. To these were added the Viridors, who presided in the forest courts of attachment and swainemote as a kind of initiative tribunal, leaving it to the judges to ratify or to annul their decisions. To complete the judicial array, there were added twenty-four Regardors, or jurors, knights of the forest, chosen by virtue of the king's writ, and elected, like the Viridors, by the freeholders in full county. The presentments for killing and taking deer are in the usual style, and amounted at this assize to forty-eight in number. The most remarkable is the plea set up by Nich. de Lee, who, in justification of his conduct in hunting in the king's forest, urges the chartered privileges (those granted by King John especially) of the knights and freeholders of Lancashire,[6] of whom he was doubtless one. These proceedings show that the sanguinary character of the forest-laws had been gradually ameliorated ever since the time of Canute, by the charters of King John, Henry III., and Edward I.; and, instead of expatriation and death, we find the heaviest punishments inflicted at this memorable assize to consist of fines and imprisonment, and those of a very moderate nature. In a word, the forest-laws, so severely condemned, were less rigorous under the Plantagenets than were the game-laws of more modern times.

The Lancaster forests, in days of yore, answer with great accuracy to the description given by Manwood, the elaborate writer on the Forest-Laws, when he says—"A forest is a certaine territory of woody grounds and pastures, privileged for wild beasts and fowls of forest, chase, and warren, to rest and abide in under the protection of the king, for his princely delight and pleasure." The forest-laws, as administered at the assize of the forests of Lancaster and of Pickering, are quoted by this authority as the most perfect model of forest jurisprudence. "The Earl of Lancaster," says he, "in the time of Edward II. and Edward III. had a forest in the counties of Lancaster and York, in the which he did execute the forest-laws as largely as any king in this realm did. And even at this day (A.D. 1580) there are no records so much followed as those which were executed by the said earl in his forests."[7]

[1] Duchy Rolls, Rot. f. 12.
[2] Ex Pet. in Parl., 18 Edward II., No. 17.
[3] The legal distinction between a *forest* and a *chase* is this—the latter is under the common law, the former under the forest-laws. Blackstone says, "A forest in the hands of a subject is properly the same thing with a chase, being subject to the common law, and not to the forest-laws. But a *chase* differs from a *park*, in that it is not enclosed, and also in that a man may have a chase in another man's ground as well as in his own, being indeed the liberty of keeping beasts of chase or royal game therein, prohibited even from the owner of the land, with a power of hunting them therein."—*Com.* ii. 38.
[4] "The cruel and insupportable hardships which the forest-laws created to the subject occasioned our ancestors to be as jealous for their reformation as for the relaxation of the feudal rigours and the other exactions introduced by the Norman family, and accordingly we find the immunities of *Carta de Foresta* as warmly contended for, and extorted

from the king with as much difficulty, as those of *Magna Charta* itself. By this charter, confirmed in Parliament (9 Henry III.), many forests were disafforested or stripped of their oppressive privileges, and regulations were made in the regimen of such as remained; particularly, (cap. 10) killing the king's deer was made no longer a capital offence, but only punishment by a fine, imprisonment, or abjuration of the realm. And by a variety of subsequent statutes, together with the long acquiescence of the Crown without exerting the forest-laws, this prerogative is now become no longer a grievance to the subject."—*Blackstone Com.* ii. p. 416.
[5] Duc. Rot. 15 Edw. I. f. 12.
[6] See John's Charter, p. 99.
[7] See *Manwood on the Forest Laws*, p. 72, a work which may be consulted with advantage by those who wish to obtain more than a popular acquaintance with this subject.

In much later times we have had an English monarch displaying his solicitude for the preservation of the "vert and venison" in the forests of Lancashire. The following royal warrant, addressed to the Master Foresters, Bow-bearers, and Keepers of the Forests, Parks, and Chases, in the county palatine of Lancaster, and in other parts of the duchy, bearing the signature of King William III., and countersigned by the chancellor and auditor of the duchy, will form a not inapt conclusion to this digression :—

WILLIAM R.

Whereas Complaint has been made to Us that great Destruction has been made of Our Deer in severall of Our Forrests, Chaces & Parks within Our Duchy & County Palatine of Lancaster, and that some of you have refused to give an Account thereof : Our Royall Will and Pleasure is, that you and every of you, do from time to time, as often as it shall be required of you, give a true and just Account To Our Right Trusty and Right Well-beloved Cozen & Counsellor, Thomas Earle of Stamford, Chancellor of Our Duchy & County Palatine of Lancaster, or Chancellor for the Time being, Of All Our Deer within the Forrests, Chases & Parks where you are respectfully concerned, and of what Destruction has been made thereof. And at the Close of every Season you also give a particular and true account what Number of Our Deer have been killed, by whom, for whom, and by whose Order or Authority, and of what Stock is or shall be remaining in Our Forrests, Chases, and Parks wherein you are concerned as aforesaid, that all abuses and ill practices may be remedied, and Our Deer better preserved for the future. And hereof you are not to faile, as you will answer the contrary at your Perill.—Given at Our Court at Kensington the 23d day of December 1697, and in the Ninth year of Our Reign,

By his Majesty's Command.

STAMFORD,
p Jo. Bennett, Aud.

Enrolled in the Office of the Auditor of the Lord the King that now is, of his Duchy of Lancaster, in the South Parts, 20 Dec. 9 Wm. III. 1697.

The act of Magna Charta, so recently granted by John, was confirmed and ratified by Henry III., to whom an aid of one-fifteenth of all the movables of his people was given by Parliament in return for this favour, with the reservation that those only who paid the fifteenth should be entitled to the liberties and privileges of the charter. To give increased stability to the obligations of this engagement between the king and his people, all the prelates and abbots were assembled, with burning tapers in their hands, and the great charter being raised in their presence, they denounced the sentence of excommunication against all who should henceforth violate this fundamental law. Then, throwing down their tapers on the ground, they exclaimed—"May the soul of every one who incurs this sentence so stink and corrupt in hell!" To which the king, who took part in the ceremony, added—"So help me God. I will keep these articles inviolate, as I am a man, as I am a Christian, as I am a knight, and as I am a king crowned and anointed."[1]

The trial by ordeal, introduced by the Saxons, and continued through so many successive ages, to the outrage of justice and the scandal of the nation, could now no longer be tolerated. The Church of Rome, never prone to innovation, was the first to protest against a standard so fallible. And accordingly we find royal letters of the reign of Henry III. (1219) addressed to the itinerant judges in the counties of Lancaster, Cumberland, and Westmorland, the north-western circuit of that day, announcing to the judges that because it was not determined previous to the opening of the circuit what form of trial they should undergo who were charged with robbery, murder, arson, and the like, "since the ordeal of fire and water had been prohibited by the Roman Church," it had been provided by the king in council that the judges should proceed in the following manner with persons accused of these crimes, viz., that those charged with the greater crime, and to whom violent suspicion attached, should be held and safely confined in prison, but not in such a manner as to incur peril of life or limb; that persons accused of other crimes, and to whom, had it not been prohibited, the ordeal of fire and water might have been sufficient, should be required to quit the realm; and that those charged with minor offences should be liberated on bail. These directions, it was felt, were very vague and general; but as they were all that the council could at the time provide, the judges were left at liberty to follow their own discretion, and to act according to the dictates of their consciences.

In this reign the undisputed possession of that great mass of Lancashire property, the lands between Ribble and Mersey, was conveyed by the family of Roger de Maresey to Randulf or Randle, Earl of Chester, in virtue of a compact of which the following is a translation :—

This agreement is made between the Lord Randle, Earl of Chester and Lincoln, and Roger de Maresey, viz., that the said Earl and Roger shall deliver to Sir Ralph de Bray, one forty marks [£26 : 13 : 4], and the other the charter which the said Roger makes to the lord the earl of the sale and demise of all his lands which he had or may have between the Ribble and Mersey; to wit, so that Roger shall go without delay between Ribble and Mersey, to the dispossessing himself of the said lands, and to the causing of all those (who held of him there) to do their homage to the said lord the earl, or their fealty to his bailiffs appointed in his place. Which done, the said Ralph de Bray shall render to the oft-named earl the charter already named, and to the same Roger the said forty marks. If the tenants refuse to do homage, etc., the earl or his bailiffs shall compel them to render it. And the said Roger, at the cost of the lord the earl, shall journey together with the earl's bailiffs, so far as this business requires, so that what is aforesaid may be consummated. And for the greater security, each of them to this writing in the form of a chirograph hath set his seal. Witnesses : the Lord Walter, Abbot of Chester, Sir William de Vernon, Justiciar of Chester, Ralph de Bray, Walter Dayvill, Richard de Biron, John de Lexington, Simon and John, clerks.

[From the Couchir Book of the Duchy Office, London, tome i. Comitatus Lancastriæ, fol. 77, num. 70.]

---

[1] Fœdera, vol. i. p. 146.

Notwithstanding the ratification of Magna Charta, the nation continued much agitated by the intrigues of the nobles within, and the hostility of the bordering countries from without, To meet this emergency a proclamation was issued to the sheriffs of the counties of Lancaster, Cumberland, and Westmorland, ordering them to assemble all those in their respective jurisdictions who held of the king in chief to the amount of a knight's fee, to be prepared with horses and arms, to march with the king from Chester on an expedition into Wales against Llewellyn, and other rebels. The barons, in the meantime, more anxious about the redress of their own grievances than the incursions of the Welsh, assembled in supreme council at Oxford under Simon de Montfort, Earl of Leicester, and, after insisting upon the strict fulfilment of the articles of Magna Charta, demanded that four knights should be chosen by the freeholders from each county in the kingdom, to make inquiries into the complaints of the inhabitants, and to present them at the next Parliament. They also resolved that three Parliaments should be held in every year, including burgesses, as well as barons and ecclesiastical dignitaries, the two latter of whom had alone been hitherto summoned ; that the sheriffs should be annually chosen in each county by the freeholders; that the sheriffs should have no power to fine the barons ; that no heirs should be committed to the wardship of foreigners ; that no new warrens or forests should be created; nor the revenues of any counties or hundreds let to farm. The king, feeling that the tendency of these extensive measures of reform was to abridge the royal power, strenuously opposed their introduction, and the matter was finally referred to the pope, by whose decision the great charter was ratified, but the ordinances of the supreme council of Oxford were annulled. The barons did not hesitate to resist the award of his holiness by force of arms, and Robert de Ferrars, earl of Derby, was amongst the most distinguished of the insurgents (A.D. 1263). An association was formed in the city of Worcester, consisting of the populace and the leaders of the insurgents, amongst whom were eighteen of the great barons, headed by the Earls of Leicester, Gloucester, and Derby, with Le Despenser the chief justiciary. By the terms of their compact they were never to make peace with the king, but by common consent, and with such securities for their liberties and privileges as those which were contained in the convention of Oxford. A long and sanguinary civil war ensued, and on the 14th May, 1264, Henry saw his army completely routed at Lewes by the valorous De Montfort, and himself, his son Prince Edward, and the king of the Romans made prisoners. On the following day a treaty, known as the *mise* of Lewes, was entered into, and the king was obliged to ratify the obnoxious convention of Oxford. Subsequently, Simon de Montfort, Earl of Leicester, fell in the contest at Evesham, August 4th, 1265, and at the same time the Earl of Derby was taken prisoner. This struggle was, however, essentially conducive to the establishment of the public liberties, and laid the foundation of our representative system of government, for after the battle at Lewes, De Montfort called a great council of the nation, to which were summoned not only the barons, prelates, and abbots, but also two knights from each county, two citizens from each city, and two burgesses from each borough. Thus was the democratic element—the foundation of the House of Commons—first introduced, the council being that in which we first distinctly recognise the Parliament of England. The defeat of the barons elevated the house of Lancaster. The forfeited title and possessions of Simon de Montfort devolved by royal favour upon Edmund Crouchback, the second son of Henry III., and the estates of Robert de Ferrars, Earl of Derby, were also conferred upon him by the king, with a grant of the possession of the county of Lancaster, but not to the prejudice of Roger de Lancastre.

Llewellyn, Prince of Wales, had been deeply implicated with the barons of England in their wars against their sovereign, Henry III., and when Edward I. ascended the throne, one of the first acts of his government was to summon the Wesh prince to do homage in person to the new king. With this mandate Llewellyn refused to comply, except upon the condition that the king's son, and other noblemen, should be delivered to the Welsh court as hostages for his safe custody. Edward was in no temper for parley, and accordingly we find a summons from the king calling upon Roger de Lancastre to attend upon his majesty, to proceed against the Welsh, who are represented as having risen in rebellion. This royal order was followed by a writ of military summons (dated Windsor, 12th Dec., 5 Edw. 1., 1276) from the king to Edmund, Earl of Lancaster, and the sheriff of the county, announcing that Llewellyn, son of Gryffydd, Prince of Wales, and his rebellious associates, had invaded the land of the lieges in the Marches, and committed homicides and other enormous damages, and commanding that the sheriff do forthwith assemble all that are capable of bearing arms in the hundreds, boroughs, and market towns of his shrievalty, to march to Worcester, in the octaves of St. John the Baptist, prepared with horses and arms.[1] The war was continued, with some intermissions through several successive years ; and in order to clear a passage into Wales, it appears that a mandate was issued by the king in the year 1282 to the

[1] Rot. Claus. 5 Ed. I. m. 12 d. in Turr. Lond.

sheriff of Lancashire, ordering him to provide two hundred woodcutters (*coupiatoribus*) to cut away the wood, and thereby to open passes into Wales. These men were to be powerful and active, and each of them was to come provided with a large hatchet to cut down the trees. They were to be chosen in the presence of William de Percy, who was sent specially into the county for that purpose, and were to muster at Chester, on Saturday, on the octaves of the Feast of St. Peter. For this service the sheriff was to pay, from the issues of his bailiwick, into the hands of each hewer, threepence per diem for his wages.[1] At the time when these Lancashire husbandmen, of extraordinary powers, were receiving threepence a day for their labour, the price of wheat was ninepence per bushel, and taking the average of wages in England for the six hundred years following, it will be found (unfavourable seasons apart) that the wages of labour have generally been in the proportion of a peck of wheat per day. In large towns the price of manufacturing labour has often been higher, and in some cases, especially amongst the weavers, much lower; but as a standard, none can approach nearer than the one which is here suggested. Much obscurity is thrown over historical and topographical works on the subject of money, for want of some standard of value to which the sums mentioned in different ages may be referred. No standard will be found so unerring as the prices of wheat and of labour, which, on being compared in times past with the price of those articles in our day, will always convey to the mind some definite notion, when sums of money are mentioned, of the value of those sums at the period under consideration. With this view the following table, extracted from the records in the exchequer, and collated with Paris, Walsingham, Stowe, Fleetwood, and others is constructed : —

CHRONOLOGICAL TABLE,

SHOWING THE PRICE AT WHICH THE ARTICLES THEREIN MENTIONED SOLD IN THE YEARS SPECIFIED.

A.D.			£	s.	d.
1202.	Wheat (rainy season)	per quarter	0	12	0
1248.	Thirty-seven Sheep for the King		0	18	4
1253.	Wheat fell to	per quarter	0	2	6
1256.	Brewers ordered to sell three gallons of Ale in the country for a penny.				
1272.	A Labourer's Wages	per day	0	0	1½
	A Harvest Man	do.	0	0	2
1274.	A Bible in nine vols., with a Comment		33	6	8
1275.	Rent of the Lord Mayor's House	a year	1	0	0
1280.	The Chancellor's Salary	do.	40	0	0
1283.	An English Slave and his Family sold for		0	13	4
1285.	Grinding Wheat	per quarter	0	0	0½
1286.	Wheat, after a great storm	do.	0	16	0
1288.	„ fell to	do.	0	1	8
1294.	Wheat (a grievous famine)	do.	1	0	0
	Wheat, average in the 13th century, about	do.	0	6	0
1300.	Wheat and Barley	do.	0	3	4
	Oats	do.	0	1	8
	A Primer for the Prince of Wales, now 15 years 11 months old		2	0	0
1302.	A Cow		0	6	0
	A fat Sheep		0	1	0
	A Cock or Hen	each	0	0	1½
1309.	A Pair of Shoes		0	0	4
1314.	Prices fixed by Parliament—A fat Ox		0	16	0

		£ s. d.			£	s.	d.
A Cow		£0 12 0	A Sheep		0	1	2
A fat Hog		0 3 4	A fat Goose		0	0	2½
Pair of Chickens		0 0 1	Eggs	per dozen	0	0	0½

This *maximum* increased the scarcity which it was intended to remove. The growers would not bring in provisions, and what was sold was dearer than before. The Act was therefore repealed in 1315.

A.D.			£	s.	d.
1315.	Salt (an unheard-of price)	a bushel	0	2	6
1326.	Yearly Rent of Arable Land in Kent	per acre ......3d. to	0	0	6
	Pasture Land	do.	0	0	1
	Meadow Land	do. ...... 4d. to	0	0	10
1338.	Allowance from Edward III. to 32 Students at Cambridge	per diem	0	0	2
	Wool taken by the King (a forced price)	per stone of 14 lb.	0	2	0
1342.	Wine	per gallon	0	0	4
1347.	King's Apothecary (a pension for life)	per day	0	0	6
1348.	A year of pestilence—a Horse		0	6	8
	a fat Ox		0	4	0
	a Cow		0	1	0
	a Heifer		0	0	6
1357.	Ransom of David King of Scotland		100,000	0	0
1360.	of John King of France		500,000	0	0
	A Horse for military service		1	0	0
	A Master Carpenter, 4d.—his Journeyman	per day	0	0	2
1379.	Wine, white, 6d.—red	per gallon	0	0	4

[1] Fœdera, vol. ii. p. 611.

A.D.				£	s.	d.
1385.	Assistant Clerk of Parliament	a year		5	0	0
1390.	Kendal Cloth	a piece ...3s. 4d. to		0	5	0
	Wheat, average in the 14th century, about	per quarter		0	6	0
1407.	Salt	per bushel		0	0	7½
	A Plough			0	0	10
	Wages of a Thresher	per day		0	0	2
1414.	A priest's stipend, with cure of souls	a year		5	6	8
	without	"		4	13	4
1482.	220 Draught Horses for			100	0	0
1495.	Allowance to Edward the Fourth's Daughter	a week		1	0	0
	for her eight servants	a year		51	11	8
	Oats	a quarter		0	2	0
	Wheat			0	6	0
	Wheat, average in 15th century, as estimated for rent, about			0	7	0
1547.	Income of the poor churches in York	a year		1	6	8
1562.	Wheat, conversion price	per quarter		0	8	0
	Ale, when malt was 8s. per quarter	per gallon		0	0	2
1576.	Beef and Mutton	a stone		0	0	6
	Veal	8d. to		0	1	0
	Wheat, average in the 16th century, about	per quarter		1	1	0
	Labour of a husbandman per week, in the 16th century			0	5	0

AVERAGE PRICE OF WHEAT AND MALT PER QUARTER, AT WINDSOR.

	£	s.	d.		£	s.	d.
From 1611 to 1620	£2	1	1½	From 1671 to 1680	£2	10	8½
1621 to 1630	2	5	2	1681 to 1690	1	19	1¼
1631 to 1640	2	6	10½	1691 to 1700	2	16	10½
1641 to 1650	3	12	8	1701 to 1710	2	3	2½
1651 to 1660	2	10	0	1711 to 1720	2	4	11
1661 to 1670	2	8	10½	1721 to 1731	2	1	1
Labour of a husbandmen per week, in the 17th century					0	9	0

These prices of wheat are from the Eton Books, and are for the best grain ; the measure also is above the legal standard, so that 7-9ths of the preceding quotations will form about the average price of all England.

AVERAGE LONDON PRICE IN JANUARY.

	Wheat.	Barley.	Oats.
From 1732 to 1740	£1 8 10	£0 15 1½	£0 12 5
1741 to 1750	1 5 8½	0 14 3	0 12 4
1751 to 1760	1 13 3	0 17 11	0 14 10½
1761 to 1770	1 13 11½	1 2 0	0 15 11½

AVERAGE PRICE IN ENGLAND AND WALES.

	Wheat.	Barley.	Oats.
From 1771 to 1775	£2 10 0	£1 6 9	£0 16 10½
1776 to 1780	1 19 0	1 0 0	0 16 6½
1781 to 1785	2 9 2	1 4 4½	0 16 10
1786 to 1790	2 5 10	1 3 5½	0 17 0½
1791 to 1795	2 11 11	1 10 11½	1 1 0
1796 to 1800	3 12 3½	1 17 8	1 5 2
Labour of a husbandman per week, in the 18th century			0 11 0

AVERAGE PRICE OF WHEAT IN ENGLAND AND WALES

In each period of five years from 1801 to 1885 inclusive, from the Official Returns.

	£	s.	d.		£	s.	d.
From 1801 to 1805	£4	0	0	From 1846 to 1850	£2	11	11
1806 to 1810	4	7	11	1851 to 1855	2	15	11
1811 to 1815	4	14	3	1856 to 1860	2	13	4
1816 to 1820	4	0	10	1861 to 1865	2	7	6
1821 to 1825	2	17	3	1866 to 1870	2	14	7
1826 to 1830	3	1	7	1871 to 1875	2	14	7
1831 to 1835	2	12	8	1876 to 1880	2	7	6
1836 to 1840	3	1	2	1881 to 1885	2	0	1
1841 to 1845	2	14	9				
Labour of a husbandman per week, in the 19th century					0	14	0

COINAGE.

For a further illustration of the Scale of Prices in successive ages, it is necessary to show how many pounds, shillings, and pennies have been coined out of a pound troy of silver at different times in England ; and also the degree of fineness of the standard, and the times at which the several alterations have taken place.

		Fine Silver.		Alloy.		Value of the lb. of Silver.		
		oz.	dwt.	oz.	dwt.	£	s.	d.
	Before A.D. 1300 a pound of standard silver contained.	11	2	0	18	1	0	0
1300.	28 Edward I.	11	2	0	18	1	0	3
1344.	18 Edward III.	11	2	0	18	1	2	2
1346.	20 Edward III.	11	2	0	18	1	2	6
1353.	27 Edward III.	11	2	0	18	1	5	0
1412.	13 Henry IV.	11	2	0	18	1	10	0

15

A.D.		Fine Silver.	Alloy.	Value of the lb. of Silver.
		oz. dwt.	oz. dwt.	£ s. d.
1464.	4 Edward IV	11 2	0 18	1 17 6
1527.	18 Henry VIII.	11 2	0 18	2 5 0
1543.	34 Henry VIII.	10 0	2 0	2 8 0
1545.	36 Henry VIII.	6 0	6 0	2 8 0
1546.	37 Henry VIII.	4 0	8 0	2 8 0
1549.	3 Edward VI.	6 0	6 0	3 12 0
1551.	5 Edward VI.	3 0	9 0	3 12 0
1551, end of 1552.	6 Edw. VI.	11 1	0 19	3 0 0
1553.	1 Mary	11 0	1 0	3 0 0
1560.	2 Elizabeth	11 2	0 18	3 0 0
1601.	43 Elizabeth	11 2	0 18	3 2 0
1816.	56 George III.	11 2	0 18	3 6 0 [1]

These rates of English money, except the last, are taken by Mr. Folkes from the indentures made with the masters of the Mint, and consequently may be depended upon as authentic; the last is from the Act 56 George III. cap. 68 (1816).

The mines of Lancashire were yet unexplored; and the most important of all its minerals, as constituting the principal source of its manufacturing greatness, had lain undisturbed in the bowels of the earth till the reign of Henry III., when coals, except as far as they might have been employed by the Romans, were, for the first time, used as fuel in England.[2] From that period to the present the great coalfields in the south and in the centre of the county of Lancaster have continued to be worked, but the full extent of their capacity and utility was not shown till the middle of the eighteenth century, when the agency of steam began to be brought into general operation under the powerful genius of Bolton and Watt, and the inventive faculties of Kay, Hargreaves, Arkwright, Crompton, and Cartwright, aided by the skill, enterprise, and capital of Peel, and a hundred other names that might be mentioned.

In the early ages of our history the honour of knighthood, with the military services to which it was incident under the feudal system, was often forced upon the subject, and hence we find that, in the year 1278,[3] a writ was addressed to the sheriff of Lancashire, commanding him to distrain upon all persons seised of land of the value of £20 per annum, whether held of the king *in capite*, or of any other lord, who ought to be knights, and were not, and all such were ordered forthwith to take out their patent of knighthood. Fourteen years after this a writ was issued, wherein the qualification was raised to double the amount, and a writ, dated the 6th of February, 1292, was issued to the sheriff of Lancashire, along with other sheriffs, proclaiming that all persons holding lands in fee, or of inheritance, of the value of £40 per annum, must take the order of knighthood before Christmas in that year. One of the prerogatives of the crown was to relax and to vary these services, and hence a writ, addressed to the sheriff of Lancashire, was issued, reciting "that the commonalty of England having performed good services against the Welsh, the king excuses persons, not holding lands of the value of £100 per annum, from taking the order of knighthood;" but in this writ it was directed that all holding above that amount, and not taking that order before the Nativity of the Virgin, are to be distrained upon. Subsequently, injunctions were addressed to the sheriff, commanding him to make extents on the lands of those who refused to take the order of knighthood, and to hold them for the king until further orders. It must not be supposed that this honour was always declined, or that no man's ambition led him to aspire to the distinction. Such a conclusion would be erroneous; for we find a writ to the sheriff of Lancashire, of the date of the 6th of April, 1305, directing him to proclaim that all who should become knights, and are not, must repair to London before Whit-Sunday next, to receive that distinction, if properly qualified.[4]

While the contest continued between England and Wales, a number of public officers were appointed, called commissioners of array (*arraiatores*), whose duty it was to array the troops engaged in the war, to preserve the peace in the midst of so much agitation, and to communicate the views and intentions of the government to the people. Roger de Mortimer, who enjoyed a large share of the royal favour, received the appointment of conservator of Lampaderoour (Lampeter), in West Wales, which appointment was announced by letter to the prelates and clergy, in Lancashire, through the medium of Reginald de Grey, the captain in Chester and Flintshire.

[1] In 1816 the pound of bullion was first coined into sixty-six shillings, of which, however, only sixty-two were issued; four shillings being kept at the mint as a seignorage.

[2] One of the earliest notices of coal in Lancashire is found in a deed among the muniments at Arley Hall—an assignment of dower made at Warrington, 3 Edward III. (1330), which, *inter alia*, mentions *minera carbonum* as then existing at Burnhill, in Ashton-in-Makerfield.-C.

[3] Rot. Claus. 6 Edward I. m. 8, d. Turr. Lond.

[4] Knights were called *milites*, because they formed a part of the royal army in virtue of their feudal tenures, one condition of which was, as Blackstone states (*Com.* B. 1. p. 404), "that every one who held a knight's fee immediately under the Crown, which, in Edward II.'s time (Stat. *de milit.* 1 Edward II.) amounted to £20 per annum, was obliged to be knighted, and attend the king in his wars, or fine for his non-compliance." Considerable fees accrued to the sovereign upon the performance of this ceremony, and hence the desire on the one hand to exert the prerogative, and the reluctance manifested in many instances on the other to accept the honour. Edward VI. and Queen Elizabeth appointed commissioners to compound with all persons who had lands to the extent of £40 a year, and who declined the honour and expense of knighthood. The exercise of the prerogative by Charles I., as an expedient to raise money, gave great offence, though warranted by positive statute and the recent example of Queen Elizabeth. The prerogative was abolished by 16 Charles I. c. 16.—C.

The necessities of the public treasury, in 1282, obliged the king to demand an aid by way of loan from the religious houses, and from all the merchants in the kingdom, and John de Kirkeby was enpowered to declare certain difficult and important matters with which he was entrusted, explanatory, no doubt, of the king's necessities, to the people of Lancashire. Speedily afterwards, letters patent were addressed to Robert de Harington, John Byron, and Robert de Holland, appointing them conservators of the peace, pursuant to the statute of Winton, and writs of Venire were issued for that purpose.[1]

In the spring of 1282 the fancied security of the English Government was disturbed by a general outbreak of the Welsh people. On the night of Palm Sunday, David, the brother of Llewellyn-ap-Gryffydd, Prince of Wales, surprised the castle of Hawarden, in Flintshire, captured the justiciary, Roger de Clifford, who is described in the Welsh annals as a cruel tyrant, and carried him off prisoner to the mountain fastnesses of Snowdon, his whole retinue of knights and attendants being at the same time put to the sword. The old national feeling of the people prevented them willingly adopting the English usages, or of tamely submitting to the imperious decrees of the proud justiciaries and bailiffs who claimed dominion over them. During the contest, several summonses for military service were issued in Lancashire, the number of which was probably increased by its vicinity to the seat of war. On the 6th April, 10 Edward I. (1282), as appears by the Parliamentary writs,[2] William le Boteler, described as "de Werington," was summoned to meet the king at Worcester, prepared with horse and arms, to march against the Welsh rebels; and on the 26th of May following a writ was sent to the sheriff, reciting an ordinance in council, whereby every person holding land or rents of the value of £30 a year was required to provide himself with a horse and suitable armour, and to join the king's forces against the Welsh, and even persons unfit for military service were required to find and equip substitutes. On the 30th of July, in the same year, a docket of commission issued from Rhuddlan, commanding all bailiffs and others in the county of Lancaster to aid and assist William le Boteler, de Werenton, in raising or pressing a thousand strong and able men (*ad eligendos mille homines fortes et potentes*)[3] to serve in the Welsh wars, from which it would appear that the obnoxious practice of impressing men into the navy in latter times extended then to the army. The contest with Wales was now at its crisis. On the 24th of November, a writ was addressed to the sheriff of Lancashire, requiring him to send all men capable of bearing arms to march against the Welsh; and Edmund, Earl of Lancaster, was required to furnish from his lands in Lancashire 200 soldiers. Early in the following year another levy was called for; and the earl, on the summons of the king, was required to repair with horse and arms to Montgomery. A similar summons to arms was also addressed to Roger de Lancastre; and to supply the necessary ways and means for this vast expenditure of the government, a commission was issued, constituting Henry de Newark and others collectors of the previous levy. The skill and perseverance of Edward, seconded by the zeal and constancy of his subjects, at length reduced the Welsh nation to the greatest extremities. Llewellyn, finding all his resources exhausted, his country almost depopulated by the length and severity of the contest, and famine rapidly completing the destruction which the sword had commenced, was obliged to submit to the conqueror; and the ancient Cambrians, after having for 800 years maintained their national independence, passed under the English yoke. The title of "Prince of Wales" was shortly afterwards conferred, for the first time, on a "foreign prince," and the eldest son of the sovereign of England has ever since that period borne this designation.

The wars of the Crusades, in which England took so large a share, had served to drain the treasury, and the cost of these holy contests seemed especially to belong to the Church. Pope Nicholas IV. to whom, as claiming to be the feudal lord of the church, and to whose predecessors the firstfruits and tenths of English benefices, though not generally acquiesced in, had in several dioceses for a long time been paid, granted to King Edward I. the tenth of these benefices for six years towards defraying the expenses of the Crusades. In order to ascertain the full value of the livings, a taxation by the king's precept, usually called "Pope Nicholas's Valor,"[4] was begun in 1288 and completed in the province of Canterbury in 1291, and in the province of York in the following year, under the direction of the Bishops of Winchester and Lincoln. This valuable and curious document is still preserved; and its contents, so far as regards the county of Lancaster, will be introduced in that department of our work which relates to the ecclesiastical history of the county. How far this exhibition of the wealth of the Church of England influenced the mind of the king it is impossible now to ascertain; but in this reign the celebrated Statute

---

[1] By the statute of Winton (Winchester), passed 13 Edward I. (1285) it is, amongst a number of other important enactments, provided, that every hundred shall be answerable for the robberies and other offences committed within its jurisdiction.

[2] Parliamentary writs, pp. 222, 223 L.—C.

[3] Idem, p. 228.—C.

[4] In 1253 Pope Innocent IV. gave the firstfruits and tenths, where payable, to King Henry III. for three years, which occasioned a taxation in the following year, sometimes called the "Norwich Taxation," that having been the diocese in which the claim was first submitted to, and sometimes "Pope Innocent's Valor."—C.

of Mortmain was passed, by which the clergy were prevented by law from making new acquisitions of land for the use of the church without inquiry before the Escheator and a licence in mortmain[1] being first obtained.

The conquest of Wales left the king with an impoverished exchequer, and to replenish it he had recourse to the practice of issuing *quo warrantos*, a kind of writ, so named from the first two words. These writs, which were issued in 1292, appear to have been sown broadcast, for no less than fifty-eight of them were despatched into Lancashire, and took more than a month at Lancaster to try, the object being to reap a harvest of fines from such as had usurped any franchise or had inadvertently exceeded powers of the charters they held. This county had scarcely recovered from the drain made upon its blood and treasure by the war with the neighbouring principality of Wales when it was called upon, in common with the other parts of England, to engage in another contest, still more formidable, against the combined power of Scotland and France. The causes of these long and sanguinary wars it is not the province of this history to investigate. On the breaking out of the war in 1293, writs of military service were issued to the sheriffs, announcing that the king was about to set out for Gascony, to protect his inheritance from the King of France; and all the knights, abbots, and priors, holding in chief by military tenure, or serjeanty, were required to meet the king at Portsmouth, to embark in this expedition. In the same year, letters-patent were sent to the knights and freeholders in Lancashire, announcing that collectors were appointed of the tenths in aid of the war; writs were issued in the early part of the following year, to sixty-eight persons about to embark with Edmund, Earl of Lancaster, to Gascony, exempting their goods from the payment of this impost; and, as a matter of precaution, orders from the king were issued to the sheriff of Lancashire, reciting that, through some religious foreigners, as well Normans as others, residing in this kingdom, and dwelling on the sea-coast, not a little danger had arisen to the safety of the state. He was therefore commanded to cause such persons to remove to the interior without delay, and to give up their places to religious English. The sheriffs were also commanded further to draw to land all their ships and boats, wherever they might find them, in the sea or any other water, and to cause all their furniture and cargoes to be wholly removed, so that the vessels might be of no use.

The commissioners for assessing and collecting the tenth and the seventh in 1296 were, " Magr Rich. de Hoghton, clerk," and " Rad. de Mansfield, clerk;" and that the returns might be duly made, Rich. de Hoghton and John Gentyl were earnestly required to appear in their proper persons before the treasurer and the barons of the exchequer, on the octave of the feast of St. Nicholas ensuing, to do and execute those matters which should be more fully explained to them; and this they were to do as they regarded the king's honour, and their own loss of all things, both lands and tenements, goods and chattels, and as they would avoid the king's perpetual wrath.[2] The exactions of the king to carry on the war became burdensome in the extreme; the first peers of the realm murmured against his demands upon their purse, and upon their personal services;[3] and to such an excess did their altercations arise, that the king, in requiring the reluctant services in Flanders of his constable Humphrey Bohun, Earl of Hereford, and one of the founders of the duchy possessions, and Roger Bigod, Earl of Norfolk, turned to the latter and exclaimed—" Sir earl, by God you shall either go, or hang!" and was answered by the earl with equal determination—" By God, sir king, I will neither go, nor hang!"[4] The clergy were not more disposed to acquiesce in the arbitrary exactions of the king and his ministers, than the laity; in consequence of which, numbers of them were put out of the protection of the law; but in order at once to stimulate their loyalty, and inflame their fears, writs were issued to John de Lancastre, and to the sheriffs, empowering them to appoint commissioners to reverse the recognisances of such of the clergy as wished to receive the king's protection, and to arrest and imprison all those who had promulgated excommunications and ecclesiastical censures against his ministers.

At this early period of our history newspapers were unknown, but in the 25 Edward I. (1297)

---

[1] The common law of England attached certain conditions as inseparable from the holding of land, such a thing as irresponsible being absolutely unknown, and, in fact, repugnant to the spirit of the English law, which, until comparatively recent times, never recognised a right without the accompanying responsibility and obligation. To the possession of all landed property was attached the triple condition—the *trinoda necessitas*, as it was called—viz., military service, works for the defence of the realm, and the maintenance of highways and bridges. It was held that these obligations could only be discharged by the *living hand* of a man, and hence land alienated to a corporate body, or to an ecclesiastic unable to discharge the obligations or services due, was said to be alienated to what was, in effect, a *dead hand (mort main)*. The law having been evaded and grants of land having frequently been secretly made to such " dead hands," it became necessary, in the interests of the State, to set forth in a declaratory enactment (1279) the conditions attaching to the holding of land, and the forfeitures that might follow on such alienation without licence in mortmain first obtained from the chief lord of the fee. To obtain this, it was necessary in the first instance for the intending grantor to cause a writ *ad quod damnum* to be issued to the Escheator of the county wherein the land lay, when a jury of twelve good and "law-worth" men was summoned to inquire if the proposed grant or alienation would be to anyone's injury, or impose any burden upon the country; and if they found that no harm would arise, and that sufficient land would still remain in the hands of the intending donor or grantor to insure the discharge of his obligations, the grant would not be against the law, and a licence for alienation would thereupon issue, and all licences in mortmain so obtained were recorded on the Patent Rolls, being matters that concerned the whole State.

[2] Rot. Claus. 24 Ed. I. m. 3. d. Dated Bury St. Edmunds, 15th November, 1296.

[3] Their feudal tenures did not bind them to foreign service, and their protest against the war and the financial measures by which it was carried on, took the practical form of a refusal to follow him in his expedition.—C.

[4] Rymer's Fœdera, vol. ii., p. 783.

the king addressed a mandate to John de Lancastre, sheriff of the county, announcing that his Majesty had learnt, that newsmongers ("*troveurs de novelles*," as they are called) were going about the country, sowing discord amongst the prelates, earls, and barons, as well as others of his subjects, endeavouring thereby to disturb the public peace, and to subvert the good order of the realm; which said offences the sheriffs were required to inquire into, and to take order for bringing the delinquents to justice. From enemies the Welsh had been converted into allies; and while the king was engaged in the French war an army from Wales was appointed to march against the Scots, to carry hostilities into their country. That no interruption might be given to that force, letters were addressed by the king to the sheriffs of Lancashire and Yorkshire, as well as to those of Nottinghamshire and Derbyshire, directing them, at their peril, to take care that all bakers and brewers should have a sufficient supply of bread and beer in the towns through which the Welsh army had to pass, on their march "against the Scottish rebels." In the course of this year, no fewer than three rates were imposed: the first, of an eighth; the second, of a fifth; and the third, of a ninth of the movables of the subject; and Robt. de Hoyland, Allan le Norreys, John Gentyl, and Hugh de Clyderhou, with the sheriff of the county, were appointed assessors and collectors for the county of Lancaster.[1] To reconcile the people to these accumulated impositions, and to assuage the popular discontent, letters were addressed to the sheriff of Lancashire, and the sheriffs of the other counties, directing them to take means for the redress of public grievances, the most intolerable of which probably was that of excessive taxation.

At this time the resources of the government were principally derived from the landed possessions of the people; but commerce and manufactures, to which in future ages the state was to stand so much indebted for its supplies, now began to dawn upon the country, and the establishment of the famous commercial society of "Merchant Adventurers" (in 1216), with the partial introduction of the staple manufacture of woollens, both in the west and in the north of England, laid the foundation of those mighty resources which in modern days distinguish the county of Lancaster from all other districts of the world.

In the time of the Edwards of the Plantagenet line the population of Lancashire must have been very considerable, for in this year the commissioners of array, in their precepts to Will. de Ormesby, the king's justiciary, directed that a levy of three thousand foot soldiers should be raised in Lancashire, and sent to Newcastle-upon-Tyne, by the feast of St. Nicholas, to be placed under the command of Robt. de Clifford, warder of the Scotch marches, adjoining to Cumberland. The following year a writ was directed to John de Warren, Earl of Surrey, directing him to march forthwith to Scotland, at the head of the troops raised in Lancashire and in the neighbouring counties.

The war with France having been brought to an end by the mediation of his Holiness the Pope, and the peace consummated by a double marriage, that of Edward himself with Margaret, the sister of Philip, King of France, and that of the Prince of Wales with Isabella, the daughter of the same monarch, the king was left at liberty to turn his undivided attention to the conquest of Scotland; and for the purpose of infusing fresh vigour into the operations against that country, Edward determined to place himself at the head of the English army. No fewer than three successive writs of military summons were issued during the year 1296 to the authorities of the county of Lancaster; the first to the sheriff, the second to Thomas, Earl of Lancastre, and the third to Henry, Baron de Lancastre, calling upon the levies to meet the king at Carlisle, and appointing Robt. de Clifford the king's commandant ("cheventain") of Lancashire, Cumberland, and Westmorland. The spirit of Scotland sank under the mighty array that was proceeding against that country, headed by a monarch accustomed to conquer. Robert Bruce, father and son, along with several other nobles, made their submission to Edward; but John Baliol, the king, assembled the flower of the Scotch nobility, together with a large portion of the military force of the kingdom, hoping by one mighty effort to expel the invaders and to liberate their country. For this purpose they made a general and simultaneous attack upon the English, under John Warrenne, Earl of Surrey, who were at that time besieging Dunbar with a force of twelve thousand men. Undismayed by superior numbers, the English general advanced to receive them, and a sanguinary battle ensued, which issued in the total defeat of the Scotch army with a loss of twenty thousand men. One of the first consequences of this victory was the surrender of Dunbar, April 29th, 1296, when Sir Patrick Graham and ten thousand men were slain; Roxburgh, Edinburgh, and Stirling opened their gates, and the other fortresses of Scotland soon followed the example. Baliol, the king, despairing of his country's cause, resigned his crown into the hands of the English monarch,[2]

---

[1] Rot. Parl. 25 Edward I. p. 2, m.
[2] Fordun, the Scottish historian, describes the ceremony as one in which the humiliated monarch, pulling off his royal ornaments, and holding a white rod in his hand, resigned, with his crown and sceptre, all the right he had, or might have, in the kingdom of Scotland, into the hands of the king of England.—C.

who, on his return from Scotland, conveyed with him the ancient stone of inauguration,[1] which had for so many ages been deposited at Scone, and to which tradition attached the belief, that wherever that stone was placed the monarch in possession of it would govern Scotland.

Though subdued, the spirit of the Scotch nation was not wholly broken. The severity of the English justiciary Ormesby, and the exactions of the treasurer Cressingham, rendered the yoke of the conqueror intolerable; and William Wallace, the descendant of an ancient family, whose valour and skill will be remembered through all time in Scotch history, reanimated the spirits and rallied the forces of his country. The English army under Warrenne, who had been made regent of the subjected kingdom, consisting of forty thousand men, having obtained a victory at Annandale, pushed forward to Stirling, where they were encountered by Wallace on the banks of the Forth, September 10th, 1297, and the greatest part of their number was pushed into the river at the edge of the sword. After this signal victory, Wallace, in his turn, became the invader, and the north of England, as far as the borders of the county of Lancaster, was laid waste with fire and sword. In December, writs of military summons were issued, requiring the tenants of the crown to attend the muster at Newcastle-upon-Tyne, to perform military service against the Scots. The king, on receiving the disastrous news in Flanders, hastened back to England, and having placed himself at the head of one hundred thousand men, of which Lancashire furnished its full complement, he chased the invaders into Scotland, and inflicted upon them a signal overthrow at Falkirk, July, 1298. Wallace, aided by the son of Robert Bruce, still kept the field, and, by a kind of predatory warfare, rendered the conquest of Scotland anything but secure.

No cessation was allowed to the efforts, military and pecuniary, of the inhabitants of the north of England; for, in the two following years, 1298-9, eight writs of military service were issued, appertaining to the county of Lancaster. The first directed the sheriff to proclaim the prorogation of the general military summons of the 26th September preceding; the second was a writ of military summons to Thomas, Earl of Lancaster, requiring him to appear at York on the morrow of St. Martin (Nov. 12); the third, addressed to the commissioners of array, ordering them to raise two thousand foot soldiers in Lancashire, to meet at Newcastle-upon-Tyne on the eve of St. Katharine (Nov. 24), to march against the Scots; the fourth was a writ to the commissioners of array, indicating the deteriorated state of the coinage, in which it was announced that if the soldiers levied by the preceding commissions should be unwilling to march on account of the bad money then current, or from the severity of the weather, the commissioners were to provide them a premium in addition to their pay; the fifth was a summons to Henry, Earl of Lancaster, to repair to the army; the sixth, a writ to Thomas de Banastre to raise two thousand infantry in Lancashire, to meet the king at Berwick-upon-Tweed; the seventh, a writ to the sheriff of Lancashire, directing that all prelates and other priests, and all widows and other women holding of the king, should send substitutes to Carlisle; and the eighth, a summons to Thomas, John, and Henry de Lancaster, to meet the king, to proceed against the Scots.

In the following year (1300) commissions were addressed to the sheriff of Lancashire, empowering him to summon all persons holding lands or rents of the value of forty pounds per annum and upwards, to meet the king at Carlisle; and in the same year the commissioners of array called by various writs upon Robert de Holand, Mathew de Redman, Allan Norreys, John Gentyl, and Robert de Norreys, to raise in Lancashire, by separate levies, three thousand men, to meet the king at Carlisle on the Nativity of St. John Baptist, and on the day after the Assumption. The oppressive nature of these ancient conscriptions may be collected from the royal proclamations of the same period by which Jehan de Seint Jehan (the king's commandant "cheventayne"), in all matters relating to deeds of arms in Lancashire, etc., was empowered, along with the Earl de Abingdon, to amerce those refractory persons who refused to perform services, either in defence of the marches or to act against the Scots. These frequent summonses to attend the king at places distant and oftentimes far apart from each other must have been very harassing, at a time when, in Lancashire especially, the roads were bad, the rivers often without bridges, and the country in many places almost inaccessible; and it is probable the vassals to whom they were addressed not unfrequently echoed Falstaff's querulous complaint—"It were better to be eaten to death with rust than scoured to death with perpetual motion."

The writs to the sheriff of Lancashire, in the two following years (1301 and 1302), relate principally to the assessment and collection of the fifteenths, which both the clergy and the laity were called upon to pay to the knights appointed to make the collections.

Jehan de Seint Jehan having been superseded in his command in Lancashire by John Butterte, letters of credence were addressed to the inhabitants, clerical and laical, requiring them

---

[1] The sacred stone, or "stone of destiny," an oblong block of limestone, which legend affirmed to have been the pillar of Jacob, as angels ascended and descended upon him, and on which the older sovereigns of Scotland had been installed, was enclosed by Edward's order in a stately seat in the Abbey at Westminster, which became from that time the coronation chair of the English monarchs.—C.

to give full faith to the king's clerk, Ralph de Mounton, and to Richard le Brun, who were commissioned to declare to them certain weighty matters touching the safety of the country, not
explained in the letters of credence, but which, it appears, related to the king's determination to
undertake a fresh expedition against Scotland. One of the first consequences of this confidential
communication was a call upon the commissioners of array, William de Dacre, Henry de Kygheley,
and Robert de Hephale, requiring them to raise seven hundred men in Lancashire, and to send
them to Lancaster after the feast of the Invention of the Cross (May 3, 1303); and all prelates,
women, and others unfit to bear arms, but who were willing to pay the fine (twenty pounds for a
knight's fee, and so on in proportion to their possessions), for the services done to the king in Scotland, were to appear before the treasurer at York on the morrow of the Ascension (May 17), or
otherwise by substitute, with horse and arms at Berwick. Aided by a large army, and a no less
powerful fleet, Edward marched victoriously through Scotland, and laid the country at his feet.
Amongst his trophies, the gallant William Wallace became his prisoner, and instead of obtaining
that respect to which he was entitled by his courage and patriotism, he was conveyed in chains to
London, where he was tried and executed as a traitor, August, 1305. The head of the great
patriot, crowned in mockery, with a circlet of oak leaves, as a king of outlaws, was placed upon
London Bridge. The execution had been determined on before the mock trial, and it was the
one blot on Edward's clemency.

The disorganisation of society produced by so much intestine war exhibited itself on every
hand. Crimes were greatly multiplied, and Peter de Badbate, Edmund Deyncourt, William de
Vavasour, John de Island, and Adam de Middleton were judges under a commission of *Trailbaston*
appointed to hear and determine all offences against the peace in the counties of Lancaster and
Westmorland, as well as in eight other counties. The number of offenders rendered necessary the
utmost promptitude in the administration of justice; and the proceedings of the judges, under
these commissions, are said to have been so summary as not to exceed the time in which their staff
of justice, or baston, could be trailed round the room.[1]

One formidable enemy still remained in Scotland—viz., Robert Bruce,[2] the grandson of that
Robert who, in the time of Baliol, was a competitor for the crown. Animated by those principles
of resistance to foreign sway which had inspired the breasts of so many of his countrymen, this
ambitious young nobleman collected a strong army in Scotland, by means of which he was enabled
to expel a large portion of the English from that country, and to drive their principal army across
the borders. Edward, roused to desperation by this renewed revolt, when he considered his
conquest secure, determined to take signal vengeance upon the Scottish nation. On his march to
the north he took the route of Lancashire, and for some time fixed his head-quarters at Preston.
From this place the king addressed a letter to his Holiness the Pope, complaining of the wrongs he
had sustained from the Archbishop of Canterbury, and claiming redress. The tidings of a new war
were communicated to John de Lancastre, by a writ, dated the 5th of April, 1306, which recites
that "Robertus de Brus," late Earl of Carrick, and his accomplices, have raised war against the
king, with the intention of usurping the kingdom of Scotland. To resist this aggression, Henry
de Percy was appointed commander-in-chief under the king, and John de Lancastre was required
to assist him with all the horses and arms in his power. At the same time two writs were addressed
to the sheriff of Lancaster: the first requiring him to make purveyance of corn, &c., for the
king's army, at the public cost; and the second a letter to the sheriff, archbishops, and other
prelates, as well as to women who owed military service, ordering them to send their substitutes to
Carlisle, in fifteen days from the Nativity of St. John Baptist (*i.e.*, before 9th July), or to appear at
the exchequer and make fine for the same. In the midst of all this hostility the Scots and the
English were not indisposed to indulge in their ancient games of the jousts and the tournaments.
The indulgence in these pastimes was thought by the king to indicate a degree of levity and
familiarity inconsistent with the relative situation of the two countries; and hence two proclamations were addressed to the sheriff of Lancashire, requiring him to announce that any persons who
should engage in these sports until the Scottish war was terminated would be liable to arrest, and
that their lands and goods would be seized into the king's hands. From Preston the king marched
at the head of one of the most powerful armies ever seen in Lancashire, to Carlisle, and from thence
into Scotland. The final conflict now approached. Bruce met the English army at Methven, in

[1] According to Sir Edward Coke, the judges of trailbaston were a sort of Justices in Eyre; and it is said they had a baston or staff delivered to them as a badge of their office; so that whoever was brought before them was *trailé ad baston, traditus ad baculum*; whereupon they had the name of justices *de trail baston*, or *justiciarii ad tradendum offendentes ad baculum vel baston*. Their office was to make inquisition through the kingdom on all officers and others touching extortion, bribery, and such like grievances; of intruders into other men's lands, barreters, robbers, and breakers of the peace, and divers other offenders;

by means of which inquisitions some were punished with death, many by ransom, and the rest flying the realm, the land was quieted, and the king gained riches towards the support of his wars. (*Mat. Westm. anno* 1305.) A commission of *trailbaston* was granted to Roger de Gray and others his associates, in the reign of King Edward III.—*Spelm.*

[2] Robert Bruce, the idol of the Scottish people, was the grandson of Robert le Brus, lord of Annandale, by Isabella, younger sister and coheir of John Scott, last Norman Earl of Chester. John Baliol was grandson of Margaret, eldest sister of John Scott.—C.

Perthshire, where a general engagement took place, which ended in the entire overthrow and dispersion of the Scots. A number of the most distinguished men in the country were taken by the English, and executed by order of Edward as traitors; but Robert Bruce escaped with his life, and took shelter, along with a few of his followers, in the Western Isles. To complete the conquest of Scotland, Robert de Lathum, Nicholas de Leyburn, Will. Gentill, Alan le Norreys, and John de Kirkeby, clerk, commissioners of array for the county of Lancaster, were ordered to levy one thousand foot soldiers in this county, one hundred and fifty of them from the liberty of Blackburn- shire, and the remainder from the other parts of the county. This force, when collected, was ordered to advance in pursuit of Robert de Brus, into the marches of Scotland, where he was lurking. But in the meantime the king, in the midst of all his glory, was seized with a mortal sickness at Carlisle, and died at Burgh-on-the-Sands, July 7th, 1307.[1]

One of the legacies left by Edward I. to his successor was the recently-subdued kingdom of Scotland; and amongst the first acts of the new monarch we find writs of military service (1307-8) addressed to the sheriffs of the counties of Lancaster, Westmorland, Cumberland, and Northumber- land, as well within their franchise as without, commanding them to assist the custos, John of Brittany, Earl of Richmond, the king's lieutenant in Scotland, with horses and arms, for the purpose of resisting the malice and insolence of "Robertus de Brus," and his accomplices. Summonses of a still more urgent nature were addressed in the following year (1308-9) to "Willielmus de Acre," "Mattheus de Redeman," and the sheriff of the county of Lancaster, urging them to assemble together, with the men of the county, as well horse as foot, and to take order for the defence of the Scotch marches, under the command of "Gilbertus de Clare," Earl of Gloucester and Hereford.

The pay of the forces was made with so much irregularity as to disincline the conscripts to the service; but in 1310 a commission of array was addressed to "Robertus de Leyburne" and "Mattheus de Redman," along with the sheriff of the county, ordering that three hundred foot soldiers should be "elected," to muster on the feast of the Nativity of the Virgin at Berwick-upon- Tweed, and from thence to march against the Scots; their wages to be paid to them by the sheriff, from the day that they marched from the county of Lancaster until their arrival at the place of muster.

The war with the Scots, so long protracted, was now drawing to a crisis. Edward II. had placed himself at the head of the English army, and the commissioners of array called upon the inhabitants of Lancashire for a fresh levy of five hundred men, while Yorkshire was required to contribute four thousand, Derbyshire one thousand, Nottinghamshire one thousand, Northumber- land two thousand five hundred, and the other counties in a similar proportion, regulated, no doubt, in some degree, by their wealth and population. After due preparation, the two armies met at Bannockburn (June 25, 1314). At first the event of the conquest seemed dubious, but the English having got involved amongst a number of covered pits prepared by Bruce for their reception, their forces fell into disorder; and the disasters of years, suffered by the Scots during the reign of the first Edward, were retrieved in a single day. The throne of Scotland was re-established by this remarkable victory, Robert Bruce reaped the reward of his valour in the loyalty and affection of his people, and Edward returned to London to coerce his refractory barons, who appeared as little disposed to submit to his sway as were the people he had so lately left in the north.

The harvest of 1314 was deficient, and the price of corn, in consequence, becoming excessive, Parliament in ignorance of, or with a disregard of, ordinary economic laws, fixed a maximum rate at which provisions should be sold. The succeeding year was still more disastrous, for, in addition to the failure of crops, there was a murrain among cattle, and a general pestilence among the starving people. The nobles expelled from their castles the hungry retainers for whom they were unable to find food, and the country necessarily swarmed with vagrants and plunderers. While the country was in this horrible condition of pestilence and famine, the Scots crossed the border, harassed the northern towns, and plundered and destroyed wherever their power could reach, neither leaders nor people in their depressed condition showing much disposition to resist. At the same time a war was being carried on in Ireland between the English and the Scots. Edward, the brother of Robert Bruce, who had become King of Scotland, had landed at Carrickfergus in 1315 with the intention, in concert with the native chiefs, of driving the English settlers out of the island, and after several conflicts caused himself to be crowned King of Ireland, and reigned for a time in Ulster. And, to add to the general state of anarchy and demoralisation, the Welsh formed an alliance with the Irish, and rose in revolt in the Principality. The description given of the state of the county of Lancaster, as well as of other parts of the country, at this period, in the

<hr/>

[1] As an evidence of the slowness with which the news of events travelled in England at that time, it may be mentioned that a period of eighteen days elapsed before the intelligence of the king's death reached the chancellor in London, and up to the 25th July he continued to affix the great seal as usual to writs in the name of the monarch who was then no more. (*See Campbell's Lives of the Lord Chancellors, vi. p. 187*).—C.

royal proclamations, serves to show to what an extent insubordination and lawless outrage were carried. According to these documents, malefactors of all classes, as well knights as others, were accustomed to assemble unlawfully by day and by night, in large bodies, and to commit assaults, and even murders, with impunity. To put an end to these excesses, commissioners were appointed in Lancashire, under the designation of conservators of the peace; and as a healing measure, a letter of credence was issued by the government to " Nigellus Owhanlam," chief of escheats, requiring him to obtain full faith for "Edmundus le Botiller," justiciar; "Ricardus de Beresford," chancellor; and "Magister Walterus de Jeslep," treasurer of Ireland, who were empowered to explain to the principal inhabitants certain matters relating to the king and the kingdom. Similar letters were also addressed to " Walterus de Lacy," " Hugo de Lacy," "Thomas Botiller," and others, whose influence was necessary to maintain the public peace, under the combined pressure of war and of famine, with both of which the county was at that time afflicted. The tide of invasion seemed now about to pour from the north to the south, and, instead of the levies being raised to march into Scotland, a commission was appointed, whereby " Johannes de Maubray " was empowered to raise all the able-bodied men in Lancashire, between the ages of sixteen and sixty, for the purpose of resisting the Scots, in case they should invade this kingdom. Shortly after the institution of this commission, a command was issued to "Thomas," Earl of Lancastre, and to one hundred and twenty-eight other individuals, usually considered barons, or tenants *in capite*, ordering them to appear at Newcastle, prepared with horses and arms, to proceed against " Robertus de Brus." In the same year (1316-17), a writ of summons was addressed to Thomas, Earl of Lancastre, and twelve other barons, convening them to meet at Nottingham, to hold a colloquium, to deliberate upon matters of state with the pope's legate.

The state of society in Lancashire at this juncture called loudly for the appointment and intervention of conservators of the public peace. A species of civil war existed in the heart of the county. Adam Banastre, of the house and family of Thomas Earl of Lancaster, in order to ingratiate himself with the king, and to avert the consequences of his own crimes, invaded the lands of the earl. Having erected the royal standard between the Ribble and the Mersey, in opposition to his feudal lord, he declared that the earl wished to control the king in the choice of his ministers, which he disapproved; and numbers of others, friends to high prerogative, embarked in his cause. Having entered the earl's castles, they supplied themselves with money and arms, which had been deposited there for the use of the soldiers who were appointed to march against the Scots. In this way about eight hundred armed men were collected, when the earl, hearing of the hostile enterprise, immediately ordered his knights and vassals into the field. This force did not exceed six hundred men; but they marched without delay against the insurgents, and, having come up with them in the neighbourhood of Preston, they divided themselves into two bodies. The force under Banistre did not wait to be attacked, but fell furiously upon the first division of the earl's men, which began to give way, when, the second division coming up, the fortune of the day was changed, and Adam and his followers took to flight, many of them having been killed by wounds in their back, received in their precipitate retreat. For some time De Banistre, their leader, concealed himself in his barn; but being closely beset by his enemies, and abandoning all hope of escape, he took courage from despair, and boldly opposed himself to his foes, of whom he killed several, and desperately wounded many others; at length, finding it impossible to take him alive, his assailants slew him, and having cut off his head, presented it to the earl as a trophy.[1] According to an ancient indictment, the battle between Adam de Banistre and his adherents and the adherents of the Earl of Lancaster took place near Preston, in the valley of the Ribble; and the victors so far forgot their duty to their lord, and their allegiance to the king, that they entered the hundred of Leyland, and robbed and despoiled various of the inhabitants of property to the amount of five thousand pounds—an immense sum in the fourteenth century, when, as we have seen, a bushel of wheat sold for ninepence, and the yearly value of good arable land did not exceed sixpence per acre.

The necessities of the state still continued urgent, and a commission of array was issued, for levying the following bodies of foot soldiers in the north: In Lancashire, 1,000; Cumberland, 1,000; Northumberland, 2,000; Westmorland, 1,000; Yorkshire, 10,000—or for five counties, 15,000. To support these enormous levies it became necessary to resort to extraordinary means, and writs were addressed to the mayors of Lancaster, Preston, and Wigan, as well as to all the other principal towns in the kingdom, soliciting them to send the king as much money as they could possibly afford, to carry on the almost interminable war with Scotland. This corporate contribution was

---

[1] "Adam Banester, a Bachelar, of Lancastreshire (probably a cadet of the house of Bank), movid Ryot againe Thomas of Lancastre, by crafte of King Edwarde: but he was taken, and behedid by the commaundement of Thomas of Lancastre." (*Leland's Calledanea*, i., 546.) "Eodem anno (1316) miles quidam Adam Banastre de comitatu Lancastriæ movit guerram contra Dominum suum comitem Lancastriæ; sed circa S. Martini idem Adam captus est et decollatus." (*Calledanea*, i., 249.)—Q.

independent of the collection of the eighteenths, which was proceeding along with it contemporaneously; for we find in the records a writ, addressed to the collectors and assessors of the rates, directing them to stay the collection in Lancashire, as to those persons who had their property destroyed from the invasion of the Scots, but specifically providing that they alone should be exempted. The levy for the scutage, in respect of the general summons of the array against the Scots, was also continued, and fixed at the rate of two marks (£1 6s. 8d.) for each shield or knight's fee in Lancashire.

In the turbulent and disastrous reign of the second Edward, the invasion of the enemy from without was aggravated by the wars of the barons directed against the royal favourites within the kingdom. We have already seen, in that department of our history of Lancashire which relates to its ancient barons, that Thomas, Earl of Lancaster, after having headed the barons against Piers Gaveston, made a further attempt, by force of arms, to remove the De Spencers from the royal councils. The earl, who is described as "a man bustling without vigour, and intriguing without abilities," was of a turbulent disposition, and had taken upon him, without the king's consent, to summon a large body of the nobles and others his retainers to meet him in a kind of little parliament, to take counsel for the redress of grievances. The meeting was appointed to be held at Doncaster on the 29th November, 1321, but being in open defiance and usurpation of the king's authority, a monition was issued on the 12th November previous, to the nobles and others, expressly forbidding their attendance. In spite of the prohibition, the meeting was held, and the disaffected had recourse to arms, with the result that a commission was issued (1321) to arrest and take "Thomas," Earl of Lancaster, and ten others, his principal associates in rebellion; and a writ was at the same time adressed by the king to the sheriffs of Nottingham and Derby, commanding them to raise the "hue-and-cry" against the Earls of Lancaster and Hereford, and other rebels their adherents, and to bring them to condign punishment. The Earl of Lancaster had entered into an alliance with Robert Bruce by which the Scotch army was to enter England, but without laying any claim to conquest. Edward, after taking Leeds Castle, in Kent, led his forces northwards; Lancaster retired into Yorkshire, in the expectation of being joined by his allies from Scotland, but no army came. Here he was encountered by a strong force under the governors of York and Carlisle, and the fatal battle of Boroughbridge (1322) surrendered him and his followers into the king's possession. The earl was conducted a prisoner to his own castle at Pontefract, where but a short time before he had jeered at his king with bitter scorn as he passed on his return from the siege of Berwick. He was adjudged guilty by the king without trial of his peers, and on the 22nd March (1322) the hand of the executioner, with the delinquent's face turned to Scotland, to indicate that he was in league with the Scotch rebels, terminated his career, without allaying the general discontent.

Although it does not appear that the county of Lancaster was the actual scene of any of the conflicts between the barons and the king's forces, yet levies of troops were called for in the county to aid the earl's enterprise; and, in a memorandum of the delivery of the prisoners confined in the king's marshalsea, and in the castle of York, some of whom had been taken in arms against the king, and others had surrendered at discretion, in all about two hundred principal men, it is stated, that "Nicholas de Longford," of the county of Lancaster, was fined two hundred marks (£133 6s. 8d.), and that "Ricardus de Pontefracte," "Robertus de Holand," "Johannes de Holand," and "Ricardus de Holand," found security for their good behaviour. There is also preserved an ancient inquisition, taken at Wigan, of which the following is a copy, tending still further to show that neither the laity nor the clergy of the county of Lancaster were indifferent spectators of the contest by which the kingdom was at that time agitated :—

Rot. plac. coram ⎫
R. Mich.   ⎬   INQUISITION taken before the king at Wigan, in the county of Lancaster,
17 Edw. II. [1323]⎪   in his presence, and at his command.
p. 2. m. 19.   ⎭

WEST DERBY.—The jurors of the Wapentake present that "Gilbertus de Sutheworth," 15 Ed. II. [1321], sent two men-at-arms at his own expense, to help the Earl of Lancaster against the King—viz., "Johannes filius Roberti le Taillour de Wynequik," and "Ricardus de Plumpton," and that he also abetted many other persons in aiding the earl against the king. The said "Gilbertus," being in court, puts himself upon the country, and is acquitted by the jury.

The jurors present that "Robertus de Cliderhou," parson of the church of Wygan, who for thirty years was a clerk of the Chancery, and afterwards escheator "citra Trentam," has committed the following offences : That he sent two men-at-arms, well armed—viz., "Adam de Cliderhou," his son, and "Johannes fil. Johannis de Knolle," to assist the Earl of Lancaster against the king, and with them four able-bodied foot soldiers, armed with swords, daggers, bows, and arrows. That on a certain high festival he preached to his parishioners and others, in his church at Wygan, before all the people, telling them that they were the liege men of the earl, and bound to assist him against king, the cause of the earl being just, and that of the king unjust. By means of which harangues many persons were incited to turn against the king, who otherwise would not have done so. And the said "Robertus," being present in court, and arraigned, says, that on a certain feast-day, when preaching in his church, he exhorted his parishioners to pray for the king, and for the peace of the kingdom, and for the earls and barons of the land ; and he denies sending any men-at-arms or foot soldiers ; and he puts himself upon the country—he is found guilty by the jury of the offences charged in the indictment—and is committed to prison. Afterwards, thirteen manucaptors undertake to produce him on Monday after the Octaves of St. Martin, under the penalty of 1,000 marks, and they also undertake to answer for any fine, &c. On which day the said " Robertus" appears in court, and submits to a fine of £200.

Though a truce had been concluded between England and Scotland, the war was continued with little intermission; and in a commission for raising fresh levies in this and the other counties (1322), it is said, that, after the conclusion of the truce, the Scots had invaded the kingdom, and that Thomas, late Earl of Lancaster, and his adherents (" whose malice was now quelled"), had entered into treasonable conspiracy with them. The commissioners of array for the county of Lancaster, under the commission, were, "Richard de Hoghton," "Johan Travers," and "Thomas de Lathum," to whom the duty was confided of arming the forces of the county and marching them to their destination.

The disorders of the times had filled the prisons of Lancashire with inmates, and writs were addressed from Kirkham to the constables of the castles of Liverpool, Hornby, and Clitheroe (but not of Lancaster), directing them to keep the prisoners in their respective castles in safe custody. At the same time a commission was issued, under the royal seal, whereby Johannes de Weston, jun. marshal of the household, was empowered to pursue, arrest, and take "Willielmus de Bradshagh' and "Ricardus de Holland," the leaders of disorderly bodies of armed men, who committed great depredations in the county of Lancaster. This Willielmus de Bradshagh soon after appears to have been restored to the royal favour; for in the following year we find a writ addressed to him, stating that the king has ordained that "Johan," Earl of Warrenne, and others, shall proceed to Lancashire with an armed force, for its protection (against the Scotch invaders, no doubt), and that "Bradshagh" shall be one of the commissioners of public protection. The return of the sheriff to a writ issued for that purpose, serves to show that the great landed proprietors were, at the early part of the fourteenth century, very few in number. It is as follows: "In Lancashire 13 knights and 51 men-at-arms. All the above hold lands to the amount of £15 per annum." According to a presentment made in the hundred of West Derby, it would appear that the sheriffs, in those days, were often remiss in their duty, and that ",Willielmus de Gentil," and "Henricus de Malton," his predecessor in office, suffered certain notorious thieves to be set at liberty upon manucaption, though their crimes were not mainpernable according to law; and that, owing to the laxity of their administration of the law, several persons in the wapentake avoided making presentment of other notorious thieves, to the injury of the peace, and the danger of the property of their honest and well-disposed neighbours. Nor was this all: they returned certain persons as jurors, and on inquests, without giving them warning; and "Gentil" so far presumed upon his office as to arrogate to himself the election of knights of the shire; "whereas," as the instrument charging him with these manifold delinquencies very properly observes, "they ought to have been elected by the county."

The intrigues of the barons were still actively at work against the king and the royal favourites, the De Spencers; and Henry, Earl of Lancaster, the brother and heir of Earl Thomas, entered into that conspiracy by which Edward was dethroned. The ill fortune of this weak monarch having precipitated him from a throne to a prison, the Earl of Lancaster became his gaoler in the castle of Kenilworth. The mildness and humanity of the earl's character ill suited him for this office, which he was ordered by Mortimer, the gallant of the perfidious queen Isabella, the "she-wolf of France," as she has been styled, to surrender into the hands of Sir John Maltravers and Sir Thomas Gournay; under whose direction, if not actually by their hands, the wretched Edward, after having been exposed to every possible insult and privation, was thrown upon a bed, and a red-hot iron having been forced into his bowels in a way to avoid all external evidence of the cruel deed, he was consigned to death, under agonies so excruciating that his shrieks proclaimed the atrocious deed to all the guards of the castle (Sept. 21, 1327).

One of the first acts of Edward III. was to reverse the attainder of Thomas, Earl of Lancaster, and to place his brother Henry in possession of the princely inheritance of that illustrious house.

But here we must pause, to take a survey of the landed property of the county of Lancaster, and the tenures by which it was held in the early part of the fourteenth century, as deduced in the "TESTA DE NEVILL." Of this book it is said, in the records published by the Crown commissioners, that—

"In the king's remembrancer's office of the Court of Exchequer are preserved two ancient books, called the Testa de Nevill, or Liber Feodorum,[1] which contain principally an account—
"1st. Of fees holden either immediately of the king or of others who held of the king *in capite*.
"2nd. Of serjeanties holden of the king.
"3rd. Of widows and heiresses of tenants *in capite*, whose marriages were left in the gift of the king.

[1] This document, which is not strictly speaking a feodarum, but an inquisition, bears internal evidence of having been taken about the year 1322, and was probably the inquisition taken after the death of Thomas, Earl of Lancaster, who, as previously stated, was beheaded in that year. —C.

"4th.   Of churches in the gift of the king, and in whose hands they were.
"5th.   Of escheats, as well of the lands of Normans as others, in whose hands the same were.
"6th.   Of thanage, forestry, and other peculiar services and tenures.
"The entries specifically entitled *Testa de Nevill* are evidently quotations, and form comparatively a very small part of the whole. They have in all probability been copied from a roll bearing that name, a part of which is still extant in the chapter-house at Westminster, consisting of five small membranes, containing ten counties, of which Lancashire is one. The roll appears to be of the age of Edward I., and these books to have been compiled near the close of the reign of Edward II., or the commencement of that of Edward III., partly from inquests on presentments, and partly from inquisitions on writs to sheriffs."

The following is a tolerably copious extract and analysis of the contents of the Testa de Nevill, so far as relates to the county of Lancaster, which may answer any popular purpose. The full entries are cited in the various local histories.

1. FEES HELD IN CHIEF OF THE KING, ETC.

"Agnes de Clopwayt in Blothelay, Alex. de Kyrkeby, Orm de Kelet, Henr. de Waleton, in Waleton, Adam Girard, Luke P'oitus de Dereby, in Dereby, Adam de Helmelesdal in Crosseby, Quenilda de Kirkdale, in Forneby, Robert Banastr, Robert de Clyton, in Leyland Hundred, Alward de Aldholm in Vernet, Hug. le Norrays, in Blakerode, Edwin Carpentar in Kadewaldesir, Rich. de Hilton, in Salford Hundred, Alan de Singleton, in Blackburn Hundred, and Amoundernesse, Rich. Fitz Ralph in Singleton, John de Oxeclive in Oxcumbe, Roger Carpentar in Lancaster, Robert Scertune in Sutherton, Ra. Barun, John Oxeclive in Oxeclive, Robert, the constable of Hofferton, in Hofferton, Adam Fitz Gilemichel in Seline, Rog. Carpentar in Lancaster, Bob. son of Roger de Shertnay, in Skerton, Rad. Balrun in Balrun, W. Gardinar in Lancaster, Walter Smith in Hefeld, Rog. Gernet in Halton, Wiman Gernet in Heschin, Will. & Benedict, sons of Walter de Gersingham, in Gressingham, Margery, widow of Barnard Fitz Barnard, in Gressingham.

"The Earl of Ferrars, in the wapentake of Derby (and he has sub-tenants), Almaric Butler, who has the following sub-tenants —Henry de Tyldesley in Tyldesley, Gilb. de Kulchet in Culcheth, Alan de Rixton in Rixton and Astley, Will. de Aderton in Atherton, Robt. de Mamelisbury in Sonky, Roger de Sonky in Penketh, Earl de Ferrars in Hole Hulesale and Wyndul, Will. de Waleton & Will. de Lydyathe in Lydiate & Hekergart, Rich. Blundea in Hyms and Barton, Ad. de Molynous & Robt Fitz Robt. in Thorinton ; the heir of Robert Banaster in Makerfeld, Waleton, & Blakeburnshire, and has sub-tenants ; Will. de Lanton and Rich. de Golborn in Langton, Keman & Herbury ; the Earl of Lincoln (Randolph Earl of Chester) in Appleton and Crouton, of the Earl Ferrars' fee ; of the same fee are, Will. de Rerisbury in Sutton & Eccleston, Robt. de Lathum in Knowaley, Huyton, and Torbock, Ad. de Molyneus in Little Crossby, Robt. de Rokeport, Rog. Gernet and Thom de Bethum in Kyrkeby, Sim de Halsale in Maghul, Will. de Waleton in Kirkdale, Will. le Koudre and the heir of Rob. de Meols, in North Meols, Thom. de Bethum and Robt. de Stokeport in Raven Meols.

"Waren de Waleton in Waleton, Ric. Banastre, Walt. de Hole, Ric. de Thorp, Will. de Brexin, Thom de Gerstan, Sim. del Pul in Bretherton, Robt. de Cleyton in Clayton & Penwortham, the abbot of Cokersand in Hoton, Robt. Russel in Langton, Leyland, and Eccleston, Robt. Banastre's heir in Shevington, Charnock, and Welsh Milnefltte.

"John Punchardun in Little Mitton, Ad. de Blakeburn and Roger de Archis in Wisewall and Hapton, Henr. Gedleng in Tunley, Caldcoata, & 'Sn. Odiswrth,' [Snodiswrth], Ad. de Preston in Extwistle, Ra. de Mitton in Altham, Mearley, and Livesay, Robt. de Cestr' in Downham, John de Grigleston in Kokerig, Will. Marshall in Little Mearley, Gilb. Fitz Henry in Rushton, Hugo Fitun in Harewood, Thos. de Bethum in Warton, Will. Deps' in Prees & Newton ; Ric. de Frekelton in Frekelton, Quintinghay, Newton, & Eccleston, Gilb. de Moels, Rog. de Nettelag & Will. de Pul in Frekelton, Alan de Singilton and Iwan de Frekelton in Frekelton, Waren de Quitinghay & Robt. de Rutton in Quitinghay, Alan de Singilton in Quitinghay, Newton, & Elswick, Warin de Wytingham in Elswick—The heir of Theobald Walter in Wytheton & Trevele, John de Thornul, Will. de Prees, Rog. de Notesage, Ad. de Bretekirke, Will. de Kyrkeym, Robt. Fitz Thomas & Will. Fitz William in Thistledon, Prees, & Greenhalgh. Will. de Merton in Marton ; Rog. Gernet, Thos. de Bethum and Robt. Stokeport in Bustard Rising.

"Adam de Bury in Bury, Robt. de Midelton in Middleton, Gilb. de Warton in Atherton, the heir of Rich. Hilton in Pendleton ; Thomas de Gresley's tenants ; Gilbert Barton in Barton,

Matthew Haversage in Withington, Robt. de Lathum in Childwall, Parbold, and Wrightington, Rich. le Pierpoint in Rumworth, Will. de Worthinton in Worthington, Rog. de Pilkinton in Pilkington, Thos. le Grettley in Lindesbey, in the honor of Lancaster.

"Will. de Lancaster in Ulverston, Matthew de Redeman and Robt. de Kymers in Yeland, Lambert de Muleton in Routheclive, Rog. Gernet in Little Farleton, Robt. de Stokeport in Gt. Farlton, Ad. de Eccliston, Will. de Molineus, Hug. de Mitton, Ric. de Katherale, Hen. de Longeford in Eccleston, Leyrebreck, and Catterall, Ad. de Werninton in Wennington, Hug. de Morwyc in Farleton & Cansfield, Henr. de Melling in Melling, Rich. de Bikerstat in Helmes & Stotfaldechage ; Adam Fitz Richard in Bold & Lawerke, Rich. Fitz Martin in Ditton, Rich. Fitz Thurstan in Thingwall, Thos. de Bethum in Bootle, Rich. de Frequelton in Thorp. Rog. de Lacy, 5 knts. fees of the fee of Clithero, Walter Fitz Osbert, Will. de Wynewyck, Peter de Stalum, Elya de Hoton, the heir of Rog. de Hoton, Alan Fitz Richard & John de Billesburgh, tenants of the king, but no place mentioned ; Will. de Neville in Kaskenemor, Marferth de Hulton in Pendleton, Roger de Midleton in Chetham, Edwin Carpentar in Cadwalesate, Ada de Prestwych in Prestwych and Failesworth, Hugh de Blakerode, by charter in Blakerode, Elias de Penilbury in Pendlebury and Chadderton, Robt. de Clifton in Clifton, Gospatric de Cherleton in Chorleton, Henry de Chetham in Chetham, Will. de Bothelton, Gilbt. de Tonge in Tonge, Randle Fitz Roger, Rich. de Edburgham, the Abbot of Furness in Furness, Ad. Fitz Orm in Middleton, Walt. de Parles in Pulton, Will. de Hest in Middleton, the Prior of Lancaster in Newton .and Aldcliff, the Burgesses of Lanc. in Lancaster, and Nich. de Verdon in Kirkby.[1]

2. SERJEANTIES HOLDEN OF THE KING.

"Orm de Kellet in Kellet, Rich. de Hulton, Wapentake of Salford, Roger Carpentar in Lancaster, Roger Gernet in Fishwick, Lonesdale, & Wapent. of Derby, Alan de Singleton, Will. de Newton ; Ad. Fitz Orm in Kellet, Thos. Gernet in Hesham, John de Oxeclive in Oxcliffe, Robt. de Overtou in Overton, Rog. de Skerton, Rog. Blundus in Lancaster, le Gardiner in Lancaster, Rad. de Bollern in Bolrun, Thos. Fitz Ada in Gersingham, Will. & Benedict in Gersingham, Margery, widow of Bernard Fitz Bernard ; Walter Underwater holds Milneflet. Ad. Fitz Richard in Singleton, by serjeanty of Amounderness, 'Willoch' & 'Neuton' in Newton, Ad. de Kelleth, son of Orm, in Kellet, Henr. de Waleton in Walton, Wavertree and Newsham's, Edwin Carpentar in Cadwalslete, Hamo de Macy and Hugo de Stotford in Scotforth, Rog. White & Gilbert Fitz Matthew in Lancaster, Will. Fitz Dolphin & Will. Fitz Gilbert in Gersingham. The places are not mentioned after the following names : Henry Fitz Siward, Robt. de Middleton, Rich. Fitz Henry, Gilbt. de Croft, Hugo de Croft, Robt. the reeve, Adam de Relloc & Rog. Fitz John ; Roger Gernet in Halton, Rog. le Clerk in Fishwick, Baldewin de Preston in Fishwick, John Fitz John in Fishwick, Alan and Rich. de la More in Fishwick, Rog. Fitz Viman in Hesham, Thomas Gernet in Hesham, John de Toroldesholm in Torrisholme, Adam Gerold in Derby, Ad. de Moldhall in Crosby, Robert de Curton in Querton, Rog. de Assart in Fishwick, Will. Wachet in Fishwick, Will. & Agnes de Ferrars, Salford, Clayton, and Newshams, Gervas Fitz Simon in Oxcliffe, Abbot of Cockersand in Bolrun, Brothers of St. Leonard at York in Bolrun, the widow Christiana de Gersingham, Robt. & Will. de Bolrun, the Prior of Lancaster, Will. le Gardiner and Adam Gernet in Bolrun, Rog. Fitz William, Will. Fitz Thomas, Will. & Matilda de Parles in Torrisholme.

---

[1] The "Testa de Nevill" mentions several tenants-in-chief, whose lands, though held of the honor, are not in the county of Lancaster, and which are omitted here.

3. WIDOWS AND HEIRESSES OF TENANTS IN CAPITE, WHOSE MARRIAGES WERE IN THE GIFT OF THE KING.[1]

"Alicia dr. of Galfr. de Gersingham, Christiana dr. of same Alicia & Thomas de Gersingham, Lady Elewisa de Stutevill, Oliva wid. of Rog. de Montbegon, Quenilda wid. Rich. Walens. Margaret wid. Ad. de Gerstan, Waltania wid. Rich. Bold, Beatrix de Milton, Quenilda wid. Rog. Gernet, Matilda de Thorneton, Avicia wid. Henr. de Stotford, Avicia wid. Rog. de Midelton, Eugenia wid. Will. de Routhclive, Eva de Halt, Matilda dr. Nicholas de Thoroldeholm, Alicia the wid. of Nicholas, Emma the wid of Nicholas, Sarra de Bothelton, Alicia wid. Rich. Fitz Robert, Cecilia wid. Turstan Banastr, Quenilda dr. Richd. Fitz Roger, Matilda de Stokeport, Lady Ada de Furneys ; wid. of Gamell de Boelton, Matilda de Kellet, Agnes de Hesham, wid. of Hugo de Oxeclive, wid. Will. Gernet.

4. CHURCHES IN THE GIFT OF THE KING, ETC.

"Lancaster ; Earl Roger de Poictou gave it to the Abbot of Sees.

"Preston ; King John gave it to Peter Rossinol, who died, and the present King Henry gave it to Henry nephew of the Bishop of Winton. Worth 50 marks *per an.*

"St. Michael upon Wyre ; the son of Count de Salvata had it by gift of the present King, and he says, that he is elected into a bishoprick, and that the church is vacant, and worth 30 marks *per an.*

"Kyrkeham ; King John gave 2 parts of it to Simon Blundon, on account of his custody of the son and heir of Theobold Walter. Worth 80 marks.

5. ESCHEATS OF THE LANDS OF NORMANS AND OTHERS.

"Merton, Aston, 'Henry de Nesketon holds of the king's escheats in the counties of Warwick & Leicester, Nottingham and Derby, Lancashire, Cumberland, Westmorland, and Northumberland.' Fourteen bovates of land in Haskesmores, which Willm. de Nevill held as escheats of our lord the king.

"Hugo le Norreys holds a carucate of land in Blakerode, which is an escheat of the king, to whom he pays a yearly rent of 20s.

6. THANAGE,[2] FORESTRY, AND OTHER PECULIAR SERVICES AND TENURES.

"Thomas & Alicia de Gersingham, by keeping the king's hawks in Lonsdale ; Luke, the constable of Derby, by being constable and keeping the castle ; Adam de Hemelesdale, by constabulary at Crosby ; Quenilda de Kirkdale, by conducting royal treasure ; Richd. Fitz Ralph, by constabulary of Singleton ; John de Oxeclive, by being carpenter in Lancaster castle ; Adam Fitz Gilmighel, by being the king's carpenter ; Roger Carpentar, by being carpenter in Lancaster castle ; Rad. Barun, by being mason in Lancaster castle ; Rad. Balrun the same ; Wm. Gardener, by finding pot-herbs and leeks for the castle ; Walter, son of Walter Smith, by forging iron for carts ; Roger Gernet, by being chief forester ; Willm. Gernet, by the service of meeting the king on the borders of the country with his horn and white rod, and conducting him into and out of the county ; he holds 2 carucates of land in Heskin ; Willm. & Benedict de Gersingham, by forestry and by keeping an aery of hawks for the king ; Gilbert Fitz Orm, by paying annually 3d., or some spurs to Benedict Gernett, the heir of Roger de Heton, in thanage ; Heir of Robt. Fitz Barnard, in thanage ; Rog. de Leycester, by paying 8s. & 2 arrows yearly ; Adam Fitz Rice & Alan Fitz Hagemund, in drengage ; Richd. de Gerard, in drengage ; Gillemuth de Halitton, in drengage ; Adam de Glothie, Will. de Nevilla, Reyner de Wambwaile, Gilbert de Notton, Rog. de Midelton, Alex. D. Pikington, Will. de Radeclive, Adam de Prestwich, Elias de Penilbury, Will. and Rog. Fitz William, Henr. de Chetham, Alured de Ives, Thomas de Burnul, Adam de Pemberton, Adam de Rulling, Gilbert de Croft, Gilbert de Kelleth, Matilda de Kelleth, Thos. Gerneth, William de Hest, and William, son of Rich. de Tatham, all in thanage ; John de Thoroldesholm, by lardenery : Rog. de Skerton, by provostry ; Robt. de Overton, by provostry ; Rog. White and Edward Carpenter, by carpentry ; Gilbert Fitz Matthew, by gardenery ; Rad. de Bolran, by masonry ; the burgesses of Lancaster, in free-burgage and by royal charter ; the prior and monks of Seaton, by royal charter ; Thomas Fitz Adam, Will. Fitz Dolfin, & Willm. Fitz Gilbert, by forestry ; Henr. de Waleton, by being head serjeant or bailiff of the hundred of Derbyshire ; Galfr. Balistrar', by presenting two cross-bows to the king ; the serjeanty of Hetham, which Roger Fitz Vivian holds, by 'blowing the horn before the king at his entrance and exit from the county of Lancaster ; Thomas Gernet, in Hesham, by sounding the horn on meeting the king on his arrival in those parts."

In addition to these peculiar services and tenures of the feudal times, many of which sound strangely in modern ears, several religious houses are enumerated which held in pure frank alms; and a still larger number of persons who held by donation, in consideration of annual rents, as will be seen on reference to the "TESTA DE NEVILL."

[1] If the landholder left only daughters, the king had the profits of relief and wardship ; and had also, if they were under the age of fourteen, the right of disposing of them in marriage. This power was said to be vested in the king in order to prevent the heiresses that were his tenants from marrying persons that were of doubtful affection to him, or that were incapable and unfit to do the services belonging to the land. He had also a power of disposing of his male wards in marriage, whose parents had died when they were under twenty-one, though without such good resons for it. But this power of disposing of wards of either sex in marriage, as well as the right of wardships, was afterwards very much abused, and was therefore taken away by the statute of 12 Car. II. (1660), together with the tenure itself by military, or (as it was usually called) knight's service.

[2] THANAGE SERVICE.—Thane, from the Saxon *thenian, ministrare*, was the title of those who attended the Saxon kings in their courts, and who held their lands immediately of those kings ; and therefore were indiscriminately called *thani et servientes regis*, though, not long after the Conquest, the word was disused ; and instead thereof, those men were called *Barones Regis*, who, as to their dignity, were inferior to earls, and took place after bishops, abbots, barons, and knights. There were also *thani minores*, and these were likewise called barons : these were lords of manors, who had a particular jurisdiction within their limits, and over their own tenants in their own courts, which to this day are called Courts

Baron ; but the word signifies sometimes a nobleman, sometimes a freeman, sometimes a magistrate, but more properly an officer or minister of the king. "Edward King grete mine Biscops, and mine Earles, and all mine Thynes, on that shiren, wher mine Prestes in Paulus Minister habband land." (*Chart. Edw. Conf. Pat.* 18 H. VI. m. 9, *per Inspect.*) In an Anglo-Saxon writ of William the First, quoted by Spelman from an Abbotsbury MS., the term *Thegena* occurs in the same sense. In *thanage of the king* signified a certain part of the king's lands and property, whereof the ruler or governor was called thane. (*Cowell.*) In the early periods of the history of this country, the payments of the thanes were made regularly into the public treasury by the sheriffs, distinctly in the name of this class ; hence we find that in 13 Henry III. (1229), the thanes of the county of Lancaster, through the sheriff, paid a composition of fifty marks (£33 6s. 8d.), to be excused from the taillinge or assessment which the king, in the exercise of his absolute authority, had imposed upon his people. (*Mag. Rot. 13 Hen. III. titulo Lancaster.*) The same sheriff (Wm. de Vesci) rendered an account of fourscore and sixteen pounds (£96) of the gift of the knights and thanes. (*Mag. Rot. 5 Hen. II. Rot. 2, b. Tit. Northumberland. Nova Placita & Novæ Conventiones.*) In 3 John (1201) the "Theigni and fermarii" of the honor of Lancaster had a composition of fifty marks to be exonerated from crossing the sea. (*Mag. Rot. 3 John, Rot. 20, a.*)

CHAPTER VIII.

E have now arrived at that period when the representative system began to prevail in the English Parliament, and when this county, by its freeholders and burgesses, obtained the privilege of returning members to the senate, charged with the duty of making known the public will in that assembly, in order to promote the interest of the great community for which it legislates. None of the English counties presents a more interesting representative history than the county of Lancaster; and yet this subject has hitherto been either entirely neglected, or has been treated in so vague and desultory a manner as to have neither uniformity nor connection. To supply this deficiency much labour has been required in examining and collating the public records; but that labour has been amply rewarded by the mass of facts which these documents contain, from the fountain-head of authentic information.

So early as the Saxon heptarchy a species of Parliament existed, as we have already seen, under the designation of the Witena-Gemot, or "Council of Wise Men," by whom the laws were enacted. This assembly consisted of the comites or earls, the hereditary representatives of counties, assisted by the prelates and abbots, and the tenants *in capite* of the crown by knight's service. The disposition of such an assembly would naturally incline them to sanction the edicts of the sovereign; and it is highly probable that his will generally served as their law. After the Conquest, the first William and his immediate descendants called to their "great council" the Norman barons and the dignified clergy, with the military tenants. This Council, or "King's Court," as it was called (the term parliament not having then come into use),[1] assembled three times in the year—namely, at Christmas, Easter, and Whitsuntide. The barons and other tenants-in-chief of the king, enumerated in Domesday Book, amount to about seven hundred. These persons possessed all the land of England in baronies, except that part which the king reserved in his own hands, and which was called "Terra Regis," and has since been called the "ancient demesne" of the crown. These tenants-in-chief, *per baroniam*, as well the few who held in socage as those who held by military service, composed the great council, or Parliament, in those times, and were summoned by the king, though they had a right to attend without summons. In the main the constitution of Parliament, as it now stands, was marked out so long ago as 17 John (1215), in the great charter granted by that sovereign, wherein he promises to summon all archbishops, bishops, abbots, earls, and great barons personally, and all other tenants-in-chief under the crown by the sheriffs and bailiffs, to meet at a certain place, with forty days' notice, to assess aids and scutages when necessary; and this constitution has subsisted, in fact, at least from 49 Henry III., there being still extant writs of that date to summon knights, citizens, and burgesses to Parliament. The landowners of the second, third, and other inferior classes, being all tenants, or vassals, of this upper class of landholders, though by free and honourable tenures, similar to those by which their lords themselves held of the king, were bound by the decisions of their superior lords. The landed interest was for a long time alone represented in the national councils, there being no representatives, either of the cities or boroughs, or of the trading interest, which were considered too insignificant to be represented in the great council.[2] The representation of such places was an innovation

---

[1] Professor (now Bishop) Stubbs remarks that "the name given to the sessions of council (under the early Norman kings) was often expressed by the Latin *colloquium*; and it is by no means unlikely that the name of Parliament, which is used as early as 1175 by Jordan Fantosme ("sun plenier Parlement"), may have been in common use. But of this we have no distinct instance in the Latin chronicles for some years further, although when the term comes into use it is applied retros-

pectively; and in a record of the twenty-eighth year of Henry III., the assembly in which the great charter was granted is mentioned as the "Parliamentum Runimedæ." . . . It is first used in England by a contemporary writer in 1246, namely, by Matthew Paris. It is a word of Italian origin, and may have been introduced either through the Norman or through intercourse with the French kingdom."—C.

[2] Archæologia, vol. ii. p. 310.

introduced in the early part of the fourteenth century by Simon de Montfort and the reforming barons of his day. It is true that these barons were actuated in some degree by ambitious motives, and that their conduct partook of the revolutionary turbulence of the age in which they lived; but they were the legitimate descendants of those illustrious patriots who wrung from King John the charter of British freedom. The reforms they introduced were parts of the same system; the one the natural effect of the other, and both flowing from that spirit of "popular encroachment" which does not, and which ought not, to rest till its fair claims are satisfied. In this way the dictation of the barons and the discontents of the subordinate orders of society were overcome; and, though in an age of comparative darkness, Edward I., the "Justinian of England," whose sagacity enabled him to mark the signs of the times, did not hesitate to declare in his writs to the sheriffs for the return of burgesses to Parliament, "that it was a most equitable rule, that that which concerns all should be approved of by all." By this temperate extension of the popular rights, the visionary projects of John Ball and Wat Tyler, which soon after arose, were defeated; and the representative system of England has remained ever since essentially unaltered, till successive enlargements of the elective franchise were rendered necessary by the altered state of society in commerce and in manufactures.

In the time of Henry III. abuses in the government had been suffered to accumulate, till, according to the contemporary historians, "justice itself was banished from the realm; for the wicked devoured the righteous, the courtier the rustic, the oppressor the innocent, the fraudulent the plain man, and yet all these things remained unpunished. Evil counsellors whispered into the ears of the princes that they were not amenable to the laws. The subject was oppressed in various ways, and, as if these sycophants had conspired the death of the king, and the destruction of his throne, they encouraged him to disregard the devotion of his people, and to incur their hatred rather than to enjoy their affection."[1] In addition to these grievances, the kingdom was deeply involved in debt, and the king stood in need of fresh contributions to carry on his wars, which the barons refused to grant till the public grievances were redressed. Overwhelmed with difficulties, Henry issued his mandate for holding a Parliament at Oxford. Of this Parliament, so celebrated in history, and particularly in the representative history of England, it is recorded that "the grandees of the realm, major and minor, with horses and arms, were convened at Oxford, June 11, 1258, together with the clergy, to make provision and reformation, and ordination of the realm; and on their oath of fidelity were exhibited the articles which in the said realm stood in need of correction." This Parliament, owing to the popular excitation under which it was assembled, and to all the members coming dressed in armour, and mounted as for battle, obtained the name of *parliamentum insanum*, or "The Mad Parliament," though it would have been well for England if all Parliaments had been equally sane; but there was a method in their madness, and one of their first acts was to ordain that four knights should be chosen by each county, whose duty it should be to inquire into the grievances of the people, in order that they might be redressed, and that they should be returned to the next Parliament, to give information as to the state of their respective counties, and to co-operate in enacting such laws as might best conduce to the public good. Some approach had been made towards this state of things in the time of King John, when the knights were appointed to meet in their several counties, and to present a detail of the state of those counties to the great council; but here they were not only to present their complaints, but, by being made a component part of the legislative body, they were to contribute from their local knowledge to the removal of those wrongs which it was their duty to present.

In this Parliament at Oxford twenty-four persons were elected—twelve on the part of the king, and as many on the part of the community—for the reformation of public abuses, and the amendment of the state of the realm.

"*On the part of the king*—
The lord bishop of London.
The lord (bishop) elect of Winton.
Sir Henry, son of the king of Almaine.
Sir John, earl of Warrenne.
Sir Guy de Lesignan.
Sir Wm. de Valence.
Sir John, earl of Warwick.
Sir John Mansel.
Friar John de Derlington.
The abbot of Westminster.
Sir Hugh de Wengham.
 [The twelfth is wanting.]

"*On the part of the barons*—
The lord bishop of Worcester
Sir Simon, earl of Leicester.
Sir Richard, earl of Gloucester.
Sir Humphrey, earl of Hereford.
Sir Roger Mareschal.
Sir Roger de Mortimer.
Sir Geoffry Fitz-Geoffry.
Sir Hugh le Bigot.
Sir Richard le Grey.
Sir William Bardulf.
Sir Peter de Montfort.
Sir Hugh Despenser."

[1] Ann. Burton, anno 1258, p. 424.

Amongst a variety of other decrees, the twenty-four enacted that the state of the holy church be amended; that a justiciar be appointed for one year, to be answerable to the king and his council during his term of office; that a treasurer of the exchequer be also appointed, to render account at the end of the year; that the chancellor shall also answer for his trust; that shire-reeves be provided in every county, trusty persons, freeholders, and vavasors,[1] of property and consequence in the county, who shall faithfully and honestly treat the people of the county, and render their accounts to the exchequer once every year; and that neither they, nor their bailiffs, take any hire; that good escheators be appointed, and that they take nothing from the goods of the deceased out of the lands which ought to be in the king's hands; that the exchange of London be amended, as well as all the other cities of the king, which had been brought to disgrace and ruin by talliages, and other extortions; and that the household of the king and queen be amended.

Of the Parliaments, they ordain:—

"That there be three Parliaments in the year: the first, upon the octave of St. Michael (Oct. 6); the second, on the morrow of Candlemas (Feb. 3); the third, June 1. To these three Parliaments shall come the counsellors-elect of the king, though they be not commanded, to provide for the state of the realm, and to manage the common business of the realm, when there shall be need, by the command of the king." "That the community do choose twelve prode men ("*prud'hommes*," men of probity and prudence), who shall go the Parliaments, and attend at other times when there shall be need, when the king or his council shall command, to manage the business of the king, and of the realm; and that the community hold for stable that which these twelve shall do; and this to spare the cost of the commons. Fifteen shall be named by the earl mareschal, the Earl of Warwick, Hugh de Bigot, and John Mansel, who are elected by the twenty-four, to name the aforesaid fifteen, who shall be of the council of the king; and they shall be confirmed by them, or by the greater part of them; and they shall have power from the king to give them counsel in good faith concerning the government of the realm, and all things belonging to the king and kingdom; and to amend and redress all things which they shall see want to be amended and redressed, and to be over the high justiciar, and over all other persons; and if they cannot all be present, that which the greater part shall do shall be firm and stable."

It has been the fashion to consider the "Provisions of Oxford," as they were called, as the rash innovations of an ambitious oligarchy, but the principle of the securities then required from the crown was adopted from the Great Charter; and the appointment of a supreme council of state was one of the conditions imposed upon John, with the more stringent demand that the twenty-five barons, who were then to control the executive, should be elected without the concurrence of the king. The unconstitutional power assumed, of choosing the responsible ministers of the crown—for in no other light can the functions of these "twelve prode men" be considered—gradually fell into disuse, though the time when that authority ceased is not very accurately defined in history. In November of the same year (1258), after the dissolution of the memorable Parliament of Oxford, writs were issued from the king's chancery to the sheriffs of England, commanding them respectively to pay "reasonable wages" to the knights delegate for their journey to Parliament, upon the affairs touching their several counties. This is the first known writ "*de expensis*," and it is of the same tenure as that of subsequent times, when it became essential to Parliament to have in it the representatives of the counties, chosen by the freeholders; but the writ for Lancashire issued on this occasion, is lost, and with it the names of the knights returned for the county.

The king and his courtiers, headed by his brothers, and countenanced by his son Edward, the heir-apparent of the crown, resisted to blood the attempts made to reform the Parliament, and to redress the public grievances, accompanied, as these attempts were, with measures for subverting the royal prerogative, and establishing an aristocratical oligarchy. The progress of reform in the constitution of Parliament was not, however, materially retarded by this resistance. It had always been the avowed intention of Simon de Montfort, Earl of Leicester, and Robert de Ferrers, Earl of Derby, to confine the executive power within the limits of the law, and to have all the acts of the king confirmed, as well by the representatives of the county as by the barons spiritual and temporal;[2] and in the Parliament of Worcester, called "Montfort's Parliament," held in 49 Henry III. (1265), it was enacted, that each sheriff throughout England should cause to be sent to the Parliament two knights elected by the freeholders, with two citizens from each of the cities, and two burgesses from each of the boroughs throughout England. By these means the respective orders in the state had an opportunity of expressing the public will; and in an assembly so constituted, and of which the lords spiritual and temporal formed a part, the due consideration of the public good was effectually secured.[3] This national council, which, Hume says, "was on a more democratic basis than any which had been ever summoned since the foundation of the monarchy," was the

---

[1] Vavasors were persons who held lands by military tenure of other persons than the king.

[2] According to Selden there were, in 1262, one hundred and fifty temporal and fifty spiritual barons, summoned to Parliament to perform the service due to their tenures.

[3] In former times both Lords and Commons sat together in one house in Parliament, says Sir Edward Coke, in his 4th Institute, 23; but this is

clearly a mistake, as is shown by Sir Robert Cotton and others, and as is decidedly proved by 6 Edward III. (1332), n. 3. Parl. Rot., where it is said—"The Bishops by themselves, the Lords by themselves, and the Commons by themselves, consulted, and advised the King touching the war with Scotland." In 17 Edward III. (1343), the Prelates and Lords met in the Chambre Blanche, and the Commons in the Chambre Peynte; and both afterwards united in the Chambre Blanche.—*Rot. Parl.*

first in which we distinctly recognise the Parliament of England. It happened, however, that in these early Parliaments the expense incurred by the communities of the counties, cities, and boroughs from the attendance of their members in Parliament was often considered oppressive; and hence we find that many poor boroughs, particularly in the county of Lancaster, had no members,—the reason alleged being that they were unable to pay their expenses, on account of their debility and poverty. The boroughs for which returns were made were principally "walled towns," held of the king in ancient demesne; and the only places in Lancashire entitled to the privilege, if that could be considered a privilege which was felt as a public burden, were Lancaster, Preston, Liverpool, and Wigan. The inhabitants of the boroughs, under the feudal system, were, for the most part, villeins, either in gross or in relation to the manor in which the town stood, and belonged to some lord.[1] The former held houses, called burgage tenures, at the will of the lord, and carried on some trade, such as carpenter, smith, butcher, baker, clothier, or tailor, and the election of members was in the inhabitants of the burgage tenures, so far as they were free agents. There were also in these boroughs certain free inhabitants who held burgages, and were in consequence invested with the elective franchise. In incorporated cities and boroughs the right of election was generally in the corporate body, or freemen as they were called, subject to such limitations, however, as the charters imposed. When the wages of the members representing the cities or boroughs were paid out of the rates, the election was in the inhabitant householders paying those rates, and the right of election was hence designated "scot and lot suffrage." In treating the subject of the county representation from the first return to Parliament made by the sheriff of Lancashire to the present time, the most clear and satisfactory mode will be to take the reign of each of the early kings separately, and connect with the lists in each reign such other historical matter as may be presented on the subject: and 1st.—Of the parliamentary history of the reign of

EDWARD I.

Although the return of knights and burgesses summoned to Parliament by writ commenced as early as 49 Henry III.[2] (1265), no original return made by the sheriff for this county, or for its boroughs,[3] is found in any of the public records till 23 Edw. I. (A.D. 1295). The first return of members for this county is to the Parliament at Westminster, appointed to assemble on *Sunday* next after the feast of St. Martin (Nov. 12); and it announces that "Matthew de Redman" and "John de Ewyas"[4] were elected knights for the county of Lancaster, by the consent of the whole county, who have full and sufficient power to do for themselves, and for the commonalty of the county aforesaid, what our lord the king shall ordain by his council.

"That the aforesaid Matthew was guaranteed to come on the day contained in the writ, by Thomas, son of Thomas de Yeland ; Thomas Fitz Hall ; William Fitz Adam ; and William son of Dake" (in confirmation of which they affix   +
their marks, the manucaptors or sureties for the members not being able probably to write their own names).   +
"And that the aforesaid John was guaranteed by John de Singleton, Richard de Grenel, Roger de Boulton, and Adam de Grene-bulles." The sheriff's return adds, "There is no city in the county of Lancaster." It then proceeds to say "that Lambert le Despenser and William le Dispenser, burgesses of Lancaster, are elected burgesses for the borough of *Lancaster*, in manner above said. And the aforesaid Lambert is guaranteed by Adam de le Grene and John de Overton ; and the aforesaid William is guranteed by Thomas Molendinar and Hugh le Barker." That "William Fitz Paul and Adam Russel, burgesses of Preston, are elected for the borough of *Preston* in Amounderness ; and the aforesaid William is guaranteed to come as above by Richard Banaster and Richard Pelle. And the aforesaid Adam is guaranteed by Henry Fitz Baldwin, and Robert Kegelpin." That "William le Teinterer, and Henry le Bocker, burgesses of Wigan, are elected for the borough of *Wygan* in the manner above said. And they are guaran-teed to come by John le Preston of Wygan, Adam de Cotiler, Roger Fitz Orme, and Richard Fitz Elys." That Adam Fitz Richard and Robert Pinklowe, burgesses of Liverpool, are elected for the borough of *Liverpool*. And they are guaranteed to come, in the time specified in the writ, by John de la More, Hugh de Molendino, William Fitz Richard, and Elias le Baxster."[5]

There is a copy of a writ and return, in 1294, for Cumberland, and amongst the persons returned for that year are—Matthew de Redman[6] and Richard de Preston, as knights of the shire.

In the Parliament of 1296, no original writ for Lancashire appears, nor is there any enrolment of writs de expensis for this county on the rolls.

[1] *Archæologia*, vol. ii. p. 315.
[2] Prynne's Enlargement of his 4th Institute.
[3] In a return presented to Parliament by order of the House of Com-mons in 1879, giving the names of members of the lower house and their constituencies "from so remote a period as it can be obtained," the earliest Parliaments mentioned are the following: (1) 15 John (1213), summoned to meet at Oxford. Writs addressed to all the sheriffs, re-quiring them each to send all the knights of their bailiwicks in arms ; and also four knights from their counties, " *ad loquendum nobiscum de negotiis regni nostre*." (2) 10 Henry III. (1226) summoned to meet at Lincoln. Writs addressed to the sheriffs of eight counties, requiring them each to send four knights, elected by the *milites et probi homines* of their bailli-wicks, to set forth certain disputes with the sheriffs. (3) 38 Henry III. (1254), summoned to meet at Westminster. Every sheriff required to send two knights, to be elected by each county, to provide aid towards carrying on the war in Gascony (4) 45 Henry III. (1261), summoned to

meet at Windsor. The Bishop of Worcester, the Earls of Leicester and Gloucester, and other magnates, having ordered three knights from each county to attend an assembly at St. Albans, the king enjoins the sheriffs to send the above-mentioned knights also to him at Windsor. (5) 49 Henry III. (1264-5), summoned to meet at London. This appears (says the return) to have been the first complete Parliament consisting of elected knights, citizens, and burgesses. In each of these cases no returns of names could be found.—C.
[4] Matthew de Redman served the office of Sheriff of the county from 1245 to 1249; the other representative of the shire in this Parliament, Sir John D'Ewyas, married Cecily, the eldest of the three daughters and co-heirs of Sir William de Samlesbury, and, in her right, had half of the manor of Samlesbury. He died before 1311.—C.
[5] Petitt MSS. vol 15, fol. 88. Inner Temple Libr.
[6] This is probably the same person that was returned for Lancashire in the following year.

17

The first parliamentary writ extant, addressed to the sheriff of Lancashire, is of the date of 25 Edward I. (6th October, 1297) in the Tower of London, and requires that knights only (not citizens and burgesses) shall be sent from this county to Parliament, for the confirmation of Magna Charta and the Charter of Forests. This writ, which is of the nature of a bargain between the king and his people, recites that, in relief of all the inhabitants and people of the kingdom for the eighth of all the goods of every layman, and the most urgent necessity of the kingdom, the king has agreed to confirm the great charter of the liberties of England, and the charter of the liberties of the forest; and to grant by letters patent that the said levy of the eighth shall not operate to the prejudice of his people, or to the infringement of their liberties; and he commands and firmly enjoins the sheriff that he cause to be elected, without delay, two of the most able and legal, or most honest and lawworthy (" probioribus et legalioribus ") knights of the county of Lancaster, and send them with full powers from the whole community of the said county, to his dearest son Edward, his lieutenant in England (the king being then abroad, engaged in the war with France), on the octaves of St. Michael next ensuing (6th Oct., 1297), to receive the said charters and the king's letters patent for the said county.[1]

The members returned in the Parliament of 1297, called for the purpose of raising money for the invasion of France, were " Henricus de Kigheley " and " Henricus le Botiller," vel " Botiler."[2] In the Parliament of 1298, the return in the original writ is " Henricus de Kigheley " and " Johannes Denyes," (? de Ewyas), knights of the shire. The Parliament of the following year (1299) produces no original writ, nor any writ de expensis, for this county. The same observation applies to the Parliament of May, 1300, and to the Parliament of 1305.

To the Parliament of March 6th, 1299-1300, " Gilbertus de Singleton " and " Robertus de Haydok " were returned for this county; in January, 1300-1, " Henricus de Kigheley " and " Thomas Travers; "[3] in September, 1302, " Willielmus de Clifton " and " Gilbertus de Singleton ; " in February, 1304-5, " Willielmus de Clifton,' vel " de Clyffedone," and " Willielmus Banestre ; "[4] in January, 1306-7, " Gilbertus de Syngilton " and " Johannes Travers " were elected to the same honour. These returns to the frequent Parliaments,[5] in the latter part of the reign of Edward I. completes the writs for that period, so far as regards this county. During the same reign, four returns were made to Parliament of members for the borough of Lancaster, two for the borough of Liverpool, five for Preston, and two for Wigan; each of which will be treated of in its proper place.

The number of counties, cities, and boroughs making returns to Parliament at this time amounted to one hundred and forty-nine,[6] in the list of which we find ten members for Lancashire, namely, two for the county, and two for each of the above-named boroughs. In the 24 Henry VI. (1446), the number of members was reduced to 274, all the boroughs of Lancashire having then disappeared from the list, and the only members returned for this county consisting of the knights of the shire.

Although these early Parliaments were frequent, the period of their sitting was of short duration. In 49 Henry III. (1265), the Parliament which assembled to settle the peace of the kingdom, after the barons' wars, accomplished its duty in thirty-two days, and then dissolved; and yet this was reputed an incredible delay. The Parliament, 28 Edward I. (1300), which confirmed the great charter and made articuli super cartas, was summoned to meet on the second Sunday in Lent, and ended the 20th day of March, on which day the writs for the knights' and burgesses' expenses were dated, making a session of three weeks. The famous Parliament at Lincoln, 28 Edward I. (Jan. 20th, 1301), wherein the king and nobles wrote their memorable letters to Pope Boniface, claiming homage from the kings of Scotland to the kings of England, sat but ten days.[7] The Parliament of 35 Edward I. was summoned to meet at Carlisle on the 20th of January

[1] Rot. Claus. 25 Ed. I, m. 6 d. Orig. in Turr. Lond.
[2] Henry de Kighley was seneschall or steward of Blackburnshire 16 Edward I. (1287-8) His colleague was the eldest son of William Fitz-Almeric le Pincerna or le Boteler, seventh baron of Warrington; he died in the year of his election, and in the following year John D'Ewyas, who had sat in the Parliament of 1295, was returned with Henry de Kighley as a knight of the shire.—C.
[3] Thomas Travers, who obtained Nateby in Garstang by deed of gift from his brother, Lawrence Travers, of Tulketh, was coroner for Furness (c. 1292), high sheriff of the county (1301-4), and keeper of the forests of Lancaster and Amounderness, and collector of scutages for the county. He died before August, 1334.—C.
[4] Of Clifton-with-Salwick and Westby, his colleague, William de Singleton, being of the house of Singleton in Kirkham parish; William Banastre, who was elected to the same honour with William Clifton in 1304, died in 17 Edward II. (1323-4), seized of " the hamlet of Singleton Parva " in Kirkham.—C.
[5] It is evident that no fixed rule was adhered to in summoning these Parliaments, except that which arose out of the king's want of either money or counsel, or both. The order of the Parliament of Oxford, that three Parliaments should be held in one year, does not appear ever to have been acted upon with uniformity, and this enactment was probably

intended only to fix the times at which the Parliaments were to assemble, till the reforms then contemplated were completed.
[6] Pryune's Brev. Parl.
[7] In June, 1299, Pope Boniface addressed a letter to Edward, demanding that every controversy between England and Scotland should be referred to the decision of the pontiff. Edward returned for answer that he should submit the matter to his Parliament. The independence of England was threatened by these inordinate pretensions, and the king never showed greater sagacity than in this resolve to summon the representatives of the nation that they might speak the voice of the nation. In that Parliament three hundred persons—prelates, abbots, barons, knights, and burgesses—were present, and whatever might be their opinions as to the rights claimed by their sovereign over the kingdom of Scotland, they were unanimous in resisting the claim set up by the pontiff, and returned as their answer: " It is, and by the grace of God shall always be, our common and unanimous resolve, that with respect to the rights of his kingdom of Scotland, or other temporal rights, our aforesaid lord the king shall not plead before you, nor submit in any manner to your judgment, nor suffer his right to be brought into question by any inquiry, nor send agents or procurators for that purpose to your court."—C.

(1307), when the king expected Cardinal Sabines; but the cardinal not arriving, as was expected, the king prorogued this Parliament by another writ till the next Sunday after Mid-lent (March 12), and on Palm Sunday the Parliament ended, having sat only fifteen days, whereof three were Sundays,[1] it being in those times the general practice to assemble the Parliaments on the Sunday, and so far to disregard the Sabbath as to hold their sittings continuously, without any intermission, on that day.

EDWARD II.

No fewer than twenty-seven Parliaments were held during the twenty years' reign of Edward II. There are no writs extant for Lancashire in ten of that number—namely, in 1308 and 1309; in November, 1311; in the first Parliament of 1312; in the Parliaments of 1313 and 1316; and in those of 1317, 1318, and 1323. Mr. Palgrave, in his second volume of Parliamentary Writs and Writs of Military Summons, published by direction of the commissioners of public records, has given a very complete list of the returns made to Parliament by the sheriff of Lancashire during this reign; and from that source the following returns, from 1307 to 1327, are derived. In 1307, it appears from the original writ for this county, that "Matheus de Reddeman, miles," and "Willielmus le Gentyl, miles," were returned. In August, 1311, "Thomas de Bethum," vel "Bethume, miles," and "Willielmus le Gentylle," vel "Gentyl, miles," were returned to the Parliament on the 8th of August. The writ de expensis for the attendance at Parliament, from the return-day until the feast of St. Dionysius, together with their charges coming and returning, is tested at London on the 11th of October. It is remarkable that an individual named Thomas de Bethun, or Bethom, is also returned for Westmorland in the same Parliament; and it is highly probable that the electors in some cases economised their expenses by returning the same member to represent two counties. This Parliament is remarkable for the desertion of its public duty, from a cause which strikingly indicates that ancient members of Parliament had much less patience than their successors of the present day. So exhausted were the lords, the king's counsel, the knights, and the burgesses, by their sitting of nine weeks, that most of them departed from Parliament without license, as the writs and summons attest, and the remainder petitioned the king to adjourn, and thus obtained licence to return to their homes. The original writ for the county of Lancaster, in the Parliament of August, 1312, returns "Henricus de Trafforde, miles," and "Ricardus le Molineaux de Croseby, miles." No enrolment of writ de expensis appears on the rolls, but the entries of such writs are incomplete. "Dominus Willielmus de Bradeschagh, miles," and "Dominus Edmundus de Dacre, miles," are returned in the original writ of March 18, 1313. In the writ of July 8, in the same year, Radulphus de Bykerstathe, miles," and "Willielmus de Slene, miles," are returned. No manucaptors were found by these knights. To the Parliament of the 23rd September, in the same year, "Henricus de Feghirby vel Fegherby, miles," and "Thomas de Thornton vel Thorneton, miles," are returned. The writ de expensis for "Henricus de Fegherby," and "Thomas de Thorneton," for attendance at Parliament, from the return day (September 23) until Thursday next after the feast of St. Michael (November 15), amounts to £21 12s. at the rate of four shillings each per diem, together with their charges coming and returning. To the Parliament of April, 1314, there is no return from the county. In the Parliament of September, 1314, "Thomas Banastr', miles," and "Willielmus de Slene, miles," appear in the original writ, as well as in the writ de expensis. "Willielmus de Bradeshagh, miles," and "Adam de Halghton, miles," are returned 20th January, 1315, and £19 4s., at the rate of four shillings each per diem, is awarded to them by the writ de expensis. In 1316, "Johannes de Lancastr'" and "Willielmus de Walton" are returned on the 27th of January. In the Parliament of April, in the same year, no writ for the county is found, but " Rogerus de Pilketon, miles," and " Johannes de Pilketon, miles," are returned by the original writ of 29th July following, and their charges allowed at the usual rate in the writ de expensis. To the Parliament summoned to meet at Lincoln, January 27th, 1318, no return appears, but "Edmundus de Nevill', miles," and " Johannes de Horneby, miles,' are returned by the original writ of October 20th in the same year, on which it is observed that no manucaptors were found by these knights. At this period an advance took place in the wages allowed to the county members for their services in Parliament, and the allowance in the writ de expensis is five shillings each per diem, instead of four as hitherto. In 1319, "Willielmus de Walton, miles," and "Willielmus de Slene, miles," are returned in the original writ for the county; but it is much torn and defaced, and rendered almost illegible. From some cause, the members' wages were again reduced to four shillings each per diem. In 1320, "Gilbertus de Haydok, miles," and "Thomas de Thornton, miles," appear in the original writ, and in the writ de expensis; but it was alleged that they were

---

[1] Prynne's Enlargement of his 4th Institute.

returned by Willielmus le Gentil, the sheriff, on his own authority, and without the assent of the county. No original writ for this county is found for the Parliament of 1321,[1] but the names of "Johannes de Horneby junior," and "Gilbertus de Heydok," are inserted in the writ de expensis, tested at Westminster on the 22d of August. "Edmundus de Nevill, miles," and "Johannes de Lancastria, miles," were returned to the Parliament of 1322.[2] By this writ the sum of one hundred and seven shillings and fourpence is awarded to the two knights for seventeen days' attendance in Parliament at York, and six days coming and returning; Edmundus de Neville receiving sixty-nine shillings, at the rate of three shillings per diem, and Johannes de Lancastria thirty-eight shillings, at the rate of twenty pence per diem; but why the latter received lower wages than the former for his parliamentary services is not stated. In the original writs of election and proclamation for this county, in the Parliament summoned to meet at Ripon on the 14th of November, 1322 (altered afterwards to York), "Richard de Hoghton, miles," and "Gilbertus de Singilton' vel Sengilton, miles," were returned. From the writ de expensis it appears that the original rate of wages was re-established, and the sum of £8 8s. for fifteen days' attendance in Parliament, and three days coming and three days returning, was awarded to the knights.

In 1324 the original writ for this county returns the names of "Edmundus de Nevill', miles," and "Gilbertus de Haidok, miles." The names of "Edmundus de Nevyll'" and "Thomas de Lathum," "per. iiii dies," are found in the enrolment of the writ de expensis, and on the original pawn or docket, as knights appearing for this county. The writ de expensis directs that sixteen marks for twenty days' attendance at Parliament, and four days coming and four days returning, at the rate of three shillings and fourpence each per diem, should be paid to the knights. No reason is assigned for the substitution of the name of "Thomas de Lathum" for that of Gilbert de Haidok. At another Parliament in this year "Willielmus de Slene, miles," and "Nicholaus le Norrays vel Norreys, miles," appear in the original writ for this county, returned by Gilbertus de [Sothe] worth, sheriff. No manucaptors were found by these knights. In the writ de expensis, £7 15s. is awarded to the members for twenty-one days' attendance in Parliament, and five days coming, and five days returning, at the rate of two shillings and sixpence each per diem. There is a peculiarity in this original writ. Usually the citizens and burgesses of the county are required to send members; but in this case the summons is confined to knights of the shire. In 1325 "Willielmus de Bradeshaghe, miles," and "Johannes de Horneby vel Hornby" are returned. No manucaptors were found by these knights. In the writ de expensis, £7 14s. is awarded for twenty-two days' attendance in Parliament, including coming and returning; "Willielmus de Bradeshaghe" to be paid at the rate of four shillings per diem, a knight's wages, and "Johannes de Horneby" at the rate of three shillings per diem, an inferior rate of wages. In 1326-7 "Edmundus de Nevyll, miles," and "Ricardus de Hoghton, miles," appear in the writ of expenses, the original writ not being found. The sum awarded to the two knights is £28 8s. for seventy-one days' attendance in Parliament, coming and returning, at the rate of four shillings each per diem.

During this reign four returns are made for the borough of Lancaster, and two for the borough of Preston, but none for either Liverpool or Wigan. The rate of wages paid to the borough members appears to have been fixed at two shillings each per diem. Lancaster, Preston, Liverpool, and Wigan were the only towns in the Palatinate called upon to return members to Parliament, but so little value did our ancestors place on the elective franchise, that they were only too anxious to be relieved of their privileges, the appreciation of the honour of being represented diminishing as the exactions of the sovereign increased. The members deemed it a waste of time, and the burgesses looked on it as a profitless luxury that might be advantageously dispensed with. Every year the number of members decreased, and some boroughs petitioned against, and even went so far as to buy themselves from, their enforced privilege. So burdensome was representation felt that, as we learn from a note to "Blackstone," from the 33 Edward III. (1359) uniformly through the five succeeding reigns, a period embracing very nearly a century, the sheriffs of Lancashire returned that there were no cities or boroughs in the county that ought, or were used, or could, on account of their poverty, send any citizens or burgesses to Parliament.

[1] In this Parliament, called the "Parliament de la Bond," from the barons coming armed against the Despensers and wearing coloured bands upon their sleeves for distinction, which met at Westminster three weeks after midsummer, an indemnity was granted against all men, of whatsoever state or condition, who had done what might be noted for trespasses and against the king's peace "in pursuing and destroying Hugh le Despenser, the son, and Hugh le Despenser, the father."—C.

[2] In the Parliament, which was held at York three weeks after Easter, the statute of indemnity granted in the preceding year was repealed, it being shown that "it was sinfully and wrongfully made and granted," and that the assent "of the prelates, earls, barons, knights of shires, and commonality" then given was "for dread of great force

which the Earl of Hereford and the other great confederates (including Thomas, Earl of Lancaster) suddenly brought to the Parliament of Westminster, with horse and arms, in affray and abasement of all the people." In the short period of eight months there had been a counter-revolution, the Earl of Lancaster had been beheaded, and a mighty change had been wrought as evidenced by the fact that in the same Parliament at York the exile of the Despensers was annulled: the "ordinances" made ten years previously were revoked for the reason "that by the matters so ordained the royal power of our lord the king was restrained on divers things, contrary to what it ought to be;" and all provisions "made by subjects against the royal power of the ancestors of our lord the king" were ordered to cease and lose their effect for ever.—C.

By an assumption of power which is scarcely to be credited, the high sheriff of the county, in 17 Edward II. (1324), arrogated to himself, as we have already seen, the right of superseding the privileges of the electors, and returning members for the county by his own appointment. The presentment made to the grand jury of the hundred of West Derby against this ostentatious and arbitrary sheriff has already been referred to, but it may not be unacceptable to have the document entire :—

> LANCASTER. { "The Grand Jury of the Wapentake of West Derby present, That ' *Willielmus le Gentil*,' at the time when he was sheriff, and when he held his Tourn in the said Wapentake, ought to have remained no longer in the Wapentake than three nights with three or four horses, whereas he remained there at least nine days with eight horses, to the oppression of the people ; and that he quartered himself one night at the house of ' Dūs de *Turbat*,' and another night at the house of one ' *Robertus de Bold*,' another at the house of ' *Robertus de Grenlay*,' and elsewhere, according to his will, at the cost of the men of the Wapentake. They also present, that the said ' *Willielmus*' allowed one ' *Henricus* fil. *Roberti le Mercer*,' indicted of a notorious theft, to be let out upon manucaption ; whereas he was not mainpernable according to the law ; in consequence of which the men of the Wapentake avoided making presentments of notorious thieves ; and that ' *Henricus de Malton*' did the same when he was sheriff. That the said ' *Willielmus*' and ' *Henricus*' returned certain persons on inquests and juries without giving them warning. That the said ' *Willielmus le Gentil*,' when sheriff, had returned ' *Gilbertus de Haydok*' and ' *Thomas de Thornton*,' knights of the shire (14 Edward II., 1320), without the assent of the County, whereas they ought to have been elected by the County ; and had levied twenty pounds for their expenses ; whereas the County could, by their own election, have found two good and sufficient men who would have gone to Parliament for ten marks or ten pounds, and the sheriff's bailiffs levied as much for their own use as they had levied for the knights. Also, that ' *Henricus de Malton*,' when he was sheriff, had returned ' *Willielmus de Slene*' and ' *Willielmus de Walton*' as knights (12 Edward II., 1318), in the same manner."
>
> "The said ' *Willielmus Gentil*' is enlarged, upon the manucaption of four manucaptors."—(*Rot. Plac.* 17 *Edw. II. m.* 72.)

EDWARD III.

In the first Parliament of Edward III. (1327), "Michael de Haverington" and "Will'us Laurence" were returned knights of the shire for the county of Lancaster. "Willielmus de Bradshaigh" and "Edmundus de Nevill" were elected in February, 1327-8, and were succeeded by "Thomas de Thornton," and "John de Horneby," who were succeeded in turn in the same year by "Willielmus Laurence" and "Thomas de Thornton." In 1329, "Nicholaus le Norreys" and "Henry de Haydok" attended the adjourned Parliament, and were succeeded by "Will'us de Saperton" and "Henricus de Haydok." "Willielmus de Bradeshagh (or de Bradeshawe)" and "Johannes de Lancastr'" were their successors in the year 1330. At the election of these members, the sheriff, by order of the king, proclaimed that if any person in the county had suffered wrong from any of the servants of the crown, they were to come to the next Parliament and make known their complaints. "Will'us de Bradshawe" and "Oliverus de Stanesfield" were returned in 1331. "Adam Banastr'" and "Robertus de Dalton" were elected in March, 1332, and in September of the same year "Robertus de Dalton" and "Johannes de Horneby," jun., were returned. In December, 1332, "Edos (Edmundus) de Nevill" and "Johannes de Horneby," jun., were elected ; and in the writs de expensis it appears that the wages of the knights were then four shillings per diem. "Edmundus de Nevill" and "Robertus de Dalton" were returned in February, 1334, and they were succeeded in the same year by "Robertus de Radeclyf" and "Henricus de Haydok." In 1335 "Robertus de Shirburn" and "Edmundus de Nevill" were elected. In 1336 "Johannes de Shirburn" and "Henricus de Haydok" were returned ; and in the same year "Johannes de Horneby," jun., and "Henricus de Haydok." In 1337 "Robertus de Irland" and "Henricus de Haydok" were returned, and they were succeeded in the same year by "Ric'us de Hoghton" and "Edmundus de Nevill."

The changes made in the county members seem at this period to have been very frequent, but whether that arose from the fickleness of the constituents, from the inadequate payments made to the knights of the shire, or from the unproductive nature of parliamentary influence, and the very diminutive size of the pension list, does not appear.

The return to the writ of summons in February, 1337-8 contained the names of "Robertus de Billisthorpe" and "Robertus de Radeclif," and in that of July in the same year "Johannes de Hornby" and "Johannes de Clyderhowe," as knights of the shire, to whom, by the writ de expensis, dated at Northampton on the 2nd of August, the sum of £7 4s. was awarded for coming to, remaining in Parliament, and returning to their houses, being a payment of four shillings each per diem for eighteen days. The writ for 1339 was issued by the guardian of the kingdom, and the king's council, in his Majesty's absence ; and the knights returned to Parliament for the county of Lancaster were "Robertus de Clyderhowe" and "Henricus de Bykerstath." In the same year "Nich'us de Hulm" and "Robertus de Prestecote" were returned. "Johannes de Radecliffe" and "Robertus de Radecliffe" were returned in 1340, and in the same year "Robertus de Dalton" and "Johannes de Dalton" were elected and returned to Parliament, with the usual allowance of four shillings per diem.

During the remainder of this reign the Parliaments continued to be held almost every year ; and it is clear, from the continually-varying names returned for the county of Lancaster, that each session was a new, and not an adjourned Parliament. It is equally clear that no argument in favour of any precise duration of Parliament can be founded upon the practice of these early times, seeing that there was frequently more than one Parliament in the year; and that at other times the assembling of Parliament was intermitted for two, three, or four years.

In the 4th of Edward III. (1330) it was enacted that Parliaments should be held once a-year, and oftener, if necessary. The 36 Henry VI. (1458) requires a Parliament to be held every year. By 16 Charles II. (1664) it is enacted that Parliaments shall be triennial; confirmed by 6 William and Mary (1694); but by 1 George I. (1714) the time of their continuance, if considered necessary by the king and his advisers, was rendered septennial. So that our parliamentary history affords all the precedents from three Parliaments in the year to one Parliament in seven years.

The following is a list of the members for the county of Lancaster during the remainder of the reign of Edward III., with the date of the Parliaments in which they sat, and the amount of wages they received from the county:—

MEMBERS (KNIGHTS).	PARLIAMENT AT	WAGES.
No writ found	Westminster, April 23, 1341	
Joh'es de Haverington .... Joh'es Ungton .... }	Westminster, Monday, 15 days of Easter (April 24, 1343)	£13 : 12s. for 34 days.
	Claus. 17 E. III. P. 1. m 1 dorso.	
Nich'us le Botiller .... Will'us fil. Rob. de Radecliff... }	Westminster, Monday after Octaves of Holy Trinity (June 7, 1344)	£12 : 16s. for 32 days.
	Claus. 18 E. III. P. 2 m. 26.	
Joh'es de Cliderhowe .... Adam de Bredekirk .... }	Westminster, Monday after Feast of Nat. Blessed Mary (Sep. 11, 1346)	£7 : 4s. for 18 days.
	Claus. 20 E. III P. 2 m. 14 d.	
Adam de Hoghton .. .. Joh'es Cokayn .... {	Westminster, Monday after Dominica day Middle Quadragesima (March 31, 1348)	£9 : 4s. for 23 days.
	Claus. 22 E. III. P. 1 m. 21 d.	
Rob'tus de Plesyngton .... Rob'tus de Prestcote .... {	Westminster, Morrow of St. Hillary (Jan. 19, 1347-8)	£15 : 4s. for 38 days.
	Claus. 22 E. III. P. 1. m. 33 dorso.	
Otto de Halsale .... Will'us de Radecliff .... {	Westminster, Octaves of the Purification (Feb. 9, 1351)	£13 : 4s. for 33 days.
	Claus. 25 E. III. Pars unica m. 27 dorso.	
No writ found	Westminster, Tuesday, Feast St. Hillary.	
	26 E. III. (1352).	
Joh'es de Haveryngton, Chivaler	Westminster, Morrow[1] of the Assumption (Aug. 16, 1352)	£4 : 4s. for 21 days.
	Claus. 26 E. III. m. 10 d.	
Will'us Careles .... ("Duchy of Lanc.") .... {	Westminster, Monday after St. Matthi. Apost. (Sep. 23, 1353)................	£6 for 30 days.
	Claus. 27 E. III. m. 5 d.	
Will'us Careles .... Ric'us Nowell .... {	Westminster, Monday after St. Mark Evang. (April 28, 1354)	£13 : 12s for 34 days.
	Claus. 28 E. III. m. 21 d.	
Rog. de Far'ndon .... Robt. de Horneby .... {	Westminster, Monday after St. Edmund, Martyr (Nov. 12, 1355)	£7 : 12s. for 19 days.
	Claus. 29 E. III. Pars unica m. 3 d.	
John de Haverington .... Robt. de Singleton .... {	Westminster, Monday in Easter week (April 7. 1357)	{ £7 : 12s. for John for 38 days, and for Robt. £6 : 4s. for 31 days.
(Addressed to the Duke.)	Claus. 31 E. III. m. 19 d.	

The writs de expensis for the knights of the shire for the county of Lancaster are directed, not to the sheriff, but to the Duke of Lancaster himself. The knights for the counties generally had two distinct writs, some of them for six, others for seven, and one for eight days' expenses; but the writs for Lancashire were issued to the Duke of Lancaster himself, or his lieutenant, by the title of Duke and Duchy of Lancaster:—

MEMBERS (KNIGHTS).	PARLIAMENT AT	WAGES.
Roger de Faryngton .... Robert de Horneby............... }	Westminster, Monday after Purification B. M. (Feb. 5, 1358)	£13 : 12s. for 34 days.
	Claus. 32 E. III. m. 31 d.	
Willielmus de Heskyth, miles Rogerus de Faryngton .... }	Westminster (May 15, 1360)	
Will'us de Radeclyf .... Ric'us de Tounlay .... }	Westminster, Sunday before Conversion of St. Paul (Jan. 24, 1261)	£15 : 4s. for 38 days.
	Claus. 35 E. III. m. 38 d.	
Edmundus Laurence .... Mattheus de Rixton .... }	Westminster, 15 days of St. Michael (Oct. 13, 1362.)	
	36 E. III.	

---

[1] This was called the "Great Council" for "settling the Staple" or manufacture of the kingdom, to which Lancashire sent only one member for the county, and none for its boroughs; but were such a council to be held in the present day, it is highly probable that this county would return, at least its full complement of members.—B. To this Parliament writs were sent to all the sheriffs, to send *one knight* only, "of the most advanced, discreet, and most exempt, in that respect, as men who would be least withdrawn from autumnal occupation." Writs were also issued (for the first time) to Henry, Duke of Lancaster, to send the same (one knight) from his county.—H.

At this period a singular piece of presumption was practised in the return to Parliament of members for the county of Lancaster. The deputy-sheriffs, instead of returning the members elected by the county, returned themselves, concealing the writ, and levying the expenses, which they appropriated to their own use. Upon complaint made to the king, he issued two writs: the first to the sheriff of Lancashire, and the second to the justices of the peace of the county, directing them to examine into the merits of the election, and to certify the facts to him in chancery. In the meantime, the levying of the expenses was suspended till further orders upon these "unparalleled writs," as they are called by Prynne. In the writ to the sheriff (17th Nov., 1362) that officer is informed that the greatest agitation exists in Lancashire respecting the election of the knights for that county in the last Parliament; and his Majesty, wishing to be more fully informed about the election, commands the sheriff to assemble the knights and other good men of the commons of the said county, and to make inquiry whether "Edrus Laurence" and "Matthew Risheton," who have been returned in the writ to Parliament as knights of the said county, or other persons, were duly elected; and if, upon deliberation and information, he should find them to have been elected by the common assent of the county, then to cause the said Edrus and Matthew to have £18 16s. for their expenses incurred in coming to the Parliament, remaining there, and then returning—that is to say, for forty-seven days—each of the aforesaid Edrus and Matthew receiving four shillings per diem; but if other persons have been elected knights of the said county, then the sheriff is to render information of their names, under his seal, into the king's chancery, and to remit the writ to his Majesty, conformably to the directions already given. The king's writ to the justices is addressed to his beloved and faithful Godefr. Folejambe, and his fellow-justices of the peace, in the county of Lancaster, on the 5th of February, 1363; and it states roundly that the said Edrus and Matthew, who are the sheriff's lieutenants, have made a false and deceptive return; in consequence of which, the jurors are required to call before them, at their next session, the knights and other good men of the same county, and take diligent information and inquisition on the above premises, and to return the same into the king's chancery; the sheriff of Lancashire being at the same time commanded to supersede the levy of the wages, until he shall have further directions from the king in his mandate respecting them. The result was, that the election was declared void, and the sheriff's lieutenants were unseated by the king's authority. The proceedings under these memorable writs, which were the first of the kind that were issued, serve to show that the king in these early times, and not the Commons House of Parliament, examined and determined on disputed elections; and that the king, by special writ issued to the sheriff, or to the justices of the peace, caused the merits of the elections to be inquired into, and certificate to be made of their legality or illegality. But, to resume the returns of the list of members for the county :—

KNIGHTS.	PARLIAMENT AT	WAGES.
Adam de Hoghton .... Rogerus de Pylkynton ... }	Westm. (Oct. 6th, 1363)....................................	*Cl.* 37 *E. III.*
Adam de Hoghton ... . Roger de Pylkynton .... }	Westm. Octaves of St. Hilary (Jan. 20, 1365)	£17 : 4s. for 43 days. *Cl.* 38 *E. III. m.* 31 *d.*
Joh. le Botiller, *Miles*...... Will. fil. Rob'ti de Radeclyf }	Westm. Monday, the morrow of the Invention of the Cross (May 4, 1366)	£8 : 16s. for 22 days. *Cl.* 40 *E. III. m.* 23 *d.*
Rog de Pylkyngton, *Chiv.* Rog. de Radeclyf, sen. ... }	Westm. 1st of May (1368)	£14 for 35 days. *Cl.* 42 *E. III. m.* 14 *d.*
Joh'es de Dalton, *Chivaler*} Joh'es de Ipre, *Chivaler*...}	Westm. Octaves of Trinity (Sunday, June 3, 1369)	£8 : 16s. for 22 days. *Cl.* 43 *E. III. m.* 13 *d.*
Joh'es de Ipre............... Ric'us de Tounley .... }	Westm. Monday (Feb. 24, 1370-1)	£19 : 12s. for 51 days. *Cl.* 45 *E. III. m.* 34 *d.*
Joh'es de Ipre...............	Wynton, Monday in Octaves of Trinity (June 8, 1371)	£4 : 4s. for 21 days. *Cl.* 45 *E. III. m.* 22. *d.*
Johannes Botiller. *Miles*... Nich. de Haverynton...... }	Westm. Morrow of All Souls (Wednesday, Nov. 3, 1372)	£6 : 12s. for 33 days. *Cl.* 46 *E. III. m.* 4 *d.*
Will'us de Atherton ...... Joh'es de Holcroft .... }	Westm. Morrow of St. Edmund (Nov. 21, 1373)..........	£12 : 8s. for 31 days. *Cl.* 47 *E. III. m.* 1 *d.*
Joh'es Bottiler, *Chivaler*... Rog. de Brokhols............ }	Westm. Monday after St. George (April 28, 1376)[1]	£34 : 8s. for 86 days. *Cl.* 50 *E. III. P.2. m.* 23 *d.*
Joh'es Botiller............... Rog. Pilkington .... }	Westm. in fifteen days of St. Hilary (Jan. 27, 1377)......................	£18 : 16s. for 47 days. *Cl.* 51 *E. III. m.* 12. *d.*

---

[1] This Parliament has been called "The Good Parliament," in consequence of the ordinances it passed against the corruption of the court and government. Several of the ministers were impeached, and the king's mistress, Alice Perrers, was made the subject of a special censure by the Commons. The increasing activity of the Commons in this Parliament derived much encouragement from the Black Prince, whose death, however, ensued soon after, when John of Gaunt, Duke of Lancaster, obtained a new Parliament, which undid much of the work of its predecessor.—Q.

In the 20 Edward III. (1346) the number of the temporal peers summoned to the Parliament held at Westminster, at the head of whom stood Henry, Duke of Lancaster, amounted only to fifty-four, from which it may be inferred that the hundred and fifty barons in Parliament of 47 Henry III. (1263) mentioned by Selden included the minor barons, at that time the only representatives of the commonalty of the land; and that not by delegation, but by a common interest. The fixed number of abbots and priors to be summoned to Parliament was determined in the reign of Edward III., but it will be seen by the following list that in the twenty-six religious houses to which this privilege was adjudged none of the Lancashire monasteries are included :—

1. St. Albans.	8. Evesham.	15. Shrewsbury.	22. Malmesbury
2. Glastonbury.	9. Winchelcombe.	16. Gloucester.	23. Cirencester.
3. St. Austin's, Cant.	10. Crowland.	17. Bardney.	24. St. Mary, York.
4. Westminster.	11. Battell.	18. Bŏnet in Holm.	25. Selby.
5. St. Edmondsbury.	12. Reading.	19. Thorney.	26. Prior of St. John of
6. Peterborough.	13. Abingdon.	20. Ramsey.	Jerusalem, first
7. Colchester.	14. Waltham.	21. Hide.	baron of England.

Although the boroughs of Lancaster, Preston, Liverpool, and Wigan, all returned burgesses to represent them in Parliament in the reign of Edward I., only the two former of these places sent members in the reign of the second Edward, and so early as the ninth year of Edward III. we find the return made by the sheriff of the county, in answer to the parliamentary writ of summons, states that, " There is not any city or borough in my bailiwick [or county]." It is to be observed that the writs do not particularise the boroughs that are to return members, but merely require the sheriff to return two citizens for each city, and two burgesses for each borough, within his county. In the 36th of Edward III. (1362), the sheriff, in his return, writes upon the writ, " There is not any city or borough in his county from which citizens or burgesses ought, or are accustomed, to come as this writ requires." In the 38th of Edward III. (1364), the reason for this negative return is rendered—" There are not any cities or boroughs (in Lancashire) that ought, or any of the citizens or burgesses of which are wont, to come to the said Parliament, on account of their debility or poverty." In the following year (1365) the case is still more strongly put—" There is not any city or borough from which any citizens or burgesses are able or accustomed to come, according to the tenor of the writ, by reason of their debility and poverty." In the 2d of Richard II. (1378-79), when the parliamentary writs were addressed to the Duke of Lancaster, this plea of debility is not confined to the county, but is extended to the whole duchy; and it is stated that there are not any burgesses in the duchy of Lancaster who were accustomed to come to our lord the king's Parliament because of their poverty. In the last year of this king's reign (1399) the plea of poverty is again reduced within the limits of the county, and it is said that there are not any citizens or burgesses within the county of Lancaster who have been accustomed in times past to come to any Parliaments. Our ancestors, so far from aspiring to an increase in their boroughs, were anxious, in the language of modern legislation, to merge those they had in schedule A, conceiving the cost of their borough members, though limited to the very moderate sum of two shillings a-day [1] during Parliaments of comparatively short duration, not sufficiently repaid by the support of their local interests. On the subject of the payment of wages to the members of Parliament, considerable light is shed by a petition presented to the king in 8 Henry VI. (1430), by the Commons, and which is expressed in these words—" The Commons pray, that all cities, boroughs, towns, and hamlets, and the residents within them, except the lords spiritual and temporal coming to Parliament, and the ecclesiastics, and those cities and boroughs which find citizens or burgesses for Parliament, shall henceforth for ever contribute to the expenses of the knights elected, or to be elected, to Parliaments."

For two hundred and fifty years—that is, from the end of the thirteenth to the middle of the sixteenth century, about one hundred and twenty, or one hundred and thirty, cities and boroughs in England returned members pretty constantly to Parliament; and about thirty others returned them only occasionally, amongst which were the Lancashire boroughs, the sheriffs having taken upon themselves to dispense with the attendance of members for those boroughs, for the reasons stated in the writs.

[1] The wages to be received by members of Parliament were fixed by the 16th Edward II. (1322) at the low rate of four shillings a day for a knight of the shire, and two shillings a day for a citizen or burgess. There are, however, some instances in which a less sum than that established by statute was allowed; and it is on record that in 1463 Sir John Strange, the member for Dunwich, agreed with his constituents to take a cade and half a barrel of herrings as a composition for his wages. The last formal payment of wages to a member occurred in 1681, when Thomas King, who had been member for Harwich, obtained from the Lord Chancellor a writ de expensis bergensium lerandi. After notice to the Corporation of Harwich, Lord Campbell, in his life of Lord Chancellor Nottingham, cites this case, and expresses an opinion that the writ might still be claimed, without a new enactment to revive the former usage. The practice had fallen into disuetude some time before this, for Pepys, in his Diary, under date March 30th, 1668, writes: " At dinner we had a great deal of good discourse about Parliament: their number being uncertain and always at the will of the king to increase, as he saw reason to erect a new borough. But all concluded that the bane of the Parliament hath been the leaving off the old custom of the places allowing wages to those that served them in Parliament, by which they chose men that understood their business and would attend it, and they could expect an account from, which now they cannot: and so the Parliament is become a company of men unable to give account for the interest of the place they serve for."—C.

The following petition, presented by the Commons to the king in the same year, shows that the very moderate remuneration of the members was withheld, to their impoverishment, and to the detriment of the state :—

"Whereas the citizens and burgesses elected to Parliament have, from antient time, been accustomed to have of right, for wages and expenses each day during the sitting of Parliament, two shillings ; and for which wages each of them had from antient time, and of right ought to have, their writ to the sheriffs of the county where such cities or boroughs are, for them to levy and deliver to them the said wages, in the same manner as the knights of shires have had and used.　And whereas these wages are now withheld, and divers notable and wise persons, elected to Parliament, cannot attend without their utter ruin, and the national loss ; the Commons of this present Parliament pray the king to grant them the said wages, of two shillings each, every day, during the Session of Parliament."

Prynne has preserved a register of the time allowed to members of Parliament for travelling from Lancashire to certain places, when the Parliaments were held in those cities, from which it appears that two, and sometimes three days, were allowed for travelling to York, four days to Coventry, and five or six to London, in ordinary seasons; but in a snow or "foul weather" eight days was the *maximum* allowance for travelling from hence to a Parliament sitting at Westminster. In 7 of Henry VI. (1429) it is asserted in the sheriff's return, notwithstanding the fact to the contrary, that there is not any city or borough within the county of Lancaster, which was accustomed in times past to send any citizens or burgesses to Parliament, on account of their poverty and want of means, and therefore no mention is made of citizens and burgesses, as appears in the indenture annexed to the writ.[1]　Similar language is held in all the returns from Lancashire till 1 Edward VI. (1547), when Lancaster, Preston, Liverpool, and Wigan, resumed their elective franchise ; and in 1 Elizabeth (1558-59) Newton and Clitheroe were added to the boroughs of the county.　During the Commonwealth two returns were made by Manchester, but that town ceased to return members at the Restoration.

RICHARD II.

In the first year of the reign of Richard II. (1377), the king, in his writ of summons for the duchy of Lancaster, addressed to John of Gaunt, Duke of Lancaster, and King of Castile and Leon, after announcing that Charles of France had overrun Flanders, and was meditating an attack upon the English city of Calais, informed his beloved uncle, that, for the better defence of his kingdom, and of the Anglican church, and to afford succour to his allies, he designed to embark for the Continent; and for the good government of the kingdom while he was absent, the duke was commanded to send from his duchy two knights from the county palatine of Lancaster, two citizens from each city, and two burgesses from each borough, within the same, to Parliament, having full power, from him (the duke) and the commons of the duchy, to take the necessary measures therein.　This writ is preserved in the archives of the duchy of Lancaster.[2]

The members returned to Parliament (Westminster, October 13, 1377) as knights of the shire for the county of Lancaster, in virtue of the writ, were "Joh'es Boteler" and "Nich. de Haveryngton," who, after a session of sixty-six days, received a writ de expensis to the amount of £26 8s.; but no citizens or burgesses were returned from any city or borough of the duchy or county of Lancaster.　In the second year of Richard II. (1378) "Joh'es Botiller, Chivaler," and "Rad'us de Ipre," were returned for the county of Lancaster, at the Parliament which met at Gloucester, October 20, 1378, as appears from the Roll Cl. 2 Rich. II. m. 22 d., on which Prynne observes that the writ in this roll was issued to the Duke of Lancaster, and to his vicegerent, for the knights of the duchy ; that in the writ to the duke this clause, "as well within the liberties as beyond," is omitted, and this clause of exception (inserted in all other writs for knights' expenses in other counties), "the cities and boroughs of which the citizens and burgesses to our Parliament, etc., shall come, so far as excepted," because the sheriffs of Lancashire then and before returned, "There is not any city nor any borough within the bailiwick from which any citizens or burgesses to the said Parliament ought (or are wont) to come, because of their weakness or poverty ;" and in this very year made this return, "And there are not any citizens or burgesses in the aforesaid duchy who have been wont to come to any Parliament, because of their poverty and debility."

The other knights of the shire returned for the county of Lancaster during the reign of Richard II. are enumerated in the following list :—

KNIGHTS.	PARLIAMENT AT	WAGES.
Nicholaus de Haryngton ...... Robertus de Urcewyk ....}	Westminster (April 24, 1379)	
Joh'es Botiller, Chivaler ...... Thos. Sutheworth, Chivaler ...}	Westminster, Monday after St. Hilary (Jany. 16, 1380)	£24 for 60 days.
		Cl. 3 R. II. m. 18 *d.*

---

[1] The sheriffs seem to have erected, nominated, returned, omitted, discontinued, revived, and recontinued boroughs, at their own will and pleasure.　Under the three first Edwards, thirteen sheriffs returned members thirteen times for Lancaster and six times for Preston ; yet in twenty-six intervening years, other sheriffs make returns to the effect set forth in the text.—*Parliaments and Councils of England*, p. 30.

[2] Roll. A, 6. m. 16.

KNIGHTS.	PARLIAMENT AT	WAGES.
Joh'es Botiller, Chivaler ...... Thos. de Suthworth, Chivaler...	Northampton, Monday after all Saints (Nov. 5, 1380)	£19 : 12s. for 49 days
		Cl. 4 *R. II. m.* 20 *d.*
Will de Athirton................. Robt. de Urcewyk	Westminster, Morrow of All Souls (Nov. 3, 1381)	£38 : 8s. for 96 days.
		Cl. 5 *R. II. m.* 22 *d.*
Roger de Pylkynton, Chivaler. Robt. de Clifton.................	Westminster, Morrow of St. John (May 7, 1382)	£10 for 25 days.
		Cl. 5 *R. II. m.* 5 *d.*
Joh'es Assheton .... Robert Usewick	Westminster, Monday, Octaves of St. Michael (Oct. 6, 1382)	£10 : 16s. for 27 days.
		Cl. 6 *R. II. p.* 1 *m.* 17 *d.*
Ric'us de Hoghton............... Robt. de Clifton	Westminster, Monday, three weeks of Quadragesima (Feb. 23, 1383)........	£10 : 8s. for 36 days.
		Cl. 6 *R. II. p.* 2 *m.* 13 *d.*
Walterus Urswyk, Chivaler ... John Holcroft.....................	Westminster, Monday before All Saints (Oct. 26, 1383)	£8 : 16s. for 40 days.
		Cl. 7 *R. II. m.* 23 *d.*
Roger de Pilkington, Chivaler Thos. Gerard	New Sarum, Friday after St. Mark (April 29, 1384)	£16 for 40 days.
		Cl. 7 *R. II. m.* 1 *d.*
Robt. Ursewick, Chivaler ...... Will. de Tunstall, Chivaler ...	Westminster, Morrow of St. Martin (Saturday, Nov. 12, 1384)	£18 for 45 days.
		Cl. 8 *R. II. m.* 27 *d.*
Robt. Ursewyk, Chivaler ...... Thos. de Radecliffe...............	Westminster, Friday after St. Luke (Oct. 20, 1385)...........................	£23 : 4s. for 58 days.
		Cl. 9 *R. II. m.* 22 *d.*
Nic. de Haveryngton, Chivaler Robt. de Workesley	Westminster, 1st October (1386)	£28 for 71 days.
		Cl. 10 *R. II. m.* 16 *d.*
Joh. le Botiller de Weryngton, Chivaler .... Thos. Gerard	Westminster, Morrow of the Purification B. Mary (Monday, Feb. 3, 1388)[1]	£46 for 115 days.
		Cl. 11 *R. II.*
Joh. de Asheton, Chivaler...... Joh. de Croft, Chivaler	Cantebrigge, Morrow of Nat. B. Mary (Sept. 9, 1388)	£18 : 8s. for 46 days.
		Cl. 12 *R. II. m.* 14 *d.*
Rad. de Ipres, Chivaler .... Joh. de Assheton, Chivaler ..	Westminster, Monday after St. Hillary (Jan. 17, 1390)	£22 for 56 days.
		Cl. 13 *R. II. p.* 2 *m.* 7 *d.*
Joh. de Ursewyk, Chivaler ... Joh. de Croft, Chivaler	Westminster, Morrow of St. Martin (Saturday, Nov. 12, 1390) ....,.....	£30 : 12s. for 34 days.
		Cl. 14 *R. II. m.* 30 *d.*
Robt. de Ursewike, Chivaler... Robt. de Workesley	Westminster, Morrow of All Souls (Friday, Nov. 3, 1391)	£17 for 40 days.
		Cl. 15 *R. II. m.* 26 *d.*
Robt. de Ursewik, Chivaler ... Rad. de Ipre, Chivaler	Wynton, Octaves of St. Hillary (Monday, January 20, 1393)	£23 for 38 days.
		Cl. 16 *R. II. m.* 19 *d.*
Robt. de Ursewyke, Chivaler.. Thos. Gerard, Chivaler	Westminster, fifteen days of St. Hillary (Tuesday, Jan. 27, 1394)	£21 for 71 days.
		Cl. 17 *R. II. m.* 9 *d.*
Robt. de Ursewike, Chivaler... Thos. de Radecliff	Westminster, fifteen days of St. Hillary (Wednesday, Jan. 27, 1395)........	£12 : 16s. for 32 days.
		Cl. 18 *R. II. m.* 6 *d.*
Robt. de Ursewyke, Chivaler.. Ric. Molyneux.....................	Westminster, Feast of St. Vincent (Monday, Jan. 22, 1397)	£30 : 12s. for 34 days.
		Cl. 20 *R. II. p.* 2 *m.* 2 *d.*
Joh. Botiller de Weryngton, Chivaler .... Rad. de Radecliff	Westminster, Monday after Exalt. of Cross (Sept. 7, 1397), and adjourned to Shrewsbury (Monday, Jan. 28, 1398)	£16 : 8s. for 41 days.
		Cl. 21 *R. II. p.* 2 *m.* 9 *d.*

HENRY IV.

The duchy of Lancaster being now united with the crown, by the duke having become King of England, the parliamentary writs of summons, in the first and second years of the reign of Henry IV., were addressed to the sheriff of Lancaster, and not to the duke.   The members for the county returned in this reign were :—

[1] This Parliament has been called by some historians "The Parlia-ment that Wrought Wonders," and by others "The Merciless Parliament."   In it articles of high treason were exhibited against the king's ministers who were, accordingly, sentenced to death or banishment.—C.

KNIGHTS.	PARLIAMENT AT	WAGES.
Robt. de Ursewyk, Chivaler ... Hen. de Hoghton, Chivaler ... }	Westminster, Morrow of St. Michael, summoned by Richard II. (Sep. 30, 1399)	£26 : 16s. for 71 days. *Cl. 1 Hen. IV. P. 1 m. 21 d.*

The king (Richard II.) abdicated on the 29th September; the Parliament met on the 30th, but only sat for a single day, whence it is oftentimes called "The Shortest Parliament." Another Parliament was summoned to meet at Westminster, October 6th, 1399. (1 Henry IV.)

Robt. de Ursewyke, Chivaler.. Nich. de Atherton, Chivaler ... }	Westminster, Octaves of St. Hillary (Jan. 20, 1401)	£34 : 16s. for 66 days. *Cl. 2 H. IV. P. 1 m. 3 d.*
No returns found......	Westminster (Jany. 30, 1402)	*3 H. IV.*
Rich. de Hoghton, Chivaler ... Nic. de Haveryngton, Chivaler }	Westminster, Morrow of St. Michael (Sept. 30, 1402)	£27 for 69 days. *Cl. 4 H. IV. m. 34 d.*
Rad. de Radeclyff, Chivaler ... Robt. Laurence .... }	Westminster, Morrow of St. Hillary (Jan. 14, 1404).....................	£31 : 12s. for 69 days. *Cl. 5 H. IV. P. m. 10 d.*
Jac. Harryngton, Chivaler...... Rad. Staveley, Chivaler .... }	Coventry (6th of October, 1404)	£8 : 8s. for 46 days. *Cl. 6 H. IV. m. 5 d.*

Will. Botiller ....
 Rob't. Lawrence .... }
	Westminster (Monday, 1st March, 1406)....................................... ... ..
	     Adjourned to 25th April ....
	     Adjourned to 4th June ....
	     Adjourned to 25th Oct. ....
	     Adjourned to 22nd Dec. ... . }
		£71 :12s. for 189 days.
		 Cl. 8 H. IV. m. 7 d.

Henr. Hoghton, Chivaler ...... Rad. de Staneley, Chivaler ... }	Gloucester (20th October, 1407)........	£21 :12s. for 54 days. *Cl. 9 H. IV. m. 8 d.*
No returns found	Westminster (Jan. 27, 1410)	*11 H. IV.*
Johannes de Assheton, Chivaler .... Johannes del Bothe .... }	Westminster (Nov. 3, 1411)	*13 H. IV.*

To the Parliament held at Coventry in the sixth year of this monarch's reign (1404), the sheriffs were commanded not to return any lawyers—persons learned in the law. Lord Chancellor Beaufort, in framing the writs of summons, illegally inserted a prohibition that any apprentice or other man of the law should be elected, and hence this Parliament was called "The Lack-learning Parliament" (*Parliamentum Indoctum.*). Lord Campbell says the recklessness of the Commons may have arisen from their not having a single lawyer among them.

HENRY V.

The first return made in this reign (1 Henry V., May 14, 1413) of the knights of the shire for Lancashire transmits the names of "Joh. Assheton and Joh. de Stanley, chivalers." By a striking singularity the indenture mentions only the name of Sir John Stanley, and entirely omits that of his colleague, stating that Nich. Longford, knight, and all others named in the indenture after him, with unanimous consent and agreement, have made a free election, and given to John Stanley the younger full power to become a knight in the Parliament to be held at Westminster, to answer for themselves and all theirs, and for all the commons in the county of Lancaster, in those matters which, under favour of the king, shall happen to be ordained in Parliament. The corresponding indenture is lost.

In the next Parliament, "Rad. de Radcliff" and "Nich. Blundell" are returned as knights of the shire for this county January 29, 1414. (2 Henry V.)

2 Henry V.	Johannes de Stanley, Robertus Lawrence, *per indent*...............	(November 19, 1414.) [1]
3 Henry V.	No returns found	(October 21, 1415.)
3 Henry V.	do.	....	(March 16, 1416.)
4 Henry V.	do.	....	(October 19, 1416.)
5 Henry V.	do.	....	(November 16, 1417.)
7 Henry V.	Nicholaus Botiller de Rouclif, Johannes Laurence	(October 16, 1419.)
8 Henry V.	Ricardus de Shirburne, Johannes del Bothe	(December 2, 1420.)
9 Henry V.	Thomas de Radclyf, *miles*, Thomas de Urswyk.....................	(May 2, 1421.)
9 Henry V.	Johannes Byrom, Chivaler, Ricardus de Sherburn	(December 1, 1421.)

[1] At this election, eighteen electors, in full county court, with other "honest men and lieges" of the county of Lancaster, elected the knights *Parliaments and Councils of England*, p. 28.

HENRY VI.

The members returned to represent the county of Lancaster in this reign were—

1 Henry VI.	Thos. de Urswyk, Johannes Gerard del Bryn, armig.	(November 9, 1422.)
2 Henry VI.	Thomas de Radclyf, chiv., Radulphus de Radclyf del Smethelles	(October 20, 1423.)
3 Henry VI.	Radulphus fil. Necholai de Longford, miles, Ricardus de Radclyf de Radclyf, armig.	(April 30, 1425.)
4 Henry VI.	Johannes Botiller de Beausee, Nicholaus Botiller de Raucliff......	(February 18, 1426.)[1]
6 Henry VI.	Radulphus de Radclif, chiv., Thomas de Stanley	(October 13, 1427.)
8 Henry VI.	Johannes Byron, miles, Robertus fil. Roberti Laurence, miles ...	(October 13, 1429.)
9 Henry VI.	Johannes de Morley, Willielmus Gernet	(January 12, 1431.)
10 Henry VI.	Willielmus de Assheton, miles, Thomas de Haryngton	(May 12, 1432.)
11 Henry VI.	Thomas de Stanley, chiv., Thomas de Radclif, chiv.	(July 8, 1433.)
14 Henry VI.	Henricus de Halsall, Thomas Laurence	(October 10, 1435.)
15 Henry VI.	Thomas de Haryngton, Henricus de Halsall	(January 21, 1437.)
18 Henry VI.	No returns found	(November 12, 1439.)
20 Henry VI.	Thomas de Stanleigh, miles, Thomas de Haryngton de Hurnebe	(January 25, 1442.)
23 Henry VI.	No returns found	(February 25, 1445.)
25 Henry VI.	Thomas Stanley, knight, Thomas Harrington, Esq., *per indent.* ..	(February 10, 1447.)
27 Henry VI.	The same persons	(February 12, 1449.)
28 Henry VI.	Thomas Stanley, Johes. Butler, knights, *per indent.*	(November 6, 1449.)
29 Henry VI.	Thomas Stanley, Ricardus Haryngton, knights, *per indent.*	(November 6, 1450.)
31 Henry VI.	No returns found	(March 6, 1453.)
33 Henry VI.	Thomas Stanley, Alexander Radcliff, knights	(July 9, 1455.)
38 Henry VI.	Richus. Harrington, knight, Henry Halsall, *per indent.*	(November 20, 1459.)[2]
39 Henry VI.	Richd. Haryngton, knight, Henry Halsall	(October 7, 1460.)

In the seventh year of this king's reign (1428-9) the qualification of electors for counties, which had hitherto been undefined, was fixed by an Act of Parliament, which ordains that "the knights shall be chosen in every county by people dwelling and residing in the same county, whereof every one of them shall have land or tenement of the value of forty shillings by the year, at the least, over and above all charges," which is explained, by an Act of the 10th (1431-2) of the same king to mean freeholds of that value within the county for which the election is to be made. Hitherto all the freeholders, without exception, had claimed the right of voting for county members, in consequence of which, it is alleged, great outrages had arisen, "whereby manslaughter, riots, batteries, and divisions among the gentlemen and other people of the said counties shall very likely arise and be, unless convenient and due remedy be provided in this behalf." From the reign of Henry VI. to the present time [1886], no change has been judged necessary in this qualification, though the nominal money equivalent has in the meantime greatly increased.[3]

The agitation of the kingdom at this period, arising out of the wars between the houses of York and Lancaster, seems to have given rise to a violent stretch of the royal prerogative, the king having, of his own authority, summoned members to Parliament; and hence an Act of indemnity was passed 23 Henry VI. (1445), which provides, "that all such knights of any county, as are returned to the Parliament by virtue of the king's letters, without any other election, shall be good, and that no sheriff, for returning them, do incur the pains therefore provided."[4]

EDWARD IV.

The members returned for the county of Lancaster in this reign were—

1 Edward IV.	No returns found	(November 4, 1461.)
3 Edward IV.	No returns found	(April 29, 1463.)
7 Edward IV.	James Haryngton, Knt., William Haryngton, Knt.	(June 3, 1467.)
9 Edward IV	No returns found	(1469.)
10 Edward IV.	No returns found	(November 26, 1470.)
12 Edward IV.	Robert Harynton, John Assheton	(October 6, 1472.)
17 Edward IV.	George Stanley, Knt., James Haryngton, Knt...	(January 16, 1478.)
22 Edward IV.	No returns found	(1483.)

From 17 Edward IV. (1478) to 37 Henry VIII. (1545) all the returns, with the exception of a few fragments of those of the Parliament of 1542-4, have hitherto been supposed to be irretrievably lost. Within that period seventeen Parliaments were summoned and dissolved, viz., the 17 and 22

---

[1] Called "The Parliament of Bats," from the circumstance that orders were sent to the members that they should not wear swords, so they came to the Parliament, which met at Leicester, with long staves, and when these staves or bats were prohibited they had recourse to stones and leaden plummets.—C.

[2] "The Diabolical Parliament," in which it was enacted that all such knights of any county as were returned to the Parliament by virtue of the king's letters, without any other election, should be good, and that no sheriff, for returning them, should incur the penalties therefor provided by the 23 Henry VI. The queen, Margaret of Anjou, and her party carried all before them, from which circumstance, and the measures carried, it was called *Parliamentum diabolicum.*—C.

[3] In the original edition Mr. Baines states that since the reign of Henry VI. "the value of money has in the meantime *increased* tenfold." The error is in using the term "value" instead of "nominal equivalent." The truth is, that £5 in the reign of Henry VI. would have purchased 15 quarters of wheat, which, for 20 years before 1707 (when Fleetwood wrote his *Chronicon Preciosum*) cost £30. In other words, from Henry VI. to 1707 the value of money had *decreased* sixfold, instead of *increasing* tenfold. What is meant is, that the equivalent of £5 *temp.* Henry VI. was £30 in 1707—a sixfold increase in nominal amount.—H.

[4] Sir Robert Cotton's Abridgement, p. 664.

· Edward IV.; 1 Richard III.; 1, 3, 7, 11, and 12 Henry VII.; and 1, 3, 6, 14, 21, 28, 31, 33, and 37 Henry VIII. Fortunately a list of the Parliament of 21 Henry VIII. (1529-36) has within recent years been found among Lord Denbigh's papers, which happily preserves the names of that historical assembly, and this has been included in the Blue Book returns issued by order of the House of Commons, March, 1878. Since the publication of that volume a discovery has been made of the greater part of the returns of Henry VIII.'s last Parliament, which was originally summoned to meet at Westminster, January 30, 1544-5, but by prorogation was adjourned to Westminster, October 15, 1545, thence by further prorogation to New Windsor, November 23, 1545, and by final writs to meet at Westminster instead of New Windsor, November 23, 1545. It was dissolved in consequence of the king's death, January 31, 1546-7. From these recently-discovered documents we get the following returns of the members elected for Lancashire:—

21 Henry VIII.	Henricus Faryington, armiger, Andreas Barton, armiger	(November 3, 1529.)
37 Henry VIII.	Thomas Holcroft, miles, Johannes Kechyn, armiger	(November 23, 1545.)

From 1 Edward VI. (1547) to 16 Charles I. (1640) the writs are regular, and the following are the members returned as knights of the shire for Lancashire:—

1 Edward VI.	Thurstan Tyldesley, Esq.—John Kechyn, Esq.	(November 4, 1547.)
7 Edward VI.	Richard Houghton (in whose place Robert Worsley, Knt.)—Tho. Butler, Esq.	(March 1, 1553.)
1 Mary	Richd. Sherborne, Knt.—John Rygmayden the Elder, Esq.	(October 5, 1553.)
1 Mary	Tho. Stanley, Knt.—Tho. Langton, Knt.	(October 2, 1554.)
1 & 2 Philip and Mary	Tho. Stanley, Knt.—John Holcroft, Knt.	(November 12, 1554.)
2 & 3 Philip and Mary	Tho. Stanley, Knt.—Will. Stanley, Knt.	(October 21, 1555.)
4 & 5 Philip and Mary	Tho. Talbot, Knt.—John Holcroft, sen., Knt.	(January 20, 1558.)
1 Elizabeth	John Atherton, Knt.—Rob. Worseley, Knt.	(January 23, 1559.)
5 Elizabeth	Tho. Gerard, Knt.—John Southworth, Knt.	(January 10, 1563.)
13 Elizabeth	Tho. Butler—John Radcliffe, Esq.	(1571.)
14 Elizabeth	John Radcliff, Esq.—Edm. Trafford, Esq., Master of the Rolls	(May 8, 1572.)
27 Elizabeth	Gilbert Gerard, Knt.—Rich. Molineux., of Sefton	(November 23, 1584.)
28 Elizabeth	John Atherton, Esq.—Rich. Holland, Esq.	(October 15, 1586.)
31 Elizabeth	Tho. Gerard, son of Sir Gilbert Gerard, Knt.—Tho. Walmesley, serjeant-at-law	(November 12, 1588.)
35 Elizabeth	Tho. Molineux, Knt.—Tho. Gerard, jun., Knt.	(February 19, 1593.)
39 Elizabeth	Tho. Gerard, jun., Knt., of Astley, Marshal of the Household.—Robt. Hesketh, Esq., of Rufforthe	(February 9, 1598.)
43 Elizabeth	Rich. Houghton, Knt.—Tho. Hesketh, Attorney of the Court of Wards	(October 27, 1601.)
1 James I.	Rich. Molineux, Knt.—Rich. Houghton, Knt.	(March 19, 1604.)
12 James I.	Gilbert Houghton, Knt.—John Radcliff, Knt.	(April 5, 1614.)[1]
18 James I.	John Radcliff, Knt.—Gilbert Houghton, Knt.	(January 16, 1621.)
21 James I.	John Radcliff, Knt.—Tho. Walmesley, Knt.	(February 12, 1624.)
1 Charles I.	Rich. Molineux, Bart.—John Radcliff, Knt.	(May 17, 1625.)
1 Charles I.	Rob. Stanley, Esq.—Gilbert Houghton, Knt.	(February 6, 1626.)
3 Charles I.	Rich. Molineux, Knt. and Bart.—Alex. Radcliff, Knight of the Bath	(March 17, 1628.)
16 Charles I.	Gilbert Houghton, Knt. and Bart.—Will. ffarrington, Esq.	(April 13, 1640.)[2]
16 Charles I.	Ralph Ashton, Esq.—Roger Kirkby, Esq.—Rich. Houghton, Esq., vice Roger Kirkby, disabled to serve	(November 3, 1640.)[3]

In 15 Henry VIII. (1523) Sir Thomas More, then chancellor of the duchy of Lancaster, held the office of speaker of the House of Commons. The learned chancellor's connection with the duchy has led to the mistake that he represented Lancashire in Parliament, and consequently that this county has had the honour to supply a member to the speaker's chair; but this is an error.

In 1 Edward VI. (1547) writs of parliamentary summons were issued to Lancaster, Preston, Liverpool, and Wigan; and each of these places at that period, if not earlier, resumed, by royal authority, the elective franchise. Queen Elizabeth, in the first year of her Majesty's reign, made a further accession to the Lancashire boroughs by the addition of Newton and Clitheroe; and all these six boroughs regularly returned members to Parliament from that time until the passing of the Reform Act of 1832, when Newton was disfranchised and Clitheroe deprived of one member; but by the same Act it was provided that two members should be given respectively to Manchester, Oldham, Bolton, and Blackburn, and one each to Salford, Ashton-under-Lyne, Bury, Rochdale, and Warrington.

[1] Prior to the meeting of this Parliament certain of the King's ministers, among them Bacon and Somerset, undertook to manage the Commons so as to secure the passing of the votes desired. The promise became known out of doors, and the ministers, in consequence, were nick-named "undertakers." It was summoned in the expectation that it would grant supplies, but instead of this the members insisted on the previous discussion of grievances, and as it proved obdurate, it was dissolved on the 7th June, without having passed a single bill, and from this circumstance was called "The Addled Parliament."—C.

[2] Called "The Short Parliament," from its being dissolved after a session of three weeks.—C.

[3] "The Long Parliament," which many thought "would never have had a beginning, and afterwards that it would never have had an end." When the members were about to meet, on the 6th December, 1648, Colonel Pride surrounded the House with two regiments, and excluded 160 members. "Pride's Purge," as it was called, was followed by the arbitrary act of Cromwell, who, on the 20th April, 1653, violently dispersed the members, and called upon Col. Charles Worsley, afterwards member for Manchester, who had command of the soldiery, to "take away the bauble." After many vicissitudes, in which fragments of this Parliament were called together again and again for special purposes, the appearance of legal dissolution was given by a bill for "Dissolving the Parliament begun and holden at Westminster, 3rd of November, 1640, and that the day of dissolution shall be from this day, March 16th, 1659" (-60).—C.

It appears that nomination boroughs were perfectly familiar so early as the reign of Elizabeth; and it is probable that both Newton and Clitheroe always partook of this character; but the most flagrant instance of the kind upon record in these early times is to be found in a bundle of returns of parliamentary writs in 14 Queen Elizabeth (1572), which, though unconnected with the county of Lancaster, may not inaptly be introduced in this place. The document is in the chapel of the Rolls, and is expressed in the following terms:—

"To all Christian people to whom this present Writing shall come : I, Dame Dorothy Packington, widow, late wife of Sir John Packington, Kt., Lord and Owner of the Town of Aylesbury, send greeting. KNOW ye Me, the said Dame Dorothy Packington, to have chosen, named, and appointed my trusty and well-beloved Thomas Litchfield and George Burden, Esqrs. to be my Burgesses of my said town of Aylesbury. And whatsoever the said Thomas and George, Burgesses, shall do in the Service of the Queen's Highness in that present Parliament, to be holden at Westminster the Eighth day of May next ensuing the Date hereof, I, the same Dorothy Packington, do ratify and approve to be my own Act, as fully and wholly as if I were or might be present there. In WITNESS whereof, to these presents I have set my Seal this Fourth Day of May, in the Fourteenth Year of the Reign of our Sovereign Lady Elizabeth, by the Grace of God, of England, France, and Ireland Queen, Defender of the Faith, etc."

In the 26th year of this queen's reign (1584) a very extraordinary claim was set up to parliamentary nomination by Sir Ralph Sadler, "a knight of noted virtue," in respect of his office of chancellor of the duchy of Lancaster, which was no less than the right to nominate both the members to represent the borough of Leicester in Parliament. The account given in the archives of the borough of this claim, and of the manner in which it was disposed of, is as follows:—

"Nov. 12, 26 ELIZ.—At a common hall, the sheriff's precept being read, and after that Sir Ralph Sadler's letter for nomination of both our burgesses, and other letters ; it is agreed, that Sir Ralph Sadler, knight, chancellor of the duchy of Lancaster, shall have the nomination of one of the burgesses; who thereupon nominated Henry Skipwith, Esq. ; and the other chosen was Thomas Johnson, one of her Majesty's serjeants-at-arms ; and either of them promised to bear their own charges."

On what authority the chancellor grounded his pretensions to nominate members for Leicester, except that it is within the duchy of Lancaster, does not appear, nor does it appear that any similar claim was ever made by any other chancellor, either before or since. It may be inferred from the corporation record that members began about this time to serve without wages; and it is probable that the practice was gradually discontinued, till at length it wholly ceased.

COMMONWEALTH.

The following are the names of the members for the county of Lancaster elected during the Commonwealth:—

1653. Will. West, John Sawry, Rob. Cunliss. (July 4.)
[The name of "PRAISE GOD BAREBONE," occurs in this Parliament in the list of London members.]
1654. Rich. Holland, Gilbert Ireland, Rich. Standish, Will. Ashurst. (Sep. 8.)
1656. Sir Rich. Houghton, Bart. Col. Gilbert Ireland, Col. Rich. Holland, Col. Rich. Standish. (Sep. 17.)
1658-9. George Book [? Rooke], Bart. ; Alex. Rigby, Esq. (Jany. 27.)[1]

11 CHARLES II.[2] TO 30 VICTORIA.

The Parliament of 1653 was a packed Parliament, returned by Cromwell, the Lord Protector, and consisted of only one hundred and twenty-one members, of whom one hundred and ten were for England, five each for Scotland and Ireland, and one for Wales. In 1654 the right of election was again partially restored, the number of members being augmented to four hundred, of whom two hundred and seventy were chosen by the counties; the remainder were elected by London and other considerable corporations and towns, Manchester and Leeds being amongst the number. To the Parliament of 1653 neither Lancaster, Preston, Liverpool, Wigan, or Clitheroe sent any members, but the county returned three; to those of 1654 and 1656 Lancaster, Preston, Liverpool, and Wigan sent each one member, and the county four. To the Parliament of 1658-9 Lancaster, Preston, Liverpool, Wigan, and Newton sent two members each; and the county two; but no return was made for Clitheroe during the whole period of the Commonwealth. Though the Government professed to be popular, the elective franchise was very much abridged during this period, and an estate of two hundred pounds value was necessary to confer the right of voting. In other respects the elections were unobjectionable except that all those who had carried arms against the Parliament, as well as their sons, were prohibited from voting at the elections.

[1] This was the only Parliament summoned in the name of Richard Cromwell, "by the grace of God Protector of the Commonwealth of England, Scotland, and Ireland, and the dominions thereto belonging." It has a unique character, for, whereas Oliver Cromwell had by his own authority reformed the composition of the House of Commons, his son Richard, by a similar assumption of power, undid the work of his predecessor and restored the representation to its former condition. The small boroughs which had recently been disfranchised regained their lost privilege ; Manchester, Leeds, Halifax ceased to return members; and the county of York was again limited to two knights. Macaulay says the change was extremely popular, as being the restoration of a system which, however anomalous, had its origin in law and prescription.—C.

[2] The reign of Charles II. is dated from the death of his royal father, in 1649, in the calendars ; and that chronology is adopted in this list, though his reign did not commence de facto till 1660.

List of the knights of the shire for the county of Lancaster, from the Restoration to the present time:—

12 Charles II.	1660.	Sir Roger Bradshaw	Edward Stanley.
13 Charles II.	1661.	The same	The same.
29 Charles II.	1678.	Peter Bold	Charles Gerrard.
31 Charles II.	1679.	Charles Gerard	Sir Charles Hoghton.
33 Charles II.	1681.	Sir Charles Houghton	The same.
1 James II.	1685.	Sir Roger Bradshaw	James Holt.
3 James II.	1688.	Lord Brandon	Sir Charles Houghton.
2 William and Mary	1690.	James Stanley, Charles, Lord Brandon..	Ralph Assheton, vice Chas. Lord Brandon, called to Upper House as Earl of Macclesfield.
7 William III.	1695.	The same	The same.
10 William III.	1698.	The same	Fitton Garrerd.
12 William III.	1701.	The same	Robert Bold.
13 William III.	1701.	The same	The same.
1 Anne	1702.	The same	The same.
4 Anne	1705.	The same	Richard Shuttleworth of Gawthorpe.
7 Anne	1708.	The same	The same.
9 Anne	1710.	The same	The same.
12 Anne	1713.	Sir John Bland, of Hulme	The same.
1 George I.	1715.	The same	The same.
8 George I.	1722.	The same	The same.
1 George II.	1727.	Sir Edward Stanley	The same.
3 George II.	1734.	The same	The same.
15 George II.	1741.	Lord Strange	The same.
21 George II.	1747.	The same	The same.
27 George II.	1754.	The same	Peter Bold of Bold.
1 George III.	1761.	The same	James Shuttleworth.
2 George III.	1762.	J. Smith (Lord Strange)	James Shuttleworth, Esq.
8 George III.	1768.	The same	Lord Arch. Hamilton.
		Richard L. V. Molyneux	Sir Thomas Egerton, Bart.
15 George III.	1774.	Edward Smith Stanley (Lord Stanley)..	The same.
		Hon. Thomas Stanley, vice Edward Smith Stanley, called to the Upper House.	
		Thomas Stanley, of Cross Hall, Esq., vice Thomas Stanley, deceased.	
21 George III.	1780.	The same	Sir Thomas Egerton, Bart., of Heaton
24 George III.	1784.	The same	John Blackburne, Esq., of Hale.
30 George III.	1790.	The same	The same.
36 George III.	1796.	The same	The same.
41 George III.	1801.	The same	The same.
42 George III.	1802.	The same	The same.
46 George III.	1806.	The same	The same.
47 George III.	1807.	The same	The same.
53 George III.	1812.	Lord Stanley	The same.
58 George III.	1818.	The same	The same.
1 George IV.	1820.	The same	The same.
7 George IV.	1826.	The same	The same.
1 William IV.	1830.	The same	John Wilson Patten, Esq.
1 William IV.	1831.	The same	Benjamin Heywood, Esq.

Of all the old Lancashire boroughs Liverpool may be said to have risen most into eminence; and for this distinction it seems indebted rather to the local advantages of its marine situation than to its chartered privileges. Preston has at all times occupied a high station amongst the towns of the county; but for several centuries it was perfectly stationary in its wealth and population; and it was not till its corporate restrictions were materially relaxed that it began to increase in either. The other old boroughs of the county have not undergone any material changes in the lapse of ages, while a number of the other towns of Lancashire have sprung into existence and been increasing within the last century in a ratio altogether unexampled.

For many years, and indeed for some ages before the Reform Act of 1832, the political character of the county representation displayed itself in a division of the return of members between the Stanley family, as the head of the Whig party, and the Blackburnes, of Hale Hall, as representing the Tory interest; but at the general election in 1831 the disposition of the county in favour of the then pending reform bill (of which the most conspicuous features were its disfranchising the decayed boroughs, and conferring the elective franchise on many of the populous unrepresented towns of the county) was so strong, that this tacit arrangement was no longer acted upon, but two members were returned, both of them in favour of the new system.

That "poverty and debility," which for so long a period induced the inhabitants of all the parliamentary boroughs in the county of Lancaster to suffer their elective rights to sink into abeyance now no longer exists, but has given place to an amount of wealth and population which fully entitles most of its boroughs and several other towns in the county to send their representatives to the national councils. By the provisions of the Reform Act of 1832, 2 Will. IV cap. 45, passed 7th June, the representation of the county of Lancaster and its boroughs stood thus :—

	Members.
Lancaster, Preston, Liverpool, and Wigan (2 members each, and unaltered)	8
Newton (disfranchised)	0
Clitheroe, instead of two members, to return	1
Lancashire, instead of two members, to return—	
North Lancashire	2
South Lancashire	2

New Boroughs.

Manchester..	2
Ashton-under-Lyne	1
Bolton-le-Moors..	2
Blackburn	2
Bury	1
Oldham	2
Rochdale..	1
Salford	1
Warrington	1
	—
	26

Before the Reform Act, Lancashire and its boroughs returned 14 members to Parliament; so that the increased number for the county and boroughs by that Act was 12, or nearly double.

MEMBERS ELECTED SINCE THE PASSING OF THE REFORM ACT, 1832.

Since the passing of the Reform Act in 1832, there have been fourteen Parliaments, the general elections for which were in December 1832, January 1835, August 1837, July 1841, August 1847, July 1852, March 1857, April 1859, July 1865, November 1868, February 1874, April 1880, November 1885, and July 1886. The first two of these Parliaments were in the reign of William IV., the last twelve in that of her present Majesty; and the Parliament elected in July, 1886, is styled the twelfth Parliament of Queen Victoria. As in 1832 a new Parliamentary era commenced, we give the numbers of registered electors in 1832 and 1865, and the number of votes polled for each candidate at every contested election. By the Reform Act the county of Lancaster was separated into two divisions for representative and electoral purposes, usually termed North and South Lancashire.

Lancashire, North (Two Members).
Electors in 1832, 6,593—in 1865, 13,006.

Elections.

1832, Dec.	Right Hon. E. G. Stanley........	(L)
	John Wilson Patten	(C)
	On Mr. Stanley becoming Colonial Secretary :	
1833, March.	Right Hon. E. G. Stanley......................	(L)
1835, Jan.	Lord Stanley	(L)
	John Wilson Patten	(C)
1837, Aug.	Lord Stanley	(L)
	John Wilson Patten	(C)
1841, July.	Lord Stanley	(C)
	John Wilson Patten	(C)
	On Lord Stanley again becoming Colonial Secretary :	
1841, Sept.	Lord Stanley	(C)
	On Lord Stanley's accepting the Chiltern Hundreds and being then created a peer :	
1844, Sept.	J. Talbot Clifton ....(Protec.)	
1847, Aug.	J. Wilson Patten	(C)
	James Heywood...........	(L)
1852, July.	John Wilson Patten	(C)
	James Heywood.................................	(L)
1857, March.	John Wilson Patten	(C)
	Lord Cavendish..............................	(L)
1859, April.	John Wilson Patten	(C)
	Marquis of Hartington	(L)
1865, July.	John Wilson Patten	(C)
	Marquis of Hartington	(L)
	On Mr. Patten accepting the Chancellorship of the Duchy of Lancaster :	
1867, July.	John Wilson Patten	(C)

Lancashire, South (Two Members).
Electors in 1832, 10,039—in 1865, 21,555.

Elections.

1832, Dec.	George W. Wood	(L)	5694
	Viscount Molyneux ....-........	(L)	5575
	Sir T. Hesketh, Bart......................	(C)	3082
1835, Jan.	Lord Francis Egerton	(C)	5620
	Hon. R. Bootle Wilbraham	(C)	4729
	Viscount Molyneux	(L)	4626
	George W. Wood	(L)	4394
1837, Aug.	Lord F. Egerton........................	(C)	7822
	Hon. R. Bootle Wilbraham...........	(C)	7645
	Edward Stanley.........................	(L)	6576
	Charles Towneley	(L)	6044
1841, July.	Lord Francis Egerton	(C)	
	Hon. R. Bootle Wilbraham	(C)	
	On decease of Mr. Wilbraham :		
1844, May.	William Entwisle	(C)	7571
	William Brown	(L)	6973
	On Lord Francis Egerton becoming Earl of Ellesmere :		
1846, June.	William Brown	(L)	
1847, Aug.	William Brown	(L)	
	Hon. C. P. Villiers......................	(L)	
	On Mr. Villiers electing to sit for Wolverhampton :		
1847, Dec.	Alexander Henry	(L)	
1852, July.	William Brown	(L)	
	John Cheetham.....	(L)	
1857, March.	William Brown....................... ...	(L)	
	John Cheetham...........	(L)	

Elections.	Lancashire, South—con.		
1859, April.	Hon. Algernon F. Egerton	(C)	7470
	William John Legh	(C)	6983
	John Cheetham	(L)	6835
	J. Pemberton Heywood	(L)	6753
	A third seat having been granted to this constituency :		
1861, Aug.	Charles Turner	(LC)	9714
	John Cheetham	(L)	8898

Elections.	Lancashire, South—con.		
1865, July.	Hon. Algernon F. Egerton	(C)	9167
	Charles Turner	(C)	8801
	Right. Hon. W. E. Gladstone	(L)	8786
	William John Legh	(C)	8476
	H. Yates Thompson	(L)	7703
	James P. Heywood	(L)	7653

Under the provisions of the Representation of the People Act, 1867, the county was divided into four separate constituencies, viz., North, North-east, South-east, and South-west Lancashire, two representatives being assigned to each. By the same Act an additional member each was given to Liverpool, Manchester, and Salford; Lancaster was deprived of its two representatives (for bribery), one each being given to Burnley and Stalybridge, the last-named borough being partly in Lancashire and partly in Cheshire.

After the passing of the Representation of the People Act, 1867, the elections for the several divisions of the county were as under :—

Elections.	North Lancashire :		
1868, Nov.	Capt. Hon. Fredk. A. Stanley	(C)	6832
	Rt. Hen. John Wilson-Patten	(C)	6681
	Marquis of Hartington	(L)	5296
1874, Feb.	Capt. Hon. F. A. Stanley, Unopposed	(C)	
	Rt. Hn. J. Wilson-Patten, Unopposed	(C)	
	On Mr. Wilson-Patten being created Baron Winmarleigh, a new writ was issued :		
1874, March.	Thomas Henry Clifton, Unopposed .	(C)	
1880, April.	Right Hon. Fredk. A. Stanley	(C)	8172
	Major-Gen. Randle Joseph Feilden...	(C)	7505
	Thomas Storey	(L)	6500

Elections.	South-East Lancashire :		
1868, Nov.	Hon. Algernon Fulke Egerton	(C)	8290
	John Snowdon Henry	(C)	8012
	Right Hon. Frederick Peel	(L)	7024
	Henry Yates Thompson	(L)	6953
1874, Feb.	Lieut.-Col. Hon. Algernon F. Egerton	(C)	9187
	Edward Hardcastle	(C)	9015
	Peter Rylands	(L)	7464
	John Edward Taylor......	(L)	7453
1880, April.	Robert Leake	(L)	11313
	William Agnew	(L)	11291
	Hon. Algernon Fulke Egerton.........	(C)	10569
	Edward Hardcastle	(C)	10419

Elections.	North-East Lancashire :		
1868, Nov.	James Maden Holt......	(C)	3612
	J. P. Chamberlain Starkie	(C)	3594
	Sir Ughtred Jas. Kay-Shuttleworth .	(L)	3463
	William Fenton	(L)	3441
1874, Feb.	James Maden Holt	(C)	4578
	J. P. Chamberlain Starkie	(C)	4488
	Sir Ughtred Jas. Kay-Shuttleworth	(L)	4401
	Lord Edward Cavendish	(L)	4297
1880, April.	Marquis of Hartington	(L)	6682
	Frederick William Grafton	(L)	6513
	William Farrer Ecroyd......	(C)	5231
	J. P. Chamberlain Starkie	(C)	5183

Elections.	South-West Lancashire :		
1868, Nov.	Richard Assheton Cross	(C)	7729
	Charles Turner	(C)	7676
	Rt. Hon. Wm. Ewart Gladstone	(L)	7415
	Henry R. Grenfell......	(L)	6939
1874, Feb.	Richard Assheton Cross, Unopposed	(C)	
	Charles Turner, Unopposed	(C)	
	On the death of Mr. Charles Turner, a new writ was issued :		
1875, Nov.	Col. John Ireland Blackburne, Unop.	(C)	
1880, April.	Rt. Hon. Sir R. A. Cross, G.C.B. ...	(C)	11420
	Colonel John Ireland Blackburne ...	(C)	10905
	William Rathbone...... ..	(L)	9616
	Hon. Henry H. Molyneux......	(L)	9207

Under the Redistribution of Seats Act, 1885 (48 and 49 Vic. c. 23), the distribution of seats was changed, and the aggregate representation increased from 33 to 57 members. Under its provisions the borough of Clitheroe ceased to return a member, and became merged in its division of the county; the borough of Wigan was deprived of one member, and an increased number of representatives was given to the boroughs of Liverpool (six), Manchester (three), and Salford (one); and Barrow-in-Furness and St. Helens were created parliamentary boroughs with one member each. The county now returns 23 members, viz., one each for the North Lonsdale, Lancaster, Blackpool, and Chorley divisions of North Lancashire; one each for the Darwen, Clitheroe, Accrington, and Rossendale divisions of North-east Lancashire; one each for the Westhoughton, Heywood, Middleton, Radcliffe-cum-Farnworth, Eccles, Stretford, Gorton, and Prestwich divisions of South-east Lancashire; and one each for the Southport, Ormskirk, Bootle, Widnes, Newton, Ince, and Leigh divisions of South-west Lancashire. The boroughs return 34 members, viz., Liverpool (nine), Manchester (six), Salford (three), Blackburn, Bolton, Oldham, and Preston (two each); and Ashton-under-Lyne, Barrow-in-Furness, Burnley, Bury, Rochdale, St. Helens, Warrington, and Wigan (one each).

Since the passing of the Act the elections for the several divisions of the county have been as follows :—

Elections.	Div.	North Lancashire.		
1885, Nov.	North Lonsdale. (one)	W. G. Ainslie	(C)	4166
		Sir Farrer Herschell ...	(L)	3941
1886, July.		W. G. Ainslie	(C)	4063
		W. M. Edmunds	(GL)	3263

Elections.	Div.	North Lancashire—con.		
1885, Nov.	Lancaster	Major G. B. H. Marton	(C)	4387
		J. C. M'Coan	(L)	3530
1886, July.		J. Williamson	(GL)	3886
		Col. G. B. H. Marton...	(C)	3691

19

Elections.	Div.	North Lancashire—con.		
1885, Nov.	Blackpool	Colonel Rt. Hon. Fredk. A. Stanley, Unop. ...	(C)	
1886, July.		Colonel Rt. Hon. Fredk. A. Stanley, Unop. ...	(C)	
		Accepted the Chiltern Hundreds on being created a peer.		
1886, Aug.	Blackpool	Sir Matthew White Ridley, Bart.	(C)	6263
		J. O. Pilkington	(GL)	2513
1885, Nov.	Chorley	Lieut.-Gen. R. J. Feilden	(C)	5867
		H. Wright	(L)	2808
1886, July.		Lieut.-Gen. Randle J. Feilden, Unopposed .	(C)	

North-East Lancashire:

Elections.	Div.			
1885, Nov.	Darwen	Viscount Cranborne ...	(C)	5878
		John Gerald Potter ...	(L)	5873
1886, July.		Viscount Cranborne ...	(C)	6085
		John Slagg	(GL)	5350
1885, Nov.	Clitheroe........	Sir Ughtred Jas. Kay-Shuttleworth	(L)	6821
		J. O. S. Thursby.........	(C)	4462
1886, April.		Sir U. J. Kay-Shuttleworth	(L)	
		On appointment as Chancellor of the Duchy of Lancaster re-elected unopposed.		
1886, July.	Clitheroe........	Sir U. J. Kay-Shuttleworth, Unopposed ...	(GL)	
1885, Nov.	Accrington......	F. W. Grafton	(L)	5320
		R. T. Hermon Hodge ...	(C)	4842
1886, July		R. T. Hermon Hodge ...	(C)	4971
		Joseph F. Leese	(GL)	4751
1885, Nov.	Rossendale	Marquis of Hartington	(L)	6060
		W. Farrer Ecroyd	(C)	4228
1886, July.		Marquis of Hartington	(LU)	5399
		Thomas Newbigging ...	(GL)	3949

South-East Lancashire:

Elections.	Div.			
1885, Nov.	Westhoughton..	Frank Hardcastle	(C)	6011
		E. Cross	(L)	3741
1886, July.		F. Hardcastle, Unop. ...	(C)	
1885, Nov.	Heywood	Isaac Hoyle..............	(L)	4538
		J. Kenyon	(C)	3955
1886, July.		Isaac Hoyle	(GL)	4206
		J. Grant Lawson........	(C)	3962
1885, Nov.	Middleton	Colonel Salis Schwabe .	(L)	5882
		T. Fielden	(C)	4885
1886, July.		T. Fielden	(C)	5126
		C. H. Hopwood, Q.C....	(GL)	4808

Elections.	Div.	South-East Lancashire—con.		
1885, Nov.	Radcliffe-cum-Farnworth	{ Robert Leake	(L)	5092
		W. W. B. Hulton	(C)	4579
1886, July.		Robert Leake	(GL)	4695
		Sir Fredk. Milner, Bart.	(C)	4559
1885, Nov.	Eccles	Hon. A. G. J. Egerton..	(C)	4559
		Vernon Kirk Armitage.	(L)	4312
1886, July.		Hon. A. G. J. Egerton..	(C)	4277
		Ellis D. Gosling	(GL)	3985
1885, Nov.	Stretford........	William Agnew	(L)	4860
		J. W. Maclure...........	(C)	4676
1886, July.		J. W. Maclure...........	(C)	4750
		William Agnew	(GL)	4011
1885, Nov.	Gorton	Richard Peacock......	(L)	5300
		D. J. Flattely	(C)	3552
1886, July.		Richard Peacock........	(GL)	4592
		Vist. Grey de Wilton...	(C)	4135
1885, Nov.	Prestwich	Abel Buckley	(L)	5414
		R. G. C. Mowbray	(C)	4686
1886, July.		R. G. C. Mowbray	(C)	4843
		Abel Buckley	(GL)	4704

South-West Lancashire:

Elections.	Div.			
1885, Nov.	Southport	G. A. Pilkington, M.D...	(L)	3741
		J. E. Edwardes-Moss ...	(C)	3581
1886, July.		Hon. G. N. Curzon......	(C)	3723
		G. A. Pilkington.........	(GL)	3262
1885, Nov.	Ormskirk	A. B. Forwood	(C)	5133
		Professor J. P. Sheldon	(L)	2343
1886, July.		A. B. Forwood, Unop. ...	(C)	
1885, Nov.	Bootle...........	Col. T. M. Sandys	(C)	6715
		S. H. Whitbread........	(L)	3915
1886, July.		Col. T. M. Sandys, Unop.	(C)	
1885, Nov.	Widnes	T. C. Edwardes-Moss ...	(C)	4527
		E. K. Muspratt	(L)	2650
1886, July.		T. C. Edwardes-Moss ...	(C)	3719
		A. Birrell....	(GL)	2927
1885, Nov.	Newton	Rt. Hon. Sir Richard A. Cross, G.C.B.	(C)	4414
		Col. M'Corquodale	(L)	4031
1886, July.		Rt. Hon. Sir Richard A. Cross, G.C.B.	(C)	4302
		Sir Geo. Errington, Bt.	(GL)	3486
		Sir R. A. Cross accepted the Chiltern Hundreds on being created a peer.		
1886, Aug.	Newton	Thos. Wodehouse Legh	(C)	4062
		D. O'C. French	(GL)	3355
1885, Nov.	Ince.....	Colonel Blundell......	(C)	4271
		C. McL. Percy...........	(L)	3725
1886, July.		Colonel Blundell	(C)	43C8
		G. P. Taylor	(GL)	3228
1885, Nov.	Leigh	Caleb Wright	(L)	4621
		Lees Knowles	(C)	3275
1886, July.		Caleb Wright	(GL)	3297
		W. H. Myers	(C)	3134

CHAPTER IX.

NE of the most spirit-stirring periods in the early annals of Lancashire is that comprehended in the long reign of Edward III., at which, in the order of our history, we have now arrived. In this reign, the estates of the House of Lancaster, forfeited by the defection of the head of that house, were restored and augmented; the ducal dignity was conferred upon Henry, the first Duke of Lancaster, and the second duke created in England; the county was erected into a palatinate jurisdiction, with *jura regalia;* and John of Gaunt, the distinguished ornament of the ducal house, flourished in princely splendour in the exercise of regal functions. To add to the interest of this portion of our history, the public records of the kingdom abound with authentic materials; and our difficulty has arisen, not from the deficiency, but from the redundancy of those materials, which, being too copious to be published in detail, can only be presented in selection, and often by close abridgement.

One of the first acts of Edward III., on ascending the throne, was to relax the severity of those decrees under which Thomas, Earl of Lancaster, by the advice of the vindictive Despensers, had been doomed to the block, and the estates of the earl, as well as of his followers, to confiscation. Edmund de Nevill, by petition laid before the king in council, humbly represented that at the command of Thomas, Earl of Lancaster, in whose service he was, he had arrayed certain persons to arrest Hugh le Despenser and others of the counsellors of the late king, for which offence he had been fined one hundred marks; of this fine he had paid thirty marks into the exchequer, which he prayed might be accepted in discharge of his fine, and which request the king was pleased graciously to grant.[1] An order from his majesty in council to the sheriff of Lancashire, issued in 1327, directs that the lands of Sir Robert de Holand, Richard de Holland, and others, who had been engaged in the quarrel of Thomas, Earl of Lancaster, against the Despensers, should be restored and delivered into their hands; and the king, by the assent of Parliament, ordered writs to be directed to the treasurer and barons of the exchequer for releasing from fines and confiscation those who had joined Thomas, Earl of Lancaster, against his majesty's deceased father, in the battle of Boroughbridge.[2] Sir Robert de Holland, who married Maud, one of the two daughters and co-heirs of Alan, Lord la Zouche, great-grandson of King Henry II., by the Fair Rosamond de Clifford, had filled many positions of trust. He fought in the wars in Scotland in 1303, served the office of Chief Justice of Chester and of Wales, with the custody of the king's castles of Chester, Rhuddlan, and Flint, as well as that of Beeston, was held in great esteem by the Earl of Lancaster, who appointed him his secretary, and for his services bestowed upon him divers manors and extensive tracts of land in Lancashire and elsewhere.[3] When the earl made a second attempt to remove the Despensers from the royal councils, Sir Robert was despatched into Lancashire to raise a body of men to support the earl's enterprise, and to join him with the levy on the banks of the Trent, where, at Burton Bridge, he had placed a body of men to prevent the king's forces crossing the river. At Burton the earl found himself outmanœuvred, and was obliged to retreat[4] northwards to Boroughbridge, where a battle was fought which ended fatally for the insurgent army.

---

[1] 1 Edw. III. (1327), p. 1. m. 21, Turr. Lond.

[2] The roll of the battle of Boroughbridge, in possession of C. W. W. Wynn, Esq., published in Division II. of the Parliamentary Writs, and Writs of Summons (Append. 188), serves to show the extent of this rebellion, and the quality of the rebels. No fewer than three hundred and fifty barons and knights had arrayed themselves under the banners of Thomas, Earl of Lancaster, in this memorable insurrection, of whom many were killed or taken prisoners, exclusive of a great number of knights of somewhat inferior note, who were captured, and their lands confiscated by Edward II., but principally restored by his successor.

[3] Among the muniments preserved in the Record Office is an exemplification of a grant from Thomas, Earl of Lancaster, &c., to Robert de Holland, of divers lands, &c., viz., the manor of Yoxhale, with the advowson; the manors Tongetwistle (Tintwistle) and Motteram in Longedendale, with the advowson of Motteram; the manor of Broughton, in the county of Bucks; the mannor of Westderby, nere Liverpoole, with the demesnes of Croxtath: and the mannors of Torisholme and Kellett, with the bailiwick of Lonesdale, Fournays (Furness) and Kertmell (Cartmel), and Forester (ship) in *Com. Lanc.* : the lands in the Hope, nere Manchester, and the bailiwick of Salford; with a release of severall mannors and advowsons in the county of Northampton (Division xxv., B. 8).—C.

[4] The king crossed the Trent at Walton, lower down the river than Burton, and by this means turned the earl's flank, compelling him to retreat across the Dove, a movement that was executed in such haste that the army chest, containing 100,000 silver pieces, fell into the river, where it remained for fully five centuries, having been fished up so recently as the year 1831.—C.

The earl was captured and beheaded a day or two afterwards at Pontefract, but Sir Robert, who had surrendered, escaped the penalty of death, though the whole of his vast possessions were confiscated to the crown, as were also those of his kinsmen, "Johannes de Holand" and "Ricardus de Holand," who had shared in the rebellious enterprise, and so remained until the accession of Edward III., when, with the assent of Parliament, their respective estates were ordered to be re-delivered into their hands. But the consummation of all this clemency was in the reversal of the attainder, and the cessation of all proceedings against Thomas, Earl of Lancaster, on the petition of his brother and heir, Henry, the now earl, to whom all the estates forfeited by his deceased brother were restored by a special act of grace, dated the 3rd of March, 1328. The order of restoration of the lands, profits, castle and honor of Lancaster to Henry, Earl of Lancaster, is directed to John de Lancaster, warden or keeper of the honor of Lancaster; Geofrey de Werburton, sheriff of Lancaster; Edmund de Assheby, keeper of the fees of the honor of Lancaster; and to the various other officers of that honor.[1] As if it had been intended to propitiate the manes of the deceased earl, a brief was issued from York to Robert de Weryington, clerk, enabling him to collect alms in various parts of the kingdom to defray the cost of the erection of a chapel, to be built on the site where Thomas, Earl of Lancaster, had been recently beheaded.

The war with Scotland still continued, and the incursions of the Scots exposed the inhabitants of the northern counties of England to the most severe suffering. The young king, anxious to avenge the wrongs committed upon his subjects, placed himself at the head of his army; to increase which he directed his mandate to the commissioners of array[2] of cavalry and infantry in the county of Lancaster, announcing that the Scots were preparing to invade the kingdom, and ordering them to prepare with arms all the men in the county, between the ages of sixteen and sixty, to join the king at Durham.[3] The Scots had driven Edward II. from the very gates of Edinburgh, and out of Scotland, and pursued him with such activity into his own kingdom that he narrowly escaped falling into their hands. Emboldened by their successes they advanced to within twenty miles of York, plundering the towns and abbeys and laying waste the country on their way. After his deposition an attempt was made, on the night of the coronation of the young King Edward III., to surprise and take Norham Castle, a fortified stronghold on the English side of the Tweed, and immediately afterwards a formidable invasion of England was planned by Bruce. In June (1327), an army of twenty-four thousand men, under Randolph, Earl of Moray, and Lord Douglas, assembled on the marches, crossed the border, and ravaged Cumberland. The young Edward, with a precocious heroism, put himself at the head of a great army of English knights and archers, and of foreign soldiers under John of Hainbault, which had assembled at York; on the 15th July he was at Durham, and immediately moved forward in pursuit of the enemy, whose track was discernable by the smoke of burning villages in the defiles of that mountainous country. Froissart gives a vivid description of this his first journey against the Scots, marching "through marshes and savage deserts, mountains and dales," looking in vain for the enemy, and eventually compelled to give up the pursuit in despair, when he returned to Durham, and thence to York. This was the first lesson in warfare of the great Edward, and it is recorded that he wept when he found that the enemy had silently escaped by a night march, and that he was circumvented by the skill of an army inferior in numbers.[4] The effect of this expedition was, however, to free the country from the invaders; and the death of Robert Bruce, King of Scotland, which occurred on the 7th of June, 1329, prevented any further active hostility between the two countries for some years. At this time the county of Lancaster was much disturbed; large bodies of armed men assembled in the hundreds of Salford and West Derby, to the alarm of the peaceable inhabitants, and the insecurity of their property and lives. To put an end to this state of things, the king addressed his warrant (in 1328) to the sheriff of Lancashire, commanding him to make public proclamation, that whoever should in future assemble in this way would be subject to imprisonment and the loss of their arms.[5] This measure does not appear to have had the desired effect. It was found necessary in 1329 to appoint a commission, consisting of John de Haryngton, Thomas de Lathom, Richard de Houghton, Richard de Kigheley, and Gilbert de Warburton, as guardians of the public peace. In the proclamation by which this commission was accompanied it is stated that great multitudes of vagabonds and others assemble illegally together, by day and by night,

[1] 2 Edw. III. p. 1. m. 18. Turr. Lond.

[2] Hume erroneously affirms that the "first commission of array which we meet with in English history" was that of Henry V., before his departure for France to engage in the memorable battle of Agincourt (1415). This commission, which marks an important revolution in the military system of England, for it was no less than a substitution of a national militia for the ancient feudal force of armed retainers under the command and banner of their respective lords, is traceable as far back as the reign of Henry II., but it was not until later, and after much complaint, that the form of the commission was settled by statute.—C.

[3] Rot. Scot. 1 Edw. III. m. 4. Turr. Lond.

[4] Among the "Chamberlains' and Ministers' Accounts (Lancashire)," in the Record Office, is an "Account of Robert de Holand (1 Edw. III., 1327), late justiciary, of expenses in wages, &c., incurred under the King's Writs of Privy Seal, and arranged under the heads of wages paid to carpenters and others in the Castle, costs of carters and carts, costs of sailors' apparel, and purveyance of the king towards Scotland.—C

[5] Claus. 2 Edw. III. m. 20 d. Turr. Lond.

watching the passes through woods and other places, both public and private, and that these banditti waylay travellers, beating, wounding, and abusing them; killing some of them, maiming others, and robbing all of them of their property. The functions of the guardians of the peace were very extensive; they were no less than the powers of inquiring into offences, and of correcting and punishing the offenders at their own discretion. While the government were punishing the outrages of the lawless, they were not unmindful of the oppressions and delinquencies practised by their own servants; and hence we find that in 1330 a writ was issued by the king's authority to the sheriff of Lancashire, reciting that, in consequence of the representation that divers oppressions and hardships had been inflicted on the inhabitants by men in authority, he was to make proclamation that whoever had suffered oppression and injustice, contrary to the laws and usages of the realm, should make known their grievances to the next Parliament through the two knights of the shire to be sent from this county to that Parliament.[1]

The country was now threatened with a fresh war. The regency, by which the Scotch nation was governed during the minority of the prince, declined to recognise the claims of Edward Baliol, whose cause the English king had espoused, and taillage was levied of a fifteenth, to enable him to carry on the war, of which William de Denum, Thomas de Banenburgh, and Robert de Tughole, were appointed the assessors in the northern counties of Lancaster, Northumberland, Cumberland,

THE OLD BRIDGE, BERWICK, BETWEEN ENGLAND AND SCOTLAND.

and Westmorland; while Henry de Percy was appointed warden of the marches. The demands upon Lancashire were not confined to money: a levy of four hundred archers and one hundred *hobelers*, very strong and able-bodied men, fully accoutred, was required from this county, and John de Denum, Edward Nevil, and Robert de Shireburn, were appointed to array the levy.[2] At the same time a writ of summons was addressed to Henry, Earl of Lancaster, directing him to join the king at Newcastle-upon-Tyne, on the Feast of the Holy Trinity (Sunday, June 14, 1332). In the meantime, the Scotch forces had penetrated into the northern counties, and spread so much alarm by their homicides and devastations that a writ was issued to the sheriff of Lancashire, announcing that the king, for the protection of the inhabitants, permitted them to withdraw themselves, with their goods and cattle, out of the county into the southern parts of the kingdom, and there to remain, wherever they chose in the king's woods, forests, and pastures, during their pleasure, and to graze their cattle in the same without making any payment for so doing. It was also announced that similar commands had been given to the Bishop of Durham, and to the sheriffs of Northumberland, Nottingham, and Derby.[3] Encouraged by the discontent of the English lords, many of whom claimed to own lands in Scotland, Edward Baliol made an attempt to recover the Scottish throne. There is good reason to believe that Edward approved of the enterprise, though he gave no aid, and even went so far as to forbid the passage of armed men through the northern

[1] Claus. 4 Edw. III. m. 18 d. Turr. Lond.   [2] Pat. 6 Edw. III. p. 3. m. 18. Turr. Lond.   [3] Claus. 7 Edw. III. p. 1. m. 18. Turr. Lond.

counties, a procedure that necessitated Baliol and his associates taking ship from the Humber. They landed on the coast of Fife in August, 1332; repulsed, with immense loss, an army which attacked them near Perth; and on the 27th of the following month Baliol was crowned at Scone, when, in response to the demand of Edward, he acknowledged his sovereignty to be a fief held under the crown of England. If his success had been rapid, his reverse was not less so, for his acknowledgement of the abandoned suzerainty proved fatal to himself, and he was at once driven from his realm, and Berwick, which he had agreed to surrender, was strongly garrisoned. The king, who was then at Pontefract, at the head of a powerful army, on his way to the north, marched forward to Berwick, in which garrison the regent Douglas had fortified himself. After a protracted siege, a general battle ensued at Halidon Hill (July 19, 1333), in which Douglas, with many earls and barons, was killed, and nearly thirty thousand of the Scots troops fell in the action, in which, according to Knyghton, the loss of the English amounted only to one knight, one squire, and thirteen private soldiers!—a loss, as the historian Hume observes, so small as almost to be incredible. The picturesque old border town of Berwick, which had been the scene of so many struggles, was surrendered, and at a Parliament at Edinburgh a large portion of the south of Scotland was annexed to England.

The taillage, or tallage,[1] collected in this reign, as mentioned above, was a kind of occasional property-tax. In the 11 Henry III. (1226-7) a taillage was made in Lancashire, which serves as a barometer by which to measure the relative importance of the principal towns of the county in the thirteenth century. The impost was assessed by "Master Alexander de Dorsete and Simon de Hal," and the payments were for—

			Marks.	s.	d.
The town of Lancaster	[£8 : 13 : 4]	....	xiij.	...	...
The town of Liverpool	[7 : 14 : 4]	....	xj.	vij.	viii.
The town of West Derby	[5 : 1 : 0]	....	vij.	vij.	viii.
The town of Preston	[10 : 0 : 6]	....	xv.	...	vj.

The tenants in thanage paid 10 marks (£6 13s. 4d.) to have respite, that they might not be taillaged.[2] It is remarkable that neither Manchester nor Salford is mentioned in this early return to his Majesty's exchequer, and that Wigan, though one of the ancient boroughs of the county, is also omitted.

On the marriage of the king's sister, Alionora, to the Earl of Gueldres, an order was issued to the abbot of Furness and to the priors Burscough, Upholland, and Hornby, as well as to the abbot of Whalley and to the priors of Kertmell and Conigshead, requiring them to levy the subsidy on their respective houses, towards the maritagium, an impost of early times, which ceased with the feudal system.[3] This order the priests were slow to obey, in consequence of which another letter was issued by the king from Pontefract, reminding them of their neglect, and ordering them to communicate their intention to the proper authority. No further documents appear on the subject; and it may be presumed that this second application produced the desired effect. The abbot of Peterborough, in order to show his attachment to the king, and to secure the favour of the noble family whose influence at this time prevailed in his Majesty's councils, presented Edward with a splendid service of plate, amongst which was a silver-gilt cup with a *scuchon*, on which were engraved the arms of "Lancaster."

The danger of invasion from the Scotch, which prevailed so frequently during the reign of Edward III., induced that monarch to issue an order to Robert de Shireburn and Edmund de Neville, directing them to enforce, in the county of Lancaster, the statute of Winton, for arming and arraying the inhabitants according to their respective estates in land.[4] The Scots, who certainly deserved the praise of persevering patriotism, and, moreover, had justice on their side, were a cause of unceasing anxiety to their English neighbours. The king's needs being urgent, he issued a warrant, dated at Nottingham, March 27th, 9th Edward III. (1335), to his beloved and faithful Thomas, Earl of Norfolk, Marshal of England, and to a great number of nobles, knights, and esquires (including William le Boteler, of Warrington, and others in Lancashire), reciting that in the Parliament lately holden in Westminster it was agreed by the peers and commons there assembled

---

[1] Taillage, or tollage, was a special contribution levied on the burgesses for the lord's behalf, in the same way that "aids" were exacted by him of his land-tenants, and was after the nominal rate of 2s. 8d. in the pound for goods, those of aliens being charged in double proportion.—C.

[2] Mag. Rot. 11 H. III. Rot. 1. a. Lancastre.

[3] Claus. 7 Edw. III. p. 1. m. 23. Turr. Lond.

[4] The statute of Winchester, or Winton, as it is commonly called, passed 13 Edward I. (1285), enforced and extended the provisions of the 27th Henry II. (1181). It required that all persons between the ages of fifteen and sixty, possessing fifteen pounds in land, or upwards, and chattels of the value of forty marks, shall keep armour, and provide themselves with a haberject or habergeon (a steel or leather breastplate, haberjonem), an iron cap, a sword, a cultel (dagger-knife), and a horse; of ten pounds in land, and chattels value twenty marks, a habergeon, sword, and cultel; of one hundred shillings in land, a purpoint, iron cap, sword, and cultel; of forty shillings in land and more, up to a hundred shillings, a sword, a bow, arrows, and cultel; and he who had less than forty shillings in land, to be sworn to keep falchions, gisarms, knives, and other small-arms. The hand-gisarm was a short bill with serrated edges.—C.

that, "for the defence and safety of the kingdom, the lands in the marches, and the people there," it was the king's duty to march against the Scots, and that with certain of his faithful subjects he had accordingly at a great cost repaired thither, and, "with the help of heaven," proposed to be at Newcastle-on-Tyne on Trinity Sunday next, with a great army, prepared to advance against the enemy and repress their malice; wherefore he enjoined all his faithful subjects that, laying all excuses aside, they should be with him at the above time and place, prepared with horse and arms to move against the enemy.[1]   Two years later (March 29th, 11 Edward III.) he issued another warrant from Westminster, addressed to his beloved and faithful "William le Boteler de Weryngton," and Thomas de Lathum, in which, after reciting that to keep the Scots in check a great body of archers was immediately required, he commanded the said William and Thomas, jointly and severally, to raise fifteen hundred archers in the county of Lancaster, and with all speed to march them at the king's expense to Scotland.

England being again involved in war with France, the king determined to embark for the Continent, partly to direct its operations, but principally to animate by his presence that extensive confederacy which he had organised against Philip, the French king.   This intention was announced in Lancashire by a writ directed to John de Haryngton, Edmund de Nevill, and Richard de Hoghton, knights, by which they were directed, along with other knights, to be in their proper persons "present before the king in council at Westminster, the day after Easter (1338), to hear what he had to expound to them for their conduct during his absence on most urgent business, in parts across the sea," and with the further purpose of receiving instructions to preserve the peace inviolate during his absence.[2]   Although Parliaments had then been only very recently instituted upon the model of popular representation, the royal influence began already to exert itself to obtain the return of such members to the House of Commons as would best secure the king's purpose, by granting him large supplies out of the public revenue; and this appears to have been the object of Edward in summoning these knights by the authority of his own writ. Though disliking the French war, the Parliament which was convened on the recommendation of this council (March 27, 1340) made a grant for two years of the ninth sheaf of corn, the ninth lamb, and the ninth fleece, on their estates; from the citizens and burgesses, of a ninth of their goods and chattels, at the true value; the like from the foreign merchants which dwelt not in cities or boroughs; and of the people that dwelt in the forests, one fifteenth.[4]   The same Parliament also granted a duty of forty shillings on each sack of wool exported, on each three hundred woolfells, and on each last of leather, for the same term, declaring, however, that this grant was not to be drawn into a precedent.   But in order to facilitate the supply, and to meet the king's urgent necessities, they agreed that he should be allowed twenty thousand sacks of wool, the amount to be deducted from the movables when they were levied.   Local treasuries became necessary as depositories for the sum collected in the respective counties, and the abbot of Furness accordingly received a command to provide a suitable house in his abbey for "the custody of the king's pence."   A writ of summons was directed to the sheriff of Lancashire, ordering him to arrest the ships in the ports, and to man and equip them for action.[5]   With the fleet, consisting of two hundred and forty sail, principally collected in this way, the king set sail for Flanders on the 22nd of June, 1340, and the next day at evening gained the splendid victory, off the harbour of Sluys, over the navy of France, in which two hundred and thirty French ships were taken, and thirty thousand Frenchmen killed, along with their two admirals, while the loss of the English was comparatively inconsiderable.[6]   The day after the victory, Edward proceeded to Ghent, where he found that his queen, Philippa, almost within sound of the roar and shouts of the battle, had just given birth to a prince, who, from his being born on St. John the Baptist's Day, was called John, and from being born at Ghent, was called "of Ghent."   The child grew to manhood, and was afterwards famed in history as John of Gaunt, "time-honoured Lancaster."

Although this signal victory gave to the navy of England a superiority which it has never since lost, the alarm of invasion spread very generally, and, amongst other preparations made to repel the invaders, it was ordered (in 1339) that fifty men-at-arms, three hundred armed men, and three hundred archers, should be raised in this country, of which number twenty-five men-at-arms and one hundred and twenty archers were to be contributed by the following gentlemen :[7] "John de Haryngton, for himself and his father, ten men-at-arms and forty archers; Robert de Radeclif, five men-at-arms and forty archers; and Henry de Trafford, ten men-at-arms and forty archers."

The warlike spirit of the king had involved him in hostilities both with Scotland and France; and in the following year a writ of military summons was issued to Gilbert de Clyderowe and to

[1] *Rot. Scotiæ*, v. 1. pp. 332, 333.—C.
[2] *Ibid*, v. 1. pp. 486, 417.—C.
[3] Claus. 12 Edw. III. p. 1 m. 37 d. Turr. Lond.
[4] In pursuance of this enactment, inquisitions upon the oath of the parishioners were taken in every parish within the realm.—C.

[5] Rot. Aleman. 12 Edw. III. p. 1 m. 23, Turr. Lond.
[6] Froissart, liv. i. chap. 51.
[7] Rot. Parl. 13 Edw. III. vol. II. p. 110.

Robert de Radeclyf, ordering them to assemble the men-at-arms and archers under their command to meet the king at Carlisle, by Quadragesima Sunday (March 5, 1340), to repel the invasion of the Scots.[1] These successive demands upon the military tenants were very harassing, and their oppressiveness was increased by the difficulty of obtaining payment from the constituted authorities. A warrant, dated at Langley, March, 1541, and addressed to the Bishop of Durham and others, recites that William le Boteler, a Lancashire man, and others, had represented to the king that though they had been a long time in the garrison at Berwick-upon-Tweed, a great part of their wages remained still due and unpaid, whereupon the king gave commandment to the bishop and his colleagues to examine the accounts of the claimants, and see them forthwith paid out of the money levied by the nonetax.[2] On the 13th August following, the king issued another warrant from Shene (Richmond), commanding John de Thynden, receiver of the nones north of the Trent, to pay out of such moneys the wages of William le Boteler and others for their services either in the marches or elsewhere in Scotland, for such time as they should remain after the 12th of March, 1341.[3] At the same time, John de Helleker, the king's receiver for Lancashire, was ordered to send money to Carlisle, towards repairing the fortresses of that city, and the abbot of Furness was commanded to provide a suitable house in his abbey for the custody of the king's pence. To the joy of the people, a proclamation was this year (1340) received in Lancashire and in the other counties of England, commanding the sheriff to publish a truce between the king and Philip de Valois, and between the English and the Scotch. Little reliance, however, appears to have been placed upon the permanent restoration of tranquillity, for in 1341 the sheriff of Lancashire was ordered to provide one hundred bows and one thousand sheaves of arrows, for the expedition into France.[4] This was speedily followed by another to the sheriff, directing him to provide a thousand sheaves of steel-headed arrows and a thousand bowstrings.

In the war with France, which was speedily renewed, Henry, Earl of Derby, son of the Earl of Lancaster, greatly distinguished himself;[5] and the events of this war, in which the French king was taken prisoner, shed an imperishable renown on the military character of England. For the prosecution of the contest large levies were raised in all the counties of the kingdom; and an order was directed by the king to the sheriff of Lancashire (1345), commanding him to make proclamation that all barons, bannerets, knights, and esquires in the county, between the age of sixteen and sixty, should be forthwith prepared, with horses and arms, to attend the king across the sea, to enable him to put a speedy and successful termination to the war.[6] Not only the noble, but the ignoble also, were embarked in this service, and the sheriff received soon after a writ of military service, commanding him to make public proclamation that all persons in his county who had been found guilty of felonies, homicides, robberies, and other offences, and had been pardoned by the king's clemency, should provide themselves with arms and accoutrements, and march to join the royal army on its embarkation at Portsmouth for France. All these preparations and all these attacks upon the French kingdom were, however, but the preludes to the great effort of 1346, which culminated on the field of Crescy, when the steady courage that was the result of the comparatively free condition of the yeomen of England was first asserted on a great scale.

The Scotch, under David Bruce, availing themselves of the opportunity which the absence of the English forces afforded, prepared to invade the northern counties, on which a writ was addressed by the king to the sheriff of Lancashire (1345), announcing the danger of the country, and ordering him to make proclamation that all the men of the county should remove their live stock to the forest of Galtres, in the county of York, where they might be preserved in safety, and where the flocks and herds would enjoy pasturage free of charge.[7] The King of England being engaged in the French wars, aided by his youthful son the Black Prince, and by the Earl of Derby, who by his father's death, September 22nd, 1345, had now succeeded to the earldom of Lancaster, Queen Philippa assembled a body of soldiers to repel the Scotch invaders, who had entered Cumberland, taken the fortress called "the Pyle of Liddel," and after beheading the governor had advanced into the bishopric of Durham, plundering and slaughtering. This force, under the command of Lord Percy, met the army of Bruce at Neville's Cross, a mile or two west of Durham (1346), with the determination to avenge the insults which had been offered to the country, and to put an end to the violations which had been committed upon the property of the inhabitants. Animated, in that chivalrous age, to the highest pitch of enthusiasm by the presence of the queen, who rode along their ranks previous to the battle, the English troops, though not numerically amounting to one-fourth of the number of the Scotch, fought like lions.

[1] *Ibid*, 18 Edw. III.
[2] *Rot. Scotiæ*, v. i. p. 606.—C.
[3] *Ibid*, v. i. p. 611.—C.
[4] The price of bows is fixed in the government order at one shilling each, which sum is also to be allowed for a sheaf of arrows, except when they are guarded with steel (*accratœ*), and then the charge is to be one shilling and twopence.
[5] See c. iv. p. 86.
[6] Rot. Franc. 19 Edw. III. p. 2 m. 12, Turr. Lond.
[7] Claus. 19 Edw. III. p. 2 m. 10 d. Turr. Lond.

The enemy was broken and driven off the field, and fifteen thousand of them were made to bite the dust, amongst whom was the Earl Marshal of Scotland.[1] To crown this memorable victory, David Bruce, the Scotch king, was made prisoner, and conveyed to London, along with a number of his captive nobles, in triumph.[2] The number of prisoners taken in this battle was so large as to fill all the prisons of Lancashire. The inhabitants, in order to relieve themselves from the burden of the support of so many prisoners, liberated a number of them, in the hope that they would return to their own country; but instead of pursuing this course, they began to commit depredations; on which the government instituted a commission, consisting of Thomas de Latham, John de Haryngton the younger, and Nicholas le Botiller, to make inquisition into the alleged liberations, and to announce that the persons guilty of this offence against the public safety would be liable to the forfeiture of life and limbs (1346).[3]

In order to reinstate the English navy in its former strength, after the splendid victory of Sluys, a tax somewhat resembling that attempted to be imposed by Charles I., though unattended by its disastrous consequences, was levied in the seaports of Liverpool and Chester, under the authority of an order from the king, by which the collectors of the ship-money were directed to collect the subsidy of two shillings the sack on wool, and sixpence the pound on movables, for sixty large ships of war *(grossis navibus de guerra)*, and to deliver the money so assessed to the admiral of the fleet of those ports. A contribution was also made in Lancashire, in favour of Edmund Baliol, King of Scotland, the nominee of Edward, King of England; and Richard Molineaux and his associates, collectors of the triennial tenths recently granted to the king, were ordered to transmit one hundred and eighty-four pounds, in two instalments, out of the sums collected for the king's exchequer (1349).[4]

At this time the "Black Death," a pestilence of the most fatal character raged in the country, and is said to have extended to Lancashire. So malignant were its effects that of the three or four millions who then formed the population of England more than one-half became its victims. It first appeared at Dorchester, and according to Stowe, the annalist, fifty thousand persons died of this plague in the city of Norwich; an equal number were interred in the burial-ground where now stands the Charter House, in the city of London, and it is recorded that more than one-half of the priests of Yorkshire perished (1348-9). The labours of husbandry were neglected; no courts of justice were opened; Parliament was prorogued; and men, intent only on their own safety, slighted every call of honour, duty, and humanity.

On the 19th September, 1356, the great battle of Poictiers was fought, Henry, Earl of Lancaster, the "good earl" as he was called, was, at the time, leading another expedition in France, and only just missed the glory of sharing in the victory by being a day's march from Poictiers. "Going from Tours," wrote the Black Prince to the city of London after the battle, "we had the intention of meeting our most dear cousin, the Duke of Lancaster, of whom we had most certain news that he would make haste to draw near us." The brilliant career pursued in France by Henry, Earl of Lancaster and Derby, had determined the king to confer upon him a signal mark of the royal favour by creating him Duke of Lancaster.[5] The origin of this title is thus represented by the heralds:—

"The first creation of the title of duke, as distinct from that of earl (for in the elder times they were oft synonymous with us), was in the eleventh year of Edward the Third (1337), when in Parliament he conferred upon his eldest son, being then Earl of Chester, the title of Duke of Cornwall. The investiture of this first duke was only by girding him with the sword, although some learned men, confounding, it seems, the ceremonies of his being afterwards made prince of *Wales*, with this creation into the title of duke, say he was invested by a ring, a rod, and a coronet, all of which indeed together are mentioned in some patents of the following times, that seem to create the eldest sons Dukes of *Cornwall*, as well as Princes of *Wales*, and Earls of *Chester*. The same investiture also, by the sword only, is mentioned in the creation of *Henry*, the first Duke of *Lancaster*, about fourteen years after this first creation of the Duke of Cornwall. He was created for life in Parliament, and the clause of investiture in the charter is only *nomen ducis Lancastriæ inponimus & ipsum de nomine ducis dicti loci, per cincturam gladii praesentialiter investimus;* and the county of *Lancaster* as a county palatine, with reference to that of *Chester*, for example of jurisdiction, is given to him as the body of his duchy.[6] Afterward, in 36 (26) Edw. III., on the last day of the Parliament, *Lionel*, Duke of *Clarence*, and *John*, Duke of *Lancaster*, both sons to the king, were honoured with those titles, *Lionel* being then in *Ireland*; but the other being present, had investiture by the king's girding him with a sword, and his putting him on a cap of fur, *desus in cercle d'or & de peres*, as the roll says—that is, under a coronet of gold and stones."

Soon after the first establishment of the duchy of Lancaster heavy complaints were made by the inhabitants in consequence of the twofold pressure of taxation—first for the support of the state, and next for the maintenance of the institutions of the duchy. To alleviate their burdens the king addressed a mandate to the Duke of Lancaster, or to his lieutenant and chancellor, wherein it was directed that all general inquisitions concerning felonies and trespasses in every

---

[1] The battle was fought on the hill just outside the city of Durham, and the site is still marked by a broken shaft of stone, the remains of a cross erected by Ralph, Lord Neville, to commemorate the victory in which he had such a distinguished share.—C.

[2] Froissart, liv. i. c. 130.

[3] Rot. Scot. 20 Edw. III. m. 4 d. Turr. Lond.

[4] 23 Edw. III.

[5] 25 Edw. III. (1351).

[6] See c. iv. p. 54.

part of the kingdom should cease, so long as the people remained peaceable, and particularly that the people in the duchy of Lancaster, who had been impeded in their business, and reduced to great poverty, by the inquisitions made in the duchy, should no longer be burdened in this way. The duke was therefore ordered to supersede all such proceedings within his duchy, and to administer the law in the same manner as in other parts of the kingdom. The same year the king addressed a proclamation to all admirals, their lieutenants and sheriffs, appointing Roger del Wych, John Syword, John Cruys, and William, son of Adam de Lyverpol, to arrest as many ships in Liverpool and Chester, and other ports, as were necessary to convey Thomas de Rocheby, the king's justiciary of Ireland, into that country. The difficulty of procuring labourers in husbandry after the country had been so much thinned of its population by the plague [of 1349] disinclined the working classes to take the usual rate of wages for their labour. It was the period of transition from serfdom [1] to free labour, in which the labourers asserted their own importance somewhat beyond the limits of discretion, and an Act was in consequence passed " to restrain the malice of servants," who insisted upon extravagant wages (*outrageouses lowers*). The standard of wages fixed by this Act was that which had prevailed voluntarily before the plague broke out, when corn was tenpence a bushel and wages fifteenpence a week. This law being in opposition to the general principle of trade, which causes the supply and the demand to regulate the price, failed in its object, and the labourers left their usual places of abode to seek more profitable employment, which they easily found from home. The whole organisation of labour was thrown out of gear; for a time cultivation was almost impossible—the fields were left untilled—and the scarcity of hands, consequent on the course of industrial employment being so rudely disturbed, made it difficult for the minor tenants to perform the services due for their lands, and it was only by a temporary abandonment of half the rentals that the landowners could induce their tenants to retain their farms. It was the first great struggle between capital and labour. Repressive measures became necessary, the strong arm of the law was again called in, and it was enacted that no servant should in summer go out of the town or parish where he usually dwelt in winter, if he could obtain employment there, with a proclamation dispensing with the law in favour of the labourers in the counties of Lancaster, Stafford, and Derby, and in the districts of Craven and the marches of Wales, who were allowed to go in the month of August—the season of harvest—to work in other counties; and persons refusing to obey this proclamation were to be put in the stocks by the lords and stewards, or, if that discipline did not prove sufficient, they were to be sent to the next prison, and there confined for three days (1359). [2] As compared with the south of England, or even the adjoining county of York, Lancashire at this period was but ill-cultivated. The huge tracts of bog and swampy morass that stretched along its southern boundary would scarcely afford a pathway for travellers, much less land for tillage or pasture; the bleak moorland wastes and sterile hills that separated it from Yorkshire on the eastern side yielded but a poor return for the labour of the husbandman; and a large portion of the western border, sloping to the sea, was covered with loose sands, driven by the drifting winds, to the destruction of vegetation beneath. Much of the country was forest and wild woodland, retaining their primeval features, and in which the animals of the chase roamed at will. But land was gradually being reclaimed from the waste, and agriculture was making progress, especially in Ribblesdale and the district of Furness, where the two great abbeys had been established, and the Cistercians had taught their neighbours and dependents to plough the fertile vales and to pasture their flocks and herds on the green slopes of Pendle and the fells of Cartmel.

During the king's absence in France, Henry, Duke of Lancaster, was summoned to attend the council, which duty he performed with his usual fidelity. This was amongst the last public acts of that venerable peer, for on the 24th of March in the following year, 1361, he died of the plague, without male heirs, on which his honours and princely possessions descended to his two daughters, Maud and Blanche, whose names, however, are not even mentioned in his will.

WILL OF HENRY, DUKE OF LANCASTER.

In this will, dated at the Castle of Leicester, 15th March 1360, his titles are set forth as Duke of Lancaster, Earl of Derby, of Lincoln, and of Leicester, Steward of England, Lord of Bruggerak [Brigerac] and of Be[a]ufort. After long directions as to his funeral and burial in the Collegiate Church of the Annunciation of our Lady at Leicester, the duke devises all his goods, silver plate, and all other movables, to pay his debts and to "guerdon" his poor servants, each according to merit and estate, and to fulfil his bequests to the Church, etc. He appoints, as his executors, "John [Sinwen or Gynwell], Bishop of Lincoln, the honourable home of holy religion, William, Abbot of Leicester, our dearest sister the Lady Wak, our dearest cousin of Walkynton, Robert la Mare, John de Bokelande, Sir John de Charnele, Sir Walter Power, Sinkyn Simeon, and John de Neumarche." He devises all his goods,

---

[1] The last recorded sale of slaves in Lancashire was about forty years before this time. It occurs in the muniments of Whalley Abbey, where, in 1309, the abbot sold, for one hundred shillings sterling, "one native, with all his family and all his effects."—O.

[2] Clause 38 Edw. III. m. 5 d. Turr. Lond.

beyond what suffice to pay his debts and reward his servants, and fulfil his bequests to the Church, to be applied "to the profit of our soul," by the advice and consent of the executors. The will was proved the 3d of the Kalends of April [March 30], 1361, in the castle of Leicester, before John, Bishop of Lincoln ; and again before Sir William de Witlesoye, official of the Court of Canterbury, at London, on the 7th of the Ides of May [9th May] 1361.—*Regist. Islip.* fol. 172 a b, *in the Archiepiscopal Registry at Lambeth.*

The extent and magnitude of the possessions of the first Duke of Lancaster, forming as they do the principal part of the duchy, may be in some degree estimated from the following enumeration exhibited in the *Inquisitio Post Mortem* taken in 36 Edw. III. (1362).

INQUISITION POST MORTEM

OF THE POSSESSIONS OF THE FIRST DUKE OF LANCASTER.

"*In the County of Lancaster.*—Lancaster castle & honor—Pleas of the county of Lancaster—West Derbyshire bailiwick—Lonesdale wapentake—Lancaster vill—Lone Water, fishery near Prestwait—Overton manor—Slyne vill—Skerton lands, &c.—Quernemore park—Wiresdale vaccary—Blesdale vaccary—Caldre vaccary—Grisdale vaccary—Amunderness wapentake—Preston—Singleton—Riggeby vill with le Wray—Hydil park—Cadilegh—Fulwode wood—Kylaneahalghe—Broughton—Mirestagh park—Wiggehalgh—Baggerburgh—Clyderhoo castle—Blakebornshire wapentake—Ightenhull manor—Colne manor, with members—Woxton—Penhulton vill—Chateburne vill—Acrinton vill—Huncotes—Haselingden vill—Penhull chace—Trogden chace—Rossendale chace—Totinton manor & chace—Hoddesden wood—Rachdale manor—Penwortham manor—Widnes manor—Ulleswalton manor—Ecclesston vill—Leylond vill—Lyverpoll castle—Westderby manor & Salford manor (as of the honor of Tuttebury)—Horneby castle & manor—Werington manor—Laton manor.

"*In the County of Leicester.*—Leycester castle & honor extended—Frithe wood—Hynkeley manor extended—Schelton manor extended—Derford manor extended—Selby, five views of frank-pledge—Carleton, four views of frank-pledge—Schulton, two views of frank-pledge—Derford, two views of frank-pledge—Hynkeley, two views of frank-pledge.

"*In the County of Dorset.*—Kyngeston Lacy manor—Winterborn Minster—Wimbourne Holt chace—Bradbury hundred—Shapwyk manor—Maiden Neuton hundred.

"*In the County of Southampton.*—Kyngesomborne manor—Pernholt wood & chace—La Lond wood—Staunden—Earle—Elleden—Huld—Pernholt—Tymbrebury—Compton Houghton—Sumborne Parva—Upsomborne (land, &c.)—Stockbrigg vill—Langesdale manor—Weston manor, near Odiam—Herteley manor.

"*In the County of Warwick.*—Kenelworth castle and manor extended—Asthull manor—Wotton rent—Waddesley—Lapworth rent—Mershton Boteler—Brinkelowe (lands and tenements)—Ilmedon, view of frank-pledge.

"*In the County of Wilts.*—Colingborne manor extended—Everlee manor extended—Lavyngton manor extended.

"*In the County of Berks.*—Esgarston manor extended—Poghele—Hungerford—Sandon—& Kentebury (land, &c.).

"*In the County of Derby.*—Melborne castle & manor.

"*In the County of York.*—Pontefract castle & honor, with members, viz.—Slaikeborne manor—Bowland manor, with forest—Snaith vill, with soke—Pykering castle, vill, and honor—Scalby manor—Hoby manor—Esingwald manor—Bradeford manor—Almanby manor—Ledes manor—Berewyke manor—Roundhaye manor—Scoles manor—Hypax manor—Allerton manor—Rothewell manor—Altoftes manor—Warnefield manor—Ackworth manor—Elmesdale manor—Camesale manor—Custon'—Tanehelfe manor—Knottingleye manor—Boghall manor, with the free court of Pontefract—Divers lands and tenements, &c., in Maningham Barnboghe—Woodhouse—Potterton—Hillum—Saxton—Roundhaye—Secroft—Thornore—Scole—Muston—Kypax manor—Ledeston—Allerton—Ayer (Ayre) fishery—Rothewell—Flete mill—Wridelesford—Kildre fishery. Divers lands and tenements, &c. Warnefeld—Crofton—Akeworth—Elmesle—Kerkeby Mensthrop—Suthelmsale—Coteyerd—Ellerker—Camesale—Balnehoke—Hargincrofte—Bernesdale—Custon—Holnhirst—Carleton Castleford mill—Hardewike—Knotingley—Beghale—Beghelker—Beghallund—(*All the aforesaid belong to the Honor of Pontefract*)—Slaykeborne in Bouland, with the forest—Bremund pasture—Roudon—Ap Aldington—Maukholes—Brombewell—Holme—Baxsterhay—Browesholme—Berkholme—Eghes—Latheringrime Bernardscless—Nicolshey—Wardeslegh—Hogeking—Heighe—Crepingwarde—Benteley Close—Graistanley—Lekherst—Peinleghes—Coswayne—Chipping Crosdale—Neuton—Hamerton Witton—Grimlington—Salley mill—Bradeford in Bouland—Blakshelfe in Mitton—Withikill—Smithecrofte—Cowyke vill, belonging to the soke of Snaythe—Roucliffe moor—Acre water fishery—Pikering castle, forest, &c., with the fees appertaining, viz.—Middleton—Levesham Finhilwode—Gotherland—Aleintoftes—Thwaite—Lingthwaite—Rumbald—Haretoft—Folketon marsh—Ednesmershe—Brumpton—Scalby—Hobye—Esingwolde—Credeling manor. *Divers rents and reprises issue out of the manors aforesaid.*

"*In the County of Northumberland.*—Dunstanburgh castle—Staunford barony, with its members—viz. Emaldon—Dunstan—Burton—Warndam—Shipplay—Crauncestre—Fenton—Newton-on-the-Moor & Cartington.

"*In the County of Huntingdon.*—Huntingdon rent—Gomecestre rent.

"*In the County of Rutland.*—Tye, two leets—Casterton Magna, two leets.

"*In the County of Northampton.*—Higham Ferrers—Raimdes vill—Russheden vill—Irchestre vill—Hegham hundred as of the honor of Tuttebury—Davintre manor—Esthaddon, two leets—Helmingden—Lylleborne—Dodeford, two leets—Wedonbeck, as of the honor of Leycester.

"*In the County of Surrey.*—Erwell, the tenement called Hertegrave.

"*In the County of Middlesex.*—London, the messuage called the Savoye, with shops & rents appertaining.

"*In the County of Lincoln.*—Lincoln county, 14 fees in the same belonging to the castle Lancaster—Retrecombe court.

"*In the County of Stafford.*—Newcastle-under-Lyne manor, castle & borough, with members, viz.—Clayton vill—Wolstanton—Shelton vill—passage of the church—Stoke, advowson of the church—Cliff wood—Bradenef lands & tenements.

"*In the County of Hereford and Marches of Wales.*—Monemouthe castle, vill, & demesne—Grossemont castle—Skenfrithe lands, &c.—Album castle & demesne—Karakenmyn castle—Oggemore castle—Ebbothe manor—Iskennin commote—Kedwellye demesne—Carnwathlon demesne or lordship.

"*In the County of Gloucester and Marches of Wales.*—Roddell manor—Eccelowe—Minsterworthe manor—Monemuthe castle—Berton lands, &c.—Blakmorles pasture—Kedwelly castle, vill, & demesne.

"*In the Counties of Gloucester, Hereford, and Marches of Wales.*—Carnewathlan lordship—Lananthir vill—Kaerkennyn castle Iskennyn commote—Ogemore castle & lordship—Ebbothe manor—Shen castle, with Barton—Album castle, with Barton—Tyburton manor—Minstreworth manor—Rodleye manor—Monemouthe castle & lordship—Grosmonde castle & lordship—Whitcastell castle & lordship—Kedwelly lordship—Carnwathlan lordship—Ogemore castle—Ebbothe manor.

FEES.

"*In the County of Bucks.*—Tappelowe—Chalfhunt St. Peter—Saundesdron—Weston Turvile—Broughton Parva—Penna.

"*In the County of Bedford.*—Suthmulne—Middleton Erneys.

"*In the County of Cambridge.*—Grauncete.

"*In the County of Worcester.*—Bruites Morton.

"*In the County of Lincoln.*—Twelve Knights' Fees each of which renders yearly 10ˢ for the castle-ward of Lancaster.

"*In the County of Somerset.*—Redene—North Overe.

"*In the County of Dorset.*—Shapewike—Swinetolre—Mayden Nyweton—Upaydelinge.

"*In the County of Kent.*—Strode—Godwinestone—Clyve Hastinglegh—Braborne—Chelefeld manor—Horton—Caulstoke Haashe.

"*In the County of Sussex.*—Scheffeld Parva—Kirsed—Kindale—Charlaxton—Fleoching—Chiffeld—Hothore—Est Grinstede—Hertefelde—Claverham—Erlington—Raketon—Torreuge—Westdene—Megham—Bethington—Telton—Cheleworth—Chiffeld manor in Fleoching—Folyngton—Wennoke—Excete—Ratton.

"*In the County of Oxon.*—Churchull—Clapwell—Dene—Chalkeford—Fyffhyde ¹—Chadlyngton—Broughton—Nywenton—Lyllingeston—Bagerugg—Pyriton—Hasele—Thomele—Brightwell—Shupton upon Charewell—Blechdon—Wighthull—Lynham—Childeston & Sewell near Goldnorton.

"*In the County of Berks.*—Fyffehide—Kingeston—Southdenchesworth—Loking—Cherleton near Wantynge—Staunden—Hanrethe—Staunford—Westhildesle—Wolhampton—Northstanden chapel—Hungerford chapel of St. John.

"*In the County of Wilts.*—Choldrington, half-a-fee—Chitterne, half-a-fee—Elcomb, half-a-fee—Merevedene, one fee—Wrichford, half-a-fee—Hordenehuuishe, one fee—Checkelowe, one fee—Berewike manor, one fee.

"*In the County of Southampton.*—Chalghton—Katerington—Erleston—Somborne—Fyffhide near Andover—Schalden—Bellum—Avenetum—Hertele—Langestoke—Weston—Estden—Semborne.

"*In the County of Devon.*—Hemly—Portheleg—Shillingford—Ferdon—Kerdogis—Ivelegh—Chilton—Coleton Ralegh—Fursan—Whithem—Whiston—Hoddesworth—Maneton—Prank-arawike—Southwyk—Sprayton—Woreslegh—Whitnealegh—Wollegh—Wrix-aton—Godelee—Kippingiscote—Uppecote—Witherige—Hole Meleford—Clompton—Clift St. Lawrence—Hordelisworth—Milleford—Deandon—Bourdouliston—Yowe—Hogeland & Heanis.

"*In the Counties of Gloucester, Hereford, & Marches of Wales.*—Landingate—Longehope—Dounameney—Huntelege—Wisham—Walbykney—Parthir—Dile—Cunstone—Dixton—New Castle—Cothitham—Monimouthe—Garthe—Rakenill—Holywell—Grosemound—Chesterton—Asperton—Mayneston—Lanwarthin—Lanknethin—in the lordship of Kedwelly—Penbray—Witewike—Hope Maloisell, Llanelthye church, St. Ismael church, Lanconar church—In the lordship of Ogmore, the under-written fees—viz., Dourenen—Deynell—Pyncote—Lanforte—Colewinstone—Frogg Castell—Ewerdon—Puttes—Le Wike—Southdone & St. Bridget.

"*In the County of Lancaster.*—Walton in Blakebornshire—Crointon—Apulton—Sutton—Eccleston—Rainhull—Knowselegh—Torbok—Hyton—Maghull—Crosseby Parva—Kirkebye—Kirkedale—Northmeles—Argameles—Ulneswalden—Bretherton—Hoghton—Claiton—Whelton with He`arge—Wytherhull with Bothelesworthe—Hoton—Longeton—Leilond—Enkeston—Chenington—Chernoke—Walshewhithull—Warton in Amoundernesse—Prees—Neuton—Frekelton—Witingham—Etheleswike—Bura in Salfordshire—Middleton with members—Chatherton—Totinton—Mitton Parva—Wiswall—Hapton—Townlay Coldecotes—Snoddeworthe—Twiselton—Extwisell—Aghton—Merlaye—Lyvesay—Donnom Fobrigge—Merlaye Parva—Rossheton—Billington—Alnethan—Clayton—Harewode—Crofton Horneby—Ulideston—Warton in Lonesdale—Gairstang with members—Thiselton—Prees—Kelgrimesarghe—Brininge—Merton Magna—Middelton in Lonesdale—Neuton—Makerfeld—Lauton—Keinan—Erbury—Goldeburne—Sefton—Thorneton—Kerdon—Halghton—Burgh—Lee—Fishwicke—Dalton in Furness—Stayninge—Midhope—Chernoke.

"*The under-written fees are held of the Honor of Tutebury.*—Hagh Parva—Bolton—Brightmet—Compton—Burghton—Childerwell—Barton in Salfordshire—Asphull—Brokholes—Dalton—Perbald—Withington—Lostock—Romworthe—Pilkinton—Worthington—Hoton [Heaton] under Herewiche—Tildeslegh—Sulthithe—Rixton—Asteley—Atherton—Sonky—Penkythe—Ines—Blundell—Barton—Halsale—Windehulle—Lydegate—Egergarthe—Lancaster priory, advowson—St. Michael-on-Wire church—Preston church—Mary Magdalen chapel—Chypin church—Ribcaster church—Whalley, abbey of.

"FOR THE DEAN & CHAPTER OF THE CHURCH OF [ST.] MARY OF LEICESTER.—Preston, advowson of the church.

"FOR THE ABBOT & CONVENT OF WHALLEY.—Romagreve in the chace of Bouland near Blakeborne, lands & tenements—Penhulton, lands & tenements—Cliderhow, the tenement called Standen—Hulcrofte & Grenelache—Standen, 'faltag' lands, &c.—Cliderhoo manor, lands, &c., as of the castle of Lancaster."

To this inquisition we are enabled to add a condensed transcription, from the rolls of the duchy of Lancaster (not before published), extending through the whole period of the first ducal administration, and which, while it sheds much light upon the early history, as well as upon the landed possessions in the county, serves to illustrate the nature of the *jura regalia* exercised by the Dukes of Lancaster in this "kingdom within a kingdom:"—

ANNO 1 DUCATUS, 26 EDWARD III. [1351-2]. ²

(*Office Reference* A1.)

Intituled, "Pleas at Preston of three sessions of the Justices of the lord the Duke of Lancaster, in the first year of the lord the duke that now is."

This roll contains the essoigns taken at Preston, before Hugh de Berewyk and his associates, justices of our lord the Duke of Lancaster, Wednesday next before the feast of St. Margaret the Virgin, in the year of his duchy the 1st (July 13, 1351).

It contains pleadings of lands between parties, plaintiffs, and defendants, pleadings of assize mortis antecessoris, novel disseisin,

---

¹ This word, which occurs in three counties in this document, may not be a local name, but simply denotes five hides of land.—H.

² As the ducal years of Henry, first duke, are neither conterminous with the regnal years of the reigning sovereign, nor with the year of our Lord, the following tables are appended. The regnal years of Edward

III. are from 25th Jan. to 24th Jan. The *ducal* years of Henry, first duke, are from 6th March to the 5th March. About ten months of every ducal year consequently fall in one regnal year, and the last two months of the ducal year fall in the next regnal year.—H

DUCAL YEARS OF HENRY FIRST DUKE OF LANCASTER.				REGNAL YEARS OF EDWARD III. IN THE SAME PERIOD.			
1st.	6th March 1351	to 5th March	1352	25th.	6th March 1351	to 24th Jan.	1352
2nd.	,, 1352	,,	1353	26th.	25th Jan. 1352	,,	1353
3rd.	,, 1353	,,	1354	27th.	,, 1353	,,	1354
4th.	,, 1354	,,	1355	28th.	,, 1354	,,	1355
5th.	,, 1355	,,	1356	29th.	,, 1355	,,	1356
6th.	,, 1356	,,	1357	30th.	,, 1356	,,	1357
7th.	,, 1357	,,	1358	31st.	,, 1357	,,	1358
8th.	,, 1358	,,	1359	32nd.	,, 1358	,,	1359
9th.	,, 1359	,,	1360	33rd.	,, 1359	,,	1360
10th.	,, 1360	,,	1361	34th.	,, 1360	,,	1361
11th.	,, 1361	to 23rd March 1361 when the duke died.		35th.	,, 1361	to 23d March 1361 when the duke died	

pleas of debt, account, and trespass, and other claims to liberties, rights, etc., all as arising in the county palatine of Lancaster, with the judgments thereof given (*inter alia* as follows) :—

"John of Winwick, parson of the church of Wygan, and lord of the borough of Wygan, appears by Robert de Prestcote or John de Lanfield, to plead damage and the prosecution of all liberties of his vill and borough of Wygan, according to the form of the charter which the lord the king granted to him thereof."

On the second portion of the roll, and on the first skin of such roll, after reciting the grant by King Edward III., in the 25th year of his reign (1351), to Henry, Duke of Lancaster, Earl of Derby, Lincoln, and Leicester, and steward of England, of his dukedom of Lancaster, as therein set forth, are recorded the letters-patent to Hugh de Berewyk and others, by the said Henry, appointing them justices of assize for his said duchy, and of pleas as well of the crown as others within the said duchy, to hold, hear, and determine, according to the law and custom of the kingdom of England, saving to him amercements, &c. Tested at the Savoy, 7th March, in the first year of his said duchy (1351).

In continuation of the roll are recorded a multiplicity of pleadings between various parties, to the following effect (anglicised from the roll) :—

"John Molyneux against John Blundell of Crosseby, touching the lands upon marriage.

"John Knody of Cliderow against William de Horneby, parson of the church of Ribchester, touching lands in Cliderowe.

"John Blounte of Hazlewood, Robert Legh, and Thos. Strangeways, came on their recognizance, at the suit of John Radclif, touching a tenement and lands in Salford. John Blounte answering that the premises were of the manor of Ordesale, and that Henry, late Earl of Lancaster, father of Henry the duke, was seised of the lands, and granted the same by charter to the said John Blounte, as of the manor of Ordesale."

And thus the pleadings are continued throughout the entire roll ; and, as evidences of that early period, they are applicable to the most considerable part of the places and manors in the county palatine of Lancaster, and the early possessors' rights and premises there.

There is a second roll distinguished A.1.a, and containing the essoigns taken at Preston before William de Fynche, or Fyncheden, and his associates, justices of the said duke's bench, in the tenth year of his dukedom (1360-61), and in its nature similar to the preceding roll.

ANNO 2 ET 3 DUCATUS [1352-54].

A 2 contains pleadings and essoigns, taken at Preston before Hugh de Berewyk and others, in the second year of the said duke and of the same nature and effect as those of the preceding rolls, and is very copious, the proceedings in many cases being fully set out.

A.2.a contains pleadings and essoigns of the like nature, as taken both at Lancaster and Preston in the fourth year of the same duke.

A.2.b is properly considered as a roll of finest letters close and patent, and as containing charters of the fourth year of Henry, Duke of Lancaster, being the twenty-eighth year of the reign of King Edward III. ; and the following outline comprises the general matters, or subjects, with several of the names of persons and places applicable thereto :—

No. on Roll.	Principal Matters.	Persons.	Places.
1.	Proceedings before the Justices at Preston as to right of Fishing.	Richard Aghton *v.* Roger Bondesson and John Stelle, the Defendants justifying in right of William de Heskayth, Thomas de Litherland, the Prior of Burscogh, the Abbot of Cockersand, and Richard de Aghton.	Merton Meer, Le Wyck, Northmeles.
2.	Account of Fines paid to the Duke as Lord for Writs of Assize.	John de Haconshou	Hamelton.
		Richayd Bradshagh	Perbald.
	William Jerard and Wife	....	Asheton-in-Makerfield.
	Peter Jerard and Wife	....	{ Wyndhull Manor. Raynhull Manor.
	William Careles...............................	....	{ Torbock Manor. Walshwittell Manor. Dalton Manor. Wrightynton. Cophull.
	William Lawrence..........	....	{ Thorneton. Laton Magna. Laton Parva. Ribleton Manor. Asheton, near Preston Manor.
	Henry de Ditton	....	Ditton.
	William de Exceatre, Parson of Crofton Church	....	North Meyles.
	John Culpeper	....	Mamcestre.
3.	Grants by The Duke to William de Heghfield, in perpetuity, 28 Acres of Land in Salford Waste, at 14s. Rent, and Tenants to do suit at the Lord's Mill.		Salford Waste.

Several other grants were made to persons specified, but cancelled, as the premises became leased by the duke's charter to John de Radclif.

4. A fine of 3s. 4d. to the duke as lord for a Writ of Pone, concerning an agreement—Cecilia Orulshagh and Hugh de Ines.

5. The duke to Richard de Walton, the duke's approver in the parts of Blackburnshire.

"Grant of a messuage and lands in Colne and Merclesden, held by the custom of the manor and castle of Clithero, and other premises in Trowden, Mithum, and Trowden Chace.

Fines to the Lord for Writs.

6. "John de Radclif, parson of the church of Bury, to the duke—Half-a-mark [6s. 8d.] for lands in Asheton-under-Lime.
"Robert de Legh and Matilda his wife to the duke—13s. 4d. [a mark] for the moiety of the manor of Flixton.
"Clarissa de Bolton to the duke—Half-a-mark for tenements in Newton-in-Makerfield and Walton-in-the-Dale.
"Robert de Legh and Matilda his wife to the duke—13s. 4d. for the manor of Ordeshale."

This course is pursued through thirteen other instances of fines of the like nature, paid by various persons in different places in the county palatine.

DE ANNO 4TO DUCATUS (IN DORSO) [1354 55].

Recognisances of Debts.

Otho de Halsale and	John de Radclif	
Richard de Rixton	John de Asheton and ors	100 marks (£66 : 13 : 4).
John, son of Adam de Claxton	Sir Adam de Hoghton, Knt.	17 marks (£11 : 6 : 8).
Otho de Halsale	The Duke	100 marks.

Grants, &c.

The Duke to Geoffrey de Langholt and Robert de Gikellswyk of Tadecastre, for the Abbot and Convent of Sallay.—Licence to Alien in Mortmain Lands in Bradeford in Bouland, held in socage by fealty and service, and as by inquisition taken by the Duke's command,
The Duke to Adam de Hoghton.—Acquittance of serving on juries, &c.
The Duke to John de Haverington of Farleton.—Lease of the Manor of Horneby and its demesnes, the Castle, Deer and Chace of Rebrundale (Advowsons, &c., excepted).
The Duke to Matthew de Southeworth.—Pardon of a debt owing to the Duke's Father, Henry, Earl of Lancaster.
The Duke to John de Dyneley and Heirs.—Grant of Dunham Manor by Homage and Fealty, and £12 : 6 : 7 per Ann. with 2s. for the Ward of Lancaster Castle. The above are all tested at Preston.
The Duke to the King.—Precept to John Cokayn and others to levy in the Duchy the remainder of Aid, granted by Parliament to King Edward III., to knight his eldest son, according to the King's Mandate, and also a Mandate of the Sheriff of Lancaster to assist therein. As tested at Lancaster.
William de Stoklegh and Avisia de Bretargh.—Inrolment of a deed of the manor of Hyton. Tested at Preston.
Pleadings at Lancaster of a similar nature to A.2.

Other Grants, from the 4th to the 11th Henry, Duke of Lancaster, comprising 29th Edward III. (1356) and 36th Edward III. (1363).

The Duke to William de Hegbfeld and his Heirs.—Grant of 23 [? 28] Acres of Waste in Salford, at a Rent of 11^s 6^d reserved, and remainder to Thomas Strangwas. Tested by Henry de Walton, Archdeacon of Richmond, Lieutenant of the Duchy of Lancaster.
The Duke to Richard de Dynesargh, of Liverpool, and his Heirs.—Grant of a Messuage and Appurtenances in Castle Street, Liverpool, which formerly belonged to Benedict le Stedeman, late Constable of Liverpool Castle, at 4^s Rent p. ann., and by Services, as the other Tenants of that Town did for their Messuages.
The Duke to Henry le Norreys.—Grant of Free Warren in Speek.
The Duke to John del Monkes.—Grant of the Wardship and Lands of Henry de Croft.
Divers Fines to the Lord for Writs of Assize.—For Lands and Tenements in Hopton, Tildesley, Ditton near Torbok, and in Chorlegh.
The Duke to John de Perburn.—Letters of protection while abroad with the Duke in the King's Service, and similar Letters of Protection to various other Persons.

Among numerous other entries on the Roll are various instruments by licence, warrant, writ, grant, or appointment—viz. For holding pleas and complaints ; for keeping the statute of weights and measures ; the statutes of servants, artificers, &c., and the record of various fines for writs of assize, &c., and therein the Writ de Conspiratione.
A Writ, diem clausit extremum, of the Lands of John de Rigmayden, in the Duchy of Lancaster.
An Exemplification of the Proceedings between Thomas de Abnay of the High Peake, and Thurstan de Holand of Salfordshire returned in the Duke's Chancery, concerning the Manor of Denton under Downeshagh.
A Mandate to John Haverington and others to equip the Men-at-Arms in the Duchy, with 300 Archers and others, to be dispatched to Newcastle-upon-Tyne, to march with the King against the Scotch.
Another Mandate on behalf of the King, as to the Alienations and Possessions of Lancaster Priory, taken with other Alien Priories, by reason of the War with France.
Appointments to the Office of Escheator, inquiries of the conduct of Bailiffs of the Wapentakes, appointment of Justices to hear and determine Trespasses within the Duchy, and Mandates to the Sheriff to assist in all such Premises.
A Lease of the Herbage of Musbury Park.
Grant of the Hospital of St. Leonard's at Lancaster, to be annexed to the Priory of Seton, if the Burgesses of Lancaster consent.
The Appointments of Keeperships of Forests.
Pardon of a Suit by the Duke for an Assault committed.
Grant and Confirmation of the Advowson of Wygan Church, and Letters of Protection to various Persons, while staying with the Duke in the King's Service in the Parts of Brittany.

ANNO 7° DUCATUS [1357-58].

Divers Fines for Writs of Assize of Lands and Tenements in Longtre, Hepay, and Dokesbury, Great Penhulton, Great Merley, Bury, Middleton, and Penhulton, in Salfordshire.
Grant of Land and Turbary in Salford, and divers Fines for Premises in Westlegh, Flixton, Whitton, Weryngton, Sonckey, Penketh, Burtonwood and Laton, Great Merton, Bispham, Pynington, Bold, Lydiat, Thornetou near Sefton, Culcheth, Tildesley, Glasebrook, Bedeford, Halsale, Wyndhull, Ines near Crosby, and Ines Blundell, including the Writs Post Disseasin, forma Donationes, Dedimus Potestatem, and the Writ de Ingressu.
A Mandate by the Duke for the King, to William de Horneby and Richard de Townley, to Collect and levy the tenths and fifteenths within the Duchy of Lancaster.
A Pardon by the Duke of the Suit of Peace against Hugh le Machon of Abingham, indicted for Housebreaking at Chorley.

ANNO 8° DUCATUS [1358-59].

The Duke's Mandate to Justices assigned to try certain Malefactors, against whom the Parson of the Church of Wygan, and the Lord of the Town, had complained regarding the hindrance of his Bailiffs in the performance of their duties, and his Mandate to the Sheriff of the Duchy to assist therein.

Divers Fines for Writs de Conventione, &c., concerning Lands in Culcheth, Mamcestre Manor, and the Advowsons of the Churches of Mamcestre and Assheton ; Lands in Chippyn, Eggeworth Manor ; Lands in Liverpool, Penhulton in Salfordshire, Culchith and Hyndelegh Manors, Croxteth Park, Flixton Manor, Kenyan, and the Manor of Huyton.

A Grant of the Herbage of the Foss of Lancaster Castle, and of the place called Bernyard in Lancaster.

An Acquittance of serving the Office of Juror, Escheator, Coroner, or Bailiff.

A Release of Rent for Lands held by John Baret in Derby, Liverpool, Everton, and elsewhere within the Duchy.

A Pardon by the Duke to John de Etheleston, indicted for extorting money and other offences, and a Pardon to William de Twys, of Transgressions.

A Lease of the Fishery in the River Ribble at Penwortham, with the Meadows there. Tested by the Duke at Preston.

ANNO 9° DUCATUS [1359-60].

Appointment of Justices in Eyre for Pleas of the Forests.

Precepts to the Sheriff to make a Proclamation for holding Sessions at Preston, and to summon Persons to attend before the Justices there.

Pardons for Trespasses of Vert and Venison in Duchy forests, and other Trespasses.

Grant of Free Warren in Halsal and Rynecres.

Lease of the Herbage called Veden and Mufden.

Grant of a Yearly Rent of 20ˢ to William de Liverpool, out of the Manor of West Derby.

Licence to take Gorse from Toxteth Park.

Pardons for Trespasses in the Duchy Forests, and in Toxteth Park.

Pardon upon Indictment for Offences against the Statutes of Servants and Labourers.

Divers Fines upon Writs for Lands in various places.

The Duke, in behalf of Roger la Warre.—Commissioners appointed to inquire into the said Roger's Petition, showing that he held the Town of Mamcestre as a Boro' and Market Town, and enjoyed certain Liberties there, and in the Manor and Hamlets, and that the Duke's Bailiffs had interfered to levy Amerciaments, &c.

A Licence to Alien in Mortmain Lands in Lancaster.

Grant of Lands in Salford to Thomas del Olera, and others.

Grant of a Messuage in Preston escheated to Henry, Earl of Lancaster, by Felony.

A Mandate to the Escheator of the Duchy to interfere no further in a Chapel and Lands in Andreton, which had been seized into the Duke's hands by the late Escheator, it being found, by Inquisition, that the Church of Standish was endowed therewith.

ANNO 10ᵐᵒ DUCATUS [1360-61].

The Duke to Adam de Skilyngcorn.—Licence to take with him a Body Guard within the Duchy of Lancaster, for the Defence and Protection of his Person.

Pardon to Agnes del Birches, for producing a forged Charter before the Justices, in an Action as to Tenements in Astelegh.

Grant of Lands in Penhulton.

Mandate to the Escheator of the Duchy for Livery of Seisin of Lands held by an Outlaw for Felony in Chipyn, the Duke having had his Year, Day, and Waste.

Mandate to Collect and Levy within the Duchy the tenth and fifteenth granted by Parliament, to defray the Expenses of War.

Appointment of Bailiff of the Manor of Derby for Life, at twopence a-day for his Wages.

Appointment of Keeper of Toxteth Park for Life, with the Grant of Skeryorderock within the Sea, to construct a Fishery there.

Mandate to the Duchy Escheator to interfere no further as to Land in Kirden [Cuerden], seized into the Duke's hands upon Felony.

Appointment of Keeper of Quernmore Park.

Mandate to the Duchy Escheator to deliver Lands which had been seized into the Duke's hands upon the Marriage of one of the Duke's Maidens, a legal Divorce having subsequently taken place.

A Pardon upon Indictment for catching Fish at Heton Norres.

Fines for Lands in Hunersfeld and Stalmyn.

Grant of a Messuage and Lands in Salford, which came to the Duke's hands by the death of Richard de Tetlowe, who was a Bastard, and died without Heir—Remainder to Thomas de Strangwas.

Grant of Lands in Ingoll.

Grant of an Escheat in Salford.

Divers Fines for Writs de Attincta, Writs of Assize, and the Writ de Debito.

Grant of 20 Marks [£13 6s. 8d.] yearly out of the Manor of West Derby.

Grant of Wardship and Marriage of William de Warton.

Appointment of Justices to try Malefactors for Trespasses in the Chases of Bowland, Penhull, Trowden, Rochdale, Rossendale, and Romesgrene.

Grant of the Wardship and Marriage of Thomas de Haverington.

Grant of Lands and Tenements in Gosenargh, escheated by Felony.

Lease for 20 Years of the Foreign Wood of Myerscough.

Mandate to the Duchy Escheator to interfere no further in Premises at Ribblechester, seized into the Duke's Hands on the Felony of Roger de Allele.

An Indenture of Agreement concerning Tenements in Romesgrene and the towns of Penhulton and Cliderowe, between the Duke and the Abbot and Convent of Whalley.

Grant of the Bailiwick of Derby Wapentake for Life.

Mandate to the Duchy Escheator not to interfere further as to Messuages and Lands in Asteley and Hyndeley, seized into the Duke's Hands by reason of the Felony of Richard de Atherton.

On the back and in continuation of this Roll to the following effect :—

The Duke to Adam Skillingcorn.—A Lease of a Place called Hoddesdone for 12 Years, at £2 6s. 8d. per Ann. Henry Le Norres of Speek, and others, for the Duke.

Recognisances of Debts and divers other Recognisances of Debts.

A Lease by the Duke to William, son of Adam of Lyverpull, and More de Lyverpull, and others de Lyverpull, of the Town, with all the Mills of the same Town, together with the Rents and Services, and the Passage of the Water of Merese, with the Turbary of Toxteth Park and the stallages as therein particularised. [The Instrument, as enrolled, is very obscure. It is tested, Henry de Walton, Lieutenant of the Duchy, at Lancaster, 24th March, 11th Year of the said Duke—1361.] [1]

---

[1] The duke died the day before this date. —H.

Mandate to John Haverington and others, to raise Soldiers, Men-at-Arms, and Archers, in the Wapentakes of Amounderness, Fourneys, and Lonsdale, within the Duchy, to march against the Scotch. And like Mandates to others for Derbyshire, Salfordshire, Blakeburnshire, and Leylondshire Wapentakes, with a distinct Mandate to the Sheriff to assist.

Grant of a yearly Rent of £10 to Henry Ditton out of the Lands of Thomas Ditton.

Grant of Wardship and Lands and Marriage of William the son of Robert de Prees.

The Duke's Pardon of Suit for Trespass and Hunting at Blakelegh Park.

Grant of Holtefeld in Salford.

Pardon of Peace to the Vicar of Kirkham Church for mal-administration in his Office of Dean of Amounderness.

Mandates to raise 300 Archers, to accompany the Duke to Brittany, from the various Wapentakes.

Grant of a Paviage for Preston, and for Customs on Merchandise in aid thereof.

Admissions of Attorneys to plead in the Duchy Courts.

Justices assigned for observing the Statute of Weights and Measures.

Permission to inquire of lands in Hornclyve.

Grant of the Wardship of Lands of Adam de Mondesley.

Paviage for the Town of Lyverpull for two Years.

Mandate to the Duchy Escheator for Livery of Seisin of Lands in Radeclif, as forfeited by Felony, the Duke having had year, day, and waste.

Confirmation of a Grant of Henry, Earl of Lancaster, to William Norreys, of Lands in Derby.

Writ of the Disseisin of Dokesbury [Duxbury] Manor.

The like of Lands in Chorley.

Mandate to the Escheator for Land in Penwortham, seized for withdrawing of the service of a Boat over the River Ribble.

Writ of the Disseisin for Lands in Ellale.

Grant of the Site of Ulneswalton Manor to Richard de Hibernia, the Duke's Physician, with Liberty to be Toll free and Hopper free at the Duke's Mills.

Grant of Allowance to the Town of Overton to grind Corn at the Duke's Mill at Lone.

Grant of the Custody of St. Mary's Chapel at Syngleton.

Pardon for Trespasses in the Duchy Forests.

Pardon for Non-Appearance in Court.

Justices assigned to keep the Waters in which Salmons are caught.

Justices to inquire of Stoppages in the Duchy Rivers, and chiefly the Ribble, to the injury of Penwortham Fishery.

Appointments of Stewardships.

Pardon of a Fine pro Licentia Concordandi, as to Tenements in Mamcestre.

Inquisition and Letters Patent touching the Manor of Mamcestre as a Market Town and Boro' with the Hamlets thereto.

The Duke to Thomas de Lathum and Wife.

Licence to hold Knouselegh Park.

Agreement touching the Wardship of Lands and the Marriage of Richard de Molyneux of Sefton.

Divers Letters of Protection for Persons serving the King abroad.

Confirmation of a Lease of the Manor of Aldeclif to the Prior of Lancaster.

Warrant to levy 520 Marks (£346 : 13 : 4) from the Freeholders of Quernmore Forest and the Natives of Lonsdale, as their portion of £1,000 Fine for Trespasses against the Assize of the Forest.

Several Mandates to the Escheators concerning various Lands seized.

Divers pardons for Trespasses and Assaults.

Exemplification of Proceedings touching the Intail of the Manor of Bury.

The like as to Lands in Harewode, the Water of Hyndeburne, and Clayton on the Mores.

[The other Records of the Annals of the Duchy are marked A.4. and A.5., and are similar in their contents to A.1. These Rolls terminate the Records of the first Duke, who died in the year 1361, without male issue.]

So rich an inheritance as the dukedom of Lancaster could not remain long in abeyance. The marriage of John of Gaunt, the fourth son of the reigning monarch of England, to Lady Blanche, the youngest daughter of the deceased duke, produced the almost immediate revival of the title, and the subsequent death of lady Maud, her elder sister, without issue, invested Duke John with the whole of those extensive possessions which the first duke had left to his children. The confidence reposed by the king in this, his favourite and most highly-gifted son, conferred upon him everything but sovereign power ; and his second marriage with Constance, the eldest daughter of Peter the Cruel, obtained for him the title of King of Castile and Leon. In this character he obtained the right to coin money, and several pieces were struck bearing his superscription. The wars in which he was engaged have already been adverted to,[1] and the history of this munificent duke shortly portrayed. His claim to the throne of Sicily, founded on no just pretension. produced a strong remonstrance on the part of his holiness Pope Urban V., who issued on the occasion one of those bulls at the bare name of which princes and kings were accustomed to tremble. This bull is still preserved, though divested of its seal. The inquiry upon what legitimate ground the Duke of Lancaster founded his pretensions to the kingdom of Sicily he was not able to answer to the Pope's nuncio, and from that time this claim seems to have been abandoned.

The Continental wars in which the English were engaged did not prevent them from embarking on a crusade against Ireland, that unfortunate country which has for so many centuries been the scene of oppression and misgovernment. In a writ addressed to the sheriff of Lancashire by the king, the Irish people are characterised as " our enemies, and rebels ; " and it is announced to the sheriff that Lionel, Duke of Clarence, the king's son, is on his way to Ireland to coerce the " rebels " into subjection, and the ports of Liverpool and Chester are required to send ships, properly manned, to support the expedition, (1361).[2] That the object of this armament was not very speedily accomplished may be inferred from the fact that, two years afterwards, a proclamation was issued

[1] See chap. iv.   [2] Pat. 35 Edw. III. p. 2. m. 24, Turr. Lond.

by the king for seizing eighty ships, of thirty tons burden and upwards, wherever they could be found, on the western coast, between Bristol in Somersetshire and Furness in Lancashire, which ships were to be sent to Lyverpole, before the feast of St. Peter ad Vincula (Aug. 1), to assist Prince Lionel in carrying on the war against Ireland. At that time the exports of Liverpool were very subject to the restrictions of orders in council. In 1362 the bailiffs of Liverpool and John, Duke of Lancaster, both received orders from the government to prohibit the exportation of provisions of various kinds, as well as of dyewares and other commodities, which prohibition extended to cloths called "worstedes,"[1] and to sea-coal, then recently discovered as an article of fuel; and similar interdicts, soon after issued, extended the prohibition to horses, linen, woollen yarns, jewels, and the precious metals. Liverpool was at that period rising, though slowly, into importance; and an order was issued by the king to the admiral on the station, as well as to the sheriff of the county, and the mayor and bailiffs of the borough, to rebuild (de novo construere) a bridge over the Mersey within their lordship. The alarm of invasion was again spread with great assiduity, and the royal proclamations of 1369 diligently propagated these apprehensions, in order to quicken the transmission of the public supplies. Adam de Hoghton, Roger de Pilkinton, William de Atherton, Richard de Radclyf, and Matthew de Rixton, commissioners of array for the county of Lancaster, were appointed, by royal mandate (1369), to press and enrol four hundred archers in Lancashire, to accompany John, Duke of Lancaster, to Aquitaine;[2] and the archbishops, bishops, abbots, priors, dukes, marquesses, earls, barons, and castellans, were informed that the king had appointed his son, the Duke of Lancaster, his captain and lieutenant in "Guynes and Caleys," the Black Prince having then returned to England broken in health. In the following month the sheriff of Lancaster was commanded to array, by himself or his deputies, all men in the county capable of bearing arms between the ages of sixteen and sixty years, and to cause them to be in readiness, and properly equipped, to resist the French, who threatened to invade England, to obstruct the passage of merchants and merchandise, and to abolish the English language![3] By a subsequent proclamation it was ordained that the men-at-arms, hobelers, and archers in the county of Lancaster should be in complete readiness by Palm Sunday (April 7, 1370), and William de Risseby, John Blake, clerk, Matthew de Rixton, and Richard ap Llewellyn Vaughan, had confided to them the power to arrest all ships, from twelve to forty tons burthen, in the ports of Lyverpull, and all other places from thence to Chester, that port included, and to send them to the ports of Southampton and Plymouth by Sunday next before the feast of Pentecost (Sunday, May 26), with a sufficient equipment of sailors for the passage, to embark in the expedition of John, Duke of Lancaster, and others in his company, going to Gascony.[4] To prosecute all these hostile operations the king, this year, by the authority of Parliament, levied upon the parishes of England a tax of fifty thousand pounds, each parish being required to pay five pounds fifteen shillings, the greater to help the less. From this return it appears that there were then eight thousand six hundred and thirty-two parishes in England, and that the contribution of

				£	s	d
Lancashire, for its 58 parishes, was				336	8	0
Westmoreland,	32	„	„	185	12	0
Cumberland,	96	„	„	556	16	0
Middlesex, exclusive of London, 63 parishes, was				365	8	0
London,	110 parishes, was			638	0	0
Yorkshire,	540	„	„	3132	0	0

But it was in vain that John of Gaunt marched through France from Calais to Bordeaux; the French were ready to harass him by skirmishes, but not to fight in any general engagement, and as a consequence no great battle occurred.

By an indenture, made in 1371, between the king and his son John, Duke of Lancaster, King of Castile and Leon, the duke grants to his father the county, castle, town, and honor of Richmond, in exchange for the castle, manor, and honor of Tykhill, castle and manor of High Peak, with knights' fees, together with the advowson of the churches of Steyndrop and Brannspath, the free chapels of Tykhill and High Peak, the church and free chapel of Marsfeld, the free chapel of Pevenese, the priory of Wylmyngdon, the priory of Whitiham, and the house of St. Robert of Knaresborough, with the castle, manor, and honor of Knaresborough, the hundred or wapentake of Stayncliff, in Yorkshire, and the manor of Gryngeley and Whetebury.[5] At the same time an order was issued by the king to the freemen, and all other tenants on the exchanged possessions, ordering them to obey John, Duke of Lancaster; and similar orders were given by the duke "to the venerable fathers, all and singular his archbishops, bishops, and other prelates of churches,

---

[1] This well-known woollen fabric derived its name from Worstead, then a busy town, but now an unimportant village about a dozen miles north of Norwich, where the manufacture was carried on.—C.
[2] Rot. Vascon. 43 Edw. III. m. 5. Turr. Lond.
[3] Rot. Vascon. 43 Edw. III. m. 3, Turr. Lond.
[4] Rot. Franc. 44 Edw. III. m. 25, Turr. Lond.
[5] Rot. Pat. 1 Rich. II. p. 1. m. 11 per inspex. Turr. Lond.

21

and to his earls, viscounts, barons, and others holding of the castle, honor, and county of Richmond," announcing that he had granted to his royal father and lord the county of Richmond, and commanding that all vassals and feudatories should perform homage, fealty, and all other services and duties to the king. [1]

The prerogatives of *jura regalia* conferred upon John of Gaunt in his duchy and county palatine of Lancaster were greatly enlarged by the royal bounty, by which he was appointed the king's especial lieutenant and captain-general of "our kingdom of France," and in Aquitaine and the parts beyond the sea.[2] This authority was still further enlarged by the memorable charter granted to the duke in the early part of the reign of his royal nephew (June, 1379), of which charter it may be said in a few words that it gave the largest powers possible to a subject to John of Gaunt, both upon the sea and in France, Aquitaine, and "elsewhere in all parts beyond the sea."

The persons embarked with the duke in his foreign expeditions were privileged by royal authority, and letters of protection were granted by the king, directing that all noblemen and others attached to the expedition should cross the sea without delay, so that none of them should be found in this country after the approaching feast of St. John the Baptist (June 24, 1379). Amongst others engaged in this expedition, and to whom letters of protection were addressed, we find the names of Robert, son of William de Clyfton; William de Barton, of Ridale; Adam del Darn; Henry Fitzhenry, son of Thomas de Alkeryngton; John de Ribelton, of Preston, in Amondernesse; Hugh de Tyldesley; John Redeman; and Adam, son of Adam de Lancaster.

Ireland was still treated as a conquered country, and each successive lord-lieutenant, instead of sailing for that island in the character of a messenger of peace, was armed with a strong naval and military force, as if embarking against a hostile state. Accordingly, we find an order from the king to the sheriffs (1373), announcing that he had appointed Simon Charwelton, clerk, and Walton de Eure, to arrest ships of from twenty to two hundred tons burthen in Bristol and the other western ports as far as Lyverpole, at which latter place they were to rendezvous, for the passage of William de Wyndesore, "governor and warden of the land of Ireland."[3]

In these early days, amongst all the restrictions on commerce, we find no laws against the importation of grain, but there are frequent interdicts against the exportation of that article; and hence we have, in the year 1375, a precept to the sheriff of the county of Lancaster, directing him not to allow the exportation of wheat, barley, or other grain from this county.

The reign of Edward III., though a period of war and military renown, terminated in peace. For the restoration of this blessing the country was indebted to John of Gaunt, Duke of Lancaster, who, in virtue of the powers with which he was invested, concluded a treaty of peace with Flanders, and also a truce with France, which, after having been prorogued from time to time, terminated finally in an adjustment of the differences between the two nations. In the last year of this king's reign (1377) a grant, as we have already seen, of chancery in the county palatine of Lancaster was made by the Duke of Lancaster;[4] and the reign concluded, as it had begun, with favours and privileges to the ducal house, which had long held the first station amongst the peers of the realm, and was speedily to be advanced to sovereign power.

[1] Ex. origin. in Turr. Lond.
[2] Rot. Franc. 47 Edw. III. m. 19, Turr. Lond.
[3] Pat. 47 Edw. III. p. 2. m. 24, Turr. Lond.
[4] See chap. iv.

CHAPTER X.

OHN OF GAUNT, Duke of Lancaster, had now attained his meridian power, and the reign of Richard II. may not inaptly be called the regency and vice-royalty of the duke. Though the king swayed the sceptre, his noble uncle guided the arm that wielded it; and all the principal measures of his reign were supposed by the people, and not without cause, to emanate from the palace of the Savoy or the castle of Lancaster. No subject of the realm had by any means equal power in this kingdom; and, as the representative of the king in foreign countries, he exercised prerogatives seldom confided to a subject. The wealth of the duke was immense, but the splendour and state which he maintained absorbed and even anticipated his princely income. The arts were then slowly emerging from the night of the middle ages; the dogmas of the schools and the superstitions of the monasteries were shaken by the rising spirit of inquiry; poetry, hitherto almost unknown in this island, except in the effusions of the Welsh bards and of Caedmon, began to be cultivated; and "time-honoured Lancaster" was amongst the most munificent patrons of genius in his age and nation.

In the "process and ceremony of the coronation" of Richard II. (July 16, 1377), who was now but eleven years of age, we find the names of John, Duke of Lancaster, Roger le Strange de Knokyn, John la Warre, Henry de Grey de Wilton, and Archibald de Grelly, all names connected with the county of Lancaster, and attached, for the purposes of this ceremony at least, to the king's court. This "process" John, King of Castile and Leon, Duke of Lancaster, and high steward of England, delivered with his own hand into the king's court of chancery.[1] The ceremonial, which was one of unusual splendour, was performed almost as soon as the obsequies of the late king were ended, and was doubtless hastened by the fact that apprehensions were entertained of the ambitious designs of John of Gaunt, who, as eldest surviving son of Edward III., expected to be sole regent. The Parliament assembled in October of the same year, when, at the request of the Commons, the Lords, in the king's name, appointed nine persons, of whom the Duke of Lancaster was one, to be a permanent council of the king, and further resolved that, during the king's minority, the appointment of all the chief officers of the crown should be with the Parliament. The decision was a grievous disappointment to the duke, and his feelings must have been ill-concealed, for there is upon the rolls of Parliament a speech that he made, in which he demanded the punishment of those who had spoken of him as a traitor. But the times were serious for England, and men's minds were exercised less by the doings in Parliament at home than by the prospect of impending danger abroad. The wars of Edward III. had produced no permanent advantage, but had engendered a spirit of revenge that threatened the safety of the country. The truce with France had expired, and Charles V., acting in concert with Spain, had lost no time in renewing hostilities; the Scots, ever restless, were again in arms, and had succeeded in burning Roxburgh and capturing Berwick. There were, in fact, enemies all round; commerce was interrupted, the seaports were ravaged, and the Isle of Wight had been plundered. The high reputation of the duke pointed him out as the mediator of differences, whether of a national or a domestic kind; and after having settled the quarrel with France and with Belgium, we find him appointed a commissioner to compose the ancient differences between the gallant Earls of Northumberland and Douglas.[2] In 1378 the prerogatives of *jura regalia* were renewed in favour of "King John," Duke of Lancaster, as he was called, on going abroad, and rendered as extensive as they were in the time of King Edward III. The privilege of coining money in the city of Bayonne and other places was at the same time renewed.[3] In the same year the duke's eldest son, Henry of Bolingbroke, whose name figures so prominently in later history, was deemed of sufficient age to receive the honour of

[1] 1 Richard II. claus. 1. m. 44.　　　[2] Scot. 1 Richard II. m. 7.　　　[3] 2 Richard II., Vasc. 3. R.

knighthood, and his father, in accordance with custom, in the second year of his regality (1378), issued a summons to Richard de Townley, the sheriff, to levy the usual aid to make him a knight. The following year plenary power was given to the duke in the marches of Scotland. While clothed with these powers the duke concluded a peace with Scotland, which was confirmed by the king, his nephew, at Northampton, and proclaimed in this county, under the designation of the "Great Truce," by the sheriff of Lancaster, at the end of the year 1380. The insurrection of Wat Tyler and his confederates, in which the house of the Duke of Lancaster, situated in the Savoy in London, was destroyed,[1] interrupted the proceedings of the court of justice at Westminster; on which occasion a proclamation was issued by the king to the Duke of Lancaster, ordaining that on account of the unheard-of and horrible commotions and insurrections of the people in the kingdom of England, and for averting the dangers arising from the incursions of foreign enemies, as well as for other reasons, all the pleadings in the Court of King's Bench stood adjourned; and all writs and mandates delivered to the duke, his chancellors, justiciaries, sheriffs, or other ministers, within the county of Lancaster, should be returned on the octaves of St. Michael (Oct. 7, 1380), instead of at the usual period.[2] The seditions which originated in the neighbourhood of London spread into the provinces; and rumours were very extensively circulated that these disturbances were fomented by the Duke of Lancaster and other peers, in order to procure the deposition of the king, that they might usurp the royal authority. To these rumours it was judged proper to give the most positive and solemn contradiction, in consequence of which a proclamation was issued by the king to all archbishops, prelates, and others, wherein it was announced that a hateful rumour, which wounded and grieved the royal heart beyond measure, had been diffused throughout divers parts of the kingdom, representing that the detestable disturbance in certain counties of England, against their allegiance to the king and the public peace, had been instigated by John, Duke of Lancaster, and certain others, prelates and faithful subjects; which rumours the proclamation denounced as wicked inventions, and declared the duke had always been faithful and zealous for the honour and safety of the country (1381).[3] These sinister rumours, notwithstanding, at length became so prevalent as to endanger the personal safety of the duke; and a proclamation was in consequence issued to Henry de Percy, Earl of Northumberland, and to John, Lord de Nevyll, appointing them to raise a bodyguard for the duke, with all possible despatch, both men-at-arms and archers, to protect him against the violence of his enemies. A mandamus was also directed to the sheriff of Lancashire to make proclamation within the duchy of the ordinances against unlawful assemblies, &c., as recited in the royal mandate of June 18, 4 Rich. II. (1380).[4] The duke was at the same time appointed the king's justiciary, to inquire, on oath, within the counties in his duchy, and the county palatine of Lancaster, into depredations, robberies, homicides, burnings, and rapes, with power to punish the offenders. That these crimes had attained to a frightful magnitude in Lancashire may be inferred from a species of royal proclamation issued by the king and duke (King of Castile and Duke of Lancaster) to the sheriff of the county of Lancaster, preserved in the archives of the duchy,[5] in which, after ordaining that the "holy Anglican Mother Church" shall have all its liberties whole and unimpaired, and fully enjoy and use the same, and that the great charter and forest charter shall, according to the statute 6 Rich. II. cap. 6 (1382), be firmly observed, proceeds to say that so licentious had become the public manners, that the female character was treated with the greatest disrespect, and "ladies and other noble maids and women," were frequently violated by force, and that the resentment of the persons subject to these outrages was so slight that numbers of them married their ravishers; for remedy of which it was ordained, that if after such outrage the parties contracted marriage, they should both of them be disabled, *ipso facto*, from maintaining any inheritance, dowry, or conjoint feoffment, or from receiving any bequest from their ancestors, and that the inheritance should descend to the next in blood.[6] The crime of abduction at this time was of frequent occurrence, and the carrying off a wife by force was by no means uncommon among knights and gentlemen as well as those of the meaner sort. The frequent wars at home and abroad, with the absence of any settled police, seem to have emboldened the young gallants of the day in the evil practice, in which they easily found lawless followers to help them.

For the purpose of interposing a barrier against the progress of the Scots in their future attempts to invade the northern counties of England, a treaty was entered into and ratified between John of Gaunt, Duke of Lancaster, and Henry de Percy, Earl of Northumberland (1383), in which it was stipulated that the freemen of the counties of Lancaster and Durham should be charged by

---

[1] See chap. iv. p. 40. The Savoy palace was built by Peter, Earl of Savoy and Richmond, on whose death it escheated to the crown; and Henry III. conferred it on his son, Edmund Crouchback, through whom it became a possession of the Earls of Lancaster.
[2] Claus. 4 Richard II. m. 1.
[3] Pat. 5 Richard II. p. 1. m. 32.
[4] Patent Rolls Richard II.—C.
[5] Roll A 6, m. 16.
[6] Scot. 7. Richard II. m. 1.

the lord to assemble, and to come with all their power, whenever proclamation was made by the Earl of Northumberland that the Scots had laid siege to any castle in the allegiance of the king. The stipulations of this treaty were soon brought into active operation, for on the 17th March, 1384, a mandate was addressed to Ralph de Radclyf, sheriff of Lancashire, to meet the Duke of Lancaster at Newcastle-on-Tyne, on the 24th March "next," with all the men-at-arms and archers arrayed within the duchy for the defence of the realm against the Scotch.[1] The Scots, aided by a body of French cavalry, renewed their incursions into Cumberland, Westmorland, and Lancashire, where they committed the most extensive outrages, on which the King of England, having assembled an army of 60,000 men, issued an order to the Duke of Lancaster to meet him with horse and arms at Newcastle, on the 14th of July (1384).[2] With this army the young king penetrated into Scotland, and, after having burnt the capital and laid waste all the towns and villages through which he had to pass, advanced as far as Dundee. This signal act of retributive justice put an end to the invasions of the Scots, and restored peace to the two countries.

A charge of high treason, in compassing the death of the king, and usurping his throne, was this year made, by John Latimer, B.D., an Irish Friar of the Franciscan order, against the Duke of Lancaster, which charge the duke, who had then just returned from his expedition into Scotland, vehemently denied, and required to be confronted with his accuser; but on the eve of the trial, according to Kennett,[3] "Lord John Holland, the king's half-brother, and Sir Henry Green, two of the duke's friends, entered the friar's lodgings, and cruelly put him to death with their own hands, by hanging him up by the neck and privy members, and laying a great stone upon his breast, which broke his neck; and, as if they had perpetrated this enormity by public authority, they drew his dead body through the streets the next day, as being deservedly punished as a traitor. This cruel action brought upon the duke much dishonour, and, though it ridded him of a false accuser, as was thought till the friar was so illegally put to death, yet it rendered his innocence more suspicious than before; and many believed him really guilty who before thought him falsely accused." This, to be sure, was a monstrous infraction of law and justice, and might well subject the duke to suspicion, if the fact could have been established that he was a party to the murder, in which light the punishment of the friar must be viewed; but we do not find in the records of the day any evidence of this fact. It was an unfortunate trait in the king's character that he surrounded himself with ministers who were ready to foment the feeling of jealousy he entertained towards his uncles. The Duke of Lancaster was unpopular, and was generally suspected of the most ambitious and criminal designs; he appears, however, to have possessed many of the high qualities of a statesman—prudent, but not an enemy to improvement—generous without prodigality—possessing great wealth and influence, but there is no evidence of his ever having employed his power in any act of disloyalty to his nephew. While the duke was in France (August, 1384), with a grand retinue to renew the negotiations for peace, the king's ministers took advantage of his absence to bring his great partisan, John Northampton, late lord mayor of London, to trial, confiscated his estates, and sentenced him to perpetual imprisonment a hundred miles beyond the city, and, encouraged by their success, they formed the bold design of bringing the duke himself to trial for treason before Sir Robert Tresillian, chief justice of the King's Bench—a design as impudent as it was illegal. The duke, informed of their intention, retired to his castle at Pontefract, and everything seemed to threaten a civil war, when the king's mother, with much difficulty, patched up a kind of reconciliation between the king and Lancaster.

The war with Scotland being ended, and the Duke of Lancaster feeling that his possessions in the duchy and county palatine were secure, he prepared to enforce his claim, in right of his wife, to his inheritance in Spain,[4] leaving his son Henry, Earl of Derby, as his *locum tenens* in his absence. In this expedition, the most splendid of the age, he was accompanied by his chancellor, William de Ashton, Esq., Thomas de Ashton, Esq., John de Eccleston, of Lyverpole, Esq., and Thomas Holcroft, Esq., all of the county of Lancaster, with a number of knights and gentlemen, to whom letters of protection were given by the king.[5] On the 12th March, in the tenth year of his regality, Robert de Urswyk, escheator, Ralph de Radclyf, sheriff, John Croft, of Dalton, chr., and Thomas de Radclyf were appointed commissioners, by authority of a royal warrant, to elect a thousand of the best archers in the duchy, to proceed with the duke to Spain when summoned.[6] Previous to his departure, the duke entered into an engagement with the king his nephew that he would not make any treaty with the crown of Spain unless upon the condition that the King of Spain should pay to the King of England 20,000 gold doubloons; and the duke further engaged

[1] Patent Rolls (Duchy Records) 7 Richard II.—C.
[2] Claus. 8. Richard II. m. 3. d.
[3] Vol. i. p. 252.
[4] See chap iv.
[5] Patent Rolls (Duchy Records) 9 Richard II.—C.
[6] *Ibid.*—C.

that he would repay to the king 20,000 marks (£13,333 6s. 8d.), which he had borrowed to defray the expenses incident to the fitting out of this expedition. The duke was accompanied on his expedition by his wife and his two daughters, Philippa and Katharine. The fleet in which they and their large force (the flower of English chivalry) embarked set sail in July, and the expedition remained abroad for some time, but the result was partly a failure and partly a success. The duke failed in securing the coveted crown of Castile, but he succeeded in finding a royal match for each of his daughters. The eldest, Philippa, he married to John I., King of Portugal, and the other, Katharine, was united to Henry, Prince of the Asturias, who, on the death of his father, became King of Spain—thus, though he lost himself a crown, he seated his descendants on the two thrones of Spain and Portugal.[1] After securing these advantageous alliances for his daughters and a large sum of money for himself he relinquished all claim to the crown of Castile and to any title to be called king of that country. Of this mission the following account is given in an ancient manuscript chronicle in the Harleian collection, in the British Museum.[2] [We have modernised the spelling.]

"And in the eleventh year of the reign of King Richard II. (1387), Sir John of Gaunt, Duke of Lancaster, went over the sea into Spain to challenge his right that he hath by his wife's title to the crown of Spain, with a great host of people, of lords, and knights, and squires, men-of-arms, and archers; and had the duchess his wife and his three daughters over the sea with him in Spain. And there they were a great while, till at last the King of Spain began [to] treat with the Duke of Lancaster; and as they were accorded together, through their sooth counsels, that the King of Spain should wed the duke's daughter of Lancaster that was heir to Spain, and the King of Spain gave to the Duke of Lancaster of gold and silver that were cast into great ingots, as much as eight chariots might carry, and many other rich jewels and gifts; and every year after, during the life of the Duke of Lancaster and of the duchess his wife, 10,000 marks of gold,[3] and that by her [their] own adventure, costs, and charges, they of Spain should bring these 10,000 marks every year, yearly, into Bayonne, to the duke's assigns, by surety made. And the Duke of Lancaster wedded another daughter of his unto the King of Portingale, well and worthily, and left there his two daughters with their lords their husbands, and came him home again into England with the good lady his wife, Duchess of Lancaster."

During the duke's absence in Spain "a submission of award" was entered into between the honourable "Prince, King, and Duke," as he is designated in this document,[4] on the one part, and William Pargrave and Igden Slingsby, Esq., on the other part, relating to the manors of Scotton, Breareton, and Thonge, in the county of York, to determine how far the latter parties, in right of their wives, the daughters of William de Westfield, were entitled to certain privileges in these manors, the award to be made by twenty knights and esquires, the most sufficient that could be found near to the manors in litigation.

In the year 1388 the alarm of Scotch invasion was again very prevalent in this country, on which the king issued a proclamation to the Duke of Lancaster, or his chancellor, announcing that the Scots and their adherents had assembled a great army, and had hastily invaded the kingdom of England, burning, destroying, and horribly slaying men, women, and children, and had almost advanced to the gates of York. To repel this cruel invasion, the duke was required to make proclamation in all cities, boroughs, and market-towns, and other places in the county and duchy of Lancaster, that all lords, knights, esquires, and others competent to bear arms should repair with all speed to join the king's army.[5] Before the return of the duke from Spain, in 1389, the battle of Otterbourne, on which the ballad of "Chevy Chace" was founded, had been fought, Douglas had been made to bite the dust, and the Scots had been driven back into their own country, but the public mind still continued agitated in the extreme by the intrigues of the Duke of Gloucester and his adherents, who sought to usurp the royal prerogatives, and to use them for their own aggrandisement. The presence of the Duke of Lancaster served to check the turbulent and ambitious spirit of his brother of Gloucester, and to restore tranquillity to the State.

Although by Magna Charta it was declared that uniform weights and measures should be used throughout the whole kingdom, to guard against those impositions to which the people were exposed from the arts of fraudulent dealers, the provisions of the charter had hitherto not been enforced; it was now ordained by the authority of the king, on petition of the Commons, that a standard measure and weight should be established for the whole kingdom, and that any person convicted of using any other should not only make satisfaction to the aggrieved parties but should also be imprisoned for six months without bail. The county of Lancaster was, however, exempt from this enactment, "because," as the king says in his answer to the Commons, "there has always been a larger measure used in Lancashire than in any other part of the kingdom."[6]

The earliest enactments in the statutes of the realm for regulating the salmon fisheries of this kingdom are those of the statute of Westminster 2, of which the confirmations relate to the Lancashire rivers, the Lune, the Wyre, the Mersey, and the Ribble; and by a statute, 13

[1] Hume's Hist. Eng., v. iii. p. 113.—C.
[2] Harl. MSS. Cod. 266 fo. 98 b.
[3] 10,000 marks, in the ordinary money of account, equals £6,666 : 13 : 4. But the "mark of gold" (the expression used in the MS.) was equal to 20 marks of silver; so that if the term be taken literally, that sum must be increased twenty-fold. It is more probable that it means 10,000 ordinary marks, paid in gold.—H.
[4] Harl. MSS. Cod. 266, fo. 50.
[5] Claus. 12 Rich. II. m. 42.
[6] Rot. Parl. vol. iii. p. 270.

Richard II. c. 19 (1389-90), it is enacted, "That no young salmon be taken or destroyed by nets, at mill dams or other places, from the middle of April till the Nativity of St. John Baptist;" and " it is ordained and assented that the waters of Lon, Wyre, Mersee, Ribbyl, and all other waters in the county of Lancaster, be put in defence, as to the taking of salmons, from Michaelmas Day to the Purification of our Lady (Feb. 2), and in no other time of the year, because that salmons be not seasonable in the said waters in the time aforesaid; and in the parts were such rivers be, there shall be assigned and sworn good and sufficient conservators of this statute." This Act was amended by 17 Richard II. c. 9 (1393-4), which enacts " that the justices of the peace shall be conservators of the recited statute, with under-conservators appointed by them, and that the said justices shall inquire into the due execution of the law at their sessions;" and further amended by 1 Eliz. c. 17 (1559), which, amongst other things, provides that the meshes of the nets used in taking salmon shall be two inches and a half broad, and that the fish shall not be taken by any other means.[1]

    "In 1393, John, Duke of Lancaster, son of the King of England, Duke of Guienne, Earl of Derby, Lincoln, and Leicester, and steward of England," as he is styled in the parliamentary records, and Thomas, Duke of Gloucester, constable of England, "complained to the king that Sir Thomas Talbot, knight, with others his adherents, conspired the deaths of the said dukes in divers parts of Cheshire, as the same was confessed and well known, and the dukes prayed that Parliament might judge of the fault. Whereupon the king and the lords in Parliament adjudged the said Thomas Talbot guilty of high treason, and awarded two writs— the one to the sheriffs of York and the other to the sheriffs of Derby, to take the body of the said Sir Thomas, returnable in the King's Bench in the month of Easter then ensuing ; and open proclamation was made in Westminster Hall that upon the sheriffs' return at the next coming in of the said Sir Thomas he should be convicted of treason, and incur the loss and penalty of the same." [2]

Notwithstanding all these court intrigues the honours and privileges of the Duke of Lancaster continued to accumulate; and by an act of royal favour he was allowed to hold Aquitaine in liege homage of the king; and all prelates, earls, viscounts, and others were commanded to pay homage to the duke. The viceroyalty of Picardy was soon after conferred upon him, at which time the privilege was conceded to him of importing sixty casks of wine, duty free, for the use of his household.[3]

    The scandal raised at court by the marriage of John of Gaunt, the king's uncle, to his mistress Catherine Swinford,[4] was somewhat abated by the king's patent, which legitimised her four children by the duke. These children were surnamed Beaufort, from the place of their birth, the patent of legitimation bearing date on the 10th of February, 1397.[5]

    In the following year (1398) the quarrel between the Duke of Lancaster's eldest son, Henry of Bolingbroke, Duke of Hereford, and Thomas Mowbray, first Duke of Norfolk which terminated in the banishment of both these knights, took place.[6] The death of the illustrious and venerable Duke of Lancaster was precipitated by this event;[7] and the deposition of Richard II., "unking'd by Bolingbroke," speedily followed.[8] On the death of his father, the Duke of Hereford returned to England, ostensibly to claim his paternal inheritance of the duchy of Lancaster, but really, through the public power, and his own daring, to assume the still higher possession of the throne. Amongst the most powerful of the adherents of the Duke of Lancaster were Henry de Percy, Earl of Northumberland, and his son Henry Hotspur, to whose services he was essentially indebted for his elevation; and one of the first acts of the new king's reign was to present the earl with a grant of the Isle of Man, to hold by the feudal service of bearing the *curtana*, called the "LANCASTER SWORD," on the day of the coronation,[9] at the left shoulder of the king and his heirs, which sword had been borne by John of Gaunt at the coronation of Richard II. This grant is represented, in the document by which it is made, as the inadequate reward of the earl's magnificent and faithful services to the State. The island, castle, peel, and lordship of Man, the possession of William le Scrope, Earl of Wiltshire, had been seized by the king, on the execution of the earl for misgoverning the kingdom in the time of Richard II.; and the whole of these possessions, together with the regalia, royal jurisdictions, franchises, liberties, and the patronage of the bishopric, as well as the goods and chattels of the unfortunate earl, were conferred upon the Earl of Northumberland in perpetuity. The restless spirit of Northumberland, who thought himself inadequately rewarded by the Isle of Man, while he had secured for his sovereign the kingdom of England, urged him on to acts of rebellion against King Henry, as he had before rebelled against his predecessor. Less fortunate in his second than in his first revolt, the reward of his perfidy to Richard overtook him, and he lost, in the sequel, his son young Hotspur, his possessions, and his life. By the attainder of the Earl of Northumberland, the Isle of Man, after six years, again fell into the possession of the

---

[1] The subsequent statutes for the regulation of these fisheries are 4 and 5 of Anne, c. 21 (1706); 1 George I. stat. ii. c. 18 (1714); 23 George II. c. 26 (1749-50); 43 George III. c. 61 (1802-3).
[2] See chap v.
[3] The duty on wine at this time was 3s. per cask, with an ad valorem duty of 5 per cent upon its introduction into the port of London.

[4] See chap. iv. p. 60.
[5] Rot. Parl. vol. iii. p. 343.
[6] See chap. v. p. 64.
[7] P. 65.
[8] P. 66.
[9] Pat. 1 Hen. IV. p. 5 m. 35

Crown, and was seized for the king's use by Sir William and Sir John Stanley;[1] on which the king, by letters patent (dated 4th Oct., 1405), of his especial grace and favour, granted to Sir John Stanley the island, castle, peel, and lordship of the Isle of Man, and all the islands and lordships thereto belonging, together with regalia, regalities, franchises, and liberties, and all other profits and commodities annexed thereto, to have and to hold for the term of his life.[2]

On the 6th of April, 1406, the king so far extended his bounty as to grant the Isle of Man to Sir John Stanley in perpetuity, in as full and ample a manner as it had been held by any former lord of the crown of England, *per homagium legium*, but altering the tenure, which was now, instead of bearing the Lancaster sword at the coronation, to pay to the king a cast of falcons at the coronation, after homage made in lieu of all demands and customs. By this grant the Stanleys obtained an absolute jurisdiction over the soil, and became, with the exception of a few baronies, immediate landlord of every estate in the island, a semi-regal position which, save a brief interregnum during the Commonwealth period, they retained until the death, without male issue, of James Stanley, in 1736, when the lordship passed to the House of Athole, James Murray, the second duke, being descended from a daughter of James, the seventh Earl of Derby.

The annals of the duchy, during the whole period of the life of John of Gaunt, will at all times rank amongst the most interesting records in the early history of the county palatine of Lancaster; but though they are all before us, they are much too voluminous to be inserted in detail, and can only be given in summary, with such references as may enable those who wish to consult particular documents to find them with facility. These annals being resumed from the period of the death of the first Duke of Lancaster, and brought down to the demise of the last subject duke, comprehend the whole period of the history of the duchy, from its creation to the time when it merged in the Crown, not indeed by absolute union, for the duchy of Lancaster has always been considered a separate inheritance, but by actual possession—the Kings of England and the Dukes of Lancaster having been the same persons ever since the time when Henry of Bolingbroke ascended the throne, to the present day.

EXTRACT FROM CLOSE ROLL, A.6.

John, Duke of Lancaster—viz. 1377 (51 Edw. III.) to 1389 (12 Rich. II.)

(From the Duchy Records in the Record Office).

PERSONS.	MATTERS.
The two introductory instruments are as follow :— 51 Edw. III.	
John the Duke to Thomas de Thelwall	[2] Appointment of Chancellor of the Duchy and County Palatine, and delivery of the Great Seal of the Royalty.
Also, the Duke to the Sheriff of the County....................	Proclamation of Pleadings of Assize, &c.
1. John Hodelleston and Wife to the Duke	Fine for Writ of Assize de Nov. Dis. 20s. paid to the Hanaper.
Nicholas de Syngleton to the Duke	Fine of 10s. for a Writ de Conventione.
2. The King and Duke for Robert, son of Sir John de Harryngton, Knt.	Mandate to Roger de Brokholes, the Duke's Escheator, for delivery of Lands formerly held in Capite.
3. The King and Duke for Henry de Ferrarijs	Mandate to the Escheator to deliver Lands formerly held in Capite.
4. The King and Duke for Walter Pedwardyne and others......	Like Mandate for Advowsons of Churches, &c. Conyngshead Priory and Wharton Church.
5. The King and Duke for William de Brottrieux, Ellalle, Scotforde, Assheton, and others.................................	The like for delivery of a Moiety of Knight's Fee and Appurtenances in Right of Thomas de Thweng.
6. The King and Duke for the Duke : Adam de Hoghton, Keeper of Quernemore Forest	Warrant to cut Timber for Repairs of Lancaster Castle.
7. The King and Duke for the Duke	Precept to the Mayor and Bailiffs of Lancaster and other Persons, to proclaim prohibition against Persons congregating with an armed power to impede the Sessions at Lancaster.
8. Various Fines paid for Writs.	
9. The King and Duke for the Duke	Writ to the Escheator to seize the Lands of Nicholas de Prestwyche.
10. The King and Duke for John Boteler and Nicholas de Haveryngton..	Precept to the Sheriff for paying them £26 8s. as Knights elect for the Commonalty of the Duchy, for Expenses in coming to the King's Parliament.

[1] Writs dated Pountfreyt Castle, 3d July, 6 Hen. IV.
[2] Claus. 8 Henry IV. m. 42.
[2] This appointment is dated at Westminster, 16th April 51 Edw. III. (1377), and states that John, King of Castile and Leon and Duke of Lancaster, in the presence of Robert de Wylington and Thomas de Hungerford, knights, and others of the king's household, in the chapel within the palace, appointed Thomas de Thelwall, clerk, his chancellor within the duchy and county of Lancaster, who took his oath to the same king, and his great seal for the administration of the regalities of the county palatine of the same, with his own hand to the said Thomas delivered, etc. Afterwards, the chancellor having received the seal, the said king, on the 20th

April in the first year of his regality (1377), by writ directed to the sheriff of Lancashire, assigned William de Skipwyth, Roger de Fulthorp, and William de Nessefeld to be his judges for all pleas, etc., in the county, ordered that the said justices should hold their sessions at Lancaster on the Monday after Ascension day, and that due proclamation should be made in full court and in various market-places of the suits or pleas to be prosecuted before the same justices, taking then and there twenty-four of the discreet, lawworthy, and honest men, from every wapentake or hundred in the said county, for the further fulfilling of the mandate. The sheriff to return the names of the twenty-four men and this writ.

PERSONS.	MATTERS.
11. The King and Duke for King Richard	Precept for Proclamation that all Foreign Mendicant Friars within the Duchy quit the Realm, according to the King's Mandate.
12. The King and Duke for the Prior and Convent of St. Mary's, Leicester	Precept to the Escheator not to interfere in the Manors and Possessions of the Abbey of St. Mary de Pratis, during the avoidance of the Abbot's death.

Here ends the first Year of the Royalty (1377), on the first side of the Roll. [1]

13. John, King of Castile, &c., for the Abbot of Furnes	Precept to the Sheriff, commanding the Executors of John Raton to pay £55 to the Abbot.
14. Fines paid to the Duke for various Writs, and attested by the Custos Regalitatis, William Wetherley, Vicar of Blakeburn Church·	
15. The King and Duke for the Abbot of Evesham	Mandate to the Barons of the Exchequer concerning the Fishery of Hoghwyk in the River Ribble, claimed by the Abbot, and seized by the Deputy-Steward of the Manor of Penwortham.
16. The same for the King and Duke	Mandate to the Sheriff to Levy Aid, according to the Statute, to make his eldest Son a Knight.
17. The same for the Duke and other Magnates of his Retinue going abroad in the King's service	Letters to the Abbots of Furneys, Whalley, Cockersand, and other Abbots, Priors, Archdeacons, and Proctors, to offer prayers and sacrifices to God for the success of the expedition.
18. The same for the Duke	Mandate to the Duke's Escheator to seize the Lands, &c., of Otho de Halsale.
19. The same for Richard de Townelay, Sheriff	Mandate to the Barons of the Exchequer to pay his Account of Charges for Parchment, &c.
20. The same for John Boteler and Ralph de Ypre.................	Precept to the Sheriff to pay the Knights elected for the Commonalty of the Duchy £16 for their Expenses in coming to Parliament at Gloucester.

This ends the second Year of the Royalty (1378).

21. 2 Rich. II. (1378-9). The King and Duke for Alan Wilkeson and Wife	Mandate to the Barons of the Exchequer to inquire of a Messuage and Lands seized into the Duke's hands, for the Felony of John de Leyland at Kirkeby, in Derbyshire.
22. Various Fines paid to the Duke for Writs.	
23. The King and Duke for the Duke	Mandate to the Justices to adjourn Sessions.
24. The same for the Abbot of Whalley	Mandate to the Barons to inquire of Tithes seized by the Escheator, as belonging to William Talbot, an Outlaw, touching the Tithes of the Church of All Saints of Whalley, at Alvetham.
25. The same for the King	Precept to the Sheriff to proclaim within the Duchy the Ordinance made as to the Goldsmiths' mark.
26. The same for Nicholas de Haryngton and Robert de Urswyk	Precept to the Sheriff to pay the Knights of the Commonalty their Expenses to Parliament at Westminster.
27. The same for the Duke	Precept to the Sheriff to elect a Coroner in the room of Thomas de Fasakereley.
28. The same for the Duke	Precept to eject Verderors for Derbyshire, Amounderness, and Lonsdale.
29. The King and Duke for John de Eccleston	Precept to the Sheriff to give Seisin (i.e. possession) of a Messuage and Lands taken by the Duke for the Felony of Robert de Raynhull.
30. The same for the Abbot of Evesham Monastery	Mandate to the Escheator to deliver Temporalities to Roger de Yatton, Abbot-elect.
31. The same for the same	Mandate to the Barons of the Exchequer to surcease demands upon the Abbot, and to answer for the Issues according to the Award of the Great Council.
32. The same for the Duke........	Mandate to the Escheator to seize the Lands, &c., of Sir Thomas Bannastre, Knight.

The end of the 3d Year of the Royalty (1379).

33. 3 Rich. II. (1379-80). The King and Duke for the Duke ...	Precept to the Sheriff for election of a Coroner.
34. The same for John de Boteler and Thomas de Southworth	Precept to the Sheriff to pay them as knights for the Commonalty, £24, for Expenses in coming to Parliament at Westminster.

Anno Quarto Regalitatis, John, Duke of Lancaster (1380).

3 Ric. II. (1379-80).	
35. Fines pad to the Lord for Writs.	
36. The King and Duke for John de Haydock........................	Precept to the Escheator to give seisin of the Lands of Willm. Botiller in Laton Magna, Laton Parva, Bispham, Warthebrek, and Great Merton ; and Rents in Atherton, Westlegh, Pynnyngton, Bolde, Lydegate, Thornton, Culcheth, Egergarth, Tildealegh, Glassebroke, Bedford, Halsall, Ives, and Wyndhull ; Great Sonkey Manor, and Werington Manor.
37. The same for John Botiller	Precept to give seisin of Lands and Mill in Burtonwood, and the Manor of Weryngton, with Advowson of the Church.

---

[1] The first year of the royalty or regality of John of Gaunt was the 17th year of his dukedom.—H.

PERSONS.	MATTERS.
38. The same for the Duke..	Precept to seize the Lands of William Botiller. The like of John Byron. The like of Richard Radclif.
39. The same for Gilbert de Gorfordsyche	Writ of Re-disseisin as to the Turbary in Scaresbrek.
40. The like for the Tenants of Worston Township..................	Mandate to the Barons of the Exchequer, relating to the Tenants of Worston, and Pasturage of Common and the Inclosure by William Nowel.
41. The same for John Botiller and Thomas de Southworth	Precept to the Sheriff to pay Knights for the Commonalty of the Duchy, £19 12s., their Expenses in coming to Parliamt. at Northampton.
42. The King and Duke for the Duke	Mandate to the Escheator to seize the Lands and Tenements of Peter Gerard. The like of Ellen de Birewayth. The like of Wm. de Bradshagh of Hagh. The like of Richd. de Caterall. The like of Gilbert de Kyghley. The like of Isabella de Eton.
43. The same for John Radecliffe	Mandate to give Seisin of the Manor of Urdesale [Ordsall], 3 parts of Moiety, of the Town of Flixton, Tenements in Le Hope, Shoresworth, Le Holynhed, in Tokholes, Salford, the Bailiwick of Rochdale, and ⅓ of moiety of the Town of Flixton.
44. The same for Isabella Bradeshagh	Mandate to assign Dower of Lands seized into the Duke's Hands by reason of the minority of Thomas Bradeshagh.

Writs of Diem Clausit Extremum.

45. The King and Duke for the Duke	Mandate to the Escheator to take the Lands of John de Skerton. And the like Mandate for several others upon deaths.
46. The same for Sir Roger Pilkington, Knight....................	Writ of Post Disseisin to the Sheriff for a Tenement in Rediche.
47. The King and Duke for the Abbot of Cokersand	Mandate to the Barons of the Exchequer to inquire of Rent of Hands in Mellyng, held by Hy. Chaderton, as seized for Debt.
48. Fines paid for various Writs to the Duke, as acknowledged by	William Horneby, Clerk of the Hanaper.
49. The King and Duke for the King	Precept to the Sheriff to take William Greenhil, an Outlaw, in the King's Court within the Duchy, according to the King's Mandate therein recited.
50. The same for same..	Precept to the Mayor and Bailiffs of Liverpool to proclaim the King's Mandate prohibiting Exportation of Corn.

Anno Sexto Regalitatis (1382).

51. The King and Duke for John de Warren	Mandate to the Escheator to give Seisin of Wood Plumpton Manor, as in Fee, by Sir John Davenport, Knt. to Robert de Eton.
52. The same for William de Atherton and Robert de Urcewyk.	Precept to the Sheriff to pay the Knights of the Commonalty of the Duchy for their expenses to Parliament at Westminster.
53. The King and Duke for the King	Precept to the Mayor and Bailiffs of Liverpool to proclaim the King's Mandate touching the Exportation of Corn.
54. The King and Duke for the King of Scotland	Precept to the Sheriff to distrain Persons in Liverpool possessing several Casks of Wine taken in the Port of Inchgalle by some Persons in the County of Chester, contrary to the Truce with Scotland, and to pay 10 Marks (£6 13s. 4d.) for each Cask.
55. The same for the King of England...	Precept to the Sheriff to publish the King's Proclamation within the Duchy relative to Charters of Pardon by the King's Subjects (except certain Persons named, and the Men of the City of Canterbury, of the Towns of Cambridge, Bridgwater, St. Edmund's, Beverley, and Scarboro')
56. The same for Sir Roger de Pilkington, Knt. and Robert de Clifton	Precept to pay the Knights elected for the Duchy Commonalty £10 for their Expenses to Parliament at Westminster.
57. Fines to the King and Duke for Writs.	
58. The King and Duke for the King of England	Precept to Liverpool as to Exportation of Corn.

Writs of Diem Clausit Extremum.

59. The King and Duke for the Duke	Mandate to the Escheator to take the Lands of Edward Lawrence and the Land of Thomas Lathum.
60. The King and Duke for the King of England	Precept to Liverpool as before.
61. The same for the Poor Fishermen in the Duchy	Precept to the Sheriff to publish the King's Prohibition against preventing the Fishermen from setting their nets in the Sea, and catching Fish for their Livelihood.
62. The same for Matilda Waryng	Writ of Re-disseisin to the Sheriff of a Messuage and Lands in Chippyn.
63. The same for Thomas de Knoll	Mandate to the Barons of the Exchequer to inquire of Lands in Chippendale, seized into the Duke's hands on the Felony of John de Knoll, as purchased after the King's Charter of Pardon.
64. The King of England for the King..................................	Writ addressed to the King of Castile and Duke of Lancaster, to cause to be elected and to come to Parliament 2 Knights for the Commonalty of the Duchy, and of every City 2 Citizens, and of every Boro' 2 Burgesses. Witness the King at Westminster, 7th January, 6 Ric. II. (1383).

PERSONS.	MATTERS.
65. The King and Duke for the King	Precept to the Sheriff to make Proclamation of the Statutes and Ordinances made in the Parliam⁺ of the 6ᵗʰ Year of King Richard (1383), as recited in the King's Mandate addressed to the Duke of Lancaster, or his Lieutenant. Witness the King at Lancaster, 8ᵗʰ Febry. (1383.)
66. The King and Duke for Margery Bannastre	Writ of Post Disseisin as to Dower of Lands in Walton in le Dale.
67. The same for the Owners of the Ship called Carrak, wrecked on the Duchy coast	Precept to the Sheriff to make Proclamation that all the Duke's Officers, Ministers, and Tenants of the Duchy, abstain from taking the Goods of the said Ship, the Crew having escaped alive.

Anno Septimo Regalitatis (1383).

68. The King and Duke for the Duke	Writ of Diem Clausit Extremum¹ upon the death of John de Kirkby, Chivaler.
69. The same for same..................	The like, upon death of David de Irland.
70. The same for same......	Precept to the Sheriff to elect a Verderor for Amounderness, instead of Adam Bradkirk.
71. The like	The like for Derbyshire, vice Richard de Aynscough.
72. The like	Do. to elect a Coroner for the County, vice Adam de Skylicorne.
73. The same for the Abbot of Cockersand	Do. to give Seisin of Lands in Billynge, seized by King Edward for the Felony of William de Falyngge.
74. Fines to the King and Duke for Writs.	
75. The King and Duke for Richard de Bareweford and Agnes, his Wife	Writ of Re-disseisin concerning Lands at Chorlegh.
76. Fines to the King and Duke for Writs.	
77. The King and Duke for the Duke	Writ of Diem Clausit, &c., directed to Robert de Ursewyk on the death of Hugh de Bradshagh.
78. The King and Duke for John Pilkington and Wife	Writ de Dote Assignanda directed to the Escheator, for Margaret de Bradshagh.
79. The same for same	Writ of Diem Clausit Extremum upon the death of Hugh de Dacre. Do. on the death of Thomas de Rigmayden. Do. of Thomas de Lathum. Do. of Richard de Balderston.
80. Fines paid to the Duke for Writs.	

Anno Octavo Regalitatis (1384).

81. The King and Duke for the Duke.............................	Precept to the Sheriff for Proclamation, that all the Men of the Duke's retinue meet him at Newcastle-upon-Tyne, to march into Scotland.
82. The same for Adam de Prestall of Salfordshire	Precept to the Sheriff not to put the said Adam on Juries, &c., he being deaf.
83. The same for Johanna Rigmayden	Writ de Dote Assignanda, addressed to the Escheator.
84. The King and Duke for the Duke.............................	Writ of Diem Clausit Extremum, on the death of Matthew de Twisalton. —— of John Kekwyk, of Derby. —— of William Barton.
85. Fines paid to the King and Duke for Writs.	
86. The King and Duke for the Duke........................	Mandamus to the Escheator, upon the death of Thomas de Rigmayden. —— of Thomas Banaster. —— of Edward Banastre.
87. The same for John Daunport (Davenport)	Mandate of William de Horneby, Receiver of the County of Lancaster, to pay the secondary Justice in the Duchy 20 Marks, for his Fee of 20s. for his Clerk for two last Sessions.
88. Fines paid to the King and Duke for Writs.	
89. The King and Duke for the King of England.................	Precept to the Sheriff to get ready the Men-at-Arms and Bowmen within the Duchy, to march agst the Scotch, according to the King's Mandate.
90. The same for the Abbot of Cockersand	Precept to give Seisin of Lands in Billynge, as seized into King Edward's Hands for the Felony of William de Falyng.
91. The King and Duke for Isabella Lathum.......................	Writ de Dote Assignanda out of Lathum Manor.
92. Fines paid to the King and Duke for Writs.	
93. The King and Duke for Roger de Fazackrelegh and Wife...	Writ de Procedendo in an Assize of Novel Disseisin before the Justices, as to Tenements in Knowslegh, Childwall, Roby, and Anlasargh.
94. The same for Johanna Kekewyk	Writ de Dote Assignanda.
95. The same for the Duke	Mandamus to the Escheator, upon the death of Thomas de Lathum.

¹ The "Inquisition" or "Inquest of Office," commonly called an *Inquisitio post mortem*, was an inquiry held on oath before a jury summoned by virtue of a writ directed to the escheator, coroner, or other officer of the king, to inquire on the death of any tenant holding lands *in capite*, or in chief, whether by knight's service or in soccage, (1) of what lands he died seized, (2) by what rents or services the same were held, and (3) who was the next heir and of what age. They were further to enquire whether the tenant was attainted of treason, or an alien, in either of which cases the lands reverted to the crown; if the heir was a minor, the king had the wardship or custody of the body and lands, with the profits accruing, until proof of legal age, and if there was no heir the lands became the king's by escheat, from which circumstance these documents are sometimes, though incorrectly, called *escheats*. The finding of the jury with the writ of enquiry was returned to the king's chancery, whence a transcript was sent to the exchequer in order that the proper officers might levy the services and duties due. The heir, on attaining the age of 21 if a male, or 16 if a female, might sue out their livery or *ouster le main* (*i.e.*, take off the hand) and obtain delivery of their lands out of their guardian's hands.—C.

PERSONS.	MATTERS.

Hic incipit Annus Nonus Regalitatis (1385).

96. The King and Duke for the King and Duke	Writ of Diem Clausit, &c. on the death of Henry de Dyneley.
	—— Geoffrey Workesley.
	—— Adam de Hoghton.
97. The same for the Duke	Precept to elect a Coroner for the County of Lancaster, vice
98. Fines paid to the Lord for Writs	John Skilicorn, deceased.
99. The King and Duke for John de Pilkyngton, Parson of the Church of Bury	Writ of Re-Disseisin as to the Manors of Le Lee, Grymsargh, Hoghton, Quylton, Ravenemeles, and Whytyngham, and Messuages and Lands in Lee, Goosnargh, Assheton, Grymesargh, Quytyngham, Frekilton, Caterall, Hoghton, Quilton, Withenhall, Hephay, Lynesey, Plesyngton, Wrightyngton, Ravenmeles, Goldburn, Preston, Sourby, Whittill in the Wodes, Walshwhittill, Eccleston, Chernock Richard, and Ribchester; and Moieties of Chernok Richard Manor and Whittill in the Wodes; two parts of Asheton and Gosenargh Manors, and the 4th part of Caterall and Wrightynton Manors.
100. The King and Duke for the King	Mandate to the Justices to adjourn Sessions.
101. The same for the Duke	Mandate to the Escheator to seize into the Hands of the King and Duke the Lands of Thomas Banastre in Ethelswyk, Freculton, Claughton in Amounds. Billesburgh, Halghton, Syngleton Parvā, Thornton le Holmes, Sowerby, Hamylton, Stalmyn, Crofton, Farryngton, Thorpe, and Brethirton.
	Like Mandate for the Lands of Edmond Banastre in Dilworth, Broghton, Preston in Amounderness, Wodeplumpton, with the More Hall and Gosenargh.
102. Fines paid to the Lord for Writs.	
103. The King and Duke for Isabella Lathum	Precept to the Sheriff to give Seisin of Tenements in Lathum Manor, vizt. Horskarre, Demedowe near Rughford, Robynfeld de Horskarre, Calverhay, Watton, Ryding, and 8 Marks (£5 6s. 8d.) Rent of Freeholds in Newburgh.
104. Fines paid to the Lord for Writs.	
105. John de Radclif to the Duke	Recognisance for Rent of Lands in Oldham, Chatherton, and Wytton, near Plesyngton.
106. The King and Duke for Margaret de Ines	Writ of Assignment of Dower to Margaret Bradeshagh, of a Water Mill in Westlegh, in the Duke's Hands by Minority of the Heir.
107. The same for Jas. Botiller, Earl of Ormond.....	Precept to the Escheator for Seisin of Rent of the Manor of Wetherton, notwithstanding no Process as to proof of Age, nor his being called on the Inquisition taken.
108. The same for Roger Fazackerlegh	Mandate to the Justices on the Bench to proceed on Novel Disseisin as to Tenements of Sir Thomas Lathum, Knt. in Knowslegh, Childwall, Roby, and Anhlesargh, and on no Accot to give Judgmt withot the Duke's advice.

Anno Decimo Regalitatis (1386).

109. Fines paid to the King and Duke.	
110. The King and Duke for Margaret de Radclif	Precept to the Receiver of the Duchy to pay a yearly Rent for Lands in Oldom, Chatherton, and Witton, near Plesington.
111. The same for Robert de Barton......	Writ of Re-disseisin for Messuages and Lands in Lathum.
112. Fines paid to the King and Duke.	
113. The King and Duke for the Duke...	Precept to the Sheriff to Levy £20 of the Lands of John de Radclif in Oldom, Chatherton, and Wytton, for Arrears.
	Witnessed by Henry, Earl of Derby, Custos of the Duchy.

Anno Undecimo Regalitatis (1387).

114. Fines paid to the King and Duke for Writs.	
115. The King and Duke for William Ward..........................	Writ to Walter de Urswyk, Keeper of Lancaster Forest, to accept Bail for the said William, detained in Lancaster Castle, for a Trespass on the Forest.
116. The King and Duke for the Duke..............................	Writ of Diem Clausit Extremum upon the deaths of Jno. de Wareyn, Thomas Strangways, Thomas Sotheworth, Richard Torbock, Thomas Holand, William Tunstall, Petronilla Banastre, Thomas Molyneux, and William Aghton.
117. The same for same	Precept to the Sheriff to elect a Coroner, vice Edward Frere.
	Do. vice Hugh de Ines, they being both incompetent to their Offices.
118. The same for same	Precept to the Sheriff to elect a Verduror for Quernmore and Wyresdale, vice John Croft, made Steward of Lonsdale.
	The like, vice Robt. Caunsefeld, he being in Spain with the Duke.
119. Fines paid to the King and Duke for Writs.	
120. Ralph de Radclif, Sheriff of Lancaster, for the King and Duke	Recognisance of Debt for the Sheriff to pay £80 for his office for one Year.
121. The same for same	Like Recognisance for a faithful Account of his profits.
122. The King and Duke, for John de Ines...........................	Precept to the Escheator to supersede the demand of £34 14s. 4d. of Lands, &c., in Wythyngton and Harewode, and other Moneys, till the next Sessions.

PERSONS.	MATTERS.

Anno Duodecimo Regalitatis (1388).

123. Fines paid to the King and Duke for Writs.	
124. The King and Duke for the Duke...............................	Mandate to the Justices to adjourn Sessions.
125. The same for same	Writs of Diem Clausit Extremum upon the deaths of Jno. de Haydok, of Alice de Legh, and John de Nevill.
126. The same for Milicent de Aghton	Writ to the Escheator for Assignment of Dower.
127. Fines paid to the King and Duke for Writs.	
128. The King and Duke for Ralph de Nevill	Precept to the Escheator for Livery of seisin of the Advowson of Prescote Church, and for Payment of Relief and for Respite of Homage till the Duke's return to England.

DUCHY OF LANCASTER.

CONTINUATION OF ABSTRACT OF THE CLOSE ROLL A. 6, 1ST TO 12TH YEAR OF THE ROYALTY OF JOHN OF GAUNT, DUKE OF LANCASTER.

(The Interior Part of the Roll having been already Abstracted, the following are from the same Roll in Tergo.)

First Year (1377).

Grantors and others.	Grantees and others.	Matters and Premises.
No. 1. dors. { Edmund, son of Alan de Folifayt	Edmund Lorence, son of John Lawrence, of Assheldon	Enrolment of the Deed of Release and Quit Claim of all Right to the Manor of Folifayt, near Tadcaster, 50 Ed. III. (1376). The like of Lands which Elizabeth Folifayt, widow, held in dower, 51 Ed. III. (1377). Other Deeds relative to the Manor.
No. 2. dors. { John de Assheton-under-Lime	John de Kirkeby........	Recognisance of the Receipt of £40 in part payment of a Debt of 140 Marks (£93 6s. 8d., 1 Rich. II. (1377-8). Other Deeds relating thereto.
No. 3. dors. { Thomas Lathum	Robert de Breton, Vicar of the Church of Huyton, and Thomas de Ryding, Chaplain	Enrolment of Deed by Release and Quit Claim at Crossehalle, in Lathum, and all other Lands granted in Lancashire, 49 Ed. III. (1375).
Annus Secundus (1378). *In Tergo.*		
No. 4. dors. { Robert de Washington and others	For William de Horneby, Parson of the Church of St. Michael-upon-Wyre.....	Recognisance of Debt of £8. Aᵒ 2do Regalitatis.
No. 5. dors. { Thomas de Lamplogh and others	For Edmund Lorence.....................	Recognisance of Debt, £40.
No. 6. dors. { Adam of Lancaster	For Thomas Mirreson of Lancaster ...	Recognisance of Debt, £10.
No. 7. dors. { William de Heton	Ralph de Ipre and Peter de Bolrun ...	Enrolment of Grant of Lands in Heton, Broune, Molebek, Urwike, and Lancaster, 51 Ed. III. (1377).
No. 8. dors. { Richard de Massy, Knt......	For John de la Pole, Justice of Chester	Recognisance of Debt of £5.—Witness, Henry, Earl of Derby (son of the Duke of Lancaster, afterwards Henry IV.), Custos of the Royalty. And various other Recognisances of Debts.
Annus Tertius (1379). *In Tergo.*		
No. 9. dors. { John de Plesyngton	Hugh de Dacre, Knt., Lord of Gillesland	Enrolment of Grant of the Manors of Halton in Lonesdale, and Eccleston in Leylandshire, in Com. Lanc., with all their Members and Appurtenances, 2 Rich. II. (1378-9). Release and Quit Claim by Feoffees.
Annus Quartus (1380). *In Tergo.*		
No. 10. dors. { Various Recognisances of Debt.		
Annus Quintus (1381). *In Tergo.*		
No. 11. dors. { John Botiller, Knt......... ..	Henry de Bispham and Richard de Carleton, Chaplains.....................	Enrolment of the Grant of the Manors of Great Laton, Little Laton, Bispham, and Wardebrek, Lands in Great Merton, and the whole Lordship of Merton Town, 4 Rich. II. (1381).
No. 12. dors. { Henry de Bispham and Richard de Carleton	John Botiller, Knt., and Alice his wife	Enrolment of Grant of the above Manors, Lands, and Lordship, in Fee Tail special, 4 Rich. II. (1380-1).

Grantors and others.	Grantees and others.	Matters and Premises.
Annus Sextus (1382). *In Tergo.*		
No. 13. dors. } Recognisances of Debts		
No. 14. dors. } Robert de Wasshyngton ...	For William de Hornby, Parson of St. Michael-upon-Wyre, and William le Ducton	Enrolment of Grant of Lands, &c., in Carleton in Amounderness, for a Rose Rent per Ann. 8 Years, and increased Rent £20 per Ann., 5 Rich. II. (1381-2).
No. 15. dors. } Roger de Fasacreley	Edward de Lathum, Henry de Scaresbreck, and others.	Memorandum of Agreement as to Dower of Tenements in Wrightiuton.
No. 16. dors. Adam de Hoghton, Chivr. Nicholas de Haryngton, Chivr. .... And Richard, son of Adam Houghton	For the King and Duke	Recognisance of Debt of 200 Marks, upon a seizure into the Duke's hands, on the death of James Botiller, Earl of Ormond.
Annus Octavus (1384). *In Tergo.*		
No. 17. dors. } Richard de Hoghton	For William de Horneby, Parson of St. Michael-upon-Wire	Enrolment of Grant of the Wardship of Lands of Henry de Kighley, Knt., in Lancashire and Yorkshire, and the Marriage of his Son, 7 Rich. II. (1383-4).
No. 18. dors. } The King and Duke	For John Nowell.........	Precept to the Sheriff to supersede taking the Body of John Nowell, to answer before the Justices of the Duchy for the death of John de Holden, upon Appeal of Murder.
The like. dors. } The King and Duke	William de Rigmayden	Precept to the Sheriff to supersede the Outlawry for Trespasses in the Duchy Chases.
No. 19. dors. } The King and Duke	For Hugh, son of John de Partyngton, of Irwelham	Precept to the Sheriff to supersede an Outlawry, King Richard II. having granted him pardon. Similar Writs for William Crist and John de Leylond, Souter, of Wigan.
No. 20. dors. } The King and Duke	For Adam de Hoghton and others ...	Precept to the Escheator to supersede Levy of Rent of 100 Marks (£66 13s. 4d.) out of Wetheton Manor.
No. 21. dors. } The King and Duke	For Thomas Smith, Nayller, of Cholle	Precept to the Sheriff to supersede Outlawry, Defendant having found Bail to appear at Sessions.
Annus Nonus (1385). *In Tergo.*		
Various Recognisances of Debts and Writs de Supersedendo, addressed to the Sheriff.		
Annus Decimus (1386). *In Tergo.*		
Recognisances of Debts, &c.		
No. 22. dors. } John de Walton...............	Robert de Saureby and John de Birkeheved, Chaplains......................	Enrolment of Grant of Lands, &c., in Lancaster, Bare, and Kertmell, 9 Rich. II. (1385-6).
No. 23. dors. Robert de Saureby and John de Birkeheved, Chaplains	John de Walton and Rosa his Wife ...	Grant of the above Lands, &c., in Fee Tail, special.
No. 24. dors. Agnes Banastre	For William de Horneby, Parson of the Church of St. Michael-upon-Wyre ..	Recognisance of Debt of 500 Marks (£333 6s. 8d.) for Infeoffment of Lands, seized into the Duke's hands by the minority of Constance Banastre.
Annus Undecimus (1387). *In Tergo.*		
Recognisances of Debts and Writs de Supersedendo as to Debts.		
No. 25. dors. } William de Dutton	For William Molen, Robert Dyryng, John de Cornay, and others, Chaplains	Enrolment of Grant of Lands, &c., of William de Dutton in Ribchester, Bispham, Northebrok, and all his Burgages and Lands and Tenements in Preston, in Amounderness, 11 Rich. II. (1387-8).
Annus Duodecimus (1388). *In Tergo.*		
No. 26. dors. } Gilbert de Halsall and others	For the King and Duke	Recognisance of Debt of £700 for payment to William de Hornby, Receiver, of £237 14s. 0¾d. for his Account of the Time he was Sheriff. Witness, Henry, Earl of Derby, Custos of the Duchy, 12 Rich. II. (1388-9).
No. 27. dors. } Robert de Standysah and others	For the King and Duke	Recognisance of Debt of £200 for the said Robert, to render Account of his Office of Sheriff.

"From the 7th year of King Richard II. (1383-4) there are no Books nor Rolls extant to the 1st of Henry IV. (1399)."—*E Libro Great Ayloffe*[1] (1692) ; *page* 159, *in John of Gaunt's Chancery of the Duchy (Record Office).*

[1] This venerable index, which, by the munificence of Her Majesty, has become public property, and is now preserved in the Record Office, is, as described in the schedule of Ayloffe's will, "a book giving an account of all or most of the records in the dutchy office, and how to find them ;" it was commenced in 1684, and, as the author himself informs us, occupied thirty years in the compilation, a period during which Benjamin Ayloffe, the industrious compiler, filled the office of clerk and keeper of the records of the duchy of Lancaster. The most important entries of the "Great Ayloffe" relating to Lancashire and Cheshire have lately been published by the Record Society (vol. viii.) under the editorship of Walford D. Selby, Esq., of Her Majesty's Record Office.

In the " Originalia Memoranda," on the Lord Treasurer's side of the Exchequer, we find the following Records relating to the county and duchy of Lancaster, from the period when the ducal house first rose into distinction to the time when the third Duke of Lancaster ascended the throne, with the letters-patent of Henry IV. and Henry V.

LANCASTER.—The Duke of Lancaster's charter, enrolled in Memoranda 9 Edw. I. (1281) ; and Records of St. Hilary, 19 Edw. II. (1325-6).

Chart. of Henry, E. of Lanc., enrolled, Recds. St. Hil. 6 Edw. III. (1327)—Roll.
D. of Lanc.'s liberty of replevying to the Morrow of Easter Term, in Co. York.   Recs. St. Mich. 26 Ed. III (1352)—Roll.
Unjust claim of Henry, late E. of Lanc., Duke of Lanc., in Co. Derby.   Recs. St. Hil. 26 Edw. III. (1352)—Roll.
Charter of Duke of Lanc. respecting divers liberties granted to him in the city of London.   Recs. Hil. 27 Edw. III. (1353)—Roll.
Charter of the D. of Lanc. for receiving £40 under the Honor of the Earl of Derby and Lincoln, in equal parts, in Co. Leicester. Mich. Records, 23 Edw. III. (1354)—Roll.
Duke of Lancaster's claim in Co. Leicester.   Easter Recs. 28 Edw. III. (1354)—Roll 1.
Charter of D. of Lanc. in Co. Leicester, enrolled Mich. Recs. 29 Edw. III. (1355)—Roll.
Cognisance of Rich. Michel, sheriff of Not. and Derby, for the D. of Lanc. in Co. Derby.   Hil. Recs. 32 Edw. III. (1358)—Roll.
D. of Lanc.'s claim in Co. Linc. for working fines.   Mich. Recs. 33 Edw. III. (1359)—Roll.
Charter of John, D. of Lanc.   Mich. Recs. 38 Edw. III. (1364)—Roll 24.
Charter of John, Duke of Lancaster.   Mich. Recs. 38 Edw. III. (1364)—21.
Record sent to the King's chancellor in the county of Lancaster.   Mich. Recs. 38 Edw. III. (1364)—Roll.
Charter of J., D. of L, for liberties granted to him.   Hil. Recs. 39 Edw. III. (1365)—Roll 16.
D. of Lanc.'s claim of divers sums.   Mich. Recs. 42 Edw. III. (1368)—Roll 20.
D. of Lanc.'s Charter, 47 Edw. III. (1373)—Roll.
Charters of John, Kg. of Cast. and Leon, D. of Lanc., enrolled Mich. Recs. 1 Ric. II. (1377-8)—Roll 2.
Charter of John, D. of Aquitaine and Lanc., of liberties granted to him by the king.   Mich. Recs. 21 Ric. II. (1397-8)—Roll 13.
The Duke of Lancaster's claim of divers sums charged upon the sheriffs of the Counties of Somerset, Dorset, Lincoln, and York. Mich. Recs. 21 Ric. II. (1397-8)—Roll.
John, Duke of Lancaster's claim of divers sums charged upon the sheriff of the County of Linc.   Mich. Recs. 22 Ric. II. (1398-9)—Roll 34.
The claim of John, D. of L. for divers sums.   Mich. Recs. 21 Ric. II. (1397-8)—Roll 21.
The claim of John, D. of Lanc. for divers sums upon the sheriff of Lincoln's accountant.   Mich. 23 Rich. II. (1399)—Roll 34.
The King's Letters Patent touching the Duchy of Lanc. enrolled Mich. Recs. 1 Hen. IV. (1399-1400)—Roll 14.

*   *   *   *   *   *

Two Letters Patent made to John Leventhorp, under the seal of the Duchy of Lancaster, enrolled Mich. Recs. 1 Henry IV. (1399-1400)—Roll 15.

*   *   *   *   *   *

Divers sums claimed by our Lord the King's Attorney-Gen. of his Duchy of Lanc., to be placed to the same King as for his Duchy of Lanc. in Co. Derby and elsewhere.   Trinity Records, 5 Henry IV. (1403-4)—Roll 16.

*   *   *   *   *   *

The King's Letters under his privy seal of the Duchy of Lanc. enrolled Mich. Recs. 6 Hen. V. (1418-19)—Roll 19.

Of the illustrious John of Gaunt, Duke of Lancaster, it has been observed that he was the son of a king, the father of a king, and the uncle of a king, and could have said as much as Charles of Valois had he been the brother of a king.   His children were as follows:—

By Blanche, youngest Daughter and co-heir of Henry, Duke of Lancaster, his first Wife—

HENRY of Lancaster, surnamed Bolingbroke, afterwards Henry IV. of England.   The first king of the Lancastrian line.
PHILIPPA of Lancaster, married John I., King of Portugal.
ELIZABETH of Lancaster, married, 1st, to John Holland, K.G., Earl of Huntingdon, and Duke of Exeter, and, 2nd, to Sir John Cornwall, K.G.

By Constance, eldest Daughter and co-heir of Peter, King of Castile and Leon, his second Wife—

KATHERINE of Lancaster, married Henry III., King of Castile and Leon.

By Catharine Swynford, Daughter and co-heir of Sir Payne Roelt, Knt., and Widow of Sir Hugh de Swynford, afterwards third Wife—

JOHN BEAUFORT, Marquess of Somerset and Dorset, married Margaret, daughter of Thomas Holland, Earl of Kent.
HENRY BEAUFORT, Cardinal of St. Eusebius, Bishop of Lincoln (1397) and Bishop of Winchester (1426).
[1] THOMAS BEAUFORT, Duke of Exeter.
[1] JOAN BEAUFORT, married, 1st, Robert, Lord Ferrers of Wemme, and, 2nd, Ralph Neville, Earl of Westmorland.

[1] In the pedigree of the Earls and Dukes of Lancaster, pp. 62-3, by the accidental omission of the marks of descent, the three younger children of John of Gaunt by Catharine Swynford—Henry, Thomas, and Joan Beaufort—appear as the issue of John Beaufort instead of John, Duke of Lancaster.

Raised to the throne by a Parliamentary revolution, and holding power by the will of the Parliament, the son of John of Gaunt had too equivocal a title to admit of his resuming the struggle for independence on the part of the crown, and the grounds even on which he rested his claim to the sovereignty—by conquest and by inheritance[1]—were in themselves contradictory, and hence his rule was marked by a ready compliance with the prayers of the two Houses of Parliament, whose powers were, perhaps, never more frankly recognised at any time in the country's history. But the throne of a usurper is never a bed of roses, and the reign of Henry IV., short though it was, was agitated by violent animosities: one conspiracy broke out after another, the peace was continuously disturbed by the struggles of contending factions, and on the third day of his first Parliament, in the week of his coronation,[2] no less than forty challenges were given and received, and forty gages thrown down by the angry and excited barons. The insurrection of the Earls of Rutland, Kent,

JOHN OF GAUNT, DUKE OF LANCASTER.

and Huntingdon, which had for its object the restoration of Richard, was followed by an insurrection in Wales; and a royal proclamation, addressed to the "Chancellor of the King's County Palatine of Lancaster," announced that Owyn Glyndourdy, and other rebels, had lately

[1] Froissart (iv. p. 669) says he claimed on three grounds, viz., conquest, right of birth, and the resignation of Richard—reasons that are thus set out by Gower in his doggerel chronicle—
Regnum *conquestat* que per hoc sibi jus manifestat;
Regno *succedit* hæres nec abinde recedit
Insuper *eligitur* a plebeque sic stabilitur (Pol. Songs i. 449);
and Chaucer recognises the threefold claim when, in his "Compleynte" to his purse (p. 22) he thus addresses him—
　　　　O *conqueror* of Brutes Albyoun,
　　　Which that *by lygne* and free *eleccioun*
　　　　　Ben verray Kynge.—C.

[2] With the object of strengthening his position, and perhaps with the hope of eventually superseding the older Order of the Garter, many of the knights of which were uncertain in their allegiance, Henry, at his coronation, instituted a second military order, the knights of which, from the custom of washing the body on the eve of great religious ceremonies, were styled "Knights Companion of the Bath." There is no early complete register of the Order, but among the forty-six knights made at the institution were three Lancashire men—Sir John Ashton, of Ashton-under-Lyne, Sir John Arden and Sir William Boteler, of Bewsey.—C.

risen against the king in great numbers, to resist whom the chancellor was required to proclaim within his jurisdiction that all knights and esquires able to bear arms in person, and archers who received annual fees from the king, should repair to Worcester by the 1st of October, to join the other levies raised to put down this insurrection (1400-1401).[1] Owyn Glyndourdy, or Owen Glendower, as we now write it, who claimed to be the great-grandson of Llewellyn and the rightful Prince of Wales, had made inroads on the garrisons of Ruthin, Oswestry, and other places on the Welsh marches. The flame of insurrection spread fast, and from his mountain fastnesses the leader was able to defy the power of England. Mortimer, whom he had made prisoner, from being an enemy, became his friend and ally, and ultimately he was joined by the Percies, who had turned their arms against the Lancastrian king. A long and sanguinary civil war ensued, in which Henry had by turns to fight against his English subjects, under the Earl of Northumberland—who, from being his friend, had become his deadly enemy—the Welsh under their native princes, and the Scotch under Robert III. of that kingdom; but by his courage, skill, and prudence he overcame his enemies, and established that throne by the power of the sword, which appeared at first to have been erected upon the affections of his people. The writ to raise troops in the county of Lancaster was followed by another addressed to the chancellor of the duchy, commanding him to proclaim that William Atherton and Edmund de Dacre were appointed to collect the "reasonable aid" of twenty shillings for the marriage-portion of Blanche of Lancaster, the king's eldest daughter, to the Duke of Bavaria, and for the knighting of the king's eldest son, Henry of Monmouth (Dec. 12th, 1402).[2]

The wounds inflicted upon the pride of France by the conquests made in that country by the Black Prince and the Earl of Derby (son of Henry, Earl of Lancaster), formed a never-ending source of hostility between the French and English nations; and the Duke of Orleans did not fail to avail himself of the difficulties by which Henry IV. was surrounded. His attacks were directed against the English castles and fortresses, both in the south and north of France, at Bordeaux and at Calais. To prevent these possessions from falling into the hands of the French, the king issued a proclamation to the chancellor of the duchy and of the county palatine of Lancaster, as well as to the sheriffs of other counties, commanding him to proclaim, in all proper places within his jurisdiction, that all knights, esquires, valets, and other persons competent for defence, having any fees or annuities, lands, tenements, gifts or grants, or other donations, held by gift of the king or his progenitors, should personally appear in the king's presence at London within fifteen days from the date of the proclamation (1407).[3] These demonstrations were of themselves sufficient to preserve the English possessions without striking a blow; and the contest between the Duke of Burgundy and the Duke of Orleans—in which the King of England, in a proclamation to the chancellor of the county palatine of Lancaster, inhibited the people of England from taking any part so much engaged the French armies—that they would not prosecute their hostility against the English cities of France.[4] Sir Thomas Beaufort had been appointed admiral of the north, but even while negotiations for peace were going on with France piracy continued, and plundering parties from the opposite coasts were organised with greater completeness than before. At Harfleur privateers were fitted out on the pretence of serving under the King of Scotland, though negotiations for a treaty of peace were at the time pending between the English and the Scots. These privateers preyed upon English merchandise, and it was estimated that property of the value of £100,000 was captured nominally by the Scots, but really by the subjects of the King of France. It must not, however, be supposed that the French were the only offenders, or that the English were more sinned against than sinning, for every port along the southern coasts of England was a haven for pirates and desperadoes to whom filibustering was as profitable as it was an exciting employment, and they were not always very discriminating as to whether the vessels attacked belonged to an enemy or to a friendly neighbour.

That the commerce of this county, in its infant state, was at this period greatly injured and impeded by the depredations of the hostile powers by which England was assailed, may be inferred from a petition to the Commons House of Parliament from the inhabitants of Lancashire, Cheshire, and Cumberland, in which they allege that several robberies and depredations have been committed on their coast by their enemies of France and Scotland, and by the rebels of Wales, who

---

[1] Claus. 2 Henry IV. p. 2, m. 1, d. A commission of array on the "rebellion of Owen Glyndourdy," dated 10th August 3 Henry IV., was directed to Richard de Hoghton, Nicholas de Harrington, Ralph Radclif, Thomas Tunstall, Thomas Gerard, William Botiller, Robert Standyssh, William de Athiston (? Atherton), John de Assheton, John Sotheworth, Gilbert Halsall, John del Bothe, Ralph Standyssh, Robert Lawrence, and Richard de Radcliff.—C.

[2] Fin. 3 Henry IV. m. 16. The "reasonable aid" was the feudal form of raising money from the king's tenants. The dower promised with the lady was 40,000, of which 16,000 nobles were to be paid down on the solemnisation of the marriage, and the balance by instalments

extending over two years. The winter preceding the wedding was spent in preparing the outfit, and the Issue Rolls of the Exchequer record payments to the amount of £1,840 on this account alone for woollen cloth, embroidery, furs, skins, saddles, and other necessaries of a great lady's trousseau. Among the items is a payment of £100 "for cloth of gold and other wares" at the establishment of the great London mercer, Richard Whytington, who had then just been made an alderman—the preparatory step to his becoming "thrice Lord Mayor."—C.

[3] Claus. 8 Henry IV. m. 17 d.

[4] Claus. 13 Henry IV. m. 22 d.

23

have seized and taken their vessels, owing, as they allege, to no admiral or keeper of the seas being upon the station, to the great destruction, ruin, and oppression of the said counties; for remedy whereof they pray that protection may be afforded to them. To which petition the king replied that an admiral should be appointed for the safeguard of the seas of the north-western coast (1410).[1]

The contest for the papacy, which at this time agitated all Christendom, was felt so strongly in England that a proclamation was issued by the king to the sheriff of the county of Lancaster, and to other counties, wherein it was announced that Peter de Luna, *alias* Benedict XIII., and Angelo Corario, *alias* Gregory XII., were rashly contending for the papal chair, and both of them being pronounced and declared notorious heretics and schismatics by the definitive sentence of the holy and universal synod canonically congregated at Pisa, the most reverend father in Christ, the Lord Petro de Candias, on account of his merits, was elected by the same authority to the pontificate, by the title of Alexander V., and the sheriff was commanded to make proclamation in all places within his jurisdiction that the said Alexander V. was the true Roman pontifex (1410).[2]

The life of King Henry IV., though only in the meridian of his years, was now drawing fast to a termination. The scenes through which he had passed on his way to the throne, and the disquietude with which he was assailed from so many quarters, while in the possession of that giddy eminence, preyed upon his constitution and shortened his days. Worn out by the troubles of his reign, he died at Westminster on the 20th March 1413, in the forty-seventh year of his age and the fourteenth of his reign. Had it been his fate to remain in the sufficiently elevated but more humble state of Duke of Lancaster it is highly probable that his life would have been more happy and his death less early. By his will (dated Jan. 21, 1408), which breathes a spirit of remorse characteristic of the state of the royal mind, he bequeathed the duchy of Lancaster as an endowment to his consort the queen, in these words: " I will that the queen be endowed of the duchy of Lancaster."

The reign of Henry V., the second British king of the Lancastrian line, presents one of the most splendid periods in the military annals of England. During this short but eventful reign, France was once more laid prostrate at the feet of her ancient rival; and the capital of that kingdom, as well as the power of its government, was held by the British monarch with a tenacity which was not relaxed even in the hour of death. At home all was tranquillity; the cabals of the court, which had embittered the last days of Henry IV., were hushed by the frank and fascinating character of his once profligate son, and the scenes of domestic discontent were confined altogether to the contests between the early reformers of the Church of Rome.

The first English martyr in the cause of the Lollards was William Sautré, rector of Osythes, in London, who was consigned to the flames in 1401, at the instance of the Church, in virtue of a writ issued by Henry IV., whose father, John of Gaunt, had been the early patron and firm friend of John Wycliffe, the founder of the obnoxious sect in England. Henry V., more influenced probably by a wish to preserve the peace and harmony of his kingdom, than by any strong predilections, espoused the cause of the Church of Rome; and it would appear from a royal proclamation, issued in the first year of his reign, to the sheriff of the county palatine of Lancaster, that the new schismatics had spread into this county. In this proclamation the king announced that certain preachers, not privileged by law, or licensed by the diocesan of the place, or permitted by the Church, of the new sect of Lollards, preach in public places, contrary to the ordinances of the Church, and, under colour of preaching the word of God, foment and disseminate discord among the people, and the pestiferous seed of evil doctrine. For remedy of which, and to protect the Catholic faith, the sheriff is commanded to make proclamation that no chaplain shall hold, dogmatise, preach, or defend this heresy and error, under pain of imprisonment and forfeiture of goods; and if any persons shall be found publicly or privately infringing these orders, by holding conventicles, or congregations, or receiving the preachers of the obnoxious doctrines, or shall be really and vehemently suspected of so doing, they shall be committed to prison without delay, to remain there until they shall obey the mandates of the diocesan in whose diocese they have preached, to be certified by the diocesan himself (1413).[3] The demand for reformation in the doctrine and the discipline of the Church was far too loud and too widely extended to be silenced by proclamations; and hence we find from another royal mandate, addressed to the chancellor of the county palatine of Lancaster in the following year (1414), that divers of the liege subjects of the king, on the incitement and instigation " of a most cunning and subtle enemy," Sir John Oldcastle (Lord Cobham), holding and teaching various opinions manifestly contrary and obnoxious to the Catholic faith, and to sound doctrine, stood charged with wickedly imagining and conspiring the king's death, because

---

[1] Rot. Parl. 11 Henry IV. *item* 52, vol. iii. p. 639.   [2] Claus. 11 Henry IV. m. 31 dors.   [3] Claus. 1 Hen. V.

he and his counsellors would not assent to these doctrines. The accused parties, too conscientious to plead not guilty of an offence which they had actually committed, or under some other influence which it is now difficult to discover, confessed their guilt; and the king of his special grace pardoned all the offenders, except Lord Cobham, Sir Thomas Talbot, knight, and ten other persons of inferior station. This pardon the chancellor was required to proclaim through the whole of his jurisdiction; and the reformers, with the above exceptions, some of whom had taken refuge in the places of sanctuary—Manchester and Lancaster being of that number—were allowed to plead the royal pardon before the feast of the Nativity of St. John the Baptist (June 24) next ensuing.[1] A number of the Lollards forfeited their lives to the dictates of their conscience—for it is impossible to impute to the great mass of them any sinister motive; and Lord Cobham, the most zealous and distinguished of their number, who had escaped from the Tower, was, three years later (1418), recaptured while the king was in France, and hung up by the middle upon a gallows erected in St. George's Fields, where he was consumed alive in the fire, under the declaration of the archbishop and his provincial synod that he was an incorrigible heretic. These terrible examples checked for a time the spread of Lollardism; but the fires only smouldered, and, in the reign of Henry VIII., under sanction of the king, they burst forth with a force so irresistible as to destroy the whole power of the "Holy Anglican Mother Church."

At this period a large accession of wealth and power was made to the duchy of Lancaster, by the union of the rights and possessions of the county of Hereford to the duchy, under the sanction of the following royal ordinance (2 Hen. V. 1414):—

"The king, by the assent of Parliament, declares, grants, and ordains, that all the honors, castles, hundreds, manors, lands, tenements, reversions, rents, services, fees, advowsons, possessions, and lordships, as well within the kingdom of England as in parts of Wales and other places, within the king's lordships, which have descended, or shall descend inheritably to the king, after the death of Dame Maria, one of the daughters and heirs of Humphrey de Bohun, formerly Earl of Hereford, Essex, and Northampton, and Constable of England, as to the son and heir of that Dame Mary; also, that all the rights, liberties, franchises, and frank customs, to the same inheritance appertaining or regarding, be severed from the crown of England, and adjoined, annexed, united, and incorporated to and with the said king's duchy of Lancaster, perpetually to remain to the same king, as being so adjoined, united, annexed. and incorporated; and further, that all the honors, castles, hundreds, wapentakes, manors, lands, tenements, and reversions aforesaid, and all other things to the said inheritance regarding, and the vassals and tenants to it appertaining, be also entirely enfranchised, and by the officers treated, guarded, and governed, in all respects, as possessions to the said duchy appertaining, and the vassals and tenants to the same duchy regarding, are enfranchised, treated, guarded, and governed for ever; and this, according to the form, force, and effect of the words contained in a schedule passed in this Parliament; and by the king, with the assent of the Lords aforesaid, and the authority aforesaid, fully affirmed. [Then follows an enumeration of the possessions at great length.[2]]

Scarcely had the chancellor of the duchy of Lancaster proclaimed, by royal command, the truce between England and Castile and Leon when the King of England, having renewed the old claim to the crown of France, and desiring to quarter the cities of that kingdom with the three lions of England, resolved on invading the French king's dominions, and embarked at Southampton with an army of six thousand cavalry, and twenty-four thousand foot, principally archers, and landed at Harfleur, August 14th, 1415. After carrying the garrison of that town, and leaving a number of his troops to defend that fortress, Henry, at the head of his troops, marched for Calais, but on his way he was interrupted by a hostile army of fourteen thousand cavalry and forty thousand infantry, under the command of the Constable of France, and obliged to come to battle on the plains of Agincourt.[3] Here the glories of Cressy and Poictiers were renewed, and the cry of "A Derby" or "An Edward," was not more piercing in the ears of the discomfited French army on those fields of English glory than was the cry of "A Henry" on the field of Agincourt. The loss of England in this memorable battle (fought Oct. 25, 1415), which destroyed the military power of France, was incredibly small—some of the contemporary authorities say not exceeding forty men—amongst whom were Edward, Duke of York, and the Earl of Suffolk.[4] That this number is much underrated cannot be doubted, and if the nature of the engagement did not establish that fact, it might be inferred from the proclamation to the chancellor of the duchy of Lancaster, issued by the king soon afterwards, for the purpose of recruiting his army, by which all knights, esquires, and valets, holding fees or annuities of the king for term of years, or for life, were required, under forfeiture of the same, to appear in their own persons at Southampton, to cross the seas to France arrayed and furnished with supplies for three months (1416).[5]

[1] Claus. 2 Henry V. m. 24.
[2] Rot. Parl. vol. iv. p. 46. While speaking of this Act, Sir Edward Coke says—"For the great roialties, liberties, privileges, immunities, quitances, and freedoms, which the Duke of Lancaster had for him and his men and tenants, see Rot. Parl. die Lunæ post octav. Sancti Martini an. 2 Henry V., all which are established, ratified, and continued by authority of Parliament, necessary to be known by such as have any of these possessions."—Fourth Institute, p. 210.
[3] The "Roll of the men-at-arms that were at the Battle of Agincourt" and "The Retinue of Henry V. in his first voyage," published in Sir N. H. Nicholas's History of the Battle of Agincourt, exhibit very

clearly the nature of the force that landed at Harfleur, and the extent to which the chivalry of Lancashire shared in the glories of that memorable St. Crispin's Day.—C.
[4] The estimates of the English loss are very conflicting. Our own chroniclers make it absurdly small, but it must have been some hundreds. Monstrelet puts the loss of the English at sixteen hundred, and another French historian, St. Remy, gives the same number. Of the chivalry of France the flower perished. Seven princes of the blood fell, with eight thousand gentlemen, of whom a hundred and twenty were nobles bearing banners.—C.
[5] Claus. 4 Henry V. m. 21 d.

Before the departure of the king for France he instituted commissions of array in this and the other counties of England, to take a review of all the freemen able to bear arms, and to divide them into companies, that they might be kept in readiness to resist an enemy. "This," says Mr. Hume, "was the first commission of array which we meet with in English history." How a writer of so much research should have fallen into the error of supposing that there had existed in England no commission of array till the time of Henry V. it is not easy to imagine : commissions of this nature had been instituted two centuries before, and the number of them in operation in the reigns of the Edwards, in the county of Lancaster alone, it is difficult to estimate.

The necessities of the state had plunged the king into great pecuniary difficulties; and although the county of Hereford, with its land revenues, had recently been added to his hereditary possessions, he was obliged, before he could embark his troops for France, to raise supplies by pledging the crown jewels. The loans obtained in this way had been contracted for with so much precipitation, and the regalia had been so widely dispersed, that a proclamation was issued by the king to the chancellor of the duchy of Lancaster, wherein it was announced that certain royal jewels, of no little value, had been committed and pledged, for the greater expedition of the king's voyage lately made to France, to certain of his liege subjects retained in the expedition, for the payment of their wages, which jewels it was now proper should be restored; the chancellor was therefore commanded to proclaim, that all persons within his jurisdiction, who had received such pledged jewels, should present them in person at the public treasury, in order that they might be redeemed; in default whereof, the offending parties were rendered liable to forfeit all their goods (1416).[1]

In anticipation of a continuance of the war with France, a commission, dated April 28th 6 Henry V. (1418), was issued for the muster and training of those capable of bearing arms within the several hundreds of the county palatine, when the following persons were named as commissioners to take the chief direction :—

John Stanley William de Atherton John Gerrard Nicholas de Harrington Henry de Kyghley Robert de Halsall Nicholas Blundell Thomas Bradshaw de Hagh	} Within the Wapentake (Hundred) of West Derby.
Lawrence de Standish William de ffarington Christopher de Standish Ralph de Clayton John de Coppull William de Worthyngton de Worthyngton	} Within the Wapentake of Leyland.
Richard de Hoghton Thomas Urswicke Nicholas Butteller Richard Butteller de Kyrklond Nicholas Singleton Richard de Katerall Thomas Rigmayden James de Pykering John Brokholes	} Within the Wapentake of Amounderness.
John Pylkington, Knt. John Byron, Knt. John de Hilton de ffarnworth John del Bothe Randle de Radcliffe Richard de Radclife de Radclife Robert del Holt Edmund de Trafford	} Within the Wapentake of Salford.
Henry Hoghton, Knt. Richard Radclife Richard Shirburne Henry de Longton Richard de Townley Thomas de Southworth Thomas de Osbaldeston	} Within the Wapentake of Blackburnshire.
Robert Laurence, Knt. William Tunstall Walter de Curwen Nicholas de Crofts John de Mosley John Lawrence	} Within the Wapentake of Lonsdale.
Richard Kirkby, Knt. Thomas ffleming, Knt. John Pennyngton John Broghton John Harrington de Cartmell Henry de Guype	} Within the Wapentake of ffourneys (Furness)

The career of King Henry V. was as short as it was brilliant. When his glory had nearly reached its summit, and both crowns were just devolving upon him, a mortal malady seized him at the age of thirty-four years, and consigned the conqueror of France to the tomb on the 31st August, 1422. His principal care in his last illness was to provide for the secure possession of his French conquest to his infant son Henry VI., then but nine months old, whom he commended to his brother, the Duke of Bedford, desiring that the Earl of Warwick might be his tutor—little suspecting that this unfortunate child would not, in his mature years, be able to maintain even his English possessions, and that, in his person, the Lancaster line would be pushed from the throne of his fathers.

[1] Claus. 4 Henry V. m. 11. dors.

The will of Henry V. bears date (in 1417) three years before his marriage to the Princess Catharine, and four years before the birth of his only son. By that will the royal testator bequeaths his duchy of Lancaster to his two brothers, John, Duke of Bedford, and Humphrey, Duke of Gloucester, in these terms:—

"I will and pray the aforesaid feoffee, &c., in the castles and manors of Halton and Clitheroe, and in all other lordships, manors, lands, tenements, rents, services, and other possessions, &c., do depart, as evenly as ye may, in two parts equal, the same castles, lordships, manors, &c. And inasmuch as you may goodly, ye do assign in the t'one of the said two parts, castles, lordships, &c., in the south coasts, and in the t'other, do assign castles, &c., in the north coasts of England ; [in the latter to] enfeoff my brother John, Duke of Bedford, and his heirs-male ; [in the south to] enfeoff my brother Humphrey, Duke of Gloucester, to him and his heirs-male, &c." [1]

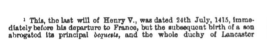

---

[1] This, the last will of Henry V., was dated 24th July, 1415, immediately before his departure to France, but the subsequent birth of a son abrogated its principal *bequests*, and the whole duchy of Lancaster descended to Henry VI. The will concludes with these words in his own autograph: "This is my last will, subscribed with my own hand, R. H. Jesu, mercy and gremercy, Ladie Marie, help."—C.

CHAPTER XI.

ALTHOUGH few periods in English history afford so many materials for the pen of the general and local historian as that comprehended in the reigns of Henry VI., Edward IV., and Richard III., during which time the wars between the houses of York and Lancaster raged with so much fury, and that of the reign of Henry VII. when these intestine broils were happily composed by the union of the rival houses in the persons of Henry VII. and his queen, yet there is no time, from the reign of King Stephen, so destitute as this of authentic records. The savage and murderous contests of the court and of the people appear so to have disorganised society that the usual communications between the authorities in the provinces and the government were neglected; or, if proclamations and edicts were issued in the several counties, they perished with many of those to whom they were addressed, the usual depositories being found almost destitute of these documents. This paucity of official information is the more extraordinary, seeing that the art of printing, that great engine of multiplication, was introduced into England by William Caxton in 1471, during the Wars of the Roses.

Many of the conquests made in France by Henry V. were lost during the regency appointed for the government of England, in the nonage of his successor. In June, 1429, the French, led by Joan of Arc, defeated the English at Jargeau and at Patay. From being attacked they in turn became the aggressors. Victory followed victory, until at length the Dauphin was crowned at Rheims, as Joan had predicted. The Duchy Rolls contain frequent entries of subsidies granted for the carrying on of the war, but the English cause was irretrievably lost, and in spite of the pompous coronation of the boy-king, at Paris, 1430, the Duke of Bedford had to abandon all hope of retaining France, and contented himself with securing Normandy, where, at Rouen, Henry for a a time held his court. When in his twenty-third year Henry was united in marriage with Margaret of Anjou, daughter of Regnier, titular king of Sicily, Naples, and Jerusalem, Duke of Anjou, and brother of Charles V. (22nd April, 1445). The commanding and masculine talents of his royal consort would, it was conceived, compensate for the weakness and effeminacy of the king; and though she brought no possessions, the French province of the Maine, then a part of the English territory, was, by a secret treaty, ceded to Charles, her uncle, on the consummation of the royal marriage. By a singular coincidence, the king had, seven years before this event, changed the title of "*Anjou king of arms*," in the English Heralds' College to that of "*Lancaster king of arms;*" and in a list of new-year's gifts presented by King Henry VI., in 1436, to the Lancaster Herald, as well as to a person who was then created a pursuivant of arms, by the title of Collar, there is a silver bell each, but for what purpose it is difficult to comprehend.[1]

No sooner had the queen arrived in the English court than she entered into all the intrigues by which it was agitated. The Duke of Gloucester, uncle to the king, having become obnoxious to the predominant party, at the head of which stood Cardinal Winchester and the Dukes of Buckingham, Somerset, and Suffolk, he was marked out as their victim. In 1440 the Duchess of Gloucester, Eleanor, the daughter of Lord Cobham, a lady of haughty carriage and ambitious mind, being attached to the prevailing superstitions of the day, was accused of the crime of

[1] Cotton. MSS. Cleop. F, iv. fo. 103 (Orig.)

witchcraft ; and it was alleged against her and her associate, Sir[1] Roger Bolingbroke, a canon of St. Stephen's Chapel, and Margery Jourdain, the witch of Eye, that they had in their possession a wax figure of the king, which they melted by a magical device before a slow fire, with the intention of wasting away his force and vigour by insensible degrees. This story partakes of the nature of the kindred superstition which prevailed a century and half afterwards, and of which Ferdinando, Earl of Derby, was the subject, if not the victim ; and we find that the wax figure in witchcraft takes its date at a period antecedent to the wars of the houses of York and Lancaster. The imbecile mind of Henry was sensibly affected by this wicked invention ; and the duchess on being brought to trial, and found guilty of the design to destroy the king and his ministers by the agency of witchcraft, was sentenced to do public penance, and to suffer perpetual imprisonment, while her confederates were condemned to death and executed. After enduring the ignominy of her public penance, rendered peculiarly severe by the exalted station from which she had fallen, the duchess was banished to the Isle of Man, where she was placed under the ward of Sir Thomas Stanley. On her way to the place of exile she was confined for some time, first in Leeds castle, and afterwards in the castle of Liverpool.[2] Events so congenial with the imagination of our great dramatic poet could scarcely fail to find their way into his historical plays ; and hence we find, in the second part of his "Henry VI.," a small stream of historical fact running through an ample meadow of poetic fiction, in which the duchess is exhibited and detected in the midst of these works of darkness.[3] After remaining in the Isle of Man some years, it would appear that this unfortunate lady was transferred to Calais, under the ward of Sir John Steward, or, as he describes himself, "Johannes Seneschallus, miles, filius Johannis Seneschalli, aliter dicti Scot Angli." From the will of this knight it appears that he was a resident and had an important command in Calais, in the mother church of which town he desires to be buried. He names John Roos as his confessor ; bequeaths to his eldest son, Thomas, all his harness of war, and his ship, the Grace de Dieu, which his master, the Duke of Bedford, had given him, together with his lands in the marches of Calais. To Sir Thomas Criell he leaves " a ring with a diamond, which Eleanor Cobham, Duchess of Gloucester, gave me while she lived with me as my prisoner."

The Duke of Gloucester, if possible more unfortunate than his lady, was accused of high treason, in aspiring to the throne, and summoned to take his trial before the High Court of Parliament at Bury St. Edmunds ; but, on the eve of the investigation, he was found dead in his bed, without marks of violence, though by no means without strong suspicion that he had fallen a victim to the cruel devices of his relentless persecutors. His great adversary, Henry Beaufort, a son of John of Gaunt, died six weeks after him at the age of eighty years. His deathbed scene has been depicted by Shakspere with a terrible power, which the soberer statement of the chronicler will not obliterate. There is little doubt the death of the Duke of Gloucester was accomplished by secret murder. Hall, on the authority of Beaufort's chaplain, says, " the queen, minding to preserve her husband in honour, and herself in authority, procured and consented to the death of this noble man, whose only death brought to pass that thing which she would most fain have eschewed, and took from her that jewel which she most desired ; for if this duke had lived, the Duke of York durst not have made title to the crown ; if this duke had lived, the nobles had not conspired against the king, nor yet the commons had not rebelled ; if this duke had lived, the house of Lancaster had not been defaced and destroyed, which things happened all contrary by the destruction of this good man."

About this time two Lancashire knights at the head of the principal families in the county were actively engaged in the delusive science of alchemy, and transmutation of metals—that *ignis fatuus* which has conducted so many ingenious men to their ruin. The king, who was in serious straits for money, and credulous enough to believe that by this means he could rid himself of the debts by which he was encumbered, had on a former occasion commissioned three philosophers to make the precious metals, without receiving any return from them in gold and silver : his credulity, however, like that of many wiser men, was unshaken by disappointment, and he issued a pompous grant in favour of three other alchemists, who boasted that they could not only transmute the inferior metals into gold and silver, but that they could also impart to man perpetual youth, with unimpaired powers of mind and body, by means of a specific called " The Mother and Queen of Medicines—The inestimable Glory—The Quintessence, or the Elixir of Life." In favour of these three "lovers of truth and haters of deception," as they modestly styled themselves, Henry dispensed with the Act passed by his royal grandfather,[4] a very unnecessary Act against the undue multiplication of gold and silver, and the only one, it is said, which has never been

---

[1] Sir was the customary prefix to the name of a beneficed ecclesiastic.—C.
[2] Wilhelmi Wyrcestrii Annales Rerum Anglicarum, pp. 460, 461.
[3] Shakspere, *Henry VI.* part ii. act i. scene 4.
[4] 5 Henry IV. c. 4. (1404).

violated—and empowered, not enabled, them to transmute the inferior into precious metals. This extraordinary commission had the sanction of Parliament, and two out of the three commissioners were Sir Thomas Ashton of Ashton-under-Lyne, and Sir Edmund Trafford of Trafford; the latter of whom had assisted at the coronation of the king, and received the honour of Knight of the Bath on that occasion. These sages, imposing probably upon themselves as well as upon others, kept the king's expectations wound up to the highest pitch, and he actually informed his people that the hour was approaching when, by the means of the *stone*, he should be enabled to pay off all his debts! It is scarcely necessary to add that this philosopher's stone never gave forth its expected virtues, and the king's debts must have remained unpaid had not his Majesty pawned the revenue of the duchy of Lancaster to satisfy the demands of his clamorous creditors. A patent for transmuting the inferior metals into gold and silver was granted by the king to these two Lancashire alchemists in the 24th year of his reign (7th April, 1446), in which they were encouraged to prosecute their experiments, and by which all the king's servants and subjects were interdicted from giving them any molestation.[1] As this document, which was found by Fuller, the historian, in the Tower, throws considerable light on the weakness and credulity of the age, and the belief in a *quasi* science that is now from the nature of things only an obsolete and forgotten lore, we give the translation:—

"The King to all unto whom, &c., greeting,—Know ye, that whereas our beloved and loyal Edmund de Trafford, Knight, and Thomas Ashton, Knight, have, by a certain petition shown unto us, set forth that although they were willing by the art or science of philosophy to work upon certain metals, to translate (transmute) imperfect metals from their own kind, and then to transubstantiate them by their said art or science, as they say, into perfect gold or silver, unto all manner of proofs and trials, to be expected and endured as any gold or silver growing in any mine; notwithstanding certain persons ill-willing and maligning them, conceiving them to work by unlawful art, and so may hinder and disturb them in the trial of the said art and science. We, considering the premises, and willing to know the conclusion, of the said work or science, of our special grace have granted and given leave to the same Edmund and Thomas, and to their servants, that they may work and try the aforesaid art and science lawfully and freely, without any hindrance of ours, or of our officers, whatsoever; any statute, act, ordinance, or provision made, ordained, or provided to the contrary notwithstanding. In witness whereof, &c., the King at Westminster, the 7th day of April."

The madness of party rage rendered the government of England indifferent to the retention of foreign possessions; and the whole province of Bayonne, which had been obtained three centuries before, at the price of so much blood and treasure, was ceded to France, with as little ceremony as in modern times a gold snuff-box would be presented to a plenipotentiary. The indifference of the court was not shared by the people. They beheld this curtailment of their ancient possessions with that disgust which it was so well calculated to excite. The embers of discontent were easily blown into a flame by Richard, Duke of York—the representative of two sons of Edward III., Lionel and Edmund—and his adherents. And the Duke of Suffolk, the favourite of the king, and the reputed paramour of the queen, after having been impeached (March 17, 1450) on a charge of ceding the province of the Maine to Charles of Anjou without authority, and surrendering the province of Bayonne without a struggle, was banished the kingdom for five years. To prevent the duke, whose friends were numerous and powerful, from ever again resuming the helm of state, he was seized by a band of pirates, employed by his enemies, on his voyage from Ipswich to Calais, and his head struck off and thrown into the sea.[2] The popular insurrection of Jack Cade was a part of the same system of hostility towards the house of Lancaster; and the Duke of York at length openly advanced his claims to that sceptre which the feeble representative of the house of Lancaster was unable to wield.

The seeds of this contest, though apparently sown in the time of King Edward III., may, in fact, be traced back to the time of Henry III., who died a century before, leaving two sons, Edward I. and Edmund Crouchback, Earl of Lancaster, the founder of that house, whose inheritance afterwards, in a fourth descent, fell on Blanche, married to John of Gaunt, the fourth son of Edward III., who, in right of his wife, was Duke of Lancaster; and whose son, Henry of Bolingbroke, afterwards Henry IV., dethroned Richard II., pretending, amongst other things, that Edmund Crouchback was the elder son of Henry III., and unjustly set aside from the crown because he was crook-backed. The crown remained, as we have seen, in the house of Lancaster for three descents, when Richard, Duke of York, descended from Edmund Langley, younger brother of John of Gaunt, made claim to the crown, by title of his grandmother, who was heir of Lionel, Duke of Clarence, elder brother of John of Gaunt. The pedigrees of these rival claimants have at all times formed matter of discussion in English history, though some of our ablest historians, Mr. Hume among

---

[1] Pat. 2. Num. 14.
[2] In the Paston Letters (letter xxvii.) a very circumstantial account is given of the murder of this unfortunate nobleman in a letter written from London on the 5th of May. When the duke was taken on board the Nicholas, the master saluted him with "Welcome, traitor." He was then "arraigned in the ship on their manner, upon the impeachments, and found guilty, and in the sight of all his men he was drawn out of the great ship into the boat, and there was an axe and a stock, and one of the lewdest (meanest) of the ship bade him lay down his head, and he should be fairly ferd (dealt) with, and die on a sword; and took a rusty sword and smote off his head within half-a-dozen strokes, and took away his gown of russet, and his doublet of velvet mailed, and laid his body on the sands of Dover; and some say his head was set upon a pole by it."—C.

them, have fallen into some errors on the subject; this is the more to be wondered at, as the descents are exhibited with great clearness and perspicuity in the Rolls of Parliament, 1 Edward IV. (1461), No. 8.

Upon this ground the Duke of York founded his claim, by succession, to the throne of England, and was supported by a number of the most powerful nobles of the land. Amongst his partisans, the duke had the fortune to number the Earl of Warwick, a man of unbounded influence, combined with great decision of character, and whose future achievements in this memorable quarrel obtained for him the name of the "king-maker." The duke's first demand was for a reform of abuses in the administration of public affairs. An alarming disease by which the king was attacked at this juncture, and which totally incapacitated him from taking any share in the government, of which he had long been only the nominal head, suggested the necessity of a regency; and the Duke of York, by the authority of Parliament, though in contravention of the wishes of the queen, who desired to have the whole rule of the land, to appoint all the officers of the government, and to fill up all the benefices of the church, was appointed regent (February 14, 1453), under the designation of " Protector and Defender of the realm of kingdom."

On the recovery of the king (February, 1455), the Duke of York was expelled from the regency, but his thirst for regal power, combined with a consciousness of the legitimacy of his hereditary claims,[1] fixed his wavering purpose. Having levied an army in the north, the duke marched to St. Albans, where the first battle between the houses of York and Lancaster took place. In this battle, which was fought on the 22nd of May, 1455, the Lancastrians suffered a severe defeat, and about five thousand of their troops remained dead upon the field, amongst whom were the Duke of Somerset, the Duke of Buckingham, the Earls of Northumberland and Stafford, Lord Clifford, and a number of other persons of distinction. The king himself fell into the hands of the Duke of York, who, with the sanction of Parliament, assumed the power of governing the state but rather in the capacity of regent than of sovereign.

The blood spilt in the battle of St. Albans was the first that flowed in that fatal contest— "the convulsive and bleeding agony of the feudal power," as Barante calls it.[2]—which was not terminated in less than thirty years—which was signalised by thirteen pitched battles, and in which the nobility of the land suffered more than any other order in the state. The people, divided in their affections or led by their superiors, took different symbols of party; the partisans of the house of Lancaster chose the Red Rose as their badge, while those of York took the White Rose as their mark of distinction; and the civil wars were known over Europe by the name of the quarrel between the two roses. In addition to the red rose the house of Lancaster exhibited on state occasions a mound or sphere with the Lancaster arms emblazed in the upper part of the circle; they had also a feather and scroll worn in the hats of the more elevated classes, and broom-pods by those of the inferior orders. The paper manufactured for their use in their communications with each other, and for their public documents, bore a peculiar water-mark, and it was only necessary to look through the sheet on which the Lancastrians wrote to discover which side of the quarrel the writers had espoused.[3]

The affairs of the conflicting parties had not yet proceeded to the last extremity; the nation was kept some time in suspense; the vigour and spirit of Queen Margaret, supporting her small power, still proved a balance to the great authority of Richard, which was impaired by his ill-defined objects, sometimes aspiring to the immediate and at other times to the reversionary possession of the crown on the death of the present king. The Parliament again appointed the Duke of York protector (November 19th, 1455), owing to one of those relapses into mental indisposition to which Henry was subject; but the queen soon produced her husband before the House of Lords, where he declared his intention to put an end to the protectorate and to resume the government. The Archbishop of Canterbury, in the discharge of his duty as a Christian prelate, endeavoured to mediate in the differences between the two houses, and thus to prevent the further effusion of blood; but though these attempts were received by both parties with an appearance of cordiality, and though the Duke of York passed in procession through the streets of London, hand in hand with Queen Margaret, to the altar of St. Paul's (March 25th, 1458), on which the existing animosities were all to be sacrificed, it soon became evident that the reconciliation was of the most transient kind, and a trifling difference between one of the king's retinue and another of the Earl of Warwick's, which, on the 9th of September in the same year, brought on a combat between their respective partisans, blew it all into air.

The Duke of York, having joined his sons at Ludlow Castle, was silently collecting forces to

---

[1] The position of York as heir presumptive to the crown had ceased with the birth of a son to Henry in the month of October, 1453, "whose noble mother," as Fabyan affirms (p. 628. Ed. 1811), sustained not a little slander and obloquy of the common people saying that he was not the natural son of King Henry, but changed in the cradle."—C.   [2] *Revue Française*, March, 1829.—C.   [3] For representations of these badges and emblems see page 178.

maintain his claims, when the Earl of Salisbury, who had mustered a force of nearly four thousand men at his Castle at Middleham, in Yorkshire, marched southward, advancing through Craven to Manchester, where their numbers were augmented by the addition of a thousand men from the Duke of York's Yorkshire estates, and thence by way of Congleton and Newcastle-under-Lyme to the neighbourhood of Market Drayton.   While on his march to join the duke, Salisbury was overtaken at Bloreheath, on the borders of Staffordshire and Shropshire, by Lord Audley, at the head of a superior force of the Lancastrians, which he had raised in Cheshire and the parts adjacent, where the Lancastrian interest prevailed.   The battle, which was fought on the 23rd of September

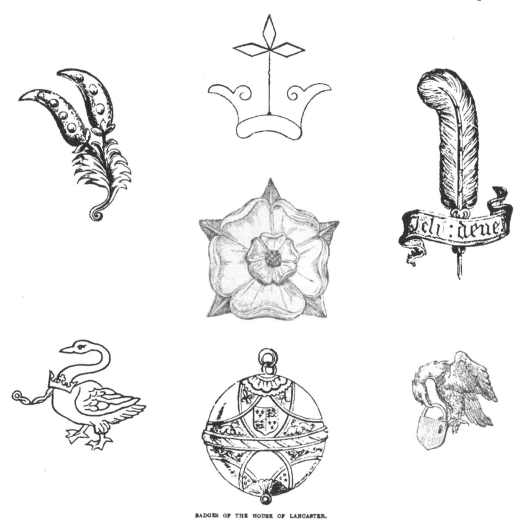

BADGES OF THE HOUSE OF LANCASTER.

(1459), was long and sanguinary, but victory at length declared in favour of the Yorkists, and the Lancastrians left two thousand four hundred men dead on the field, many of whom were from Lancashire and Cheshire ; and amongst the slain was Sir R. Molyneux, of Sefton, son-in-law of Sir Thomas Stanley, the king's chamberlain.   The Duke of York had now openly declared his intention to expel the princes of the Lancastrian line, and this was the first battle avowedly fought for the crown.   After this victory the Earl of Salisbury marched to join the Duke of York at Ludlow, which he succeeded in doing, but the king's army advanced rapidly and encountered the Yorkists on the 13th of October, when Sir Andrew Trollope, who was really attached to the house of Lancaster, deserted to the king with the troops under his command; others, induced by a proclamation of pardon, followed his example, when the Duke of York, struck with consternation, disbanded his army and fled through Wales into Ireland.

The list of proscriptions which followed the battle of Bloreheath sufficiently indicates that the men of Lancashire were by no means unanimous in their support of the house of Lancaster. Long and undisturbed possession, as well as a distinctly legal title by a free vote of Parliament, was in favour of the house of Lancaster, but the persecutions of the Lollards, the disfranchisement of the voter, the interference with elections, the odium of the war, the shame of the long misgovernment, told fatally against the weak and imbecile king, whose reign had been a long battle of contending factions.[1] A kind of packed Parliament having assembled at Coventry, six weeks after the battle was fought, attainders were exhibited against Richard, Duke of York, and his adherents, and amongst the persons attainted of high treason for the part they took at Bloreheath, we find the names of Thomas Nevill, John Nevill, Thomas Haryngton, Thomas Parre, and William Stanley, to which list was added the name of Robert Boulde, the brother of Harry Boulde, Knight, accused with others of having industriously circulated a report that the king was dead. It further appears that the Commons House of Parliament charged Thomas, the second Lord Stanley, with certain heavy offences, both of omission and commission, as set forth in a declaration to the following effect:—[2]

"That when Lord Stanley was required by the king to join him with such forces as he could collect, he came not; but his brother, Sir William Stanley, with many of the lord's servants and tenants, joined the Earl of Salisbury, and were with him at Bloreheath. That when Edward Prince of Wales summoned Lord Stanley to come to him in all haste, his lordship delayed, saying he was not ready, though he had been commanded to hold himself ready with his troops at a day's warning; such delay and absence being a great cause of the loss (of the Lancastrians) at Bloreheath. That Lord Stanley was within six miles of the place, accompanied by 2,000 men, and stayed three days after at Newcastle, but six miles from Eccleshall, where the queen and Prince of Wales were. That the morning after the battle he sent a letter of excuse for not going to them, as required. That Lord Stanley, after the battle, in a letter, thanked God for the success of the Earl of Salisbury, and trusted that he should be with the earl in another place, to stand him in as good stead as if he had been with him there. That when the prince, in obedience to the king, sent for Lord Stanley's tenants in the hundreds of Wirrall and Macclesfield, Cheshire, they were let [hindered] by Lord Stanley, so that they could not come. That a cook of Lord Stanley, in Sir William Stanley's troops, being wounded at Bloreheath, and left behind at Drayton, declared to divers gentlemen that he was sent to the Earl of Salisbury, in the name of Lord Stanley, with more of his fellowship. That various persons wearing the livery of Lord Stanley were taken at the forest of Morff, Shropshire, and before death confessed that they were sent by Lord Stanley to attend on Sir William, to assist the Earl of Salisbury. To the prayer of the commons that the king would have Lord Stanley committed to prison, to abide trial, the king returned a refusal in the courtly terms of 'Le Roi s'avisera.'"

Throughout this bitter struggle Lord Stanley pursued a course of watchful dexterity, remaining neutral when neutrality was deemed the safer policy, and casting in his lot with whichever side, at the moment, had the prospect of victory. He had married Eleanor, daughter of Richard Nevill, Earl of Salisbury, who commanded the Yorkists at Bloreheath, and the sister of Warwick—"the king-maker"—an alliance that naturally brought him under the suspicion of the Lancastrians. When, after the battle, he wrote to the victorious Salisbury, "thanking God for the good speed of the said earl," it was natural, to his father-in-law, but when he added that he "trusted to God he should be with the earl in other places, to stand him in as good stead as he should have done if he had been with him (at Bloreheath)," it was treason. There is reason to believe he had given the earl private assurance of his sympathy, and that he had, moreover, encouraged his tenants to serve under his brother William, who had "plucked the pale and maiden blossom" and declared himself upon the White Rose side. It is remarkable that, although the battles fought between the houses of York and Lancaster for the crown were so numerous, the county of Lancaster was not the scene of any one of these contests, neither Lancastrian nor Yorkist, as it would seem, caring to make an enemy of the head of the powerful house of Stanley, whom the people would always follow, and hence the peaceable inhabitants of this county escaped many of the horrors that intestine wars never fail to inflict in the immediate scene of their operation. The contamination of public morals was, however, felt here, as well as in other parts of the kingdom. According to a solemn declaration of Parliament, the complaints upon this subject were loudly made throughout every part of the kingdom, of robberies, ravishments, extortions, oppressions, riots, unlawful assemblies, and wrongful imprisonments. To aggravate these evils the offenders were aided and abetted by persons of station in the country, whose badges or liveries they wore, and by whom the administration of justice was continually interrupted. Amongst the most notorious of the offenders five-and-twenty are mentioned by name, and in this list we find "Robertus Pylkyngton, nuper de Bury in Com. Lanc', Armiger"[3] (the only Lancashire name), and other persons of equal respectability. These flagitious outrages originated with the civil wars, the

<hr>

[1] J. R. Green (History of the English People, p. 278).—C.   [2] Rot. Parl. 38 Hen. VI. (1459), vol. v. p. 369.
[3] Rot. Parl. 38 Henry VI. (1459), vol. v. p. 368.

greatest of all national curses, and continued till those wars were at an end, when the laws resumed their dominion.

The defection of the large body of veteran troops brought over from Calais by the Earl of Warwick, which deserted to the royal standard along with their commander, Sir Andrew Trollop, seemed for a time to extinguish the hopes of the Yorkists; but they speedily recovered, and, led by the Earl of Warwick, encountered the king's forces near Northampton. Here a desperate and sanguinary conflict took place (July 10, 1460), which resulted in the Lancastrians being utterly routed, owing to the treachery of Lord Grey of Ruthin, who commanded King Henry's van, and who deserted to the enemy. The loss on both sides amounted to ten thousand men, comprehending a large proportion of the nobility and gentry, against whom the Earl of Warwick and the Earl of March principally directed their hostility. Queen Margaret and her son escaped, but the unhappy Henry was found in his tent almost alone; the victorious earls, who treated him with great respect, carried him first to Northampton and then to London, where, on the 16th July, he was lodged in the bishop's palace.[1]

In the session of Parliament which followed, a kind of compromise of the conflicting claims was adopted, under the sanction of the legislature, by which Henry, who had been taken prisoner at the battle of Northampton, was to enjoy the crown of England and the duchy of Lancaster for life, but at his death they were to descend to the Duke of York, or to his heirs in perpetuity. The queen could ill brook an arrangement by which the title of her only son to the crown of England was extinguished. To support this title, she collected a numerous army from the counties of Lancaster and Chester, and took up her station in the neighbourhood of Wakefield, in the county of York. No sooner had the Duke of York heard of this formidable array of hostile troops than he marched to the north, and took possession of Sandal Castle. Conceiving that his courage would be compromised if he refused to meet a woman in battle, he quitted his strong station and advanced into the plain, where the queen, aided by Lord Clifford, had the skill to place his troops between two fires; and though the duke performed prodigies of valour, his army was completely routed, and he himself was numbered amongst the slain (Dec. 31st, 1460). The Queen, proud of such a trophy, ordered the duke's head to be struck off and placed upon the gates of York, adorned with a paper crown to indicate the frailty of his claims—

> "Off with his head, and set it on York gates;
> So York may overlook the town of York."

An unfeminine speech, that did not cause her much feeling of remorse, for afterwards, when gazing upon the terrible spectacle as she entered the city, she is represented as exclaiming to Henry—

> "Welcome, my lord, to this brave town of York:
> Yonder's the head of that arch enemy.
> Does not the object cheer your heart, my lord?"

Lord Clifford—the "black-faced Clifford," as he has been called—still more sanguinary than his royal mistress, plunged his sword, after the battle was over, into the breast of the Earl of Rutland, the duke's youngest son, in revenge, as he alleged, for the death of his father, who fell in the battle of St. Alban's, while fighting against the Yorkists. From this time the scabbard was cast aside, and the Earl of March, now become Duke of York, determined to avenge the death of his father and brother, and to obtain the crown, or to perish in the attempt. The battle of Mortimer's Cross, fought on the second of February, 1461, with the loss of four thousand men to the Lancastrians, seemed to open the way to the gratification of young Edward's ambition; but the second battle of St. Albans,[2] fought thirteen days afterwards (Feb. 17, 1461), in which Margaret, attended by the king, held the command, and in which the Earl of Warwick was worsted, changed the aspect of these ever-varying campaigns, though it did not prevent Edward from marching to London and taking possession of the throne. Although Henry VI. was dethroned, and Edward IV. seated in his place, the civil wars were by no means at an end. Margaret, having returned to her favourite county of York, assembled an army of sixty thousand men; and King Edward, with his celebrated general, the Earl of Warwick, hastened into that county with forty thousand, to give her battle. The hostile armies met at Towton, near Tadcaster, on Palm Sunday (March 29, 1461). In this memorable battle, while the Yorkists were advancing to the charge, there happened a heavy fall of snow, accompanied by wind, which drove full in the faces of the Lancastrians. Lord Falconberg, who led the van of Edward's army, improved this event by a stratagem; he ordered a body of infantry to advance before the line, and, after having sent a volley or flight of arrows among the enemy, immediately to retire. The Lancastrians, imagining that they had got within reach of the opposite army, discharged all their arrows, which fell short of the Yorkists. After their quivers

---

[1] Hall fo. 94. Stow, p. 409.—C.

[2] The second battle of St. Albans was fought at Barnard's Heath, on the high ground a mile north of the town.—C.

were emptied, Edward advanced his line, and did execution with impunity on the dismayed Lancastrians. The bow, was, however, soon laid aside, and the sword decided the combat, which ended in the total overthrow of King Henry's forces. Edward had issued orders, before the battle, to give no quarter, and the routed army was pursued with dreadful slaughter. The flying troops shaped their course to Tadcaster bridge, but, despairing of reaching it, they turned aside to a place where the Cock, a small rivulet, discharges itself into the Wharfe. This was done with so much hurry and confusion that the bed of the river was soon filled with dead bodies, which served as a bridge for the pursuers and the pursued to pass over. The slaughter at this point was tremendous. According to the historians of the period, thirty-six thousand seven hundred men fell in the battle and pursuit, and the waters of the Wharfe were deeply crimsoned with the blood of the victims. The heralds who numbered the dead upon the field state the number of slain at twenty-eight thousand, and under the sign-manual of King Edward they give the following: If the battle at Wakefield Green had been disastrous to the House of York, it proved no less disastrous to the Lancastrians, for the cruelties perpetrated by the black-faced Clifford were repaid with tenfold vengeance at Towton. The carnage in that terrible conflict was appalling, and if the statements of contemporary writers may be accepted, the blood stood in puddles, and stagnated in the gutters for weeks afterwards. Well might Warwick, dealing out a poetic justice, then say to the victorious Edward—

> "From off the gates of York fetch down the head—
> Your father's head, which Clifford placed there ;
> Instead whereof let this supply the room,
> Measure for measure must be answered."

LIST OF THE NOBLEMEN AND KNIGHTS SLAIN IN THE BATTLE OF TOWTON.

NOBLEMEN.
Henry Percy, Earl of Northumberland.
Thomas Courtney, Earl of Devonshire.
William Beaumont, Viscount Beaumont.
John Clifford, Lord Clifford.
John Neville, Lord Neville.
Randulf, Lord Dacre.
Lord Henry Stafford, of Buckingham.
Lionel Welles, Lord Welles.
Anthony Rivers, Lord Scales.

Richard Welles, Lord Willoughby.
Sir Ralph Bigot, Knight, Lord de Malley.

KNIGHTS.
Sir Ralph Gray.
Sir Richard Jeney.
Sir Harry Bellingham.
Sir Andrew Trollop.
With twent-eight thousand numbered by the Heralds.

The Parliament, which met on the 4th of November, 1461, employed itself in the usual work of proscription, and "Henry of Derbie, otherwise Duke of Lancaster, and the heirs of his body coming, were utterly disabled from enjoying any inheritance, estate, or profits, within this realm or dominions of the same for ever." A number of noblemen and gentlemen were attainted for the vague offence of being present at the death of the Duke of York, slain in the battle of Wakefield, amongst whom were Richard Tunstall, Henry Bellingham, and Robert Whittingham, knights. By the same Parliament it was enacted that the attainder of Henry VI. should subject him to the forfeiture of all the lands and possessions belonging to the duchy and county palatine of Lancaster ; and that King Edward and his queen should enjoy the duchy and liberties to the same belonging, separate from the crown ; and that the tenants of the said duchy and county should enjoy all their liberties and franchises unimpaired. The battle of Towton Field seemed decisive of the wars between the houses of York and Lancaster. Henry escaped into Scotland, while his more fortunate rival repaired to London to meet his Parliament, by which his title was recognised, and he was declared king by right from the death of his father. Margaret, whose spirit and perseverance remained unsubdued, sailed for France, to supplicate the French monarch to grant her forces for the purpose of reasserting the claims of her house. With this request Louis so far complied as to place at her disposal two thousand troops, with which she embarked for England. For a time she retired into Scotland, but having resolved on making an effort to recover the crown, she, accompanied by her husband and son, crossed the Border about the middle of April, and marched to Hexham, where she was joined by a number of volunteers from Scotland, and from Lancashire and the other northern counties of England ; an engagement took place there, on a plain called the Levels, on the 15th May, 1464,[1] between the queen's troops and the Yorkists, now become the royal army, under Montacute, which issued in the total defeat of the Lancastrians, and the capture of the Duke of Somerset and Lords Roos and Hungerford, who were all three tried by a court-martial, convicted of high treason, and immediately beheaded. In that decisive battle the fortunes of the House of Lancaster sank to the lowest point of hopelessness, as if "never to rise again." "The fate of the unfortunate royal family of the Lancastrian house after this defeat,' says Mr. Hume, "was

[1] In February, 1464, the Parliament was prorogued in consequence of the commotions in various counties. On the 1st March, John Paston writes to his father (Paston Letter ccxxx.), "The commons in Lancashire and Cheshire were up to the number of ten thousand or more; but now they be down again; and one or two of them was (be)headed in Chester as on Saturday last past."—C.

singular. Margaret flying with her son into a forest, dwelt sometime concealed there, and was at last conducted to the sea-coast, when she made her escape into Flanders. She passed thence into her father's court, where she lived several years in privacy and retirement. Her husband was not so fortunate or so dexterous in finding the means of escape. Some of his friends took him under their protection, and conveyed him into Lancashire, where he remained concealed during a twelve month; but he was at last detected, delivered up to Edward, and thrown into the Tower." The place of his concealment was Waddington Hall, in the parish of Mitton Magna, in the north-eastern part of the county; and the person by whom he was betrayed was Sir John Talbot, who, as a reward for his perfidy, or, as the grant terms it, "in consideration of his good and faithful service in the capture of our great adversary," &c., received a grant of twenty marks (£13 6s. 8d.) a year from Edward IV., confirmed to his son by his successor Richard III. (26th June, 1484), and made payable out of the issues and revenues of the county palatine of Lancaster. In addition to defraying their costs and charges, Sir Thomas Talbot, who was the principle in the apprehension, received the sum of £100, and a yearly pension of £40, which was confirmed to him by the next and last Yorkist sovereign, Richard III.;[1] and Sir John Tempest and Sir James Harrington each received one hundred marks (£66 13s. 4d.). Sir James Harrington also received a grant of Thurland Castle, and other estates from Edward, "not only for his good and gratifying services, often performed, but especially for his great and laborious diligence about the taking and keeping of the great traitor, our rebel and enemy, Henry, lately called Henry VI."

Considering himself now securely seated on the throne, Edward surrendered himself up to those voluptuous pleasures to which he was naturally so much inclined. His vices did not prevent him from meditating a marriage with Bona, the sister to the Queen of France, and Warwick was sent to negotiate the alliance. While the earl was engaged in this mission, Edward became enamoured of Elizabeth Wydville, the widow of Sir John Grey, Lord Ferrers, of Groby, whose husband fell in the second battle of St. Albans, while engaged on the side of the house of Lancaster. Finding that the only way to the lady's chamber was through the church he was privately married to her; and hence the remark "that he married his wife because she would not become his mistress, and took the wife of another man (Shore) as his mistress." Warwick could not brook this insult. He complained loudly of the king's conduct towards him, and associated himself with such malcontents as seemed disposed to question and to overthrow the king's authority.

The earl being joined by the Duke of Clarence, they collected a number of their adherents, and marched into Lancashire, where they importuned Lord Stanley, who had married Eleanor, the Earl of Warwick's sister, to embrace their cause. To this application Lord Stanley, who was at the time negotiating a marriage between his eldest son and the daughter of the new queen's sister, though strongly urged by his brother-in-law Warwick, who visited him at Manchester for the purpose, was too astute to compromise himself with either faction, returned a peremptory refusal to strike a blow for king or king-maker, and the project of his rising in arms to displace his royal master was for the present abandoned by the Earl of Warwick. The "king-maker" was, however, of a spirit too intrepid to be diverted from his purpose by a disappointment of this nature. In the month of September, 1470, the attempt was renewed, and the earl and the duke, availing themselves of the zeal of the Lancastrian party, and of the general discontent which Edward's extravagance and imprudence had excited, raised the standard of revolt in the centre of the kingdom, supported by an army of 60,000 men. Edward hastened to encounter this formidable enemy, and the two armies approached each other near Nottingham. On the eve of the battle Edward was surprised in the night by the cry of "War!" when, supposing that all was lost, he fled into Norfolk, by the advice of his chamberlain, and from thence escaped with difficulty to Holland. As a natural consequence of this royal panic and temporary abdication, Henry VI. was released from his confinement, and again seated on his precarious throne, under the auspices of Clarence and Warwick, who did not fail to vest all the regal power in their own hands as regents. When Edward had been driven into exile, Lord Stanley abandoned his neutrality, and accompanied the Bishop of Winchester to release the captive Henry from his keepers in the Tower, and convey him "with great pomp, and apparelled in a long gown of blue velvet," through the streets of London to the Palace of Westminster, when he was restored to the crown. The adherents of the House of York followed the king's example, and his queen, who had just been delivered of Prince Edward,

<hr />

[1] Waddington Hall, now a dilapidated farmhouse, but retaining traces of antiquity, was an occasional residence of the Tempests, but Bracewell, their chief abode, Whalley Abbey, and Bolton, as well as Waddington, occasionally afforded Henry an asylum while a fugitive in this part of the country. Of the capture of the poor king the Warkworth Chronicle gives the following account: "Also the same year (1465) Kinge Henry was taken bysyde a house of religione in Lancasbyre (Whalley), by the mene of a blacke monke of Abyntone, in a wode called Clitherwode, bysyde Bungarley Hyppynge stones by Thomas Talbott, of Bashall, and

John Talbott his cosyne of Colebery (Salesbury), withe other moo; whiche disseyvide (? discryvide i.e., descried) beynge at his dynere at Wadyngtone Hall, and caryed to Londone on horse bake, and his lege bownde to the styrope, and so brought through Londone to the Toure, where he was kept long time." Mr. Halliwell, who edited the Chronicle for the Camden Society, referring to the "blacke monke," says "the name of the rascal" was William Cantlow. The Thomas Talbot, who was a principal in the capture of Henry, was son-in-law of Sir John Tempest. —C.

was amongst the fugitives. Queen Margaret, who was still abroad, received the intelligence of the improved prospects of her house with rapture ; but before the winds, inconstant as her own fortune, could waft her to the shores of England, the sun of the house of Lancaster had set, never more to rise in her family.

A supply of two thousand troops having been granted by the Duke of Burgundy to Edward, he returned to England, and disembarked, as Henry of Bolingbroke, Earl of Derby and Duke of Lancaster, had done at Ravenspur, in Yorkshire (on the 16th March, 1471), declaring, as that duke had done, that his object was not to challenge the throne but merely to obtain his paternal inheritance. By one of those unaccountable anomalies, which the absence of records and the vagueness of contemporary history disqualify us from explaining, Edward was allowed by the regents to present himself, without molestation, in considerable force before the gates of London, into which he was admitted without a struggle, and to reascend the throne, Henry having very peaceably retired to the Tower. The battle of Barnet, fought April 14, 1471, three days after the entrance of Edward into London, in which he commanded in person, terminated fatally for the house of Lancaster ; and Warwick himself, after having performed prodigies of valour as a foot-soldier, when he ought to have been directing the operations of his army as a general, was numbered amongst the slain. Queen Margaret reached the shores of England, accompanied by her son Edward, now eighteen years of age, just in time to hear of the death of Warwick and the defeat of his army. This lion-hearted woman seemed now to bow to her fate, and sought the privilege of sanctuary ; but being urged by Tudor, Earl of Pembroke, and others of the adherents of her house, to make another effort for the throne, she marched through Devon, Somerset, and Gloucester, to Tewkesbury, daily accumulating fresh forces on her route ; here she was overtaken by King Edward, April 19th, 1471, and after a sanguinary battle overthrown. The queen fell into the hands of the victors ; her boy fell on the field, stabbed, as was affirmed, by the Yorkist lords, after Edward had met his cry for mercy by a buffet from his gauntlet ; and to consummate the disasters to the royal house of Lancaster, Henry VI. died *suddenly* a few days after in the Tower, to which place Margaret was committed as a state prisoner, and after remaining six years in confinement, she was ransomed by Louis, King of France, at the price of fifty thousand crowns. The queen survived her captivity four years, having spent the evening of her life in solitude and exile. The reign of Edward, after the overthrow of the house of Lancaster, presents no subjects connected with the history of this county, with the exception of a fruitless expedition into France to regain the lost conquests of England, in which Lord Stanley and several Lancashire knights were engaged, but which terminated in nothing better than an ostentatious display of military strength.

A copy of the will of Edward IV., made by Rymer, is deposited in the Rolls Chapel,[1] by which document the king directs " that all the revenues, issues, proffits, and commodities, commyng and growing of oure countie palatine of Lancastre, and of alle our castelles, lordshippes, manoirs, lands, tenements, rents, and services in the countie palatine and shire of Lancastre, parcell of oure said duchie of Lancastre, with their membres and appurtenances," &c., shall be applied "towards the marriages of our doughtres." This will is of considerable length, and bears date the 20th June, 1475.

In the last year of the reign of Edward IV. (1482) a petition was presented to Parliament which had been promoted in the south-eastern part of Lancashire, where the manufacture of hats has prevailed for many ages to a great extent. This document serves to date, with tolerable accuracy, the period when alarms from the consequences of improved machinery first began to manifest themselves in this county. The allegations of the petition are in these terms :—

"PRAYEN youre Highnes the Comons of this present Parliament assembled. That whereas Huers,[2] Bonettes, and Cappes, aswele sengle as double, were wonte truly to be made, wrought, fulled and thikked by the myght and strength of men, that is to say, with hande and fote ; and they that have so made, wrought, fulled and thikked such Huers, Bonettes, and Cappes, have well and honestly afore thys goten their lyvyng therby, and therupon kept apprentices, servauntes, and good housholdes. It is so, that ther is a subtile mean founde now of late, by reason of a Fullyng Mille, whereby mo Cappes may be fulled and thikked in one day, than by the myght and strengthe of four-score men by hand and fote may be fulled and thikked in the same day : The which Huers, Bonettes, and Cappes, so as it is aforesaid by the said Milles fulled and thikked, ben brosed, broken and deceyvably wrought, and may in no wise by the mean of eny Mille be truly made, to the grete hurt of your seid Highnesse, and of all your subjetts which daily use and occupie the same, and to the utter undoyng of suche your subjettes, as ben the makers of the same Huers, Bonettes, and Cappes, and wolde and entende to lyve by the true making of the same ; withoute youre most gracious helpe be shewed to theim in this behalf."

The petitioners conclude with a prayer that Parliament will interdict, for two years at least, the use of these fulling-mills ; to which the reply is—" Le Roy le voet " (The King wills it).

The intrigues of the court which followed on the death of Edward IV. were unbounded. The ancient nobility, with the Duke of Gloucester as protector at their head, opposed by every means

---

[1] Excerpta Historica, p. 366.   [2] Huers or pillions were a head-covering of cloth worn by priests and graduates.—H.

in their power the relations of the queen, who were considered as aspiring upstarts; and Earl Rivers, her brother, Sir Richard Grey, one of her sons, and Sir Thomas Vaughan, an officer in the king's household, were, by the authority of the duke, committed to Pontefract Castle—the same Pontefract where, before, Thomas, Earl of Lancaster, had been beheaded, and within whose walls Richard II. had fallen beneath the murderous battle-axe of Piers Exton—for "setting variances amongst the states, to subdue and destroy the noble blood of the realm;" on which vague charge all three, without being brought to legal trial, were executed by Gloucester's order. Their real offence, however, consisted in standing in the way of the duke's assumption of the crown, and no quantity of blood was thought too large to be shed for the purpose of removing the impediments to his elevation. Lord-chamberlain Hastings shared the same fate, for venturing to doubt whether the protector's arm, which had been withered from his birth, was diseased by the sorceries of his queen-sister and Shore's wife. Lord Stanley escaped with difficulty, but not without a severe contusion, a murderous blow being levelled at his head by the ruffians introduced into the council-chamber in the Tower, at Gloucester's bidding, to seize Hastings and hurry him away to execution.[1] Stanley was kept prisoner in the Tower for a time, but his usual luck attended him. Gloucester visited him, set him free, and ere a month had passed he stood beside the usurper at Westminster, a trusty counsellor, bearing the mace, while the circle and symbol of sovereignty was placed on Richard's head. On the same day (June 26, 1483) he was constituted one of the commissioners for executing the office of Lord High Steward of England, and before the close of the year he had been invested with the Order of the Garter and made Constable of England for life. The duke had evidently fixed his eye upon the throne, and was determined to ascend it at whatever price. To consummate his purpose, his two nephews, Edward V. and his brother Richard, Duke of York, were—as is commonly affirmed, though the question is involved in much obscurity[2]—smothered in the Tower, whilst sleeping in their bed, by three assassins of the name of Dighton, Forest, and Slater, under the direction of Sir James Tyrrel, a creature of the duke's. Having thus removed the obstacles in his way to power, the coronation, which appeared to be preparing for Edward V., was appropriated by the Duke of Gloucester to his own purpose and that of his queen. The ceremony was of the most splendid kind, that the gorgeousness of the scene might conceal the blood which contaminated the track to the throne. Lord Stanley, who had just been liberated from the Tower, was placed in the humiliating situation of bearing the mace before the king, and the "Lady of Rychemond" bore the queen's train. The other Lancashire peers present were Lord Grey of Wilton and Lord Morley; and among the knights were Sir William Stanley, Sir Edward Stanley, Sir Charles Pilkington, Sir Rafe Ashton, and Sir William Norris;[3] also Sir James and Sir Robert Harrington.[4]

During the short reign of Richard III. a considerable number of letters-patent were granted by the king. These documents, in Latin and in English, are preserved in what is styled "a very valuable book," belonging to the lord treasurer Burghley, in the Harleian collection of the British Museum; and the following are their titles, so far as they relate to the county and duchy of Lancaster:—

HARL. MSS. Cod. 433. [Temp. Rich. III.]

ART.

14 To John Howard, knt., the Office of Chief Steward of the duchy of Lanc. South of Trent.

21 To Henry Stafford, Duke of Buckingham, the offices of constable, steward, and receiver of the castle, manor, and town of Monmouth, in S. Wales, and of all the other castles, lordships, manors, towns, &c., which are parcels of the Duchy of Lanc. in S. Wales. The duke is also appointed keeper or head forester of the forest and chace of *Hodewake*, and of all the other forests and chaces being parcels of the Duchy aforesd in S. Wales.

43 To Sir Richd Huddlestone the office of receiver of the lordps, manors, lands, & tenemts in Cumberld & Lancasl.e which were formerly Thos Grey's (Marquis of Dorset).

63 A Writ appoints Guy Fairfax, knt., and Milo Metcalf, Chief Justiciaries of Lanc.

70 Royal Letters for the advowson of the Parish church of Gayton, parcel of the Duchy of Lanc.

86 Letters Pat. to Thos Metcalfe, the office of Chancellor of the Duchy of Lanc. and the custody of the seal for the same office.

87 Ditto.

92 To Guy Fairfax, knighte, th' office of Chieff Juge of Lancastre.

93 To Miles Metcalfe the office of one of the Juges at Lancastre.

94 To Thomas Molineux the office of king's Serjeant and Attorney at Lawe, in all his courtes within the county palatyne of L.

---

[1] According to Sir William Dugdale, quoting from Stow, this catastrophe might have been avoided if Lord Hastings had given heed to a dream of Lord Stanley's on the preceding night, in which his lordship beheld a boar, the cognisance of Gloucester, goring with his tusks Hastings and Stanley till the blood ran about their shoulders. Shakspere had evidently heard the story, for he introduces it in the third act of *King Richard III.*, scene 2.

[2] The historian of Croyland, a contemporary writer, says that it was set abroad that the two sons of Edward IV. were deceased, but by what manner of violence was unknown. The "Chronicle of the Grey Friars of London," the register book of that fraternity, has this simple and impressive entry, under date 1 Richard III. (1483) "And the two sons of King Edward were put to silence."—C.

[3] Harl. MSS. 2115, f. 152.

[4] Hollinshed's Chron. vol. iii. p. 398.

ART.
99 To Henry Stafford, D. of Buck., the office of constable, stuarde, and receivour of the castles, mannors, & townes of
Mounemouthe and Kydwelly, of all castles, lordshps, townes, &c., in Wales, and the Marches parcels of the Duchie of
Lanc. & thoffice of Pananaster (?)[1] Forster and Maister of the Game in all the forests and chaces of Wales and Marches of
the same, belonging to the said duchie.
102 To John Howard, D. of Norfolke, the office of Chief Steward of the Duchy of Lanc. South of Trent.
103 To Thomas Pylkyngtone, knight, the office of Sheriff of the county of Lanc[r] and the county Palatine.
106 To John Dudley, Esq., the office of Stew[d] of the Duchy within the counties of Berks and Southampton.
107 To Sir John le Scrop—chamberlain of the Duchy.
113 To Sir Ric[d] Huddlestone receiver ut supra.
116 To therle of Surry the Stewardsh[p] of the Duchie.
130 To Thomas Kebell thoffice of Generall Attourney of the Duchie of Lanc. in Engl[d] & Wales.
171 To W. Castby thoffice of Steward of Daventre, Higham Ferys, Paverells Fee, &c.
177 To Ad[m] Nelsone th office of Messagere of the Duchie, and Ushere of the councelle house ordeyned for the same.
178 To Ric[d] Pottyerr the Attorneyshp of the Duchie.
179 To therle of Surry ut supra.
276 To John Fitz Herbert the Baillieff of the newe Franchesie of the Duchie of Lanc. in the countie of Derby.
327 "To John, Duc of Norfolke, thoffice of chieffe Steward," as above in the Latin patent.
518 To Nicholas Gardyner, thexecutor of John Gardyner, Licence to found a chauntrie in our Ladie church of Lanc. & to mortize
12 b. of land there.
519 To Morgan Kidwelly the Stewardship of all the lordshps of the Duchy of Lanc. or otherwise belonging to the king in the
co. of Dorset.
824 To Thom[s] L[d] Stanley, Lord Strange, many castles, lordships, manoirs, to hold by knight's service whereof part of them belonged
to Roger Tocot, Henry Stafford Duc of Buckingham, &c.
1628 "Comission to the Lord Stanley, constable of England, to sease vnto the kinges use the Manoir of Brightmeed in the counte of
Lancaster, that late was of Thomas Seint Legere his, rebelle. Yeven at London the 16th day of Dec. an[o] primo." Several
other comissions to the same to seize upon lands belonging to the above Sir Thomas S[t] Leger and Henry Stafford, D. of
Buckingham, are found here.
2001 Warrant for the Maire, &c., of Lanc., to reteigne 20 marks (£13 : 6 : 8) of the fee firme of their towne which the king hath
given unto them. Yeven at Stoney Stratforde y[e] 6th of Nov[r] a[o] 2do. (1484).
2210 Letter patent from Edw 5 to Tho[s] Kebeele for the attorneyship of the Duchy (1483).
2366 Fees & Wages of officers.
2377 Fees payable to officers in the Rape of Pevensey and parcel of the Duchy of Lancaster.

The following is the warrant or commission (numbered 1628) from Richard III. to Lord
Stanley to seize the lands of Sir Thomas St. Leger, who had married Anne, the king's eldest sister,
but who had revolted against his authority, and suffered the punishment of death in 1483.

Commission for Seizing the Lands of a Rebel in Lancashire. [1 Rich. III. 1483.]

The Lord }   "Ricardus. To our right trusty & right welbeloued Cousin & Counsellor the Lord Stanley, Constable of
Stanley. { England, greting. We wil and charge you and by these presentes yeue you ful auctorite & power to sease into our
handes the manoir or Lordship of Brightmede in our Countie of Lancastre that late was of Th. Seintleger our Rebell and thisseues
Rentes and Reuenues thereof from Michelmesse last passed to take & perceyue to our vse & behaves, yeuing straitly in
commaundement to the officer and tenauntes of the said maner or lordship and to all others our officer treue liegeaunces and
subjettes that vnto you and your assignees in thexecucion of the premisses they be attending aiding fauouring & assisting as it
apperteineth. Yeuen at London the xvj day of December Anno primo (1483).

[Ten other commissions follow the above ; or, rather, ten memoranda of such commissions, addressed to "The Lord Stanley,"
to seize lands and manors belonging to Sir Thomas St. Leger and the Duke of Buckingham, forfeited by rebellion, and situated in
the counties of "Wilts, Warre, Leicestre, Chester, Beds, Hertford, Somers, Rutland, and Oxford."]

A Warrant, or Commission. [2 Rich. III. 1485.]

The Lorde   }   "A commission directed to al knightes Squiers gentilmen and al other the kinges subjecttes of the Counte
Stanley &   } of Chester. Shewyng that the king hath deputed the Lord Stanley, the Lord Straunge and S[r] Willm Stanley to
Strange &   } have the Rule and leading of al psones appointed to do the king service when they be warned ageinst the kyng's
S[r] W[m] Stanley. } Rebelles Charging them therefore to provyde effectual attendaunce. And if any Rebelles arryue in thoose
partes than al the power that they can make be ready to assist the saide lorde and knight, Vpon theirs faiths and 'legeaunces, &c.
Yeven at Windesore, &c. (Jan. 13, 1485.)

The same }   "A lyke Commission to the knightes Squiers gentilmen and other of the Countie of Lancastre to geve their
lorde. } attendaunce vpon the Lorde Stanley & Straunge to doo the kinge grace service ageinst his Rebelles in whatsoever
place within this Royme thay fortune tarryue, Vpon theire feithe & leigeaunces. Yeuen at Westm'r the xiiij day of Januer.
A[o] ijdo (1485).   [*Fol.* 201, *b.*]

The first article in this volume of the Harl. MSS. Cod. 592 is headed "PRO DUCATU
LANCASTRIE," and consists of a patent, by which the king (supposed to be Edward IV., though it is
not so expressed, the style being simply "*Edwardus Dei gratia*," &c.) confirms to himself and
heirs, being kings of England, in perpetuity, all the liberties, privileges, customs, &c., of the county
palatine and duchy of Lancaster, previously granted by his ancestors, kings of England, by
charters, which are here recited. This article is an inspeximus, tested thus : "Witness the
king at Westminster, November 4." No date of the dominical or regnal year. It consists of
twenty-four very large folio pages.

In order to reconcile Lord Stanley to Richard's usurpation he was constituted steward of his
household, as well as Constable of England for life ; but these acts of royal favour failed to secure

___
[1] This word is thus marked with the (?) in the Harl. catalogie. There is no doubt of its accuracy, and that it is the name of the officer
who superintended forest-panage.

25

his fidelity. After the coronation, and while, as tradition affirms, the young princes were being "put to silence" in the Tower, Richard made a triumphal progress to the north, Lord Stanley accompanying him. While the king and Stanley were being feted by the citizens of York, the Duke of Buckingham was busy concocting a plot for the overthrow of Richard. Communications passed between him and the Countess of Richmond, Lord Stanley's wife, with the avowed object of placing her son, Henry of Richmond, upon the throne; and messengers passed to and fro between the countess and her son, who was then an attainted exile in Brittany. Lancashire was in a state of ferment; and there is extant a letter written at the time by Edward Plumpton, the secretary of Lord Stanley's eldest son, Lord Strange, which gives a curious side-glance at the condition of things. Writing from Lathom on the 18th of October, 1483—the day fixed by Buckingham for the uprising—he says: "People in this country be so troubled in such commandment as they have in the king's name and otherwise, marvellously that they know not what to do. My Lord Straung [Strange] goeth forth from Lathom upon Monday next with XM. [ten thousand] men, whither we cannot say. The Duke of Buckingham has not so many as yet." He significantly adds, "[it] is sayd here that he is able to go where he wyll, but I trust he shall be right withstanded and all his malice and els were great pyty."[1] The king, whose suspicions never slumbered, was fully aware of Buckingham's intention; and that he might have the more secure hold on the allegiance of Lord Stanley, and prevent him from inciting an insurrection in Lancashire and Cheshire, where his power and influence where almost unlimited, Richard insisted that George, Lord Strange, the son and heir of the house of Stanley, should remain in his hands as a hostage. These suspicions were increased by the circumstance of Lord Stanley having, about the year 1473, married for his second wife Margaret, the widow of Edmund, Earl of Richmond, half brother of Henry VI., by whom she had issue Henry, Earl of Richmond, the representative of the house of Lancaster, whom Buckingham was seeking to place upon the throne. Lord Stanley's wife was implicated in the abortive insurrection; but as his lordship had prudently kept in the background, he could not be directly impeached, and with his customary good fortune he managed to profit by the transaction, for on the day that Buckingham's head rolled away from the axe Richard bestowed upon him "the castle and lordship of Kimbolton, late belonging to the great rebel and traitor, Humphrey Stafford, Duke of Buckingham." Richard's displeasure was, however, subsequently marked by an act of attainder against the Countess of Richmond, in which it is set forth that

"Forasmuch as Margaret, Countesse of Richmond, Mother to the Kyngs greate Rebelle & Traytour, Henry, Erle of Richemond, hath of late conspired, confedered, & committed high Treason agenst oure Soveraigne Lorde the King, Richard the Third, in dyvers & sundry wyses, & in especiall in sendyng messages, writyngs & tokens to the said Henry, desyrng, procuryng, & stirryng hym by the same, to come into this Roialme, & make Werre agenst oure said Soveraigne Lorde; to the which desyre, procuryng, & stirrynge the said Henry applied hym, as it appereth by experience by hym late shewed in that behalf. Also the said Countesse made chevisancez of greate somes of money, as well within the Citee of London, as in other places of this Roialme to be employed to the execution of the said Treason & malicious purpose; & also the said Countesse conspired, confedered, & imagyned the destruction of oure said Soveraigne Lord, and was assentyng, knowyng, & assistyng Henry, late Duke of Buckingham."

The punishment for "high treason" was of course public execution, but Richard "of his grace and favour," as he alleges, but under the influence of his fears, as is more probable, and in consideration of "the good and faithful services done and intended to be done by Thomas, Lord Stanley, husband of the countess,"[2] remitted the death penalty. But at the same time he declared all her property forfeited to the crown, whether in fee-simple, fee-tail, or otherwise; but not to the prejudice of Thomas, Lord Stanley, or any other person or persons, with the exception of the Countess of Richmond. It does not appear that the countess was ever removed from Lathom House for trial, though it was ordered that she should be kept in ward by her lord, in private apartments, and not suffered to hold any communication with the king's enemies. One of the first acts of the next reign was to annul this act of attainder, and fully to reinstate the "noble princess Margaret, Countess of Richmond, in all her possessions."[3] Margaret, Countess of Richmond, was the only daughter and heir of John Beaufort, first Duke of Somerset, the grandson of John of Gaunt and Catharine Swynford. This lady had married Edmund, Earl of Richmond, and Henry, the present earl, was the only issue of that marriage. She had afterwards married Sir Henry Stafford, and at his death espoused Thomas, Lord Stanley. The present Earl of Richmond had long been a source of disquietude to the reigning family of the house of York, who had spared no pains to obtain possession of his person, for the purpose of administering those murderous remedies for the cure of a disputed title which they so well knew how to apply. But he survived all their machinations, and an alliance, suggested by the Marquis of Dorset and the Bishop of Ely, between the Earl of Richmond and Elizabeth, the eldest daughter of Edward IV., promised to effect a

[1] Plumpton Papers, pp. 44-5, Camden Soc.—C.   [2] Rot. Parl. vi. p. 250.—C.   [3] Ibid 1 Henry VII. (1485) vol. vi. p. 286.

union between the Red and the White Roses, for which the nation had long panted with ardent desire. The first attempt to accomplish this object by the agency of the Duke of Buckingham failed, and the duke and a number of his friends became the victims of the premature enterprise.[1]

Retarded in the attainment of his object by the failure of the Duke of Buckingham's enterprise, but by no means discouraged from pursuing it, the Earl of Richmond, "England's hope," embarked from Harfleur, in Normandy (August 1st, 1485), with a small army of two thousand men, with which, on the 17th of the same month, he landed at Milford Haven, where he was joined by Sir Richard Rice ap Thomas, who had been entrusted with a command in Wales by the tyrant Richard. In his march into the interior of the country he was joined by the powerful family of Shrewsbury, as well as by Sir Thomas Bourchier and Sir Walter Hungerford, and a large number of persons of inferior note. Richard, aware of the storm by which he was menaced, had collected a well-appointed army in Nottinghamshire, and towards this point the Earl of Richmond directed his course, by way of Tamworth.

Richard, knowing that he had forfeited all claim to the confidence of his people, that the enormities he had committed for the attainment of the throne had withdrawn from him the flower of his nobility, and that those who feigned allegiance to his person and government panted for an opportunity to betray and desert him, became more suspicious of his friends than alarmed by his enemies. The persons of whom he entertained the greatest suspicion, and those who had the power more than any others to decide his fate, were Lord Stanley and his younger brother, Sir William Stanley, of Holt, in Denbighshire. By a strange infatuation the king commissioned Lord Stanley to raise an army in the counties of Lancaster and Chester. The number of soldiers under the command of the Stanleys was so considerable that the decision of the approaching battle, on which a kingdom depended, was placed in their hands. Two days before the battle commenced Richard marched from Nottingham to Leicester at the head of his army, and entered that town with a countenance strongly characteristic of the gloomy state of his mind. He took up his quarters for the night at the principal inn,[2] the Blue Boar, but then called the White Boar, his cognisance, and concentrated his outposts, in preparation for the approaching engagement.

The dawn of the following day found the two hostile armies on Bosworth Field—Richard in the command of twelve thousand men, and Richmond with about half that number. Lord Stanley had placed himself near the neighbouring village of Atherstone, six miles from the field of battle, with a force differently estimated by historians, but probably amounting to about five thousand men. Even now the determination which his lordship had taken was not generally known in the conflicting armies, though the commanders, no doubt, had sagacity enough to discover that he had abandoned Richard, and was determined to support his rival to the throne. The sword suspended over the neck of Lord Strange, who was in Richard's camp as a hostage, hung only by a hair, and it was only averted by an opportune intervention.

Richard, extending his troops as widely as possible, to intimidate his enemy by an impression of the great strength of the army to which they were opposed, gave the command of the vanguard to the Duke of Norfolk and the Earl of Surrey; he himself led the centre, which was guarded on the flanks by the horse and led on by the bowmen. Richmond having placed his bowmen in front, under the command of the Earl of Oxford, gave the command of the right wing to Sir Gilbert Talbot and of the left to Sir John Savage. The command of the horse he took upon himself, aided by his uncle the Earl of Pembroke. Richmond having, by a successful manoeuvre, possessed himself of a path which intersected a swamp, and thrown the glare of the sun in the face of the enemy, the battle commenced. The first shock of the two armies showed sufficiently the different spirit by which they were animated. For a while, however, the contest hung in suspense; but the

---

[1] Amongst others, a gentleman of the name of William Colingbourne, who had been high sheriff of Wiltshire and Dorsetshire, suffered death for having written the following whimsical *jeu d'esprit*, in allusion to the names of the two royal favourites, Ratcliffe and Catesby, and to the crest of Lovel, which was a dog, and that of Richard, which was a boar:—

"The Rat, the Cat, and Lovel the Dog,
    Rule all England under a Hog."

[2] Richard slept at the Blue Boar Inn, and the bedstead whereon he is supposed to have lain is still preserved, and its history is thus handed down: "In the year 1613, Mrs. Clark, keeper of that inn, was robbed by her servant-maid and seven men, and the relation is thus given by Sir Roger Twisden, who had it from persons of undoubted credit, who were not only inhabitants of Leicester, but saw the murderers executed: 'When King Richard III. marched into Leicestershire against Henry, Earl of Richmond, afterwards Henry VII., he lay at the Blue Boar Inn, in the town of Leicester, where was left a large wooden bedstead, gilded in some places, which, after his defeat and death in the battle of Bosworth, was left, either through haste, or as a thing of little value (the bedding being all taken from it), to the people of the house; thenceforward, this old bedstead, which was boarded at the bottom (as the manner was in those days), became a piece of standing furniture, and passed from tenant

to tenant with the inn. In the reign of Queen Elizabeth, this house was kept by one Mr. Clark, who put a bed on this bedstead, which his wife going to make hastily, and jumbling the bedstead, a piece of gold dropped out. This excited the woman's curiosity; she narrowly examined this antiquated piece of furniture, and, finding it had a double bottom, took off the uppermost with a chisel, upon which she discovered the space between them filled with gold, part of it coined by Richard III. and the rest of it in earlier times. Mr. Clark (her husband) concealed this piece of good fortune, though by degrees the effects of it made it known, for he became rich from a low condition, and, in the space of a few years, mayor of the town; and then the story of the bedstead came to be rumoured by the servants. At his death, he left his estate to his wife, who still continued to keep the inn, though she was known to be very rich; which put some wicked persons upon engaging the maidservant to assist in robbing her. These folks, to the number of seven, lodged in her house, plundered it, and carried off some horse-loads of valuable things, and yet left a considerable quantity of valuables scattered about the floor. As for Mrs. Clark herself, who was very fat, she endeavoured to cry out for help, upon which her maid thrust her fingers down her throat and choked her; for which fact she was burnt, and the seven men, who were her accomplices, were hanged at Leicester some time in the year 1613.'"

appearance of Lord Stanley, the arbiter of the battle of Bosworth Field, who declared in favour of his son-in-law, decided the fate of the day. The king's forces fought without spirit, and seemed more anxious to secure their own safety than to obtain victory. In this emergency Richard was advised to quit the field, and a horse was provided for the purpose; but he had placed his all upon the issue, and he fought like a hero. His only remaining hope was now in the death of Richmond; and in a desperate onset to accomplish that object he slew Sir William Brandon, the earl's standard-bearer, with his own hands, and at the next moment dismounted Sir John Cheyney. The commanders of the two armies were now on the point of coming in personal collision, an event of which they both seemed ambitious; but at the moment when the combat was about to take place, Sir William Stanley broke into the line with his three thousand tall men, and surrounded Richard, who still continued to fight with all the courage and desperation of his nature; but at length, sinking under the superior force by which he was assailed, fell dead on the field, pierced with innumerable wounds, and covered with gore, his last words being, "Treason! Treason! Treason!"[1] The numbers of the slain in the battle of Bosworth Field, like the numbers engaged in the contest, are differently estimated. Some accounts rate them as low as a thousand and others as high as four thousand. The loss, however, fell principally upon the Yorkists, as Sir William Talbot, in an account written to his friends immediately after the battle, says that the number of slain on the part of the Earl of Richmond did not exceed ten persons! The Duke of Norfolk, Lord Ferrars of Chartley, Sir Robert Ratcliffe, Sir Robert Piercy, and Sir Robert Brackenbury, were all numbered with the dead; and Sir William Catesby, the ready instrument of all Richard's crimes, being taken prisoner, was beheaded with several others at Leicester two days afterwards. After the battle, Lord Stanley, who, with his brother, Sir William, had contributed so much to the success of the day, took the crown which adorned the chapeau of estate Richard had worn upon his salad or head-piece, and placing it upon the head of the Earl of Richmond crowned him on the field by the title of King Henry VII. A large portion of the spoils of the field fell into the hands of Sir William Stanley, and were allowed by the king's permission to enrich that gallant knight. "Richard's body being stripped naked, all tugged and torn, and not so much as a clout left to cover his shame, was trussed behind a pursuivant-at-arms like a hog or a calf; his head and arms hung on one side the horse and his legs on the other, all besprinkled with mire and blood, and was so carried to Leicester." "No king," says Mr. Hutton, "was ever so degraded a spectacle; humanity and decency ought not to have suffered it." Mr. Carte says, "They tied a rope about his neck, more to insult the helpless dead than to fasten him to the horse." After lying exposed to the inspection and insults of the populace, the tyrant's body, at the end of the second day, was taken to the church of the Grey Friars, and there buried in a stone coffin."[2]

Thus ended the wars between the houses of York and Lancaster, so far as the members of the house of York were concerned, in which from eighty to ninety thousand Englishmen were slain. Three kings, several princes of the blood, sixty-two nobles, one hundred and thirty-nine knights, four hundred and forty-one esquires, and six hundred and thirty-eight of the gentry of the kingdom, fell in these memorable wars.[3] The contest between the rival houses was not, however, an unmixed evil; probably it was more beneficial in its remote consequences than injurious in its immediate effects. Up to that time the property as well as the power of the nation was chiefly divided amongst the king, the nobility, and the clergy. The great mass of the people of England were, as they had been from the time of the Scandinavian invasion, serfs, dependent upon the will of their lords, transferable like cattle, and held in nearly the same estimation. Such was their degradation that the *honour* of hazarding their lives to settle a quarrel between the Red and the White Roses was too great for them to enjoy; but as every lord was obliged, by a kind of moral necessity, to take part in this widely-extended contest, either on the one side or the other, it became necessary for his own safety to seek the aid of his vassals; and before those vassals could be allowed to take the field it was necessary that they should be emancipated and become free men. In this way the feudal system, introduced before the Conquest, and consolidated by the Conqueror, was shaken to its centre; trade and commerce hastened its downfall; villeinage was virtually at an end as early as the reign of Edward VI.; and in the twelfth year of Charles II. (1660) the name itself was erased from the statute-books.

[1] It is commonly said that Lord Stanley placed the crown upon the head of the victorious Richmond, but it is an absurd mistake to suppose that Richard wore the royal crown upon his helmet during the battle; he was too experienced a soldier to put on such headgear, even supposing the crown could have been attached to his helmet. The story probably arose from his wearing a circlet of gold or some other distinguishing ornament of estate resembling a crown, such as was worn by Henry V. upon his helmet at the battle of Agincourt, and which then served to break the force of the stroke of the Duke of Alençon's battleaxe.—C.

[2] A monument was subsequently erected to his memory, with his "picture," as Sandford calls it, "in alabaster;" and, ten years afterwards, Henry VII., on his Lancashire progress, paid £10 1s. to James Keyley for this erection, which perished with the dissolution of the monastery in the following reign.

[3] "In my remembrance," says Philip de Commines, "eighty princes of the blood royal of England perished in these convulsions. Those that were spared by the sword renewed their sufferings in foreign lands. I myself saw the Duke of Exeter, the king's brother-in-law, walking barefoot after the Duke of Burgundy's train, and earning his bread by begging from door to door." Sir John Fenn, in his preface to "Original Letters," written during the reigns of Henry VI., Edward IV., and Richard III., says that every individual of two generations of the families of Somerset and Warwick fell on the field, or on the scaffold, as victims of those bloody contests.

When Henry of Richmond came out of the field of Bosworth a victor, it was to rule over a nation weak, impoverished, and bleeding at every pore. The fierce struggles of the Roses destroyed the power of the nobles and weakened their influence by sweeping away the heads of the principal families. The power of the barons had been too great for the safety of the sovereign. In the long contest they had sought to extend their own privileges and to restrict those of the crown and the freemen. Their ambition failed of its object, and when the great "king-maker" sank overpowered upon the field of Barnet, their sun may be said to have gone down. But if that contest weakened the power of the crown and the oligarchy, it was at least productive of one national benefit, inasmuch as it precipitated that social change which ultimately led to the complete overthrow of the social system: it re-established the *liberi homines* or freemen, relieved the middle class of the system of vassalage to which they had been subjected, and virtually extinguished the system of serfdom that had prevailed in England from pre-Norman times.

One of the first acts of Henry on succeeding to the crown was to reverse the attainders passed against the adherents of the house of Lancaster.[1] This was followed by an act of confiscation against the property of the adherents of the tyrant Richard, amongst whom were Sir Thomas Pilkington, Sir Robert Harrington, and Sir James Harrington, all of the county of Lancaster, whose estates were principally awarded to the Stanley family for their services at the battle of Bosworth Field. Besides their forfeited possessions Lord Stanley had bestowed the lands of Pooton of Pooton, Bythom of Bythom, and Newby of Kirkby, all in Lancashire, "with at least twenty gentlemen's estates more." Among the duchy records is an enumeration of these properties, which include, among others, Holland, Nether Kelleth, Halewood, Samlesbury, Pilkington, Bury, Cheetham, Cheetwood, Halliwell, Broughton-in-Furness, Bolton-in-Furness, Underworth, Shuttleworth, Shipplebotham, Middleton, Oversfield, Smithells, Selberthwaite, Tottington, Elswick, and Urswick; he had also a grant from the king of Burford St. Martin, in Wiltshire. As a further reward, his lordship was created Earl of Derby, elected a member of His Majesty's Privy Council, appointed a commissioner for exercising the office of lord high steward of England, and shortly afterwards had conferred upon him the great office of Constable of England for life. At the same time an arrangement was concluded between the earl and his wife, Margaret, Countess of Richmond and Derby, the king's mother, in recompense of her jointure and dower, and ratified by the sanction of Parliament.[2] A considerable augmentation was made to her possessions six years afterwards, by the grant of the lordships and manors of Ambursbury and Winterbourne, in the county of Wilts, and the manors of Henxstrigge and Charlton Canvile, in the county of Somerset, of which Henry VII. was seised, and which had been granted to Henry Beaufort, then Cardinal Beaufort and Bishop of Winchester.[3] Henry VII., in compliance with the prayer of the commoners, "that in consideration of the right to the realms of England and France being vested in his person and then heirs of his body, by the authority of the said Parliament, he would be pleased to espouse the Lady Elizabeth, daughter of King Edward IV., which marriage they hoped God would bless with a progeny of the race of kings," he in January, 1486, married that princess, and thus was accomplished the union, so long wished for by an exhausted nation, between the houses of York and Lancaster.[4]

A disease hitherto unknown, which, from its symptoms, was called the "sweating sickness," prevailed at this time (1485) in Lancashire and in other parts of the kingdom. Happily the malady, which was most fatal, was of short duration, having made its appearance about the middle of September and run its course before the end of October in the same year. "The complaint was a pestilent fever," says Lord Verulam, "attended by a malign vapour, which flew to the heart and seized the vital spirits; which stirred nature to strive to send it forth by an extreme sweat. If the patient were kept in an equal temperature, both for clothes, fire, and drink, moderately warm with temperate cordials, whereby nature's work were neither irritated by heat nor turned back by cold, he commonly recovered, and the danger was considered as past in twenty-four hours from the first attack. But infinite numbers of persons died suddenly of it before the manner of the cure and attendants were known. It was conceived not to be an epidemical disease, but to proceed from a malignity in the constitution of the air, gathered by the predisposition of seasons; and the speedy cessation declared as much." Fifteen years afterwards this county was visited by the plague, which spread extreme alarm through the country, and the king, to escape the danger of contagion, sailed with his family to Calais. This sweating sickness had so completely subsided in London that the ceremony of the coronation, which had been fixed for the 30th of October, 1485, took place according to appointment; on which occasion only two elevations and one new

[1] Rot. Parl. 1 Henry VII. vol. vi. p. 273.
[2] Rot. Parl. 1 Henry VII. vol. vi. p. 311.
[3] Rot. Parl. 7 Henry VII. vol. vi. p. 446.
[4] The desire for the union was a popular sentiment, but, though Henry had sworn at Vannes to marry the Lady Elizabeth, he showed no alacrity in performing the oath, "his aversion to the house of York being so predominant," says Bacon, "as it found place not only in his wars and councils but in his chamber and bed." Hist. Henry VII. p. 16.—C.

creation were made in the peerage, and the parties so honoured were Jasper, Earl of Pembroke, the king's uncle, created Duke of Bedford; Thomas, Lord Stanley, created Earl of Derby; and Edward Courtney, created Earl of Devon.

The partiality in favour of the House of York was still felt in the north of England, and particularly in that city which gave its name to the party of the White Rose. The king, to conciliate the affections of his subjects, determined to make a progress into the north of England. On his way thither he learned that Viscount Lovel, with Sir Humphrey Stafford and Thomas his brother, had quitted the sanctuary at Colchester, in which they had taken refuge, and were again in the field at the head of a body of insurgents. To meet the impending danger a small force was immediately collected under the Duke of Bedford, which Lord Lovel finding himself unable to resist, dispersed his army and fled into Lancashire, where he took up his residence in secret under the roof of Sir Thomas Broughton, of Brougton-in-Furness. Having remained here for some time, and arranged a secret correspondence with the knight, he at length embarked for Flanders, the seat of all the intrigues against the existing English dynasty, carried on under the fostering care of Margaret, Duchess of Burgundy, sister of the fallen tyrant Richard III., and widow of Charles the Bold. An opinion prevailed, propagated by the malcontents, that one of the sons of Edward IV., said to have been murdered in the Tower by order of his uncle, the Duke of Gloucester, still survived; and that his murderers, smitten with remorse when they had despatched one of the children, suffered the other to escape. Richard Simons, a priest living at Oxford, had as his pupil the son of a baker, named Lambert Simnel, of the age of about fifteen years, a prepossessing youth of princely presence, whom Simons concluded would fitly personate the young prince.[1] To aid the enterprise this juvenile pretender was sent over to Ireland, where he found many supporters of his claims, and where he was crowned as Edward VI.; but his principal friend was the Dówager Duchess of Burgundy, whose hatred to the house of Lancaster was implacable, and who, though possessed of many good qualities, seemed under the restraint of no moral principle when engaged in attempting the subversion of the throne of Henry VII. With the aid of the duchess, by whom Simnel was provided with two thousand troops, under the command of Martin Swart, a German mercenary, he embarked for England in suitable vessels, commanded by Captain Thomas Gerardine, and accompanied by a large number of Irish adventurers, who seemed well inclined to forget the danger to which they exposed themselves when a crown was the prize to be gained by the successful party in the contest. Simnel and his followers landed at the Pile or Peel of Fouldrey, in the bay of Morecambe, in the county of Lancaster. Here he encamped on a common, subsequently called Swart or Swarth Moor, in Furness, where he drew together a number of adherents, charmed with the chivalrous character of the enterprise, and, amongst others, Sir Thomas Broughton, of Broughton-in-Furness, the friend and correspondent of Lord Lovel. On the breaking up of the camp, the insurgents, under John de la Pole, Earl of Lincoln, marched southward through Yorkshire into Nottinghamshire, where they were joined by Lord Lovel, the devoted servant of the fallen tyrant Richard III. The king, with his usual promptitude and decision, hastened to give the insurgents battle, and having been reinforced by six thousand men, under the Earl of Shrewsbury and Lord Strange,[2] accompanied by seventy knights and persons of distinction, the hostile armies met at Stoke Field, near Newark. The battle, which was fought on the 4th June, 1487, on the south side of that village, was fierce and obstinate, and continued for three hours, but at length victory declared in favour of the king. All the leaders in the rebel army were killed upon the field, including the Earl of Lincoln, Earl Kildare, Martin Swart, Sir Thomas Pilkington, and Sir Thomas Broughton.[3] The number of the rebel troops slain amounted to four thousand, and of the king's forces to about half that number. Amongst the prisoners was the pretended Edward Plantagenet, *alias* Lambert Simnel, and the wily priest Simons, his tutor. The youth, beneath the resentment of Henry, found his level as an assistant-cook in the king's kitchen, more happy, probably, than if he had worn the king's crown; and as a reward for his merits he was afterwards

---

[1] At one time he assumed the title of Edward Plantagenet, Earl of Warwick, son of the late Duke of Clarence; and at another the title of Richard, Duke of York, second son of Edward IV.

[2] Lord Strange had, according to Edward Plumpton, "a great host, enough to have beaten all the king's enemies only, of the Earl of Derby's folkes and his own" (Plumpton Papers, 89-90, Camden Soc.)—C.

[3] In the original edition Mr. Baines affirms Francis Lord Lovel was slain at Stoke Field and the statement has been repeated by Mr. Harland. Elsewhere he says that after the battle of Bosworth this devoted servant of Richard III. was drowned while attempting to ford the river at Ince, in order to pass to his house at Halewood in Childwall parish (the present seat of the Ireland-Blackburnes); but another account represents that after the action at Stoke Field, Lord Lovel, who had been engaged with the other insurgents, made his escape after the battle, and was seen on horseback endeavouring to swim the river Trent. A rumour prevailed that he fled to some place of retirement, and was starved to death by the treachery or neglect of those in whom he confided, a report that would seem in later times to have been confirmed by a circumstance narrated

in the following letter from William Cowper, Esq., Clerk of the Parliament, concerning the supposed finding of the body: "Hertingfordbury Park, 9 August, 1737. Sir,—I met t'other day with a memorandum I had some years ago, perhaps not unworthy your notice. You may remember that Lord Bacon, in his 'History of Henry VII.,' giving an account of the battle of Stoke, saia of the Lord Lovel, who was among the rebels, that he fled & swame over the Trent on horseback, but could not recover the further side, by reason of the steepnesse of the banke, & so was drowned in the river. But another report leaves him not there, but that he lived long after in a cave or vault. Apropos to this, on the 6th May, 1728, the present Duke of Rutland related in my hearing, that about twenty years then before, viz., in 1708, upon the occasion of new laying a chimney at Munster Luvel (the family seat in Oxfordshire), there was discovered a large vault or room underground, in which was the entire skeleton of a man, as having been sitting at a table, which was laid before him, with a book, paper, pen, &c., &c. In another part of a room lay a cap, all much mouldered and decayed, which the family and others judged to be the Lord Luvel, whose exit has hitherto been so uncertain."—C.

promoted to the office of one of his Majesty's falconers. As for Simons, he was committed to prison, and doomed to perpetual incarceration. The king rewarded the services of Lord Strange by conferring upon his father, Lord Stanley, the confiscated estates of Sir Thomas Broughton. " With this unhappy gentleman the family of Broughton, which had flourished for many centuries, and had contracted alliances with most of the principal families in these parts, was extinguished in Furness."[1]

After the battle of Stoke the king made another journey into the northern counties, but it was rather an itinerant circuit of justice, to try and sentence the rebels, than a royal progress. Strict inquisition was made into the conduct of the offenders, whether they had been principals or abettors in the late rebellion. Many persons were sentenced to death and executed, but the prevailing punishment was by fine and confiscation, which spared life, but raised money—at all times the distinguished characteristic of King Henry's policy.

In the reign of Richard III. Sir William Stanley became seised of certain royal demesne lands, " as a fee of the manors of Pykhill, Sessewyke, and Bedewall, the moite of the manors of Istoid, Hewlyngton, Cobham, Hem, Wrexham, Burton, Alyngton, Esclusham, Eglosecle, Ruyaban, Abynbury, Dynull, Morton, Fabror', Minere, Osbaston, Sonford, Oseleston; the moite of the castell, lordship, and manor of Dynasbran; castell, lordship, and town of Lyone, otherwise called the Holte; the moite of the lordship, manors, and lands of Hewelyngton, Bromfeld, Yale, Wrexham, and Almore, with the advowsons of the moite of the churche of Grefford, in Wales, and marche of Wales, unto the countie of Shropshire adjoining." This grant was made to the gallant knight partly, no doubt, of the royal bounty, but not wholly so, as other manors and lands, as well as money, were given by him to the crown on the grant being ratified to Sir William. After the change of the dynasty it became a matter of doubt whether the grant made by King Richard was of sufficient validity to confer an undisputed title; and for the purpose of removing all uncertainty on the subject an Act was passed in the fourth year of the reign of Henry VII. (1488) confirming the royal grant to Sir William Stanley and to his heirs for ever.[2] Sir William had secured for himself all the riches and treasure which Richard had brought to Bosworth. He was afterwards made Chancellor of the Exchequer, and, as a further honour, had the Garter confirmed upon him. Lord Bacon says he was "the richest subject for value in the kingdom," having in his castle of Holt, in Denbighshire, " 40,000 marks in ready money and plate, besides jewels, household stuff, stocks upon the ground, and other personal estate exceeding great. And for his revenue in land and fee, it was £3,000 a year old rent, a great matter in those times."

The crime of abduction, rendered somewhat memorable in Lancashire in modern times, prevailed as early as the reign of Henry VII., and by an Act of that monarch the taking and carrying away of a woman forcibly and against her will (except female wards and bondwomen) was made a capital offence, Parliament conceiving that the obtaining of a woman by force, whatever assent might afterwards follow, was but a rape drawn forth in length, because the first force drew on all the rest.[3]

The failure of the pretensions of Lambert Simnel served only to whet the invention of his noble patroness, the Duchess of Burgundy, who, with an assiduity and malignity that belonged to her character, got up a new tragedy, in which Perkin Warbeck, an adroit youth, the son of a renegade Jew, of Tournay, was to act the principal part, as the young Duke of York, a son of Edward IV. After passing through Portugal he landed at the Cove of Cork, in Ireland, where he asserted his claims to the throne of England; and after visiting France he repaired to Flanders, where the duchess declared him to be her nephew, the Duke of York, and named him " The White Rose of England." Attracted by the news of this regal star which had risen on the Continent, Sir Robert Clifford embarked for Flanders, to ascertain the identity of the young prince; and after

[1] West's Furness, synopsis of families, p. 210.
[2] Rot. Parl. 4 Henry VII. vol. vi. p. 210.
[3] Lord Verulam's History, p. 65. The crime of abduction had been prevalent in Lancashire for generations. So common had it become that, as we have already seen (chap. x.), John of Gaunt thought it necessary to issue a proclamation in which he gave express command to the sheriff to deal severely with all such malefactors and stealers of the wives and daughters as well as of the nobles or others he might find; and he added that the crime was more common in Lancashire than elsewhere, and that "the ladies and others thus ravished were wont (as a very natural denouement) to marry their ravishers." We read in Rymer's Fœdera that on Good Friday in the year 1346, Sir Thomas de Ardern and Sir Thomas de Dutton with Thomas Litherland, prior of Burscough, in Lancashire, and a number of armed followers, entered the manor house of Boaumys, near Reading, and forcibly carried off the lady of the house and compelled her to marry Gerard de Lisle. In 1387, Thomas, son of Ralph Vernon, was indicted for having with a number of others forcibly entered the house of Margaret Caryngton, a widow, and with having violated her and carried her away (Cheshire Records). In July, 1437, William Pulle, late of Liverpool, but then of Wirral, "gentleman," with "many other felons, misdoers, and disturbers of the peace," riotously broke into the house of

the widowed Lady Isabel Boteler, at Bewsey, near Warrington, and having violated her carried her away, first to Birkenhead, and then to Bidston Church, where, by menaces, he compelled her to marry him. The offence seems in that year to have become epidemic, for on the 4th December, as we learn from the Privy Council Proceedings (v. xxvi.), writs were issued to the sheriffs of London and of twenty-four English counties; setting forth that the king had been informed of "divers great robberies, rapes of women," &c., for the suppression of which the sheriffs were enjoined to see that the provisions of the statutes of Winchester were strictly carried out. A few years after this (1452), as appears by the Parliamentary Rolls (vol. v. pp. 114-269) Edward Lancaster, gentleman, with a band of fifty persons, entered the house of the widow of Sir Henry Beaumont. Lancaster placed the lady on horseback behind one of his accomplices, making her fast with a towel, and conveyed her to a church, where a priest was in waiting to marry her to the said Edward. She refused to repeat the words of matrimony, alleging that she was contracted to Charles Nowell, Esq., and therefore his wife, but in spite of her protests she was by coercion wedded to Lancaster. Finding the mild measures of Henry VI. of little effect, Henry VII. determined on more vigorous measures, and in the third year of his reign an Act was passed visiting the offenders with condign punishment.—C.

having examined him with great minuteness he wrote to England to say that he knew Richard Duke of York as well as he knew his own son, and this was unquestionably that prince, and the indubitable "White Rose." The king, though a silent was by no means an inactive observer of the drama which was acting, and in which he had so deep an interest. His inquiries at home and his emissaries abroad convinced him that young Warbeck was an impostor, and he determined to seize several of the persons in this country by whose aid the young pretender was partly upheld and supported. Amongst a number of others, both of the laity and clergy, Sir Simon Radcliffe, Lord Fitzwalter, Sir Simon Montford, Sir Thomas Thwaites, and William Dawbigney, were arrested on a charge of high treason and brought to trial, and being found guilty of conspiring to dethrone the king they were sentenced to death and beheaded. It was now ascertained that Sir Robert Clifford had been induced to embark in the king's service as a state informer.[1] On his return to England from Flanders he sought an audience of the king in council, and affecting great contrition he fell down at his sovereign's feet, and besought his forgiveness—of which he had already been assured. As a return for the royal clemency he declared his readiness to communicate all that he knew of the parties who had been in league with Warbeck, and amongst others he accused Sir William Stanley, the king's chamberlain, who was at that moment in the royal presence.

The king received this information with every semblance of amazement! Clifford was requested to reconsider his charge, and warned of the consequences of repeating a false accusation : he persisted, however, in his assertions and offered to justify his accusations upon his soul and upon his life. The next day Sir William was examined before the lords of the council, when he neither denied nor attempted to extenuate his guilt. His reliance for pardon, it is said, rested principally upon his former services, and upon the intercession of his brother, the Earl of Derby, but both these hopes failed him. In about six weeks from the time when the accusation was first preferred by Sir Robert Clifford, Sir William Stanley was arraigned of high treason, and being found guilty was condemned to suffer the utmost penalty of the law, and soon after beheaded (16th February, 1495).[2] The specific crime charged against Sir William Stanley has never been satisfactorily ascertained ; but it is said that in a conversation with Sir Robert Clifford he observed, "that if he were sure that Perkin Warbeck was King Edward's son he would never bear arms against him." This the judges construed into conditional treason ; and the preference that the expression implied for the claims to the crown of the house of York over that of the house of Lancaster stung Henry to the quick. The true cause, however, of the extreme severity towards Sir William Stanley was probably his wealth, as he was one of the richest subjects in England, there having been found in his castle of Holt forty thousand marks (£26,666), exclusive of plate, jewels, and other effects, to which are to be added three thousand pounds a year in land. This was a temptation too alluring for a monarch of the king's disposition to resist ; and the general opinion is that Sir William Stanley was quite as much the victim of Henry's cupidity as of his own alleged treason. Some disquietude, it is said, lurked in the mind of Sir William, whose ambition had prompted him to aspire to the vacant earldom of Chester, the ancient dignity of Randle, Viscount Bayeux, the Norman baron. This request having been refused, his allegiance is supposed to have been shaken ; and the king, having become suspicious that his love was turned into hate, was glad of an occasion to remove from his court and person one to whom he was under infinite obligation. It is by no means clear that Sir Robert Clifford, the state informer, was not from the beginning an emissary of the king, who maintained a widely-extended system of *espionage*, and that he did not go over to Flanders with his consent, and by his connivance. This supposition Bacon (Lord Verulam) rejects, on the ground that Sir Robert never afterwards received that degree of confidence with the king which he enjoyed before he left England ; but this is a slender foundation on which to hazard the conjecture, seeing that spies and their employers must, in the nature of things, generally appear to stand in a state of alienation, if not of actual hostility. The Parliament which assembled in the same year (1495) passed an act of attainder against Sir William Stanley, by which all his honors, castles, manors, lordships, and other possessions, were confiscated and forfeited to the king, and thus swept into the general mass of forfeitures which filled the royal coffers.[3]

In the midst of all the cares of state Henry found sufficient leisure in the summer, after the execution of Sir William Stanley, to visit his mother, for whom he always cherished the most affectionate regard, and his step-father, the Earl of Derby, at Knowsley, and at Lathom, in this

---

[1] There is no doubt that Clifford was in the service of the king in the capacity of a spy. There is a significant entry in the Privy Purse expenses of Henry, under date January 20th, 1495—"Delivered to Sir Robert Clifford, by the hand of Master Bray, £500."—C.

[2] In the Privy Purse Expenses of Henry (*Excerpta Historica*, p. 101), are certain items of expenditure incurred at the time of the execution of Sir William Stanley—

	£	s.	d.
Money given to Sir William Stanley at his execution (supposed to be a reward to the headsman)	10	0	0
Paid for Sir William Stanley's buriall at Syon (a convent of Bridgetine nuns, on the banks of the Thames, at Isleworth)	15	19	0
Paid to Simon Digby, in full payment for the buryall of Sir Wm. Stanley	2	0	0

[3] Rot. Parl. 11 Henry VII. vol. vi. p. 503.   —C.

county. The visit was ostensibly for the purpose of manifesting the king's confidence in the Earl's fidelity, but in reality to ascertain from personal observation in what heart the head of the Stanleys had taken his brother's tragic death. Whatever may have been Lord Derby's private feelings, he prudently resolved to sink the brother in the subject, and so far was he from expressing any hostility towards the king on account of the recent execution that he gave all possible effect to the royal progress, and entertained his guest with a splendour and hospitality such as has had seldom been witnessed in these parts. To promote the king's accommodation the noble lord built a substantial bridge of stone over the Mersey at Warrington, for the passage of himself and his suite; which bridge has been found of so much public utility as to afford a perpetual monument of the visit of Henry VII. to Lancashire. The Countess of Richmond and Derby not only returned her sons's affection but she extended also her love to the queen and her children; and the following letter (spelling modernised), written by her to Thomas Boteler, Earl of Ormond, chamberlain to the queen, while he was on a foreign embassy, is strongly characteristic of her maternal affection :—

"My Lord Chamberlain,—I thank you heartily that ye list so soon remember me with my gloves, the which were right good, save they were too much [large] for my hand. I think the ladies in that parts [sic] too great ladies all, and according to their great estate they have great personages. As for news here, I am sure ye shall have more surety than I can send you. Blessed be God, the king, the queen, and all our sweet children be in good health. The queen hath been a little crazed; but now she is well, God be thanked. Her sickness is [? not] so good as I would, but I trust hastily it shall, with God's grace; whom I pray give you good speed in your great matters, and bring you well and soon home.—Written at Sheen, the 28th day of April.
    "To my lord the Queen's Chamberlain.

(M. Rychemound.")

The progress of the king on his northern tour to Lancashire commenced on the 20th of June, 1495, and terminated on the 3rd of October in the same year. In the account of the "privy purse expenses of Henry VII." the charges incurred on this journey are enumerated with great particularity, and the successive stages of the royal route, both going and coming, are marked with the king's accustomed precision, in the following terms :—

"*June* 21. At Wicombe. 22. At Notley. 25. At Wodestok. 28. For making the King's bonefuyer, 10s.   *July* 1. At Cleping-norton. 2. At Evesham. 3. At Tukesbury. 4. At Wours. 5. To Brom riding to Northamptonshire and Ruteland with five lettres, 10s.   9. To a preste that was the King's scolemaster, £2.   To a tumbler upon the rope in rewarde, 3s. 4d.   10. At Biewdeley. 12. At Ludlow. 15. At Shrewsbury. 16. At Cumbemere Abbey.   To an archer of th' archeduc in rewarde, £4.   17. At Holte. 18. At Chester. To Topliff the Juge of Ireland, £2.

"23. To John Reding for vitailling, waging of four shipps at Fowey and Plymouth, with 470 [men] for six weeks to be opon the sea, £350 2s. 9d.   For his costs riding theder with the money, £6 13s. 4d.   To Sir Geffrey for vitailling, hiring of shippes, hiring of horses, for his olde costs, & for his costs now, in grosse, £42 17s. 4d.   To the Pycard of Chester hired for a moneth, to carry men into Ireland, £4 13s. 2d.   To a Spanyard for carrying seventy men over into Irelande at one tyme, £10.   To William Damport for four tun of bere, with the carriage and empty pipes, £4 11s. 2d.   At Vaile Roiall Abbey.   To one that leped at Chestre, 6s. 8d   For the wags of eleven pety captanes for fourteen days, every of them 9d. by day, £5 15s. 6d.   [Equal to about six shillings per day at the present time.]   For their conduyt money, £1 9s. 3d.   To the wags of 149 Fotemen for fourteen days, every of them 6d. by day, £101 10s. 6d.   To their condyt money, £26 6s. 8d.   For 142 jackets, at 1s. 6d. the pece, £13 11s.   To fifty-five crosset men, every of them 1s., £2 15s.

"*July* 18. At Whonwick (Winwick).   20. At Lathom. To Sir Richard Pole for 200 jacquetta, price of every pece 1s. 6d., £15 [Husband of Margaret Plantagenet, daughter of George, Duke of Clarence, and afterwards Countess of Salisbury.]   For the wages of 100 horsemen for fourteen days, every of them 9d. by day, £52 10s.   For their conduyt for 3 days, every of them 9d. by day, £11 5s.   For the wages of 100 fotemen for fourteen days, every of them 6d. by day, £35.   [To swell the King's retinue.]   For their conduyt for four days, every of them 6d. by day, £10.   For shipping, vitailling, and setting over the see the foresaid 200 men with an 100 horses, £13 6s. 8d.   To the shirif awayting upon Sr Sampson for the safe conduyt of the foresaid souldeours, £2.

"*Aug.* 2. To Picard, a herrald of Fraunce, in rewarde, £6 13s. 4d.   To the women that songe before the Kinge and the Quene in reward, 6s. 8d.   [From which it appears that the king was accompanied in this progress by the queen.]   3. At Knowsley.   4. At Warington.   5. At Manchestre.   6. At Maxfeld.   8. At Newcastell.   10. At Strafford.   11. At Lychefeld.   12. At Burton.   13. At Derby.   28. At Lughburgh.   29. At Leye.

During the king's residence at Lathom, Perkin Warbeck, having collected a considerable armament, attempted a landing on the coast of Kent; but this enterprise, like all the others in which he embarked, utterly failed. He next sailed for Scotland, where he was received with great favour by the Scotch king. Here he told his pathetic story with much effect, representing that "one Henry Tudor, the son of Edmund Tudor, had usurped that throne of which he had been deprived by his uncle, Richard of Gloucester. Henry, not content with displacing him from the throne, had laboured to compass his death and ruin. The justice of his cause, however, was so manifest to his Most Christian Majesty Charles, King of France, and to the lady Duchess of Burgundy, his dear aunt, that they not only acknowledged his title to the English crown, but were ready to assist him in obtaining it." The Scotch king so far supported the claims of his interesting young guest that he allowed him to take to wife Lady Katherine Gordon, daughter of the Earl of Huntly, a lady of great beauty and of high accomplishments. The next step was to penetrate into England by the northern borders, and to erect his standard in Northumberland. Here Perkin issued a "royal proclamation,"[1] inviting all loyal subjects to repair to his standard, and holding out the most alluring promises to those who embraced his cause. This expedition ended in a precipitate retreat, but not till the Scotch had plundered and laid waste the county of Northumberland. His next and final attempt was upon the coast of Cornwall, where a recent insurrection, which terminated in the defeat of the rebels upon Blackheath, seemed to have prepared the people for his reception. The first appearance of Perkin was at Bodmin, where he was joined by about three thousand of the inhabitants of that town and the neighbouring district. Thus encouraged, he marched to the city of Exeter, which he summoned to surrender in the name of "Richard IV., King of England." The king lost not a moment in despatching the lord chamberlain, Lord Brook, and Sir Rice ap Thomas, with a light force, to Exeter, to relieve the city, charging them to announce that he was on his march in person, at the head of the royal army. All these preparations were rendered unnecessary by the gentry of the county having collected a force sufficient to alarm the invaders, who suddenly raised the siege of Exeter, and marched to Taunton. From this place Perkin Warbeck fled in the night, attended by about sixty horsemen, to Beaulieu, in the New Forest, where he shut himself up for safety in the sanctuary of that place (September 21, 1497), alleging that he foresaw the carnage that would ensue, and he could not endure to see the blood of his subjects spilt! Lady Katherine Gordon, who had followed the fortunes of her husband, whom she tenderly loved, was captured at St. Michael's, in Cornwall, by the king's troops, and, being taken to court, she was treated by the queen with great kindness, and even affection. Her beauty was the theme of general admiration, and, being extremely fair, the title given to her husband by the Duchess of Burgundy was transferred to his lady, who was thenceforth called "The White Rose." The pretender, Perkin, on a promise of pardon from the king, surrendered himself into his hands. On being brought to London he confessed the imposture, and became an object of scorn rather than of loyal regard. Having formed a conspiracy, as was alleged, with Edward Plantagenet, Earl of Warwick, the eldest son of the late Duke of Clarence, who had been kept a prisoner in the Tower from his infancy, he was brought to trial for high treason, found guilty, and afterwards executed at Tyburn. The Earl of Warwick, his accomplice, was also convicted, and beheaded on Tower Hill, in whom fell the last of the male line of the Plantagenets.

The king, no longer exposed to the danger of losing his throne, surrendered himself to that passion which, when inordinately cherished, strengthens with age, and outlives all other vices.[3] The annual revenue from the royal estates and the properties which had lapsed to the crown were estimated at about one hundred and seventy thousand pounds, of which forty thousand were derived from customs. The sums which flowed into the royal coffers from the arbitrary exactions and extortions under obsolete laws of Empson and Dudley, who wrested the law to do the same work of plunder as had been accomplished by the sword and the fetter in the days of baronial tyranny were immense; and the strictness with which the account of the king's privy purse was kept is at once amusing and instructive. In these accounts, from the year 1491 to 1505, amongst an immense number of other items of expenditure, the following appear:—

	£	s.	d.
Paid to Robert Suthewell for horses, sadells, and other necessarys bought for the conveyance of my Lady Kateryn Hunt-leye (The White Rose)	7	13	4
Paid to my Lord Strange in reward	40	0	0
Paid to Sir Edward Stanley in reward	26	13	4
Paid for making of the bonefuyer	2	0	0
Paid to Sir Gilbert Talbot going on an embassade to Rome, for his costs	5	0	0

Towards the close of his reign, the king displayed great anxiety to bring a "celestial honour," as it was called, into the house of Lancaster. To accomplish this object he sent an embassy to Rome, to importune the new pope Julius II. to canonise Henry VI., but upon what ground, except that he had, when Henry VII. was a boy, predicted that he should one day fill the throne of England, it is difficult to conjecture. His Holiness referred the matter to certain cardinals, to take the verification of the deceased monarch's holy acts and miracles; but these were not sufficiently

---

[1] Sir Robert Cotton's MSS.

[2] Contemporary historians describe this young prince, in their strong but homely terms, as reduced to the most abject state of imbecility by his long confinement, and by his almost entire exclusion from human intercourse. "He was," says Holinshed, "a very innocent." Hall says, "Being kept for fifteen years without company of men, or sight of beasts, he could not discern a goose from a capon."

[3] Among other modes of raising money the king had frequently recourse to subsidies. A levy of this kind was made in 1496, when the persons appointed to be commissioners for Lancashire, along with the

justices of the peace, were Edmundus Trafford Mil', Johes Talbot Mil', Thomas Lawrence Arm', and Thomas Hesketh Arm'. It is due to the king, however, to say, that he did from time to time award allowances from the revenues of the duchy of Lancaster for the relief of the public burdens, as appears by the following items in the acts of the first and eleventh years of his reign:—

First, of the General Receivour of the Duchie of Lancastre (1485) .... £2303 : 14 : 5½

First, of the General Receyvour of the Duchie of Lancastre (1495) .... £2303 : 14 : 6½

in
st,
y-
is

r

(1)
Eleanor, dau. of For mar. Alexander III., King of Castile, in Scotland ; died Nov. 27, 1290.

Beatrice, born June 25, 1242 ; m. 1260, John, Duke of Brittany, and Earl of Richmond ; died 1272.

EDWARD II., born April Jan. 25, 132 1327.

nry of Monmouth, restored to = Maud, d. and h. of Sir he Earldom of Leicester, 1324; rd Earl of Lancaster and eicester, and Steward of ngland on the reversal of is brother's attainder, 1327 ; ied 1345.

Patrick Chaworth, Lord of Kidwelly.

John, Lord of Beaufort, in France ; d. unmar.

EDWARD III., " born Nov. 1 21, 1377. 1

Henry, Earl of Lancaster and = Isabel, dau. of Henry Leicester, Steward of England, cr. Earl of Derby, March 16, 1337 ; Earl of Lincoln, Aug. 20, 1349 ; and Duke of Lancaster, March 6, 1351 ; K.G. ; d. March 24, 1360.

Bellomont, or Beaumont, Lord of Folkingham.

Blanche.
Maud.
Joan.

Isabel.
Eleanor.
Mary.

(3)
Edward, Prince of W the "Black Prince," June 15, 1330 ; cr. Ear Chester, May 18, 11 Duke of Cornwall, M 13, 1337 ; d. July 8, 137

Katharine, dau. of Sir John Payne Roet, of Hainault, and w. of Sir Otes Swynford, Kt., m. Jan. 13, 1395 ; d. May 10, 1403 (issue while a concubine).

Edmund of Langley, = Isabel, younger dau. Earl of Cambridge, 1362 ; DUKE OF YORK, Aug. 6, 1385 ; b. June 5, 1341 ; m. (2) Joan, d. of Thomas Holland, Earl of Kent, but by her had no issue ; died Aug. 1, 1402.

and coh. of Peter the Cruel, King of Castile and Leon.

Thomas of Woodstock, b. Jan. 7, 1354 ; cr. Earl of Buckingham, 1377 ; Duke of Gloucester, 1385 ; mar. Eleanor, dau. of Humphrey de Bohun, Earl of Hereford, Essex, and Northampton, and had issue Humphrey, Earl of Buckingham, and 3 daughters ; d. Sept. 8, 1379.

Isabel.
Joan.
Blanche.
Mary.
Margaret.

Edward of Angouleme, 1365 ; died young.

(1)
Mary de Bohun, youngest d. and co-h. of Hum phrey, E. of Hereford, Essex, and Northampton, Constable of England ; mar. 1380 ; died 1394.

, Earl o of Exc Earl of rmandy, nd, Cap d Chan argaret, Neville, Robert aby, co. 27, 1426.

Joan, mar. (1) Robert, s. of Robt. Ferrers, Ld. of Wemme, county Salop ; and (2) Ralph Neville, Earl of Westmorland ; died Nov. 13, 1440.

(1)
Edward, 2ND DUKE OF YORK, K.G., cr. E. of Rutland and Duke of Albemarle ; m. Philippa, 2nd d. and co-h. of John, Ld. Mohun, of Dunster ; slain at Agincourt, Oct. 25, 1415, s.p.

Anne, dau. of = Roger Mortimer, Earl of March, 2nd s. of Lionel, D. of Clarence, 3rd son of Edward III.

Richard, cr. Earl of Cambridge, 1414 ; beheaded Aug. 6, 1415.

= Maud, dau. of Thomas, Lord Clifford ; remar. John, Lord Latimer.

Constance, mar. Thos. le Despenser, cr. E. of Gloucester, 1397 ; attainted 1399 ; by him had a son and two daughters.

(1)
HENRY V., King = K a t h of England, b. youn Aug. 9, 1388 ; ain, Earl and Mar mar. June 3, of Cl ruis of Dorset, El 1420 ; d. Aug. f nd Duke of Som 31, 1422. Jan. rset ; m. Eleano

ward, Earl of Mor f Clarence, nd dau. and coh. f Richard Beauhamp, Earl of Varwick, and had sue ; slain at first attle of St. Albans, May 22, 1455.

Thomas.

Joan, m. James J. of Scotland ancestor of James IV., who m. Margaret, dau. of Henry VII., of England.

Margaret, m. Thos. Courtenay, 7th E. of Devon, and had issue.

R I C H A R D, 3RD = Cecilia, youngest DUKE OF YORK, E. of Cambridge and Rutland, Lord Tindale, E. of Ulster and March, Lord of Wigmore, Clare, Trim, and Connaught ; slain at Wakefield, Dec. 31, 1460.

dau. of Ralph Neville, Earl of Westmorland, by Joan Beaufort, dau. of John of Gaunt, Duke of Lancaster ; died May 31, 1495.

Isabel, mar. Hy. Bourchier, Earl of Essex.

HENRY VI., King of Eng land, b. Dec. 6, 1421 ; d. about May, 1471.

rl of slain ield, 60.

George, Duke of = Isabel, elder d. and Clarence, Earl of W a r w i c k and Salisbury ; said to have been drowned in a butt of malmsey in the Tower, Feb. 18, 1478.

coh. of Richard Neville, E. of Warwick, b. Sept. 5, 1451 ; m. July 11, 1469 ; d. Dec. 12, 1476.

RICHARD III., K. of = Anne, d. and coh. England, b. Oct. 21, 1450 ; cr. Duke of Gloucester ; elected King, June 18, 1483 ; slain at Bosworth, August 22, 1485.

of Rich. Neville, Earl of Warwick, the "kingmaker," and w. of Edward, Prince of Wales, son of Henry VI. ; m. July 12, 1472 ; d. March 16, 1485.

Anne, w. of Henry Holland, Duke of Exeter ; d. 1475.
Elizabeth, m. John de la Pole, Duke of Suffolk ; d. 1503.
M a r g a r e t, mar. Charles, last Duke of Burgundy, of the French line ; d. 1503, s.p.

Edward, Duke of Corn wall, cr. P. of Wales and E. of Chester ; b. Oct. 13, 1453 ; slain after the battle of Tewkesbury, May, 1471, s.p.

ke of York, orfolk, Earl ham, and E. , b. Aug. 17, an. 15, 1478, y d. and h. Lord Mow of Norfolk, o have been d with his dward V., , s.p.

George, Duke of Bedford, died young.

Edward, E. of Warwick, last heir male of the Plantagenets ; beheaded, Nov. 28, 1499. (With him ended the line of Plantagenet, 345 years after it had come to the English throne.)

Margaret, cr. Countess of Salisbury, 1513 ; m. Sir Rich. Pole, K.G. ; beheaded May 27, 1541.

Henry Pole, Lord Montague, beheaded Jan. 9, 1539.

Reginald Pole, Dean of Exeter, Archbp. of Canterbury, and Cardinal ; d. Nov. 17, 1558.

obvious to entitle him to the dignity of the calendar, and the negotiation was abandoned in despair.   A MS. in the Harleian Collection,[1] found amongst the papers of Fox, the martyrologist, entitled " *De Miraculis Beatissimi Militis Xpi Henrici Vj*," consisting of about 150 folio closely-written pages, contains an account of a vast number of reputed miracles performed by this monarch, of which the following may be taken as specimens :—

> " How Richard Whytby Priest of Mount St. Michaels was long ill of a Fever, & at last miraculously cured by journeying to the Tomb of Henry VI."   [Folio 113 b.]
> " How John called Robynson, who had been blind ten years, recovered his sight by visiting Henry's Tomb."   [Folio 97 *b.*]
> " How Henry Lancaster, afflicted with Fever, was miraculously cured in three days by the appearance of that blessed Prince Henry VI. in the sky."   [Folio 98.]
> " How a girl called Joan Knyght, who was nearly killed with a bone sticking in her throat, and considered dead, on the bystanders invoking Henry VI., vomited the bone & was restored to health."   [Folio 119 *b.*]

One of the last acts of the last Parliament of Henry VII. was to answer a demand for two "reasonable aids;" the one for making a knight of his eldest son Arthur, "now deceased," and the other for the marriage of his eldest daughter Margaret (from which marriage sprang the Stuart dynasty in England) to the King of Scotland, and also for the "great and inestimable charges" which he had incurred for the defence of the realm.   Parliament having duly considered these demands, and being fully aware of the difficulty and discontent which would arise from the aids being levied according to the ancient tenures of the kingdom, compounded for them by presenting the king with forty thousand pounds, towards which sum the contribution for Lancashire, and the commissioners employed in its collection, were as follows: Thomas Boteler, Knyght; John Bothe, Knyght; Pears Lee, Knyght; Richard Bold, Knyght; John Sowthworth, Knyght; Thomas Laurence, Knyght; William Thornborough, Esquyer; and Cutberd Clyfton, Esquyer—£318 2s. 3¾d.

The death of the king, at Richmond Palace (April 21st, 1509), put the usual termination to the accumulation of wealth.   "He left," says Lord Verulam, "mostly in secret places, vnder his own Key and keeping at Richmond, treasure of store, that amounted (as by Tradition it is reported to have done) vnto the Summe of neare Eighteene hundred thousand pounds Sterling; a huge Masse of Money, even for these times."

From the time of Henry VII. the distinction of the Roses, as a badge of party, fell entirely into disuse.   The origin of this distinction may be traced back to the time of John of Gaunt, whose device was a *red* rose, and Edmund of Langley, whose device was a *white* rose.   "These two factions," says Selden, "afterwards, as for cognisance of their descent and inclinations, were by the same flowers distinguished," till the white rose and the red were united, on the marriage of Henry VII. with the Princess Elizabeth.

[1] Cod. 423.

CHAPTER XII.

HE sixteenth century, during almost the whole of which period the throne of England was occupied by Henry VIII. and his children, affords abundant materials for both the general and the local history of the county of Lancaster. A great religious movement, the seeds of which, under the fostering influence of John of Gaunt, were sown in the fourteenth century, and moistened in succeeding ages by the blood of the followers of Wycliffe, attained its maturity in the reign of Henry VIII. The great national revolution was doubtless due, in some degree, to the arrogance and oppression of the church in its expressed form, ecclesiasticism, which provoked an English sense of wrong, and a consequent determination to resist in material things, but still more to the increase of knowlege among the laity consequent upon the invention of printing. About the year 1450 the first printed Bible appeared in Latin, and thus a mighty enemy to despotism and superstition was raised. The change in religious thought gradually gained strength and power, until it had so leavened the mind of the nation as to prepare for those changes in the teaching and ritual of the national church, the meaning of which is tersely comprehended in the one word that identifies that memorable epoch—the Reformation. Monastic life had become corrupted, and irregularity and self-indulgence generally prevailed. The heads of the religious houses had succeeded in obtaining for their establishments a large portion of the rectorial endowments; and hence, in a very many instances, the parishes were left to the spiritual care of vicars, who were willing to accept the small tithes as a miserable means of subsistence. As a rule they belonged to the inferior clergy, men with little learning and less piety—"mass-priests, who could read their breviaries and no more"—and who, in their lives, oftentimes manifested the gross habits of the class from which they sprang. The services of the church, too, were read in an unknown tongue, so that the common people (to use the words of the preface to the Book of Common Prayer), "heard with their ears only, and their heart, spirit, and mind were not edified thereby;" whilst to the comparatively few who were able to understand, "the manifold changes of the service" were so perplexing that "to turn the book only was so hard and intricate a matter that many times there was more business to find out what should be read than to read it when it was found out." Observances and practices had crept into the services of the church which were unknown in primitive times, preaching was neglected, and the religious training of the young was but little cared for. Copies of the Scriptures were so costly as to be beyond the reach of the great mass, and consequently they were left to glean such little knowledge of Holy Writ as they could from the scenes and incidents—the "stories," as they were commonly called—painted on the walls of the churches, and from the so-called miracle-plays performed therein for their edification and amusement.

The ancient habit of implicit obedience to authority was passing away, and earnest men were beginning to think and to talk of the principles of government both in Church and State. Their "lack of faith," as Fisher phrased it, weakened their belief in the doctrine of infallibility, and led them to seek a higher guide to duty than the absolute direction of an ecclesiastic, so that when Parliament was prorogued in December, 1529, after effecting certain reforms in the church, their exultation was so great that, as Mr. Froude says, "lay England celebrated its exploits as a natural victory." In 1533 the English Parliament passed the Statute of Appeals,[1] repudiating the authority and jurisdiction claimed by the sovereign-pontiff, and thus the connection between the Church of England and that of Rome was dissolved. Being free from the control and interference of the Holy See the church advanced step by step to the rejection of all those doctrines associated with the office and pretensions of the pontiff. Shortly afterwards the Bible was ordered to be translated and printed in English, and a copy was directed to be set up publicly in every church throughout the kingdom, to be read by all who pleased, without hindrance or discouragement; and thus a spirit of inquiry was diffused among the people.

The real character of Cromwell's ecclesiastical policy was more clearly seen in the attitude he assumed towards the monastic orders. The Lollard cry for their suppression had died away, but monasticism had relaxed its discipline, the monks had outlived the work they were created to perform, and a general carelessness prevailed in regard to the religious objects of their trust. In 1535 the conflict between monarchy and monasticism began; the visitation of the religious houses— the preparatory step to their suppression—was followed in the succeeding year by the insurrection under the northern monks, known as "The Pilgrimage of Grace." A Lancashire man, John Paslew, the Abbot of Whalley, appeared in the foremost rank of this perilous enterprise, and when the expedition ended in the discomfiture of its promoters, Paslew was arraigned at Lancaster on the charge of high treason, condemned, and hanged in a field called the "Holehouses," at Wiswall, opposite the house of his birth, and almost within sight of his own monastery. The houses of Whalley and Furness were the first to bow before the blast, but the other conventual establishments were soon involved in the common ruin, the whole of them being doomed to suppression before the close of the year 1540.

The Reformation is commonly attributed to Henry VIII., but it had really little concern with his personal character or the motives of his conduct. For his own purposes he abolished the jurisdiction claimed by papal bishops, and made his own courts supreme; and to replenish his exhausted exchequer he plundered the religious houses of their endowments, and thus unconsciously prepared the way for the doctrines which his successor maintained and protected. He accomplished all that such an instrument could be expected to do: he rooted up the weeds and prepared the ground for the seed sown by his successor. In this way he effected the rough work of the Reformation, but at his death "he left a church which was little but a ruinous heap, its revenues dissipated, its ministers divided, its doctrines unsettled, its laws obsolete, impracticable, and unadapted to the great changes it had sustained."[2] The confiscation of the monastic estates enabled many of the Lancashire gentry, as well as those in other parts of the kingdom, to make considerable additions to their patrimonial lands on very reasonable terms. The Stanleys were not negligent of the golden opportunity, and the Braddylls, the Asshetons, the Holcrofts, the ffarringtons, the Hollands, and many other families, added largely to their hereditary possessions. With the wealth which poured into his coffers the king was enabled (in part fulfilment only of his promise) to found six new bishoprics, one of which was established at Chester, creations that could not fail materially to affect the ecclesiastical institutions of that county, which previously had been included in the more remote see of Lichfield. The persecutions on account of the ever-varying religion of the governing power created a degree of public excitement that has seldom had a parallel in British history; in the north of England the impression produced by these changes was deeper than in the south; and in Lancashire, where the recusants were more numerous than in any other county, both the clergy and the laity awaited the result of the contest of the rival churches of England and Rome with an anxiety fully commensurate with the important interests it involved. Nor were the military and naval events of this period less interesting. The battle of Flodden Field, the wars with France,, the almost incessant contests with Ireland, and the menaced invasion of this country by Spain, which terminated in the destruction of the "Invincible Armada," filled the whole nation with military ardour; and the ample official correspondence between the lieutenancy in the county of Lancaster and the successive ministers of state[3] shows that this county took its full share in the great events by which the destiny of the nation was fixed and its independence for ever secured.

No prince ever ascended the throne of England under circumstances more auspicious than

[1] The preamble to this statute, declaring the independence of the sovereignty of England, presents a fine example of the strength of the English language, and is expressed in words terse and vigorous as our early mother tongue could make it: "Where, by divers sundry old authentic histories and chronicles, it is manifestly declared and expressed that this realm of England is an empire; and so hath been accepted in the world, governed by one supreme head and king, having the dignity and royal estate of the imperial crown of the same; unto whom a body politic, compact of all sorts and degrees of people, divided in terms and by names of Spirituality and Temporality, be bounden and owing to bear, next to God, a natural and humble obedience; he being also institute and furnished by the goodness and sufferance of Almighty God with plenty, whole, and entire power, pre-eminence, authority, prorogation, and jurisdiction, to render and yield justice and final determination to all manner of folk, residents or subjects, within this his realm, in all causes, matters, debates, and contentions happening to occur, insurge, or begin within the limits thereof, without restraint or provocation to any foreign prince or potentate of the world."—C.

[2] Blunt's *Sketch of the Reformation*, p. 184.—C.

[3] See Mr. Harland's *Lancashire Lieutenancy under the Tudors*, &c. (vols. 49 and 50 of the Chetham Society's series).

those which attended the elevation of Henry VIII. At peace with all foreign nations, in the enjoyment of an undisputed title to the throne, with a treasury full almost to repletion, and in possession of the affections of his people, while himself yet "in the flower of pleasant youth," he had nothing to wish for, and nothing to dread, except the impetuosity of his own passions. His venerable grandmother, the Countess of Richmond and Derby, had survived her son Henry VII., and offered her valuable council and assistance in the formation of the young king's cabinet, at the head of which stood the Archbishop of Canterbury. The countess lived to see the hope of her old age married to Catherine, daughter of Ferdinand of Arragon—the "virgin widow" of his deceased brother Arthur, and died soon after the consummation of that unhappy union, a union that Henry, under pressure from his advisers, reluctantly entered into on account of the doubtful position of that princess, and the questions of legitimacy that might in later times arise, notwithstanding that the contract of marriage had, in 1503, been legalised by a Papal decree.[1] The coronation took place at Westminster on the 24th June, 1509, and there is preserved a copy of the coronation oath, altered and interlined by Henry's hand, which is interesting as showing the tendency of his mind, even at that early period of his reign, to assert the independence of the crown in matters of church government.[2]

A few years served to engage the king in a war with France, and to awaken the dormant feelings of hostility entertained towards England by the Scottish nation. To prosecute his operations with success, James IV., King of Scotland, on the 22nd August 1513, while Henry was encamped before Teronenns, passed the English frontier west of Berwick, at the head of fifty thousand men,[3] and menaced the adjoining shores with his invading army. After being invested for six days the castle of Norham surrendered, and shortly afterwards three other border strongholds—Wark, Etall, and Ford—yielded. The report of this plundering raid fired the ardour of the English people. Large levies, principally of the tenantry of the great landed proprietors, were raised in the northern counties, which were placed, by the direction of the queen regent,[4] under the command of Thomas Howard, Earl of Surrey.[5] The Lancashire men made a ready response when the war-note was sounded. The knights and esquires summoned their retainers and burnished and made ready their arms and armour. As the rhyming chronicle has it, they mustered—

> "From Warton unto Warrington,
> From Wigan unto Wyersdale,
> From Weddicar to Waddington,
> From Ribchester unto Rochdale."

The forces consisted chiefly of archers, the "good yew bow" and the "clothyard shaft," of which latter there was a notable manufactory at Warrington,[6] being the staple weapons. After mustering under the banners of their respective leaders, they marched, as we learn from an old rhyme, first to Hornby Castle, where, with the men from Cheshire, they placed themselves under the command of Sir Edward Stanley, a younger son of the Earl of Derby, and then advanced to join the forces of the Earl of Surrey, which, with these additions, numbered twenty-six thousand men. The earl having marched from Pontefract by the route of Bolton Castle, the two armies met on the field of Flodden, near the foot of the Cheviot Hills, on the margin of the vale of Tweed. The Earl of Surrey, having divided his forces into two parts, confided the vanguard to the command of his son,

Lord Howard, the lord admiral, and the rear he headed himself. Sir Edmund Howard commanded the right wing and Sir Edward Stanley the left wing of the English army. On leading his followers to the field, the earl exclaimed, "Now, good fellows, do like Englishmen this day!" The right wing of the vanguard, under Sir Edmund Howard, overwhelmed by a large body of Scottish spearmen, commanded by Lord Home, narrowly escaped annihilation by the timely arrival of the Bastard Heron, with a numerous body of outlaws, who maintained a dubious contest, till the Lord Dacre, with a reserve of fifteen thousand horse, charged the spearmen, and put them to flight. The English vanguard, under the lord admiral, fought like heroes, and, after slaying the Earls of Errol and Crawford, dispersed their forces in every direction. The commanders of the conflicting armies, the Earl of Surrey and the Scottish king, with the chosen warriors of their respective armies, were opposed to each other. James fought on foot, surrounded by thousands of his men, cased in armour, which resisted the arrows of the English archers. Marching with a steady step towards the royal standard of England, he conceived this trophy of victory to be almost within his grasp, and was congratulating himself on the glories that awaited him, when Sir Edward Stanley, leading the left wing of the English army, composed principally of the Lancashire, Cheshire, and Yorkshire levies, defeated the Earls of Argyle and Lennox, and turned the fortune of the day. The Scottish ranks, harassed by the murderous discharges of the archers, and the tremendous blows of the bill-men, fell into disorder; when Stanley, seizing the moment of panic, chased them over the hill, and, wheeling to the right, led his followers against the rear of the main Scotch army under King James, and thus placed him between two fires. In vain did the gallant monarch endeavour to penetrate the hostile ranks by which he was environed: the moment of his destiny was at hand, and he fell a lifeless corpse upon the field, within a spear's length of the feet of the Earl of Surrey. The battle, which began about five o'clock in the afternoon of the 9th September 1513, terminated at night-fall, and the pursuit was continued for only four miles. On the part of the Scotch, ten thousand warriors were slain, amongst whom were not only the king, but his natural son the Archbishop of St. Andrews, with two other bishops, two abbots, twelve earls, thirteen barons, five eldest sons of barons, and fifty other men of distinction,[1] including the French ambassador and the king's secretary. "Scarce a family of eminence," says Scott, "but has an ancestor killed at Flodden." Six thousand horses were taken, with the whole park of the Scotch artillery, and about eight thousand prisoners. The English loss was very severe, the number slain being estimated at seven thousand, but the men of rank who fell were not nearly so numerous. There is perhaps no event in the annals of the county that has been the subject of so much exultation on the part of Lancashire men, or that has formed the groundwork of so many traditions and formed so fruitful a theme for ballad writers as the victory of Flodden Field. That their favourite leader, Sir Edward Stanley, should, by his skill and courage, have contributed so essentially to turn the fate of the day, and that those other gallant knights, Sir William Molyneux of Sefton, Sir William Norris of Speke, Sir Richard Ashton of Middleton, "young Sir John Stanley," Sir Thomas Boteler of Bewsey, Sir Bryan Tunstall of Thurland, and Holt of Stubley, should have co-operated so efficiently with their leader, will long be mentioned with praise by those who cherish the memory of gallant deeds at arms, and combine with them the localities of the respective contingents. The records of the day are full of the achievements of the heroes of Flodden Field, which are celebrated in prose and in rhyme; and an ancient MS. in the Harleian collection in the British Museum,[2] records these valiant deeds in a strain of high eulogium. The poem is in nine fits, or cantos, occupying sixty-six closely-written quarto pages, and opens with the following argument:—

"Heare is the Famous historie or Songe called Floodan Field; in it shalbe declare how whyle King Henrie the Eighth was in France, the King of Scoots called James, the Fowerth of that name, Invaided the Realme of England, And how he was Incountred wᵗʰ all att a place called Branton, on Floodan Hill, By the Earle of Surrey Live Tennant General for the Kinge, wᵗʰ the sonne Lord Thomas Haworth, the great Admirall of England wᵗʰ the Helpe of dyvers Lords & Knights in the North Countrie, As the Lord Dakers of the North, the Lord Scrope of Bolton, wᵗʰ the most Corragious Knight Sʳ Edward Standley, whoe for his prowis and valliantnes shewed att the said Battell, was made Lord Mount Eagle as the Sequell declareth." [3]

The poet narrates the progress of the battle, and ends with celebrating the victory. After the battle the victorious army penetrated into Scotland; and Speke Hall, the seat of Sir William Norris, has ever since been enriched with trophies of this memorable campaign, brought from the

[1] Lord Thomas Howard's official account.
[2] Harl. MSS. No. 3526. "Yonge John Stanley"—"that child so young," as Weber calls him in one of his ballads—was an illegitimate son of James Stanley, Warden of Manchester and afterwards Bishop of Ely. He commanded a contingent composed mainly of troops raised in Lancashire and Cheshire by his father, who is said to have "put in more power than any other prelate," and contributed materially to the victory at Flodden, receiving, as the reward of his bravery, the honour of knighthood on the field.—C.

[3] This is the earliest known transcript of the ballad, and the date of the MS. is about 1636. Mr. Henry Gray has lately published a version of the ballad "taken from an ancient manuscript which was transcribed by Mr. Richard Guy, late schoolmaster of Ingleton, Yorkshire." It is accompanied by annotations and various readings, and historical and descriptive notes, with a list of the Craven men who fought at Flodden, from the pen of Mr. Chas. A. Federer.—C.

palace of the Scottish king. The English monarch, who was then in France,[1] accompanied by Henry, Earl of Derby, and engaged in the great expedition in which Tournay was won, in the ardour of his gratitude, on his return to England in November, addressed a congratulatory letter to Sir Edward Stanley. Similar letters, *mutatis mutandis*, were sent to Sir William Molyneux, Sir William Norris, and Sir Richard Ashton, and, as a still further mark of his Majesty's gratitude, Sir Edward Stanley, who was the fifth son of Thomas, Earl of Derby, was created Lord Monteagle, in allusion to the family crest. The Earl of Surrey was restored to the family title of Duke of Norfolk, while his son, Lord Howard, was honoured with the title of the Earl of Surrey. Wolsey, then the king's favourite minister, was created Bishop of Lincoln ; and Lord Herbert obtained a step in the peerage as Earl of Worcester.

About this period, the ancient commission of array, for levying and organising troops in the different counties of the kingdom, to guard against foreign invasion and domestic tumult, began to be superseded by a new local authority, called the lieutenancy,[2] at the head of which, in this county, was placed the Duke of Norfolk, who was succeeded in the office by the Earl of Shrewsbury, and subsequently by Edward, Earl of Derby ; and although not a hereditary honour, the office of lord-lieutenant of the county palatine of Lancaster has been filled almost ever since its institution by the head of the Stanley family.

The baneful connection formed by Scotland and France served again to embroil our northern neighbours in a fresh war with England, and preparations were made for invading the northern counties. To repel this invasion a royal mandate was issued to the high sheriff of the county of Lancaster, commanding him to make proclamation in these words :—

"Forasmuche as the King's Highnes has learned of an intention to invade England at or before the beginning of September, formed by the Scots at the instigation of the French king ; his grace, therefore, by advice of his counsel, charges all and singular his subjects, of whatsoever rank, &c., between the ages of 60 and 16, inhabitants within the county of Lancaster, that from henceforth they, uppon oon Houres Warnyng, be in arredynes defensiblie arrayed with Harnes and Wepyns apte and mete for the Warres, to attend the Earl of Shrewsbury, his Lieutent general of the North against Scotland," &c. [3]

The Scotch, sensible at length of the injustice of being so frequently called upon to sacrifice their own peace and prosperity to foreign interests, expressed their reluctance to advance into England ; and the Duke of Albany, brother to James III., who had assumed the regency, and under whose command the French auxiliaries and the Scottish chiefs were to fight, observing this disinclination and being told that a great force was advancing from England, concluded a truce with Lord Dacre, warden of the English marches,[4] which did not, however, prevent Scotland from being entered by the Earl of Surrey, 1522, at the head of his army, who ravaged Merse and Teviotdale, and burnt the town of Jedburgh. From these terrible inflictions the Scotch were glad to escape by an alliance with England instead of France, not without a remote expectation of a contract of marriage between Lady Mary, heir-presumptive to the throne of England, and the young Scotch monarch, at that time in his nonage.

The seeds of the Reformation, which had been sown in the time of John of Gaunt, Duke of Lancaster, cherished by the Lollards in succeeding ages, and occasionally moistened by their blood, attained to maturity in the time of Henry VIII. Martin Luther, a monk of the order of St. Augustine, and a professor in the university of Wittemberg, had raised the standard of reformation in Saxony, by preaching and writing against the indulgences granted, with so lavish a hand, by the Church of Rome, and his works had attracted sufficient notice to induce the King of England to enter the polemical lists against him. Henry sent his answer in reply to Luther, whom he denominated "the arch heretic," to Leo X., and his Holiness was so much gratified by its perusal, either from the strength of the argument or the dignity of the advocate, that he rewarded the royal controversialist with the appellation of "Defender of the Faith,"[5] by bull dated October 11, 1521. The fickleness of the king's affections induced him, soon afterwards, to put the friendship of the head of the church to a severe test. Doubts had been suggested by the scrupulous as to the legality of the king's marriage with Catherine of Arragon, the widow of his brother ; and it was held by them that the degree of consanguinity was such as to vitiate the marriage. These scruples,

---

[1] The queen, in her letter to the king, announcing the victory of Flodden Field, says : "The victory has more honour than if he (the king) should win all the crown of France."—1 Ellis's *Original Letters*, p. 88.

[2] 15 Rymer, 75.

[3] Pat. 14 Hen. VIII. p. 2. m. 8d. The ancient "commission of array" may be traced as far back as the reign of Henry II. In 1415, Henry V., before his departure for the memorable battle of Agincourt, appointed commissioners of array in every county in England, to take a review of all the freemen able to bear arms, to divide them into companies under able captains and officers, and to keep them in readiness to march against an enemy. It was this county militia that afterwards became, in Lancashire and elsewhere, the "trained bands," levied, drilled, and exercised, till they were expert and disciplined soldiers, and then employed for national defence in quelling rebellions whether in England, Scotland, or Ireland, and even

in foreign wars. The Earl of Shrewsbury was, at the time, the king's lieutenant-general of the north, and when, a few years later, "His Majesty's Council in the northern parts" was instituted, a court that was almost vice-regal, the earl was appointed the first president.—C.

[4] When Wolsey heard of the truce he described Albany's conduct as that of "a coward and a fool."—C.

[5] King Henry's jester, finding his royal master transported with unusual joy, asked him the cause of his hilarity, to which the king replied that the pope had honoured him with a style more exalted than that of any of his ancestors—the title of "Defender of the Faith :" to which the fool replied, "O, good Harry, let thou and I defend one another, and let the faith alone to defend itself." The copy of Henry's reply to Luther, sent by the king himself to the pope, with the royal autograph in the title page, is preserved in the library of the Vatican, and exhibited amongst its literary curiosities.

as Henry alleged, began to disturb his own mind ; and to relieve himself from so great a burden he applied to Rome for a divorce, which Clement VII., who now filled St. Peter's chair, was inclined to grant, had not the fear of offending the emperor Charles V., the nephew of Catherine, and who wished to espouse Mary, the queen's daughter, restrained his inclinations. The impetuosity of Henry's temper could ill brook the delay of episcopal hesitation, and the beauty of Anne Boleyn, a maid of honour to the queen, to whom he had made an offer of his hand, induced him to disavow the papal jurisdiction and obtain, from his own ecclesiastical courts, a dissolution of the marriage with Catherine. His clergy, not less obedient to the royal wish than the laity, determined, in convocation, that an appeal to Rome was unnecessary. The Parliament, when it next assembled, passed the Statute of Appeals, and declared the "Defender of the Faith" to have pre-eminence, authority, and jurisdiction over the church "within this his realm,"[1] and thus dissolved the connection between the Church of England and the Church of Rome. A number of the clergy, and many of the laity, amongst whom there was probably a majority in the county of Lancaster, adhered to the faith of their fathers, but the great body of the nation were disposed to go much further than the king: they acted upon principle, he was influenced by passion, and remained as much a friend to indulgences, after he had espoused the beautiful maid of honour, as he was when he first married her mistress. Neither the Catholics nor the Protestants satisfied him. In the plenitude of his power, and to gratify his sanguinary temper, he inflicted the punishment of death upon persons of both persuasions, and he promoted the Reformation only so far as it could be made subservient to the gratification of his voluptuousness and as it administered to the demands of his prodigality.

Such is the perverting influence of religious persecution that Sir Thomas More, the mild, equitable, and enlightened chancellor of the duchy of Lancaster, on his elevation to the chancellorship of England (in 1534), inflicted the torture upon James Bainham, a member of the Inner Temple, and finally consigned him to the flames in Smithfield, in 1531, for no other offence but because he followed the example of the court by favouring the doctrines of the Reformation. More himself having, a few years after, refused to acknowledge the king's supremacy—saying that it was a two-edged sword: if he was in favour of that doctrine, it would confound his soul, and if he was against it, it would destroy his body—was, for this offence, brought to trial on a charge of high treason, and, being found guilty, was beheaded on Tower Hill[2] (July 6, 1535), the king, "of his mercy," remitting the disgusting quartering of the quivering flesh because of his "high office."

In the twenty-sixth year of the king's reign the Lords and Commons humbly requested Henry, as their "most gracious Sovereign Lord, upon whom and in whom dependeth all their joy and wealth," to receive the firstfruits of all spiritual dignities and promotions; and also an annual pension of one-tenth part of all the possessions of the church. The firstfruits, or profits of the first year of benefices, was a tribute that appears to have been gradually, by little and little, imposed upon the clergy, and for a time was confined to the see of Norwich. Popes Clement V. and John XXII. attempted to make it universal, but it was long before the claim in this country was generally admitted. The tenths, or *decimæ*, were the tenth part of the annual profit of each living which was also claimed by the Holy See, but this latter claim of the pontiff met with a vigorous resistance from the English Parliament, and a variety of Acts were passed to prevent and restrain it, particularly the statute 6 Henry IV. c. 1, which calls it a horrible mischief, a damnable custom; but the clergy, blindly devoted to the will of the Pope, still kept it on foot—sometimes more secretly, sometimes more open and avowedly—so that in the reign of Henry VIII. it was computed that in the compass of fifty years 800,000 ducats had been sent to Rome for firstfruits only. As the clergy had been willing to contribute so much of their incomes to the acknowledged head of the church, it was thought proper, when the papal power was abolished, to annex this revenue to the crown, which was done by statute 26 Henry VIII. c. 3, after which a new *valor beneficiorum* was made, by which the clergy are at present rated. In 1534 a royal commission was issued to ascertain the value of all the ecclesiastical property and the amount of all the benefices in the kingdom. The book containing the latter of these returns is called *Liber Regis*, and is a beautiful manuscript, transcribed, it is said, by a monk of Westminster, for the king's library. The office for the receipt of tenths and firstfruits was instituted upon the visitation of these commissioners, whereby the *Decimæ Decimarum* were appointed to be paid to the King of England, instead of being paid, as hitherto, to the pope. The report of the commissioners forms a kind of ecclesiastical Domesday Book.[3]

[1] Statutes at Large, 26 Henry VIII. c. 1.
[2] State Trials, i. 59.
[3] The state of the inferior clergy in the county of Lancaster, as well as in the other parts of the province of York, was at this time most deplorable, whether considered as to their acquirements or their stipends.

According to Archbishop Lee, in a letter addressed to Cromwell, "their benefices were so exile, of £4 5s. 6d. per annum, that no learned man would take them. Therefore they were fain to take such as were presented, as that they were of honest conversation, and could competently understand what they read, and minister sacrments. In all

The great visitation of monasteries was commenced in the autumn of 1535,[1] when Cromwell, chancellor of the exchequer and first secretary to the king, filled the office of vicegerent and vicar-general. The visitation of the Lancashire monasteries was made by Dr. Thomas Legh and Dr. Richard Layton, and their original reports are in the Record Office, under the custody of the Master of the Rolls. The resolution to dissolve the monasteries had already been taken. The spirit in which this visitation was made clearly indicated that the reports were meant to form the groundwork for the dissolution of those institutions, and the consequent appropriation of their lands and revenues to the use of the crown. It cannot be denied that the monastic institutions were subject to great abuse; and that, under the specious appearance of devotion to God, some of the first duties to man were neglected or perverted; but it must also be admitted that the collecting of *ex parte* evidence by stipendiary emissaries, and the making of that evidence a ground for plundering the property of the church, was a proceeding full of injustice, and an example that no future age can imitate with impunity. The questions proposed by the royal commissioners on their Lancashire visitation were reduced to the following heads: (1) As to the incontinence of the heads of each monastery; (2) the name of the founder; (3) the estate of the convents; (4) the superstitions practised in them; (5) the debts they had incurred; (6) the names of the votaries who wished to be discharged from their vows.[2]

How far the deplorable picture of monastic life exhibited in this report is faithful we have not the means of discovering.[3] So far as the great monasteries are concerned it is at variance with the declaration of an Act of Parliament passed in the following year, wherein it is said, "that in divers and great solemn monasteries of this realm religion is right well kept and observed." The great monastery of Furness does not appear to have been entitled to this flattering character, if the report of the visitors is to be credited; and of Whalley the particulars are so few as to convey no information on this head. The returns of the commissioners served as an apology for dissolving the lesser monasteries, to which the king and his minister, the vicar-general, had a strong predisposition. In the following year (1535) a bill was passed through Parliament, with very little deliberation, for dissolving all monastic establishments in England whose clear yearly income did not exceed £200, in the preamble to which bill it is said, that—

"Forasmuch as manifest sin, vitious, carnal, and abominable living, is daily used and committed commonly in such little and small abbeys, priories, and other religious houses of monks, canons, and nuns, where the congregation of such religious persons is under the number of twelve," &c., "whereupon the Lords and Commons, by a great deliberation, finally be resolved, that it is and shall be more to the pleasure of Almighty God, and for the honour of this his realm, that the possessions of all such religious houses, not being spent, spoiled, and wasted for increase of maintenance of sin, shall be used and converted to better uses, and the unthrifty religious persons so spending the same be compelled to reform their lives; be it therefore enacted, that his majesty shall have to himself and to his heirs for ever, all and singular monasteries, the yearly value of which do not amount to £200."

By this Act, about three hundred and eighty communities were dissolved, and an addition of thirty-two thousand a-year (of the value in our money of upwards of £160,000) was made to the royal revenue, exclusive of £100,000 in money, plate, and jewels. According to Fuller, "ten thousand persons were, by this dissolution, sent to seek their fortunes in the wide world: some had twenty shillings given them at their ejection, and a new gown, which needed to be of strong cloth, to last till they got another. Most were exposed to want; and many a young nun proved an old beggar." Whalley and Furness fell before the general dissolution, but the other monastic or conventual establishments did not long survive, the whole of them being doomed to suppression before the close of the year 1540; the College of Manchester, with the whole of the chantries in the county, to the number of fifty-seven, being swept away a few years later, and their lands alienated to the crown.

his diocese he did not know twelve that could preach." The Irish clergy at the same time were in a still lower condition. Their new archbishop wrote of them to the lord privy seal, "As for their secular orders, they be in a manner as ignorant as the people, being not able to say a mass, or to pronounce the words, they not knowing what they themselves say in the Roman tongue." So in 1530, "A bird may be taught to speak with as much sense as several of them do in this country." Harrison says that before the Reformation "many of the clergy went either in divers colours, like players, or in garments of light hue, as yellow, red, green, with their shoes piked, their hair crisped, their girdles armed with silver, their apparel for the most part of silk, their caps laced and buttoned with gold; so that to meet a priest in those days was to behold a peacock that spreadeth his tail when he danceth before his hens." There could only have been very few of these clerical peacocks, however, to dance before the bewitching "hens" of Lancashire, for with the exception of a few richly endowed offices, as the wardenship of Manchester and the rectories of Wigan and Winwick, the benefices within the county were very poor, and many of them not worth more than four or five pounds a year. The stipend of a clerk "to serve in the chapel at Litherpool" was then £4 17s. 5d. a year; of a clerk and schoolmaster at Manchester, £4 0s. 2d.; of a clerk and schoolmaster at Preston, £2 18s. 2d.; so that other ways had often to be resorted to by the secular clergy to eke out their small wage.—C.

[1] Before this date the house of the Austin Friars at Warrington, founded by one of the Botelers, had for some cause or other been closed.—C.

[2] The report is in Latin, and its statements as to incontinence, &c., would not bear translation. It is therefore omitted. The following statements in the report are, however, worth preserving:—*Furness*, yearly rent or income, £900—*Cartmell*, yearly rent, £100; here they have a portion of the Holy Cross—*Conished*, yearly rent, £113; here they have the girdle of the Virgin Mary (as it is thought), to bless the pregnant (from one of the abbeys he visited, the worthy commissioner, Dr. Layton, sent to Cromwell, as a curiosity, "the girdle of Mary Magdalene")—*Cokersand*, yearly rent, £200—*Whalley*, £541—*Lytham*, £55—*Hornby*, £16—*Penwortham*, £27—*Burscough*, £200—*Upholland*, £65—*Kersal Cell*, £9; the house owes 20 marks (£13 6s. 8d.)—*Stanlaw*, £10—*College of Manchester*, £200.

[3] It is alleged by the Roman Catholics that young men were employed to corrupt and defame the nuns. Fuller mentions a story, upon the authority of Sir William Stanley, from which it appears that two young gentlemen, under the pretence of the royal permission to visit a convent, remained there three days and three nights, where they were received with that hospitality and decorum which ought to have inspired in them nothing but gratitude; but that, in return for these favours, they falsely accused the nuns of licentiousness, and in that way a pretence was obtained for dissolving the convents.—Fuller's *History of Abbeys*, p. 315.

A CERTIFICATE of the ANNUAL VALUE and other PARTICULARS of a number of the
RELIGIOUS HOUSES in LANCASHIRE.[1]

County of Lancaster.—The Breviate of the brief Certificate, upon the new Survey of the Religious Houses within the County Palatine of Lancaster, given to the King's Highness by Act of Parliament, and within the case of dissolution.

Religious Houses.	First Value.	Second Value.	Bells, Lead, and Goods.	Woods worth to be sold.	Debts owing by the House.	Religious persons.	Servants and others having livings.	Offer for redemption to be paid at days.
Cokersand	£157 14 0½	£224 7 7½	£343 18 5	40s.	£108 9 8	22	17	£3 3 0
Cartmell	91 6 3	212 12 10¼	274 13 9½	16l.	59 12 8	10	38	3 4 0
Conishead	97 0 2	161 5 9	333 6 3½	12l.	87 17 3¼	8	41	3 4 0
Burscough	80 7 6	122 5 7	418 10 10	25l.	86 3 8	5	42	3 4 0
Holland	53 3 4	78 12 9	132 2 8	40l.	18 18 10	5	26	200 4 0

The following progress of a suffragan, entitled *Progressus Dni Suffraganij*, indicates the order in which the visitation of the Lancashire monasteries, from the centre to the northern part of the county, was made. From the obscurity of the writing, and the manner in which the MS. is bound up with other papers in the Codex, the transcript has been made with considerable difficulty, and probably with some inaccuracy on that account. The report (of which we have modernised the spelling, &c.) is without date, but it appears to have been made about the year 1538, to Cromwell, the vicar-general, by one of the visitors.[2]

IN COUNTY [OF] LANCASTER.

Whalley.—Item to Whalley in Lancashire, of the Cistercians, out of one diocese, under the Bishop of Chester, the which convent was first founded in the county of Chester, at a place called Stanlaw, by Sir John Lascy, knight, and that was A.D. 1172. But after Lord Henry Lascy, the third and last Earl of Lincoln of the name, removed them[3] with the bodies of his ancestors John and Roger Lascy, knights, unto Whalley, that was A.D. 1296. Umylsa, prior.

Cokersand.—Item to Kokersand, canons of the Premonstratensians, of the foundation of a certain hermit, named Hugh Garthe, in King John's time, 24 miles from the other.

Lancaster.—Item to Lancaster, to the friars preachers, of the foundation of Sir Hugh Harrington, knight, 5 miles from the other.

Cartmel.—Item to Cartmel, Canons of St. Austin order, of the first foundation of Lord William Marshall, the Earl of Pembroke, A.D. 1202, before his death 17 years' 3d King John, 10 miles off the other.

Conishead.—Item to Conishead, canons of St. Austin, of the first foundation of Gamel Pennyngton, knight, which founded there a place of three or four canons, which was in strife for a season, by reason that they builded upon the ground of Lord William Lancaster, Baron of Kirby-Kendal and Overstone; but this first foundation was A.D. 1067, from the other 5 miles.

Furness.—Item to Furness, of the Cistercians, of the foundation of Lord Stephen, then the Earl of Boulogne, before he was king of England nine years, and 26th year of the reign of King Henry I. (1125-6), as appeareth by the following: [This is an imperfect and unintelligible piece of Latin.

Coupland.—Item to Cowdre, of the Cistercians, of the first foundation of Lord Reginald Meschines, then lord of Coupland, that was A.D. 1134 in Henry I.'s time, 19 miles from the foresaid place.

St. Bees.—Item to St. Bees, monks of the order of St. Benet, of the foundation of the foresaid Lord Meschines, 5 miles from the other (fol. 106).[4]

[Notes at the end.]

"In all these we have been in, beside divers others more, both in Durham bishopric and also Carlisle; with many good towns and villages, as well in my lord's grace's liberty as in others. And thus Jesus preserve your Mastership."

[In another hand.]

"These notes belong unto me.—THO. LOVELL. 1592." (Fol. 108.)

The religious feelings, as well as the temporal interests, of a large body of men were deeply involved in the suppression of the lesser monasteries, which measure was considered, with much justice, as the precursor of a still more sweeping appropriation of church property. The families of distinction, whose ancestors had founded monasteries, or whose sons were provided for by spiritual offices, complained of being deprived of their patronage and emoluments; and the poor, for whom there was then no parochial provision in infancy or in old age, and whose wants had been supplied at the doors of the convents, were equally loud in their complaints; while persons under the influence of higher motives felt shocked and outraged by the spoliation and overthrow of the altars of their fathers. Agrarian discontent and the love of the old religion united in a stubborn resistance to Cromwell's projects of change. The discontents of the people first broke out in acts of open rebellion in Lincolnshire, where the prior of Oxney and a leader named Melton, who assumed the character of a mechanic, collected an army of twenty thousand men, of which Melton took the lead, under the name of "The Captain Cobbler." A proclamation of pardon from the king was found of sufficient force to disperse this irregular army, while the doctor himself and a number of its other leaders, among whom was Lord Hussey, were consigned to public execution. On the 13th of October, 1536, the "brute and beastly" rebels of Lincolnshire, as Henry called them,

---

[1] Harl. MSS. in Brit. Mus. cod. 604, fol. 91.
[2] Harl. MSS. codex 604.
[3] That is from Stanlaw.
[4] Coupland, or Copeland, and St. Bees are both in Cumberland.

dispersed when Thomas Myller, the Lancaster Herald, who had read and posted up his proclamation at Louth, went on to Pontefract, where he found a less easy task before him.

Immediately after the suppression of the Lincolnshire outbreak a more formidable insurrection sprang up in the northern counties, under the designation of the "*Pilgrimage of Grace*," and Robert Aske, a gentleman of family, residing upon his patrimonial estate at Aughton, in the East Riding of the county of York, who had been at Lincoln, was placed at its head. The insurrectionary spirit spread far and wide, from the Tweed on the north to the Humber and the Ribble on the east and the west. The insurgents rendezvoused in Yorkshire, and to excite the enthusiasm of their followers, and to induce the people to join their ranks, a body of priests marched at their head with the banner of the cross, on which was depicted the figure of the Saviour, with the chalice and the host. Each of the soldiers wore on his sleeve, as the emblem of his holy cause, a representation of the five wounds of Christ, with the name "Jesus" marked in the centre. An oath or covenant was enjoined upon the pilgrims, by which they declared "that they entered into this pilgrimage for the love of God, the preservation of the king's person and issue, the purifying the nobility, and driving away all base-born and ill councillors; and for no particular profit of their own, nor to do displeasure to any, nor to kill any for envy; but to take before them the cross of Christ, his faith, the restitution of the churches, and the suppression of hereticks and their opinions."

On the 16th October York received the rebels, after their having carried the town of Hull. Their next operation was directed against the castle of Pontefract, which was in possession of Lee, the Archbishop of York, and Lord Darcy, whose slumbering loyalty the king attempted to awaken by a letter written from Northampton,[1] in which he desires Lord Darcy to proclaim as false certain traitorous, slanderous, and untrue reports. The reports alluded to, and so strongly denounced by the king, were contained in a mandate issued by one of the rebel chiefs, assuming the name of "the Earl of Poverty," which alleged that the king and his heretical ministers had determined, first, that no infant should be baptised without a tribute to be paid to the king; second, that no man with an income of less than £20 a year should either eat bread made of wheat, or capons, or chickens, or goose, or pig, without paying a tribute; and third, that for every plough-land the king would have a tribute. The Earl of Shrewsbury, then residing at Sheffield Castle, animated by a zeal which outstripped the king's commands, raised a force to resist the progress of the rebellion; and the Duke of Norfolk, the Earl of Derby, and other noblemen, followed his example. On arriving before Pontefract the rebels summoned the castle. With this summons the Archbishop of York and Lord Darcy readily complied by surrendering the fortress without resistance. On the 20th of October, Myller, the Lancaster Herald, arrived at Pontefract with a proclamation from the king; but when he rode into the town to fix it on the market cross he was prevented, and commanded to go to the castle, where he was received by Aske, the captain of the rebellious host, seated on a kind of throne, with the Archbishop of York on his right and Lord Darcy on his left, attended by Sir Robert Constable, Sir Christopher Danby, and others; but the hopes of the rebel general were then too much elevated to warrant an expectation of that submission which the proclamation required. According to Wilfred Holme, a writer of that age, residing at Huntington, near York, the following lines were often recited by the pilgrims of grace, from the antiquated quiddities of Merlin:—

> " Foorth shall come a worme, an *Aske* with one eye,
> He shall be the chiefe of the mainye ;
> He shall gather of chivalrie a full faire flock
> Halfe capon and halfe cocke :
> The chicken shall the capon slay,
> And after that shall be no May."

From Pontefract the rebel army marched to Scawsby Lees, near the left bank of the river Don, with the intention of fording the river, and taking the ancient town of Doncaster, then in possession of the Duke of Norfolk, the leader of the vanguard in the battle of Flodden Field, on whom the king had conferred the command of the royal army.

The ardour of the priests and their devoted followers, in this northern rebellion, was most striking. The abbots of Whalley, Salley, Jervaux, Furness, Fountains, and Rivaulx, with all the persons they could influence, either joined the main army or made diversions in its favour in their respective districts. In a word, the whole of the north of England was in a state of alarm and agitation. The Earl of Derby, with commendable zeal for his sovereign's interest, called out the militia of Lancashire and Cheshire, and by his promptitude and activity in securing Whalley Abbey, and other houses of treasonable resort, kept in check the rising in Cumberland and Westmorland, and the northern parts of Lancashire. The king, in his emergency, issued warrants to

Harl. MSS. cod. 283, fol. 80.

his devoted followers, importuning them to join the Earl of Derby in his endeavours to repress this wide-spreading rebellion.

The originals of two of these documents are preserved in the Harleian Collection,[1] and are expressed in similar terms. Both are dated Windsor Castle, 28th Oct., 28th year·of the reign (1536)—one being addressed to Sir Rodger Bradshawe, Knt., and the other to Sir Thos. Langton, Knt. The following is a transcript of the one addressed to Sir Roger Bradshawe :—

BY THE KING.

Trusty and wellbeloved we grete you well. And forasmuche as we be credibly aduertised how that most like a trew and feithfull suiect you haue assembled all your Force and Joyned the same w^t our right trusty and right wellbeloved Cousin therle of Derbye for the rep'ssion of certayne traitors and rebells in those p'ties, like as for the same we gyve vnto you our most hertie thanks. Soo we thought as well cõnvenyent to requier you to p'sist and contynue in your faithfull towardnes in the companey of our said cousin tyll the said traitors shalbe vtterly subdued, as to signifie that we shall not onely considre your charges therein, But likewise so remembre your s'uice in the same as you shall haue cause to say you haue well emploied your labours paynes and trayvaills in that behalf. Yeuen vnder our signett at our castell of wyndsoure the xxiijth day of octobre in the xxiijth yere of o^r reigne.

(signature)

Indorsed—"To o^r trusty and wellbeloved s'unt Sr Roger Bradshawe knyght."

The warmth of the king's thanks for the service rendered to the royal cause by Sir Roger Bradshawe and Sir Thomas Langton, and the solicitude expressed by him that they should continue their services, sufficiently indicate the sense he entertained of the danger attending this rebellion, not only to the peace and tranquillity of the county of Lancaster but also to the stability of his throne. The scene of hostile operations in Lancashire was principally on the eastern boundary, adjoining to the county of York; and the Earl of Cumberland, emulating the example of the Earls of Shrewsbury and Derby, gallantly repulsed the rebels in an attack made upon Skipton Castle. The main army of the insurgents now prepared to advance to the south, and with that view they proposed to ford the Don at the point where the Earl of Shrewsbury was posted by direction of the Duke of Norfolk; but a sudden rising of the waters of that river, though proceeding from causes purely natural, served to awaken the susceptible superstition of the followers of Aske, who, viewing this impediment as an evil omen, were prevailed upon to disperse, partly to repair the deficiency in their commissariat department and partly to afford time to conduct a negotiation between the government and the insurgent chiefs. The Duke of Norfolk was placed in a situation of great difficulty. The impetuosity of the king's temper disinclined him to make any concessions to his subjects in arms; and the demands of the rebels were such as to preclude his compliance with them without compromising the royal dignity. They claimed that a royal pardon should be granted without exception of persons; that a parliament should be held at York, and courts of justice established there, so that no suitor on the north side of the Trent should be required to go to London upon any suit at law. They further demanded a repeal of several Acts of Parliament, specifying particularly those for the last subsidy, and the statute of uses, with the statute which made words without overt acts misprision of treason; and the statute requiring the clergy to pay their tenths and firstfruits to the king. They further desired that the Princess Mary, the king's daughter by Catherine of Arragon, might be restored to her right of succession, the pope to his wonted jurisdiction, and the monks to their houses again; that the Lutherans might be punished; that Audley, the lord chancellor, and Cromwell, the lord privy seal, might be excluded from the next Parliament; and that Doctors Lee and Layton, who had visited the northern monasteries, might be imprisoned for bribery and extortion. After an interval of a month the "Pilgrims of Grace" again assembled in greater strength than before, and once more prepared to ford the Don; but again the waters rose suddenly, and a second time prevented that operation. The negotiations were renewed, under the management of Sir Ralph Ellerker and Sir Robert Bowas, on the side of the insurgents, and of the Duke of Norfolk for the king. The duke was empowered to offer pardon to all the rebels, with the exception of ten; six of them to be named, and four unnamed; but this offer, from the uncertainty which it involved, was refused. It was next proposed by the duke that a kind of congress should assemble at Doncaster, consisting of three hundred representatives chosen from the men of the different wapentakes, to negotiate with the duke and the lord admiral, who was a Fitzwilliam of Aldwark. For some time the duke, by the direction of the privy council, insisted on the king exercising the right to except ten persons from the general amnesty, but finding it impossible to obtain these terms he at length agreed that the royal clemency should be extended to the whole of the rebel army without exception. On these terms the pilgrimage was dissolved (Dec. 9), but the king, on the dispersion of the insurgents, read them a lecture, in a royal manifesto, of a nature which would, in these days, rather have raised than suppressed a rebellion. In answer to that part of their petition which related to the removal of his ministers, who were charged with a design to subvert the religion of the state, and to enslave the people, the king says, "And we, with our whole council, think it right strange that ye, who be but brutes and inexpert folk, do take upon you to appoint us who be meet or not for our council; we will therefore bear no such meddling at your hands, it being inconsistent with the duty of good subjects to interfere in such matters."

In the interval between the dispersion of the insurgent army of the north and their reassembling an attempt was made by the rebels to take the abbeys of Whalley and Salley, which the Earl of Derby was preparing to resist, when he received the king's command at Preston to disperse his forces. These orders he obeyed, but finding, on the reassembling of the rebels, that the danger was imminent, he again collected his troops, and marched to Whalley, when he succeeded in securing the monastery, and in restoring the public tranquillity. The following despatch to the king from the earl was written on the 1st of November, four days after the repulse of the rebels from Skipton Castle, and details the operations with sufficient particularity:—

LETTER OF THE EARL OF DERBY TO THE KING (HENRY VIII.) ON THE TAKING OF WHALLEY ABBEY.[1]

"Pleas it your magestye to be adurtysed that vpon Munday last past I being at your town of preston in Lancash their accompanyed and in other townes and villages nere thereabouts wt the moost part of your true & faithfull subjects of the same Shir was then in aredynes to have advansed forward toward Salley to have executed your graces cōmandment. And the said Munday at nyght I had appoynted to have loged at the Abbey of Whalley whiche is but iiij myles from Salley. And about ix of clok of the same Munday came on Berwyke your Herald[2] at armes vnto me. And hauing your Cote armure on his body delyu'ed me a £re dyrected vnto me frō my Lord the Erle of Shrewisbury your g'ces lieutenātt and my Lord of Rutland and my Lord of Huntyngdon. Theffect of whiche £res wᵃ this (they certifyed me by the same yt my Lord of Norfolk and they had stayd the cōmons of Yorkshir and that eu'y man was sparpoled and retyred home vnto their own howses. And that my said Lord of Norfolk was dep'ted to your Highnes. And that they were informed from the Lord Derby that I wt my retynue had appointed to be on the said Munday at Whalley Abbey. And forsomvche as all things was well stayd as they dyd write therefor they desired and prayd me and nevertheless in yor graces name charget me that I shuld sparple my said Company wt out doing any hurt or molestacion to the saides cōmons or any of theym. And that I shuld not fayle hereof as wold answar to your Highnes at my p'ill. And like the charge your herald did giff vnto me in your graces name. And after the Recyt of the said £re & after Counsaill taken wt the Lord Montegle then present and wt a great nomber of the gentlemen of the same Shir and wt their assents I and they thynkyng the said £re & comandment to be in effect as your comandment considering it did come from your said lieutennt dyd immediately sparple the said Company so assembled as is aforesaid and soo departed whomwards. And the same Munday in the moro the comons of the borders of Yorkeshir nere to Salley wt sume of the borders of Lancashir nere to theym assembled theym together and wt force they vnkowen to me sodenly toke the said Abbey of Whalley wher I had intended to have loged that nyght. And when they herd and knew how yt I had receyved such a £re or comandment as is aforesaid then they sparpoled their Cumpeny the same Daye. And truly all thoghe the ways and passages to Whalley & Salley be vere cumberous strayt full of myre impediments by warters & otherwyse yet I wt the power of yor true subgetts soo assembled wold have put all oᵣ bodyes in the aventure to have executed your former comandment if the said £re had not cumon to my hands. And wt godds g'ce I haue no dowt but in conclusion all thogh a great fray had thereof insued as it was lyke to have byn venquyshed. And wher their hath byn lately another insurrecion and Rebellion in the borders of Westm'land Cumb'land and in that part of Lancashir northward from yor town of Lancaster and now sparpoled who had intended as it is to be suspected and as I do verely beleve to haue cumen through this Shir if they had not byn affrayd of me and other your true subgetts soo assembled as is aforesaid at Preston. The circustance whereof I feare were to tedious for your grace here to put in w'tyng of all that I have herd and knowen thereof wt the fals and feaned £res & deuyses that hath byn feaned by that assemble and other whiche £res & deuyses they sparple abrode amongᵃ your subiects by settyng theym on Churche Dores and otherwise. Therfor I have made a byll of Artycles therof sumthing breifly made signed wt my hand which I delyu'd to yor s'unt Henry Acres who was wt me and eight persons wt hym to have s'ued your grace in my Cumpeny And can instruct yor grace thereof. And in thise affairs and all other accordyng to my bonden dutye I shall always during my liff as yor true subget be redy wt hert & hand to do you such pore s'ues as lyeth in my power wt asmoche obedyens as I can ymagin. As oᵣ Lord God knoes who p'sue your magestye in high honoᵣ and excellencie. Written at my manoᵣ of Lathom on all saincts Daye abowt iiij of clok after none.

"Yoᵣ most obedyent seruant & subict,

In dorso

"To THE KINGS MAGESTIE.—My Lord of Derbye to the Kings highnes certifying the king in what redynes he was wᵗʰ Lancashire against the Rebelles in the North."

---

[1] This dispatch forms part of the code entitled "Letters, Papers," &c., relating to the disturbances in the north of England.

[2] Thomas Myller, the Lancaster Herald, had been deprived of his office. When in the presence of Aske, at Pontefract, he had bent the knee to the rebel chief, and this act cost him his life. He was indicted for high treason in kneeling down before traitors with the king's most honourable coat-of-arms upon his back, and so encouraging and comforting them, and he suffered death at York in the following year.— *Stat. Papers* vi., p. 435.—C.

The following documents cast still further light on these transactions, and serve to show to how great an extent the religious houses in Lancashire, and their heads, were implicated in this rebellion, one object of which was to repossess the monks of the monasteries:—

PART OF THE FIRST DRAUGHT OF HENRY VIII.'s LETTER TO THE EARL OF SUSSEX, &c., CONCERNING THE REBELLION IN THE NORTH. (It seems to be of Thomas Crumwell's hand.—*Harl. Cat.*)

" Right trusty and wel-beloved Cousins and trusty and well-beloved (counsellors) we greet y⁰ wel. And lating y⁰ w˙t that having receved yᵒʳ sondry £res we doo right wel p'ceyve by the contents of the same yʳ circūspecte proceedings and diligent endeuoʳs in the trial of our traitors and Rebelles of these p'ties and the trayning cf the rest of r affaires there to such frame as maye be to r satisfaction for the whiche we geve vntoyowr moatharty thanks. And to make vnto youe p'ticuler answers to the p'ticuler points of yʳ said £res. First forasmuche as by such examynacons as yoᵘ have sent vnto vs It appereth that thabbot of Furnes and di'use of his moncks have not been of that truthe towards vs that to their dieuties apperteyned. We desire and pray yoᵘ wt all the dexteritie yoᵘ cann to deuise and excogitate to vse all the meanes to yoᵘ possible to enserche and trye out the veray truth of their proceedings and wt whom they or any of them have had any Intelligence, For we thinke veraylie that yoᵘ shall fynde thereby such matier as shall shewe the leght of many things yet vnknowen. And r pleasure is that yoᵘ shall vₚpon a furtљer examynacon Comytt the said Abbot and such of his Monks as yoᵘ shall suspecte to have been offendoʳs to warde, their to remayn tyl y⁰ shall vppon the signification vnto vs of such other things as by yoʳ wisdome yoᵘ shall trye out knowe further of r pleasure. Secunde we sende vnto yoᵘ herewᵗ certain £res according to yᵒʳ desire for the bestowinge of the Monks wᵗ uij or uij Blankes to be directed to suche other houses as yoᵘ shall think mete, w other Mon' Neu'theles we thinke it necessary that yoᵘ shall not only duely examyn them all befor yoᵘ shall dismisse any of that sorte that shall goo to other houses, as well for that we think some of the houses mentioned in yoʳ bill of their names be not wel hable to recyve their number set vpon them as for that the house of Gervayse is in some daunger of suppression by like offence as hathe been comytted (at or in) Whalley ; but also that yoᵘ shall retayne John Estgate who wold goo to Methe, tyl we may p'ceyve the cause whye he shuld desire to goo more to that place thenne to any other. And as touching the rest that desire capacities if yoᵘ shall thinke them men mete tᴏ be suffred to goo abrode, we be content yoᵘ shall give them their Bedding and chamber stuff wᵗ suche money as yoᵘ shall by yʳ wisedoes thinke mete, the capacities for whom we shall send vnto yoᵘ by the next messenger. Thirde wheras yoᵘ have sent vnto vs the copie of the £re writen from r cousen of Norff (Norfolk) to Lord Darcye after his first dep'ture from Doncaster Which yoᵘ found in the Vicar of Black Burnes chamber Forasmoche as by the same it appereth that there hathe been great Intelligence amougs such p'sonnes as were of that naughty inclinacon entent and conspiracye, We desire and praye yoᵘ as wel by the straite examinacon of the said Vicar as by all other meanes that yoᵘ canne possibly deuise strongly to enserche howe the said copie was conveyed thether Who was that Messenger Who was of counsel and how many £res or writings of that sorte or any other weir in that tyme conveyed in to those p'ties to whom from whom and of what effect. For iu the ernest folowing of this matier yoᵘ maye doo vnto vs as highe and as acceptable s'uice as canne be deuised. Finally we desire and pray yoᵘ to sende vppe in sauftie vnto vs Richard Estgate late Monke of Salleye. Our s'unt sʳ Arthur Darcy hathe writen that he doubteths not to declare suche matier against him at his repayr vnto vs as shall conveye some things to r knowleuge whiche for r affaires shalbe very necessary to be knowen. Which things being ones conduced to some p'fection we shall signifie r pleasure vnto yoᵘ touching the return of r cousin of Sussex to r presence.

" Indorsed—The Mynute of the £res to my Lord of Sussexe xith Marcij xxviij yeare of H. 8."   " T. C."

THE ANSWER OF   TO CERTAIN ARTICLES ADMINISTERED TO HIM TOUCHING THE SAME REBELLION (TEMP. HEN. VIII.)[1]—*Harl. Cat.*

Fower articles whervpon   was to Answere vnto touchinge the Rebellyone in   the   yeare of H. 8.

1. Firste whether yoᵘ wrotte any l'res to the Prior of Conished or Cartemell or to any Religeous persone.
2. Item. What motyon or at whose Request or interpellation yoᵘ wrott them.
3. Item. Of what tenor or forme such l'res were that yoᵘ wrotte.
4. Item. What daye or place yoᵘ wrott them.

1. To the firste I graunte I wrott a letter to the priorᵉ of Cartemell, as hereafter shalbe declared, but neuer to the prior of Conishid or any other religeous p'son touchinge any thinge of the insurrection in my life, otherwise then is vnderwritten.

3. To the third I saye I cannot perfectely remember the very tenor or forme of the saide letter, for I kepte no coppye therof, but as farre as I canne now remember it was of this effecte : That, forasmuch as all religeouse p'sonnes in the North partes had entered their houses by puttynge in of the comones, and as I am enformed yoᵘ meaninge the Prior of Cartemell, being required so to enter doe wᵗdrawe yrselfe. I thinke yoᵘ may safly enter and doe as other doe, keepings yoʳselfe quiete for the season, and to praye for the kinge. And at the next Parliamente then to doe as shalbe determyned, and I have no doubte but so doinge yoᵘ may contynewe in the same wᵗʰ the grace of God, who keepings yoᵘ, &c. And if I sawe the origenall letteres or a coppie thereof I would truly confesse my deede.

2. To the second I say I wrotte the sayᵈ letters to the Prior of Cartemell at the requeste and desire of one Collenes, baylif of Kendall, wᶜʰ Collenes at my beinge at pomfret shewed me that all the Chanoncs of Cartemell were entered the house excepte the foolishe prior, who would not goe to them onlie for his owne profite, desiringe me to write a letter to him to exhort him to goe in likewise as his brethren had done. And I graunted him to write the same l're when I come to Yorke, wᶜʰ was the morowe after the Conceptyon of our Ladye, and I deferred the tyme because I would hear howe the matters proceeded in the communication at Donkester, the meane space after that Collenes came to Yorke eftesoones desiringe the same letter. At whose onlye mocon requeste and interpellacon I wrot the same letter of suche effecte as is vnderwritten, beinge the boulders so to write for somuch as at my departynge from pomfret it was openly proclaymed, as I hard saye, and also at yorke when I came there it was voyced in euery manes mouth that the Abbeyes should stand in such maner as they were put in vnto the nexte parliamente, and after my coming home to Kirkeby, in the presence of Sʳ Henry Gascoine, knight, and other, desired me to exporte suche of the wiseste men as were Channones of Sᵗ Ageathes by Richemonde whom I knewe to be contente (leaste they or the country should thinke strange thereat) to be put forthe of their houses by the kinges authoritie, and to be taken in againe by the same. And so to remaine vnto the determenacon of the nexte parleamente, saying it was concluded at the communicacon at Doncaster it should so be. At whose de(sire) I spake to one Coke, prior of the same howse, to be contente wᵗʰ the premisses, and he promissed to be for his parte, and

to exhorte his brethren to the same. And this manner of puttynge out and takynge in was comonly spoken of to be true after our returne from Pomfret in all those partes as well wth gentlemen as other vnto the cominge of the Duke of Norfolke in these parts as farre as euer I hard of any man.

4. To the fourthe I saye I wrot the said l'res at yorke, the Satordaye or Sondaye followinge the Conceptyon of our lady wch was vpon a fridaye, wch daye I departed from Pomfret homeward, one fortenyght before the publycacon of the pardon wch was published at Richemond, iij myles from the place where I dwell, on a market daye, beinge Saturdaye the xxiij day of December, and not, as I remember, a   letter concerninge the insurrection. I never wrot so   ma   ex(cepte) that the   thereof large wch was wthin   of the firste beginninge of the insurrectyon in Richemondsheire, to the Abbot there, Mr. Siggeswicke, Mr. Witham, gentleman. And I all together wrotte lettres to the Abbotte of Fountaines and other preastes for a poste horses, and one other to Sr Christofer Danby, knight, to desire him to subscribe his name to his Letter, wch wee receaved from him, the Coppie of wch lettres doe remayne yet, as I suppose, in Jervaux abbaye aforesaid, and from the tyme of writynge the said lettrees vnto the priore of Cartemell wch was wthin two dayes after the conceptyon of o^{r} Ladye, as it is above Expressed vnto this daye I never wrotte ne sente vnto him any letter or messuage for anythinge, ne I haue hard anythinge by worde or writynge from him at any tyme sithen.—(Fol. 85.)

The rebel army of the north was dispersed, but the cause of their discontent was in no degree removed. Several of the monks and others, who had repossessed themselves of the religious houses during the time of the insurrection, were again ejected, and a fresh rebellion broke out on the northern extremity of Lancashire, under Musgrave and Tilley. The career of the insurgents was short and humiliating, and their only military operation consisted in besieging the city of Carlisle, in which they entirely failed. The Duke of Norfolk, having put their army to flight, made prisoners of all their officers with the exception of Musgrave. Threescore and fourteen of them were brought to trial by martial law, and being found guilty of treason and rebellion they were all hanged on the walls of Carlisle. Similar risings took place at Hull, and in some other places, but without success; and the king, in the heat of his indignation, seemed to consider these fresh revolts as a justification for the infraction of the act of amnesty granted by his authority at Doncaster, though many of the accused who afterwards became sufferers were not, and could not be, concerned in the latter rebellion. Aske, the leader of the Pilgrimage of Grace, was tried and executed, with the unfortunate Lancaster Herald, at York, as were also Sir Robert Constable at Hull, Sir John Bulmer and Sir John Percy at Tyburn, Sir Stephen Hamilton, Nicholas Tempest, and William Lumley. Many others were thrown into prison, and most of them shared the fate of their leader. The plea of compulsion set up by Lord Darcy for the surrender of Pontefract did not avail him, neither did his advanced age of eighty years, though many of them had been spent in the service of his country.[1] The inexorable monarch, after his condemnation, refused to extend to him the royal clemency, and he was executed on Tower Hill. "Being now satisfied with punishing the rebels the king published anew," says Lord Herbert, "a general pardon, to which he faithfully adhered; and he created a patent court of justice at York for deciding on suits in the northern counties, a demand which had been made by the rebels." It appears, however, that the arms of justice was *not* yet stayed, for at the spring assizes at Lancaster, in 1536-7, John Paslew, D.D., Abbot of Whalley, was arraigned, convicted, and sentenced to death for high treason,[2] on account of the part he had taken in the northern rebellion, and suffered the extreme penalty of the law on a gallows erected in front of the house of his birth, in a field called the Holehouses, at Wiswall, in Whalley;[3] while William Trafford, Abbot of Salley, and the prior of the same place were executed at Lancaster two days before, along with John Eastegate and William Haydocke, monks of Whalley. Adam Sudbury, Abbot of Jervaux, with Ashbeed, a monk of that house, and William Wold, prior of Burlington, also suffered death for the same offence.

The part taken by the monks in the rebellion of the north, and the encouragement they had given to their dependants and tenants to join in that insurrection, served as a reason for the dissolution of the larger monasteries, of which it had been declared by Parliament that "in divers of them religion was right well kept and observed." This character, however, did not save them from the rapacious grasp of the spoiler; and the sagacity which suggested that the dissolution of the smaller monasteries would soon be succeeded by the sequestration of the property of the larger establishments was soon made manifest. A new commission, with the Earl of Sussex at its head, was appointed to investigate the conduct of the existing monasteries, and the commissioners spent

[1] On being led to execution, Lord Darcy accused the Duke of Norfolk, the commander-in-chief of the king's forces, of having encouraged the rebellion of the north; but this charge was disregarded by the king, and seems to have had no better foundation than the anxiety of the duke to spare the lives of the rebels. Near the close of Henry's reign, the duke and his son, the Earl of Surrey, fell into disgrace, owing to the intrigues of their enemies at court, and to the fickleness of the king's disposition. The accomplished and lamented son perished on the scaffold; and his father was indebted for his life rather to the death of the king than to the services he had rendered to his country, by his achievements on the ocean, his gallantry in the battle of Flodden, and his still more distinguished service in dispersing an army of 40,000 men without the effusion of blood.

[2] There does not appear to be any indictment of Paslew among the Lancaster records, but the probability is that he was tried before the

famous Sir Anthony Fitzherbert, as he is known to have been at Furness a few days after the event, along with Richard Radcliffe, Earl of Sussex, then lord-lieutenant of Lancashire.—C.

[3] Dr. Whitaker gives the date of Paslew's execution variously as the 10th and 12th March. Stowe names the 10th, which is probably correct, but he is inaccurate in saying the execution took place at Lancaster. Haydocke was executed on the 12th. Concerning these events the following memorandum appears among the Cotton MSS.:—

1536. 6 idus Martii dominus Johannes Paslew in theologia baccalaureus 25 abbas et ultimus domûs de Whalley.

4 idus Martii eodem anno suspensus fuit Willielmus Haydocke, monachus abbatiæ de Whalley (*marginal note*). In campo vocato *Parvo Imps.*

Ricardus Eastgate (a monk of Salley who had fled to Whalley), monachus de Sauley suspensus fuit apud (*the rest wanting*).—C.

nearly four years in going from house to house, by turns soliciting and compelling the heads of those houses to surrender them, with their lands and revenues, into the hands of the king. Though these appropriations were so numerous in the reign of Henry VIII., only one original surrender of any religious house is to be found, and that is the surrender of the abbey of Furness, in the county of Lancaster, and though the monks of Furness had obtained the repute of being more treasonable talkers and more inveterate conspirators than the brethren of Whalley, they contrived in their sequestered glen to furnish a very small amount of legal evidence available on a trial for high treason. Roger Pyle, the abbot, was wary, the monks were cautious, and the servants were discreet, so that Sussex was constrained to admit there were only two of the fraternity whom he "could fynde faultye." Warned by the fate of Paslew, the abbot was "very facile and ready-mynded," and as he set some value upon his life, and the earl upon the abbey lands, an agreement was speedily arrived at—the earl obtained the surrender of the abbey, the lands of which were attached to the duchy of Lancaster; the abbot secured for himself the rectory of Dalton, hard by, and the "bredren of misorder" were fain to content themselves with small pensions for their lives. The "byll" or instrument of surrender is dated the 5th of April, 1537, from which it appears that the annual value of the monastery was £960, and that thirty monks

FURNESS ABBEY.

were attached to that house. It is signed *Per me Rogerum abbatem Furnesii*, in the presence of the Earl of Sussex and of "Sir Thomas Butler, Sir William Leyland, Johan Cladon, clerk, Sir Johan Beron (Byron), and Sir Anthony Fitz-Herbert, one of the king's justices, beying of the kynges counsell within the said countie." The surrender of Furness Abbey will serve as a specimen of the proceedings under this new commission.[1]

"All the members of the community, with the tenants and servants, were successively examined in private ; and the result of a protracted inquiry was, that, though two monks were committed to Lancaster Castle, nothing could be discovered to criminate either the abbot or the brotherhood. The commissioners proceeded to Whalley, and a new summons compelled the abbot of Furness to reappear before them. A second investigation was instituted, and the result was the same. In these circumstances, says the earl, in a letter to Henry, which is still extant, 'devising with myself, if one way would not serve, how and by what means the said monks might be rid from the said abbey, and consequently how the same might be at your gracious pleasure, I determined to assay

---

[1] See original papers in the British Museum, Cleop. E. iv. 111, 244, 246. See also West's *Furness*, Appendix x. 4-7.

him as of myself, whether he would be contented to surrender, give and grant unto (you) your heirs and assigns the said monastery; which thing so open to the abbot fairly, we found him of a very facile and ready mind to follow my advice in that behalf.' A deed was accordingly offered him to sign, in which, having acknowledged 'the misorder and evil rule both unto God and the king, of the brethren of the said abbey,' he, in discharge of his conscience, gave and surrendered to Henry all the title and interest which he possessed in the monastery of Furness, its lands and its revenues. Officers were immediately despatched to take possession in the name of the king; the commissioners followed with the abbot in their company, and in a few days the whole community ratified the deed of its superior. The history of Furness is the history of Whalley and of the other great abbeys in the north. They were visited under pretext of the late rebellion, and, by one expedient or other, were successively wrested from their possessors and transferred to the crown."[1]

As an inducement to their superiors to surrender their monasteries, tempting offers of a permanent provision were made to the brotherhood; and to such as withheld their consent, either no allowance whatever was granted, or that allowance was so small as to leave them in a state of abject penury.[2]

The progress of the Reformation kept pace with the dissolution of the papal institutions, and in the year 1538 the Scriptures[3] were for the first time printed entirely in English, under the sanction and authority of the Government, and all incumbents were enjoined to provide a copy and set it up publicly in the church, and not to hinder or discourage the reading of it. Pope Clement, incensed by all these acts of disobedience to the Romish church, was at length induced to issue his celebrated bull of excommunication, by which the King of England was declared an apostate, the whole kingdom was put under an interdict, his subjects were required to rise up in arms against his authority, foreign potentates were charged to make war upon him, and he was expelled from the pale of the Holy Catholic Church. So far were the thunders of the Vatican from arresting the king in his sacrilegious career that, in the following year, a bill was brought into the English Parliament vesting in the crown all the movable and immovable property of the monastic institutions which either had already been or should hereafter be suppressed, abolished, or surrendered. The heads of the twenty-eight mitred abbeys, and the two priors of Coventry and St. John of Jerusalem, having been divested of their revenues, lost the seats which they had hitherto enjoyed in the House of Peers; but the county of Lancaster did not in this way suffer any diminution of parliamentary influence, seeing that none of those highly-privileged houses were situate in this county. The abbots, masters, and priors of the religious orders in Lancashire, however, frequently received writs of summons to Parliament; and it appears from the Close Rolls that from 49 Henry III. to 23 Edward IV. (1264 to 1483) the heads of the Premonstratensian Abbey of Cockersand alone received upwards of one hundred of these parliamentary writs. From this period (1539-40) is to be dated the dissolution of all the monastic institutions in the county of Lancaster; and the following is a concise history of their original foundation, the religious orders to which they were attached, and their estimated income, according to Dugdale and to Speed, at the time of the visitations, which took place in the interval between 1534 and 1540:—

"At BURSCOUGH was a Priory of Austin, or Black Canons, founded by Robert Fitz-Henry, Lord of Lathom, in the reign of Richard I. St. Nicholas was the tutelar saint of this house, which had a prior, and five religious, and forty servants, and was endowed at the dissolution with £80 7s. 6d. per annum, according to Dugdale; according to a second valuation, £122 5s. 7d; according to Mr. Speed, with £129 1s. 10d.

"At COKERHAM there was a Priory.

"At COCKERSAND, a Premonstratensian Abbey.[4] Here was first a hermitage, and then an hospital for several infirm brethren, under the government of a prior, dedicated to St. Mary, and subordinate to the Abbey of Leycestre, founded, or chiefly endowed, by William of Lancastre, in the time of Henry II.; but about the year 1190 it was changed into an Abbey of Premonstratensian Canons, to which there seems to have been united another abbey of the same order, which Theobald, brother to Hubert Walter, Archbishop of Canterbury, some years after, built, or designed to build, at Pyling, to the honour of the blessed Virgin. The Abbey of Cockersand consisted, about the time of the dissolution, of twenty-two religious, and fifty-seven servants, and was then found to be worth £157 14s. per annum, Dugd.; £228 5s. 4d., Speed; £282 7s. 4d. according to a second valuation. The site was granted, 35 Henry VIII. (1543), to John Kechin.

"At CONISHEAD, a Priory of Austin Canons. Gabriel Pennington built, in the time of Henry II., upon the soil, and by the encouragement of William of Lancastre, Baron of Kendal (who was a very great benefactor), an hospital and priory of Black Canons, to the honour of the blessed Virgin Mary; which priory consisted of a prior, and seven religious, and forty-eight servants, and was valued at £124 2s. 1d. per annum, Speed; £97 0s. 2d. Dugd., which was the first valuation; but, upon a second valuation, £161 5s. 9d.

"At FURNESS, a Cistercian Abbey. The monastery, begun at Tulketh, A.D. 1124, for the monks of Savigny, in France, was, after three years (viz. A.D. 1127), removed to this valley, then called Bekangsgill.[5] Stephen, the Earl of Morton and Bologne,

---

[1] Lingard iv. 256.
[2] The pensions to the superiors varied from £266 to £6 per annum. The priors of cells received generally £13. A few whose services had merited distinction obtained £20. To the other monks were allotted pensions of six, four, or two pounds, with a small sum each as a departure fee, to provide for his immediate wants. The pensions to nuns averaged about £4. "It should, however, be observed," says Dr. Lingard, from whom we quote, "that these sums were not in reality so small as they appear, as money was, probably, at that period, of *ten times* more value

than it is now." This, however, is an over-estimate, taking the price of wheat as the criterion.
[3] This was the Coverdale Bible, printed anew in Paris by Coverdale and Grafton. Another edition of the Bible was printed in 1538, known as "Cranmer's," or "The Great Bible." These Cranmer appointed to be sold at 13s. 4d. each one, or if Cromwell would give the printers exclusive privilege, at 10s. each.—C.
[4] This monastery, by favour of the king, outlived for a short time the general dissolution.
[5] The Vale of the Deadly Nightshade.

(afterward King of England), was the founder of this abbey, which was of the Cistercian order, and commended to the patronage of the blessed Virgin Mary. It was endowed at the dissolution with £805 16s. 5d. per annum, Dugd. ; £766 7s. 10d., Speed.

"At Up Holand, a Benedictine Priory. Here was, in the chapel of St. Thomas the Martyr, a college or chantry, consisting of a dean and twelve secular priests, who were changed (A.D. 1319) by Walter, lord bishop of Litchfield, at the petition of Sir Robert Holand, then patron, and, as I conceive, original founder, into a prior and Benedictine monks. Here were, about the time of the suppression, five religious, and twenty-six servants. This house was valued at £53 3s. 4d. per annum, Dugd. ; £61 3s. 4d., Speed ; and at £78 12s. according to a second valuation. It was granted, 37 Henry VIII. (1545), to John Holcroft.

"At Hornby, a Premonstratensian Cell.[1] An hospital or cell of a prior and three Premonstratensian canons to the abbey of Croxton, in Leicestershire, of the foundation of the ancestors of Sir Thomas Stanley, Lord Monteagle, to whom the site and domains of this priory (as parcel of Croxton) were granted, 36 Henry VIII. (1544). It was dedicated to St. Wilfred, and endowed with lands to the value of £26 per annum.

"At Kershall or Kyrkshawe, a Cluniac Cell. King Henry II. granted, and King John, anno regni I. (1199), confirmed, to the monastery of Nottinghamshire, the hermitage here, which thereupon became a small house of Cluniac monks, and a cell to that priory was granted, 32 Henry VIII. (1540), to Baldwin Willoughby.

"At Kestmel or Cartmele, a Priory of Austin's Canons. William Mareschall the elder, Earl of Pembroke, founded here (A.D. 1188) a priory of regular canons of the order of St. Austin, which was dedicated to the blessed Virgin, and rated, 26 Henry VIII. (1534), at £91 6s. 3d. per annum, Dugd. ; £124 2s. 1d., Speed ; £212 11s. 10d. second valuation. Herein, about the time of the dissolution, were reckoned ten religious, and thirty-eight servants. The site of this monastery was granted, 32 Henry VIII. (1540), to Thomas Holcroft.

"At Lancaster—(1) an Alien Priory. Earl Roger of Poictiers gave (A.D. 1094) the Church of St. Mary, with some other lands here, to the abbey of St. Martin de Sagio, or Sees, in Normandy, whereupon a prior and five Benedictine monks were placed here, who, with three priests, two clerks and servants, made up a small monastery, subordinate to that foreign house, which was endowed with the yearly revenue of about £80 sterling. After the dissolution of the alien priories this, with the land thereunto belonging, was annexed by King Henry V. or his feoffees to the abbey of Syon, in Middlesex. (2) An hospital for a master chaplin and nine poor persons, whereof three to be lepers, was founded in this town by King John, while he was Earl of Morton, which was afterwards, by Henry, Duke of Lancaster, annexed to the nunnery of Seton, in Cumberland, about 30 Edward III. (1356), It was dedicated to St. Leonard. (3) A priory for Black Friars. Here was a house of Dominican or Black Friars, founded about 44 Henry III. (1260) by Sir Hugh Harrington, Knight, which was granted, 32 Henry VIII. (1540), to Thomas Holcroft. (4) A Friary for Grey Friars. A Franciscan Convent near the bridge.

"Langrigh, now Longridge. An ancient hospital under Longridge Hills, of a master and brethren, dedicated to the Virgin Mary and our Holy Saviour.

"At Lythom or Lethum, a Benedictine Cell. Richard Fitz-Roger, in the latter end of the reign of King Richard I., gave lands here to the church of Durham, with intent that a prior and Benedictine monks might be settled here, to the honour of St. Mary and St. Cuthbert. Its annual revenues at the suppression were worth £48 19s. 6d., Dugd.; £53 15s. 10d., Speed. The site as parcel of Durham was granted, 2 Mary (1554), to Sir Thomas Holcroft.

"At Manchester, a College.[2] Thomas de la Ware, clerk, some time rector of the parish church here (having the barony and estate of his brother, John Lord de la Ware, without heirs), obtained leave of the king, 9 Henry V. (1421), to make it collegiate, to consist of a warden and a certain number of priests. It was dedicated to the blessed Virgin, and endowed with revenues to the yearly value of £200, or, as they were returned into the firstfruits office, 26 Henry VIII. (1534), £226 12s. 5d. in the whole, and £213 10s. 11d. clear. This college was dissolved in 1547 by King Edward VI., but re-founded, first by Queen Mary, and afterwards by Queen Elizabeth (A.D. 1578), and again by King Charles I. (A.D. 1636), for a warden, four fellows, two chaplains, four singing men, and four choristers ; being incorporated, as they were before by Queen Elizabeth, by the name of 'the Warden and Fellows of Christ Church, in Manchester.'

"At Penwortham, a Benedictine Priory. Warine Bussel, having given the Church and tithes of this place, with several other estates in this county, to the abbey of Evesham, in Worcestershire, in the time of William the Conqueror, here was shortly after a priory erected, and several Benedictine monks from Evesham placed in it. This priory was dedicated to the Virgin Mary, and rated, 26 Henry VIII. (1534), at £29 18s. 7d. per annum, as Dugdale in one place, and £99 5s. 3d. as he saith in another ; and at £114 16s. 9d. per annum, as Speed. The site was granted, 34 Henry VIII. (1542), to John Fleetwood.

"At Preston—(1) An ancient Hospital, dedicated to St. Mary Magdalen, occurs in the Lincoln taxation (A.D. 1291). The mastership was in the gift of the king. (2) A Friary, for Grey Friars. The original builder of the Grey Friars' College, on the north-west side of this town, was Edmund, Earl of Lancaster, son to King Henry III., the site of which was granted, 32 Henry VIII. (1540), to Thomas Holcroft.

"At Warrington, a Friary for Austin Friars. At the bridge-end of this town was a priory for Augustine Friars, founded before A.D. 1370 which, 32 Henry VIII. (1540), was granted to the often-mentioned Thomas Holcroft.

"At Whalley, an Abbey for Cistercians. Henry Lacy, Earl of Lincoln, having given the advowson of the parish to the White Monks of Stanlawe, in Cheshire, they procured the same to be appropriated to them, whereupon (A.D. 1296), they removed their abbey hither, and increased the number of their religious to sixty. There was another removal proposed to a place called Tocstathe, by Thomas, Earl of Lancaster (A.D. 1316), but it seems not to have taken effect. Whalley was dedicated to the blessed Virgin Mary, and, at the suppression, had revenues to the yearly value of £321 9s. 1d., Dugd. ; £551 4s. 6d., Speed. It was granted to Richard Ashton and John Braddyll, 7 Edward VI. (1553).

"At Wyersdale, a Cistercian Abbey. A colony of Cistercian monks from Furness, for some time fixed here ; but about A.D. 1188 they removed over into Ireland, and founded the abbey of Wythney."

The lands and revenues of the monasteries of Furness, Cartmel, Conishead, Burscough, and Up-Holland, were confided by Parliament to the officers of the duchy of Lancaster, to be administered for the king's use.[3] The king also annexed to the duchy of Lancaster property of the yearly value of £769 4s. 2½d., subject to an annual pension to chantry priests of £126 2s. 4d. This appropriation was made through the medium of the Court of Augmentation, which court was established in year 1535, for the purpose of ordering, surveying, selling, or letting, all manors, lands, tithes, and other property belonging to the monasteries. The number of monasteries suppressed in England and Wales amounted in the whole to six hundred and forty-five, exclusive of ninety-six colleges, two thousand three hundred and seventy-four chantries and free chapels, and one hundred and ten hospitals,[4] the value of which property has been variously estimated, but,

---

[1] This cell was resigned before the visitation in 1535.
[2] This college escaped the general dissolution, or was speedily restored.

[3] 32 Henry VIII. (1540) c. 20.
[4] Camden's Brit. i. cxci.

according to the *Liber Regis*, it yielded annually £142,914 12s. 9¼d.,[1] which, taken at twenty years' purchase, would produce £2,858,290,[2] worth in our money, £28,582,900. The revenues of the church before the dissolution of the monasteries is said to have equalled about one-fourth of the whole landed income of the kingdom.[3] According to the records in the Augmentation Office[4] the process pursued by the commissioners on the dissolution of each of the monasteries was as follows: (1) The commissioners broke its seal, and assigned pensions to the members. (2) The plate and jewels were reserved for the king, the furniture and goods were sold, and the money was paid in to the Augmentation Office. (3) The abbot's lodgings and the offices were left standing, for the convenience of the next occupant; the church, cloisters, and apartments for the monks were stripped of the lead and every other saleable article, and then left to fall to ruins. (4) The lands were by degrees alienated from the crown by gift, sale, or exchange. A revenue so immense as that yielded by the monasteries might, under judicious application, have extinguished all the public burdens both for the support of the state and the relief of the poor, and expectations of this kind were held out to the people.[5] But they were soon undeceived: pauperism became more extensive than ever, and within one year from the period of the last appropriation a subsidy of two-tenths and another of two-fifteenths were demanded by the king, and granted by Parliament, to defray the expenses of religious reforms.[6] Henry VIII., like his predecessor, was rapacious—with this difference, however, that the father collected money to save, while the son amassed wealth to supply the demands of a licentious profusion. Much of the church property was disposed of to the king's favourites, by grants or by indulgent sales, one of the conditions of which was, that the new proprietors of the abbey lands should keep up the ancient hospitality; but as this was in some degree voluntary, the practice soon fell into disuse. A portion of the monastic revenues was appropriated to the advancement of religion, though much less than Cranmer had projected and the king had originally promised. His first purpose, as appears from documents under his own hand, was to found eighteen new bishoprics, but the number declined from time to time till it was at last reduced to six. Westminster was the first, in which he endowed a bishopric, a deanery, twelve prebendaries, a choir, and other officers. The year after this he endowed Chester (which included Lancashire and Richmondshire in Yorkshire), Gloucester, and Peterborough; but in these cathedrals he only endowed six prebendaries. Two years after he likewise endowed Oxford and Bristol. He also converted the priories of Canterbury, Winchester, Durham, Worcester, Ely, Rochester, and Carlisle into collegiate churches, consisting of deans and prebendaries.[7] Anciently there had been a bishop's see at Chester, but it had merged in the diocese of Lichfied. But none of these were in this county. That the endowments might not be too rich, each chapter had imposed upon its ecclesiastical revenue the obligation of contributing annually to the support of the resident poor, and to the repair of the highways.[8] The order of the Knights of St. John of Jerusalem, including the Knights Templar and the Hospitallers, after having existed for four hundred and thirty-six years, was doomed to suppression by legislative enactment (1540); and the Universities of Oxford and Cambridge, happily for learning in future ages, escaped, though narrowly, the same fate. The chantries in the monasteries and churches of this county were very numerous at the period of the Reformation, as may be inferred from the following List of Chantries, which we find in the records of the office of the duchy of Lancaster:—

1. Warton Church stipend, no date.
2. Kirkeby Irelath. Chantry.
3. Leverpole Chapel.
4. Leverpole Chapel.
5. Eccleston. Chantry.
6. Sefton. Chantry.
7. Croston. Chantry.
8. Manchester College. Tithes.
9. Manchester. Tithes in Moston, Norton [? Gorton or Newton], Kirkemanshulme, Cromeshall.
10. Burscoughe Priory, the Manor.
11. Ormskirke. Chantry.
12. Eccles. Chantry.
13. St. Michael's-on-Wyre. Chantry.
14. Manchester, Beckwith's. Chantry.
15. Manchester College. Tithes of Trafford, Stratford, and Chollerton.
16. Halsal Church. Chantry.
17. Yerleth. Parcel of the Monastery of Furnes.
18. Beamonde. Parcel of the Monastery of Furnes.

---

[1] ANNUAL REVENUE OF ALL THE MONASTIC HOUSES CLASSED IN THE ORDERS.

No. of Houses.	Orders.	Revenue. £	s.	d.
186	Benedictines	65877	14	0
20	Cluniacs	4972	9	2¼
9	Carthusians	2947	15	4¼
101	Cistercians	18691	12	6
173	Austins	33027	1	11
32	Premonstratensians	4807	14	1
25	Gilbertines	2421	13	9
3	Fontefraud Nuns	825	8	6½
3	Minoresses	548	10	6
1	Bridgetines	1731	8	9¼
2	Bonhommes	859	5	11¼
	Knights Hospitallers	5394	6	5¼
	Friars	809	11	8¼

[2] Bishop Burnet says "the valued rents of the abbey lands, as they were then let, was £132,607 6s. 4d., but they were worth above ten times as much in true value." (*History of the Reformation*).—C.

[3] Lord Herbert, p. 396.

Burnet's Records, i. 151.

[5] Coke's Inst. iv 44.

[6] Henry's enormous expenditure is easily accounted for by the fact that his principal employment was gambling.—*Privy Purse Expenses of Henry* VIII. p. xxiii.

[7] Burnet.—C.

[8] Rymer xv. 77.

19. St. Michael's-on-Wyre. Chantry.
20. Manchester College. Tithes of Grain of Bradford, Ardewick and Openshaw.
21. Ballie. Chantry in the Chapel within the Parish of Mitton, Yorkshire.
22. Chantry in Lancaster.
23. Hollingfare Chapel, in Warrington.
24. Standish Church. Chantry.
25. Warrington Church. Butler's Chantry.
26. Halsall Church. Chantry.
27. Preston Church, St. Mary's Chapel.
28. Ribchester Church. Chantry.
52. Pickering Lythe. Parcel of the Manor, in Yorkshire. Windell Chapell in Prescot. Chantry.
53. Beckingshaw Chapel in Croston, and a tenement in Preston, parcel of the possession of College of New-warke, Leicester.
54. Silverdale, Bolton, Hest, parcel of the Monastery of Cartmell.
55. Clitherow Chapel, in Whalley. Chantry.
56. Manchester Church, Trafford's Chapel. Chantry.
57. Eccles Church. College of Jesus.

The condition of the people appears to have suffered with the suppression of the monastic institutions. No fewer than four separate statutes were passed between the years 1535 and 1544, setting forth lists of decayed cities and towns in different and in almost all parts of the kingdom, wherein it is declared, " That there hath been in times past many beautiful houses in those places which are now falling into ruin," and amongst the towns mentioned in the Act of 1544 are, " Lancaster, Preston, Lyrepool, and Wigan, in Lancashire."

The privilege of *sanctuary* was one of the evils of the monastic system, though its date is anterior to the foundation of monasteries. In virtue of this privilege certain places became cities of refuge—"*seats of peace*," as they were called; and the inviolability of these asylums in early times is sufficiently indicated by the answer of Cardinal Bourchier, when importuned by the creatures of the Duke of Gloucester to bear away his ill-fated nephew, young Richard of York, from the sanctuary of Westminster:—

" God in heaven forbid
We should infringe the holy privilege
Of blessed *sanctuary* ! Not for all this land
Would I be guilty of so deep a sin."
SHAKSPERE'S *Rich. III. Act* iii. *Scene* 1.

"These sanctuaries were first instituted and designed for an asylum or place of safety to such malefactors as were not guilty of any notorious crimes. . . . There were many of them in this kingdom before the Conquest ; and they became so numerous after, and so scandalous (divers of them having obtained protection for those that were guilty of high treason, murder, rape, felony, &c.), that, being complained of in Parliament, 1540, immediately after the dissolution of the religious houses, the greatest part of them were suppressed, and those few that remained reduced to their first institution." [1]

By an Act passed 32 Henry VIII. (1540-1) it was decreed that all sanctuaries, with the exception of certain places named, should be "utterly extinguished." Manchester and Lancaster were the places so excepted in Lancashire ; but when trade began to extend itself, the nuisance of a harbour for thieves and other delinquents became intolerable, and by an Act passed 33 Henry VIII. (1541-2) Manchester, by reason of the presence of the sanctuary men being, as was alleged, prejudicial to the wealth, credit, good occupyings, and good order of the town, was allowed to forego its privilege, and to transport all the refugees within its jurisdiction to Chester, which, being poor, could not lose much by their irregularities.

The position of religious parties in Lancashire in the closing years of Henry's reign may be briefly stated. The progress of the Reformation kept pace with the dissolution of the Papal institutions ; but in the northern and western, the less populous parts of the county, the new doctrines advanced but slowly, many of the more influential families adhering to the old form of faith. The Earl of Derby having enriched himself considerably out of the spoils of the suppressed monasteries, and being, moreover, as he professed himself, a believer in the "religion of good luck," was an ardent supporter of the Reformation ; and many others, who had in like manner profited by the wholesale confiscations, were influenced by the same prudent considerations. But the esquires and lesser gentry, who had gained nothing, cared little for the new services, and in many instances their attachment to the old religion was strengthened by jealousy of their more fortunate neighbours. In the south-eastern parts of the county, the Salford Hundred—which included the manufacturing and trading towns of Manchester, Bolton, Bury, and Rochdale, with their busy, industrial inhabitants—the reformed faith had many zealous adherents, and eventually gained complete ascendancy, though not without many religious conflicts and the manifestation of much bitterness of feeling.

The king survived the dissolution of the monasteries seven years, but no event occurred, in that period, of public interest in the history of Lancashire. During his last sickness he revoked his former wills, and ordained that, after his death, his three children, Edward, Mary, and Elizabeth, should succeed him in the sovereign power, the son as male heir, and the daughters in the order of primogeniture. He died at Westminster on the 28th of January, 1547. His death was concealed for three days, but when at length the solemn sound was heard from the bell towers of England proclaiming the fact, it not only announced his decease but the downfall also of the Romish system in this country.

[1] Burton's MSS.

CHAPTER XIII.

VERY year during the "infant reign" of Edward VI. the Reformation continued to advance with a steady step; but no events of any distinguished public interest occurred within this period connected with the county palatine of Lancaster. In the first year of this reign, Francis, Earl of Shrewsbury, was constituted lord-lieutenant of the counties of Lancaster, York, Chester, Derby, Stafford, Salop, and Nottingham, and in the following he was made justice of the forests north of the Trent.[1] Under the inhibition of a proclamation,[2] issued by the Lord-protector Somerset, in the name of the king, all places of public worship belonging to Dissenters, as well Protestant as Catholic, in this and the other counties of England, were closed; and any preacher, of whatsoever persuasion, who took upon himself to preach in an open audience, except such as were licensed by the lord-protector, or by the Archbishop of York, became obnoxious to the sovereign will. The avowed object of this intolerant proclamation was "to produce an uniform order throughout the realm, and to put an end to all controversies in religion." At the same time there was a board of commission formed for advancing the Reformation, of which Edward, Earl of Derby, was a commissioner. This document was founded upon an Act of Parliament, by which the Archbishop of Canterbury, "with other learned and discreet bishops and divines," was directed to draw up an order of divine worship, called a liturgy, or book of common prayer. The result of its labours was the production of an English form of communion, and further, by November, 1548, it had drawn up a complete *English Service Book*, now known as the *First Prayer-Book of Edward VI.*[3] This duty having been performed to the satisfaction of the king and his Parliament, it was enacted that from the feast of Whitsunday, June 9th, 1549, all divine offices should be performed according to the prescribed ritual, and that such of the clergy as should refuse to conform, or should continue to officiate in any other manner, should, upon conviction, be imprisoned six months, and forfeit a year's profit of their benefices; for the second offence, forfeit all church preferment, and suffer a year's imprisonment; and for the third offence, suffer imprisonment during life. And all that should write or print anything against this liturgy were to be fined, for the first offence, ten pounds; for the second twenty pounds; and for the third forfeit all their property, with imprisonment for life. Against this act, the Earl of Derby and eight of the bishops entered their protest on the journals of the Lords. In the same arbitrary spirit a law was made against vagabonds, by which it was enacted that any persons who should be found three days together, loitering without work, or without offering themselves to work, or that should run

---

[1] Lodge's Illustrations, i. p. xiv.
[2] Dated September 23, 1548.
[3] With some variations in a subsequent edition of 1552, which was called the "*Second Book* of King Edward VI.," this Liturgy is not

essentially different from that of the present day. It was based upon the ancient Catholic services, which had been handed down from the primitive ages of the Church: and which the English people had for generations heard sung or said, without comprehending the meaning.—C.

away from work, and resolve to live idly, should be seized on; and whosoever should present them to a justice of the peace was to have them adjudged to be slaves for two years, and they were to be marked with the letter V imprinted with a hot iron on their breast.[1] Two years afterwards (1550), this cruel statute was repealed,[2] and provisions were made for relieving the sick and impotent, and for setting such of the poor who were able to work; on which law the celebrated statute of the 43rd Elizabeth (1601) was grounded. That the Earl of Derby and several of the bishops should have protested against the Act of Uniformity, and its impracticable provisions, which Act presumptuously assumed "to be drawn up by the aid of the Holy Ghost," could not be matter of wonder; but why his lordship, and the Earls of Rutland and Sussex, the Viscount Hereford, and Lords Monteagle, Sands, Wharton, and Evers,[3] should enter a protest against an Act passed prohibiting all simoniacal pactions for reservation of pensions out of benefices, and the granting of advowsons while the incumbent was yet alive, it is difficult to discover, unless upon the supposition that his lordship headed an opposition alike hostile to all the measures of the existing administration, whether good or bad. The Act for Legalising the Marriage of the Clergy passed in the same year, and was also protested against by the Earl of Derby, by the Earls of Shrewsbury, Rutland and Bath, and by the Lords Abergavenny, Stourton, Monteagle, Sands, Wharton, and Evers. Edward VI., or rather the regency by which his government was directed, imitating the example of his royal father, instituted a visitation, by which the chantries of Lancashire were inspected by two lay gentlemen appointed for that purpose, and by a civilian, a divine, and a registrar, in order to ascertain the state of the chantries, and to apply their revenues to the king's use, to be expended, as was alleged, in the endowment of schools, the maintenance of the poor, and the erection of colleges. These visitations became general throughout the provinces of Canterbury and York, and the suppression of chantries followed as a matter of course.[4] Subsequently, Lord Paget, the chancellor of the duchy of Lancaster, was charged with having appropriated large sums out of the revenues of the suppressed chantries to his own use, and with other acts of malversation, of which charges he was convicted, on vague and unsatisfactory evidence, and fined in the enormous sum of six thousand pounds. Nor did the severity of his lordship's sentence end here: he was degraded from his rank as a Knight of the Order of the Garter, because he was not a gentleman by descent, either from his father or his mother. His real offence, however, consisted in his steady adherence to the fallen protector, the Duke of Somerset, by which he became obnoxious to his successful uncle, the Duke of Northumberland.

"His Majesty's Council in the Northern Parts," an institution arising out of the demands of the Pilgrims of Grace, for the purpose of facilitating the administration of justice, without subjecting suitors in the north to the trouble and cost of repairing to the metropolis, was organised in this reign, and the Earl of Shrewsbury was appointed to the office of lord president of the council. This court, which was in some degree viceregal, consisted of a council, with the president at its head, assisted by Henry, Earl of Westmorland, Henry, Earl of Cumberland, Cuthbert, Bishop of Durham, Lord William Dacres of the north, John, Lord Conyers, Thomas, Lord Wharton, John Hind, knt., one of his majesty's justices of the common pleas, Edmund Molyneux, knt., serjeant-at-law, Henry Savel, knt., Robert Bowes, knt., Nicholas Fairfax, knt., George Conyers, knt., Leonard Becquith, knt., William Bapthorp, knt., Anthony Nevill, knt., Thomas Gargrave, knt., Robert Mennell, serjeant-at-law, Anthony Bellasis, John Rokeby, doctor of law, Robert Chaloner, Richard Morton, and Thomas Eynis, esqrs. The sum of a thousand pounds a year was granted to the lord-president for the better entertainment of himself and his council, with divers revenues to the stipendiary members, who were required to be in continual attendance upon the council, except at such times as a certificate of absence was granted to any of them by the lord president. The council was furnished with powers to decide cases between plaintiffs and defendants in their bill of complaint, without replication, rejoinder, or other plea of delay, with power and authority to punish such persons as in anything should neglect, contemn, or disobey their command, or the process of the council, and all other that should speak seditious words, invent rumours, or commit such like offences (not being treason) whereof any inconvenience might grow, by pillory, cutting the ears, wearing of papers, imprisonment, or otherwise, at their discretion; or to assess fines of all persons who might be convicted of any riot; and to assess costs and damages, as well to the plaintiffs

---

[1] The wholesale evictions consequent upon the break-up of the feudal system, and the suppression of the religious houses, where, previously, the poor had been principally relieved, led to a large increase of vagrancy, to restrain which many enactments were made in the reign of Henry VIII., some of extreme severity. The Act here referred to (1 Edward VI., cap. 3) recites the increase of idle vagabonds, and after prescribing the punishment for offenders, directs that impotent persons be removed to the place where they had resided for three years, and allowed to beg, and further, that a collection be made in the churches every Sunday and holiday, after reading the Gospel of the day, the amount to be applied to the relief of bedridden poor.—C.

[2] The Act 5 and 6 Edward VI., cap. 2, directs the parson, vicar, curate, and churchwardens to appoint two collectors to distribute weekly to the poor. This Act was renewed and extended by 2 and 3 Philip and Mary, and the 5th, 14th, 18th, and 39th Elizabeth, and in 1601 the Act 43 Elizabeth, cap. 2, made assessment compulsory.—C.

[3] Journals of the Lords, 1552.

[4] See the Rev. Canon Raines's History of the Chantries within the County Palatine of Lancaster (vols. 59 and 60 of the Chetham Society's series).—H.

as to the defendants. And for the more certain and brief determination of causes, it was ordained that the lord-president and council should keep four general sessions or sittings in a year, each of them to continue by the space of one month—one at York, another at Hull, the third at Newcastle, and the fourth at Durham, within the limits whereof the matters arising there should be ordered and decreed.[1] In fixing upon these places for holding the periodical sessions of the council, the convenience of the eastern rather than of the western counties of the north seems to have been consulted; and it is difficult to say why Lancaster was not fixed upon, in making the arrangement, in preference to either Durham or Newcastle. That the suitors might not be oppressed with heavy bills of costs, it was directed "that no attorney should take, in one sitting or sessions, above twelve pence, nor any counsellor more than twenty pence, for one matter." A fatal malady soon afterwards seized the young monarch, who, in his last sickness, was entrusted to the charms and medicines of a female empiric. On the 6th of July, 1553, he expired, with the reputation of high talents for government, had time suffered them to be fully developed. He was succeeded, after an ineffectual effort in favour of the unfortunate Lady Jane Grey, the victim of the ambition of others, by his sister the Lady Mary, only daughter of Catherine of Arragon.

The reign of Queen Mary is known in the history of Lancashire, as it is in the other parts of the kingdom of England, more by the bloody persecution which stained it than by any other circumstance. The reproach of the loss of Calais, the last remaining stronghold of England in France, is almost obliterated by the streams of blood which flowed to satiate an embittered mind, the abode of superstition and the slave of priestly domination. A period of nearly three hundred years has scarcely been found sufficient to wash away these sanguinary stains from the religious community to whom they attach, though they were the crime of the age in which it was the destiny of this unhappy queen to live, and her father and her sister both shared her guilt in a mitigated degree. In the less accessible parts of Lancashire the Reformation had made but little progress, and in other districts many of the people showed no great reluctance to return to the religious observances of their fathers. The Earl of Derby, who was the moving spirit of the county, was of the number. The queen was a Papist, and the earl's religious opinions were sufficiently elastic to enable him without much difficulty to accommodate himself to the changed circumstances of the times. Under Edward he had been a commissioner for the advancing of the Reformation; under Mary he became an orthodox Catholic, ready to persecute heretics, and to do everything good Catholics should, except restore to the Church the ecclesiastical property that had fallen into his possession. One of the first acts of Queen Mary was to re-establish the Roman supremacy, to crush the leaders of the Reformation, and to trample under foot the newly-acquired liberties of the English Church; and in furtherance of that object the abolished chantries were immediately restored, and though she could not prevail upon her Parliament to order the relinquishment by their then possessors of the confiscated lands of the dissolved abbeys, she set a not ignoble example by at once restoring those lands which had been attached to the crown from such sources. The following list contains the names of the parish churches in Lancashire whose chantries were restored in the first year of the queen's reign (1553-4), with stipends allowed to the chantry priests, which were from £1 10s. to £6 per annum: Ashton-under-Lyne, Childwall, Croston (St. John and St. Trinity), Goosnargh, Halsall (St. Nicholas and St. Mary's), Holme, Kirby, Kirkham 2, Lancaster 2, Manchester Collegiate Church 7, Mawdline, St. Michael-on-Wyre, Ormskirk, Prestwich, Rufford, Blackburn, Tarleton, Standish 2, Tunstal, Thurland Castle, Ulverstone, Walton 2, Warrington 3, Warton, Wigan, and Winwick 2. During the life of her father, Mary had written a penitential letter, expressing her contrition for not having submitted herself to his "most iust and virtuous laws," in the matter of the Reformation, and putting her conscience under his royal and paternal direction. The letter is preserved in the Harleian Collection.[2] The subsequent death of the king, and the possession of the royal power on the part of his daughter, obliterated the remembrance of these solemn protestations, and she became still more fixed than before in her attachment to the ancient faith. Her matrimonial alliance with Philip, King of Spain, strengthened her previous partialities; and the presence of Cardinal Pole, legate of the pope, one of the most learned of the clergy, and one of the most devoted disciples of the church of Rome, conspired to fix this attachment. An Act for reviving the statutes of 5 Richard II., 2 Henry IV., and 2 Henry V. against heretics (the Lollards) was hurried through the Parliament, and gave the sanction of law to the executions which speedily followed.[3] The first martyr in this reign was John Rogers, one of the translators of the Bible in the time of Henry VIII.,[4] a Lancashire man, educated at Cambridge,

[1] Bishop Burnet's Collection of Records, book i. p. ii., No. 56.
[2] Cod. 282. See also Cotton MSS. lib. Otho, C.X.
[3] This Act (1 and 2 Philip and Mary, c. 6), for the punishment of heresies, directs that "every article, branch, and sentence contained in the same three several Acts, and every of them, shall from the 20th day of January then next coming be revived, and be in full force, strength, and effect, to all intents, constructions, and purposes for ever."—C.
[4] In the dedicatory epistle of that Bible this divine signs himself Thomas Matthew.—C.

and one of the first theological scholars of the age.   The offence with which he was charged was
that of holding a meeting near Bow Church, in London, where a minister of the name of Ross had
administered the communion according to the rites of the English book of service, and had openly
prayed that God would either change the heart of the queen or take her out of the world.   The
tribunal before which he was condemned sat on the 28th of January, 1555, and consisted of the
Bishops of Winchester, London, Durham, Salisbury, Norwich, and Carlisle; and sentence was
passed both upon Hooper, the silenced Bishop of Gloucester, and Rogers; but the utmost severity
of the law was only executed on the latter, the former having at that time been merely degraded
from the order of the priesthood.   Seven days after the sentence of condemnation was passed
(Feb. 4), Rogers was called to make ready for Smithfield, where he was sentenced to be burnt at
the stake for heresy.   When brought to Bonner, Bishop of London, to be degraded, he asked
permission to see his wife, in order that he might, through her, convey his dying blessing to his
ten children; but the request was peremptorily refused, with the insulting taunt that he was a
priest, and could not possibly have a wife.   When fastened to the stake, a pardon was brought,
and offered to him, on condition that he would recant; but, with an intrepidity which nothing
but religious principle can inspire, he rejected the proffered clemency, and assumed the crown of
martyrdom.   Hooper was afterwards sent to his former episcopal city of Gloucester, and on the
9th February was burnt at the stake in front of the cathedral.

The next Lancashire martyr executed in Smithfield was John Bradford, born at Manchester,
who had in early life been a man of the world, and filled the office of secretary to Sir John
Harrington, the treasurer of Henry VIII. and Edward VI.   At a subsequent period he became a
divine of exemplary piety,[1] of mild and diffident manners, but of a character so decided that he
did not hesitate to lay down his life for the truth of that religion which he had embraced from
strong conviction.   To so high a pitch had religious hostility attained, that Bourn, a canon of St.
Paul's, and afterwards Bishop of Bath, while preaching a sermon in favour of the Catholic faith,
had a dagger hurled at him by one of the congregation.   From this violence he was happily
rescued by Bradford, who assuaged the storm of popular tumult.   But this was made a charge
against him; and it was alleged that his power to allay the storm proved that he could direct
the elements of which it was composed.   Though a prebendary of St. Paul's, he preached much
in Lancashire, his native county, where his piety and zeal rendered his ministry peculiarly
acceptable.   Being sent to the King's Bench Prison, he was tried along with Dr. Rowland Taylor
for denying the doctrine of transubstantiation, or the corporeal presence of Christ in the sacrament,
and asserting that wicked men do not partake of Christ's body in that ordinance.   In vain was
his fear appealed to.   He would admit of no tenets or practices but such as were contained in the
Holy Scriptures; and being found "incorrigible" he was deemed a heretic, first excommunicated,
and then condemned.   For some months he was confined in Newgate, in the hope that he would
retract his "heretical errors;" but instead of abjuring, he employed himself in promulgating
them, particularly amongst his friends in Lancashire; and the Earl of Derby, in declaiming against
him in the House of Lords, informed their lordships that Bradford had done more hurt by the
letters he had written while he was in prison than he could have done by preaching, had he been
at large and at liberty to preach.[2]   "With Bradford," says Bishop Burnet, "one John Lease, an
apprentice of nineteen, was led out to be burnt, who was also condemned upon his answers to the
articles exhibited to him.   When they came to the stake, they both fell down and prayed.   Then
Bradford took a fagot in his hands, and kissed it; and so likewise kissed the stake, expressing
thereby the joy he had in his sufferings, and cried, 'O England, repent, repent, beware of
idolatry and false anti-christ!'   But the sheriff hindering him from speaking any more, he
embraced his fellow-sufferer, and prayed him to be of good comfort, for they should sup with
Christ that night.   His last words were, 'Strait is the way, and narrow is the gate, that leadeth
into eternal life, and few there be that find it.'"   (July, 1555.)[3]

George Marsh, a native of the parish of Dean, was the third and last Lancashire martyr who

[1] When he became religious, "he sold," says Simpson, his intimate friend, "his chains, rings, brockets, and jewels of gold, which before he used to wear, and did bestow the price of this his former vanity in the necessary relief of Christ's poor members."

[2] These letters breathed the most ardent spirit of piety, combined with an invincible heroism; and in one of them, addressed to the inhabitants of "Lancashire and Cheshire," written from his prison a short time before his martyrdom, he thus expresses himself: "Turn unto the Lord, yet once more, I heartily beseech thee, thou Manchester, thou Ashton-under-Lyne, thou Bolton, Bury, Wigan, Liverpool, Mottram, Stopport, Winsley [?Worsley], Eccles, Prestwich, Middleton, Radcliff, and thou city of West-Chester, where I have truly taught and preached the word of God.   Turn, I say unto you all, and to all the inhabitants thereabouts; turn unto the Lord our God, and he will turn unto you; he will say unto his angel, 'It is enough, put up thy sword.' And that he do this, I humbly beseech his goodness, for the precious

blood sake of his dear Son, our Saviour Jesus Christ.   Ah! good brethren, take in good part these my last words unto every one of you.   Pardon me mine offences and negligences in behaviour amongst you.   The Lord of mercy pardon us all our offences, for our Saviour Jesus Christ's sake Amen."

[3] It is said that Lord Derby interceded with the queen to spare the life of Bradford, and that one of his servants proposed to assist Bradford to leave the kingdom on conditions which the martyr declined (*Lancashire: its Puritanism and Nonconformity*).   The council at first resolved that he should be committed to the Earl of Derby, in order that he might be burnt in Manchester, but the authorities, from some cause or other changed their purpose, and ordered him to be burnt in Smithfield.   Probably the Earl of Derby felt some reluctance to undertake the burning of the great preacher, whom he had himself encouraged to preach the doctrines of the Reformation.—C.

29

suffered in the reign of Queen Mary. This single-minded man had been brought up as a farmer with his father, who was a Lancashire yeoman, but he afterwards embraced the profession of a divine, and to his duties of a curate added those of an instructor of youth. The obscurity of his station did not preserve him from persecution. He was charged with propagating heresy and sowing the seeds of sedition; and finding that he had become the object of suspicion, he surrendered himself to the Earl of Derby at Lathom House. Here he underwent various examinations,[1] and several attempts were made to prevail upon him to espouse the Catholic faith, but as they all proved unsuccessful, he was at length committed by his lordship to Lancaster Castle, where he was again advised and entreated to recant. While in this situation, endeavours were made to extract from him information, whereon to found charges against other persons in the county; but no motives of fear or reward could induce him to endanger the lives or liberties of his fellow-christians. After remaining some time in confinement at Lancaster, he was removed to Chester, and placed in the bishop's liberty. The bishop's (Dr. Coates's) endeavours to "reclaim" him having proved ineffectual, he was remanded back to prison, and, in a few days, summoned before the spiritual court, assembled in the Lady Chapel of the cathedral church at Chester, where, in the presence of the mayor, the chancellor, and the principal inhabitants of the city, he was accused of having preached most heretically and blasphemously in the parishes of Dean, Bolton, Bury, and Eccles, as well as in other parishes in the bishop's diocese, not only against the pope's authority but against the church of Rome, the holy mass, the sacraments of the altar, and the articles of the Romish faith. To these charges he modestly answered he had preached neither heresy nor blasphemy, and that the doctrines which he believed and had propagated were those sanctioned by royal authority in the reign of Edward VI. On the subject of the power of the pope he did not hesitate to declare that the bishop of Rome ought to exercise no more authority in England than the Archbishop of Canterbury ought to exercise in Rome. This answer raised the Bishop of Chester's indignation to the highest possible pitch, and the torrents of his wrath flowed out with so much fury that he stigmatised his prisoner as "a most damnable, irreclaimable, and unpardonable heretic." After some further endeavour made by the chancellor to reclaim this "irreclaimable heretic," the bishop proceeded to pass sentence upon him, when "the holy church," which never puts anyone to death, delivered him to the secular authorities, and he was consigned to the Northgate Prison, where he remained till the 24th of April, 1555. On this memorable day he was led to execution amidst a crowd of spectators, agitated by conflicting feelings. The scene of this horrible tragedy was a precinct of Chester called Spital Broughton, within the liberties of the city. After the exhibition of a conditional pardon, as was the prevailing practice, from the queen, by the vice-chancellor, Mr. Vawdrey, and the refusal of the martyr to retract his faith, the people, roused to indignation by the barbarous scene that presented itself, attempted to rescue Marsh from the hands of his sanguinary murderers, and sheriff Cowper, sharing the public feeling, joined in the attempt, but he was beaten off by the other sheriff and his retainers. The most composed man in the assembly was the victim about to be sacrificed to his principles. He exhorted the multitude to remain strong in the faith, and the fagots being lighted around him, he surrendered his spirit into the hands of his Redeemer. While these revolting scenes were acting in the north the powers of persecution raged in the south with undiminished fury, and the distinguished martyr, Cranmer, Archbishop of Canterbury, shared the fate of so many of his order. The effect of these sanguinary persecutions was to spread the doctrines they were meant to destroy; and it may be fairly doubted whether ever so many converts were made to the Protestant faith in the same time as during those years, when the seeds of the church were thus watered by the blood of the saints.

In the early part of this reign a muster of soldiers was made in the county palatine of Lancaster, from the respective hundreds, of which the following is the abridged record, from a MS. temp. Elizabeth, among the Birch Evidences:—

LANCASHIRE MILITARY MUSTER.—MARY, 1553.

"DERBY HUNDRED to raise 480 men. These were the commanders of them:—

"Edward, Earl of Derby, Sir Richard Molyneux, Sir Thomas Gerrard, Sir Peers Legh, Sir John Holcroft, Sir John Atherton, Sir William Norris; Thomas Butler of *Bewsey*, George Ireland of *Hale*, William Tarbock of *Tarbock*, Lawrence Ireland of *Lydiate*, Esquires.

"SALFORD HUNDRED—350 men.

"Sir Edmund Trafford, Sir Wm. Ratcliffe, Sir Robert Longley, Sir Thomas Holt, Sir Robert Worseley; Robert Barton, Edward Holland, Ralph Ashton, Esqs.

---

[1] In the course of one of these examinations, Marsh gave the earl the following well-deserved reproof: "It is strange that your lordship, being of the honourable council of the late King Edward, consenting and agreeing to acts concerning faith towards God and religion, should so soon after consent to put poor men to a shameful death for embracing the same religion."

"LEYLAND HUNDRED—170 men.

"Sir Thomas Hesketh; Edward Standish, John Fleetwood, Roger Bradshaw, John Langtree, Peers Anderton, and John Wrightington, Esqs.

"AMOUNDERNESS HUNDRED—300 men.

"Sir Thomas Hesketh, Sir Richard Houghton; George Brown, John Kitchen, Richard Barton, William We[s]tbie, and Wm. Barton, Esqs.

"BLACKBURN HUNDRED—400 men.

"Sir Richard Shireburn, Sir Thomas Langton, Sir Thomas Talbot, Sir John Southworth; John Townley, Thomas Catterall, John Osbolston, John Talbot, Esqs.

"LONSDALE HUNDRED—350 men.

"The Lord Monteagle, Sir Marmaduke Tunstall; Thomas Carus, George Middleton, Thomas Bradley, Hugh Dicconson, and Oliver Middleton, Esqs.

"HUNDRED OF WEST DERBY.

The Parish of Ormskirk ....men 28	The Parish of Sefton ....men 30	The Parish of Leigh ....men 36
The Parish of North Meols .... „ 9	The Parish of Walton .... „ 36	The Parish of Warrington .... „ 25
The Parish of Aughton............... „ 12	The Parish of Wigan ... . „ 52	The Parish of Childwell .... „ 27
The Parish of Altcar .... „ 9	The Parish of Prescot .. .. „ 67	The Parish of Huyton .... „ 16
The Parish of Hallsall .... „ 28	The Parish of Winwick .... „ 34	

"THE HUNDRED OF LEYLAND.

The Parishes of Leyland............men 36	Brindle Parish, cum villa ....men 14	Parochia de Eccleston ....men 19
The Parish of Croston .... „ 36	Parochia de Chorley et vill .... „ 9	Penwortham Parish .... „ 17

"THE HUNDRED OF AMOUNDERNESS.

Warton ....men 6	Pulton ....men 3	Elston and Huddersall ....men 5
Carleton .... „ 8	Weton .... „ 3	Goosenargh .... „ 7
Hardhome-with-Clifton .... „ 8	Threleye... .... „ 6	Much Singleton........................ „ 7
Much Eccleston .... „ 5	Houghton .... „ 5	Whittington .... „ 5
Clifton .... „ 6	Little Eccleston and Larbreke ... „ 6	Haighton .... „ 5
Bispham and Norbreke .... „ 5	Upper Rawolliffe and Tornecard ... „ 1	Elson .... „ 2
Scalnew and Straynowe .... „ 7	Little Singleton and Grange ...... „ 5	Fryswicke .... „ 3
Freckleton .... „ 5	Westby and Plumbton............... „ 8	Grymsawre and Unkefall............ „ 5
Thilston .... „ 8	Rigby and Wraye .... „ 8	Ribbleton .... „ 3
Warton .... „ 4	Elliswicke .... „ 5	Lea .... „ 3
Newton and Scales .... „ 3	Kelmyne and Brininge .... „ 5	Plumpton .... „ 11
Ashton, Ingbill, and Cottom ...... „ 8	Kirkham .... „ 3	Billesburghe .... „ 6
Out Rawcliffe.......................... „ 4	Wassed .... „ 1	Barton's Newisame .... „ 2
Thornton .... „ 8	Lithum .... „	Parish of Garstang....... .... „ 45
Layton and Warbrick .... „ 8		5	

"THE HUNDRED OF BLACKBURN.

The Parish of Blackburn ....men 113	The Parish of Ribchester ....men 20	Pendle Forest ....men 86
The Parish of Whalley .... „ 175		Rossendall Forest .... „ 86

"THE HUNDRED OF LONSDALE.

Cockeram ....men 8	Barwicke ....men 3	*Furness*
Ellall .... „ 11	Carnford................................. „ 3	Bayliwicke of Hawshead............men 17
Wiersdale .... „ 6	Marton .... „ 6	Bayliwicke of Milthwaye .... „ 8
Wiremore .... „ 4	Silverdale .... „ 2	Ditto of Colton .... „ 8
Turnham .... „ 4	Healand .... „ 4	Ditto of Grisdale .... „ 7
Ashton and Stodley .... „ 2	Hutton .... „ 3	Ditto of Smithwick .... „ 10
Scotford .... „ 7	Dalton .... „ 3	Ditto of Clayfe .... „ 7
Buke and Alkelefe.................... „ 8	Gressingham .... „ 2	Dalton in Furness...................... „ 21
Lancaster .... „ 7	Whittington .... „ 5	Bardsay .... „ 2
Skerton .... „ 2	Newton .... „ 1	Kirkby Irelith .. .. „ 8
Taisholme, Pulton, and Bare ...... „ 4	Docker .... „ 1	Lanckewicke .... „ 5
Leisham .... „ 2	Tunstall .... „ 1	Norland and Egton Ulverston...... „ 13
Overton .... „ 2	Camffeild .... „ 1	Osmunderly .... „ 4
Middleton .... „ 2	Barrow .... „ 8	Pennington............................. „ 8
Hayton and Oxcliffe .... „ 4	Loeke .... „ 2	Torwarbboth .... „ 7
Halton and Aughton .... „ 5	Irebie .... „ 1	Hamlet of Cromston.................. „ 4
Sline and Heste....................... „ 2	Thatum .... „ 4	Doversdale Broughton .... „ 7
Bolton .... „ 6	Hornbye .... „ 7	Much Land .... „ 27
Nether Kellet .... „ 5	Claughton ....•.................. „ 2	Broughton cum Membris, with
Over Kellet .... „ 5	Caton .... „ 5	Township of Cartmell .... „ 16
Compyne Wraye .... „ 1		Cartmell, Holcar, and Alithwaite.. „ 15

"SALFORD HUNDRED, no particular returns."

Four years afterwards, when England had become involved in that war which expelled her from the continent of Europe, a royal proclamation was issued by the king and queen to Nicholas, Archbishop of York, Chancellor of England, commanding him to cause commissions to be issued under the great seal to the justices of the peace and sheriffs of the counties of Lancaster, Suffolk, and Norfolk, with full powers to array, inspect, and exercise all men-at-arms and men capable of bearing arms, as well archers as horse and foot men, so that from the present time, and in time to come, they might be arrayed in arms ready to serve their country.[1] In the same year a levy was made within the county of two hundred soldiers, all archers, "to serve the Queenes Matie under the conduction of Sr Rob^te Worsley, Knight (of Booths), and Edward Tildesley, Esq. (of Tyldesley and Morley)," the quota for each hundred being as follows:—

Hundred of West Derby		men	42	
„	Salford	„	36	
„	Leyland	„	17	} 200 archers.[2]
„	Amoundernes	„	30	
„	Blackburn	„	39	
„	Lonsdale	„	36	

Every archer to be allowed ten shillings in money over and besides his furniture, though whether the sum named was intended for bounty, marching money, or rations is not stated. All this preparation was unavailing: a siege of eight days, under the Duke of Guise, rendered the French masters of Calais, a fortress which it had cost the conquerors of Cressy eleven months to acquire, and which, for two hundred years, had been held by this country as the key to the dominions of the French king.

Shortly before the fall of Calais, the Scots, influenced by French counsels, began once more to move on the Border, and to threaten the northern counties of England with invasion. At this juncture the Earl of Derby, as lord-lieutenant of the counties palatine of Lancaster and of Chester, addressed a despatch to the Earl of Shrewsbury, lord-president of the north, apprising his lordship of the measures that had been taken to array the levies in Lancashire and in Cheshire against "the Scottish doings,"[3] of the number of the forces, and of the captains by whom they were to be commanded. The despatch is of the date of the 29th of September, 1557, and the following are the

"CAPTEYNS IN THE COUNTY OF LANCASTER.

"Sir Richard Molynexe (of Sefton), K. [knight], or his son & heire ; a feeble man himself	200
"Sr Thom"s Gerrard (of Bryn), K.	200
"Sr Thom"s Talbot (of Bashall), K.	200
"Sr Richard Hoghton (of Hoghton Tower), K. not hable himself, but will furniah an hable Gent. to be Capteyn : Bycause he is not hable to goo himself doth furnish but	100
"Sr Thom"s Heaketh (of Rufford), & others with hym.	100
"Sr Thom"s Langton (of Walton-le-Dale, Baron of Newton-in-Makerfield), Knt. Sr Will"m Noresse (of Speke), Knt., neyther of them hable, but will furniahe an hable Capteyn	100
"Sr Will"m Radclif (of Ordsal), or his son and heire Alex^r, who is a handsome Gent. & Sr John Atherton joened w^t him	100
"Frauncis Tunstall (of Thurland), & others	100
"Sr John Holcroft (of Holcroft), or his son and heire—Richard Asheton of Mydd[elton], and others	100

"It"m, The rest appoynted in Lancashire be of my retynnue.

In January, 1558, an expedition under the Duke of Guise was directed against Calais. The city, which had been in the possession of England for over two hundred years, was attacked, and after a short siege capitulated, January 7th. The loss filled the whole kingdom with murmurs. England, it was said, had fallen. The queen was in despair, and with her latest breath exclaimed that the loss of Calais would be found written on her heart. Disappointed in all her hopes, Mary's spirits sank under her accumulated disasters, and at the age of forty-two years she descended childless to the grave, leaving the throne to the possession of her half-sister Elizabeth, whose masculine habits and discriminating mind much better fitted her to wield a sceptre.

The death of Queen Mary, on the 17th of November, 1558, found the Lady Elizabeth, now become Queen of England, at Hatfield; and a summons was immediately sent by the queen's council to the Marquis of Winchester, the Earl of Shrewsbury, the Earl of Derby, and other noblemen, requiring them to repair thither, to conduct the queen to London. Amongst the nobles assembled to perform this first act of loyal duty were the Duke of Norfolk, Lords Audley and Merley, Lord Dacres of the north, Lord Monteagle, Lord Vaux, Lord Wharton, and many others. In Parliament, the annunciation of Elizabeth by the Archbishop of York was hailed with acclamation, and the general cry of "God save Queen Elizabeth," not merely from the courtiers, but also

---

[1] Pat. 3 and 4. Phil. and Mary (1556-7), p. 5. m. 11 dors.
[2] Harl. MS. (1926, Art. 6. f. 23).—C.
[3] Queen Mary having, at the instigation of her husband, Philip of Spain, declared war against France, the Queen Dowager and Regent of Scotland, Mary of Guise, was urged by the French court to make a diver-

sion in their favour ; but though the Scottish nobles refused to enter on a war during their sovereign's minority, there was a furious outbreak of the Scottish borderers, and raids were made in the name of the northern counties.—C.

from the patriots, gave promise that a new and more happy era had already commenced. The state religion was soon destined to undergo another change, but instead of being rapid and violent it was conducted with great prudence; and that the feelings of the Catholics might not be outraged by a sudden transition, the queen retained a number of her Catholic ministers, taking care to have a sufficient number of the reformed faith to overrule their deliberations. Notwithstanding his acquiescence in Mary's policy, the Earl of Derby had ordered his movements so adroitly as to win the confidence of the new queen. On her accession he was sworn of the Privy Council, and in the following year was made chamberlain of Chester and one of the commissioners of the north. To further the great work of ecclesiastical reform, the queen set on foot a royal visitation throughout England, and appointed commissioners to visit each diocese, whose business it was to inquire into the late persecutions, to ascertain what wrongs had been done, what blood had been shed, and who were the persecutors. They were further directed to minister the oath of recognition, and to enjoin the new book of service,[1] which was to come into general use on the festival of John the Baptist. Another of their duties was to examine such as were imprisoned and in bonds for religion, though they had already been condemned, and to liberate them from prison. The commissioners for the north (1559) were, Francis, Earl of Shrewsbury, president of the council in the north, Edward, Earl of Derby, Thomas, Earl of Northumberland, lord warden of the East and Middle Marches, Thomas, Lord Evers; Henry Percy, Thomas Gargrave, James Crofts, Henry Gates, knts.; Edwin Sandys, D.D., Henry Harvey, LL.D., Richard Bowes, George Brown, Christopher Escot, and Richard Kingsmel, Esqrs.

The northern visitation commenced at St. Mary's, Nottingham, on the 22nd of August, 1559, and was continued throughout the dioceses of Lincoln, York, Chester, and Durham. The commissioners received the complaints of many clergymen, who had been ejected from their livings during the last reign for being married; and in almost all cases they were restored. Dr. Edwin Sandys, a representative of the ancient family of Sandys of Hawkshead-in-Furness, who had acquired a great reputation for learning and ability in the University of Cambridge, of which he had been vice-chancellor in King Edward's time, was one of the visitors for the northern parts, preached against the primacy of the pope, and did much by his zeal to spread the reformed doctrines;[2] he also endeavoured to prepare the clergy to take the oath of supremacy to the queen, which was required of them, and to which most of them conformed, though in Lancashire there were many who declined to take the oath, and who staunchly supported the doctrine of the real presence in the sacrament.

In these times of religious and political excitement the clergy were naturally prone to mix up secular subjects in their discourses, and to convey to the royal ear, when occasion presented itself, the views of the preachers on the administration of government. This species of preaching a certain great man at court (probably Lord Burghley) writing to Dr. Chadderton, afterwards Bishop of Chester, thought proper to rebuke. "The queenes majestie," saith he, "doeth mislike that those who preach before her should enter into matters properlie appertaining to matter of government." They were therefore required to abstain from such preaching—not that her majesty wished to close her ears against the advice of those who were moved to desire amendment in things properly belonging to herself, but, on the contrary, was willing to hear any that should, either by speech or writing, impart their sentiments, but she did not wish to be lectured in public, nor to have the affairs of government animadverted upon before the vulgar.[3]

It having been enacted that the oath of supremacy should be taken to the queen, her majesty issued a proclamation to Sir Ambrose Cave, Knt., Chancellor of the Duchy of Lancaster, dated at Westminster, on the 23rd of May, 1559, directing that this oath should be taken throughout his jurisdiction, both by the clergy and laity.[4] At the same time she directed that all the chantries should conform themselves to the practice of her own chapel, and in that (though much of popish ceremony was retained) she forbade that the host should be elevated, and commanded that the Lord's Prayer, the Creed, and the Gospels, should be read in the vulgar tongue. In the following year a number of new bishops were consecrated, amongst whom were Edward Scrambler, D.D., for Peterborough, and James Pilkington, B.D., for Durham, both Lancashire men, and both firm adherents of the reformed religion. Soon after his inauguration, Dr. Pilkington preached before the queen at Greenwich, on the mission of a fanatic from the county of Lancaster of the name of Ellys, calling himself Elias. The Bishop of London had, however, so little regard for the northern prophet and his "warning voice" that he ordered him, three days afterwards, to be put in the pillory in Cheapside, from whence he was committed to Bridewell, where he soon after died.[5]

[1] This was the *Second Book of Edward VI.*, with some slight alterations, which was issued as *The Prayer Book of Elizabeth*, by the authority of Convocation and Parliament. It was used for the first time in the queen's private chapel, May 12, 1559.—C.

[2] The services of Sandys were subsequently rewarded by his elevation, first to the see of Worcester and eventually to that of York.
[3] Chadderton's MS. fo. 32 a. Peck's Desid. Cur. p. 83.
[4] Pat. 1 Eliz. m. 32 dors.
[5] Strype's Ann. of ye Reformation, i. 506.

The bishopric of Chester having become vacant, in consequence of Cuthbert Scott, "a ferocious papist" as he has been styled, refusing to take the oath of supremacy, the queen issued her mandate to the Chancellor of the Duchy of Lancaster, announcing that the dean and chapter, with her majesty's license, had elected William Downham to be their bishop and pastor, and commanding the chancellor to cause to be delivered up without delay the temporalities belonging to the episcopal see within his bailiwick, together with the issues and profits thereof, from the feast of St. Michael the Archangel.

The Queen Regent of Scotland having been won over to the designs of the house of Guise for the re-establishment of the Roman Catholic religion, and as a necessary consequence the pulling down of the reformation in Scotland which was then being promoted by John Knox, and ultimately to effect the removal of Elizabeth from the throne of England, a force of three hundred men, of whom seventy-eight were to be archers, was, on the 21st December, 1559, ordered to be raised in Lancashire, and to be under the conduct of Sir John Southworth,[1] of Samlesbury, to serve the queen's majesty at Berwick, the fortifications of which had then been recently strengthened. The following is the apportionment:—[2]

Hundred of	Men.	Of whom Archers.
West Derby	63	16
Salford	59	13
Leyland	15	7
Blackburn	55	15
Lonsdale	58	15
Amounderness	50	12
	300	78

In the month of January following another levy of two hundred soldiers and two hundred and sixty-seven pioneers[3] was raised in Lancashire for service at Leith,[4] to be under the command of Thomas Boteler, of Bewsey, and others, the several hundreds providing the quotas named:—[5]

Hundred of	Soldiers.	Pioneers.
West Derby	40	53
Leyland	17	22
Salford	37	48
Blackburn	36	48
Amounderness	32	43
Lonsdall-with-Furness	39	52
	200	267

That the nation might be put in a posture of defence, a muster of troops was ordered in the several counties of the kingdom, and the following is the

GENERAL MUSTER, IN JANUARIE, 1559-60,[6]

CERTIFIED WITHIN THE COUNTY OF LANCASTER.

BLACKBURNE HUNDRED—407 harnessed men, unharnessed men 406.
AMOUNDERNESS HUNDRED—213 harnessed, unharnessed 369.
LONDESDALL HUNDRED—356 harnessed, unharnessed 114.
LEYLONDE HUNDRED—80 harnessed, unharnessed 22.
SALEFORDE HUNDRED—394 harnessed, unharnessed 649.
WEST DERBY—459 harnessed, unharnessed 418.
Sum Total of harnessed men, 1,919.
Sum Total of unharnessed men, 2,073.[7]

Hollinworth says "there was a sore sicknesse" in Lancashire in 1565, which was probably some remains of the plague contracted by the English army at Newhaven, in 1562, at which time, Stowe avers, 17,404 persons died in London alone in one year.

Although the progress of the Reformation was rapid in many parts of the kingdom, in the county of Lancaster it was retrograde. The Catholics multiplied, the mass was usually performed, priests were harboured, the Book of Common Prayer and the service of the church established by law were laid aside, many of the churches were shut up, and the cures were unsupplied unless

[1] Sir John Southworth was a zealous Roman Catholic, and in later life suffered imprisonment as a recusant. In a letter from Lords Eure and Wharton to Francis, Earl of Shrewsbury (president of the council of the north), dated October 22, 1557, the writers state that "Sir John Southworth had made request that we would be a means to your lordship that he might continue in service here with his hundred men. He says he is a young man, and desires to know service in war, and as we think him to be commended therein, being a toward and tall gentleman, we require your lordship to favour this his honest suit." Three hundred men were, on this recommendation, entrusted to his command, to march to Berwick. A lengthy notice of Sir John Southworth is given in The History of the Ancient Hall of Samlesbury.—C.
[2] Harl. MS. 1926, Art. 7. fo. 23.—C.

[3] These were in the nature of a force of army labourers, their duties being to level the roads, throw up works, dig trenches, and sink mines so as to destroy the enemy's fortifications. The name is derived from the French pionnier, a contraction of piochnier from piocher, to dig.—C.
[4] Leigh is the place named in the MS., but Leith is evidently intended. (See Froude's Hist. Eng., v. vii. p. 189.) Leigh in Lancashire is pronounced locally as if spelled Leith.—C.
[5] Harl. MS. 1926, Art. 8. fo. 28 b. There is a slight error in the addition, though the aggregate is correct, the totals being 201 and 266 respectively.—C.
[6] Harl. MSS. cod. 1926, fo. 4 b.
[7] This document is printed in the original edition from the Harl. MS. 1926, Art. 2. fo. 4 b, but the numbers are inaccurate.—C.

by the ejected Catholic priests.   This was thought the more extraordinary, as the queen had instituted an ecclesiastical commission, with the bishop of the diocese at its head, for the promotion of religion.   Downham, who had been appointed Bishop of Chester in succession to Scott, and in whose diocese the larger number of the Lancashire parishes lay, was a Protestant of a very mild type, and not much troubled with earnest scruples of any kind, so that Papists and Puritans were left to pursue their several courses without much episcopal interference.   As might be anticipated, under so negligent a bishop the Reformation progressed but slowly.   Romanism held its own, and the gentry openly defied the Act of Uniformity, or complied with it only to such an extent as would save them from trouble.   To stimulate the zeal of the prelate, the queen addressed to him, in 1567, a letter of remonstrance, couched in her usual tone of decision, reminding him of his duty, and requiring of him its more vigilant performance.   "We think it," says the queen, "not unknown, how, for the good opinion we conceived of your former service, we admitted you to be bishop of the diocese ; but now, upon credible reports of disorders and contempts, especially in the county of Lancaster, we find great lack in you.   In which matter of late we write to you, and other our commissioners joined with you, to cause certain suspected persons to be apprehended, writing at the same time to our right trusty and well-beloved the Earl of Derby for the aid of you in that behalf.   Since which time, and before the delivery of the said letters to the Earl of Derby, we be duly informed that the said earl hath, upon small motions made to him, caused such persons as have been required to be apprehended, and hath shown himself therein, according to our assured expectation, very faithful and careful of our service."[1]   In conclusion, the bishop is required to make personal visitation, by repairing to the most remote parts of his diocese, and especially into Lancashire, and to see to it that the churches be provided with honest men and learned curates, and that there be no more cause to blame him for his inattention and neglect.   At a subsequent period, the lords of the council wrote to the bishop, complaining that many persons in the counties of Lancaster and Chester absented themselves habitually from church, and from places of public prayer, and requesting that the bishop would take measures to enforce their attendance.   To this intimation his lordship replied that he had made diligent inquisition into the matter of complaint, that some of the gentry and others had promised to be more conformable in future, but that others had disregarded his admonitions, and that he had enclosed a list certifying the names of those who remained obstinate, and of those who promised to conform.[2]   The zeal of the Earl of Derby in favour of the reformed faith, so warmly eulogised by the queen, was the zeal of a convert, and therefore perhaps the more lively.   In the last reign, his lordship embraced the cause of popery, and the committal of the intrepid George Marsh to that dungeon from which he was liberated only to be conducted to the stake serves to show that sudden changes in religious faith were not confined to priests, but that they were extended to nobles, and to a certain extent pervaded the whole people.   In the county of Lancaster there was more of consistency than in other parts of the kingdom ; and this is a principle which excites respect, even though it should be a consistency in error.   The queen's admonitions to the bishop, as the head of the ecclesiastical commission, produced an immediate effect.   The bishop entered upon his visitation with all convenient despatch ; many of the popish recusants, as they were called, were detected in plots to subvert the established religion, and to substitute their own in its stead ; and the county was engaged in a kind of religious warfare, which is described with considerable animation, and probably with as much accuracy as can be expected, by an author having a strong bias towards the Protestant cause :—[3]

"And first," says our author, "to give some account of the Bishop's Visitation. Which proved thus, according to the Relation he made of it himself to the Secretary in a Letter to him, dated Nov. 1, 1568, 'That he had the last Summer visited his whole Diocess, which was of Length above six score Miles ; and had found the People very tractable ; and no where more than in the farthest Parts bordering upon Scotland.   Where as he said, he had the most gentle Entertainment of the Worshipful to his great Comfort.   That his Journey was very painful by reason of the extreme heat ; and if he had not received great Courtesy of the Gentlemen, he must have left the most of his Horses by the way ; Such Drought was never seen in those Parts.'   The Bishop also now sent up, by one of his Servants, a true Copy of all such Orders as he, and the rest of his Associates, in the Queen's Commission Ecclesiastical, had taken with the Gentlemen of Lancashire.   Who (one only excepted, whose name was John Westby), with most humble Submissions and like Thanks unto the Queen's Majesty, and to her Honourable Council, received the same ; Promising that from henceforth they would live in such sort, that they would never hereafter give occasion of Offence in any thing concerning their bounden Duty, as well towards Religion as their Allegiance towards their Prince.   But notwithstanding their Promises, the Commissioners bound every of them in Recognizances in the sum of an Hundred Marks for their Appearances from time to time, as appeared in the abovesaid Orders.   And certain Punishments inflicted upon some of them had done so much good in the Country, that the Bishop hoped he should never be troubled again with the like.   Nowel, Dean of S. Paul's, London, was a Lancashire man, and was now down in that Country.   Who with his continual preaching in divers Places in the County, had brought many obstinate and wilful People unto Conformity and Obedience, and had gotten great Commendation and Praise (as he was most worthy) even of those that had been great Enemies to his Religion.

"But now to set down particularly what had been detected and discovered among these Lancashire Papists, and the Negligence, or Lothness of the Bishop to prosecute them. Information was brought into the Bishop by one Mr. Glasier, a Commissioner, and

[1] Pap. Office, Strype's Ann. i. 544-5.   [2] Harl. MSS. cod. 286, fo. 28.   [3] Strype's Ann. i. 546-552.

another named Edmund Ashton, that great Confederacies were then in Lancashire. And that Sundry Papists were there lurking, who had stirred divers Gentlemen to their Faction, and sworn them together, not to come to the Church in the Service time, now set forth by the Queen's Authority, nor to receive the Communion, nor to hear Sermons; but to maintain the Mass and Papistry. And after this Information, Glasier advised the Bishop to go to the Earl of Darby, and to execute the Commission in Lancashire; or else it could not be holpen but many Church Doors must be shut up, and the Curates hindered to serve as it was appointed to be used in the Church. And that this Confederacy was so great, that it would growe to a Commotion, or Rebellion. The Bishop hereupon sent for those Offenders by Precept, but declined to go yet to execute the Commission in Lancashire. Again, Sir Edward Fytton informed the Bishop, that Mr. Edmund Trafford spake of these Matters before to him as a Commissioner, for to have redress thereof. Whereupon Mr. Gerrard said, that if the Bishop would not go to Wygan in Lancashire, or such like Place, and sit to execute the Commission, and move the Earl of Darby to be there (who had assured them he would sit and assist), he knew that a Commotion would ensue; and that he knew their Determination was thereunto. For that his Kinsman and Alliance to his Remembrance (naming Mr. Westby) had told him, He would willingly lose his Blood in these Matters. Also he said further, that from Warrington all along the Sea Coasts in Lancashire, the Gentlemen (except Mr. Butler) were of the Faction, and withdrew themselves from Religion; as Mr. Ireland, Sir Wm. Norris, and many others more. So that there was such a Likelihood of a Rebellion or Commotion speedily, that for his Part, if the Bishop would not go to execute the Commission in Lancashire, he would himself within twelve Days inform the Privy Council. And yet he had desired the Bishop to deliver the Commission unto him, and Fytton to execute: but the Bishop refused, saying he would send for the Offenders. But afterward, the Bishop and Gerrard signed Precepts for divers Papistical Priests and some Gentlemen to appear before the Commissioners concerning the Premises.

"Again, one Edmund Holme made this Discovery; That there was a Letter written from Dr. Saunders [Nicolas Saunders] to Sir Richard Molineux and Sir William Norris; the Copy of which Letter was ready to be shewed. The Contents of it, as it seems, were, to exhort them to own the Pope supreme Head of the Church; and that they should swear his Supremacy, and Obedience to him, before some Priest or Priests appointed by his Authority; who should also absolve them that had taken any Oath to the Queen as supreme, or gone to Church and heard Common Prayer. Hereupon Sir Richard Molineux did make a vow unto one Norrice, otherwise called Butcher, otherwise called Fisher, of Formeby; and unto one Peyle, otherwise called Pyck (who reported that he had the Pope's Authority), that he would do all things according to the Words of the said Letter. And so did receive Absolution at Pyck's hand; And he did vow to the said Pyck, that he would take the Pope to be the supreme Head of the Church. And the said Molineux's Daughters, Jane, Alice, and Anne, and his son John, made the like Vow as their Father had done. And then they took a Corporal Oath on a Book. And so did John Mollin of the Wodde, and Robert Blundel of Inse, and Richard Blundel of Christby, and Sir Thomas Williamson, and Sir John Dervoyne, and John Williamson. These were some of those Popish Gentlemen of Lancashire; and these were their Doings. But the Commission Ecclesiastical, roundly managed, had pretty well reduced them, as we heard before. In what Form the Submission ran, to which these Popish Gentlemen subscribed, before they made their Peace, I know not. But I find this Year one Form offered to Sir John Southworth, of these Parts (who had entertained Priests, and absented from the Church), by order of the Privy Council; which was as followeth :—

"'Whereas I, Sir John Southworth, Knt., forgetting my Duty towards God and the Queen's Majesty, in not considering my due Obedience for the Observation of the Ecclesiastical Laws and Orders of this Realm, had received into my House and Company, and there relieved, certain Priests, who have not only refused the Ministry, but also in my hearing have spoken against the present State of Religion, established by her Majesty and the States of her Realm in Parliament, and have also otherwise misbehaved myself in not resorting to my Parish Church at Common Prayer, nor receiving the Holy Communion so often times as I ought to have done :

"'I do now, by these Presents, most humbly and unfeignedly submit myself to her Majesty, and am heartily sorry for mine Offence in this Behalf, both towards God and her Majesty. And do further promise to her Majesty from henceforth, to obey all her Majesty's Authority in all Matters of Religion and Orders Ecclesiastical; and to behave myself therein as becometh a good, humble, and obedient Subject; and shall not impugn any of the said Laws and Ordinances by any open Speech, or by Writing, or Act of mine own; nor willingly suffer any such in my Company to offend, whom I may reasonably let or disallow: Nor shall assist, maintain, relieve, or comfort any Person living out of this Realm, being known to be an Offender against the said Laws and Orders now established for godly Religion, as is aforesaid. And in this doing, I firmly trust to have her Majesty my gracious and good Lady, as hitherto I, and all other her Subjects, have marvellously tasted of her Mercy and Goodness.'

"But this knight refused to subscribe the submission, any further than in that point of maintaining no more those disordered persons."

Mary, Queen of Scots, having at this time been expelled from her throne by her subjects, under the authority of the Earl of Murray, regent of the kingdom of Scotland, sought an asylum in England, but before she could be admitted to the court it became necessary that she should justify herself from the charge of having been accessary to the murder of her husband. In this she failed—indeed, her agents refused to proceed with the investigation, when the evidence of her guilt became conclusive; and instead of being admitted to the court of Elizabeth she was ever after kept as her prisoner, first in Bolton Castle, afterwards at the castle of Sheffield, then at Tutbury, and finally at the castle of Fotheringay. Several of Mary's adherents now fled out of England from Lancashire and other parts of the kingdom, and it was discovered in the course of the year (1568) that sums of money were sent to them from hence, to promote the invasion of England and to re-establish the ancient religion. The recently-created bishopric of Chester was amongst the lowest of the livings in the English Church, not exceeding in value three hundred and fifty pounds a year; and yet such was the hospitality at this time kept up by the bishops that Dr. Downham, in his application to the Queen for the extension of his *commendam*, represented that he supported every day, in virtue of his office, "forty persons, young and old, besides comers and goers."[1] The bias of the queen's mind was towards the ancient religion, with all its forms and ceremonies, so far as was consistent with that supremacy which she claimed as the head of the church; and though the real presence was openly denied by the reformed church she openly thanked one of her preachers for a sermon he had preached in favour of that doctrine.[2] Celibacy in the ministers of religion was always viewed by her with favour; and all the influence of her favourite minister Cecil was necessary to prevent her from interdicting the marriage of the clergy.

[1] Bishop Downham's Letter to the Secretary of State, 1568.   Heylin, p. 124.

While this was the disposition of the queen several of her ministers conceived that the reform in the religion of the state was by no means sufficiently radical; and not only Cecil, but Leicester, Knolles, Bedford, and Walsingham, favoured the Puritans, who derived their origin from those exiled ministers that, during the reign of Queen Mary, had imbibed the opinions of Calvin, the reformer of Geneva. Their historian[1] describes the Puritans as objecting to the assumed *supremacy* of the bishops, and the jurisdiction of the ecclesiastical court; to the frequent repetition of the Lord's Prayer in the liturgy, to the responses of the people, and to the reading of the apocryphal lessons; to the sign of the cross in the administration of baptism; and to the ring and the terms of the contract in marriage; to the observance of the festivals in the calendar, the chaunt of the Psalms, and the use of musical instruments in the cathedral services; and, above all, to the habits, "the very livery of the beast," enjoined to be worn by the ministers during the celebration of divine services. Dean Nowell, one of the queen's chaplains, so celebrated for his preaching in Lancashire, his native county, was understood to favour the Puritanical doctrines, which was probably one of the causes of his popularity in this county; and when, in a sermon preached before his royal mistress, he spoke disparagingly of the sign of the cross, she called aloud to him in the congregation, and ordered him "to quit that ungodly discussion, and to return to his text."

From this period, through a succession of ages, the county of Lancaster continued much divided on subjects of religion and politics—the Catholics assuming the high church and the monarchical principles, and the Puritans the low church and democratic principles, while the Established Church held the balance between the two, by turns favouring the former or the latter, as best accorded with the objects and views of the existing government; and not unfrequently restraining and even persecuting both. In no county in the kingdom have the distinctions been so marked as in Lancashire, and in none will this observation be found so unerring an index whereby to account for the local feuds and for the party animosities.

Throughout the reign of Elizabeth there were frequent plots and conspiracies to deprive her of her crown and life. Both Mary, Queen of Scots, and her son James were suggested as occupants of the throne to be forfeited, and the Earl of Derby was also named, if only he would once more turn Catholic. Mary of Scotland fully relied on his adherence to her cause; but had the opportunity offered, it is doubtful whether he would not have considered the title of a Stanley, in whose veins coursed the blood of Henry III., better than either that of Elizabeth Tudor or Mary Stuart. In 1568 secret conferences were held at York between the Bishops of Ross and Liddington, friends of the Scottish queen, and the Duke of Norfolk, to procure the queen's liberty, and secure the duke's marriage clandestinely with her, to which certain Lancashire men were believed to have been privy. Several of the leading families of the north, anxious to re-establish the Catholic religion, and to place Mary, Queen of Scots, on the throne of England, entered into a conspiracy for this purpose, at the head of which stood the Earls of Northumberland and Westmorland. One of their first objects was to liberate Mary from her confinement in Tutbury Castle, and Sir Thomas and Sir Edward Stanley, sons of the Earl of Derby, along with Sir Thomas Gerrard and other Lancashire gentlemen, favoured the enterprise. In furtherance of this object the Earls of Northumberland and Westmorland put forth the following proclamation:—

"THE DECLARATION OF THE EARLS AT THE RISING IN THE NORTH.[2]

"We, Thomas Earl of Northumberland, and Charles Earl of Westmorland, the Queen's true and faithful subjects, to all that came of the old and Catholic Religion, Know ye that we with many other well-disposed persons, as well of the Nobility as others, have promised our Faith to the Furtherance of this our good meaning, Forasmuch as divers disordered and evil-disposed persons about the Queen's Majesty have by their subtle and crafty dealings to advance themselves, overcome in this Realm the true and Catholic Religion towards God, and by the same abused the Queen, disordered the Realm, and now lastly seek and procure the destruction of the Nobility: We therefore have gathered ourselves together to resist by force, and the rather by the help of God and you good people, to see redress of these things amiss, with the restoring of all ancient customs and liberties to God's Church, and this noble Realm ; lest if we should not do it ourselves, we might be reformed by strangers, to the great hazard of the state of this our country, whereunto we are all bound.

"God save the Queen."

The influence of the leaders of the insurrection, and the attachment of the people to the Catholic faith, drew together an army of four thousand foot and six hundred horse. To strengthen their force the Earls of Westmorland and Northumberland addressed a letter to the Earl of Derby (Nov. 27, 1569), requesting him to join their standard, and to procure for them such aid and assistance as his lordship could collect in "all parts of his terrytoryes, to effect their honorable and godly enterprises."[3] The rebel earls appear to have had every hope of his lordship's support, and even Sir Francis Leek seems to have had some misgivings as to how far his loyalty could be relied on, for in one of his letters to Cecil he remarks, as if mistrusting the earl, that "all the keyes of Lancashire do not at present hange at the Earl of Derby's owlde gyrdell."[1]   The northern earls were out of their reckoning when counting on Lord Derby's support; Catholic though he might be in heart, the family instinct was prominently developed, and, to remove any possible doubt of his sincerity, he redoubled his efforts in harassing and imprisoning the Catholics in his county. Seven days before the date of the rebellious earls' despatch, he had received a commission from the queen, appointing him lord-lieutenant of the county of Lancaster; and his lordship, without loss of time, inclosed the treasonable invitation to the queen, accompanied by the following despatch:—

"THE EARL OF DERBY TO THE QUEEN'S MAJESTY.

"My most humble and obedient duty done. It may please your Majesty to understand, that this Day, being the 29th of this Month, one *Walther Passelewe* brought to my Howse a Letter from the Earls of *Northumberland* and *Westmorlande*, together with a Protestation of their undutiful Meaning and rebellious Attempt (as may appear), which the said *Passelewe* prayed one of my Servants, might be delivered to me : The which after I had received, perceiving the same to be unsealed, and, upon perusing, finding the matter to swerve so far from the Duty of any good Subjects, thought it my Part to give the same to be understanded of your Majesty, and so have sent them enclosed as I received them. The Bearer, because I could not safely send him without Guard, I have sent to come with more leisure, but with as much speed as conveniently may be used. I found with him the like Letter and Protestation sent to my Lord *Mounteagle*, which I have also sent enclosed. And resting your Majesty's assured at Commandment, beseeching God long to prosper your Majestie, and make you victorious over your enemies, I humbly take my Leave.

"From *Lathom*, my House, the 29th *November*, 1569.—*Your Majesty's most humble and obedient Subject and Servant,*
"EDWARD DERBY."

The "Rising of the North," as it was called, occurred in November, under the leadership of Percy, Earl of Northumberland. As the old ballad expresses it—

> "Erle Percy there his ancyent spred,
> The half-moone shining all soe faire ;
> The Nortons ancyent had the crosse,
> And the five wounds our lord did beare."

A more ill-concerted and more disastrous enterprise was never engaged in.   Lord Derby mustered the forces of Lancashire and Cheshire, but the rebellion, to use the words of the historian, " flashed in the pan," and the earl and his men were not required to take part in its suppression.   The queen and her council, ever alive to their duty and the public safety, assembled an army of seven thousand men, at the head of which the Earl of Sussex was placed, attended by the Earl of Rutland, and the Lords Hunsdon, Evers, and Willoughby.   The royal army having overtaken the insurgent force in the bishopric of Durham, the Earls of Northumberland and Westmorland retreated to Hexham, where, on hearing that the Earl of Warwick and Lord Clinton were advancing against them, they dispersed their forces without striking a blow.   The destruction of lives and estates which followed was wide and sweeping enough.   The Earl of Northumberland was executed, and the princely house of Neville was overwhelmed in utter and irretrievable ruin. This abortive effort of treason was succeeded soon after by another rebellion in the north, raised by Leonard Dacres, which was suppressed by Lord Hunsdon, at the head of the garrison of Berwick, without any other assistance.   Great severity was exercised against such as had taken part in these rash enterprises.   Sixty-six constables were hanged[2] for neglect of duty, and no fewer than eight hundred persons are said to have suffered by the hands of the public executioner. Fifty-seven noblemen and gentlemen of the counties of Northumberland, York, Durham, &c., implicated in this rebellion, were attainted by Parliament in the following year; but the list of proscriptions does not contain any Lancashire names.[3]   To guard against the recurrence of rebellion, and speedily to suppress any attempt to disturb the public tranquillity, the levies of troops, armour, and money were very abundant this year in the county of Lancaster; and amongst the original certificates preserved in these returns the following autographs appear:—

"Edward Derby, F. Stanley, Thomas Butler, Thos. Gerrard ; Hundred of West Derby.—Thomas Hoghton, Cuthbert Clifton : Hundred of Amounderness.—Thomas Hesketh, Edwarde Standysshe ; Hundred of Layland.—Rich. Shyrburn, Sir Rychard Assheton, John Braddyll ; Hundred of Blackburn.—Wyllum Mountegle ; Hundred of Lonsdale.—Robert Worseley, Edmund Trafford, John Radclyff, Robt. Barton, Edward Holand, Raffe Assheton, Francis Holt ; Hundred of Salford."

In the course of the same year a memorable search had been instiued in the county of Lancaster, by order of the lords of the council, which was simultaneously made in the other parts of the kingdom, for vagrants, beggars, gamesters, rogues, or gipsies, which was commenced at nine o'clock at night on Sunday, the 10th of July, 1570, and continued till four o'clock in the afternoon of the following day, and which resulted in the apprehension of the almost incredible number of thirteen thousand "masterless men,"[4] many of whom had no visible mode of living, "except that which was derived from unlawful games, especially of bowling, and maintenance of archery, and

---

[1] Sharp's Memorials of the Rebellion in 1569, p. 374.—C.　　　　[3] Harl. MSS. cod. 309, fol. 201 b.
[2] Camden, p. 423.　　　　[4] Strype's Ann. vol. i. p. 572.

Edward Derby

Thomas ...

F. Stanley

Edward Standyshe

Thomas Butler

Richard Assheton

John Talbott

Thomas Holcroft

Thomas Hoghton

William Montegle

Cuthbert Clifton

Robert Langton

Edmund Trafford

John Radcliff

Robert Barton

Edward Holland

Francis Gott

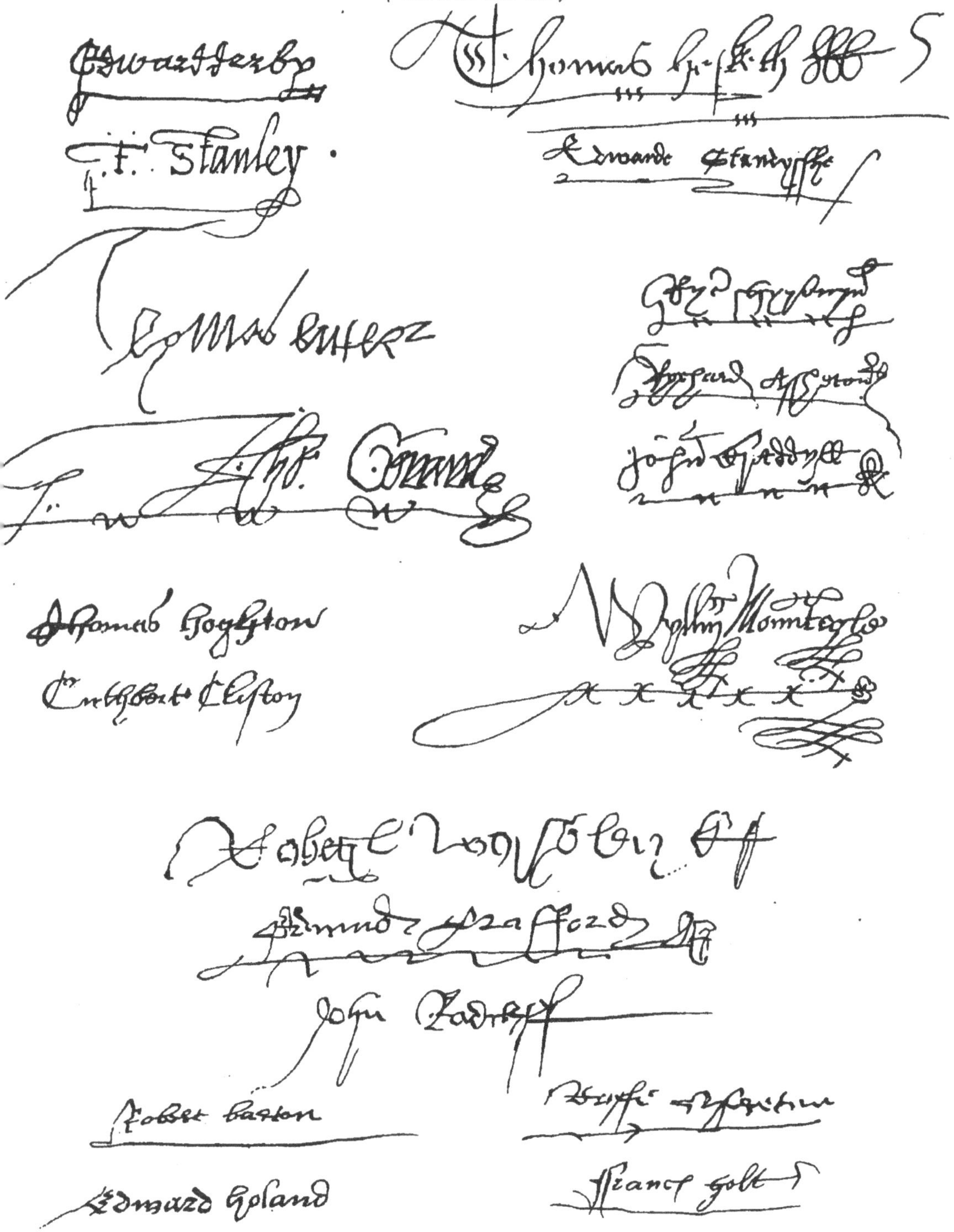

who were all passed to their own counties, under the direction of the magistrates." The effect of this vigorous measure of police, which was continued monthly till the November following, was to diminish the numbers that would otherwise, in those unsettled times, have swelled the insurgent force and endangered the stability of the government.

The Earl of Derby, in the discharge of his duty as the head of the lieutenancy in Lancashire and Cheshire, assembled the justices of the peace in the palatine counties, in their respective divisions, for the purpose of arranging their forces, and for adjusting the assessments to which they should respectively be liable. These arrangements being completed, they were transmitted to the lords in council, accompanied by the following despatch:—

ORIGINAL LETTER OF THE EARL OF DERBY.

"Right honorable my very good Lords according to the Queen her ma^tes pleasure unto me and others signified by yor letter and articles, I have caused the Sheriffs, commissioners of the musters, and Justices of the peace of the Counties of Lancaster and Chester (where I am her majesty's lieutenant), to assemble in their accustomed divisions sundry times for the execution of the same : Who have made inquisition as well touching such sums of money as have been assessed or taxed since the date of her ma^tes last commission for musters, for provision of armour, weapons, shot, and such like. As also for taxations, collections, and assessments of money for the furniture of Soldiers for her ma^te service with other things in the said letters and articles contained, and have sent unto yor L. herew^th all the said certificates of both Shires, whereof the last came to my hands so latelye as upon Friday last. W^ch was the cause of so long tract of time of both certificates. Thus wth my very hearty Commendations unto yor good L. I take my leave of you. From Lathom my howse the 7th of September 1570.—Yo^r good L. very loving Friend assured

"EDWARD DERBY.

Indorsed.—"To my very good Lords of the Queen her mate honorable privy Council give these."
In another hand.—   "1570 7° 7bris
"The Earl of Derby to the Council wth certificates out of the counties of Lancaster and Chester touching money collected for provision of Armour and Weapons." [1]

Devoted as the Earl of Derby had shown himself to the service of the queen, yet suspicion was entertained, and that in high quarters, that his loyalty was of a dubious kind, and that it would scarcely withstand the temptations to which it was exposed from the wicked counsellors by whom he was surrounded. Under the influence of these suspicions it is probable that Margaret, Countess of Derby, after the earl's death, had been apprehended, and placed in confinement; for, from a letter addressed by her ladyship to Mr. Secretary Walsingham, it appears that she was at one time a state prisoner, labouring under the accumulated pressure of bodily affliction and pecuniary embarrassments. The suspicions against the Earl of Derby were communicated to the queen's secretary of state by the Earl of Huntingdon, in a letter, intended to have been consigned to the flames as soon as it was read, but which has outlived its original destiny. A number of suspicious circumstances were accumulated against the Earl of Derby, and amongst others he was strongly suspected of keeping a conjuror in his house! The letter was in these terms:—

THE EARL OF HUNTYNGDON TO SECRETARY CECIL. [2]

"Sir,—I am bolder to write to you of weighty matters, than I dare be to some others ; the Cause I leave to your Consideration, and so to you only I am bold to impart that I hear. The Matter in short is this : Amongst the Papists of Lancashire, Cheshire, and the Cousins, great Hope and Expectation there is, that Derby will play as fonde a Part this year, as the two Earls did the last Year. I hope better of him for my Part, and for many Respects, both general and particular, I wish him to do better. I know he hath hitherto been loyal, and even the last Year, as you know, gave good Testimony of his Fidelity, and of his own Disposition ; I think will do so still ; but he may be drawn by evil Counsel, God knoweth to what. I fear he hath even at this time many wicked Councillors, and some too near him. There is one Browne a Conjuror[3] in his House, kept secretly. There is also one Uphalle, who was a Pirate and had lately his Pardon, that could tell somewhat, as I hear, if you could get him: He that carried my Lord Morley over was also there within this Se'nnight kept secretly. He with his whole Family never raged so much against Religion as they do now ; he never came to common Prayer for this Quarter of this year, as I hear, neither doth any of the Family except five or six Persons. I dare not write what more I hear, because I cannot justify and prove it ; but this may suffice for you in Time to look to it. And surely, in my simple opinion, if you send some faithful and wise Spy that would dissemble to come from D'Alva, and dissemble popery, you might understand all ; for if all be true that is said, there is a very fond Company in the House at this Present. I doubt not but you can and will use this Matter, better than I can advise you. Yet let me wish you to take heed to which of your Companions (though you be now but five together) you utter this Matter, ne forté it be in Latham sooner than you would have it, for some of you have Men about you and Friends attendinge on you, &c., that deal not always well. I pray God save our Elizabeth, and confound all her Enemies ; and thus I take my leave, committing you to God his Tuition.

"From Ashby the 24th of August 1570.   "Your assured poor Friend,
                                                                                                "H. HUNTYNGDON.

"P.S.—Because none there should know of my Letter, I would not send it by my Servant, but have desired Mr. Ad to deliver it to you in Secret : When you have read it I pray you to burn it, and forget the name of the Writer. I pray God I may not hear any more of your coming to ——"

The Earl of Derby's loyalty remained unshaken through another ordeal. A new conspiracy was formed by the Duke of Norfolk, in concurrence with Mary, Queen of Scots, whom the duke proposed to marry, in which he was aided by the Duke of Alva, the Spanish general, and the court of Rome, the object of which was to deprive Elizabeth of the throne, and to elevate Mary to that

---

[1] Harl. MSS. Cod. 302, fo. 104.
[2] Lord Burghley's State Papers i. 603.
[3] Conjuring was another term for witchcraft, a practice of which the earl was himself suspected. He was celebrated for his skill in setting bones and in surgery, and this qualification probably gave rise to the

belief that he practised the black arts, for in the Boyle MSS. there is a memorandum written by Richard Boyle, first Earl of Cork, in which he says, "Mumford resorteth to Stanley's house in Lancashire, within six miles of Leerpoole. There he is to be had. There he lately cast out divels."—C.

distinction. The vigilance and sagacity of Secretary Cecil, now become Lord Burghley, discovered the treasonable confederacy, and the duke was brought to trial before a commission of twenty-six peers, amongst whom were " Arthure Grey, Lord Wylton," and " William West, Lord de Laware."[1]

A unanimous sentence of death was passed against the duke, which was carried into execution in the middle of the following year (1572); and the Earl of Northumberland, for the part he had taken in the northern rebellion, shared the same fate. Against the Queen of Scots, though her prisoner, Elizabeth did not venture yet to proceed to the utmost extremity, but she sent Lord Delaware, Sir Ralph Sadler, Sir Thomas Bromley, and Dr. Wilson, to expostulate with her on her intended clandestine marriage with the Duke of Norfolk, on her concurrence in the northern rebellion, on the encouragement she had given to Spain to invade England, and on the part she had taken in procuring the pope's bull of excommunication against Elizabeth, and particularly upon allowing her friends abroad to give her the title of " Mary, Queen of England." These charges Mary denied, and justified herself either by repelling the allegations or by casting the blame on others over whom she had no control.[2] The queen was by no means satisfied with these apologies; and the temper of Parliament, as expressed in the application for the immediate trial and execution of Mary, showed that a storm was gathering, by which that unfortunate princess was speedily to be overwhelmed. The evidence of the Bishop of Ross, exhibited in the Burghley State Papers,[3] shows that Mary was, as early as the year 1571, in negotiation with the ambassadors of both France and Spain, for her escape from Sheffield Castle to the Continent, and that she was aided in her design by several Lancashire gentlemen. The bishop says the queen wrote a letter by a little priest of Rolleston's, that Sir Thomas Stanley, Sir Thomas Gerrard, and Rolleston, desired a " cypher for her, and that they offered to convey her away, and willed this examinate to *ax* the duke (of Norfolk)'s opinion herein." He further says that Hall told him that if the queen would get two men landed in Lancashire, Sir Thomas Stanley and Sir Edward Stanley (the Earl of Derby's son and grandson), along with Sir Thomas Gerrard and Rolleston,[4] would assist her escape to France or Flanders, and that the whole country would rise in her favour.

The death of Edward, the munificent Earl of Derby, with whom, says Camden, " the glory of hospitality hath in a manner been laid asleep," took place at Lathom House, on the 24th of February in the year 1572; and he was succeeded in his title and estates by Lord Strange, a nobleman honoured with the special favour of Queen Elizabeth, and for whose family she entertained the highest regard.[5]

The progress of public improvement in the county of Lancaster appears to have been slow up to the time of Elizabeth, as may be collected from an expression contained in a petition from Dean Nowell, the founder of the free school of Middleton, for the better encouragement of learning and true Christianity, who, in speaking of the people, designates them as " the inhabitants of the rude country of Lancashire."

During this reign the military strength of the kingdom was taken with great accuracy, and from the muster or order of government in 1574 it appears that Lancashire then ranked amongst the first counties in the kingdom in military strength, furnishing 6,000 able men, 3,600 armed men, 600 artificers and pioneers, 12 demi-lances[6] and 90 light horse, and that in number of able-bodied men it was only exceeded by Cornwall, Devonshire, Sussex, Somerset, Norfolk, Oxford, Dorset, Bucks, Kent, Yorkshire, and probably Middlesex, of which the return is only partially given. The population of Yorkshire, when compared with Lancashire, was then in the proportion of nearly seven to one, though now the population of Lancashire is larger than that of Yorkshire. Of the other counties, Lancashire exceeds the highest of them except the metropolitan county of Middlesex.[7]

The country was kept for years in a state of agitation by religious feuds, and the unceasing efforts of the Jesuits and other emissary priests, sent into the country for the purpose of fomenting sedition, and alluring the people from their allegiance to the queen. To guard against the recurrence of rebellion, and the more speedily to suppress any attempts to disturb the public tranquillity, levies of troops, armour, and money were made, and the military strength of the kingdom fully ascertained.

On the 14th March, 1573-4, instructions were issued for the execution of the commission, directed to all the justices of the peace in every shire, for the general musters and training of all manner of persons, able for war, to serve as well on horseback as on foot. In the month of June in

[1] Harl. MSS. cod 542. fo. 77.
[2] Camden, p. 442.
[3] Vol. ii. pp. 20 and 112.
[4] Sir Thomas Stanley, Sir Thomas Gerrard, and Rolleston, were apprehended, and committed to the Tower as state prisoners.—*Lord Burghley's Papers* ii. 771.
[5] Burghley's State Papers ii. 184.

[6] This name, from the demi or half lance which they used as a weapon, was by the Act 4 and 5 Philip and Mary (1558) given to a class of soldiers who, having previously been light horse, had become heavy cavalry, supplying the place of the men-at-arms.—C.
[7] By the population returns of 1881 the numbers stand thus:—
Inhabitants of Lancashire 3,454,441
Middlesex 2,920,485
Yorkshire................. 2,880,564

that year, an abstract was made of all the certificates of the number of able and unable men within the shires of England and Wales, the total number of able men in England being returned at 202,004. The Lancashire muster, of which the following is a copy, was in August, 1574:—

MUSTER OF SOLDIERS IN THE COUNTY OF LANCASTER IN 1574. [1]

"The numbers of demy-lances, horses, geldings for light horsemen, armo^r, munition and weapons put in Readiness wthin the County of Lancaster, as well by force of the statute as granted of good Will, by persuasion of the Commissioners of the general musters. And of the particular names and surnames of them wch do furnish, have and keep the same for her Mat^{ies} Srvice wch were Certified into her Hon. Privy Council, conjoined wth the general musters by force of the First and Second Commissions of the said musters the month of August 16th Eliz. Reginæ."

HUNDRED OF DERBY.	Demi Lances.	Light Horses.	Corslets.	Almayne Rivets or Plate-Coats.	Pikes.	Long Bows.	Sheaves of Arrows.	Steel Caps or Skulls.	Calivers.	Morions.	Bills.
These are to furnish :—											
Henry, Earl of Derby (3 lances to be horsemen)..	6	10	10	40	10	30	30	30	20	20	20
Sir Tho. Stanley, Knt	..	2	3	3	3	3	3	3			
Sir Tho. Gerard, Knt....	1	2	10	10	10	8	8		3	3	
Richard Bold, Esq.	1	2	3	3	3	3	3	3	2	2	
Tho. Butler, Esq...	..	2	3	3	3	3	3	3	3	3	
Sir John Holcroft, Knt...	..	1	1	2	2	2	2	2	1	1	
Geo. Ireland, Esq	..	2	2	2	2	2	2	2	1	1	
Henry Halsall, Esq	1	2	3	..	3	3	3	3	2	2	
Roger Bradshaw, Esq.	..	1	2	2	2	2	2	2	1	1	
Edward Tyldesley, Esq	..	1	2	2	2	2	2	2	1	1	
Edward Scarisbrick, Esq...	..	1	2	2	2	2	2	2	1	1	
Wm. Gerard, Esq	..	1	2	2	2	2	2	2	1	1	
Edw. Norrys, Esq..	..	1	2	2	2	2	2	2	1	1	
Richard Massye, Esq.	..	1	2	2	2	2	2	2	1	1	
Peter Stanley, Esq	..	1	2	2	2	2	2	2	1	1	
Henry Ecclesby, Esq...	..	1	2	2	2	2	2	2	1	1	
John Byron, Esq.	..	1	2	2	2	2	2	2	1	1	
John Moore, Esq.	..	1	1	...	1	..	..	..	...	1	
Richd. Blundell, Esq.	..	1	1	...	1	..	..	..	..	1	
John Kylshawe of Culcheth, Esq.	..	1	1	...	1	..	..	..	..	1	
Barnaby Kitchen Esq..	..	...	...	1	1	1	1	1	1	1	
John Bold, Esq	..	...	...	1	1	1	1	1	1	1	
Bartholomew Hesketh	..	...	...	1	1	1	1	1	1	1	
Mr. Langton, de Lee	..	1	1	..	1	..	..	..	..	1	
Adam Hawarden	..	1									
Richard Urmston.....	..	1									
Edmund Hulme (of Male)	..	1									
Thos. Ashton	..	...	...	1	1	1	1	1	1	1	
J. Molyneux (of Melling), Geoff. Holcroft, Rob. Blundell (Ince), Tho. Lancaster, John Rysley—same as Tho. Ashton.											
Hamlet Ditchfield	..	...	...	1	1	1	..	1	...	1	1
Humphrey Winstanley	..	...	...	1	1	1	..	1	...	..	1
John Bretherton, Tho. Molineux, John Ashton, Tho. Abrahams, Fras. Bold, Rd. Eltonhead, Rob. Fazackerley, Wm. Ashehurst, Lambert Tildesley, John Crosse, and Ellis Kigheley—the same as Humphrey Winstanley.											
Nicholas Fleeteroft to furnish	..	...	...	1	..	1	1	1	...	..	1
Richd. Holland, Wm. Naylor, Jas. Lea, Wm. Molineux, Adam Bolton, Rd. Bould, Rd. Howarde, Ralph Sekerston, Rob. Corbett, and Rd. Mosse —the same as Nicholas Fleeteroft.											
Summary for the Hundred of West Derby...	9	39	85	118	111	106	105	90	54	71	45
HUNDRED OF LEYLAND.											
Sir Tho. Hesketh, Knt., to furnish (and 2 harquebuts)...	1	2	3	3	3	3	3	3	...	2	
Edwd. Standish, Esq...	..	2	2	2	2	2	2	2	1	1	
Wm. Farington, Esq. (for goods) to furnish	..	1	..	..	..	1	1	...	1 harquebut		
Tho. Standish, Esq. (for lands) „	..	1	..	...	..	1	1	..	1 ditto		
Rd. Lathom Esq........................	...	1									
Tho. Ashall, Rob. Charnock, Rd. Ashton—same as Rd. Lathom.											
Henry Banister, Esq..	..	1	..	..	..	1	1	1	1 harquebut		
John Adlington, Esq.	...	1	...	..	..	1	1	1	1 ditto		
Peter Farington, wife of Jno. Charnock, Wm. Chorley, John Wrightington, Gilbt. Langtree, Edw. Worthington, Lawrence Worthington—same as Jno. Adlington.											

[1] Harl. MSS. Cod. 1926, foll. 5-19a.

Hundred of Leyland—*continued*.	Demi-Lances.	Light Horses.	Corslets.	Almayne Rivets or Plate-Coats.	Pikes.	Long Bows.	Sheaves of Arrows.	Steel Caps or Skulls.	Calivers.	Morions.	Bills.
Wm. Stopford	...	..	...	1	.	1	1	1			
John Butler	..		...		...	1	1	1			1
The following 47 persons, each same as J. Butler]:—											
Thomas Stanynawght, George Norres, Richard Todde, Richard Jevum, Rich. Hoghe, John Clayton, Tho. Solome, Wm. Tarleton, John Stones, John Stewerson, John Lightfoote, Wm. Forshawe, Edmunde Parker, Willm. Tayler, Henry Farington, Rich. Fore.te. Robert Cowdrye, Henry Sherd'ey, Rawffe Caterall, Thomas Sharrocke, Thomas Gellibronde, Alexander Brende, Roberte Farington, Wm. Cowper, Oliver Garstange, John Cuerdon, Robert Molyneux, Edward Hodgson, Richard Withrill, Laur. Garstange, Gilberte Howghton, James Browne, Thomas Dickonson, Laur. Finche, Vx. Thurston Hesketh, John Wakehelde, Seth Forester, James Tompson, Thomas Chisnall, Laur. Nightgall, Vx. Roberte Charnocke, Richard Nelson, James Prescote, Rich. Tompson, Robert Forster, John Lawe, Roger Brodhurste.											harquebuts
Summary for the Hundred of Leyland	1	11	5	11	11	70	70	70	10	10	49 · 4

Hundred of Blackburn.

	Demi-Lances.	Light Horses.	Corslets.	Almayne Rivets or Plate-Coats.	Pikes.	Long Bows.	Sheaves of Arrows.	Steel Caps or Skulls.	Calivers.	Morions.	Bills.
Sir Rd. Sherburne, Knt., to furnish	1	2	3	3	3	3	3	3	2	2	
John Towneley, Esq.	1	2	2	2	2	2	2	2	1	1	
Sir John Southworth, Knt.	...	2	2	2	2	2	2	2	1	1	
John Osbaldeston, Esq.		2	2	2	2	2	2	2	1	1	
Tho. Caterall, Esq.	...	1	...	...		1	1	1	...	...	1 harq.
Tho. Nowell, Esq.	...	1	...	...		1	1	1	...	...	1 ditto
Rd. Ashton, Esq.	...	1	2	2	2	2	2	2	1	1	
Jno. Talbot, Esq.	...	1	2	2	2	2	2	...	1	1	
Nicholas Banester, Esq.	...	1									
John Rishworth, Esq.	...	1									
Rd. Grymeshaw, Esq.	...	...	...	1		1	1	1	1	...	1
Tho. Walmysley, Esq., Jno. Braddyll, Esq., Hy. Towneley, Tho. Aynsworth, Nich. Parker—same as Richd. Grymeshaw.											
Alex. Houghton, gent	...	...	1	1	1	1	1	1	1	...	1
Roger Nowell, Esq.	...	...	...	1	..	1	1	1	1	...	1
Wm. Barecroft, Hy. Banester, Tho. Watson, Ilvan Heydock, Edw. Starkie, Rob. Moreton, Olin Birtwisle, Jno. Greenacre, Nicholas Hancock—same as Roger Nowell.											
Tho. Astley, to furnish	...		...	1		1	1	1	...	...	1
Tho. Whittacre, Geo. Shuttleworth, Francis Gartaide—same as Tho. Astley.											
Rob. Smith						1	1	1	...		1
[The following 70 persons to furnish same as Rob. Smith.]											
John Ashowe, Nicholas Robinson, George Seller, Nicholas Halstidd, Wm. Langton, Bryan Parker, Laurence Whitacre, John Ormrode, Rawffe Haworth, Richard Cunlyffe, Rich. Parker, Wm. Barker, Adam Bolton, George Talbot, Thomas Lassell, Thomas Isherwoode, Richard Haberiame, Wm. Starkye, Rich. Harrison, Rich. Crounlowe, Tho. Honghim, Rich. Shawe, Rich. Bawden, Alexander Lyvesaye, William Churchlowe, Rawffe Talbotte, Edwarde Carter, Rich. Woodde, Tho. Holliday, Roger Nowell, Hughe Shuttleworth, Hughe Halsted, Henry Speake, Tho. Enot, Henrie Shawe, Peter Armerode, Thomas Walmysley, Thomas Dewhurst, Olin Ormerode, John Nuttall, Gilberte Rishton, Nicholas Cunliff, Henrie Barecrofte, Laur. Blakey, John Hargreve, James Fieldes, James Hartley, Thomas Ellys, Thurston Baron, Roberte Caruen, George Elston, Barnarde Townley, Oliver Halsted, John Seller, John Pastlowe, John Whittacre, John Aspinall, Roberte Cunliff, Richard Charneley, Geffrey Ryshton, Roberte Seede, Thurstone Tompson, Richard Bawden, Tho. Osbaldeston, John Holden, Gyles Whitacre, Richard Tattersall, Roberte Smithe, Nicholas Duckesburie, William Merser.											
Summary for the Hundred of Blackburn	2	13	14	34	14	112	112	109	26	27	90

Hundred of Amounderness.

	Demi-Lances.	Light Horses.	Corslets.	Almayne Rivets or Plate-Coats.	Pikes.	Long Bows.	Sheaves of Arrows.	Steel Caps or Skulls.	Calivers.	Morions.	Bills.
John Rigmaiden, Esq., to furnish	...	1	2	2	2	2	2	2	1	1	
Cuthbert Clifton, Esq.	...	1	...	1	1	2	2	2	1	1	
John Westby, Tho. Barton, Wm. Skillicorne—same as Cuthbert Clifton.											
Richd. Traves	...	...	...	1	...	1	1	2	1	1	1
Jas. Massey, Geo. Alane—same as Rd. Travers.											

HUNDRED OF AMOUNDERNESS—continued.	Demi-Lances.	Light Horses.	Corslets.	Almayne Rivets or Plate-Coats.	Pikes.	Long Bows.	Sheaves of Arrows.	Steel Caps or Skulls.	Calivers.	Morions.	Bills.
Rob. Mageall	..	...	...	1	..	1	1	2	...	...	1
Thos. Ricson	..	...	...	1	..	1	1	2	...	...	1
Wm. Hodgkinson	...	...	...	1	1	1	1	1	...	1	1
Wm. Banester, Tho. Breres, Roger Hodgkinson, Laurence Walles— same as Wm. Hodgkinson.											
Wm. Hesketh to furnish of goodwill											
Rob. Plesington, Tho. Whyttingham, Wm. Singleton, John Veale, Evan Heydock, Wm. Burrell— same as Wm. Hesketh.				..	..	..	..	..	1	1	
Henry Kyghley		..	..	1	..	1	1	1			
Summary for the Hundred of Amounderness........	1	5	2	17	11	22	22	27	15	20	10
HUNDRED OF LONSDALE.											
Wm. Lord Monteagle ....*One to be a horse	2*	3	20	20	20	15	15	15	6	6	
Rob. Dalton, Esq.	1	1	1	2	3	3	3	3	1	1	
Fras. Tunstall, Esq. .		2	2	2	2	2	2	2	1	2	
Geo. Middleton, Esq., Roger Kirbie, Esq.—same as Fras. Tunstall.											
Wm. Fleming	..	1	1	1	1	1	1	1	1		
Tho. Carus	..	1	1	1	1	1	1	...	1	1	
Rob. Byndlowes	..	1	1	1	1	1	1	...	1	1	
Tho. Curwen—a light horse furnished.......	..	1									
Wm. Thornborowe, do. do.	..	1									
Gabriel Croft	..	...	1	1	...	1	1	1	1		
Nicholas Bnulsey	..	...	..	1	1	1	1	1	1	1	
George Southworth	..	...	..	1	..	1	1	1	1	1	
Jas. Ambrose, Wm. Redman, Marmaduke Blackburne, Anthony Knipe, Tho. Stanfilde—same as Geo. Southworth											
John Preston, Esq.	..	1	2	2	2	2	2	2	1	1	
Fras. Tunstall	..	...	..	1	..	1	1	1	1	1	
Nicholas Hudleston, Rd. Curwen, Rd. Redman—same as Fras. Tunstall.											
Edward North (or Corthe)			..	1	..	1	1	1	..	..	1
Jno. Tompson, Rob. Banz jun , John Gibson, Tho. Poker, Mr. Newton, of Whittingham, Tho. Puker,—same as Edward North [or Corthe].											
John Calvert	..	...	..	1	..	1	1	1	..	..	1
Rd. Reder, Chr. Skerrowe, Rd. Hynde, Elenor Singlet, Lee Parkinson, Chr. Thornton, John Proctor, Geoffrey Batson, Tho. Widder, Wm. Thornton, Chr. Battye—same as Jno. Calvert.											
Summary for the Hundred of Lonsdale	3	17	33	52	35	57	57	?29	25	30	13
HUNDRED OF SALFORD											
Edmund Trafford, Esq., to furnish	1	2	10	10	10	8	8	8	3	3	
Jno. Radcliffe, Esq.	1	2	3	3	3	3	3	3	2	2	
Rob. Barton, Esq..	...	2	2	2	2	2	2	2	1	1	
Rd. Holland, Esq., Fraunce Holt, Esq., John Bothe, Esq.—same as Rob. Barton.											
Edmund Prestwich, Esq., a light horse furnished	..	1									
Chr. Anderton, Rob. Worsley, Edwd. Rawstorne—same as Edmund Prestwich.											
Charles Holte, Esq.	...	1	..	1	..	..	..	..	1	1	
Edmd. Ashton, Esq	..	1	..	..	..	..	..	..	1	1	
Wm. Hilton, Esq., Jas. Browne, Esq., Ralph Ashton, Esq, T. Greenhalghe, Esq, Alexr. Barlowe, Esq.—same as Edmund Ashton											
John Orrell, Esq.	..	1	1	1	1	1	..	..	...	1	1 Harq.
George Halghe............			..	..	1	1	1	1	..	1	1
Jas. Bradshaw, Allen Hilton, Edmd. Heywood, Roger Browne, Rd. Leaver, Geo. Longworth—same as Geo. Halghe											
Bradshawe of Bradshawe			..	..	1	1	1	1	..	..	1
Alexr. Warde, Wm. Holland, Tho. Mascie, Rob. Holte, Chas. Radcliffe, Edw. Butterworthe, Cuthbert Schofild, Arthur Ashton, Tho. Lees, Jas. Ashton, Geo. Gregory, Ellis Aynsworth, Tho. Crompton—same as Bradshawe.											
Geo. Pylkinton to furnish	...	..	1	..	..	..	..	..	1	1	
Jas. Hulme	..	..	..	1	..	1	1	1	1	1	1
Rd. Radcliffe	..	..	..	1	..	1	1	1	1	1	1
Tho. Chatterton	..	..	..	1	..	2	2	2	1	1	1
Dane Eliz. Biron	...	..	..	1	..	2	2	2	...	1	1
Wm. Tatton, Esq.	..	..	1	..	..	1	1	1	1	1	1
Adam Hill			..	1	..	1	1	1	..	..	1

HUNDRED OF SALFORD—*continued.*	Demi-Lances	Light Horses	Corslets	Almayne Rivet or Plate-Coats	Pikes	Long Bows	Sheaves of Arrows	Steel Caps or Skulls	Calivers	Morions	Bills
Tho. Ashton				1	...	1	1	1	1	1	1
Morris Ashton				1	...	1	1	1	1	1	1
Wm. Radcliffe		..		1	..	1	1	1	1	...	1
Laur. Tetlowe, Wm. Hyde, Rob. Hyde, Ralph Holme, Tho Byron, Rob. Holme, Tho. Willott, Alex. Rigbie,—same as Wm. Ratcliffe.											
John Sharples				...	1	1	1	1	..		1
John Marten, John Bradshawe, Edwd. Hopkinson, Wm. Brown, Hugh Westmough, Edmd. Brodhurst, Roger Hymlley, Geo. Lathom, Tho. Valentyne, John Parr, Otes Holland, Edmd. Seeadie, Hy Tonge, Robert Hodge, Jno. Nowell, Ralph Cowoppe, James Anderton, John Robert, Rd Meadowcroft, Thos Aynsworth, Edmd. Taylor, Rob. Barlowe, John Wright, Rd. Lavesay, Hum Worthington, Tho. Buckley, Rob. Haworth, Edmd. Whytehead, Jno. Chadwick, Hy. Sledge, Ellis Chadwick, Rob. Butterworth, Peter Heywood, Roger Hoalt, Wm Bamford, Thos. Barlowe, Wife of Edwd. Symond, Roger Lay, Fras. Barlowe, Thurstan Hayner, Rob Blaguley, Anthy. Elcock, Tho. Birch, Edwd Saddell, Rob Skelmesden, Tho Nicholson, Tras. Pendleton, Humphrey Houghton, Wm. Blaguley, Geo. Birch, Geo. Prowdlove, Geo. Holland, Laur. Robinson, Nichs. Mosley,—same as John Sharples.											
Adam Hill				1	..	1	1				1
Jas. Guillame, Jas Chetame, Edw. Holme,—same as Adam Hill.											
The Town of Manchester were contented of goodwill to furnish and have in readiness				6	...	6		...		2	2
Summary for the Hundred of Salford	2	24	30	58	28	118	118	123	33	35	97
Sum of all the furniture within County of Lancaster	18	108	159	224	213	490	490	490	163	173	305

Men furnished by the Statute, and of goodwill, the number of 1230.

The total number of men, both by statute and voluntary contribution, for the county of Lancaster is here stated to be 1,230. Their arms, armour and furniture are stated above; but the following table will show the contribution thereto of each hundred in every kind of weapon and armour, though there are some slight discrepancies between the aggregate of the items and the totals given in the summary:—

	Derby.	Leyland.	Blackburn.	Amounderness.	Lonsdale.	Salford.	Total.
Demi-Lances	9	1	2	1	3	2	18
Light Horses	39	11	13	5	16	24	108
Corslets	85	5	14	2	33	30	169
Coats of Plate, &c.	118	14	34	17	52	58	293
Pikes	111	14	14	11	35	28	213
Long Bows	106	70	112	22	62	118	490
Sheaves of Arrows	106	70	112	22	62	118	490
Steel Caps or Skulls	90	70	109	27	59	123	490
Calivers	54	10	26	15	25	33	163
Morions	71	10	7	20	30	36	174
Bills	45	49	90	10	13	97	305

A CERTIFICATE of a general Muster taken within the County of Lancaster in August aforesaid, 16th Eliz. Reg. (1574), wherein was certified, over and beside the 1,230 men furnished by force of the Statute for armours, the number of 2,375 able men furnished by the countrey [which be armed]; and also the number of 2,415 able men to serve her Majestie, and which be unarmed. [Total, 6,020.]

HUNDRED OF [WEST] DERBY.

Archers, being able men furnished by the country with bows, arrows, steel caps, sword, and dagger... 140 ⎫ 564
Bill men, being able men furnished by the country with jack, sallet, bill, sword, and dagger .... 424 ⎭

Archers, being able men unfurnished .... 140 ⎫ 530
Bill men, being able men unfurnished .... 390 ⎭

HUNDRED OF LEYLAND.

Archers, being able men furnished by the country with bows, arrows, steel caps, sword, and dagger ...　59 ⎫
Bill men, being able men furnished by the country with jack, sallet, bill, sword, and dagger ....　200 ⎬ 259
Archers, being able men unfurnished ....　40 ⎫
Bill men, being unfurnished ....　90 ⎬ 130

HUNDRED OF BLACKBURN.

Archers, being able men furnished by the country with bows, arrows, steel caps, sword, and dagger ...　126 ⎫
Bill men, being able men furnished by the country with jack, sallet, bill, sword, and dagger ....　251 ⎬ 377
Archers, being able men unfurnished ....　20 ⎫
Bill men, being able unfurnished... ....　402 ⎬ 422

HUNDRED OF LONSDALE.

Archers, being able men furnished by the country with bows, arrows, steel cap, sword, and dagger ...　112 ⎫
Bill men, being able furnished by the country with jack, sallet, bill, sword, and dagger .. ..　344 ⎬ 456
Archers, being able men unfurnished ....　76 ⎫
Bill men, being able unfurnished...　267 ⎬ 343

HUNDRED OF AMOUNDERNESS.

Archers, being able men furnished by the country with bows, arrows, steel cap, sword, and dagger ..　108 ⎫
Bill men, being furnished by the country with jack, sallet, bill, sword, and dagger ....　152 ⎬ 260
Archers, being able unfurnished ....　120 ⎫
Bill men, being able unfurnished...................................... ....　459 ⎬ 579

HUNDRED OF SALFORD.

Archers, being able men furnished by the country with bows, arrows, steel cap, sword, and dagger ...　60 ⎫
Bill men, being able furnished by the country with jack, sallet, bill, sword, and dagger ....　294 ⎬ 354
Archers, being able unfurnished ....　72 ⎫
Bill men, being able unfurnished..　309 ⎬ 381

Sum ⎰ Sum Total of the men furnished with arms at the charges of the country ....　2375
　　⎱ Sum Total of the able men, and being unarmed, certified in this general muster ....　2495
　　　　　Under that there was certified, also of labourers or pioneers unarmed.........　600

This return is sufficiently interesting to give in a more intelligible form, though here again there are discrepancies between the sum of the hundreds and the totals given in the text.

Hundred.	Archers.		Billmen.		Soldiers.		Total.
	Furnished.	Unfurnished.	Furnished.	Unfurnished.	Furnished.	Unfurnished.	
Derby	140	140	429	390	569	530	1099
Leyland..................	59	40	200	90	259	130	389
Blackburn..............	126	20	251	402	377	422	799
Lonsdale	112	76	344	267	456	343	799
Amounderness........	108	120	152	459	260	579	839
Salford	60	72	294	309	354	381	735
Total for the county	605	468	1670 .	1917	2275	2385	4660

In the same year that these returns were made, a declaration was promulgated of the ancient tenth and fifteenth chargeable throughout the county, of which the following is a summary :—

[Harl. MS. Cod. 1926.]

" A Declaration of the Ancient Tenth and Fifteenth chargeable within the county of Lancaster, with a note also of the Deductions set down by Sir Peter Leighe and Sir Peter Gerrard, Knights, Thomas Kighley, Esq., and others Commissioners for the same Deductions, by virtue and force of a Commission to them directed in the twenty-fifth year of the reign of King Henry VI. (1446-7), with a note also of the remaine and declaration of the certain tenth and fifteenth now payable and chargeable through every hundred and part of the said county of Lancaster [xvi. Eliz. Reginæ, 1574].

SUMMARY.

HUNDRED.	Tenth and Fifteenth.			Deductions.			Remainder.		
	£	s.	d.	£	s.	d.	£	s.	d.
Leyland Hundred	36	10	4	5	17	8	30	12	8
Blackburn	48	8	6	11	3	0	37	5	6
Salford	48	9	4	6	15	0	41	14	4
[West] Derby	125	8	7	18	19	1	106	9	6
Amounderness	66	17	0	16	8	8	49	17	8
Lonsdale..	50	18	2	12	8	10	39	4	0

" Sum of the ancient tenth and fifteenth within the county of Lancaster, as the same is before particularly set down
　　and expressed, amounteth unto the sum of ....　£376 11 11½

" Whereof there was deducted by force of a commission under the great seal of England, directed to the commissioners
　　before named, bearing date as before, the sum of ....　71 7 3½

" And so remaineth payable to the Queen's Majesty for a tenth and fifteenth within the said county of Lancaster,
　　the sum of................................... ....,................................ ....　£305 4 8

31

This is the earliest notice on record of "the ancient tenth and fifteenth" chargeable on each hundred of the county of Lancaster. The taxes called by these names were originally the tenth and fifteenth part of the value of movable goods. They were originally assessed on each individual, but in the reign of Edward III. a taxation was made upon all cities, boroughs, and towns by compositions, and then the fifteenth became a fixed and certain amount—the fifteenth part of the then existing value of the movable property of the place.

While these financial arrangements were proceeding, the county was much agitated by religious feuds; and the ministers of religion were not only threatened with but actually exposed to the dagger of the assassin. At Manchester serious disputes occurred between the ecclesiastics of the Collegiate Church and the townsmen, induced partly by the unpopularity of the warden and partly by the lurking attachment evinced by a large portion of the people to the tenets of the Roman Catholic religion. The clergy of the church were frequently beaten by the populace, and it is recorded that in Mid-Lent, 1574, one of the preachers, a bachelor of divinity (Oliver Carter), while on his way to perform divine service at one of the parochial chapels, was assailed by one William Smith, of Manchester, who drew out a dagger and inflicted on him no less than three separate wounds.[1] In the month of November, in the same year, the Privy Council addressed a communication to Downham, Bishop of Chester, respecting the neglect of worship and of the "godlie exercises of religion" in Lancashire and Cheshire, and requiring him to furnish a list of persons refusing to attend the services of the church. The bishop's reply, which is preserved among the Harleian MSS.,[2] is dated February 1st, 1575-6. The "Certificate of the Papists" referred to does not accompany the reply, but is doubtless the one given on page 241, and is interesting as furnishing the names of the principal Roman Catholic families in Lancashire at the time.

In November, 1577, Downham, Bishop of Chester, died, and with the view of carrying on a more vigorous crusade against Romanism in its stronghold, a distinguished Lancashire puritan, William Chaderton, a native of Nuthurst, near Manchester, was appointed to succeed him. Shortly afterwards he was preferred to the wardenship of the collegiate church at Manchester, holding it *in commendam*. Almost immediately after he had entered upon possession of his new dignities he was appointed one of the Ecclesiastical Commissioners for the counties of Lancaster and Chester, whose province it was to establish the tenets of the Reformation, and prevent the inhabitants from again degenerating into Popery. As his personal friend and counsellor, Henry, Earl of Derby, was at the time residing at his house at Aldport Park, on the confines of Manchester, the bishop also fixed his abode in the town, and with the earl commenced an active opposition to Romanism. Following his example, several of the magistrates within the diocese set themselves to hunt out seminary priests, to stop their secret masses, and to imprison recusants, particularly those of the leading families, who refused adherence to the reformed religion. New and more severe measures were adopted; fines were levied against those who did not appear at Church; and this proving ineffectual, the principal offenders were ordered to be imprisoned at Halton Castle, in Cheshire. Subsequently, in December, to suit the convenience of the earl and the bishop, they were removed to Manchester, and there confined, some in the chapel built by Thomas del Bothe on Salford Bridge, which had been converted into a prison, others in the fortified residence of the Radcliffes, called The Pool, the greater number, however, being lodged in a building contiguous to the collegiate residence (the present college or Chetham Hospital) at Hunt's Bank, called the New Fleet. The open insolence of the Jesuit missionaries, who did not even dissemble the fact that their purpose was to absolve all the queen's subjects from their allegiance and obedience, giving absolution under the seal of confession, and acting in all under the direct authority of the pontiff, called forth the Act 23 Elizabeth, c. 1, "An Act to retain the Queen's Majesty's subjects to their due obedience." It declared those to be guilty of high treason whosoever should persuade subjects from their obedience to their queen and from the religion established in England, and should propose to reconcile them to the Church of Rome. Saying mass was to be punished by a fine of 200 marks; hearing it by a fine of 100 marks (with, in each case, a year's imprisonment); absence from the parish church was to be punished by a fine of £20 a month, and if continued a year two sureties of £200 each were to be given for future good behaviour. This enactment, as may be supposed, produced consternation throughout the country, and in Lancashire, the great stronghold of the Romish party, caused much ill-feeling, which now and then broke out into open violence. Abstractedly it would appear that the remedy was most severe, and fell hardly on innocent persons, and the measure has been stigmatised as an isolated and unprovoked enactment. Severe though it was, its administration was tempered with mercy, and the French historian, Rapin, has affirmed that "as long as the court

[1] Warden Herle's letter to the lord treasurer "concerning some injuries offered some of the College by Papists," dated 27th April, 1574, and printed by Strype in the *Life of Archbishop Parker*, v. iii., pp. 185-7.—C.

[2] Harl. MSS. Cod. 286, fol. 28.—C.

imagined that these men only administered the sacraments in private to those of their own religion, no notice seemed to be taken of it."[1] The urgency and necessity of the times required severe measures. Loyal subjects knew their necessity, and, with few exceptions, they were only resisted and evaded by the traitorous and disloyal.[2]

The voluminous correspondence of Dr. Chaderton, Bishop of Chester, preserved by Mr. Peck in his *Desiderata Curiosa*, extending from the year 1580 to 1586, details with considerable minuteness the proceedings of the ecclesiastical commission in the county of Lancaster during that period, and the object of which commission was to prevent the inhabitants from degenerating again into popery, as well as to punish those recusants, particularly of the leading families, who refused to adhere to the reformed religion. These objects are stated in the following

"LETTER FROM THE LORDS OF THE QUEEN'S COUNCIL TO HENRY HASTINGS, EARL OF HUNTINGTON
[*Lord-President of the North*].[3]

"1. After our right hartie comendations unto youre good lordship.

"2. Upon notice given unto her Majestie of the falling awaie in matters of religion in sundry of her subjects of good qualitie & others within the countie of Lancaster; for the avoiding of further inconveniences like to grow thereof, yf speedye redresse be not had, shee hath thought meete at this present to graunt out the ecclesiasticall commission for the diocease of Chester, directed to our verie good lords the lord archbishoppe of that province, the Earl of Darbie, your lordship, the lord bishoppe of Chester, and others; whereby you are auctorised to proceed with the saide parties soe fallen away for the reducinge of them to conformitie, or to punishe them acordinge to such direction as you shall receive by the saide commission warranted by the lawes of the realme:

"3. And forasmuch as this infection, the longer it shall be suffered to reigne the more yt will be spred & become dangerous; therefore yt behoveth that all expedition be used in the execution of the said commission; which, being presentlye sent to the earle of Darbie, her majesties pleasure is,

"4. That youre lordship, with the saide Earle of Darbie & Bishoppe of Chester, doe forthwith consider & take order for the time & place of your firste meetinge; & thereof to geve knolege unto the rest of the commissioners, that they may be readie to meete & assist you at the time & place to be appointed.

"5. And as this defection is principallie begun by sundrye principoll gentlemen of that countie, by whom the meaner sort of people are ledd and seduced; soe it is thought meter that in theexecution of the commission you begin first with the best of the said recusants. For that we suppose that the inferior people will thereby the soner be reclaymed & brought to obedience; which, in oure opinions, will be not a little furthered, yf you shall, at the place of youre assemblies, cause some learned minister to preach and instruct the saide people duringe the time of youre staye in those places.

"6. And soe referinge the care and consideration of all other thinges that maye appertaine to the furtherance of this her majesties service to the good consideration of you the Commissioners, wee bid you right hartelie farewell. From the court at None such, the x. of June, 1580.

"T. Bromley, Canc.	J. Sussex.	Ro. Leceater.	James Crofte.
W. Burgheley.	A. Warwicke.	Henry Hunsdon.	Fra. Walsingham.
E. Lincoln.	F. Bedford.	Chr. Hatton.	Tho. Wilson.

"To our verie good lord the Earle of Huntington."

This despatch is followed by two others, the first of which (June 29, 1580) directs that no question whether this ecclesiastical commission supersedes the former shall prevent them from proceeding with their duty; and the latter (July 3) directs that the penalties against the recusants for not coming to church shall be advanced, and that the chief of their number shall be imprisoned in Halton Castle, in the county of Chester, with the diet to be allowed them after the manner of the Fleet Prison in London. The next communication from the lords of the council (July 15) signifies that the queen having granted the fines laid upon certain popish recusants in Lancashire to Mr. Nicholas Annesley, and he having been obliged to take out a *distringas* on their lands and goods, the commissioners are to see that the said *distringas* is duly executed by the sheriff, and the forfeitures paid to Mr. Annesley. This is followed by a letter from Lord Burghley to Dr. Chaderton (July 23), touching the ill state of Lancashire at the time when the high commission first repaired thither, in which it is announced that the queen has sent a letter of thanks to the Earl of Derby for his zeal in endeavouring to reform the county. His lordship, at the same time, expresses his wish to obtain a proper person to whom he may entrust the care of the tenants of Manchester College; and after giving the bishop hopes that his firstfruits may be remitted, he gives him this statesman-like advice as to his behaviour both to great men and to poor: "And nowe, good my lorde, that you are once entered into the way of reformation, remember S. Paul, *tempestivè, intempestivè.* Somewhere you must be as a father, somewhere [as] a lord. For so the diversitie of your flocke will require. With the meanest sort, courtesie will serve more than argument; with the higher sort, auctoritie is a match." From a subsequent despatch (July 26) from the lords of the council to the Bishop of Chester, it appears that the people of Lancashire had much disputing about the bread of the holy sacrament—whether it should be common bread or of the wafer kind, on which point their lordships decided that the communicants in each parish should use that which they liked best till the Parliament had taken further order in the matter. To the Parliament was also referred the question whether fairs and markets should be continued on the Sabbath days or they should be discontinued. In a letter of July 31 from Sir Francis

[1] Tindal's "Rapin," v. ix. p. 620, ed. 1729.   [2] History of Samlesbury, pp. 60, 61.—C.   [3] Peck's Desid. Cur. p. 85.

Walsingham to the Bishop of Chester, the queen's resolution was communicated to deal with the recusants, and it was at the same time stated that good preachers were wanted in Lancashire.[1] In a despatch of the 29th of September, from the queen to the Bishop of Chester, his lordship and the dean and chapter are required to furnish out three light horsemen for Ireland; and, at the same time, the rectors of Wigan, Winwick, and Middleton are required by the council to furnish out three more light horsemen, being each one. Two following despatches of November 12 required that certificates of the recusants should be returned from Lancashire, if not as perfect as possible yet as perfect as they can be made. The prevailing evil of young gentlemen being educated abroad in popish countries is dwelt upon, and divers gentlemen in the diocese are required to be called before the bishop, and to give bonds for calling their children home in three months. In a communication from Edwin Sandys, Lord Archbishop of York, to William Chaderton, Lord Bishop of Chester, an account is given of an "exercise" lately held in Yorkshire, probably on account of the great earthquake of the 6th of April, 1580.

In the following year (1581) the prosecutions against the popish recusants were still more strongly pressed by the lords of the council; and Sir John Southworth, Lady Egerton, James Labourne, Esq., John Townley, Esq., Sir Thomas Hesketh, the lady of Mr. Bartholomew Hesketh, Campion the Jesuit, James Aspden, John Baxter, Richard (a priest), William Wickliffe, and Richard Massey, are mentioned as of that number, all of whom were placed in confinement, and subjected, as the correspondence sufficiently indicates, to heavy penalties and to personal privations. As is usual in times like these, pretenders to supernatural gifts were abroad in the county; and one Elizabeth Orton made no small stir by two feigned visions which she pretended to have had, and accounts of which were spread abroad amongst the Catholics and other ignorant people, to mislead the vulgar, and unsettle the minds of the well-affected. This unfortunate girl was publicly whipped (July 22), in order to extort from her a confession; and the experiment at first succeeded, but she afterwards retracted her declaration, made before the bishops and the other ecclesiastical commissioners. That confession was, however, thought too valuable to be lost, and, notwithstanding her retractation, it was publicly read in the parish church, and in other places where the fame of her visions had been divulged. In addition to Halton Castle, in the county of Chester, the new Fleet at Manchester, which had been erected specially for the purpose, was used as a prison for the recusants; and Sir John Southworth was kept in confinement there, under the wardship of Mr. Robert Worsley, of Booths, an active public officer. In the course of this correspondence, the lord president of the north (December 7) commends the design of the Bishop of Chester to live at Manchester, and wishes him to set up a lecture there, to commence every morning at six o'clock, and every evening at seven o'clock.[2] Notwithstanding all this vigilance, the lords of the council still complained to Mr. Richard Holland, high sheriff of the county (December 14), that though an Act had been passed in the last session of Parliament for all recusants to be proceeded against at the quarter sessions, yet nothing was done in Lancashire; and they required the justices of the peace to meet and cause the rural deans, ministers, and churchwardens to present all such recusants upon oath at the next quarter sessions, or, in case of neglect, to return the names of all absent justices, and other defaulters, to the Privy Council.[3]

Amongst the most distinguished of the recusants was Father Edmund Campion, the Jesuit already mentioned,[4] who openly "exhorted the queen's women to commit the like against the queen as Judith had done with commendation against Holofernes."[5] After having passed through

---

[1] Owing to the impoverishment of the Church at the time of the Reformation, and the inadequacy of the endowments of many of the benefices, there was much spiritual neglect in the parishes, and a great lack of learned men to preach the reformed doctrines. To remedy the evil, certain itinerant ministers were appointed, called King's or Queen's Preachers, whose duty it was to preach the reformed doctrines in out-of-the-way places, in this then out-of-the-way county. The office seems to have been originally instituted when the College of Manchester was dissolved in the early part of the reign of Edward VI, when the Earl of Derby, to whom the College-house and lands were transferred, was required, as a condition, to appoint and maintain four such preachers, not only to solemnise the parochial services at Manchester but to visit and preach in the several churches and chapels in the neighbourhood. The original grant was £40 a year to each. In Elizabeth's reign, and at the commencement of each succeeding reign until the crown lands were subjected to the authority of Parliament, a sum of £200 a year was voted for the payment of four preachers, either as itinerant or as officiating in poor chapelries. After that time the annual grants of Parliament were substituted for the royal bounty. The office was regulated by James I., "out of zeal to God's glory and care to the souls of many thousands of His Majesty's subjects in this county of Lancaster, there being great want of maintenance for preachers in most places of that shire." The number was continued at four, who were to preach among the impropriations subject to the appointment of the Bishop. During the Commonwealth period the amount paid was largely increased, and the form of grant was altered; but after the Restoration the original payments were re-established.—C.

[2] Dodd affirms that Bishop Chaderton gave orders to the clergy of Manchester to read prayers in the apartments where the prisoners were confined, especially at mealtimes, so that they had the pleasant alternative of taking theological nourishment with their food, or going without victuals altogether; and the more scrupulous elected to be deprived of their meals rather than endanger the health of their souls by taking in a nourishment, as they conjectured, to poison their better part.—C.

[3] The Parliament of January, 1581, declared the crime of absolving or withdrawing others from the established religion high treason, and adjudged that the penalty of saying mass should be increased to two hundred marks and one year's imprisonment; of hearing mass, to one hundred marks and imprisonment for the same period; that the fine for absence from church should be £20 a lunar month; and if extended to a year, the offender to find two sureties for his future good behaviour in £200 each; and to prevent the concealment of priests as tutors or schoolmasters in private families, every person acting in such capacity, without the approbation of the ordinary, was liable to a year's imprisonment, and the person who employed him to a fine of £10 per month. 23 Eliz. c. 1.

[4] A letter from Campion to the privy council, offering to avow and to prove his Catholic religion by disputation, before the doctors and masters of both universities, concludes in a strain worthy of an ancient martyr: "If," says he, "those my offers be refused, and my endeavours can take no place; and I, having run thousands of miles to do you good, shall be rewarded with rigor, I have no more to say, but to recommend your case and mine to Almighty God, the searcher of hearts, who send us of his grace, and set us at accord before the day of payment. To the end at last we may be friends in heaven, where all injuries shall be forgotten."

[5] Camden's "Annals Elizabeth," p. 262, edit. 1635.—C.

the counties of York and Lancaster, disseminating the Catholic doctrines, he was apprehended in London and committed to the Tower, where, by the operation of the rack, he was brought to divulge the names of the persons by whom he had been entertained, and in which number the following inhabitants of Lancashire appear: "Talbot, of ———, Esq.; Thomas Southworth, Gent.; Bartholomew Hesketh, Gent.; Mrs. Allen, Widow; Richard Hawghton, of the Park, Gent.; ——— Westby, Gent.; ——— Rygmaiden, Gent." It further appeared that he was in these places between Easter and Whitsuntide last past; and that during that time he resided in Lancashire, at Mr. Talbot's and Mr. Southworth's. On the 12th of November Campion was brought to trial in London, along with seven other persons, before Sir Christopher Wray, the lord chief justice, charged with conspiring the death of the queen's majesty, the overthrow of the religion now professed in England, and the subversion of the state. On the trial a letter was produced, written by Campion, the prisoner (in 1581), to a person of the name of Pound, a Catholic, in which the writer said, "It grieveth me much to have offended the Catholic cause so highly as to confess the names of some gentlemen and friends in whose houses I have been entertained: yet in this I greatly cherish and comfort myself, that I never discovered any secrets there declared, and that I will not, come rack, come rope." Though the prisoners, particularly Campion, defended themselves with great ability, they were all found guilty, and the Jesuit, and three of his fellow-prisoners—namely, Thomas Cotton, Robert Johnson, and Luke Finley—were executed.[1] The lords of the council, in a despatch to Henry Stanley, Earl of Derby, and William Chaderton, Lord Bishop of Chester, thanked them in the queen's name for their brisk proceedings against the recusants, and desired them to go on; thanking them also for removing such as were prisoners at Chester to the new Fleet in Salford, and expressing their sorrow that priests were lurking about the country under the name of school-masters, whom they wished to have apprehended and brought to punishment. In another despatch from the Archbishop of York to the Bishop of Chester, the bishop is required to reform Mr. Wigington, a young Puritanical minister, or, if that is not practicable, to prevent him from preaching in his diocese. The expense of supporting the recusant prisoners could not be defrayed out of the monthly forfeitures levied in the diocese on the recusants, and therefore the collection of eight-pence per week in every parish, allowed by the statute of 14 Elizabeth for the relief of other poor prisoners, was ordered by the lords of the council to be converted to this use, and letters were written to the Earl of Derby, the Bishop of Chester, and the justices of the peace in Cheshire and Lancashire (June 24, 1582), to give orders for that collection to be made forthwith. It was also ordered that Sir Edmond Trafford, the late sheriff of Chester, should pay the sum of one hundred marks, levied by way of fine in his shrievalty on James Labourne, Esq., a recusant, to Robert Worsley, keeper of the new Fleet, in Manchester, for the diet and other charges of the priests and other poor recusants in that prison. To save charges, Sir Francis Walsingham, in a letter to the Earl of Derby (June 30), requested that the most inoffensive poor recusants, as women and such like, might be discharged upon their own bonds. The collection of this parish assessment, though amounting to only eightpence weekly for each parish, appears to have been attended with great difficulty, to obviate which, Mr. Worsley transmitted a proposal to Government (Dec. 3), wherein he offered, if he might have a year's collection beforehand, to erect a general workhouse for the whole county of Lancaster, there being then none in existence. This scheme the lords of the council strongly approved, and recommended that Mr. Worsley's proposal should be acceded to, both in Lancashire and Cheshire, but the undertaking seems to have failed.

The following letter, having reference to the objections which had been urged against the weekly payment of eightpence from each parish, occurs in "Strype's Annals":—

The lords of the council to the Earl of Darby and Bishop of Chester, concerning the weekly collections to be made in his diocese for maintenance of popish recusants in prison.

After our hearty commendations to your good lordships.

Whereas, by direction from us heretofore by sundry letters written unto you, you have proceded to the levying of a certain contribution by 8d. by the week upon every parish within the diocess of Chester, levy-able by the statute of the xiv year of her majesty's reign, for the feeding and maintenance of prisoners committed to the common gaols of the counties within that diocess; which contribution not having been, sithence the stablishing of that statute, collected, and (as we have been informed) we did conceive that the same might have been gathered, and employed in the maintenance of such prisoners, as being persons dangerous to the state, and committed to safe custody, to the end they should not pervert her majesty's subjects with *popery* and disobedience; but that certain of the justices of the peace in the counties of Lancaster and Chester have been here with us, and declared unto us, that the inhabitants of either county do murmur and find themselves grieved with the payment of that contribution, as well for that the same is conceived not to be agreeable with the meaning of the statute, as that it is not indifferently laid among them in respect of the parishes, being of unequal numbers of householders; some containing many, and some but a few; and yet the tax equal, both to the great and to the less.

---

[1] According to the *Theatrum Crudelitatis Hæreticorum in Anglia*, there were executed of priests and others of the popish religion, in Queen Elizabeth's reign, from 1570 to 1517, thirty-one priests and thirteen lay-men. In Henry VIII.'s reign, from 1537 to 1543, according to the same authority, there were executed fifty-two priests, including one cardinal, nine abbots, and three priors, besides thirty-two Franciscans that died in several prisons; in addition to which, there were six laics, one of whom was Sir Thomas More, late lord chancellor, and another the Countess of Salisbury.

Upon consideration whereof, we think it not convenient to lay any charges upon her majesty's subjects more than the law may warrant, or the necessity of her majesty's service, with regard to her prerogative, may be allowed. So in case of such necessity as this is, the same tending to the benefit of her majesty and her estate, we did little expect any such disliking of the inhabitants of the said counties, as by some of the justices hath been declared unto us. And so much the less, because we never understood thereof from your lordships, and the greatest number of the best affected of the justices of those counties : who, as we are informed, did joyne with your lordships in the assessing of the said collections, of whom many have lately written unto us for the continuance thereof, shewing the benefit already grown thereby. Considering also, that by yielding thereunto, the whole diocese was to have been eased of the number of rogues, vagabonds, and masterless persons wandering and pestering the same, who, by the erecting certain houses of correction, were to have been set on work, and employed in honest and commendable arts and exercises.

And albeit upon this information upon the pretended grievance of her majesty's subjects, wee do think it convenient to have the said collection of 8d. by the week to be stayed ; yet before we could give any direction thereunto, not knowing what your lordships and the rest, by whom the same hath chiefly been dealt in by our directions, can say to the information in that behalf delivered unto us, we have thought good first to acquaint you therewith, that we might receive your answer, knowledge, and opinion thereof : which we pray you to certify with as convenient speed as you may. And so we bid your good lordships right hrtily farewel. From the court at Greenwich the 6. of July, 1583.

(Signed) THO. BROMLEY, Canc. W. BURGHLEY, A. WARWIKE, ROB. LEYCESTER, and divers more.

Lord Burghley, and the other lords of the council, in a letter (Jan. 18, 1583) to the Earl of Derby and the Bishop of Chester, thanked them in the queen's name for the pains they had taken in the examination of James Labourne, a layman, about whom they had ordered the queen's council to consider how far he might be punished for his lewd speeches, which punishment speedily ensued. Labourne, having been brought to trial, was convicted and executed, on a charge of having conspired to subvert the queen's government, and to overturn the religion of the state. The lords of the council, though not disposed entirely to liberate either Sir John Southworth or John Townley, Esq., from their confinement in the Fleet at Manchester, submitted to the Earl of Derby and the Bishop of Chester (Feb. 22) whether they might not relax the severity of their imprisonment. The expense of the prison establishment in Manchester at this time was so considerable that Mr. Worsley brought in a Bill (July 6) for the diet of sixteen recusants to the amount of six hundred and fifty pounds, which neither the fines, which were very large, nor the collections of eightpence per week from the parish, which were very small, and deemed to be illegal, were equal to pay. The justices of Lancashire, therefore (Oct. 7), made an offer of a year's contribution to meet this expense, which example the lords of the council urged the justices of Cheshire to imitate. At this time many Jesuits and other priests were abroad in the county of Lancaster, the antidote for which pest, the lord-president of the council of the north conceived, was best to be found in zealous Protestant preachers, and, in particular, he hoped a good one would be placed at Preston, which, being a central part of the county, it was desirable should be well supplied.

At the same time, Archbishop Sandys composed a monitory letter, which he addressed to Dr. Chaderton, and the other bishops of his province, urging them to take the sword and armour of the Spirit to defeat the common enemy, and to defend the faith even to blood and death. The fibres of superstition had, he said, taken deep root in the land. To these he urged them to apply the sharp sickle of God's word, to build up the walls of Jerusalem, and with all earnestness to shake down the cruelty and tyranny of Antichrist, to check the stubborn and contentious enemies of the Church with a rod of iron, and to restrain them from infecting the sound with their leprosy.[1]

An obscure letter, from Sir Francis Walsingham to the Earl of Derby (Nov. 30), communicated the fact that Mr. Cartwright, a Puritan minister, and a number of Popish rescuants, were in Lancashire, for remedy of which he recommended good preachers. In this letter it is stated that Somerville entertained the disloyal intention of assassinating the queen, and that, in order to avert the consequences of his treason, he had feigned himself to be mad, but it appeared on examination that he was not labouring under any mental distraction.

The parochial weekly collection, though yielding little revenue, was still pressed on by the lords of the council; and those gentlemen who opposed it, especially Mr. Bold, were ordered (Dec. 2) to be sent up to London, to enter into recognisances to appear before the council, as well as those who subscribed their names both for it and against it, and those who promised to join with the Earl of Derby and the Bishop of Chester, but yet forsook them. Ferdinand Stanley, Lord Strange, in order to show his zeal in the prosecution of recusants, addressed a letter of congratulation (Dec. 16) to the Bishop of Chester on the good opinion entertained of his behaviour by the lords of her majesty's council, and also on the good opinion they entertained of his father the Earl of Derby.

As a further act of grace to Sir John Southworth, the lords of the council addressed a letter to the Earl of Derby (23 Feb., 1584), the Bishop of Chester, Sir John Byron, and Sir Edmund Trafford, signifying their wish that Sir John might, at the instance of his son, have the liberty or certain walks, which he had formerly been permitted to take, but which Mr. Worsley had refused to grant him, on account of Sir John not being present at the saying of grace, and refusing to

[1] Libr. Conv. and Caius Con.

read the Bible. By another dispatch (March 22), permission was granted to Mr. Townley, a prisoner for religion at Manchester, to repair to London for medical advice, at the request of Dean Nowel, Mr. Townley's brother-in-law. In a despatch (March 22) to the Earl of Derby and the Bishop of Chester, the lords of the council signify that there being several popish priests now prisoners at Manchester, for perverting the queen's subjects from their allegiance, it is thought good that they should be tried for the same, *in terrorem*, at the next assizes; and that lay gentlemen recusants, their prisoners, be made to pay for their diet, or be put upon prison allowance. The zeal of the council against the recusants was not confined to one sex, for, in a letter (May 2) addressed by Sir Francis Walsingham to the Bishop of Chester, his lordship is desired to cause Mr. Bartholomew Hesketh's wife, a daughter of Sir John Southworth, and a busy recusant, to be apprehended. He is also desired to inquire into the reason why " Sir John Southworth is minded to disinherit his son," and to take care to prevent his so doing.[1] Robert Dudley, Earl of Leicester, in a letter to the bishop (June 5), expresses his approval of the recognisance of Sir Thomas Hesketh, and intimates his intention shortly to visit his cousin the Earl of Derby. It appears that some apology was thought necessary to be made by Her Majesty's Council to the ecclesiastical commissioners for the removal of Sir John Southworth and Mr. Townley from Manchester to London. Their lordships therefore stated to the Earl of Derby and the Bishop of Chester that these gentlemen, having paid their fines according to the late statute, could not any longer remain justly committed, and moreover that they would do less mischief in London than in Lancashire ; but that if the commissioners thought it absolutely necessary for the ends of good policy, or for their own sake, they should be sent back to Manchester. To turn the disloyalty of the subject to the advantage of the state, the lords of the council wrote to the sheriffs and justices of Lancashire, requiring the recusant gentlemen in that county to set forth certain horsemen for the queen's service, or, in lieu thereof, to pay a composition in money of twenty-four pounds for every horseman ; and the queen, whose zeal for the military service was not less active than that of her ministers, addressed a letter to the sheriff of Lancashire, ordering him to levy two hundred footmen in that county for the Irish service, without parade; the said men to be ready at three days' warning, to march under Edmund Trafford, Esq., whom she had appointed to be their captain, all furnished with calivers, corslets, bows, and halberts, to which were afterwards added swords, daggers, doublets, hose, and cassocks.

In a letter from the lords of the council (June 25, 1585) to Ferdinand Stanley, Lord Strange, the Bishop of Chester, and the justices of Lancashire and Cheshire, it is signified that several libels having been formerly published against the queen, and now a vile book (" Leicester's Commonwealth ") against Robert Dudley, Earl of Leicester, the queen cannot forbear rebuking some for their great slackness in not suppressing the former libels, and requiring them to be more diligent in taking care of this last, both the queen and they knowing the Earl of Leicester to be clear of the aspersions contained in it.

The last public letter in the series of the Chaderton MSS. is from the queen to the Bishop of Chester (Jan. 23, 1586), signifying that her majesty, being resolved to assist the Hollanders against the King of Spain[2] with a thousand horse, besides foot, and the clergy, in case the King of Spain should prevail, being in as great danger as herself, she had thought good that they should provide some of the said horse, or allow twenty-five pounds for each horse and furniture to buy them abroad—the Bishop of Chester, and his clergy in particular, to fit out as many horse as directed in the following schedule, sent with the queen's letter :—

SCHEDULE.

1. The bishoppe, 3 ; 2. The deane, 1 ; 3. The chapter, 2 ; 4. Edward Fleetwood, parson of Wigan, 1 ; 5. John Caldwell, parson of Wynwicke, 2 ; 6. Edward Ashton, parson of Middleton, 1 ; 7. John Nutter, prebendarie parson of Sefton, of Aughton, and Bebington, 1 ; 8. Rd. Gerrard, prebendary in Southwell, and parson of Stopport in Cheshire, 2—total, 13.

In the "Harleian Collection of Manuscripts"[3] in the British Museum, we find a number of original papers relating to " recusants and others," from which are made the following extracts relating to the county of Lancaster :—

PAPERS RELATING TO RECUSANTS AND OTHER RELIGIOUS CRIMINALS.

(Originals.)

Fo. 76. gñt.]

This ys the names of all the bishops doctors priests that were prisoners in the Fleet for religion synce the fyrste yere of the raygne of quene Elizabethe, A.D. 1558.

[There are 18 entries on this paper, of which the 17th is Mr. Prestwick, gentleman, 16 of December, 1562. [Fol. 7 b.

---

[1] Sir John Southworth's eldest son had become a convert to the reformed religion—an act that there was some fear would cost him his inheritance: hence the Bishop of Chester was directed to inquire into the matter, that "in case the bad father have so ill a meaynge towards his eldest and best soon, some order may be taken to stay his purpose, and to preserve the inheritaunce for its right heire."—C.

[2] Elizabeth was very slow in consenting to enter upon this expedition, for to support subjects against their sovereign appeared to her to be little less than treason against the rights of monarchs. Eventually, however, her scruples were overcome by the combined counsels of Burleigh, Walsingham, and her special favourite, Leycester.—C.

[3] Cod. 360.

Persons to be sought for.

[The names of these persons are written under each other in one column, and opposite most of the names are remarks stating the quality and condition of the person, his haunts, &c. The following appear to be Lancashire gentlemen, but there are no remarks :]

The sonne of Sr Ths. Gerrard ; Bouth, geⁿ ; Stanley, geⁿ.

[The above seem to have been suspected of implication in Babington's Plot, for under one remark is written, "whereof the servants of Babington can further shewe."]

10 Sep. 1586.

A Collection of Sundry Persons as well Priests as other ill-affected to the State.

N.B.—There is no Lancashire gentleman under this head, but in the two following, which are lists of names, and styled in the Catalogue, " Advertisements touching others," and "discovering more of the same Gang," there are these :—

Mr. Charnock of Ashby ; Mr. Hilton [Hulton] of Hilton Park ; Sr. John Ratclyffe, a daungerous Temporiser ; Burton, a Priest remayning with the wyfe of Sr. Thomas Gerott's [Gerard's] base son, being a Fleming born, and a very great harborer of the ill-fated gent. in those parts,—she remaineth for the most part at Checkerbent in the house of Ralfe Holme, a Recusant ; Mr. Standish of Standish ; Mr. Haughton of Haughton Tower ; Henry Davys, sometime very inward with Shelley. [Fol. 14.]

Names of such as are detected for receiptinge of Priests, Seminaries, c., in the County of Lancaster.

This appeareth by the presentment of Ralph Serjeant, Churchwarden of Walton in Ledale.—Jane Eyves of Fishwick, widow, receipt the Sr. Evan Banister, an old Priest ; Sr. Richard Banister, an old Priest, is receipted at the house of one —— Carter, nere to Runcorn Boat.

This appeareth by the presentment of the Vicar of Garstang.—One named little Richard receipted at Mr. Rigmaden's of Weddicar, by report.

This appeareth by the presentment of Law : Procter, sworne man of Brihilt.—One Duckson, an old priest, continueth in Samlesburye by common Report.

This appeareth by the presentments of the Curate of Burnley, and the Churchwarden of the Church.—Robt. Woodroof, a seminary Priest, receipted at the house of Jenet Woodroof of Banktop in the parish of Burnley within this half-year, by common report.

This appeareth by the presentment of the Vicar of Whalley.—John Lawe, a seminary priest, receipted in divers parts of Lancashire as specially in the parishes of Ormskirk, Preston, Blackburne, and Whalley.

This appeareth by the presentment of the Parson of Wigan :—
1. Henry Fairehurst of Winstanley, yeoman ; 2. Thomas Orrell of Winstanley, yeoman ; 3. Thomas Berchall of Billinge yeoman ; 4. James Winstanley of Billinge, yeoman ; 5. John Roby of Orrell, yeoman ; 6. Henrie Laithewaite of the Medowes, gent. ; 7. John Culchethe of Abram, gent. ; 8, 9. Myles Gerrerde of Ince, esquire, and his wyfe.

These Persons are presented (by great and Common fame and reporte) to be receipters of Priests hereafter named, viz.—
Bell ;   Burton ;   Mydelton ; Alex. Gerrard, brother to Miles Gerrard of Innce, esquire ; James Foord, son to Alex. Fourd of Swindley, gent. ; John Gardner, brother to Robt. Gardner of Aspull, gent. ; Alex. Markland, son to Matthew Markland of Wigan ;   Pilkington, born in Standish Parish ;   Worthington, born in the same parish ; Stopforth.

This appeareth by the presentment of the Curate of Chippin.—Guile, a Priest receipted at the house of James Dewhurst of Chippin by the report of John Salesburie of Chippin.

This appeareth by the presentment of the Vicar of Deane.—Divers Priests harboured at the house of Ralphe Holme of Checkerbent.

This appeareth by the presentment of the Curate of Sephton.—James Darwen, a seminary priest, receipted at the house of Richard Blundell of Crosby esquire by common report.

This appeareth by the presentment of the Vicar of Kirkham.—Richard Cadocke, a seminary priest, also Diev. Tytmouse, conversant in the company of two widows, viz., Mistress Alice Clyfton and Mistress Jane Clyfton, about the 1st of October last, 1580, by the report of James Burie.

This also appeareth by the presentment of the Vicar of Kirkham.—Richard Brittain, a priest receipted in the house of William Bennet of Westby, about the beginning of June last, from whence young Mr. Norrice, of Speke, conveyed the said Brittain to the Speke, as the said Bennet hath reported.
The said Brittain remayneth now at the house of Mr. Norrice, of the Speke, as appeareth by the deposition of John Osbaldston (by common report).

Fo. 32 b.—This appeareth by the presentment of Tho. Sherples.—James Cowper, a seminary priest, receipted, relieved, and maintained at the lodge of Sr. John Sowthworthe, in Samlesburie Park, by Mr. Tho. Sowthworth, one of the younger sons of the said Sr. John. And at the house of John Warde, dwellings in Samblesburie Park side. And the said priest sayeth mass at the said lodge and at the said Warde's house. Whither resorte Mr. Sowthworthe, Mistress Ann Sowthworth, John Walmesley, servante to Sr. John Sowthworthe, Tho. Sowthworthe, dwelling in the Park, John Gerrerde, servant to Sr. John Sowthworthe, John Singleton, John Wrighte, James Sherples junior, John Warde of Samblesburie, John Warde of Medler the elder, Henry Potter of Medler, John Gouldon of Winwick, Thomas Gouldon of the same, Robt. Anderton of Samblesburie, and John Sherples of Stanleyhurst, in Samblesburie.

This appeareth by the presentment of Tho. Sherples.—At the house of William Charnocke of Fulwood, gent., was a Mass done on our Lady Day in Lent last by one Evan Bannister, and these persons were at it:—William Harrison of Fulwood and his wife, Richard Harrison and his wife, James Sudale of Haighton, Thomas Sudale and his wife, George Berley and his wife, Jeffraye Wirdowe of Owes Walston and his wife.

This also appeareth by the presentment of Tho. Sherples.—At the house of James Sherples in Samblesburie was a Masse done on Candlemas Day by one Henry Dueson, alias Harry Duckeson, and these persons were at it:—John Sherples of Stanleyhurst in Samblesburie and his wife, and his son Thomas and his daughter Ann, and Rodger Sherples and his wife, and Richard Sherples, and the wife of Harry Sherples, and the wife of Hugh Welchman, and Thomas Harrisson and the wife of Thomas Welchman the elder, the wife of John Chitome, Robt Blackehay, Thomas Duckesson of Houghton, James Duckeson, the wife of Harrie Bonne.

Fo. 33. At the lodge in Samblesburie Parke, there be masses daily and seminaries, diverse resorte thither, as James Cowpe Harrison Bell, and such like. The like unlawfull meetings are made daily at the house of John Warde, by the Park side of Samblesburie, all whiche matters, masses, resorte to masses, receiptinge of seminaries, will be justified by Mr. Adam Sowtheworthe, Thomas Sherples, and John Osbaldston.

Diocese of Chester.

Com. Lanc. Amounderness Deanery.	Cuthbe Clifton (of Clifton), Esq. John Westone, Esq. Alexander Houghton (of Hoghton), gent. Leonard Houghton and his wife Mres ——— Burton, widow Thomas Burton, her son Wm. Skellicorne (of Prees in Kirkham), gent., and his wife (Jane daughter of Thos. Houghton of Hoghton). Bridgett Browne, widow Garge Clarkson, gent. John Hotherall, gent. Thomas Dicconson (of Ecclesto), gent.		Com. Lanc. Blackburn Deanery.	Ellen Bannister, wife of Robte Banester, gent. Anne Townley, wife of Henrie Townley, gent. Jenet Paslowe, wife of Francis Paslowe, gent. John Rishton, gent. John Rishton, husbandman Randle Ferrand Richard Wodde Richard Hinley

Obstinate   Willm. Hesketh (of Aughton), gent.
              George Walton, gent.
              Thomas Coston (? Croston) and his wife
              Wm. Hardock (? Haydock), junior, and his wife
              Wm. Easton, gent.
              John Singleton (of Stayning), gent.
              George Houghton, gent.
              James Eues
              Richard Eues
              George Butler
              John Hothersall, husbandman
              Thomas Walmesley
              Rogerson, widow, and her children
              Robte Midgeall, gent.

Conformable   Arthur Houghton, gent.
              Wife of George Sothworthe, gent.
              George Copell, gent., and his wife
              Thomas Cowell
              Thomas Cradon

*   *   *
Conformable   Wm. Rishton, gent., and his wife
                     Ellen Rishton, widow
                     Gilbert Rishton, gent., and his wife
                     Lun. Whittacre, gent.
*   *   *

Warrington Deanery
                     Hamlet Holcrofte (of Little Wolden), gent., and his wife
                     Dame Margaret Atherton, widow
                     Tho. Mollinex, gent.
                     Matthewe Travys
                     John Mollinex, "schalerner"
Obstinate   Elizabeth Hesketh, widow
                     Eliz. Sutton, widow
                     Eliz. Kighley, gone
                     Stanley, widow, and Anne her daughter
                     One Bineston, her servant
                     Wm. Fletcher
                     Kat. Marsh, wife of Humfrey Marsh
                     Henry Richardson
Conformable   Edward Chawner (? Challenor)

Blackburn Deanery
              John Sothworth (of Samlesbury), Knt., and
                  the lady (Mary, daughter of Sir Richd.
                  Assheton of Middleton) his wife
              Thomas Sothworth, his son and heir
              John Sothworth, gent., sonne to John Soth-
                  worth, Knt.
              Anne Sothworth, his daughter
              Dorothie Sothworth, his sister
              John Talbott, Esq.
              John Townley, Esq., and his wife
              Tho. Catherall, Esq., and his wife
              Henrie Lowe, junior
              Margaret Lowe, widow
Obstinate   James Hargreues
              Lucie Townlie
              John Yate, son to John Townley, Esq.

Manchester Deanery
                     Wm. Hulton (of the Park), Esq., and his wife, obstinate

[Several names follow, belonging to the county of Chester, after which are—]
Com. Lanc.   † John Sothworth (of Samlesbury), Knt.
Item.   † Cuthbert Easton, Esq.
                     † John Talbot (of Basball), Esq.
                     † John Townley (of Townley), Esq.
                     † Thom. Caterall (of Caterall and Little Mitton), Esq.
                     † Alexander Houghton (of Hoghton), gent.
                     † Thomas Mollinex, gent.
                     † John Hothersall (of Hothersall), gent.
                     † Matthewe Travis, yeoman
Com. Cest.   John Whitmor, Esq.
                     Wm. Houghe, Esq.

Of all the rest these twelve[1] are in or opinions of longest obstinacy against Religion, and if by your Lordships' good wisdomes they could be reclaymed we think the other wold as well follow their good example in embrasinge the Queen's Majesty's most godly proceeding as they have followed their evil example in "contemprisinge" their duty in that behalf.

Indorsed—Feb. 9th [or 7th], 1575.

In the Elizabethan age, when taxation had not attained its present perfection, the counties were called upon to supply their monarch with the substantial viands which graced even the breakfast table of her majesty. [2] The county of Lancaster, by an agreement entered into at Wigan

[1] There are only eleven names here.

[2] EXPENSES OF QUEEN ELIZABETH'S TABLE.

The Queen's Majesty booke signed with her hand.

BREAKFAST.

		The Queen's Majesty's diet, as she hath been daily served.	
Cheat and mancheat	6d.	Cheat and mancheat, 8	8d.
Ale and beer	3½d.	Ale and beer, 6 gallons	10½d.
Wine, 1 pint	7d.	Wine, 1 pint	7d.
Flesh for Pottage.		*Flesh for Pottage.*	
Mutton for the pot, 3 st.	18d.	Mutton for the pot, 4 st.	2s.
Long bones, 2 st.	6d.	Long bones, 4 st.	12d.
Ise bones, 2 st.	2d.	Ise bones, 3 st.	3d.
Chines of Beef, 1 st.	16d.	Chines of beef, 1 st.	16d.
Short bones, 2 st.	4d.	Chines of mutton, 2 st.	2s.
		Short bones, 1 st.	2d.
Chines of beef, 1 stone	14d.	Chines of veal, 3 st.	6d.
Conies [rabbits] 2 stone	8d.	Chickens for gruel, 2	7d.
Butter, 6 dishes	6d.	Veal, 2 stone	2s.
		Chines of beef, 1 [? stone]	16d.
		Butter, 2 lb.	8d.
Sum...... 8s. 6½d. (rather 7s. 8½d.)		Sum...... 13s. 11½d.	
Surcharged...... 5s. 5d.		ELIZABETH R.	

by the Earl of Derby, the Bishop of Chester, Lord Strange, and a number of the justices of the peace there assembled, compounded, on behalf of the inhabitants of the county, for the provision of oxen and other cattle for Her Majesty's household; and Sir Richard Shirburn and Alexander Rigby, Esq., on their resort to London during the ensuing term, were authorised to ratify the agreement with "Mr. Treasurer, Mr. Controwler, and Mr. Cofferer," with whom it was agreed that the county of Lancaster should yield yearly for that purpose forty great oxen, at fifty-three shillings and fourpence apiece, to be delivered at her majesty's pasture at Crestow. This grave matter being adjusted, the following award was made from each hundred, in ratification whereof the undersigned affix their hands:—

[West] Derby Hundred, £26; Amounderness, £16 10s.; Lonsdale, £16 10s.; Salford, £16 10s.; Blackburn, £16 10s.; Leyland, £8. Total, £100.—If the sum shall come to more or less, the same to be increased or abated after this rate.

	H. Derby.	W. Cestr.	Fer. Strange.	
Richard Shirburne	Richard Brereton	James Ashton	Christopher Anderton	Tho. Eccleston
John Byron	Richard Holland	Edw. Tyldesley	Robert Worsley	Nicholas Banester
John Radcliffe	Wm. Farington	Richard Ashton	Robert Langton	John Bradley

For the Provision of Oxen for the Queen's Majesty's Household.

These contributions, which were reduced to a money charge, having subsequently fallen into arrear, a purveyor was sent down by the government to execute the commission by seizing the oxen in the county; but the Earl of Derby, aided by his treasurer, took order for enforcing the payment of the composition, and in any case where the money could not be had the commissioners were directed to take in lieu thereof, "for her mate provision, Bacon, and such lyke thinges."[1] The exactions of these purveyors "for her majesty's household and stables" had become so notorious, that in the year 1590 a commission was instituted in Lancashire to investigate these delinquencies, and to certify the same to the queen's government.

A manuscript book of correspondence relating to the lieutenancy of the county of Lancaster, from the year 1582 to the end of Queen Elizabeth's reign, is deposited in the Harleian Collection in the British Museum,[2] and serves to show with how much diligence the affairs of the queen were administered during that period. These documents, though many of them highly interesting, and calculated to shed much light upon the early history of the county, are too voluminous to be comprised in the limits of a county history, and can therefore only be interwoven into the general history in abstract. In Folio 54 of this manuscript a despatch appears from the lords of the council, signed Tho. Bromley, Canc. E. Lyncoln, R. Leicester, W. Myldmaye, F. Bedford, Chr. Hatton, J. Crofte, Wm. Burghley, F. Walsingham, R. Sadler, addressed "to the justices of the peace inhabiting within the hundred of Salford," apprising them that her majesty's service in Ireland requires to be supplied with fifty soldiers from this county, and directing that the levies be made, so that the men may be at Liverpool ready to embark on the 15th of December, prepared with such arms and accoutrements as are necessary for their complete equipment, or that the sums necessary for that purpose be forthcoming. The number of men to be provided from the respective hundreds in the following quotas:—

"Men to be made forth of these hundreds following: Derby hundred, 10½ men; Lonsdale, 9½ men; Salford, 9 men—£38 6s.; Blackburn, 9½ men; Amoundernes, 7 men; Leylond, 4½ men. Total 50."

On the receipt of this mandate a letter was addressed by "Ric Holland, Vic." from Heaton House, summoning Sir Edmund Trafford, and the other justices of the county, to meet at Ormskirk, on Saturday, 1st of December (1582), to take the necessary order for carrying her majesty's commands into effect.[3]

This series of official documents illustrates the correspondence contained in the Chaderton MS., and here we find the proceedings adopted against the recusants, as detailed in a despatch of the 20th of June, wherein the sheriff and justices of the county of Lancaster are directed to proceed against the principal offenders, forbearing for the present to prosecute those of the meaner sort, but to call before them, at their quarter sessions, recusants being of the quality of gentlemen and upwards, and ladies and gentlewomen widows, and to take bonds and securities of them for their personal appearance at the next assizes for the county of Lancaster, that conviction and judgment may ensue. To guard against remissness in the discharge of this duty, they are warned to take care to answer her majesty's expectations, and the trust committed unto them, seeing that the judges of assize had received directions to examine and take account of their doings, and to report the same in writing to the council.

In the following year (1583) her majesty's service in Ireland required that Lancashire, instead

---

[1] Codex 1926. See also Mr. Harland's Lancashire Lieutenancy under the Tudors, c. (vols. 49 and 50 of the Chetham Society's series).

[2] Ibid.

[3] Cod. 1926, fo. 72 b.

of fifty, should send two hundred able-bodied men to that country, to be in readiness to meet at Chester on the 10th of September, to embark from thence for Ireland.[1] To obviate a complaint that had been made to the queen and her council, to the effect that the men, when placed under the command of strangers, were not treated with "that love and care" that appertained to them, her majesty, by her letters, recommended that they should be placed under the son of Sir Edmund Trafford, and that they should be furnished with "swords and daggers, and likewise convenient doublets and hose, and also a cassock, or some motley or other sad green colour or russet." The hundred of Salford furnished one-fourth of the whole number, and the letter of Sir Thomas Preston, summoning the levy to muster at Preston, required that they should come provided with weapons as follows : "20 wth calivers, 10 wth corslet and pikes, 10 wth bows and arrows, and 10 wth halberds or good black bills." The urgency of the occasion is strongly indicated by the superscription of the letter, which runs thus : "Deliver this Letter to the next justice of peace of the hundred aforesaid, and he to break it open, and aft^r the perusal thereof to be sent from one justice to another, that no delay be in the service wthin contained."[2]

In the year 1585-6 the county was visited by a famine and by a murrain amongst cattle, which was felt with great severity in the north; and her majesty, in her royal solicitude, directed the lords of the council to address a letter to the sheriff and justices of the peace in the counties of Lancaster and Chester,[3] requiring that the gentry of those counties should strictly abstain from killing and eating flesh in the time of Lent, and other prohibited days, not only from the effect that the abstinence of their own families would produce, but from the benefit of the example amongst those of a meaner sort. These orders were addressed to the sheriff of Lancashire by the lords of the queen's council, and were generally diffused throughout the county.

The violation of the Sabbath had long been complained of in Lancashire, and one of the objects of the ecclesiastical commission sent down by Queen Elizabeth into this county was to remedy these enormities. For the same purpose a letter was promulgated by the magistrates of the county signed by Jo. Byron, James Asshton, Edm. Hopwood, Robte Worsley, Ric. Shirborn, Bryan Parker, Th. Thalbotte, Tho. Talbot, Edm. Trafforde, Ric. Brereton, John Bradshawe, J. Wrightington, Nicholas Banester, Ric. Asshton, Alex. Rigbie, and Edm. Fleetewoode.

The complaint was, that the Sabbath was profaned by "Wakes, fayres, markettes, bayrebayts, bull baits, Ales, Maygames, Resortinge to Alehouses in tyme of devyne service, pypinge and dauncinge, huntinge and all maner of vnlaw^{ll} gamynge." For reformation whereof it was ordered to give in charge at the quarter sessions to all mayors, bailiffs, and constables, as well as to other civil officers, churchwardens, &c., to suppress by all lawful means the said disorders of the Sabbath, and to present the offenders at the quarter sessions that they might be dealt with for the same according to law. It was also directed that the minstrels, bearwards, and all such disorderly persons, should be immediately apprehended and brought before the justices of the peace, and punished at their discretion ; that the churchwardens should be enjoined to present at the sessions all those that neglected to attend divine service upon the Sabbath Day, that they might be indicted and fined in the penalty of twelve-pence for every offence ; that the number of alehouses should be abridged, that the ale-sellers should utter a full quart of ale for a penny, and none of any less size, and that they should sell no ale or other victuals in time of divine service ; that none should sell ale without a licence ; that the magistrates should be enjoined not to grant any ale-licence but in public sessions ; and that they should examine the officers of the church and of the commonwealth to learn whether they made due presentment at the quarter sessions of all bastards born or remaining within their several precincts ; and that thereupon a strict course should be taken for the due punishment of the reputed parents according to the statute ; as also for the convenient keeping and relief of the infants.[4]

This rigid moral discipline was much complained of by some of the gentry, and still more by the labouring classes ; and when, at a subsequent period, King James, in his progress, visited the county of Lancaster, he not only rescinded the orders but he founded upon that Act his book of Sabbath sports, the consequence of which was felt for succeeding ages. But of this more in its proper place.

The plots against the queen, and against the established Protestant Church of England, both foreign and domestic, awakened in the nation a spirit of fervent loyalty; and an association of Lancashire gentlemen, on the model of the Earl of Leicester's association, was formed for the defence of Queen Elizabeth against the machinations of Mary Queen of Scots and the other enemies of the state. In the declaration promulgated by this association[5] the doctrine of the divine right of kings and queens is strongly insisted upon, and the associators pledged themselves in the most solemn manner to defend the queen against all her enemies, foreign and domestic, in confirmation of which they took a solemn oath upon the holy Evangelists, and in witness whereof they affixed their hands and seals as follows :—

[1] Harl. MSS. cod. 1926, fo. 103 b.
[2] The ancient practice of England was not only to permit but absolutely to require that every able-bodied freeman under sixty years of age should be taught the use of arms and enjoined to keep his arms and armour ready for use, and in accordance with the provisions of the statute 33 Henry VIII., c. 9, butts were provided in every tithing, village, and hamlet, for shooting, at times convenient. The cross-bowmen and harquebussiers of Lancashire were long the pride of the English army, and the high character borne by these stalwart soldiers in fight, as well as the close proximity of their county to Ireland and Scotland, led to frequent and heavy levies upon the flower of the peasantry during the disturbed period of Elizabeth's reign, for the purpose of putting down the rebellion in Ireland, resisting the incursions of the Scots, or guarding the kingdom against the threatened invasions of the Spaniards.—C.
[3] A letter of similar import addressed by the queen to the sheriff of Lancashire is contained in the Chaderton MSS.
[4] Harl. MSS. cod. 1926, fol. 80.
[5] Harl. MSS. cod. 2219.

Hen. Derby	Adam Langhe	Willm. Massye	John Grenalghe
W. Cestren :	Robt. Charnocke	Edward Tarbucke	Henry Banestr
Fer. Stranghe	Richard Ormeston	Peter Stanley	Nycholas Banestr
Rychard Sherburne	Willm. Holton	Thomas Talbott	Thomas Lancaster
John Radclyffe	William Thorneborowe	John Bradley	Rychard Eltonheade
Thomas Houghton	Edward Stanley	John Culcheth	Robt. Holt
Edward Butler	Edmund Chaderton	John Ryahley	Edward Chaderton
Rychard Ashton	Gilbt. Langtree	George Ireland	Frances Tunstall
Edward Norres	John Croft	Charles Holt	Willm. Skillicorne
Thomas Holcroft	Thomas Leighe	Thomas Goodlowe	Edmund Prestwiche
Edward Osbaldeston	Edward Braddle	Thomas Morley	John Singleton
Rychard Holland	John Wrightington	Thomas Ashton	Henrye Butler
Rychard Boolde	Edward Rawstorne	Alexander Barlowe	Thomas Brockholes
Edward Scaresbrecke	James Browne	Fraunces Holt	John Massye
Thomas Hesketh	Barnabie Kilchin	James Ashton	William Redman
John Holcroft	Edward Halsall	Henry Eccleston	Alen Holton
Richard Mollineux	Edward Tildisley	Alexander Rigbye	Willm. Kirbye
Rauffe Ashton	Henry Stanley senior	James Anderton	William Radclyffe
Robt. Langton	Willm. Farrington	Barth. Hesketh	Edward Worthington
Myles Gerrard	Henry Stanley	Lawrence Ireland	Thomas Woofall
Willm. More	John Byrome	Thomas Lathome	

In this list of loyal and patriotic Lancashire men occur the names of many who still adhered to the ancient faith, a circumstance that would seem to justify the boast sometimes made by Roman Catholics of the loyalty of their forefathers to a Protestant queen on the approach of the Spanish Armada. Undoubtedly many of them were faithful to the crown, and it is not less certain that the best of the old Catholic peers and gentry were out in the Armada year; but there was a special feature of this eventful period that must not be overlooked in considering the forces which then disturbed the kingdom. There were at the time two parties in the Roman Church, both of them the objects of popular distrust, though each had very different aims in view. There was the English Catholic, who, while bent upon destroying the government of the queen, was yet loyal to the queen herself, though his loyalty was often sorely tempted by intriguing ecclesiastics; and there was the Roman Catholic whose disloyalty was stimulated and encouraged by Jesuits and other foreign emissaries, who, resolved upon subverting the religion and liberty of England, had prevailed with their disciples to accept a foreign purpose and a foreign prince. The former reverenced Rome as the oldest of the Latin sees, but he was proud of his English birth, and loving his country as other men loved it, was prompt to march when a foreign enemy threatened to profane its soil; he clung to ancient forms, and was desirous of seeing them restored, but he was in every other sense an Englishman, and imbued with the grand old spirit of patriotism which recoiled with aversion from an act that would imperil the greatness or welfare of his fatherland. Whilst the latter was only English in name, Spain was his only country, and Philip his only king and the Roman Church, if the Pope was its head and his cardinals its officers, was undoubtedly with him in abetting the Spaniard in his projected invasion. Many of the Catholics acted traitorously towards their country, and were ready to go to any extreme of perfidy and treason if only they could thereby serve the church; but it should also be remembered that there were very many among them who, amid the social disabilities and persecutions to which they were subjected, never wavered in their patriotism or in their loyalty to the crown.

Upon this declaration of loyalty an Act of Parliament was framed, by which, after reciting that sundry wicked plots had lately been devised and laid, as well in foreign parts as within this realm, to the great endangering of her majesty's royal person, and for the utter ruin and subversion of the commonwealth, it was ordained, that if at any time, after the end of the then present session of Parliament, any open invasion or rebellion should be had or made of her majesty's dominions, or any act attempted leading to the hurt of her majesty's royal person, by or for any person that shall or may pretend title to the crown of this realm, or if anything be compassed or imagined tending to the hurt of her majesty's royal person, by any person, or with the privity of any person that shall or may pretend title to the crown, then, by her majesty's commission under her great seal, the lords and others of her majesty's privy council, and such other lords of Parliament, to be named by her majesty, as with the said privy council shall come up to the number of twenty-four at the least, shall, by virtue of this Act, have authority to examine all such offences, and thereupon to give sentence or judgment as upon proof shall appear to them meet.

Mary Queen of Scots had long been a prisoner in England; and it requires no sagacity to perceive that this Act was passed specially to bring her and her adherents to trial before a new species of tribunal. The occasion was not long wanting. The conspiracy, formed in the year 1586, by Anthony Babington, a young man of fortune, residing at Dethick, near Winfield, in Derbyshire, where Mary was then a prisoner, and which had for its object to assassinate Elizabeth, and to elevate Mary to the throne of England, followed so speedily upon the passing of the new Act as to raise the surmise that the plot had been arranged to promote the interest of Mary's enemies, rather than to advance her cause. Babington found little difficulty in organising a band of assassins. At the head of these fanatics stood John Savage, a man of desperate courage, who wished to monopolise the glory of despatching the heretical queen; next in order followed Babington himself, and he had associated with him Barnwel, a man of noble family in Ireland; Charnock, a gentleman of Lancashire, and Abington, whose father had been cofferer to the queen's household. Walsingham, the queen's secretary, whose vigilance never slept, and who had engaged Maud, a Catholic priest, and a party in the plot, as his spy, became perfectly acquainted with all the proceedings of the conspirators; and when the proofs against Mary had sufficiently accumulated, she was arraigned and brought to trial, October 12, 1586, charged with having, with others, compassed the queen's death and the subversion of the established religion of the realm. After much hesitation, she consented at length to plead, and declared herself not guilty. Amongst the forty commissioners appointed under the authority of the Great Seal to sit in judgment in this case were Sir Thomas Bromley (Lord Chancellor), the Earl of Shrewsbury, the Earl of Derby, Lord Grey de Wilton, and Sir Ralph Sadler, Chancellor of the Duchy of Lancaster, with Sir Christopher Wray, the Lord Chief Justice, and four other judges.

The correspondence of Babington and Mary, carried on in cypher, and proved by her secretaries, Nau and Curle, was laid before the commissioners, from which it appeared that Babington had informed her of the designs laid for a foreign invasion, the plan of an insurrection at home, the scheme for her deliverance, and the conspiracy for assassinating Queen Elizabeth, by "six noble gentlemen," all of them his private friends, who, from the zeal which they owed to the Catholic church and her majesty's service, would undertake the tragical deed. To this, Mary replied that she approved highly of the design, that the gentlemen might expect all the rewards which it would be in her power to confer, and that the death of Elizabeth was a necessary circumstance, before any attempts were made either for her own deliverance or for an insurrection.[1] It was also proved that she had allowed Cardinal Allen, a native of Lancashire, but long resident in Rome, to treat her as Queen of England, and that she had kept up a correspondence with Lord Paget, for the purpose of inducing the Spaniards to invade this kingdom. It was further proved that Cardinal Allen and Parsons the Jesuit had negotiated by her orders, at Rome, the conditions for the transfer of the English crown to the King of Spain, and for disinheriting her heretical son, James VI. of Scotland. The trial, as might have been expected, terminated in the conviction of Mary. When the verdict of "guilty" was given, which, under the provisions of a recent statute, annihilated her claim to the crown, the streets of London blazed with bonfires, and peals rang out from steeple to steeple. On sentence of death being passed, the Queen of England hesitated long whether to inflict the utmost sentence of the law or to extend the royal clemency to her unfortunate kinswoman; but the force of public opinion was carrying all before it. The unanimous voice of the people, the importunity of Parliament, and probably the queen's own secret inclinations, at length decided that Mary should be executed. When Elizabeth sullenly consented, and flung the warrant, signed, upon the floor, the Council took upon themselves the responsibility of executing it, and the Earl of Shrewsbury, the Earl of Kent, the Earl of Derby, and the Earl of Cumberland, attended by two executioners, went down to Fotheringhay, in Northamptonshire, for the purpose of seeing the sentence of the law carried into effect.[2] Mary received the fatal intelligence without dismay, and suffered on the scaffold (February 8, 1587) with a degree of heroism which proved that she considered herself rather as a martyr to the holy Catholic religion than as a traitor to the state.

While these transactions were pending, the alarm of Spanish invasion spread through the kingdom. In a letter from the Earl of Dudley, as lord lieutenant of the county of Lancashire, to the deputy lieutenants, they were warned that advices had been received, from sundry parts beyond the seas, of foreign forces assembled to invade this realm, and it was the special command of her majesty that order should be taken in every part of the country, that the principal inhabitants should furnish themselves without delay with armour and weapons, and take care that

---

[1] State Trials, vol. i. p. 123.

[2] The extent to which Elizabeth was implicated in the death of the Queen of Scots has been variously estimated. The preponderance of evidence, however, goes to show that her hand had been forced by her ministers, and that when the fatal warrant was signed, her "commandment," as expressed in the charge against Davison, who carried it to the Council (Sir W. H. Nicolas, "Life of Davison," p. 95), was "not to put it in execution before the realm shall be actually invaded by some foreign power." The "commandment," if given, was disregarded. The Commission which ordered the execution of the helpless captive was sent by the Council to the Earl of Shrewsbury at Orton Longueville, near Huntingdon, where he was at the time staying, by a "Mr. Robert Beale, whom your L(ordship) knoweth to be honest, wise, and trustye." The letter accompanying the Commission, which, it must be admitted, in no way compromises Elizabeth, is preserved among the papers in the posses-

sion of the Marquess of Bath, at Longleat, in Wiltshire, and by the courtesy of his lordship, the editor of this edition of the History of Lancashire had the opportunity of examining it, with other documents, while staying at Longleat a year or two ago. It is addressed "To our veary good Lord the Erle of Shrewsbury, Erle Marshall of England," and commences "The Council to the Earl of Shrewsbury, 3 Feb." The document is endorsed in the Earl's own hand, in the usual business-like form, but, considering the tragic nature of the contents, with a cold-blooded curtness that is perhaps unexampled. It reads: "Broughte by Mr. Beale with the Comysion ye vjth of February 1586(7) at Orton Longvile: with him came Sir Drew Drewrye; and the vijth day went to Fotheringham, and the viijth of Februarie 86 executed the Scotts Quene accordinge to my said Comyssion. Mr. Androwes, the Shereff of Northamp-sheere, I sent to bring her downe to execution, and so I charged him with her both lyvinge and with her dead corpse."—C.

all their tenants and followers be also provided and in readiness to repel the common enemy. By another despatch from his lordship, of the same date, addressed to the justices of the county, they are charged to provide their proper quota of horsemen, to be ready at the shortest notice to resist the invaders. At this critical period it became essential that the magistracy of the county should be sound and well affected, and although the Earl of Derby, in his confiding temper, did not conceive any material change to be necessary, the lord treasurer, on the suggestion of the Rev. Edward Fleetwood, rector of Wigan, and others, caused a new commission to be issued, in which the names of several fresh magistrates were introduced, and a considerable number of those who were thought favourable to the recusants omitted. The consequence was, that at the summer assize in 1587, no fewer than six hundred recusants were presented on oath, eighty-seven of whom were indicted, and a notification was made of twenty-one vagrant priests usually received in Lancashire, and twenty-five notorious houses of receipt for them.[1] The Puritans, though pursued with rigour, had become extremely obnoxious to the High Church party, and the scurrilous libels against the prelacy, clandestinely issued from the press in Manchester and other places[2] at this period, under the assumed name of MARTIN MARPRELATE, tended to aggravate the difference and to excite the animosity of the queen and her court.

The ambition of Philip, King of Spain, and his anxiety again to introduce the Roman Catholic religion into England, had involved the two countries in active hostility, and preparations had for some time been making by the Spanish government to invade this country. In the midst of these preparations and alarms the Queen of England and the King of Spain contemplated the negotiation of a peace; and the Earl of Derby, Lord Cobham, Sir James Croft, and others were appointed commissioners on the part of England, to meet certain Spanish commissioners at Bourbourg, near Calais. The negotiations continued for some time, but without any relaxation on the part of Philip for attack, or of Elizabeth for defence. The haughty Spaniard, having at length become impatient, ordered the "Invincible Armada," by which presumptuous name his fleet was distinguished, to prepare for sea; and although Santa Crux, by whom the fleet was commanded, objected to the danger of navigating a narrow and tempestuous sea, without the possession of a single harbour capable of affording shelter, and the Duke of Parma, the commander of the Spanish land forces, wished to reduce the port of Flushing previously to the depature of the expedition, their prudent counsel was rejected, as was also the advice of Sir William Stanley, who had devoted himself to the Spanish cause, and had sacrificed his patriotism and his integrity by the sale of Deventer and the transfer of its garrison to the enemy.[3] The preparations of Spain were beyond all former example, and the invading fleet consisted of seventy-two galliasses and galleons, forty-seven second-rate ships of war, and eleven pinnaces, carrying two thousand eight hundred and forty-three pieces of ordnance, eight thousand and ninety-four seamen, and eighteen thousand six hundred and fifty-eight soldiers; while the English fleet, by which this immense armament was to be resisted, consisted only of thirty-four ships of war, and a number of vessels principally furnished by opulent individuals and by communities, but by no means equal in weight or appointment to those to which they were to be opposed. In this emergency the queen issued a proclamation to Henry, Earl of Derby, as lord lieutenant of the county of Lancaster, urging his lordship, and the county over which he presided, by every consideration of social and domestic security, to call forth the united energies of the county, in common with the nation in general, to resist the meditated attack upon the throne and the altars of their country.

In a scarce volume, printed by Messrs. Leigh and Sotheby, in 1798, is given, from a contemporary manuscript, "The Names of the Nobility, Gentry, and others who Contributed to the Defence of this Country at the Time of the Spanish Invasion, in 1588," the following being the list for the county of Lancaster:—

	£		£
Edward Norris, 16 die Marcii	25	Henry Bannester, armiger, eodem.	25
George Ireland, eodem die	25	Barnabie Kitchen, armiger, eodem	25
Edward Scaresbeck, armiger, eodem	25	Richard Blundell, eodem	25
James Worseley, armiger, eodem	25	James Anderton, eodem	25
William Massye, armiger, eodem	25	Richard Bold, eodem	25

[1] See letter of Edward Fleetwood, dated 7th September, in Cotton MSS.

[2] Printing at this time was restricted to London and the two universities, and all candidates for licences to print were placed under the supervision of the Company of Stationers. Under these restrictions the extreme Puritans provided a press and engaged itinerant printers, who, like strolling players, went from one place to another to exercise their art and mystery, finding refuge from the royal pursuivants in the country houses of the gentry. They began at Kingston, in Surrey; removed to Fawsley, in Northamptonshire; thence successively to Norton, Coventry, and Woolston, in Warwickshire; they had a brief sojourn at Warrington; and finally their press was discovered in a house in Newton Lane, Manchester, when the Earl of Derby—who was residing at the time at Alport Park, on the outskirts of the town—decided to make short work by destroying the press and putting the type into the melting-pot. It does not appear that any of the Lancashire Puritans had any direct connection with the printers of these mysterious publications; but the suspected authors, Penry, a young Welshman, and a minister named Udall—who seem to have sought only a temporary shelter in the county—were seized and charged with the offence. One of them died on the scaffold and the other in prison.—C.

[3] The advice of Sir William was to take possession of Ireland, as a preliminary measure for the conquest of England.

	£
Richard Mollineux, armiger, eodem	25
John Cultheath (Culcheth), armiger, eodem	25
Lawrence Ireland, armiger, eodem	25
Thomas Lancaster, armiger, eodem	25
Myles Gerrarde, armiger, eodem	25
William More, armiger, eodem	25
Adam Harden, armiger, eodem	25
Thomas Standishe, Esq., eodem	25
Sir Edmonde Trafford, miles, 14 die Marcii	100
Sir Jo. Radcliffe, miles, eodem	100
Raphe Asheton, armiger, eodem	25
Richard Hollande, armiger, eodem	25
Richard Asheton, armiger, eodem	25
James Asheton, armiger, eodem	25
Thomas Leigh, armiger, eodem	25
Christofer Anderton, armiger, eodem	50
George Lathom. gen., eodem	25
Edward Brewerton (Brereton), armiger, eodem..	25
Humfry Houghton, gen., eodem	25
Richard Tipping, gen., eodem	25
Giles Hilton, gen., eodem	25
Roberte Heskeeth, armiger, eodem	50
Edward Standishe, armiger, eodem	50
John Fletewood, armiger, eodem	50
Serjant Walmesly, gen., eodem	25
Robert Charnocke, armiger, eodem	25
Henrie Eccleston, armiger, eodem	25
Richard Brewerton, armiger, eodem	25
John Cowerden, gen.. eodem	25

	£
Roger Diconson, eodem	25
Thomas Clayton, eodem	25
Richard Worseley, eodem	25
William Farrington, armiger, eodem	25
Sir John Southworth, miles, 20 die Marcii	25
Nicholas Banester, armiger, eodem	25
Edward Osbaldston, armiger, eodem	25
Roger Nowell, armiger, eodem	25
Richard Walmsly, gen., eodem	25
John Talbot, eodem	25
John Lowe, eodem	25
Serjant Shutleworth, 16 die Marcii	25
John Dewhurst, 20 die Marcii	25
Thomas Houghton, armiger, eodem	100
* Henrie Butler, armiger, eodem	25
* John Singleton, armiger, eodem	25
* Thomas Eccleston, armiger, eodem	25
Thomas Preston, armiger, eodem	50
Christopher Preston. armiger, eodem	25
William Fleminge, armiger, eodem	25
John Bradley, armiger, eodem	25
George Midleton, armiger, eodem	25
William Crofts, armiger, eodem	25
* Robert Bindlowes, eodem	25
* William Thorneborough, eodem	25
* John Westbie, armiger, 26 Aprilis	25
* Roger Breers, armiger, eodem	25
* John Byrom, armiger, eodem	25

* Not charged.

Similar proclamations were sent to the lords lieutenant in all the other shires, and the country was animated to a degree of enthusiasm never before witnessed. The beacons in every part of the county were ordered, by a mandate from Ferdinando, Lord Strange, to be kept in continual readiness; and it appears, from a note of taxation in the archives of the hundred of Salford, that the following charges were made for watching the beacon at Rivington Pike, from the 10th of July to the 30th of September, 1588: Manchester division, £3 8s. 10¼d.; Bolton division, £2 6s. 10¼d.; Middleton division, £2 6s. 10¾d..—Total, £8 2s. 8¼d.[1]

Amongst the precautionary measures for the defence of the kingdom was one of considerable rigour, which the necessity of the times seemed to suggest. A letter was addressed to the Earl of Derby and the other lords lieutenant of counties and commissioners of musters, requiring that because the enemy made his boast that he should have assistance of the Catholic subjects of this land, that all the horses belonging to the recusants should be seized and committed to the custody of some well-affected gentlemen, their neighbours, that their services might be used if there should be occasion; and in the meantime that they should be kept and maintained at the charge of the owners, to be restored again when the danger was past. This document recommends that care should be taken of the beacons, and that persons who spread false rumours and reports should be arrested and committed to prison; and that assistance should be given to the clergy, whose special province it was to find out a certain number of horse and foot, who were to meet for the guard and defence of her majesty's person, because it might fall out that they should stand in need of men to ride their horses and to wear their armour. Amongst other places mentioned for the landing of the invading army was the Pile of Fouldrey, in the county of Lancaster—the place where Martin Swart landed with Perkin Warbeck in the reign of Henry VII.; and the reason of this arrangement was that it was the best harbour for large shipping in all the western coast of England, "betwene Mylforde Haven in Walls and Carliell on the borders of Scotlande," that the deputy-steward of the Pile was Thomas Preston, a Catholic, or "a papyshe Atheiste," as he is designated, who commanded the "menredes" (i.e., dependents or retainers) of Furness Abbey, and that Dr. Allen, who was born at no great distance,[2] and had infected the inhabitants with his "Romish poyson", was likely to direct the attention of the Spaniards to this harbour.[3] The magistrates, gentry, and freeholders of the county were required to meet Lord Strange at Preston on the 13th of July, in order to complete the preparations for the defence of the country; and in the mandate issued by his lordship, in virtue of orders from the queen, the very significant words are used of "Fayle not at youre vttermost peril." By means of these vigorous preparations a force was collected of one hundred and one thousand and forty men, trained and untrained, in the different divisions of the kingdom, including thirteen thousand eight hundred and thirty-one pioneers, lances, light horse, and petronels, of which Lancashire and Cheshire furnished the following numbers:—

[1] Harl. MSS. 1926.—O.
[2] Cardinal Allen was born at Rossall, near Fleetwood, within sight of the Castle or Pile (i.e., Peel) of Fouldrey.—O.
[3] Landsdowne MSS. cod. 56, endorsed "Towchinge a place called ye Pille, in Lancashire, a dangerous place for Landinge, 1588."

" An Abstract of the Certificates returned from the Lieuftenants of the able, trayned, and furnished men in the seu'all Counties, vpon Letters from the Lordes, reduced into Bandes under Captaines, and howe they were sourted with weapons, in Aprill, A.D. 1588 :—

Warre 1588 Lancastre	Trained and Untrained.	Men	Shot.	Corslets.	Bows.	Bills.	Lances.	Light Horse.
		1170	700 Calivers	300	80	20	20	50

The provision of these two Counties is not certified.

Cheshire	Trained and Untrained.	Men.	Shot.	Corslets.	Bows.	Bills.	Lances.	Light Horse.
		2189	420 Calivers 39 Muskets	500	80	80	30	50

" The Abstract of the numbers of Everie sorte of the armed men in the Counties through the Kingdom, taken an° 1588 :—

Counties.	Able Men.	Armed.	Trained.	Untrained.	Pioneers.	Lances.	Light Horse.	Petronels.
Lanckeshire	...	1170	1170	...	...	64	265	...
Cheshire	...	2189	2189	...	...	20	50	91

Among the MSS. in the possession of Dr. Crompton, of Cranleigh, Surrey, formerly of Manchester, is a " declaration of the accompts of Sir John Byron, Knighte," which throws some light upon the preparations going on in Lancashire at this time. It is headed :—

A Declaration of the Accompts of Sir John Byron, Knighte, the one of the deputie Lyveten'nts withn the Countie of Lancaster, wherein is declared what sev'all somes of money the saide Sir John Byron hath receyved and standeth charged wth, what he hath paide and disbursed as well by warrante from the Right Hon'able the Earl of Darbie, L. Lyveten'nt of the saide Countie as otherwyse, and the remaynes in the said Sir John Byron his handes, to be answered the fifte day of Januarye. Aa. R. R. Elizabeth, &c., tri'cessimo sco 1589.

RECEIPTS.

	li.	s.	d.
Derbie—Ffyrste receyved wth'in the hundredth of Derbie by my saide L., his direction for the furnishinge and tranyinge of the vi.c (600) trayned souldires required to be in readynes by his L. of the xiiijth of Maye, 1586, the some of three hundreth fyftie eight poundes too shillings threepence halfpeny	ccclviii	ij	iii ob
Salford—Also receyved within the hundreth of Salford the some of too hundreth and twentie pounds eleven shillings and fouerpence	ccxx	xj	iv
Leylonde—Receyved also within the hundreth of Leylonde for the use of afforesaide, the some one hundreth fourtie neene pounds neene shillings fouerpence	cxlix	ix	iiij
Sm viic.xxviij^{ll}. ij^s. xi^d. ob			

PAYMENTS.

To Mr. Stanley—Paide to Henrye Stanley, Esquier, towards the p'vision of armore & weapon for the furnishinge of the saide vjc souldiars	vcxiiij	x	
Paide to the saide Mr. Stanleye for preste moneye	vi		
To my L.—Paide to my saide L. for p'vision of powder	xxx		
To Mr. Doughtie—Delyvered to Mr. Michell Doughtie	vi	xiij	iiij
Beacons—Paide to Richarde Molenex, Esquier, for the erectinge of a beacon	xx		

PAYMENTS—Continued.

	li.	s.	d.
Beacons—Paid to Rob'te Pilkington[1] at too seu'all tymes for repayringe and kepinge the beacon at Ryven (Rivington) Pyke	v	xvij	iiij
Paide for wage of ccc souldia' trayned too dayes in March, 1587, at seu'all places	xx		
Paide for powder at Ormskirk the saide tyme of trayninge	iiij		
Paide the xxiiij daye of May for wage for too dayes trayninge of the said ccc souldiars at Manc.ester	xx		
Paide the same tyme for ccx$^{ll.}$ of powder for the saide too dayes trayninge	xiiij		
Paide for xviij rowles of matches		x	viij
Delyvered to Captain Morgan for his paynes in traninge	vi	xiij	iiij
Armor for Irelande—Also paide as appereth by a byll of charge for kepeinge, dressing, and recariadg from Chester of such armour as was left there by Mr. Delves, appointed for Irish service	vi		iiij
Sm t. vic.liiij$^{ll.}$ v^s.			

REMAYNES.

Remayneth in the hands of the saide Sir John Byron, Knight, to be repayd and answered upon this accompt as by the p'ticulars of receipts and payments hearby at lardg, y^t doth and maye appeare, the some of	lxxviiij	xvij	xi ob

In the midst of these preparations the Spanish Armada sailed from the Tagus, and after encountering various disasters entered the English Channel, and formed in the shape of a crescent, the horns of which lay some miles asunder. The sight was grand beyond conception, but the

---

[1] Robert Pilkington was doubtless the eldest son of George Pilkington, of Rivington.

events which soon after followed were infinitely more gratifying.[1]   The command of the English fleet had been confided to Lord Howard of Effingham (a Catholic), the lord high admiral, whose want of naval skill was supplied by the Earl of Cumberland and the Lords Henry Seymour, Thomas Howard, and Edmund Sheffield, with Sir William Winter, Sir Francis Drake, Sir Robert Southwell, Sir John Hawkins, Sir Henry Palmer, Sir Martin Frobisher, Sir George Beeston,[2] and others.   By this able council the plan of operations was determined upon, and before the Spanish fleet had been two hours arrayed in order of battle, the cannonade was commenced by the English with a spirit which showed that the determination existed to save England, or, if she was to fall, to let her fleet be the first sacrifice.   A succession of engagements took place, in all of which, though none of them decisive, the advantage was on the side of England, till the finishing blow was given by a masterly manœuvre, practised on the 29th July, 1588.   On that memorable night the sea on a sudden became illuminated by the appearance of eight vessels in flames, drifting rapidly in the direction of the Armada, which was then moored off Calais.   A loud cry of horror burst from the Spaniards on the appearance of these engines of destruction; and in the midst of the panic they cut their cables and ran out to sea, inflicting upon each other more damage than they had hitherto received from their intrepid enemies.   The fire ships burnt harmlessly on the edge of the beach, but a furious gale blowing from the west, the Armada was dispersed along the coast from Ostend to Calais, and the guns of the British fleet completed what the skill of their manœuvres and the fury of the elements had begun.   The want of ammunition compelled the English admiral to return to port, otherwise the Spanish fleet would have been annihilated.   Within the Armada itself, however, all hope was gone.   The crowded galleons were mere slaughter houses.   The scattered remnant of the fleet, with torn sails and shattered masts, unable to return, took the only course open—a circuit round the Orkneys.   Drake followed close in the wake of the flying squadrons, and, like a true British sailor, wrote to Walsingham, " We have the army of Spain before us, and mind, with the grace of God, to wrestle a fall with them.   There was never anything pleased me better than the seeing the enemy flying with a south wind to the northwards."   But the work of destruction was reserved for a mightier foe than Drake, for no sooner had the remnant of the fleet reached the Orkneys than the storms of the northern seas broke on them with a fury before which all concert and union disappeared.   The shores of Scotland and Ireland, in which direction the enemy steered, were covered with the wrecks of their vessels, and strewn with the dead bodies of their mariners; and when the Duke of Medina, the successor of Santa Cruz, terminated his unfortunate voyage in the port of St. Andero, he acknowledged the loss of thirty ships of the largest class and 10,000 men.

The English nation was filled with exultation by this signal deliverance and most memorable victory.   The expressions of thankfulness were not confined to the heroes by whom it was achieved, but rose to that Being without whose providential aid all their efforts must have been in vain. A medal was struck by the Queen's orders, with the inscription " *Afflavit Deus, et dissipantur,*" and the nation, wishing to bear in perpetual memory " this signal deliverance from the malice, force, and cruelty of their enemies," celebrated a general thanksgiving by royal proclamation, which was announced to the county of Lancaster by the Earl of Derby in the following terms:—

" After my very hearty commendations: Whereas I am credibly informed that it hath pleased God to continue His goodness towards our prince, church, and country, as in the late overthrow of our enemies taken upon the coasts of Ireland, it may appear by this calendar here inclosed,—I have thought it expedient, in respect of Christian duty, we should fall to some godly exercise of thanksgiving for the same by prayer and preaching.   Willing you so to commend the business to the clergy of your hundred in their several charges, as our God, by mutual consent, may be praised therefor.   And this not to be omitted nor delayed in anywise, but to be put in execution at or before the next Sabbath.   And thus, desiring God to bless Her Majesty with long life and continual victory over all her enemies, bid you farewell.   Lathome, my house, this 24th of September, 1588.—Yours assuredly,

H. Derby

" To my very loving friends, Sir John Byron, Knight, one of my deputy-lieutenants for Lancashire, and to the rest of the justices of peace."   [Here follows a list of the " Ships and men, sunk and drowned, killed and taken, upon the coast of Ireland," on the side of the Spaniards."]

---

[1] From a manuscript in the Harleian Coll. cod. 286, it would appear that the first notice of the sailing of the Armada from Spain was communicated to the government by Homfraye Brooke, a Liverpool merchant; but the dates do not correspond with the official details, and we are unable to reconcile them.   The document, however, is curious, and as such will be inserted in the West Derby Hundred History, under the head of Liverpool.

[2] Sir George Beeston was of the family of that name of Beeston, in Cheshire, and was 89 years of age when he so gallantly aided in the defeat of the Armada.   His monument with the recumbent effigy upon it is still to be seen in the chancel of Bunbury Church.—O.

[3] Harl. MSS. cod. 1296, fo. 88.

Although the pope, Sextus V., had fulminated a new bull of excommunication against Elizabeth, absolving her subjects from their allegiance, and had published a crusade against England, with plenary indulgences to any one that engaged in the invasion, and although Dr. Allen had received a cardinal's hat to qualify him as legate to England, yet the Catholic subjects of the queen, both in this and other counties, remained faithful to their allegiance, and were amongst the most active in equipping ships and placing them under Protestant commanders to repel the invaders.[1] Amongst a number of others, Sir Thomas Gerrard, Sir Thomas Vavasour, and Sir Charles Blount distinguished themselves by their zealous and disinterested service in their country's cause.

In Ireland the war seemed interminable, and no sooner was the Armada disposed of than an order was issued, through Sir Richard Sherburne and Sir John Byron, to the magistrates of Lancashire, requiring them to levy another hundred soldiers, in addition to those before sent, to proceed to Ireland, properly furnished and equipped, to assemble at Chorley, and to proceed from thence to their destination. In a subsequent letter, the gentry and principal freeholders of the county are advertised that all the demi-lances and light horse within the respective hundreds are to appear before the lord lieutenant for his inspection; which mandate awards to each the number he is to furnish. It appears that in the former year the inspection did not take place, and the Earl of Derby, in a communication of the 19th of February, notifies that it is the queen's pleasure that they should be furnished and equipped, and ready at one hour's warning, and that the money assessed for the levies should be paid into the hands of his receiver, Richard Holland, Esq., at his house at Heaton.

The authority of the law was at this time so little regarded in the county of Lancaster that Thomas Langton, of Walton-le-Dale, the Baron of Newton, on Sunday evening, November 21, 1589, assembled his tenants and retainers, to the number of eighty, in front of the house of Mr. Thomas Hoghton, of Lea, in the parish of Preston, and challenged him to combat, ostensibly because he had impounded a number of cattle belonging to the widow of one Singleton, but really to avenge an ancient feud. Finding himself menaced in his own mansion, he sallied forth at the head of a band of thirty men, when a regular engagement ensued, in which Mr. Hoghton and Richard Bawdwen, one of his followers, were left dead on the field. The Earl of Derby, as lord lieutenant of the county, to vindicate his authority, caused a watch to be instituted day and night that the offenders might be detected and brought to justice; and a species of magisterial assize was appointed to be held at Preston, to inquire into the circumstances of the riot and murders. The magistrates could only pursue one course, and that was to direct that all the parties engaged in the homicides should be indicted at the ensuing assizes on a charge of wilful murder. The Earl of Derby, foreseeing the consequences that would ensue, addressed an earnest petition to Lord Burghley, the queen's high treasurer, beseeching his lordship to use his influence to obtain a pardon from the queen, as very many of the ruder sort engaged in the riot could not read, and being unable to take the benefit of clergy must lose their lives, while those who were of more distinction must be burnt in the hand, and thereby a dangerous quarrel would arise amongst the gentlemen of the county, of an extent and duration that would involve the most serious consequences. This application, which was accompanied by a petition from forty-seven of the offenders for the queen's pardon, and was supported by a petition from the widow of Mr. Hoghton, seems so far to have prevailed that the murder was compromised by the heir of the deceased gentleman receiving from the principal offender, as a compensation for his father's death, the valuable estate and manor of Walton-le-Dale, the future scene of one of Cromwell's most splendid victories. Some documents on this subject, characteristic of the times of Elizabeth, will be found in their proper place in the Hundred history.

In the preceding century a less fatal but more licentious outrage was perpetrated upon one of the principal families of Lancashire: "On the Monday next after the feast of St. James the Apostle," as the official documents express it (i.e. July 30, 1436), William Pulle, of Liverpool, in the county of Lancaster, and of Wyrall, in the county of Chester, gentleman, with a great number of others, repaired to the house of Isabell, the widow of Sir John Boteler of Bewsey, and feloniously and most horribly ravished the said widow, and carried her off in a state of nudity, except "her kirtyll [petticoat] and her smokke," into a wild and desolate part of Wales, for which offence he was indicted at Lancaster. But of this also more in its proper place.

The loyal conduct of the Catholics, when this country was menaced with invasion, did not stay the persecutions to which they were exposed. A commission under the great Seal of England was issued in 1591 for the apprehension and discovery of seminary priests and Jesuits, and for reducing the recusants to conformity. To give effect to this commission the churchwardens in the

[1] Stowe's Ann. p. 747.

various parishes of Lancashire were required to meet the magistrates, and to bring with them lists in writing, containing the Christian and surnames of all the householders in their respective parishes, both men and women, with all their inmates above the age of sixteen years, certifying whether they repaired to the church to hear divine service, that, in case of neglect, they might be dealt with accordingly. The rigorous proceedings against the Catholics, not in this county only, but in the country generally, may be inferred from the facts mentioned by Challoner, who states, that for the vague offences of harbouring priests, or of receiving ordination beyond the seas, or of admitting the supremacy of the pope, and denying that of the queen, sixty-one priests, forty-seven laymen, and two gentlewomen, suffered capital punishment, by laws recently enacted, and unknown to the ancient constitution of the country; and that in one night fifty Catholic gentlemen, in the county of Lancaster, were suddenly seized and committed to prison, on account of their non-attendance at church. As a test of their fidelity to the reformed faith, all the justices of the peace were required openly and publicly to take the oath of supremacy in special sessions, and an order from the lords of the queen's council, of the date of the 22nd of October 1592, addressed " To our verie Lovinge frends the highe Sheriff & Custos Rotulorum of the County of Lancaster Sr John Byron & Sr Edward Fytton, knights, Richard Asheton, Richard Brereton, & Richard Holland esquiers, and to every of them,"[1] directs that sessions of the peace shall be holden "before the 20th day of November next," at the accustomed places in the county, at which every justice of the peace present shall take the said oath, and that any person having hitherto filled that office, who shall refuse or forbear to take the oath, shall be removed out of the commission of the peace; or any justice of the peace who does not repair to the church or chapel where the common prayer is used, or whose wife, living with her husband, or son and heir, living in his father's house, or within the county where his father dwells, refuses or does not usually go to church, the husband or father of such recusant shall cease to exercise the office of justice of the peace during the time of such recusancy. The high sheriff and other persons named in the writ of *Dedimus Potestatem* are themselves first required to take the oath, and then to administer it to the justices, saving that the lords of Parliament are excepted.

The Puritans, at least that part of them called Brownists, who deemed every species of communion with the Established Church unchristian, fared little better than the Catholics. Five of them were arraigned in the year 1593, on a charge of writing and publishing seditious libels; and though the publishers were spared, Barrow and Greenwood, the writers, were condemned and executed, notwithstanding their plea that the obnoxious passages were directed against the bishops, and not against the queen. Penry, the "Martin Marprelate" of Manchester, was sentenced to death under the provisions of the statute 23 Elizabeth, c. 3, on a pretence that a number of papers, containing disjointed sentences, intended as a petition to the queen, were treasonable; and to prevent the populace from interposing any obstacles in the way of his execution, he was suddenly taken from prison, and hanged at the door of Sir Thomas Waterings. Penry, as previously stated, was a native of Wales, and his execution gave rise to the following lines :—

"The Welshman is hanged   "And tho' he be hanged,
Who at our kirke flanged,   Yet he is not wranged ;
And at her state banged,   The de'ul has him fanged
And brened are his bucks.   In his kruked kluks."

The alarm of Spanish invasion was revived in 1593, and the queen addressed a letter to the Earl of Derby, as lord lieutenant of the palatine counties of Lancaster and Chester, announcing that troubles had been stirred up in Ireland, and that it had come to the knowledge of her majesty's council that certain Spanish ships of war were to be sent, by the way of Scotland, to aid the insurgents in that country. To repel this invasion, levies were to be made in the different counties of the kingdom, and the counties of Lancaster and Chester were each required to furnish one hundred and thirty-eight able men, properly equipped, to proceed to Liverpool or Chester, to be embarked in that service. To enforce this order, a letter was addressed by the Earl of Derby to Sir Richard Shirburn, Knt., Richard Hollande, Esq., and the other deputy lieutenants of the county, in which his lordship was pleased to state, "that her majesty, in her princely wisdom, having resolved, by God's assistance, to withstand and suppress this wicked force treacherously brought against her highnesses most excellent and godly government," required that consultation might be had, and the utmost promptitude used, in carrying the measures into effect. A subsequent letter from his lordship, dated on the 14th of June in the same year, represents that "general greffe and mislyke" have been conceived in the county, and not without good cause, if he is rightly informed, from the manner in which the county has been assessed for the Irish service. In consequence of these alleged malversations, the magistrates for the hundred of Salford were

[1] Harl. MSS. cod. 1926, fo. 109 a.

required to assemble at Manchester, and to make out an account of the sums of money which had been collected in their respective jurisdictions for this service during the last eight years, in order that justice might be done to the county. From the nature of this official correspondence, it would appear that the alarm of invasion soon subsided,[1] for in the month of September in the same year the lords of the council directed that the beacon watches should be discontinued, and that the inhabitants of the county of Lancaster should forthwith be discharged from the necessity of contributing to this service.

At this period of our history the hospitals of Chelsea and Chatham did not exist, neither did the chests out of which disabled soldiers and mariners, who have served their country, are relieved; but unfortunate persons of this description, when they were discharged from the public service, received a certificate, addressed to the justices of the peace in the counties where they were born or had been impressed, recommending them to the humane consideration of the churchwardens and constables. These certificates were given by men high in office, and amongst others we find one, signed by no fewer than nine members of her majesty's council, in favour of Nicholas Whittacre, a poor soldier, having done good service and bearing office as a lieutenant in her majesty's wars, directing that he might receive such benefit from the general collections of the county of Lancaster, where he was born or impressed, as was given to others of the same description.[2]

An event which agitated the county of Lancaster—"the superstitious county of Lancaster"—in the most extraordinary manner, happened to the head of its principal family soon after the death of Henry, Earl of Derby, which occurred at Lathom, September 25th, 1594. His son and successor, Ferdinando, was seized "in the flower of his youth," with a violent sickness, at Knowsley, on the 4th of April, 1595, which was attributed to witchcraft, both by himself and his attendants, and of which he died at Lathom House twelve days afterwards. The cause of his death was inexplicable to his medical attendants. Being inexplicable, it was by them conveniently assigned to sorcery and witchcraft, and in a report drawn up at the time many absurd stories were related of the "strange dreams" and "divinations" that preceded his end. Everybody believed he was either consumed by the witches or poisoned by the Papists; and while his physicians attributed his mortal sickness to the former, his chaplain, who had a horror of Popery, was equally confident in assigning the cause to the wickedness of the latter. The late Dr. Ormerod, in his prefatory memoirs to the "Tracts Relating to the Military Proceedings of Lancashire," says, though he gives no evidence in support of the statement, "It is well known that Jesuitical intrigue led to his death by poison." He is said to have been tampered with by a member of the Hesketh family to assume the title of king in right of his grandmother. The supposition is that, having indignantly rejected the proposition, he was poisoned by the conspirators.

It appears that this country was visited in the years 1595 and 1596 by a severe dearth, amounting almost to famine, owing to a succession of unfavourable seasons. In the following year, the lords of the council issued a letter to the justices of the peace in the county of Lancaster, congratulating them on the return of plenty; but at the same time directing them to cause diligent inquisition to be made in all the divisions of their county for such persons as kept up the price of provisions, by buying or bargaining for corn or other victuals, except in open market, or for their private use, and directing that they should apprehend all engrossers and compel them to revoke their bargains.

In the list of Queen Elizabeth's annual expenses, civil and military, in the year 1598, the following items occur:—

The County Palatine of Lancaster.	£	s.	d.
Chamberlaine, fee	20	0	0
Clerk of the crown, fee	40	0	0
And his diet when he rides, esteemed	40	0	0
Clerk of the pleas, fee	40	0	0
Clerk of the extreats, fee	20	0	0
Barons of the exchequer (2), fee apiece	40	0	0
Attorney, fee	6	13	4
Messenger, fee	2	0	0
And his riding expenses			
Crier, fee	2	0	0

The Duchy of Lancaster.	£	s.	d.
Chancellor, fee and allowance of £4 for paper, parchment, and ink	140	10	0
Surveyor, fee	63	13	4
Attorney, fee and allowance	45	0	0
Receiver-general, fee and allowance	38	10	0
Clerk in the court of the duchy, fee and allowance	27	10	4
Messenger, fee and his charges when he rideth	40	0	0

[1] The threat of a second armada was met by a descent of the English forces on Cadiz. The town was plundered and burnt to the ground; thirteen vessels of war were fired in its harbour, and the stores accumulated for the expedition utterly destroyed. In spite of this crushing blow, a Spanish fleet gathered in the following year and set sail for the English coast, but, as in the case of its predecessor, storms proved more fatal than the English guns, and the ships were wrecked and almost destroyed in the Bay of Biscay.—History of the English People, p. 430.—C.

[2] A statute of Elizabeth, passed shortly after this time, provided that "all parishes within this Realm of England and Wales shall be charged to pay weeklie such sume of monie towardes the reliefe of sicke, hurte' and maimed souldiers and mariners soe as no Parishe be rated above the summe of tenne pence, nor under the sume of two pence weeklie to be paide." This Act was confirmed by a decree of the Commonwealth, May 28th, 1647, but the amount collected under its provisions being found inadequate, owing to the long continuance of the war and the consequent increase in the number of applicants for relief, an increased rate not to exceed 2s. 6d. per week from each parish was sanctioned by Parliament August 10th, 1647.—C.

At this time the tide of recent triumphs seemed to have taken a turn. In Ireland disorder had resumed its sway, and a defeat of the English forces in Tyrone led to a general rising of the northern tribes. The efforts made for the suppression of the rebellion failed through the vanity and disobedience of the Queen's lieutenant, the Earl of Essex, and it soon became evident that strong measures for the suppression of the revolt must be taken if Ireland was to remain to the English crown. Fresh levies were called for, and in the order for raising men to go to Ireland, in 1599, the magistrates of Lancashire were cautioned "not to send any vagabonds or disorderly persons, but men of good character, and particularly young men, who were skilled in the use of the hand gun."

The numerous levies that had been made for the queen's service in Ireland enabled the English general, Mountjoy, to effect the subjugation of that country, though the rebels so-called were aided by an invading army of six thousand Spaniards, which had landed at Kinsale. The new lieutenant, Mountjoy, although without military experience, soon restored obedience to the English authority. All open opposition was speedily crushed out by his energy and ruthlessness. A line of forts secured the country as the English mastered it. Hugh O'Neile, who had roused Ulster to revolt, was made prisoner. A famine, which followed, completed the devastating work of the sword, and eventually the work of conquest was accomplished. But the long and eventful reign of Elizabeth now drew to a close. The queen, in the midst of all her splendour and success, fell into a state of irrecoverable melancholy. "She held in her hand," says one who saw her in her last days, "a golden cup, which she often put to her lips; but in truth her heart seemed too full to need more filling." Gradually her mind gave way, her memory failed, and at length, at three o'clock on the morning of the 24th of March, 1603, in the seventieth year of her age, having bequeathed her crown to her lawful successor, James the Sixth of Scotland, the eldest son of the unfortunate Mary Queen of Scots, a life so great, yet so lonely in its greatness, ended—the great Elizabeth passed quietly away—a woman who had reigned like a man, to be succeeded by a man who reigned like a woman!

Immediately on the death of the queen a letter was addressed by the lords of the council to the sheriff of Lancaster (and the other sheriffs) announcing that "As much as it has pleased God to take out of this life to His mercy our dearly-beloved sovereign Queen Elizabeth, it has become necessary, for the maintenance of the safety of the realm, forthwith to proclaim James VI., King of Scotland, and now James I. King of England, France, and Ireland." For this purpose, their lordships had sent a proclamation, which the sheriff was requested to publish in his County of Lancaster, and which proclamation announced that the imperial crown had, by the death of the high and mighty princess Elizabeth, descended on the high and mighty prince, James, lineally and lawfully descended from the body of Margaret, daughter of the high and renowed prince Henry VII., King of England, his great grandfather, the said Lady Margaret being the daughter of Elizabeth, daughter of King Edward IV., by which happy conjunction both the houses of York and Lancaster were united, to the joy unspeakable of this kingdom, formerly rent and torn by the large dissension of bloody and civil wars.

This proclamation met with a prompt, loyal, and dutiful response from the principal gentry of the county of Lancaster, to which the following names were subscribed:—

John Ireland, sheriff	Robt Dalton of Pilling	Christopher Carus	Edward Standish
Sʳ Rychard Mollineux	Roger Bradshaw	John Cansfild	John Traves
Sʳ Rychard Hoghton	Roger Nowell	John Calvert	Henry Butler
Sʳ Cuthbert Halsall	Nycholas Banister	Edmund Fleetwood	Edward Rigbie
Sʳ Edward Warren	Myles Gerrard	Edward Rawstorne	Edward Langtrie
Sʳ John Radclyffe	Edward Stanley	Willm Hvlton	Robt More
Thomas Preston	Barnabie Kitchin	James Browne	Thomas Tildisley
Francis Tunstall	Sʳ Nycholas Moseley	Alexander Barlow	Thomas Ireland
Randle Barton	Thomas Walmysley	John Greenhaugh	Alexander Standish
Rychard Holland	Thomas Gerrard	Alexander Reddish	Roger Downes
Thomas Sothworth	Thomas Langton	Edmund Hopwood	John Crosse
John Osbaldeston	John Townley	John Braddill	John Wrightington
Willm Thorneborrow	Richard Sherburne	Thomas Barton	Robt Pilkington
George Preston	James Anderton of Lostock	James Westby	Thomas Gidlow
Edward Tarbucke	James Anderton of Clayton	John Massye	Willm Chorley
Alexander Standish	Robt Charnock	Edward Norres	Rychard Ashton
James Ashton	Thomas Ashton	Richard Ashton	Willm Clayton
John Middleton of Leyton	Rychard Fleetwood	Rychard Bold	Roger Bradshawe
Willm Farrington	Henrye Banister	Raufe Ashton	—— Winstanley
Robt Dalton de Thurnam	Roger Kirkby	Robt Hesketh	

CHAPTER XIV.

 UEEN ELIZABETH was no sooner consigned to the tomb of her royal progenitors than her successor, James I., entered upon his progress from Edinburgh, by way of York, to London. But having now arrived at times comparatively modern, we shall pause to take a short retrospective view of the ancient manners and customs of the people of Lancashire, and in some degree of the kingdom in general, which, on being collated with the customs and manners of modern times, will often afford instructive lessons, and exhibit by turns striking contrasts and close resemblances.

From the time of the Norman Conquest the inhabitants of the county of Lancaster have been much addicted to the chase. The extent of their forests has attached them to this pursuit; and their skill in archery, for which they have been famed, both in war and in their sports,[1] had given them a taste for the chase, which displayed itself as early as the reign of King John, and was at its height in the reign of Henry VIII. The laurels gained on the field of Flodden by the levies under Sir Edward Stanley were principally owing to their dexterity in the use of the bow and the bill.[2] According to Holinshed, the skill of the archers must have been in great request, for, says he, "the whole countie of Lancaster hath beene forrest heretofore;" but this is an error of the venerable chronicler, as is shown with sufficient clearness by the domesday survey of William the Conqueror. It is true that when the Lacies, and the successors of the ducal house of Lancaster, sported over their vast domain, from the castle of Clitheroe to the castle of Pontefract, the right of free warren was exercised over all the intervening country without control; but it is also true that the tract was studded with towns and villages, more numerous even in the days of John of Gaunt than in the reign of Henry VIII.[3]

The nobles of Lancashire, in their baronial halls, were distinguished for their ancient munificence; and the successive Barons, Earls, and Dukes of Lancaster set the example for which Edward, Earl of Derby, the model of hospitality, was celebrated. The knights, the gentry, and the yeomen, each in their station, were also famed for their hospitality and manly exercises; and Camden, speaking of the Lancashire men generally, without distinction of rank, says, "You may determine the goodness of the country by the temperament of the inhabitants, who are extremely comely."[4]

The dress of the ladies in the time of the Ferrers, first Earls of Derby, is described as at once simple and graceful: they were clothed in modest, elegant habits, consisting of a loose gown girdled round the waist, which reached to the ground, and was surmounted with a veil over the head. The unmarried ladies were distinguished by an additional robe over the gown, which hung down before, and resembled the sacerdotal robe. The dress of the men of the higher order was a flowing robe; and the common people wore a kind of tunic girt round the loins, which seldom

---

[1] See chap. vii.
[2] Chap. xii. The English chiefly depended upon the force of their infantry, and the bravery and expertness of the archers, which was as much relied upon in our ancient warfare as is the *charge* in modern British tactics. The archers were protected by body armour, the arms being left perfectly free; except when they wore a brigandine of mail, which came before them like an apron; their arms were a long bow, a sheaf of arrows, a sword, and a small shield. The bill-men, so called from their weapon, which resembled a small bill, or hooked axe, were sometimes armed in brigandines of mail, but at other times they were scarcely protected at all by armour.

[3] Description of England in the reign of Elizabeth, written by Wm. Harrison, and affixed to Holinshed's Chronicles, new edit. p. 324. See also chap. vii. of this work.

[4] Britannia, iii. 877.

reached lower than to the knees. Nothing could be more vain and ridiculous than the fashions which prevailed in the reign of the last sovereign of the Lancaster line, and which seemed to combine all the fantastical costumes of former reigns. In the reign of Henry VII. there was an affectation of feminine attire in the men, and the lord chamberlain is described in the Boke of Kervynge as saying, "Warme your soverayne hys petycote, his doublet, and his stomachere; and then put on hys hosen, and then his schone or slyppers, then stryke up his hosen mannerlye, and tye them up, then lace his doublet hole by hole," &c. Of the garbs of the priests just before the Protestant Reformation, Harrison, an author of great fidelity, who wrote in that century, says that

" 'They went either in diverse colors like plaiers, or in garments of light hew, as yellow, red, greene, &c., with their shoes piked, their haire crisped, their girdles armed with silver; their shooes, spurres, bridles, &c., buckled with like mettall; their apparell (for the most part) of silke, and richlie furred, their cappes laced and buttoned with gold; so that to meet a priest in those daies, was to beholde a peacocke that spreadeth his taile when he danseth before the henne.' These clerical beaux must have been the dignitaries of the church, and not the inferior clergy of the county of Lancaster, who are described by Archbishop Lee as in the possession of benefices not yielding them more than four guineas per annum.[1] In the reign of Elizabeth the dress of the clergy was more becoming their sacred order, and the showy colours, the 'piked' shoes, and the glittering girdles, were discarded. The head-dress of the laity was as various as the cut of their beards, 'which were sometimes shaven from the chin like those of Turks, sometimes cut short like the beard of marques Otto, sometimes made round like a rubbing brush, other with a *pique devant;* and now and then suffered to grow long.' As the men imitated the fashions of the women, so did the women imitate the fashions of the men, to a degree offensive alike to good taste and to modesty; and Harrison, in describing the ladies of the *ton* in his days, says, 'Thus it is now come to pass, that women are become men, and men are transformed into monsters.' Randle Holme, one of our county collectors, says that, about the fortieth year of Elizabeth (1598), the old fashions, which were used in the beginning of her reign, were again revived, with some few additions made thereto, as guises, double ruffs, &c. The men likewise, besides the double use of the cloak, had a certain kind of loose hanging garment, called a *mandeville,* much like to our old jackets or jumps, but without sleeves, only having holes to put the arms through; yet some were made with sleeves, but for no other use than to hang on the back. Early in the reign of Elizabeth, the wearing of great breeches was carried to a very absurd and ridiculous length, together with the peas-cod doublets, as they were called. These slops, or breeches, or trunk-hose, it was their custom to stuff with rags, or such like materials, till they brought them to an enormous size—so enormous that it was deemed necessary to legislate for their regulation. The legislators themselves, however, seem to have fallen into the same absurdity; for in the Harleian Collection, No. 980, a paper is preserved, from which it appears that in the reign of Elizabeth a scaffold was erected round the inside of the House of Commons, for those members to sit in who used the wearing of great breeches stuffed with hair, and bulging out like woolsacks. Bulver, in his pedigree of the 'English Gallant,' speaks of a man whom the judges accused of wearing breeches contrary to the law, when he, for his excuse, drew out of his slops the contents—'as, first, a pair of sheets, two table-cloths, ten napkins, four shirts, a brush, a glass, a comb, with night-caps,' and other useful articles. The ladies, that they might not be outdone in grotesqueness of attire, invented the large hoop farthingales as a companion to the trunk-hose, and the women who could not purchase these expensive commodities supplied their place with bum-rolls."

The description of a fine lady's dress in the time of Queen Elizabeth, as breathed in the wishes of Miss Margaret Hardman, while she was under the influence of *possession* (apparently by a *spirit* of pride), in the house of Mr. Nicholas Starkie, of Leigh, in the county of Lancaster, is too graphic to be withheld:—

" ' 'Come on, my lad,' said she, for so she called her familiar—'come on, and set my partlett on the one side, as I do the other. I will have a fine smock of silk, with a silk petticoat garded a foot high; it shall be laid with good lace, it shall have a French body, not of whalebone, for that is not stiff enough, but of horne, for that will hold it out; it shall come low before, to keep in my belly. I will have a French farthingale; I will have it low before and high behind, and broad on either side, that I may lay my arms upon it. My gown shall be black wrought velvet; I will have my sleeves set out with wire, for sticks will break, and are not stiff enough. I will have my perewincke so fine; I will have my cap of black velvet with a feather in it with flewes of gold, and my hair shall be set with pearls. I will have a busk of whalebone; it shall be tied with two silk points; and I will have a drawen wrought stomacher embossed with gold, and a girdle of gold. I will have my hose of orange colour, this is in request; and my cork shoes of red Spanish leather. I will have a scarf of red silk, with a gold lace about the edge. I will have a fan with a silver steel, and a glass set in it. Bring me a pair of gloves of the finest leather that may be, with two gold laces about the thumb, and a fringe on the top, with flewes and red silk underneath, that I may draw them through a gold ring, or else I will have none of them.' " [2]

The general diffusion of wealth in Elizabeth's reign led to an ostentatious display of luxury that spread by the force of the imitative principle through every class of society, and the pride of apparel was scarcely less obtrusive in men than in women. The sumptuary laws which were passed in the reign of Henry VIII.[3] to prevent "the subversion of good and politic order in knowledge and distinction of people, according to their estates, pre-eminences, dignities, and degrees," had ceased to be regarded. Those who were gaining wealth by manufacture, and trade, and industry, refused to be bound by statute as to what they should and what they should not wear, and the queen and her council wisely left the regulation of such matters to the tastes of the people and their ability to gratify them.

When King James came to the crown, most of the old fashions used in the days of Elizabeth were again revived, and the large breeches, with the hoop farthingales amongst the rest, came once more into fashion. Expensive garters and curious shoe-roses were worn very generally, and the ladies kept pace with the other sex in costly ornaments.

"In the comedy of the 'City Madam,' a lady says, 'These roses would show well, an 'twere the fashion for the garters to be seen.' But of all the ridiculous fashions, that of the men wearing stays was, perhaps, the most so; and the Earl of Somerset, when so equipped, may be supposed to have served as a model for men of fashion of a much more recent period. The manufacturers were not much behind the courtiers, and the opulent clothier's widow of Newbury is thus described: 'She came out of the

---

[1] See chap. xii. p. 201, note 3.   [2] Tract of the Rev. Geo. More, published in 1600.   [3] 24 Henry VIII., c. 13.—C.

kitchen in a fair train gown, stuck full of silver pins ; a white cap on her head, with cuts of curious needlework under the same, and an apron before her as white as the driven snow ;' while the spruce master tailor, her suitor, wore 'a new russet jerkin, and a tall sugar-loaf hat clapped on the side of his head.' The spinning or factory girls of that day are thus described :—

> " ' And in a chamber close beside
> Two hundred maidens did abide,
> In petticoats of flannel red,
> And milk-white kerchers on their head,
> Their smock sleeves like to winter's snow,
> That on the western mountains flow,
> And each sleeve with a silken band
> Was fairly tied at the hand.
> Which pretty maids did never lin,
> But in that place all day did spin,' " &c.

The young gentleman was distinguished by his gay suit of apparel, his cloak, and rapier ; the merchant's dress at that time was a plain grave suit of clothes, with a black cloak ; and the rustic, when in his Sunday attire, had a leathern doublet with long points, and a pair of breeches primed up like pudding-bags, with yellow stockings and his hat turned up with a silver clasp on the leer side.[1] These fashions were not confined to any particular district, they extended to the whole kingdom. 'The manners and customs of the inhabitants of Lancashire,' says John De Brentford, 'are similar to those of the neighbouring counties, except that the people eat with two-pronged forks. The men are masculine, and in general well made ; they ride and hunt the same as in the most southern parts, but not with that grace, owing to the whip being carried in the left hand. The women are most handsome, their eyes brown, black, hazel, blue, or grey ; their noses, if not inclined to the aquiline, are mostly of the Grecian form, which gives a most beautiful archness to the countenance, such indeed as is not easy to be described. Their fascinating manners have long procured them the name of *Lancashire Witches*.'[2] Leland says, 'The dress of the men chiefly consists of woollen garments, while the women wear those of silk, linen, or stuff. Their usual colours are green, blue, black, and sometimes brown. The military are dressed in red, which is vulgarly called scarlet.' According to Randle Holme, hats were not used in Lancashire, nor indeed in England, till the time of Charles II. This is obviously a chronological mistake. The hatting business existed in the south-east part of this county in the time of Henry VI., and probably much earlier, as we have a petition to Parliament in that reign from the hatters, complaining of the introduction of machinery into their business, and representing that 'hats, caps, &c., were wont' to be fulled by manual labour ; but that, of late, fulling-mills had been introduced, to effect this operation, to the prejudice of the workmen, and the deterioration of the fabric. Silk stockings were not worn till the year 1560, when Queen Elizabeth, on being presented with a pair made by Mrs. Montague, her silk woman, as a New Year's gift, declared that she liked them so well that she would not wear any more cloth hose,[3] which persons of the highest distinction had hitherto worn."

In the reign of Elizabeth there were few houses of stone in the county of Lancaster except those of the nobility and the highest rank of gentry. The houses of the middle and lower class were principally built with wood. Those of the better order had large porches at the principal entrance, with halls and parlours; the framework was constructed with beams of timber of such enormous size that the materials of one house, as they were then built, would make several of equal size in the present mode of building. The common method of making walls was to nail laths to the timber frame, and strike them over with rough (clay) plaster, which was afterwards whitened with fine mortar, and this last was after beautified with figures and other curious devices.[4] Some had houses built with bricks, but these were rare, and of modern date. The inner walls were either hung with tapestry, arras-work, or painted cloth, whereon were different devices, or they were wainscoted with oak, and in that way made warm and ornamental. The cottages of the poor were slightly set up with a few posts, and plastered over with clay, not very dissimilar to the rustic cottages of the present day. The houses in the cities and towns were built each story jutting over that beneath it, so that where the streets were not wide the people in the top storeys, from opposite houses, might not only converse with each other, but even shake hands together. The houses were covered with tiles, shingles, slates, or lead. The streets of Manchester, Preston, Liverpool, and other towns of the county were unpaved, and were generally narrow, the smallness of the carriages and the diminutive intercourse not requiring spacious streets. At the period of the wars between the houses of York and Lancaster, the windows principally consisted of lattice or wicker work, and sometimes of panes of horn; but in the reign of Elizabeth glass had become plentiful, and was generally used in small squares set in lead. A still further improvement took place in the buildings about this period. Till the time of Henry VIII. the houses were generally erected without chimneys; and in many of the first towns of the realm not more than two or three chimneys were to be seen, the fires being made in a recess in the wall, where the family dressed their victuals, and left the smoke to make its escape as it does at present out of the Irish cabins. Valleys were generally preferred for the sites of towns and villages, the buildings in the early times of Britain being mostly of a construction too slight to encounter the boisterous elements of the climate to which they were exposed. The outbuildings, such as the dairy, stables, and brewhouse attached to the mansions, were at a little distance from the house, and yet sufficiently near, says Harrison, " that the goodman lieng in his bed may lightlie heare what is donne in each of them with ease, and call quicklie vnto his meinie if anie danger should attack him."

The houses of the great and opulent possessed much the same character, but in Lancashire a

---

[1] Strutt's Ancient Manners and Customs of the English, iii. 98.
[2] Bodleian Collection, 1602.
[3] Stow's Chronicle, fo. 867.
[4] Harrison's Description of Britain.

style of architecture prevailed, remarkable for massiveness, and which, if not peculiar to the county, was nowhere else practised so commonly or on so large a scale. The great difference between the timber mansions of Lancashire and those of other parts of the kingdom were, that while using a material common to all, the former were distinguished by their extravagant solidity and their strength and ingenuity of construction. The timbers were more commonly exposed on the outside than in the case of houses in the southern counties, and the ponderous framework, than which stone itself could not longer be expected to resist time, or more firmly withstand the stroke of injury, with the massive bracing ribs and panels wrought in the semblance of tracery, exhibited a rude magnificence that, if lacking the delicacy and elaboration of detail observable in the more stately fabrics of brick and stone erected in other parts of the kingdom, are yet deserving the careful investigation of the architect and antiquary. Of the many picturesque halls and manor houses erected during the Tudor reigns, many excellent examples fortunately still remain comparatively uninjured. The centre and most important feature of such houses was the great hall, and on it the disposition of the other apartments mainly depended. Here the general business of the household was transacted, and what may be called the public life of the family was carried on. It was the general rendezvous of the servants and retainers, who lounged about when duty or pleasure did not call them to other offices or to the field. In it the lord of the soil held his court by day, and his male servants and men-at-arms stretched themselves and slept, how they could, on the rush-covered floor at night. The walls of the apartment were hung with armour, pistols and petronels, swords and spears, and other implements of warfare. The screen and the "musycians" gallery were garnished with the antlers of the deer and other trophies of the chase, and in the more opulent houses the upper end was draped with tapestry of elaborate design. Before the spread of refinement had necessitated the addition of a private room, where the more honoured guests could be entertained apart from the clatter of the throng, the great hall was the place where all had their meals together. Round the "hie-board" or "table dormant" on the daïs, assembled daily the family and guests, placed according to their rank above the salt, whilst the retainers, and those of inferior degree, sat at the benches, placed mostly on trestles, and ranged "banquet-wise" along each side of the apartment. Dinner was then, as now, the principal meal of the day, and in the better houses was usually conducted with much ceremony, and certain well-established rules of courtesy were strictly observed. Our forefathers were by no means insensible to the pleasures of the table. The family usually assembled about ten o'clock, and, unless called upon by urgent matters to the field or the council, dinner was enjoyed with leisurely deliberation. The parlours and private dining-rooms were fitted up with more regard for elegance, and were more luxuriously furnished than the banqueting hall: the floors were carpeted, and the chairs, stools, and other articles of furniture, were often adorned with coverings of needlework. The dormitories had their complement of truckle beds and ponderous "four-posters," and in addition there were arks, and coffers, and presses, wrought in oak and carved elaborately.

While the upper classes were living in the full enjoyment of their wealth, the thrifty manufacturers in the prosperous inland towns were accumulating riches, becoming themselves small landowners, and by their enterprise establishing a new world of commercial energy; but, though trade increased, and their gains were large, it was long before refinement and luxury found their way into their dwelling-places, and in their habits and education they were little removed from the common people, who were ignorant and superstitious, but as merry and boisterous as they were illiterate and rude.

In the time of Edward I. orchards and gardens were much in use, but they afterwards grew into neglect, so that from John of Gaunt's days to the end of the reign of Henry VII. little attention was paid to these delightful and ornamental appendages to the gentlemen's mansions. This was owing to herbs, fruits, and roots being little in use for the purpose of human food; but in the beginning of the reign of Henry VIII. not only the poor but the rich began to use melons, radishes, skirrets, parsnips, carrots, cabbages, turnips, and salad herbs, the latter of which were served as delicacies at the tables of the nobility, gentry, and merchants. Hops in times past had been plentiful, but they also grew into disuse, and the cultivation of them was neglected till a few years before the Reformation, when they were imported from the Low Countries;[1] and hence the couplet—

"Hops, Reformation, Bays, and Beer
Came into England all in a year;"

---

[1] Hops were not imported until 1524, other bitters having previously supplied their place, but it is evident that as early as 1440, when the *Parvulorum Promptorium* was compiled, their use was not altogether unknown, though Mr. Albert Way is of opinion that at that time hopped beer was either imported from abroad or brewed by foreigners, a supposition that is certainly supported by the *Promptorium.* "The manifold virtues in hops," says an ancient writer, "do manifestly argue the wholesomeness of *beer* above *ale.*"—C.

or, as another ancient rhyme expresses it—

> "Turkeys, Carps, Hops, Piccarel, and Beer
> Came into England all in one year."

Ale, a thick, sweet, unhopped liquor, however, had been drunk in England long before, and was a favourite beverage amongst the working classes, when they were all good Catholics. The number of fasts in Catholic times somewhat diminished the consumption of flesh-meat, which would otherwise, as the sustenance of the people was chiefly animal food and milk, have been very great; but when it became lawful for every man to feed upon what he was able to purchase, except upon the weekly fast-days, which were observed by all long after the Reformation, it was necessary to resort to herbs, roots, and bread, to diminish the consumption of cattle.

"In number of dishes and change of meat, the nobilitie of England," says Harrison, "doo most exceed, sith there is no daie in maner that passeth over their heads, wherein they have not onelie béefe, mutton, veale, lambe, kid, porke, conie, capon, pig, or so manie of these as the season yieldeth; but also some portion of the red or fallowe déer, beside great varietie of fish and wild foule, and sundrie other delicacies. The chiefe part of their daily provision is brought in before them (commonlie) in siluer vessell, if they be of the degrée of barons, bishops, and vpwards, and placed on their tables, whereof, when they haue taken what it pleaseth them, the rest is reserued, and afterwards sente downe to their seruing men and waiters, who féed thereon in like sort with conuenient moderation, and their reuersion also being bestowed vpon the poore, which lie readie at their gates in great numbers to receiue the same."

This species of hospitality prevailed to a vast extent at Lathom House and Knowsley, in the time of Edward, Earl of Derby; and the bishop of the diocese, Dr. Downham, entertained every day forty persons, besides comers and goers.[1] To guard against intemperance each guest at the table of his noble host called for a cup of such liquor as he preferred, which, when he had satisfied himself, he returned to the servant.

"By this device," says our author, "much idle tipling is cut off, for if the full pot should continuallie stand at the elbow or near the trencher, diuers would alwaies be dealing with it, whereas now they drinke seldome and onelie when necessitie urgeth, and so auoid the note of great drinking, or often troubling of the seruitours with filling of their bols. Neuerthelesse, in the noblemen's hals this order is not vsed, neither in any man's house commonlie vnder the degrée of a knight or esquire of great reuenues. The gentlemen and merchants keepe much about one rate, and each of them contenteth himselfe with foure, fiue, or six dishes, when they haue small resort, or peradventure with one or two, or thrée at the most, when they haue no strangers to accompanie them at their tables."

Before the suppression of the monasteries the heads of the two religious houses of Furness and Whalley were the most important personages in the county. Their establishments were maintained with regal splendour, and each had a retinue of servants that a prince might envy. The Stanleys were their great rivals in magnificence and the display of sumptuous hospitality. The records of Furness, the chartulary of Whalley, and the household books of the Earls of Derby, reveal the magnitude of their domestic establishments, and furnish a vivid picture of the condition of life and the profusion and rude magnificence that prevailed in the households of the great. The head of the great Cistercian house at Furness lived in a state of lordly ease. In addition to his great monastery at Beakansgill, he had his "spacious hall" in Lonsdale, his "stately grange" in Craven, and his "great inn" at York. The retinue of the Abbot of Whalley included ninety servants, who were tabled in the house; but the Earl of Derby surpassed them both, for it appears from the "checkrowle" of his establishment that, in 1587, "Mr. Steward," "Mr. Comptrowler," and "Mr. Receiver" had each three servants, seven "gentlemen waiters" had one servant each, and "Sir" Gilbert Townley, the chaplain, had one also. There were in the earl's retinue, in addition, nineteen "yeomen ushers," six "grooms of the chamber," two "sub-grooms," thirteen "yeomen waiters," two "trumpeters," besides inferior servants, making in all, one hundred and eighteen persons, among them being "y⁰ foole," to provoke mirth, and a "conjuror," to cast out devils. The tables of each were supplied with game and venison, and with every delicacy that could be procured. The consumption of animal food was enormous, and laymen and ecclesiastics seemed to have rivalled each other in the extent of their libations. Ale and beer were the common beverages. The Earl of Derby provided fifteen hogsheads every week, and in addition, it is said, thirteen and a half tuns of wine were drank at Lathom in one year; while at Whalley eight pipes of red wine a year were consumed, besides much larger quantities of what, in the chartulary, are called "sweet wines." In the houses of the knights and lesser gentry, though carried out upon a smaller scale, the same spirit of profuseness and lavish hospitality was maintained.

The potato, though now so familiar, especially in Lancashire, was not then known in England, except as a foreign root obtained with much difficulty and cost, and therefore the more desired. The wine most in estimation was called *theologicum*, because it was had from the clergy and religious men, whose cellars were well replenished. March beer was also much esteemed at the tables of the nobility and gentry, but it was required to be at least a year old. The household ale was not drunk till after it had been brewed a month.

The artificers and husbandmen had their festivities, as well as their betters, "especiallie," says Harrison, "at Bridales [i.e. Bride Ales], purifications of women, and such odd méetings, where it is incredible to tell what meat is consumed and spent, ech one bringing such a dish. or so many, with him, as his wife and he doo consult vpon, but alwaies with this consideration, that the léefr fréend shall haue the better prouision. This also is commonlie séene at their bankets, that the good man of the house is not charged with anything sauing bread, drink, sauce, houseroome and fire. But the artificers in cities and good townes deale far otherwise, for albeit that some of them doo suffer their iawes to go before their clawes, and diuers of them making good cheer doo hinder themselves and other men ; yet the wiser sort can handle the matter well enough in these iunkettings, and therefore their frugalitie deserueth commendation. Both the artificer and the husbandman are sufficientlie liberall and verie friendlie at their tables, and when they méete, they are so merry without malice, and plaine without inward Italian or French craft and subtiltie, that it would doo a man good to be in companie among them." [1]

The more opulent classes generally used wheaten bread at their own tables, while their household and poor neighbours were forced to content themselves with rye or barley, and in times of scarcity with beans, peas, or oaten bread, the latter of which was then in general use amongst the middle and lower classes in Lancashire and in Yorkshire, and is by no means entirely banished from these counties in the present day. According to the same authority the difference between summer and winter wheat was not known in his time by the husbandmen in many counties; but in the north, about Kendal, and we presume about Lancaster also, the spring wheat was cultivated, and called March wheat. In Elizabeth's time the practice of sitting long at meals grew into disuse, and two meals a day, dinner and supper, were thought sufficient. The nobility, gentry, and students usually dined at eleven o'clock in the forenoon, and supped between five and six o'clock in the afternoon. The merchants seldom dined before twelve at noon, and supped at six at night. The husbandmen and artisans dined at high noon, as they called it, and supped at seven or eight. In the universities the students, out of term-time, dined at ten o'clock in the morning.

In those early days, when coffee and tea, with various other slops, were unknown, or not used in England, it was no uncommon thing for the chief lords and ladies of the court to breakfast, as we have already shown,[2] upon a fine beefsteak and a cup of ale, and that at eight o'clock in the morning; and that the hour of supper was early in Queen Mary's time may be inferred from Weston's promise to Bradford, the Lancashire martyr, that he would see the queen, and speak to her on his behalf after supper; but, adds he, "it is to be thought that the queen has almost supped at present, for it is past six of the clock." In the reign of King James early hours were still kept by people of quality, for we learn from the king's history of the "Powder Plot," that the letter cautioning Lord Monteagle against going to Parliament was delivered in the evening, between six and seven o'clock, when his lordship was just going to supper.

During the wars of the Roses, the domestic accommodations of the people in this and the other counties of the kingdom were as scanty and deficient as their historical records.

"There are," says Harrison, "old men dwelling in the village where I remaine, which have noted three things to be marvellouslie altered in England within their sound remembrance : One is, the multitude of chimnies latelie erected, whereas in their yoong daies there were not aboue two or three, if so manie, in most vplandish townes of the realme (the religious houses and manour places of their lords alwaies excepted, and peraduenture some great personages), but ech one made his fire against a reredosse in the hall, where he dined and dressed his meat. The second is the great (although not generall) amendment of lodging, for (said they) our fathers (yea and we our selues also) haue lien full oft vpon straw pallets, on rough mats couered onelie with a shéet vnder couerlets made of dagswam or hopharlots (I vse their owne termes) and a good round log vnder their heads in steed of a bolster or pillow. If it were so that our fathers, or the goodman of the house, had within seuen yeares after his marriage purchased a matteres or flockbed, and thereto a sacke of chaffe to rest his head vpon, he thought himselfe to be as well lodged as the lorde of the towne, that peraduenture laie seldome in a bed of downe or whole fethers ; so well were they contented, and with such base kind of furniture ; which, also, is not verie much amended as yet in some parts of Bedfordshire, and elsewhere further off from our southerne parts. Pillowes (said they) were thought méete onelie for women in childbed. As for seruants, if they had anie shéet aboue them, it was well, for seldome had they anie vnder their bodies, to keepe them from the pricking straws that ran oft through the canuas of the pallet, and rased their hardened hides. The third thing they tell of, is the exchange of vessell, as of treene platters into pewter, and wooden spoones into siluer or tin. For so common were all sorts of treene stuffe in old time, that a man should hardlie find foure péeces of pewter (of which one was peraduenture a salt) in a good farmer's house, and yet for all this frugalitie (if it may so be iustly called) they were scarce able to liue and paie their rents at their daies without selling of a cow, or an horse, or more, although they paide but foure pounds at the vttermost by the yeare."

On the union of the houses of York and Lancaster, under the prudent government of Henry VII., the degrading and impoverishing feudal system having been virtually abolished,[3] the condition of all classes began to improve ; and in the reign of Elizabeth they attained to comparative opulence, as would appear from the same authority.

"The furniture of our houses," adds our author, "also exceedeth, and is growne in maner euen to passing delicacie ; and herein I doo not speake of the nobilitie and gentrie onlie, but likewise of the lowest sort. Certes in noble men's houses it is not rare to see abundance of Arras, rich hangings of tapistrie, siluer vessell, and so much other plate as may furnish sundrie cupbords to the summe oftentimes of a thousand or two thousand pounds at the least ; whereby the value of this and the rest of their stuffe dooth grow to be almost inestimable. Likewise in the houses of knights, gentlemen, merchantmen, and some other wealthie citizens, it is not geson [rare] to behold generallie their great prouision of tapistrie, Turkie worke, pewter, brasse, fine linen, and thereto costlie

[1] Description of England.
[2] See chap. xiii. p. 181.
[3] "As for slaves and bondmen, we have none ; and if any come hither, so soon as they set foot on land they become so free of condition as their masters."—Description of England in Elizabeth's Time.

cupbords of plate worth five or six hundred or a thousand pounds, to be deemed by estimation. But as herein all these sorts doo far exceed their elders and predecessors, and in neatness and curiositie, the merchant all other ; so in time past the costlie furniture staied there, whereas now it is descended yet lower, euen vnto the inferiour artificers and manie farmers, who, by vertue of their old and not of their new leases, haue for the most part learned also to garnish their cupbords with plate, their ioined beds with tapistrie and silke hangings, and their tables with carpets and fine naperie, whereby the wealth of our countrie dooth infinitelie appear."

Formerly the accommodation at the principal inns, even in the towns, was very deficient, but in the time of Elizabeth they had so much improved as to become great and sumptuous; and Holinshed, in his Itinerary from Cockermouth to London, enumerates amongst these places Kendale, Burton, Lancaster, Preston, Wigan, and Warrington, where the inns were well furnished with "napierie, bedding, and tapisserie. Each commer," says he, "is sure to lie in cleane sheets wherein no man hath been lodged since they came from the landresse. If the traueller haue an horse his bed dooth cost him nothing, but if he go on foot he is sure to paie a penie for the same ; but whether he be horseman or foote, if his chamber be once appointed, he may carie the kaie with him, as of his owne house, so long as he lodgeth there." It appears, however, that he was subject to great impositions at these plausible houses of entertainment, and if he was not upon his guard, his " budget " would be pillaged both by his host and by the servants. The penny for the lodging, when the comparative value of money is considered, was pretty much the same in amount in the time of Elizabeth as that which is now paid by travellers for similar accommodation at respectable inns. Henry VIII., indeed, had debased the coinage so much as to unsettle its value, but Elizabeth restored it by utterly abolishing the use of copper coin, which she made into cannon, and using only silver even in her halfpence and farthings, and silver groats were as common in her day as silver shillings are in ours.

Before the Reformation education had made but little progress. When the first of the Tudor sovereigns ascended the throne there was not a single public school from one end of the county to the other ; and had Shakspeare's Jack Cade been then living, he would have had no cause to reproach the Lancashire men, as he did Lord Say, with having " most traitorously corrupted the youth of the realm in erecting a grammar school." When the Reformation had been accomplished only three such schools had been founded—Farnworth in 1507, Manchester in 1515, and Warrington in 1526—but before the close of Elizabeth's reign the number had been increased to twenty-four. For the boy of " pregnant wit," as Hugh Oldham, the founder of the Manchester school phrased it, there were the schools attached to the monasteries, where he might obtain some kind of learning, better or worse, and be trained for the priesthood ; but those of the middle class had little chance, unless they had the good fortune to be admitted to the houses of the nobles and better born, when, with the younger members of the family, they might receive scholastic teaching from a properly-appointed teacher, and be fitted for the Universities. As a consequence there were few of the trading classes in the towns who could read, and still fewer who could write. Colonel Fishwick, in his " History of Kirkham," tells us that, so late as Elizabeth's reign, of the thirty sworn men who had control of the affairs of that parish only one could write, and that when he failed to attend the meetings the business had to be suspended.

The religious condition of the people, both before and after the Reformation, was little better. The parochial clergy were few, and their parishes were extensive, justifying to some extent the remark which Fuller made a century later, that " some clergymen, who have consulted God's honour with their own credit and profits, could not better desire for themselves than to have a Lincolnshire church as best built, a Lancashire parish as largest bounded, and a London audience as consisting of the most intelligent people." The heads of religious houses had succeeded in obtaining for themselves the larger portion of the rectorial endowments, and consequently the parishes were left to the spiritual care of vicars, generally men of little learning, who were willing to accept the small tithes as a miserable means of subsistence. The " parson " of Wigan was a great man in his way, and it is recorded that on one occasion, at his house in London, " he feasted two kings and two queens, with their attendants, seven hundred messes of meat scarce serving for the first dinner." But with the exception of the Rectors of Wigan and Winwick, the Vicar of Rochdale and the Warden of Manchester, there were few of the parochial clergy who were not rude and illiterate, and sprung from the lowest of the people.

After the Reformation the condition of things was but little better, and the state of the clergy was positively worse. James Pilkington, the first reformed Bishop of Durham, a Lancashire man, on visiting his ancestral home at Rivington, found the state of things in the county so deplorable that he in 1564 addressed a letter of remonstrance to Archbishop Parker, who was patron and rector of the three large parishes of Rochdale, Blackburn, and Whalley. " Your cures," said the Bishop, " all, except Rochdale, be as far out of order as the worst in all the country. The old Vicar of Blackburn resigned for a pension, and now liveth with Sir John Biron. Whalley hath as ill a vicar as the worst. And there is one come thitherto that hath been deprived or changed his name, and now teacheth school there; of evil to make them worse. If your grace's officers list, they might amend many things. I speak this," he adds, "for the amendment of the country, and that your grace's parishes might be better spoken of and ordered." The state of the church was lamentable. The Archbishop of York had covenanted with Downham, the Bishop of Chester, a man not over-burdened with scruples of any kind, for the visitation of the diocese; and Downham, good easy man, was content to receive the visitation fees, which were collected for him by a deputy. The Vicar of Rochdale was an avowed Papist, who kept out of the way, and retained a deputy to officiate for him. The Vicar of Blackburn eventually resigned on account of his ignorance, and the "ill vicar" of Whalley, as Pilkington designated him, is said to have been a man of low habits, loose morals, and so little learned that he was unable to read intelligibly. In the chapelries the complaint of ignorance, drunkenness, and licentiousness was general. The Curate of Stretford, in Manchester parish, kept an alehouse; his neighbour, the lector or reader of Chorlton, eked out a scanty subsistence by doing a little pawnbroking privately, but happening to be found out he was required to pay two shillings to the poor's box as the penalty for his offence; and Colonel Fishwick, in his "History of Kirkham," tells us that the Curate of Singleton, in that parish, was presented for, among other things, that "There is not servyce done in due tyme. He kepeth no hous nor releveth the poore. He is not dyligent in visitinge the sycke. He doth not teach the catechisme. There is no sermons. He churcheth fornycatours without doinge any penaunce. He maketh a dongehill in the chapell yeard, and," to crown his delinquencies, " he hath lately kepte a typlinge hous and a nowty woman in it."[1]

The endowments of these small chapelries were very inadequate, many of the benefices being worth no more than £4 or £5 a year. The Curate of Blackley, near Manchester, when prosecuted, in 1581, for teaching without a licence, pleaded poverty, and affirmed that his stipend was only £2 3s. 4d. a year; the Vicar of Rochdale paid the " preste " of his chapel of Saddleworth £3 every half year, and thought he had done handsomely; while many had to depend on the voluntary principle, and be content with the small offerings of their respective flocks. In many other places the clergy were equally ill-paid and the people as badly served—a condition of things that justified the commissioners in reporting to the Privy Council, in 1591, that in Lancashire the people " lack instruction, for the preachers are few. Most of the parsons are unlearned, many of those learned not resident, and divers unlearned daily admitted into good benefices." The churches on Sundays and holy days are reported as " being empty," and, it is added, what will hardly excite surprise, that there are " multitudes of bastards and drunkards," that " people swarm in the streets and ale-houses during service time," and there are "many lusty vagabonds."

With such laxity in the church it is no wonder that immorality should have prevailed to a large extent among the people, the masses of whom, it is to be feared, were neither very refined nor very virtuous. Delighting in cruel sports, such as bull-baiting and bear-baiting, and given to all manner of unlawful gaming, lewdness, and boisterous revelry, the alehouses, to which the more dissolute resorted, and they were innumerable, were the scenes of riots and feuds, which not only caused annoyance and scandal to the more well-disposed, but endangered the public peace to a greater degree than we can now easily conceive, and in the interests of morality it became necessary for those in authority to suppress by all lawful means such disorderly proceedings, and to punish all itinerant bearwards, vagrants, and other such disorderly persons. In August, 1585, the magistrates of Lancashire passed a series of resolutions respecting the government of alehouses, the principal of which were that no alehouse should be kept without a licence being first obtained at the quarter sessions, a rule not before observed. No ale was allowed to be sold for more than one penny for a quart. " Rogues and valiant beggars," and "strange beggars of forren shires," were forbidden to exercise their vocation in the county, and warning to this effect was to be " geven openlie in all parish churches" within the county; and none were to have license to beg except in their own hundred, and none were to use " begginge" who were able to work. No licences were henceforth to be granted for begging except at the general quarter sessions, in order that the Edie Ochiltrees of Lancashire might be restrained, if not suppressed.

The sports and pastimes of our ancestors consisted of hawking, hunting, and archery, to which the nobles added the jousts and tournaments; theatrical amusements of various kinds and music were also in vogue, to which the rustics added bull-baiting and bear-baiting, with their various gambols at the wakes and fairs. The theatrical performances consisted of sacred mysteries derived from the Holy Scriptures, of comedies, and of masques, which prevailed in the time of Elizabeth, when Shakspere lived, and in the times of James I., when Ben Jonson composed his celebrated masques for the royal amusement. Up to this time the players were deemed vagrants, and in 6

<hr />

[1] Chester Presentments at York quoted in Fishwick's *History of Kirkham*, pp. 45-6.—C.

Edward III. (1332), it was ordained by Parliament that they should be whipped out of London, notwithstanding their endeavours to entertain Prince Richard and his uncle the Duke of Lancaster. Their dramas, though sacred, were so ridiculous as to bring the histories of the New Testament into contempt, and to encourage libertinism and infidelity.[1] The wakes, though arising from the dedication of churches, soon degenerated into a species of rustic fairs, often kept on the Sunday, but totally devoid of any religious character. The waits or wakes, who were a species of nocturnal musicians, went through the streets at midnight, about Christmas time, playing their music, which is still partially continued; but in earlier times they were accustomed to sing carols and Christmas hymns. The minstrels were less stationary: they strolled about the country to feasts, fairs, and weddings, and these *cantabanqui* were accustomed to mount upon benches and barrel-heads, where they sang popular songs for the amusement of the rustics at the price of a groat a fit or canto, their matter being for the most part stories of past times.[2] Thus, in "The Blind Beggar of Bethnal Green" is the following verse :—

"Then give me leave, nobles and gentles each one, And if that it may not win good report,
One song more to sing, and then I have done ; Then do not give me a *groat* for my sport."

The second Randle Holme, who seems to have been a better antiquary than poet, has preserved the names of a number of the prevailing games of Lancashire in the following metrical enumeration :—

"AUNTIENT CUSTOMS IN GAMES USED BY BOYS AND GIRLES, MERILY SETT OUT IN VERSE.

"Any they dare chalenge for to throw the sledge,
To jumpe, or leape ovir ditch, or hedge ;
To wrastle, play at stoole ball, or to runne,
To pitch the barre, or to shoote of a gunne ;
To play at loggets, nine holes, or ten pinnes,
To trye it out at foote ball by the shinnes,
At tick tacke, seize nody, maw and ruffe,
At hot cokles. leape frogge, or blind man's buffe :
To drink the halper pottes, or deale at the whole cann,
To play at chess, or pue [? put] and inke horne ;
To daunce the moris, play at barley brake,
At al exploits a man can think or speak :
At shove groate, venter poynte, or cross and pile,
At beshrew him that's last at any stile ;
At leaping over a Christmas bonfire,
Or at the drawynge dame [? dunne—*i.e.* a dun horse] out of the myer;
At shoote cocke, Gregory, stoole ball, and what not,
Picke poynt, toppe, and scourge to make him hot."

The arts, as the coucher books of Whalley and Furness sufficiently show, had made considerable progress in the time of the first Duke of Lancaster. The art of engraving in wood and on copper had also advanced, as is evident from the remaining prints of Andrea Mantegna; and we have already seen that these ornamental accomplishments were crowned by an invention, the most important of any age or country, that of the art of printing, made by Guttenburg at Mentz, and introduced by Caxton, our countryman, into England.[3]

The administration of the laws in these early times was often extremely lax, as is instanced in the frequent and systematic arrests of the inhabitants of the county and duchy of Lancaster, under the colour of law, in the reign of Henry VI.; in the abduction of Lady Butler in the same reign; and in the killing of Mr. Hoghton at a still later period. When vagrants, pedlars, and strumpets were to be dealt with, the punishment was sufficiently severe and certain; the first, on conviction, were doomed to be grievously whipped, and burnt through the gristle of the right hand with a hot iron of an inch square; the next were condemned to the pillory, for the second offence against the monopolising borough shopkeepers; and the third were immersed by the ducking-stool, which was also appropriated to the correction of those domestic disturbers known by the name of notorious scolds.[4] Trial by combat or wager of battle, so prevalent in these early days, served to encourage the strong against the weak; this relic of a semi-barbarous age long outlived the trial by ordeal, which, as we have shown, was abolished on the northern circuit;[5] and, doubtless, in all other circuits in the kingdom, as early as the reign of Henry III. In the times of religious persecution the terrors of the rack were resorted to for the purpose of extorting confession for

[1] The first stage performances were in the churches, and on the Sabbath-day ; but this profanation of the sacred edifices was interdicted by Bonner, Bishop of London, in 1542.—*Warton's Hist. of Eng. Poetry.*
[2] Puttenham s Art of English Poesy, p. 69.
[3] It is conjectured, though the fact cannot be ascertained with certainty, that Manchester was the first town in Lancashire into which the printing press was introduced.
[4] The ducking-stool, though now wholly discarded, was in use in Manchester and in Preston within comparatively recent times. In the *Shuttleworth Accounts* (Chet. Soc.) there occur the entries—"January,

1601—for makinge a new pare of stocks and cockstool." "February 1611. Habergham Eaves—half a xv th for the cookestoole at Burneley." "August 1620—the Constable of Habergham Eaves, a xv th towards the cooke-stole and whipp-stocke to be made in Burnely—viiJ. ob." The Manchester Court Leet Records contain many entries relating to the cuck-stool. In 1648 the retiring constables were fined for neglecting to duck Mary Kemp, "a common scold," and their successors were ordered to see her ducked !—C.
[5] Chap. vii.

crimes that had sometimes never been committed; and as the duchy of Lancaster had its star-chamber, so also it had its rack.

Though grammar schools had been founded in various parts of the county long before the close of Elizabeth's reign, their effect was only gradually manifested on the general population. Education made but comparatively little progress, and the men of Lancashire, though the merriest of Englishmen, were as ignorant and superstitious as they were merry. Nowhere was the belief in witchcraft and supernatural agency more rife than in the palatinate. The shaping power of the imagination clothed every secluded clough and dingle with the weird drapery of superstition, and made every ruined or solitary tenement the abode of unhallowed beings, who were supposed to hold their diabolical revelries within it. The doctrines of necromancy and witchcraft were in common belief, and it is doubtful if there was a single person in the county who did not place the most implicit faith in both. The belief in these abominations was not confined to any one class of the people, or to the professors of any one form of faith. On the contrary, Churchmen, Romanists, and Puritans were alike the dupes of the loathsome impostors who roamed the country, though each in turn was ready to upbraid the others with being believers in the generally-prevailing error, and not unfrequently with being participators in the frauds that were practised. The bishops gave authority and a form of licence to the clergy to cast out devils; Romish ecclesiastics claimed a monopoly of the power; and the Puritan ministers, not to be outdone, tried their hands at the imposture. The Earl of Derby was reputed to keep a conjuror in his house; the Warden of Manchester, Dr. Dee, was a professor of the black art; and the criminal records of Lancashire tell of the number of wretched old women who were tried for having, according to the popular belief, sold themselves and sworn to do the devil's service, and of the monstrous fictions and horrible attestations that were made against them. Happily, with a more liberal administration of the laws, witch-finding became less reputable, and also less remunerative. The light of knowledge gradually dispelled the shades of the once generally-prevailing delusion, and the belief is now finally exploded, except among the most ignorant and vulgar. In Lancashire the term "witch" has long since lost its original opprobrium, and is now transferred to a gentler species of fascination which is exercised by the fairer sex in the palatinate without fear of judge or jury—a fascination so potent that few are able to escape the spell, and still fewer desire to do so.

Of the laws against witchcraft we shall have occasion to treat at some length; and it may suffice to say in this place that in the administration of those laws in Lancashire impartial justice and royal clemency were of rare occurrence.

But we must now resume our history with the reign of James I. at the commencement of the seventeenth century. On the king's arrival in York, on his first progress to London, he was met by persons of distinction from all the northern counties of England, charged with the duty of declaring the loyalty and allegiance of those counties to his majesty, without stipulating, however, for the loyalty of the king to the free institutions of the country. From the county of Lancaster Sir Edmond Trafford and Sir Thomas Holcroft attended, both of whom received the honour of knighthood in the garden of the palace at York, on Sunday the 17th of April, 1603; on the following day his majesty conferred the same honour on Sir Thomas Gerrard of Bryn, at Grimstone; and on the arrival of the royal suite at Worksop, Sir John Biron, of Newstead Abbey, in the county of Nottingham, and of Rochdale, in the county of Lancaster, father of John, the first Lord Biron, and Sir Thomas Stanley, of Derbyshire, were also dubbed knights. After the king's arrival in London, Sir Thomas Hesketh, Sir Thomas Walmsley, Sir Alexander Barlow, Sir Edward Stanley, Sir Thomas Langton, and Sir William Norris, all of the county of Lancaster, received the honour of knighthood; and in the following year (1604), Sir Gilbert Hoghton of Hoghton Tower, a distinguished favourite of the king, obtained the same honour. In this year Sir John Fortescue, knight, Chancellor of the Duchy of Lancaster, was appointed a member of a royal commission for the extermination of the Jesuits.

The plague, which had broken out in London in the first year of the king's reign, and carried off thirty thousand of its inhabitants, when the whole population of that city did not exceed one hundred and fifty thousand, spread the following year into Lancashire, and became so extremely fatal, that in Manchester alone one thousand of the inhabitants[1] died of that malady in 1605, which was probably equal to one-sixth of its population. The chaplin of the collegiate church, Mr. Kirke, his wife, and four children fell victims to the disease. With heroic fortitude the Rev. William Bourne, one of the fellows, continued to preach through the visitation, says Hollinworth, "in the towne so longe as he durst by reason of the unruliness of the infected persons, and want of government, and then he went and preached in a field near to Shorter's (? Shooter's) Brook, the townspeople being on one side of him and the country people on the other." In accordance with

---

[1] Hollinworth's Mancuniensis MS.

an arrangement come to with the lord of the manor, and in settlement of a dispute with the towns-men, six acres of land, part of the common at Collyhurst, were devoted to cabins for the reception of plague patients, many of whom were also buried there. At this time it was not usual to inter the dead of the lower class of people in coffins, and the bodies were probably often insufficiently covered with earth, which might conduce to the spread of the pestilence; indeed, as late as 1628 it was no unusual thing to bury the poor without coffins.[1]

This pestilence having greatly subsided in London, it was appointed that the first parliament in the new reign should assemble on the 5th of November; but while the preparations were making a plot was discovered, the most atrocious that "the tongue of man ever delivered, the ear of man ever heard, the heart of man ever conceived, or the malice of devils ever practised"[2]—a plot which had for its object to destroy at one blow the king and queen, and their family, with the lords and the commons of the realm congregated in parliament. Some of the actors in this tremendous drama stand connected with the county of Lancaster, but happily rather has conservators than destroyers. The letter by which the treason was disclosed is supposed to have been written by a lady, a descendant by the female line of Sir Edward Stanley, the Lancashire hero of Flodden Field,

FAC-SIMILE OF THE LETTER TO LORD MOUNTEAGLE.

to her brother, Lord Monteagle, a Roman Catholic.[3] Overtures had been made by the conspirators to Sir William Stanley, who was then in Flanders, to become a party in the treason, but Sir William in some degree retrieved his character by declining to take part himself, and by discountenancing an intended application to foreign Catholic powers to aid the conspiracy. The plot originated with Robert Catesby, a descendant of the noted favourite of Richard III., a man of fortune, in the enjoyment of the family estate at Ashby, in Northamptonshire, and with Thomas Percy, a gentleman-pensioner to the king, and a descendant of the illustrious house of Northumberland, both of them Roman Catholic recusants; its object being to destroy the Protestant reigning family, and to substitute a Catholic dynasty. Having increased their numbers by the addition of Robert Winter, Thomas Winter, John Wright, and Christopher Wright, and

---

[1] Sir Henry Spelman's Treatise De Sepulturâ, p. 173.
[2] Sir Edward Philip's speech on the trial of the conspirators engaged in the gunpowder treason.
[3] Father Juvenci, in his Hist. Societatis Jesu, l. xiii. s. 45, says that "Tresham, one of the conspirators, sent to Lord Monteagle, his friend, the letter revealing the conspiracy."

embarked Guido Fawkes, a Yorkshireman, and a soldier of fortune passing under the name of Johnson, in the enterprise, Percy, who had rented the vault under the Houses of Parliament as a fuel cellar, there accumulated thirty-six barrels of gunpowder to perpetrate the intended explosion. Sir Everard Digby, Ambrose Rookwood, Esq., Francis Tresham, Esq., Thomas Habington, Esq., John Grant, and Robert Keys, gentlemen, became also members of the conspiracy, though less actively employed in the treason.[1] To bind the conspirators to secrecy and to perseverance in the treasonable design, Gerrard, a Jesuit, administered an oath to Catesby and Percy, and to others of their fraternity, in these terms:—

"You shall swear by the blessed Trinity, and by the sacrament you now purpose to receive, never to disclose, directly or indirectly, by word or circumstance, the matter that shall be proposed to you to keep secret, nor desist from the execution thereof, until the rest give you leave.

Ten days before the time appointed for the assembling of Parliament, Lord Monteagle, son and heir to Lord Morley, being in his lodgings in London, ready to go to supper, between six and seven o'clock at night, one of his footmen, on returning from an errand across the street, delivered to him a letter, without either date, signature, or superscription, which had been put into his hand in the dark by a man unknown, who charged him to give it to his master, and which letter was expressed in these terms:—

"To the ryght honorable The Lord monteagle,—my lord, out of the loue I beare To some of youere frends, I haue a caer of youer preseruacion, Therefor i would advyse youe as you Tender youer lyf To deuyse some exscuse to shift of youer attendance at This parleament, for god and man hathe concurred To punishe the wickednes of This Tyme, and Thinke not slightlye of this advertisment but reteyre youre self into youre contri, wheare yowe maye expect the euent in safti, for Thowghe Theare be no apparance of anni stir, yet I saye they shall receyue a Terrible blowe this parleament, and yet they shall not seie who hurts Them. This counsel is not To be a contemned because it maye do yowe good, and can do yowe no harme, for The dangere is pased as soon as yowe have burnt The letter, and I hope god will give yowe The grace to mak good use of it, To whose holy proteccion I comend yowe."—(See p. 264 for facsimile.)

After pondering over the letter for some time, doubtful whether the writer was in jest or in earnest, his lordship repaired to the king's palace at Whitehall, and there delivered the letter to the Earl of Salisbury, the principal secretary of state,[2] who has himself given an account of what followed; and we prefer quoting his own words, because they involve a point of history which has been misrepresented for the purpose of courtly adulation.

"When I observed the generality of the advertisement and the [style of the letter], I could not well distinguish whether it were a frenzy or sport. For, from any serious ground, I could hardly be induced to believe that it proceeded, for many reasons. First, because no wise man would think my Lord to be so weak as to take any alarm to absent himself from Parliament vpon such a Loose Advertisement. Secondly, I considered that if any such thing were really intended, that it was very improbable that only one Nobleman should be warned and none other. Nevertheless, being loth to trust my own judgement alone, being always inclined to do too much in such a Case as this, I imparted the letter to the Earl of Suffolk, Lord Chamberlain, to the end I might receive his opinion. Wherevpon perusing the words of the letter and observing the writing, *That the blow should come without knowledge who had hurt them*, we both conceiued that it could not be more proper than the time of Parlement; Nor by any other way like to be attempted, then with Powder whilst the King was sitting in the assembly. Of which the Lord Chamberlaine [thought] ye more probability Because there was a great Vault vnder the said Chamber wch was neuer used for anything but some wood and coal belonginge to ye Keeper of ye Old Palace. In which consideration, after we had imparted the same to the Lord Admiral, the Earl of Worcester and the Earle of Northampton and some other, We all thought fit to forbear to impart it to the King, vntill some three or four days before the Session. At which time we shewed his Matie the letter, rather as a thing we would not Conceal (because it was of such a nature) than any way perswading him to give any further Credit to it, vntill the place had been visited, wherevpon his Matie (who hath a naturall habit to Contemn all false fears and a Judgmt so strong as never to doubt anything which is not well warranted by reason) concurred only thus far with vs, That seeing such a matter was possible, That should bee done which might prevent all danger, or else nothing at all. Herevpon it was moved, That till the night before his coming nothing should be done to interrupt any purpose of theirs that had any such devillish practice, But rather to suffer them to go on till the Eve of the day. And so on Monday in the afternoon accordingly the Lord Chamberlain, whose office it is to see all places of Assembly put in readiness when the King's person should come, taking with him ye Lord Mounteagle, went to see all ye places in ye Parliament House. And took also a slight occasion to peruse that Vault, where finding only Piles of Billets and faggots heaped vpp, His Lordshipp fell into inquiring onely who owned the same wood, Observing the proportion to be somewhat more than ye Howse Keeper was likely to lay in for his own use. And when Answer was made that it belonged to one Mr. Percy, His Lordship straight conceiued some suspicion in regard of his person; And the Lord Mounteagle taking some notice that there was great profession between Percy and him from which some inference might be made that it [was] the warning of a friend. My Lord Chamberlaine resolved absolutely to proceed in a search though any way returned being returned to the Court about five a Clock took me up with him to the King, and told him yt although they were hard of belief that any such thing was thought of yet in such a case as this whatsoever was not done (to put all out of doubt) was as good as nothing. Wherevpon it was resolved by his Matie that this matter should be so carried as no man should be scandalized by it, nor any alarm taken for any such purpose. For the better effecting whereof The Lord Treasurer, the Lord Admiral, the Earl of Worcester, and we two agreed That Sr Tho. Knevett should, under a pretext of searching for stolen and imbezilled goodes, both in that place and other houses thereabouts, remove all that wood, and so to see the plain ground vnder it. Sr Tho. Knevett going thither (vnlooked for) about Midnight into the Vault, found that fellow Johnsonne [Fawkes] newly come out of the Vault, and without any more questions stayed him, And having no sooner removed the wood, he perceived the Barrells, and so bound the Caitiff fast, who made no difficulty to acknowledge the fact, nor to Confess clearly that the morrow following it should have been effected. And thus have you a true narration from the beginning," &c.

[1] Works of King James I. p. 241.

[2] Letter from (Cecil) the Earl of Salisbury, dated November 9, 1605, to Sir Charles Cornewallyes. Harl. MSS. cod. 1875.

35

From this letter, which was written by Tresham, a relation of Lord Monteagle, it appears that the sagacity of first penetrating the mystery, imputed to the king by historians, and by senators,[1] and for which he himself takes credit in his work on the "Powder Treason,"[2] was not his. After some delay, and with considerable difficulty, Fawkes, the incendiary, was brought to confess, in the presence of the privy council, that the plot was first communicated to him about Easter, in the year 1604, when he was in the Low Countries, by Thomas Winter, and that on his arrival in England he conferred upon it with Catesby, Percy, and John Wright, and that they and he laboured in the mine to penetrate from the adjoining house through the walls into the vault under the House of Lords, which work was abandoned when Percy got the vault itself into his possession. On the rumour of the discovery of the plot, several of the conspirators hurried down into Warwickshire, where they made a fruitless attempt to raise an insurrection, in which Percy and Catesby were killed, and Digby, Rookwood, and the others, being taken prisoners, were brought to London, tried, and executed on the thirtieth of January, 1606, along with Fawkes. The Catholics as well as the Protestants condemned this diabolical treason in the most unqualified terms; and so strongly was the king impressed with the conviction that it was the conspiracy of a few fanatical individuals, and not of a Christian community, that, in his speech at the opening of Parliament, he deprecated the injustice of involving the Roman Catholics, as a body, in such enormous barbarities. Lord Monteagle, whose promptitude and undeviating loyalty had, through the blessing of Providence, saved all the estates of the realm, was rewarded for his communication by a grant of crown lands and a pension; and as a further mark of the king's favour towards him, the life of his brother-in-law, Thomas Habington, Esq., of Hendlip, in Worcestershire, the husband of the lady who is conjectured to have written the mysterious letter which afforded the clue to the discovery, was saved, on condition that he should not quit the county of Worcester. The debt of public gratitude due to Lord Monteagle from his country has been thus commemorated:—

> "Lo, what my country should have done (have raised
> 　An obelisk, or column, to thy name,
> Or, if she would but modestly have praised
> 　Thy fact, in brass or marble writ the same)
> I, that am glad of thy great chance, here do I
> 　And, proud my work shall out-last common deeds,
> Durst think it great and worthy wonder too,
> 　But thine, for which I do't, so much exceeds.
> My country's parents I have many known,
> 　But saver of my country thee alone."
> 　　　　　—BEN JONSON's *Epitaph on Lord Monteagle.*

Sir William Stanley, with two other popish recusants of the names of Owen and Baldwin, were placed under arrest at Brussels, on suspicion of having been concerned in the gunpowder treason; but in the cool language of Sir Thomas Edmonds, the English ambassador, "Sir William was not yet so deeply charged concerning this last treason" as to be put upon his trial. According to a monument in St. Ann's Church, Aldersgate, London, Peter Heywood, Esq., of Heywood (then spelt Heiwood), a magistrate of the county of Lancaster, having probably accompanied SirThomas Knevett, apprehended Guido Fawkes with his dark lantern coming forth from the vault of the Houses of Parliament on the eve of the gunpowder treason; and on the same authority it appears that this vigilant magistrate was stabbed in Westminster Hall, five-and-thirty years afterwards, by John James, a frantic Dominican friar, for urging him to take the oaths of supremacy and allegiance.[3] That the Stanley family stood in high estimation with the king may be inferred from the fact of the mutual interchange of New Year's gifts in 1606[4] between his majesty and the Earl of Derby, and from the present of plate given to the earl on the christening of his son and heir, James, the future Earl of Derby, who was destined to die on the scaffold in the cause of the Stuarts.

Among the "Domestic State Papers"[5] is a letter from Sir Nicholas Mosley and Richard Holland, dated Tetlow, 20th November, 1605, and addressed to the constables of Manchester, in which occurs the following passage:—

"For better accomplishment of His Majesty's commands by the late proclamation for detecting and apprehending divers traitors therein mentioned, or others suspected of having had any hand in that horrible treason, we command you to cause watch and ward to be duly kept in Manchester for staying and examining all strangers and others suspected of having been privy to the said detestable enterprise, and to cause them to be forthwith brought before the next Justice of the Peace to be examined and searched for letters, &c., and we command you and all others to do your best endeavours, upon pain of your allegiance, and as you tender His Majesty's high indignation."

[1] In the preamble to the act for public thanksgiving on the anniversary of the 5th of November, it is said, that "the conspiracy would have turned to the utter ruin of this whole kingdom, had it not pleased Almighty God, by inspiring the king's most excellent majesty with a divine spirit to interpret some dark phrases of a letter, shewed to his majesty, above and beyond all ordinary construction, thereby miraculously discovering this hidden treason."

[2] Works of King James I. p. 227.
[3] Stowe's Survey of London, vol. i. p. 605. Clarendon's *Hist. of Reb.* i. 387.
[4] Nichols's *Progresses of King James* I. vol. i. p. 598.
[5] *Domestic State Papers*, v. xxxiii. No. 42.—C.

A knightly dignity of inheritance more elevated than that of the knights banneret[1] was instituted by the king, in 1611, for the ostensible purpose of defending and reforming the province of Ulster, in Ireland. It was the boast of King James and his courtiers that he had done more in nine years towards ameliorating the condition of the people of Ireland than had been accomplished by his predecessors in the four hundred and forty-years which had elapsed since the first conquest of that country.[2] To carry on these improvements, and to preserve the peace of the country, the baronets were created, each of whom had a bloody hand, in a field argent (the arms of Ulster), superadded to his family arms. The stipulations entered into by the recipients of the new honour were that they should be aiding towards the building of churches, towns, and castles; should hazard their lives and fortunes in the performance of their duty; and that, when any spark of rebellion or other hostile invasion should threaten to disturb the peace of the kingdom or province, they should be ready to defend it; and that each of them should maintain and keep thirty foot soldiers there at 8d. a day for three years. None were at first admitted to the new honour except those descended, at least, from a grandfather, on the father's side, who had borne arms, and who had a clear income in land of £1,000 per annum. At the institution of the order, it was intended that the number should not exceed two hundred, that number to be filled up as the titles became extinct. In the first batch of baronets, created on the 22nd of May, eighteen knights were honoured with this hereditary degree, amongst whom were the names of Sir Richard Molineux of Sefton; Sir Richard Hoghton of Hoghton Tower; and Sir Thomas Gerrard of Bryn,[3] all in the county of Lancaster; and Sir George Booth of Dunham Massey, in the county of Chester.[4] Up to this time, the honourable ancient dignities were only eleven in number, but they were now increased to twelve, ranking in the following order: First the king, second the prince, third the duke, fourth the marquis, fifth the earl, sixth the viscount, seventh the baron; and these seven are called princely, and allowed to wear coronets. The other five are noble—as, first the knight baronet, second the knight banneret, third the knight bachelor, fourth the esquire, and fifth the gentleman.

This was the age of witchcraft; and no county in the kingdom was more scandalised by the degrading superstition than the county of Lancaster. In the present day, when the term "Lancashire Witches" serves only to excite feelings of gaiety and admiration,[5] it is not possible to conceive how different were the sentiments produced by these magical words in the seventeenth century, when the "Solomon of the North" ascended the throne of England, and when, on the proclamation of a general pardon, the crime of "wytchcrafte" was excepted from the common amnesty. A petition from Dr. Dee, warden of the Collegiate Church of Manchester, of the date of the 5th of January, 1604, praying to be freed from this revolting imputation of witchcraft, even at the risk of a trial for his life, sufficiently indicates the horror excited by the charge. "It has been affirmed," says the doctor, "that your majesty's supplicant was the conjuror belonging to the most honourable privy council of your majesty's predecessor, of famous memory, Queen Elizabeth; and that he is, or hath been, a caller or invocater of devils, or damned spirits: these slanders, which have tended to his utter undoing, can," he adds, "no longer be endured; and if on trial he is found guilty of the offence imputed to him, he offers himself willingly to the punishment of death; yea, either to be stoned to death, or to be buried quick, or to be burned unmercifully."[6] Conjuror or not, the reverend warden sported with conjuror's weapons, and his predictions on the fortunate day for the coronation of his royal mistress, and his pretensions to render innoxious the waxen effigy of Queen Elizabeth found in Lincoln's Inn Fields, very naturally subjected him to those suspicions which, combined with other circumstances hereafter to be mentioned, proved his utter undoing. The doctor's connections, too, were of the most suspicious kind. For some years he was the friend and associate of Edward Kelley, *alias* Talbot, a notorious English alchemist and necromancer, who, for some delinquencies, coining it is said, had had his ears cut off at Lancaster. It was the practice of Kelley to exhume and consult the dead to obtain a knowledge, as he pretended, of the fate of the living; and upon a certain night, in the park of Walton-le-Dale, in the county of Lancaster, with one Paul Wareing, of Clayton Brook, his fellow-companion in such

[1] The last knight banneret created was Sir Ralph Sadler, chancellor of the duchy of Lancaster, on the field of Musselburgh, in the year 1547.
[2] King James's Works p. 259.
[3] Each baronet paid a patent fee of £1,000 on his creation; but this sum was returned to Sir Thomas Gerrard, in consideration of his father's sufferings in the cause of the king's mother, Mary Queen of Scots.
[4] Dr. Peter Heylin, in his *Help to English History*, published in 1671, gives a list of the baronetcies created from the institution of the Order to the time of issue, in which the following Lancashire names appear :—
1611. May 22.—Sir Thos. Gerard, of Bryn, Knight.
1620. June 28.—Ralph Ashton, of Lever, Esq.
1627. June 26.—Edward Stanley, of Bickerstaffe, Esq.
1641. Aug. 16.—Rob. Bindloose, of Borwick, Esq.
1644. April 1.—John Preston, of the Manour in Furnesse, Esq.
1644. April 25.—Thomas Prestwich, of Holme (Hulme), Esq.

1660. June 7.—Sir Orlando Bridgeman, of Great Lever, Knight, Chief Baron of the Exchequer.
1660. Aug. 17.—Sir Ralph Ashton, of Middleton, Knight.
1660-1 Mar. 4.—Thomas Clifton, of Clifton, Esq.
The list is, however, incomplete, the following names being omitted :—
1611. May 22.—Sir Richard Molyneux, of Sefton, Knight.
1611. May 22.—Sir Thomas Houghton, of Hoghton Tower, Knight.
1640. July 20.—Edward Mosley, of Ancoats, Esq.
1642. June 24.—George Middleton, of Leighton, Esq.—C.
[5] Mackenzie mentions a case of a fine girl, condemned to die in Scotland for witchcraft, whose crime in reality was that she had attracted too great a share, in the lady's opinion, of the attention of the laird. This in modern times would have been called a *real* Lancashire witch.
[6] Lansdowne MSS. cod. 161.

deeds of darkness, he invoked one of the infernal regiment, to know certain passages in the life, as also what might be known by the devil's foresight of the manner and time of death, of a noble young gentleman in Wareing's wardship.[1] This ceremony being ended, Kelley and his companion repaired to the churchyard of Walton-le-Dale, sometimes called Law Church, where they dug up the body of a poor old man recently interred, and whom, by their incantations, they made to deliver strange predictions concerning the same gentleman, who was probably present, and anxious to read a page in the book of futurity.[2] After these feats, which were no doubt performed by a kind of ventriloquism, Seer Edward went abroad, accompanied by Dr. Dee, where they found the celebrated elixir, or philosopher's stone, in the form of a powder, by which, amongst other transmutations, they converted the bottom of a warming-pan into good silver, only by warming it at the fire ; and so plentiful were the precious metals that their children played with golden quoits![3] The fame of the alchemists having reached Queen Elizabeth, she sent a messenger, Captain Peter Gwinne, secretly, for Kelley, who had got himself immured in one of the prisons of the Emperor Rodolphus II. in Prague. But he was doomed to die in a foreign land, for in an attempt to escape out of the window of the castle he received a mortal bruise—the elixir not being able, as it should appear, to communicate immortality to its possessor.

The first distinct charge of witchcraft in any way connected with this county is that (in 1447) of the wife of the good Duke Humphrey, Duchess of Gloucester, the associate of Roger Bolingbroke the priest and Margaret Jourdan,[4] who, after having been hurled by her ambition and inquisitive credulity from the highest elevation to the lowest degradation, became the prisoner of Sir Thomas Stanley, in the Isle of Man, and for some time suffered confinement in the castle of Liverpool.[5] The arts of the Lancashire alchemists, and Sir Edward Ashton, though partaking of the nature of witchcraft, prefer no claim to supernatural agency, but may rank amongst the eccentric phenomena of the human mind.[6]

In the Stanley family, Edward, Earl of Derby, had the reputation, on the authority of a minister of state, of entertaining a conjuror in his house ; and Margaret Clifford, Countess of Derby, lost the favour of Queen Elizabeth for a womanish curiosity (from which the queen herself was not entirely free) and consulting with wizards and cunning men ; while Ferdinando, Earl of Derby, died, as we have seen, under the impression that he was bewitched, in which belief " very many, and some of them very learned men, concurred." During his last sickness " a homelie wise-woman, about fifty years old, was found mumbling in a corner in his honour's chamber, but what God knoweth. . . . About midnight was found by Mr. Halsall an image of wax, with hair like unto the hair of his honour's head, twisted through the belly thereof; and he fell twice into a trance, not able to move hand or foot, when he would have taken physic to do him good. In the end, he cried out often against all witches and witchcraft, reposing his only hope of salvation upon the merits of Christ Jesus his Saviour."[7]

Connected with these impositions and this infatuation was the doctrine and practice of demoniacal possession and dispossession, on which subject an almost interminable controversy arose, which divided public opinion in the county of Lancaster for many years, and which, like witchcraft itself, was at lenth exploded by the progress of knowledge.

Amongst the first cases of this kind is that of "Ann Milner, a maiden of Chester, eighteen years of age," to whom an evil spirit appeared suddenly, on the 16th of February, 1564, in the form of a " white thing compassing her roundabout," while she was bringing her father's kine from the field. The following morning she took to her bed, where she fell into a succession of trances, from which she was not recovered till, on the bidding of Master Lane, a clergyman, she said the Lord's Prayer and *Te Deum*, and was immediately dispossessed, after more than a month's affliction, at which the whole city stood astonished. The judge of assize, John Throgmorton, Esq., high justice, heard a sermon from Master Lane, on the occasion, and Sir Wyllyam Calverley, knight, Richard Harlestone, Esq., and John Fisher, attested the veracity of the narrative.[8]

Another case of demoniacal possession, much more extensive and varied in its circumstances, took place at Cleworth, now called Clayworth, in the parish of Leigh, in the county of Lancaster, thirty years afterwards. The facts are related by the Rev. John Darrell, a minister of religion, and himself a principal actor in the scene. According to the narrative published by this divine, there

---

[1] Weever's Ancient Funeral Monuments, p. 45.
[2] It is not known with certainty when this circumstance occurred, but a local historian, anxious to supply the omission, gives the date August 12, 1560, and says that Dee was present. This, however, is clearly an error, for Kelly could then only have been about five years of age, and Dee did not make his acquaintance until long afterwards.—O.
[3] With this "powder of projection," or "salt of metals," as it was variously called, Dee and his associate were enabled to coat the baser metals with silver or gold, having, as it would seem, hit upon the process which, a century and a half later, Joseph Hancock introduced into Sheffield—that of electro-plating. Ashmole, in his MS., 1790, fol. 58,

says, " Mr. Lilly told me that John Evans informed him that he was acquainted with Kelly's sister in Worcester, that she showed him some of the gold her brother had transmuted, and that Kelly was first an apothecary in Worcester."—O.
[4] Margaret Jourdan, the Witch of Eyee, was burnt to death in Smithfield.
[5] See chap. xi. p. 175.
[6] See chap. xi. p. 176.
[7] Harl. MSS. cod. 247.
[8] From a black-letter copy in the British Museum, transcribed and obligingly furnished by George Ormerod, Esq.

lived in the year 1594 (? Jan. 1596-7), at Cleworth, one Nicholas Starkie,[1] who had only two children, John and Anne, the former ten and the latter nine years of age. These children, according to our authority, became possessed with an evil spirit; and John Hartley, a reputed conjuror, was applied to, at the end of from two to three months, to give them relief, which he effected by various charms, and the use of a magical circle with four crosses, drawn near Mr. Starkie's seat, at Huntroyde, in the parish of Whalley. Hartley was conjuror enough to discover the difference between Mr. Starkie's table and his own, and he contrived to fix himself as a constant inmate in his benefactor's family for two or three years. Being considered so essential to their peace, he advanced in his demands, till Mr. Starkie demurred, and a separation took place; but not till five other persons, three of them the female wards of Mr. Starkie, and two other females, had become possessed through the agency of Hartley, "and it was judged in the house that whomsoever he kissed on them he breathed the devil." According to the narrative, all the seven demoniacs sent forth such a strange and supernatural voice of loud shouting as the like was never before heard at Cleworth, nor in England. In this extremity Dr. Dee, the warden of Manchester College, was applied to to exorcise the evil spirits; but he refused, telling them he would practise no such unlawful arts as they desired, but, instead, advised that they should "call in some godlye preachers, with whom he would consult concerning a public or private fast." At the same time he sharply reproved Hartley for his fraudulent practices. Some remission of violence followed; but the evil spirits soon returned, and Mr. Starkie's house became a perfect bedlam. John Starkie, the son, was "as fierce as a madman, or a mad dog;" his sister Anne was little better; Margaret Hardman, a gay, sprightly girl, was also troubled, and aspired after all the splendid attire of fashionable life, calling for one gay thing after another, and repeatedly telling her *lad*, as she called her unseen familiar, that she would be finer than him.[2] Eleanor, her younger sister, and Ellen Holland, another of Mr. Starkie's wards, were also "troubled;" and Margaret Byrom, daughter of Adam Byrom, a wealthy "merchaunt" of Salford, a woman thirty-three years of age, who was on a visit at Cleworth, became giddy, and partook of the general malady. The young ladies fell down as dead, while they were dancing and "singing and playing the minstrel," and talked at such a rate that nobody could be heard but themselves.

The preachers being called in, according to the advice of Dr. Dee, they inquired how the young demoniacs were handled, to which the possessed replied by a strange and absurd rhapsody. On the 16th of March, Maister George More, pastor of Cawke (Calke), in Derbyshire, and Maister John Darrell, afterwards preacher at St. Mary's, in Nottingham, came to Cleworth, when they saw the girls grievously tormented. Jane Ashton, the servant of Mr. Starkie, howled in a supernatural manner, Hartley having given her kisses and promised her marriage. The ministers having got all the seven into one chamber, gave them spiritual advice; but on the Bible being brought up to them, three or four of them began to scoff and called it, "Bib-le Bab-le, Bible Bable." The next morning they were got into a large parlour and laid on couches, when Maister More and Maister Dickens, a preacher (and their pastor), along with Maister Darrell and thirty other persons, spent the day with them in prayer and fasting, and hearing the word of God. All the parties afflicted remained in their fits the whole of the day. Towards evening, every one of them, with voice and hands lifted up, cried to God for mercy, and He was pleased to hear them, so that six of them were shortly dispossessed, and Jane Ashton in the course of the next day experienced the same deliverance. At the moment of dispossession some of them were miserably rent, and the blood gushed out both at the nose and the mouth. Margaret Byrom said that she felt the spirit come up her throat, when it gave her a "sore lug" at the time of quitting her, and went out of the window with a flash of fire, she only seeing it; John Starkie said his spirit left him like a man with a hunch on his back, very ill-favoured; Eleanor Hardman's was like an urchin; Margaret Byrom's like an ugly black man with shoulders higher than his head; and the others were equally hideous. This occurred on the 9th January, 1596-7. Two or three days afterwards the unclean spirits returned, and would have re-entered had they not been resisted. When they could not succeed, either by bribes or entreaties, they threw some of them violently down, and deprived others of the use of their legs and other members; but the victory was finally obtained by the preachers, and all the devils banished from Mr. Starkie's household. In this state of turmoil and confusion Mr. Starkie's house had been kept for upwards of two years, but in the meantime Hartley, the conjuror, who seems to have been a designing knave, after undergoing an examination before two magistrates, was committed to Lancaster Castle, where he was convicted, on the evidence

---

[1] Nicholas Starkie was the head of the family of that name, of Huntroyde, near Padiham, in Whalley parish. He married at Leigh, August 5th, 1578, Anne, widow of Thurston Barton, of Smithells, and daughter and sole heir of John Parr, of Kempnough and Cleworth, and in her right became possessed of Cleworth, where he was residing at the time of the events narrated. Of the two children of the marriage, John, the eldest, married, in 1604, Margaret, daughter of Thomas Leigh, and from him descends the present owner of Huntroyde, Le Gendre Nicholas Starkie. Anne, the daughter, who was baptised at Leigh, May 22, 1608, became the wife of Thomas Dyke, of Westwick, co. York, Esq.—C.

[2] See p. 255.

of Mr. Starkie and his family, of witchcraft, and sentenced to be executed, principally, as it is stated, for drawing the magical circle, which seems to have been the least part of his offence, though the most obnoxious to the law. In this trial, *spectral evidence* was adduced against the prisoner, and the experiment was tried of saying the Lord's Prayer.[1] It does not appear that any of the Lancashire witches or wizards were tried by *swimming*. When it no longer served his purpose, he endeavoured to divest himself of the character of a conjuror, and declared that he was not guilty of the crime for which he was doomed to suffer. The law, however, was inexorable, and he was brought to execution. On the scaffold he persisted in declaring his innocence, but to no purpose. The executioner did his duty, and the criminal was suspended. While in this situation the rope broke, when he confessed his guilt; and being again tied up, he died the victim of his own craft, and of the infatuation of the age in which he lived.[2] On the appearance of Mr. Darrell's book, containing the relation of these marvellous events, a long controversy arose on the doctrine of demonology, and it was charged upon him by the Rev. Samuel Harsnet, afterwards Bishop of Chichester, Norwich, and York, that he made a trade of casting out devils, and that he instructed the *possessed* how to conduct themselves, in order to aid him in carrying on the imposition. Mr. Darrell was afterwards examined by the queen's commissioners; and, by the full agreement of the whole court, he was condemned as a counterfeit, deposed from the ministry, and committed to close confinement, there to remain for further punishment. The clergy, in order to prevent the scandal brought upon the church by false pretensions to the power of dispossessing demons, soon after introduced a new canon into the ecclesiastical law, expressed in these terms: "That no minister or ministers, without licence and direction of the bishop, under his hand and seal obtained, attempt, upon any pretence whatsoever, either of possession or obsession, by fasting and prayer, to cast out any devil or devils, under pain of the imputation of imposture, or cozenage, and deposition from the ministry." Some light is cast upon these mysterious transactions by " a discourse concerning the possession and dispossession of seven persons in one family in Lancashire," written by George More, a Puritanical minister (the Vicar of Calke or Cawc), who had engaged in exorcising the legion of devils. This discourse agrees substantially with Darrell's narrative, but adds some facts that are worthy of mention—amongst others, that he, Mr. More, was a prisoner in the Clink for nearly two years, for justifying and bearing witness to the facts stated by his fellow-minister. Speaking of Mr. Starkie's family, he says that Mr. Nicholas Starkie having married a gentlewoman that was an inheritrix, and of whose kindred some were Papists—these, partly for religion and partly because the estate descended not to heirs-male—prayed for the perishing of her issue, and that four sons pined away in a strange manner; but that Mrs. Starkie, learning this circumstance, estated her lands on her husband, and *his* heirs, failing issue of her own body, after which a son and daughter were born, who prospered well till they arrived at the age of ten or twelve years. In this disordered state of the public mind a work of King James's, under the title of " Dæmonologie," alike distinguished for its vulgar credulity and for its sanguinary denunciations, was issued from the press, and read with avidity. The sapient author, after having imagined a fictitious crime, placed the miserable and friendless objects of conviction beyond all hopes of royal clemency. Having laboured to open the door for the most unjust convictions, the royal fanatic adds that all witches ought to be put to death, without distinction of age, sex, or rank.[3]

It has been said that witchcraft came in with the Stuarts, and went out with them, but this is an injustice to the memory of the author of " Dæmonologie," for the belief in sorcery, witchcraft, enchantment, demonology, and practices of a kindred nature, were, as we have seen, widely prevalent long ere King James ascended the English throne. Henry VIII., in 1531, granted a formal licence to "two learned clerks," " to practise sorcery, and to build churches," a curious combination of evil and its antidote; and ten years later he, with his accustomed inconsistency, issued a decree making "witchcraft and sorcery felony, without benefit of clergy."

A few years after the royal author of the sanguinary commentary upon the demoniacal code of Henry VIII. and Elizabeth ascended the English throne a discovery took place of an alleged convention of witches, held at Malkin Tower[4] (a ruined and desolate farmhouse), in Pendle Forest, in the county of Lancaster. It has been justly observed by Dr. Hibbert-Ware that witchcraft was generally the most rife in wild and desolate parts of the country, and this observation is borne out

---

[1] Dr. Hutchinson's Historical Essay on Witchcraft, p. 33.

[2] Darrell's narrative of the strange and grievous vexation by the devil of seven persons in Lancashire. One of his most famous acts of dispossession was exercised on William Somers, of Nottingham.

[3] The infliction of death for witchcraft in England has been generally, if not universally, by hanging; but in Scotland, in 1608, "some women were taken in Broughton as witches, and put to an assise, and convicted, albeit they persevered constant to the end, yet they were burned quick [alive] after such a cruel manner, that some of them died in despair, renouncing and blaspheming God; and others, half-burnt, brake out of the fire, and were cast quick in it again, till they were burned to the death."—*The Earl of Mar's declaration, quoted in Sir W. Scott's Demonology,* p. 315.

[4] Malkin is a north country name for a hare, but in this instance the name is more probably derived from *maca,* an equal, a companion. *Malkin* is the name of a familiar demon in Middleton's old play of " The Witch."—C.

in Lancashire, for no district in the county is more wild and desolate than certain parts of the parish of Whalley, in which parish almost all the witch scenes of the county have been performed. The persons accused of holding the convention at Malkin Tower were a poor wretched old woman, of the name of Southernes, and Anne Whittle, each of them fourscore years of age and upwards, with several of their neighbours and relations, all of the same rank. No fewer than nineteen of these persons were tried at the assizes at Lancaster in the autumn of 1612, charged with the crime of witchcraft, of whom the following is a list :—

WITCHES OF PENDLE FOREST.—Elizabeth Southernes, widow, *alias* Old Demdike; Elizabeth Device (probably Davies), *alias* Young Demdike, her daughter; James Device, the son of Young Demdike; Alizon Device, the daughter of Young Demdike; Anne Whittle, widow, *alias* Chattox, *alias* Chatter-box, the rival witch of Old Demdike; Anne Redferne, daughter of Ann Chattox; Alice Nutter; Katherine Hewytt, *alias* Mould-heeles; Jane Bulcock, of the Mosse End; John Bulcock, her son; Isabel Robey; Margaret Pearson, of Padiham.

The last-mentioned of whom was tried—1st, for murder by witchcraft; 2nd, for bewitching a neighbour; 3rd, for bewitching a horse; and being acquitted of the two former charges, was sentenced for the last to stand upon the pillory, in the markets of Clitheroe, Padiham, Colne, and Lancaster, for four successive market-days, with a printed paper upon her head, stating her offence.

WITCHES OF SAMLESBURY.—Jennet Bierley, Ellen Bierley, Jane Sowthworth, John Ramsden, Elizabeth Astley, Alice Gray, Isabel Sidegraves, Lawrence Haye.

The sensation produced by these trials in this and the neighbouring counties was great beyond all former example;[1] and Thomas Potts, Esq., the clerk of the court, was directed by the judges of assize, Sir Edward Bromley, Knight, and Sir James Altham, Knight, to collect and publish the evidence, and other documents connected with the trial, under the revision of the judges themselves. According to this authority, Old Demdike, the principal actress in the tragedy, was a general agent for the devil in all these parts, no man escaping her or her furies, that ever gave them occasion of offence, or denied them anything they stood in need of. The justices of the peace in this part of the country, Roger Nowell and Nicholas Bannister, having learnt that Malkin Tower, in the forest of Pendle, the residence of Old Demdike and her daughter, was the resort of the witches, had ventured so far to brave the danger of their incantations as to arrest their head, and a number of her followers, and to commit them to the castle at Lancaster. Amongst the rest of the voluntary confessions made by the witches, that of Dame Demdike is preserved, and is to the following effect :—

"That about twenty years ago, as she was coming home from begging, she was met near Gouldshey, in the forest of Pendle, by a spirit, or devil, in the shape of a boy, the one-half of his coat black and the other brown, who told her to stop, and said, that if she would give him her soul, she should have anything she wished for; on which she asked him his name, and was told that his name was *Tib*; she then consented, from the hope of gain, to give him her soul. For several years she had no occasion to make any application to her evil spirit; but one "Sunday morning, having a little child upon her knee, and she being in a slumber, the spirit appeared to her in the likeness of a brown dog, and forced himself upon her knee, and begun to suck her blood under her left arm, on which she exclaimed, 'Jesus, save me!' and the brown dog vanished, leaving her almost stark mad for the space of eight weeks." On another occasion she was led, being blind, to the house of Richard Baldwyn, to obtain payment for the services her daughter had performed at his mill, when Baldwyn fell into a passion, and bid them to get off his ground, upbraiding them with being whores and witches, and said he would burn the one and hang the other; on which *Tib* appeared, and they concerted matters to revenge themselves upon Baldwyn, but it does not appear what was the nature of that revenge. This wretched creature, who appears, like her compeer Chattox, to have been a poor mendicant pretender to the powers of witchcraft, might have read the work of her sovereign King James; for in her examination she says that the surest way of taking man's life by witchcraft is to make a picture of clay like unto the shape of the person meant to be killed, and when they would have the object of their vengeance to suffer in any particular part of his body, to take a thorn, or pin, and prick it into that part of the effigy; and when they would have any of the body to consume away, then to take that part of the figure and burn it; and when they would have the whole body to consume, then to take the remainder of the picture and burn it, by which means the afflicted will die."

A number of other examinations follow, principally those of the witches themselves, amounting in substance to this, that Old Demdike persuaded her daughter, Elizabeth Device, to sell herself to the devil, and that she took her advice; and that she, in her turn, initiated her daughter, Alizon Device, in her infernal arts. When the old witch had been sent to Lancaster Castle, a grand convocation, consisting of seventeen witches and three wizards, was held at Malkin Tower on Good Friday, which was by no means observed as a fast, and at which it was determined to kill M'Covell, the governor of the castle, and to blow up the building, for the purpose of enabling the witches to make their escape, which certainly would have been a very effectual way of accomplishing that object, seeing that the persons meant to be rescued were in the building which it was intended to destroy! The object of this witch-council was threefold: first, to christen the familiar of Alizon Device, one of the witches who had been taken to Lancaster; second, to concert a plan for blowing

[1] Potts's Preface to the Trials of the Lancashire Witches in 1612. This has been reprinted, with Notes, &c., by the late James Crossley, Esq., F.S.A. (vol. 6 of the Chetham Society's series).

up the castle and murdering the gaoler; and third, for bewitching and murdering Mr. Lister, a gentleman residing at Westby, in Craven, in Yorkshire. The business being ended, the witches, in quitting the meeting, walked out of the barn, which was dignified with the name of a tower, in their proper shapes; but no sooner had they reached the door than they each mounted their spirit, which was in the form of a young horse, and quickly vanished out of sight. Before the assizes Old Demdike, worn out by age and trouble, escaped the hands of the executioner by her death in prison, but the other prisoners were brought to trial.

The first person arraigned before Sir Edward Bromley (Aug. 18, 1612), who presided in the criminal court, was Ann Whittle, alias Chattox, who is described by Mr. Potts as a very old, withered, spent, and decrepit creature, eighty years of age, and nearly blind—a dangerous witch of very long continuance, always opposed to Old Demdike; for whom the one favoured the other hated deadly, and they envied and accused one another in their examinations. This witch was more ready to do mischief to men's goods than to themselves, her lips ever chattered as she walked (and hence, probably, her name of Chattox, or Chatter-box), but no man knew what she said; her abode was in the forest of Pendle, amongst the wicked company of dangerous witches, where the woollen trade was carried on, and she, in her younger days, was a carder of wool. She was indicted for having exercised various wicked and devilish arts called witchcrafts, enchantments, charms, and sorceries, upon one Robert Nutter, of Greenehead, in the forest of Pendle, and, by force of the said witchcraft, having feloniously killed the said Robert Nutter. To establish this charge, her own examination was read, from which it appeared that fourteen or fifteen years ago a thing like "a Christian man" had importuned her to sell her soul to the devil, and that she had complied with his request, giving to her familiar the name of *Fancy*; and on account of an insult offered to her daughter Redfern by Robert Nutter, they two conspired to place a bad wish upon Nutter, of which he died. Amongst other charms was that of an incantation used over drink, in the process of brewing, when it failed to work, of which the following is a copy:—

"A CHARM.

"Three Biters hast thou bitten,
The Hart, ill Eye, ill Tonge ;
Three bitters shall be thy Roote,
Father, Sonne, and Holy Ghost, a God's name.
Fiue Pater-nosters, fiue Auies, and a Creede,
In worship of fiue wounds of our Lord."

It was further deposed against the accused that John Device agreed to give Old Chattox a dole of meal yearly if she would not hurt him; and that when he ceased to make this annual payment he took to his bed and died. To which were added two other crimes of smaller magnitude; first, that she had bewitched the drink of John Moore; and, second, that she had, without the operation of the churn, produced a quantity of butter from a dish of skimmed milk! In the face of this evidence, and no longer anxious about her own life, she acknowledged her guilt; but humbly prayed the judges to be merciful to her daughter, Anne Redfearne. This prayer, so natural from a mother, was vain. Bent, as was the court before which she was tried, on blood, they knew not how to appreciate this touching trait of maternal magnanimity.

Against Elizabeth Device, the testimony of her own daughter, a child nine years of age, was received, and the way in which her evidence was given, instead of filling the court with horror, seems to have excited their applause and admiration. According to our authority, the familiar of the prisoner was a dog, which went by the name of *Ball*, and by whose agency she bewitched to death John Robinson,[1] James Robinson, and James Mitton; the first of the victims having called her a strumpet, and the last having refused to give Old Demdike a penny when she asked him for charity. To render her daughter proficient in the art, the prisoner taught her two prayers, by one of which she cured the bewitched, and by the other procured drink. The prayer for drink was in these terms: "*Crucifixus hoc signum vitam Eternam.* Amen." The charm for curing the bewitched, thus:—

"A CHARM.

"Vpon Good Friday, I will fast while I may,
Vntil I heare them knell
Our Lord's owne Bell,
Lord in his messe
With his twelue Apostles good,

"What hath he in his hand !
Ligh in leath wand :
What he in his other hand ?
Heauen's doore key.
Open, open Heauen's doore keyes,
Sneck, sneck hell doore," &c.

The person of Elizabeth Device, as described by the clerk of the court, seems to have peculiarly qualified her for an ancient witch: "She was branded," says he, "with a preposterous mark in

[1] The ancient Rabbins held that the devils most frequently appeared in the shape of *Seghuirim*, rough and hairy goats; but none of the familiars of the Lancashire witches were of this classical description.

nature; her left eye standing lower than her right, the one looking down and the other up, at the same time." Her process of destruction was by modelling clay or marl figures, and wasting her victims away along with them—another proof of the king's sagacity, which, no doubt, the judges, who seem to have been more solicitous to obtain the favour of their royal master than to administer impartial justice to his subjects, would not fail to make known at court. James Device was convicted principally on the evidence of his infant sister, of bewitching and killing Mrs. Ann Towneley, the wife of Mr. Henry Towneley, of the Carr, by means of a picture of clay, and both he and his sister were witnesses against their mother. This wizard, whose spirit was called *Dandy*, is described as a poor, decrepit boy, apparently of weak intellect, and so infirm that it was found necessary to hold him up in court on his trial. Upon evidence of this kind no fewer than ten of these unfortunate people were found guilty at Lancaster, and sentenced to suffer punishment of death; eight others were acquitted, though for what reason it is difficult to imagine, for the evidence against some of them, at least, appears to have been equally strong; or, to speak more properly, equally weak and absurd, as against those who were convicted. The persons sentenced to death, and afterwards executed, were Ann Whittle, *alias* Chattox, Elizabeth Device, James Device, Ann Redferne, Alice Nutter, Catherine Hewytt, John Bulcock, Jane Bulcock, Alizon Device, and Isabel Robey.

Mr. Crossley, in his introduction to Potts's "Discovery of Witches," remarks that "the main interest in reviewing the miserable band of victims will be found to centre in Alice Nutter. Wealthy, well-conducted, well-connected, and placed probably on an equality with most of the neighbouring families, and the magistrate before whom she was brought and by whom she was committed, she deserves to be distinguished from the companions with whom she suffered, and to attract an attention which has never yet been directed to her. That James Device, on whose evidence she was convicted, was instructed to accuse her by her own nearest relatives, and that the magistrate, Roger Nowell, entered actively as a confederate into the conspiracy, from a grudge entertained against her on account of a long-disputed boundary, are allegations which tradition has preserved, but the truth or falsehood of which, at this distance of time, it is scarcely possible satisfactorily to examine. Her mansion, Rough Lee, is still standing, a very substantial and rather fine specimen of the houses of the inferior gentry *temp.* James I., but now divided into cottages."[1]

Against Jane Bierley, Ellen Bierley, and Jane Southworth of Samlesbury, charged with having bewitched Grace Sowerbutts at that place, the only material evidence adduced was that of Grace Sowerbutts herself, a girl of licentious and vagrant habits, who swore that these women, one of them being her grandmother, did draw her by the hair of the head, and lay her upon the top of a hay-mow, and did take her senses and memory from her; that they appeared to her sometimes in their own likeness, and sometimes like a black dog. She further deposed that by their arts they prevailed upon her to join their sisterhood; and that they were met from time to time by "four black things going upright, and yet not like men in the face," who conveyed them across the Ribble, where they danced with them, and then each retired to hold dalliance with their familiar, conformable, no doubt, to the doctrine of *Incubi* and *Succubi*, as promulgated by the royal demonologist. To consummate their atrocities, the prisoners bewitched and slew a child of Thomas Washman's, by placing a nail in its navel; and after its burial they took up the corpse, when they ate part of the flesh, and made "an unxious ointment" by boiling the bones. This was more than even the capacious credulity of the judge and jury could digest, and, after listening with all gravity to this farrago, the judge demanded of the accused what answer they could make, when they "desired him for God's cause to examine Grace Sowerbutts, who set her on, or by whose means the accusation came against them." The simple question wrung from the prisoners on the verge of anticipated condemnation demolished the whole fabric of imposture, and laid open the plot even to the dull comprehension of Sir Edward Bromley. The taint of Papistry was known to rest upon Grace Sowerbutts and her supporters, and it was rumoured, moreover, that she had been under the training of one Thompson, a seminary priest or Jesuit, whose real name was Southworth, formerly a connection of one of the accused, Jane Southworth, who had lately become a convert to Protestantism, and for that reason was likely to be hated by her Popish relative. The judge's faculties seem to have been sharpened by his horror of Popery, and though he hardly relished the release of even Protestant witches, he doubtless found some solace in the assurance that his sagacity had unravelled imposture and unearthed a dangerous Jesuit, whom he would have been willing to string up in the plain belief that he was thereby doing a just and righteous work. Leading the principal witness step by step to a denial of all she had asserted, having first delivered himself of the opinion "that if a priest or a Jesuit had a hand in one end of it, there would appear to be knaverie and practise on the other end of it," he got her to confess that she was a cheat and an impostor, and that every article of her accusation was a falsehood and invention from beginning to end ; that "Master Thompson, who she took to be Master Christopher Southworth, to whom she had been sent to learne her prayers, did persuade, counsell, and advise her to bring the horrible charge she had against her grandmother, aunt, and Southworth's wife." In short, this precocious prodigy of wickedness was compelled to play a losing game, and, as a consequence, her intended victims escaped with a stern exhortation from the judge. The Samlesbury witches were therefore acquitted, and the seminary priest Thompson, *alias* Southworth, who was suspected by two of the county magistrates,[1] to whom the affair was afterwards referred, of having instigated Sowerbutts to make the charge, escaped for want of confirmatory evidence. John Ramsden, Elizabeth Astley, Alice Gray, Isabel Sidegraves, and Lawrence Haye were all discharged without trial.

The relationship which the Southworths who were concerned in the trial bore to each other has not until recent years been ascertained, but a careful examination of the muniments at Samlesbury Hall, which the Editor of this edition was permitted to make some few years ago, enabled him to identify with tolerable certainty the principal of the Samlesbury witches.[2] The supposed chief instigator of the plot, the priest Thompson, otherwise Christopher Southworth, was, no doubt, Christopher, the fourth son of Sir John Southworth, the noted recusant—a Romish ecclesiastic who was undergoing imprisonment for recusancy in the castle of Wisbeach at the time of Sir John's decease in 1595, and must have been fifty-four years of age at the time these accusations were preferred. Jane Southworth, the intended victim of this arch-conspirator, was the widow of John Southworth, a grandson of Sir John, the recusant, and nephew of the *soi-disant* Thompson. Upon her the chief interest in this extraordinary trial gathers. Unlike the great majority of those accused of holding communion with the evil one, she was no poor, houseless mendicant, or aged beldame with gobber tooth and stooping gait ; nor had she " the wrinkles of an old wiue's face," which was accepted as " good euidence to the jurie against a witch," but a lady well connected and of considerable property—

> "Of an unquestion'd carriage, well reputed
> Among her neighbours, reckoned with the best."

She was the daughter of a Lancashire knight of great influence and large possessions, Sir Richard Sherbourne, of Stonyhurst, and herself the mother of the future lord of Samlesbury. She was, moreover, young, and, it may be reasonably supposed, not without personal attractions, and had become a widow only a few months before the charge of witchcraft was brought against her, a circumstance, it might have been expected, that would have spared her the persecution of her deceased husband's Jesuitical kinsman. The other persons named were all dependents of the Southworth family, or tenants on the Samlesbury estate.

The judge, Sir Edward Bromley, in addressing the convicted prisoners, when sentence of death was passed upon them, made a parade of clemency and impartial justice, which was only to be discovered in his words : " You," said he, " of all people, have the least cause of complaint ; since on the trial for your lives there hath been much care and pains taken ; and what persons of your nature and condition were ever arraigned and tried with so much solemnity ? The court hath had great care to receive nothing in evidence against you but matter of fact !³ As you stand simply (your offences and bloody practices not considered), your fate would rather move compassion than exasperate any man ; for whom would not the ruin of so many poor creatures at one time touch, as in appearance simple, and of little understanding ? But the blood of these innocent children, and others his majesty's subjects, whom cruelly and barbarously you have murdered and cut off, cries unto the Lord for vengeance. It is impossible that you, who are stained with so much innocent blood, should either prosper or continue in this world, or receive reward in the next." Having thus shut the door of hope, both in this life and the life that is to come, the judge proceeded to urge the victims of superstition to repentance ; and concluded by sentencing them all to be hanged. It would, probably, have occurred to the judges, that persons possessed of the power to kill their enemies, and endowed with a capacity of locomotion that enabled them to fly over the land or the sea, might have slain their prosecutors, or mounted their familiars and taken flight, had not the dogma promulgated by King James answered this objection *in limine* : " When the witches are apprehended and detained by the lawful magistrates," says the royal commentator, " their power is then no greater than before that ever they meddled with these matters."[4] This, indeed, is a

---

[1] The Rev. William Leigh, and Edward Chisnall, Esq.

[2] A more detailed account of the "Samlesbury witches" will be found in "The History of the Ancient Hall of Samlesbury," by James Croston.

[3] *Nothing but matter of fact !*—Why, to prove the guilt of one of the prisoners, evidence was received that it was the opinion of a man, not in court, that she had turned his beer sour ; and to prove the charge of murder, it was thought sufficient to attest that a sick person had declared his belief that he owed his approaching death to the maledictions of the

prisoner. The bleeding of the corpse on the touch of the sorceress, one of the absurd and now exploded superstitions insisted upon by King James, was advanced on oath, on the trial of Jennet Preston, as an incontrovertible evidence of guilt ; and yet the judge upon the bench declares that no evidence was received against the prisoners but matter of fact. His lordship would have approached much nearer the truth if he had said that nothing but fiction was heard in evidence.

[4] King James's "Dæmonologie," chap. vi.

necessary part of the doctrine, otherwise Elizabeth Device and her associates might as easily and as invisibly have conveyed themselves from the bar of the castle of Lancaster, as from the witch convention at Malkin Tower. At the appointed time all these poor wretches died by the hands of the public executioner—victims, no doubt in part, of their own fraudulent arts, resorted to for the purpose of eking out a miserable subsistence—but, much more, sacrifices offered upon the altars of ignorance and superstition.

At the assizes at York, in the summer of the same year (1612), Jennet Preston, of Gisborn, was brought to trial before Sir James Altham, charged with having attended the great witch meeting at Malkin Tower, in Lancashire, on the Good Friday preceding, and with having murdered Thomas Lister, Esq., of Westby, in Craven, by witchcraft. In support of these charges it was deposed by Anne Robinson, probably one of the family of the Lancashire witch-finders, that when Mr. Lister was lying in extremity upon his death-bed, he cried out to them that stood about him, "Jennet Preston is in the house, look where she is! take hold of her; for God's sake shut the doors, and take her! Look about for her, and lay hold on her, for she is in the house!" and so crying, he departed this life. Other witnesses deposed that after Mr. Lister was dead, and laid out in his winding sheet, Jane Preston was brought to touch the dead body, on which fresh blood presently gushed out in the presence of all those that were in the room. This appears to have been the only evidence against the prisoner, except that which was contained in the examination of James Device, the grandson of Old Demdike, who deposed before Roger Nowell and Nicholas Bannister, two Lancashire magistrates, that Jennet Preston, the prisoner, was present at the great witch meeting at Malkin Tower on the memorable Good Friday, and that she came to the meeting mounted upon a spirit like unto a white foal, with a black spot in the forehead; that at this meeting she asked the aid of the witches and wizards assembled to kill Mr. Thomas Lister, and that they consented to entangle him in the meshes of their net of enchantment, and in the end to destroy him; on which she gave them an invitation to attend another witch feast on the next Good Friday on Romeles (Rombald's) Moor, and then mounting her spirit she took flight through the air, and became invisible. This strange mass of absurdities satisfied the judge of the prisoner's guilt, who summed up the evidence, if evidence it could be called, strongly against her; but the jury, somewhat more scrupulous, spent the greatest part of the day in deliberation; in the end, however, they returned a verdict of guilty, and the poor unfortunate wretch ended her life on the gallows, denying firmly her guilt, and accusing, with a great deal of truth, her prosecutors of the crime of murder. It does not appear that the rack was resorted to in Lancashire, but if the rack was not applied the gallows was in frequent use; and a man of the name of Utley, a reputed wizard, was hanged at Lancaster about the year 1630, for having bewitched to death Richard, the son of Ralph Assheton, Esq., of Downham, and lord of Middleton.[2]

At the assizes at Lancaster, in 1633-4,[3] another batch of reputed witches, consisting of seventeen in number, was brought to trial from the usual resort in Pendle Forest. The informations were laid before Richard Shuttleworth, of Gawthorpe, Esq., and John Starkie, Esq., on the 10th of February, 1633-4, the latter of whom had figured as one of the possessed amongst the seven demoniacs at Cleworth, in the year 1597. The principal evidence against the prisoners was Edward Robinson,[4] the son of Edmund Robinson, of Pendle, mason, who deposed that two greyhounds had been transformed into witches. That one of the witches there, Dickonson's wife, had conveyed him before her on horseback to a meeting at Hoarestones, where a convocation of witches, amounting to threescore or thereabout, had assembled to regale themselves; that one of them, Loynd's wife, he had seen sitting upon a piece of cross wood in his father's chimney; that afterwards he had met and fought with a boy, who turned out to have a cloven foot; that in a neighbouring barn he had seen three witches taking pictures, into which they had stuck thorns; and that, at the meeting at Hoarestones, all the persons now in confinement for witchcraft were present. The only evidence that appears in confirmation of this testimony is that of Edmund Robinson, the father, who had himself been a witness against the Lancashire witches of 1612, which amounts merely to this—that he heard his son cry pitifully, and that the boy told him all that was contained in his deposition.

It ought to be generally known that the blood is congealed in the body for two or three days after death, and then becomes liquid again in its tendency to corruption; and that the air being heated by a number of persons coming into the room, the blood will flow when murderers are absent as well as when they are present. This test ought therefore to be exploded.

[2] Dr. Whitaker's "History of Whalley," p. 528.

[3] Among the MSS. in the State Paper Office is a letter addressed by Sir William Pelham to Lord Conway, dated May 16, 1633-4, in which he says:—"The greatest news from the country is of a huge pack of witches, which are lately discovered in Lancashire, whereof, 'tis said, 19 are condemned, and that there are at least 60 already discovered, and yet daily there are more revealed: there are divers of them of good ability (i.e., good social status) and they have done much harm. I hear it is suspected that they had a hand in raising the great storm, wherein his Majesty (Charles I.) was in so great danger at sea in Scotland." Charles, accompanied by Laud, then Bishop of London, had paid a visit to Scotland in the summer of 1633-4, and was then crowned at Holyrood.—C.

[4] The prototype of Matthew Hopkins, the south-country witchfinder. Sir Walter Scott, in his preface to "The Wonderful Discovery of Witches in Lancashire," in Lord Somers' Tracts, has fallen into an error by confounding the Pendle Forest witches of 1612 with those of 1633.

[5] Hoarestones is an ancient farmhouse still remaining in Pendle Forest.—C.

Upon this evidence all the seventeen prisoners were found guilty, and sentenced to be executed. But the judge very properly respited the execution; and on the case being reported to the king in council, the Bishop of Chester, Dr. Bridgman, was required to investigate the circumstances. This inquiry was instituted at Chester, and four of the convicted witches— namely, Margaret Johnson, Frances Dickonson, Mary Spencer, and the wife of Hargraves—were sent to London, and examined, first, by the king's physicians and surgeons, and afterwards by the king himself. Charles I., less prone to credulity than his father, having satisfied himself that the charge against these poor creatures was groundless, extended to them the royal clemency, and so well was the case of those left behind represented by the singular delegation that all the seventeen received a free pardon. It is not the least extraordinary part of these most extraordinary transactions that, previous to the trial, Margaret Johnson, of Marsden, one of the prisoners, had been so acted upon by the terrors of her situation, that she actually made a confession of her own guilt, attended with circumstances which would, if true, have ended in her execution. According to this deposition, Johnson had sold her soul to a spirit, or devil, in the similitude of a man, to whom she gave the name of *Mamilian*, who had promised to supply all her wants. It is difficult to imagine how voluntary confessions of crimes never committed could be obtained from persons who were liable to forfeit their lives, and frequently did forfeit them, on their own accusation. But the fact is undeniable. Sir George Mackenzie, himself a believer in witchcraft, and who, as the king's advocate, had conducted many trials in Scotland for that crime, speaking upon the judicial confession of the criminals themselves, says—

"Those poor persons who are ordinarily accused of this crime are poor ignorant creatures, and oft-times women, who understand not the nature of what they are accused of, and many, mistaking their own fears and apprehensions for witchcraft, when they are defamed, become so confounded with fear, and the close prison in which they are kept, and so starved for want of meat and sleep (either of which wants is enough to disorder the strongest reason), that hardly wiser or more serious people than they would escape distraction; and when persons are confounded with fear and apprehension, they will imagine things very ridiculous and absurd. Most of those poor creatures are tortured by their keepers, who, being persuaded they do God good service, think it their duty to vex and torment poor prisoners. I went," continues Sir George, "when I was a justice-depute, to examine some women who had confessed judicially, and one of them, who was a silly creature, told me, under secrecy, that she had not confest because she was guilty, but being a poor creature, who wrought for her meat, and being defamed for a witch, she knew she would starve, for no person thereafter would either give her meat or lodging, and that all men would beat her, and hound dogs at her, and that, therefore, she desired to be out of the world; whereupon she wept most bitterly, and upon her knees called God to witness what she said."

The account of these transactions given by Dr. Webster, in his "Display of Witchcraft," serves to show the consternation and alarm which must have been felt in those days, particularly amongst the old and decrepit, from the machinations of the witch-finders. Of the boy Robinson he says—[1]

"This said boy was brought into the church at Kildwick [in Yorkshire, on the confines of Lancashire], a large parish church, where I, being then curate there, was preaching in the afternoon, and was set upon a stool to look about him, which moved some little disturbance in the congregation for a while. After prayers I inquired what the matter was. The people told me that it was the boy that discovered witches; upon which I went to the house where he was to stay all night, where I found him and two very unlikely persons, that did conduct him and manage the business. I desired to have some discourse with the boy in private; but that they utterly refused; then, in the presence of a great many people, I took the boy near me and said, 'Good boy, tell me truly and in earnest, didst thou see and hear such strange things at the meeting of witches as is reported by many that thou didst relate?' But the two men, not giving the boy leave to answer, did pluck him from me, and said he had been examined by two *able* justices of the peace, *and they did never ask him such a question*. To whom I replied the persons accused had therefore the more wrong." As government spies multiply traitors, so professional witch-finders create witches. "The boy Robinson," says Dr. Webster, "in more mature years, acknowledged that he had been instructed and suborned to make these accusations against the accused persons by his father and others, and that, of course, the whole was a fraud. By such wicked means and unchristian practices divers innocent persons lost their lives; and these wicked rogues wanted not greater persons (even of the ministry too) that did authorise and encourage them in their diabolical courses; and the like in my time happened here in Lancashire, where divers, both men and women, were accused of supposed witchcraft, and were so unchristianly and inhumanly handled as to be stript stark naked, and laid upon tables and beds to be searched for their supposed witch-marks, so barbarous and cruel acts doth diabolical instigation, working upon ignorance and superstition, produce."[2]

Not only persons of the ministry but the king himself, as we have seen in the last reign, authorised and encouraged these diabolical courses, not omitting the witch-mark in his descriptions.[3]

[1] Webster's "Display of Witchcraft," p. 276.

[2] The cruel process was to strip the supposed witch naked, and thrust pins insensible to various parts of the body, to discover what the royal demonologist called the "witch-mark," or the devil's stigma—that is, a part of the body insensible to pain, and which was supposed to be possessed by the devil as a sign of his sovereign power, and as the place at which the imps sucked! Sometimes the accused were thrown into a river, or pond, having their thumbs and toes tied together, where, if they sank, they were held innocent, but if they swam, were dragged forth to prison. On other occasions the suspected witch was bound cross-legged on a stool, there to be watched, and kept without meat or sleep for the space of four-and-twenty hours, within which time it was supposed that her imp would make her a visit, and in that way betray her.

[3] Bishop Jewel, when preaching a sermon before Queen Elizabeth, exhorted her majesty to use her authority to check the "tremendous operations of the devil by exterminating his agents—the witches and wizards, who were then very numerous." In the "Covntrey Ivstice"

(1618), by "Michael Dalton, Lincoln's Inn, Gent."—who was probably a Lancashire man—there are some passages that have reference to this combined delusion and imposture: "Now, against these witches," says this legal luminary, "the Iustices of peace may not alwaies expect direct euidence, seeing all their workes are the workes of darknesse, and no witnesses present with them to accuse them: and therefore, for their better discouerie, I thought good here to insert certaine obseruations out of the booke of discouery of the witches that were arraigned at Lancaster, Ann. Dom. 1612, before Sir Iames Altham and Sir Edw. Bromely, Iudges of Assize there.

"1 They haue ordinarily a familiar, or spirit, which appeareth to them.

"2. Their said familiar hath some bigg or place vpon their body, where he sucketh them.

"3 They haue often pictures of clay, or waxe (like a man, &c. found in their house.

"4. If the dead body bleed vpon the witches touching it.

It must not, however, be supposed that all who countenanced these impositions were themselves fools or impostors, for amongst the judges of the land who gave into the delusion we find the venerable name of Sir Matthew Hale.[1]

One of the Lancashire witches having, as it appears, quitted her native county, and wandered into Worcestershire, in consequence of the distress occasioned by the civil wars, which the poor are always the first to feel, this wretched mendicant, a more fit object of compassion than of terror, was found by a wicked boy, who protested that she had by her sorceries deprived him of speech. On what kind of evidence this charge was raised may be easily conjectured; and though the fate of the poor woman is not distinctly stated, there is but too much reason to suppose, from the avidity with which witches were in those times pursued, and the relentless cruelty with which they were persecuted, that on this evidence she was tried and executed.

Although trials for witchcraft were by no means unusual in the time of the Commonwealth, and though no fewer than three hundred reputed witches were tried, and the major part of them executed, in the period between the deposition of Charles I. and the death of his son and successor, in the southern counties of England, yet we only find two cases of this kind of judicial homicide in the county of Lancaster within that agitated period, and these are mentioned somewhat vaguely by Dr. Webster, who say, "I myself have known two supposed witches to be put to death at Lancaster within these eighteen years[2] that did utterly deny any league or covenant with the devil, or even to have seen any visible devil at all. And may not the confession of those (who both died penitent) be as well credited as the confession of those that were brought to such confessions by force, fraud, or cunning persuasion and allurement?"

But there was a very memorable case of supposed demoniacal possession and dispossession in the close of the seventeenth century, with which we shall conclude this very curious portion of our county history. The case to which we refer is that of Richard Dugdale, the Surey demoniac, and the story, though a very long one, may be told in a few sentences. Dugdale, it appears, was a youth just rising into manhood, a gardener by trade, living with his parents at Surey in the parish of Whalley, addicted to pleasure and distinguished even at school as a posture-master and ventriloquist. During his possession he was attended by six Dissenting ministers, the Rev. Messrs. Thomas Jolly, Charles Sagar, Nicholas Kershaw, Robert Waddington, Thomas Whally, and John Carrington, who were occasionally assisted at their meetings, held to exorcise the demon, by the Rev. Mr. Frankland, Mr. Pendlebury, and the Rev. Oliver Heywood. According to the narration put forth under the sanction of these names, which is called—

"An account of Satan's acting in and about the body of Richard Dugdale, and of Satan's removal thence through the Lord's blessing of the within-mentioned Ministers and People;" when Dugdale was about nineteen years of age he was seized with an affliction early in the year 1689, and from the strange fits which violently seized him he was supposed to be possessed by the devil. When the fit was upon him "he shewed great despite," says the narrative, "against the ordinary of God, and raged as if he had been nothing but a devil in Richard's bodily shape; though, when he was not in his fits he manifested great inclination to the word of God and prayer, for the exercise of which in his behalf he desired that a day of fasting might be set apart as the only means from which he could expect help, seeing that he had tried all other means, lawful and unlawful."[3] Meetings were accordingly appointed of the ministers, to which the people crowded in vast numbers. These meetings began on the 8th of May, and were continued about twice a month till the February following. At the first meeting the parents of the demoniac were examined by the ministers, and they represented "that at Whalley rush-burying [or bearing], on the James's-tide, in July 1688, there was a great dancing and drinking, when Richard offered himself to the devil on condition that he would make him the best dancer in Lancashire." After becoming extremely drunk he went home, where several apparitions appeared to him and presented to him all kinds of dainties and fine clothing, with gold and precious things, inviting him at the same time "to take his fill of pleasure." In the course of the day some compact or bond was entered into between him and the devil, and after that his fits grew frequent and violent. While in these fits his body was often hurled about very desperately,[4] and he abused the minister and blasphemed his Maker. Sometimes he would fall into dreadful fits, at other times he would talk Greek and Latin, though untaught. Sometimes his voice was small and shrill, at others hollow and hideous. Now he was as light as a bag of feathers, then as heavy as lead. At one time he upbraided the ministers with their neglect, at others he said they had saved him from hell. He was weather-wise and money-wise by turns; he could tell when there would be rain and when he should receive presents. Sometimes he would vomit stones an inch and a half square, and in others of his trances there was a noise in his throat as if he was singing psalms inwardly. But the strongest mark of demoniacal possession consisted in a lump which rose from the thick of his leg, about the size of a mole, and did work up like such a creature towards the chest of his body till it reached his breast, when it was as big as a man's fist, and uttered strange voices.[5] He opened his mouth at the beginning of his fits so often that it was thought spirits went in and out of him. In agility he was unequalled, "especially in dancing, wherein he excelled all that the spectators had seen, and all that mere mortals could perform; the Demoniac would, for six or seven times together, leap up so as that part of his Legs might be seen shaking and quavering above the heads of the People, from which heights he oft fell down on his knees, which he long shivered and traverst on the ground at least as nimbly as other men can twinkle or sparkle their Fingers, thence springing up in to's high leaps again, and then falling on his Feet, which seem'd to reach the Earth, but with the gentlest and scarce perceivable touches when he made his highest leaps." And yet the divines by whom he was attended most unjustly rallied the devil for the want of skill in his pupil after this fashion:

"5. The testimony of the person hurt, vpon his death.
"6. The examination and confession of the children or servants of the witch.
"7. Their owne voluntary confession, which exceeds all other evidence."—C.

[1] At the assizes at Bury St. Edmunds, in 1664, Amy Dunny and Rose Cullender were tried before Sir Matthew, and, being convicted, were hanged, both protesting that they were innocent.

[2] The Doctor's book is dated Feb. 23, 1673, so that it is probable the execution took place about the year 1654. We have attempted, but without success, to ascertain the date from the Criminal Records in Lancaster Castle, which are very defective.—B.
[3] "The Surey Demoniac," pp. 1, 2.
[4] Ibid, p. 4.
[5] Ibid, p. 60.

"Cease, Dancing Satan, and be gone from him," says the Rev. Mr. Carrington, addressing himself to the devil. "Canst thou Dance no better, Satan? Ransack the old Records of all past times and places in thy memory, Canst thou not there find out some other way of finer trampling? Pump thine invention dry! Cannot that universal Seed-plot of subtile Wiles and Stratagems spring up one new method of cutting capers! Is this the top of skill and pride to shuffle feet and brandish knees thus, and to trip like a Doe and skip like a Squirrel, and wherein differs thy leapings from the hoppings of a Frog, or bounces of a Goat, or friskings of a Dog, or gesticulations of a Monkey? And cannot a Palsey shake such a loose Leg as that? Dost not thou twirle like a Calf that has the turn, and twitch up thy Houghs just like a spring-hault tit?" In some of his last fits he announced that he must either be killed or cured before the 25th of March. This, says the deposition of his father and mother and two of his sisters, proved true, for on the 24th of that month he had his last fit, the devil being no longer able to withstand the means that were used with so much vigour and perseverance to expel him, one of the most effectual of which was medicine, prescribed in the way of his profession, by Dr. Chew, a medical practitioner in the neighbourhood.

The Rev. Zachary Taylor asserts that the preachers, disappointed and mortified at their ill success in Dugdale's case, gave it out that some of his connections were witches, and in contact with the devil, and that they supposed was the cause why they had not been able to relieve him. Under this impression they procured some of the family to be searched, that they might see if they had not teats or the devil's mark, and they tried them by the test of saying the Lord's Prayer. Some remains of the evil spirit seemed, however, still to have possessed Richard, for though after this he had no fits, yet once, when he had got too much drink, he was after another manner than drunken persons usually are.[1] In confirmation of which feats not only the eight ministers but twenty respectable inhabitants affixed their attestation to a document prepared for the purpose ; and three of the magistrates of the district—namely, Hugh Lord Willoughby, Ralph Egerton, Esq., and Thomas Braddill, Esq.—received depositions from the attesting parties. This monstrous mass of absurdity, superstition, and fraud—for it was beyond doubt a compound of them all—was exposed with success by the Rev. Zachary Taylor, the Bishop of Chester's curate at Wigan, one of the king's preachers in the county of Lancaster ; but the reverend divine mixed with his censures too much party asperity, insisting that the whole was an artifice of the Nonconformist ministers in imitation of the pretended miracles of the Catholic priests, and likening it to the fictions of John Darrell, B.A., which had been practised a century before upon the family of Mr. Starkie in the same county. Of the resemblance in many of its parts there can be no doubt, but the names of the venerable Oliver Heywood and Thomas Jolly form a sufficient guarantee against any imposition on their part ; and the probability is that the ministers were the dupes of a popular superstition in the hands of a dissolute and artful family.

Within living memory the superstitious terrors of witchcraft have prevailed in Lancashire to an extent that has embittered the lives of the persons supposing themselves subject to this grievous visitation. These, however, were only the remains of the popular mythology. During the sixteenth century the whole region, in some parts of the county, seemed contaminated with the presence of the witches ; men and beasts were supposed to languish under their charm ; and the delusion, which preyed alike on the learned and the vulgar, did not allow any family to suppose that they were beyond the reach of the witch's wand. Was the family visited by sickness, it was believed to be the work of an invisible agency, which in secret wasted the image made in clay before the fire, or crumbled its various parts into dust ; did the cattle sicken and die, the witch and the wizard were the authors of the calamity ; did the yeast refuse to perform the office of fermentation either in the bread or in the beer, it was the consequence of a *bad wish* ; did the butter refuse to *come*, the familiar was in the churn ; did the ship founder at sea, the wind of Boreas was blown by the lungless hag, who had scarcely sufficient breath to cool her own pottage ; did the Ribble overflow its banks, the floods descended from the congregated sisterhood at Malkin Tower ; and the blight of the season, which consigned the crops of the farmer to destruction, was the saliva of the enchantress, or the distillations from the blear-eyed dame, who flew by night over the field in search of mischief. To refuse an alms to a haggard mendicant, was to produce for the family that had the temerity to make the experiment an accumulation of the outpourings of the box of Pandora. To escape from terrors like these, no sacrifice was thought too great. Superstitions begat cruelty and injustice. The poor and the rich were equally interested in obtaining a deliverance ; and the magistrate who resided in his mansion at Read, and the peasant who occupied the humblest cot amongst the hills of Cliviger, were alike interested in abating the common nuisance.[2]

Nor was the situation of the witch more enviable than that of the individuals or the families over which she exerted her influence. Linked by a species of infernal compact to an imaginary

[1] "Surey Demoniac," p. 62.

[2] According to Gaule, there were eight classes of witches distinguished by their operations : first, the diviner, gipsy, or fortune-telling witch ; second, the astrologian, star-gazing, planetary, prognosticating witch ; third, the chanting, canting, or calculating witch, who works by signs or numbers ; fourth, the venefick or poisonous witch ; fifth, the exorcist or conjuring witch ; sixth, the gastromantick witch ; seventh, the magical, speculative, sciential, or arted witch ; eighth, the necromancer.

"The Lancashire witches" were principally fortune-tellers and conjurors. The securities against witchcraft were numerous, but the most popular was the horseshoe ; and hence we see in Lancashire so many thresholds ornamented with this countercharm. Mr. Roby, in his "Traditions of Lancashire," has treated the subject with great vivacity and spirit ; and his legendary tales serve to convey to the mind a vivid impression of the effects of the popular superstition in other times.

imp, she was shunned as a common pest, or caressed only on the principle that certain of the Indian tribes pay homage to the devil. The reputed witches themselves were frequently disowned by their families, feared and detested by their neighbours, and hunted by the dogs as pernicious monsters. When in confinement, they were cast into the ponds, by way of trial; punctured by bodkins, to discover their imp-marks; subjected to deprivation of food, and kept in perpetual motion, till confessions were obtained from a distracted mind. On their trials they were listened to with incredulity and horror, and consigned to the gallows with as little pity as the basest of malefactors. .Their imaginary crimes created a thirst for their blood; and people in all stations, from the highest to the lowest, attended the trials at Lancaster, as we have seen from Mr. Pott's record of the criminal proceedings there, with an intensity of interest that their mischievous powers, now divested of their sting, so naturally excited.

The belief in witchcraft and demoniacal possession was confined to no particular sect or persuasion. The Roman Catholics,[1] the members of the Established Church of England, the Presbyterians and Independents, and even the Methodists, though a sect of more recent standing, have all fallen into this delusion; and yet each denomination has upbraided the other with gross superstition, and not unfrequently with wilful fraud. Since the light of general knowledge has chased away the mists of this once generally prevailing error, we all smile at these bitter criminations and recriminations, which ought to guard us against the commission of similar faults. It is due, however, to the ministers of the Established Church to say that they were amongst the first of our public writers to denounce the belief in witchcraft, with all its attendant mischiefs; and the names of Dr. Harsnet, afterwards Archbishop of York; Dr. John Webster, the detector of Robinson, the Pendle Forest witch-hunter; of Zachary Taylor, one of the king's preachers for the county of Lancaster; and of Dr. Hutchinson, chaplain in ordinary to His Majesty George I., are all entitled to the public gratitude for their efforts to explode these pernicious superstitions, though their merit is in some degree tarnished by an overweening solicitude to cast the imputation of ignorant credulity from their own community, and to fix it exclusively upon others.[2] For upwards of a century the sanguinary and superstitious laws of James I. disgraced the English statute-book; but in the 9th year of George II. (1735-6) a law was enacted repealing the statute of James I., and prohibiting any prosecution, suit, or proceeding against any person or persons for witchcraft, sorcery, enchantment, or conjuration. In this way the doctrine of withcraft, with all its attendant errors, was finally exploded, except amongst the most ignorant of the vulgar.[3]

To return to the chronological order of our history. In the year 1617, James I., on his return from Scotland to London, passed through the heart of Lancashire, and there, in the midst of joy and hilarity, sowed the seeds of discontent so wide and deep as to shake the stability of the throne. Having arrived at Brougham Castle, on the 6th of August, he proceeded by way of Appleby and. Wharton to Kendal. Here he stopped two nights, when, entering Lancashire, he reached Hornby Castle[4] on the 11th, and from thence proceeded to Ashton Hall, the mansion of Thomas, first Lord Gerard. Having remained here one night he advanced to Myerscough, where the royal retinue stopped two days, to enjoy the pleasures of the chase in the forest. Then, taking the route through Preston, he went to Hoghton Tower, where he sojourned for three days. Thence he proceeded to Lathom House, where he became the guest for two nights of the Earl of Derby; and from thence proceeded by Bewsey and Vale Royal, by easy stages, to London. Of the royal tour through Lancashire, Nicholas Assheton, Esq. of Downham, in the parish of Whalley, has preserved the following account in his private journal :—[5]

"[1617] June 1, Sunday. Mr. C(ristopher) P(arkinson) moved my brother [in-law] Sherborne from Sir Richard Hoghton, to do him such favour, countenance, grace and curtesie, as to weare his clothe, and attend him at Hoghton, at the King's coming in August, as divers other gentlemen were moved and would. He likewise moved mee. I answered I would bee willing, and readie to doe Sir Richard anie service.

---

[1] See the Bull of Pope Innocent VIII. to the inquisitors of Almain, empowering them to detect and burn witches. The Romish church appointed penances for converted witches; and Cranmer, the Protestant Archbishop of Canterbury, in his articles of visitation, directs his clergy, in 1549, to inquire after any persons that use "charms, sorcery, enchantments, witchcraft, soothsaying, or any like craft, invented by the devil," which instructions were renewed in Elizabeth's reign, with the addition, "especially in time of women's travail." Richard Baxter, a divine in deserved estimation amongst the nonconformists, was a firm believer in the possession and dispossession of devils, and his "World of Spirits" abounds with proofs of his firm conviction of the reality of this popular delusion.

[2] Among the letters in the State Paper Office is one dated May 10, 1634, and addressed by Sir William Pelham to Lord Conway, in which the following passage occurs: "The greatest news from the country is of a large pack of witches which are lately discovered in Lancashire, whereof 'tis said 19 are condemned, and that there are at least 60 already discovered, and yet daily there are more revealed: there are divers of them of good ability, and they have done much harm. I hear it is suspected that they had a hand in raising the great storm, wherein his majesty (Charles I.) was in so great danger at sea in Scotland."—C.

[3] CODE OF WITCHCRAFT.—By the 33 Henry VIII. cap. 8 (1541) persons practising witchcraft are declared guilty of a capital felony. This Act was repealed by 1 Edw. VI. (1547). By the 5th of Eliz. cap. 16 (1562), persons using invocations of spirits, &c., by which death shall ensue, are made liable to be punished with death; otherwise liable to fine and imprisonment. By 1 James I. cap. 12 (1603), persons invoking or consulting with evil spirits, taking up dead bodies for purposes of witchcraft (Seer Edward Kelley's offence), or practising witchcraft, to the harm of others, are declared guilty of a capital felony: by the 21st of the same king, cap. 28 (1623), the crimes of declaring by witchcraft where treasure is hidden, procuring unlawful love, or attempting to hurt cattle or persons, are rendered punishable for the first offence by pillory, and for the second by death. By 9 Geo. II. cap. 5 (1735), all the statutes against witchcraft are repealed.

[4] Mr. Nichols, in his "Progresses of King James I." has mistaken the ancient seat of the Monteagles for Hornby Castle in Yorkshire, the seat of the Duke of Leeds, and described the latter instead of the former.

[5] This *Journal* has since been edited by the Rev. Canon Raines, and printed for the Chetham Society, as vol. 14 of their series.—H.

"August 11. My brother (in-law) Sherborne his taylor brought him a suit of apparall, and us two others, and a livery cloake from Sir Richard Hoghton, that we should attend him at the King's coming, rather for his grace and reputation, shoeing [showing] his neibors' love, than anie exacting of mean service.[1]

"August 12. Coz(en) Townley came and broke his fast at Dunnoe (near Slaidburn), and went away. To Mirescougb. Sir Richard gone to meet the King; we after him to ——. There the King slipt into the [Myerscough] Forest another way, and we after, and overtook him and went past to the Yate; then Sir Richard light [alighted]; and when the King came in his coach, Sir Richard stept to his side, and tould him ther his Majestie's Forrest began, and went some ten roodes to the left, and then to the Lodge. The King hunted, and killed a buck.

"August 13. To Mirescough, the Court. Cooz(en) Assheton came with as gentlemanlie servants as anie was ther, and himself excellentlie well appointed. The King killed five bucks. The King's speeche about libertie to pipeing and honest recreation. We that were in Sir Richard's livery had nothing to do but riding upp and downe.

"August 14. Us three to Preston; ther preparation made for Sir Gilbert Hoghton, and other Knights. Wee were desyred to be merrie, and at nyght were soe. Steeven Hamerton and wyffe (of Hellifield Peel), and Mrs. Doll Lyster supped with us att our lodging. All Preston full.

"August 15. The King came to Preston. Ther, at the Crosse, Mr. (Henry) Breares the lawyer (Recorder of Preston) made a Speche, and the Corporation presented him with a bowle; and then the King went to a Banquet in the Town Hall, and soe away to Houghton; ther a speche made." After the delivery of the Speech, as Mr. Assheton continues, the King "hunted, and killed a stag. Wee attend on the Lords' table [i.e. at dinner].

"August 16. Hoghton. The King hunting; a great companie; killed affore dinner a brace of staggs. Verie hott; so he went in to dinner. Wee attend the Lords' table, and about four o'clock the King went downe to the Allome-mynes,[2] and was ther an hower, and viewed them preciselie, and then went and shott at a stagg, and missed. Then my Lord Compton had lodged two brace. The King shott again, and brake the thigh-bone. A dogg long in coming, and my Lord Compton shott again, and killed him [the stag]. Late in to supper.

"August 17. (Sunday) Hoghton. Wee served the Lords with biskett, wyne, and jellie. The Bushopp of Chester, Dr. Morton, preached before the King. To dinner. About fower o'clock, ther was a rush-bearing and pipeing afore them, affore the King in the Middle Court. Then to supper. Then, about ten or eleven o'clock a Maske of Noblemen, Knights, Gentlemen, and Courtiers, afore the King, in the middle round in the garden. Some Speeches; of the rest, dancing the Huckler, Tom Bedlo, and the Cowp Justice of Peace.

"August 18. The King [after knighting, at Hoghton Tower, Sir Arthur Lake, of Middlesex, and Sir Cecil Trafford, of Lancashire] went away about twelve to Lathome. Ther was a man almost slayne with fighting. Wee back with Sir Richard. He to seller, and drunk with us, and used us kindlie in all manner of friendlie speche. Preston; as merrie as Robin Hood and all his fellowes.

"August 19. All this morning wee plaid the Bacchanalians.",

At Lathom House, the seat of William, sixth Earl of Derby, the king rested two nights; and on the 20th of August, before his departure, knighted Sir William Massey, Sir Robert Bindloss, of Borwick, Sir Gilbert Clifton, Sir John Talbot, of Preston, Sir Gilbert Ireland, of The Hutt, and Sir Edward Osbaldeston, of Osbaldeston, all of Lancashire.

The king then proceeded to Bewsey Hall, the seat of Thomas Ireland, Esq., on whom his majesty, before his departure, conferred knighthood, as he did on Sir Lewis Pemberton, of Hertfordshire.[3]

On that Sunday on which the king was at Hoghton Tower (August 17) a petition was presented to his majesty, signed principally by the Lancashire peasants, tradespeople, and servants, representing "that they were debarred from lawful recreations upon Sunday, after evening prayers, and upon holy days, and praying that the restrictions imposed in the late reign might be withdrawn." The origin of this complaint, as we have seen,[4] was laid in the time of Elizabeth, who, in order to reform the manners of the people, instituted a high commission in the year 1579. The commissioners were—Henry, Earl of Derby, Henry, Earl of Huntington, William, Lord Bishop of Chester, and others; and at their sittings, which were held at Manchester, they issued orders throughout the county against "pipers and minstrels playing, making and frequenting bear-baiting and bull-baiting, on the Sabbath days, or upon any other days in time of divine service; and also against superstitious ringing of bells, wakes, and common feasts; drunkenness, gaming, and other vicious and unprofitable pursuits." These restrictions the royal visitor thought incompatible with the privilege of his subjects, whose complaints, as he says, "We have heard with our own ears, and which grievances we promised to redress." In the fulfilment of this pledge he issued a proclamation,[5] "against withholding recreation from the people on Sunday afternoon and evening," of which the following is a copy:—[6]

"BY THE KING.

"Whereas upon our returne the last yeere out of Scotland, Wee did publish Our pleasure touching the recreations of Our people in those parts vnder Our hand: For some causes Us thereunto moouing, We have thought good to command these Our directions then given in Lancashire with a few words thereunto added, and most appliable to these parts of Our Realmes to be published to all Our Subjects.

"Whereas We did iustly in Our Progresse through Lancashire, rebuke some Puritans and precise people, and tooke order that the like vnlawful cariage should not be vsed by any of them hereafter, in the prohibiting and vnlawful punishing of Our good people

[1] Although the gradations of society were then such that the gentry of England disdained not, on occasions like the present, to wear the livery of the rank immediately above them, yet there is an urgent anxiety in Mr. Assheton's mind to have it understood that his appearing in Sir Richard Hoghton's livery was merely as a token for good-will.— Dr. Whitaker.

[2] The alum mines, which appear to have been held by the Hoghtons under a lease from the crown, were situated within a short distance of Hoghton Tower. Webster, in his "History of Metals" (1672), says: "Sir Richard Hoghton set up a very profitable mine of allum nigh unto Hoghton Tower in the Hundred of Blackburn, within these few years, where store of very good alome was made and sold."—C.

[3] Nichols's "Progresses of King James," vol. iii. p. 405.
[4] Chap. xiii.
[5] May 24, 1618.
[6] From a rare tract in Smeeton's Collection in the Manchester Free Public Library.—C.

for vsing their lawful Recreations and honest exercises vpon Sundayes and other Holy dayes, after the afternoone Sermon or Seruice : Wee now find that two sorts of people wherewith that Countrey is much infested (Wee meane Papists and Puritanes) haue maliciously traduced and calumniated those Our iust and honourable proceedings. And therefore lest Our reputation might vpon the one side (though innocently) haue some aspersions layed vpon it, and that vpon the other part Our good people in that countrey bee misled by the mistaking and misrepresentations of Our meaning : We haue therefore thought goode hereby to cleare and make Our pleasure to be manifested to all Our good People in those parts.

"It is true that at Our first entry to this Crowne and Kingdome, Wee were informed, and that too truly, that Our County of Lancashire abounded more in Popish Recusants than any Countie of England, and thus hath stil continued to our great regreet, with little amendment, saue that now of late, in Our last riding through Our said County, Wee find both by the report of the Judges, and of the Bishop of that diocesse that there is some amendment now daily begining which is no small contentment to Vs.

"The report of this growing amendment amongst them, made Vs the more sory, when with Our owne Eares wee heard the generale complaint of Our people, that they were barred from all lawful recreation, and exercise vpon the Sundayes afternoone, after the inding of all Divine Seruice, which cannot but produce two euils : The one, the hindering of the conuersion of many, whom their Priests will take occasion hereby to vexe, perswading them that no honest mirth or recreation is lawfully or tollerable in Our Religion, which cannot but breed a great discontentment in Our peoples hearts, especially of such as are peraduenture vpon the point of turning ; The other inconuenience is that this prohibition barreth the common and meaner sort of people from vsing such exercise as may make their bodies more able for Warre, when Wee or Our Successors shall haue occasion to use them ; and in place thereof sets up filthy tiplings and drunkennesse, and breeds number of idle and discontented speaches in their Alehouses. For when shall the common people haue leaue to exercise, if not vpon the Sundayes and Holidayes, seeing they must apply their labour and winne their liuing in all working dayes ?

HOGHTON TOWER.

"Our expresse pleasure therefore is that the Laws of Our Kingdome, and Canons of Our Churches bee as well obserued in that County, as in all other places of this Our Kingdom. And on the other part that no lawful Recreation shall be barred to Our good People, which shall not tend to the breach of Our aforesaid Lawes, and Canons of Our Church ; which to expresse more particularly, Our pleasure is that the Bishop, and all other inferior Churchmen, and Churchwardens, shall for their parts be carefull and diligent both to instruct the ignorant, and conuince and reforme them that are misled in religion, presenting them that will not conforme themselues, but obstinately stand out to Our Judges and Justices : whom We likewise command to put the Law in due execution against them.

"Our pleasure likewise is that the Bishop of that Diocese take the like straight order with all the Puritans and Precisians within the same, either constraining them to conforme themselues, or to leaue the Countrey, according to the Lawes of our Kingdome, and Canons of our Church, and so to strike equally on both hands, against the contemners of our Authoritie, and aduersaries of our Church. And as for our good peoples lawfull Recreation, Our pleasure likewise is, that after the end of Diuine Seruice, our good people be not disturbed, letted or discouraged from any lawfull Recreation ; such as dauncing, either men or women, Archerie for men, leaping, vaulting, or any other such harmless Recreation, nor from hauing of May-Games, Whitson-Ales, and Morris-dances, and the setting up of May-poles and other sports therewith used, so as the same be had in due and conuenient time, without impediment or neglect of diuine service. And that women shall have leaue to carry rushes to the Church for the decoring of it, according to their old custome. But withall we doe here accompt still as prohibited all vnlawfull games to bee vsed vpon Sundayes onely, as Beare and Bull-baitings, interludes, and at all times in the meaner sort of People by Law prohibited, Bowling. And likewise Wee barre from this benefit and libertie all such knowne Recusants—either men or Women, as will abstain

37

from coming to Church or diuine seruice, being therefore vnworthy of any lawfull recreation after the said seruice, that will not first come to the Church and serue God : Prohibiting in like sort the said Recreations to any that, though conforme in Religion, are not present in the Church at the Seruice of God, before their going to the said recreations. *Our* pleasure likewise is, That they whom it belongeth in Office, shall present and sharply punish all such as in abuse of this Our libertie, will vse these exercises before the ends of all diuine Seruices for that day. And we likewise straightly command, that euery person shall resort to his owne Parish Church to heare diuine seruice, and each Parish by it selfe to vse the said recreation after diuine seruice. Prohibiting likewise any Offensive weapons to be carried or vsed in the said times of recreation, and Our pleasure is, That this our Declaration shall be published by order from the Bishop of the Diocesse, through all the Parish Churches, and that both Our Judges of our Circuit and our Justices of Our Peace be informed thereof.

"Giuen at our Mannour of Greenwich the foure-and-twentieth day of May in the sixteenth yeere of our Raigne of England, France, and Ireland, and of Scotland the one and fiftieth.

GOD SAUE THE KING."

Subsequently his majesty further said "that his loyal subjects in all other parts of the kingdom did suffer in the same kind, though perhaps not in the same degree, as in Lancashire, and he did therefore publish a declaration to all his loving subjects, concerning lawful sports to be used on Sundays and festivals," which was printed and published by his royal command in the year 1618, under the title of "The Book of Sports," which the bishops were ordered to cause to be read and published in all the parish churches of their respective dioceses, on pain of punishment in the high commission court. Against this profanation of the sanctuary, Abbot, the intrepid Archbishop of Canterbury, was amongst the first to enter his protest ; and being at Croydon on the day that it was first to be read in the churches, he positively forbade the officiating minister to obey the royal command.

In the early part of the reign of Charles I. that monarch, uninstructed by events, thought fit, "for the ease, comfort, and recreation of his well-deserving people, to ratify and republish this his blessed father's declaration ;" and the reason assigned was, "because of late, in some counties of the kingdom, his majesty finds that, under pretence of taking away abuses, there hath been a general forbidding, not only of ordinary meetings, but of the feasts of the dedication of churches, commonly called *wakes*." His Majesty therefore expressed his royal will and pleasure that these feasts, with others, should be observed ; and that the justices of the peace, and the judges of assize, should make known his gracious intentions, and that the bishops should cause his will to be published in all the parish churches of their several and respective dioceses. The dissatisfaction felt by some of the clergy and many of the laity in Lancashire, and in all other parts of the kingdom, at these reiterated injunctions to violate, as they considered it, the sanctity of the Sabbath, was one of the causes of the civil wars, the approach of which was already foreseen by men of political sagacity. By others the licence was hailed as a privilege. The effects of the "Book of Sports," at the end of two centuries, are still visible in Lancashire ; and, as Dr. Whitaker has truly observed, there is scarcely a village in the county which does not exhibit symptoms of obedience to the injunction of "honest recreation."

In addition to the honours already mentioned as conferred upon the gentry of the county of Lancaster by King James, that sovereign knighted Sir Thomas Tildesley, on 15th of June, 1616, at Wimbledon. The same year, Sir Hugh Parker, son of Lord Monteagle, was made a Knight of the Bath, in honour of the creation of Prince Charles. Sir Gilbert Gerrard, of Harrow-on-the-Hill, a junior branch of the family of Gerrard of Bryn, in Lancashire, was in 1620 advanced to the rank of a baronet ; and Sir Ralph Ashton, of Lever, and Sir John Boteler attained the same honour in the summer of that year. For Sir Richard Hoghton the king had the highest esteem. The name of this gentleman appears in many of the royal masques and public entertainments ; and amongst the archives of the family a note, with the royal autograph, is preserved.

It does not appear that the paternal government of King James, combined as it was with the creation of the baronets of Ulster, had placed Ireland in a state of tranquillity, or even of security ; for, near the end of this king's reign, we find the lords of the council writing a letter to the Earl of Derby, as lord lieutenant, requiring that all Irishmen, passengers from any port in Lancashire or Cheshire to their own country, should take the oath of allegiance, on pain of being sent to London, in safe custody, for contumacy.

CHAPTER XV.

N the 27th March, 1625, after a reign over England of twenty-two years, the first of the Stuart kings—"the wisest fool in Christendom," as he has been styled— died of a tertian ague at the palace of Theobalds. It was Mid-Lent Sunday, Laud was preaching at Whitehall when the news reached London, and on the afternoon of the same day the proud but dignified Charles was proclaimed successor to the throne of his vain and vulgar father. Few princes have succeeded to the crown under circumstances that seemed more to foreshadow a reign of felicity; none have encountered greater difficulties or experienced greater misfortunes. "The face of the court," we are told, "was much changed in the change of the king," but if so, it could only have been a forced homage to the decency and personal demeanour of the sovereign, for Buckingham still reigned supreme. The possessor of the crown was changed, but the administration of government was unaltered. The Parliament, which met for the first time on the 18th of June, received the new king with every demonstration of loyalty, and Charles in turn made a "fair speech," in which he assured the members that he had been "trained at the feet of Gamaliel (meaning his faith), and all the world should see that none were more desirous to maintain the religion he professed than himself." "We can hope everything from the king who now governs us!" exclaimed Sir Benjamin Rudyerd—the "Silver Trumpet" of the Long Parliament—in an outburst of enthusiasm. But there were men in that assembly with cooler heads than Sir Benjamin Rudyerd, men who tempered their loyalty with caution, the old opponents of absolute kingship, who were by no means sanguine as to the nature of the lessons of Gamaliel, and in whose minds grave misgivings had arisen in the brief interval between the accession to the throne and the meeting of Parliament. Charles inherited his father's inordinate notions of kingly power, and he resolutely shut his eyes to the fact that he had to deal with an entirely different state of public opinion. The accession of the Tudors had been followed by the break-up of the feudal system and the effacement of many of the old landmarks of English society. A new class had sprung into existence, eager for the acquirement of political freedom, and the king was unable or unwilling to recognise the changed condition of things; through no fault of his own he had fallen among masterful circumstances, which it was impossible for him, with his narrow views and hereditary prejudices, to mould to any safe issue, and his weak point, if not his damning fault, was that he could not see, as other rulers have seen, that submission to the inevitable may often give a new lease of authority. The power of the sovereign had waned, but that of the people had increased ; Parliament, while bent upon abridging the ancient prerogative of the crown, was equally resolute in the extension of its own. The king persisted in his determination to reign and govern by "divine right," and the attempt to stretch the royal authority beyond its due limits led to resistance by force. Charles refused to yield anything, and in the fierce struggle which his obstinacy provoked he fell. The assent to the Petition of Right in the third Parliament, though it won the grant of a subsidy, came too late to restore confidence. Had that confirmation of the liberties, which were already the birthright of Englishmen, been less tardily given and accepted as a final measure by the strong-minded men who framed it, the kingdom might have been spared the calamity of civil slaughter; but when, on the one hand, popular leaders made that just and reasonable enactment the vantage ground for direct attacks upon the ancient prerogative of the crown, and, on the other, a distrustful sovereign withdrew in effect what he had previously, to the great joy of the nation, conceded, a breach was made between king and people; the trumpet-blast of discontent swept over the country; the seeds of strife were sown and nurtured both by king and Parliament, until eventually distrusting and wearied of each other neither cared for peace. The ill effects arising from the neglect of that clear understanding which ought to have taken place between his predecessor and the people of England, on the change of the Tudor for the Stuart dynasty, soon became manifest. The evils of this great political blunder were exhibited in the arbitrary levy of ship-money without the authority of Parliament; in the revival of the forest laws, the cause of so many prosecutions, and of so much contention in ancient times in Lancashire; and in the mistaken policy of the new king in ratifying and enforcing the obnoxious Book of Sports, which served, both here and in several other counties of the kingdom, as a touchstone to distinguish, and as an apple of discord to divide, the high-church party and the Puritans. To sustain these extraordinary proceedings, and to put down all opposition, the council-table and the star-chamber[1] enlarged their jurisdiction to a vast extent,[2] "holding (as Thucydides said to the Athenians) for honourable that which pleased, and for just that which profited." The king and the ardent friends of prerogative wished to govern the country without a Parliament, so deep was their disgust at the resistance made to the king's demands for grants from the people; and the supporters of the privileges of Parliament resolutely determined to uphold these bulwarks of the national liberties, and persevered in doing so till the sword was drawn, and they came to govern without a king. That Charles should have no liking for Parliaments is not surprising. He was by no means unacquainted with history, and it must be confessed there was little in the conduct of the Parliaments of previous sovereigns to inspire admiration or command respect. A representative body that had permitted itself to become the passive instrument of the tyrannical oppression of the Tudor princes could not appeal to the imagination with the same result that it can now after more than two centuries of free action. Charles, having exhausted every expedient to raise money by his own authority, was obliged, after an intermission of eleven years, to issue his writs, calling together a Parliament, which assembled, according to summons, on the 13th April, 1640—the first since the dissolution in 1629. Robert Holt was sheriff of the county at the time, and the writs under his hand bear date March 5th, 1639 (-40). There were dark whispers of coming troubles, and for the first time in the history of the Lancashire boroughs indifference to the franchise gave place to enthusiastic interest in the principles of the candidates chosen. Instead of proceeding to grant supplies, the Parliament, which was composed principally of country gentlemen, made it their first business to demand a redress of grievances, and nothing but a speedy dissolution, after it had existed for three weeks, prevented them from stopping that part of the public supplies which arose out of ship-money.[3] The king and his ministers struggled on for six months longer without Parliamentary aid; but on the 3rd of November, fresh writs having been issued in the meantime, the Long Parliament was convened, and their first business was to renew the cry of grievance and the demand for redress. This assembly, so memorable in English history, consisted of five hundred members, and the following is a list of the county and borough members for Lancashire:—

Lancashire.—Ralph Ashton, Esq., and Roger Kirby, Esq.
Lancaster.—John Harrison, Knt., and Thomas Fanshaw, Esq.
Preston.—Richard Shuttleworth, Esq., and Thomas Standish, Esq.
Newton.—William Ashurst, Esq. and Roger Palmer, Knt.
Wigan.—Orlando Bridgman, Esq. and Alexander Rigby, Esq.
Clitheroe.—Ralph Ashton, Esq. and Richard Shuttleworth, Gent.
Liverpool.—John Moore, Esq. and Richard Wyn, Knt. and Bart.

One of the first acts of the House of Commons was to determine "whether the king should be permitted to govern the people of England by his sole will and pleasure, as an absolute monarch, and without the assistance of Parliament, as he had lately done, or whether he should be compelled to admit the two houses of Parliament to a participation in the legislative authority with him, according to the constitution of England ever since the first institution of the House of Commons

[1] A riot, not very dissimilar to that which occurred in 1589, took place at the manor-house of Lea, in the parish of Preston, in 1633, for which the offenders were prosecuted in the court of Star Chamber, where Sir Richard Hoghton was fined £100, and other two of the rioters £50 each.

[2] Clarendon's "Hist. of the Rebellion," book i.

[3] The first writ for levying ship-money was issued by Charles I. in 1636, and the quotas required to be contributed by the several places afford some standard whereby to estimate the wealth and importance of those counties, cities, and towns, nearly two centuries ago. The contribution of Lancashire was one ship of 400 tons, 160 men, and £1,000 in money; borough of Preston, £40; borough of Lancaster, £30; borough of Liverpool, £25; borough of Wigan, £50; borough of Clithero, £7 10s.; borough of Newton, £7 10s. Yorkshire contributed two ships, 600 tons, and £12,000; Hull, £140; Leeds, £200; Bristol, 1 ship, 100 tons, 40 men, and £1,000; and London contributed seven ships, 4,000 tons, 1,560 men, and six months' pay. This impost, with some modifications, continued for three successive years, and the arrears due from Lancashire at the end of that period were £172 10s. In this year (1636) a levy of troops was made upon ten of the counties in the north and centre of England, amounting to 10,483 foot and 1,233 horse, to which Lancashire was required to contribute 420 foot and 50 dragoons, and Yorkshire 6,720 foot and 60 horse.

in the reign of Henry III." The decision of the house it was not difficult to anticipate. It declared that the two houses of Parliament formed an integral part of the government of the kingdom, and that to attempt to govern without them was an arbitrary and unconstitutional exercise of the royal authority.[1]

In the same spirit an Act was passed wherein it was declared that the court of Star Chamber was an arbitrary and tyrannical tribunal, unknown to the ancient laws of the country, and in violation of the provisions of the great charter, and that it should be finally and for ever abolished from and after the 1st of August, 1641. By the same Act it was declared that the jurisdiction used and exercised in the Star Chamber[2] of the duchy of Lancaster, held before the chancellor and council of that court, should also be abolished on the 1st of August.[3] The abolition of the court of Star Chamber was followed by an Act in which the county of Lancaster was almost equally interested. This was the Act defining the limits of the forests in England, and thereby terminating the exactions so long existing of the justices in eyre. In this way the tyrannical operation of the forest laws in this county was brought to an end, and the people were no longer subjected to have their estates and even their houses invaded by that odious jurisdiction.

The complaint of grievances was not confined to the House of Commons but extended also to the constituent body, and the knights, squires, merchants, gentlemen, and freeholders of this county presented a petition to Parliament, representing that a gross breach of privilege had taken place at the election of knights of the shire for the county of Lancaster, unparalleled at any election in the kingdom.[4] The petitioners also complained, as they had done twelve months before, of other grievances, and prayed that such persons as were found to have been instrumental in bringing on arbitrary and insolent government might make reparation to their country, and from henceforth be excluded from the exercise of that authority.[5] This petition was entrusted to a delegation of gentlemen from the county of Lancaster, who were, contrary to the usage of the present time, admitted to the house to present it, and informed by the speaker that the house found this document to contain many weighty considerations, with great expressions of care and affection to the commonwealth, and that the contents should be taken into serious consideration.[6]

The Parliament had already assumed the prerogative of nominating both the lords-lieutenant and the deputy-lieutenants of the counties; and hence we find that, in the same year that the Lancashire petition was received, Lord Strange (eldest son of the Earl of Derby) was nominated by that authority lord-lieutenant of the county palatine of Chester, and Lord Wharton lord-lieutenant of the county palatine of Lancaster; and the names of Sir George Booth, Mr. John Moore, Sir Thomas Stanley, Mr. Alexander Rigby, of Preston, Mr. Dodding, Mr. Egerton, Mr. Ralph Ashton, of Middleton, Mr. J. Hales, Sir William Brereton, Mr. Thomas Standish, of Duxbury, Sir Ralph Ashton, of Downham, Mr. Robert Hide, Mr. Thomas Byrch, Mr. Edmund Hopwood, and Mr. Jo. Bradshaw, were added, by nomination of the house, to be deputy-lieutenants of the county palatine of Lancaster.[7]

The storm, which had been long gathering, was now ready to burst; and in this portentous year (1641) Mr. Ashton, Mr. Shuttleworth, Mr. Rigby, and Mr. Moore, members of Parliament, were enjoined by the House of Commons to proceed into Lancashire to see the ordinance of the militia put in force in the county. These orders were speedily followed by others to put the county in a state of defence, for which purpose forces were sent into Lancashire, and directions were given to the deputy-lieutenants, and other officers in the county, to disarm and secure all recusants and other "malignants." That offices of public trust might be filled by men devoted to the Parliament, Edward Lord Newburgh, chancellor of the duchy of Lancaster, was directed by the House of Commons forthwith to issue out commissions of peace to Sir Ralph Assheton, Bart.; Ralph Assheton, of Middleton, Rich. Holland, John Bradshaw, William Radcliffe, Rich. Shuttleworth, John Braddyll, John Starkie, Esquires; Sir Tho. Stanley, Bart.; Jo. Holcrofte, Tho. Standish, Geo. Dodding, Tho. Fell, and Peter Egerton, Esquires. And it was further ordered that his lordship should immediately discharge Sir Gilbert Hoghton, Knight and Baronet; Robert Holt, of Stubley,

[1] The 15 of Edward II. declares the necessity of obtaining the consent of Parliament to all laws, and there is no instance on record of the statute having been abrogated.—C.

[2] The Star Chamber—so named from the gilded stars with which the ceiling of the chamber is said to have been anciently ornamented—was instituted by Henry VII. in contravention of the provisions of Magna Charta. It was composed of a committee selected from the Lords of the Council, a tribunal that was bound by no law, but which decided cases brought before it that involved the security of life and property. It was through the instrumentality of this court that the Tudors and the earlier Stuarts perpetrated most of their arbitrary enactments.—C.

[3] Rot. Parl. 16 Charles I. p. 2. nu. 6.

[4] In allusion to an illegal interference in the return of members, by Lord Strange.—"Lancashire's Valley of Achor," p. 2.

[5] Treatise in the King's Collection in the British Museum, inscribed "Gift of George III." This collection contains, among other treasures,

all the books and pamphlets from the beginning of the year 1640 to the coronation of Charles II. (1661), and nearly one hundred manuscripts never yet in print, the whole comprising 30,000 books and tracts uniformly bound, consisting of 20,000 volumes, the catalogue of which is contained in twelve small folio volumes, each treatise being dated according to the day of its publication. This accumulation of tracts was formed with great pains and at much expense, and so privately as to escape the most diligent search of the Protector, who anxiously wished to obtain them. To prevent discovery they were sent into Surrey and Essex, and finally lodged with Dr. Barlow, the library-keeper at Oxford, to whom the collectors confided them. On his suggestion they were removed to the king's library, as their most fit depository, and presented finally by the royal munificence to the British Museum.

[6] Journals of the House of Commons, March 12, 1641.

[7] Ibid, 1641.

Alexander Rigby, of Burgh, John Greenhalgh, Edm. Assheton, Sir Alexander Radcliffe, William Farington, Orlando Bridgman, Sir Edw. Wrightington, and Roger Kirkeby, Esquires, from being further employed as commissioners of the peace within the said county.[1]

That the garrison in the interest of Parliament in Manchester might be supplied with ordnance, Mr. Ralph Assheton was furnished with the speaker's order for the conveyance of four small pieces of brass cannon to that place, with one similar piece for the safety of his own house at Middleton. It was further ordered that one thousand dragoons should be raised for the safety of the county of Lancaster,[2] in compliance with the wishes and desires of the well-affected people of that county, who, foreseeing the danger with which they were menaced, petitioned Parliament for protection and support against "the papists and other malignants" [the king and his confidential advisers and adherents being virtually, though not expressly, included in the number] "who had associated and raised great forces, both horse and foot, to oppress and distress the well-affected subjects in the counties of York, Northumberland, Westmorland, and Cumberland, and in the counties palatine of Durham, Chester, and Lancaster." For carrying this purpose into effect, it was ordered by the House that all lords-lieutenant, deputy-lieutenants, colonels, and other inhabitants of these counties, should associate themselves, and mutually aid and assist one another by raising forces of horse and foot, and leading them into places which should be most convenient and necessary; and, by all other good ways and means whatsoever, suppress and subdue the popish and malignant party in these counties, and preserve the peace of the kingdom according to the order and declarations of Parliament.[3] The preparations for civil war being now nearly matured, it was ordered that lord-general the Earl of Essex, commander of the Parliamentary forces, should be requested by Parliament to appoint Lord Fairfax the commander-in-chief of the northern counties, in the absence of his excellency, with power to make and appoint other officers. All these preparations naturally required the sinews of war; it was therefore ordered that money should be borrowed for the defence of Lancashire, and that such money or plate as Mr. Thomas Case, or any other person duly qualified, should underwrite for the defence of this county, and the reduction of the malignant party here, should have the public faith pledged for its repayment, with eight pounds per cent. per annum interest—the money to be issued for the use of the county by warrants under the hands of any four members of the House of Commons serving for this county.[4] Bills to the amount of four hundred thousand pounds, to be disbursed for the protection of Lancashire and Cheshire, were then issued, with the strict injunction that no part of this money should be employed against the Parliament, but preserved sacredly for its service. Instructions to this effect were sent to the deputy-lieutenants of Lancashire, and the same instructions, *mutatis mutandis*, were sent to those of Cheshire. Although the greatest exertions had been made to reinforce the English troops in Ireland, and Mr. John Moore had been sent down by Parliament with express instructions to Sir William Brereton, enjoining him to transport the horse troops that were in Lancashire and Cheshire without delay to that country, the rebellion and massacre, so memorable in the history of Ireland, took place this year (1641), and a great number of the refugees sought an asylum in Lancashire. The fugitives, naked and destitute, found their way to Liverpool, told their harrowing tales of robbery and murder, and sought the hospitality and charity of the county.[5] In the height of party rage the king was charged by his enemies with being accessory to these atrocities; and this rumour, though totally unfounded, served still further to alienate the affections of his subjects in all parts of the kingdom, and to aggravate the popular ferment in Lancashire. The Puritans exclaimed that the multitudes of Papists dwelling among them would repeat within the county the bloody scenes which had been transacted in the sister kingdom, seeing that they were actuated by like hellish principles. A request was therefore made to Lord

[1] Journals of the House of Commons, October 24, 1641.
[2] The king, in himself, had no power of calling upon his subjects to bear arms, except in restoring order and for the defence of the realm against a foreign enemy, but on the other hand such a power had never been exercised by the two Houses of Parliament without the assent of the king, and when he refused consent to the Militia Bill, which would have given the command of the national force in every county to men devoted to the Parliamentary cause, he was only acting in accordance with constitutional precedent. Both parties broke through that constitutional precedent—the king in levying forces by royal commissioners of array, and the Parliament in appointing lords lieutenant of the militia, by the ordinance of the two Houses without the assent of the Crown.—C.
[3] Journals of the House of Commons, Nov. 17, 1641.
[4] *Ibid*, Nov. 22, 1641.
[5] The atrocities committed during this insurrection in Ireland are almost without parallel in history. Froude, in his "English in Ireland," has given a graphic description of the scenes enacted. Sir John Temple was so affected by the terrible spectacle passing under his own eyes that his language in describing it rises into a tone of profound and tragic solemnity. "Multitudes of English," he says, "daily came up in troops, stripped and miserably despoiled; persons of good rank and quality, covered over with old rags, and even without any covering but a little twisted straw to hide their nakedness. Wives came lamenting the

murder of their husbands, mothers of their children—barbarously destroyed before their faces. Some, over-wearied with long travel, and so surbated, came creeping on their knees; others, frozen with cold, ready to die in the streets. The city was thus filled with the most lamentable spectacles of sorrow, which, in great numbers, wandered up and down all parts, desolate, forsaken, having no place to lay their heads on, no clothing to cover them, no food to fill their hungry bellies. The popish inhabitants refused to minister the least comfort to them, so as those sad creatures appeared like ghosts in every street. Barns, stables, and out-houses were filled with them, yet many lay in the open streets; and these miserably perished." Of the numbers that perished it is rash to offer so much as a conjecture. In the midst of excitement so terrible extreme exaggeration was inevitable, and the accounts were more than usually hard to check, because the Catholics, in their first triumph, were as eager to make the most of their success, as the Protestants to magnify their calamity. In the first horror it was said that 200,000 persons had perished in six months. For these enormous figures the Catholic priests were responsible. They returned the numbers of the killed in their several parishes up to March, 1642, as 154,000. To these may have been conjecturally added the crowds who died of exposure, want, or the plague in Dublin and the other towns. Sir John Temple considered that 150,000 perished in two months, or 300,000 in two years. At the trial of Lord Maguyre the figures were sworn at 152,000.—C.

Strange, the lord lieutenant of the county, that the Protestants might be furnished with arms and ammunition, as the means under God, of their lawful defence against their malignant enemies, the expenses of which they proposed to discharge out of the county levies.

The king, having despatched his queen, with the Prince of Orange and the young Princess Mary, to Holland, now quitted London, and repaired to York, which city he reached on the 19th March, 1642, leaving Parliament sitting. This measure produced the most alarming apprehensions in every part of the country. Petitions from all quarters were presented to his majesty, and, amongst others, one from the county palatine of Lancaster, drawn up by Richard Heyrick, warden of Manchester, and subscribed by sixty-four knights and esquires, fifty-five divines, seven hundred and forty gentlemen, and of freeholders and others about seven thousand, was presented the 31st of May. In this document the petitioners, after expressing their assurance of his majesty's zeal for the Protestant religion, add—

"You have at once provided against all popish impieties and idolatries, and also against the growing danger of Anabaptists, Brownists, and other novelties; all which piety, love, and justice, we beseech God to reward into your own bosom. But yet, most gracious sovereign, there is one thing that sads our hearts, and hinders the perfection of our happiness, which is, the difference and misunderstanding between your majesty and your Parliament, whereby the hearts of your subjects are filled with fears and jealousies; justice neglected, sacred ordinances profaned, and trading impaired, to the impoverishment of many of your liege people; for the removal whereof we cannot find any lawful means, without your majesty's assistance and direction."

To this dutiful and loyal address his majesty replied from his court at York, on the 6th of June—That it was a great contentment to him to find so many true sons of the Church of England; and that he took in very good part their desire of a good understanding between his majesty and the two Houses of Parliament, which it had always been his wish to maintain. About the same time a petition from the knights, esquires, ministers, gentlemen, and freeholders of the county of Lancaster was sent to the king at York, by the party attached to the Parliament, in which, after pointing out to his majesty the great evil that was likely to arise to the kingdom from his absence from Parliament, they entreat his majesty, for the honour and safety, as well as for the peace and welfare of his dominions, "to return to his great council, in whom the nation had so far confided, that they had entrusted them with their lives, liberties, and estates." To this petition the answer of the king was, that he had not gone from his Parliament, but that he had been driven from them. The Parliament, anxious to possess themselves of the prerogatives of the crown, as well as of their own privileges, requested the king to remove Sir John Byron from the lieutenancy of the Tower, and to place the militia of the kingdom at their disposal. To the first of these requests the king replied that he had confided the lieutenancy of the Tower to a gentleman of unquestionable reputation and known fortune, and that he did not expect to have been called upon to remove him without any particular charge against him; and as to the militia, that force was, in virtue of the royal prerogative, subject to the king's command, though he should be ready to listen to any well-digested proposition on the subject that might be submitted to him.[1] Notwithstanding this answer, the Parliament so far usurped the royal functions as to issue an ordinance for assuming the power over the militia of the kingdom. A strong party still existed in Lancashire in favour of the king, to check which an ordinance was issued by Parliament for levying money on the estates of the "malignants," and Mr. Assheton was appointed to prepare the necessary documents. At the same time it was declared, by a species of anticipation, but on no less an authority than that of the two Houses of Parliament, that many desperate and ill-disposed persons in the county of Lancaster had been in actual war and rebellion against the Government; it was therefore ordered, that the committee formerly named to be assessors should be authorised to seize and take all rents, moneys, houses, goods, and plate of the malignants, rendering an account to Parliament;[2] and it was further ordered that the tenants and debtors of the malignants should pay their rents and debts into the hands of the committees appointed by Parliament, whose receipts shall be a full and legal discharge of the debts.

On the 28th of June, 1642, Sir John Girlington, the high sheriff of Lancashire, convened a meeting, by the king's command, to be held at Preston, for the purpose of promulgating the Lancashire petition, and the king's answer, together with his declarations. At this meeting, Lord Strange (the royalist lord-lieutenant) and Lord Molyneux attended, along with Sir George Middelton of Leighton, Sir Alexander Radcliffe, Sir Edward Fitton of Gawsworth, Mr. Tildesley of Myerscough, Mr. William ffarington, and many others of the king's party; and Mr. Alexander Rigby and Mr. Shuttleworth, who had been sent into the county by Parliament as members of the committee for the House of Commons, with several of the new deputy-lieutenants appointed by Parliament, also appeared. The meeting being too large to be contained in any of the public buildings in the town, it was adjourned by the sheriff to Preston Moor. Here the Parliamentary

---

[1] Lord Clarendon's "History of the Rebellion," book iv.   [2] Journals of the House of Commons, February 15, 1642.

committee demanded that the sheriff should deliver up to them the royal commission and warned him against the execution.   The proceedings soon became so tumultuous, that the sheriff departed with about four hundred of his friends, exclaiming, "All those that are for the king, go with us"— "for the king! for the king!"[1]   Mr. Rigby and his friends, in reply, exclaimed, "For the king, and for the Parliament!" which appears to have been the more popular cry.   Here the terms *Cavalier* and *Roundhead* were first applied in Lancashire, and they soon became as familiar here as they had for some time been in London.[2]   While these proceedings were taking place upon the moor, Mr. ffarington conveyed away several barrels of gunpowder, which had been collected at Preston.   Soon afterwards the high sheriff and Lord Strange, by virtue of the commission of array,[3] seized the magazines of the county of Lancaster, appointed for the use of the Lancashire militia, which they determined to detain, in contravention of a resolution of the House of Commons, requiring them to deliver them up into the hands of the deputy-lieutenants.[4]   At the same time an attempt was made by Sir Alexander Radcliffe and Mr. Thomas Prestwich, two of the commissioners of array, and by Mr. Nicholas Moseley, and Mr. Thomas Danson, the under-sheriff, to seize a quantity of ammunition stored in the college at Manchester, for the use of the royal party; but in this they were disappointed, owing to the vigilance of Mr. Assheton of Middleton, Sir Thomas Stanley of Beckerstaffe, and several of the deputy-lieutenants, who removed the powder and match to a place of security, and in that way preserved them for the use of the Parliamentary forces.   At Liverpool the Cavaliers were more successful, having a few days before seized thirty barrels of powder in that port.   The two houses of Parliament, in order to mark their sense of the conduct of Sir John Girlington, Sir Geo. Middleton, and Sir Edward Fitton, summoned them all to London as delinquents; and Lord Strange was, by the same authority, required to deliver up into the hands of the deputy-lieutenants, that part of the magazine of the county of Lancaster which had been seized by his lordship.   The march of the king, at the head of his troops, from York to Hull, where Sir John Hotham closed the gates and refused to admit him into the garrison, was considered as the commencement of the civil wars; and the Parliament, with that prudent foresight for which they were so much distinguished, issued an ordinance directing that forty barrels of gunpowder should be sent from the stores of the Tower of London, for the service of their supporters in the county of Lancaster.   James, Lord Strange, who was then at York in attendance upon the king, was appointed by his majesty lord-lieutenant of the counties of Lancaster and Chester, and was required forthwith to repair to the seat of his lieutenancy, to put in force the commission.   These hostile measures, under the commission of array, were taken in contravention of an express order of the two houses of Parliament, by which the high sheriff of the county of Lancaster, and the sheriffs of other counties, were commanded to suppress the rising or coming together of any soldiers, horse or foot, by any commission from his majesty, without the consent of Parliament, and all persons whatsoever were forbidden to exercise any such commission or warrant for levying soldiers, or gathering them together, without their consent.

On the return of Lord Strange from York to Lathom House on the 4th of July, his lordship determined to secure the town of Manchester for the king, and with this view he required the inhabitants to give up the magazine which they had accumulated against the approaching storm; but this they declined, on the ground that if they surrendered their arms and ammunition in these perilous times, they would be deprived of the means of defending their own persons and property. The proposal that the stores should be placed under the charge of magistrates of both parties was also refused, and finding that his object was not to be obtained, he retired.   It has been stated that afterwards he had recourse to force of arms, and that a skirmish ensued, in which his lordship lost twenty-seven of his men, after killing eleven of the inhabitants, but the story is confused and unsupported by any trustworthy evidence.   The 15th of the same month was also a memorable day in the annals of Lancashire.   On that occasion, Lord Strange was invited to a public entertainment by the loyal party of Manchester, designated as the Cavaliers.   Here the high sheriff read the commission of array, though interdicted by the Parliament.   He came with his retinue as lord-lieutenant and accompanied by the high sheriff; while the company were in the banqueting-room, Captain Holcroft and Captain Birch, deputy-lieutenants of the county, of the Parliamentary or *Roundhead* party, entered the town with their forces, and beat to arms.   His lordship quitted the repast to muster the troops by which he was attended, and a skirmish took place, in which a man

---

[1] Mr. Alexander Rigby's letter, dated June 24, 1642.

[2] Before the king left London, his palace at Whitehall was frequently beset with petitioners, some of whom expressed their complaints in strong terms of discontent. To allay the ferment, the complainants were frequently struck, and sometimes wounded, by a kind of voluntary royal guard, composed of disbanded soldiers, who rallied round his majesty, waiting for military employment. The haughty carriage of the guards procured for them the name of *Cavaliers*, while the persons who surrounded the palace, owing to their plain attire and undressed hair, were called *Roundheads*. In time, these terms became party names; the king's supporters being styled *Cavaliers*, and the adherents of the Parliament *Roundheads*. The term Malignants was also applied to the loyalists, when they were in a state of active hostility against the Parliament.

[3] This commission was issued by the king on the 10th July, 1642. The Parliament was so strongly opposed to the measure that they stigmatised the commission as against the laws, and denounced the commissioners as the betrayers of the liberty of the subject.

[4] Resolution of the House of Commons, June 27, 1642.

of the name of Richard Percivall of Kirkman's Hulme, a linen webster (weaver), was killed by the royalists.[1] This was the occasion on which the "first blood" was shed in those civil wars that for several years spread destruction through the country, and brought in the end both Lord Strange and his sovereign to the block. The affray, which partook of the nature of a street row, was greatly exaggerated, and though two or three over-zealous Parliamentarians were the real offenders, the chief instigator being Sir Thomas Stanley of Bickerstaffe, an anti-royalist and distant connection of the Stanleys of Lathom, it was made the excuse for impeaching Lord Strange, who, by a strange perversion of facts, was charged with "levying war against the king, Parliament, and kingdom." The details of what actually occurred are thus given in a rare tract published at the time and reprinted by the Chetham Society :—

"My Lord Strange being invited the 15 of this moneth to the towne of Manchester by neare twenty of the chiefe men and officers there unto a banquet that afternoone, he being then accompanied with the high sheriff of Lancashire, the Lord Molineux, Sir Gilbert Haughton, Sir Alexander Radcliffe, Mr. Holt of Stubley, Mr. Farrington, Mr. Prestwich, Mr. Tilsley, and other gentlemen of the best ranke in the shire, accepted the loves of the towne, and his lordship, in his coach, attended by some thirty of his own horse, being but his ordinary attendance, and met with at least a hundred horse of the said towne, being the inviters and their friends. At the entrance to the towne were divers expressions of joy from the inhabitants, as continued acclamations, bonfires, the streets strewed with flowers, &c. His lordship being with all the chiefe men at Manchester in the house of Mr. Greene at the banket, his lordship staid not a quarter of an houre, but word was brought of Mr. Holcroft marching in the towne with souldiers, armed with pikes and muskets, with their matches lighted and cockt, also a drum beating before them to assemble more companie (their muskets also were charged with bullets, as appeared by those which were taken from them), who presented themselves in the street in a warlike posture, and at the time two other companies in like manner assembling in two severall streets of the said towne, environed his lordship. Mr. Sheriffe, understanding this plot and practice while he was in the chamber with his lordship, ran hastily downe for prevention of the pretended inconvenience, but finding my lord's horse before his owne, made use thereof, he found Mr. Holcrofte neere the Crosse, with divers armed men, whereupon the sheriffe did command him and the rest in his majestie's name to lay downe their armes, keepe the peace and cease the tumult, but Mr. Holcroft, unwilling at the first, notwithstanding the proclamation according to the statute, charg'd him with disobedience to his majestie's lawes. My lord observing the sheriffes long stay, and desiring to assist for the preservation of the peace, and missing his owne horse or any other, was forc't to goe along the street afoot without any of his ordinary servants, and made his owne way through the people, until at the end of the streete he met a horse of Sir Alexander Radcliffe, and in his passage was shot at with two pistols out of a window by Sir Thomas Stanley, and another by him, as will be deposed, but, God be thanked, they both missed ; he was also seen at the said window, charging his pistoll ; there was also a muskett shot at his lordship from a shop in the streete, which was seen to hit the wall neare by him. My lord, with the sheriffe going their intended way, met a new company, who thronged the streets, and endeavoured to stop the passage with pikes and muskets. Their captaine, one Birch, bad them give fire; but the raine being so great, put out most of their matches, and being resolutely commanded to advance their pikes were much afraid, and some obeyed, especially their captaine, who hid himself under a cart which stood in the streets ;[2] the men seeing themselves overcome, submitted and retired. The place being cleared, his lordship with the rest were going out of the towne, but suddenly some came in the reare, and cutt a gentleman on the head and struck him off his horse. A son of that gent, rescuing his father, was also wounded ; it is thought one of them is in great danger ; the man that struck the old gent was shot, but not yet known by whom. This bloody assassinate was followed with great cunning and eagernesse by Sir Thomas Stanley and Mr. Holcroft, both his lordship's knowne enemies. They be men of decayed fortunes and much indebted, ready to leave the country, whereof they thought convenient to build some hopes on others' ruines, assuring themselves if that towne were on good tearmes with my lord, it would end all their hopes, thinking by this divelish plot to master the country by taking away his lordship's life, as may appeare by testimony offer'd to produce the party so hired to murther his lordship, affirming if the towne were so kind then unto his lordship to entertain him with a banquet, they would give him a second to breake the peace. When the gentlemen of Manchester did invite my lord into the towne, his lordship did acquaint them with an information that Sir Thomas Stanley and Holcroft had bin very busy that morning among divers armed souldiers, whereof his lordship did aske them if they would not like that his lordship might come into the towne with his ordinary attendance, of which they seem'd most desirous, and prepared a banquet for those of his lordship's servants, as they are ready to arrive. Next morning the chiefe of the townsmen repaired to his lordship, but lodged but a mile off, at Sir Alex. Radcliffe's (Ordsal Hall), with a protestation of great griefe at this accident, and all of them under their hand did give his lordship a declaration that Sir Thomas Stanley, Holcroft, and Birch were the disturbers of their peace, and the only occasion of their treachery, so as my lord and the towne are on very faire termes, and the other three by these means, God be thanked, discovered themselves to the world, so as no just, wise, religious person will hereafter give them any countenance."

This document is followed by the signatures of those who made the declaration.

On the departure of Lord Strange from York, it had been determined by the king in council that the royal standard should be raised at Warrington; and after the affair at Manchester, his lordship mustered the county in three places—on the heath at Cockey Moor by Bury, Houghton Moor near Ormskirk, and Fulwood Moor near Preston—at each of which places large bodies of men appeared, most of them armed with pikes, muskets, or other weapons. His lordship was proceeding into Cheshire and North Wales to effect the same service, when he was checked in his career by an intimation from the king's council that these noisy musters which he had made were pre-indications of his own ambitious design, and that it was not safe for his majesty to intrust him with so much power.[3] To add to the indignity, his lordship was divested of the lieutenancy of Cheshire and North Wales, and it was proposed to unite Lord Rivers, who had recently been made an earl, with him in the lieutenancy of Lancashire. Suspicions had been insidiously expressed as to his sincerity in the royal cause, and it was feared that his near alliance to the crown might make him a dangerous person to be entrusted with any considerable military power. Though indignant at

---

[1] The burial of Percivall is thus recorded in the register of the Collegiate (now Cathedral) Church at Manchester : "1642, Julie 18. Richard Percivall of Grindlowes."—C.

[2] Seacombe, in his "House of Stanley," referring to this incident,

says the "inveterate malice" of Birch was due to the fact of his lordship's having "trailed him under a hay-cart at Manchester, by which he got, even among his own party, the deserved epithet of Lord Derby's carter." P. 133. —C.

[3] Seacombe.

these reflections on his patriotism and honour, his loyalty never flagged and his fidelity never wavered; but the distrust of the king's advisers had a depressing effect upon many of the loyal inhabitants of Lancashire, and in a corresponding degree encouraged the boldness of the disaffected. It was a fatal mistake, and one to which many of the disasters that followed may be traced. Charles, with his usual policy, endeavoured to conciliate him, made him General of the Forces in Lancashire and Cheshire, and directed him to recover the town of Manchester, which had then been put in a state of defence and become the stronghold and rallying point of the anti-royalist party. From this time the intention of erecting the royal standard in Lancashire was abandoned. and on the 22nd of August his majesty, attended by Prince Rupert, and a large cavalcade of military and citizens, erected the standard on a hill near Nottingham Castle, amidst cries of "God save the king," that mingled with the hoarse voice of the storm and the tempest, the omen of coming disaster. The war soon after became general. Not only all religious denominations but almost every class of persons interested themselves deeply in the issue. The nobility, for the most part, with many of the higher order of the gentry, were for the king, and the principal part of their tenantry espoused the same cause. The yeomanry or freeholders in general took the side of the Parliament, and the manufacturers and traders were to a large extent of the same party. With few exceptions the peers ranged themselves on the side of the king, but there is no reliable data by which it is possible to fix accurately the proportion of the gentry in each fold. The "Royalist Composition Papers"[1] furnish a tolerably complete list of the landed men who espoused the Royalist cause, but there is no corresponding list of those who took the side of the Parliament. The Royalists, though adhering to the king from different motives, were practically one body, and were dealt with as such, but in the ranks of their opponents were men of widely different aims— thoughtful, but brave, strong-minded Englishmen, impressed with a stern unflinching love of justice, and a determination to maintain those liberties they held to be their birthright; and turbulent and aggressive fanatics, impatient of uniformity in rites and ceremonies and the decorous adjuncts of a national church, who, by their violent appeals to the passions of the people preached them into rebellion. It is impossible to class men like Essex and Cromwell together, or to place in the same category with the latter such wild enthusiasts as Lilburne, and Wildman, and Peters. The army, which consisted principally of a kind of trained band or militia, inclined most to the Parliament; and of the religionists, all the high churchmen, and a large majority of the Catholics, were on the side of the king; while the Puritans in the church, and the Presbyterians and Independents out of it, espoused the popular cause. It has been observed that in the civil wars between the houses of York and Lancaster this county was not the scene of a single battle; but during the contest now before us no county in the kingdom was more distinguished than Lancashire.

After the Reformation, those Catholics who refused to take the oath of abjuration were stigmatised as recusants and deprived of their arms, under an apprehension that they might be applied to an improper purpose;[2] but these persons, by one of the revolutions in parties which frequently take place, now espoused the cause of loyalty with great zeal, and a number of the leading Catholics of Lancashire petitioned the king to have the arms which had been taken from them re-delivered, or that they might furnish themselves with competent weapons, to be used in these times of war and danger for the defence of the king and the security of their country and families. Amongst these petitioners we find the names of Sir William Gerard, Bart., Sir Cecil Trafford, Knt., Thomas Clifton, Charles Townley, Christopher Anderton, John Cancefield, and others, Esquires, in the county of Lancaster. The petition, which has been printed by the Chetham Society, is in the following terms:—

"To the King's Most Excellent Majesty.—The Humble Petition of us, the inhabitants of Lancashire, whose names are hereunder written in the behalf of ourselves and divers others of the said county, your majesty's most loyall subjects are disarmed, and not sufficiently provided for the defence of your Royall person and our families. Our most humble supplication to your Majestie is that we may be received into your most gracious protection from violence, have our Armes taken from us redelivered in this time of actuall war, and by your Majesty's speciall directions may be enabled further to furnish ourselves with competencie of weapons for the security of your royall person (if we be thereunto required), our countries, and families, who now are not only in danger to the common disturbance, but also menaced by unruly people to be robbed ; And when, by the Almightie's assistance, your Majesty's Kingdom shall be settled, in case we be again disarmed, that a full value in money in lieu thereof to us may be restored."

The answer returned by the king was of course most gracious, and communicated the royal will and pleasure that they should, with all possible speed, provide sufficient arms for themselves, their servants, and tenants, which they were authorised and required, during the war raised against the

[1] "The Royalist Composition Papers" contain the proceedings of the committee for compounding with delinquents, and are of the greatest interest and value in elucidating the family history and ascertaining the actual landed and personal property of individuals during the Commonwealth period. The original papers, arranged in counties, are preserved in the Record Office, and may be referred to by the MS. Indexes, the Lancashire portion giving alphabetically the names of the compounders as contained in volumes 98 to 101.—C.

[2] On the 25th of May a number of Catholics and others had assembled in a tumultuous manner on a plain about seven miles from Lancaster, armed with swords and other offensive weapons, on which the high sheriff, being called in, dispersed the assembly and disarmed the Catholics.

king, to keep and use for his defence, and for the defence of themselves and their country, against all forces and arms raised against the authority of the crown by any ordinance or authority whatever. The petition of the Lancashire recusants and the compliance of the king with its prayer was immediately met by the despatch of Sir John Seaton, in the interests of the Parliament, into the district from which the petition had emanated, with an order authorising the suppression of associations of Catholics in Lancashire, Cheshire, and the five northern counties. Lord Strange, whose devotion to the royal cause was not to be extinguished by ingratitude on the one hand or by alluring offers on the other, continued to exert himself to the utmost in order to sustain the interests of his sovereign; and Lord Molyneux, equally zealous in the same cause, raised a regiment in Lancashire, of which he was made colonel; but many of the other principal men in the county actively engaged in the war were, as we have already seen, in favour of Parliament. The zeal and ability displayed by Lord Strange, though ill requited by his friends, brought upon him the decided hostility of his enemies; and Parliament, in a proclamation of the 16th of September, stigmatised him as a rebel, guilty of high treason, and ordered him to be so denounced by the clergy and constables in all the churches and towns of Lancashire and Cheshire; while "all sheriffs, and other his majesty's subjects, were required to apprehend the said Lord Strange, and bring him up to Parliament, there to receive condign punishment." On the same day articles of impeachment against his lordship were drawn up, and voted by the Commons; and it was, among other charges, alleged against him, "that upon the 15th day of July in the present year, he did maliciously, rebelliously, and traitorously summon together a great number of his majesty's subjects at Manchester, and did there invite, persuade, and encourage them to levy war against the king, parliament, and kingdom, and did on that occasion kill, murder, and destroy one Richard Percivall; for which matters and things the knights, citizens, and burgesses in parliament assembled impeached the said James, Lord Strange, of high treason."[1] At this crisis Lord Strange was urged by the king to muster all the forces in his power in Lancashire, and to march at their head to join the royal army then assembled at Shrewsbury. Long before the messenger who was the bearer of this despatch, under the king's own hand, arrived at Lathom, the force assembled in virtue of the commission of array had dispersed; but his lordship lost no time in issuing his warrants for the appearance of his tenantry and dependants. The summons was promptly obeyed, and three regiments of foot, with three troops of horse, armed and clothed at his lordship's own charge, were raised in the month of August, and marched under his command to Shrewsbury. The report made to the king of the state of Lancashire was, that the county was much divided in its attachments, and that Manchester was in the hands of the Parliamentary forces. To secure a station of so much importance, his lordship was ordered to return again to the seat of his lieutenancy, and by all means to secure the town of Manchester, which had then been put in a state of defence and strongly fortified with posts and chains, and barricades of mud at the ends of its ten streets, under the direction of a German colonel of engineers—John Rosworm or Rosswurm—who had been trained in the wars of the Low Countries, and had been hired by the townsmen for that purpose.[2] In obedience to these orders, his lordship, assisted by Lord Rivers, Sir Gilbert Gerard, Lord Molyneux, and other gentlemen of the county, marched from his rendezvous at Warrington, at the head of a force of 4,000 foot, 200 horse, and seven guns, and on Sunday morning, the 25th September, 1642, arrived before Manchester. The main body took up a position on the south side of the Irwell, in the grounds of Sir Edward Mosley, the lodge in Alport Park affording head quarters to Lord Strange. The other division took up a position on the Salford side of the river, the inhabitants of that borough being favourably inclined to the royal cause. On the following day the siege commenced, and was prosecuted with great vigour, but with little success, during the whole week, at the end of which time his lordship received two despatches, each of which had probably some influence in inducing him to raise the siege.[3] The first of these communications was of a domestic nature, and announced that his venerable father, William, Earl of Derby, had paid the debt of nature, his death occurring at Chester, on Thursday, the 29th September, and that his lordship, as heir-apparent, was elevated to the earldom; the other stated that the Earl of Essex was marching from London to give his majesty battle, and the earl, for such he had now become, was required to march with his whole force to the head-quarters of the royal army at Shrewsbury. In compliance with the commands of his sovereign, the Earl of Derby drew off his ill-equipped and hastily-levied forces, quitted Manchester, and marched without

[1] Rushworth's Coll. iv. 680.

[2] This mercenary adventurer, who resembled in some respects the famous Dugald Dalgetty of Drumthwacket, was ready to be employed by either party, and had agreed with Warden Heyricke and the Presbyterians of Manchester to superintend the defences of the town for a period of six months for the modest sum of £30. A faithful and valuable servant he proved, but a provokingly ill-tempered one, for when

he found that the Royalists would have been willing to make more liberal terms, he never ceased to bewail the beggarly remuneration he had agreed to accept from the Roundheads, or to rail at the "despicable earthworms," as he, not unjustly, styled those who had offered it, and when the danger was passed, refused to pay even the scanty pittance he had bargained with them for.—C.

[3] See Manchester.

delay to join the king. This "deliverance" of Manchester, as it was called, was considered by the Parliamentary party in Lancashire as "a visible manifestation of God's goodness towards them," and a public thanksgiving was ordained by Parliament throughout the country, in token of the general gratitude. From Shrewsbury the Earl of Derby marched with his forces into Warwickshire, where he made an unsuccessful attempt to take the town of Birmingham. The force by which he was opposed was the trained bands or militia; and in the desperate rencontre which took place within about a mile from Birmingham, the earl is represented, in the despatches to Parliament,[1] to have lost six hundred men in slain, and the same number of prisoners; while, according to the same authority, the Warwickshire men lost only one hundred and twenty of their trained band. After this unfortunate engagement the earl returned by way of Shrewsbury into Lancashire, and again established his rendezvous at Warrington, satisfied that he had "discharged a good conscience in all," and that his "honour was safe in spite of his worst detractors." "The county of Lancaster," says the letter of a Roundhead, who was himself actively engaged in the civil wars, "is grievously disturbed and divided into two factions, the papists and malignants, whereof there are many in Lancashire, taking one part, and the well-affected Protestants another. The Earl of Derby, the great ringleader of the papist faction, keeps his rendezvous at Warrington, whither great multitudes of ill-affected people, both out of Lancashire and Cheshire, daily resort, it being upon the frontiers of both these counties. They make daily great spoil in the country, which has so much incensed the people that they are determined, tide death tide life, to endure it no longer." The counterpart of this representation is given by Arthur Trevor, the Cavalier, who, in a letter to the Marquis of Ormonde,[2] says, "North Wales and South Wales, except a very few, are his majesty's. Cheshire hath agreed upon a cessation of arms for a month. I confess, my lord, that I do not like this measuring out of treason by the month. Manchester is the very London of these parts, the liver that sends the blood into all the counties thereabouts, and until it be cleansed or obstructed, I cannot imagine that there can be any safety in this neighbourhood. It is much hoped that my lord of Newcastle will take the part of Yorkshire that joins to Lancashire, and is poisoned by it, on his way to Manchester." Of Manchester Lord Clarendon says "it had from the beginning (out of that factious humour which possessed most corporations, in the pride of their wealth) opposed the king, and declared magisterially for the Parliament." Unhappily for his lordship's comparison, Manchester was not a corporation; nor was pride, except indeed spiritual pride, the characteristic of the Parliamentary party. The Earl of Newcastle was still delayed from proceeding into Lancashire, as his intention was, with his overwhelming force of 12,000 men, and in the meantime a skirmish took place at Leigh and Lowton Common, between the Earl of Derby's troops and the country people (Nov. 27), of which one of the latter gives the following relation :—

"The last Sabbath," says he, "as we were going towards the church, a post rode through the country informing us that the earl's troops were coming towards Chowbent; whereupon the country people rose, and before one of the clock on that day we had gathered together 3,000 horse and foot, encountering them at Chowbent aforesaid, and beating them back to Leigh, killed some, and wounded many; where you would wonder to have seen the forwardness of the young youths, farmers' sons. We drove them to Lowton Common, where they, knowing our foot to be far behind, turned face about, and began to make head against us, whereupon began a sharp although a short encounter; but when they perceived our full and settled resolution, they made away as fast as their horses could carry them, and we after them, killing, wounding, and taking prisoners about two hundred of them; and we never lost a man, only we had three of our men wounded, but not mortally. The nailers of Chowbent, instead of making nails, have busied themselves in making bills and battle-axes; and also this week the other part of the country meet, and not only intend to stand upon their guard, but to disarm all the papists and malignants within their precincts, and to send them prisoners to Manchester, to keep house with Sir Cecill Trafford, who is there a prisoner. The men of Blackburn, Padiham, Burnley, Clitheroe, and Colne, with those sturdy churls in the two forests of Pendle and Rossendale, have raised their spirits, and are resolved to fight it out rather than their beef and fat bacon shall be taken from them. The last week Sir Gilbert Hoghton set his beacon on fire, which stood upon the top of Hoghton Tower, and was the signal to the country for the papists and malignants to arise in the field, and in Leyland hundred; whereupon great multitudes accordingly resorted to him at Preston, and ran to Blackburn, and so through the country, disarming all and pillaging some, which Mr. Shuttleworth, a Parliament man, and Mr. Starkie hearing of, presently had gotten together about 8,000 men, met with Sir Gilbert and his Catholic malignants at Hinfield Moor, put them to flight, took away many of their arms, and pursued Sir Gilbert so hotly that he quitted his horse, leapt into a field, and by the coming of the night escaped through fir-bushes and bye-ways to Preston, and there makes great defence by chaining up Ribble bridge, and getting what force he can into the town for his security; out of which the country people swear they will have him, by God's help, with all his adherents, either quick or dead. Oh, that the Parliament had but sent down their 1,000 of dragooners into the country! We would not have left a mass-monger nor malignant of note but we would have provided a lodging for him. It is reported by some about the Earl of Derby that he is very melancholy and much perplexed about the unadvised course he has run; for the last Thursday at Warrington, at dinner, he said he was born under an unfortunate planet, and that he thought some evil constellation reigned at the hour of his birth, with many such other words of passion and discontent."

In the southern part of the county, Bolton—the "Geneva of Lancashire" as it was called—was the school and the centre of Puritanism, and consequently a thorn in the flesh of "malignant" Wigan; and equally the roystering Cavaliers of Wigan were a standing menace to the austere Roundheads of Bolton. The desire of each was to capture and destroy the other, and the opportunity for conflict was not far to seek. Early in December a smart engagement took place,

---

[1] Dated Nov. 23, 1642.   [2] Dated ultimo Decembris, 1642.

when the companies of Captain Bradshaw and Captain Venables, having issued from Bolton, were met at Hindley, near Wigan, by the Loyalist troops, when a considerable number were slain and the rest made prisoners. The alarm in the country now spread on every side; civil war had never before been seen by the inhabitants; the different classes of society were suspicious of each other, and the intention was entertained of raising the *levy en masse*, by ringing alarm-bells in the hundred of Salford. The language of the Cavaliers was haughty and menacing, that of the Roundheads sarcastic and insolent. Confidence amongst neighbours was banished; trade was greatly interrupted; and scarcity and even absolute want prevailed to an alarming extent. The religious predilections of one party were outraged by the other. The Loyalists, who were characterised by irreligion and profanity, to show their contempt for the sanctimonious character of the Puritans, dismantled their sanctuaries, and carried their irreverence to sacred things so far as to play at cards in the pews of their chapels;[1] while, on the other hand, monuments of antiquity, to which the name of popish could be attached, were frequently consigned to destruction by a fanatical populace;[2] and visionaries were not wanting to call for an agrarian law. In this excited state of the public mind, a meeting was held at Preston for the purpose of recruiting the king's forces, and raising the necessary supplies for their support. In this assembly the Earl of Derby, "lord-general of the county of Lancaster," as he was styled, presided, and Sir John Girlington, the high sheriff of the county, Alexander Rigby, Esq., of Burgh, Robert Holt, Roger Kirby, and William Farrington, Esquires, with many others, attended. A series of resolutions was adopted, the principal of which was that the sum of £8,700 should be raised by a rate on the county of Lancaster, to be employed for the payment of 2,000 foot and 400 horse soldiers, and to provide magazines and ammunition for the use and safety of the county, under the direction of a council, to be held at Preston, for the assistance of the lord-general; the council to consist of Sir John Girlington, Knt., Adam Morte, gentleman, Mayor of Preston, and James Anderton and Robert Kirby, Esquires, with power to call to their assistance Sir Gilbert Hoghton, Knt. and Baronet, Thomas Clifton, William Farrington, and John Fleetwood, Esquires, or any other of his majesty's commissioners of array within the county of Lancaster, so often as they should see occasion. At the same meeting it was agreed that the following should be the pay of the Lancashire troops *per diem* :—

Foot.	s.	d.	*Horse.*	s.	d.	*Dragooneeres.*	s.	d.
Captain	10	0	Captain	16	0	Captain	12	0
Lieutenant	4	0	Lieutenant	8	0	Lieutenant	6	0
Ancient	3	0	Cornet	6	0	Cornet	4	0
Sergeant	1	6	Corporal	4	0	Sergeant	3	0
Drummer	1	3	Trumpeter	5	0	Corporal	2	0
Corporal	1	0	Private	2	6	Dragooneere	1	6
Private	0	9				Kettledrum	2	0

And to every Commissary 5s.

The horrors of civil war banished the festivities of Christmas. The hundreds of Salford and Blackburn, the principal seat of hostilities, were actively employed in preparing for attack or for defence. On Christmas Eve, 1642, the Earl of Derby, at the head of several thousand men, provided with three field-pieces, marched from Wigan against the town of Blackburn. On arriving before the town the earl demanded that they should give up the place, and surrender their arms to the king. To this the militia replied that they were trustees for the king and for the Parliament, that the town was in their keeping, and that they should not surrender their trust. Finding them deaf to his summons, the earl endeavoured to prevail by the thunder of his cannon, but, night coming on, he was obliged to withdraw his forces, to his severe mortification, and to the joy of the inhabitants, who were unprepared for a renewal of the contest. The expectation entertained by the Earl of Derby that his influence in the counties of Lancaster and Chester, where he was supposed to have more command over the people than any subject in England had in any other quarter,[3] would render the most important service to the king, was grievously disappointed. This large and populous county was already nearly lost to the royal cause; and though the king had sent into Cheshire Sir Nicholas Byron, a soldier of great command, with a commission of "Colonel-General of Cheshire and Shropshire, and Governor of Chester," that county was placed in a situation of the most imminent peril, measuring out its loyalty by monthly portions. The estimate formed by Lord Clarendon of the Earl of Derby's talents and devotion to the royal cause, is as much too low as Secombe's estimate is too high. Speaking of the earl, his lordship says :—

[1] News from Manchester, dated Dec. 17, 1642.
[2] Commissioners were this year sent by Parliament into Lancashire and the other counties, to take away all images, superstitious pictures, and relics of idolatry, out of churches and chapels, wherever they might be found.
[3] Clarendon's "Hist. of the Rebellion," book vi.

"The restless spirit of the seditious party was so ready to be engaged, and punctually to obey, and, on the other hand, the Earl of Derby so unactive and so uncomplying with those who were fuller of alacrity, and would have proceeded more vigorously against the enemy ; or, through want of experience, so irresolute, that, instead of countenancing the king's party in Cheshire, which was expected from him, the earl insensibly found Lancashire to be almost possessed against him, the rebels every day gaining and fortifying all the strong towns, and surprising his troops without any considerable encounter. And yet, so hard was the king's condition, that though he knew these great misfortunes proceeded from want of conduct, and of a vigorous and expert commander, he thought it not safe to make any alterations, lest that earl might be provoked, out of disdain to have any superior in Lancashire, to manifest how much he could do against him, though it appeared he could do little for him. Yet it was easily discovered that his ancient power there depended more upon the fear than upon the love of the people, there being very many now in this time of liberty engaging themselves against the king, that might not be subject to that lord's commands. However, the king committed Lancashire still to his lordship's care, whose fidelity, without doubt, was blameless, whatever his skill was."[1] Speaking of the inferior classes, the noble historian is more correct in his description. "The difference in the temper of the common people of both sides," says he, "was so great, that they who were inclined to the Parliament left nothing unperformed that might advance the cause ; and were incredibly vigilant and industrious to cross and hinder whatsoever might promote the king's ; whereas they who wished well to him thought they had performed their duty in doing so, and that they had done enough for him, in that they had done nothing against him."[2]

Lord Clarendon's error in these passages, which contain much of truth, consists in his not having adverted to the origin of the quarrel between the court and the country, and in his having forgot that the first violation of our free constitution was on the part of the former. Hence the alienation of the affections of the people, as also the want of power in the Earl of Derby to rouse them into a state of active loyalty. It should, moreover, be remembered that any apparent inactivity on the part of Lord Derby was due, not so much to his want of judgment or resolution as to the obstacles that were continuously placed in his way by those about the king's person who distrusted his purpose; and hence it was, that while his zeal irritated those on the Parliament side it failed to secure for him the confidence of those who should have been his political friends, and his readiness to recognise the loyalty and accept assistance from the Roman Catholics of the county only intensified the bitterness of the ultra-Protestant party.

The war in other parts of the kingdom, though still in its pristine vigour, produced no very important result during the year 1642. Early in the year 1643 Sir Thomas Fairfax, son of Ferdinando, Lord Fairfax, "the hero of the Commonwealth," quitted Yorkshire, and repaired to Manchester, where he established his headquarters, and infused into the Lancashire campaign of that year a great degree of vigour. The first operation was undertaken by Sir John Seaton, a Scotch knight, and major-general of the Parliamentary forces. On the 10th of February Sir John marched from Manchester at the head of a body of troops, and taking the route by Bolton and Blackburn, at each of which places his force was considerably augmented, advanced to Preston. This ancient borough was then garrisoned by the king's troops, supported by a number of the neighbouring gentry, and headed by the mayor, a zealous supporter of the royal cause. The town was prepared for the visit, and was well fortified with an outer and inner wall. The attack was, however, made with so much vigour and promptitude, that the place was carried after a combat of two hours, and the gallant mayor, Adam Morte, Esq., Captain Hoghton, brother of Sir Gilbert, and a number of other officers, were numbered amongst the slain. In the rapidity of their advance from Blackburn to Preston, the Parliamentary forces had left behind them the fortress of Hoghton Tower, the seat of Sir Gilbert Hoghton ; but no sooner had Preston surrendered than three troops were despatched by Sir John Seaton, most of them Blackburn men, to take this tower. Having discharged a shot against the walls a parley was obtained, which terminated in the surrender of the place (Feb. 14). Captain Starkie and his company then marched into the garrison, where they found three large pieces of ordnance, with a good supply of arms and ammunition; but while they were congratulating themselves on their easy conquest the tower blew up, and the captain, with sixty of his men, either perished or were dreadfully maimed by the explosion. In the accounts sent to Parliament this disaster is represented as an act of perfidy on the part of the Cavaliers, but their is no satisfactory evidence to establish the charge ; and, for anything that appears to the contrary, the sacrifice of life may have been occasioned by the precipitancy which was manifested in demolishing the tower.

In the absence of the main part of the Parliamentary troops, the Earl of Derby despatched a strong force from Wigan to take possession of Bolton, where Colonel Ashton commanded. After a furious assault at the Bradshawgate-gate entrance to the town, the garrison was obliged to retreat to a mud wall two yards thick, which had been erected for the security of the place, and was guarded at the entrance by a chain. Here the battle was resumed with great obstinacy, but in the end the assailants were obliged to retreat, bearing along with them two or three cartloads of their dead soldiers slain in the engagement (Feb. 16). Two hundred club-men from Middleton, Oldham, and Rochdale, came soon after to the assistance of the place, accompanied by two hundred soldiers from Manchester under the command of Captain Radcliffe.

[1] Clarendon's History of the Rebellion, book vi.   [2] Ibid.

In the meantime Captain Birch proceeded from Preston to Lancaster, which proved an easy conquest (Feb. 17); and the castle, in which were Mr. Roger Kirkby, one of the knights of the shire, and Sir John Girlington, also surrendered, but not till these gentlemen had effected their escape. At the same time, twenty-one pieces of ordnance, taken from a Dunkirk ship, which had been stranded on the shores of Morecambe Bay, were brought to the castle, and served to enhance the value of the victory.

The campaign was now destined to take a more auspicious turn for the royal cause. The Earl of Derby, accompanied by Sir John Girlington and the brave Sir Thomas Tyldesley, by command of the king, presented himself at the head of a strong force before Lancaster, and immediately summoned the mayor and burgesses to surrender both the town and castle into his hands, on pain of the severest infliction.[1] To this summons the mayor replied that all their arms had been taken, under the command of officers within the town, for the king and Parliament; and, as to the castle, it had never been in possession of the mayor and burgesses. This answer was considered so unsatisfactory by the earl, that he set fire to the town, and ninety houses and eighty-six barns, or other buildings of a similar description, were consumed (March 18).[2] An attempt was made from Preston by the Parliamentary forces, under Colonel Ashton, to relieve Lancaster, but it failed; and the Earl of Derby, after taking Lancaster with a severe carnage, in which men, women, and children were slain,[3] returned to the south and took Preston by assault (March 21), and slew about six hundred of the enemy. The men of Bolton held " a solemn fast and humiliation " for the fall of Preston, and Lord Derby, elated with his success, determined on making another effort to reduce that Puritan stronghold. From Preston he marched to Blackburn, which also surrendered, and advanced to Bolton on the 28th of March, the day after the fast which had been kept at Manchester to deprecate the judgments of Heaven. On receiving the summons to surrender in the name of the king, the garrison replied that they should keep the town for the king and Parliament, and then went composedly to prayers. The end of the prayers was the beginning of a renewed assault upon the town, which the inhabitants resisted with so much success as again to drive off the assailants (March 28). The Boltonians were eager to repay the compliment of attacking by making an attack on Wigan. While that town proudly held its own, Bolton, which had been twice attacked, was accounted an inferior rival. The idea of inferiority was not to be endured, and hence a besieging force, aided by the train bands from Manchester, under Sir John Seaton, was despatched with the object of accomplishing the overthrow. Wigan was equal to the occasion. Earthworks were hastily thrown up, the walls were manned, and every preparation made to give the enemy a warm reception. After a short parley the town was stormed, and a breach having been unexpectedly made in the walls, the Boltonians rushed in, and, fired by a spirit of revenge, sacked the town and carried all before them; but a report arriving that the Earl of Derby was advancing with a considerable force to the relief, they secured what booty they could, and then beat a retreat (April 1), the Manchester men hurrying to Warrington, where, in an attempt to take the town, they suffered a defeat (April 5).

Lord Molyneux, after having fought at Edge Hill on the side of his majesty, had returned into Lancashire to recruit his regiment; and by his aid the towns of Lancaster and Preston had been reconquered. To consummate the campaign, it was determined to march to Manchester, then the stronghold of the Parliamentary force in the county, and to secure the place for the royal cause. Animated to renewed exertions by the remembrance of his former defeat before that place, the Earl of Derby declared that he would, if properly supported, either reduce the town or lay his bones before it; but on the very eve of the meditated attack, Charles had again recourse to the fatal policy of drafting. On the arrival of the royal army at Chorley, Lord Molyneux was summoned by a messenger from the king to repair forthwith to Oxford with his regiment, there to join the main army. This was a grievous disappointment to the Earl of Derby, who entreated his stay in Lancashire but for four days longer, in order to make the assault upon Manchester. The orders of the king were not, however, to be disobeyed; the earl's auxiliaries set out on their march for Oxford without delay. The following week was observed as a national fast by order of Parliament; but in the midst of their devotions the arts and practice of war were by no means neglected. The Earl of Derby was strongly entrenched at Wigan, the head-quarters of the Cavaliers, as Manchester was of the Roundheads. Bent upon following up the moral advantage gained by the unsuccessful attack of the Parliament forces of that town, the earl, gathering a force, said to consist of " eleven troops of horse, seven hundred foot, and infinite clubmen," marched from Preston, crossed the Ribble at Ribchester, and proceeded to Whalley with the intention of clearing Blackburn hundred of the Parliamentary forces. Being met by Colonel Shuttleworth, at the head of a number

---

[1] Summons of the Earl of Derby, dated March 18, 1643.   [2] Lancashire's " Valley of Achor," p. 25.

[3] "Lancaster Massacre," p. 2.

of troops supported by a hasty levy, a running fight took place near Ribchester, which was continued down to the Ribble at Salesbury, and ended in the repulse of the earl. The victory was deemed of so much importance to the popular cause that Parliament ordered a day to be set apart for a public thanksgiving. On the 28th of April, the Parliamentary forces, taking the route of Wigan, Ormskirk, and Preston, again advanced to Lancaster, where they succeeded in relieving the castle, which had been besieged by the king's forces. The siege of Warrington by the Parliamentary forces, under Colonel Ashton, was commenced on the 23rd of May. As a preliminary to the siege, the church of Winwick was taken possession of, and five days after Warrington capitulated (May 28). At this time a ship was taken at Liverpool which had been sent to the Royalists to supply them with reinforcements both of men and of ammunition. An effort was made by the Earl of Derby to regain the magazines at Liverpool; but, by the determined resistance of Mr. Moore and his Parliamentary adherents, the earl's designs, though supported by a formidable force, were entirely frustrated.

The Parliament, pressed by their necessities, passed an ordinance this year for the sequestration of the estates of "notorious delinquents" in the several counties of the kingdom, on the alleged ground that those who had raised the unnatural war should be made to defray its expenses. At the same time, sequestrators were appointed to seize the property of those who were hostile to the Parliament, and in this way to replenish their exhausted revenues (April 1).[1] The sequestrators in Lancashire were Sir Ralph Ashton and Sir Thomas Stanley, baronets; Ralph Ashton of Downham, Ralph Ashton of Middleton, Richard Shuttleworth, Alexander Rigby, John Moore, Richard Holland, Edward Butterworth, John Bradshaw, Wm. Ashurst, George Dodding, Peter Egerton, Nicholas Cunliffe, John Starkie, Gilbert Ireland, Thos. Birch, and Thos. Fell, esquires; and Robert Hyde, Robert Cunliffe, Robert Curwen, John Newall, and John Ashurst, gentlemen. On the 6th of September in this year an order passed the House of Commons empowering the deputy-lieutenants in the palatine counties of Lancaster and Chester to choose auditors charged with the duty of keeping perfect accounts of all such moneys, goods, and profits as might be taken or seized by virtue of any order or ordinance of either Houses of Parliament; and also to choose a treasurer, into whose hands such money should be paid; and it was subsequently ordered that Ralph Ashton, Richard Shuttleworth, John Moore, and Alexander Rigby, esquires, all Members of Parliament, should act as auditors in Lancashire.[2]

The disasters of this short but active campaign, with the treatment that the Earl of Derby had received from the king and his advisers, had a deadening influence upon the royal cause in Lancashire; and the earl, at the earnest solicitation of the queen, proceeded to the Isle of Man, to secure that island from the dangers with which it was menaced by the king's enemies, who, favoured by a confederacy within, had formed a project for taking possession of the island. His lordship was not insensible to the danger attendant upon this step, both towards the county and towards his own family. Previous to his departure he took all possible precautions to supply his house at Lathom, which was in itself a complete fortress, with men, cannon, and provisions; and to place the garrison under the command of a heroine whose name will ever rank amongst the most gallant and illustrious of her sex.[3]

At the same time that the queen commanded the Earl of Derby to proceed to the Isle of Man, her majesty wrote to the Earl of Newcastle from York (May 8), informing him that she had sent Wm. Murray to communicate with him on the state of Lancashire, and exciting him, by the honour that would await him, to recover for the king this "lost county." In another letter from the queen to the earl, on the following day, her majesty informs him that she has received further news from Lancashire, which the bearer is commissioned to communicate. In obedience to the queen's commands, the Earl of Newcastle, after his victory at Adwalton Moor[4] (June 30th, 1643), despatched a declaration and summons from his headquarters at Bradford to the town of Manchester, requiring them to lay down their arms, to avoid the further effusion of "Christian blood," under an assurance that, on their prompt obedience, his majesty's grace and mercy should be extended towards them, at the same time apprising them, that if they presumed to reject this offer, the blood shed in consequence of such rejection would fall upon their heads. To this imperious mandate Manchester replied, by the messenger who brought the earl's despatch, that they had at all times shown themselves desirous to maintain the king's prerogatives and the liberties of the subject, but that they had resolutely resisted those who, under colour of his majesty's commission, endeavoured to overthrow the Protestant religion. As to his lordship's threats, they were nothing dismayed by

[1] Rushworth's Collections, vol. v. p. 309.
[2] The king had also his commissioners of sequestration, and in "Instructions" to Prince Rupert, dated February 5th, 1643-4, he directs that the estates and goods of persons in rebellion against him shall be seized into their hands, and the revenues used for the support of his forces.—Harl. MSS. cod. 2135.
[3] The Lady Brilliana Harley, in a letter to her son Edward, dated 30th June, 1643, writes: "All Lancashere is cleared, only Latham howes. My Lord of Darby has left that county, which they take ill."—"Letters of Lady Brilliana Harley" (Camden Soc.), p. 205.—C.
[4] Situate between Leeds and Bradford, and more commonly known as Adderton or Atherston Moor.—C.

them, but hoped that God, who had been their protector hitherto, would so direct their force that they should be able to return the violence intended into the bosoms of those who should become their persecutors. The earl never found a suitable opportunity to prosecute his intended operations against the county of Lancaster, but was obliged to content himself with sending a small force of two hundred horsemen to occupy Blackstone Edge, the chief pass over the Pennine range into Lancashire; as, however, the Manchestrians had taken the precaution of placing a garrison of twelve hundred soldiers in Rochdale, and had sent a further contingent of eight hundred men to guard the foot of the pass over the Edge, the small force despatched by the Earl of Newcastle was completely routed, while the holders of the pass were enabled to raid the Craven district with impunity. For some months afterwards hostilities ceased in this county, though the civil wars still raged in the north, the south, and the east, and the blood of Englishmen continued to flow without any prospect of termination. In the northern parts of Lancashire, near its junction with Westmorland and Cumberland, a battle was fought between the Parliamentary army under Colonel Rigby, and the Royalist troops under Colonel Huddlestone, one of the

BLACKSTONE EDGE.

commissioners of array, which terminated in a "great victory" (Oct. 1). The last remaining stronghold of the king in the northern part of this county was Thurland Castle, which was at that time defended by Sir John Girlington, and which had sustained a siege of eleven weeks without receiving any relief, though the king's forces in Westmorland lay within view of the castle. At length it was determined to make a desperate effort to relieve the garrison: and the Westmorland and Cumberland forces, united with that from Cartmel and Furness, assembled over the sands, to the number of sixteen hundred men; Mr. Roger Kirby and Mr. Alexander Rigby of the Burgh leading the Lancashire forces. To defeat this operation, Colonel Rigby marched in the middle of October, at the head of a strong detatchment of the besieging army in front of Thurland Castle, into Furness, on Saturday; and on Sunday morning, after committing his troops to God's protection in prayer, the colonel commanded his men to attack the enemy. In this engagement, if such it could be called, the word of the Cavaliers was, "In with Queen Mary," while that of the Roundheads was, "God with us." An instant panic seized the Royalists, who fled in all directions, and instead of a battle it became a rout.

"At our first appearance," says Colonel Rigby, in his official despatch to the speaker of the House of Commons,[1] "God so struck the hearts of these our enemies with terrour, that, before a blow given, their horse began to retreat, our foot gave a great shout, our horse pursued, their's fled ; their foot dispersed, and fled ; they all trusted more to their feet than their hands ; they threw away their arms and colours, deserted their magazine drawn with eight oxen, and were totally routed in one quarter of an hour's time ; our horse slew some few of them in the pursuit, and drove many of them into the sea. Wee took their Colonel Hudleston, of Millam, two captains, and an ensign, and about foure hundred prisoners, six foot colours, and one horse colour ; and their magazin, and some horses, and more arms than men ; and all this without the losse of any one man of ours ; wee had only one man hurt by the enemy, and only another hurt by himselfe with his own pistoll, but neither mortally ; upon the close of the business, all our men with a great shout, cryed out, ' Glory be to God ;' and wee all, except one troop of horse, and one foot company, which I left to quiet the countrey, returned forthwith towards our siege at Thurland."

After this engagement the colonel pressed the siege of Thurland with so much vigour that in two days the castle surrendered by capitulation.[2] Following up the usual system, the fortress was immediately demolished, and Colonel Huddlestone was sent prisoner to London, to be dealt with by the Parliament. This year (1643) that mischievous publication "The Book of Sports," the fruitful parent of so much disaster to the house of Stuart, was denounced in Parliament, and, in virtue of a vote of the House, was consigned to the flames by the common hangman.[3] The king, finding his authority entirely superseded, and that the people and the militia, in many places which his troops summoned to surrender, professed to act under the sanction of Parliament, declared that the two houses were not a free Parliament, and in effect denied their authority, as they had denied his. The convocation had already been abolished by an ordinance of Parliament, which declared that government by archbishops and bishops was evil, and that the same should be taken away ; and a solemn league and covenant was now entered into between the Scotch and the English, by which it was stipulated that the Protestant religion should be sustained in Scotland, according to the form already established in that country, while a reformation should be effected in England, agreeable to the word of God and the example of the best reformed churches.[4] To secure the fidelity of the army to the cause of Parliament in this Catholic county, it was ordered that such officers and commanders in Lancashire in the service of Parliament as should refuse to take the covenant, on its being tendered to them, should be discharged of their command and kept in custody, if the committees of the county should so determine.[5]

An assembly of divines for the English counties, now divided into separate dioceses, was also constituted, and formed into Classis, or provincial synods, which were formally settled in this county in the year 1647 ;[6] and to the end that the maintenance provided or disposed of by Parliament for preaching ministers might only be given to godly and learned and orthodox divines, it was ordained by Parliament that no minister within the county should hereafter receive a benefice without a certificate of his fitness for the ministerial office under the hands of two or more deputy-lieutenants in the said county; and under the hands of Mr. Herle of Winwick, Mr. Heyricke of Manchester, Mr. Hyett of Croston, Mr. Horrocks of Dean, Mr. Ambrose of Preston, Mr. Shaw of Aldingham, Mr. Angier of Denton, Mr. Johnson of Ashton Mersey Bank, Mr. Ward of Warrington, Mr. Shawe of Liverpool, Mr. Gee of Eccleston, Mr. Latham of Douglas [Standish], Mr. Harper of Bolton, Mr. Hollinworth of Salford, Mr. Wright of Gargreave, and Mr. Johnson of Rochdale, or any seven or more of them.

Parliament, fully aware of the danger by which the county of Lancaster was menaced, issued an order that Mr. James Wainwright, under the superintendence of the committee of safety, should send forty barrels of powder into this county, for its better security and defence;[7] and in the course of the same month a letter was despatched by the speaker of the House of Commons to the gentlemen in Lancashire, in acknowledgment of their great and good services. It was the policy of Parliament to dismantle and demolish all the fortresses in the country, and on the 8th of July (1643) an order was sent from the Commons to the Lords, directing "that the castle of Hornby be forthwith so defaced, or demolished, that the enemy may be prevented from making any further use thereof to the annoyance of the inhabitants," and the deputy-lieutenants were required to give an account of their service in the execution thereof.

The strength of the conflicting armies was now swelled to a large amount. Sir Thomas Fairfax was made general of the north by Parliament, with a force of 21,000 men, including 6,000 horse and 1,000 dragooneers ; while Prince Rupert and Prince Maurice, the king's nephews, commanded an army of equal strength, on behalf of the king, with the Earl of Derby in Lancashire, and Sir Marmaduke Langdale and Lord Byron,[8] Baron of Rochdale, in Cheshire, Shropshire,

[1] Dated Preston, in Lancashire, Oct. 17, 1643.
[2] This victory, says Whitelock, was the more discoursed of because Rigby was a lawyer.
[3] The spirit in which some of the clergy had complied with the royal injunction to read the "Book of Sports," may be conceived from the remark of one of them, who, after having read the declaration, said, "Dearly beloved, you have heard now the commandments of God and man, obey which you please."

[4] Journals of the Lords, Sept. 18, 1643.   [5] Ibid.
[6] The Manchester Classis held its meetings in the Refectory of the College. The first meeting was held February 16th, 1646-7, and minutes were taken of its proceedings, which extend to August 14th, 1660.—C.
[7] Journals of the Commons, June 1, 1643.
[8] Sir John Byron, for his services at Edge Hill, Roundway Down, and elsewhere in the Royalist cause, was created Baron Byron of Rochdale, in the county palatine of Lancaster, Oct. 24, 1643.—C.

and Wales. The preparations on both sides were such as might be expected at the commencement of a campaign which was intended to terminate the contest. Towards the close of the last year (Dec. 26) the king's forces, under Lord Byron, had obtained an important victory at Nantwich, and obliged their enemies to seek refuge in Lancashire, where, according to the plan of the campaign, the Earl of Newcastle was to have attacked them, but the unexpected advance of Sir Thomas Fairfax into Staffordshire disconcerted the plan of operations by drawing the earl's attention to that quarter. The Lancashire forces, to the number of 2,000 foot, and a large body of cudgellers, finding themselves secure from the earl, effected a junction with Fairfax and Sir William Brereton near Nantwich, in front of which the Royalists, under Lord Byron, were posted, and after a gallant action his lordship was defeated with great loss (Jan. 25, 1644), and obliged to seek shelter for his discomfited forces in Chester.[1] After the battle of Nantwich the united forces, under Sir Thomas Fairfax, accompanied by the regiments of Colonel Rigby, Colonel Egerton, Colonel Ashton, and Colonel Holcroft marched to Lathom House, the seat of the Earl of Derby, where they arrived on the 28th of February. The withdrawal of Lord Derby to the Isle of Man had had a depressing influence on the Royalist cause in Lancashire.   Victory after victory was gained by the Parliamentarians, and fortress after fortress was demolished by their orders. Manchester had scorned the summons of Prince Rupert ; Warrington had yielded ; Wigan—"faithful Wigan"—could no longer hold its own ; Thurland Castle, the last remaining stronghold in North Lancashire, had capitulated ; and Lathom House, the princely seat of the Earl of Derby, alone held out. The winter of 1643-4 was employed in strengthening the defences of the several towns in the county, all of which were then in the hands of the king's enemies, and vast preparations were made for the renewal of the conflict. On Saturday, the 24th of February, 1643-4, a council of Parliamentary officers—the Holy State, as it was called—was held at Manchester, when it was finally resolved that an attack on Lathom should be made. Sir Thomas Fairfax undertook the command, with the assistance of Colonel Assheton of Middleton, Colonel More of Bank Hall, and the irrepressible Colonel Rigby, who, in the interest of the Parliament, was head, and heart, and hand, and almost everything else of importance in the county. This mansion, which the dangers of the times had converted into a fortress, was, in the absence of the earl, defended by Charlotte Tremouille, the Countess of Derby, assisted by Major Farmer and the Captains Farington, Charnock, Chisenhall, Rawstorne, Ogle, and Molyneux.   On the arrival of his army before Lathom House, Sir Thomas Fairfax obtained an audience with the countess, who had disposed her soldiers in such a way as to impress the Parliamentary general with a favourable opinion of their numbers and discipline. The offer made to the countess in this interview by Sir Thomas was that, on condition of her surrendering the house to the troops under

TOWER—HORNBY CASTLE.

his command, herself and her children and servants, with their property, should be safely removed to Knowsley, there to remain, without molestation, in the enjoyment of one-half of the earl's estates.   To this alluring proposal her ladyship mildly but resolutely replied that a double trust had been confided to her—faith to her lord and allegiance to her sovereign ; and that without their permission she could not make the required surrender in less than a month, nor then without their approbation.   The impetuous temper of the Parliamentary army could not brook this delay, and after a short consultation it was determined to besiege the fortress rather than attempt to carry it by storm.   At the end of fourteen days, while the works were constructing, Sir Thomas Fairfax sent a renewed summons to surrender, but with no better success, the reply of the countess being that she had not forgot her duty to the Church of England, to her prince, and to her lord, and that she would defend her trust with her honour and with her life.   Being ordered into Yorkshire, Sir Thomas confided the siege to Colonel Peter Egerton and Major Morgan, who, despairing of success from negotiation, proceeded to form the lines of circumvallation with all the formality of a German siege.   The progress of the besiegers was continually interrupted by sallies from the garrison, which beat the soldiers from their trenches, and destroyed their works.   At the end of three months a deep trench was cut near the moat, on which was raised a strong battery, where

---

[1] Lord Byron's letter to the Marquis of Ormonde, dated Chester, Jan. 30, 1643-4.

a mortar was planted for the casting of grenades. In one of these discharges the ball fell close to the table at which the countess and her children were sitting, and broke part of the furniture to atoms. A gallant and successful sally, under Major Farmer, and Captains Molyneux, Radcliffe, and Chisenhall, destroyed these works, killed a number of the besieging army, and captured the mortar. The countess not only superintended the works and commanded the operations, but frequently accompanied her gallant troops to the margin of the enemy's trenches. The Parliament, dissatisfied with all this delay, superseded Colonel Egerton, and confided the command to Colonel Rigby. Fresh works were now erected, but they shared the fate of their predecessors; and Colonel Rigby, on the approach of Prince Rupert into Lancashire, was obliged to raise the siege at the end of four months, and to seek shelter for himself and his army in Bolton. Prince Rupert, after the battle of Newark, marched towards Lancashire, at the head of a powerful army, with the intention of raising the siege of Lathom House—in which he succeeded—and to recover the "lost county" of Lancaster, in which he failed most deplorably. On his arrival at Stockport (*Stopworth*, as it was then called), seated on the banks of the river Mersey, where the Parliament had a strong garrison, commanded by Colonels Dukinfield and Mainwaring, he found the hedges lined with musketeers, who disputed his passage. To secure the entrance of his troops, his highness despatched Colonel Washington, at the head of a party of dragoons, to scour the hedges, which service the colonel performed with so

AUTOGRAPH OF CHARLOTTE DE LA TRÉMOILLE, COUNTESS OF DERBY.

much success that the musketeers were driven from their station, and the prince, with his horse, followed at their heels, pell-mell, into the town, which he took, with all the cannon and ammunition and some hundreds of prisoners (May 25). Prince Rupert, without suffering his progress to be arrested by the garrison at Manchester, advanced to Bolton. On his arrival before that place, on the 28th of May, he was joined by the Earl of Derby, who had returned from the Isle of Man, and was at the head of a considerable force, breathing vengeance against the assailants of his house, when the resolution was taken, in a council of war, to carry the town by storm. The assault was immediately commenced, but the resistance from the garrison was so vigorous that the assailants were repulsed with the loss of two hundred men. Irritated, but not dispirited, by this failure, another attack was resolved upon, which was led by the Earl of Derby, at the head of two hundred chosen Lancashire men, chiefly of his lordship's tenantry. The fury of this assault was irresistible, and the town fell into the hands of Prince Rupert. Colonel Rigby, who, on hearing of Rupert's advance, had abandoned the siege of Lathom and fallen back upon Bolton, with a number of his troops, escaped from the town, and, crossing the Yorkshire hills, marched to Bradford. Unfortunately for his own character, and for the life of his noble companion in arms, Prince Rupert refused to give quarter to the vanquished, and twelve hundred persons were put to the sword after the battle was won. So great was the slaughter that, it has been said, there was scarcely a Puritan family for miles round Bolton, that had not to mourn the loss of some member who had fallen in the fight. It was a fatal day for Bolton, and, in the end, no less fatal to the head of the House of Stanley, for the cruelties then practised were repaid with vengeance in a few years later in the Market Place of the town. The siege of Lathom began on the 6th March, and hostilities were carried on with varying fortunes until the 27th of May, on the morning of which, while the dawn was deepening into day, Rigby in hot haste withdrew his forces from before the walls. In the evening, the sun, as it went down in the west, shed its warm rays upon the plumed helmets and glistening corslets of a triumphant army crossing the drawbridge, with drums beating and colours flying, to tell the story of victory, and to proclaim relief to the heroic countess and the gallant defenders of the "seven towered Lathom." The trophies of this day, consisting of the colours taken at Bolton, were sent by the Earl of Derby to Lathom House, and were received by the countess with great exultation.

The prince, without delay, advanced to Liverpool, where there was a strong garrison under the command of Colonel Moore,[1] the governor of the town, and Member of Parliament for that borough. His highness, whose sanguine disposition frequently hurried him on to hasty conclusions, did not hesitate to pronounce that the place was too feeble to resist the prowess of his arms for a single day; but, though the siege was prosecuted with great vigour, the fortress did not surrender in less than three weeks from the time that the Royalist army brought their cannon to bear upon the works. Before the garrison surrendered, they shipped off all the arms, ammunition, and portable

SIR ALEXANDER RIGBY.

effects; and most of the officers and soldiers went on shipboard, while a few made good the fort, which they rendered to the prince upon quarter, but they were all put to the sword.[2] Having thus secured two of the most important places in Lancashire, Manchester excepted, Prince Rupert paid a hasty visit to his noble relative, the heroine of Lathom House, where he gave instructions for strengthening the fortress by adding to the towers, bastions, and counterscarps. He then continued his march, by way of Blackburn, to York, at the head of 20,000 men, where he joined the Marquis of Newcastle. The day after his arrival before that city, the great and decisive battle of Marston Moor was fought (July 2). This engagement was obstinately disputed between the most numerous armies that were engaged during the whole course of these wars. Eighty thousand British troops were here led to mutual slaughter. Prince Rupert, who commanded the right wing of the Royalists, was opposed to Oliver Cromwell, who commanded the left of the Parliamentary army. The Marquis of Newcastle commanded on the left, and was opposed to Sir Thomas Fairfax and Colonel Lambert. For some time the scale of victory hung in suspense, and both parties in

---

[1] The Moores, or Mores, had been wealthy burgesses of Liverpool from early times. One of the family, John de le More, appears first on the list of burgesses who, in 1295, guaranteed the payment of the wages of the member returned as the representative of Liverpool in Parliament.

They had prospered as merchants, were accounted the leaders of the Presbyterian party in the town, and had become powerful rivals and bitter enemies of the Stanleys.—C.

[2] Whitelock's Memorials, p. 91.

turn thought that the day was their own; but, after the utmost efforts of courage and skill, the rout of the royal army became general, Prince Rupert's train of artillery was taken, and his whole army pushed off the field of battle.[1] The Earl of Derby had accompanied Prince Rupert, and was in the thick of the fight at Marston Moor. Three times, we are told, he rallied his men, but at Marston, as at Edge Hill, the rash impetuosity of the prince turned victory into disaster, and the king's cause was lost.

The civil wars were not now at an end, but their issue was no longer doubtful. The Marquis of Newcastle, whose counsel had been disregarded, quitted the kingdom with mixed feelings of disgust and despair, and Prince Rupert drew off the wreck of his army into Lancashire, where he had the mortification to see the strongholds which he had recently obtained speedily reconquered.

After the battle of Marston Moor it was determined by Lord Fairfax to send 1,000 horse into Lancashire, to form a junction with the Parliamentary forces from Cheshire and Derbyshire, for the purpose of watching the motions of Prince Rupert, who marched to join the king's forces in Cumberland and Westmoreland. Parliament had, in the meantime, passed an ordinance for a grant of £3,000 to the forces of Lancashire;[2] and a plan was devised for the committees of Parliament, in Derbyshire and Lancashire, to join the association of the northern counties. One of the objects of this association was to supply the forces of Lancashire with money to carry on the war.[3] To mitigate the miseries of the sufferers in Lancashire, an ordinance was passed, that all officers

GREENHALGH CASTLE.

and soldiers under the command of Colonel Alexander Rigby and Colonel Richard Shuttleworth, at Bolton or in other places, by the loss of limbs, &c., and such women and children whose husbands or fathers had been slain, or died in the service, should be pensioned "out of the several sequestrations of papists and delinquents, within the respective hundreds of Blackburn, Leyland, and Amounderness, or out of assessments provided for that purpose; but that no person should receive, by way of maintenance, more than four shillings and eightpence per week."[4] The return of Prince Rupert into Lancashire was the signal for a renewal of hostilities, deserving the name of little more than skirmishes, though some of them are dignified in the despatches of the day as "great victories." Fights took place near Ormskirk, Up-Holland, and Preston, in the last of which Lord Ogleby and Colonel Ennis were made prisoners.[5] The Lancashire campaign of this year was terminated by the surrender of Liverpool to the Parliamentary forces under Sir John Meldrum (November 1), the Earl of Derby having failed in an attempt to relieve that place, with a loss of 500 men killed and taken prisoners.[6] Lord Byron, too, was little less unfortunate; for, in a letter to the Marquis of Ormonde, dated November 15, 1644, he says, "My brother Robin is now a prisoner at Manchester, with some of his officers, the rest being disposed of to other garrisons of

the rebels, and I am so unfortunate at this time as to have no exchange for him here.[7] Liverpool is lost through the treachery of the common soldiers, who, not pressed with any other want but of loyalty and courage, most basely gave up the town and the officers to the mercy of the rebels."[8] The county remained for a time in a state of comparative tranquillity, though occasionally harassed in the Fylde district by Sir Thomas Tyldesley. With the object of dislodging this resolute and uncompromising partisan, Sir John Meldrum set out with a force from Manchester, and a fierce encounter took place at Freckleton Marsh, on the estuary of the Ribble, near Kirkham. Tyldesley rallied and reformed his men, but his efforts being unavailing, he crossed the Ribble and marched on towards Meols.[9] Victory followed victory. One position after another was forced and one detachment after another dispersed, until, as Rushworth wrote, "there remained of unreduced garrisons belonging to the king in Lancashire only Latham House and Green (halgh) Castle," the latter an embattled and moated structure which had been built on the banks of the Wyre in 1490 by the First Earl of Derby.

In the midst of all this "unsuccessful and successful war," the condition of the inhabitants of Lancashire, owing to the spoil, rapine, and cruelty, which never fail to attend civil wars,

[1] Rushworth, vi. 634.
[2] Commons Journals, June 25, 1644.
[3] Ibid, July 1.
[4] Ibid, Aug. 5.
[5] Col. Shuttleworth's Despatch, dated Whalley, Aug. 1644.
[6] Whitelock's Memorials, p. 103.
[7] Carte's Original Letters and Papers, i. 70.
[8] Ibid, p. 71.
[9] Chetham Soc. v. lxii. p. 56.—C.

was most deplorable. In some parts of the county the people had scarcely anything left to cover their nakedness. They and their children were without bread to eat; and their misery was so extreme, that an order was issued by Parliament that, upon the 12th day of September, being the day appointed for a solemn fast throughout the country, one half of the public collections to be made in all the churches within the cities of London and Westminster, and within the line of communication, should be employed for the relief of the poor distressed people in the county of Lancaster, the money to be paid into the hands of the Rev. Mr. Herle and the Rev. Mr. Case, members of the Westminster Assembly of Divines, to be by them forwarded to Mr. John Hartley, of Manchester, and disbursed through the medium of Mr. Heyricke, warden of Manchester; Mr. Harper, minister of Bolton; Mr. Wood, minister of Warrington; Mr. Lathom, minister of Douglas; Mr. Ambrose, minister of Preston; Mr. Shaw, minister of Aldingham; and Mr. Hipworth, minister of Whalley; or any four of them.[1] The people, growing impatient from the protracted miseries of war, began to demand its speedy termination; and surmises were entertained that the contest was prolonged for the profit it afforded in places and pensions bestowed upon the members of the House of Commons. To remove all suspicion on this head, an Act called "The Self-denying Ordinance" was introduced and passed, by which all members of either House of Parliament were prohibited from holding any command in the army.

The extensive revenues and patronage of the duchy of Lancaster having become objects of contest between the conflicting parties, the duchy seal, by which the proceedings in court obtained their ratification, was forcibly taken from Christopher Banister, the vice-chancellor of the county, by the troops raised against the Parliament, without which seal neither sheriff nor justice of the peace could be constituted, nor could common justice be administered to the inhabitants. To repair this loss, the two Houses of Parliament ordained that a new duchy seal should be made; that it should have like power and validity as that formerly used, and that all acts done by the former seal, since it was taken from the vice-chancellor, "should be utterly void, frustrate, and of no effect."[2] One of the first documents to which the new duchy seal was attached was the patent of John Bradshaw, Esq., as high sheriff of the county of Lancaster.[3] This year the Parliament assumed the patronage of the ecclesiastical benefices of the duchy, and exercised that patronage by conferring the living of the hospital of Leicester upon Mr. Grey, the brother of the Earl of Kent.

All the strong places in Lancashire were now in possession of the Parliamentary forces, with the exception of Lathom House, and grants of money and munitions of war continued to be dispensed by Parliament for the maintenance of these possessions.[4] The garrison at Lathom having made itself especially obnoxious by the "daily roberyes and plundering" of neighbouring Round-heads, its submission was resolved upon. At the outset negotiations were entered into with the Earl of Derby, who was then in the Isle of Man, with the view of securing the withdrawal of the force stationed there without recourse to arms, but this coming to nothing, it was determined to make another attempt to sieze the stronghold which had so long been a refuge and safe protection for the cavaliers of Lancashire. For this purpose a besieging force was placed under the command of Colonel Egerton, of Shaw; Alexander Rigby, however, being again the moving spirit who directed the operations. The battle of Naseby, fought June 14, 1645, where the king commanded on one side, aided by his nephews, Prince Rupert and Prince Maurice, and Fairfax on the other, aided by Cromwell, proved most disastrous to the royal cause, and disabled the Cavaliers from prosecuting the campaign in the northern counties. After that disastrous day the king marched to Chester, with the intention of carrying the war into Lancashire, and of relieving Lathom House, which was at that time again besieged by the Parliamentary forces. His majesty's ill-fortune still pursued him, and he was doomed to sustain another defeat on Rowton Heath, in the neighbourhood of Chester. The renewed siege of Lathom was commenced in the month of July, 1645, under the command of General Egerton, at the head of 4,000 men. The Countess of Derby and her family having retired to the Isle of Man, the command of the garrison was confided to Colonel Rawstorne, aided by Major Munday and Captain Key, commanders of horse, and Captain Charnock, Captain Farington, Captain Molyneux Radcliffe, Captain Henry Noel, Captain Worral, and Captain Roby. For five months the siege was sustained with great spirit, in the hope that the king's troops would be able to relieve the garrison; but this expectation having been utterly disappointed, Colonel Rawstorne and his brave companions in arms, who had become reduced to the last extremity, were obliged to surrender this ancient and venerable edifice into the hands of the enemy on the 2nd

[1] Journals of the Commons, Sept. 11, 1644.
[2] Ibid, Nov. 25.
[3] Godwin, in his "History of the Commonwealth," says the sheriff was "president" Bradshaw, but this is an error which has gained currency by frequent repetition. The person on whom the shrievalty was conferred when Parliament in 1644, exercising the Royal functions, assumed the powers of the Duke of Lancaster, and in contravention of the Act of 28 Edward III., retained it for four successive years, was John Bradshaw, the head of the line of Bradshaw in the parish of Bolton, and therefore only remotely connected with president Bradshaw.—C.
[4] Journals of the Commons, April 5 and July 9, 1645.

of December. The fall of Lathom House was the occasion of rejoicing in every Puritan town in Lancashire; The horns of the "great beast were all broken," and Parliament considered the event of sufficient importance to call for a thanksgiving in the cities of London and Westminster. This service being over, the House of Commons proceeded to consider what was to be done with the fortress, when it was determined that it should be demolished; and in virtue of this resolution the towers and all the strong works were razed to the ground, and the house of Lathom, once the pride and glory of Lancashire, was dismantled and ruined. The earl, on receiving intelligence of the ruthless destruction wrought by the fanatical soldiers of Rigby, expressed himself in sorrow more than in anger, and nothing can be more touching than his reflections upon the loss, or more apposite than the texts of Scripture he, at the time, entered in his book of "Private Devotions": "Our holy and our beautiful house," he wrote, "where our fathers praised Thee, is burned with fire; and all our pleasant things are laid waste" (Isaiah lxiv., 11); "I have forsaken mine house; I have left mine heritage; I have given the dearly-beloved of my soul to the hand of her enemies. Mine heritage is unto me as a lion in the forest, it crieth out against me'" (Jeremiah xii., 7-8).

From the first breaking out of the troubles Chester had been secured by the commission of array for the service of the king, but the besieging army under Sir William Brereton having been reinforced by the Parliamentary troops from Lathom House, this ancient city was obliged to surrender by articles of capitulation, between Lord Byron, the governor, and Sir William Brereton, on the 3rd of February, 1645-6. The royal cause had now become hopeless, and the Scottish army having marched into the centre of England, as the allies of the Parliamentary force, the king surrendered himself into their hands at Newark on the 5th of May. The pressure of so large an army as that maintained by Parliament fell heavily upon the public treasury; and, in order to replenish the finances, the two houses issued an ordinance for raising £60,000 per month for the support of the forces, to which the county of Lancaster was required to contribute £529 3s. 2d., and the county of Chester £39 13s. 11d. Immense sums of money were exacted from such persons of property as had favoured the royal cause, and it was alleged that this was the only effectual means of reaching the feelings of the "heart-malignants," by which name the partisans of the king were distinguished by their enemies. Three years before this time Parliament had issued ordinances, as we have already seen, for sequestrating "the estates of delinquents, papists, spies, and intelligencers" throughout the kingdom, wherein it was directed that all bishops, deans, or other persons, who have raised or shall raise arms against the Parliament, or shall be in actual war against them; or shall have contributed any money, arms, &c., towards the force of the enemy, shall have their property sequestrated into the hands of sequestrators and committees in this order named.[1] The king, who could afford to his friends no protection against these exactions, consented that they should pay such compositions as might be agreed upon between them and the Parliament; but when the Parliament demanded a bill of attainder and banishment against seven persons—the Marquis of Newcastle, Lord Digby, Lord Byron, Sir Marmaduke Langdale, Sir Richard Granville, Sir Francis Doddington, and Judge Jenkins—he absolutely refused compliance. A power was in this way given to the committee of sequestration to allow "the delinquents, papists, and others" to compound for their estates, on payment of a specific sum into the public treasury; and the following is

A CATALOGUE

Of the Lords, Knights, and Gentlemen of Lancashire who compounded for their Estates in the years 1646, &c., with the sum affixed at which each Freeholder contracted:—

	£	s.	d.		£	s.	d.
Ambrose Wm., of Lowick, gent.	129	0	0	Brownelow Randal, of Pemberton, husbandman	15	0	0
Ashton Thomas, of Penketh	192	8	4	Baxter Charles, of Newton	21	0	0
Ashton Thos., of Heatbank, yeoman	16	4	0	Brabarn Thomas, of Whittington	122	17	0
Adkins Nathaniel, of Broughton	31	0	0	Butterworth Alex., of Belfield	3	6	8
Brown Ralph, of Aspeh [? Astley or Aspull]	11	0	0	Byrom John, of Salford, gent.	201	16	6
Bate John, of Warbreck	11	0	0	Byrom Edward, of Salford, gent.	2	6	8
Barker James, of Blackrod	10	0	0	Bowker Adam, of Salford	16	13	0
Bridgeman Edward, of Warrington	100	0	0	Bowker Peter, of Manchester	12	0	0
Bowden Edward, of Kirbie	40	0	0	Beckingham Rowland, of Hornby	16	0	0
Baylcon Wm., of Barmaker	70	0	0	Carus Thos. of Halton, gent.	516	10	0
Breres Launcelot, of Whittle	10	0	0	Chisenhall Ed., of Chisenhall, Esq.	480	0	0
Bretherton John, of Leigh, gent.	150	0	0	Charnoke Robert, of Astley, Esq.	260	0	0
Breres Alex., of Martin, gent.	82	4	5	Cowling Thurstan, of Chorley	10	13	0
Brown Wm., of Wigan	20	12	0	Collier James, of Rainford	36	8	0
Brown Edward, of Woodplumpton	127	8	0	Cooling James, of Chorley, mower	9	0	0
Bower Wm., of Latham, yeoman	25	0	0	Croston Richard, of Heath-Charnock	12	0	0
Brockelesse John, of Lancaster, gent.	151	0	0	Charnock Thomas, of Leyland, gent.	58	0	0

[1] The mere fact of professing the Roman Catholic religion subjected "the delinquent" to forfeit two parts out of three of his whole estate, and two parts of his goods. The sittings of the committee of sequestration for Lancashire were usually held at Preston.

	£	s.	d.
Cotterell [? Catterall] John, of Brindle	20	9	6
Dawson [? Danson] Thomas, of Rosthwaite, gent.	45	0	0
Dewhurst Wm., of Dewhurst, gent.	186	10	0
Forth William, of Wigan	40	0	0
Fearnley Ann, of Warrington	21	0	0
Fleetwood Joseph, of Penwortham, Esq.	641	3	4
Fincham Ralph, of Cottam, gent.	125	0	0
Farington Wm., sen., of Werden, Esq.	536	0	0
Foxcroft Henry, of Claughton	2	0	0
Foster Robert, of Coppull, tanner	8	15	0
Farington William, the younger, of Werden, gent.	117	13	4
Garside Gabriel, of Rochdale	28	0	0
Gerrard Thomas, of Ince, gent.	209	0	0
Gerrard, Thos., of Aughton, gent.	80	0	0
Gerrard Richard, of Bryn, Esq.	100	0	0
Gerrard William, of Pennington	2	10	6
Gregson John Wood, of Plumpton	51	7	0
Holt Robert, of Castleton, Esq.	150	0	0
Holt Richard, of Ashworth, gent.	551	0	0
Hough Robert, of Moston	25	0	0
Hey Ellis, of Eccles, gent.	309	0	0
Hancock John, of Clithero, yeoman	5	5	0
Hesketh Robert, of Rufforth, gent.	45	18	9
Heap Thos., of Pilkington, gent.	101	0	0
Haughton Richard, of Ridley, gent.	60	0	0
Haughton Thomas, of Haughton	2	10	0
Hind Rd., of Overton, yeoman	34	0	0
Hodginson Luke, of Preston	15	0	0
Halsworth Thos., of Heath-Charnock	18	0	0
Haydock Roger, of Heapy	3	15	0
Heywood Peter, of Heywood	351	0	0
Higham Thos., of Lancaster, deceased	70	10	0
Jackson John, of Overton, gent.	6	0	0
Kirby John, of Kirby, gent.	36	5	4
Kitson Thomas, of Warton, gent.	390	0	0
Livesey Rd., of Broadhalgh, gent.	10	0	0
Leckonby Richard, of Elswick	58	6	0
Moseley Nichols, of Ancotes, gent.	170	0	0
Moseley Sir Edw., of Ancotes	4874	0	0
Mosley Francis, and Nicholas, his son, of Collyhurst, gent.	200	0	0
Morley Francis, of Wennington, gent.	160	0	0
Morte George, of Blackrod, Esq.	46	10	0
Middleton Sir George, of Layton, Knt. and Bart., with £60 per annum settled	855	0	0
Mollineux Robt., of The Wood, gent.	240	0	0
Norris John, of Bolton	50	0	0
Norris Alexander, of the same	15	0	0
Nuttall Joshua, of Church	20	0	0
Nowell Roger, of Read, Esq.	736	4	6
Nicholson Francis, jun., of Poulton, yeoman	133	3	4
Norris Robt., of Kirby, yeoman.	107	11	8
Norris Thomas, of Speak, Esq.	508	0	0
Ogle Cuthbert, of Whiston, gent.	120	0	0
Orrell Rd., of Farrington, gent.	22	10	0
Pendleton Henry, of Manchester	80	0	0
Prescott William, of Upholland	27	0	0
Prestwich Sir Thomas, and Thomas, his son, of Hulme	330	0	0
Preston George, of Natby	30	0	0
Preston Thomas, of Holker, Esq., with £120 per annum settled	186	17	0
Potter Alexander, of Manchester	4	5	0
Pilkington John, of Adlington	7	10	0
Pilkington Richard, of Coppull	11	5	5
Prescot Robert, of Standish	8	0	0
Pilkington Richard, of Wigan	29	5	0
Rascoe John, of Aspeth [? Aspull]	10	0	0
Ryly Thomas, of Chatburn	50	0	0
Robinson Edmund, of Newland	40	0	0
Rigby Alex., of Burgh, Esq.	381	3	4
Rawlingson Robt., of March-Grange	8046	0	0
Rivington James, of Euxton	14	12	6
Radcliffe William, of Balderston	15	0	0
Raphson Edmund, of Ince-Blundell	11	1	0
Rogerson William, of Coppull	10	5	0
Raincars Nicholas, of Hindley	21	11	10
Rogerson John, of Manchester	4	18	4
Seddon John, of Hentley [? Hindley]	10	0	0
Slaughter Henry, of Lightcocks	130	0	0
Shartock [? Sharrock] Ralph, of Wolson [? Walton].	50	0	0
Stanley Ferdinando, of Broughton	150	0	0
Sherrington Francis, of Boothes, Esq.	373	10	0
Summer John, and Wm., his son, of Leyland	805	0	0
Shaw Henry, of Langrope [? Langroyd]	23	0	0
Sandis Wm., of Easthwaite, gent.	50	0	0
Stanley Wm., of Woodhall, gent.	46	13	0
Southworth John, of Samlesbury	358	18	9
Talbot Sir John, of Salop, Knt.	444	0	0
Trevillian Robt., of Didsbury, yeoman	50	0	0
Twiford Rich., of Didsbury, yeoman	44	0	0
Tempest William, of Wigan	7	14	0
Taylor John, of Oldham	10	0	0
Townson Robert, of Causfield	2	5	0
Twiford Robt., of Didsbury, gent.	45	15	4
Valentine John, of Beaucliffe, in the parish of Eccles, gent.	255	4	9
Woodward Alex., of Shevington	44	0	0
Walker William, of Kirkham, gent.	175	0	0
Wall Thomas, of Prescot	20	0	0
Wakefield John, of Standish, mower	20	0	0
Walmesley Edward, of Banister Hall	114	0	0
Welshman Hugh, of Samlesbury	3	10	0
Widdowes John, of Lawton, gent.	34	14	0
Westfield Richard, of Overton	34	0	0
Wood John, of Prestwich	0	10	0
Wood Francis, of Gressingham	51	15	0
Whittingham Richard, of Clayton	118	10	0
Wildbore Augustus, of Lancaster, D.D.	132	2	6
Winckley Wm., of Billington, gent.	26	0	0
Windresse Wm., of Nether-Wiersdale	30	19	9
Wignall John, of Halsall	12	3	0

The foregoing "Catalogue," which is very incomplete, and certainly not remarkable for accuracy, appears to have been copied by Mr. Baines from a small and scarce volume printed in 1655,[1] "for Thomas Dring, at the signe of the George, in Fleet Street, neare Clifford's Inne, London." An accurate list of the Lancashire compounders, with the particulars of their estates and the results of their "delinquencies" consequently remains a work of the future, but the want has been in part supplied by the Record Society in the exceedingly useful volumes edited by Mr. Walford D. Selby, of the Record Office, in which is given a list derived from a contemporary index of the compounders' names digested into counties, and containing nearly all the names of the Lancashire delinquents, with those of Cheshire also. As this index supplies many omissions in the list given in previous editions of this work, we give it entire :—

Ambrose William, Lowicke
Anderton Hugh, Euxton
Anderton James, Birchley
Anderton William, Anderton

Ashton Edmund, Chatterton
Ashton Thomas, Penketh
Ashton Thomas, Heatbanck
Atkins Nathaniel, Broughton

Baines Jonathan, Nether-Wiersdale
Barker James, Blackroad
Barnes Thomas, West Darby
Bate John, Warrington

[1] A reprint of this volume was issued to subscribers resident chiefly in Lancashire and Cheshire in 1733, with the following title page: "A Catalogue of the Lords, Knights, and Gentlemen, that have Compounded for their Estates. To which are added, some Gentlemen's names, which were omitted in the former Edition. London: Printed by Thomas Dring, 1655; and Chester: Re-printed by R. Adams, 1733. (Price Bound Two Shillings.)"—C.

The estates of Thomas Eccleston, of Eccleston, Esq., deceased, were also sequestrated, but an allowance was made to his widow and children of the fifth part of those estates for their maintenance.[1]   The extensive estates of the Earl of Derby shared the same fate; but on a petition of Charles, Lord Strange, Edward and William, the earl's sons, and the ladies Henrietta-Maria, Catherine, and Amelia, his daughters, a fifth part of the earl's estates was allowed for their maintenance, and the manor of Knowsley, with the house and lands belonging to it, formed part of that allowance, with a strict injunction that no timber should be felled upon the lands, but that the same should be preserved according to the order of sequestration.[2]

The national religion, so far as regarded its government, was now changed; Presbyterianism had superseded episcopacy, and the Presbyterian Parliament of England became more violent for conformity than the Court of High Commission which the Parliament had destroyed.   The arbitrary imposition of the covenant upon every minister of the Anglican Church was the first result, and numbers of incumbents were ejected from their livings for their refusal to sign this obligation.[3]   The Independents, however, were the ascendant party in Parliament; and though their principles reject all ecclesiastical establishments and all human interference in matters of religion, they so far sacrificed their own views as to submit to a temporary trial of "Presbyterial church government."   Parliament had chosen an assembly of divines to obtain their advice in settling the government, liturgy, and doctrine of the church; and this synod, usually called The Assembly of Divines, met at Westminster, in Henry VII.'s Chapel, for the first time on the 1st of July, 1643, to secure the government and liturgy of the Church of England; some of the counties having two, and others only one member.   Lancashire had two—namely, Richard Heyricke, M.A., warden of Manchester, and Charles Herle, M.A., rector of Winwick.   The assembly consisted of thirty laymen, viz., ten peers and twenty commoners, and one hundred and twenty-one divines and three scribes.   Their first duty was to draw up the confession of faith, and the larger and shorter catechism still in use amongst the evangelical dissenters.   As soon as the Assembly had prepared the "Directory for Public Worship," Parliament ordered the Book of Common Prayer to be set aside, and on the 23rd August, 1645, enjoined that all ministers should read the "Directory" to their people on the next Lord's Day after receiving it, and that henceforward persons using the Book of Common Prayer, in public or in private, should be fined for the first offence £5, for the second £10, and for the third a whole year's imprisonment.   In London and Lancashire the "Humble Advice of the Westminster Assembly of Divines" concerning church government was promptly adopted.   The plan recommended was to divide England and Wales into provinces, and annual conferences were appointed for the regulation of ecclesiastical affairs.   Preston,[4] from its central situation, was selected as the place for holding the first meeting of the Lancashire Classis,[5] which were formed according to the following:—

ORDINANCE OF PARLIAMENT.

LANCASHIRE CLASSICAL PRESBYTERIES.

Die Veneris, 2d October, 1646.

The County of Lancaster is divided into the nine classical Presbyteries following:—

I. CLASSIS.

Parishes of Manchester, Prestwich, Oldham, Flixton, Eccles, and Ashton-under-Lyne.

MINISTERS.	LAYMEN.	
Mr. Richd Heyricke } Manchester R^d Hollinworth }	Robert Hyde of Denton, Esqr	Thomas Smith of Manchester } Gentn. Peter Serjant of Pilkington } Robert Leech of Ashton }
John Angier of Denton	Richd Howorth of Manch^r, Esq.	John Wright of Bradford }
Wm Walker of Newton	Robt. Ashton of Shepley, Esq.	W^m. Peake of Worsley } Yeomen.
Toby Furnes of Prestwich	Thos. Strangeways of Gorton, Esq.	Thos. Taylor of Flixton }
Humphrey Barnet of Oldham	Wm. Booth of Reddish } Gentmn.	Thos. Barlowe of Eccles }
John Jones of Eccles	John Gaskell of Manch^r }	Peter Seddon of Pilkington }
John Harrison of Ashton-under-Lyne	Edw. Sandiforth of Oldham } John Birch of Openshaw }	James Jollie of Droylsden }

[1] Ordinance of Parliament, July 11, 1645.
[2] Order of the Committee, dated Manchester, Sept. 24, 1647.
[3] The number of Church clergy ejected has been variously estimated. Neal, the historian of the Puritans, puts it at one thousand six hundred, while Walker, in his "Sufferings of the Clergy," names eight thousand, though this latter is palpably an overstatement; the petition presented to General Sir Thomas Fairfax in 1647 opens thus—"The humble petition of many thousands of the poor Clergy of England and Wales, &c." The probability is that the number sequestered for refusing the covenant was from five thousand to six thousand, but be the number what it might, the tyranny of the proceeding was odious as coming from men who had themselves clamoured for liberty and struggled against religious persecution.—C.

[4] The meetings of the Provincial Assembly were held seventeen times in Preston, twice in Wigan, twice in Bolton, and once in Blackburn. The first meeting was held in Preston, in August, 1648, when Isaac Ambrose preached and Mr. James Hyett was appointed moderator.— Minutes of the Manchester Classis.—C.
[5] The "Minutes of the Manchester Classis" are in the possession of the Trustees of Cross Street Chapel, Manchester, but an accurate transcript is preserved in the Chetham Library.—C.

II. CLASSIS.

Parishes of Bolton, Middleton, Bury, Rachdale, Dean, and Radcliffe.

MINISTERS.	LAYMEN.			
Mr. John Harper of Bolton	Ralph Ashton of Middleton		James Stot of Healey	
Wm. Ashton of Middleton	John Bradshaw of Bradshaw		Robert Pares of Ratchdale	
Wm. Alte	Edm. Hopwood of Hopwood		Hy Molyneux of West Houghton	
Andrew Lathom	Robt. Leaver of Darcy Leaver	Esquires.	John Bradshaw of Darcy Leaver	Gent.
John Scholfield of Bury	Edw. Butterworth of Belfield		John Scolfield of Castleton	Yeomen.
Robert Bathe of Ratchdale	Ralph Worthington of Smithells		Gyles Green of West Houghton	
Alexander Horrocks	John Andrews of Little Leaver		Henry Seddon of Heaton	
John Tilsley	Robt. Heywood of Heywood	Gentlemen.	Roger Hardman of Radcliffe	
James Walton of Dean	Peter Holt of Heape		Rich. Dickonson of Aynsworth	
Thomas Pyke of Radcliffe	Arthur Smeathurst of Heape		Emanl Thompson of Ratchdale, Clothr	
	Thos. Eccersall of Bury		Samuel Wilde of Ratchdale, Mercer	

III. CLASSIS.

Parishes of Blackburn, Whalley, Chipping, and Ribble Chester.

MINISTERS.	LAYMEN.			
Mr. Adam Boulton of Blackburn	Sir Ralph Ashton, Bart.		Nicholas Cunliffe of Wycollar	
Rt. Worthington of Harwood	Rich. Shuttleworth, Sen.		Robt. Cunliffe of Sparthe	
Rich. Redman of Low Church	Rich. Shuttleworth, Jun.		John Cunliffe of Hollins	
Wm. Walker of Whalley	John Starkie		Nicholas Rishton of Anteley	
Henry Morrice of Burnley	John Parker	Gent. Esquires.	Roger Geliborn of Bedwood	Gentlemen.
John Bryers of Padiham	Rich. Ashton of Downham		Wm. Yates of Blackburn	
Wm. Ingham of Church	John Livesay of Livesay		John Howorth of Clayton	
John King of Chipping	Thos. Barcroft of Barcroft		Thos. Whalley of Rishton	
			Chas. Gregory of Haslinden	

IIII. CLASSIS.

Parishes of Warrington, Winwick, Leigh, Wigan, Holland, and Prescot.

MINISTERS.	LAYMEN.			
Mr. Chas. Herle of Winwick	Wm. Ashurst of Ashurst		Jeffrey Birchall of Orrel	
Thos. Norman of Newton	Peter Brook of Sankey	Esqs.	John Latham of Whiston	
James Woods of Ashton	Wm. Vernon of Shakerley		Wm. Barns of Sankey	
Wm. Leigh of Newchurch	John Dunbabin of Warrington		John Marsh of Bold	
Hen. Atherton of Hollinfaire	Thos. Risley of Warrington		Thurstan Peak of Warrington	Gentlemen.
Bradley Hayhurst of Leigh	Robt. Watmough of Winwick		Edw. Heaton of Billing	
Thos. Crompton of Astley	Gilbert Eden of Winwick		George Aynsworth of Newton	
James Bradshaw of Wigan	John Ashton of Newton		Arthur Leech of West Leigh	
Thos. Tonge of Hindley	Jas. Pilkington of Ashton	Gentlemen.	Peter Smith of West Leigh	
Henry Shaw of Holland	Rich. Astley of Tildesley		Thomas Guest of Astley	Yeomen.
Wm. Plant of Farnworth	Henry Morrice of Atherton		Geo. Dean of Rainhill	
Rich. Modesley of Ellins	Alex. Tompson of Wigan		John Rylands of Sutton	
Timothy Smith of Rainforth	Peter Harrison of Hindley		Roger Topping of Dalton	
John Wright of Billinge	Thos. Sephton of Skelmersdale		Peter Leyland of Haydock	

V. CLASSIS.

Parishes of Walton, Hyton, Childwell, Sephton, Altker, North-Meals, Halsall, Ormskirk, and Aughton.

MINISTERS.				
Mr. Wm. Ward of Walton	Mr. Wm. Dune of Ormskirk		Hugh Cooper of Ormskirk	
John Fog of Liverpool	James Worral of Aughton		Peter Blundell of Scarisbrick	
Robert Port of Toxteth			Jas. Cross of Aughton	Gentn.
Rich. Pickering of Kirkeby	**LAYMEN.**		Nicholas Cooper of Kirkdale	
Wm. Norcot of Darby	John Moor	Esqrs.	Edw. Chambers of Liverpool	
Wm. Bell of Hyton	Gilbert Ireland		Henry Woods of Kirkby	
David Ellison of Childwall	Jn. Wilkinson Sen. of Liverpool		Thos. Thomason of Darby	
Benry Bolton of Hale	Jerh. Aspinwall of Toxteth		Thos. Tyrer of Hyton.	
Josh. Tompson of Sephton	Peter Ambrose of Toxteth		Bryan Soothworth of Tarbocke	Yeomen.
John Kid of Crosby	Henry Mercer of Darby	Gentlemen.	John Williamson of Woolton	
Robert Seddon of Altker	Wm. Plomb of Woolton		Thos. Rothwell of Ince	
James Starkie of North Meals	James Moss of Crossend		Wm. Watkinson of Blowick	
Thos. Johnson of Halsal	Thos. Hesketh of Halsal		Wm. Wilson of Lidyate	
	Thos. Bootle of Melling			

VI. CLASSIS.

Parishes of Croston, Leyland, Standish, Eccleston, Penwortham, Hoole, and Brindle.

MINISTERS.	LAYMEN.			
Mr. James Hyett of Croston	Sir Richard Houghton, Bart.		Edward Doughty of Adlington	
Paul Lathom of Standish	Peter Cateral of Crook, Esqr.		John Pincock of Euxton	
Edward Gee of Eccleston	Thos. Wilson of Wrightington		Alex. Chisnal of Whittle	
Henry Welch of Chorley	John Cliffe of Brotherton	Gentn.	Geo. Dandy of Croston	Yeomen
James Langley of Leyland	John Benson of Winnel		Thos. Wasley of Chorley	
Ralph Marsden of Brindle	Ralph Leaver of Chorley		John Crane of Eccleston	
	Roger Haddock of Chorley, yeoman.		John Cowdray of Longton	

VII. CLASSIS.

Parishes of Preston, Kirkham, Garstang, and Poulton.

MINISTERS.	LAYMEN.	
Mr. Isaac Ambrose } Preston Robert Yates } Preston Ed. Fleetwood of Kirkham Thos. Cranage of Gosenargh Chr. Edmondson of Garstange John Sumner of Poulton	Aldern. { Alexander Rigby } Esqrs. William Langton } Esqrs. Matthew Addison of Preston Wm. Sudal of Preston Wm. Cottam of Preston Edwd. Downs of Wesam } Gentn.	Thos. Nickson of Plompton Robt. Crane of Leaton Wm. Latewise of Catteral } Gentn. Richd. Whitehead of Garstange Edward Veal of Langton, Esq. Richd. Wilkins of Kirkham } Yeomen. Edmd. Turner of Gosenarg } Yeomen.

VIII. CLASSIS.

Parishes of Lancaster, Cockerham, Claughton, Melling, Tatham, Tunstal, Whittington, Warton, Bolton, Helton, and Husom.

MINISTERS.	LAYMEN.	
Mr. Nehmh. Barnet of Lancaster John Sill of Gressingham Peter Atkinson of Ellel Nicholas Smith of Tatham Rd. Jackson of Whittington Richd. Walker of Warton John Jaques of Bolton Thomas Whitehead of Halton	Henry Porter of Lancaster Wm. West of Middleton Wm. Turner of Melling Thos. Rippon of Lancaster Wm. Gardner of Glasson Thos. Toulson of Lancaster Geo. Toulson of Lancaster Thos. Clayton of Wiersdale } Gentlemen. Robert Lucas of Kellet, yeoman.	Robert Curwen of Kellet, Gent. Wm. Greenbank of Halton James Thornton of Melling Wm. Wither of Brownedge Edmd. Barwick of Highfield Robt. Eskrigg of Whittington } Yeomen. Henry Storry of Storry Christopher Shearson of Ellel Henry Holme of Kellet.

IX. CLASSIS.

Parishes of Aldingham, Ursewick, Ulverstone, Hauxhead, Coulton, Daulton, Cartmel, Kirkby, and Wennington.

MINISTERS.	LAYMEN.	
Mr. Thomas Shaw of Aldingham Philip Bennet of Ulverstone (William) Kemp of Hauxhead Bryan Willow of Coulton John Marigold of Cartmel	Thomas Fell } Esqrs. Edward Rigby } Esqrs. Adam Sands of Booth John Sawry of Plympton } Gentn. Wm. Knipe of Cartmel	Robt. Rawlinson of Greenhead Thos. Fell of Scarthwaite } Gentn. Wm. Rawlinson of Graithwaite Thomas Dawson of Lear } Yeomen. Richd. Ayres of Belefe } Yeomen.

Resolved, by the Lords and Commons assembled in Parliament,—

That they do approve of the division of the County of Lancaster into the nine Classical Presbyteries, represented from the said County.

Resolved,—That the said houses do approve of the Ministers and other persons represented from the County of Lancaster, as fit to be of the several and respective Classes into which the said County is divided.

JE: BROWN, Cler. Parliamentorum.
HEN. ELDYNGE, Cler. Parl. D. Com.

Despite the vigilance and exertions of the Presbyterian ministers and elders, the principles of Independency made considerable progress, and were embraced by nearly the whole of the Lancashire forces. Frightened out of their calm thoughts by the threatened rivalry, they denounced with one voice toleration both in its modified and its unmitigated form, and as early as March 3rd, 1647, a month after the first meeting of the Classis, we find them preparing an address to Parliament, to which 8,500 signatures were obtained, calling upon the House to put down "Anabaptists, Brownists, Heretics, Schismatics, and Blasphemers," and stigmatising the sectarian spirit of the times as a "fretting leprosie and eating leprosie.' The Independents are not named, but it is probable they were included among the Schismatics, in which case it must be admitted that the efforts of the signatories were of small avail. After the example of their brethren in London and in some of the counties, the Lancashire ministers, in the early part of 1648, adopted and signed "The Harmonious Consent," which appears to have been drawn up by Heyricke, and in which all kinds of sectaries are vehemently denounced. This extraordinary document was subscribed by nearly all the Presbyterian ministers of the county,[1] the following being the signatories to it—eighty-four in all:—

Richard Heyricke, warden of Christ Colledg in Manchester
Richard Hollingworth, fellow of Christ Colledg in Manchester
Robert Yates, pastor of the Church at Warrington
Bradley Hayhurst, preacher of the word at Leigh
Alexander Horrocks, minister of the Gospel at Deane
John Tilsley, pastor of Dean
John Harper, pastor of Bolton
Richard Goodwyn, minister of the Gospel at Bolton
Richard Benson, minister of Chollerton

William Alt, min. of Bury
Robert Bath, pastor of Rachdal
William Assheton, pastor of Middleton
John Harrison, pastor of Ashton-under-Lyne
Thomas Pyke, pastor of Radcliff
John Angier, pastor of Denton
John Walker, minister of the Gospel at Newton-Heath chapel
Toby Furnesse, minister of the Gospel (Bury ?)
John Joanes, min. of Eccles

[1] A similar "Attestation" was agreed to by the ministers of Cheshire, May 2, 1648, and signed at their meeting at Northwich on the 6th of July following.—C.

Edward Woolmer, min. of Flixton
Robert Gilbody, preacher at Holcome
Jonathan Scholefield, min. at Heywood
Thomas Holland, min. of Ringley
Thomas Clayton, min. of Didsbury
Robert Constantine, min. of Ouldham
Peter Bradshaw, min. of Cockey
John Brierley, preacher at Salford
Thomas Johnson, min. of the Gospel at Halsal
William Bell, pastor of Hyton
William Dun, min. of the Gospel at Ormeskirk
James Worrall, pastor of Aughton
William Aspinwal, preacher of God's Word at Mayhall (Maghull)
John Mallison, min. of God's Word at Melling
Robert Seddon, min. of God's Word at Alker (Altcar)
Will. Norcot, minister of West Derby
Will. Ward, min. of the Gospel at Walton
Nevil Kay, pastor at Walton
Henry Boulton, preacher at Hale
John Fogge, pastor of Leverpoole
Joseph Tompson, min. of Sephton
Jo. Kyd, min. of Much-Crosby
James Bradshaw, pastor of the Church at Wigan
James Starkey, pastor of North-meoles
James Wood, preacher of the Word at Asheton in Makerfield
Thomas Norman, pastor of Newton
Timothy Smith, preacher of the Word at Rainforth
John Wright, pastor of Billinge
Henry Shaw, pastor of Holland
Thomas Crompton, min. of the Gospel at Astley
William Bagaley, min. of the Gospel at Burtonwood
William Leigh, preacher of the Word at Newchurch
Richard Mawdesley, pastor of Ellins (St. Helens)

James Hyet, pastor of Croston
Thomas Cranage, pastor of Brindle
Edward Gee, minister of the Gospel at Eccleston
Paul Latham, pastor of Standish
Samuel Joanes, pastor of Hoole
Henry Welch, min. at Chorley
Wil. Brownsword, preacher at Dugglas
James Crichely, preacher at Penwortham
Edward Fleetwood, pastor at Kirkham
Isaac Ambrose, pastor of Preston
William Addison, lecturer at Preston
William Ingham, minist. at Goosenarghe
Matthew Moore, minister at Broughton
Christopher Edmundson, pastor at Garstang
Thomas Smith, preacher at Garstang chapel
John Breres, minister at Padiham
Richard Jackson, pastor at Whittington
Nicolas Smith, pastor of Tatham
Robert Shaw, pastor at Cockerham
James Scholecroft, minister at Caton
Thomas Whitehead, pastor at Halton
Peter Atkinson, minister at Ellel
John Jaques, minister of Bolton (le Sands)
Richard Walker, minister of Warton
Philip Bennet, minister of Ulverston
William Smith, minister of Over-Kellet
Brian Willan, minister of Coulton
Peter Smith, minister of Shireshead (Shire-Side)
Edward Aston, minister of Claughton
Thomas Denny, minister of Wiersdalle (Wyersdale)
Thomas Fawcet, minister of Overton
Will. Garner, preacher of the Gospel
John Smith, minister of Melling

In the course of this year a memorable petition, subscribed by 12,500 "well-affected gentle-men, ministers, freeholders, and other inhabitants of the county palatine of Lancaster," was sent to the two Houses of Parliament, expressive of the ardent desire of the petitioners for the settlement of the religion of the state, according to the solemn covenant, and for the suppression of schism, heresy, and blasphemy, and for the continued union and good correspondence between England and Scotland. To this it was replied that Parliament held themselves obliged by the zeal of the petitioners in favour of these important objects, and particularly by their attachment to the solemn league and covenant. On the 9th of December Parliament resolved that the several Classis in Lancashire should form one province; and on the same day it was announced that Sir Richard Hoghton, Colonel Edward Rosseter, Colonel Edmond Harvey, Colonel Thos. Wayte, Mr. Henry Arthington, Mr. Robert Clive, Sir John Fenwick, Mr. Robert Charlton, Mr. Thos. Broughton, Sir Francis Drake, Colonel George Booth, Mr. Alex. Thistlethwayte, Mr. John Spelman, Mr. Walter Kirle, Sir Richard Skeffington, Mr. E. Crymes, Mr. John Dixwell, Mr. John Lloyd, Mr. Wm. Crowther, Sir James Harrington, Col. Edward Harley, Mr. Robert Parker, Mr. Humphrey Edwards, Mr. Edmund Fowell, Col. John Birch, had taken the solemn league and covenant.

Although the king was a prisoner, and the royal cause for the present seemed utterly hopeless, another attempt was made in 1648 to re-light the embers of civil war. General Langdale, an officer in the interest of the king, had assembled a considerable force in the northern counties, near the Scotch frontier, and an army was collected in Scotland, to be placed under the command of the Duke of Hamilton, which was intended to penetrate into England, to retrieve the fortunes of the Stuarts. The approach of this force produced a deep sensation in Lancashire, and repeated meetings of the county were called, to provide the necessary force to resist the invaders, and to secure the persons and property of the inhabitants. The House of Commons, fully aware of the approaching danger, despatched Col. Ashton, Major Brooke, and Mr. Fell, members of that house, into Lancashire, with instructions from the committee at Derby House to employ their best endeavours for the safety and preservation of the county;[1] and Peter Bold of Bold, Esq., and John Anderton of Anderton, Esq., were added to the committee of Lancashire. Early in May Colonel Rigby convened a general meeting of the gentry at Bolton, at which it was agreed to raise forthwith all the forces of the county, and warrants were issued for that purpose. On the following Monday, another general meeting was held at Preston, when it was resolved that all the forces of the county that could be raised in time to the south of Garstang should march to Lancaster, to co-operate with the forces of the hundred of Lonsdale, stationed at that place; and the forces of the hundred of Amounderness, with horse and foot, under the command of Lieut.-Colonel Alexander Rigby, marched

---

[1] Journals of the Commons, May 17, 1648.

without delay.[1]   An additional brigade was ordered to be raised in the county, the command of which was confided to Colonel Ralph Ashton, now advanced to the rank of Major-General of the Lancashire forces, with the "entertainment" of forty shillings per diem, over and above his pay of colonel of horse, and colonel of foot, with instructions to join Major-General Lambert, in the service of the north.   For the purpose of infusing the requisite vigour into these military preparations, a month's pay in advance was ordered for the officers and soldiers of the county of Lancaster, and £4,000 was directed to be paid out of the sequestrations of Westmoreland for that purpose, with £10,000 out of the grand excise for their further payment.   The officers and soldiers of the county of Lancaster in May put forth a declaration, in which they protested that "they owned the solemn league and covenant of the three kingdoms;" that they would support the established government of "king, lords, and commons, according to the laws of the land and the declarations of the present Parliament;" that as to "papists, popish persons, malignant abettors of former innovations, usurpations, or oppressions, or other disaffected persons, they detested them from the bottom of their hearts, and would resist them with their lives and fortunes."   At this period the danger was considered so imminent that the assizes for the county palatine were adjourned *sine die*, and the judges were ordered to postpone the assizes in the whole of the northern circuit.[2]   All eyes were now turned upon this part of the kingdom, and reports were made from Lancashire to the Parliament almost at every sitting, indicating the approach of the enemy, and the state of preparation in which the county stood for their reception.   A committee was appointed in Parliament, under the designation of "The Committee of Lancashire," which sat at Derby House; and by this body it was ordered that four colonels of foot and two of horse, with their regiments, then in readiness in the northern part of the county, should join Major-General Lambert.   Colonel Alexander Rigby

THE HODDER BRIDGE.

commanded one of the regiments of horse, and Colonel Nicholas Shuttleworth the other; while Colonel Dodding, Colonel Standish, Colonel Ashton, and Colonel Ughtred Shuttleworth were placed in command of the foot regiments.   The campaign opened on the 4th of July with an engagement between Colonel Lilburne, at the head of a party of 600 horse, and Sir Richard Tempest, with a superior force, which terminated in favour of the colonel, who captured 600 of the enemy's horse and made 300 prisoners.[3]   At length it was announced that the Duke of Hamilton had entered England at the head of 17,000 troops, and that it was his purpose to march from Cumberland along the western coast, while General Sir Marmaduke Langdale advanced in a parallel direction from Northumberland, keeping to the east, but so arranging their plan of operation that they might be able to form a speedy junction, when, by the nature of the service, it might be required.   The force under General Lambert was found wholly insufficient to arrest this torrent from the north, and Oliver Cromwell was ordered by Parliament to march out of Yorkshire into Lancashire to resist their further progress.   These orders he promptly obeyed, and advancing on the 16th of August to Hodder Bridge, close by Stonyhurst, he was joined by Major-General Ashton with the Lancashire force, the united strength being 12,000 men.   "After a tedious and weary march of much endurance and difficulty, and passing through unseasonable weather and extreme hardness of ways," wrote one in the Parliament army, "the Lieutenant-General, Cromwell, came on Monday night, the 14th, to Skipton, within ken of the enemy; Tuesday to Gisborn; Wednesday we marched to Stronghurst (Stonyhurst); Thursday, very early, our army marched towards Preston, whither the enemy lay." A council of war was assembled at the Hodder Bridge, and Cromwell learned that the Scotch

[1] Rushworth's Recollections, viii. 1123.
[2] Journals of the House of Commons, Aug. 1, 1648. In the year 1650 a discussion arose in Parliament upon the propriety of holding the Lan-

cashire assizes at Preston, but the decision was finally in favour of Lancaster.
[3] Journals of the House of Commons.

troops, under the Duke of Hamilton, had been joined by an Irish force under General Monroe, and that they were also in communication with Sir Marmaduke Langdale's division. Early in the morning of Thursday, the 17th of August, Cromwell advanced from Stonyhurst towards Preston, where he found the forces under Sir Marmaduke Langdale drawn up upon Ribbleton Moor, while the principal part of the Duke of Hamilton's force had passed over Ribble bridge, and were posted in Walton-le-Dale, between the Ribble and the Darwen. By a most extraordinary oversight the duke not only suffered Sir Marmaduke's forces to be beaten without affording them any assistance,[1] but he allowed the Parliamentary troops to fall back upon their flanks, and to cut off the communication between the Scotch and the English army. Sir Marmaduke, finding it impossible to resist the advance of the enemy, retreated before them into the town of Preston, where the duke was quartered, and a sanguinary engagement took place in the streets, which terminated in favour of Cromwell, who, having forced the bridge of the Ribble, advanced over the Darwen, and passed the night within musket-shot of the duke's forces. On the 17th August Cromwell addressed a letter to the committee sitting at Manchester, informing them of the victory. "We lay," he says, "the last night at Mr. Sherburne's, of Stonihurst,[2] nine miles from Preston, which was within three miles of the Scots' quarters. We advanced by times the next morning towards Preston, with a desire to engage the enemy, and by the time our forlorn (hope) had engaged the enemy we were about four miles from Preston; and thereupon we advanced with the whole army, and the enemy being drawn out upon a moor betwixt us and the town, the armies on both sides engaged, and after a very sharp dispute, continuinge for three or four houres, it pleased God to enable us to give them a defeat, which I hope we shall improve, by God's assistance, to their utter ruin." Notwithstanding the great superiority of the duke's army in point of numbers they retreated during the night through Chorley to Wigan, and took up their quarters in that town. Here they were closely pursued on the following day. On Saturday they resumed their march towards Warrington, but being overtaken near Winwick, a desperate engagement took place, which served to complete their overthrow. At Warrington, a large division of the Scotch army, under General Bayley, capitulated on the hard condition that the general should surrender himself and all his officers and soldiers prisoners of war, with their arms, ammunition, and horses upon quarter for life. The duke afterwards fled, with the wreck of his army towards Nantwich, but the country people fell upon the stragglers, and the duke himself was made prisoner, and subsequently beheaded. In this campaign of three days the Royalist army of 21,000 men was defeated and almost annihilated by a force of little more than one-third their number, and with a loss on the part of Cromwell of scarcely fifty men.[3] The official despatches, containing the history of this short but memorable campaign, from the pen of Cromwell, are strikingly characteristic of the language and spirit of the age.[4] This was Charles's

[1] According to the opinion often afterwards expressed by Sir Marmaduke Langdale to Lord Clarendon, if the Duke of Hamilton had sent him one thousand foot to reinforce his troops upon Ribbleton Moor, Cromwell must have been defeated.

[2] In his despatch to the Speaker of the House of Commons, Cromwell writes: "That night quartered the whole army in the field by Stonyhurst Hall, being Mr. Sherburn's house, a place nine miles distant from Preston;" and Captain Hodgson, an officer who accompanied him, writes: "We pitched our camp at Stonyhares Hall, a Papist's house, one Sherburn's." Tradition still points to the old oaken table in the entrance at Stonyhurst, and affirms that Cromwell slept on it, while his men bivouacked in the grounds; but the story may well be doubted, for the stern warrior was hardly likely to put up with so indifferent a couch, when the "Papist's house" afforded so much better accommodation.—C.

[3] Lord Clarendon's History, iii. p. 246. It is stated by Noble that Cromwell's son Henry, a captain in Harrison's regiment of horse, fell in the battle of Preston; but this is a mistake, nor does it appear that any officer of distinction in the Parliamentary army, with the exception of Colonel Thornhaugh, was numbered amongst the slain.

[4] LIEUTENANT-GENERAL CROMWELL'S LETTER TO THE SPEAKER OF THE HOUSE OF COMMONS.

"Sir,—After the conjunction of that Party which I brought with me out of Wales, with the Northern Forces about Knaresbrough and Wetherby, hearing that the Enemy was advanced with their Army into Lancashire, we came the 6th instant to Hodder Bridge over Ribble, where we had a Council of War; and upon Advertisement the Enemy intended Southward, and since confirmed, that they resolved for London it self, and Information that the Irish Forces under Monroe, lately come out of Ireland, which consisted of 1,200 Horse and 1,500 Foot, were on their march towards Lancashire to join with them; it was thought to engage the Enemy to fight was our Business: And accordingly marching over the Bridge that Night, quartered the whole Army in the Fields. Next Morning we marched towards Preston, having Intelligence, that the Enemy was drawing together thereabouts from all his Out-Quarters, we drew out a Forlorn of about 200 Horse and 400 Foot; these gallantly engaged the Enemy's Scouts and Out-guards, until we had opportunity to bring up our whole army. So soon as our Foot and Horse were come up, we resolved that Night to engage them if we could; and therefore advancing with our Forlorns, and putting the rest of the Army into as good a Posture as the ground would bear (which was totally inconvenient for our Horse, being all Inclosure and miery Ground), we pressed upon them through a Lane, and forced them from their ground, after four Hours Dispute, until we came to the Town; into which four Troops of

my Regiment first entred; and being well seconded by Coll. Harrison's Regiment, Charged the Enemy in the Town and cleared the Streets. At last the Enemy was put into Disorder, many Men slain, and many Prisoners taken: The Duke with most of the Scots' Horse and Foot retreated over the Bridge; where, after a very hot Dispute betwixt the Lancashire Regiments (part of my Lord General's and them being at push of Pike), they were beaten from the Bridge, and our Horse and Foot, following them, killed many, and took divers Prisoners; and we possessed the Bridge over Darvent and a few houses there, the enemy baing drawn up within musquet shot of us, where we lay that Night, we not being able to attempt farther upon the enemy, the Night preventing us. In this posture did the Enemy and we lie most part of that Night; upon entering the Town, many of the Enemy's Horse fled towards Lancaster, in the Chase of whom we had divers of our Horse, who pursued them near Ten Miles, and had Execution of them, and took about Five hundred Horse, and many Prisoners: We possessed in the Fight very much of the Enemy's Ammunition; I believe they lost Four or Five Thousand Arms; the number of the slain we judge to be about a Thousand, the Prisoners we took near about 4,000.

"In the Night they marched away, 7 or 8 Thousand Foot, and about Four Thousand Horse; we followed them with about Three Thousand Foot, and about Two Thousand Five Hundred Horse and Dragoons; and in this Prosecution that worthy Gentleman, Coll. Thornhaugh, pressing too boldly, was slain, being run into the Body, Thigh, and Head, by the Enemy's Lancers; Our Horse still prosecuted the Enemy, killing and taking divers all the way; but by that time our Army was come up, they recovered Wigan before we could attempt any thing upon them. We lay that Night in the Field close by the Enemy, lying very dirty and weary, where we had some skirmishing, &c. We took Major-General Van Druske, Col. Hurrey, and Lieut.-Col. Ennis.

"The next morning the Enemy marched towards Warrington, made a stand at a Pass near Winwick; we held them in some Dispute untill our Army was come up, they maintaining the Pass with great Resolution for many Hours; but our Men, by the Blessing of God, Charged very home upon them, beat them from their Standing, where we killed about a Thousand of them, and took (as we believe) about Two Thousand Prisoners, and prosecuted them home to Warrington Town, where they possessed the Bridge. As soon as we came thither, I received a Message from Lieut.-General Bailey, desiring some Capitulation; to which I yielded, and gave him these Terms: That he should surrender himself and all his Officers and Soldiers Prisoners of War, with all his Arms, Ammunition, and Horses, upon Quarter for Life, which accordingly is done. Here we took about Four Thousand complete Arms, and as many Prisoners: And thus you have their infantry ruined.

last appeal to arms, and when intelligence of the disaster reached him in the Isle of Wight he told Colonel Hammond, the governor, that "it was the worst news that ever came to England." For the king it was; for there is little doubt that Cromwell's victory hastened the action of the Republicans, and precipitated that event which the world has ever since condemned.

This splendid victory was celebrated as a day of general thanksgiving throughout the whole kingdom, by order of Parliament, and commissions passed the great seal to commissioners in the counties of Lancaster, York, &c., to inquire into the losses that had been sustained by the inhabitants in consequence of the invasion of the Scots under the Duke of Hamilton, and to make satisfaction for those losses. In furtherance of this object, an order was issued by Parliament that a collection should be made on the day of general thanksgiving in all the churches and chapels in the kingdom, and that the money collected should be employed, one moiety "for the relief and support of the wounded soldiers in Lancashire," and the other for the distressed people in that county,[1] who were suffering at this time under the combined visitation of the sword, pestilence, and famine.[2]

Part of Sir Marmaduke Langdale's horse, having effected their escape to the north after the battle of Preston, engaged in the siege of Cockermouth, but Major-General Ashton, by whom they were pursued, having raised the siege at that place, marched to Appleby, where the Royalist force capitulated on his summons, and upwards of 100 officers of various ranks, five pieces of cannon, 1,200 horse, and 1,000 stand of arms, fell into his hands.[3] The danger of the renewal of the war was now considered so entirely at an end that an order was issued by Parliament for disbanding all the officers and soldiers, both horse and foot, in the county of Lancaster, and this duty was confided to Major-General Lambert. On the disbanding of the Lancashire forces an order was issued by Parliament for the demolition of Clitheroe Castle, and at the same time the council of state met to consider what castle should be demolished. Some faint hopes still existed of a reconciliation between the king and the Parliament, and as late as the 13th of November in this year a negotiation was on foot for that purpose. With this view, an act of oblivion was to be passed, which should provide for the forgiveness of all offenders except seven, and it was agreed by the two houses that the seven persons to be excepted from the clemency of the government should be Lord Digby, Sir Marmaduke Langdale, Sir Richard Greenhill, Judge Jenkins, Sir Francis Dodrington, the Earl of Derby, and Lord Byron. These persons were doomed to be sent into banishment, and an ordinance was drawn up for that purpose; but the negotiation failed, the Parliament insisting that the bishoprics should be dissolved, and that their lands should revert to the crown, and the king refusing to acquiesce in that proposal.

The catastrophe was now fast approaching, and the moderate party in the House of Commons having been forcibly excluded by a military outrage in the name of freedom and justice commonly designated as "Pride's Purge," on the 4th of January, 1649, a high court of justice was instituted by the "Rump Parliament," for the trial of the king. Of this tribunal, John Bradshaw, serjeant-at-law, was elected lord president.[4] The trial, if such it could be called, commenced on the 20th, but the king three several times denied the jurisdiction of this court. When he was called up the fourth time, several witnesses were examined; and the court, having come to the unanimous decision that he was guilty of high treason and other high crimes, adjudged him to be executed by severing his head from his body. This sentence was carried into effect on the 30th of January, 1649, in front of the banquetting room, Whitehall. The king met his fate with a dignity and composure that awakened the sympathy even of his enemies. The English monarchy, after existing for eight centuries, was thus transformed into a Commonwealth, but without any of the substantial advantages of representative government.

"The Duke is marched with his remaining Horse (which are about 3000) towards Namptwich, where the Gentlemen of the Country have taken about 500 of them ; the Country will scarce suffer any of them to pass, but bring in and kill divers as they light upon them. I have sent Post to my Lord Grey and Sir Edward Roades, to gather all together with speed for their Prosecution ; Monroe is about Cumberland, with the Horse that ran away, and his Irish Horse and Foot ; but I have left a considerable Strength, I hope, to make resistance, till we can come up to them.

"Thus you have the Narrative of the Particulars of the Success. I could hardly tell how to say less, there being so much of God, and I was not willing to say more, least there should seem to be any thing of man ; only give me leave to add one word, shewing the disparity of the Forces of both sides, that so you may see, and all the world acknowledge, the great Hand of God in this Business. The Scots' Army could not be less than 12,000 Foot well armed, and 5,000 Horse ; Langdale not less than 2,500 Foot. and 1,500 Horse ; in all, One and Twenty Thousand : In ours, in all, about 8,600 ; and by Computation about 2,000 of the Enemys slain, betwixt Eight and Nine Thousand Prisoners, besides what are lurking in Hedges and private Places, which the Country daily bring in or destroy.

"Your very humble

"August 20, 1648.   "OLIVER CROMWELL."

[1] Journals of the Commons, August 23, 1648.

[2] In a memorial entitled, "A true Representation of the present sad and lamentable condition of the County of Lancaster, and particularly of the Towns of Wigan, Ashton, and the parts adjacent, verified by James Hyet, Richard Hollinworth, Isaac Ambrose, and John Tilsley, Ministers of the Gospel," it is said—"There is very great scarcity and dearth of all provisions, especially of all sorts of grain, particularly that kind by which the country is most sustained (oats), which is full six-fold its usual price ; all trade is utterly decayed ; it would melt any good heart to see the numerous swarms of begging poor, and the many families that pine away at home, not having force to beg ; very many now craving alms at other men's doors, who were used to give alms at their own doors ; and some of them, already being at the point to perish through famine, have fetched in and eaten carrion and other unwholesome food, to the destruction of themselves and increase of the infection."

[2] Official despatches, dated Appleby, Oct. 11, 1648.

[3] President Bradshaw was descended from an ancient Lancashire family, subsequently settled at Marple, in Cheshire. A few months after the king's death, the president received the appointment, from the authorities of the Commonwealth, of chancellor of the duchy of Lancaster.

On the day following the execution of Charles, the serjeant-at-arms, accompanied by pursuivants, and surrounded by cavalry, proceeded to Cheapside, and there read to the assembled crowd the proclamation that whosoever should proclaim a new king without the authority of Parliament should be deemed a traitor. The proclamation was ordered to be read in every market town, and there is preserved among the Tanner MSS.[1] the original letter from Sir Gilbert Ireland, the then High Sheriff of Lancashire, to William Lenthal, Speaker of the House of Commons, acknowledging the order of Parliament, and reporting the days on which the proclamation was read in the several towns of the county, the first intimation that many of the Lancashire people had heard of the dark tragedy enacted at Whitehall[2] and notwithstanding that the House of Commons had ordered the post to be stayed for a day, there must have been considerable despatch, for the document reached the Sheriff on the 2nd February. The letter is as follows :—

Sr,—According to your Commands received ye 2 of this instant, by my vndersherriffe and deputyes I have caused ye act and proclamacon you then sent mee to bee proclaimed and published within all ye publique townes and places within this county, and taken ye opportunity of all ye markett dayes I could possibly in such a tyme. And in further obedience to your order I doe here vnto annexed prsent you with an account of such tyme and tymes, place and places, as the same have been proclaimed and published. And am very forward further to serve the Common wealth wherein I shall bee commanded.

       Sr, I am your most humble servant,   G. IRELAND, vic. com. Lancr.

ffebruary 11th, 1648 (1649).

An account of ye Townes, dayes, & houres ye Act for prohibiting the proclaiming of any person to be King of England or Ireland or the Dominions thereof was proclaimed and published. 1648. Com. Lancr. :—

Townes.	day of ye month.	houre.	Townes.	day of ye month.	houre.
Leigh	ffebruary 5e	12 clocke.	Wigan	ffebruary 9e	11 a clocke.
Bolton	ffebruary 5e	4 clocke aft noone.	Newton	ffebruary 9e	3 aftrnoone.
Bevney (? Bury)	ffebruary 6e	8 a clocke.	Chorley	ffebruary 6e	1 a clocke.
Rotchdale	ffebruary 6e	12 a clocke.	Garyton (? Garstang)	ffebruary 8e	12 a clocke.
Manchester	ffebruary 6e	4 aftrnoone.	Preston	ffebruary 10e	10 in ye morning.
Warrington	ffebruary 7e	1 a clocke.	Lancaster	ffebruary 10e	2 in ye afternoone.
Prescott	ffebruary 7e	5 in ye aftrnoone.	Blackburn		
Liverpoole	ffebruary 8e	9 a clocke.	Clitheroe		The said act is to be published vpon
Ormskirke	ffebruary 8	9 aftrnoone.	Poulton		Munday and Tuesday next.
Holland	ffebruary 9e	8 a clocke.	Kirkeham		

For the Honnorable William Lenthall, Speaker of ye Right Honnorable House of Commons, these.

When intelligence of the beheading of Charles reached Lancashire the authorities, both civil and religious, were filled with horror and amazement, and boldly avowed their detestation of the act that had been perpetrated, Presbyterian and Independent joining with each other in expressing their reprobation of the impious deed, and asserting their freedom from "the blood-stain of the Lord's anointed." The dissolution of monarchy followed, as a natural consequence, the execution of the king, and the supreme authority was declared to be vested in the representatives of the people. A new seal for the county was made ; the forms of all public business were changed ; the Court of King's Bench became the Court of Public Bench, and proceedings, instead of being in the king's name, ran in that of "The Keepers of the Liberties of England." The writ appointing the Sheriff of Lancaster in 1652, which is in the possession of the editor of this edition, is expressed as follows :—

The Keepers of the Libertie of England by Authoritie of Parliamt. To our trustie and wellbeloved Alexander Barlowe (of Barlow) Esquire, Sheriffe of the County Palatine of Lancaster, greeting. Whereas we haue Comitted to oure trustie and well-beloved John Parker (of Extwisle) Esquire, the office of Sheriffe of the Countie aforesaid, of and in the Countie Palatine of Lancaster aforesaid, to be kept and houlden during our pleasure as in our Letters Patent to him thereof now made is more fully conteyned. We Command you that to the same John Parker, Esquire, the office of Sheriffe aforesaid, and the Countie aforesaid to the same belonging, together with all Rolls, Writts, Remembrances, and all other things to the said office belonging, and of, and in your Custodie, being by an Indenture thereof betweene you and him, the said John Parker, Duely to be made, you Deliver. Witness our selves, at Lancaster, under the Seale of the Countie Palatine of Lancaster, the Nyne and Twentieth Day of November, in the yeare of our Lord One thousand Six hundred ffiftie two.   GERARD.

Appended to this document is the seal of the county palatine, which, as a curious example of puritan heraldry, may be here described. The obverse is almost identical with that of the great seal of the Commonwealth voted by the Commons on the 9th January, 1648-9, and represents the House of Commons sitting with the Speaker in the chair and the clerks at the table, the whole being encircled with the legend,

"IN THE YEAR OF FREEDOM BY GOD'S BLESSING RESTORED, 1648."

On the reverse are two shields united under a festoon of foliage ; the dexter, *argent*, a cross *gules* for St. George of England ; and the sinister, *azure*, a harp *or* for Ireland. Surrounding it is the inscription,

"THE SEAL OF THE COUNTY PALATINE OF LANCASTER, 1648."

[1] Tanner MSS. 57 2, J. 522.—C.
[2] Henry Newcome, of Manchester, the noted Puritan divine, in his "Autobiography," writes—"This news came to us when I lived at Goos-

tree (in Cheshire), and a general sadness it put upon us all. It dejected me much (I remember), the horridness of the fact ; and much indisposed me for the service of the Sabbath next after the news came."—C.

The substitution of the Presbyterian for the Episcopal form of church government was followed by an attempt on the part of the dominant power to control the ecclesiastical revenues, and to regulate their expenditure. An ordinance of the Parliament, dated March 29th, 1649, abolished the "name, title, dignity, function, and office of Dean, Sub-dean, Dean and Chapter," and all other titles and offices belonging to any college or collegiate church in England and Wales. This order was, of course, followed by the sequestration of the college property at Manchester. The Fellows, in disgust, renounced their sacred functions, but the Warden remained firm at his post, and shortly afterwards having the opportunity of preaching before the members of the House of Commons, he did so with so much force and effect, and pleaded his case so pathetically, that the college was reinstated in the possession of part at least of its revenues, though upon the condition that such of its members as hesitated to take the National Covenant should be ejected. But Heyrick's troubles did not end here. By virtue of an Act of Parliament passed June 8th, 1649, "for the providing of maintenance of preaching ministers and other pious uses," commissioners were appointed in each county to report upon the state of each parish. The Lancashire commission is dated March 29th, 1650, and the commissioners appointed were, in addition to the Justices of Assize in the county and the Attorney-General of the Commonwealth, John Moore, Thomas Fell, John Sawrie, William West, George Towluson, Thomas Whittingham, George Pigott, Jerehiah Aspinwall, Robert Maudesley, Richard Standish, Richard Shuttleworth, John Starkie, Peter Holt, James Ashton, Alexander Barlowe, John Hartley, Thomas Birche, Gilbert Ireland, John Atherton, and Peter Bold, esquires; and Thomas Cubham and Robert Glest, gentlemen. In due time these gentlemen, or a portion of them at least, visited Manchester, with the result that the college was ordered to be dissolved, and the church lands in the parish appropriated to the use of the Commonwealth, a small provision of £100 a year being reserved for Mr. Heyrick, and a yearly stipend of £80 each for Mr. Hollinworth and Mr. Walker, who were reported as "godly p'chers." Heyrick was indignant, and the contention became bitter and exasperating. He had declaimed with vehement sarcasm against Papists and prelates to find he had only exchanged King Log for King Stork, and that the sectaries, or schismatics as he called them, who had helped to pull down episcopacy, had neither sympathy with him nor toleration for his opinions. Manchester was made to feel the power of the Republican party. In the summer of 1649 the sequestrators intimated their intention of dealing with the property of the collegiate church. The Presbyterians were alarmed at the threat, declared that "the hand of God had gone out against them," and resolved on keeping a day of public humiliation. A resistance on the part of the Warden[1] and his friends was anticipated. Colonel Thomas Birch, of Birch Hall—Lord Derby's carter, as the Cavaliers contemptuously styled him—was deputed to enforce the order. Heyrick, maintaining the authority of ancient charters, refused to surrender, whereupon Birch ordered his men (Nov. 5th, 1649) to break open the doors of the chapter house, and finding, on their entrance, the muniment chest, he directed it to be sent unopened to London. Not content with seizing the deeds and writings of the college, the fanatical soldiery set about defacing the costly architecture of the church, breaking the painted windows, and demolishing the carved screens and sculptured monuments. "The most beautiful ecclesiastical edifice in Lancashire," says Dr. Halley, "which by the prudence and high character of its catholic wardens, Collyer and Vaux, had been protected through the perils of the Reformation, and afterwards, by the influence of its Presbyterian warden, Heyrick, through the perils of civil war, was bereaved of its rich ornaments and time-hallowed memories by the fanaticism of an ignorant and preaching soldiery."[3]

The Lancashire commissioners appointed under the provisions of the Act of June 1649, held their first inquisition in Manchester on the 17th of June, 1650. Three inquisitions were taken in that town, six at Wigan, three at Lancaster, three at Preston, and one at Blackburn—sixteen in all. These surveys, which have been lately printed by the Record Society, under the able editorship of Lieut.-Colonel Fishwick, F.S.A.,[4] show that there were then in the county 63 parish churches (exclusive of Meols, which is omitted), and 118 chapels, of which no less than 38 were without ministers, chiefly for want of "maintenance." The commissioners wisely recommended the subdivision of many of the larger parishes, and that some of the chapels remote from the mother church should have separate parishes assigned them. These surveys are further valuable

[1] Heyrick retained his title of Warden, but as the chapter was dissolved and he officiated on a salary, he could only be regarded as a parochial minister.—C.

[2] Walker states ("Sufferings of the Clergy," pt. ii. p. 88) that on the 5th November, 1649, the college chest was broken open by a mob of soldiers, and the deeds and writings of the college seized and sent to London, where they afterwards perished in the great fire. Such has been the tradition to the present day, and the late Canon Wray supposed that there had been two attacks made upon the chapter house, one in 1641 and the other in 1649; but upon a careful examination of the collegiate records in 1840, these documents are supposed to be still in the safe custody of the chapters, and that if they had been seized in Heyrick's time and sent to London, they had also been afterwards returned to their proper repository. On the 3rd June, 1672, "all the ancient charters of foundation were remaining in the chapter house." ("Coll. Reg.," Vol. I. See also "Wardens of Manchester," pt. ii. p. 129, Chet. Soc. Vol. VI., new series.)—C.

[3] "Lancashire: Its Puritanism and Nonconformity." Second edition, page 282.—C.

[4] Record Society's Publication, v. 1.—C.

from the fact that they give the name of the minister of each church and chapel, and in many instances the names of important householders in the respective districts.

Under the Commonwealth rule, marriage, as a religious ceremony, was forbidden, and became merely a civil contract entered into before the civil magistrate, who had authority to ratify and register the contract, the Act of 1653 declaring that "no other marriage whatsoever within the Commonwealth of England, after the 29th day of September, 1653, shall be held or accounted a marriage according to the laws of England." The banns were usually published at the market cross or other place of public resort, and in some instances they are certified as having been published by the bellman. In Lancashire, Edward Hopwood, a Puritan magistrate, seems to have been especially engaged in this service and to have been accounted a sort of Parliamentary high priest. According to the register of Bolton he proclaimed the banns at the market cross there in 1659; in 1655 he performed the same service at Radcliffe; and according to the register of Whalley "the agreement of marriage between Roger Kenyon, gent., and Mrs. Alice Rigby, was duly published at the market town of Clitheroe on three market days."

In the course of the year 1649 an overture was made by Parliament through their commissary-general, Ireton, for the surrender of the Isle of Man, upon the condition that the Earl of Derby should be permitted to retire peaceably to England, and that the fine on his estate should be greatly mitigated by the sequestrators. To this offer the earl replied that he abhorred with his soul the perfidiousness of disloyalty, and that he never would be instrumental in casting such an odium as this surrender implied upon the house of Derby. "I scorn," said he, "your proffer, I disdain your favour, I abhor your treason, and so far from delivering up this Island to the Parliament, I shall keep it for the King to the utmost of my Power; and if you trouble me with any more messages of this nature, I will burn the paper and hang the Messenger." The determined spirit of loyalty manifested in this answer was celebrated by the Cavaliers in prose and in rhyme, and one of their happiest efforts is expressed in the following stanza:—

> "The Isle of Man is yet our owne,
> Brave Darby safe and sound;
> 'Tis he that keepes the English Crown,
> Why then should hee compound?"

The death of Charles I. does not close the melancholy history of the civil wars in Lancashire: another illustrious victim was yet to follow, whose fate remains to be related. Although monarchy had been abolished in England, and the government of a commonwealth decreed, Charles II., son of the late king, appeared in Scotland towards the end of the year 1650. On the 3rd of September, Dunbar—Cromwell's "crowning mercy"—was fought and lost. Having succeeded in rallying his supporters, Charles received the circle and symbol of sovereignty at Scone on the 1st January, 1651; and on the 31st July following he set out from Stirling on his march southward, taking the western road by Carlisle. In August the royal standard was floated once more over the battlemented tower of old John of Gaunt—"time-honoured Lancaster"—and Charles was proclaimed king. On the 16th of August the royal Scotch army, under the Duke of Hamilton and General Leslie, headed by the king, reached Preston, from whence they advanced by a rapid march to the south, crossing the bridge of Warrington, which General Lambert had been directed to break down, and in this way to arrest their progress till the Parliamentary force under Cromwell, which was in close pursuit, came up. Had this order been executed, it is highly probable that the fate of Charles II. might have been determined, as was that of his royal father, in the hundreds of Amounderness and West Derby, three years before. Cromwell, at the head of 10,000 infantry, advanced through Lancashire within two days' march of the royal army, and was joined between Lancaster and Preston by General Lambert and General Harrison, at the head of 8,000 horse. The king, in order to strengthen his cause, had summoned the Earl of Derby from the Isle of Man, where he had hitherto maintained his independence. Prompt on all occasions to obey the call of his sovereign, this gallant nobleman, accompanied by Sir Thomas Tyldesley, who had sought safety there, embarked with 250 foot and 60 horse, and arrived in the Wyre Water in Lancashire,[1] August 15th, whence he hastened to Preston, while the king marched south towards Worcester. Here he issued his warrant as the king's lieutenant, commanding all those who were in favour of the royal sway to meet him in the town in arms. This call was but feebly obeyed, for though his lordship's plans were well laid, his influence had been much shaken.[2] Having collected about 600 horse,[3] which was swelled by other forces to 1,500 men, his lordship marched to Wigan. Here he was met and encountered by Colonel Lilburne, in Wigan Lane, and a desperate engagement took place, which terminated in the utter rout of the Royalists (Aug. 25). In this short but

---

[1] "Whitelock's Memorials," p. 502.   [2] Arthur Trevor's Letter to the Marquis of Ormonde.   [3] Seacombe.

sanguinary engagement the earl lost five colonels, the adjutant-general, four lieutenant-colonels, one major, four captains, and two lieutenants, taken prisoners; and Lord Widdrington, Major-General Sir Thomas Tyldesley, one colonel, and two majors, with a number of other officers slain. After displaying prodigies of valour, and receiving several severe wounds, the earl found a temporary concealment in a house in Wigan,[1] from which he escaped during the night, and pursued his route, at the head of about thirty troopers, by way of Warrington, to join his royal master at Worcester. Colonel Lilburne's "seasonable victory" over the Earl of Derby was, as usual, made the subject of a public thanksgiving by Parliament;[2] and the king's disappointment on the arrival of the earl at Worcester was extreme.

In the battle of Worcester, fought on the 3rd of September, 1651, Cromwell was again victorious: the royal army was dispersed, and the king became a fugitive. If the Earl of Derby could not replenish the king's army he was enabled to find him an asylum in the house of a loyal peasant, at Boscobel, on the borders of Staffordshire, near which stood the *Royal Oak*, the emblem of his future restoration. The earl, less fortunate than his sovereign, was captured in Cheshire on his way to Knowsley, by Major Edge,[3] to whom he surrendered on a promise of quarter. In violation of this engagement the earl was put upon his trial for high treason, before a court-martial held at Chester on the 1st of October, of which Colonel Humphrey Mackworth was president, on the charge of having corresponded with "Charles Stuart," in violation of the Act of the 12th of August preceding. To this his lordship pleaded that he had surrendered on promise of quarter, whereby he was exonerated from any charge affecting his life. Very little deliberation was thought necessary to dispose of this plea; and the sentence of the court was that he should suffer death by his head being severed from his body in the public market-place at Bolton, on Wednesday, the 15th of October. Cromwell having got his most formidable foe in his power, resolved to get rid of him by the shortest process that time and circumstances admitted, and an appeal made by the earl to him from the decision of the military tribunal was unavailing, as was also, as Whitelock affirms, an attempt made by his lordship to escape, by letting himself down by a rope from the leads of the prison;[4] and on the appointed day he was conducted to Bolton, where he had been represented as the author of the barbarities practised by order of Prince Rupert after the surrender of that place in 1644. Notwithstanding these representations the sympathy of the people was strongly excited in favour of his lordship; and when the executioner came to perform his duty, the spectators expressed their emotions by their tears. After the necessary time spent in acts of devotion his lordship laid his neck with great firmness on the block, and the executioner terminated the misfortunes of his disastrous life by severing his head from his body. Of this gallant peer Clarendon has said that "he was a man of unquestionable loyalty," of great honour, and clear courage, but that he had the misfortune not to know how to treat his inferiors; and the events of his life show but too clearly that he had imbibed no portion of that spirit of amelioration which belonged to the age in which he lived. By the special order of the earl, his George and Garter were delivered to his son, who with filial affection attended his father to Bolton on the day of his execution, and the same evening conveyed his remains to Wigan, from whence they were removed to the family burial-place at Ormskirk.[5]

Seven days before his lordship's execution the gallant Countess of Derby, who commanded in the Isle of Man during his absence, received a summons from Captain Young, of the President frigate, to surrender that island to the Parliament to which she replied "that she was charged with the duty of keeping the island by her lord's command, and without his orders she would not deliver it up." The earl, feeling that the permanent retention of the island was impossible, wrote an affectionate letter of consolation to the countess, in which he advised her to surrender the island, and by his request this ancient possession of the Stanleys passed soon after under the sway of the Commonwealth. The countess and her family were now left destitute, or dependent upon the precarious contributions of their friends; and it was not till after the Restoration that their circumstances were retrieved, and then only partially. After the battle of Worcester, the remnant of the Royalist army escaped into Chester, and from thence marched into the south-western part of Lancashire, under Lieutenant-General Lesley and Major-General Middleton. Being overtaken at Middleton, on the 10th of September, by Major-General Harrison and Colonel Lilburne, a smart engagement ensued, in which the retreating army was beaten, and General Lesley and General Middleton, with several other officers and 600 of their men, were taken prisoners. Four days previous to this engagement the Scots fugitives had lost a number of officers

---

[1] The house is traditionally said to have been the Dog Tavern, near the Market Place.—C.

[2] Journals of the Commons, Aug. 29, 1651.

[3] Oliver Edge, of Birch Hall Houses, in Rusholme, a captain in the Manchester regiment, who was also returning from Worcester.—O.

[4] "Whitelock's Memorials," p. 511.

[5] For the most full and accurate account of the circumstances of this execution, and indeed for the best memoir of the life of this gallant and unfortunate nobleman, the reader is referred to "The Stanley Papers," part iii., edited by the Rev. Canon Raines, and forming vols. 66, 67, and 70 of the Chetham Society's series.—H.

and 250 rank and file, in an affair of posts on Heaton Wood Green, between Manchester and Oldham, and their overthrow was completed by the country people, who rose upon them on their march, and dispersed them in every direction.[1]

During the latter period of the Commonwealth, while the "Lord-President Bradshaw" held the office of chancellor of the duchy of Lancaster,[2] the question of abolishing the court of the duchy and county palatine of Lancaster was frequently discussed in Parliament, and a number of conflicting resolutions were adopted by the House of Commons on the subject. By one of these resolutions it was determined that the court should continue till the 1st of April, 1652, "and no longer;"[3] by another, that the jurisdiction of the duchy and county palatine of Lancaster should be continued six months after the 1st of April; by a third, that it should be continued till the 1st of April, 1653;[4] by a fourth, that the abolition of the jurisdiction should be postponed *sine die*, on the petition of the justices of the peace and two grand juries assembled at the assizes.[5] In 1659 the subject was resumed, when it was resolved that the seal for the county palatine of Lancaster should be brought into the House on the 1st of November, and then cancelled, no more to be used, and that the profits of the seal should be sequestrated for the use of the Commonwealth. In February, 1660, the vote touching the cancelling of the seal of the county palatine was made null and void,[7] and an Act was introduced, and subsequently passed, for "reviving the jurisdiction of the Counties Palatine of Lancaster and Chester,[8] and the court of the Duchy Chamber of Lancaster."

After dissolving the Long Parliament by "push of pike," April 20th, 1653,[9] Cromwell, having been appointed "LORD PROTECTOR" of the Commonwealth (Dec. 16th, 1653), summoned a new Parliament on his own authority, without the intervention of the freeholders or other electors, as appears from the following document addressed to William West, Esq., the representative of Lancashire in the "Barebones Parliament:"—

"Forasmuch as upon the dissolution of the late parliament it became necessary that the peace, safety, and good government of this Commonwealth should be provided for; and in order thereunto persons fearing God and of approved fidelity and honesty are by myself, with the advice of my Council of Officers, nominated, to whom the great charge and trust of so weighty affairs is to be committed; and having good assurance of your love to and courage for God, and the interest of his cause, and of the good people of this commonwealth:—

"I, Oliver Cromwell, captain general and commander-in-chief of all the armies and forces raised and to be raised within this Commonwealth, do hereby summon and require you, William West, Esquire (being one of the persons nominated), personally to be and appear at the Council Chamber, commonly known or called by the name of the Council Chamber in Whitehall, within the city of Westminster, upon the 4th day of July next ensuing the date hereof, then and there to take upon you said trust, unto which you are hereby called and appointed to serve as a member for the county of Lancaster, and hereof you are not to fail. Given under my hand and seal the 6th day of June, 1653.

In 1657 an Act of Parliament was passed for "an assessment upon England at the rate of £60,000 by the moneth for three moneths, from the 25th day of March, 1657, to the 24th day of June then next ensuing." Each county was assessed in a certain sum per month, and a body of commissioners was appointed in each county who had to superintend the collection of this amount of money. The county of Lancaster was assessed in the sum of £800 per month, the commissioners[10] being—

Sir Richard Houghton, baronet; Richard Shuttleworth, Gilbert Ireland, Richard Holland, Ralph Ashton, Peter Bould, Richard Standish, Edmund Hopwood, Lawrence Rostern, John Starkey, Thomas Braddil, Richard Haworth, Edward More, Richard Radcliff, John Bradshaw, Tho. Birch, Jeremiah Aspinwal, Robert Maudsley, Edward Robinson, John Fox, Peers Leigh, James Duckenfield, Nicholas Shuttleworth, William Hilton, Henry Porter, Thomas Fell, William West, esquires; Edmund Werden, William Patten, Evan Wall, Christopher White, George Piggot, Thomas Clayton, gent; Richard Ashton, esq; Alexander Norres, Roger Gillibrand, gent; John Nowell, Ralph Livesey, esquires; Jo. Livesey, Peter Sergeant, William Knipe, Thomas Cole (*sic*), Adam Sands, gent; Randle Sharples, esq.; John Case, Thomas Westmore, Hugh Cooper, John Cliff, William Swarberick, Thomas Jones, gent.

---

[1] For many details of the civil war as relating to Lancashire, see the "Civil War Tracts, &c., 1642-1651," edited by Geo. Ormerod, Esq. (vol. 2 of the Chetham Society's series).

[2] The Act constituting Bradshaw Chancellor of the Duchy of Lancaster was passed July 19th, 1649, and the office, when others were abolished elsewhere, was, on his account, specially retained, and on the 2nd April, 1652, secured to him. On the 16th September, 1653, Parliament further enacted that the continuance of the palatinate power of Lancaster should be vested in him.—C.

[3] Journals of the House of Commons, Nov. 26, 1651.

[4] Journals of the House of Commons, Jan. 1, 1652-3.

[5] April 8, 1653.

[6] August 5, 1659.

[7] Feb. 27, 1659-60.

[8] March 14, 1659-60.

[9] This was the memorable occasion when Cromwell having displaced the Speaker, pointed to the mace lying on the table of the House, and ordered Lieut.-Colonel Charles Worsley, who had entered with two files of musketeers, to "take away that bauble." Worsley was a Lancashire man, who resided at Platt, in Rusholme, and was nominated by Cromwell as representative for Manchester in the Parliament summoned to meet on Sept. 3rd, 1654. It is not stated what became of the mace, but as the Journals of the House of Commons show that when Parliament reassembled a message was sent to Lieut.-Colonel Worsley for it, there is every probability that it had remained in his custody.—C.

[10] "Local Gleanings Lanc. and Ches.," v. ii. p. 153-4.—C.

By another Act passed in the same session, it was enacted that an assessment at the rate of £35,000 per month should be raised throughout England, commencing on the 24th June, 1657. Of this the county of Lancaster was to raise £466 13s. 4d. per month. The same commissioners were appointed for Lancashire, with the addition of Colonel Edward Salmon.

The assumption of more than regal powers by Cromwell became the subject of strong animadversion, while it was justified by the devoted creatures of the Lord-Protector, who carried their adulation so far as to make him an offer of the crown. He had too much policy to fall into this snare; but the evening of his life was clouded with painful apprehensions of plots and treasons, the general attendants upon usurped power; and, after a short sickness, he expired on the 3rd of September, 1658. On the death of the Lord-Protector, Sept. 3rd, 1658, President Bradshaw was elevated to the seat of President of the Council, and on the 3rd June, 1659, was appointed, with Serjeants Fountain and Tyrrel, a Commissioner of the Great Seal, an office from which he asked to be relieved on account of his growing infirmities. During his last illness he adhered steadily to his former principles, and declared that, were the king to be tried again, he

PRESIDENT BRADSHAW.

would be the first man to sit as his judge. Having survived to the eve of the great changes that were now approaching, he died on the 31st of October, 1659, on which day his death was thus announced in the "Diurnalls:"—

"WHITEHALL, Oct. 31, 1659.—This day it pleased God here to put a period to the life of the Lord *Bradshaw*, after a year's lingering under a fierce and most tedious quartan ague, which in all probability could not have taken him away yet a while, had he not by his indefatigable affection toward the public affairs and safety, in time of danger, wasted himself with extraordinary labours."[1]

President Bradshaw was pompously interred in Westminster Abbey; but after the restoration his remains were exhumed, and exposed on the gibbet in company with those of Cromwell and Ireton.

The feeble sway of Richard Cromwell, the successor of his father, revived the prospects of the Stuarts, which had never been wholly extinguished. An extensive league was formed amongst the Cavaliers in different parts of the kingdom, the object of which was to make a simultaneous effort to recover the crown for King Charles. With this object, the son of Sir Marmaduke Langdale was

[1] Harl. MSS. cod. 1929, fo. 26.

appointed to command in Lancashire and the other northern counties; Major General Massey in the midland counties; and Lord Byron in the south; but in none of these places did the enterprise succeed. Sir George Booth, of Dunham Massey, a zealous supporter of the Parliamentary interest in the early stages of the civil wars, and one of the deputy-lieutenants for Lancashire, issued a declaration about the same time in Cheshire, for " a free Parliament, legally chosen " by the votes of the electors, not called by individual summons, and for a government upon a settled foundation of "religion, liberty, and property." To this end Sir George entered into correspondence with Mr. Ireland, Mr. Holland, and Mr. Brookes. The Earl of Derby and Sir Thomas Middleton also seconded his endeavours; and such of the gentry of Lancashire and Cheshire as desired it were allowed to assist in the deliberations[1] for restoring the monarchy. Wearied with the unsettled state of society, upwards of a thousand volunteers marched through Warrington, to rally round the standard of revolt, and Sir George was, through the influence of Mr. Cooke, a Presbyterian minister, enabled to make himself master of the city, though not of the castle, of Chester. Here he might have remained in a state of security, till the friends of the king, and the enemies of arbitrary rule, under the name of Commonwealth, had collected their forces; but in an evil hour he marched out of the city to meet General Lord Lambert. A sanguinary engagement, fought on the 19th of August, 1659, ensued at Winnington Bridge, near Northwich, which ended in the overthrow of Sir George, and his Cavaliers, whom Adam Martindale likened to "Mahomet's Angellical Cockes, made up of fire and snow," the whole force being driven from the field. One part of the fugitive army marched to the neighbourhood of Manchester, where they were dispersed; and the other to Liverpool, where an engagement took place in the public streets, equally unfavourable to the royal cause. To crown these disasters, Sir George Booth was taken prisoner, and the young Earl of Derby, who had shared in the enterprise, and whose followers, by their "boisterous merriment and profanity," are said to have given offence to Booth's "Angellical Cockes," was also captured, "in the habit of a serving man," and kept in confinement till the eve of the Restoration.

Many of the Presbyterians of Lancashire knew of the contemplated rising, but prudently abstained from committing themselves to the measures of Sir George Booth, or openly avowing sympathy with his action. Adam Martindale, himself a Lancashire man, but then rector of Rostherne, wrote—"Had I been so affected I could easily have spoiled all the sport, for I knew of it a good while before, as my revered brother, Mr. Henry Newcome, of Manchester, very well knows, and could, with a post letter, easily have prevented all." The enterprise failed through the distrust and the conflicting interests of the Episcopalians and Presbyterians engaged in it, but it nevertheless revealed the preparations that many parties were silently making for great changes, and new hope filled men's minds in consequence.

When the remnant of Booth's army reached Lancashire, bringing news of the disaster at Northwich, the leaders of the Presbyterian party were much depressed, and the Classis resolved that a public exercise, which had been appointed at Manchester, should be turned into a day of fasting and prayer. But the check was only momentary, and it was not long ere the voice of lamentation was changed to that of rejoicing and thanksgiving, for the Cheshire rising or the Cheshire race, as it had been wittily called, was soon followed by the accomplishment of the design it failed in. On the return of Lambert and his victorious army to London, a schism broke out between the officers and the Parliament, which was followed by one of those outrages upon the liberties of the House with which the country had become only too familiar. Lambert and his troops surrounded the House, which Lenthall, the speaker, and the other members were prevented by the soldiery from entering (October 13, 1659). General George Monk, "the sly fellow," as Cromwell called him, who was at the time in Scotland, on hearing of this procedure, marched with a large force to Coldstream,[2] on the Scottish border, and thence towards London. The cry of " A Free Parliament" ran like fire through the country. Not only Fairfax, who appeared in arms in Yorkshire, but the people who crowded the streets of the capital, and the sailors who manned the fleet lying in the Thames, caught up the cry. On the 3rd February, 1659-60, Monk entered the city, and from that moment the restoration of the Stuarts was inevitable. The army of the Commonwealth was rendered powerless by an adroit dispersion of the troops over the country; the secluded members of the Long Parliament—the victims of "Pride's Purge"—were restored, and that Parliament which many had thought would never have had a beginning, and afterwards that it would never have an end, was dissolved (March 16, 1659-60). The news of these events caused great rejoicing among the loyalist Presbyterians of Lancashire, and the Manchester Classis ordered a day of public thanksgiving in the churches of Manchester, Ashton-

[1] Lord Mordaunt's Letter to Charles II.
[2] It was at Coldstream that, in December, 1659, General Monk's regiment, which had been recruited chiefly among the Puritans of Scot- land, was disbanded as soldiers of the Commonwealth, and recruited as the Coldstream Guards, when the famous march began to London to effect the restoration.—C.

under-Lyne, Oldham, and Eccles, "for the late great and wonderful changes and deliverance began by God for his people in these nations." A new House of Commons—the Convention Parliament—assembled April 25th; the Declaration of Breda, in which Charles promised a general pardon, religious toleration, and satisfaction to the army, was received with a burst of national enthusiasm; and the old constitution was restored by a solemn vote of the Convention—"that according to the ancient and fundamental laws of this kingdom, the government is, and ought to be, by King, Lords and Commons." Immediately the vote was passed an invitation was sent to the exiled king to return to his people and receive his crown.[1] Within a month, Charles, after an exclusion of twelve years, had landed in England, and made a triumphal progress through the streets of London, amid the deafening cheers of a people almost delirious with joy. The shouts that rent the air were but the expression of a nation's belief that law and order would be restored, and that the government of the country at length rested upon a foundation on which peace and security, religion and liberty, might be established. Abundant favours were poured down upon General Monk (who had been the main instrument in effecting the restoration), who, by patent, dated July 7, 1660, was advanced to the dignity of the dukedom of Albemarle, and he received from his sovereign, as a further mark of his royal bounty, the ancient honor of Clitheroe, parcel of the duchy of Lancaster.

Every one rejoiced to see a calm after so long a storm, confident that the tranquillity sought for in vain during the previous twenty years of calamity and confusion would now be enjoyed. In no part of the kingdom was the exuberance of joy greater than in Lancashire, where Prelatists and Puritans, Episcopalians and Presbyterians, alike forgot their controversies, their animosities, and their jealousies, and men who had fought for and upheld the republic marched side by side with those who had bled and suffered for the king, in the excess of their newly-awakened loyalty. In Manchester it was ordered that the king should be publicly proclaimed and prayed for (May 12th), to the infinite joy of the townsmen—one of whom, John Hartley, of Strangeways, in the fullness of his liberality, gave £10 for his majesty's use—but to the great mortification of some of the Cromwellian soldiers who had been billeted upon the inhabitants. Henry Newcome, who a week before, as he tells us, had prayed for the king "by periphrases," delivered a fervid address in the Collegiate Church, in which he exhorted his hearers "to carry their rejoicings carefully," and prayed that the joy of that great and glorious day "might not be blemished by the intemperance of a single person," words that were remembered, and had a chastening influence on those who heard him. The example of Manchester, so far at least as the demonstrations of loyalty were concerned, was followed by Ashton-under-Lyne, Bolton, Bury, Rochdale, and other towns, though it is doubtful if the same degree of sobriety was manifested by the people in their festivities, for the "malignants" of Wigan drank the loving cup to its very dregs, and the whilom republicans of Rochdale, in a frenzy of delight, killed a luckless drummer-boy, by, as they said, "the miscarriage of their muskets;" and even the inhabitants of Puritan Manchester, a few months later, in spite of the pious exhortations of Newcome and the stern remonstrances of the warden, Heyricke, made the occasion of the coronation "an engine to intemperance and excess," and in their delirium of joy "fell a-drinking of healths" to testify their love and loyalty to the restored king.

[1] In its eagerness to secure the restoration of the king the Convention Parliament irrevocably committed the destinies of the country to the guidance of Charles, without any condition for securing the liberties of the people. "To the king's coming without conditions," says Burnet, in the "History of his Own Times," "may well be imputed all the errors of his reign, and, it may be added, many mischiefs that followed afterwards."—C.

CHAPTER XVI.

 HE restoration of the Stuarts produced a strong sensation in the county of Lancaster, where the contest between prerogative and privilege had been carried on with a degree of zeal scarcely equalled in any other part of the kingdom. The effort to establish a commonwealth had gradually fallen into discredit. Presbyterian church-government lost its sway, and the balance of opinion, in this and in the other counties of the kingdom, once more inclined to monarchy in the government of the state, and to episcopacy in the government of the church. The return of Charles II., as already stated, was received in Lancashire with every demonstration of joy, the Presbyterians rivalling the Episcopalians in their exultations, and in the cordiality of the welcome offered to the returning sovereign. The coronation was made the occasion of extravagant rejoicings. The men of Manchester, who had been so lately in open resistance to their king, could hardly set bounds to their enthusiasm, and in their town wine flowed from the conduit, the gutters were filled with strong beer, and bonfires blazed for a whole week. To prevent the Presbyterians from possessing local power or authority, and to establish more firmly the security of the throne, the Corporation Act was passed, ordaining that in all cities, corporations, boroughs, cinque ports and other ports in England and Wales, every mayor, alderman, and common councilman, and all other corporate officers, should be obliged, in addition to the ordinary oath of allegiance and supremacy, to make a particular declaration against the solemn league and covenant, and to declare on oath that it was not lawful, on any pretence whatever, to take arms against the king; and the person making this oath was further required to aver that he abhorred that traitorous position of taking arms by the king's authority against his person, or against those commissioned by him. A more deadly blow was dealt at the Puritans in the renewal of the Act of Uniformity. That no Nonconformist might exercise the authority of a magistrate, it was required that no person should be elected or chosen into any office or place in such corporation who should not have, within one year before such election, taken the sacrament of the Lord's Supper, according to the rites and ceremonies of the Church of England.

On the 19th of May, 1662, the Act of Uniformity was passed, by which every minister, on pain of losing his ecclesiastical preferment, was obliged to conform to the worship of the Church of England, according to the Book of Common Prayer, before the feast of St. Bartholomew (Aug. 24), and to sign a declaration affirming his assent and consent to everything contained and presented by it. During the civil war episcopacy was abolished and presbyterianism established in its stead. Large numbers of the clergy—some six thousand or more—had been driven from their benefices, and their places supplied by ministers who abhorred episcopacy and rejected the government and ritual of the Church of England. On the arrival of St. Bartholomew's Day two thousand of these ministers resigned their benefices, preferring poverty with a clear conscience to affluence with a mind tortured by the reproach of having sacrificed what they conceived to be their duty to their Maker to their worldly advancement. The following form of ecclesiastical ejectment was sent by the Lord Bishop of Chester to the churchwardens of Garstang, for the removal of the Rev. Isaac Ambrose, and similar notices were served upon the churchwardens in the other parishes or chapelries where the minister had refused to conform:—

"Whereas in a late Act of Parliament for uniformitie, it is enacted that every parson, vicar, curate, lecturer, or other ecclesiasticall person, neglecting or refusing, before the Feast Day of St. Bartholomew, 1662, to declare openly before their respective congregations, his assent and consent to all things contained in the booke of common prayer established by the said act, *ipso facto* be deposed, and that every person not being in holy orders by episcopall ordination, and every parson, vicar, curate, lecturer, or other ecclesiasticall person, failing in his subscription to a declaration mentioned in the said act to be subscribed before the Fast Day of St. Bartholomew, 1662, shall be utterly disabled, and *ipso facto* deprived, and his place be void, as if the person so failing be naturally dead. And whereas Isaac Ambrose, late vicar of Garstang, in the county of Lancaster, hath neglected to declare and subscribe according to the tenor of the said act, I doe therefore declare the church of Garstang to be now void, and doe strictly charge the said Isaac Ambrose, late vicar of the said church, to forbear preaching, lecturing, or officiating, in the said church, or elsewhere in the diocese of Chester. And the Churchwardens of the said parish of Garstang are hereby required (as by duty they are bound) to secure and preserve the said parish church of Garstang from any invasion or intrusion of the said Isaac Ambrose, disabled and deprived as above said by the said act, and the churchwardens are also required upon sight hereof to show this order to the said Isaac Ambrose, and cause the same to be published the next Sunday after in the Parish Church of Garstang, before the congregation, as they will answer the contrary.—Given under my hand this 29th day of August 1662.

"GEO. CESTRIENS.

"To the Churchwardens of Garstang, in the County Palatine of Lancaster."

The ejected and silenced ministers in Lancashire amounted to sixty-seven, of whom the following are the names:—

The Rev. Robert Towne, Alkrington ; Rev. Thomas Jollie, Altham ; Rev. James Talbot, Alkholme ; Rev. Thomas Crompton, Astley Chapel, parish of Leigh ; Rev. John Harrison, Ashton-under-Lyne ; Rev. James Woods, Ashton-in-Makersfield ; Rev. John Wright, M.A., Billinge ; Rev. Robert Birch, Birch Chapel ; Rev. Thomas Holland, Blackley ; Rev. Richard Astley, Blackrod ; Rev. Richard Goodwin, M.A., vicar of Bolton ; Rev. Robert Park, Bolton ; Rev. Samuel Mather, M.A., Burton Wood ; Rev. Mr. Dury, Bradshaw ; Rev. Philip Bennett, Cartmel ; Rev. Mr. Camerford, Cartmel ; Rev. Henry Welch, Chorley ; Rev. James Woods jun., Chowbent ; Rev. John Leaver, Cockey Chapel ; Rev. Mr. Lowe, rector of Croston ; Rev. James Hiet, Croston ; Rev. Thomas Whitehead, vicar of Dalton ; Rev. John Tilsley, M.A., vicar of Dean ; Rev. John Angier, Denton ; Rev. James Holm, Denton ; Rev. Jonathan Schofield, Douglas Chapel ; Rev. Edmund Jones, vicar of Eccles ; Rev. Peter Atkinson, sen., Ellel Chapel ; Rev. Peter Atkinson, jun., Ellel Chapel ; Rev. Isaac Ambrose, vicar of Garstang ; Rev. Wm. Leigh, M.A., Gorton Chapel ; Rev. Mr. Bullock, Hambleton ; Rev. James Walton, Horwich ; Rev. Mr. Sandford, Harwood ; Rev. Peter Aspinall, Heaton ; Rev. George Thomasson, Heywood Chapel ; Rev. James Bradshaw, Hindley, Wigan Parish ; Rev. William Bell, M.A., vicar of Huyton ; Rev. Henry Pendlebury, M.A., Holcombe Chapel ; Rev. Peter Naylor, Haughton Chapel ; Rev. Nehemiah Ambrose, vicar of Kirkby ; Doctor William Marshall, vicar of Lancaster ; Rev. Thos. Drinckal, Lindale Chapel ; Rev. John Fogg, Liverpool ; Rev. Timothy Smith, Longridge Chapel ; Rev. Joseph Harrison, Lund Chapel ; Rev. Henry Newcome, M.A., Manchester ; Rev. Mr. Richardson, Manchester ; Rev. John Mallinson, vicar of Melling ; Rev. Thomas Gregg, St. Helens Chapel ; Rev. Mr. White, Melling ; Rev. Nathaniel Baxter, M.A., vicar of St. Michael-le-Wyre ; Rev. Mr. Kippax, New Church in Rossendale ; Rev. John Walker, Newton Heath Chapel ; Rev. Robert Constantine, Oldham ; Rev. Nathaniel Heywood, vicar of Ormskirk ; Rev. Thomas Pyke, rector of Radcliffe ; Rev. Roger Baldwin, Raynford ; Rev. Samuel Newton, Rivington ; Rev. Robert Bath, vicar of Rochdale ; Rev. Richard Holbrook, Salford ; Rev. Joseph Thompson, Sefton ; Rev. Cuthbert Harrison, Singleton ; Rev. Paul Latham, Standish ; Rev. Nicholas Smith, Tatham ; Rev. Thomas Crompton, M.A., Toxteth Park ; Rev. [Zach.] Taylor, Turton ; Rev. Mr. Lampitt, Ulverstone ; Rev. Henry Finch, vicar of Walton ; Rev. Robt. Eaton, Walton ; Rev. Michael Briscoe, Walmsley Chapel ; Rev. Robert Yates, rector of Warrington ; Rev. Charles Hotham, rector of Wigan.[1]

At the time when the Act of Uniformity took effect, there were several candidates for the ministry in this county, who had no fixed place, but who continued Nonconformists. These were Mr. Thomas Waddington, Mr. James Haddock, Mr. Cuthbert Halsall, Mr. John Eddlestone, Mr. Thomas Kay, afterwards at Hoghton Tower, and Mr. John Crompton, afterwards minister of Cockey Chapel.

The passing of the Act of Uniformity effected greater and more sudden changes in the religious aspect of the Church than had occurred at any former period. The Reformation was accomplished gradually and without any great displacement of the clergy, and the expulsions during the civil war period, though much more numerous, extended over a series of years; but that on St. Bartholomew's Day was sudden and complete—it was the definite exclusion of a great party, that, among much fanaticism, included in its ranks many eminent divines and earnest painstaking men, who had diffused through the country a greater amount of religious vitality than had perhaps ever been experienced before.

That the laity of the Nonconformist persuasion might not stand upon a more advantageous footing than their clergy, Lord-Chancellor Clarendon, to whom the age in which he lived, and after ages, were mainly indebted for these rigorous enactments, procured a bill to be passed into law, called the Conventicle Act (1664), by which every person above the age of sixteen years, being present at any meeting or conventicle for religious purposes, when more than five persons were assembled and where the service was performed in any other manner than according to the liturgy used by the Church of England, became liable to a penalty of £5, or three months' imprisonment, for the first offence; £10, or six months' imprisonment, for the second offence; and transportation to the plantations for the third offence, unless a fine of £100 was paid; and persons suffering conventicles to be held in their houses or outhouses were liable to the same punishment. This Act operated with great severity in Lancashire, and the sufferings of the people in many districts were extreme. Assemblies were often held at midnight, to escape the rigours of the law; and as five persons assembled together for prayer constituted a conventicle, it frequently happened that the members of the family were obliged either to forego their duty or to subject themselves to the persecution of the times. The thirst for revenge had been roused by the tyranny of the

[1] The venerable Oliver Heywood, a name held in high estimation amongst the Nonconformists, was a native of Little Lever, in the parish of Bolton, in this county ; but at the time of the passing of the Act of Uniformity he was settled at Coley Chapel, in the parish of Halifax, and was ejected from that place.

Presbyterians in their hour of triumph, and to fill up the measure of intolerance the Five-mile Act[1] was introduced in 1665 (17 Car. II. c. 2) by which any Nonconformist minister, of whatever denomination, was prohibited from dwelling or coming within five miles of any corporate town, or other place where he had been minister, or had preached, after the Act of Oblivion, unless he first took the following oath: "I do swear that it is not lawful, upon any pretence whatsoever, to take arms against the king,[2] and that I do abhor the traitorous position of taking arms by his authority, against his person or against those that are commissioned by him, in pursuance of such commissions; and that I will not at any time endeavour any alteration of government, either in Church or State." It was further enacted that any schoolmaster who should refuse the oath should be incapable of teaching any public school, and any two justices were empowered to commit to prison any person infringing the enactments of this rigorous law.[3] The sufferings of the ejected ministers and their people were extreme, and large numbers of persons suffered on account of their religion in different parts of the kingdom. Manchester seems, however, to have been exceptionally favoured, for from the circumstance that it was neither a corporate town or borough returning a member to Parliament, it escaped to some extent the disabilities imposed by the Act, and became consequently a place of refuge for ejected ministers from other parts of the county. In Lancashire, where the Catholics were so numerous, a preponderance was given to that party, and the dissenting interest was reduced to the lowest point of depression. Several of the ministers, incapable of enduring the privations to which they were exposed, or disinclined to subject themselves to the penalties of the law, conformed to the requirements of the Church, and of that number were the following in Lancashire: Mr. Bradley Hayhurst, of Leigh; Mr. Joshua Ambrose, of West Derby; Mr. William Cole, of Preston; Mr. William Colburn, of Ellinburgh [? Ellenbrook]; Mr. William Loben, of Oldham; Mr. James Booker, of Blackley; Mr. William Aspinwall, of Formby; Mr. Briars, of Heapy; Mr. Fisher, of Kirkham; Mr. Jacques, of Bolton-le-Sands; Mr. Jessop, of Winwick; and Mr. Robert Dewhurst, of Whitworth Chapel.[4] "The great body of the Dissenters, however, remained steadfast to their principles," says Neale, "and the Church gained neither reputation nor numbers." So hot was the persecution that the Lancashire Classis discontinued their meetings from the first year of the new king's reign; and those assemblies which had been held so frequently in the period between 1646 and the dissolution of the Commonwealth (1660) were not resumed till 1693, when they were held under the designation of Meetings of Ministers of the United Brethren within the county of Lancaster, the Rev. Henry Newcome filling the office of moderator, and Charles Sager that of scribe, at the first of the resumed meetings for the parishes of Manchester, Prestwich, Flixton, Eccles, and Ashton-under-Lyne.

The passing of the Act of Uniformity dispelled the anticipations of toleration which Charles II.'s declaration from Breda had seemed to foreshadow. For nearly ten years the sequestrated ministers were exposed to the danger of fine and imprisonment, and excited by alternate hopes and fears, though many of them were sheltered under the protection of powerful friends. But better days were in store, and after the fall of Clarendon, who had been their chief persecutor, the king issued a declaration of indulgence in religion (15th March, 1671-2), in which he declared his "will and pleasure to be, that the execution of all and all manner of penal laws in matters ecclesiastical, against whatsoever sort of Nonconformists or recusants, be immediately suspended, and they are hereby suspended." The declaration was an exercise of the kingly prerogative, for Parliament was not sitting at the time, and the Nonconformists were consequently placed in a somewhat perplexing position. They yearned for religious freedom, but they had loudly proclaimed their adherence to Parliamentary government. To their minds the suspension of the law by the royal prerogative was an unconstitutional proceeding, and to avail themselves of it was to admit the dispensing power of the king. A ferment immediately arose. Some of the more intolerant believed they saw in it an opening for the introduction of Popery, and the eminent Nonconformist, Philip Henry, wrote that the clemency of the king had put him in a "trilemma." The scruples of the Lancashire ministers seem to have been readily overcome. The king's declaration was made on March 15th, intelligence of it reached the county on the 18th, and on the 15th April following the first licence in Lancashire was taken out for Henry Newcome, of Manchester, first for his own house and afterwards, on account of its incapacity, for a barn in the neighbourhood of Shudehill. Altogether about 3,500 licences were issued, of which 185 were for Lancashire,[1] the last of them being for the house of Mr. Buxton, in Manchester, dated February 3, 1672-3. The great majority of the applications were for Presbyterian teachers or places of meeting, and thus, says Dr. Halley, "amidst many fears, anxieties, and prayers was founded what may be called the 'old dissent of Lancashire.'" The following copy of a licence issued for a place of meeting in Warrington will serve as an illustration of the printed form used, the words in italics being written in :—

"CHARLES, by the Grace of God King of England, Scotland, France, and Ireland, Defender of the Faith, &c. To all Mayors, Bayliffs, Constables, and other Our Officers and Ministers, Civil and Military, whom it may concern, greeting. In pursuance of Our Declaration of the 15th of March, 1671-2, We have allowed, and We do hereby allow of *a Roome or Roomes in the Court house of Warington in Our County of Lancaster* to be a Place for the Use of Such as do not conform to the Church of England who are of the Perswasion commonly called *Presbyterian* to meet and assemble in, in order to their publick Worship and Devotion. And all and singular Our Officers and Ministers, Ecclesiastical, Civil and Military, whom it may concern, are to take due notice hereof: And they and every of them are hereby strictly charged and required to hinder any Tumult or Disturbance, and to protect them in their said Meetings and Assemblies. Given at Our Court at Whitehall the *30th* day of *Septembr* in the 24th year of Our Reign,[3] 1672.—By His Majesties Command,   "ARLINGTON."

On the restoration of Charles II. the intention was formed to institute a new order of knighthood, as a reward to the faithful adherents of the house of Stuart during the period of their adversity;[4] and the following persons in the county of Lancaster were judged fit to be made "Knights of the Royal Oak," each of whom was in possession of an estate of the estimated annual value affixed to his name :—

Thomas Holt, Esq.	£1000	Thomas Preston, Esq.	£2000
Thomas Greenhalgh, Esq.	1000	Thomas Farington of Worden, Esq.	1000
Colonel — Kirkby of Upper Rawcliffe	1000	Thomas Fleetwood of Penwortham, Esq.	1000
Robert Holte, Esq.	1000	John Girlington, Esq.	1000
Edmund Asheton, Esq.	1000	William Stanley, Esq.	1000
Christopher Banester, Esq.	1000	Edward Tyldesley of Fox Hall, Esq.	1000
Francis Anderton, Esq.	1000	Thomas Stanley, Esq.	1000
Col. James Anderton	1500	Richard Boteler of Out Rawcliffe, Esq.	1000
Roger Nowell, Esq.	1000	John Ingleton, Esq., sen.	1000
Henry Norris, Esq.	1200	—— Walmesley of Dunkenhalgh, Esq.	2000

This order was intended by Charles as a reward to several of his followers, and the knights were to wear a silver medal, with a device of the king in the oak, pendant to a ribbon about their necks; but, on reflection, it was thought proper to abandon the intention, from the apprehension that such an order of knighthood might create heats and animosities, and open those wounds afresh which it was thought prudent should be healed.[5]

The time had now arrived when the feudal system, which had existed for upwards of six hundred years,[6] with various modifications, was to be finally undertaken, and by the 12th of Charles II., cap. 24 (1660), the tenures of knights' service, chivalry, escuage, petit serjeanty, villeinage, &c., were taken away, and the tenures of fee-simple, fee-tail, and copyhold, substituted in their place. The land was relieved of its charges, and in lieu of the revenue raised in the Court of Ward and Liveries duties were imposed on beer and ale.[7] In the same reign the militia laws were so far altered as to place that great constitutional citizen-military body more immediately under the power and control of the crown than they had been in times past" (1661). In 1761 the aggregate number of the militia was swelled to thirty thousand eight hundred and forty,[9] of which Lancashire was required to furnish eight hundred; and in 1802 the total number of the militia was increased to forty thousand nine hundred and sixty-three,[10] the quota for Lancashire being then fixed, as it now stands, at two thousand four hundred and thirty-nine. The land-tax, originally a monthly assessment imposed in the time of the Commonwealth, was occasionally levied in the reign of Charles II. In 1692, a new valuation of estates was made throughout the kingdom, when it was fixed that Lancashire should be charged with five in 518 parts. In the year 1798 this annual tax was made perpetual, subject to redemption and purchase by the owners of estates.

On Friday the 6th of February, 1685, Charles II. died at Whitehall, poisoned, as some people believed, but more probably from apoplexy, the consequence of his excesses, "leaving nothing for

[1] The number of licences granted for the neighbouring county of Chester was 83.—C.
[2] "Puritanism and Nonconformity in Lancashire," 2 edit. p. 411.—C.
[3] It was the practice to count the regnal year from the death of Charles I., in 1649.—C.
[4] Noble, in his "Memoirs of the Cromwell Family," says that Henry Cromwell, "first cousin, one remove, to Oliver, Lord Protector," was among the number, and adds that "as he knew the name of Cromwell would not be very grateful in the court of Charles the Second, he disused it and styled himself plain Henry Williams, Esq., by which name he was set down in the list of such persons as were to be made Knights of the Royal Oak."—C.

[5] Banks's *Honores Anglicani*, from which it appears that the total number of knights meant to have been created in all England was 687.
[6] See chap. ii.
[7] The statute which accomplished this change is described by Blackstone as "a greater acquisition to the civil property of this kingdom than even Magna Charta itself, since that only pruned the luxuriances that had grown out of military tenures, and thereby preserved them in vigour; but the statute of King Charles extirpated the whole, and demolished both root and branches.—C.
[8] 13 Charles II. cap. 6.
[9] 1 Geo. III.
[10] 43 Geo. III. cap. 90.

immortality but the fame of weakness even in vice." Idler and voluptuary as he had been, the politeness of the gentleman continued to the last, and with almost his last breath he apologised to the watchers for the trouble he was giving in keeping them around him.   His reign was marked by many legislative enactments of the gravest kind, and forms an important era in the county and the kingdom.   If, under his rule, Parliament sanctioned the Act of Uniformity, the Five Mile Act, and the Test Act, it should also be remembered that it abolished the more odious features of feudalism, enacted special laws for the advancement of commerce, and added a new security for the personal freedom of Englishmen in the Habeas Corpus Act.   When the Duke of York ascended the throne under the title of James II., to allay the scruples of the nation, he solemnly promised the Privy Council to preserve the laws inviolate, and maintain the government in Church and State as by law established, a pledge that was welcomed by the whole country with enthusiasm, and in Lancashire, as Macaulay tells us,[1] the people of Wigan, true to the traditions of their town, made themselves conspicuous not only by the extravagance of their loyalty, but by the boldness of their address, in which they assured the king that they would defend him "against all plotting Ahithophels and rebellious Absaloms."   "We have the word of a king, and a king was never worse than his word" was the general cry; but the worthlessness of James's word was soon apparent, for within three days of his accession to the crown, his government had committed an illegal act.   The arbitrary measures of the sovereign excited alarm and distrust among the people at large, and their indignation found vent when, on the 8th June, 1688, the seven bishops, of whom one—John Lake, Bishop of Chichester, was identified with Lancashire, having been previously rector of Prestwich and incumbent of the parochial chapelry of Oldham— having declined to publish an illegal Declaration, and championed the cause of the national faith and the national freedom, were conveyed to the Tower between lines of weeping men and weeping women, who prayed aloud for their safety and knelt to receive their blessing, and a few days later appeared as criminals at the bar of the King's Bench.   This incident in the struggle of England against the aggression of England's king served to hasten the impending crisis, and thoughtful men—Conformists and Nonconformists alike—began to look with earnest desire to the accession of Mary, the elder daughter and heiress of James, then espoused to the Prince of Orange.   Ere long communications more or less direct were opened with the prince by those who had found refuge at his court, and ultimately an invitation to appear in England with a body of troops was given.   A side light is thrown upon the state of feeling in Lancashire at the time by some of the entries in Henry Newcome's diary.   Thus we read:—

1688. October 7. Now was the amazing news of the Prince of Orange designing to come among us.
    October 8. I went to Grange this day, and met my Lord Delamere at Hulme.—They none of them minded the news, and seem to be less concerned and less afraid than I am.
    October 16. Things are dark and in great confusion. The Lord be merciful to us!
    November 9. The news came this morning of the landing of the Dutch in the west. An astonishing providence. Our refuge is in God, and in Him only.
    November 14. We heard whispers of sad things to-day.
    November 16. We had a private day on the sad occasion of the confusion in the nation and country. Lord Delamere came to town soldier-like. I was affected with a great passion of tears to see my Lord Delamere ride by.
    November 28. Lord Delamere with his company went from Nottingham in a sad season. I was discouraged this night on the probable cause for it, in the news about his being set upon, and either killed or wounded.
    November 30. We heard the news, amazing and surprising, of the general revolt of most of the great ones from King James.
    December 2. We heard the news of a treaty, which was what we prayed for, and the only way likely to heal us.
    December 24. We waited upon my Lady Bland (of Hulme) to see my Lord Delamere, whom we found preserved, and wonderfully revived upon this strange revolution.

The brief reign of James II. was terminated by his abdication and the "peaceful revolution" which placed William of Orange and the Princess Mary upon the throne.

The progress of William III. on his way to Ireland, previous to the battle of the Boyne, lay through the southern part of Lancashire; on the 11th of June, 1690, his majesty, attended by Prince George of Denmark, the Duke of Ormond, the Earls of Manchester, Oxford, and Scarborough, and other persons of distinction, arrived in Liverpool, whence, with the troops that had been encamped at Wallasey Leasowes, on the Wirral shore at the opposite side of the Mersey, he embarked three days later, and landed at Carrickfergus, from which place he advanced southwards, and on the 1st July defeated James II. on the banks of the Boyne; a battle momentous in its consequences, and ever memorable in Irish history.   The expulsion of the Stuarts by the House of Orange produced violent discontent amongst the subjects of the new king of the Roman Catholic persuasion, and in no part of the country was that feeling more powerful than in Lancashire.   The doctrine of "killing no murder" inculcated so freely by the Royalists during the latter part of the protectorate of Oliver Cromwell, was now revived, and a conspiracy was formed, called "The

[1] Macaulay's History of England vi., p. 476.—C.

Lancashire Plot," for removing King William from the throne by the hand of the assassin. The history of this event is involved in considerable obscurity, and even the existence of the plot has been called in question. Suspicion had been excited by the landing of several Irishmen on the coast, and by the discovery of arms in transit from London to Lancashire. The Catholics of the county opened communications with the Irish supporters of King James, and Lord Molyneux, Sir William Gerard, Sir Thomas Clifton,[1] and other of the leading Papists, set about arming their tenantry in defence of the cause of the absent king. On hearing of this, Lord Delamere issued a proclamation calling upon the friends of liberty and the new government to meet him on Bowdon Downs, when nearly forty thousand armed men, partly Low Churchmen and partly Nonconformists, responded to the call—a demonstration that quelled the spirit of revolt among the Jacobites, and preserved the tranquillity of Lancashire. The Irish party in favour of James II., having received encouragement from the French ministry, engaged a man of the name of Dumont to assassinate the reigning monarch of England; and a party in Lancashire, more distinguished for their daring than for their strength, swelled the number of the conspirators. As early as the 18th of October, 1689, a communication was made to the Secretary of State for the Home Department, by the magistrates assembled at quarter sessions of the peace, held by adjournment in Manchester, to the effect that many of the branches of the Roman Catholic families in this county had absconded, and that in their absence several boxes, with scarlet cloaks, pistols, and swords, intended for their use, had been received in Lancashire.

On the 16th of May, 1690, Robert Dodsworth, of Crosby Ravensworth, in the county of Westmorland, deposed upon oath, before Lord Chief Justice Holt, that certain Roman Catholic gentlemen and others in Lancashire and the neighbourhood, whom he named, had entered into a treasonable conspiracy to make war against the Government, with a design to restore King James, and that the following officers were known to him as having received commissions for the purpose of raising troops to carry out the enterprise:—

UNDER COLLONEL THOMAS TILDESLEY[2] (of Myerscough Lodge).
Lieutenant Collonel Girlington, a Protestant (of Thurland Castle).
Capt. Thomas Tildesley (of Fox Hall[3]—nephew of Colonel Tyldesley).
Capt. Ralph Tildesley (younger brother of Colonel Tyldesley).
Capt. Richard Butler (of Rawcliffe).
Capt. Henry Butler (son of Richard of Rawcliffe).
Capt. Alexander Butler, a Protestant.
Capt. Thomas Carus (of Halton).
Lieut. William Westby (third son of Thomas Westby of Mowbreck).
Mr. Goodwin, the Priest, was to raise a Troop at his own Charge, and to put in Officers.
Lieut. George Carus, of Sellet (son of Chris. Carus, of Halton).
Lieut. Thomas Butler (younger son of Henry of Rawcliffe).
Cornet Knipe, Protestant.
Cornet Coale, Protestant (of Beaumont Cote).

UNDER COLLONEL TOWNLEY (of Townley).
Lieut. Coll. Standish (of Standish).

Capt. Burley or Barlow.
Cornet Woolfall (Richard Woolfall of Woolfall in Huyton).
Quarter Master Duckett.

UNDER COLLONEL MOLYNEUX.
Lieut. Coll. Gerrard (son to Sir William Gerrard of Bryn).
Capt. Westby (of Mowbreck).
Capt. Harrington (of Huyton-hey).
Capt. Molyneux (? of New Hall in Huyton).
Capt. Massey (of Puddington).
Capt. (George) Penny.
Capt. Carus, Protestant.
Lieut. Richard Stanley (of Great Eccleston).
Lieut. Penalt (? Pennant), or such like Name, he lives in Wales, and came into my Place.
Cornet Carus.
There is also one Coll. Tempest (? of Bracewell), in Yorkshire.

UNDER COLL. DALTON, I know none.

Several of these Officers I have it from their own Mouths, the others only by hearsay.

According to Bishop Burnet, a conspiracy was formed contemporaneously with this Lancashire " plot" by the Earl of Clarendon, the Bishop of Ely, Lord Preston, Mr. Graham, and William Penn, the celebrated Quaker, to restore the deposed king; and Lord Preston, Mr. Ashton, and Mr. Elliot were despatched to France to communicate to him the design and to obtain his co-operation. The Government having come to the knowledge of this mission the parties engaged in it were arrested on shipboard, and amongst their papers were found " a declaration to be published when the French should have succeeded at sea," and " the result of a conference between certain lords and gentlemen for the restoration of King James." In January, 1691, Lord Preston and Mr. Ashton were brought to trial at the Old Bailey on a charge of high treason, and, being both convicted, were sentenced to be executed as traitors. Mr. Ashton, who displayed an uncompromising firmness, underwent the penalty of the law; but Lord Preston contrived to make his peace with the court and was pardoned. Against Mr. Elliot no legal proof could be adduced; Lord Clarendon, who was afterwards seized, was merely confined to his own house in the country; and the Bishop

[1] The following Treasury order, signed by William III., throws some light upon the affair:—
"At our Court at Kensington, the 1st day of February, 1694, in the sixth year of our reign.
"To Robert Lord Lucas, governor of our Tower of London, in satisfaction of so much expended and disbursed by him in sending down the gentlemen (late prisoners in the Tower) into Cheshire and Lancashire—to wit, Caryl Lord Visc. Molyneux, Sir Thomas Clifton, Sir William Gerard, Sir Rowland Stanley, Peter Lea of Lyme, Bartholomew Walmsley, and William Diccenson, Esq.—and all other charges and expenses of the guards and attendants."—C.

[2] Second son of Sir Thomas Tyldesley, the distinguished Royalist soldier who fell at Wigan Lane in 1651.—C.

[3] Fox Hall, a mansion of which scarcely a vestige now remains, stood within a few yards of the pier at South Shore, Blackpool. Within the hall was a secret chamber, which formerly went by the name of the "King's Cupboard," and which is traditionally said to have been made for James II. during the supposed plots of 1690 and 1694.—C.

of Ely, Mr. James Graham, and William Penn absconded. In the meantime a correspondence had been kept up between the deposed monarch and some of the Roman Catholics in Lancashire and Cheshire, which was conducted through the medium of one Bromfield, a Quaker, residing at Redland, near Chester, in the house of a person of the name of Wilson, who was also engaged in the conspiracy. These parties having absconded, the former to Ireland, and the latter into Lancashire, the management of the intrigue was committed to three adventurers of the names of Lunt, Gordon, and Threlfall, who had come over from Ireland with a commission from King James—Lunt being appointed to Staffordshire, Cheshire, and Lancashire; Threlfall to Yorkshire; and Gordon to Scotland. Subsequently Lunt was committed to the castle of Lancaster on a charge of high treason, founded principally upon the evidence of the captain of the ship who brought him over from Ireland, and who found some of the commissions of King James amongst the papers which he had inadvertently left in the vessel. A person of the name of Dodsworth, of whom mention has already been made, was also a witness against Lunt. Owing to a deficiency in the evidence, Lunt was acquitted at Lancaster, and the joy and exultation of the Jacobites were extreme. Uninstructed by the danger he had escaped, he became a messenger to the deposed monarch, who was then fitting out an expedition at the Hague, and on his return to England he was sent into Lancashire, plentifully supplied with arms. Having become alarmed at his own situation, he communicated all the particulars of the conspiracy to assassinate the king to his majesty's ministers; and some time after this treachery he was sent down into the country with Captain Baker to secure the conspirators. A strict search was immediately instituted at the residence of Captain Standish, of Standish Hall, where the meetings had been principally held, and in many of the houses of the other suspected persons. Here there was found a quantity of firearms and ammunition, but whether to such an amount as to indicate an intention to levy war against the king's government does not appear. According to Tindall there was found in Mr. Standish's closet the draft of a remonstrance or declaration to be printed and published on the landing of King James. When the trials came on at Manchester, to which place the assizes had been adjourned, the witnesses deposed that the persons whom they accused had received commissions from King James II. to levy troops—that they had enlisted soldiers and formed them into bodies with a design to assist the French, who were making preparations to land in this country—and that the Roman Catholics in Lancashire and Cheshire contributed towards the subsistence of the enemy, in addition to having accumulated ammunition in their own houses. In proof of these charges a witness of the name of Taffe, an Irish renegade priest, was called, who had been engaged in the conspiracy and had turned informer; but instead of giving the evidence that was expected from him he declared that the pretended "Lancashire Plot" was a villainous contrivance, concerted between Lunt and himself, to ruin certain gentlemen in this county; and the prosecution so entirely failed that the witnesses who were to support the allegations were committed to Newgate upon a charge of perjury, and of having conspired against the lives and estates of the Lancashire gentlemen.[1] The subject of the existence or non-existence of the conspiracy was afterwards brought under the consideration of Parliament, before whom both Taffe and Lunt, with a great number of other witnesses, were examined; and after an investigation, continued for ten weeks, the house resolved, "That it does appear to this house that there were sufficient grounds for the prosecution and trials of the gentlemen at Manchester. That, upon the informations and examinations before this house, it does appear that there was a dangerous plot carried on against the king and his government."[2] The majority in favour of this decision was, however, very small, the numbers being—for the resolution 133, against it 97. A similar decision was come to by the House of Lords, though the Earls of Rochester and Nottingham contended strenuously that the government had not sufficient cause to prosecute the Lancashire and Cheshire gentlemen, and entered their protest against the decision of the house. In the meantime a proclamation was issued by the Government, but without success, to apprehend Mr. Standish, of Standish, who had absconded. Notwithstanding these Parliamentary decisions, Lunt, Womball, and Wilson, three of the witnesses against the accused parties, were tried at Lancaster assizes for perjury against the Lancashire and Cheshire gentlemen, and found guilty of the charge preferred against them; and they were afterwards indicted for a conspiracy against the lives and estates of those gentlemen, but the accusers having refused to furnish the king's attorney and solicitor-general with witnesses to prove the conspiracy, the prosecution dropped, and Lunt, Womball, and Wilson were discharged. The spirit of party ran so high that Dodsworth, one of the Government witnesses, was murdered after the discovery he had made of the conspiracy; and Redman, another Government witness, shared the same fate two days afterwards.[3]

[1] John Lunt, who appears to have taken a leading part in attempting to fasten the charge of treason upon the Lancashire men, was a miscreant of the most infamous type and actuated by the basest motives; he had been a highwayman, one of his accomplices was a cattle lifter, and at the time of the trial he made such a ridiculous figure that the jury were compelled to treat his evidence as altogether unworthy of belief.—C.

[2] Journals of the House of Commons, Feb. 6, 1694-5.
[3] For details of this "Lancashire Plot" see "Jacobite Trials in Manchester in 1694," edited by Wm. Beamont, Esq., and "The Trials at Manchester in 1694," edited by the Right Rev. Alex. Goss, D.D.—being vols. 28 and 61 of the Chetham Society's series.— H.

The reign of Queen Anne, though sufficiently agitated by foreign wars was not disturbed by domestic commotions. Her successor, the Elector of Hanover, on whom the crown devolved in accordance with the provisions of the Act of Settlement, and who assumed the title of George I., was less fortunate. At the time of his accession a great change had come over the feeling of many of the Lancashire people, and the descendants of those who had resisted the authority of Charles I. were no less resolute in their determination to support the cause of his grandson, the exiled James. When George I. ascended the throne the Jacobites were very numerous, and those who were favourable to the Hanoverian succession had, on the whole, but a sorry time of it. Liverpool was the head-quarters of the Whigs, but Manchester had become the great stronghold of the Tory party. The Roman Catholics of the county consistently maintained their adherence to the exiled Stuarts; the high Churchmen and ecclesiastical Tories were greatly incensed against the Whig party which was then dominant at Court, and the Nonjurors—those who had refused to take the oath of allegiance to the new dynasty after the revolution and had been obliged to resign their preferments in the Church in consequence—were bitter in their denunciations and affirmed that under Whig administration heresy and impiety were daily gaining ground. The preaching of Dr. Sacheverell had fanned the flame of discontent; in no part of the kingdom had the preacher more determined partisans than in Lancashire; and, as a consequence, the Whigs and the Nonconformists who were in favour of the Hanoverian succession became common objects of persecution. The cry of "The Church in danger!" was raised, the cry was re-echoed from town to town; in Lancashire it was reiterated with even greater vehemence than by the Lord Mayor's chaplain, and in what had been the stronghold of Puritanism, excited mobs roamed the streets, attacked the Dissenters, plundered their homes and pulled down their meeting houses, professedly in the Church's defence.

On the 10th June, 1715, the birthday of Prince James Francis Edward (the Old Pretender), a riotous mob, headed by Thomas Syddall, a blacksmith, or according to some authorities, peruke maker, paraded the town of Manchester, wrecked the Dissenting chapel there, proclaimed the Pretender as King James the Third, and afterwards demolished the meeting-houses at Blackley, Greenacres, Monton, and other places. For these offences Syddall, the ringleader, was placed in the pillory, and afterwards imprisoned in the castle at Lancaster. About the same time a rebellion broke out in the north, and the county of Lancaster once more became involved in the horrors of civil war. The restoration of the unfortunate house of Stuart and the re-establishment of the Catholic religion were the ostensible causes of the approaching contest. To effect these objects a small army was raised in Scotland, and the Earl of Derwentwater, with a number of other peers and Scottish lairds, engaged in the desperate enterprise. The Earl of Mar was at the head of the insurgent army in Scotland, but the division which penetrated into England was led by the Earls of Derwentwater, Winton, Nithsdale, and Carnwath; and Mr. Forster, a gentleman of Northumberland, received from the Earl of Mar the command of this forlorn hope, with the commission of general. The invaders took the route of Jedburgh, but five or six hundred of the Highland foot soldiers refused to cross the frontier, and returned to the Highlands. The strong admonition conveyed by this defection in the rebel army was disregarded by its devoted leaders, and on the 31st of October, 1715, they marched to Langtown, in Cumberland, to the music of the bagpipes, at the head of a few hundred men.[1] On the 2nd of November they advanced to Penrith, on the 3rd to Appleby, on the 5th to Kendal, on the 6th to Kirkby Lonsdale, and on the 7th to Lancaster. At each of these places the Chevalier de St. George, son of James II., was proclaimed king by the style and title of James III. At Lancaster, where the rebel army remained two days, they caused the Pretender to be prayed for as king of England, and here they seized six pieces of cannon on board one of the ships in the bay. Syddall, who was undergoing imprisonment for the outrage at Manchester, was liberated, and joining the force marched southwards with it. The burgesses of Lancaster, with scarcely an exception, were favourable to the king de facto, but many of the Catholic gentry in the neighbourhood came with their tenantry and dependants to aid the cause of the Stuarts, among them Dalton of Thurnham, Hodson of Leighton, Tyldesley of Myerscough, Butler of Rawcliffe, and Walton of Cartmel. On Wednesday, the 9th of November, the horse arrived at Preston, and on the 10th they were joined by the infantry, who had halted at Garstang the preceding day. On their arrival at Preston their force had increased to about 1,600 men. They all wore cockades, the Scotch blue and white, and the English red and white. Grown confident by their uninterrupted advance they prepared to march for Manchester and Warrington; but the country had begun to rise in their front, and a congregation of Protestant dissenters, headed by their minister the Rev. James Woods,[2] had actually marched from Chowbent to Walton-le-Dale, where they were drawn up in battle array to dispute the passage of the Ribble.[3]

[1] Proceedings befor the House of Lords.   [2] Mr. Woods had been ejected from Ashton-in-Makerfield.
[3] Toulmin's "Hist. of the Dissenters.

43

Woods had concerted measures with Sir Henry Hoghton to raise and arm the Nonconformist peasantry in his neighbourhood, and had received authority to act in his Majesty's service, as appears by the following communication:—

"To the Rev. Mr. Woods, in Chowbent, for his Majesty's service.—CHARLES WILLS."

"The officers here design to march at break of day for Preston. They have desired me to raise what men I can to meet us at Preston to-morrow, so desire you to raise all the force you can—I mean lusty young fellows, to draw up on Cuerden Green, to be there by ten o'clock; to bring with them what arms they have fit for service, and scythes put in straight poles; and such as have not, to bring spades and bill-hooks for pioneering with. Pray go immediately all amongst your neighbours and give this notice.—I am, your very faithful servant,   "H. HOGHTON.
"Wigan, Nov. 11th, 1715." [1]

These heroes were armed with the implements of their husbandry, and, reversing the ancient prediction, they made swords of their ploughshares and spears of their pruning-hooks. Headed by their minister Woods they marched to Preston where they were met by similar bodies headed by the Rev. John Walker of Horwich and the Rev. John Turner of Preston.[2] Positions were assigned them by General Wills, and Woods and his people disputed the passage of the rebels across the Ribble, keeping them in check until news arrived that the king's forces were approaching, when the first care of the rebels was to barricade the streets of Preston. About mid-day on Saturday, November 12th, General Wills attacked the town with great vigour, but in the first instance with little success. On Sunday, General Carpenter, at the head of three regiments of dragoons, appeared before the town, and General Forster, finding himself completely invested, and considering his situation to be desperate, sent Colonel Oxborough with a trumpeter to sue for a capitulation. Owing to some disagreement between the Scotch and the English forces as to the surrender, the negotiation was not concluded that night, but in the meantime Lord Derwentwater and Mr. Mackintosh were delivered up as hostages, and on Monday morning, November 14th, the whole of the rebel army made an unconditional surrender.

The rebellion was now at an end, but its penalty remained to be paid. No fewer than seven lords and 1,500 men, including officers, fell into the hands of the king's forces; and the gaols of Lancaster, Preston, Manchester, Liverpool, and Chester were filled with state prisoners. Courts-martial sat upon a number of the leaders; and James Radcliffe Earl of Derwentwater, William Earl of Nithsdale, Robert Earl of Carnwath, George Earl of Winton, William Lord Widdrington, William Viscount Kenmure, and William Lord Nairn, were all impeached before the House of Lords, and found guilty of high treason. Of these noblemen, the Earl of Derwentwater and Lord Kenmure were beheaded on Tower Hill on the 24th February, 1716; Earl Nithsdale and Earl Winton escaped the blow, having found means to get out of the Tower; and Lord Widdrington, Lord Nairn, and the Earl of Carnwath were reprieved, and afterwards pardoned. Forty-nine other prisoners were convicted, and forty-seven of them paid the price of their treason by the forfeit of their lives; but General Forster and Mr. Mackintosh had sufficient address to escape out of Newgate and make their way to the Continent. Captain Charles Murray, son of the Duke of Athole, was condemned by a court-martial, but he was afterwards reprieved. Of the prisoners condemned at the "Bloody Assize," as it was called at Lancaster, sixteen were hanged at Preston, five at Wigan, five at Manchester—among them the blacksmith or peruke maker Syddall—four at Garstang, four at Liverpool, and nine at Lancaster; and Colonel Oxborough, Mr. Gascoigne, the Rev. Mr. Paul, and John Hall, Esq., were hanged at Tyburn.[3]

On the day of the surrender of the insurgent forces at Preston a great battle was fought at Dunblane, between the Duke of Argyle and the Earl of Mar, in which, as in most engagements of doubtful issue, both armies claimed the victory; and on the 22nd of December, 1715, the Chevalier de St. George, under an expectation that all the subjects of the realm were ready to take up arms in his favour, landed from the Continent in Scotland. This hope was woefully disappointed, for after spending a month in issuing proclamations, by one of which it was announced that his coronation would take place on the 23rd January, he found it expedient to quit the kingdom. The most convenient point for embarkation was Montrose, and from this port he sailed in a small French vessel, accompanied by the Earl of Mar and sixteen other persons of distinction of the Jacobite party. The followers of the Stuarts, being thus left without leaders, dispersed on the approach of the Duke of Argyle, and the claims of that house were doomed to remain in abeyance for another generation.

The oaths of supremacy and allegiance to the reigning family were now strongly urged, both upon the clergy and the laity of this kingdom, and an Act of Parliament was passed, wherein, amongst other matters, it was directed that all Roman Catholics, nonjurors, and others, who refused

---

[1] Toulmin's "Life of Mr. John Mort."—C.
[2] In acknowledgment of their services the government granted pensions of £100 a year to Woods and Walker, the former of whom was afterwards known as "General" Woods. See Rev. Franklin Baker's "Discourses on the Life and Times of the Rev. James Woods," 1859, p. 15. —C.
[3] For many interesting particulars as to this rebellion, see "Lancashire Memorials of the Rebellion of 1715," edited by the late Dr. Hibbert-Ware (vol. 5 of the Chetham Society's series).

to take these oaths, should transmit to commissioners, appointed for the purpose, a register of their estates, setting forth in what parish and township the lands were situated, by whom they were occupied, the annual value at which they were estimated, and the names, titles, additions, and places of abode of their owners. Under the operation of this Act returns were made to the commissioners of estates in the various counties of England to the yearly amount of £358,194 5s. 3¾d., of which sum the estates in Lancashire yielded £13,158 10s. in the following proportions: 73 estates of Catholics, nonjurors, &c., in Amounderness Hundred, £2,660 1s. 3d.; 29 estates in Blackburn, £972 10s. 2d.; 54 estates in Leyland Hundred, £1,463 13s. 1½d.; 25 estates in Lonsdale, £1,432 8s.; 17 estates in Salford, £721 1s. 3d.; 122 estates in West Derby, £5,901 16s. 2½d.

By the Act just quoted this mass of landed property was placed in jeopardy, but it does not appear that the owners were dispossessed of their estates, or that any use was ever made of the registers, except that they were published in the year 1745, "with a view to assist the magistrates and other officers entrusted with the execution of the orders of Government, for suppressing the growth and unhappy effects of the insurrection in the north." At this period a contest, conducted with great vigour and asperity, prevailed both in the county of Lancaster and in several of the other counties of England, involving the doctrine of *the divine right of kings*, in which the nonjurors insisted that no pretence whatever could justify an insurrection against the sovereign; that the Stuarts, being kings of England *de jure*, could not be legally displaced; and consequently that no other king but the descendants of James II. could claim from them an oath of allegiance. On the other hand, it was contended that the people had a right to cashier a sovereign, when that sovereign aimed at the subversion of the religion and constitution of the realm; and that the house of Hanover being in possession of the throne *de facto*, and by the general though not the universal will of the nation, allegiance was justly due to that house, and not to the family that had been expelled. The contest became too warm to be settled in the closet, and in the reign of George II. another appeal was made to arms. Prince Charles Edward, the Young Chevalier as he was called by the partisans of the Stuarts, or the Young Pretender (son of the Pretender) as he was more generally designated, animated with the hopes of a throne, and misled by the sanguine representations of his friends, quitted his exile in France, and on the 2nd of August, 1745, landed in the Hebrides. France had promised substantial support, not because France had any particular liking for the Stuarts, but because she was not unwilling to pay off some old scores by finding employment for her traditional foe. The prince having assembled about 1,200 men in the neighbourhood of Fort William, hostilities immediately commenced. From thence he proceeded to Edinburgh, and, owing to the energy and activity of his friends and the apathy of his enemies, he was enabled to take possession of that ancient capital. Aware that the blow, to be successful, must be struck in England, and entertaining confident expectations of being joined by numbers wherever the standard of the Stuarts was planted, he resolved to advance into the heart of the country and to hazard all upon the issue. On the 6th day of November the young prince, at the head of his small army, crossed the western border, and invested Carlisle, which in less than three days surrendered. Here he found a considerable number of arms and plenty of ammunition, and to encourage his followers his father was proclaimed king of Great Britain, and himself regent, by the magistracy of that city. The ministers of George II. now began to bestir themselves, and an army was assembled in Staffordshire, under Sir John Ligonier, to arrest the career of the invaders. Unintimidated by these hostile preparations, and confident in his own resources, the young adventurer advanced by the route of Penrith into Lancashire, marching on foot in a Highland garb at the head of his forces. But the expectation of being joined by the inhabitants of the country through which he passed was not realised. His enterprise was considered desperate, and the people in general proved well affected to the house of Hanover. Charles Edward, at the head of the vanguard of his army, reached Lancaster on the 24th of November, wearing a light plaid belt, with a blue sash, and mounting a blue bonnet, with a white rose, the badge of the house of York, in front. The numbers of his army have been variously represented, but according to the testimony of MacDonald,[1] himself one of the rebels, it did not exceed 5,600 men when marching through Lancashire. The troops were principally of the Highland clans, who, led by their chiefs, marched to the music of the Highland pipes and drums.[2] On their banners were inscribed the words, "Liberty and Property—Church and King." The arms of the majority were the broadsword, the dirk, and the shield, and a small number were musketeers. The prince was their commander-in-chief, and the Dukes of Perth and Athol, and Marquises of Montrose and Dundee, with twelve other Scotch and English noblemen, and thirteen knights, mostly from the Highlands,

[1] State Trials, ix. 546   [2] "The King shall enjoy his own again" was one of their favourite tunes.

who had received their titles from their intrepid leader, swelled the number, and conferred dignity on the desperate enterprise. Generally the most rigid discipline prevailed, but in some cases the invaders seized the horses of the farmers, and used them partly for mounting their cavalry and partly for conveying their baggage.

Francis Townley, a scion of an old Lancashire family, who had figured at the court of Louis XV., and seen service and earned distinction abroad, was entrusted with a colonel's commission from the French king. The commission authorised him to raise forces on behalf of the prince, and with that object he repaired to Manchester, the reputed stronghold of the Jacobite party, to beat up for recruits. The town was excited; the bolder spirits were jubilant and eager in their desire to don the white cockade; some money was raised, and more was promised but never paid; and what is known to history as the "Manchester Regiment" was enrolled. On the 27th of November the prince arrived at Preston, and by a forced march by way of Wigan reached Manchester on Saturday the 29th, where quarters were ordered for 10,000 troops. Here the force was joined by about 200 Englishmen, who had been formed into a regiment commanded by Colonel Townley, under the designation of the "Manchester Regiment." In the civil wars of his great grandfather Charles I., Manchester had, as we have seen, been the head-quarters for many years of the Parliamentary party in Lancashire; but from some cause which it might not be difficult to explain the mass of the people had changed from Roundheads to Jacobites, and the arrival of Prince Charles was celebrated by illuminations and other public demonstrations of joy. "His Majesty King James the Third" was proclaimed at the Market Cross; receptions were held by the prince at which Jacobite damsels, wearing tartan favours, strove with one another for the privilege of kissing his hand; and in the evening bonfires were lit and merry peals rang from the steeple of the "old church." The next day, after a special service in the church, the troops were reviewed, and on the Monday, the Highlanders, augmented by the Manchester Regiment, set forward on their march southwards, advancing in two divisions, by different routes, to Macclesfield, where they were again united. Thence they advanced, on the following day, by way of Congleton and Leek, to Derby, where they received intelligence that General Wade's army was in Yorkshire, and that the Duke of Cumberland, brother of King George, was at the head of a considerable force of veterans in the neighbourhood of Lichfield. The danger of being hemmed in between two armies, each of them more numerous than his own, awakened the apprehension of the young prince, who immmediately summoned a council of war. Lord Nairn and some of the most sanguine of the rebels insisted upon the propriety of marching directly to London, but the majority determined to retreat to Scotland with all possible expedition, and Prince Charles reluctantly acquiesced in this determination. That retreat tolled the knell of the hopes of the Stuarts! Derby was accordingly abandoned on the 6th of December, and on the 9th the vanguard arrived at Manchester, when the regiment raised by Townley was broken up, though Townley himself, with some of his more ardent supporters, determined on sharing the fortunes of the prince. On the 12th the remnant of the army entered Preston by way of Wigan, and continuing the route by Lancaster, reached the Scotch frontier on the 20th, having performed this memorable retreat of nearly two hundred miles, at midwinter, in fourteen days, and without any material loss of either men, baggage, or cannon.

The speedy arrival of the Duke of Cumberland in Lancashire contributed essentially to the re-establishment of the public peace and confidence; and a number of stragglers from the fugitive army, who had loitered behind for the purpose of plunder, were taken prisoners by General Oglethorp's dragoons on the 16th Dec., and committed to Lancaster Castle. During the winter great exertions were made to strengthen the hostile armies. The Duke of Cumberland repaired to the north at the head of a numerous and well-appointed force, and the time was approaching when the crown of Great Britain was to be contended for upon the plains of Scotland. Early in the month of April the belligerents drew towards Inverness-shire, and on the 16th of that month they met on the heath of Culloden. Here an engagement took place which, prostrating in the dust the hopes of the house of Stuart, will be for ever memorable in the history of these islands. After the destruction of his army, the Prince Pretender wandered as a fugitive in the Highlands for several months, with a reward of £30,000 fixed upon his head, enduring the extremity of personal privation; but at length he escaped into France, and the tranquillity of the British dominions was restored. A considerable number of his English partisans, principally officers in the "Manchester Regiment," were conveyed to London and tried for high treason. At the head of these unfortunate men stood Francis Townley, Esq., of Carlisle, nephew of Mr. Townley, of Townley Hall, in Lancashire, who was himself tried for being concerned in the rebellion of 1715, but acquitted. The trials took place on the 15th, 16th, and 17th of July, 1746, before a special commission assembled at the court-house of St. Margaret's Hill, Southwark; and the facts of the rebellion and the participation of the prisoners being fully established, they were pronounced

guilty and adjudged.   " To be severally hanged by the neck, not till they were dead, but cut down
alive, then their bowels to be taken out and burnt before their faces, their heads to be severed
from their bodies, and their bodies severally divided into four quarters, and these to be at the
king's disposal."   The number of persons tried was seventeen, and of that number Francis
Townley, colonel of the Manchester Regiment; Thomas Theodorus Deacon, James Dawson, John
Barwick, George Fletcher, and Andrew Blood, captains in the Manchester Regiment; Thomas
Chadwick, lieutenant; Thomas Syddall, adjutant in the same regiment, a son of Thomas Syddall,
the peruke maker, who was hanged for his share in the rebellion of 1715; and David Morgan,
a barrister-at-law, and a volunteer in the Pretender's army, were executed on Kennington Common,
on the 30th July, with all the horrid accompaniments prescribed by the law.   As they mounted
the scaffold each of the prisoners made a sort of confession of faith, seven out of the nine
professed themselves to be of the reformed religion,[1] and in general they resigned themselves to
their fate with a degree of heroic constancy worthy of a better cause.   The heads of Colonel
Townley and Captain George Fletcher were placed upon Temple Bar; but the heads of all the
other prisoners were preserved in spirits and sent into the country to be placed in public
situations in Manchester or in Carlisle—the heads of Thomas Syddall and Thomas Theodorus
Deacon remaining for years spiked upon the Manchester Exchange.   The following prisoners,
chiefly Lancashire men and officers or volunteers in the Manchester Regiment, were also convicted,
but they were reprieved and afterwards pardoned: Alexander Abernethy, James Gadd, Thomas
Furnivall, Christopher Taylor, William Brettargh, John Sanderson, Charles Deacon, and James
Wilding.   Bills of indictment for high treason arising out of this rebellion were also found by the
county of Surrey against the Earls of Kilmarnock and Cromartie, and against Arthur, Lord
Balmerino, and these three peers were impeached before the House of Lords on the 28th of July,
1746.   Conviction speedily followed accusation, they were all three pronounced guilty, and the
Earl of Kilmarnock and Lord Balmerino suffered on the block.   The titular Earl of Derwentwater,
having been taken in a ship bound to Scotland, suffered the same fate; and Lord Lovat, though
turned fourscore years of age, was consigned to the block for traitorously conspiring to raise
and levy war against the king.   In the country, nine persons concerned in this rebellion were
executed at Carlisle, six at Brompton, near Penrith, and eleven at York.   About fifty were
executed as deserters in different parts of Scotland, and eighty-one suffered as traitors in that
country.

In both these rebellions the county of Lancaster displayed a firm attachment to the reigning
family—the Catholics as well as the Protestants.   The instances of defection were very rare; and
when they occurred they were rather imputable to some peculiarity in the situation of the
delinquents than to any party or religious feelings.   The romantic attempt of the Young Chevalier,
as displayed in the rebellion of 1745, had in it something imposing to ardent and enthusiastic
minds; and those who embraced his cause on the south of the Tweed were principally young men
of warm temperament, whose imaginations were dazzled by the chivalrous character of the
enterprise.   The defeat at Culloden ended a dynastic contest of more than fifty years in less
than fifty minutes.

Since the final overthrow of the Stuarts, the incidents that go to make up the history
of Lancashire have been associated more with commercial progress than chivalric enterprise.
Though the voice of the county has not unfrequently been heard directing the advancement of
national wealth and greatness, and occasionally it has been conspicuous for its agitations—social,
educational, and political—it has in the main devoted itself to the cultivation of the peaceful
arts and the practical business of life.   For a century or more it has gone on inventing and
advancing, signalising itself more by its mechanical skill and ingenuity than by its deeds of
daring and military prowess.   Discovery and invention—the disclosure of the secrets of nature
and the application of them to the uses of man—were born almost together, and have gone on
hand in hand until they have changed almost entirely the aspects of the county.   The last
hundred years present a marvellous retrospect of the progress of mechanical invention, and their
history is little more than a continuous record of industrial activity and commercial enterprise.
" Before the reign of the second George had drawn to a close, labouring artisans began to exercise
their inventive faculties on the rude appliances then in use.   Practical observation enabled them
to elaborate their mechanical contrivances step by step, and thus a series of progressive inventions
followed each other.   For five centuries and more the county had been famed for its manufactures, which have contributed to the wealth of its people and the prosperity of the nation,
but for long ages it made little or no progress in improving the machinery, if we may call it
such, employed in the production of its wares.   The soil had grown its flax and cotton, the

---

[1] Colonel Townley and Captain Blood were the only Roman Catholics.

sheep had yielded its wool, and the worm had spun its silk, but as late almost as the days of our great grandmothers the spinning wheel and the loom were as simple and as primitive in their construction as those used by the Hindoo. The cotton trade had long formed the staple industry, but until 1738 the weaver was accustomed to throw his shuttle from hand to hand between the threads that formed his warp. In that year Kay invented the fly shuttle, which enabled one man to do the work of two; in 1767, James Hargreaves, of Blackburn, constructed his first spinning jenny; and in the same year a reed maker, named Highs, invented a machine for the spinning of cotton twist by rollers, to which he gave the name of the water frame throstle. Scarcely had he completed his work than Richard Arkwright, a Bolton barber of a mechanical turn, obtained a model of it, improved the construction, and with the assistance of the Strutts, of Belper, established a cotton mill, the first in the kingdom, and thereby laid the foundation of his fortune and the rapid extension of the cotton trade. While these things were being accomplished, Samuel Crompton, a young man residing at Hall-i'th'-wood, near Bolton, was secretly giving practical form to an idea that had floated through his brain, and in 1779 produced his spinning mule, a machine so named from the circumstance of its combining the principles of the two inventions of Hargreaves and Arkwright to produce a third more effective than either. In 1787, Bolton and Watt's rotative steam engine was brought into action at Warrington, and about the same time Cartwright introduced his power loom, the most important of the inventions for diminishing manual labour in the cotton manufacture. By the aid of these inventions, and with the product of its great coal-fields, which have yielded their treasures to help the industry of the artisan and facilitate his labours, the commerce of Lancashire has extended itself with marvellous rapidity, the wealth and population have been augmented in a corresponding degree, and the changes in the appearance of the county have been such as might compare with the fictions of Eastern romance."[1]

The labour of a producing population cannot be sustained without facilities of transit for the articles produced. The primitive modes of intercourse were altogether inadequate to the growing energies of the people, and without improved means of communication the industry of the county could not be maintained, or its wealth and prosperity increased; hence, Lancashire, which had been the birthplace of so many mechanical inventions, became also the cradle of the canal system and led the way in the construction of that system of artificial water ways which subsequently spread like a network over the country. At a later date, under the wand of the magician Steam, the railway system was called into existence, and as the county has the credit of giving birth to the canal system, so also may it claim the credit of having initiated the railway system, for, though the Stockton and Darlington line was formed a few years previously, the Liverpool and Manchester was the first railway on which the powers of the steam locomotive for the purposes of traction were fully established. Since then it has spread its ramifications over the entire face of the county, until, as is estimated, there are now over 600 miles of roadway. "Onward" may be said to have been the watchword of the county, but its efforts have been devoted for the most part to the practical business of life, and for the last hundred years or more its annals are little else than a continuous chronicle of mechanical enterprise, ingenuity, and skill.

Having brought down the general history of the county to the middle of the eighteenth century, the more recent historical events will be treated in the hundred and parish histories; but it will be proper here to take a general survey of the gentry of the county, and, preliminary thereto, to give a catalogue of the heralds' visitations in chronological order, as they are exhibited in the British Museum:—

LANCASHIRE VISITATIONS.

Date of Herald's Visitation. *Name of Herald.*

1533. Thomas Benoilt, Clarencieux, by his deputy, William Fellow, Lancaster Herald; entitled "A Visitac'on made in Lancashire and in a p'te of Chestershyre,[2] p' Lancast'r Heraulde in ye xxiiiith yeare of o'r Soveraigne Lord Kinge Henry viiith, by a Speciall Com'cion of Thom's Benoilt, alias Clarencieux, King of the same Province."—(Harl. MS. 2076, fol. 11.)[3]

---

[1] "Lancashire, Descriptive and Historical," by Jas. Croston, F.S.A., pp. 44-5.—C.
[2] Vide a long note on this MS. in Bibliotheca Heraldica, p. 582. It appears from this visitation that only one Cheshire family declined to make an entry, while many of the Lancashire families refused even to be spoken with by the herald; and others, who condescended to grant an audience, dismissed the heraldic "visitant with the utmost rudeness." Two examples of the conduct of knightly families in the latter county are given, with his usual simplicity, by Mr. Fellows: "Sir Richard Hoghton, Kt., hath putt away his ladye and wief, and kepeth a concobyne in his howse, by whom he hath divers children, and by the Lady he hath Ley Hall, w'ch armes he bereth quartred with his in the first quarter. He says that Mr. Garter licensed him so to doe, and he gave Mr. Garter an angell noble, but he gave me nothing, nor made me good cheer, but

made me proud wordes." (Harl. MSS. 2076, f. 12 b.) "Sir John Townley, kt., had to his first wief one who was daughter to Sir Charles Apillyadon, etc. I wot not what her name is, nor I made no greate inquisition, for he would have no note taken of him, saying, there was no more gentlemen in Lancashire but my lords of Derby and Monteagle. I sought hym all the day ryding in the wyld country, and his reward was ije. w'ch the guyde hadd the most p'tt, as I had as evill a jorney as ever I hadd."
[3] Mr. Baines held the opinion, in which the late Mr. Harland shared, that the copy in the British Museum was the original, but it is not so. The original, which was in the possession of William Pierpoint, of Thoresby, co. Notts, in 1688, was destroyed by fire at that mansion in 1745. The copy in the Harl. MSS. is a transcript coeval with the duplicate in the College of Arms, and includes ordinaries of Lancashire and Cheshire arms not contained in the office copy.—C.

Date of Herald's Visitation.	Name of Herald.
1567.	William Flower, Norroy.—Harl. MS. 2086. [This MS. is neatly written in the hand of the celebrated Glover, Somerset Herald, who accompanied his father-in-law, Flower, in the Visitation. It is in tabulated form and has some continuations by other hands.]
——	Another copy of the same Visitation, written narratively.—Harl. MS. 891,[1] fol. 59.
——	Another copy of the same Visitation, in tables.—Harl. MS. 1468,[2] fol. 12.
——	Another copy of the same Visitation, entered alphabetically, with some continuations.—Harl. MS. 1549.
——	Another copy of the same Visitation, written and augmented in 1598 by William Smith, Rouge Dragon Poursuivant; "a work" stated in the Harl. Catalogue to be "carefully executed, but unfinished." The arms are all neatly coloured.—Harl. MS. 6159. [There is also a copy of Flower's Visitation in the Manchester Coll. Lib., based apparently upon Smith's transcript.]
1613.	"Many, if not most of the loose papers" of the Visitation, by Richard St. George, Norroy.—Harl. MS. 1437.

Descents registered at the Visitation of 1613.—Harl. MS. 1549, fol. 108.
Pedigrees, supposed to be copied from the Visitation of 1567, by Thomas Knight, Chester Herald.
Arms of Families of Lancashire and Cheshire blazoned.—Harl. MS. 893.
Pedigrees apparently copied from the Visitation of 1567.—Harl. MS. 1158.
"Lancashire Pedigrees, supposed to be copied from the Visitation of 1567, with continuations by the two last Randle Holmes, so low as the year 1704."—Harl. MS. 1987.
Funeral Certificates of the Counties of Lancaster, Cheshire, Shropshire, and North Wales, begun 1st March 1600.—Lansdowne MS. 879.
Funeral Certificates of the counties of Lancaster, Chester, and North Wales, begun 28th May 1606.—Lansdowne MS. 2041.
Randle Holme's Collections for Lancashire, chiefly consisting of extracts from deeds.—Lansdowne MS. 2042.
Ibid.—Lansdowne MS. 2112.
Collections, Historical, Heraldical, and Juridical, principally relating to Lancashire.—Lansdowne MS. 7386.

There is here one important omission, arising out of the last and most authentic visitation of the county not having yet found its way into the British Museum; this is the visitation of Lancashire made by Sir William Dugdale, knight, himself a descendant of a Lancashire family long settled at Clitheroe, and some time Garter Principal King-of-arms. Sir William's visitation is deposited in the Heralds' Office, Doctors' Commons, London; and the following extracts from the diary of the venerable antiquary fixes the dates with precision when the entries were made:—[3]

[*Visitation of Lancashire.*] [4]

September 1664.—8. To Manchester. 12. To Blackburn. 14. To Garstang. 15. To Lancaster. 17. To Preston. 21. To Rufford, Mr. Molineux house. 22. To Ormeskirke. 24. To Knowsley, the Earle of Derby's. 26. To Tabley in Chesh. Sʳ Peter Leicester's. 28. To Stone. 29. Home to Blythe Hall.

March 1665.—9. From Blythe Hall to Stone. 10. Manchester. 11. To sit at Manchester. 13. To ride to Preston. 14. To sit at Preston. 15. Lancaster. 16. To sit at Lancaster.

April 1665.—4. To Rydale (neere Ambleside), Mr. Fleming's house. 5. Lancaster. 6. Preston. 7. Ormskirk. 8. To sit at Ormskirk. That night to my Lᵈ Molineux.

In addition to the herald's visitations and other MSS. in the British Museum, copies of many of the Lancashire wills and inventories, funeral certificates, and *Inquisitiones post mortem* have been printed by the Chetham and Record Societies.

Persons assuming to be gentlemen, but who were not entitled to the honour of bearing arms, were subject to the following indignities on their names being struck from the former visitations: "Their names being written on a sheet of paper," says William Flower, Norroy king-of-arms, "with fayre greate letters, was carryed by the Bayliff of the Hundred, and one of the Herauldes men to the Chiefe Towne of that hundred, where, in the chiefe place thereof, the herauldes man Redd the names (after crye made by the Baylife and the people gathered) And then pronounced openly by the said Bayley Every man's name severally contained in the said bill: that done, the Bayley sett the said Bill of Names on a poste fast with wax where it may stand drye, so it be as aforesaid in the Chiefest place of the said Towne." When Sir William Dugdale made his visitation, some whose ancestors had long borne arms disclaimed their right altogether, and the Nonconformist families generally appear to have disregarded his summons, disdaining the "noble science" and treating with contempt its terrestrial distinctions and dignities.

Amongst the MS. collections in the Chetham Library, Manchester, are the following:—

No. 6694.—A copy of Flower's Visitation, bearing the date of 1567, and the following years, transcribed from a book of parchment in the hands of Robert Cooke, Clarencieux king-of-armes, in 1583.
No. 6719.—Another copy of the Visitation of 1567, transcribed, &c., by Wm. Smith, Rouge Dragon.
A great variety of pedigrees and genealogies of Lancashire families, &c., many of the armorial bearings curiously emblazoned, others sketched with the pen, interspersed with numerous historical memoranda. By Thomas Barret.[5]

---

[1] This MS. contains also the Visitation of Suffolk, and other pedigrees.
[2] This MS. likewise contains the Visitation of Middlesex in 1664.
[3] Hamper's Life of Sir William Dugdale, pp. 117, 118. Sir William was knighted by Charles II. May 25, 1677.
[4] The Visitations of Lancashire, by Benolt (1533), Flower (1567), St. George (1613), and Dugdale (1664-5), have been printed by the Chetham Society.—C.
[5] These will be found in the MS. vols. numbered 8017, 8019, 8020, 8022, 8024, and 1826.—H. Mr. Grogson mentions an original copy of the Visitation of Lancashire, A.D. 1662, in this library, supposed to be in Dugdale's own handwriting, containing two hundred and eighty-four entries of arms and genealogies, but we do not find any such MS., nor was there any Visitation of Lancashire made by Dugdale in that year.—B. There is no such MS. in the library. Dugdale's Visitation of Lancashire was not in 1662 but in 1664 and 1665, of which the office copy (C 37) is preserved in the Heralds' College.—H.

FAMILIES WHICH ENTERED THEIR DESCENTS AT THE LANCASHIRE VISITATIONS OF
1533, 1567, 1613, AND 1664-5

Family	1533	1567	1613	1664-5
Adlington of Adlington	1533	1567	1613	1664-5
Ainsworth of Pleasington	—	1567	1613	1664-5
Allen of Broughton	—	—	—	1664-5
Ambrose of Ambrose Hall	—	1567	—	—
Ambrose of Lowick	—	—	—	1664-5
Anderton of Anderton	—	—	—	1664-5
Anderton of Birchley	—	—	—	1664-5
Anderton of Euxton	—	—	—	1664-5
Anderton of Lostock	—	—	—	1664-5
Andrews of Little Lever	—	—	—	1664-5
Ashawe of Hall-on-the-Hill	1533	1567	1613	—
Asheton of Asheton	—	1567	1613	1664-5
Asheton of Chadderton	—	1567	—	1664-5
Asheton of Great Lever	1533	1567	1613	1664-5
Asheton of Middleton	1533	1567	1613	1664-5
Asheton of Penketh	—	1567	1613	—
Asheton of Shepley	—	1567	—	1664-5
Ashton of Bamfurlong	—	—	1613	—
Ashton of Croston	—	—	1613	1664-5
Ashton of Preston	—	—	—	1664-5
Ashurst of Ashurst	—	—	1613	1664-5
Astley of Stakes	—	—	1613	1664-5
Atherton of Atherton	1533	—	—	1664-5
Aughton of Adlington	—	1567	—	—
Bamford of Bamford	—	—	1613	1664-5
Banastre of Altham	—	—	—	1664-5
Banastre of Bank	1533	1567	1613	1664-5
Banastre of Darwen	—	1567	—	—
Banastre of Preston	—	—	—	1664-5
Bankes of Winstanley	—	—	—	1664-5
Barcroft of Barcroft	—	—	—	1664-5
Barlow of Barlow	—	1567	—	1664-5
Barton of Barton	—	1567	—	—
Barton of Smithells	1533	1567	—	—
Beck of Manchester	—	—	—	1664-5
Beconsall of Beconsall	1533	1567	—	—
Billinge of Billinge	—	—	—	1664-5
Bindloose of Borwick	—	—	—	1664-5
Birch of Ardwick	—	—	—	1664-5
Birch of Birch	—	—	—	1664-5
Birtwistle of Huncoat	—	1567	—	1664-5
Blackburn of Newton	—	—	—	1664-5
Blundell of Ince Blundell	—	1567	1613	1664-5
Blundell of Little Crosby	—	1567	—	1664-5
Blundell of Preston	—	—	—	1664-5
Bold of Bold	1533	1567	1613	1664-5
Booth of Barton	1533	1567	—	—
Booth of Booth	—	—	—	1664-5
Booth of Salford	—	—	1613	—
Bootle of Melling	—	—	—	1664-5
Brabyn of Docker	—	—	—	1664-5
Braddyll of Brockholes	—	1567	1613	—
Braddyll of Whalley	—	—	—	1664-5
Bradley of Bradley	—	1567	—	—
Bradley of Bryning	—	—	—	1664-5
Bradshaw of Bradshaw	—	—	1613	1664-5
Bradshaw of Darcy Lever	—	—	—	1664-5
Bradshaw of Haigh	1533	1567	1613	1664-5
Bradshaw of Pendleton	—	—	—	1664-5
Bradshaw of Pennington	—	—	—	1664-5
Bradshaw of Preesall	—	—	—	1664-5
Breres of Chorley	—	—	1613	—
Bretherton of Hey	—	—	—	1664-5
Brettargh of Brettargh's Holt	—	—	—	1664-5
Brockholes of Clayton	—	—	—	1664-5
Brockholes of Heton	—	—	1613	—
Bruche of Bruche	1533	1567	—	—
Bryers of Walton	—	—	—	1664-5
Buckley of Buckley	—	—	—	1664-5
Burron of Warrington	—	—	—	1664-5
Bushell of Kuerden	—	—	—	1664-5
Butler of Bewsey	1533	1567	—	—
Butler of Kirkland	—	1567	1613	1664-5
Butler of Rawcliffe	1533	—	—	1664-5
Butterworth of Belfield	—	—	1613	1664-5
Byrom of Byrom	—	—	—	1664-5
Byrom of Manchester	—	—	—	1664-5
Byrom of Salford	—	—	1613	1664-5
Byrom of Clayton	1533	1567	—	—
Calvert of Cockerham	—	—	1613	—
Carus of Asthwaite	—	1567	—	—
Carus of Halton	—	—	—	1664-5
Case of Hayton	—	—	—	1664-5
Catherall of Mytton	—	1567	—	—
Catterall of Crooke	—	—	—	1664-5
Chaddock of Chaddock	—	—	—	1664-5
Chaderton of Leghes	—	—	1613	—
Chadwick of Chadwick	—	—	—	1664-5
Chadwick of Healey	—	—	1613	—
Chadwick of Taunton	—	—	—	1664-5
Charnock of Charnock	—	1567	1613	—
Charnock of Leyland	—	1567	1613	—
Chetham of Chetham	—	—	—	1664-5
Chetham of Crumpsall	—	—	1613	—
Chetham of Nuthurst	—	—	—	1664-5
Chetham of Turton	—	—	—	1664-5
Chisnall of Chisnall	—	1567	1613	1664-5
Chorley of Chorley	—	1567	1613	1664-5
Chorley of Ormskirk	—	—	—	1664-5
Chorley of Preston	—	—	—	1664-5
Clayton of Clayton	—	—	1613	—
Clayton of Crooke	—	—	—	1664-5
Clayton of Lentworth	—	—	—	1664-5
Clayton of Little Harwood	—	—	—	1664-5
Clifton of Clifton	—	—	—	1364-5
Clifton of Westby	—	1567	1613	—
Cole of Coat	—	—	—	1664-5
Cooper of Carnford	—	—	—	1664-5
Cottom of Tornaker	—	—	1613	—
Crombock of Clarke Hill	—	—	—	1664-5
Cross of Liverpool	—	1567	—	—
Cudworth of Werneth	—	1567	1613	1664-5
Culcheth of Abram	—	—	—	1664-5
Culcheth of Culcheth	—	1567	—	1664-5
Curwen of Poulton	—	—	1613	—
Dalton of Bispham	—	—	1613	—
Dalton of Thurnham	—	—	—	1664-5
Daniell of Wigan	—	—	—	1664-5
Davenport of Salford	—	—	—	1664-5
Dewhurst of Alston	—	—	—	1664-5
Dewhurst of Dewhurst	—	—	1613	—
Dichfield of Ditton	—	1567	1613	—
Dickinson of Writinton	—	—	—	1664-5
Doding of Conishead	—	—	1613	1664-5
Downes of Wardley	—	—	1613	1664-5
Dukinfield of Hindley	—	—	—	1664-5
Eccleston of Eccleston	—	1567	—	1664-5
Egerton of Shaw	—	—	—	1664-5
Eltonhead of Eltonhead	—	1567	1613	1664-5
Entwistle of Foxholes	—	—	—	1664-5
Eyves of Fishwick	—	—	—	1664-5
Farington of Farington	1533	1567	—	—
Farington of Lingard	—	1567	—	—
Farington of Ribbleton	—	1567	1613	1664-5
Farington of Worden	—	—	1613	1664-5
Fazakerley of Fazakerley	—	—	1613	1664-5
Fazakerley of Kirby	—	—	—	1664-5
Fleetwood of Penwortham	—	1567	1613	1664-5
Fleetwood of Rossall	—	—	1613	1664-5
French of Preston	—	—	—	1664-5
Fyfe of Wedacre	—	—	—	1664-5
Gartside of Rochdale	—	—	—	1664-5
Gerard of Astley	—	1567	—	—
Gerard of Bryn	1533	—	—	1664-5
Gerard of Ince	—	1567	1613	—
Gerard of Newton	—	—	—	1664-5
Gilibrand of Chorley	—	—	1613	1664-5
Gilibrand of Peel	—	—	1613	1664-5

Family	1533	1567	1613	1664-5
Gilibrand of Ramsgreve	—	—	—	1664-5
Girlington of Thurland	—	—	1613	1664-5
Goodlaw of Aspull	—	—	1613	—
Gorsuch of Gorsuch	—	—	—	1664-5
Greenhalgh of Brandlesholme	—	—	—	1664-5
Gregory of Highhurst	—	1567	—	—
Grimshaw of Catterall	—	—	1613	—
Grimshaw of Clayton	—	1567	—	1664-5
Halsall of Halsall	1533	1567	1613	1664-5
Halsall of Melling	—	—	—	1664-5
Harrington of Huyton	—	—	1613	1664-5
Hartley of Strangeways	—	—	—	1664-5
Hawarden of Appleton	—	—	1613	—
Hawarden of Widnes	—	—	—	1664-5
Hawarden of Wolston	—	1567	—	—
Haydock of Cottom	—	—	1613	—
Haye of Chorlton	—	—	—	1664-5
Heaton of Heaton	1533	1567	—	—
Hendley of Hendley	—	1567	1613	—
Hesketh of Aughton	—	—	1613	1664-5
Hesketh of North Meols	—	—	1613	—
Hesketh of Poulton	—	—	1613	1664-5
Hesketh of Preston	—	—	—	1664-5
Hesketh of Rufford	1533	1567	1613	—
Heyrick of Manchester	—	—	—	1664-5
Heywood of Heywood	—	—	—	1664-5
Heywood of Walton-on-the-Hill	—	—	—	1664-5
Hilton of Millwood	—	—	—	1664-5
Hodgkinson of Preston	—	—	—	1664-5
Hoghton of Park Hall	—	—	1613	1664-5
Holcroft of Holcroft	1533	1567	—	1664-5
Holden of Holden (?)	—	1567	1613	1664-5
Holland of Clifton	1533	1567	—	—
Holland of Denton	—	1567	—	1664-5
Holland of Heaton	—	—	—	1664-5
Holland of Sutton	—	1567	—	1664-5
Holt of Ashworth	—	—	—	1664-5
Holt of Bridge Hall	—	—	—	1664-5
Holt of Grislehurst	1533	1567	1613	1664-5
Holt of Stubley	1533	1567	1613	1664-5
Hopwood of Hopwood	1533	1567	—	1664-5
Hothersall of Hothersall	—	—	—	1664-5
Houghton of Houghton	—	1567	1613	1664-5
Houghton of Lea	1533	—	—	—
Howorth of Howorth	—	—	1613	1664-5
Howorth of Thurcroft	—	—	—	1664-5
Hulme of Hulme	—	—	—	1664-5
Hulton of Farnworth	—	1567	—	—
Hulton of Hulton	1533	1567	—	1664-5
Hulton of Thorpenaty	—	—	—	1664-5
Hyde of Denton	—	1567	1613	1664-5
Hyde of Hyde	—	—	1613	—
Hyde of Urmston	—	1567	—	—
Ince of Ince	—	—	—	1664-5
Ireland of Hutt	—	1567	1613	1664-5
Ireland of Lydiate	—	1567	—	—
Johnson of Preston	—	—	—	1664-5
Kenyon of Peele	—	—	—	1664-5
Keurden of Keurden	—	1567	—	1664-5
Keurden of Preston	—	—	—	1664-5
Kighley of Inskip	1533	1567	—	—
Kirkby of Kirkby	—	—	1613	1664-5
Kirkby of Upper Rawcliffe	—	1567	—	—
Knipe of Boughton	—	—	—	1664-5
Lacy of Longworth	—	—	—	1664-5
Lancaster of Rainhill	—	1567	1613	1664-5
Langley of Agecroft	1533	1567	—	—
Langton of Broughton Tower	—	—	—	1664-5
Langton of Lowe	—	—	—	1664-5
Langton of Newton	1533	1567	—	—
Langtree of Langtree	1533	1567	—	—
Latham of Irlam	—	—	1613	1664-5
Latham of Mosborough	—	—	1613	—
Lathom of Parbold	—	—	—	1664-5

Family	1533	1567	1613	1664-5
Lathom of Whiston	—	—	—	1664-5
Lawe of Preston	—	—	—	1664-5
Legh of Bradley	1533	—	—	1664-5
Legh of Bruche	—	—	—	1664-5
Leigh of Preston	—	—	—	1664-5
Leigh of Barton	—	—	—	1664-5
Leigh of Singleton Grange	—	—	—	1664-5
Lemon of Preston	—	—	—	1664-5
Lever of Little Lever	—	1567	1613	—
Lever of Kersall	—	—	—	1664-5
Leyland of Morleys	1533	—	—	—
Lightbown of Manchester	—	—	—	1664-5
Livesay of Sutton	—	—	—	1664-5
Livesey of Livesey	—	—	1613	1664-5
Longworth of Longworth	—	1567	1613	—
Longworth of Upper Rawcliffe	—	—	—	1664-5
Lowde of Kirkham	—	—	—	1664-5
Maghull of Maghull	—	—	—	1664-5
Markland of Wigan	—	—	—	1664-5
Mascy of Carlton	—	1567	—	—
Mascy of Layton	—	—	1613	—
Mascy of Rixton	1533	—	—	1664-5
Maudesley of Leyland	—	—	—	1664-5
Maudesley of Maudesley	—	—	1613	1664-5
Medowcroft of Smethurst	—	—	—	1664-5
Mercer of West Derby	—	—	—	1664-5
Midleton of Leighton	—	1567	1613	1564-5
Molyneux of Haughton	—	—	—	1664-5
Molyneux of Hawkley	—	1567	—	—
Molyneux of Melling	—	1567	—	—
Molyneux of New Hall	—	—	—	1664-5
Molyneux of Sefton	1533	1567	1613	1664-5
More of Bankhouse	1533	1567	—	—
Morecroft of Ormskirk	—	—	—	1664-5
Morley of Winnington	—	—	1613	—
Mort of Damhouse	—	—	—	1664-5
Mort of Preston	—	—	—	1664-5
Mosley of Ancoats	—	—	—	1664-5
Mosley of Hough	—	—	1613	—
Mossocke of Kenniscough	—	—	—	1664-5
Mynshull of Manchester	—	—	—	1664-5
Nelson of Fayrehurst	—	—	—	1664-5
Newport of Lichfield [1]	1533	—	—	—
Newsam of Newsamhall	—	1567	—	—
Newton of Newton	—	—	—	1664-5
Norreys of Middleforth	—	—	—	1664-5
Norreys of Speke	—	1567	—	1664-5
Norreys of Tarleton	—	—	—	1664-5
Norreys of West Derby	—	—	—	1664-5
Nowell of Great Mearley	—	1567	—	—
Nowell of Little Mearley	—	1567	—	—
Nowell of Reade	—	—	1613	1664-5
Nuthall of Tottington	—	—	—	1664-5
Ogle of Whiston	—	—	—	1664-5
Oldham of Manchester	—	—	—	1664-5
Orrel of Turton	1533	—	1613	1664-5
Osbaldeston of Osbaldeston	1533	1567	1613	1664-5
Osbaldeston of Sunderland	—	—	—	1664-5
Parker of Bradkirke	—	—	—	1664-5
Parker of Extwisle	—	—	—	1664-5
Parkinson of Falsnape	—	—	1613	—
Parr of Kempnough	—	1567	—	—
Patten of Warrington	—	1567	1613	1664-5
Penketh of Penketh	—	1567	1613	—
Pennington of Pennington	—	—	—	1664-5
Pennington of Wigan	—	—	—	1664-5
Pigot of Preston	—	—	—	1664-5
Pleasington of Dimples	—	1567	1613	—
Porter of Lancaster	—	—	—	1664-5
Preston of Holker	—	—	1613	1664-5
Preston of the Manor (Furness)	—	—	—	1664-5
Preston of Preston	—	—	1613	1664-5
Preston of Preston-Patrick	—	—	1613	—
Prestwich of Hulme	—	1567	1613	—
Prestwich of Prestwich	1533	—	—	—

[1] No trace of this family is found in any of the other Visitations of Lancashire.—C,

	1533	1567	1613	1664-5
Radcliffe of Manchester	—	—	1613	—
Radcliffe of Ordsall	1533	1567	—	—
Radcliffe of Radcliffe	—	—	—	1664-5
Radcliffe of Todmorden	—	—	—	1664-5
Radcliffe of Wimerley	—	1567	1613	—
Ratcliffe of Leigh	—	—	—	1664-5
Rawlinson of Carke	—	—	—	1664-5
Reddish of Reddish	1533	1567	—	—
Ridge of Manchester	—	—	—	1664-5
Rigby of Burgh	—	—	1613	—
Rigby of Hareoke	—	1567	1613	1664-5
Rigby of Layton	—	—	—	1664-5
Rigby of Middleton	—	—	—	1664-5
Rigby of Wigan	—	—	1613	—
Rigmaiden of Wedacre	—	1567	—	—
Rishton of Dunishope	—	—	—	1664-5
Rishton of Ponthalghe	—	—	—	1664-5
Rishton of Rishton	1533	—	—	—
Risley of Risley	—	—	—	1664-5
Rixton of Sankey	—	1567	—	—
Robinson of Buckshaw-in-Euxton	—	—	—	1664-5
Rogerley of Park Hall in Blackrod	—	—	1613	—
Rosthorn of New Hall	—	—	—	1664-5
Rushton of Antley	—	—	—	1664-5
Rushton of Dunkenhalgh	—	1567	1613	—
Rushton of Sparth	—	—	1613	—
Ryley of the Green	—	1567	—	—
Sale of Hope Carr	—	—	—	1664-5
Sandford of High Ashes & Nuthurst	—	—	—	1664-5
Sandys of Graythwaite	—	—	—	1664-5
Sawrey of Plumpton	—	—	—	1664-5
Scarisbrick of Bickerstaffe	1533	—	—	—
Scarisbrick of Scarisbrick	—	1567	—	—
Schofield of Schofield	—	1567	—	1664-5
Sclater of Light Oaks	—	—	—	1664-6
Sharples of Freckleton	—	—	—	1664-5
Sharples of Sharples	—	1567	—	1664-5
Sharrock of Walton	—	—	—	1664-5
Shaw of Bulloghe	—	—	—	1664-5
Shaw of Heath Charnock	—	—	—	1664-5
Shaw of Heyside	—	—	—	1664-5
Shaw of Preston	—	—	—	1664-5
Shaw of Shaw Place	—	—	—	1664-5
Sherbourne of Little Mitton	—	—	—	1664-5
Sherbourne of Ribbleton	—	—	1613	—
Sherbourne of Stonyhurst	—	1567	1613	1664-5
Sherbourne of Twisleton	—	—	—	1664-5
Sherbourne of Wolfhouse	—	—	—	1664-5
Shuttleworth of Asterley	—	—	—	1664-5
Shuttleworth of Bedford	—	—	—	1664-5
Shuttleworth of Gawthorpe	—	1567	—	1664-5
Shakerley of Shakerley	1533	1567	—	—
Singleton of Brockhall	—	1567	1613	—
Singleton of Steyning	—	—	—	1664-5
Skillicorne of Preece	—	1567	—	—
Sorocold of Barton	—	—	—	1664-5
Southworth of Samlesbury	1533	1567	—	1664-5
Spencer of Ashton Hall	—	—	—	1664-5
Standish of Burgh	—	—	1613	1664-5
Standish of Duxbury	1533	1567	1613	1664-5
Standish of Standish	1533	1567	—	1664-5
Standish of West Derby	—	—	—	1664-5
Stanley of Bickerstaffe	—	—	1613	1664-5
Stanley of Broughton	—	—	—	1664-5
Stanley of Crosshall	1533	1567	—	1664-5
Stanley Earl of Derby	1533	—	—	1664-5
Stanley of Eccleston	—	—	—	1664-5
Stanley of Hornby Castle	—	—	—	1664-5
Stanley of Moor Hall	—	—	—	1664-5
Starkie of Aughton	—	—	—	1664-5
Starkie of Huntroyde	—	—	—	1664-5
Strangeways of Strangeways	—	—	1613	—
Talbot of Carr	—	—	—	1664-5
Talbot of Salebury	1533	1567	—	1664-5
Tarbock of Tarbock	1533	1567	—	—
Tatlock of Cunscough	—	—	—	1664-5
Tetlow of Werneth	—	—	1613	—
Thornton of Thornton	—	—	1613	—
Townley of Barnside	—	—	—	1664-5
Townley of Dutton	—	—	—	1664-5
Townley of Hurstwood	—	—	—	1664-5
Townley of Oakenhead	—	—	—	1664-5
Townley of Royle	—	—	1613	1664-5
Townley of Stinehedge	—	—	—	1664-5
Townley of Townley	1533	—	1613	1664-5
Tonge of Tonge	—	—	—	1664-5
Trafford of Trafford	1533	1567	1613	1664-5
Travers of Nateby	—	—	1613	—
Tyldesley of Garret	—	—	—	1664-5
Tyldesley of Morleys	—	1567	—	1664-5
Tyldesley of Wardley	—	1567	1613	—
Urmston of West Leigh	1533	1567	—	1664-5
Valentine of Bentcliffe	—	—	—	1664-5
Veale of Methop	—	—	1613	—
Veale of Whinneyheys	—	—	—	1664-5
Wadsworth of Hayton	—	—	—	1664-5
Wall of Preston	—	1567	—	1664-5
Walmsley of Banister	—	—	—	1664-5
Walmsley of Caldcotes	—	—	—	1664-5
Walmsley of Dunkenhalgh	—	—	1613	1664-5
Walmsley of Showley	—	—	—	1664-5
Walton of Walton	—	—	—	1664-5
Watmough of Myclehead	—	—	1613	—
West of Borwick	—	—	—	1664-5
Westby of Mowbreck	—	1567	—	—
Westby of Myerscough	—	—	—	1664-5
Westby of Rawcliffe	—	—	—	1664-5
Westby of Westby	—	—	1613	—
Whalley, Abbey of (Founder)	1533	—	—	—
Whittacre of Whittacre	—	1567	—	—
Whittingham of Whittingham	—	1567	1613	1664-5
Winkley of Winkley	—	—	1613	—
Winkley of Preston	—	—	—	1664-5
Wood of Turton	—	—	1613	—
Woodward of Shevington	—	—	—	1664-5
Woolfall of Woolfall	—	—	—	1664-5
Worsley of Booths	1533	1567	—	1664-5
Worsley of Platt	—	—	—	1664-5
Worsley of Worsley Mains	—	—	1613	—
Worthington of Blainscough	—	1567	—	1664-5
Worthington of Croshawe	—	—	1613	1664-5
Worthington of Shevington	—	—	—	1664-5
Worthington of Worthington	—	—	1613	1664-5

Of the principal nobility and gentry of the county we shall have to treat in the respective hundreds; but the following list, extracted from a MS. in the author's possession, collated with Blore's List, published in 1673, forms a useful and compendious catalogue for more general reference :—

FAMILIÆ LANCASTRIENSES,

Or, a List of the Nobility and Gentry in the County Palatine of Lancaster, from the time of Henry VII. to the Accession of William III., from Original Records and the MSS. of Sir John Byron, Sir George Booth, Mr. John Hopkinson, and others, with the Orthography preserved of both Persons and Places.

Abraham of Abraham	Ambrose of Ambrose Hall	Andrews of Little Lever	Aspden of Aspden
Adlington of Adlington	Anderton of Lostock	Appleton of Appleton	Ashton of Ashton-under-Lyne
Allen of Rosshall	Anderton of Birchley	Ashaw of Hethe Charnock	Ashton of Middleton
Allen of Broughton	Anderton of Anderton	Ashfield of Ashfield	Ashton of Chatterton
Ambrose of Lowick	Anderton of Euxton, Clayton, &c.	Ashurst of Ashurst	Ashton of Shepley

Longworth of Upper Raw-
cliff
Lovel of Halewood
Lowde of Kirkham
Lowe of Preston
Maghull of Maghull
Markland of Wigan
Markland of the Meadows
Mason of Clitherow
Massey of Rixton
Massey of Carlston
Maudsley of Maudsley
Meadowcroft of Smethurst
Meales of Meales
Melson of Fairhurst, &c.
Melton of Melling
Mercer of West Derby
Mereland of Mereland
Merton of Melling
Middleton of Leighton
Minshull of Manchester
Mitton of Mitton
Molyneaux of Sephton
Molyneaux of Thornton
Molyneaux of Thornton, &c.
Molyneaux of Rainhill and
Hawksley
Molyneaux of Wimberley
Molyneaux of Thorpe
Molyneaux of Combscough
Molyneaux of Shipton
Molyneux of Larbrick, &c.
Molyneaux of Kirton
Molyneaux of Crosby and
Woodhouse
Molyneaux of New Hall
Montbegon of Hornby Castle
Moore or More of Bank Hall
More of Leverpoole
Morecroft of Ormeskirk
Morley of Morley
Morley of Wennington
Mort of Highfield, Dapilton,
and Damhouse
Mort of Preston
Moseley of Hough-end
Moseley of Manchester, An-
cotes, and Garrett
Mosley of Holme
Mossoake of Kenniscough
Mowbrick of Mowbrick
Nelson of Maudsley
Netby of Netby
Neville of Hornby Castle
Newsome of Newsome
Newton of Newton
Newton of Lancaster
Norris of Sutton and Speke
Norris of Tarleton and
Middleforth
Norris of Davy Hulme
Nowell of Rede
Nuthall of Nuthall

Nuthall of Tottington
Ogle of Whiston
Ogle of Prescot
Oldham of Oldham
Oldham of Manchester
Ormeston of Ormeston
Ormrode of Ormrode
Orrill of Orrill
Orrill of Turton
Osbaldiston of Osbaldiston
Osbaldiston of Sunderland
Parker, Lord Morley and
Monteagle, Hornby Castle
Parker of Bradkirk
Parker of Entwistle
Parker of Bromlowe [? Brows-
holme]
Parker of Holland
Parr of Kempnough and
Cleworth
Patten of Warrington
Pemberton of Pemberton
Penketh of Penketh
Pennington of Wigan
Pigot of Preston
Pilkington of Pilkington
Pilkington of Rivington
Plessington of Plessington
Plessington of Pelingford
Porter of Lancaster
Preston of Preston
Preston of Holker
Preston of Mannor
Prestwich of Prestwich
Pudsey of Bolton
Radcliff of Ordsall
Radcliff of Radcliff
Radcliff of Radcliff, another
descent
Radcliff of Radcliff, another
descent
Radcliff of Chatterton
Radcliff of Todmorden
Radcliff of Leigh
Radcliff of Wimberley
Ratcliff of Edgworth
Rawlinson of Greenhead,
Tottlebank, and Carke
Rawstorne of Newhall
Reddish of Reddish
Redman of Gressingham
Ridge of Marple and Ridge
Rigby of Harrock
Rigby of Middleton
Rigby of Layton and Burgh
Rigby of Huncote
Rigby of Rigby
Rigmaden of Rigmaden
Riley of the Green
Rishton of Ponthalghe
Rishton of Antley
Rishton of Dunkenhalghe
Rishton of Rishton

Rishton of Dunnishopp
Risley of Risley
Rixton of Rixton
Robinson of Preston, &c.
Sal[es]bury of Sal[es]bury
Sale of Hop Carr
Samlesbury of Samlesbury
Sandford of Nuthurst
Sandys of Graythwaite
Sankey of Sankey
Sawrey of Plumpton
Scaresbreck of Scaresbreck
Sclater of Light Oakes
Scillycorn of Scillycorn
Scolefield of Scolefield
Shackerley of Shackerley
Sharples of Sharples
Sharples of Frickleton
Sharrock of Walton
Shaw of Bull-haghe
Shaw of Heath Charnock
Shaw of Shaw Place
Shaw of Preston
Shaw of Hey Side
Sherborne of Sherborne
Sherborne of Stannihurst
Sherborne of Wolf House
Sherborne of Ribbleton
Sherborne of Mitton
Sherborne of Twistleton
Sherrington of Sherrington
Shuttleworth of Hacking
Shuttleworth of Gawthorpe
Shuttleworth of Asteley
Shuttleworth of Bedford
Shuttleworth of Shuttleworth
Shuttleworth of Larbricke
Singleton of Singleton
Singleton of Staning
Singleton of Browcow
Slater of Light Oakes
Smith of Cuerdley
Smyth of Peel House
Sorocold of Barton
Southworth of Samlesbury
Spencer of Ashton Hall
Standish of Standish
Standish of Duxbury
Standish of Burghe
Stanley Earls of Derby
Stanley of Hornby Castle
Stanley of Stanley
Stanley of Moor Hall
Stanley of Bickerstaffe
Stanley of Crosshall
Stanley of Broughton
Stanley of Holt and Tatton
Stanley of Eccleston
Starkey of Barthington
Starkey of Huntroyd
Starkey of Aughton
Starkey of Pendle Hall
Strangeways of Strangeways

Sutton of Rixton
Talbot of Dinckley
Talbot of Sal[es]bury
Talbot of Carr
Tetlow of Cunscough
Tetlow of Oldham
Tildsley of Tildsley, Wardley
Tildsley of Garret
Tildsley of Moreleys
Tong of Tong
Torbeck of Torbeck
Townley of Townley
Townley of Barnside
Townley of Carr
Townley of Royle
Townley of Oakenhead
Townley of Stonedge
Townley of Ditton
Townley of Littleton
Townleys of Hirstwood
Trafford of Trafford
Trafford of Chatterton
Travers of Neatby
Tunstall of Thurland Castle
Tunstall of Bolton
Turton of Turton
Valentine of Bentcliff
Veale of Winneyleys
Urmaston of West Leigh
Ursewick of Lancaster
Wadsworth of Hayton
Wall of Preston and Morehall
Wall of Preston and Chingle
Hall
Walmsley of Showley
Walmsley of Caldcotes
Walmsley of Banister Hall
Walmsley of Dunkenhalgh
Walton of Walton
Watmough of Micklenhead
West of Borwick
Westby of Mirescough
Westby of Rawcliffe
Westby of Mowbreck
Whittacre of Simonstone
Whittingham of Whittingham
Winckley of Winckley
Winckley of Preston
Winstanley of Winstanley
Wood of Turton
Woodward of Shevington
Woolfall of Woolfall
Woolfall of Aughton
Woolton of Woolton
Worsley of Worsley and
Booths
Worsley of Manchester
Worthington of Worthington
Worthington of Blainsco
Worthington of Crawshaw
Worthington of Shevington
Wrightington of Wrightington

The following additional names of the gentry of Lancashire have not in our manuscript copy the residences, though they have the arms annexed: Agard, Antringham, Apleisdon, Arrowsmith, Arbrech, Ball, Bayne, Bellowe, Bewick, Bethone, Bolton, Bozona, Broughton, Brindleshaw, Brough, Bushoppe, Byron, Chantrell, Curwen, Dalton, Dansey [Dauntesey], Delamere, Delafield, Denneta, English, Fleming, Fitzwarren, Fitzwilliams, Forward, Frickleton, Garnet, Gentel, Gawen, Goldsworth, Greenham, Grassam, Halliwell, Hawksted, Haydock, Heyton, Hodgson, Ipress, Irebell, Kendall, Keswick, Kirstow, Linacres, Linsey, Magnyll, Mildmore, Morris, Mouthall, Norvana, North, Norwood, Ormesby, Peeford, Peyton, Pickering, Plumpton, Prent, Ransford, Rawsthorne, Sands, Sanupe, Scales, Smith, Strickland, Tapaler, Thompson, Thornborough, Thwaytes, Tipping, Travers, Twyford, Verdun, Weld, Werdon, Windsore, Wright.

The following names of persons connected with the county palatine are taken from **Mr.** Thompson Cooper's "New Biographical Dictionary" (1873), which contains concise notices of eminent persons of all ages and countries, and more particularly of distinguished natives of **Great** Britain and Ireland. The list, it should be added, is by no means complete, the names of many eminent Lancashire men being omitted. Of the *literati* of the county a very complete dictionary, with biographical and bibliographical notes, will be found in the admirable "List of Lancashire Authors," edited for the Manchester Literary Club by Mr. Chas. W. Sutton. Mr. Thompson Cooper's list briefly specifies dates and places of birth when given:—

Ainsworth Robert, lexicographer, 1660-1743 ; Eccles.
Alanson Edward, eminent surgeon, 1747-1823 ; Newton.
Allen William, cardinal, 1532-1594 ; born in Lancashire.
Almon John, c. 1738-1805 ; Liverpool.
Ambrose Isaac, 1604-1664 ; born in Lancashire.
Andrews Robert ; born in Lancashire (?).
Annett Peter, said to be born at Liverpool ; died 1778.
Arkwright Sir Richard, 1732-1792 ; Preston.
Arrowsmith Edward, Jesuit, c. 1586-1628 ; Haydock, Winwick.
Ashe John, chaplain to Lady Sarah Houghton, 1672-1734.
Ashton Thomas, D.D., 1716-1775 ; Lancaster (?).
Ashworth Caleb, D.D., 1722-1775 ; born in Lancashire.
Askew Ægeon, born in Lancashire about 1576.
Assheton Nicholas, 1590-1625.
Assheton William, D.D., 1641-1711 ; Middleton.
Birch Peter, D.D., ob. 1710 ; born in Lancashire.
Boardman Andrew, D.D.
Bolton Samuel, D.D., 1606-1654 ; Manchester.
Booker John, 1601-1667 ; Manchester.
Booth Barton, 1681-1733 ; born in Lancashire.
Bostock John, M.D., 1774-1846 ; Liverpool.
Bowles John, bp., —1637 ; born in Lancashire.
Bradford John, martyr, 1510-1555 ; Manchester.
Brandreth Joseph, M.D., —1815 ; Ormskirk.
Bridgeman Sir Orlando, 1674.
Brierley Roger, —1637 ; born near Rochdale.
Briggs John, poet, 1788-1824 ; born near Cartmel.
Byrom John, poet, 1691-1763 ; Kersal.
Carter Oliver, B.D., fellow of Manchester Coll. Church, —1605.
Carter Peter, born in Lancashire.
Chaderton Lawrence, D.D., c. 1537-1640 ; Chadderton.
Chaderton William, bishop, —1608 ; Manchester.
Chamberlaine Robert, poet, c. 1607 ; born in Lancashire.
Chisenhale Edward, colonel for Charles I., author ; born in Lancashire.
Christopherson John, bishop, —1558 ; Ulverston.
Clarke Henry, LL.D., 1745-1818 ; Salford.
Clowes John, 1743-1831 ; Manchester.
Cogan Thomas, M.D., —1607 ; Master Manchester Grammar School.
Cort Henry, 1740-1900 ; Lancaster.
Cottam Thomas, Jesuit, —1582 ; born in Lancashire.
Crabtree Henry, curate of Todmorden, author, c. —1685.
Crabtree William, astronomer, 1610-1644 ; born at Broughton, Manchester.
Dalton John, D.C.L., philosopher, 1766-1844 ; lived at Manchester
Dee John, LL.D., 1527-1608 ; warden of Manchester.
De Quincey Thomas, 1785-1859 ; Manchester.
Dodd Charles, 1672-1743 ; born near Preston.
Dodd Thomas, printseller in Manchester, 1771-1850.
Evanson Edward, 1731-1805 ; Warrington.
Falkner Thomas, 1710-1784 ; Manchester.
Fleetwood William, —1594 ; born in Lancashire.
Foster Henry, 1797-1831 ; Wood Plumpton.
Frankland Thomas, 1633-1690 ; born in Lancashire.
Gooden Peter, —1695 ; born near Manchester.
Greswell Edward, D.D., 1797-1869 ; Manchester.
Harland John, author, 1806-1868 ; lived in Manchester.
Harwood Edward, D.D, 1729-1794 ; born in Lancashire.
Hemans Mrs. Felicia, poetess, 1794-1835 ; Liverpool.

Henry William, M.D., 1774-1836 ; Manchester.
Heywood Oliver, 1629-1677 ; Bolton.
Holden George, vicar of Maghull, 1783-1865.
Henry Henry, D.D., 1596-1665 ; born in Lancashire.
Horrox Jeremiah, astronomer, 1619-1641 ; born at Toxteth.
Huddleston John, priest, 1608-1698 ; born in Lancashire.
Huddleston Richard, priest, 1583-1655 ; born in Lancashire.
Hutton Matthew, archbishop, 1529-1606 ; Warton.
Jones Thomas, archbishop, —1619 ; born in Lancashire.
Kemble John Philip, actor, 1757-1823 ; Prescot.
Leigh Charles, M.D., author ; Grange.
Leland John, D.D., 1691-1766 ; Wigan.
Lever Sir Ashton, —1788 ; born near Manchester.
Macdonald Archibald, monk at Liverpool, —1814.
Markland J. H., author, 1788-1864 ; Manchester.
Markland Jeremiah, 1693-1776 ; Childwall.
Neville Edmund, Jesuit, —1648 ; born in Lancashire.
Neville Edward, Jesuit, died 1709 ; born in Lancashire.
Nightingale Joseph, 1775-1824 ; Chowbent.
Nowell Alexander, c. 1507-1602 ; Read Hall.
Ogden Samuel, D.D., 1716-1778 ; Manchester.
Peel Sir Robert, 1750-1830 ; born in Lancashire.
Peel Sir Robert, 1788-1850 ; born in Lancashire.
Percival Thomas, M.D., 1740-1804 ; Warrington.
Pilkington James, bishop, 1520-1576 ; born near Bolton.
Rawlinson Christopher, 1677-1733 ; born in Lancashire.
Richmond Legh, 1772-1827 ; Liverpool.
Rock Daniel, D.D., 1799-1871 ; Liverpool.
Romney George, 1734-1802 ; Dalton.
Roscoe Henry, 1800-1836 ; Liverpool.
Roscoe Thomas, 1791-1871 ; Liverpool.
Roscoe William, 1753-1831 ; Liverpool.
Rushton Edward, priest, —1586 ; born in Lancashire.
Sanderson John, D.D., —1602 ; born in Lancashire.
Sandys Edwin, bishop and archbishop, 1519-1588 ; born in Lancashire.
Sharples Henry, D.D., R.C. bishop Lancashire district, —1850.
Shuttleworth P. N., bishop, 1782-1841 ; Kirkham.
Smyth William, bishop, c. 1450-1514 ; Prescot.
Speed John, c. 1555-1629 ; Farrington.
Stubbs George, 1724-1806 ; Liverpool.
Taylor John, D.D., 1694-1761 ; born in Lancashire.
Towers Richard, 1781-1844 ; Preston.
Townley Charles, 1737-1782 ; Townley.
Travis George, —1797 ; Royton.
Tunstall James, D.D., vicar of Rochdale, c. 1710-1772.
Turner William, D.D., 1800-1872 ; Preston.
Wakefield Gilbert, 1756-1801 ; lived at Warrington.
Walker Thomas, 1784-1836 ; Manchester.
Walmsley Charles, D.D., 1722-1797 ; born near Wigan.
Warburton John, 1682-1759 ; Bury.
Weever John, c. 1576-1632 ; born in Lancashire.
Wensleydale James Parke, Lord, 1782-1868 ; Highfield, near Liverpool.
Whewell William, D.D., 1794-1866 ; Lancaster.
Whitaker John, 1735-1808 ; Manchester.
Whitaker Thomas Dunham, vicar of Whalley, 1759-1821.
Whitaker William, D.D., 1548-1595 ; Holme, Burnley.
Wilson Anthony, 1750— ; Wigan.
Worthington John, 1618-1671 ; Manchester.

The following particulars respecting the heraldry of the twenty-eight incorporate towns of Lancashire are contained in a paper contributed by Miss Fishwick to the *Palatine Note Book*.[1] The chief aim in the choice of charges it will be seen has been either to represent the ancient families, the local industries, the public buildings, or to make an heraldic pun on the name. Three of the towns, Ashton-under-Lyne, Bolton, and Warrington, have assumed arms to which they have no legitimate claim. The local authorities, when they were incorporated, instead of following the usual legal course of petitioning for a grant of armorial ensigns, took upon themselves to manufacture the pseudo-heraldic insignia which appear on the common seals of their corporations, and which are displayed in many other ways in defiance of the laws of heraldry and of good taste. Many of the Lancashire towns received seals at a very early date, some of which afterwards received arms, and others retain their seals only. Among the former are Liverpool, Clitheroe, and Wigan ; amongst the latter, Garstang, Kirkham, and Newton. If these towns ever received arms they have fallen into disuse.

[1] *Palatine Note Book*, v. ii. pp. 118-120.—C.

1. WIGAN. Incorporated A.D. 1100.—*Azure*, the moot hall; in the dexter chief a sword erect, all proper.
2. CLITHEROE. Incorporated 1147.—*Gules*, the castle and moat, proper.
3. KIRKHAM. Incorporated 1286.—Seal: a dove, with an olive branch in its mouth.
4. LANCASTER. Incorporated 1461.[1]—*Gules*, a lion passant gardant *or*, on a chief *azure*, a fleur-de-lis of the second.
5. NEWTON-IN-MAKERFIELD. Incorporated 1558.—For the seal, see Lewis, "Top. Dict." iii. 360. Out of a ducal coronet a ram's head, holding in the mouth a sprig of laurel (the crest of the Leghs, lords of Newton).
6. LIVERPOOL. Incorporated 4th July, 1626.—*Argent*, a cormorant[2] *sable*, beaked and legged *gules*, holding a branch of laver, proper. *Motto:* Deus nobis haec otia fecit.
7. GARSTANG. Incorporated 1680.—For the seal, see Lewis, "Top. Dict." ii. 245, and Fishwick's "History of Garstang," p. 68.
8. PRESTON. Incorporated 1685.—*Azure*, a paschal lamb constant with banner, all *argent*; round the head a nimbus *or*; in base, the letters P.P.[3] of the second.
9. BOLTON-LE-MOORS. Incorporated 11th October, 1838.—*Gules*, two bendlets *or*.
10. MANCHESTER. Incorporated 23rd October, 1838.—*Gules*, three bendlets enhanced *or*, a chief *argent*, thereon waves of the sea and a ship under sail, proper. *Motto:* Concilio et labore.
11. SALFORD. Incorporated 16th April, 1844.—*Azure*, semée of bees volant; a shuttle between three garbs *or*, on a chief of the last a bale corded, proper, between two mill rinds *sable*. Granted 6th November, 1844. *Motto:* Integrity and industry.
12. ASHTON-UNDER-LYNE. Incorporated 29th September, 1847.—*Argent*, a mullet pierced *sable* (the ancient family coat of Assheton of Ashton), a crescent for difference. *Motto:* Labor omnia vincit.
13. WARRINGTON. Incorporated 1847.—*Argent*, six lioncels, 3, 2, and 1, *gules* (traditionally said to be the coat of the Vilars, early lords of Warrington). *Motto:* Dat Deus incrementum.
14. OLDHAM. Incorporated 13th June, 1849.—*Sable*, a chevron between three owls, proper; on a chief of the second, three roses proper, seeded *or*. *Motto:* Sapere aude (the arms and motto of Bishop Oldham).
15. BLACKBURN. Incorporated 1851.—*Argent*, a fesse wavy *sable*, between three bees volant, proper; on a chief *vert*, a bugle horn, stringed, *argent*, between three fusils *or*. Granted 7th February, 1852. *Motto:* Arte et labore.
16. ROCHDALE. Incorporated 9th September, 1856.—*Argent*, a woolpack encircled by two branches of the cotton tree flowered and conjoint, proper; a bordure, *sable*, charged with eight martlets of the field. Granted 1857. *Motto:* Credo signo.

17. STALYBRIDGE.[4] Incorporated 5th March, 1857.—*Argent*, a chevron ingrailed, *gules*, between, in chief, two crosses moussue and, in base, a mullet, pierced, *sable*; two flasques *azure*, each charged with a rose of the field. Granted 18th June, 1857. *Motto:* Absque labore nihil.
18. SOUTHPORT. Incorporated 1861.—*Argent*, a fesse dancette, *gules*, between, in chief, three crosslets fitchée, *sable*; and in base a lifeboat, manned, on the waves of the sea, proper. *Motto:* Salus populi.
19. BURNLEY. Incorporated 1861.—*Or*, a chevron engrailed, *gules*, between, in chief, two fusils and, in base a lion rampant, *sable*; a chief wavy of the last, thereon a dexter hand erect, couped at the wrist, *argent*, between two bees volant of the first. Granted 17th May, 1862. *Motto:* Pretium que et causa laboris.
20. BARROW-IN-FURNESS. Incorporated 13th June, 1867.—*Gules*, on a bend *or*, a bee volant and an arrow flighted, proper, between, in chief, a snake nowed, and in base a stag tripping, of the second; on a chief *argent*, a steamer on the waves of the sea, proper. Granted 13th December, 1867. *Motto:* Semper sursum.
21. ST. HELENS. Incorporated 5th February, 1868.—*Argent*, two bars *azure*, over all a cross *sable*; in the first and fourth quarters a saltire *gules*; and in the second and third a gryphen segreant of the third. *Motto:* Ex terra lucem.
22. BLACKPOOL.—No arms have been granted to this borough, but the Corporation have a seal, in which, however, but little of the spirit of heraldry is displayed. It is divided quarterly: (1) the pier and promenade, (2) a ship sailing on the sea, (3) the sands and a bathing van, and (4) a lifeboat manned.
23. BURY. Incorporated 9th September, 1876.—Per cross quarterly quartered *azure* and *argent*: first, *argent*, an anvil; second, *azure*, a golden fleece; third, two shuttles crossed; fourth, a branch of the Egyptian papyrus—all proper. Granted 28th February, 1877. *Motto:* Vincit omnia industria.
24. ACCRINGTON. Incorporated 15th February, 1878.—*Gules*, on a fesse *argent* a shuttle fesswise, proper; in the base two printing cylinders, issuant therefrom a piece of calico (parsley pattern), also proper; on a chief per pale, on *and vert*, a lion rampant *perpure* and a stag courant *or*. Granted 26th August, 1879. *Motto:* Industry and prudence conquer.
25. OVER DARWEN.—Arms not yet granted.
26. HEYWOOD. Incorporated 18th February, 1881.—*Or*, five pellets between two bendlets engrailed, the whole between as many mascles *sable*. *Motto:* Alte volo.
27. BOOTLE-CUM-LINACRE. Incorporated 1881.—*Argent*, on a chevron *azure*, between three fleurs-de-lis *sable*, three stags' heads caboshed *or*, on a chief *sable*, three mural crowns, proper. *Motto:* Respice, aspice, prospice.
28. CHORLEY.—Arms not yet granted.
29. BACUP   ditto
30. MIDDLETON   ditto
31. MOSSLEY   ditto

This county gives the title of Duke (or Duchess) of Lancaster to the sovereign; Manchester confers the title of duke on the Montagus; (West) Derby, the title of earl on the Stanleys; and, until lately, Warrington, that of earl on the Greys; the Byrons are barons of Rochdale, and Winmarleigh confers a barony on the family of Wilson-Patten; the Duke of Hamilton had a seat (Ashton Hall) on the banks of the Lune, the Earl of Ellesmere resides at Worsley, the Earl of Wilton at Heaton, Lord Petre at Dunkenhalgh, Lord Suffield at Middleton, and the Duke of Devonshire at Holker; the Earl of Sefton resides at Croxteth Park, and Earl Balcarres, Baron of Wigan, at Haigh Hall. The other seats of noble families in Lancashire are, Knowsley Hall, Earl of Derby; Lathom House, Lord Skelmersdale; Childwall Hall, Marquis of Salisbury; Holker Hall, Duke of Devonshire; Bewsey Hall, Lord Lilford; Worsley Hall, Earl of Ellesmere; Witherslack Hall, Lord Stanley of Preston; Great Lever Hall, Earl of Bradford; Peel Hall, late Lord Kenyon; Ashton-under-Lyne Hall, Earl of Stamford; Dinkley Hall, Lord Warren de Tabley; and Eccles Riggs, Viscount Cross. The Listers derive their title from the vale of one of the

[1] Lancaster appears to have been incorporated at a much earlier date than is here given. The "mayor, bailiffs, and commonalty of the ville of Lancaster" are mentioned in the charter of 37 Edw. III. (1363-4); and a charter was granted by John, Earl of Morton, which he confirmed after his accession to the crown. The arms should be—per fesse *azure* and *gules*, in chief a fleur-de-lis, and in base a lion passant guardant *or*. The placing of a chief *azure* on a field *gules*—colour upon colour—is false heraldry.—C.
[2] The bird which is graven on the corporation seal has been the subject of much controversy, and variously described as a cormorant, a dove, a shoveller duck, an eagle, and a hypothetical bird, the "liver," to which the name of the town has been traditionally ascribed. The sprig in its mouth has been interpreted as an olive branch, a branch of laver or seaweed, and a fleur-de-lis; but it is now established with tolerable certainty that it is a rude device of the eagle of St. John, the patron saint

of the king, to whom the town owed its first chartered rights. A crest and supporters, in addition to the arms, were granted in 1797, viz., Crest: A cormorant, the wings elevated, in the beak a branch of laver, all proper. Supporters: Dexter, Neptune, with sea-green mantle flowing, the waist wreathed with laver; on his head an eastern crown *or*; in his right hand his trident *sable*, the left supporting a banner of the arms of Liverpool. Sinister, a triton wreathed as the dexter, and blowing his shell, the right hand supporting a banner, thereon a ship under sail in perspective, all proper; the banner staves *or*.—C.
[3] The letters P.P. have been variously interpreted. Some facetiously read them Proud Preston, others pro patria, but the more probable meaning is pictura pacis, in allusion to the Agnus Dei, or lamb of peace.—C.
[4] The borough of Stalybridge is partly in Lancashire and partly in Cheshire.—C.

principal rivers of the county, but their seat is at Gisburne Park, in Ribblesdale, on the eastern side of the border, before the Ribble quits Yorkshire.

Before the general history of Lancashire is concluded, it may be proper shortly to advert to the geographical situation of the county, and to its agriculture and minerals, as well as to its rivers and other distinguishing characteristics.

The geographical situation of Lancashire is between 53° 20′ and 54° 25′ north latitude, and between 2° 0′ and 3° 17′ west longitude; it is bounded on the north by Cumberland and Westmorland, on the east by Yorkshire, on the south and south-east by Cheshire, and on the west by the Irish Sea. Its extreme length from N.W. to S.E., including Furness, is 75 miles, and its greatest breadth 45 miles; its circumference is 294 miles; and its surface 1,765 square miles, of which about 1,125 are comprehended in the district south of the Ribble and 650 to the north of that river. The area of the county comprises 1,219,220 acres of land, of which about 400,000 are in tillage, 450,000 in pasture, and about 400,000 in woodlands, moors, and mosses, of which 350,000 acres may be termed waste. It is divided into the six hundreds of Lonsdale, Amounderness, Blackburn, Leyland, Salford, and West Derby, and contains 69 parishes (exclusive of nine extra-parochial places), 446 townships, 16 Parliamentary boroughs, and 29 market towns. This county, as has been already seen, is palatinate, and it is the chief seat of the duchy of Lancaster. Ecclesiastically, it is in the province of York, and in the dioceses of Manchester, Liverpool, and Carlisle; and judicially, in the northern circuit, though of late years it has practically formed a circuit of itself, with assizes held at Lancaster, at Liverpool, and at Manchester; and presentments have been made recommending the formation of Lancashire into a separate circuit.

The whole of the western side of Lancashire extending from the Mersey to the river Duddon is washed by the Irish Sea, but though maritime the coast-line does not present any of those features of wild romantic grandeur observable in other parts of the kingdom, where the precipitous cliffs and rocky promontories projecting into the deep water have been cavern-hollowed and worn into fantastic forms by the constant beating of the billows. For the most part the ground, which slopes gently towards the sea, consists of pasture and meadow land, with occasionally a range of low sandhills, formed by the drifting winds. But if level, the coast is by no means monotonous. Between the estuary of the Ribble and the outlet of the Wyre, where Blackpool—the Brighton of the North, as it has been designated—faces full front to the Irish Sea, the water breaks with impetuous force upon the beach, the waves oftentimes rolling up to the very edge of the three-mile esplanade. Further north the aspect is more varied, the picturesquely-irregular shores of Morecambe Bay, where moor and fell blend pleasantly with the low-lying meadows and pastures that genius and industry have won back from the sea, presenting many a scene of interest and beauty; while beyond, where the limestone ridges that form the stony barrier of the Lake country stretch away westward from the mountain to the main, the whole extent of sea-margin is more boldly featured. A noticeable feature of the Lancashire coast is the number of its estuaries. Though not the largest, the most important is that of the Mersey, the southern side of which belongs to Cheshire. Curiously enough no mention of it is made either by Ptolemy, the Roman geographer, or in the Itinerary of Antonine; and as the vestiges of a primeval forest have been discovered where the tide now flows, the omission gives colour to the suggestion that in Celtic times the level of the estuary was higher, and the site of Liverpool little else than a swampy morass, the broad river on which now floats the sea-craft of a hundred nations being then only an inconsiderable stream. The estuary of the Ribble, where Lytham and Southport confront each other, is by far the largest of these three river outlets, and next in importance is that of the Wyre, on the edge of which stands the rising town of Fleetwood. The mouth of the Lune, which forms the port of Lancaster, has, so far as its commerce is concerned, sunk into comparative insignificance, and having become encumbered by sandbanks, the navigation is considerably impeded; and the same obstructions to commerce exist, in an equal or greater degree, in the broad estuary, where at ebb of tide the Leven winds its way through the shifting channels of the Ulverston sands.

The eastern side of the county, which borders on Yorkshire, presents a marked contrast in form and feature, the division line forming a part of the great Pennine range, a mountainous ridge—the Backbone of England, as it has been called—that stretches northwards from the Peak in Derbyshire to the Cheviots on the Scottish border. Here nature presents herself in her sternest guise, the hills in many places attaining a considerable altitude, and presenting in their ruggedness much the appearance they did after the last upheavals and convulsions of the geological period. The highest eminence in the chain is Pendle Hill, overlooking the town and castle of Clitheroe, where the limestone formation begins, which has an elevation of 1,831 feet; Boulsworth Hill reaches to the height of 1,700 feet; and the summit of Blackstone Edge, north of Rochdale, is 1,323 feet above the sea level, while Bleasdale Forest has an altitude of 1,709 feet. It is in the

Furness district, however, that the highest eminences are to be found, Coniston Old Man, the *alt maen* or high rock, being 2,577 feet, the Seathwaite Fells 2,537 feet, and Brown Pike 2,239 feet in height. The secondary elevations are Rivington Pike, a few miles north of Bolton, 1,545 feet, Caton Moor, Padiham Heights, Hambleton Hill, Longridge Fell, Woolfell Cragg, and the Cartmel and Graygrith Fells. The other principal heights are Billinge Hill, Cribden Hill, Clough Pike, Wharton Crag, Winter Hill, Grizedale Fells, Uglaw Pike, and Beacon Hill.

The southernmost part of the county is comparatively flat, the new red sandstone, of which the surface rock is for the most part composed, occasionally rising into gentle ridges but never attaining any considerable altitude. Between Liverpool and Manchester the country is almost a continuous plain, occupied at one time by peat wastes and mosses, that have, however, within the present century, been to a large extent reclaimed by drainage and cultivation, the most notable of them being Chat or St. Chad's Moss, with Barton Moss, which is essentially an adjunct, where Stephenson encountered his greatest difficulties when constructing the original line of railway between Manchester and Liverpool. Further north the scenery is more varied and picturesque, the valleys watered by the Ribble and the Lune possessing nearly all the elements of picturesque landscape in charming combination. The tributary streams which swell the affluents—the Hodder, the Calder, the Douglas, the Darwen, and the Wenning—as they descend from the higher moorlands in which they are cradled, pass through a varied country, and exhibit many picturesque reaches, as yet unspoiled by manufacturing industry ; and even the Irwell, sullen and inky as it is below Manchester, presents many sylvan features in the wooded dingles about Summerseat and in the glens nearer its source within the limits of the old forest of Rossendale.

A very large proportion of the county was at one time forest land, and long subsequent to the granting of the Forest Charter—*Carta de Foresta*—in the reign of Henry III. (1224), much of the country was wild woodland, in which the beasts of the chase roamed at will. One of these forests—the Forest of Blackburnshire—included the four chases of Pendle, Rossendale, Accrington, and Trawden, and embraced an area estimated at 50,000 acres, or nearly 80 square miles, a district in which there are places that still retain their primeval features, and in their name-survivals bear evidence of the nature of their former occupants, as for example in Wolfstones, Wolfenden, Staghills, Stacksteads (more correctly Stagsteads), Swineshaw, Hogshead, Boarsgreave, and Sowclough.

Manufacturing is, for the most part, confined to the southern half of the county, in which, in addition to the twin cities of Liverpool and Manchester, there are many populous towns. In the Fylde country, north-west of Preston, the people are chiefly employed in agiculture, and corn-growing is carried on upon an extensive scale ; but further north, in the neighbourhood of Lancaster, and upon the lower slopes of the Bleasdale Moors, the land is for the most part devoted to meadow and pasture.

Such, in brief, are the natural features of the county, which, if the latest in its formation, has yet, by the genius, the industry, and the commercial enterprise of its people, contributed perhaps more than any other to the wealth and the greatness of the common country.

Although the climate of Lancashire is humid the air is generally pure and salubrious. In the elevated and hilly regions on the north and eastern boundaries it is, of course, cold and piercing, but in the lower districts, shelving to the south and the west, it is in general mild and genial. Severe frost is seldom experienced in the low lands of Lancashire for more than a few days ; a covering of snow is generally soon dissolved by the mildness of the atmosphere, and by the saline particles wafted by the western winds from the Irish Sea and the Atlantic Ocean. Seed-time and harvest are as early here as in the neighbouring counties. They vary a little between the north and the south parts of the county, and are the latest towards the east, contiguous to the high moorlands. The winds generally veer from S. to N. by the W. point ; they are rarely easterly, and those which most prevail are the S.W. the S. and the W. As to the humidity of the climate, it must be admitted " that the hills which form the line of separation between Yorkshire and Lancashire arrest the clouds from the Atlantic Ocean in their progress, causing them to deposit their contents," and that consequently there is more rain in Lancashire than the general average of the kingdom ; but the difference is less than is imagined, and it will be shown that the opinion that Lancashire is the water-pot of England, and that " it is always raining in Manchester," is a popular error, capable of refutation from the test of meteorological observation. The average depth of rain which falls throughout England in the course of a year is about 28 inches. London appears to be subject to less rain than any other part of the kingdom ; and as we recede from the metropolis, the quantity of rain is frequently found to increase in about the same proportion, so that in Cornwall it is nearly the same as in Lancashire, where, in the mountainous districts, an average of nearly 50 inches is reached, the average for the entire county being about 35 inches. The following table, which exhibits the mean monthly and annual quantity of rain, in inches and decimal parts, at various places, for an average of many years, will serve to correct a general prejudice against the climate of this county :—

MEAN MONTHLY AND ANNUAL QUANTITIES OF RAIN AT VARIOUS PLACES, BEING
THE AVERAGES FOR MANY YEARS.

	Manchester 33 years.	Liverpool 18 years.	Chatsworth 16 years.	Lancaster 20 years.	Kendal 25 years.	Dumfries 16 years.	Glasgow 17 years.	London 40 years.	Paris 15 years.	Viviers 40 years.	General Average.
	Inch.	Inch.	Inch.	Inch.	Inch.	Inch.	Inch.	Inch.	r. Inch.	r. Inch.	Inch.
January ..	2·310	2·177	2·196	3·461	5·299	3·095	1·595	1·464	1·228	2·477	2·530
February ...	2·568	1·847	1·652	2·995	5·126	2·837	1·741	1·250	1·232	1·700	2·295
March	2·098	1·523	1·322	1·753	3·151	2·164	1·184	1·172	1·190	1·927	1·748
April	2·010	2·104	2·078	2·180	2·986	2·017	·979	1·279	1·185	2·686	1·950
May	2·395	2·573	2·118	2·460	3·480	2·568	1·641	1·636	1·767	2·931	2·407
June	2·502	2·816	2·286	2·512	2·722	2·974	1·343	1·738	1·697	2·562	2·315
July	3·697	3·663	3·006	4·140	4·959	3·256	2·303	2·448	1·800	1·882	3·115
August	3·665	3·311	2·435	4·581	5·039	3·199	2·746	1·807	1·900	2·347	3·103
September ..	3·281	3·654	2·289	3·751	4·874	4·350	1·617	1·842	1·550	4·140	3·135
October ...	3·922	3·724	3·079	4·151	5·439	4·143	2·297	2·092	1·780	4·741	3·587
November..	3·360	3·441	2·634	3·775	4·785	3·174	1·904	2·222	1·720	4·187	3·120
December ...	3·832	3·288	2·569	3·955	6·084	3·142	1·981	1·736	1·600	2·397	3·058
Year.	36·140	34·121	27·664	39·714	53·944	36·919	21·331	20·686	18·649	33·977	32·313

As the nature of the soil and the minerals which a county affords depends on the rocks and beds which underlie them, it is necessary to give a list of the strata, which may be stated in the following *descending* order.[1] The geology of the county may be broadly ranged under these nine great divisions:—

I. Drifting Deposits.
II. Trias, or New Red Sandstone.
III. Permian Series.
IV. The Coal Measures.
V. Limestone Shale.

VI. Mountain Limestone.
VII. Old Red Sandstone.
VIII. Upper Silurian.
IX. Lower Silurian.[2]

Under these we now proceed to enumerate the subdivisions, specifying the minerals contained in each subdivision, with their qualities and uses, and then briefly indicating the nature of the soils forming the surface of such subdivision.

I.—DRIFT DEPOSITS.

The four subdivisions of this great upper deposit are—

1. The VALLEY-GRAVEL.—This consists of a bed of coarse gravel, composed of various-sized azoic, palæozoic, and a few triassic rocks, well rounded, parted with layers of fine sand without pebbles, exhibiting every appearance of having been deposited by water; most frequently stratified, but sometimes unstratified. It has generally two well-marked terraces above the level of the present rivers, as well as some minor terraces. On the top of this deposit are generally found three to four feet of silty loam. The valley-gravel is about 40 feet in maximum thickness.

Soils, &c.—All the rich meadows and pasture-lands in the county are found lying on this deposit, such as those on the rivers Lune, Ribble, Darwen, Wenning, Wyre, Calder, Brock, Mersey and Roch, comprehending a very large extent of excellent land.

2. FOREST SAND AND GRAVEL.—This is a deposit of sharp forest sand, parted with layers of gravel, and the same rocks as are contained in No. 1, and having every appearance of a regular deposit by water, distinguishable only by its being found at greater elevations, containing more sand, and being generally more regularly stratified. It often contains thin beds of till and loam lying in it, as well as drifted coal. Its maximum thickness is about 90 feet.

Soils, &c.—All the soil found on the gently rising grounds in the county, reaching generally to about 800 feet above the level of the sea, and composing the sandy and loamy soils, which form good pasture and agricultural land.

3. TILL OR BOULDER CLAY.—This is a mass of strong brown clay, in which are mingled the same kinds of rock as those contained in Nos. 1 and 2, of sizes from six tons down to small

---

[1] For this admirable, clear, and concise summary of the rocks and beds, their minerals, and the soils above th m, I am indebted to the friendship of an able and eminent geologist, whom I am not permitted to name.—H.

[2] The geology of Lancashire has been very fully illustrated and described by numerous observers, a list of which, commencing as far back as the year 1667, comprising no less than 561 books, memoirs,

and papers, is given by Messrs. Whitaker and Tiddeman in the "Geological Survey Memoir on the Burnley Coal-field" (1875). Of the more modern investigators, special mention should be made of the Rev. Professor Sedgwick, whose researches extended more particularly to the country bordering upon the English Lakes; Professor Phillips, Professor Edward Hull, M.A., LL.D., F.R.S., and Mr. E. W. Binney, F.R.S.—C.

pebbles—some rounded and partly rounded, and others quite angular, especially coal-measure and magnesian limestone rocks, without any order of deposition, great and small stones being mixed together indiscriminately. It is quite impervious to water, and is well known as a valuable brick clay, and as being the deposit which yields striated or scored stones. Beds of fine laminated silt and patches of sand are sometimes found in it.

Soils, &c.—This deposit comprises the stiff clay soils on which, in the lower districts, are found thick beds of acid peat. It is also known for its thick beds of excellent brick clay. This deposit covers the greatest extent of country of any of the drift deposits, and is found from the level of the sea up to 1,200 feet above that level in some places, and is very variable in thickness.

4. LOWER GRAVEL.—This is a bed of sand or coarse gravel, having pebbles consisting of the same kinds of rocks as Nos. 1, 2, and 3, sometimes but not always well rounded, occurring under the brick clay. It often affords good springs of bright water. Its thickness is about 30 feet.

Soils, &c.—This deposit being seldom exposed at the surface, it affects but little the nature of the soils of the county.

II.—TRIAS, OR NEW RED SANDSTONE.

This division includes the KEUPER and the BUNTER strata. The KEUPER has two great beds—

1. The RED MARLS, 3,000 feet in thickness.

Soils, &c.—When uncovered by drift deposits, this bed forms strong red clay, similar to those found in Cheshire, and is remarkable for containing brine springs and beds of gypsum. It underlies a great extent of country on the west side of the county next the sea, though not exposed to view, owing to the thick beds of drift by which it is covered.

2. THE LOWER KEUPER, SANDSTONES AND WATER STONES.—This lower bed of the Keuper is about 450 feet in thickness.

Soils, &c.—It is seldom exposed in this county, but it yields beds of building stone.

BUNTER.—This has three deposits—

1. The UPPER MOTTLED SANDSTONE, 500 feet in thickness.

Soils, &c.—It is seldom exposed, but when it does form the soil it affords good warm land, and is remarkable for containing good springs of water.

2. PEBBLE BEDS, 650 feet in thickness.

Soils, &c.—These seldom afford any good building stone; but when near the surface, and uncovered by drift, they yield good, warm, and dry land.

3. LOWER MOTTLED RED SANDSTONE, 100 feet thick, but *often absent*. This is seldom exposed at the surface, and consequently has little influence on the composition of the soil.

III.—PERMIAN SERIES.

This great series may be classed in six subdivisions:—

1. LAMINATED AND FINE-GRAINED RED SANDSTONES.—These may be taken as about 300 feet in thickness.

Soils, &c.—These do not exercise much influence on the nature of the soils, but in the district about Furness Abbey they yield a good durable building stone, of which the abbey is built.

2. RED AND VARIEGATED CLAYS AND MARLS.—These are also about 300 feet thick, and contain sometimes, but not always, beds of limestone and gypsum, and bands of sandstone. The clays and limestones contain fossil shells of the genera Schizodus, Gervillia, &c.

Soils, &c.—These are seldom exposed at the surface, and consequently have little influence on the composition of the soils. The beds of limestone afford good water-setting limes, such as those of Bedford and Worsley. Other beds afford good building stone, as at Skillaw Clough, lying north-east of Ormskirk; and at Stank, in Lower Furness. Sometimes beds of fine white gypsum are met with in this deposit.

3. CONGLOMERATE OR BRECCIA.—This varies in thickness from one to a hundred feet.

Soils, &c.—The conglomerate is only exposed at two places in the county, viz., at Cheetham Weir-hole, near Manchester, and at Rougham Point, near Flookborough, in the parish of Cartmel, so that it has no effect on the soils of the county, and does not yield any building stones or useful minerals.

4. LOWER NEW RED SANDSTONE.—This is generally soft and incoherent; its thickness is about 500 feet.

Soils, &c.—It is seldom exposed to the surface, but it is met with at Collyhurst, near

Manchester; at Sutton, near St. Helens; at Grimshaw Delph, midway between Ormskirk and Wigan; at Roach Bridge, near Preston; at Cokersand Abbey; at Robshaw Point, at the mouth of the Lune, near Lancaster; and at Rougham Point, near Flookborough. It is well known from its affording most excellent moulding sand, and its yielding good springs of water.

5. RED SHALY CLAYS.—These are not seen anywhere in the county.

6. ASTLEY PEBBLE BEDS.—These, although containing the common coal plants, lie quite unconformable both to the coal measures and to the Upper Permian series. They are termed the Lower Permian, and are about 60 feet in thickness.

Soils, &c.—These beds are never exposed at the surface in this county, being only found in sinking.

IV.—THE COAL MEASURES.

These may be ranged under three subdivisions:—

1. THE UPPER COAL MEASURES.—These commence with the red shales and clays, containing beds of limestone, at Ardwick, near Manchester, and terminating with the Bradford four-foot coal. They are about 2,000 feet in thickness.

Minerals, &c.—These upper measures afford six beds of coal, which have been wrought at different places near Manchester, one of which, the lowest, the Pendleton and Bradford four-foot, is celebrated for its qualities as an iron-puddling and glass-making coal. The limestones, especially those at Ardwick, are known for their excellent water-setting properties, and (without entering into speculations as to their use by the Romans here) have been worked for the last hundred years.

2. MIDDLE COAL MEASURES.—These commence with the floor of the Pendleton four-foot, and terminate with the Riley or Arley Mine, having a thickness of 2,910 feet.

Minerals, &c.—These contain about twenty workable beds of coal, in the upper and middle parts yielding excellent steam coals, such as those of Denton, Ashton-under-Lyne, Oldham, Middleton, Burnley, Heywood, Bury, Clifton, Hulton, Worsley, Tyldesley, Atherton, Leigh, Hindley, Aspull, Blackrod, Wigan, Ashton-in-Makerfield, Haydock, Pemberton, St. Helens, Bickerstaff, &c. The lower seams yield good house and caking coals, such as the Black and the Bent mines of Ashton-under-Lyne and Oldham, and at Burnley, Cliviger, and Little Hulton; the King, the Smith, the Yard, and the Arley mines of Wigan, Hindley, Pemberton, St. Helens, and Bickerstaff. They also yield the cannels of Ashton-under-Lyne, Oldham, Hulton, Worsley, and Wigan.

3. LOWER COAL MEASURES.—These commence with the Arley Mine, and terminate with the lowest Millstone Grit, and are 3,500 feet in thickness.

Minerals, &c.—These lower measures include seven beds of coal, ranging over the greater part of the elevated parts of the county, and yield good caking and smithy coals, as well as coals suitable for household purposes. They are met with at Stalybridge, Mossley, Oldham, Rochdale, Todmorden, Bacup, Cliviger, Colne, Padiham, Accrington, Baxenden, Blackburn, Darwen, Turton, Horwich, Chorley, Wrightington, Upholland, and Newburgh. Some of the coal floors afford most excellent fireclays, which are extensively worked; and some of the most durable building stones and flag stones of the county are obtained from this group of the coal measures. The beds of shale on the high lands are known from their being covered by thick deposits of alkaline peat.

V.—LIMESTONE SHALE.

This division consists of various shales and grits, and is 2,000 feet in thickness.

Soils, &c.—It results in a surface of cold land, often covered with peat, and seldom containing minerals suitable for any useful purpose.

VI.—MOUNTAIN LIMESTONE.

This well-known series is also 2,000 feet in thickness.

Soils, Minerals, &c.—The mountain limestone forms the highlands in the north-east part of the county, giving dry pastures. It sometimes affords lead in small quantities, but is chiefly remarkable in the district of Furness for its containing the valuable deposits of hematite or red iron ore, which are found in immense masses, occupying valleys and "swallow holes" in the limestone. In some districts this limestone is used as a building stone, and all over the county is worked for the purpose of being burned into lime, and then used for building or for agricultural purposes, being well known as the best lime in the county.

VII.—OLD RED SANDSTONE.

Not seen in the county.

VIII.—Upper Silurian.

This division is about 5,000 feet in thickness.

Minerals, &c.—The Upper Silurian is known from its yielding excellent slates and flag stones, such as those at Kirkby-Ireleth, and other places, and from its forming the fells of the northern and eastern parts of the county.

IX.—Lower Silurian.

This geological stratum has a thickness of about 10,000 feet.

Minerals, &c.—The Lower does not occupy so great an extent in this county as the Upper Silurian, but it affords slates, and in the neighbourhood of Coniston mines of copper.

The above summary gives the various soils, as resulting from the strata and deposits which underlie them; but we may place in juxtaposition with this another summary of the surface lands and soils, which will afford, with a different classification and arrangement, the means of comparison and contrast, and thus enable the general reader to form a more comprehensive view of the subject in all its bearings, whether regarded from a geological or an agricultural point of view. Lancashire naturally divides itself into two distinctly-marked tracts of land :—

    1. The High Mountainous or Moory Tract ; and
    2. The Low Level or Flat Tract.

The former exhibits a sort of crescent boundary to the north, east, and south; and the latter spreads out westward to the shores of the Irish Sea.[1] These great divisions may be subdivided, in the view of cultivation, according to their different qualities, thus :—

I. The Hilly and High Moory or Heathy Division.	V. The Mersey or Southern Division.
II. The Steep Fell or High Furness Division.	VI. The Ribble and Fylde Division.
III. The Elevated Craggy Limestone Division.	VII. The Lime and Flat Limestone Division.
IV. The Valley Land Division.	VIII. The Low Furness Division.

IX. The Moss or Peaty Division.

The *First* of these subdivisions comprehends the mountainous ridges which rise in succession from the S.E. boundary to Rochdale, and end in the high felly track above Leck, and the N.E. border to the Yorkshire limits. The *Second* comprehends the Furness and Cartmel Fells. The *Third* extends from Warton and Yealand to Silverdale. The *Fourth* includes the various valleys formed by the different ranges of hills in the two first divisions, and the valleys on the Lune, Ribble, Darwen, Wenning, Wyre, Calder, and Brock, comprehending a great quantity of land of excellent quality. The *Fifth* or Mersey subdivision comprises a rich and fertile tract of flattish land from the northern bank of the Mersey to the southern bank of the Ribble in one direction, and from the sea-coast to considerably above the town of Oldham in the other. The *Sixth* contains a tract of land less extensive, but little inferior in quality, stretching from the north bank of the Ribble to the south border of the Lune in one line, and from Lytham and Bispham to near Inglewhite in another. It is of stronger quality than the other, and on the sea-coast of an alluvial nature. The *Seventh* commences on the north bank of the Lune, and runs in a narrow tract from Sunderland Point to the northern extremity of the county, by Warton and Yealand. The *Eighth* subdivision comprises a small point of land on the north side of the Sands, bounded on both sides by the sea-coast, which is usually called Low Furness. The *Ninth* comprehends the different peat and boggy tracts called Mosses, which are to be found in each of the two grand divisions of the county, but are by far the largest and of the greatest depth in the flat land division. Chat Moss, Pilling Moss, Marton Moss, Farington Moss, and Halsall Moss, are the principal tracts of peat in the county.

The lands that are included under the first four subdivisions are in a great measure employed as pasture, the more high and mountainous tracts being chiefly occupied by sheep, while the various declivities and valleys in which they terminate form the grazing and feeding grounds for neat cattle as well as sheep. In the neighbourhood of Rochdale, Haslingden, Bolton, and Chorley, the high moory lands afford pasture for cattle and horses as well as for sheep; and in some parts of this extensive range the common and even the mountain lands have undergone considerable improvements. Trade has made them valuable, and an increasing population has afforded the means of enriching the soil. The next four subdivisions (Nos. V.-VIII.) are commonly managed under a sort of mixed cultivation, but grass land is much the most prevalent, especially in the vicinity of towns. Northward, the dairy is frequently the principal object; but in low situations tillage husbandry prevails to a considerable extent. The Fylde, the Lune, and the Low Furness districts form the principal grain-tracts of the county, though in each of these there are large portions of land under grass, for pasturage and hay. The mossy or peaty tracts form a characteristic of the county of Lancaster.[2] When properly drained, this land yields good crops of potatoes, and will produce both grass and grain to remunerate the cultivator, under a proper system of drainage and improvement. The sandy marsh-land on the borders of the sea in Lonsdale is capable of being made fine land by embankment, but ages have passed away without this land having been applied to any valuable purpose of vegetable production. The soil in the more elevated parts of the hills of Lancashire is in general moory, heathy, and rocky. The lower portions of the sides of the hills, and the valleys formed by them, are commonly somewhat of the nature of holme. The flat tracts that spread at a considerable distance below them are chiefly of the loamy, clayey, or alluvial description; gravelly, and mossy or peaty portions, being found in all.

The principal *surface* distinctions of soil are Heath, Moor, Holme, Loam, Clay, Sand, and Moss or Peat; and the under strata or substances on which they are deposited are rock of various kinds, as grit or freestone, bluestone or whinstone, and limestone, fossil, coal, clay, marl, gravel, and sand. The freestone substrata are of three kinds—yellow, white, and red rock. The blue rocky stratum prevails in the fell tracts of Furness and Cartmel, the light limestone substratum at Chipping and Longridge Fell, and the dark-coloured at Duddon, Coniston, and Hawkshead. Clay and marl, both separately and mixed, frequently form the subsoil in the flat tracts; and gravel and sand are generally met with as the subsoil in low and flat tracts. The whole space between the

---

[1] Dickson.

[2] These mosses consist of a kind of moorish boggy earth, and are distinguished into white, grey, and black, from the colour of the turf. The white mosses are compages of the leaves, seeds, flowers, stalks, and roots of herbs, plants, and shrubs, accumulated through a succession of ages. The grey consists of the same substances, in a higher state of putrefaction, which in the black is at its height. The grey is harder and more ponderous than the white; the black more bituminous than either. Square pieces of these mosses are cut out in the shape of bricks, and being laid in the sun to dry, are called turf [turves] and used for fuel.—*King's Vale Royal*, p. 17.

Mersey and the Ribble, and between the sea-coast and the first risings of the high hills to the east, is a rich loamy and sandy soil. This is the finest district in the county, both for situation and quality of land. The air is mild and warm, and the soil is in general deep, rich, and productive. In proceeding to the south-east, where the county commences, opposite Stockport by Manchester, then turning to the left by Pendleton, Worsley, Leigh, Newton, Ashton, Up-Holland, Croston, and Longton, to Penwortham on the banks of the Ribble to the north-west, and returning thence above Walton-le-Dale, by Chorley, Little Bolton, Bury, Rochdale, Royton, Oldham, and Ashton-under-Lyne; the land included in this range is in general of the stiffish loamy kind. Below Manchester and at Middleton it is often mixed with sand. Between Manchester and Worsley, in one or two places very strong; it is also stiff about Hulton, Chowbent, and Leigh, and all the way to near Newton. At Newton it is rendered lighter by the intermixture of a small portion of sandy matter of a darkish colour. To the west of Haydock Lodge there is a small tract that has almost the tenacity of clay. About Ashton, and from thence to Bolton and to Wigan, in the whole breadth to the Ribble, it is commonly a moderate loam, in some places of a peaty nature, in others much mixed with vegetable matter of a dark appearance. Close round Croston it is rich alluvial sandy loam; but approaching Penwortham it has almost the stiffness of clay, particularly in Hutton. Above Bolton there is in some places a good strong loam on the red rock bottom. From Bolton to Manchester, in most of the breadth, it is commonly a good strong loam, in several places deep and rich, especially near the borders of the rivers. It is thinner about Bury, as it rises to the hills. The tract which extends from the great road by Warrington, Liverpool, and Ormskirk to the mouth of the river Douglas at Hesketh Bank, and from the banks of the Mersey and Irish Sea to the line of division just noticed, is a range of land that has great fertility, being for the most part a sandy vegetable loam of considerable depth. The little space that lies between the rivers Irwell and Mersey below Manchester is quite of this quality, rich, and often of a very black colour. The same soil is particularly conspicuous about Warrington, St. Helens, and all round Ormskirk. Above Winwick it is a stronger loam, with less vegetable matter, and continues of the same quality in a great measure nearly from Warrington by Prescot and Knowsley, till within a short distance of Liverpool, where it becomes much intermixed with reddish fine sand, which indeed almost forms the whole soil in some places; towards the borders of the Mersey it frequently presents the rich black appearance. At Allerton and Great Woolton it is mixed with sand, and the red rock sometimes appears so near the surface as to be broken by the plough. In the tract to the north of Liverpool, on both sides the great road, the soil is mostly a still stronger and stiffer loam, but in many parts much mixed, and of a dark colour. It is nearly the same quality till it approaches Ormskirk. As it advances towards the coast, it becomes of a much more sandy quality, and there are small spaces almost wholly of this nature. In this tract, white sand on clay with marl bottom is the most common substratum; the rock seldom appears. This fine extensive range of land, which, from the nature of the soil, is obviously suited to the production of almost every sort of vegetable, is in general under a sort of combined system of grass, grain, and horticultural crops. In all the range of land for some distance from the banks of the river Mersey, extending from the great road near Stockport by Warrington, considerably beyond the town of Liverpool, potatoes and a few other crops are raised in the horticultural method, along with grain and seed grass. About Stretford, and many parts of the parish of Flixton, this is the chief management, but the fields of grain are not numerous, and the crops of turnips few. It prevails still more near Warrington, and at Woolton, Allerton, Garston, and other places in the parish of Childwall. It is met with in Kirkdale, and other parts of the parish of Walton, but with less grain and fewer green crops. The same system is likewise noticeable about Ormskirk, to the west of Oldham, and in many parts of the parish of Middleton, particularly towards Manchester on the east side of the district. The same method prevails in the middle portion of the district, as about Wigan, Prescot, Leigh, &c.; patches of turnips, or other sorts of green vegetables, are in these places rarely met with. All the sorts of grain are occasionally grown in these parts, but oats and wheat are the most prevalent. Barley is, however, frequently met with on the coast. The rich grain-land called the Fylde consists of clayey loam and alluvial soil. It commences on the north bank of the Ribble, and stretches out to the south bank of the Lune, and from the sea-coast to the foot of the mountainous ridges towards the east. The soil here, though of a more stiff and adhesive quality, is in general good, and capable of affording abundant crops under suitable drainage and proper management. The top earthy layer of soil in the whole of this tract may with propriety be denominated a strong loam, more or less of the clayey kind, according to the nature of the situation and other circumstances. Southward from Preston the soil is a good moderate clayey loam, readily broken down into a proper state. But northward of Preston, and east of that place, in the direction of Ribbleton, Goosnargh, above Barton, by Claughton, and by Ashton, Lea, Salwick, Catford, above Sowerby, and Myers-cough, it is of a stronger quality. Near Lancaster the surface layer gets more of a friable nature, and approaches to the state of a strong pure loam, being much mixed with clay. In a great part of the fine valley that extends nearly to Glasson Point, the soil is of a deep, rich, alluvial quality, much mixed with black mould. The land to the west, stretching out to the southern border of the estuary formed by the Lune, is of the rich loamy clay kind, becoming alluvial as it advances towards the banks of the rivers, and principally in a state of grass.

In the northern part of the county the soil is principally of the dry, friable, and limestone kind, and divided by the sands into two parts. The first of these tracts begins on the northern border of the Lune, and stretches out from it, and that of the estuary, at its mouth near Sunderland Point, to the extreme boundary at Herring Skye; the crag at Dalton and Leighton Beck, beyond Yealand, spreading out from the sea-coast in all the distance to the hilly ranges of moorland beyond Halton, Kellets, Capern-Wray, Borwick, and Priest-Hutton. The second tract commences at the point near Rampside on the coast, and extends to above the towns of Dalton and Ulverston, rounding out to the sea in both directions. This is the tract of Low Furness, and has the islands of Walney, Old Barrow, and a few others of very small dimensions, belonging to it. There is a small portion of land of this description extending from Allithwaite to Flookborough, and bounded by the sea in its whole course. This soil is generally rather thin. The best tracts are those just above Lancaster, including the neck of land frequently termed the Little Fylde, and that of Low Furness. In all these different portions of ground, where the limestone under-stratum lies at no depth below the surface, there is commonly, when in grass, a fine close sward, that shows the limit of the limestone with great exactness.

This general description of the soil of Lancashire, drawn from the surveys of the Agricultural Society, will naturally be subject to many exceptions; but, as a whole, it may be presumed to be sufficiently accurate to convey an outline of the face of the county, and to indicate its agricultural capacities. It is a fact in husbandry worthy of remark, that the first potatoes raised in England were grown in this county, and it is still famous for producing and cooking that valuable root. A very large area is in pasturage, and dairy farming, consequent upon the large and yearly increasing population in the manufacturing towns, is carried on upon an extensive scale. The following table gives a classification of the holdings according to size in 1875 and 1880:—

Years.	50 Acres and under.		50 to 100 Acres.		100 to 300 Acres.		300 to 500 Acres.		500 to 1,000 Acres.		Above 1,000 Acres.		Total.	
	No.	Area.	No.	Area.	No.	Area.	No.	Area.	No.	Area.	No.	Area.	No.	Area.
1875	18,210	299,109	2,873	202,169	1,468	225,184	74	26,828	12	8,070	1	2,195	22,638	764,005
1880	17,423	286,009	3,027	219,412	1,552	235,174	104	31,555	13	8,532	1	2,726	22,170	783,408

According to the agricultural returns for the year ending June, 1886, the total area of land in the county under cultivation was 817,334 acres, a percentage of 67·7, as against one of 60 in 1870. The area under corn crops was 102,846 acres; under green crops, 58,909; rotation grasses, 74,230; and permanent pasture, 579,109—more than two-thirds of the whole under cultivation. Only 2,235 acres were fallow. The quantity of live stock in the county when the return was made in 1803, on the alarm of French invasion, was 648 oxen, 84,527 cows, 54,573 colts and young cattle, 80,772 sheep and goats, 30,982 pigs, 5,474 saddle horses, and 26,660 draught horses.[1] The agricultural returns for 1886 show that in that year the number of cattle was 242,053. They were chiefly polled Suffolks, red Yorkshires, and Leicesters. The total number of horses was 36,649. Sheep numbered 298,611. Pigs numbered 42,822.

According to the return made in 1872-3 the county was divided among 88,735 proprietors, possessing in all 1,011,769 acres, with an annual value of £13,878,277. Of the owners, 76,177, or 87 per cent, possessed less than one acre each, and the average value, including minerals, was £13 14s. 4d. per acre. Nineteen proprietors owned upwards of 5,000 acres, the largest proprietor being the Earl of Derby, who possessed 47,269 acres, with a rental of £156,735. Among the other chief landowners are the Trustees of the Duke of Bridgewater, the Duke of Devonshire, the Marquis de Costeja, the Earl of Stamford, the Earl of Wilton, Lord Lilford, and Lord Skelmersdale.

This county is rich in minerals, and particularly in that combustible mineral which of all others is the most important to a manufacturing community. The geology of this porti n of the kingdom is also interesting.

The western side of the county of Lancaster, bordering on the Irish Channel, from the mouth of the river Mersey at Liverpool to the mouth of the Lune, near Lancaster, is covered for several miles inland with meadows and marshy land, and presents nothing on the surface that is particularly deserving the attention of the geologist or mineralogist. Between Liverpool and Preston may be seen, on the sands at low-water, the roots and trunks of trees, the remains of ancient forests; these extend also inland, under the surface of the country, nearly on a level with the present low-water-mark.[2] Perhaps a probable explanation of the occurrence of subterranean or submarine forests on the coasts of our island below the level of the sea at high-water might be given by admitting the former action of a mighty deluge, sweeping over the surface, tearing up the trees in its course, and floating them to the coasts, intermixed with sand and mud. Few counties in England present more decisive proofs of the action of such a deluge than the county of Lancaster. Masses of stone, some of considerable size, are scattered over many parts of its surface, or buried at a small depth beneath it, imbedded in clay; and these stones consist of granite, sienite, and other primary rocks, though no rocks of a similar kind are to be seen in situations nearer than in North Wales on one side, or Westmorland or Cumberland on the other, and some of the stones appear to belong to rocks still more remote, in the mountains of Scotland. These stones are generally more or less rounded by attrition, and have evidently been transported from a great distance to the places where they are now found.

No county in England is more distinguished than Lancashire for its ancient forests.[3] Exclusive of the subterranean forest, which probably, before the Roman invasion of Britain, served as the margin for our principal rivers, and the line of coast on the west side of the county, we have to the north-east the forests of Wyresdale, Lonsdale, Quernmore, Bleasdale, Lancaster, Bowland, Pendle, Trawden, Accrington, and Rossendale; in the centre of the county the forests of Amounderness and Fulwood; and in the south-west those of Derbyshire (or Derby Hundred), Symonswood, Croxteth, and Toxteth. The north-eastern forests still retain much of the character that belonged to them in the time of King John; but in the centre and south-western part of the county, civilisation and refinement have taken from the ancient forests not only their primitive wildness but have almost deprived them of their name.

It remains only to notice the extent of mineral and other products as obtained in recent years. And first as to coal, one of the main sources of the manufacturing greatness of Lancashire. The coalfield, overlying the millstone grit, and forming the uppermost member of the carboniferous series, extends over a very large portion of the southern and eastern parts of the county, the greatest length being from Burnley in the north to Ashton-under-Lyne in the south—a distance of more than twenty miles—and from Oldham in the east to St. Helens in the west, about twenty-seven

[1] The cattle plague rendered it impossible to give a reliable return of the number of live stock in Lancashire.

[2] Speaking of this forest, Mr. Greenough, the president of the Geological Society, in his Geological Map of England, dated November, 1819, says, " There is a subterranean forest extending all the way along the coast, from the Ribble at Penwortham, near Preston, to the Mersey at Liverpool. The inner line of this forest takes in Longton Moss and Much Hoole, crosses the Douglas, continues to Rufford, in a direct line to Ormskirk, comes near to Melling, passes to Litherland, and terminates at the Mersey, opposite Everton. The parishes of Penwortham, Much Hoole, Rufford, Halsal, Altcar, and part of Walton, stand upon this forest: taking the line pretty nearly of the Lancaster canal to Crowlane, it extends to St. Michael's, and from thence keeps the canal line to Lancaster, and, including the west side of the Lune, continues along the Kendal road to Warton; at Cartmel it appears again, and extends into Furness in that neighbourhood, for a distance, say three or four miles, and a little of it is seen between Milnthorpe and the Sands."

[3] See chap. vii.

miles.   But within this area are two large outliers of millstone grit, which separate the north or Burnley district from the main coalfield of Wigan and Manchester, presenting a barren area that is about compensated for by the coal measures that extend along the eastern borders of Cheshire by way of Stockport, Norbury, Poynton, and Hurdsfield.   The thickness of the measure is very great, and as the ground is much broken by faults, and the beds dip at a high angle, the workings have extended a greater depth than in any other district, the deepest pits being at Rose Bridge, near Wigan, which have been sunk to a depth of 815 yards, and at Dukinfield, on the edge of Cheshire, where the workings of the Astley Pit have been sunk 672 yards, and the coals have been wrought to a depth of 772 yards by inclines.   The greatest thickness is observed in the Manchester district, where the total section, according to Professor Hull, is as follows:—

Upper Coal Measures, 2,013ft.	Limestone series	600ft.	Lower Coal Measures, Gannister, 1,870ft.	Black Mine to Royley Mine ...	897ft.
	To Openshaw coal	600ft.		Royley Mine to Rough Rock ..	1,370ft.
	To Yard coal	485ft.			
Middle Coal Measures, 4,247ft.	Barren measures..................	1,678ft.	Millstone grit		2,000ft.
	Unknown strata	—	Limestone shale, about..		2,000ft.
	Sod Mine to Black Mine	2,000ft.			

The thickness of the workable seams (exceeding 2ft.) is said to be 100ft., the coal being chiefly situated in the 3,000ft. forming the bottom of the middle and top of the lower measures.   In the Wigan district there are eighteen workable seams—about 65ft. in all—the total section being:—

Upper Measures, barren... 1,500ft. | Middle Measures, mass seams... 2,550ft. | Gannister Measures... 1,800ft.

In the Burnley district the lower and middle coal measures together are from 2,500ft. to 3,000ft. in thickness, the upper measures being unrepresented.   The rate of increase in the quantity "got" is very great, as will be seen, when we state that the quantity of coal raised in 1852 was 8,225,000 tons.   Mr. Edward Hull, in his "Coal-fields of Great Britain," estimated the quantity of coal raised in 1857 in Lancashire at 8,565,500 tons;[1] while Mr. Robert Hunt, F.R.S., in the "Memoirs of the Geological Survey of Great Britain," gives the total produce of coal in Lancashire in 1865 as 11,962,000 tons.   This enormous amount is thus stated in the book named (p. 95.):—

	No. of Collieries.
North and East, or Manchester District, Mr. Joseph Dickenson, Inspector	249
Western District, Mr. Peter Higson, Inspector...	93
Number of Collieries (including a much larger number of Pits) in Lancashire	342

COAL RAISED AND SOLD.

	Tons.
North and East District	6,312,000
Western District (including cannel coal)	5,650,000
Total coal produce of Lancashire	11,962,000

In 1865, the production of cannel coal in Lancashire[2] was 650,000 tons, out of a total production in England of 946,175 tons.   In the same year the total produce of coal in the United Kingdom was 98,150,587 tons, so that Lancashire produced considerably more than one-eighth of the whole production of the United Kingdom.   As to the distribution of Lancashire coal by railway, the London and North Western Railway carried in 1865 from the coal-fields of Lancashire 3,440,778 tons; and the Manchester, Sheffield, and Lincolnshire Railway received and forwarded 685,789 tons.   The shipments of Lancashire coal from the ports of Liverpool, Chester, Runcorn, Preston, Fleetwood, and Lancaster, in 1865, were, coastwise 462,472 tons, and to foreign countries 650,529 tons.   The quantity of coal raised in 1871 was 13,851,000 tons.   According to the official mineral statistics the output for the years 1873, 1874, and 1875 was—

	1873. Tons.		1874. Tons.		1875. Tons.
North and East Lancashire	9,560,000	....	8,095,570	....	8,825,798
West Lancashire	7,500,000	....	7,442,950	....	8,250,246

For several years the amount raised has exceeded 18,000,000 tons, and in 1880 it reached 19,120,294 tons, of which 9,519,858 tons were obtained from the north and east districts, and 9,600,436 tons from the west district.   The amount of coal carried from the county is about 11,000,000 tons, of which about 7,000,000 tons are shipped.

[1] In "The Coal-fields of Great Britain," by Edward Hull, M.A. (London, 1861), the following general summary is given of the extent of the Lancashire coal-fields and the quantity of available coal :—

	Square Miles.	Millions of Tons of Coals.
1. Area of the main coal-field	192	3,717
2. Area of the Manchester coal-field.........	5	.. 23
3. Area of the Burnley coal-field	20	.. 272
	217	4,012

"The quantity of coal raised in 1857 was 8,565,500 tons. Taking the future production at 9,000,000 tons, there is sufficient coal to last for 445 years. The above calculation includes the coal within a vertical depth of 4,000 feet. This coal-field contains (1857) 390 collieries—in Lancashire 359 ; in Cheshire 31, the latter producing 550,000 tons."
[2] Eight collieries in the East Lancashire or Manchester district produced in 1865 120,000 tons of cannel, and 11 collieries in the West Lancashire or Wigan district produced in that year 530,000 tons of cannel.

In the report of the Royal Commission on coal, founded upon investigations made in the years 1866-71, the probable aggregate yield of all the seams of the Lancashire and Cheshire coal-field, above one foot thick, was stated to be, within 4,000 feet, 5,546,000,000 tons; below 4,000 feet, 90,000,000 tons. At the present time the available coal supply is estimated at 5,150,000,000 tons.

The carboniferous limestone of North Lancashire is the repository of the valuable hematite iron ore, which occurs in fissures of the rock, or filling large "pockets" or caverns that appear to have been previously channels of underground waters. The iron obtained from this ore is the best suited for the manufacture of Bessemer, and its working has, within the last thirty years, given rise to a thriving industry in this part of the county. In the neighbourhood of Ulverston, in the district of Furness, there were, in the year 1865, no fewer than twenty mines of the red iron ore, or hematite, the produce of which in that year is officially stated, in the "Memoirs of the Geological Survey of Great Britain" (p. 65), as amounting in quantity to 607,439 tons, the money value of which was £303,719. As to the distribution of these ores in 1865, there were shipped at Barrow (which place, as a consequence of the working of the mines and the traffic in ores, has rapidly grown from a mere village to a large and flourishing town), 181,767 tons; sent *viâ* Ulverston, 172,880 tons; to Hindpool furnaces, 249,344 tons; to Duddon furnaces, 350 tons; shipped at the Ulverston Canal, 3,089 tons; total, 607,439 tons. There were carried in that year, by the North-Eastern Railway, to the Newcastle-on-Tyne district, 11,370 tons; to the Darlington district 11,708 tons; to the Stockton-on-Tees district, 9,365 tons; to Hull, 23 tons; total 32,467 tons. In Lancashire, in 1865, there were six ironworks, having twenty-four furnaces (16½ in blast), which produced 204,925 tons of pig-iron. These works are the Barrow Hematite, worked by a limited company; the Newland and the Backbarrow, worked by Messrs. Harrison, Ainslie, and Company; the Kirkless Hall, by the Wigan Coal and Iron Company Limited; the Furness, by the Furness Iron and Steel Company Limited; and the Carnforth Ironworks. The four furnaces at Newland and Backbarrow, all using charcoal, were only partially worked. The iron ore produced in three half years, 1866 and 1867, in the Furness district was—

	First Half Year 1866.	Second Half Year 1866.	First Half Year 1867.
	Tons.	Tons.	Tons.
Total Furness iron-ore raised	353,334	330,440	316,400
Say exported—by sea	83,651	78,122	57,608
by rail	113,254	68,572	58,467
Total sent away	196,905	146,694	116,075
Say consumed in district	156,429	183,746	200,325

At Hodbarrow, on the Cumberland side, of and under the Duddon, 131,542 tons were produced. The quantity of ore raised in the Furness district had increased in 1871 to 931,048 tons, and in 1880 it reached 1,188,543 tons. There is a mine of native oxide of iron at Warton, near Carnforth, from which, in 1880, 189 tons were raised; lead ore and zinc ore are being explored for between Clitheroe and Chatburn; and rock-salt at Preesal, near Fleetwood.

The produce of the one (Coniston) copper-mine in Lancashire, in 1865, was 1,796 tons of ore, value £12,175; making 161 tons 12 cwt. of fine copper, value £15,226; but the total quantity of ore raised in 1880 was only 442 tons.

The Whitewells mine, near Clitheroe, produces some lead, but how much does not appear from the return. In 1866, Mr. Hunt states, it produced 250 tons of lead ore, containing 750 oz. of silver. Of iron pyrites, or sulphur ores, the quantity (coal brasses) produced in Lancashire in 1865 is estimated at 2,750 tons, value £1,100; in 1879 the quantity raised was 2,000 tons, valued at £900.

Mr. Robert Hunt's "Mineral Statistics for 1865," of course, contains no return or estimate of the production of building and flag stones, or of the ordinary clay; but there are various districts in the county in which are large quarries of freestone and flagstone, the quantity raised in 1880 being 2,404 tons. A fine blue slate is obtained in Furness, and as much as 2,973 tons of hydraulic limestone was, in 1880, dug out of the Ardwick mine, near Manchester.

In 1859 Mr. E. W. Binney, F.R.S., &c., read before the Manchester Literary and Philosophical Society a paper, entitled " A Few Remarks on the Building Stones used in Manchester," the statements in which are just as true now as when first made. After, pointing out the different duration of building stone in a pure air and dry climate, and in the moist climate of Manchester, in the atmosphere of which about 40,000 tons of sulphur are yearly burnt in the coal consumed in the city, to say nothing of the gases given off by the numerous chemical manufactories, and the exhalations from half a million of human beings, Mr. Binney says : " It may be safely concluded that no quantity of good building stone, suitable for outside building in Manchester, or any like place, can be procured from the middle coal-field." He adds that "the lower coal-field and the millstone grit yield the only good building stones for Manchester. These strata comprise the beds lying under the Arley or Riley seam of coal and the limestone shale, and from their being generally found on the high land of the district are known by the name of 'High Moor Stone.'" "As a general rule, the more pure silica the rock is composed of, the better building stone it is. A mixture of mica or clay causes the rock to be more schistose or flaggy, as well as softer." In his enumeration of stones and flags, Mr. Binney names the upper flag of Upholland, Catlow, and Holy Fold (lying between the Arley and Riley coals) and the lower flag of Bradshaw and Shawforth, near Rochdale, lying under the rough rock and above the upper millstone grit. These flag-beds yield the stone generally used for parpoint work. A fine sharp-grained silicious grit is found sometimes above the Gannister coal, as at Ending Common, near Rochdale, which makes a good building stone. A stone much used in building is the Halliwell, Woodhead-Hill, or Lomax Wood rock, lying immediately under the Salts or best coal of New Mills. The rough rock, generally known as Summit and High Moor Stone (the upper millstone of the Geological Survey), a stone much used in building, is of a coarser grain than the stones previously mentioned. It is composed of grains and rounded pebbles of translucent quartz, cemented together with partly-decomposed feldspar and a little iron and manganese in the state of oxide. It is soft when first quarried, and works pretty freely, hardening when exposed to the air. As a building stone it is preferred, owing to its working much easier than the two millstones. Parbold, Horwich, Holcombe Hill, Blackstone Edge, and Werneth Lowe, are good examples of this stone. The upper millstone of Holcombe, Bank Lane, Todmorden, Saddleworth, and Tintwisle is a hard and durable sandstone, composed chiefly of silica. It is much harder to work than the rough rock, and stands the weather better; but it is not in great use, owing to its being difficult to work. The lower millstone, as seen at Roecross and Rhodes Wood, Tintwisle, and the lower part of Pendle Hill, contains some excellent building stones; but they are hard to work, and therefore they have not been much used. It is, no doubt, one of the strongest and most durable stones of the series. In the lower parts of it are some beds of fine-grained sandstone, freer to work than the upper beds. A most excellent bed of this description is found at Bailey, near Ribchester." Finally, Mr. Binney observes that, looking at the facilities afforded by railways, it might have been expected that some of the beautiful syenite of Shap, containing large crystals of feldspar, or the grey syenite of Bootle and Ravenglass, would have been used for building in Manchester; but he knows of none. [1] The soft freestones of the coal-measures are in general use, because cheap and easily worked; but durability ought always to be regarded by owners and architects rather than cheapness.

The Millstone Grit, or lowest sandstone of the coal-measures, in which workable coal is scarcely ever found, extends from the northern edge of the southern coal-field between Colne and Blackburn, and stretches northward towards Hornby, separating the northern from the Southern Lancashire coal-fields. This stratum forms a tract of mountainous moorland, in which are found Pendle Hill, Padiham Heights, Rivington Pike, Longridge Fell, Billinge Hill, and several other hills of considerable elevation. A small extent of the millstone grit, as before-mentioned, rises in the midst of the southern coal-field, and a lead-mine was formerly worked in it at Anlesargh. Here was first discovered a then unknown mineral substance, which was ascertained by Dr. Withering to be the carbonate of barytes. This mineral was for a long time supposed to be peculiar to Anlesargh, but it has since been found in the Yorkshire and Shropshire lead-mines, associated with the ores of lead. The millstone grit in this part of Lancashire covers the metalliferous limestone, and the latter comes to the surface at the bottom of Pendle Hill, and in some other parts of this tract.

The district north of the river Lune, between Lancaster and Kirkby Lonsdale, and from the latter place along the boundary of the county to Lancaster Sands, has the metalliferous limestone for its immediate substratum. It is this stratum which, in Yorkshire, Derbyshire, North Wales, and Durham, furnishes a large quantity of lead-ore, but no veins of this mineral have been discovered, or at least are worked, in the metalliferous limestone of Lancashire. In most parts of our island where the limestone abounds, as in Yorkshire and Derbyshire, it is characterised by the occurrence of large caverns within it, and there is a remarkable subterranean opening of this kind, called Donald Mill Hole, about seven miles north-east of Lancaster, near the road to Kirkby Lonsdale.[2] A small tract of country, south of Dalton in Furness, and nearly surrounded by the sea, has the metalliferous limestone for its immediate substratum.

On the northern side of Morecambe Bay there is a detached portion of the county of Lancaster called Furness. This, in a more natural division of the county, would be annexed to Cumberland or Westmoreland, which it adjoins. The mountainous ranges which form the lofty parts of those counties branch into Furness, and give it an alpine character. The most valuable mineral production of this district is red hematite, a peculiar ore of iron which is obtained near Ulverston. This is the richest ore in the United Kingdom, yielding the best and most ductile iron, suited for the purpose of wire-drawers. The ore is also sent to distant parts of England, to improve the quality of iron, by intermixing it in the furnace with the common ores of iron, to increase the ductility and tenacity of the metal. This valuable mineral occurs in beds intermixed with a red unctuous clay, which leaves a bluish metallic stain on the fingers. The ore is frequently found in large kidney-shaped masses, composed of concentric layers, which have a diverging radiated structure, and are well known in the cabinets of mineralogists. The mountains on the western side of Windermere Lake, and those surrounding the Lake of Coniston, are all situated in this district, and form some of the most magnificent features in the lake scenery of this part of our island; and they are well known to picturesque travellers and artists. The principal mountains

[1] Since Mr. Binney's report was written extensive quarries have been worked for the syenite granite at Shap, and this beautiful material has been polished and forwarded to all parts of the United Kingdom, and been largely used in the construction of several public works, including

the Thames Embankment, Albert Memorial, and many important buildings in London, Liverpool, Manchester, Glasgow, and elsewhere.—C.
[2] See "West's Guide to the Lakes."

46

in this part of the county are, Coniston Fell, in Furness, the highest part of which, called Grey Friar, or Old Man,[1] is, according to the trigonometrical measurement by Colonel Mudge, 2,577 feet above the level of the sea; and the barometrical admeasurement of Mr. Dalton approaches so near as to come within six feet of the same elevation.

Lancashire is a well-watered region, as the ancient name of the inhabitants, the *Segantii*, or dwellers in the country of the waters, sufficiently imports. The principal rivers of the county are, the Mersey, the Ribble, the Lune, the Irwell, the Douglas, the Calder, the Wyre, the Ken, the Leven, and the Duddon. The course of these rivers is described by the venerable Harrison, chaplain to Lord Cobham, with great fidelity, and though this description was written nearly three hundred years ago, it will not on that account be the less acceptable to many of our antiquarian readers; while others will be impressed with the immutability of these striking features of nature, and with the slight variation in the names of the places through which the rivers pass, or that are watered by their fertilising streams.

"The *Mersey* riseth among the Peke hills, and from thence going downe to the Woodhouse (? Woodhead), and taking sundrie rilles withal by the waye, it becommeth the confines betweene Chester and Darbyshyres. Going also toward Goitehal, it meeteth with a faire brooke increased by sundrye waters called Goyte. The *Goyte* riseth not far from the Shire meere hill (wherein the Dove and the Dane haue their original) that parteth Darbyshire and Chestershyres in sunder, and thence commeth downe to Goyte howses, Ouerton, Taxhall, Shawcrosse, and at Weybridge taketh in the Frith, and beneath Berdhall the Set that riseth aboue Thersethall and runneth by Ouersetts. After this confluence also the Mersey goeth to Goyte hall, and at Stopford towne meeteth with the *Tame*, which diuideth Chestershire and Lancastershyres in sunder, and whose head is the very edge of Yorkeshyre, and whence it goeth Southwarde to Sadleworth Firth, then to Mukelhurst, Staly hal, Ashton Underline, Dukenfield, Denton, Reddish, and so at Stockeford or Stopford into the Mersey streame, which passeth forth in like sort to Diddesbyry, receyuing a brooke by the waye, that commeth from Lime parke, by Bramhall parke and Chedley. From Diddesbyry it proceedeth to Northen, Ashton, Aiston, Flixston, where it receiueth the *Irwell*, a notable water which riseth aboue Bacop, and goeth thence to Rosendale, and in the wave to Aytenfielde it taketh in a water from Haselden. After this confluence it goeth to Newhall, Brandlesham, Bury, and aboue Ratcliffe ioyneth with y⁰ *Rache* water, a faire streame. Beying therefore past these two, our Irwel goeth on to Clifton, Hollonde, Edgecroft, Strang wayes, and to Manchester,[2] where it vniteth itselfe with the *Yrke*, that runneth thereinto by Royton, Midleton, Heaton hill, and Blackeley. Beneath Manchester also it meeteth with the *Medlocke* that commeth thyther from the north-east side of Oldham, and betweene Clayton and Garret Halles, and so betweene two parkes, falling into it about Holme. Thence our Irwel going forward to Woodsall, Whicleswijc, Ecles, Barton, & Irwelhom, it falleth neere vnto Flixton, into the water of Mersey.

"The *Rache* consisteth of sundrye waters, whereof eche one in a maner hath a proper name, but the greatest of all is the Rache it self, which ryseth among the blacke stony hilles, from whence it goeth to Littlebrough, and beying past Clegge, receyueth the *Beyle*, that commeth thyther by Mylneraw chappell. After thys confluence also, it meeteth with a rill neere vnto Rachedale, and soone after with the Sprotton [Spodden] water, and then the Sudley brooke, whereby his chanell is not a little increased, which goeth from thence to Grisehurst and so into the Irwell, before it come at Ratcliffe. The second streame is called *Bradsha*. It ryseth of two heades, aboue Tureton church, whence it runneth to Bradsha, and ere long taking in the Walmesley becke, they go in one chanell till they come beneath Bolton in the More. From hence (receyuing a water that commeth from the rootes of Rauenpike hill by the way) it goeth by Deane and Bolton in the More, and so into Bradsha water, which taketh his way to Leuermore, Farnworth, Leuerlesse, and finally into the Irwell, which I before described, and whereof I finde these two verses to be added at the last:—

"Yrke, Irwell, Medlocke, and Tame,
When they meete with the Mersey, do lose their name.

"Nowe therefore to resume our Mersey you shall vnderstande that after his confluence with the Irwell he runneth to Partington, and not farre from thence interteineth y⁰ Gles or Glesbrooke water, increased wyth sundrye arms whereof one commeth from Lodward, an other from aboue Houghton, the thyrde from Hulton Parcke, and the fourth from Shakerley: and beying all vnited neere vnto Leighe, the confluence goeth to Holcroft, and aboue Holling greene into y⁰ swift Mersey. After this increase the saide streame in lyke sort runneth to Rigston, & there admytteth the Bollein brooke water into his societie, which rising neere y⁰ Chamber in Maxwell Forest goeth to Ridge, Sutton, Maxfield, Bollington, Prestbyry, and Newton, where it taketh in a water coming from about Pot Chappell, which runneth from thence by Adlington, Woodforde, Wymsley, Ryngey, and Ashley, there receyuing the Byrkin brooke that commeth from betwene Allerton and Marchall, by Mawberly, and soone after the Marus or Mar, that cometh thereinto from Mar towne, by Rawstorne, and after these confluences goeth on to Downham, and ouer against Rixton beneth Crosforde bridge into the Mersey water, which proceeding on, admitteth not another that meeteth with all neere Lym before it go to Thelwall. Thence also it goeth by Bruche and so to Warrington, a little beneath crossing a brooke that commeth from Par by Browsey, Bradley, and Sankey on the one side, and another on the other that commeth thither from Gropenhall, and with these it runeth on to nether Walton, Acton Grange, and so to Penkith, where it interteineth the Bolde, and soone after the Grundiche water on the other side, that passeth by Preston and Daresbyry. Finallye our Mersey goyng by Moulton, it falleth into Lirepool Hauen, when it is past Rucorne. And thus much of the Mersey, comparable to the Wyuer, and of no lesse fame then most ryuers of thys Islande.

"Beying past these two we come next of all to the Tarbocke water that falleth into the sea at Harbocke, without finding any mo tyll we be past Wyrall, out of Leirpoole hauen, and from the blacke rockes, that lye vpon the north point of the aforesayd Island. Then come we to *Alt* mouth, whose fresh rysing not farre into the lande, commeth to Feston, and soone after receiuing another on the right hand, that passeth into it by Aughton, it is increased no more before it come at the sea. Neyther finde I any other falles till I meete with the mouth of the Yarrow and Duglasse, which haue their recourse to the sea in the one chanell as I take it.

"The *Duglasse* commeth from the west of Rauenspike (Rivington Pike) hill, and ere long runneth by Andertonford to Worthington, & so (takyng in two or three rylles by the waye) to Wigen, where it receyueth two waters in one chanell, of which one commeth in south from Bryn Parke, the other from the north-east. Being past thvs it receyueth one on the north side from Standishe, and another bv south from Hollond, and then goeth on toward Rufford Chappell taking the Taud with all, that discendeth from aboue Skelmersdale towne, and goeth thorow Latham Parke, belonging vnto the Earle of Darby. It meeteth also on the same side with Merton meere water, in which meere is an islande called Netholme, beside other, and when it is past the hanging bridge, it is not long ere it fall into the Yarrowe.

"The *Yarrowe* ryseth of two heades, whereof the second is called Bagen brooke, & making a confluence beneath Helbywood, it goeth on to Burghe, Egleston, Croston, and then ioyneth next of all with the Dugglasse, after which confluence the maine streame goeth forth to Banke hall, Charleton, How, Hesket, and so into the sea. Lelande, wryting of y⁰ Yarrow, saith thus: Into the

_____
[1] Old Man is a corruption of Alt Maen—i.e. (Brit.) high rock or stone.

[2] "Lelande speaketh of the Corne water aboute Manchester, but I knowe nothing of his course." [The Corn-brook.—H.]

Duglasse also runneth the Yarrow, which commeth wythin a myle or thereabout of Chorleton towne, that parteth Leland shire from Darby shire, vnder the foote of Chorle also I finde a ryll, named Ceorle, and about a myle and a half from thence a notable quarrey of stones wherof the inhabitants doe make a great bost and price.

"The *Rybell*, a riuer verie rich of Salmon and Lampreie, dooth in manner inuiron Preston in Andernesse, and it riseth neere to Ribbesdale aboue Gisburne :—

" From *Penigents* proud foot, as from my source I slide
That mountaine my proud syre, in height of all his pride,
Takes pleasure in my course, as in his first-borne Flood ;
And Ingleboro Hill of that Olympian Brood
With Pendle, of the North the highest hills that be,
Doe wistly me behold, and are beheld of me."
DRAYTON's *Polyolbion*, 27th Song, p. 131.

"It goeth from thence to Sawley or Salley, Chatburne, Woodington, Clitherow castell, & beneath Mitton meeteth with the *Odder*, which ryseth not farre from the cross of Grete in Yorkshire, and going thence to Shilburne, Newton, Radholme parke, and Stony hirst, it falleth ere long into the Ribble water. From hence the Ribble hath not gone farre, but it meeteth with the *Calder*. Thys brooke ryseth aboue Holme Church, goeth by Townley and Burnsley (where it receiveth a trifeling rill), thence to Higham, and ere long crossing one water that commeth from Wicoler, by Colne, and another by and by named Pidle brooke that runneth by Newechurch, in the Pidle : it meeteth with ye Calder, which passeth forth to Padiam, & thence (receyuing a becke ou the other side) it runneth on to Altham, and so to Martholme, where the Henburne brooke doth ioyne with all, that goeth by Alkington chappell, Dunkinbalghe, Rishton, and so into ye Calder as I haue sayde before. The Calder therefore being thus inlarged, runneth forth to Reade (where M. Nowell dwelleth), to Whalley, and soone after into Ribell, that goeth from this confluence to Salisbury hal, Ribchester, Osbaston, Sambury, Keuerden, Law, Ribles bridge, and then taketh in the Darwent, before it goeth by Pontworth or Pentworth into the sea. The *Darwent* deuideth Leland shire from Andernesse, and it ryseth by east aboue Darwent Chappell, and soone after vniting it selfe with the Blackeburne, & Rodlesworthe water, it goeth thorowe Howghtou Parke, by Howghton towne, to Walton hall, and so into the Ribell. As for the Sannocke brooke, it ryseth somewhat aboue Longridge chappell, goeth to Broughton towne, Cotham, Lee hall, and so into Ribell.

"The *Wire* ryseth eight or ten miles from Garstan, out of an hill in Wiresdale, from whence it runneth by Shireshed chappell, and then going by Wadland, Grenelaw Castle (which belongeth to the Erle of Darbie), Garstan, & Kyrkeland hall, it first receyueth the *seconde Calder*, that commeth down by Edmersey chappell, then another chanel increased with sundrie waters, the first water is called Plympton brooke. It riseth south of Goener, and commeth by Crawforde hall, and eare long receyuing the Barton becke, it proceedeth forward till it ioyneth with the Brooke rill that cometh from Bowland Forest by Claughton hall, where M. Brokehales doth lie, and so thorow Mersco forrest. After this confluence the Plime or Plimton water meeteth with the Calder, and then with the Wire which passeth forth to Michael church and the Raw cliffes, and aboue Thorneton crosseth the Skipton, that goeth by Potton, then into the Wire rode, and finally into the sea, according to his nature.

"The *Coker* from its shortnesse deserueth no description. The next is *Cowdar*, which comming out of Wire dale (as I take it) is not increased with any other waters, more then Coker.

"But beying past tnese twoo, I came to a notable ryuer called the *Lune*, or Loine, or (as the book of Statutes hath) Lonoire (Anno 13 Ric. II. c. cap. 19), and giueth name to Lancaster, Lonecaster, or Lunecaster where much Romane monie is found and that of diuerse stamps, whose course doth reast to be described as followeth :—[1]

"The Lune, saith M. More, of Catherine Hall, in Cambridge, of some commonly called the Loine, riseth at Crossehoe in Dent dale, in the edge of Richmonde shire, out of three heades. From hence it goeth to Burborne chappell, where it taketh in another rill comming from by east, then to Kyrby Lansdale, and aboue Whittenton crosseth a brooke comming from the Countie stone, by Burros, and soon after beneath Tunstal and Gretey, which descending from about Ingelborrow hill passeth by Twyselton, Ingleton, Thornetou, Burton, Wratton, & neare Thurlande castell toucheth finally with the Lune, which brauncheth and soone after vniteth it selfe againe. After this also it goeth on towarde New Parke, & receyueth the Wenny and the Hinburne both in one chanell, of which this riseth north of the crosse of Grete, and going by Benthams and Robertes hill, aboue Wray taketh in the Rheburne that riseth north of Wulferagge. After thys confluence also aboue New parke, the Lune maketh his gate by Aughton, Laughton, Skirton, Lancaster, Excliffe, Awcliffe, Stodday, Orton, and so into the sea.

"The next fall is called the *Docker*, and peradventure the same that Lelande doth call the *Kery* [Keer], which is not far from Wharton where the rich Kitson was born, it ryseth north of Docker towne, and going by Barwye hall, it is not increased before it come at the sea, where it falleth into the Lune water at Lune sands. Next of all we come to Bitham beck, which riseth not far from Bitham towne and parke, in the hilles, where about are great numbers of goates kept and maintained, and by all likelihood resorteth in the end to Linsands. Being past this we finde a forked arme of the sea called *Kensandes* : into the first of which diuers waters doe runne in one chanell, as it were from foure principall heades, one of them comming from Garrig hall, another from by west of Whinfielde, & ioyning with ye firste on the east side of Skelmere parke. The third called Sprot or Sprota ryseth at Sloddale, and coming downe by west of Skelmer parke, so that these two brookes haue the aforesayde parke betweene them, and fall into the fourth east of Barneside, not very farre in sunder. The fourth or last, called *Ken* [Kent], cometh from Kentmeres side out of Ken moore, in a poole of a mile compasse very well stored with fish, the head whereof, of all the baronie of Kendall, is in Westmorland, and going to Steuelop, it taketh in a rill from Chappelton Inges. Then leauing Colnehed parke by east, it passeth by Barueside, to Kendall, Helston, Sigarthe, Siggeswyc, Leuenbridge, Milnethorpe, and so into the sea. The other péece of ye forked arme, is called *Winstar*, ye head whereof is aboue Winstar chappell, and going downe almost by Carpmaunsell, and Netherslake, it is not long eare it fall into the sea or sands ; for all this coast, & a gulfe from the Ramside point to the Mealenasse, is so pestered with sands, that it is almost incredible to see how they increase.

"Hauing passed the *Leuen* or Conysandes or Winander fall (for all is one), I come to the *Lew* which riseth at Lewicke chappell, & falleth into the sea beside Plumpton. The *Rawther* descending out of lowe Furnesse hath two heades, whereof one cometh from Pennyton, the other by Vlverstone abbay, and ioyning both in one chanell, they hasten into the sea, whither all waters direct theyr

---

[1] In celebrating the fame of the Lune, the Shropshire poet, in his "Faerie Land," pronounces a high, though somewhat incongruous, poetic eulogium upon the fine cattle, the deep-mouthed hounds, the gallant bowmen, and the princely duchy of Lancashire :—

"Besides in all this Isle, there no such Cattell be,
For largenesse, Horne, and Haire, as these of Lancashire ;
So that from every part of England farre and neere,
Men haunt her Marts for Store, as from her Race to breed.
And for the third, wherein she doth all Shires exceed,
Be those great race of Hounds, the deepest mouth'd of all
The other of this kind, which we our Hunters call,
Which from their bellowing throats vpon a sent so roare
That you would surely thinke, that the firme earth they tore
With their wide yawning chaps, or rent the Clouds in sunder,
As though by their lowd crie they meant to mocke the thunder.

Besides, her Natiues haue been anciently esteem'd,
For Bow-men neere our best, and euer have been deem'd
So loyall, that the Guard of our preceding Kings,
Of them did most consist ; but yet 'mongst all these things
Euen almost euer since the English Crowne was set
Vpon the lawfull head of our Plantaginet,
In Honor, next the first, our Dukedome was allow'd,
And always with the greatest, reuenues was endow'd :
And after when it hapt, France conquering Edward's blood
Diuided in it selfe, here for the Garland stood ;
The right Lancastrian Line, it from York's Issue bare :
The Red rose, our braue Badge, which in their Helmets ware
In many a bloody field, at many a doubtfull fight
Against the House of Yorke, which bare for theirs the White.'

voyage. Then come we to another rill south-west of Aldingham, descending by Glaiston castell, and likewyse the fourth that ryseth neare Lyndell, and running by Dawlton castell and Furnesse abbay, not farre from the Barow heade, it falleth into the sea ouer against Wauey and Wauey chappell, except myne aduertisements misleade me.

"The *Dodon* commeth from the Shire stone hill bottome, & going by Blackhill, Southwake, s. Johns, Uffay parke, and Broughton, it falleth into the salt water betweene Kyrby and Mallum castell, and thus are we now come vnto the Rauenglasse point," where our authority quits the rivers of Lancashire.

The increase of the population of Lancashire during the present century is unequalled by that of any other county in the kingdom. The West Riding of Yorkshire makes the nearest approximation to it; but while in that riding the increase in the three decennial periods, from 1801 to 1811, from 1811 to 1821, and from 1821 to 1831, was 16, 22, and 22 per cent, in Lancashire the increase in the same periods was 23, 27, and 27 per cent, thereby swelling the total number of souls in this county from 673,486 in 1801, to 1,335,600 in 1831.[1] While the value of property assessable to the county rate in most of the other counties of the kingdom decreased within the fourteen years 1815 to 1829, it increased in Lancashire in the same period in the proportion of 25 per cent—namely, from the sum of £3,166,009, the amount in 1815, to £4,214,634, the amount in 1829.

After an interval of fifty years since 1831, Lancashire maintained its supremacy in point of population over all the English counties, as the following figures will show, taken from the Official Census for 1881:—

	1841.	1851.	1861.	1871.	1881.
Lancashire.............................	1,667,054	2,031,236	2,429,440	2,819,495	3.454,225
Middlesex	1,576,636	1,886,576	2,206,485	2,539,765	2,920,485
Yorkshire	1,592,059	1,797,995	2,033,610	2,436,355	2,886,564
The increase in the ten years ...	1831 to 1841.	1841 to 1851.	1851 to 1861.	1861 to 1871.	1871 to 1881.
Lancashire..........................	330,200	364,182	398,204	390,005	634,730
Middlesex	218,306	309.940	319,909	333,280	380,720
Yorkshire	220,093	205,936	235,615	402,745	450,209

The early period of the ecclesiastical history of Lancashire is involved in considerable uncertainty, and even the diocese to which this county appertained is not well defined[2] till the time of the Reformation, when Henry VIII., in the 33rd year of his reign (1541), in order to make some slight restitution for the spoliation he had committed upon the property of the church, erected Chester into a distinct bishopric.[3] From this time the whole county of Lancaster was, till 1847,[4] included in the diocese of Chester—the southern part in the archdeaconry of Chester and the northern part in the archdeaconry of Richmond. These divisions are more ancient than the Valor of Pope Nicholas IV., for in that important ecclesiastical document we find all the Lancashire churches which then existed under one or other of these divisions. Before the Reformation, the diocese of Lichfield, Coventry, and Chester, by each of which names the bishopric was alternately distinguished, according to the city wherein the bishop dwelt, included Staffordshire, Derbyshire, part of Shropshire, and that part of Warwickshire which is not subject to the bishopric of Worcester. "Now," say the authorities, "the diocese of Chester contains Cheshire, part of Denbighshire, and part of Flintshire, all Richmondshire, and part of Lancashire to the river Ribble." This definition, however, is not quite accurate, the whole of Lancashire being till 1847 in the diocese of Chester, as well the northern part, which is within Richmondshire, as the southern part, which in the Domesday Survey is called "*Inter Ripam et Mersham.*" Parts of the counties of York, Westmorland, and Cumberland, were also included in this diocese.

[1] The general average increase in England and Wales in these three periods is 14½, 17¾, and 16 per cent; and somewhat less in Scotland—namely, 13, 16, and 13 per cent.

[2] Hoveden says that Chester was a bishop's see whilst it was under the dominion of the Britons, and an ancient manuscript, quoted in the *Monasticon* (v. i., page 197), informs us of Egbert's intention of having his daughter, St. Edith, veiled by the then Bishop of Chester—"And the King Egbryght, for the wollenesse that was in St. Modwen, betoke to hure his dowghtr Edyth, to norych, and to kepe, and to informe hur, after the reule of Sent Benett, and after to veyle his dowghtur of the *Boschoppe of Chester*." In the manuscript Chronicle of St. Werburgh's Abbey, Willric is called also Bishop of Chester (temp. Ethelred), but these accounts are obviously fallacious, and probably allude to the Bishops of Mercia under the designation of Bishops of Chester. On the conversion of the Mercian king Peada, son of Penda, to Christianity (A.D. 656), Diuma, a Scot, went from Iona as first Bishop of the Mercians or Middle Angles, and took up his abode at Repton, near Derby, then the capital of Mercia. his diocese being co-extensive with the kingdom, of which Cheshire was a small parcel. Eleven years after Diuma's death, St. Chad transferred the seat from Repton to Lichfield, from which time there continued an unbroken episcopal line in that city, until, by doom of the canon law, all bishops were to remove to the greatest cities in their respective diocese, when Peter, Bishop of Lichfield (A.D. 1075), removed his seat from Lichfield to Chester, and was thenceforward commonly styled Bishop of Chester. In 1095 his successor, Robert de Limsey, transferred the episcopal chair to Coventry, though he continued to write himself Bishop of Chester; and in the reign of Henry I., Roger Clinton, disapproving the change, removed the seat back to Lichfield, from which time the see was commonly designated the bishopric of Lichfield, Coventry, and Chester, until Henry VIII. divided the diocese, and erected the separate and distinct see of Chester.—C.

[3] Patent (33 Henry VIII., p. 2, m. 23) dated at Walden, August 4, 1541. By a subsequent Act of Parliament (33 Henry VIII.) the see of Chester was placed within the province of York.—C.

[4] As early as the 12th December, 1838, an Order in Council was made for founding the see of Manchester, but that order not taking effect, on the 10th February, 1847, a commission was issued, under which a report was made on the 20th April following, and an Act was thereupon passed, 10 and 11 Vict., cap. 108 (23rd July, 1847), whereby the recommendations of the report were ordered to be carried into effect by her present Majesty in Council.—C.

When, in 1847, the diocese of Manchester was carved out of that of Chester, there remained within the older diocese of Chester, in the county palatine of Lancaster, the whole of the deanery of Warrington except the parish of Leigh. The diocese of Chester, until the passing of the Liverpool Bishopric Act (1878), included the archdeaconries of Chester and Liverpool; and the latter only included the Lancashire part of the diocese, which comprises six rural deaneries, viz., Liverpool (North), Liverpool (South), Prescot, North Meols, Winwick, and Wigan. In 1847, by virtue of the Act 10 and 11 Vict., c. 108, the bishopric of Manchester was created, and the collegiate church of Manchester elevated to the dignity of a cathedral and made the seat of the bishop. The diocese, roughly stated, includes the whole of Lancashire except the West Derby Hundred, which until the creation of the see of Liverpool in 1880 remained (except the parish of Leigh) in the diocese of Chester, and the Furness and Cartmel districts, north of the Sands, which are united to the diocese of Carlisle.

It was the practice of the popes in the early period of our history to make contributions towards the expenses of the holy wars, and Pope Nicholas IV., imitating the example of Pope Innocent, granted the tenths of the ecclesiastical benefices in England which he claimed and which had customarily been paid to Edward I. for six years, to defray the expenses of his expedition to the Holy Land. That this revenue might be collected to its full value, a taxation, by the king's precept, was begun in the year 1288, and finished as to the province of Canterbury in 1291, and as to that of York in 1292.

This taxation is a most important record, because all the taxes, as well of the English sovereigns as the pope's, were regulated by it, until the survey made in the 26th year of Henry VIII., when the materials for the *Liber Regis*, usually called the "King's Books," were collected; and because the statutes of colleges, which were formed before the Reformation, are also interpreted by this criterion.[1] The whole of this Valor has been published by the Commissioners of Public Records, under the editorship of Henry Ellis, Esq. (afterwards Sir Henry Ellis), and the following are extracts from it relating to the ecclesiastical benefices in the county of Lancaster :—

ARCHIDIACONAT' CESTR'.

DECANATUS DE MAINTECESTER' ET BLACKBURNE.

	Coventr' Taxatio.			Sp. Decima.		
	£	s.	d.	£	s.	d.
Ecclia. de Maincestr'	53	6	8	5	6	8
Ecclia. de Ecclis p't', &c.	20	0	0	2	0	0
Prior de Loncastr' 'pcip' in eadm.	2	13	4	0	5	4
Ecclia. de Prestwyke	18	13	4	1	17	4
Ecclia. de Burey	13	6	8	1	6	8
Ecclia. de Middelton	13	6	8	1	6	8
Ecclia. de Rakedale	23	6	8	2	6	8
Ecclia. de Aston'	10	0	0	1	0	0
Ecclia. de Flyxton	4	13	4	0	9	4
Ecclia. de Blakeburne cu' capell'	33	6	8	3	6	8
Ecclia. de Walley cu' capell'	66	13	4	6	13	4
Sma £259 6 8						
Inde decima............ 25 18 8						

DECANATUS DE WERINGTON.

Ecclia. de Werinton'	13	6	8	1	6	8
Ecclia. de Prestcote	40	0	0	4	0	0
Ecclia. de Childwell	40	0	0	4	0	0
Ecclia. de Walton	44	0	0	4	8	0

	Coventr' Taxatio.			Sp. Decima.		
	£	s.	d.	£	s.	d.
Ecclia. de Seston (Sefton)	26	13	4	2	13	4
Ecclia. de Halesale	10	0	0	1	0	0
Ecclia. de Ormeschirche	13	6	8	1	6	8
Ecclia. de Hoyton	10	0	0	1	0	0
Ecclia. de Wyneswyk	26	13	4	2	13	4
Ecclia. de Leithe	8	0	0	0	16	0
Ecclia. de Wyan	33	6	8	3	6	8
Sma ....398 mrc.						
Inde decima ... 39 mrc 10s. 8d.						
In libris £265 6 8						
Inde decima......... 26 10 8						

DECANATUS DE LEYLAND.

Ecclia. de Stanedech	13	6	8	1	6	8
Ecclia. de Eccleston	12	0	0	1	4	0
Ecclia. de Croston	33	6	8	3	6	8
Ecclia. de Peuwortham	20	0	0	2	0	0
Ecclia. de Layland	10	0	0	1	0	0
Sma £88 13 4						
Inde decima 8 17 4						

ARCHIDIACONATUS RICHEMUND.

DECANATUS DE AYMUNDERN'.

	Coventr' Taxatio.			Sp. Decima.		
	£	s.	d.	£	s.	d.
Ecclia. de Lancastr'	80	0	0	26	13	4
Ecclia. Sci Michis sup Wyrr	63	13	4	23	6	8
Ecclia. de Preston	66	13	4	23	6	8
Ecclia. de Riwecestr'	22	0	0	12	0	0
Ecclia. de Schipping	10	13	4	5	0	0
Ecclia. de Kirkhm	160	0	0	53	6	8
Ecclia. de Pulton	66	13	4	22	0	0
Ecclia. de Gayrsteng	26	13	4	10	0	0
Sma ....tol £558 6 8						

DECANATUS DE LONSDALE AND KENDALE.

	Coventr' Taxatio.			Sp. Decima.		
	£	s.	d.	£	s.	d.
Ecclia. de Halton	12	0	0	3	6	8
Ecclia. de Clahton	6	13	4	2	13	4
Ecclia. de Tatehm	6	13	4	3	6	8
Ecclia. de Melling	40	0	0	20	0	0
Ecclia. de Tunstal	26	13	4	6	13	4
Ecclia. de Heshm	10	0	0	5	0	0
Ecclia. de Warton	66	13	4	26	13	4

Lonsdale north of the Sands, including the districts of Cartmel and Furness, formed part of the county of Westmorland when the *Valor Beneficiorum* was taken; but that district now belongs to Lancashire, and the following parishes stand under the head

---

[1] Ellis on the Taxatio Ecclesiastica Angl. et Wall, auctoritate P. Nicholai iv. circa (A.D. 1291).

DECANATUS COUPLAND.

	Ebor' Sp'. Antiq. Tax'. £	s.	d.	Nova Tax. £	s.	d.
Ecclia. de Wytinghm	10	13	4	2	13	4
Ecclia. de Kertynel	46	13	4	8	0	0
Ecclia. de Aldinghm	53	6	8	10	0	0
Ecclia. de Warswythk	5	6	8	2	0	0
Ecclia. de Dalton	8	0	0	2	0	0
Ecclia. de Penigton	5	6	8	Nichil.		
Ecclia. de Wolveston	12	0	0	5	0	0

From these returns it may be inferred that the parishes of more recent date are—Altcar, Aughton, Bispham, Bolton-le-Sands, Brindle, Chorley, Coulton, Deane, Hoole, Hawkeshead, Kirkby Ireleth, Liverpool, Rufford, Radcliffe, Bolton, North Meols.

These sixty-six parishes were comprehended in the deaneries of Manchester, Warrington, Blackburn, and Leyland, in the archdeaconry of Chester: and Amounderness, Furness, Lonsdale, and Kendal, in the archdeaconry of Richmond; and the following in the ecclesiastical arrangements existing prior to the creation of the dioceses of Manchester and Liverpool:—

ARCHDEACONRY OF CHESTER.

DEANERY OF MANCHESTER.

	Value in the King's Books. £	s.	d.	Tenths. £	s.	d.
Ashton-under-Lyne, rectory, dedicated to *St. Michael*	26	13	4	2	13	4
Bolton-le-Moors, discharged vicarage, *St. Peter*	10	3	0	1	0	3½
Bury, rectory, *St. Mary*	29	11	5½	2	19	1¾
Dean, dis. vicarage, *St. Mary*	4	0	0	0	8	0
Eccles, dis. vicarage, *St. Mary*	6	8	0	0	12	9½
Flixton, curacy to an impropriation, *St. Michael*		—			—	
Manchester, Collegiate, *Christ*	213	10	11	21	7	1
Middleton, rectory, *St. Leonard*	36	3	11½	3	12	4½
Prestwich-cum-Oldham, rectory, *St. Mary*	46	4	9½	4	12	5¾
Radcliffe, rectory	21	0	5	2	2	0½
Rochdale, vicarage, *St. Chad*	11	4	9½	1	2	5¾

DEANERY OF WARRINGTON.

	£	s.	d.	£	s.	d.
Altcar, curacy to an impropriation, *St. Michael*		—				
Aughton, rectory, *St. Michael*	4	15	5	1	9	6½
Childwall, vicarage, *All Saints*	5	11	8	0	9	2
Halsall, rectory, *St. Cuthbert*	24	11	5½	2	9	1¾
Huyton, dis. vicarage, *St. Michael*	6	9	0	0	12	10¾
Leigh, dis. vicarage, *St. Mary*	9	0	0	0	18	0
Liverpool, rectory, *St. Nicholas*		—			—	
North Meols, rectory, *St. Cuthbert*	8	3	4	0	16	4
Ormskirk, dis. vicarage, *St. Peter and St Paul*	10	0	0	1	0	0
Prescot, vicarage, *St. Mary*	24	10	0	2	8	1
Sefton, rectory, *St. Helen*	30	1	8	3	0	2
Walton-on-the-Hill, rectory, *St. Mary*	69	16	10½	6	19	8¼
Warrington, rectory, formerly dedicated to *St. Elfin*, now *St. Helen*	40	0	0	4	0	0
Wigan, rectory, *All Saints*	80	10	8	8	1	0¾
Winwick, rectory, *St. Oswald*	102	9	9½	10	4	11¾

DEANERY OF BLACKBURN.

	£	s.	d.	£	s.	d.
Blackburn, vicarage, *St. Mary*	8	1	8	0	16	2
Whalley, vicarage, *St. Wilfrid*	6	3	9	0	12	4½
Brindle, dis. rectory, *St. James*	12	8	4	1	4	10
Chorley, rectory, *St. Lawrence*		—			—	
Croston, rectory, *St. Michael*, now divided into six independent parishes, viz., Croston and Hoole in 1642, Chorley and Rufford in 1793, and Tarleton and Hesketh-cum-Becconsall in 1821[1]	31	11	10½	3	3	2½
Eccleston, rectory, *St. Mary*	28	6	0½	2	17	7½
Hoole, rectory, *Holy Trinity*	6	14	0	0	13	4¾
Leyland, vicarage, *St. Andrew*	11	0	0	1	2	0
Penwortham, curacy to an impropriation, *St. Mary*		—			—	
Rufford, rectory, *St. Mary*		—			—	
Standish, rectory, *St. Wilfrid*	45	16	8	4	11	8

ARCHDEACONRY OF RICHMOND.

DEANERY OF AMOUNDERNESS.

	Value in the King's Books. £	s.	d.	Tenths. £	s.	d.
Bispham, perpetual curacy		—			—	
Chipping, rectory, *St. Bartholomew*	24	16	5½	2	9	7¼
Cockerham, dis. vicarage, *St. Michael*	10	16	8	1	1	8
Garstang, vicarage, *St. Helen*	14	3	4	1	8	4
Kirkham, vicarage, *St. Michael*	21	1	1½	2	2	1¾
Lancaster, vicarage, *St. Mary*	41	0	0	4	2	0
Lytham, perpetual curacy, *St. Cuthbert.*	22	0	0	2	4	0
Poulton, dis. vicarage, *St. Chad*	7	16	8	0	15	8
Preston, vicarage, *St. Wilfrid*	15	3	11½	1	10	4¾
Ribchester, dis. vicarage, *St. Wilfrid*	39	9	9½	8	8	11¾
St. Michael's, dis. vicarage	10	17	6	1	1	9

DEANERY OF FURNESS.

	£	s.	d.	£	s.	d.
Aldingham, rectory, *St. Cuthbert*		—			—	
Cartmel, curacy to an impropriation, *Holy Trinity*		—			—	
Coulton, curacy to an impropriation, *Holy Trinity*		—			—	
Dalton, dis. vicarage, *St. Mary*		—			—	
Hawkshead, curacy to an impropriation, *St. Michael*						
Kirby Ireleth, dis. vicarage, *St. Cuthbert*						
Pennington, curacy to an impropriation, *St. Michael*		—			—	
Ulverston, vicarage, *St. Mary*	28	18	0	2	17	9½
Urswick, dis. vicarage, *St. Michael*	7	17	6	0	15	9

DEANERY OF LONSDALE.

	£	s.	d.	£	s.	d.
Claughton, dis. rectory, *St. Chad*	9	15	0	0	19	6
Melling, dis. vicarage, *St. Peter*	7	1	10½	0	14	2¼
Tatham, rectory, *St. James*	12	5	0	1	4	6
Tunstall, dis. vicarage, *St. John the Baptist*	6	3	11½	0	12	4¾
Whittington, rectory	13	9	9½	1	6	11¾

DEANERY OF KENDAL.

	£	s.	d.	£	s.	d.
Bolton-le-Sands, dis. vicarage	4	15	0	0	9	6
Warton, *Holy Trinity*	74	10	2½	7	9	0¼
Halton, *St. Wilfrid*	20	0	7¼	2	0	0¾
Heysham, *St. Peter*	8	9	2	0	16	11

[1] Since 1835 this parish has been further divided, Bretherton being made a rectory, and Mawdesley and Bispham a rectory.—C.

ARMS OF THE SEE OF CHESTER.

Gules, three mitres, labelled, *or*.

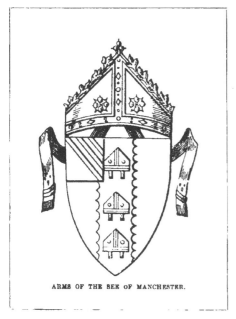

ARMS OF THE SEE OF MANCHESTER.

ARMS OF THE SEE OF LIVERPOOL.

Or, on a pale, engrailed, *gules*, three mitres, labelled, gold; on a canton of the second, three bendlets enhanced, *argent*.

Argent, an eagle with wings expanded *sable*, beaked *or*, resting its dexter claw on an ancient ink-horn ppr. A chief per pale, *azure* and *gules*, charged on the dexter with an open book of the third, inscribed with the words, "Thy word is truth," of the second, and on the sinister with a lymphad, gold.

After the dissolution of the monasteries, Henry VIII., with the consent of his Parliament, directed that the lands and manors of the monasteries and priories in Lancashire should be administered by the chancellor, officers, and ministers of the county palatine and duchy of Lancaster. This enactment, so characteristic of the age, was expressed in the following comprehensive terms: "Be it enacted, that all and singulier the liberties, fraunchises, privileges, and temporall jurisdiction, whiche the said late owners of the scites, circuites, precinctes, manors, and other pmisses of the late Monastery of Furnes, of the late Monastories and Priories of Cartemele, Conyngshed, Burscough, and Holland, lawfully had used, and exercised by them selfis or by their officers or ministres, shalbe by vertue of this acte revived and be really and actually in the Kinges Highnes, his heires, ministros of the said Countie Palatyne and Duchy of Lancastre; and that the stewards, bailiffes, officers, and Ministres of the County Palatine and Duchy of Lancast. shalbe compelled to accompt for the same bifore the said chauncelour, officers and ministers of the said Countie Palantyne and Duchie of Lancastre, as other officers and accomptauntis in the Court of the said Duchie heretofore have doon or owe to doo."

THE DIOCESE OF CHESTER.

In the succeeding year the bishopric of Chester was instituted, and the following is

A CATALOGUE OF THE BISHOPS OF CHESTER SINCE 33 HENRY VIII. (1541).

Which Bishopric was created on the Dissolution of the Monasteries.

1541		John Bird, D.D. Translated from Bangor; deprived by Queen Mary for marrying, 1554. Died at Chester, 1556.
1554		George Cotes, D.D. Died 1556.
1556		Cuthbert Scott, D.D. Deprived by Queen Elizabeth. Escaped from the Fleet, and died at Louvain.
1561	May 4.	William Downeham, D.D. Died November, 1577. Buried at Chester.
1579	Nov. 9.	William Chaderton, D.D., Warden of Manchester. Translated to Lincoln, May 24, 1595. Died April 11, 1608.
1595		Hugh Bellot, D.D. Translated from Bangor. Died May, 1596. Buried at Wrexham, Denbighshire.
1597	June —.	Richard Vaughan, D.D. Translated from Bangor; translated to London, December, 1604. Died March 30, 1607.
1604	Jan. 14.	George Lloyd, D.D. Translated from Man. Died August 1, 1615. Buried at Chester.
1616	July 7.	Thomas Moreton, D.D. Translated to Lichfield and Coventry, 6th March, 1618, and thence to Durham, 1632. Died 22nd September, 1659, aged 95.
1619	May 9.	John Bridgeman, D.D., Rector of Wigan; father of Lord Keeper Sir Orlando Bridgeman; deprived by the Cromwellian Parliament. Died at Morton, co. Salop. 11 November, 1652.
1660	Dec. 2.	Brian Walton, D.D. Died November 29, 1661. Buried in St. Paul's, London.
1661	Feb. 9.	Henry Ferne, D.D. Died shortly after consecration. Buried at Westminster.
1662	May	George Hall, D.D., Rector of Wigan. Died at Wigan, August 23, 1668.
1668		John Wilkins, D.D., Rector of Wigan. Died at London, November 19, 1672.
1672-3	Feb. 9.	John Pearson, D.D., Rector of Wigan. Died July 16, 1686. Buried at Chester.
1686	Oct. 17.	Thomas Cartwright, D.D., Rector of Wigan. Nominated to Salisbury, but died in Dublin, 1689.
1689	Dec. 15.	Nicholas Stratford, D.D., Warden of Manchester. Died Sept. 12, 1707. Buried at Chester.
1707-8	Feb. 8.	Sir William Dawes, Bart., D.D. Translated to York, 1713-14. Died April 30, 1724. Buried in Chapel of Catherine Hall, Cambridge.
1714	April 14.	Francis Gastrell, D.D. Died November 24, 1725. Buried in Christ Church, Oxford.
1726	April 12.	Samuel Peploe, D.D. [1] Died February 21, 1752. Buried at Chester. Aged 84.
1752	Mar. 22.	Edmund Keene, D.D. Translated to Ely, 1770. Died July 6, 1781. Buried at Ely.
1771		William Markham, LL.D. Translated to York, 1776. Died 1807.
1776	Dec. 31.	Beilby Porteus, D.D. Translated to London, 1787. Died 14th May, 1808, aged 78. Buried at Hyde Hill, Sandridge, Kent.
1788	Jan. 20.	William Cleaver, D.D. Translated, 1799, to Bangor, and thence to St. Asaph. Died May 15, 1815.
1800	June 14.	Henry William Majendie, D.D. Translated to Bangor, 1810.
1810	Jan. 21.	Bowyer Edward Sparke, D.D. Translated to Ely, 1812.
1812	July 5.	George Henry Law, D.D. Translated to Bath and Wells, May, 1824.
1824	June 20.	Charles James Blomfield, D.D. Translated to London, August, 1828.
1828	Sept. 14.	John Bird Sumner, D.D. Translated to Canterbury, 1848. Died 1862. Buried at Addington, Surrey.
1848	Mar. 14.	John Graham, D.D. Died 1865. Buried at Chester.
1865	Aug. 24.	William Jacobson, D.D. Resigned February 2nd, 1884, and died July 13th in the same year.
1884	April 25	William Stubbs. D.D., LL.D.

THE DIOCESE OF MANCHESTER.

The diocese of Manchester was first divided into the two archdeaconries of Manchester and Lancaster, but a third archdeaconry, called the archdeaconry of Blackburn, was afterwards constituted and formed out of the archdeaconry of Manchester. The archdeaconry of Manchester consists of the deanery of Manchester (founded August 23, 1843) and the whole parish of Leigh.

[1] It may be mentioned that during his episcopate the following churches in Lancashire were built, rebuilt, or consecrated by Bishop Peploe: St. George's, Preston (1725); Grimsargh (1726); Unsworth-in-Prestwich (1730); St. George's, Liverpool (1734); Burtonwood, Warrington (1736); Ardwick, Manchester (1741); Lees, Ashton-under-Lyne (1744); St. Mary's, Rochdale (1744); Rusland-in-Colton (1745); Poulton-le-Sands (1745); Field Broughton (1745); St. Thomas's, Liverpool (1750); All Saints', Bolton-le-Moors (1752). He also consecrated the following, which had been rebuilt between 1726 and 1752: Formby-in-Walton; Newchurch-in-Winwick; Shaw-in-Prestwich; Hambleton-in-Kirkham; Poulton-le-Fylde; Holme-in-Whalley; Sankey-in-Prescot; Westhoughton-in-Deane; Rufford; Gressingham; and Wyersdale.—C.

The parish of Leigh is detached from the deanery of Warrington, and now forms part of the deanery of Manchester.

The archdeaconry of Lancaster (founded August 10, 1847) consists of the deanery of Amounderness and so much of the deaneries of Kendal and Kirkby Lonsdale as are included in the diocese of Manchester. The aforesaid portions of the deaneries of Kendal and Kirkby Lonsdale united constitute the deanery of Tunstall.

The archdeaconry of Blackburn (founded August 13, 1877) consists of the deaneries of Blackburn and Leyland and such portions of the deanery of Manchester as are comprised within any of the new parishes in the rural deanery of Whalley.

BISHOPS OF MANCHESTER SINCE THE FOUNDATION OF THE SEE.

The Right Rev. James Prince Lee, D.D., F.R.S., the first bishop, was nominated to the see October 23, 1847, and consecrated at Whitehall January 23, 1848, by the Archbishop of York and the Bishops of Chester and Worcester. He was born in 1804, and received his education at St. Paul's School, London, and at Trinity College, Cambridge. In 1830 he became assistant master

THE RIGHT REV. JAMES PRINCE LEE, D.D., F.R.S., FIRST BISHOP OF MANCHESTER.
[From a photograph by Mr. Alfred Brothers, Manchester.]

at Rugby under Dr. Arnold; and in 1838 was appointed head master of King Edward's Grammar School, Birmingham. He died at the episcopal residence, Mauldeth Hall, Burnage, December 24, 1869, aged 65, and was buried on the 31st of the same month at St. John's, Heaton Mersey. During his episcopate he consecrated one hundred and ten new churches, exclusive of twenty churches built and consecrated in lieu of former churches. During the same period he ordained four hundred and seventy-one priests, and five hundred and twenty-two deacons. His library was bequeathed to the Owens College.

The Right Reverend James Fraser, D.D., was nominated to the see January 18, 1870, and consecrated at the Cathedral, Manchester, 25th March, 1870, by the Archbishop of York and the Bishops of Chester and Ripon. He was born at Prestbury, in Gloucestershire, in 1818, and received his education at Shrewsbury and Oxford. He died at the episcopal residence, Bishop's Court, Higher Broughton, Manchester, October 22, 1885, and was buried at Ufton Nervet, Berkshire, of which church he was formerly rector. During his episcopate he consecrated one hundred and five new churches, exclusive of twenty-one new churches built and consecrated in lieu of former churches.

47

THE RIGHT REV. JAMES FRASER, D.D., BISHOP OF MANCHESTER, 1870–1885
[From a photograph by Messrs. Elliott and Fry, Baker Street, London.]

THE RIGHT REV. JAMES MOORHOUSE, D.D., BISHOP OF MANCHESTER.
[From a photograph by Messrs Johnston and Shanassey, Melbourne.]

The Right Rev. James Moorhouse, D.D., third and present Bishop of Manchester, was born at Sheffield, November 19, 1826; educated at the Collegiate School in that town, and at St. John's College, Cambridge, where he took his degree of B.A. in 1853, and M.A. in 1860. He was ordained in 1853 appointed Hulsean Lecturer in 1865, Chaplain-in-Ordinary to the Queen, 1874, and in 1876 was consecrated Bishop of Melbourne, in Australia. He was translated from the see of Melbourne, January 30th, 1886, and confirmed at St. James's Church, Piccadilly, London, May 3rd, 1886.

The following table will show the extension of the Church of England in Lancashire during the present century:—

DEANERY.	POPULATION.					No. of Churches.				
	1801.	1821.	1851.	1871.	1881.	1801.	1821.	1851.	1871.	1881.
Manchester	304,231	459,621	981,084	1,307,752	1,789,703	76	81	158	231	284
Leyland.........	30,461	44,583	53,641	60,311	65,958	14	16	25	28	29
Blackburn.................	82,806	138,184	219,115	322,509	403,986	26	28	56	69	86
Amounderness	60,892	85,807	142,675	174,243	203,123	39	44	65	75	80
Tunstall....................	7,506	9,145	9,404	9,996	11,521	15	15	18	18	19
Total	485,896	737,340	1,405,919	1,874,811	2,474,291	170	184	322	421	498

THE DIOCESE OF LIVERPOOL.

The diocese of Liverpool was founded by order in Council, dated March 30th, 1880, pursuant to the Bishoprics Act, 1878, an endowment fund of about £100,000 having been subscribed for the purpose. The order came into operation on the 9th April in that year, the diocese created consisting of the West Derby Hundred, with the exception of so much thereof as is in the diocese of Manchester, and includes the whole of the parish of Wigan. A supplementary order, dated August 3rd, 1880, vested the patronage of the Bishop of Chester within the diocese in the Bishop of Liverpool, and founded twenty-four honorary canonries; the parish church of St. Peter being at the same time assigned as a cathedral church. Liverpool gives name to an archdeaconry, and an archdeaconry of Warrington was formed July 21st, 1880. These two arch-deaconries were rearranged July 14th, 1882, when that of Liverpool was divided into the rural deaneries of Liverpool North and Liverpool South.

The church of St. Peter—the pro-cathedral—was founded in 1700, the year following that in which Liverpool was, by Act of Parliament, severed from Walton-on-the-Hill, and constituted a separate parish. It was erected at a cost of £3,500, and consecrated June 20, 1704, and is tradi-tionally said to have been the first *parish* church built in Lancashire after the Reformation. With the older church of St. Nicholas, the rectory of Liverpool was held in medieties, one rector being assigned to each church, an arrangement that continued until the first vacancy after the passing of the Act 1 and 2 Vict. (1838), when the two churches were united in one rectory. On the foundation of St. Peter's the patronage was purchased from Lord Molyneux, the patron of the mother church of Walton, and vested in the corporation of Liverpool, in which body it remained until 1836, when it was sold to John Stewart, Esq.

Shortly after the creation of the see of Manchester, the late Mr. Harmood Banner, who was at the time churchwarden of St. Peter's, proposed that the building, which is devoid of architec-tural beauty, should be cleared away, and a structure worthy of becoming the cathedral of Liverpool erected on the site, but though a good deal of interest was awakened at the time, no practical effect was given to the suggestion. On the creation of the bishopric, in 1880, a sum of £576 was expended in making such alterations as were necessary to adapt it to the purposes of a temporary cathedral, but the erection of a new and more stately edifice is contemplated.

The following figures will show the rate of church extension within the limits of the diocese up to the time of the creation of the see: The number of churches and chapels of ease was, in 1650, 37; in 1722, 38; in 1803, 50; in 1850, 122; and in 1880, including the chapels of various public institutions, 215. The number of benefices was, in 1880, 180; the number of curates, 100; and the total population, 1,084,000.

The Right Rev. John Charles Ryle, D.D., the first and present bishop, was nominated to the see on its creation in 1880. He was born at Park House, Macclesfield, received his education at Eton and at Oxford, in which University he took a first-class in 1837, and was ordained in 1841. He was afterwards presented to the Rectory of St. Thomas's, Winchester; in 1844 to the Rectory of Helmingham, in Suffolk; in 1861 to the Vicarage of Stradbroke, in the diocese of Norwich; and in 1880 he was nominated Dean of Salisbury, a preferment he held until his appointment to the see of Liverpool in the same year.

THE RIGHT REV. JOHN CHARLES RYLE, D.D., FIRST BISHOP OF LIVERPOOL.

[From a photograph by Samuel A. Walker, Regent Street, London.]

Dr. Bird, the first Bishop of Chester, anxious, as he alleges, to execute his office and duty in planting virtue and suppressing vicious living in Manchester and its populous neighbourhood, as well as for the maintenance of hospitality, petitioned the king, his patron, that he might be made warden of Manchester, on allowing an annual pension to the incumbent warden.[1] These claims, though not admitted by Henry VIII., were granted by his daughter Elizabeth to Dr. Chaderton, who held the wardenship of Manchester *in commendam* to his bishopric.[2]

[1] Harl. MSS. cod. 604.　　　　　[2] Strype's Annals, vol. l. p. 552.

In the early periods of our history it was more the practice than it has been in modern times to impose exclusive taxes upon the clergy to alleviate the burdens of their secular fellow-subjects, and hence we find in the year 1608, when insurrections prevailed amongst the people, to prevent the country from being depopulated by letting land go out of tillage into pasturage, a rate was imposed by George (Lloyd), bishop of Chester, upon his clergy in the counties of Lancaster and Chester, of which impost the following is a copy, so far as relates to this county:—

"*Archid. Decanatus* CESTRIE ⎱ A Rayte imposed by me George Bushoppe of Chest^r vpon the Clergie within the Countye of *in Com.* LANCASTRIE ⎰ Chesshyre & Lancashyre within the Dyoces of Chestr, By vertue of l're̅s from the lordes grace of York grounded vpon + from the lordes and others of his ma̅tes most honorable privye counsell for the fyndinge of horses Armes & other furniture, the xxviiith of October, 1608.

WARRINGTON DECANATUS IN COM. LANCASTR.

Mr. Massye, pson of Wigan	a light horse furnished.
Mr. Mollineuxe, pson of Walton	a light horse furnished.
Mr. Turner, pson of Sephton	a light horse furnished.
Mr. Banister, p⁻on of Aughton ⎫ Mr. Meade, vicar of Prescott ⎬	a corslett furnished.
Mr. Hallsall, pson of Hallsall ⎫ Mr. Frenche, pson of North Meales ⎬	a petronill furnished.
Mr. Ambrose, vicar of Ormskirke ⎫ Mr. Hopwood, vicar of Childwall ⎬	a caliver furnished.
Mr. Lowe, vicar of Leighe ⎫ Mr. Hanson, vicar of Hayton ⎬	a caliver furnished.
Mr. Ryder, pson of Winwicke	a light horse furnished.

MANCHESTER DECANATUS IN COM. LANCASTRIE.

Mr. Langley, pson of Prestwitche ⎫ Mr. Watmoughe, pson of Burye ⎬	a light horse furnished.
Mr. Ashton, pson of Middleton	a petronill furnished.
Mr. Parker, pson of Ashton Vnderlyne	a petronill furnished.
Mr. Shawe, pson of Radclyffe, & ⎫ Mr. Whitle, vicar of Hayles ⎬	a musket furnished.
Mr. Warden & fellowes of Manchestr College	a petronill furnished.

LEYLANDE DECATUS IN COM. P'DICT.

Mr. Leighe, pson of Standishe ⎫ Mr. Rigbye, pson of Eccleston ⎬	a petronill furnished.
Mr. Benet, pson of Brindle ⎫ Mr. Conie, vicar of Croston, & ⎬ Mr. Brere, vicar of Leylonde ⎭	a corslett furnished.

BLACKBURNE DECANATUS IN COM. LANCASTRIÆ.

Mr. Morres, vicar of Blackburne ⎫ Mr. Ormerodd, vicar of Whalley ⎬	a corslett furnished.

AMONDERNESS DECANATUS ARCHID. RICHM.

Mr. Porter, vicar of Lancastr	a corslett furnished.
Mr. Paler, vicar of Preston ⎫ Mr. Norcrosse, vicar of Ribchestr ⎬	a musket furnished.
Mr. Whyt, vicar of Poulton & ⎫ Mr. Greenacres, vicar of Kirkham ⎬	a musket furnished.
Mr. Ayneworth, vicar of Garstange ⎫ a muskett Mr. Woolfenden, vicar of St̅t Mychaells vpon Wyer ⎬ furnished
Mr. Calvert, vicar of Cockerham ⎫ Mr. Parker, vicar of Chippin ⎬	a caliver furnished.

LONDISDAYLE ARCHID. RICHM. IN COM. LANCASTR.

Mr. Fishe, pson of Bentham............	a petronel furnished.
Mr. Sawrey, pson of Halton	a musket furnished.
Mr. Prockter, vicar of Clapham ⎫ Mr. Burrowe, vicar of Mellinge ⎬	a caliver furnished.
Mr. Waterhouse, vicar of Londisdaile ⎫ Mr. Hampton, vicar of Sedbrighe ⎬	a musket furnished.

FOURNES DECANATUS ARCHID. RICHM. IN COM. P'DICT.

Mr. Lyndoe, vicar of Vrswicke ⎫ Mr. Hey, vicar of Penington ⎬ Mr. Gardner, vicar of Dalton ⎭	a musket furnished.
Mr. Gilpin, pson of Aldingham	a corslett furnished.

"GEORGE CESTRIENSIS."—*Harl. MSS*

As already stated, the counties of Lancaster and Chester were included in the diocese of Lichfield and Coventry, until the creation of the see of Chester in 1541, and it is morally certain that the Lancashire and Cheshire wills, prior to that date, were proved at Lichfield.[1] It is commonly affirmed that these wills were transferred to Chester after the founding of that bishopric, but the statement does not seem to rest on any reliable authority, and it is not improbable that a careful search in the registry at Lichfield would show that they are still deposited there. In 1830 returns were made from which it appeared that the date of the earliest wills in the Consistory Court of the chancellor at Chester is 1521 (? 1541); in the rural dean's court, 1602; and in the commissary's court at Richmond and Lancaster, 1500; and that they extend to the present time with some chasms, principally previous to the year 1600. In the years 1826, 1827, 1828, the number of wills proved and letters of administration granted, in the diocese of Chester, amounted—*In the Consistory Court at Chester*, in 1826, to 1722; in 1827, to 1689; in 1828, to 1805. *In the Rural Dean's Court at Chester*, in 1826, to 246; in 1827, to 235; in 1828, to 124, the rural dean's jurisdiction having been inhibited during part of the year 1828. *In the Commissary's Courts at Richmond and Lancaster*, in 1826, to 475; in 1827, to 472; and in 1828, to 472. Under the able editorship of Mr. J. P. Earwaker, M.A., F.S.A., the Record Society issued, in 1879 and 1881, two volumes, containing an Index of the Wills and Inventories now Preserved in the Court of Probate at Chester, from 1545 to 1620, and 1621 to 1650, together with (1) a List of the Transcripts of Early Wills Preserved in the Consistory Court, Chester; (2) a List of Wills Printed by the Chetham Society; (3) a List of the Wills seen and noted by the Revs. J. and G. J. Piccope, and not now to be found at Chester; (4) a List of the Wills Preserved in the Harl. MS., 1991, in the British Museum; (5) a List of the Lancashire and Cheshire Wills Proved in the Prerogative Court of Canterbury, 1650-1660; and (6) a List of the Lancashire and Cheshire Administrations granted in the Prerogative Court of Canterbury, 1650-1660.

[1] Some of the early Lancashire and Cheshire wills were proved at the Prerogative Court of Canterbury, and are now to be found at Somerset House, London, as the old diocese of Lichfield and Coventry was under the jurisdiction of the Archbishop of Canterbury.—C.

A LIST OF LIVINGS IN THE GIFT OF THE DUCHY OF LANCASTER, WITH THE NAMES OF THE
INCUMBENTS—DECEMBER, 1886.

Name of the Living.	County.	Diocese.	Gross Value. £	Incumbent's Name.
Rectory of Ackworth	York	York	427	William Marcus Falloon, M.A.
Rectory of Ashen	Essex	St. Albans	368	William John Deane, M.A.
Rectory of Ashley	Wilts, Gloucester & Bristol		220	Edmund Baskerville Mynors, M.A.
Rectory of Barwick-in-Elmet	York	Ripon (nett)	800	Charles Augustus Hope, M.A.
Rectory of Beeston Regis	Norfolk	Norwich	169	W. Bosworth
Rectory of Long Bennington-with-Foston	Lincoln	Lincoln	409	William Barker.
Rectory of Castleford	York	York	560	William Thomas Mainwaring Sylvester.
Vicarage of Clare	Suffolk	Ely	307	Robert Sorabie.
Rectory of North Coates	Lincoln	Lincoln	483	Timothy Richard Matthews, B.A.
Rectory of Crofton	York	York	350	Josiah Samuel Moore, M.A.
Vicarage of Dedham	Essex	St. Albans	168	Charles Alfred Jones, M.A.
Rectory of Edingthorpe	Norfolk	Norwich	269	Joseph Lawson Sisson, B.A.
Rectory of St. Andrews, with the Vicarages of St. Nicholas and St. Mary, Hertford	Hertford	St. Albans	280	Woolmore Wigram, M.A.
Rectory of Hertingfordbury	Hertford	St. Albans	700	Frederick Burnside, M.A.
Rectory of Kirk-Bramwith	York	York	619	William Pulsford, B.A.
Rectory of Langham	Essex	St. Albans	692	David Henry Ellis, LL.D., B.D.
Rectory of Matlaske	Norfolk	Norwich	399	Herbert Wynell Mayow
Rectory of Methley	York	Norwich	375	Hon. Philip York Saville, M.A.
Rectory of Miningsby	Lincoln	Lincoln	206	Henry Caukwell, M.A.
Vicarage of Mundon	Essex	Rochester	160	William Stuart, M.A.
Rectory of Mundesley	Norfolk	Norwich	180	William Richard Croxton.
Vicarage of Needwood	Stafford	Lichfield	180	John Edward Addison Fenwick, M.A.
Vicarage of Nidd	Yorkshire	Ripon	—	John William Conway-Hughes, B.A., S.C.L.
Rectory of Owmby	Lincoln	Lincoln	315	Thomas Stamford Raffles, M.A.
Rectory of Plumstead, with Matlaske	Norfolk	Norwich	—	(see Matlaske).
Rectory of Poole Keynes	Wilts, Gloucester & Bristol		250	Benjamin Mallam, M.A.
Rectory of North Repps	Norfolk	Norwich	591	Samuel Francis Cresswell, D.D.
Rectory of South Repps	Norfolk	Norwich	654	Richard Hamond Gwyn, M.A.
Rectory of South Reston	Lincoln	Lincoln	101	Edward Fellows, M.A.
Rectory of Sidestrand (alternate)	Norfolk	Norwich	114	Forster George Simpson, B.A.
Rectory of North Somercotes	Lincoln	Lincoln	500	James Bell, M.A.
Rectory of South Somercotes	Lincoln	Lincoln	600	Peverel Johnson, M.A.
Rectory of Stambourne	Essex	St. Albans	465	Alfred Master, M.A.
Rectory of Stanford Rivers	Essex	St. Albans	750	Robert Rolleston, B.A.
Rectory of Stratford (St. Mary)	Suffolk	Norwich	356	James George Brewster, B.A.
Rectory of Swafield	Norfolk	Norwich	196	Frederick Simpson Thew, M.A.
Rectory of South Thoresby	Lincoln	Lincoln	310	Basil Arthur Galland, M.A.
Rectory of Trimingham	Norfolk	Norwich	137	William Tatlock, M.A.
Vicarage of Whitwick	Leicester	Peterborough	250	Augustus Francis Tollemache, M.A.

At the end of the year 1819 a sort of semi-official return was published of the "Catholic Chapels, with the number of their respective congregations in the county of Lancaster," of which the following is an epitome :—

	Number of Chapels.	Number in Congregations.
In the Hundred of West Derby	32	33,200
Hundred of Salford	5	15,880
Hundred of Blackburn	10	4,500 [1]
Hundred of Leyland	9	6,000
Hundred of Amounderness	16	12,650
Hundred of Lonsdale	5	1,270
Total	77	73,500

PLACES OF RELIGIOUS WORSHIP IN LANCASHIRE.

One part of the official census of 1851 was prepared under the direction of the Registrar-General by Mr. Horace Mann, and printed separately in an octavo form in 1853. It consists of a report and tables, showing the number of places of religious worship of the various denominations, and the number of sittings they contained at the time, with other particulars which we need not specify, as those already named are all that we propose to notice in this work. In his report Mr. Mann states that there are in England and Wales 35 different religious communities or sects—27 native and indigenous, 9 foreign. Besides these, there are many isolated congregations of religious worshippers, adopting various appellations; but it does not appear that any of them is sufficiently numerous and consolidated to be called a "sect." The following arrangement (which has been adhered to in the table) shows these communities or sects, under certain obvious considerable and minor classes, in the order of historical formation :—

[1] The great Catholic college of Stonyhurst is in this hundred.

PROTESTANT CHURCHES.

BRITISH.

Church of England and Ireland.
Scottish Presbyterians :—Church of Scotland (its Lancashire Presbytery is called that of Liverpool and Manchester) ; United Presbyterian Synod ; Presbyterian Church in England (exclusive of Unitarians).
Independents or Congregationalists.
Baptists :—General (Unitarian) ; Particular ; Seventh Day ; Scotch ; New Connexion General (Trinitarian).
Society of Friends (or Quakers).
Unitarians.
Moravians, or United Brethren.
Wesleyan Methodists (John Wesley) :—Original Connexion (Wesleyans) ; New Connexion (Kilhamites) ; Primitive Methodists ; Bible Chrisians (or Bryanites) ; Wesleyan Association ; Independent Methodists ; Wesleyan Reformers.
Calvinistic Methodists (George Whitfield) :—Welsh Calvinistic Methodists ; Countess of Huntingdon's Connexion.

Sandemanians, or Glassites.
New Church (Swedenborgians).
Brethren.

FOREIGN.

Lutherans.
German Protestant Reformers.
Reformed Church of the Netherlands.
French Protestants.

OTHER CHRISTIAN CHURCHES.

Roman Catholics.
Greek Church.
German Catholics.
Italian Reformers.
Catholic and Apostolic Church.
Latter-day Saints, or Mormons.

JEWS.

Mr. Mann classes "Isolated Congregations" (not connected with any particular sect) in five groups—(1) Those in which members of other sects unite in worship. (2) Those based on peculiar doctrines (Universalists, Millennarians, Predestinarians, &c.) (3) Unsectarian (Christians, New Christians, Christ's Disciples, Free Gospel Christians, &c.) (4) Where in the returns the sect is not particularised (as Protestant Dissenters, Dissenters, Protestant Christians, &c.) And (5) Missionary congregations. Beyond these there still remains a residue of congregations difficult to classify (as Free Church, Inghamites, Christian Israelites, Southcottians, &c.)

Neither the census of 1861 nor those of 1871 and 1881 included any summary of the religious denominations. That of 1851 is therefore the latest official summary of the kind, and the following are its results as to Lancashire :—

Denomination.	No. of Places of Worship.		No of Sittings.
1. Church of England	529	......	383,466
2. Church of Scotland	5	......	4,510
3. Presbyterian Church in England	12	......	9,090
4. United Presbyterian Church	5	.. ...	3,115
5. Reformed Irish Presbyterians	1	......	120
6. Independents	170	......	80,072
7. Baptists (particular 70, undefined 21)	100	......	34,068
8. Society of Friends (Quakers)	27	......	8,264
9. Unitarians	35	......	12,384
10. Moravians	2	......	1,084
11. Wesleyan Methodists	300	......	107,983
12. New Connexion do.	27	......	11,569
13. Primitive do.	107	. ...	25,812
14. Wesleyan Association do.	81	......	25,555
15. Independent do.	1	..t...	30
16. Wesleyan Reformers	4	......	900
17. Welsh Calvinistic Methodists	8	.. ...	5,141
18. Lady Huntingdon's Connexion	11	......	4,998
19. New Church (Swedenborgians)	21	......	5,544
20. Brethren	5	......	970
21. Isolated Congregations	36	......	7,466
22. Roman Catholics	114	.. ...	55,610
23 Latter-day Saints	15	......	1 379
24. Jews	7	.....	1,138

CHAPTER XVII.

LANCASHIRE, in its southern part, designated in the Domesday Survey "INTER RIPA & MERSHAM," was divided into six hundreds at the time of the Norman Conquest—namely, Derbei, Neweton, Walintone, Blackebvrn, Salford, and Lailand Hvndrets.[1] To the north of the Ribble were Agemvndrenesse, Lanesdale, and Hovgvn. Mr. Whitaker, in his "History of Manchester," thus treats of the old hundreds:—

"The hundreds of the Saxons were exactly the same with the cantrefs of the Britons. The latter consisted of a hundred townships, and the former were composed of ten tythings. These were always considerable districts, and exist to this day the great divisions of our counties. Each of them contained a hundred free-masters of families or, in other words, a hundred superiors of townships. And those of South Lancashire, which were six before the Conquest, were only three at first—Blackburne, Derby, and Salford. Newton, Warrington, and Layland, which are mentioned equally in the Domesday Survey, appear equally, from their smallness, especially the two first, to have been merely additions to the original number. And from a comparative view of the nature and extent of all, it is plain that Layland was taken out of Blackburne hundred, and Warrington and Newton out of Derby. These were all denominated from the towns or villages which were constituted the heads of their respective centuries. And those of Salford, Warrington, and Newton, Blackburne, Derby, and Layland were so constituted, because they belonged to the crown. All of them but Newton continued in its possession as late as the reign of the Confessor. All of them had been retained by the crown on the general partition of the country, the appointed demesne of the royalty. And the town of Salford has, for this reason, been ever independent of the lord of Manchester, and continues to the present time annexed to the regalities of the duchy. The whole compass of South Lancashire, which, through all the period of the Britons, probably has contained only two cantrefs, Linuis and another, now enclosed thirty tythings, thirty manours, and three hundred townships. The division of Salford, the only one of its three hundreds that has not been dismembered, had just ten manors, ten tythings, and a hundred townships within its present limits. And the custom, which is retained amongst us to this day, of making the hundred responsible for robberies committed between sun and sun, had its commencement at this period, and was a natural appendage of the Saxon system of tythings."

There are evidently no sufficient data to determine into how many hundreds South Lancashire was divided in the Roman period, and still less in the time of the aborigines; but it is perfectly clear that in the Saxon period it consisted of six hundreds, and that subsequently the hundreds of Newton and Warrington merged in that of West Derby. Henry, a monk of Malmesbury, speaking of the shires, says Lancashire had only five small shires—West Derbyshire, Salfordshire, Blackburn-shire, Leylandshire, and the territory of Lancaster, which, by a common word, are called hundreds.[2] Hundreds, though not always corresponding, as in Lancashire, with the ancient shires, are synonymous with wapentakes, which, according to Higden, take the name from the chief officer of a hundred towns resuming the arms of the vassals on the lord's arrival amongst them.[3]

"In some places (and particularly in the northern counties) hundreds are sometimes called *Wapentakes*, the reason of which denomination is distinctly mentioned in the laws of *Edward the Confessor*,[4] viz., when a person received the government of a *Wapentake* at the appointed time and usual place, the elder sort met him, and, when he was got off his horse, rose up to him; then he held up his spear and took security of all present according to custom; whoever came touched his spear with theirs, and by this touching of armour were confirmed in one common interest; and thus from *wæpnu*, weapons, and *tac*, a touch, or *taccare*, to confirm, they were called *Wapentakes*."[5]

As late as the fourteenth century the hundred of Salford was called a *Wapentake*. This appears from the following rent-roll of the Earl of Lancaster in Salford town and hundred, 10 Edw. II. (1316-17), extracted from "A Survey of Lonsdale," 25 Edw. 1. (1296-7), in the Tower of London:—[6]

---

[1] The term *hundreds* has been variously derived, either from their containing a hundred vills (portions of ground upon each of which a family was located), from their finding a hundred Fidejussores to the king's peace, from their consisting of a hundred hides of land, or from their sending a hundred men to the wars.

[2] Lel. Coll. tom. ii. p. 397.
[3] Ran. Higden, Polychron. lib. i. de Legibus, edit. Gale, p. 202.
[4] Edit. Wheloc. p. 45.
Thoresby Ducat. Leodiens. p. 81.
[6] Harl. MSS. cod. 2085, 528 b.

EXTENT [*i.e.* Survey] of the LANDS of the EARL in the WAPENTAKE of LONSDALE, Co. Lanc., 25 Edw. I. (1296-7), on the death of Edmund, Earl of Lancaster, &c.[1]—*Salford Vill in the aforesaid account by the Inquisition of* 10 *Edw. II.* (1316-17).

		£	s.	d.
Rent of assise of the Vill of Salford, with the rent of one toft near the bridge		6	14	9
Farm of the Water-mill there..		3	0	0
Toll, Stallage of the market and fair of the same place		2	6	7½
Small places [or plots] there		0	13	1¾
Pleas and perquisites of the Courts		0	2	0
Total		£12	16	6¼

SALFORD WAPENTAKE :

		£	s.	d.
Rent of assise of Burghton [Broughton]		2	8	0
Do.	of Ordesale	1	2	0
Do.	of Cadeuelheued [Cadishead]	0	4	0
Do.	of Scoresworth [Shoresworth]	0	2	0
Do.	of Tonge	0	4	0
Farm of the land of Augustine de Barton		1	6	0
Do.	of Wm. de Radcliffe	0	17	8
Do.	of Roger de Middleton, in Chetham..	0	13	4
Do.	of Alice de Prestwich, in Prestwich, Holonet, and Sholesworth [? Hollinhead and			
	Shoresworth]	1	6	8
Do.	of Roger Pilkington, in Rovington	0	10	0
Do.	of Geoffrey de Hulme, in Hulme	0	5	0
Do.	of Alice Prestwich, in Penulbery	0	10	0
Do.	of Wm. Fitz-Roger, in Radish [Reddish]	0	6	0
Do.	of Rd. Pilkinton, in Chorleton [cum-Hardy]	1	0	0
Do.	of Henry de Trafford	0	5	0
Do.	of Rd. de Byrom	1	4	0
Do.	of Hugh Meuil [Menil], in Werkslegh [Worsley] and Hulton	1	0	0
Do.	of William de Bradshagh, in Blackrod, yearly	1	0	0
Do.	of the Vill of Clifton	0	8	0
Sak-Fee of the land of Richd. Fitz-Roger...		0	10	0
Do.	half the Vill of Flixton	0	1	6
Rent of the land of John de la Ware..		4	3	6
Do.	Jordan de Crompton	0	1	1
Farm of the Serjeanty of the Bailiff [or Bailiwick] there		16	0	0
Pleas and perquisites of the Court of the Wapentake there		4	7	3
Total		£40	5	0

In 1 John (1199) the Wapentake of Salford was held by Elias Fitz-Robert, by serjeanty.—(Rot. Chartar, 1 *John* m. 5.)

Rich. de Hilton held the *Wapentake* of Salford in serjeanty, at the will of our lord the king, in the time of Edward III., as appears from the Testa de Nevill, p. 371 ; and at a much later date Hollinworth, in his MS., speaks of " the *Wapentake* of Salford, where the pole is elevated 53° 24'."

The origin of the hundred divisions has been usually traced to the time of Alfred ; but probably they may claim a higher antiquity, and were derived from the Franks or the Germans. They were at least by his order more accurately defined than in the British and Roman periods, and by him they were made subservient to the better administration of the laws, and the preservation of the lives and property of the people. The government, ecclesiastical and civil, now formed itself into a consistent and connected whole, to the perfection of which these divisions essentially administered.

"The ecclesiastical estate," says Sir Henry Spelman, "was first divided into provinces, every province into many bishopricks, every bishoprick into many archdeaconries, every archdeaconry into divers deaneries, and every deanery into many parishes. And all these committed to their several governors—parsons, deans, archdeacons, bishops, and archbishops—who, as subordinate one to the other, did not only execute the charge of their several portions, but were accountant also for the same to their superiors. The temporal government was likewise divided into satrapies or dukedoms, which contained in them divers counties ; the county divers lathes or trithings ; every trithing divers hundreds, or wapentakes ; every hundred divers towns or lordships, shortly after called baronies ; and the government of all these was committed to their several heads, viz., towns or manors to the lords thereof, whom the Saxons called theings, after barons ; hundreds to the lords of hundreds ; trithings or lathes to their trithing-greves ; counties to their earls or aldermen ; and large satrapies to their dukes, or chief princes, all which had subordinate authority one under the other, and did within the precinct of their own territories minister justice unto their subjects."

In this systematic concatenation none contributed more to the well-being of society than the government of the hundred ; and, as late as the time of Edward I., an Act was passed, called the Statute of Winton, which, amongst a number of other excellent provisions of police, enacts that every hundred shall be answerable for the robberies and other offences committed within its jurisdiction, thus giving to every citizen an interest in the person and property of his neighbour. In later times the hundred courts, which, in their early institution, were at once ecclesiastical, civil, and criminal, have sunk into courts of inferior jurisdiction ; but they have still their use, and, under a reformed system of laws, are made highly conducive to the public welfare. The hundreds of Lancashire now stand thus : (1) Salford Hundred, (2) West Derby Hundred, (3) Leyland Hundred, (4) Blackburn Hundred (between Ribble and Mersey) ; (5) Amounderness Hundred, and (6) Lonsdale Hundred, S. and N. of the Sands (North of Ribble).

[1] As Edmund Crouchback, Earl of Lancaster, died abroad at Pentecost, (May) 1266, all regnal years referring to him should be of Edward I.—H.

48

REPRESENTATION OF THE PEOPLE ACT, 1867.

In August, 1867, " An Act further to Amend the Law Relating to the Representation of the People in England and Wales " was passed, and a brief summary of such of its provisions as related to the county of Lancaster, and to the city and boroughs within the county, is consequently appended. The following were the principal clauses as to the *Franchise*:—

3. Every man shall, in and after 1868, be entitled to be registered as a voter, and, when registered to vote for a member or members to serve in Parliament for a borough, who is qualified as follows (that is to say): (1) is of full age, and not subject to any legal incapacity ; and (2) is on the last day of July in any year, and has during the whole of the preceding twelve calendar months been, an inhabitant occupier, as owner or tenant, of any dwelling-house within the borough ; and (3) has during the time of such occupation been rated as an ordinary occupier in respect of the premises so occupied by him within the borough to all rates (if any) made for the relief of the poor in respect of such premises ; and (4) has before the 20th day of July in the same year *bona fide* paid an equal amount in the pound to that payable by other ordinary occupiers in respect of all poor-rates that have become payable by him in respect of the said premises up to the preceding 5th day of January : Provided that no man under this section be entitled to be registered as a voter by reason of his being a joint occupier of any dwelling-house.

4. Every man shall, in and after 1868, be entitled to be registered as a voter, and, when registered, to vote [&c. as in clause 3] ; and (2) as a lodger, has occupied in the same borough, separately and as sole tenant, for the twelve months preceding the last day of July in any year, the same lodgings, such lodgings being part of one and the same dwelling-house, and of a clear yearly value, if let unfurnished, of ten pounds or upwards ; and (3) has resided in such lodgings during the twelve months immediately preceding the last day of July, and has claimed to be registered as a voter at the next ensuing registration of voters.

5. Every man shall, in and after 1868, be entitled to be registered as a voter, and, when registered, to vote for a member or members to serve in Parliament for a county, who is qualified as follows (that is to say): (1) is of full age, and not subject to any legal incapacity, and is seised at law or in equity of any lands or tenements of freehold, copyhold, or any other tenure whatever, for his own life, or for the life of another, or for any lives whatsoever, or for any larger estate of the clear yearly value of not less than £5 over and above all rents and charges payable out of or in respect of the same, or who is entitled, either as lessee or assignee, to any lands or tenements of freehold or of any other tenure whatever, for the unexpired residue, whatever it may be, of any term originally created for a period of not less than 60 years (whether determinable on a life or lives or not), of the clear yearly value of not less than £5 over and above all rents and charges payable out of, or in respect of, the same : Provided that no person shall be registered as a voter under this section unless he has complied with the provisions of the 26th section of the Act of the second year of the reign of his majesty William IV. cap. 45.

6. Every man shall, in and after 1868, be entitled to be registered [&c. as in clause 5] : (1) is of full age, and not subject to any legal incapacity ; and (2) is, on the last day of July in any year, and has during the twelve months immediately preceding, been the occupier, as owner and tenant, of lands or tenements within the county of the rateable value of £12 or upwards ; and (3) has, during the time of such occupation, been rated in respect to the premises so occupied by him to all rates, if any, made for the relief of the poor in respect of the said premises ; and (4) has, before the 20th day of July in the same year, paid all poor-rates that have become payable by him in respect of the said premises up to the preceding 5th day of January.

7. Where the owner is rated at the time of the passing of this act to the poor-rate in respect of a dwelling-house or other tenement situate in a parish wholly or partly in a borough, instead of the occupier, his liability to be rated in any future poor-rate shall cease, and the following enactments shall take effect with respect to rating in all boroughs : (1) After the passing of this act no owner of any dwelling-house or other tenement situate in a parish either wholly or partly within a borough shall be rated to the poor-rate instead of the occupier, except as hereinafter mentioned. (2) The full rateable value of every dwelling-house or other separate tenement, and the full rate in the pound payable by the occupier, and the name of the occupier, shall be entered in the rate-book. Where the dwelling-house or tenement shall be wholly let out in apartments or lodgings not separately rated, the owner of such dwelling-house or tenement shall be rated in respect thereof to the poor-rate : Provided as follows : (1) That nothing in this act contained shall affect any composition existing at the time of the passing of this act, so nevertheless that no such composition shall remain in force beyond the 29th day of September next. (2) That nothing herein contained shall affect any rate made previously to the passing of this act, and the powers conferred by any subsisting act for the purpose of collecting and recovering a poor-rate, shall remain and continue in force for the collection and recovery of any such rate or composition. (3) That where the occupier under a tenancy subsisting at the time of the passing of this act of any dwelling-house or other tenement which has been let to him free from rates, is rated and has paid rates in pursuance of this act, he may deduct from any rent due or accruing due from him, in respect of the said dwelling-house or other tenement, any amount paid by him on account of the rates to which he may be rendered liable by this act.

8. Where any occupier of a dwelling-house or other tenement (for which the owner, at the time of the passing of this act, is rated, or is liable to be rated) would be entitled to be registered as an occupier in pursuance of this act, at the first registration of parliamentary voters to be made after the year 1867, if he had been rated to the poor-rate for the whole of the required period, such occupier shall, notwithstanding he may not have been rated prior to the 29th day of September 1867, as an ordinary occupier, be entitled to be registered, subject to the following conditions : (1) That he has been duly rated as an ordinary occupier to all poor-rates in respect of the premises, after the liability of the owner to be rated to the poor-rate has ceased, under the provisions of this act. (2) That he has, on or before the 20th day of July, 1868, paid all poor-rates which have become payable by him as an ordinary occupier in respect of the premises, up to the preceding 5th day of January.

9. At a contested election for any county or borough represented by three members, no person shall vote for more than two candidates.

11. No elector who within six months before or during any election for any county or borough shall have been retained, hired, or employed for all or any of the purposes of the election, for reward by or on behalf of any candidate at such election, as agent, canvasser, clerk, messenger, or in other like employment, shall be entitled to vote at such election, and if he shall so vote he shall be guilty of a misdemeanour.

12. The boroughs of Totnes, Reigate, Yarmouth, and *Lancaster*, to cease to return members after the end of the present parliament.

15. Persons reported guilty of bribery or treating in Lancaster to be disqualified as voters for the northern division of the county of Lancaster, in respect of a qualification arising within the borough of Lancaster.

Part II. of the Act related to the Distribution of Seats.

17. Boroughs in schedule A (*i.e.* of less population than 10,000 in 1861) to return only one member each. [No Lancashire borough in schedule A.]

18. From and after the end of this present parliament the city of *Manchester* and the boroughs of *Liverpool*, Birmingham, and Leeds, shall each respectively return three members to serve in parliament.

19. Among the new boroughs in schedule B, to return one member each, are the following : *Burnley*, in Lancashire, including (as temporary contents or boundaries) the townships of Burnley and Habergham Eaves. *Stalybridge*, in Lancashire and Cheshire,

including the municipal borough of Stalybridge; the remaining portion of the township of Dukinfield; the township of Stayley; and the district of the local Board of Health of Mossley.

21. From and after the end of the present parliament, the borough of *Salford* shall return two members instead of one to serve in future parliaments.

23. From the end of the present parliament, each county named in the first column of Schedule D shall be divided into the divisions named in the second column, and (until otherwise directed by parliament) each of such divisions shall consist of the hundreds, wapentakes, and places mentioned in the third column of the schedule. Two members to serve for each division in the second column, to be chosen as if each such division were a separate county. Schedule D includes among the counties to be divided— NORTH LANCASHIRE into two divisions, viz., *North Lancashire*, including (temporarily) the hundreds of Lonsdale, Amounderness, and Leyland. *North-East Lancashire*, comprising the hundred of Blackburn. SOUTH LANCASHIRE into two divisions, viz., *South-East Lancashire*, comprising the hundred of Salford : and *South-West Lancashire*, comprising the hundred of West Derby. The places of election for these four divisions are to be, for North Lancashire, *Lancaster ;* for North-East Lancashire, *Blackburn ;* for South-East Lancashire, *Manchester ;* and for South-West Lancashire, *Liverpool.*

Part III. of the Act contained the following clauses :—

26. Different premises occupied in immediate succession by any person as owner or tenant during the twelve calendar months next previous to the last day of July in any year shall, unless and except as herein is otherwise provided, have the same effect in qualifying such person to vote for a county or borough, as a continued occupation of the same premises in the manner herein provided.

27. In a county where premises are in the joint occupation of several persons as owners or tenants, and the aggregate rateable value of such premises is such as would, if divided amongst the several occupiers, so far as the value is concerned, confer on each of them a vote, then each of such joint occupiers shall, if otherwise qualified, and subject to the conditions of this act, be entitled to be registered as a voter, and, when registered, to vote at an election for the county : Provided always that not more than two persons, being such joint occupiers, shall be entitled to be registered in respect of such premises, unless they shall have derived the same by descent, succession, marriage, marriage-settlement, or devise, or unless they shall be *bona fide* engaged as partners carrying on trade or business thereon.

28. Where any poor rate due on the fifth day of January in any year from an occupier, in respect of premises capable of conferring the franchise for a borough, remains unpaid on the first day of June following, the overseers, whose duty it may be to collect such rate, shall, on or before the twentieth of the same month of June, unless such rate has previously been paid, or has been duly demanded by a demand-note, to be served in like manner as the notice in this section referred to, give or cause to be given a notice in the form set forth in Schedule (E) to this act to every such occupier. The notice shall be deemed to be duly given if delivered to the occupier or left at his last or usual place of abode, or with some person on the premises in respect of which the rate is payable. Any overseer who shall wilfully withhold such notice, with intent to keep such occupier off the list or register of voters for the said borough, shall be deemed guilty of a breach of duty in the execution of the registration acts.

30. The following regulations shall, in and after 1868, be observed with respect to the registration of voters : (1) The overseers of every parish or township shall make out, or cause to be made out, a list of all persons on whom a right to vote for a county, in respect of the occupation of premises, is conferred by this act, in the same manner, and subject to the same regulations, as nearly as circumstances admit, in and subject to which the overseers of parishes or townships in boroughs are required by the registration acts to make out, or cause to be made out, a list of all persons entitled to vote for a member or members for a borough in respect of the occupation of premises of a clear yearly value of not less than ten pounds. (2) The claim of every person desirous of being registered as a voter for a member or members to serve for any borough in respect of the occupation of lodgings shall be in the form numbered 1 in Schedule (G), or to the like effect, and shall have annexed thereto a declaration in the form, and be certified in the manner in the said schedule mentioned, or as near thereto as circumstances admit ; and every such claim shall, after the last day of July and on or before the twenty-fifth day of August in any year, be delivered to the overseers of the parish in which such lodgings shall be situate, and the particulars of such claim shall be duly published by such overseers on or before the first day of September next ensuing in a separate list, according to the form numbered 2 in the said Schedule (G). So much of section 18 of the act of the session of the sixth year of the reign of her present Majesty, chapter 18, as relates to the manner of publishing lists of claimants, and to the delivery of copies thereof to persons requiring the same, shall apply to every such claim and list ; and all the provisions of the 38th and 39th sections of the same act, with respect to the proof of the claims of persons omitted from the lists of voters, and to objections thereto, and to the hearing thereof, shall, so far as the same are applicable, apply to claims and objections, and to the hearing thereof, under this section.

The remaining clauses relate chiefly to election arrangements and the settlement of borough boundaries.

Clause 36 provides that "it shall not be lawful for any candidate, or any one on his behalf, at any election for any borough, except the several boroughs of East Retford, Shoreham, Cricklade, Much Wenlock, and Aylesbury, to pay any money on account of the conveyance of any voter to the poll, either to the voter himself or to any other person ; and if any such candidate, or any person on his behalf, shall pay any money on account of the conveyance of any voter to the poll, such payment shall be deemed to be an illegal payment within the meaning of the Corrupt Practices Prevention Act, 1854."

Clause 49 runs as follows : "Any person, either directly or indirectly, corruptly paying any rate on behalf of any ratepayer for the purpose of enabling him to be registered as a voter, thereby to influence his vote at any future election, and any candidate or other person, either directly or indirectly, paying any rate on behalf of any voter for the purpose of inducing him to vote, or refrain from voting, shall be guilty of bribery, and be punishable accordingly ; and any person on whose behalf and with whose privity any such payment as in this section is mentioned is made shall also be guilty of bribery, and punishable accordingly."

The duties of the Boundary Commissioners are thus defined by clause 48 : "They shall, immediately after the passing of this act, proceed, by themselves or by assistant-commissioners appointed by them, to inquire into the temporary boundaries of every borough constituted by this act, with power to suggest such alterations therein as they may deem expedient ; they shall also inquire into the boundaries of every other borough in England and Wales, except such boroughs as are disfranchised by this act, with a view to ascertain whether the boundaries should be enlarged, so as to include within the limits of the borough all premises which ought, due regard being had to situation or other local circumstances, to be included therein for the purpose of conferring upon the occupiers thereof the parliamentary franchise for such borough ; they shall also inquire into the divisions of counties as constituted by this act, and as to the places appointed for holding courts for the election of members for such divisions, with a view to ascertain whether, having regard to the natural and legal divisions of each county, and the distribution of the population therein, any and what alterations should be made in such divisions or places ; and the said Commissioners shall, with all practicable despatch, report to one of Her Majesty's principal Secretaries of State upon the several matters in this section referred to them, and their report shall be laid before Parliament.

The following is the general saving clause : "56. The franchises conferred by this act shall be in addition to and not in substitution for any existing franchises ; but so that no person shall be entitled to vote for the same place in respect of more than one qualification, and subject to the provisions of this act, all laws, customs, and enactments now in force conferring any right to vote, or otherwise relating to the representation of the people in England and Wales, and the registration of persons entitled to vote, shall remain in full force, and shall apply, as nearly as circumstances admit, to any person hereby authorised to vote, and shall also apply to any constituency hereby authorised to return a member or members to parliament, as if it had heretofore returned such members to parliament and to the franchises hereby conferred, and to the registers of voters hereby required to be formed."

60. In the event of a vacancy in the representation of any constituency, or of a dissolution of parliament taking place, and a writ or writs being issued, before the 1st January, 1869, for the election of members to serve in the present or any new Parliament, each election shall take place in the same manner in all respects as if no alteration had been made by this act in the franchises of electors, or in the places authorised to return a member or members to serve in parliament, with this exception, that the boroughs by this act disfranchised shall not be entitled to return members to serve in any such new parliament.

In the interpretation clause it is provided that "dwelling-house shall include any part of a house occupied as a separate dwelling, and separately rated to the relief of the poor."

The following are some particulars, derived from Parliamentary and population returns, in reference to the four divisions of the county, under the Act, and all the boroughs, old and new (the latter in *italics*), in Lancashire:—

NORTH LANCASHIRE.—Area, 836·7 sq. miles, exclusive of boroughs except the borough of Lancaster (4·7 sq. miles), which is included in the above area.

NORTH-EAST LANCASHIRE.—Area, 247·1 sq. miles. The new borough of *Burnley* (9·6 sq. miles) is not included in this area.

SOUTH-EAST LANCASHIRE.—Area, 314 sq. miles. Part of the new borough of *Stalybridge* (0·9 sq. mile) is not included in this area.

SOUTH-WEST LANCASHIRE.—Area, 379·8 sq. miles. The new borough of *St. Helens*[1] (9·2 sq. miles) is not included in this area.

Taking the old division of the county into two only, North and South Lancashire, the following shows the population of each of the old boroughs within such division in 1851 and 1861, and its increase or decrease; also its gross estimated rental in 1856 and 1865, its increase or decrease, and the number of members it sends:—

NORTH LANCASHIRE.

BLACKBURN (two members).—Population in 1851, 46,536; in 1861, 63,126; increase, 16,590. Gross rental in 1856, £126,373; in 1865, £176,451; increase, £50,078.

CLITHEROE (one member).—Population, 11,480 and 10,864; decrease, 616. Rental, £34,578 and £45,327; increase, £10,749.

LANCASTER (two members).—Population, 16,168 and 16,005; decrease, 163. Rental, £50,435 and £56,285; increase, £5,850 [Disfranchised by the Act of 1867.]

PRESTON (two members).—Population, 69,542 and 82,985; increase, 13,443. Rental, £211,600 and £244,056; increase, £32,456

SOUTH LANCASHIRE.

ASHTON-UNDER-LYNE (one member).—Population, 29,791 and 33,917; increase, 4,126. Rental, £81,975 and £105,590; increase, £23,615.

BOLTON (two members).—Population, 61,171 and 70,395; increase, 9,224. Rental, £179,882 and £226,476; increase, £47,594.

BURY (one member).—Population, 31,262 and 37,563; increase, 6,301. Rental, £112,884 and £131,595; increase, £18,711.

LIVERPOOL (three members).—Population, 375,955 and 443,938; increase, 67,983. Rental, £1,680,824 and £2,655,888; increase, £975,064.

MANCHESTER (three members).—Population, 316,213 and 357,979; increase, 41,706. Rental, £1,427,600 and £1,676,785; increase, £249,185.

OLDHAM (two members).—Population, 72,357 and 94,344; increase, 21,987. Rental, £192,594 and £450.407; increase, £257,813.

ROCHDALE (one member).—Population, 29,195 and 38,184; increase, 8,989. Rental, £110,096 and £141,244; increase, £31,148.

SALFORD (two members).—Population, 85,108 and 102,449; increase, 17,341. Rental, £348,841 and £401,707; increase, £52,866.

WARRINGTON (one member).—Population, 23,363 and 26,947; increase, 3,584. Rental, £77,762 and £86,741; increase, £20,832.

WIGAN (two members).—Population, 31,941 and 37,658; increase, 5,717. Rental, £77,762 and £95,555; increase, £17,793.

The total population of *North Lancashire* (inclusive of four represented boroughs) was 460,530 and 547,469; increase, 86,939. Rental, £1,727,977 and £2,287,130; increase, £559,153.

The population of *South Lancashire* (inclusive of ten represented boroughs) was 1,557,067 and 1,871,030; increase, 313,963.[2] Rental, £6,471,124 and £9,046,578; increase, £2,575,454.

THE LANCASHIRE BOROUGHS CREATED BY THE ACT OF 1867.

1. BURNLEY included the township of Burnley (population 19,971, in 3,515 inhabited houses). and the township of Habergham Eaves (with a population of 18,013, in 3,369 inhabited houses). Total population of new borough 37,984, in 6,884 inhabited houses.

2. STALYBRIDGE included the municipal borough of Stalybridge (with a population of 24,921, in 4,864 inhabited houses) and the remaining portions of the townships of Dukinfield (15,024 persons, in 3,086 houses) and of Stayley (2,986, in 573 houses) and the district of the Local Board of Health of Mossley, of which the population (taken from "The Board of Health Officers' Almanack, 1867") was 14,000, but the number of inhabited houses is not known. With this modification the total population of the new borough was 56,931, in 8,523 houses, exclusive of those in the Mossley district.

---

[1] St. Helens was not made a new borough by the Act of 1867.—C.

[2] This is exclusive of Heaton Norris (population, 13,839; gross rental, £46,953), in the borough of Stockport, North Cheshire, and situate in this division, and inclusive of parts of Latchford and Thelwall (population, 2,897; and gross rental, £9,185), comprised in the borough of Warrington, and situate in North Cheshire.

The following will show the changes in the representation of this county and of its boroughs made by the Act of 1867 :—

COUNTY MEMBERS.

	1866.		1868.
North Lancashire	2 {	North Lancashire..	2
		N E. Lancashire	2
South Lancashire	3 {	S.E. Lancashire	2
		S.W. Lancashire	2
County Members	5		8

CITY AND BOROUGH MEMBERS.

	1866.		1868.
Ashton-under-Lyne	1	....	1
Blackburn	2		2
Bolton	2	....•....•....••...	2
Bury..	1		1
Clitheroe	1		1
Lancaster..	2	Disfranchised	0
Liverpool	2		3
Manchester	2		3
Oldham...	2		2
Preston..	2		2
Rochdale	1		1
Salford..	1		2
Warrington	1	....….........	1
Wigan	2		2

NEW BOROUGHS.

	1866.		1868.
Burnley	0		1
Stalybridge	0		1
Borough Members	22	....	25

The total representation of Lancashire in county and borough members was in 1866, 27 ; in 1867, by the new Act, it was increased to 33. The increase was three additional county and three additional borough members. It was expected that St. Helens would be one of the new boroughs, but it was not included in the new Act.

The following were the appointments (Aug. 1867) of the Assistant Boundary Commissioners, and their districts, so far as they related to Lancashire :—

NORTH-WESTERN (two sub-districts, 22 inquiries).—Sub-district A, comprising boroughs of Clitheroe, Burnley (new), Blackburn, Preston, Rochdale, Bury, Bolton, and Wigan. Counties to be divided, North Lancashire and South Lancashire (10 inquiries).

Lieut. Hozier, 2nd Life Guards.	Mr. F. W. Gibbs.

Sub-district B, comprising the boroughs of Liverpool, Manchester, Salford, Ashton-under-Lyne, Oldham, Birkenhead, Chester, Stockport, Macclesfield, Warrington, and Stalybridge (new). County to be divided, Cheshire (12 inquiries).

Lieutenant-Colonel Gordon, R.E., C.B.	Mr. P. Cumin.

THE REFORM ACTS 1884 AND 1885.

Further Acts to amend the law relating to the representation of the people of the United Kingdom were passed in 1884 and 1885. These Acts—"The Representation of the People Act, 1884," and "The Redistribution of Seats Act, 1885"—together form the third of the great changes in the constitution of the House of Commons which have taken place within the present century. The first of these important statutes, which received the Royal assent December 6, 1884, establishes a uniform household franchise and a uniform lodger franchise (as enacted by Secs. 3 and 4 of the Representation of the People Act, 1867) in all counties and boroughs throughout the United Kingdom; creates (by Sec. 3) what has been called the "service franchise," whereby an inhabitant, by virtue of any office, service, or employment, of a dwelling-house not inhabited by his master becomes entitled to vote as if he were the tenant ; declares that no fresh qualifications can in future be created by means of rent charges ; prohibits for the future the manufacture of fagot votes, and provides for their gradual extinction, while reserving to present fagot voters their personal right to vote ; and makes the occupation of any *land or tenement* (formerly land alone would not suffice in a borough) of £10 annual value a sufficient qualification in either borough or county. The £50 occupation franchise in counties is abolished as unnecessary. Overseers are required to ascertain by service of notices on rated occupiers, and to enter in a separate column in the rate-book the names of all male inhabitant occupiers other than the person rated who are entitled to be registered as inhabitant occupiers of a dwelling-house.

The Redistribution of Seats Act received the Royal assent on the 25th of June, 1885. The cardinal principles upon which it is based are as follow :—

1. The total number of members is raised from 652 to 670. The true complement of the House of Commons was previously 658, but six seats—four in England and two in Ireland—were disfranchised in 1869.

2. Of the eighteen additional seats six are given to England and twelve to Scotland, the previous representation of Wales and Ireland remaining unchanged.

3.· Boroughs having less than 15,000 inhabitants cease to return members to Parliament, and are merged in the county divisions. To this rule there are two exceptions—the borough of Warwick, which is added to Leamington, the joint borough having upwards of 15,000 inhabitants ; and Haverfordwest, which, instead of being merged in the county, is added, for Parliamentary purposes, to the Pembroke district.

4. Boroughs with less than 50,000 inhabitants in 1881 return only one member to Parliament.

5. Boroughs with populations varying from 50,000 to 165,000 return two members.

6. Boroughs with more than 165,000 are granted an additional member for about every 50,000.

7. Boroughs and counties returning more than one member are divided into two divisions, each division returning one member. Boroughs which have hitherto returned two members, and whose representation remains unchanged by the Act, are exempted from this rule.

8. The adoption of the above scale, as regards disfranchisement, made available 160 seats for redistribution. These, together with the eighteen additional seats, made a total of 178 disposable seats.

9. Of these 178 seats, ninety-six were given to county constituencies and eighty-two to the boroughs.

10. The Metropolitan boroughs (including Croydon and West Ham) were increased from twenty-two to sixty-two members.

Among the various minor provisions of the Act may be mentioned—

DIVIDED BOROUGHS.—A voter is not allowed to vote in more than one division of these boroughs, and the elections in all the divisions are held on the same day.

DIVIDED COUNTIES.—Each of the new divisions is treated as a separate constituency, and therefore a voter having property in more than one division is able to vote in each division in which he is registered.

SUCCESSIVE OCCUPATION of premises in the same Parliamentary borough qualifies a person to be registered as a voter, notwithstanding that they may be in different divisions ; but a change of occupation from one borough to another, or from a county to a borough, or *vice versâ*, or from one division of a county to another, vitiates the qualification for the year.

RETURNING OFFICERS.—In new boroughs, with a few exceptions, the returning officer—where there is no mayor—is appointed by the sheriff of the county, and must have an office within the borough. Returning officers in divided boroughs may appoint deputies.

PAID AGENTS, CLERKS, &c., if appointed in any division of a divided borough, are prohibited from voting in any other division of the same borough.

COUNTY ELECTIONS are held in such town as the magistrates in quarter sessions may appoint.

CORRUPT VOTERS, reported as guilty of offences at the election of 1880, are incapable for seven years of being registered as voters for the borough (or for the county division, if it has been merged therein) in respect of property within the borough.

Under the provisions of the Act the aggregate representation of Lancashire was increased from 33 to 57 members. The borough of Clitheroe was merged in its division of the county, and Wigan was deprived of one member ; six additional members were given to Liverpool, three to Manchester, and one to Salford ; and Barrow-in-Furness and St. Helens were created Parliamentary boroughs, and assigned one member each. By the same Act the county was divided into twenty-three separate constituencies returning one member each.

The representation of the county of Lancaster and its boroughs is now as follows :—

COUNTY.

North Lancashire.Divisions.	Members.	South-East Lancashire—cont.Divisions.	Members.
North Lonsdale	1	Eccles	1
Lancaster	1	Stretford	1
Blackpool	1	Gorton	1
Chorley	1	Prestwich	1
North-East Lancashire.		*South-West Lancashire.*	
Darwen	1	Southport	1
Clitheroe	1	Ormskirk	1
Accrington	1	Bootle	1
Rossendale	1	Widnes	1
		Newton	1
South-East Lancashire.		Ince	1
Westhoughton	1	Leigh	1
Heywood	1		
Middleton	1	Total	23
Radcliffe-cum-Farnworth	1		—

BOROUGHS.

Ashton-under-Lyne	1	Preston	2
Barrow-in-Furness	1	Rochdale	1
Blackburn	2	St. Helens	1
Bolton	2	Salford	3
Burnley	1	Warrington	1
Bury	1	Wigan	1
Liverpool	9		—
Manchester	6		34
Oldham	2		—

County Members 23
Borough Members 34

57

The Parliamentary borough of Stalybridge is located partly in Lancashire and partly in Cheshire.

TOWNS AND PLACES INCLUDED IN THE SEVERAL COUNTY DIVISIONS.

NORTH LANCASHIRE.—FOUR DIVISIONS.

1. NORTH LONSDALE DIVISION.—The sessional divisions of Barrow-in-Furness, Hawkshead, and North Lonsdale (including Cartmel), and the parishes in the sessional divisions of South Lonsdale, of Bolton-le-Sands, Borwick, Carnforth, Dalton, Nether Kellet, Over Kellet, Priest Hutton, Silverdale, Warton-with-Lindeth, Yealand-Conyers, and Yealand-Redmayne.

2. LANCASTER DIVISION.—The sessional divisions of Garstang, Hornby, and South Lonsdale (except so much as is comprised in Division 1, as above described), and the municipal borough of Lancaster.

3. BLACKPOOL DIVISION.—The sessional divisions of Amounderness, Kirkham, and Leyland (except so much as is comprised in Division 4, as below described), and the municipal borough of Preston.

4. CHORLEY DIVISION.—The sessional division of Leyland Hundred, and the parishes in the sessional division of Leyland, of Clayton-le-Woods, Cuerden, and Leyland.

NORTH-EAST LANCASHIRE.—FOUR DIVISIONS.

5. DARWEN DIVISION.—The sessional divisions of Blackburn (except so much as is comprised in Division 7), Darwen, and Walton-le-Dale, the municipal boroughs of Blackburn and Over Darwen, and the parishes in the sessional division of Clitheroe, of Aighton Bailey and Chaigley, Little Bowland, Chipping, and Leagram, and Thornley-with-Wheatley.

6. CLITHEROE DIVISION.—The sessional divisions of Burnley (except the parish of Hapton), Clitheroe (except so much as is comprised in Division 5), and Colne, and the municipal boroughs of Burnley and Clitheroe.

7. ACCRINGTON DIVISION.—The municipal borough of Accrington, and the parishes of Altham, Church, Clayton-le-Moors, Hapton, Huncoat, Oswaldtwistle, and Rishton.

8. ROSSENDALE DIVISION.—The sessional division of Rossendale, and so much of the municipal borough of Bacup as is not included in the sessional division of Rossendale.

SOUTH-EAST LANCASHIRE.—EIGHT DIVISIONS.

9. WESTHOUGHTON DIVISION.—The sessional division of Bolton (except so much as is comprised in Division 12) and the municipal borough of Bolton.

10. HEYWOOD DIVISION.—The sessional division of Bury (except so much as is comprised in Divisions 11 and 12), the municipal boroughs of Bury and Heywood, and so much of the parish of Spotland as is not included in the Local Government district of Whitworth, or in the municipal borough of Bacup, or in the municipal borough of Rochdale.

11. MIDDLETON DIVISION.—The sessional division of Middleton (except so much of the parish of Spotland as is included in Division 10, or in the municipal borough of Bacup, the municipal borough of Rochdale, and the parishes of Alkrington and Tonge, and in the sessional division of Bury so much of the parish of Hopwood as is not included in the municipal borough of Heywood.

12. RADCLIFFE-CUM-FARNWORTH DIVISION.—The parishes in the sessional division of Bolton, Farnworth, Kearsley, and Little Hulton, and in the sessional division of Bury, the parish of Pilkington, and so much of the parish of Radcliffe as is not included in the municipal borough of Bury.

13. ECCLES DIVISION.—The parishes of Barton-upon-Irwell, Clifton, Flixton, Urmston, and Worsley, and so much of the parish of Pendlebury as is not within the municipal borough of Salford.

14. STRETFORD DIVISION.—The municipal boroughs of Manchester and Salford, and so much of the municipal borough of Stockport as is situate within the county of Lancaster and the parishes of Bradford, Burnage, Chorlton-cum-Hardy, Didsbury, Harpurhey, Levenshulme, Moss Side, Newton, Reddish, Rusholme, Stretford, and Withington, and so much of the parish of Heaton Norris as is not included in the municipal borough of Stockport.

15. GORTON DIVISION.—The parishes of Denton, Haughton, and Openshaw, and so much of the parish of Gorton as is not included in the Parliamentary borough of Manchester.

16. PRESTWICH DIVISION.—The municipal boroughs of Ashton-under-Lyne and Oldham, and the parishes of Blackley, Chadderton, Crompton, Crumpsall, Droylsden, Failsworth, Great Heaton, Little Heaton, Moston, Prestwich, and Royton, and so much of the parish of Ashton-under-Lyne as is not included in the municipal borough of Ashton-under-Lyne.

SOUTH-WEST LANCASHIRE.—SEVEN DIVISIONS.

17. SOUTHPORT DIVISION.—The sessional division of Southport, the municipal borough of Southport, and the parishes of Great Crosby, Ince-Blundell, Little Crosby, and Thornton.

18. ORMSKIRK DIVISION.—The sessional division of Ormskirk, and the parishes of Aintree, Dalton, Kirkby Litherland, Lunt, Netherton, Orrell and Ford, Sefton, and Upholland, and, in the Prescot sessional division, of Croxteth Park, Knowsley, and Prescot.

19. BOOTLE DIVISION.—The municipal boroughs of Liverpool and Bootle-cum-Linacre, and the parishes of Childwall, Fazakerley, Walton-on-the-Hill, and Wavertree, and so much of the parishes of West Derby and Toxteth Park as is not included in the municipal borough of Liverpool.

20. WIDNES DIVISION.—The sessional division of Prescot (except the parish of Rainhill, and so much as is comprised in Divisions 18 and 21), and the parishes of Allerton, Garston, Hale, Halewood, Little Woolton, Much Woolton, and Speke.

21. NEWTON DIVISION.—The sessional divisions of St. Helens and Warrington, the municipal borough of St. Helens, and so much of the municipal borough of Warrington as is situate within the county of Lancaster, and the parishes of Ashton-in-Makerfield, Billinge, Higher End, Rainhill, and Winstanley, and so much of the parish of Eccleston as is comprised in the sessional division of Prescot.

22. INCE DIVISION.—The municipal borough of Wigan, and the parishes of Abram, Haigh, Hindley, Ince-in-Makerfield, Orrell, and Pemberton.

23. LEIGH DIVISION.—The sessional division of Leigh.

APPENDICES.

APPENDIX I.

THE SUCCESSION IN THE DUCHY OF LANCASTER.

(Abridged from Hargrave MSS. Brit. Mus. Cod. 327, fol. 1-50.)

The Address of the late Villiers, Lord Hyde, afterwards Earl of Clarendon in the Duchy of Lancaster.

To the King by his Majesty's most dutiful subject and servant,—HYDE.

Jan'y 20, 1772.

A LIST [abridged] of those who have held the Duchy of Lancaster under different titles of honour, succinctly showing the augmentation, the decline, and the present state of the Duchy.

Three Noblemen almost of the highest distinction bore the title of Lord of the Honor of Lancaster. Lord of an Honor was a dignity superior to that of Lord of a Manor, and in use before the Conquest. The Honor of Lancaster was of the most remote antiquity. It was composed of a number of Honors long before it was raised to an earldom, as it was successively to a dukedom.

1. Roger of Poictou stands first, but was deprived of his possessions for his disloyalty, which he probably inherited from his father, Roger de Montgomery, who got Arundel, Chichester, and the county of Salop from William I., and rebelled against William II.

2. William, Earl of Montaigne, Surry and Warren, third son of King Stephen, was next appointed Lord of the Honor of Lancaster, and put in possession of other considerable estates by his father. But Henry II. resumed what this royal earl held of the crown, and left him what came from his father before he was king.

3. John, surnamed Sansterre, notwithstanding his name, became, as Hovenden says, a tetrarch. His brother, Richard I., not weighing, as his father did, prudence against generosity, rendered him, who from ambition was too desirous of dominion, powerful by territories ; he rebelled accordingly against his benefactor, as he had done against his father, and was the murtherer of his nephew Arthur.

4. After King John, the Honor of Lancaster was raised to an earldom. Peter of Savoy, uncle to Queen Eleonora, wife of Henry III., was created by that king Earl of Lancaster. John, his predecessor, was, indeed, in the enumeration of his titles, called Earl of Lancaster as a king's son, who by the ancient laws of the crown were, as is reported, earls of course, without any particular creation or investiture. Part of the territories belonging to this earldom lay near the new temple, London. It was called a Vavasorie. Here the said earl Peter built a house, and named it from his own country "Savoy." His son being deemed an alien, the earldom escheated to the crown, and Henry III. conferred it on his son.

5. Edmond, called Crouchback, probably from his wearing a crouch or cross on his back, as was often done by votaries to pilgrimages. His mother was Eleanor, the second of the five daughters of the Earl of Provence. All of them were married to real or titular kings. From this prince is descended the royal house of Lancaster, rival to that of York. Their contest was of the longest duration and the most bloody that ever afflicted this nation. His father bestowed on him the titles and estates of Montford, Earl of Leicester, of Ferrars, Earl of Derby, and of John, Earl of Monmouth. He also inherited, by the will of his first wife Avelina, the succession of her father William, surnamed De Fortibus, Earl of Albemarle. Edmond was declared high steward of England, and procured a licence of Edward I. to turn his house (the Savoy) into a castle. Castles had distinction, rights, and powers, which houses or even manors had not. Sir William Fleetwood ranks an honor before a castle, a castle before a lordship, a lordship before a manor, and a manor before a messuage. The possessions of this earl were equal to some kingdoms. His second wife was Blaunch of Artois, the beautiful Queen of Navarre, niece to Saint Lewis, King of France, by whom he had three sons.

6. Thomas, the eldest, succeeded to his titles and estates, and was consequently Earl of Lancaster by inheritance. He was made chief of Edward II.'s privy council, but after many mutual disgusts and reconciliations he took arms against him, or rather against the Spencers, was defeated at Borough Bridge, and beheaded at Pontefract after he had underwent the scoffs of the Royalists for taking, as it was pretended he did in a letter to the Scotch, the title of King Arthur. He married Alice, daughter of Henry de Lacy, Earl of Lincoln, and added in her right the estate of Lincoln and Salisbury to his immense patrimony.

7. His brother Henry became entitled to such part only of his possessions and honours as had been settled upon him by the king, in case the last earl should die without issue, which he did ; and though the king afterwards considerably increased his estates by grants, yet he kept the greater share of the property of the late earl, which had been forfeited by his attainder. Henry further increased his estates by a large fortune with his wife Maud, heiress to her father Sir Richard Chaworth and to other relations ; by which acquisitions the Earls of Lancaster grew very considerable in Wales.

8. His son Henry, who had been created Earl of Derby and Lincoln in his father's lifetime, succeeded to his estates and honours. He added dignity to his illustrious family. He was the first Duke of Lancaster, and the second of our nobility raised to the ducal title. The Duke of Cornwall stood before him. By his patent of creation in the 25 of Edward III. (1351), the king created the county of Lancaster into a palatinate, and granted the duke *jura regalia* in that county and many other privileges. The grant by this charter was only for his life, so all these distinctions, with his dukedom, ceased at his death in 1361. In the 25th year of that reign (1351) the duke obtained in exchange for Richmondshire divers and large domains in the counties of York, Durham, Nottingham, Derby, Sussex, and Norfolk. But shortly before his death (23rd of March, 1361) he surrendered many of his privileges to the crown, which were afterwards granted to John of Gaunt.

9. John of Gaunt married his daughter Blanch, and made the house of Lancaster more royal. Maud, her eldest sister, dying without issue, all the Lancaster dominions devolved to this prince, who was first created Earl and afterwards Duke of Lancaster by his father Edward III.; which king, the 28th February, in the 51st year of his reign (1377), instituted, for the higher dignity of his son, a chancery, justices for the pleas of the crown, as well as for common law, *jura regalia*, and power of execution of writs and offices, and all other powers which were exerted by the Earl of Chester in his county palatine, but limited this institution to the duke's life, which ended in 1361.[1] The like privileges, with the same limitations, had been granted to Henry Duke of Lancaster ; but in the 13 of Richard II. (1389-90), the second duke, John, petitioned the king and Parliament at Gloucester that the late king's

---

[1] Sic in edition of 1835. It must, however, be 1399, the date of John of Gaunt's death, that is intended.—B, H,

grant to him might be extended to his heirs-male, and the king, by charter, with the assent of Parliament, extended it according to the prayer of the petition. He also obtained from King Richard a grant and release of all the forfeited estates which came to the crown by the attainder of Thomas Earl of Lancaster. This duke had his council in Lancashire before the grant to him of *jura regalia*, and in the grants and leases from the duke it is styled " Thrice Noble Council of the Thrice Noble Duke of Lancaster," &c. His council likewise took cognisance of land there before the last foundation or confirmation of the palatinate. He married, after the death of Blanch, Constantia, daughter of Peter, King of Castile, and took his father-in-law's title, but ceded it afterwards by contract, and was by Act of Parliament created Duke of Aquitaine. His recited titles are, son of the king, Duke of Aquitaine and Lancaster, Earl of Derby, Lincoln, and Leicester. His estates were greatly augmented by his father, who, in the 50th year of his reign (1376), granted to him and his heirs large domains in Hertfordshire, and at Calais, in France.

10. On his death, his son Henry de Bolingbroke, Duke of Lancaster, returned just as it was pronounced by a packed Parliament that his banishment should be perpetual. At first he only claimed his legal inheritance ; but finding a weak Government and a strong torrent of popularity, his ambition burst forth and filled every sail. He dethroned Richard II. by arms but without battle, and wore his crown by the name of Henry IV. ; but by Act of Parliament he severed the duchy from it. This act or charter is entitled " Charta regis Henrici quarti de separatione Ducatus Lancastriæ a corona." It recites all the titles and prerogatives of the duchy, and decrees that it shall be governed by its own officers, which were at that time a chancellor, an attorney-general, a receiver or treasurer, a clerk of the court, six assessors, twenty-three receivers, and three supervisors. But this is not the first institution of the duchy court, as has been erroneously imagined. The same was granted to Henry, the first Duke of Lancaster, and repeated in the charter or rescript of Edward III. for creating John of Gaunt Duke of Lancaster, and also in that of the 13th of Richard II. (1389) for extending the title and estates to his heirs-male. It has, indeed, been preserved from this reign, with little variation, to the present time. Henry IV. was so jealous of his dukedom and so zealous to preserve it that he settled it on his son, to save the title from being absorbed in that of king.

11. Henry V. enlarged (with the assent of Parliament) the dukedom by his mother's estate. She was daughter and heiress of Humphrey de Bohun, Earl or Hereford, whose estates were of great extent and value, and were situate chiefly in the counties of Essex, Middlesex, Cambridge, Norfolk, Lincoln, Bucks, Wilts, Suffolk, Surrey, Gloucester, Dorset, Hereford, and in the City of London and Marches of Wales. In this reign an Act of Parliament passed declaring that all grants of offices and estates in the duchy should pass under the duchy seal or should be void.

12. His successor Henry VI. did nothing of himself, and was made to do nothing worthy of notice that I can discover relating to the duchy.

13. The right to the dukedom next descended to John Beaufort, Earl of Somerset, son of Catherine Swinford, third wife of John of Gaunt, Duke of Lancashire, whose children by her before their marriage were legitimated in 20 Richard II. (1396) by Act of Parliament. But Edward IV. deemed the title and estate forfeited by the attainder of Henry VI., and by an Act of Parliament united the estates, " appropriated " is the expression in the act, to the crown, yet decreed at the same time that the office should remain on its former establishment. Until this period the office of chancellor of the county palatine was distinct from that of chancellor of the duchy, though often held by the same person ; nevertheless the chancellor of the county palatine was always subservient to the chancellor of the duchy, by whom all grants of offices and lands, as well in the county palatine as in the duchy at large, were made ; and if the county palatine seal was necessary to the completing the grant, the chancellor of the county affixed it by virtue of a warrant from the chancellor of the duchy. By this act the county palatine was annexed to the duchy, and the chancellor of the duchy hath ever since held the office of chancellor of the county palatine, executing the latter by his deputy or vice-chancellor. In the 12th year of this king (1472) an Act of Parliament passed for vesting a very considerable portion of the duchy estates in trustees for the use of the king's will, and the king directed the same by his will to be appropriated to diverse charitable and superstitious uses, but this trust was destroyed by an act of Henry VII. (1485), and the estates were resumed and reunited to the duchy.

14. Edward V. was not of an age to make any alterations during the short time that he was called king.

15. Richard III., though he made some excellent laws with regard to the nation, left the duchy as he found it. But,

16. Henry VII., whose right to it came from his mother, Margaret, the Countess of Richmond and Derby, daughter to John Beaufort, Duke of Somerset, who was son to the Earl of Somerset just mentioned, broke Edward IV.'s act and entail, separated the duchy again from the crown, and entailed both the crown and duchy on himself and his heirs for ever, and so it has continued distinct, though in the crown (the time of the usurpation excepted), to this day ; yet I do not perceive that any of our kings or princes have borne the title of Lancaster since Henry V., who by his father's express disposition inserted it among his other titles when Prince of Wales.

17. This wide-spreading inheritance [the duchy of Lancaster] was very greatly increased by the several acts of King Henry VIII. for the dissolution of monasteries and for erecting the court of augmentations, and by the act of Edward VI. for the dissolution of colleges and chantries, and by a charter of King Philip and Queen Mary, made in pursuance of an Act of Parliament, whereby very large estates in the counties of Hertford, Essex, Bucks, Suffolk, Sussex, and York were united to the duchy ; and so great a regard was paid by this queen to the future preservation of this her patrimonial inheritance, that she got a clause inserted in this act, declaring that all such estates as had been since the first of Edward VI., or should be at any time afterwards, granted from the duchy, and had or should revert or be forfeited to the crown, should return to the survey of the duchy court.

18, 19, 20, 21. This favourite succession, thus formed and augmented, passed through King Henry VIII., Edward VI., Philip and Mary, and Elizabeth, to James I. (notwithstanding many grants in fee were given by those sovereigns), in such good condition as to raise in the beginning of his reign an immense annual income, and to make a considerable part of the civil establishment, over and besides some very extensive and valuable domains which he granted, together with divers crown lands, to maintain his sons Henry, Prince of Wales, and Prince Charles. The king's necessities afterwards requiring extraordinary sums to be raised from his landed property, he first began with taking large fines for leases of duchy estates upon contracts for sixty years. But finding money came in slowly from this scheme, he proceeded to all who would become purchasers upon his terms ; so that when Charles I. succeeded to the throne, he found the duchy possessions reduced to very little more than the estates comprised in his own settlement and in the leases for sixty years.

22. King Charles's exigencies drove him to follow the example of his father in selling his duchy inheritance, by which he raised money to a considerable amount. No part of it was preserved except some few forests and parks and the estates which went to his queen Henrietta in jointure, and those which were comprised in the leases for sixty years granted by his father, and even many of those were sold in reversion for small sums. But upon almost all the grants in fee there were reserved to the crown fee-farm rents in the whole to a large amount. In 1649 a commission was appointed by an act of the Commons for the sale of the crown and duchy lands. The Restoration cancelled all transactions in consequence of that act.

23. King Charles II., soon after his accession, made several very extensive grants in fee of duchy estates to persons instrumental in his restoration, particularly to the Duke of Albermarle and the Earl of Sandwich, and he also made many leases for terms of ninety-nine years in reversion at small rents, some of which are still subsisting. In 1665 he settled divers fee-farm rents, and very near all the landed estate of the duchy which was not in jointure upon his mother Henrietta, upon Queen Catherine for her life ; and Queen Henrietta dying in 1671, the king added the estates comprised in her settlement to Queen Catherine's jointure ; so that the remaining revenue from the duchy to the crown sunk to a state of insignificance. In 1670 and 1672 this king had two acts to sell all the fee-farm rents, as well as those of the crown as of the duchy, and they were accordingly sold, and such as were in settlement on Queen Catherine were either surrendered by her, and an equivalent granted to her in lieu thereof by charge upon the hereditary excise, or were sold in reversion expectant on her death.

24. King James II., though a prince of more order and business, did not attempt to save this ducal part of his patrimony from ruin, and such was the reduction of its income that in 1686 the officers of the duchy agreed to reduce salaries, to make them better tally with the small production from the duchy estate.

25. William III. accelerated the decline. He granted for 99 years, after the demise of Queen Catherine in 1705, most of the estates comprised in her jointure, which were all that remained unsold, except what is not worth mentioning.

A stop was put to the devastation by an act passed in the first of Queen Anne (1702) to restrain the crown from granting leases for more than 30 years, or three lives, with impeachment of waste, and a reservation of the ancient or more usual rent or greater, or of a third part of the value; building leases only were confined to 50 years; but King William's above-mentioned grants for 99 years had absorbed so much of the duchy revenues that little or no attention through the reigns of George I. and George II. were given to the improvement of it, or even order in the office, till the Earl of Arundell was appointed chancellor. He was a nobleman who loved business and respected justice, and made confusion and partiality give place to regularity and candour. Lord Strange adopted, perfected, and enlarged his predecessor's laudable designs in the reign of George III.; but with all the advantage of their proceedings and plans, and under such auspices as ought to animate every one to do right, this revenue will not for many years be an object worthy of royal consideration; and, according to probability, never a great one, not even when the leases granted by Charles II. and those of William III., for 99 years, expire, and are renewed with increased reserved rents, which the first will in the compass of 10 or 12 years, and the latter in about 33.

The annual certain amount at present is but.................... .... £3273 13 0
And the annual disbursements.. 3558 4 8

The deficiency £284 11 8

which is made good by fines upon leases, casual rents reserved on leases for mines, sales of timber and such like. A surplus undoubtedly arises from these articles, perhaps about £2,000 a year, or rather under, but that cannot, from the nature of it, be freed.

APPENDIX II.

PERAMBULATION OF THE FORESTS.

12th Henry III. (1228).

Lansdowne MSS. Cod. 559, fol. 55 (ss.)

These are the twelve knights of the county of Lancaster who made perambulation of the forests by precept of the lord the king—to wit, Wm. Blundell, Tho. de Bethum, Adam de Bury, Wm. de Tatham, Adam de Coupynura, Adam de Molyneux, Gilbert de Kellet, Paulinus de Gairestang, Patrick de Berwyk, Henry de Lee, Grymebald de Ellale, Thos. de Burnhull, who say that the whole county of Lancaster ought to be disafforested, according to the tenor of the charter of forests, except the woods underwritten: 1st, *Quernemore*, by these bounds—to wit, as Langtwayt extends itself towards the Erlesgate, descending as far as to the bridge of Musart Siket [*i.e.*, ditch or runnel], descending as far as to the Frith Brok, following the Frith Brok descending as far as to the Lone [Lune], following the Lone ascending as far as to Esk Brok, ascending and following [it] to Mag Brigge, ascending as far as to Hankersdame, following the Siket of Hankersdame, ascending as far as to the siket which is under Ullethwayt, and descending from that siket as far as Storchag, and from Storchag as far as to the east part of the head of Brounes-gate, following Brounes-gate ascending as far as to the summit of the head of Cloghok [Clougha], and from the summit of the head of Cloghok, as far as to the summit of the head of Dameriagele, descending as far as to the siket which is between two "marbes arres" [? marked trees], following the Silcok [?] as far as to Blemes, following the siket as far as to Condone [ ], following the siket as far as to the moss under Eghlotes-heved, following that moss ascending as far as to the road of Stokthwayt, following that road ascending to the Erlesgate. And further, without these bounds, John the king gave a certain part of the forest, by his charter, to Matthew Gernet and his heirs, to render therefor yearly half-a-mark [6s. 8d.], saving to himself his venison [or hunting], and therein the king may do his pleasure. And excepting *Covet and Bleasdale* by these bounds—to wit, From the head of Calder on the south part, as far as to Ulnesty, and from Ulnesty as far as to the top of the head of Perlok [Parlick Pike], and from that summit following the Merlegh, descending as far as to where the Merlegh falls into [the] Broke at Thorpen Lees, following the Broke and descending to the duct [? path] in the east side of Wone Snape, following Wone Snape as far as to Stayngile, and from Stayngile as far as to Comistia, following Comisty and descending as far as into Calder, following and ascending as far as to the forenamed Ulnesty. And except *Fulwode*, by these bounds, from the Hay of Runisgil as far as to the way [or road] of Sepal, and thence as far as to the duct [? path] which goes from Sepedale to Fulwode, and thence so as that duct falls into Haversich-gate, and thence so as the way goes to Coleford in the Ferms, and thence so as that falls as far as to the Codelische, and thence as far as to the Hay of Ranislyt. And the men of Preston ought to have building timber for their houses and for fuel, and pasture for their cattle. [And except] *Toxtath*, by these bounds: So as where Oskeles Brok falls into Mersee, following Oskeles Brok, ascending as far as to the park of Magwom, and from the meadow as far as Bromegge, following the Bromegge as far as to the Brounlowe, and thence across as far as to the old turbaries between the two marshes, as far as to Lambisthorn, and from Lambisthorn descending as far as the Waterfall of the head of Stirpull, following and descending as far as to the Mersee, near these [bounds]. King John placed Smethdown with its appurtenances in the forest, and gave Thingwall to a certain pauper in exchange for . . . and therein the king does according to his will. Also, except the wood of *Derby*, by these bounds: From Bradi-stone in Hargun-Kar, and so by the middle of the Kar, as far as to Haselhurst, and so where the footpath goes out of the wood as far as to Longlegh, which extends from [West] Derby as far as unto Kyrkeby, and so beyond Longlegh into Mikkyll-brok, and ascending from Mykkyl-brok as far as Blak-brok, ascending from Blak-brok as far as into Throun-thornedale-brok, and so ascending as far as to the plains and the street where they have common, and herbage, and other things in the aforesaid wood. And the men of Derby have all necessaries in the aforesaid wood. Also, except *Burton Wode*, by these bounds: From Hardesti as far as to Sonky, and from Ravelslache as far as to Brade-legh-broke; so as that William Pincerna [Butler] and his heirs may have common of pasture for their beasts in store, and feeding for their swine, and building timber at his castle for his building and burning. Also we the jurors say, that *Croxtath* park was in defence [or protection] since the coronation of Henry, the grandfather of our king, and belongs to Knowslay, to the heir of Robert Fitz Henry, and ought to be disforested, according to the tenor of the charter of forests. Also we say that *Altkar* was placed in protection since the coronation of Henry, the grandfather of our king, and belongs, a certain part of it, to the vill of Ines [Ince] and the Ramsmelis [Raven-meols], and to Forneby, and to Holand, and to Lydgate, and ought to be disforested. We also say that the vill of Halis was in demesne of the grandfather of our king, and that the king placed in defence part of the wood after his coronation, from Flaxpolis to Quyntebriche. And the king gave the aforesaid vill of Halis, in its entirety and with its appurtenances, to Richard de Mide, by his charter of the forest; and it ought to be disforested according to the tenor of the charter of the forest. Also we say that *Symondeswoode* was placed in defence after the coronation of Henry, grandfather of our king, and belongs with Kyrkeby to the heir of Richard Fitz Roger, and ought to be disforested according to the tenor of the charter of forests, &c.

APPENDIX III.

THE LANSDOWNE FEODARY. [1]

KNIGHTS' FEES.

W ich were those of Henry, late Earl of Lincoln, and which, after the death of the said earl, were those of Thomas, late Earl of Lancaster, and now (to wit, in 23 Edward III., 1849) are those of Henry, Earl of Lancaster, Derby and Leicester, and Lord High Steward of England.

Salfordshire—Totington.

Roger de Midelton holds four carucates and two bovates of land in Midelton, for one knight's fee.
Margery de Radeclyve and Henry her son hold four carucates and six bovates of land in Bury, for one fee.
Henry de Trafford holds two carucates of land in Chatherton for the fourth part of one fee, where eight, &c.
Alice, who was the wife of Adam de Prestwyche, holds the manor of Akkeryngton for homage and service, and there is the twenty-fourth part of a knight's fee there.

Leylandshire—Penwortham.

Robert de Keurdale holds in demesne and service three carucates of land in Keurdale, whereof ten [? carucates] make one knight's fee.
John Feton holds in service one carucate of land in Wythenhill, one carucate of land in Hoghton, two carucates of land in Quarlton, half a carucate of land in Wythull, in woodland, for half a fee and the sixteenth part of one fee, where eight carucates make a fee.
The same John holds in service one carucate of land in Clayton, where ten carucates make one knight's fee.
William Caudray holds in demesne and service the vill of North Meols, for the fourth part of one knight's fee, where ten carucates make one knight's fee.
Adam de Walton, parson of Mitton, holds two carucates in Ulneswalton, where ten carucates, &c.
William de Faryngdon holds in demesne and service one carucate of land in Leyland, where ten carucates, &c.
Thomas de Sutton holds one messuage and three bovates of land in Penwortham, where ten carucates, &c.
The abbot of Evesham holds one bovate of land in the same place, where ten carucates, &c.
Margaret Banastre holds in demesne and service three carucates of land in Dokesbury, and . . . yngton (Adlyngton ?), six bovates of land in Hethe Chernock, half a carucate of land in Chernok Richard, two carucates of land in Standish and Longtree, and one carucate of land in Walshe Quethull [Welsh Whittle], one carucate of land in Shevengton, for one fee, where eight carucates, &c.

Amounderness.

Adam de Freckelton holds in demesne and service four carucates of land in Frekelton, two carucates of land in Etheleswyk, one carucate of land in Whytyngham, two carucates of land in Neuton, for one fee, where eight carucates make one knight's fee.
William Prese holds in demesne and service one carucate of land in Neuton, where eight [carucates], &c.
The same William holds in demesne and service two carucates of land in Prese, where eight carucates, &c.
Ralph de Bethum holds in demesne and service three carucates of land in Warton, and half a carucate of land in Neusom, and one carucate of land in Bretherton, for half a fee, where nine carucates, &c.
The heirs of Wodeplumpton hold demesne and service one carucate of land in Bretherton, two carucates of land in Claighton in Amounderness, and half a carucate of land in Neusum, where ten carucates, &c.
Adam de Hoghton, chevalier, holds in service one carucate of land and one bovate of land in Heton in Lonnesdale, where ten carucates, &c.
Robert de Holand, chevalier, holds in service three carucates of land in Eukston, where ten carucates, &c.
Nicholas de Boteler holds in demesne one messuage and eleven bovates of land in Frekelton, where seven carucates, &c. ; and that quantity is the sixth part of one fee, except besides } one twentieth part less.
Robert de Frekelton holds one messuage and two bovates and three parts of one bovate of land in Frekelton, where eight carucates, &c. ; and that quantity is the twenty-first part of a fee.
The heir of Robert Sherburne holds two bovates of land in Frekelton, and one bovate of land in Etheleswyk, where eight carucates, &c.
The heir of Adam de Banestre, chevalier, holds two bovates of land in Frekelton, and five bovates of land in Etheleswyk where eight carucates, &c.
Thomas Bredekyrk holds one bovate of land in Etheleswyk, where eight carucates, &c.
Thomas, son of Gilbert Singleton, holds one bovate of land in Frekelton, where eight carucates, &c.
The heirs of Orm Travers hold five bovates of land in Etheleswyk, where eight carucates, &c.

Syngleton.

There are in this place twenty-one messuages and twenty-six bovates of land in the hands of bonders, who render therefor yearly at the terms of Easter and Michaelmas £21 9s. 3d. And there are there eleven cottages, with so many curtilages, and one croft, and one plot of land in the hands of tenants-at-will, who render therefor yearly 21s. 6d. And all the aforesaid bonders owe tallage, [2] and give marchet [3] and heriot, and the sixth part of all the goods belonging to the deceased on the death of a husband, and not more unless he were a widower. And if any of them shall have a male pullet [or cock], he ought not to sell it without licence. And to have the aforesaid, with perquisites of court, as well for Syngleton as for Riggeby, extending to 30 yearly. Total, £24 0s. 9d.

It is to be noted that for every bovate of land aforesaid, a first rent of 2s. 6d. yearly, with the work at ploughing, harrowing, mowing the meadows at Riggeby, and carrying elsewhere the provisions of the lord at Richmond, York, Doncaster, Pontefract, and Newcastle, with twelve horses alike in summer and winter. And afterwards the aforesaid customs were released, and the aforesaid bovates demised to the aforesaid bonders holding them, viz. for each bovate, 14s. 2½d.

Ryggeby.

There are in this place twenty-one bovates of land, and a half and a fourth part of one bovate in the hands of the bonders, who render therefor yearly at each term, £19 16s. 4d. In the parking of cattle by command of the king or of the lords of Lancaster, which for the time were in the Wapentake of Amounderness, and were folded at Riggeby, and estimated at half mark yearly, to wit, for the keeping of every beast a day and a night in the winter time one penny, and for every day and night in the summer time, a halfpenny. Total, £20 3s.

---

[1] From the Lansdowne MSS. Cod. 559, fol. 23 (sa). This document (like the last) was given in the Latin, in the Appendix to the old edition. These translations I find among the late Mr. Harland's papers.—B. H.

[2] *Tallage:* Special contributions of money levied on the tenant for the lord's behalf, in the same way that *aids* were exacted by him of his land tenants.—C.

[3] Marchet, or maiden-rent, was a payment to the lord of the manor to be free from an abominable ancient privilege of manorial lords on the bridal night of a tenant's daughter.

Wro [? *Wray*].

Adam, son of Richard the clerk, holds five acres of land, and renders yearly at the two terms of the year 4d.—namely, at the feast of the Annunciation of the blessed Mary, 2d.; and at the feast of St. Michael, 2d. Roger Culvay holds three and a half acres of land, and renders yearly at the terms 9d. Adam, son of Jordan, holds one acre, and renders yearly at the terms 12d. Richard de Wro holds half a bovate of land, and renders yearly at the terms 5d. William le Harpour holds one and a half bovate of land, and renders yearly at the terms 15½d. Adam de Kilgrimshagh holds half a bovate of land, and renders yearly at the terms 4½d. Giles holds two and a half acres, and renders yearly at the terms 10d. John de Bonk holds one bovate and one and a half acre of land, and renders yearly at the terms 10½d. John le Wise holds eleven [acres], and renders yearly at the terms 6½d. William le Wogher holds six acres of land, and renders yearly at the terms 2½d. John de Bredkyrk holds half a bovate of land, and renders yearly at the terms 9d. Adam de Parys holds two bovates, which were those of John le Harpour, and renders yearly at the terms 3s. 0½d. of free farm, and two marks. And the said tenants owe suit to the court of Ryggeby twice a year, and also the heirs of the said tenants, after the decease of the said tenants, owe double farm [rents]. Total, £30 7s. 1d.

The heirs of William, son of Ellen, hold the fourth part of one bovate of land in Etheleswyk, where eight carucates make one knight's fee.

The heir of Adam de Bredeshagh holds one messuage and half a bovate of land in Neuton, where eight carucates, &c.

The heir of John de Bredkyrk holds two bovates of land in Neuton, where eight carucates, &c.

The heir of Adam Harper holds half a bovate of land in Neuton, where eight carucates, &c.

The heir of Henry de Fetherby and William de Whityngham, John de Staunford, and the heir of Richard de Mirscowe, hold the mediety of the manor of Claghton divided amongst them, by the service of the fifth part of one knight's fee.

Knights' Fees of Blakeburnshire.

Robert de Longeton, chevalier, holds in demesne and service two carucates of land in Walton-in-the-Dale, one carucate of land in Over Derwent, two carucates of land in Nether Derwent, one carucate of land in Melling and Eccleshull, and one carucate of land in Little Harewood, for one knight's fee.

The Abbot of Whalley holds in demesne and service one carucate of land in Billyngton for the eighth part of one knight's fee. John de Schotelesworth holds in demesne one bovate of land in Hunkot, where eight carucates make one knight's fee.

The heir of John de Clayton holds one bovate of land in Hunecote, where eight carucates, &c.

John de Alvetham holds in demesne and service one carucate of land in Alvetham, and one carucate of land in Clayton, where eight carucates, &c.

Brian de Thornhill holds in demesne and service one carucate of land in Folrigg, where eight carucates of land, &c.

Gilbert de le Legh holds, with the heirs of John de Caterale and Philip de Clayton, divisibly amongst them, holding in demesne and service Tounlay, Snoddesworth, and Caldecotes, for the eighth part of one knight's fee.

William de Heskaith, chevalier, holds in demesne and service two carucates of land in Great Harewode, where eight carucates of land, &c.

John de Radeclif, Joan (or Jane) his wife, hold as dower of the same Joan, of the inheritance of the heir of Thomas Talbot, two carucates of land in Russhton, where twenty carucates, &c.

William de Radeclif holds in demesne and service one carucate of land in Blakeburn, where ten [carucates], &c.

The heir of William de Chatherton holds in demesne and service one carucate of land in Mitton, where eight carucates, &c.

The heir of Margaret Banistre holds in demesne and service in Halghton one carucate of land, where eight carucates, &c.

The heirs of Adam Nouel and Richard de Morlegh hold in demesne and service two carucates of land in Morley, where twelve carucates, &c.

Gilbert de le Legh, and the heir of John de Caterale, holds in demesne and service the *vill* of Hapton for the third part of one knight's fee.

The heir of William le Heriz holds one carucate of land in Little Merley, where twelve carucates, &c.

The heir of Lore de Caterale holds one carucate of land in Little Mitton, where eight carucates, &c.

The heir of Thomas de Osbaldiston holds in service one carucate of land in Whetheley and Thorneley, where eight carucates, &c.

The Abbot of Kyrkestall holds half a carucate of land in Extwisell, where eight carucates, &c.

Robert de Blakeburn holds one carucate of land in Donnum (Downham), where twenty carucates, &c.

John de Dyneley holds half a carucate of land in the same place, where twenty carucates, &c.

The heir of John Fitz William holds two bovates of land in the same place, where twenty carucates, &c.

The heir of Hugh de Donnum holds one and a half bovate of land in the same place, where twenty carucates, &c.

The heir of Robert Spendelufe holds half a bovate of land in the same place, where twenty carucates, &c.

The heir of William Fitz Allan holds one bovate of land in the same place, where twenty carucates, &c.

The heir of Henry le Henriz holds one bovate of land in the same place, where twenty carucates, &c.

The heir of Richard le Cok holds three and a half acres of land in the same place, where twenty carucates, &c.

The heir of Hugh Fitz Ralph holds one bovate of land in Worston, where twelve carucates, &c.

The heir of Hugh Fitz Thomas holds one bovate of land in the same place, where twelve carucates, &c.

The heir of Thomas de Rede holds one bovate of land in the same place, where twelve carucates, &c.

The heir of William Fitz Hugh holds one bovate of land in the same place, where twelve carucates, &c.

The heir of William Fitz Thomas holds one bovate of land in the same place, where twelve carucates, &c.

Alice Sherburne holds two parts of two carucates of land in Wiswall, where eight carucates, &c.

The abbot of Whalley holds the third part of two carucates of land in the same place, where eight carucates, &c.

John de Dyneley holds in demesne and service one carucate of land in Twisilton, where fourteen carucates, &c.

The heir of John del Hall of Chipyn holds a certain tenement in Chepyn, for the fortieth part of one fee.

Richard Cocus [the cook] holds three and a half acres of land in Donnoum by knight service, where twenty carucates, &c.

Tenures of the Knights' Fees alienated in Alms, and of other Tenements held in fee-farm in the fee of Penwortham.

The abbot of Evesham holds in alms ten bovates of land in Penwortham, where ten carucates make one knight's fee.

John Flemyngs and William del Lee hold three carucates of land in Longeton, at fee-farm, by charter of the Lord Henry de Lasci, the last earl, paying yearly 50s. for all services, where ten carucates, &c.

Thomas de Leyland holds one bovate of land in Penwortham at fee-farm, paying yearly 13s.

Sir Adam de Hodeleston holds for the term of his life, of the grant of the Lord Henry de Lascy, the last earl, three carucates of land in Billyngton, by knight service, where eight carucates, &c., which tenement the abbot of Whalley acquired to himself and his successors for ever.

The Earl of Lancaster holds in demesne one carucate of land in Alkrington, where eight carucates, &c.

The lord Earl of Lancaster holds in his demesne six bovates of land [in] Huncotes, where eight carucates, &c.

The same earl holds in his demesne one carucate and two bovates of land in Donnoum, where twenty carucates, &c.

The same earl holds in his demesne three bovates of land in Worston, where twelve carucates, &c.

The abbot of Whalley hold in alms one carucate of land in Blakeburn, where ten carucates, &c.

The abbot of Neweby holds in alms a half carucate of land in Extwisell, where eight carucates, &c.

Robert Spendeloue holds the mediety of one bovate of land in Penwortham, by what service they know not, but will inquire.

Particular Knights' Fees, formerly of the Earl of Lincoln, in the Duchy of Lancaster.[1]

Robert de Longeton, chevalier, holds one knight's fee of the Duke of Lancaster, in Walton, in Blakeburnshire, with members, which same fee Robert Banastre lately held of the fee of the former Earl of Lincoln.

Henry, the duke, holds the fifth part of one knight's fee, in Ulneswalton, which Warin de Walton formerly held of the aforesaid fees.

Thomas Banastre del Bonk, and Thomas, son of Adam Banastre, knight, John de Thorpe and Ralph de Bykerstath, and William, son of William Banastre, hold of the said duke the twelfth part of one fee in Breth'ton, which Richard Banastre, Walter de Hole, Richard de Top, William de Breyme, Thomas de Gerstan, and Simon del Pull, formerly held of the aforesaid fees.

Adam de Hoghton, chevalier, and all his tenants, hold of the duke the third part of one knight's fee in Hoghton, Etheleswyk, and Clayton, and Whelton with Hepay, Wythenbull with Rotheleeworth, which Robert de Feton formerly held of the said fees.

The abbot of Cockersand holds the fourth part of one knight's fee in Hoton, in pure and perpetual alms of the aforesaid fees.

The heir of Robert Fitz Richard holds of the said duke the tenth part of one knight's fee in Longeton, which Robert Fitz Richard formerly held of the aforesaid fees.

Henry, Duke of Lancaster, William de Faryngton, and William de Holand, hold of the said duke the tenth part of one knight's fee in Longeton, Leyland, and Eccleston, which Robert Bushell formerly held of the said fees.

John Haveryngton and all the parceners hold of the said duke the fourth part of one knight's fee in Shevyngton, Chernok, and Walshewythull, which Robert Banastre formerly held of the said fees.

Richard de Caterhalle holds of the said duke the twenty-first part of one knight's fee in Little Mitton, which John de Pynchardon held of the aforesaid fees.

The abbot of Whalley, Richard de Sherburn, and Gilbert de la Legh, hold of the said duke the fourth part of one knight's fee in Wiswall and Hapton, which Adam de Bla[k]burn and Roger del Arches lately held of the aforesaid fees.

Gilbert de la Legh holds of the said duke the fourth part of one knight's fee in Tounley, Coldecotes, and Sudworth, which Henry Goldyng formerly held of the said fees.

Richard de Greenacres holds of the said duke the tenth part of one knight's fee in Tweyselton, which the Earl of Lincoln formerly held in his own hand of the aforesaid fees.

The abbot of Kyrkestall holds of the lord duke the tenth part of one knight's fee in Extwysell, which Adam de Preston formerly held of the said fees.

John de Haveryngton, chevalier, Thomas Dardern, and Adam de Hoghton, Richard Noel, and John de Bayley, hold the fourth part of one knight's fee in Aghton, Merlay, and Livesay, which Ralph de Mitton formerly held of the aforesaid fees.

John de Dyneley holds the fourth part of one knight's fee in Donnum of the said duke, which Robert Chester formerly held of the aforesaid fees.

Brian . . . . de Thornhull holds of the said duke the eighth part of one knight's fee in Folerigg, which John de Grigleston formerly held of the aforesaid fees.

John de Morley, Richard and John de Greenacres, hold of the said duke the tenth part of one knight's fee in Little Merlay, which William Marescall formerly held, &c.

John de Radeclif holds the tenth part of one knight's fee in Rissheton of the said duke, which Gilbert Fitz Henry de Alvetham formerly held, &c.

Henry de Clayton holds the eighth part of one knight's fee of the said duke in Clayton, which Henry de Clayton, his ancestor, formerly held, &c.

William de Hesketh, chevalier, holds the fourth part of one knight's fee of the said duke in Harewod, which Hugh Fyton formerly held, &c.

Henry, Duke of Lancaster, holds six bovates of land in Huncotes, where sixty-four bovates of land make one knight's fee of the aforesaid fees.

Henry de Clayton and John de Shotelesworth hold of the said duke two bovates of land in Huncotes, where sixty-four bovates make one knight's fee of the aforesaid fees.

Roger de Pilkyngton holds of the said duke one knight's fee in Bury in Salfordshire, which Adam de Bury formerly held, &c.

John de Rydale holds one knight's fee of the said duke in Midelton with members, which Robert de Midelton formerly held, &c.

Henry de Chaterton holds the fourth part of one knight's fee of the said duke in Chatherton, which Gilbert de Barton formerly held, &c.

Henry, Duke of Lancaster, holds the fifth part of one knight's fee of the aforesaid fee in Totyngton, which the Earl of Lincoln formerly held.

Parcels of Fees formerly of Thomas de Grelle.

The heir of Gilbert de Barton holds of John de la Ware one and a half knight's fee in Barton with members, which Gilbert de Barton formerly held of Thomas de Grelle, and he of the Earl of Ferrars, and he of the king in chief.

Thomas de Latham, chevalier, Robert de Holand, chevalier, and Thomas de Sotheworth, hold of John de Ware one knight's fee, of which Thomas de Latham, chevalier [holds] three carucates of land in Childewall, one carucate in Asphull, one carucate of land in Turton [half a carucate of land in Childewall, half a carucate of land[2]] in Brockholes, and the aforesaid Robert [Holand] and Thomas de Southworth hold one carucate in Harewode in Salfordshire, where six and a half carucates of land make one fee, which Robert de Latham holds of the said John, one knight's fee in Dalton, Parbald, and Wrightyngton, which Robert de Latham formerly held of the aforesaid fees.

The heir of John Fitz Henry de Hulton holds of the said John the third part of one knight's fee in Romworth and Lostock, which Richard Perpond formerly held, &c.

Roger de Pilkyngton holds of the said John the fourth part of one knight's fee in Pilkyngton, which Roger de Pilkyngton, his ancestor, formerly held, &c.

Fee of Lyncoln.

Henry, Duke of Lancaster, and all his tenants hold in demesne and service within the duchy of Lancaster twenty-two knights' fees, and the half the fourth part and the twentieth part of one knight's fee, which the Earl of Lincoln formerly held within the aforesaid duchy, and he, the Earl of Lincoln, never held many or any parcels there, which same fees the said earl formerly held of the honor of Lancaster, as appears above by the particulars and parcels above written.

John de la Ware holds in demesne and service five and a half fees and the twelfth part of a fee, within the said duchy, which same Thomas de Grelley held, which same Thomas formerly held of the king, as of his honor of Lancaster, as estimated twelve fees, but within the said duchy the said Thomas never held more than five fees and a half, and the twelfth part of one knight's fee, which the said John la Ware now holds, as appears by the particulars and parcels above said, and all the rest of the said twelve fees the said Thomas holds in other various counties outside the duchy aforesaid, but where and in what parcels held we know not.

---

[1] This part of the inquest must have been taken two years after the former, the date of the duchy creation being 25 Edward III. (1351).

[2] The words enclosed within brackets have been erased in the original document.

Parcels of the Fee of Hornby.

Inquisition taken at Hornby by Robert Paslew, escheator of the king in the county of Lancaster, Richard de Burgh, Benedict de Hergun, Adam de Farleton, Simon de Farleton, Adam, clerk of Claghton, Roger de Tunstall, William Aaron de Farleton, Roger de Farleton, John Fitz Eva de Tunstall, Henry de Wenyngton, Henry Fitz Robert de Wennyngton, Adam Fitz Andrew de Farleton, John Fitz Benedict de Farleton, William Fitz Roger Scocchis, Robert Fitz Waltham de Ergham, Thomas Fitz Allan de Hergun, Gilbert Fitz Huctred de Hergun, Adam Fitz Martin de Farleton, John Makeles, and Simon Fitz Thomas de Hergun.

The jury say on their oath that Hubert de Burgh holds the manor of Horneby of Henry Munden and Roger de Monte Begon, and he in chief of the king ; and they say that they know not by what service Hubert or Roger holds of Henry, nor by what service Henry holds of the king, because that barony is divided into several [or many] parts, in several [or many] counties.

Fees of Roger de Monte Begon.

Adam de Montebegon, ancestor of Roger de Montebegon, gave to Henry de Rokesby two carucates of land in Wennyngton, by knight service, where fourteen carucates make a fee.

The same Adam gave to Geoffrey de Walton six carucates of land in Farleton and Cauncefeld, by knight service.

Roger de Montebegon gave to the canons of Hornby 100 acres of land.

The same Roger gave to Thomas de Wennyngton one bovate in Farleton, by military service.

Roger de Montebegon gave to the prior of Thornholme forty acres of land and one messuage in Tunstall.

John de Haryngton de Aldyngham, John de Coupelond, and Joan, daughter and heir of John Rigmayden, and their tenants, hold one knight's fee in Ulverston, Warton in Lonsdale, and Gayrestang with members, of the Duke of Lancaster, which fee William of Lancaster formerly held of the honor of Lancaster, and no more, neither any parcel of a fee in the aforesaid duchy ; whereof the said John de Haryngton and John de Coupeland hold Ulverston in common, for the eighth part of one knight's fee of the said fee.

The same John de Coupeland and the free tenants of the manor of Warton in Lonsdale with members, to wit, in Ellale, Scotford and Kerneford, Yealand and Assheton, for the fourth part and the eighth part of one knight's fee of the aforesaid fees. And the foresaid John de Coupeland, and Joan, daughter and heir of John Rigmayden, and their tenants, hold half a knight's fee in Gayrestang with members, to wit, in Great Eccleston and Little Eccleston with Layrebreck, Caterale and Little Carleton, Great Carleton, and Uprouclif, of the said fee.

The countess of Durmund [Ormonde] and all her tenants hold [in] Wytheton, Treuels, Thistleton, and Prees, half a knight's fee of the said duke, as of the honor of Lancaster, which Theobald Walter, John de Thornhull, William de Prees, and Adam de Bredkyn, formerly held of the aforesaid honor.

Ralph de Bethum, chevalier, holds of the said duke the fourth part of one knight's fee in Kelgrymesargh and Bryning, which Roger, Thomas de Bethum, and Robert de Stopford, formerly held of the said honor of Lancaster.

William le Botyler, chevalier, holds of the said duke the tenth part and the twentieth part of one knight's fee in Great Merton, which William de Stow formerly held of the said honor of Lancaster.

The prior of St. Thomas, near Stafford, holds of the said duke the tenth part of one knight's fee in alms, as it is stated, in Penhulton in Salfordshire, which the heir of Richard de Hulton formerly held of the said honor of Lancaster.

The abbot of Cokersand, William de Nevyll, and William de Burgh de Midelton hold the fourth part of one knight's fee in Midelton in Lonesdale of the said duke, which Adam de Midelton formerly held of the said honor of Lancaster.

Robert de Langeton, chevalier, and all his tenants, hold of the said duke one knight's fee in Neuton in Makersfeld, Langeton, Kenyan, Erbury, and the mediety of Goldburn, which Robert Banastre, William de Langton, and Richard de Goldburn, formerly held of the said honor of Lancaster.

Richard le Molyneux holds half a knight's fee of the said duke in Sefton, Thornton, and Kyrden.

William de Bradshagh holds of the said duke the twelfth part of one knight's fee, which Hugh le Norreys formerly held of the said honor of Lancaster.

Roger of Little Boulton holds of the said duke the sixteenth part of one knight's fee in Little Boulton in Salfordshire, which his ancestors formerly held of the honor of Lancaster.

The heir of Robert de Holand, chevalier, and Nicholas D'ewyas, hold of the said duke the eighth part of one knight's fee in Bright Mede, a hamlet of the vill of Boulton, which their ancestors formerly held of the Earl of Ferrars and he of the king in chief.

Richard de Langley and Joan his wife hold of the said duke the fortieth part of one knight's fee in Crompton [and] Burghton, which Adam de Tetlow [formerly] held of the Earl of Ferrars.

William de Dacre holds of the said duke one knight's fee in Halton, Burgh, Leke, Fissewyk, which Roger Gernet formerly held of the king by forestry.

The abbot of Fourneys and all his tenants hold of the said duke half a knight's fee and the eighth part and the tenth part of one knight's fee in Dalton in Fourneys with members, in pure and perpetual alms.

Parcel of the Fees formerly of Thomas de Grelley.

Nicholas Langeford, chevalier, holds of John la Ware one knight's fee in Wythington, which Matthew de Haversegge formerly held of the said fees.

Hugh de Worthyngton and John de Heton hold of the said John half of one knight's fee in Worthyngton and Heton-under-Horwich, which William de Worthyngton formerly held of the said fees.

The abbot of Whalley holds the manor of Staynyng of the Duke of Lancaster, for the half of one knight's fee.

The Countess Durmund [of Ormonde] holds the tenth part of one knight's fee of the fee of Lincoln.

The heir of Henry del Cherton holds the thirty-second part of one knight's fee in Chernok.

[From this sentence to the following (in fol. 41), the *Feodary* is a counterpart of the *Testa de Nevill*, fol. 396.]

Henry the duke holds, in demesne and service, two knights' fees within the duchy of Lancaster, to wit, in Croston with members one fee, which the heir of William de Lee, chevalier, and John Flemmynges, chevalier, hold of the manor of Horneby, which fee John de Mara formerly held of the said fee of Horneby. And the said duke and his tenants hold in the manor of Horneby one knight's fee, which same fee Henry de Munden and Roger de Monte Begon formerly held of the king, but they never held any more fees, or parcels of fees, within the said duchy, but in other counties they held fees, as they [the jury] learn, but what and where they know not.

Fee of William of Lancaster.

William de Lancaster holds half one knight's fee in demesne in Ulverston, and pays to the abbot of Fourneys 30s. yearly. And the abbot [holds it] in chief of the king, and therefor he answers to the king.[1]

Matthew de Redman and Robert de Conyers hold the eighth part of one knight's fee in Yeland of the fee of the said William, and he in chief of the king.

The same William gave Grimbald de Ellale two bovates of land in Crymblis.

William the first [ ] of Gilbert gave two carucates of land in Cokyrram to the canons of Laycester in alms, whence one of his heirs now holds of the king in chief.

---

[1] *Testa de Nevill*, fol. 307.

The same William gave Grimbald de Ellale two carucates in Ellale by military service, where twenty-four carucates make one knight's fee.

The same William gave Hugh Northmore two carucates of land in Scotford by the same service.

The same William gave Ralph Thormondisholm half a carucate of land in Lancaster, and he renders 4s.

The same William gave Robert Facon two bovates of land in Carnford by military service.

The same William gave Gilbert de Assheton half a carucate of land in Assheton, and he renders service 3s. 4d. yearly.

The Fee of Michael de Fourneys.

Michael de Fourneys gave William Fitz Edward half a carucate of land in Urswick in marriage, by the service of 4s. for all, &c., by his charter.

The same gave to Adam Fitz Bernulf two bovates of land in the same vill by charter for 32d. yearly.

William Fitz Michael gave to Gilbert Fitz Reynfrid two bovates of land in Urswick for 22d. yearly.

Michael de Fourneys gave to Gamel the Forester one carucate of land in Urswick by the service of 10s. yearly. [*Vide* West, App. xi. No. 1.]

The heir of William, son of Michael de Fourneys, holds of the king in chief twenty and a half carucates of land in Fourneys, and renders therefor yearly £10.

Michael, his ancestor, gave three carucates of land in Adgarislich in marriage with his daughter Goditha.

The abbot of Fourneys holds twenty and a half carucates of land in Fourneys in alms of the gift of King Stephen.

The same abbot holds two carucates of land in Stapulthorn, and renders to the king yearly 40s.

The same abbot holds half a carucate of land in Bemond [Beaumont] in alms.

Gilbert de Croft holds two carucates of land in Dalton near Kendal, and renders yearly 10s.

Edmund de Dacre, chevalier, and his parcener, hold the fourth part of one knight's fee in Ireby and Tatham of the said duke.

Thomas de Grysyngham, William del Grene, Alan Hughson, Henry de Haybergh, Benedict Adamson, Cecilia de Southeworth, William Fitz William de Loccay, and John de Haryngton, hold the eighth part of one knight's fee in Gersyng.

[*On a piece of parchment attached to fo.* 41 *and* 42.]

Alan de Penyngton holds of the abbot of Fourneys the manor of Penyngton by knight service and by suit at the court of Dalton every three weeks, and by the service of the tenth part of a knight's fee, and by rent of 30s. yearly. And the same Alan holds of the said abbot Tilberthwayt and Langden in Fourneys by knight service and suit to the court of the aforesaid abbot in Ulverston.

John Neville holds of the abbot of Fourneys the mill of Ulverston by knight service, and renders yearly 30s. Also, the same holds of the same abbot Les Ladermanez by the same service and a rent of 12d. yearly or a sparrow-hawk. Also, the same holds of the same abbot Manscayriggs, by the same service and a rent of 12d. yearly. Also, the same holds of the same certain lands in Rosset by the same service and a rent of 3½d. yearly.

Christopher de Broghton holds of the aforesaid abbot, Staynnerll, by knight service and a rent of 2½d. yearly.

William de Heton holds of the aforesaid abbot, Rosset, by knight service and 6½d. yearly.

The Fee of Bowland.

Adam de Wamarville holds in demesne and service two carucates of land in Esyngton, and one carucate of land in Bathesby, where fourteen carucates make a fee.

Elias de Knoll holds in service one carucate of land in Bathesby, where fourteen carucates, &c.

Alan de Neuton holds in demesne two bovates of land in Neuton, where twelve carucates, &c.

Thomas de Knoll holds in demesne four bovates of land in Neuton, where fourteen carucates, &c.

John Tempest holds in demesne and service one carucate of land in Wadyngton, where fourteen carucates, &c.

Thomas le Surreys holds in demesne and service one carucate, and three bovates of land in Mitton, where fourteen carucates, &c.

William de Mitton holds in demesne seven bovates of land in Mitton, where fourteen carucates, &c.

Adam de Bury holds in demesne and service one carucate of land [in] Wythekyil, where fourteen carucates, &c.

The lord the Earl of Lancaster holds in demesne two bovates of land in Mitton, where fourteen carucates, &c.

The lord the Earl of Lancaster holds in demesne one carucate and six bovates of land in Bradford, where fourteen carucates, &c.

Adam Bot holds at fee-farm one bovate of land in Bradford by service of one collar and one hank of hair[1] for service by charter of the lord John de Lascy.

APPENDIX IV.

A LIST OF PAPISTS WHO REGISTERED THEIR ESTATES, AND THE RESPECTIVE VALUES THEREOF, IN LANCASHIRE.[2]

As reported to Parliament by the Commissioners appointed under the Act 1 George I.

	£	s.	d.		£	s.	d.		£	s.	d.
Aspenwall Richard	25	5	0	Anderton Richard	14	0	0	Bury Andrew	13	0	0
Alston John	19	7	0	Bolton Richard	2	0	0	Brown William	9	17	4
Aray Elizabeth	2	0	0	Bolton Thomas	12	0	0	Baine Edmund	0	16	0
Abbott Richard	20	0	0	Bolton William	7	12	5	Butler Elizabeth	11	10	0
Alker John	39	1	0	Blundell Robert	4	17	0	Brown Elizabeth	8	0	0
Arkwright Robert	7	0	0	Blackburne Richard	21	2	0	Barret Thomas	13	5	0
Anderton Sir Lawrence	621	16	10	Bowyer John	30	0	0	Bannister George	5	1	4
Anderton Margaret, Dame	486	8	3½	Burscough John	20	10	0	Barton John	5	0	0
Aspenwall Henry	14	0	0	Blackburn Thomas	1	6	0	Blundell Mary, Dame	200	0	0
Ashton Arthur	1	8	0	Burgess Robert	7	0	0	Bamburgh John	83	8	6
Ashton Richard	13	19	0	Bulling John	28	10	0	Bellassis Rowland	300	0	0
Abram William	10	0	0	Billing Margaret	6	0	0	Barton Roger	16	3	2
Ascough Hugh	5	1	8	Bolton William	6	15	0	Brown William	22	10	0

---

[1] These terms, "½ colerii et ½ hanc de Pilo," are obscure, and the translation can only be called conjectural.—J. H.

[2] From this list it appears that the number of Lancashire estates amounted to 465, of an annual value of £27,903 7s. 9¼d., and that those of the other counties of England amounted to £375,284 15s. 3d., while the value of the forfeited estates in Scotland was estimated at £27,771 7s. 7d.—C.

Name	£	s.	d.
Booth Richard	23	19	0
Buller John	7	5	0
Bolton John	70	5	0
Blackbourne Richard	12	0	0
Blackledge William	13	3	0
Bolton Joseph	11	0	0
Butler Thomas	0	2	3
Butler Christopher	10	19	6
Barton Henry	7	0	0
Bolton John	0	12	0
Blakey William	3	13	0
Bambur Thomas	26	10	6
Brockholes John	522	19	1
Barton Hugh	35	11	6
Blackbourn Margaret	20	0	0
Butler Mary	100	0	0
Ball Robert	1	14	0
Bordley William	0	0	6
Butler Catharine	537	0	0
Bellassis Rowland	400	0	0
Burscough Richard	10	0	0
Butler Henry	60	0	0
Blundell Nicholas	482	12	2½
Breers Bridget	10	0	0
Barlow Anthony	171	9	0
Bolton Elizabeth	25	12	0
Connell George	6	5	0
Coope James	13	0	0
Clarkson Perpetua	5	10	0
Cottam John	14	5	8
Cocker Anne	5	0	0
Cliffton Bridget	3	10	0
Charnley Paul	30	7	6
Casseney John	3	17	6
Corless Alice	27	3	6
Cottam Ellen	26	15	0
Cornwallis Mary	100	0	0
Cordwell Cuthbert	8	0	0
Crook John	14	0	0
Coope Richard	18	5	0
Catterall James	16	13	0
Cottam Lawrence	13	3	0
Charnley Thomas	4	0	0
Craven Richard	7	0	0
Charnley Anne, widow	6	5	0
Charnley Ann, spinster	5	0	0
Cottam Lawrence	27	0	0
Cragg Matthew	17	14	0
Callen Thurston	30	15	0
Clifford Hugh, Lord	163	6	10
Culchith Thomas	85	8	9
Cliffton Thomas	1548	16	10½
Culchith Mary	150	0	0
Culchith John	30	0	0
Clare Martha	10	0	0
Clare Thomas	4	10	0
Crosby Thomas	1	12	0
Case Henry	12	0	0
Case William	28	5	0
Chaddock John	3	4	0
Culcheth Roger	64	15	4
Clarkson John	10	0	0
Cropper Richard	4	18	0
Crook James	34	2	6
Curdon William	3	13	0
Cottam William and Oliver	5	15	0
Cardwell Richard	19	8	0
Cordwell John	0	15	0
Charnock Anne	1	4	0
Cowpe William	2	10	0
Caton Lawrence	6	0	0
Croft William and Margaret	18	6	0
Croskell Robert	13	0	0
Carus George	30	0	0
Carus Frances	100	0	0
Cartwright Richard	12	10	0
Chantrell Darcy	39	0	0
Critchlow Anne	25	11	0
Chadwick Mary	30	0	0

Name	£	s.	d.
Clarkson Edward	36	5	0
Curwen Henry	141	10	0
Duckworth Elzabeth	8	12	0
Derbyshire John	13	2	0
Demen Evan	8	5	0
Daniel John	17	3	0
Dobeon James	4	6	0
Diver John	1	17	0
Doubiggen Anne, Winder	9	0	0
Dennet James	37	12	6
Dickenson Agnes	200	0	0
Dandy William	24	10	0
Danson James	3	10	0
Dilworth James	6	5	6
Daniel Edward	0	14	0
Davy William	10	0	0
Dilworth Stephen	2	14	0
Eastham Edmund	9	10	0
Eccleston Thomas	341	5	11
Eccleston Eleanora	100	0	0
Erdywick Sampson	48	0	0
Eccles Thomas	19	6	6
Elscar Richard	20	0	0
Edmonson Elizabeth	31	19	11
Escourt Francis	33	0	0
Ellam Edward	2	0	0
Foster Henry	23	17	0
Fish Evan	12	4	0
Farnworth Edward	77	5	6
Finch James	15	13	0
Fisher Thomas	22	0	0
Fazakerley Robert	187	10	10¾
Faulconberg Lord Visct.	356	0	9
Fowler John	233	16	10
Fleetwood Sir Richard	1	9	9
Fisher Henry	32	5	6
Fletcher John	70	0	0
Foster Robert	39	8	0
Fletcher William	7	0	0
Felton John	2	7	6
Felton James	4	0	0
Foxcroft William	26	8	0
Grigson William	9	0	0
Gerard Mary, Dame	100	0	0
Gillibrand Thomas	40	1	6
Gillibrand John	18	7	10
Gerrard John	114	18	4
Gerard Oliver	31	0	0
Gregson Thomas	16	0	0
Gregson Catherine	4	5	0
Gerrard Evan	112	12	3
Gorsuch James	52	11	8
Gerrard Sir William	247	6	11
Guest John. jun.	30	15	4
Gerrard Richard	45	5	0
Gregory Jane	1	5	0
Glover Peter	24	0	0
Golden Thomas	128	1	11
Glover Ellis	25	10	0
Glover Ralph	5	0	0
Greenough Robert	34	15	0
Green Barbara	36	2	6
Gore Thomas	68	0	0
Gerard Thomas	345	14	2
Grimbelson Emer	12	0	0
Guest Jennett	5	10	0
Gradell Christopher	0	6	0
Gillow William	4	6	6
Gillow Richard	15	0	0
Gradwell Elizabeth	14	0	0
Gregson George	3	0	0
Green Agnes	63	3	8
Goose Thomas	0	1	0
Green Ellen	4	0	0
Gate John	25	0	0
Gate Francis	25	0	0
Grey William	4	10	0
Gerrard Richard	10	9	10
Gerrard John	20	10	0

Name	£	s.	d.
Green Margaret	36	2	6
Gooden Richard	65	14	4
Gooden Thomas	83	10	0
Gerrard Richard	150	0	0
Higson John	8	0	0
Helme William	9	10	0
Higgenson Roger	11	0	0
Hudson Alexander	5	14	0
Harrison James	15	0	0
Harrison Edward	19	8	0
Hesketh Margaret	57	0	0
Holden Richard	20	0	0
Harrison William	8	0	0
Hankinson Thomas	0	15	0
Hill John	1	12	0
Hilton Richard	1	6	8
Halsell James	6	0	0
Harrison James	22	0	0
Harrington Charles	197	3	0
Harrington Mary	200	0	6
Hodgkinson Mabell	46	5	5¼
Howard Ralph	18	0	0
Howarden Catherine	56	1	0
Harrington Mary	31	10	0
Howarden Mary	23	10	0
Harrington Dorothy	107	12	6
Howarden Mary	37	0	6
Howard Thomas	4	13	0
Holland Alexander	19	0	0
Houghton Margaret	4	10	0
Holland Thomas	0	15	0
Hodgkinson Marg. and Robt. Greenough	29	8	4
Halliwell William	89	0	6
Hawett Cecilia	80	0	0
Heatley Peter	29	0	0
Hodson Thomas	17	10	0
Holland Helen	41	10	0
Harrison Henry	6	13	0
Hesketh William	198	3	4½
Hesketh George	13	6	8
Hull Elizabeth	23	0	0
Heatly Hugh	4	5	0
Hathornthwaite John	49	3	4
Hatton Edward	0	8	4¼
Harrison William	20	0	0
Houghton Thomas	11	8	0
Howard Edward	6	10	0
Hodgkinson Anne	9	0	0
Hitchmough Edward	0	18	0
Higginson Robert	13	0	0
Johnson Richard	10	11	6
Jackson John	11	10	0
Jackson Richard	20	0	0
Ince Christopher	163	4	0
Ince Dorothy, Anne, and John Twist, &c.	5	9	6
Johnson Thomas	10	10	0
Jump Robert	33	0	0
Jump Hugh	9	0	0
Jackson John	50	8	0
Jenkinson Thomas	5	0	0
Johnson Robert	15	0	0
Juice Robert	27	0	0
Irlam Frances	5	7	0
Jackson Richard	5	0	0
Jump William	3	14	0
Knott Thomas	20	0	0
Kendal, Richard	2	15	0
Kay Elizabeth	4	2	6
Kitchen Anne	16	0	0
Lickfold John	2	15	0
Latholm William	6	0	0
Linesay Richard	8	7	6
Langtree Richard	5	4	6
Letherbarrow Thomas	11	10	0
Lurting John	11	0	0
Lancaster William	32	0	0
Lytherland Elizabeth	4	10	0

Name	£	s.	d.
Lickey Nicholas	32	10	0
Lancaster Francis	5	17	6
Lancaster Thomas	10	0	0
Leadbeater Alice	0	12	0
Leyburne James	15	0	0
Longworth John	23	13	0
Lancaster John	87	6	4
Longworth Mary	24	17	6
Langton Edward	69	6	5
Leigh Margaret and Alias	18	18	0
Lumb John	18	10	0
Langtree Thomas	5	0	0
Leckonby William	79	11	6
Leigh Emma	20	0	0
Laithwaite Anne	15	17	6
Leyburne Nicholas	10	0	0
Leyburne George	10	0	0
Lund Anthony	10	0	0
Leigh James	7	8	0
Leigh Roger	1	4	0
Molden William	0	18	0
Moulden John	24	15	0
Medcalf Christopher	0	16	0
Moorcroft William	15	0	0
Maudesley Thomas	5	0	0
Maudesley William	21	10	0
Molineux Sir William, Bart.	2346	16	2
Molineux Robert	309	8	2
Maborn Robert	29	0	0
Molineux William	80	0	0
Massey Richard	352	0	9
Mather Richard	5	0	0
Maudesley Margaret	4	17	0
Molineux Thomas	13	0	0
Martin Richard	21	0	0
Malley Thomas	6	10	0
Miller Thomas	14	0	0
Menick John	5	2	8
Morton William	7	5	0
Molineux Richard	1100	0	0
Moore Andrew	38	15	0
Miller Thomas	10	0	0
Norris Gabriel	10	10	0
Noblet John	1	15	0
Naylor Thomas	32	0	0
Nelson Maximilian	100	18	10
Neusham John	26	15	0
Nelston Edward	33	0	0
Osbalstone Edward	9	13	4
Oyle Richard	64	0	0
Orrell Humphrey	68	12	0
Osbalstone Robert	14	0	0
Osbaldiston Alexander	92	2	0
Parkinson Edward	14	17	8
Parkinson Richard	22	10	0
Platt John	1	12	6
Parker Richard	15	0	0
Pool John	1	19	0
Parker James	19	0	0
Peers Peter	5	8	0
Pennington Thomas	0	10	0
Parker Edward	28	0	0
Rowbotham John	7	10	0

Name	£	s.	d.
Richmond James	8	0	0
Rice John	23	0	0
Roscow William	42	14	6
Riding Thomas	1	10	0
Rice Percivall and Thomas.	82	13	6
Richardson Richard	11	10	6
Riddle Edward	119	3	5
Rothwell Robert	12	10	0
Richardson Richard	43	15	0
Reddish Susannah	4	13	0
Robinson John	8	10	0
Russell Richard	9	10	0
Rutter Elizabeth	1	0	0
Rycroft Lydia	24	0	0
Rice Percivall	19	1	0
Standish Alexander	28	0	0
Sanderson James	36	10	0
Sanderson John	21	0	0
Snape William	2	5	6
Smith Francis, and Catherine his wife	7	10	0
Sturzacker Jane	5	0	0
Shuttleworth Richard	8	15	0
Sanderson Nicholas	6	0	0
Scarisbrick Edward	20	0	0
Shepherd Robert	1	1	0
Spencer Edward	2	5	6
Scarisbrick Frances	320	1	6
Shirburne Sir Nicholas	1210	6	3½
Stanley Anne	118	15	0
Speakman John	8	0	0
Sanderson Ralph	14	0	0
Scott Thurstone	10	0	0
Shepherd William	14	15	0
Scott Thomas	59	5	8
Syers Thomas	37	12	0
Smith William	12	0	0
Swarbreck John	23	15	0
Slater Gabriel	11	0	0
Slater Thomas	13	0	0
Sheppard Robert	11	0	0
Shuttleworth Margaret	15	0	0
Standish Cecilia	415	0	8½
Sweetlove Thomas	1	0	0
Speakman John	8	0	0
Sweetlove William	6	19	0
Sergeant John	17	1	10
Snape Margaret	5	0	0
Speakman John	9	13	9
Sayle William	0	19	0
Sayle Alice	29	10	0
Shepperd Ellen	60	15	0
Singleton Anne	76	15	10
Thompson John	0	3	6
Trafford Richard	35	0	0
Turner James	6	10	0
Townley Mary	150	0	0
Tootell Jane	24	0	0
Townley Thomas	50	0	0
Townley Ursula	400	0	0
Townley Richard	991	13	5½
Townley Catharine	50	0	0
Turner Mary	7	0	0

Name	£	s.	d.
Tickle Richard	54	4	0
Tildesley Agatha	52	10	0
Taylor John	25	5	0
Thelwall Thomas	16	0	0
Trafford John	303	2	7
Taylor John	10	0	0
Tatlock Thomas	25	0	0
Tootell Richard	0	5	0
Thornton Gilbert	18	15	0
Thornton John	6	0	0
Tristram Edmond	35	8	4
Tarlton William	15	10	0
Taylor William	14	10	0
Turner Anne	10	0	0
Taylor Oliver	10	15	0
Thornburgh Jane	40	0	0
Tomlinson Robert	0	10	0
Taylor Alice	17	10	0
Threlfall Cuthbert	31	12	6
Tildersley Edward	720	9	2
Urmstone John	25	0	0
Urnsworth Edward	19	5	0
Urnsworth George	36	2	6
Urnsworth Thomas	0	16	0
Westby Thomas	20	0	0
Woodcock James	0	12	0
Worthington Matthew	2	5	0
Wilcock John	21	0	0
Worden George	7	2	8
Wilson Robert	5	10	0
Walmaley Richard	205	4	6
Westby Cuthbert	20	0	0
Willasey Thomas	7	7	6
Winstanley William	46	0	0
Woolfall Richard	262	3	9
Whittle Richard	55	16	3
Walker George	19	0	0
Walmaley William	35	0	0
Wilson Lawrence	28	5	0
Whalley Thomas	8	0	0
Westby John	119	11	1
Whittle John	8	7	0
Woodcock Elizabeth	16	10	0
Woodcock John	19	19	0
Worsley Jennett	5	15	0
Wilson Richard	9	0	0
Worthington Thomas	7	0	0
Williams Ellen, Alice, and Mary Woodcock	24	15	0
Woodcock Ellen	26	15	0
Whalley Thurston	12	0	8
Walker Robert	15	15	0
Walker William	7	10	0
Walmsley Mary	5	0	0
Westby John	230	5	1½
Whiteside Mary	8	10	0
Whittle Margaret	4	0	0
Whitehead Richard	6	0	0
Williamson James	13	0	0
Waring John	10	0	0
Yates Sarah	27	0	0
Yates John	7	6	8

APPENDIX V.

VARIOUS CREATIONS OF ORDERS, &c. (LANCASHIRE).

LANCASHIRE BARONETS CREATED IN THE 17TH AND 18TH CENTURIES.

Created by King James I.

1611, May   22. Sir Richard Molineux of Sefton, Knight, Irish Visc.—viz., Viscount Molineux.
            Sir Richard Houghton of Houghton Tower, Knight.
            Sir Thomas Gerard of Bryn, Knight.

1620, June   28. Ralph Ashton of Lever, Esq.

Created by King Charles I.

1627, June   26. Edward Stanley of Bickerstaffe, Esq.
1640, July   20. Edward Mosley of Ancoats. Extinct.
1641, August 16. Robert Bindloss of Borwicke, Esq.
1642, June   24. George Middleton of Leighton, Esq. Extinct.
1644, April   1. John Preston of the Mannour in Furnesse, Esq.
1644, April   25. Thomas Prestwich of Holme, Esq.

Created by King Charles II.

1660, June   7. Sir Orlando Bridgeman of Great Lever, Knight, Chief Baron of the Exchequer, then Lord Chief Justice of the Common Pleas, and afterwards Lord-keeper of the Great Seal of England.
August 1. Sir Ralph Ashton of Middleton, Knight.
1660-1, March 4. Thomas Clifton of Clifton, Esq.
1661-2, March 1. Edward Moore, of Moorehall, Esq. (*Note* that this patent to Edward Moore, though at this time the receipt was made, did not pass the Seal until 22d Nov. 1675.)
1676-7, Feb. 8. Richard Standish of Standish, Esq.
1677, October 8. Francis Anderton of Lostoke, Esq.
1679, Nov. 17. Sir Roger Bradshaigh of Haigh, Knight.

Created by King George I.

1720, June 18. Oswald Mosley of Rolleston, Co. Stafford, Esq.

Created by King George II.

1759, March 26. Sir Ellis Cunliffe of Liverpool, Co. Lancashire, Knight, with remainder, in default of issue-male, to Robert his brother.

Created by King George III. to 1797.

1761, May 12. Thomas Hesketh of Rufford, Esq., with remainder to his brother, Robert Hesketh, Esq.
1764, Jan. 22. William Horton of Chadderton, Esq.
1774, May   3. Richard Clayton of Adlington, Esq , with remainder to the heirs male of his father John Clayton, Esq., deceased.
1781, March 24. John Parker Mosley of Ancoats, Esq.
1797 Oct.   30. Richard Onslow of Althom, Esq., vice-admiral of the red.

The intended Order of the Royal Oak.

A List of Persons' Names [in the county of Lancaster] who were fit and qualified to be made Knights of the Royal Oak,[1] with the value of their estates, Ann. Dom. 1660.

This order was intended by King Charles II. as a reward to several of his followers, and the knights of it were to wear a silver medal, with a device of the king in the oak, pendant to a ribbon, about their neck ; but it was thought proper to lay it aside, lest it might create heats and animosities, and open those wounds afresh which at that time were thought prudent should be healed. As this is little known, we have judged that its publication would be as well curious as acceptable to the public.

Thomas Holt, Esq.	per ann. £1000		Thos. Preston, Esq.	per ann.	£2000
Thos. Greenhalgh, Esq	„	1000	Thos. Farrington of Worden, Esq.	„	1000
Col. Kerby, Esq.	„	1500	Thos. Fleetwood of Penwortham, Esq.	„	1000
Robert Holte, Esq.	„	1000	John Girlington, Esq.	„	1000
Edmund Ashcton, Esq.	„	1000	William Stanley, Esq.	„	1000
Christopher Banister, Esq.	„	1000	Edward Tildesley, Esq.	„	1000
Francis Anderton, Esq.	„	1000	Thomas Stanley, Esq.	„	1000
Col. James Anderton, Esq.	„	1500	Richard Boteler, Esq.	„	1000
Roger Nowell, Esq.	„	1000	John Ingleton, senior, Esq.	„	1000
Henry Norris, Esq.	„	1200	(Richard?) Walmesley of Dunkenhalgh, Esq.	„	2000

Barons and Baronesses by Tenure, Writ of Summons, or Letters Patent of creation :—
James Stanley, son and heir-apparent to William, Earl of Derby, *Lord Strange,* by summons, 3 Charles I. (in the summons Stanley de Strange). There can be no doubt but when this summons was issued it was under the presumption that the barony of Strange of Knockyn was still invested in his father. This, however, proving a mistake, the House of Lords was compelled by a certain degree of necessity to admit that this summons created a new barony, which, by virtue of the writ, afterwards passed to and was recognised in the family of Murray, Duke of Athól.

A Catalogue of such Persons as have had summons to Parliament in right of their Wives, with the dates when first summoned :—
George Stanley, son and heir-apparent to Thomas, Earl of Derby, Baron Strange (*i.e.*, of Knockyn, *jure uxoris*, Joane, daughter and heir of John Lord Strange of Knockyn), 22 Edward IV.

The Names of those Noblemen's eldest Sons who have been summoned to Parliament in the Lifetime of their Fathers (by some title which had descended to them) or by the title of their father's Barony, and had place and precedence according thereto, with the respective dates when they were so first summoned :—

Henry Stanley, Lord Strange, eldest son to Edward, Earl of Derby, 1 Elizabeth.
Ferdinando Stanley, Lord Strange, eldest son to Henry, Earl of Derby, 29 Elizabeth.
James Stanley, Lord Strange, eldest son to William, Earl of Derby, 3 Charles I.

A Catalogue of those Persons [in Cumberland and Lancashire] *who were dignified by Oliver Cromwell with the title of Lord, and called on to sit in his other, i.e. upper, House of Parliament :—*[2]

Charles Howard, of Naworth Castle, in Cumberland. [3]
Philip, Lord Wharton, Lancashire.
Sir Gilbert Gerard, Bart., Lancashire.

[1] From a MS. of Peter Le Neve, Esq., Norroy, among the collection of Mr. Joseph Ames.
[2] Dugd. *Troub.* pp. 144-5.
[3] This gentleman was created, according to Morgan (though not so ticed by Dugdale), Baron Gillesland and Viscount Howard of Morpeth, by Cromwell, July 20, 1657. He afterwards obtained from King Charles II. the dignities of Baron Dacres of Gillesland, Viscount Howard of Morpeth (Dugdale's "Baronage," vol. ii.), and Earl of Carlisle. He appears to be the only one of the lords made by Cromwell who, after the Restoration, was confirmed in the rank of peerage (General Monk excepted).

APPENDIX VI.

COTTON—ANNALS OF THE COTTON MANUFACTURE—THE COTTON FAMINE.

LANCASHIRE owes so much of its wonderful development in population and prosperity to the import and manufacture of cotton, and has made this manufacture so completely and peculiarly its own, that the history of Lancashire cannot be considered complete without a fuller account of the subject than the mere scattered references to it in the accounts of the various parishes.

As to the natural history of cotton, Mr. Randal H. Alcock, of Bury, a gentleman who is not only a cotton manufacturer but a careful and able botanist, and who has given especial attention to cotton, having himself grown all the attainable varieties, supplies me with the following account :—

"The cotton plant—*Gossypium*—belongs to the natural order *Malvaceæ*, or the Mallow tribe, of which Lindley says, 'The uniform character of the order is to abound in mucilage, and to be totally destitute of all unwholesome qualities.' The cotton plant is to a small extent used medicinally in its native countries. 'The young leaves of *Gossypium vitifolium* are employed in Brazil in dysentery, and, steeped in vinegar, are applied to the head in hemicrania.' The medicinal virtues of the cotton plant are also set forth by the older botanists, as Matthiolus, Gerard, and Dodonæus. From its seed also an oil is expressed, though not of very good quality, and the remaining oil-cake is good food for cattle, but inferior to linseed oil-cake.

"The genus *Gossypium* is distinguished by its large bracts, or epicalyx, as they are frequently called. These three large bracts completely hide the calyx proper, which is small and inconspicuous. The seeds are surrounded by the wool-like substance known as cotton or cotton wool. The species of this genus are either of small size and annuals—or more properly short-lived perennials of varying duration—or shrubs, and trees of greater stature and longer life. They are natives of Asia, Africa, America, and numerous tropical islands. The leaves are alternate and petiolate, and generally quincunx in arrangement, or five in a set, having the sixth, or first of the next series, immediately over the first of the last, and two spiral turns round the stem, being completed by the five leaves. This seems to be the general arrangement, but it is subject to considerable variation. The leaves are variously lobed or divided, according to the species—indeed few plants vary so much in the forms of their leaves, not only in different species, but also in the same species and even on the same plant. Some are entire, others three, four, five, six, or seven lobed, or more ; some have small intermediate lobes ; some are long, others short ; some acuminate, and others rounded. The whole plant is sprinkled over with blackish gland-like spots, which contain a purple colouring matter ; the other parts of the plant contain a yellow colouring matter. Another series of glands near the base of the principal ribs of the leaves secrete a saccharine fluid. These saccharine glands are also to be found not unfrequently at the base of each of the bracts on the outside, sometimes accompanied by three others at the base of the true calyx. The stipules are frequently almost linear, but in some kinds are large and foliaceous, always more or less falcate. The flower-stalk is axillary, or opposite to the leaves, sometimes by arrested development of the growing point apparently terminal, usually single flowered ; flowers large and showy, various shades of primrose, with a purple spot in some cases at the base of each petal ; some kinds are pure white, and others are reddish purple. The external whorl of the flower is composed of three large bracts, which, according to the species, are more or less united at the base, and divided or split up at the margin. The calyx is cup-shaped, obscurely, or more or less strongly, five-toothed. The corolla of five petals is hypogynous, and is convolute in æstivation. The staminal tube is dilated over the ovary, and is columnar above. The filaments are of varying length in different species ; they are simple or forked, and bear kidney-shaped anthers. The ovary is superior, and three to five celled ; the placentation is axile, and the ovules numerous, the style terminal, and the stigmas three to five. The capsule is roundish, or ovoid, and dehisces loculicidally, and the seeds are covered, in most kinds, with a downy coating. In some sorts this down is green, in others white, and occasionally it is quite absent. All cotton seeds are enveloped by the more profuse mass of hairy cellular tissue known as cotton, which varies in length, strength, and colour. The embryo is curved within mucilaginous albumen : the radicle is inferior. The cotyledons are leaf-like, and, in the same way as in the other parts of the plant, are dotted over with black spots.

"The excellence of cotton wool for manufacturing purposes depends upon the qualities of its fibre in respect to length, strength, and colour, and these qualities are not uniform, but vary greatly, in different species, in different countries, and in proportion to the care bestowed on its cultivation. Before proceeding to the consideration of the different species of cotton, it will be well to notice those peculiarities of its fibre which are common to all, and which cause it to be useful for spinning, while the cotton-like coverings or appendages of several other seeds are of no use for such a purpose. The peculiar structure of the cotton fibre was pointed out by Mr. James Thomson, of Clitheroe, in a paper which he read to the Royal Society in 1834, and he was led to the investigation of the subject by the disputed question whether the cerecloths of the Egyptian mummies were made of cotton or of flax. A microscopic examination of each kind of fibre—in which he had the assistance of the well-known microscopist Mr. Bauer—clearly showed the absolute distinctness of the two fibres, and proved that these ancient fabrics were, without exception, linen, and not cotton as had been contended. The cotton fibre is without divisions or joints. In the unripe state it is cylindrical, but shortly changes its character, and even before the capsule bursts it assumes a tape-like form, at first sight like two tubes united by a kind of web. The fibre in its ripe state is always naturally twisted, the number of twists varying from 300 to 800 in an inch. 'This form and character,' says Mr. Thomson, 'the fibres retain ever after, and in that respect undergo no change through the operations of spinning, weaving, bleaching, and dyeing, nor in all the subsequent domestic operations of washing, &c., till the stuff is worn to rags ; and then even the violent process of reducing those rags to pulp, for the purpose of making paper, effects no change in the structure of the fibre.' On the other hand, the flax fibre is always cylindrical, and jointed, something like a bamboo, and there is never any twist about it. The cerecloths of these ancient Egyptian mummies were then linen. By the application of the same microscopic test those of Peruvian mummies have been proved to be cotton.

"There is an order of plants nearly allied to the *Malvaceæ*, viz., the *Sterculiaceæ*, which in some genera, as *Bombax* and *Eriodendron*, resemble the cotton plant in having a hairy covering around their seeds ; but, as this substance has not the natural twist which I have described, it is not available for spinning, and is useful only for stuffing cushions and such like purposes. These are trees of a noble and beautiful aspect. The cotton-like fibres found about the fruit of the cotton-sedge, the thistle, the willow, and several other vegetable hairs, are unsuitable, for the same reason. It is true that flax, hemp, jute, and China grass, are spun, and have not the peculiar twist of the cotton fibre, but all these are woody tissue, which, originating in cellular tissue, has afterwards acquired additional properties.

"As to the number of the species of *Gossypium* there has been great difference of opinion. In our own country eminent scientific men do not come to the same conclusions as regards species and varieties, even in our own limited British flora, how much more must we expect differences of opinion where the native species are spread over the whole world, and the genus in question has been cultivated for thousands of years. In truth, the materials do not seem to have been yet gathered together by which the number of true species may be set down with certainty. An attempt has been made to reduce them to two, viz., black-seeded and white-seeded, while cultivators have told us they can recognise as many as 120 sorts. Practical cotton spinners of medium counts of yarn, provided they are not botanists, find no difficulty in this matter. If you will ask them, they will tell you there are two

---

[1] In vol. ii. of the original edition of this work, chapters iv. v. vi., containing 132 pages, were occupied by a "History of the Cotton Manufacture." This article, for which Mr. Baines acknowledged his indebtedness to his son, the present (Sir) Edward Baines, was superseded by a separate work, into which it was enlarged and extended ("History of the Cotton Manufacture of Great Britain." Lond. 1837). Moreover, works on the general subject (rare than Mr. Baines first wrote) are now so easily procurable that it is not deemed necessary in a county history to do more than give such an outline of the facts on the subject of the manufacture as may be valuable for reference.—B. H.

principal sorts of cotton—American and Surat; and this, indeed, is a good botanical distinction and a natural division, as the two families are so distinct that they will not inter-breed. We may then first divide the genus *Gossypium* into the two important tribes—Indian or old-world cotton, and American or new-world cotton. There are different species under each division, but the two races seem distinct and indigenous in their respective hemispheres, though by means of commerce they are now widely spread over the globe.

"According to modern authorities there are about eight usually admitted species; but in the first instance, I shall treat of five only, three of which belong to the Occidental or New World, and two to the Asiatic or Old World group. Four of these five species, there is no doubt, supply us with the chief bulk of our commercial cotton. These five principal kinds are—

Gossypium barbadense, or Sea Island.
Gossypium hirsutum, in two varieties, viz., New Orleans and Upland.
Gossypium acuminatum, Brazilian.
Gossypium herbaceum, Surats.
Gossypium arboreum, the tree-cotton of India.

"1. *Gossypium barbadense*, or the Sea Island plant, produces the finest and longest-stapled cotton grown, and is used exclusively for spinning fine yarns. It is so valuable as occasionally to have realised seven shillings a pound in the Liverpool market. The price for the best is at present (February, 1870) 4s. per pound. (The price of best Sea Island cotton in Liverpool, September 22nd, 1887, was 1s. 10d.) We obtain our chief supply from the coast of South Carolina, where its cultivation extends from the mouth of the Savannah to the mouth of the Santee rivers, a distance of about one hundred and thirty miles. Cultivated far inland, the wool loses its distinctive excellence. The seed which produces it was originally imported from Anguilla, one of the Antilles. This species is a robust, handsome plant, is glabrous, and has sulphur-yellow flowers with a large purple spot at the base of each petal. The bracts are deeply laciniated, and the leaves are, for the most part, distinctly five-lobed. The seeds are black, and generally bare—in saying bare, I mean that they are destitute of the downy epidermal covering which I have mentioned as pertaining to some species. This is, however, not a universal characteristic of the species, as many *barbadenses* have a woolly clothing. The finest Egyptian cotton, which approaches the nearest to Sea Island in quality, is also the produce of *G. barbadense*, though other kinds are grown in Egypt to some extent. In the time of Pliny, cotton was cultivated in Upper Egypt, but its cultivation was afterwards discontinued. It was recommenced by an enterprising viceroy, Mehemet Ali, as a private speculation, and we received, in consequence, cotton from Egypt of excellent quality in 1823. So recently as 1827 or 1828, Sea Island seed was first planted in Egypt, since which time it has continued to flourish. When we speak of Egyptian cotton we generally refer to the produce of a robust, hardy form of Sea Island. In common with other long-stapled cottons that of the Sea Island plant is not pure white but has a creamy tinge.

"2. The New Orleans cotton, or *Gossypium hirsutum* of Linnæus, is, as its name indicates, a hairy plant. I do not notice the discrepancies and obscurities which exist in the naming of various cottons to which the name *hirsutum* has been given. These may soon be met with by any one who examines several herbaria. The name *hirsutum* has, by different authorities, been applied to several cottons, but it is sufficiently descriptive to be very applicable to the New Orleans. The flowers of this species are various shades of pale primrose, sometimes nearly white, and without and purple mark at the base of the petals. The capsule or boll is more orbicular or less ovoid than the Sea Island species. There are two varieties of it, the New Orleans proper, and that known as Upland. The New Orleans proper has its seeds covered with a short white wool (or fuzz, as it is often called); the Upland variety has a similar down, but green. The staple of the Upland is shorter than the Orleans. *Gossypium hirsutum* supplies the most approved cotton of any species for general purposes. It comes to us generally in a clean and sound state, and is rarely adulterated by the addition of other substances to make weight, in which respects it is much superior to most Surat. The staple is, on an average, a little longer than the best East Indian cottons that we import, and also more uniform in length, with a less proportion of the short, light, and inferior fibre, technically called fly. There is also a peculiar silkiness in the American fibre which I cannot explain, but the result of all is that the American cotton has a preference over Surat, as at present imported, unless, after taking into account the greater loss and expense in working, the latter is sensibly cheaper. Previous to the American war the United States supplied us with by far the greatest part of our cotton for many years, and Middling Orleans was the chief standard of prices. Now, Fair Dhollerah is an equally important standard. American cotton is not absolutely uniform, but varies considerably in quality, some samples being longer in staple than others; some are white, some tawny, and some red. We hear sometimes also of the blue American. This peculiar shade arises chiefly from the fine sand with which the cotton is contaminated. If we examine a number of seeds from a bale of American cotton we may notice that some are covered with a thick coating of down, others more sparingly, and some may be nearly or quite bare. Bare seed or scanty fuzz in New Orleans cotton indicate a greater or less degree of 'degeneration,' as the planters express it. They call such cotton degenerate, because the plants then yield a less quantity of cotton. This state arises from faults in culture, and also from late ripening when frost has stopped the growth of the plant. The planters of New Orleans cotton renew their seed when it deteriorates from Mexico, or from the gulf hills in Mississippi, every fourth or fifth year. Dr. Forbes Royle seems to think that the staple becomes finer and longer in degenerate Orleans. It is asserted, on the other hand, that degenerated Orleans is in no way improved in staple. I may mention that some good authorities believe that *G. hirsutum* is only a form of *G. barbadense*, and not a distinct species; others believe the differences between the two forms to be specific and permanent. I incline to the latter opinion, though, so far as the seed only is concerned, the *hirsutum* is so apt to become bare. Uplands cotton is merely a variety of Orleans, very likely depending chiefly upon situation, soil, and such like circumstances. The green coating of the seeds, which I have already mentioned, is very bright and striking, but, as we have seen, this coating is a very variable feature. We find green-coated seeds in almost all our bales of American cotton. Last year I grew a plant of New Orleans, crossed by the Sea Island—a hybrid raised by Major R. Trevor Clarke, who supplied me with the seed, and to whose horticultural experience I am indebted for much information. Now the Sea Island has usually a black, bare seed, and the New Orleans is covered with a white fur, but the seed of the hybrid has a green covering like Upland. This, Major Clarke tells me, is always the case with this hybrid. Upland cotton was early cultivated in Italy and Sicily under the name of Coton de Siam, and indeed was formerly better known as the produce of these countries than of America. The older botanists, as Schwarz, Cavanilles, and others, called it by a very long and imposing name, '*Xylon Americanum præstantissimum semine virescente.*' The plant is always cultivated as an annual, but is not really one, as it will continue, under favourable circumstances, to bear fruit three years or more. Another striking and important variety of *G. hirsutum* is the kind known as Vine Cotton. This is a gigantic form of the species. The boll is of very great size, and often contains as many as thirteen seeds in each cell. It differs from the ordinary Orleans, chiefly, if not entirely, in its greater size.

"3. The next commercial cotton to be noticed is *Gossypium acuminatum* of Roxburgh. This is an arboraceous perennial. The flowers are palish yellow, large, and almost hidden by the enormous bracts. The petals are marked with a slight purple spot, and the capsule is long and large, much pointed at the apex. The specific name *acuminatum* was given to it by Dr. Roxburgh, probably on account of the pointed character both of its leaves and capsules. Botanically *G. acuminatum* is especially remarkable in having the seeds closely agglomerated together, instead of being free as in other species. By this peculiarity the species may be readily distinguished, from a mere inspection of the seeds. These are frequently called Kidney cottons. The Brazilian and Peruvian cottons are chiefly of this kind, and are much esteemed; they are included in Pernam, Maranham, Ceara, Para, Paraiba, Peruvian, and several others, though some of these cottons include other kinds than Kidney, but in less quantity. *G. acuminatum* is also to be met with in the East and West Indies, and elsewhere. The quality of its staple is excellent, and its better sorts are of more value than Orleans, as it is longer and stronger, and finer yarns can be spun from it.

"All the cottons I have been describing belong to the New World group. We now pass on to those of India. We call Indian cotton 'Surat' in consequence of that port being the principal one from which it was formally shipped to us.

"4. The Indian cotton is *Gossypium herbaceum* of Linnæus, and there are many varieties cf it cultivated in various parts of India, Rangoon, China, and Japan, and also on the shores of the Mediterranean. This species of the cotton plant is, perhaps, taking all things into account, more important to us, commercially, than any. India is one of our dependencies, and we have had during the last few years to rely upon India for the greater part of our cotton supply, and probably the greatest stay to our particular industry will still be that country. In other ways the cotton of India is interesting; the varieties are numerous, and their selection and cultivation seem capable of improvement in various ways, to the great advantage both of Lancashire cotton spinners and Indian farmers. *Gossypium herbaceum* includes all the indigenous herbaceous cotton of India, of which there are many varieties, indeed most likely the specific name *herbaceum* does service for many kinds which are true and distinct species. Unfortunately it has even come to be applied to the American Upland cotton, variously translated into 'herbaceous cotton,' 'cotone erbaceo' 'coton herbace,' &c., which has caused not a little confusion. All the cotton which comes from India does not belong to the species *herbaceum*, for others have been introduced at different times, and are to be met with in several parts, especially Brazilin and Bourbon—a kind mentioned below, and latterly New Orleans. Herbaceous cotton has a stem more or less branched, one and a half foot to two feet high, in temperate climates, but growing higher in the hotter countries. The leaves are palmate, sometimes three, but generally five, lobed. There are two well-defined varieties (or, they may be species), judging by the leaves, one having broad lobes and the other narrow. It is the former which is the *G. herbaceum* of Linnæus. In addition to its broad-lobed leaves it is peculiar in its habit of growth, the stem, and more especially the branches, not being straight, but zigzag, making an angle at each node in an opposite direction to the last. It was found by the early botanists growing in the Levant, whence, no doubt, Linnæus and others received the specimens which are to be found in their herbaria. *G. herbaceum* presents great variety of form, so great that almost every Indian village can boast of its peculiar breed of cotton. The species may be described as having the flowers axillary, generally solitary towards the extremities of the branches, petals of a lively yellow colour, with a purple spot at the base of each, more rarely white, in which case the spot is rose coloured. The segments of the exterior calyx are cordate at the base, the margins dentate, sometimes entire, the capsules ovate, and three or four celled. The seeds are free and few in number, and are clothed with firmly-adhering greyish down under the short-stapled cotton wool.

"5. There is a fifth undoubted species, which can scarcely be called a commercial cotton, as it is but little used for manufacture, though it has been employed to hybridise and improve other Indian cottons. This is *Gossypium arboreum*, the tree cotton of India. It is exemplified in what is known as Nurmah cotton. It is found everywhere in India, though not sown in fields, but generally round gardens, near ponds, and especially about the temples, for it is, seemingly, looked upon as a sort of sacred plant. It rises to the height of eight or ten feet, 'and when in flower is remarkably handsome. It is also very productive, and frequently continues to yield cotton during a period of four or five years; but is generally cultivated more for ornament than use.' I am not aware what is the reason for this, as the staple is of good quality. The leaves of Nurmah cotton are deeply lobed, and have intermediate small lobes, which were formerly supposed to constitute a specific character; more recent knowledge has, however, proved the fallacy of this supposition. Many supposed specific differences have ceased to be of any value since the plant has been carefully observed in the living state. The leaves, and all the other parts of the plants are of a pinky colour. When it first springs up from seed this is very conspicuous, the stem being of a bright red. The flower is a reddish purple, and the seed is covered with a clear green down.

"The five species which have been enumerated are undoubtedly distinct (unless we class together *G. barbadense* and *G. hirsutum*); but about all others there is a great diversity of opinion. With the exception of Bourbon, and what have been called West Indian green seeds, few are commercially important, and others are but very imperfectly known. Dr. Forbes Royle, in his 'Cotton in India and Elsewhere,' quotes Dr. Cleghorn, who writes from Edinburgh on this subject, and says that 'he had brought together all the Asiatic and American species of Gossypium to be found in the University collection (which comprised the herbaria of Hamilton, Countess of Dalhousie, &c., with additions from Wight and Campbell),' and 'the collection is large enough to illustrate the fact that there has been an excessive *confusion and multiplication of species*. I believe all the specimens in the herbarium at the University may be referred to:—(1) *G. acuminatum*, (2) *G. herbaceum*, (3) *G. arboreum*, (4) *G. barbadense*. Particularly he mentions a great multiplication of species of Indian cotton.' He says, 'of *G. herbaceum* there is a great variety of specimens, bearing I know not how many names, such as *Gossypium nigrum*, *G. nigrum lœve*, *G. vitifolium*, *G. indicum*, *G. viridescens*, *G. rubicundum*. All these,' he concludes, 'appear to me manifestly the indigenous *G. herbaceum* or country *kupas* of the Peninsular ryots.' There is, however, little doubt that there are many other species of cotton besides these four. Under these circumstances of doubt and uncertainty I shall not venture to say much about other species of cotton, though they cannot be passed by entirely.

"First, then, there is Bourbon cotton, which has generally been taken to be very closely allied to *G. barbadense*, if not identical with it, though it is probably quite a distinct species, as yet unnamed in scientific parlance. It is called Bourbon cotton from having been grown in the Isle of Bourbon, where it is supposed to have been introduced by the French from the West Indies. Its seeds were early introduced into India, in many parts of which continent it is thoroughly naturalised, particularly in the south. This sort is pretty widely distributed. A short time ago I had a lot from Puerto Cabello on the Caribbean Sea, which Major Clarke tells me is veritable Bourbon. The plant is a small pyramidal tree, with glabrous three, five, seven lobed leaves. The flower is small, and entirely pale yellow; the capsule small, smooth, roundish, ovate; the seeds naked or nearly so.

"Next there is West Indian green seed cotton, which I have just mentioned, a cotton apparently indigenous in the West Indian islands, and which formerly supplied Europe with large quantities of cotton under the name of Coton Maurice, or Mauritius cotton. It is a stout small tree bearing green seeds, and yielding a copious supply of cotton of good quality, closely resembling New Orleans.

"In books one finds a species named *religiosum*—a name given by Linnæus, but it cannot be recognised, and is supposed to have been applied to a red or tawny cotton, from hearsay evidence that it was used for some part of the raiment of priests. It is, however, now well established that many, if not all, cottons will occasionally produce this coloured fibre, as, for instance, the Nankin cotton of China, Coconada cotton, red cotton amongst the New Orleans, and also amongst the Peruvian. Such a distinction is therefore of no value.

"Other species which, according to Royle, appear to be distinct, though they yield but little of the cotton of commerce, are as follow: *G. racemosum*, said to yield the cotton of Porto Rico. This species has its peduncles supporting two or three flowers, each with a pedicel. *Tomentosum*, from the Sandwich Islands, a small cotton with tawny wool, also found wild in Fiji. It occupies a large tract on the coast. There is also a species with entire, cordate, acuminate leaves, which appears to be unnamed; it was collected on Magdalena Bay, Lower California.

"It is a point of considerable interest to endeavour to identify the commercial cottons with the plants which produce them. In the 'Liverpool Cotton Brokers' Association Weekly Circular' we find cotton classified, not botanically, but according to its value in the market, the highest priced being at the head of the list and the lowest at its foot. The kinds are divided primarily into five, viz., American, Brazilian, Egyptian, &c., West Indian, &c., and East Indian.

"In the American list we have Sea Island and Stained Sea Island, which are *G. barbadense*; then Upland, Mobile, Orleans, and Texas, which are all derived from *G. hirsutum*.

"In the Brazilian list there are Pernam and Ceara, Paraiba, Santos, Bahia, Maceio, and Maranham. These and other cottons, which, though not specified, are included under the same head, are mixed, being for the most part Kidney cotton, but also including Bourbon, varieties of Sea Island and New Orleans. Varieties of the last, or possibly true native species, are to be found in Peru very large and tree-like.

"The division 'Egyptian' includes Egyptian, Smyrna, &c., and is a very mixed lot. The finest Egyptian, and that which we receive in the greatest quantity, is from the *barbadense* or Sea Island stock; some is from the *hirsutum*, and some possibly from native sorts; the Smyrna is from herbaceous or East Indian cotton.

"The cottons included in the division 'West Indian,' are, perhaps, the most varied of all. The separate items are, West Indian, &c., Haytien, La Guayra, Peruvian, Carthagena, and African. In this list will be found Sea Island, Bourbon, Kidney, and West Indian green seeds, with a lesser sprinkling of all other Occidental cottons.

"Of the East Indian cotton, the Liverpool Cotton Brokers' Association distinguish these kinds: Sawginned Dharwar (which is acclimatised American from Louisiana), Broach, Dhollerah, Oomrawuttee, &c., Mangarole, &c., Comptah, and Scinde. These are all called Surats, and are chiefly derived from *G. herbaceum*. Then there are Tinnevelly and Western Madras, which are the native cotton with some Bourbon; and lastly, Bengal, which is *G. herbaceum*.

"A great difficulty with the English manufacturer for a time after the year 1861 was the scarcity of cotton, consequent upon the American civil war. During that war American cotton became very scarce, and advanced in price from its normal value of about 6d. a pound to 30d., and other cottons experienced a proportionate rise. This high price brought about an increased production in India, and we also received some supplies from countries which do not usually send us any; thus China, in ordinary time, not only uses all her own cotton but also imports from India, yet, during the American war we received a considerable quantity of it from China. With lower prices our imports of China cotton have again altogether ceased. Having depended many years chiefly on America for our cotton, the shorter staples of India required considerable alterations in the system of working. Attempts have been made to improve the quality of Indian cotton by the introduction of American seed, and to improve it in cleanliness by the introduction of the saw-gin for separating the cotton from the seed. However disinterested and praiseworthy these exertions have been, we are forced to admit that they have been attended with only very partial success, and have, in many cases, proved absolute failures. Experiments, with a view to improve Indian cotton, have been prosecuted with more or less vigour since 1788, yet spinners do not find that the staple of Surat cotton alters much, if at all, in character. If I am right in believing that India can produce its native cotton with greater advantage than it can foreign kinds, it would seem that improvements in quality would be best made by the selection of the best native sorts, or of such foreign kinds as have been proved to answer, such as Bourbon and Brazilian, of which the staple, in their adopted habitat, approximates to the native sorts. Abundant evidence proves that American cotton does not answer in India. The conditions of soil and climate are different in India and America, and these conditions it is impossible to modify. Efforts to improve Indian cotton in this direction are a mere waste of time and money, and might well be laid aside. Native Indian cotton can be grown, but little, if at all, inferior to Uplands American, and will answer all the purposes for which the latter is used. What the English manufacturer wants is plenty of it and cheap, the cleaner the better; and the more abundant we can get it, the better the means of conveyance, the more direct the communication between the producer and the consumer, and the fewer obstructions to trade, of whatever nature, the more advantageous will it be alike to England and to India."

The cotton plant, in one or other of its varieties, is a native of almost all tropical countries. The most ancient known seat of its manufacture is India. Herodotus (book iii. c. 106) speaks of a plant there, bearing fruit, containing a wool finer and better than that of the sheep, of which the natives make their clothes. Arrian (*Indian History*, c. 16), in his account of the voyage of Nearchus down the Indus (B.C. 327), mentions the cotton clothing and turbans of the natives made from a shrub which he calls *tala*. Strabo (book xv.) mentions the culture of the cotton plant in Persia in his day (the Christian era); and Pliny, towards the close of the first century, describes the plant as cultivated in Egypt (*Nat. Hist.* lib. xix. c. 2, Delph. edit.), and called by some *Gossypium*, but more usually *Xylon*, "from which are made the fabrics which we call *xylina*," which he describes as beautifully white and soft, and used especially as garments for the Egyptian priests. Cotton, however, had been of comparatively late introduction into Egypt, as not a shred of cotton fabric has been found among the great varieties of stuff in the mummy-wrappings of the ancient sarcophagi; and Herodotus, in describing the curious vegetable wool of India, would hardly have omitted to speak of it as used in Egypt if it had been known there in his time.

On the discovery of America, the Spaniards found the Mexicans already skilled in the manufacture of cotton, which they wrought to singular fineness and beauty; and cotton cloth was found by Lord Colchester among the mummy-wrappings in the ancient Peruvian tombs. In later times, Mungo Park and his successors in African exploration have found cotton fabrics almost universally known among the native African tribes.

From Pliny's comparing the cotton fruit to the quince it has been thought by some that the name Cotton was derived from the name of that fruit, *Cotoneum malum*. It has, however, been well shown by Dr. W. Cooke Taylor, LL.D.,[1] that this is a mere verbal coincidence, as *cotoneum* is only a corrupted form of *cydoneum*, from Cydon, a city of Crete, whence the quince was supposed to have been brought; while, on the other hand, cotton is one of the forms of the root קָטַן, *Katan*, to adhere or stick closely (a word found in all the Shemitic languages) the most strikingly characteristic of the closely-fitting cotton robes having given its name to the fabric of which they were made. And, Dr. Cooke Taylor further points out the curious fact that the word "to cotton" in the sense of associating together, as also the noun "cottons," as the name of a close-fitting garment, were used in England before the vegetable substance of that name was in this country at all. The word has probably come to us from the Arabic, in which the product is called *Kotòn*, pronounced *gootn*. The Mahommedan conquest made it known in Europe, and the name in Spanish, *algodon*, and Portuguese, *algodno*, still retains the Arabic article. The cotton manufacture, thus proved to have been known from the earliest historic times in India, and from India spreading through the East, was first introduced into Europe by the conquering Mahommedans. Cottons were among the articles taxed with import duties on admission to the seat of the Eastern Empire, by Justinian, in the sixth century, but they were then brought to Constantinople in the manufactured state. The first seat of the manufacture was Spain, where it was introduced by the Moors about the tenth century, and where the cotton plant still grows wild.

The first known mention of cotton in England is found in the accounts of Bolton Abbey, from which Dr. Whitaker (*Hist. Craven*) quotes, in the year 1298—"in *Sapo et cotoun ad Candelam*, 17s. 1d." Small quantities of cotton wool were probably imported from the Levant for this purpose, *i.e.*, for candle wicks. Next comes the mention by Chaucer (*circa* 1375), who describing the knight in the prologue to the *Canterbury Tales*, says: "Of fustian he wered a gipon," and the same stuff, a Spanish manufacture named from the Spanish word *fuste*, substance, is named by Hakluyt half a century later as a well-known article of commerce.

The manufacturer of cotton goods was not, however, introduced into England before the end of the fifteenth century, probably not till the middle of the sixteenth. "Cottons" are indeed mentioned at an earlier date among English manufactures. Leland, in 1538, says of Bolton, "Bolton upon moore markets stondith most by cottons and cowrse yarne. Divers villages in the mores about Bolton do make cottons." These "cottons," however, were in reality *woollen* fabrics imitated and named by the weavers of Lancashire from the veritable cottons which, as has been already shown, were imported from the Continent. Thus we find the Act 5th and 6th Edward VI. (1552), entitled "for the true making of *woollen cloth*," proceeds to specify "all the cottons called Manchester, Lancashire, and Cheshire cottons;" while the Acts of about the same period (33 Henry VIII. c. 15, "Touchinge the Translation of sainctuary from Manchester to Westchester" [Chester], and 8 Elizabeth, c. 11, for regulating various matters of the trade in "cottons, friezes, and rugs") speak of these cottons being "frised" and "milled," processes only applicable in the

---

[1] "Handbook of Silk, Cotton, and Woollen Manufacture," p. 93.

woollen manufacture. Camden also (1590) speaks of Manchester excelling the neighbouring towns "by the glory of its woollen stuffs, which they call Manchester cottons." A relic of the use of the word still exists in the name "Kendal cottons," by which a certain coarse woollen cloth has been known probably for five hundred years.[1]

The probability seems to be that the actual cotton manufacture was introduced about 1585, by the Flemish refugees, on the fall of Brussels, Malines, and Antwerp, before the Duke of Parma. Many of these settled at Manchester and were encouraged by the Warden and Fellows of Manchester College, who allowed them firing and wood for their looms from their woods, on paying fourpence each by the year.

By 1641, however, Manchester was known for a manufacture undoubtedly *cotton*, in the true meaning of the word, when it is described by Lewis Roberts in his *Treasure of Trafficke*, who, speaking of this town, says, "they buy cotton wool in London, that comes first from Cyprus and Smyrna, and at home work the same and perfect it into fustians, vermillions, dimities, and other such stuffs, and then return it to London, where the same is vented and sold, and not seldom sent into forrain partes." [2]

Once introduced, however, the cotton manufacture, at first chiefly fustians, and what Fuller in 1662 calls "Manchester Tickin," took firm root in the district. It was well suited to the labouring population and yeomen scattered throughout the Salford Hundred, affording many processes in which every member of their households could render some assistance. By the beginning of the last century many of the Lancashire gentry had begun to bind their sons apprentices to the cotton manufacturers, paying premiums of £50 or £60; and though Dr. Aikin tells how the young men often revolted at the hard work and coarse fare, and broke their indentures, enlisting or going off to sea, enough of them settled in the various seats of the manufacture to account, in great measure, for the curious dispersion noticeable at the present day of the old Lancashire territorial family names throughout the factory districts.

For the first century and a half after the introduction of the cotton manufacture the processes employed continued to be of a very rude description—in fact, a mere adaptation of the appliances with which the people had been for centuries familiar in the woollen manufacture. The cotton, arriving in bales from the Levant or the West Indian Islands, was carded between two hand-cards like large wire hair-brushes, spun on the common single-thread spinning-wheel, and woven, by a shuttle thrown by hand, in a rude loom, not much more efficient, though constructed with more mechanical exactness, than that which for a thousand years had been in use in India.

Various causes, however, combined to hinder the cotton manufacture from continuing permanently in the same elementary state as that of woollen cloths had done. The material employed was of an altogether finer description than the staple of the woollen fabrics, and the imports of cotton fabrics from India were a continual reproach and challenge (such as the woollen manufacturers had never had to stimulate them) to the English spinners and weavers of cotton.

As has been the case with many branches of art and manufacture, imperfect inventions and discoveries, interesting as tentative steps in the march of progress, preceded those which achieved success, and marked the great eras in the history of the cotton manufacture.

1678. As early as the middle of the sixteenth century, an ingenious Frenchman, M. de Gennes, contrived the first power loom, which is described in the *Philosophical Transactions* of the Royal Society for 1678. It did not come into practical use, however.

1697. Total import of cotton wool, 1,976,359 pounds.

1700. The importation of printed calicoes from the East Indies prohibited by law.

1721. Printed calicoes forbidden by law to be used or worn.

1738. The first distinct advance towards practical improvements in the cotton manufacture took place in this year. The fly-shuttle was invented by John Kay, a Bury man, who was engaged in cloth-weaving at Colchester, enabling the shuttle, previously thrown by hand, to be thrown to and fro between the layers of warp by the alternate jerk from side to side of a pick held in the right hand.

About the same time "stock-cards" of a much larger size than those previously held in the hand, the under card fixed and the upper movable and suspended, which had been previously in use in the woollen manufacture, were adopted for the carding of cotton.

In this year also a patent was taken out in the name of Lewis Paul for a plan of spinning by rollers invented by his partner, John Wyatt, of Birmingham, who had been occupied upon it for a dozen years. The specification[3] distinctly alludes to a succession of rollers, each set moving faster than the former; but it is doubtful whether his idea was anything more than that of adopting the processes of metal rolling to cotton, so as to compress it before being twisted in the ordinary way. He attempted to carry out the manufacture by his invention in Birmingham (1739-41), and Mr. Cave attempted it also in a spinning factory at Northampton, but without success.

1748. Lewis Paul took out two patents for carding machines, one of them by flat cards, the other for carding by cylinders. With the latter of these was a contrivance for stripping off the cotton by a stick with needles in it like the teeth of a comb. Carding by this cylinder was used by Paul at his factory in Northampton, but did not for many years after come into general use.

1758. Another patent for the spinning machine already patented twenty years before was taken out by Lewis Paul; but though some improvements were introduced, including a more complete arrangement of the cylinder for carding, it attained no practical success.

1760. A much less ambitious contrivance, that of the drop-box, enabling the weaver to use several shuttles consecutively, merely dropping them at the side till wanted again, was this year invented by Robert Kay, son of the inventor of the fly-shuttle, which now became of great importance, and was extensively introduced.

These contrivances, doubling the amount of work which a weaver could perform, at once increased the difficulty of procuring weft. The single-thread spinning wheels could not supply what was wanted, and the weaver often had to walk miles in a morning to collect weft enough to last him the rest of the day. The demand for a quicker method of spinning became more urgent than ever.

1764. The spinning jenny was invented by James Hargreaves, of Standhill, near Blackburn. This was, indeed, only a mechanical extension of the principle of the old spinning wheel, but it enabled eleven threads, and subsequently as many as a hundred, to be spun at once. After occupying some time in perfecting it, Hargreaves used it privately, without seeking any patent.

1766. Cotton wool admitted duty-free in British-built ships.

1768. Hargreaves forced to quit Blackburn by the jealousy of his neighbours. He removed to Nottingham, and went into partnership in a small spinning factory. In 1770 he patented the jenny.

---

[1] Dr. Cooke Taylor's "Handbook," etc., p. 97.
[2] Quoted at length in Mr. Baines's "History of the Cotton Manufac-ture," pp. 100, 101, where see many other extracts from early writers illustrative of the subject.
[3] Given at length in Baines's "Hist. Cotton Manuf.," p. 122.

1769. Richard Arkwright took out a patent for his spinning machine, ultimately called the water frame, the first practical application of elongation by rollers. He had been employed in maturing his invention for some years, first at Preston (where he first fitted up his machine in the parlour of the grammar-school-house), and afterwards at Nottingham. There his invention was taken up by Messrs. Need and Strutt, who entered into partnership with him. There has been great contention as to Arkwright's title to be considered the original inventor of this machine. He himself refers, in the case which he drew up in 1782, to the fact of previous attempts having been made to spin cotton by machinery, in Birmingham and Northampton (Wyatt in 1738), and his claim was also disputed by Thomas Highs, a reedmaker of Leigh. Whatever may have been his acquaintance with previous efforts of the kind, however, Arkwright seems to have been the first to see how they might be combined and turned to practical advantage. In doing this he displayed great mechanical skill, and undoubtedly to him is owing, if not the original invention, at least its perfecting into the shape which revolutionised the cotton manufacture.

1771. Arkwright's first mill built at Cromford.

1772. The carding machine was improved by the invention of the feeder by John Lees, of Manchester.

1774. Further improvements in carding by Mr. Wood and Mr. Pilkington.

1775. Arkwright took out a second patent for a series of machines, including carding, and the subsequent processes of drawing and roving, by which the sliver of cotton doffed from the cards is first repeatedly drawn out and doubled and then slightly twisted into a loose roving. Arkwright's carding machine, in this patent, embodied an important invention— the metal comb, rapidly worked with a crank to doff the cotton from the carder.

These inventions and improvements of Arkwright gave an immense impetus to the cotton manufacture. From this time the factory system dates its rise. Enterprising men from all parts of the country purchased the right to use his patents, or used adaptations of them without purchasing them. He himself prospered, both by royalties on his machines and still more by the skill with which he managed his own manufactories. In a few years, however, the infringements of his patents had become so bold and general that, in 1781, he instituted a series of actions, of which one, against Colonel Mordaunt, alone was tried. The result was that his patent was set aside on the ground that the specification was obscure and unintelligible. After vainly endeavouring to interest the Government in his "case," he again tried the issue of law in 1785. In that year he obtained a verdict in his favour, in February, in the Court of Common Pleas, but the associated manufacturers carried the cause to the King's Bench, with the effect of finally invalidating his patent in June of the same year. This, however, did not diminish his prosperity, which arose from his general skill and enterprise as a manufacturer. He was high sheriff of Derbyshire in 1786, being knighted the same year. He died August 3, 1792, at the age of sixty.

1779. Samuel Crompton, a weaver of Hall-i'th-Wood, near Bolton-le-Moors, completed his invention of the mule, so called from its combining the principles and advantages of the two great machines—the jenny and the water frame.

The water frame, with its system of rollers, spun good twist (for warps), but in the higher counts the tension caused by the drag of the bobbins was too great. Crompton combined the system of rollers with an adaptation of Hargreaves' plan for elongating the yarn by drawing out the spindles on a movable frame. He was quietly working at this invention from 1774 to 1779, and produced yarns at that time of surprising fineness, ranging as high as 80 hanks to the pound, 40's being the highest previously known. For 40's the price was 14s. per pound in 1775. Crompton was not a pushing man, and as he made no attempt to secure a patent, his invention became common property, and the only reward he received was a grant of £5,000 from Parliament in 1812, and a few hundred pounds raised on two occasions by subscription. This invention, following upon those already recorded, gave a still further impulse to invention, concentrating attention especially on the possibility of weaving by power. The same year witnessed riots in many parts of the country, directed against spinning machinery.

1780. Muslin first attempted to be manufactured in England, but unsuccessfully, the yarn not being produced fine enough. Within seven years, however, the mule had removed this obstacle, and muslin was largely manufactured.'

1785. Cotton first imported into Liverpool from America, viz. five bags !

The first patent for a power loom, taken out by Dr. Edmund Cartwright, a Kentish clergyman. He took out a second patent in 1787. This machine, however, though ingenious, and taken up by the Grimshaws, of Gorton, who stocked a mill with them at Knot Mill, did not come into any general use. Dr. Cartwright, however, received a grant of £10,000 from Parliament.

The steam engine first used in cotton manufacture by Messrs. Robinson, of Papplewick, Nottinghamshire.

1786. Total import of cotton wool during the year, 19,900,000 pounds, from the following markets : viz., British West Indies, 5,800,000 ; French and Spanish colonies, 5,500,000 ; Portuguese and Dutch colonies (East Indies), 3,600,000 ; Smyrna and Turkey, 5,000,000 ; American States, 3,000 pounds.

1787. Heavy duties imposed on the importation of all foreign cotton manufactures, ranging from 20 to 50 per cent ad valorem. These duties were augmented every few years, till, in 1813, they reached as high as 85 per cent on white calico.

1792. A self-acting mule patented by Mr. Kelly, of Glasgow.

Whitney's cotton gin invented.

1793. Fine counts, from 100's upwards, first spun by power.

1794. A power loom patented by Mr. Bell, of Glasgow.

1796. A power loom patented by Mr. Robert Miller, of Glasgow. This was tried for some years at Mr. Monteith's mills, near Glasgow, with two hundred looms, but without any success.

1797. The scutching machine invented by Mr. Snodgrass, of Glasgow, for loosening and opening the cotton preparatory to carding.

1798. Duties imposed on importation of cotton wool, varying from 4 per cent to about 6 per cent. These were, however, repealed in 1801.[1]

1801. First construction of fire-proof cotton mill, Messrs. Philips and Lee, of Manchester, first applying cast-iron beams to this purpose.

1802. The first Act of Parliament, 42 Geo. III. c. 73, promoted by the first Sir Robert Peel, passed for the regulation of the labours of apprentices in cotton mills, prohibiting their employment for more than twelve hours a day ; prohibiting night-work after June, 1804; and providing for their instruction and clothing; also for the whitewashing and ventilation of factories.

Import duties on raw cotton reimposed, slightly higher than those of 1798.

1803. A power loom patented by H. Horrocks, of Stockport.

1804. Thomas Johnson, of Stockport, by the invention of the dressing machine, patented this year, supplied the missing link in power-loom invention, for want of which the looms already mentioned, though they had shown the practicability of the principle, had failed to achieve any decisive success.

1806. Peter Marsland, of Stockport, patented a power loom with a double crank, and worked it in his own factory, though it proved too complicated for general adoption.

1813. Important improvements made in the power loom by H. Horrocks, of Stockport, which he patented. This was the machine which came into general use, for power-loom weaving, with various modifications.

---

[1] The fullest and most reliable details of the duties imposed at various times on raw and manufactured cotton are given by Mr. Edward Baines in his valuable work, "The History of the Cotton Manufacture," already referred to.

The same year the hand-loom weavers took the alarm, as the spinners had done in 1779, and the power looms were destroyed by the mob wherever they could find them. It was estimated that at this time there were not above 2,400 power looms in use ; and these, only being used for the coarser fabrics, had not at all lessened the demand for hand-loom work.

1814. The duties on the importation of white calico from the East Indies, the previous year raised to 85 per cent, reduced to 67½ per cent.

1815. Robert Owen, of New Lanark Mills, on the Clyde, began to advocate a ten hours' bill. The Act of 1802, having only contemplated apprentices, had been evaded by the employment of non-apprenticed poor children. Sir Robert Peel advocated Owen's views in Parliament.

1816. Sir Robert Peel (the first) procured the appointment of a commission to consider the state of factory children.

1817. Number of spindles employed in the United Kingdom estimated by Mr. John Kennedy at 6,645,833.

1819. Employment of children in cotton mills further regulated by Act of Parliament, 59 George III., called Peel's Act, which prohibited the employment of children under nine years of age, and limited the labour of all young people under sixteen to twelve hours a day, with other regulations.

1822. About this time double carding machines began to come into use in Oldham, and came to be known as Oldham engines. They were, however, scarcely used at all elsewhere, until the precariousness of profits in the cotton trade during and subsequent to the American war (1861-5), forced the manufacturers to avail themselves of even the slightest means of simplifying and cheapening production. They are now coming extensively into use among spinners of coarse and medium counts.

1823. Cotton first imported from Egypt, viz., 5,623 packages, averaging 500 pounds.

1825. A self-acting mule patented by Mr. Richard Roberts, of the firm of Sharp and Roberts, of Manchester. This, improved by them (for which a further patent was taken out a few years later), was a great success, and came to be the mule generally used.

A self-acting mule invented by Mr. Smith, of Glasgow, which is also very largely used.

First contrivances patented for stopping the loom on the breaking of the weft, by Messrs. Stansfield, Pritchard, and Wilkinson, of Leeds. This, however—a slight mechanism attached to the shuttle itself—did not come into any general use.

Mr. Huskisson reduced the enormous duties on foreign cotton manufactures, previously 37½ per cent, and 67½ per cent on muslins or nankeens and white calico respectfully, to a uniform duty of £10 per cent ad valorem, with 3½d. per square yard if printed.

1829. Danforth's American Throstle, patented by Mr. John Hutchinson, of Liverpool. T..e throstle is represented in some works as distinct from the old water frame, but in reality it is merely the name which was given to Arkwright's spinning machine at a later period when its construction had been simplified.

1831. Duty on raw cotton, previously 6 per cent ad valorem, fixed at 5s. 10d. per hundredweight.

Another Factory Bill brought in by Sir John Hobhouse and Lord Morpeth, to shorten the labour of all young persons under eighteen, in cotton, worsted, woollen, linen, and silk mills, to eleven and a half hours a day, and eight and a half on Saturdays. The Act as it passed, however, was limited to cotton mills, and left the term of labour at sixty-nine hours a-week.

1832. Number of spindles in the United Kingdom estimated by Mr. Baines at 9,333,000 ; number of power looms, 203,373.

The additional duty on printed calico, 3½d. per square yard, repealed.

1833. Earnest attempts were made by Mr. Sadler, Mr. John Fielden, Mr. William Cobbett, and Lord Ashley, to induce Parliament to pass a ten hours' bill. A Royal Commission was appointed, at the instance of Mr. John Wilson Patten (afterwards Lord Winmarleigh), to collect information on the condition of children employed in factories.

Duty on foreign raw cotton reduced to 2s. 11d. per cwt. ; from British possessions to 4d. per cwt.

The self-acting temple invented by Mr. William Graham, of Glasgow. This kept the cloth constantly stretched by the action of a pair of clippers It has, however, been generally superseded by the use of roller temples.

1834. On the report of the commissioners a new Factory Act, 3 and 4 William IV. c. 103, was introduced by Lord Ashley, but being carried out of his control by Government, was passed with very little improvement on the Act of 1831. It prohibited the labour of young persons under eighteen from 8-30 p.m. till 5-30 a.m. in cotton and other factories (silk factories excepted) ; limited the employment of persons under eighteen to twelve hours in one day, and sixty-nine hours a week ; and of children under eleven to nine hours a day, and forty-eight hours a week ; requiring for these last two hours' schooling a day ; and for the first time appointing inspectors.

The weft fork patented by Messrs. Ramsbottom and Holt, of Todmorden—a very ingenious contrivance, by which the breaking of the weft at once stops the loom. This, still further simplified, has come into almost universal use.

1836. Number of operatives employed in spinning and weaving factories in the United Kingdom, 237,000. (Estimate by Mr. Baines, founded upon reports of factory inspectors.)

About this year, the card-making machine invented by Mr. J. C. Dyer, of Manchester. It was exhibited at the meeting of the British Association at Birmingham in 1839.

1844. Another Act for regulating the hours of labour of women and children in factories was brought in by Sir James Graham for the Government, and passed, the amendments of the ten hours' bill party being defeated. 7 and 8 Vict. c. 15.

1844. An ingenious plan for coiling the sliver as it is run out from the carding machine, patented by Mr. John Tatham.

1845. Duty on cotton finally repealed.

1847. The Ten Hours Bill, brought in by Mr. John Fielden, M.P., passed, 10 Vict. c. 29.

1849. Mason's long collars, for steadying the spindles in roving-frames, introduced. Higgins's do., which have also come to be widely used, were introduced in 1860.

1850. The Ten Hours Act of 1847 having proved technically defective, owing to the adoption of the shift, or relay, system, which had not been provided against, an attempt was made by its promoters to procure its amendment. Meanwhile a bill was brought in by Lord Ashley, to settle the question by conceding 10½ hours a day with 7½ on Saturdays (instead of 10 hours a day with 8 on Saturdays, the settlement of 1847). This was strenuously opposed by a large proportion of the advocates of the previous Act, but was carried ; 13 and 14 Vict. c. 54. It is under this Act that until 1874 factories continued to be worked. The Act was slightly amended by 16 and 17 Vict. c. 104 (1853), and 19 and 20 Vict. c. 38 (1856) ; and in 1860 was extended to bleaching and dyeing works (23 and 24 Vict. c. 78), and in 1861 to lace factories (24 and 25 Vict. c. 117). A further agitation with respect to hours of labour was set at rest by the Factory Act of 1874 (37 and 38 Vict. c. 44), and the work of legislation was crowned by the Factories and Workshops Act 1878, by which the whole of the scattered legislation, embracing forty-five Acts, and extending over a period of 50 years, was brought into one lucid and harmonious whole.

1851. At the Great Exhibition this year, muslin exhibited, manufactured of yarn of the extraordinarily fine count, 700's, spun by T. Houldsworth of Manchester. In 1862 they showed yarn still finer.

1858. Revolving flat cards, introduced in carding, and loose boss top rollers in spinning, patents of Mr. Evan Leigh, of Manchester.

1860. Mr. R. Arthur Arnold, in his *History of the Cotton Famine*, p. 25, estimates the number of cotton mills in Great Britain at 2,650, worked by about 440,000 persons, whose wages amounted to about £11,500,000 a-year. Number of spindles, 30,387,467; number of power looms, 350,000.

For a generation past improvements have taken place in the machinery employed in the cotton manufacture, which, though in reality very considerable, have not been of a kind to be separately recorded. No great inventions have been made. No such epochs have occurred in the manufacture as those which are connected with the jenny, the water frame, the mule, the power loom, &c. The principle of the machinery has remained almost unaltered, but improved mechanical arrangements have secured greater accuracy or speed in the movements; and every maker has introduced small modifications of his own, invention following invention, until the spinner and manufacturer have great difficulty in deciding on their respective merits.

This general course of advancement has also been greatly facilitated by the great improvement which has taken place in the make of mechanical tools, lathes, drills, planing machines, &c. Hence the almost entire disuse of wood in cotton machinery, replaced by cast or wrought iron; and hence, too, constantly increasing accuracy in the fittings, and greater strength and stability, combined with lightness. So great has been this advance, that Mr. Chadwick estimates the improvements of the twenty years preceding 1860, as measured by increased production and increased economy, as follows:—

	Percentage. Increase of Production.	Percentage. Saving of Labour.
In willowing and blowing machines	20 to 25	20
In carding machines	20 to 25	20
In drawing frames	20 to 25	50
In slubbing and roving	20 to 25	40 to 45
In spinning and doubling, by increase in size	100	40
In looms	25	50

As to the rate of improvement in spinning, the late Mr. J. Kennedy, of Manchester, gives the following figures:—

	Hanks Spun per Spindle per Day.		
	1812.	1830.	1858.
Yarn No. 40's	2·0	2·75	2·75
	Cost of Labour at the Three Periods.		
Yarn No. 40's	1s.	7½d.	5d.

Speed, therefore, had almost reached its safe maximum in 1830, and the extra production since is chiefly due to the increased size of the machines.

The late Sir Thomas Bazley. Bart., M.P., in a paper read at the Society of Arts in 1862, says: "The last year of full occupation for the cotton trade was 1860. The number of spindles then employed was about 32,000,000, and the number of looms employed about 340,000. The production in the machine-making trade had doubled within ten years. Bleach, print, and dye works had been largely extended during that period. The fixed investments, including the value of land and rights to water, amounted to not less than £60,000,000 sterling, to which must be added a working capital of £20,000,000; add to these, again, the value of merchants' and tradesmen's stocks at home and abroad, the value of raw cotton and subsidiary materials, and of bankers' capital, and the grand total of capital employed in the trade will not be less than £200,000,000 sterling."

Mr. Henry Ashworth thus sums up the progress of the cotton trade, &c., of Lancashire:—

In 1760 Dr. Percival stated the value of one year's production at	£200,000
In 1860 Mr. Bazley "	£85,000,000
In 1769 the cotton imported into the United Kingdom was	3,870,000 lb.
In 1860 " "	1,083,600,000 lb.
In 1784 the value of 1lb. of 42's yarn was	10s. 11d.
In 1860 " "	11d.
In 1786 the value of 1lb. of 100's yarn was	38s.
In 1860 " "	2s. 6d.
In 1692 the real property assessed for land-tax in Lancashire was	£97,242
In 1815 " " "	£3,087,774
In 1851 " " "	£8,640,695
In 1860 " " "	£11,453,851

The cause of this immense development of the cotton trade is seen at a glance in its final result: it is the possible economy o cotton, as compared with wool and flax. In the normal condition of the cotton trade, as it existed in 1860, Mr. Ashworth says:—

1lb. of flannel would cost	3s. 1d.
1lb. of linen "	2s. 4d.
1lb. of calico "	1s. 0d.

The possibility of this economy, adds Dr. Watts, has built up the cotton industry, whilst the inventive, organising, productive, and mercantile enterprise employed upon it has done much to educate the people of this kingdom, and to carry civilisation to every country upon the earth.

During the American civil war (1861-5) the necessity of working inferior kinds of cotton, in the absence of American, gave a special direction to the mechanical ingenuity interested in the cotton manufacture. The Indian cotton, of a much shorter staple than the American, required special adaptations of the old machinery; and the precariousness of the trade, together with the extremely small profits which could, at the best, be made by the manufacturers, induced great attention to every detail in the machinery, even the slightest economising of time, labour, or friction being of great importance.[1]

A few only of the most prominent facts of the Cotton Famine, that period of intense suffering to almost every class of the community in the cotton districts, can be here noted, for which facts and figures we are indebted to Dr. Watts's book on the *Cotton Famine*.

In the United States of America, the election, in 1860, of Mr. Abraham Lincoln to be President, being a great party triumph of the Republican over the Democratic party, led to an attempt at secession by a number of the Southern states. The inevitable consequence was the blockade of the Southern cotton ports, cutting off the supply of cotton material to England, which had been too largely and exclusively derived from that source. In Lancashire, cotton mills began to run short time, or to close entirely, in October, 1861, and in twenty-eight poor-law unions in this manufacturing district[2] there were, in that month, 3,000 applications for relief more than usual at that period of the year; in November, 7,000 more presented themselves; in December the increase

---

[1] For the information of the foregoing section of cotton annals, as to the later developments of machinery in the cotton manufacture, I must acknowledge my great indebtedness to Mr. John Thornely, of Flowery Field, Hyde.—B. H.

[2] These twenty-eight unions were—Ashton-under-Lyne, Barton-upon-Irwell, Blackburn, Bolton, Burnley, Bury, Chorley, Chorlton, Clitheroe, The Fylde, Garstang, Glossop, Haslingden, Lancaster, Leigh Macclesfield, Manchester, Oldham, Preston, Prestwich, Rochdale, Saddleworth, Salford, Skipton, Stockport, Todmorden, Warrington, and Wigan.

was again 7,000 ; and the recipients of relief in January, 1862, were 12,000 (or about 25 per cent) more than in January, 1861. But these statistics were no real measure of the extent of the distress. Savings banks, the loan funds of co-operative societies, the funds of friendly societies, and the allowances of trades societies, were all largely helping to support those thrown out of work. Month after month only witnessed the rapid extension of the distress, which seems to have reached its height in the month of December 1862. The following table will show the progress of the work of relief :—

NUMBERS OUT OF WORK, NUMBERS RELIEVED, AND PROPORTIONS OF PERSONS RELIEVED TO THOSE
ENTIRELY OUT OF WORK.

	Out of Work.	Relieved.	Proportion Relieved.
1862.			
June	——	129,774	——
July	——	153,774	——
August	— —	216,437	——
September	——	277,198	——
October	——	371,496	——
November	244,616	458,441	187 per cent
December	247,230	485,434	196 „
1863.			
January	228,992	451,343	197 „
February	239,751	432,477	180 „
March	240,466	420,243	174 „
April	215,522	362,076	168 „
May	191,199	289,975	151 „
June	168,033	255,578	152 „
July	178,205	213,444	129 „
August	171,535	204,603	119 „
September	160,835	184,136	114 „
October	154,219	167,678	108 „
November	159,117	170,268	107 „
December	149,038	180,298	120 „
1864.			
January	158,653	202,785	127 „
February	153,864	203,168	132 „
March	148,920	180,027	120 „
April	124,828	147,280	117 „
May	116,550	116,088	99 „
June	105,161	100,671	95 „
July	101,568	85,910	84 „
August	102,090	83,063	81 „
September	135,821	92,379	68 „
October	171,568	136,268	78 „
November	153,295	149,923	97 „
December	126,977	130,397	102 „
1865.			
January	114,488	119,544	104 „
February	115,727	125,885	108 „
March	113,794	111,008	97 „
April	104,571	95,763	91 „
May	86,001	75,784	88 „

On the assumption that each unemployed operative represents 2½ persons, one-fifth of the whole were without relief when the proportion was at the highest. Without entering into any of the harrowing details of want, starvation, and misery, of this long period of suffering, we turn with pleasure to a few of the remarkable features of the relief so promptly, widely, and able administered. This relief was both in money and kind, in provisions, bedding, clothing, house-rent, &c. It was administered, to an extent that can never be known, by individual and private charity and sympathy ; in the shape of poor-rate it was in vastly increased ratio paid at the relief boards ; and in voluntary contributions—not only from all parts of the United Kingdom but from all parts of the civilised world—it was distributed through the agencies of great central and small local committees.

The earliest great organisation seems to have been what has been called "The Mansion House Fund," originated at a meeting of city merchants, &c., on 25th April, 1862 ; and the subscriptions for the cotton operatives, then commenced, reached ultimately the magnificent sum of £528,336, in addition to large supplies of blankets, clothing, &c.

On the 29th April, 1862, a meeting of gentlemen of Manchester, called together by the Mayor, Mr. Thomas Goadsby, was held in the Town Hall, to consider the propriety of forming a Relief Committee ; but the general opinion expressed—so little was the situation understood—was that there was no necessity for any other than existing agencies to deal with the distress. A second meeting was convened in May, and during its adjournment for a week, to give time for practical suggestions, a committee was formed, principally of Manchester men, with Mr. John Wm. Maclure as the honorary secretary, and to it were afterwards added the Mayors and ex-Mayors of all the boroughs in the cotton districts. On the 19th July a meeting of noblemen and gentlemen connected with Lancashire was held at Bridgewater House, London, and the subscription there originated reached in five hours £17,000, and ultimately amounted to £52,000. The Earl of Derby accepted the office of chairman ; Colonel Wilson Patten, M.P. (the present Lord Winmarleigh), that of treasurer ; and Sir J. P. Kay Shuttleworth that of honorary secretary of the committee. The Manchester subscription at that date was about £30,000, collected by local committees, which were afterwards allied with the central executive, and some voluntary contributions sent in without canvassing. The Bridgewater House Committee, a Special Relief Committee, and the Manchester Committee, were all formed into one central executive—the General Committee still existing, but the real work being done by the executive. A speech of Mr. Cobden stimulated the executive to enlarge their sphere of action in seeking contributions throughout the kingdom ; and by the end of January, 1863, there had been collected in Manchester and Salford, by a local collecting committee, and by various local committees in other places, not less than £130,000. Many county meetings were held, and there was scarcely a borough or parish in the kingdom which did not freely respond to the cry of distress. At the county of Lancaster meeting, on the 2nd December, 1862, a list of subscriptions was handed in of £70,000 additional to the relief fund. The

Bridgewater House Committee, in handing over the funds to the central executive for distribution, laid down the principle that they should be applied only to such operatives as were not in receipt of relief from boards of guardians. The District Provident Society was adopted as the distribution committee for the townships of Manchester and Hulme, with branches; Salford had an independent local committee; and the central executive decided to recognise only one local committee in each of the outlying towns. The scale of relief ultimately adopted by the central executive (and by the local committees in October, 1863) would average about 2s. per head per week, giving rather more to small and rather less to large families. The executive offered for adoption three specimen scales; allowing also in winter a supply of fuel and clothing—

	No. 1.		No. 2.		No. 3.	
	s.	d.	s.	d.	s.	d.
Single person	3	6	3	6	3	0
Man and wife	5	6	5	6	5	0
Man, wife, and one child	6	9	6	9	6	3
,, ,, two children	8	0	8	0	8	0
,, ,, three ,, ...	9	9	9	3	9	9
,, ,, four ,, ...	11	3	10	11	11	6
,, ,, five ,, ...	12	9	12	8	13	0
,, ,, six ,, ...	14	0	14	0	14	0

' It was thought that such a scale, varying from one-fourth to one-third of ordinary wages, would not materially lessen the inclination for any kind of work for wages, whenever such work was to be had, especially as relief was coupled with "disciplinary work," viz., outdoor labour, or elementary instruction in schools for men and boys; and instruction in sewing schools or classes for women and girls. In the winter of 1862-3 there were at one time 48,000 men and youths in attendance at these schools, many of which were also in the evening, for instruction and recreation; and in Manchester and its vicinity lectures and concerts were given. More than 41,000 females were in the sewing classes in March, 1863. The whole of the large fund from Australia, or New South Wales, was specially appropriated to schools for youth, sewing classes for females, and the payment of the school pence of children. The scheme was carefully organised and perfected, and daily tasks carried on, until the gradual increase of employment in mills and on public works, emigration to other counties, and emigration to the United States, Canada, Australia, and New Zealand drained the schools of their pupils.

The following table shows the number of persons who were relieved by the Poor-Law Guardians in the last week in November, 1861 and 1865, and by the Guardians and Relief Committees in the corresponding week in November, 1862, 1863, and 1864 :—

	1861.	1862.	1863.	1864.	1865.
Ashton-under-Lyne ...	1,827	56,363	23,568	20,638	1,417
Barton-upon-Irwell ...	663	3,910	1,230	1,220	896
Blackburn	4,110	38,104	9,457	10,012	4,083
Bolton............	3,200	19,525	8,013	6,543	3,166
Burnley	1,503	17,502	13,046	16,948	1.557
Bury	1,782	29,926	10,048	15,113	2,932
Chorley	1,350	7,527	3,409	2,471	1,155
Chorlton	2,042	15,367	9,984	5,694	3,993
Clitheroe	624	1,879	976	1,138	547
Fylde, The	633	1,282	1,086	771	699
Garstang......	567	1,026	696	807	458
Glossop	221	7,605	6,752	3,263	195
Haslingden	946	17,346	3,340	7,108	1,243
Lancaster	903	1,129	1,025	901	789
Leigh	636	2,722	1,091	901	806
Macclesfield	2,158	5,609	2,775	2,429	2,310
Manchester	4,678	52,477	13,818	9,035	5,046
Oldham	1,622	28,851	8,371	9,164	1,892
Preston	4,805	49,171	17,489	13,226	2,377
Prestwich	601	4,794	1,958	1,078	593
Rochdale..	2,060	24,961	8,132	6,243	1,789
Saddleworth	237	2,414	1,287	988	261
Salford	2,507	16,663	5,600	3,600	2,265
Skipton	1,902	2,635	1,856	2,030	1,354
Stockport	1,674	34,612	10,661	8,593	1,189
Todmorden	795	7,590	1,689	2,696	668
Warrington	1,131	1,992	1,416	1,458	1,220
Wigan	2,360	14,959	11,527	5,855	3,538
Total	47,537	458,441	170,288	149,923	48,267

An emigrants' aid society was established in Manchester in April, 1863, simply to aid such as were determined to go to the colonies. From various sources the funds reached £4,600, which assisted in the outfit of 834 statute adults, and aided the passages of 385. So far as could be ascertained from the passenger lists of the custom-house authorities the number of spinners and weavers who left the United Kingdom were: In 1861, 123; in 1862, 562; in 1863, 2,036; and in 1864, 1,187. In the three last years an average of 7,700 persons emigrated yearly, whose occupations were not specified in the lists.

The total sum distributed in relief by the central executive through the various committees was £841,809. To this the Mansion House Committee added £419,692, besides sending £53,531 to committees in Ashton-under-Lyne district, which were not recognised by the central committee; and the various committees themselves made local collections amounting to £297,008, and received direct from other sources £49,659. To the amount of local subscriptions is to be added about £80,000 collected in Manchester, and paid direct by the collecting committee into the funds of the general committee. Thus the total sum of money distributed by committees was £1,661,679; in addition to which there passed, in food and clothing, through the hands of the central executive, 16,500 barrels of flour, 997 barrels of beef, bacon, &c., 500 barrels of biscuits, 410 cases of fish, 228 sacks of potatoes, carrots, turnips, &c., 225 deer, with many hundred pheasants, rabbits, hares, &c., 28 chests of tea, 2½ pipes and 108 dozens of wine, 11,519 tons of coal, and 893 bales of clothing, blankets, and clothing materials. The whole of these contributions in kind were valued at £111,968, making the total amount of public subscriptions *one million seven hundred and seventy-three thousand six hundred and forty-seven pounds.*

The balance-sheet of the central executive to 31st December, 1864, shows the receipt of 25,999 separate individual donations, amounting to £242,865; collections at 3,093 churches and chapels of £53,265; collections from 5,403 parishes of £65,517; and collections amongst the workpeople of £15,715. Collecting committees were organised in 1,241 places in connection with the central committee at Manchester, exclusive of those in connection with the Mansion House Fund; and the exertions of those who remitted to Manchester resulted in the sum of £497,782. So that about three-fifths of the funds resulted from regular organisation and sustained effort, one-sixth from spontaneous individual benevolence, one-seventh from collections in places of worship, and about one-sixtieth from the working-people employed by various firms. The returns and balance-sheet show that the collections by local committees (in the Lancashire district), including the Manchester collecting committee, were equal to 41 per cent of the whole central fund, and to 24 per cent of the total sum, including the amount distributed by the Mansion House Committee. In other words, a district containing about 10 per cent of the population of England and Wales, whilst suffering under the paralysis of the cotton famine, which destroyed one-half of its principal industry and inflicted a large extra burden of poor-rates, yet contributed 24 per cent of the whole relief fund, in addition to the immense amount it distributed in private charity, which cannot be reduced into statistical shape. Of the whole amount of foreign and colonial subscriptions (£93,041), 55 per cent was sent from Australia, including New South Wales, a sum which, compared with the population of the colony, had no equal out of Manchester. Next on the foreign list stands the United States for £1,333 in money, and about £27,000 in provisions; and George Griswold, a merchant of New York, freighted his own ship, bearing his own name, with provisions, paid the salaries of the officers and sailors, and sent them across to Liverpool to help the distressed operatives of Lancashire.

Of the various large towns in England which, through local collecting committees, obtained and remitted sums in each case of £1,000 and upwards to the central committee to November, 1864, the following may be enumerated:—

Birmingham, £8,000 (balance in hand, £6,816); Bristol, £5,000; Bradford (Yorkshire), £10,500 (balance £11,178); Bury St. Edmunds, £1,167; Birkenhead, £1,240; Bath (to the Mansion House Committee), £2,333; Cotton Districts Relief Fund £85,732 (balance £55,955); Canterbury, £1,748; Cheltenham, £3,678; Cambridge University, £3,301; Chichester, £1,303; Chester (city) £1,675, (county) £4,405; Crewe, £1,138; Chesterfield, £1,200; Darlington, £2,500; Devonport, £1,358; Derby, £1,590; Great Malvern, £1,141; Gloucester, £5,752 (and £2,942 through other channels); Huddersfield, £2,000 (balance (£5,134); Halifax, £1,000 and £3,271 to various local committees (balance £1,977); Ipswich, £2,000 (balance £1,033); Kensington, £1,670 (balance £1,100); Kendal and Lonsdale wards, £1,900 (balance £1,600); Liverpool, £57,125 (£1,544 elsewhere, and balance £35,579); Leeds, £7,000 (balance £18,064); Leicester, £5,265; Maidstone, £1,140; Malton. £1,546; Northampton, £1,213; Newcastle-on-Tyne, £4,023; Oxford (University) £5,574, (city) £1,100 (and balance £1,000), (county) £2,098; Plymouth, £1,550; Pimlico, £3,278; Ripon, £1,162; Rotherham, £1,041; Shrewsbury, £1,603; St. Pancras, £2,739; St. Margaret's and St. John's, Westminster, £1,540; St. Marylebone, £10,000 (and balance £889); St. Helens, £2,550; Stroud (borough), £2,052; Staffordshire (county), £4,936; Southport, £3,963; Swansea, £1,800 (and balance £480); Sunderland, £1,787; Sheffield, £2,500 (and balance £8,161); Worcester, £2,000 (and balance £740); Wolverhampton, £3,616; Walsall, £1,020; Warwickshire, £6,017; Warrington, £3,060; York, £3,085 (and balance £1,930).

Ireland.—Belfast, £4,378; Cork (city) £1,800, (county) £1,550; Dublin, £25,000.

Scotland.—Aberdeen, £8,000; Arbroath, £1,136; Banff, £1,063; Dundee, £6,125; Dumfries, £4,500; Edinburgh, £34,265; Fife (county), £2,379; Montrose, £1,110; Perth (city and county), £4,023.

The Cotton Famine Fund left in the hands of the central executive about 1s., and in those of the Mansion House committee about 6d. in the pound of the respective subscriptions unappropriated.

Amongst other modes devised for relieving the pressure was the Public Works Act. In February, 1865, Mr. Robert Rawlinson (who had a special mission as to the applications for loans from Government for public works) informed the central executive that the total amount devoted to the Public Works Act was £1,850,000, the whole of which (except £3,918) had been appropriated in about 90 places, having been taken up in 155 separate loans. The larger portion of the expenditure was on sewerage and street improvement works, including the formation, paving, and flagging, channeling, and kerb-stones of streets, and also the widening, re-forming, and improvement of highways in the rural districts. The total amount of loans ordered by the Poor-law Board, under the Public Works Act, was £1,846,028; of which £370,946 was for public sewerage works, £839,007 for road and street improvements, £414,629 for water supply, £58,285 for public works and recreation grounds, 13,038 for cleansing, embanking, and pitching rivers, £12,453 for land drainage and other agricultural works, £52,550 for cemeteries, £59,139 for the erection or extension of market-places, £10,830 for gasworks, and £5,000 for public baths. The total amount to be lent to any local board or other authority was limited to one year's rateable value of the property assessable within the district for which such loan was required. The interest chargeable was 3½ per cent per annum, and the repayment was to be spread over any number of years not exceeding thirty, and to be secured by mortgage of the local rates, the loans to be subject to the approval of the Poor-law Board, and the money to be in such instalments as the Poor-law Board should direct. The cotton operatives worked most admirably at these public works, which progressed satisfactorily. In the week ending December 31, 1864, the number of unskilled factory operatives employed was 3,978, and of skilled labourers 2,741, many of the latter being originally factory operatives. The total number employed (6,719) was exclusive of at least 2,000 men getting stone in the quarries, and on other works contingent upon the Public Works Act. Dr. Watts not only pays a just tribute to the patient endurance with which the cotton operatives bore a long season of suffering and privation, but shows that amongst the women there was no sensible moral deterioration, and that, notwithstanding the pressure of distress, crime had actually decreased.

The consumption of cotton fell in 1861 to 1,007,400,000 pounds, or about 8 per cent, whilst prices rose about 13½ per cent on the average of the whole year. In 1862 the consumption was 451,700,000 pounds, but it cost more by £12,989,000 than the same quantity would have done at the average prices of 1861. Thus 44 per cent of the quantity required 86 per cent of the capital of 1861 to purchase it. Cloth was frequently sold on the same day at a less price per pound than raw cotton. The average condition of the trade is shown at a glance:—

Year.	Middling Fair Orleans.	40's Mule Twist.	39in. Shirtings.	Margin between Cotton and Cloth.
	Per lb.	Per lb.	Per lb.	Per lb.
1860	7⅛d.	11 3/16d.	14d.	6⅞d.
1861	9⅞d.	12d.	13½d.	4d.
1862	18½d.	17 13/16d.	18¼d.	minus ¼d.

Under the stimulus of high prices, running the blockade, and the Confederate cotton loan, 71,766 bales of American cotton reached England in 1862, and 131,900 bales in 1863. The bulk of the cotton consumed, however, was of course from India, and for the amount of labour employed upon it the production was more than 11 per cent less than it would have been on American cotton ; and where the Indian staple alone was used, the decreased production was fully 15 per cent as compared with American cotton, whilst the proportion of waste was very much greater. The consumption of cotton in 1863 was 508,400,000 pounds, being about 50 per cent of the quantity used in 1861, but at a cost of £44,485,000, or 141 per cent more than the cost of the same quantity at that date. The consumption of the year exceeded that of 1862 by about 33 per cent, showing that the tide was slowly turning.

In 1864 the prices of American cotton fluctuated with the varying fortunes of the war ; falling with peace rumours, till the employers of almost 13,000 hands, with liabilities amounting to £1,500,000, were chronicled amongst the failures ; and large holders of cotton were named whose stocks fell in a few weeks from £120,000 to £150,000 in value in each case. The bankruptcies registered in the court of Manchester were : In 1861, 175 ; in 1862, 370 ; in 1863, 261 ; and in 1864, 387. On the year employment was somewhat more plentiful, the exportation of cotton being 561,480,000 pounds, at a cost of £53,808,000, being 55 per cent of the quantity, and 170 per cent more than the cost, of the same quantity in 1861. Employment during 1864 averaged about 20 per cent more than in 1863, the weekly exportation of cotton being 26,500 against 22,030 bales.

In the appendix to Dr. Watts's book, various tables show the expenditure for in-maintenance and outdoor relief by boards of guardians, in the twenty-eight distressed unions of the cotton districts, for the years (ended Lady-day) 1861-2-3-4 and 5. We give the totals only :—

	In Maintenance.	Outdoor Relief.	Rate of Expenditure in the £ on Assessment.
1861	£64,382	£126,719	7⅔d.
1862	76,024	155,298	9¼d.
1863	87,136	573,395	4s. 10⅝d.
1864	82,693	494,675	3s. 9¼d.
1865	83,839	308,237	1s. 11¼d.

Such are some of the chief facts of the disastrous five years' cotton famine, as regards Lancashire. In 1866 the dearth of cotton had ceased, the supply from all sources, under the pressure of extraordinary prices, being nearly equal to that of 1860, the most prosperous year before the war.

The following statistics, which exhibit at a glance the varying fortunes of the cotton trade in the various branches of its raw material, are compiled, by permission, from the valuable tables in the annual cotton circular of Messrs. George Holt and Co., Liverpool, and in that of their successors, Messrs. Ellison and Co.

RAW COTTON IMPORTED INTO GREAT BRITAIN.

Year.	Bales American.	Bales Brazil.	Bales Egyptian	Bales East India.	Bales China.	Bales West India.	Total Import in Bales.	Total Estimated Import in lb
1701-1705	...		Yearly	average	on the five	years	...	1,200,000
1716-1720	...	...		...	...		...	2,200,000
1771-1775	...	.	..	...	. .	.	..	4,800,000
1776-1780	.			...	. .		...	6,700,000
1781-1785	.		...	...	. .		...	10,900,000
1786-1790	...		..	.	...		...	25,400,000
1791-1795	.		.	...	...		...	26,700,000
1796-1800	.		.	...	...		...	37,300,000
1801	...	...	.	...	...	...	...	56,000,000
1802	.		. .	...	.		...	60,300,000
1803	...	..		. .	.	...	...	53,800,000
1804	.		...		. .	...	...	61,900,000
1805		...		...	. .		...	59,700,000
1806	124,939	51,034	..	7,787	...	77,978	261,738	58,200,000
1807	171,267	18,981		11,409	...	81,010	282,667	74,900,000
1808	37,672	50,442	...	12,512	. .	67,512	168,138	43,600,000
1809	160,150	146,927		35,764	...	103,511	440,382	92,800,000
1810	216,759	142,846	..	79,382	.	92,186	562,173	136,500,000
1811	128,192	118,514	.	14,646	.	64,879	326,231	91,600,000
1812	95,331	98,704	.	2,607	.	64,563	261,205	63,000,000
1813	37,720	137,168	...	1,429	. .	73,219	249,536	51,000,000
1814	48,853	150,930	...	13,018	.	74,860	257,661	60,100,000
1815	203,051	91,055		22,357	..	52,840	369,303	99,300,000
1816	166,077	123,450		30,070	...	49,295	369,432	93,900,000
1817	199,669	114,518	..	120,202	...	44,872	479,261	124,900,000
1818	207,580	162,409	..	247,659	...	50,991	668,729	177,800,000
1819	205,161	125,415	..	184,259	...	31,300	546,135	149,700,000
1820	302,395	180,086	...	57,923	...	31,247	571,651	143,900,000
1821	300,070	121,085	...	30,095	...	40,428	491,678	129,000,000
1822	329,906	143,505	. .	19,263	...	40,770	533,444	142,200,000
1823	452,538	144,611	5,623	38,393	...	27,632	668,797	188,100,000
1824	282,371	143,310	38,022	50,852	..	25,537	540,092	143,700,000

RAW COTTON IMPORTED—*Continued.*

Year.	Bales American.	Bales Brazil.	Bales Egyptian.	Bales East India.	Bales China.	Bales West India.	Total Import in Bales.	Total Estimated Import in lb.
1825	423,446	193,942	111,023	60,484	...	31,988	820,883	222,400,000
1826	395,852	55,590	47,621	64,699	...	18,188	581,950	171,500,000
1827	646,776	120,111	22,450	73,738	...	30,988	894,063	271,100,000
1828	444,390	167,362	32,889	84,855	...	20,056	749,552	219,800,000
1829	463,076	159,536	24,739	80,489	...	18,867	746,707	221,800,000
1830	618,527	191,468	14,752	85,019	...	11,721	871,487	261,200,000
1831	608,887	168,288	38,124	76,764	...	11,304	903,367	280,500,000
1832	628,766	114,585	41,183	109,298	...	8,490	902,322	287,800,000
1833	654,786	163,193	3,893	94,698	...	13,646	930,216	304,200,000
1834	733,528	103,646	7,277	89,098	...	17,485	951,034	320,600,000
1835	763,199	143,572	43,721	117,965	...	22,796	1,091,253	361,700,000
1836	764,707	148,715	34,953	219,493	...	33,506	1,201,374	410,800,000
1837	844,812	117,005	41,193	145,174	...	27,791	1,175,975	408,200,000
1838	1,124,800	137,500	29,700	107,200	...	29,400	1,428,600	501,000,000
1839	814,500	99,300	33,500	132,900	...	36,000	1,116,200	388,600,000
1840	1,237,500	85,300	38,000	216,400	...	22,300	1,599,500	583,400,000
1841	902,500	94,300	40,700	273,600	...	32,900	1,344,000	489,900,000
1842	1,013,400	87,100	19,600	255,500	...	17,300	1,392,900	528,500,000
1843	1,396,800	98,700	48,800	182,100	...	17,700	1,744,100	667,000,000
1844	1,246,900	112,900	66,700	237,600	...	17,500	1,681,600	644,400,000
1845	1,499,600	110,200	82,000	155,100	...	8,800	1,855,700	716,300,000
1846	932,000	84,000	59,600	49,500	...	9,000	1,184,100	480,500,000
1847	874,100	110,200	20,700	222,800	...	4,900	1,232,700	465,000,000
1848	1,375,400	100,200	29,000	227,500	...	7,900	1,740,000	686,500,000
1849	1,477,700	163,800	72,600	182,200	...	9,100	1,905,400	754,300,000
1850	1,184,200	171,800	79,700	307,900	...	5,700	1,749,300	685,600,000
1851	1,393,700	108,700	67,400	328,800	...	4,900	1,903,500	760,100,000
1852	1,789,100	144,200	189,900	221,500	...	12,600	2,357,300	925,200,000
1853	1,532,000	132,400	105,400	485,300	...	9,100	2,264,200	902,300,000
1854	1,665,800	106,900	81,100	308,300	...	10,400	2,172,500	886,600,000
1855	1,623,600	184,700	114,800	396,100	...	8,900	2,278,100	901,100,000
1856	1,758,300	121,600	113,900	463,000	...	11,400	2,468,200	1,021,000,000
1857	1,482,000	168,900	75,900	680,500	..	11,300	2,418,600	976,100,000
1858	1,863,300	106,200	105,600	361,000	...	6,500	2,442,600	1,025,500,000
1859	2,086,300	124,900	101,400	510,700	...	6,800	2,830,100	1,190,800,000
1860	2,580,700	103,300	109,500	563,200	...	9,800	3,366,500	1,435,800,000
1861	1,841,600	100,000	97,800	986,600	...	9,700	3,035,700	1,261,400,000
1862	71,766	133,824	146,562	1,072,439	...	20,477	1,445,068	533,100,000
1863	131,900	137,900	248,700	1,223,700	167,000	23,000	1,932,200	691,800,000
1864	197,800	212,200	318,900	1,399,500	399,100	59,600	2,587,100	896,100,000
1865	461,910	340,280	413,890	1,266,520	141,610	331,100	2,755,310	966,400,000
1866	1,162,740	407,650	200,220	1,847,770	18,840	111,820	3,749,040	1,353,800,000
1867	1,225,690	437,210	198,170	1,508,750	1,940	129,020	3,500,780	1,273,800,000
1868	1,269,060	636,890	201,440	1,452,070	...	100,650	3,660,110	1,292,000,000
1869	1,089,720	514,200	226,640	1,496,410	...	105,640	3,382,610	1,196,000,000
1870	1,664,010	402,760	219,920	1,063,540	...	112,100	3,462,330	1,321,100,000
1871	2,249,290	514,750	271,850	1,235,940	...	133,590	4,405,420	1,676,100,000
1872	1,403,470	717,230	304,880	1,288,120	...	166,440	3,880,140	1,372,900,000
1873	1,897,790	471,540	328,470	1,068,690	...	137,750	3,904,240	1,508,500,000
1874	1,958,210	497,620	300,430	1,040,920	...	117,810	3,914,990	1,519,800,000
1875	1,859,280	423,630	281,340	1,054,570	...	89,210	3,708,030	1,458,600,000
1876	2,074,520	331,590	331,920	775,660	...	69,790	3,583,480	1,459,900,000
1877	2,006,740	316,050	293,150	522,270	...	59,880	3,198,090	1,306,200,000
1878	2,232,660	126,470	183,940	432,160	...	40,610	3,015,840	1,305,700,000
1879	2,427,480	77,490	256,190	506,180	...	91,940	3,359,230	1,449,500,000
1880	2,633,940	122,610	240,100	569,610	...	73,530	3,639,790	1,588,100,000
1881	2,741,740	288,760	271,520	537,650	...	57,360	3,837,030	1,676,100,000
1882	2,592,070	300,610	229,800	1,052,160	...	60,220	4,234,860	1,769,200,000
1883	2,747,770	280,750	267,250	688,400	..	£0,520	4,034,690	1,742,100,000
1884	2,765,170	245,820	292,300	801,450	...	49,960	4,154,700	1,791,600,000
1885	2,392,590	209,980	285,150	366,620	...	50,710	3,305,060	1,465,289,950
1886	2,902,120	196,700	256,800	329,760	...	56,390	3,941,770	1,744,838,830

⁎ APPENDIX VII. to the original edition consisted of a catalogue of Roger Dodsworth's MS. Collections in the Bodleian Library, so far as they relate to the county of Lancaster. Mr. Brook Herford collated this Appendix, with a full catalogue of Dodsworth's MSS. in the Bodleian (162 vols.), printed by the Rev. Jos. Hunter, in a volume entitled "Three Catalogues," &c. (London, 1838), and found so many inaccuracies in that of Mr. Baines that it is unnecessary, indeed useless, to reprint what could only mislead. Students and antiquaries are therefore referred to Mr. Hunter's volume, as containing a far more full and accurate catalogue as to Lancashire.

APPENDIX VII.

ELECTORAL STATISTICS OF LANCASHIRE.

*** These are based upon the census of 1881 (for population), and on the Parliamentary register for 1886 for the numbers entitled to vote. In cases where by-elections have occurred since the general election in 1886 the statistics are given below.

COUNTY CONSTITUENCIES.

Constituency.	Population.	Number of Electors on Register.	Number of Votes Polled.	Candidates.	Party.	Members Returned.
LANCASHIRE, NORTH.						
North Lonsdale	50,338	9,219	4,063	W. G. Ainslie	C.	W. G. Ainslie
			3,263	W. M. Edmunds	G.L.	
Lancaster	53,970	8,961	3,886	J. Williamson	G.L.	J. Williamson
			3,691	Col. G. B. H. Marton	C.	
Blackpool	56,055	11,903	unopposed	Col. Rt. Hon. Sir F. A. Stanley	C.	Col. Rt. Hon. Sir F. A. Stanley [1]
Chorley	59,384	9,881	,,	Lieut.-Gen. R. J. Feilden	C.	Lieut.-Gen. R. J. Feilden
LANCASHIRE, NORTH-EAST.						
Darwen	61,092	12,629	6,085	Viscount Cranborne	C.	Viscount Cranborne
			5,350	John Slagg	G.L.	
Clitheroe	65,476	12,698	unopposed	Rt. Hon. Sir U. J. Kay-Shuttleworth	G.L.	Rt. Hon. Sir U. J. Kay-Shuttleworth
Accrington	62,721	10,797	4,971	R. T. Hermon-Hodge	C.	R. T. Hermon-Hodge
			4,751	Joseph F. Leese	G.L.	
Rossendale	69,887	11,450	5,399	Marquis of Hartington	L U.	Marquis of Hartington
			3,949	Thos. Newbigging	G.L.	
LANCASHIRE, SOUTH-EAST.						
Westhoughton	62,543	10,625	unopposed	Frank Hardcastle	C.	Frank Hardcastle
Heywood	56,254	9,269	4,206	Isaac Hoyle	G.L.	Isaac Hoyle
			3,962	J. Grant-Lawson	C.	
Middleton	67,009	11,748	5,126	T. Fielden	C.	Thomas Fielden
			4,808	C. H. Hopwood, Q.C.	G.L.	
Radcliffe-cum-Farnworth	63,086	10,433	4,695	Robert Leake	G.L.	Robert Leake
			4,559	Sir Frederick Milner, Bart.	C.	
Eccles	59,088	9,781	4,277	Hon. A. G. J. Egerton	C.	Hon. A. G. J. Egerton
			3,985	Ellis D. Gosling	G.L.	
Stretford	49,768	11,140	4,750	John William Maclure	C.	John William Maclure
			4,011	William Agnew	G.L.	
Gorton	61,960	10,334	4,592	Richard Peacock	G.L.	Richard Peacock
			4,135	Viscount Grey de Wilton	C.	
Prestwich	67,617	11,156	4,843	R. G. C. Mowbray	C.	R. G. C. Mowbray
			4,704	Abel Buckley	G.L.	
LANCASHIRE, SOUTH-WEST.						
Southport	57,643	8,437	3,723	Hon. G. N. Curzon	C.	Hon. G. N. Curzon
			3,262	Dr. G. A. Pilkington	G.L.	
Ormskirk	54,491	8,714	unopposed	A. B. Forwood	C.	A. B. Forwood
Bootle	53,167	14,663	,,	Col. T. M. Sandys	C.	Col. T. M. Sandys
Widnes	53,951	8,223	3,719	T. C. Edwardes-Moss	C.	T. C. Edwardes-Moss
			2,927	A. Birrell	G.L.	
Newton	52,816	9,344	4,302	Rt. Hon. Sir R. A. Cross, G.C.B.	C.	Right Hon. Sir Richard Assheton Cross, G.C.B. [2]
			3,486	Sir Geo. Errington, Bart.	G.L.	
Ince	52,607	9,157	4,308	Colonel Blundell	C.	Colonel Blundell
			3,228	G. P. Taylor	G.L.	
Leigh	51,816	8,572	3,297	Caleb Wright	G.L.	Caleb Wright
			3,134	W. H. Myers	C.	

[1] Accepted the Chiltern Hundreds on being created a peer. A new election August, 1886. Sir Matthew White Ridley, Bart. (C.) 6263, J. O. Pilkington (G. L.) 2,513.

[2] Accepted the Chiltern Hundreds on being created a peer. A new election August, 1886. Thos. Wodehouse Legh (C.) 4,062, D. O'C. French (G. L.) 3,355.

BOROUGH CONSTITUENCIES.

Constituency.	Population.	Number of Electors on Register.	Number of Votes Polled.	Candidates.	Party.	Members Returned.
Ashton-under-Lyne	43,630	6,553	3,050	John Addison, Q.C.	C.	John Addison, Q.C.
			3,049	Alex. Butler Rowley	G.L.	
Barrow-in-Furness	47,100	6,063	3,212	W. S. Caine	L.U.	W. S. Caine
			1,882	J. Ainsworth	G.L.	
Blackburn (2)........................	104,014	16,329	unopposed	Wm. Coddington	C.	Wm. Coddington
				Wm. Henry Hornby	C.	Wm. Henry Hornby
Bolton (2)	108,963	16,063	7,779	H. Shepherd Cross	C.	H. Shepherd Cross
			7,669	Col. Hon. F. C. Bridgeman	C.	Col. Hon. F. C. Bridgeman
			6,460	J. C. Haslam	G.L.	
			6,230	R. C. Richards	G.L.	
Burnley	63,638	9,638	4,209	Peter Rylands	L.U.	Peter Rylands [1]
			4,166	Ald. J. Greenwood	G.L.	
Bury	53,240	8,214	unopposed	Rt. Hon. Sir H. James, Q.C.	L.U.	Rt. Hon. Sir H. James, Q.C.
Liverpool, Kirkdale	69,361	8,346	3,084	G. Baden-Powell	C.	G. Baden-Powell
			2,172	Ralph Neville.................	G.L.	
„ Walton	58,201	7,683	2,872	J. G. Gibson, Q.C.	C.	J. G. Gibson, Q.C.
			1,681	C. H. Bromley	G.L.	
„ Everton	78,569	9,439	unopposed	Edward Whitley	C.	Edward Whitley
„ West Derby	67,727	8,873	3,604	Lord Claud J. Hamilton ...	C.	Lord Claud John Hamilton
			2,244	Serjeant Hemphill, Q.C. ...	G L.	
„ Scotland	70,606	7,076	2,911	T. P. O'Connor	P.	T. P. O'Connor
			1,431	A. Earle	L.U.	
„ Exchange	72,007	8,171	2,920	D. Duncan	G.L.	D. Duncan
			2,750	L. R. Baily...................	C.	
„ Abercromby.............	67,551	9,137	3,583	W. F. Lawrence.............	C.	W. F. Lawrence
			2,804	Sir Thomas Brassey	G.L.	
„ East Toxteth	52,180	8,003	unopposed	Baron H. de Worms	C.	Baron H. de Worms
„ West Toxteth	64,848	7,684		„	C.	T. B. Royden
				T. B. Royden	C.	
Manchester, North-West	67,407	12,685	5,489	W. H. Houldsworth	C.	W. H. Houldsworth
			4,453	Henry Lee	G.L.	
„ North	70,043	8,703	3,476	C. E. Schwann	G.L.	C. E. Schwann
			3,350	J. F. Hutton	C.	
„ North-East	71,067	8,579	3,680	Rt.Hon.Sir Jas. Ferguson,Bt.	C.	Rt. Hon. Sir. J. Ferguson, Bt.
			3,353	C. P. Scott	G.L.	
„ East	76,217	9,779	4,160	Rt. Hon. A. J. Balfour	C.	Rt. Hon. A. J. Balfour
			3,516	J. H. Crosfield	G.L.	
„ South	67,346	8,534	3,407	Sir Henry Roscoe	G.L.	Sir Henry Roscoe
			3,072	Lieut.-Col. Thomas Sowler..	C.	
„ South-west	72,147	8,890	3,570	Jacob Bright	G.L.	Jacob Bright
			3,459	Lord Frederick Hamilton...	C.	
Oldham (2)...........................	152,513	25,600	11,606	J. M. Maclean	C.	J. M. Maclean
			11,484	Elliott Lees	C.	Elliott Lees
			10,921	Rt. Hon. J. T. Hibbert......	G.L.	
			10,891	J. M. Cheetham.............	G.L.	
Preston (2)...........................	100,262	14,876	7,491	W. E. M. Tomlinson	C.	W. E. M. Tomlinson
			7,276	R. W. Hanbury..............	C.	R. W. Hanbury
			4,982	Capt. Pilkington	G.L.	
			4,771	George Potter	G.L.	
Rochdale...........	68,866	10,808	4,738	Thomas Bayley Potter	G.L.	Thomas Bayley Potter
			3,481	J. A. R. Marriott	C.	
Salford, North	56,355	7,728	3,327	Edward Hardcastle	C.	Edward Hardcastle
			3,168	Arthur Arnold	G.L.	
„ West.....................	54,397	8,197	3,399	Lees Knowles.................	C.	Lees Knowles
			3,283	Benjamin Armitage	G.L.	
„ South	65,483	8,717	3,645	Henry Hoyle Howorth	C.	Henry Hoyle Howorth
			3,488	William Mather..............	G.L.	
St. Helens	57,403	8,291	3,621	H. Seton-Karr	C.	H. Seton-Karr
			3,404	A. Sinclair	G.L.	
Warrington.....	45,253	7,730	3,717	Sir Gilbert Greenall, Bt. ...	C.	Sir Gilbert Greenall, Bt.
			3,216	J. Crosfield...................	G.L.	
Wigan...........	48,194	6,988	3,371	Francis Sharpe Powell	C.	Francis Sharpe Powell
			2,780	C. M. L. Percy	G.L.	

[1] On the death of Peter Rylands a new writ issued Feb. 14, 1887. John Slagg (H.R), 5,026 ; J. O. S. Thursby (C.), 4,481.

APPENDIX VIII.

THE CHETHAM SOCIETY.

THIS Society has added so largely to the available historical materials relating to the counties of Lancaster and Chester, that a history of Lancashire would be incomplete without some reference to its labours and to those by whom they have been carried on. It was commenced in the year 1843 by a private proprietary of three hundred and fifty members, for the purpose of publishing in a continuous yearly series the "Historical and Literary Remains connected with the Palatine Counties of Lancaster and Chester," of which rich MS. treasures were known to be in existence. Its first president was the late Dr. Edward Holme, M.D.; but for many years the mainspring of its activity was the late James Crossley, Esq., of Manchester, who, on Dr. Holme's death, was chosen the president, a position he continued to occupy until his decease, August 1st, 1883, when the Worshipful Richard Copley Christie, M.A., chancellor of the diocese of Manchester, was elected his successor. The members of the first council in 1843 were as follows: Edward Holme, Esq., M.D.; Rev. Richard Parkinson, B.D., Canon of Manchester; The Hon. and Very Rev. William Herbert, Dean of Manchester; George Ormerod, Esq., LL.D., F.R.S., F.S.A., F.G.S.; Samuel Hibbert-Ware, Esq., M.D., F.R.S.E.; Rev. Thomas Corser, M.A.; Rev. George Dugard, M.A.; Rev. C. G. Hulton, M.A.; Rev. J. Piccope, M.A.; Rev. F. R. Raines, M.A.; James Crossley, Esq.; James Heywood, Esq., F.R.S.; William Langton, Esq.: William Fleming, Esq., M.D. The following are the members of the council for the year 1887-8: The Worshipful Richard Copley Christie, M.A., chancellor of the diocese of Manchester (president); The Right Rev. the Lord Bishop of Chester, D.D. (vice-president); James Croston, Esq., F.S.A.; J. P. Earwaker, Esq., M.A., F.S.A.; Lieut-Colonel Fishwick, F.S.A.; Henry H. Howorth, F.S.A., M.P.; Rev. John Howard Marsden, B.D., F.R.G.S., late Disney Professor; Rev. James Rayne, M.A., Canon of York; Frank Renaud, Esq., M.D., F.S.A.; J. P. Rylands, Esq., F.S.A.; Rev. Richard Tonge, M.A., hon. canon of Manchester; A. W. Ward, Esq., Lit.D., M.A.; J. Joseph Jordan, Esq. (treasurer); John E. Bailey, Esq., F.S.A. (hon. secretary). The best testimony to the value of their labours will be found in the following list of the publications of the Society (comprised in one hundred and twenty-five volumes) which have already appeared:—

PUBLICATIONS.

Travels of Sir William Brereton, 1634-5. Edited by Edward Hawkins, F.R.S., &c. (1)

Civil War Tracts of Lancashire, 1641-51. Edited by George Ormerod, D.C.L., &c. (2)

Chester's Triumph, an old play performed in 1610. Edited by Rev. Thomas Corser M.A. (3)

Life of Adam Martindale. Edited by Canon Parkinson (4)

Lancashire Memorials of the Rebellion in 1715. Edited by Samuel Hibbert-Ware, M.D., &c. (5)

Pott's Discovery of Witches (of 1613). Edited by James Crossley (6)

Iter Lancastrense, a poem of Rev. Richard James in 1636. Edited by Rev. Thomas Corser, M.A. (7)

Notitia Cestriensis: Bishop Gastrell's notes on the parishes in the diocese of Chester, 1720-23. Edited by Canon Raines. Vol. I. (Cheshire) pp. i.-xvi. and 1-396 (8.) Vol. II. (Lancashire) Part I. 1-160 (19.) Part II. 161-351 (21.) Part III. (with Index) 353-621 (22.)

The Norris Papers. Edited by Thomas Heywood, F.S.A. (9)

Coucher Book (or Chartulary) of Whalley Abbey. Edited by W. A. Hulton. Vol. I. pp. i.-xl. and 1-338 (10.) Vol. II. p. 339-636 (11.) Vol. III. pp. 637-936 (16.) Vol. IV. pp. 937-1314 (20)

The Moore Rental [of estates in Liverpool in 1667]. Edited by Thomas Heywood, F.S.A. (12)

Dr. John Worthington's Diary, &c. Edited by James Crossley. Vol. I. pp. i.-viii. and 1-398 (13.) Vol. II., Part I., pp. 1-248 (36.) Vol. II. Part II. Edited by Chancellor Christie. pp. xii. 249-384; Index 15 (114)

Nicholas Assheton's Journal. Edited by Canon Raines (14)

The Holy Lyfe and History of Saynt Werburge. Edited by Edward Hawkins (15)

Warrington in 1465 [an old Rent-roll of the Legh family]. Edited by William Beamont (17)

Rev. Henry Newcome's Diary, 1661-1663. Edited by Thomas Heywood, F.S.A. (18)

A Golden Mirrour, from the original edition of 1589. Edited by Rev. Thomas Corser, M.A., &c. (23)

Chetham Miscellanies, Vol. I. (24.) [Other volumes are 37, 57, 83, 96, and 103.]
  Papers connected with Milton and his family. Edited by J. F. Marsh. 46 pp.
  Epistolary Reliques of Lancashire and Cheshire Antiquaries, 1653-73. Communicated by George Ormerod. 16 pp.
  Calendars of the Heraldic Visitations in Lancashire. By George Ormerod. 26 pp.
  A fragment illustrative of Sir William Dugdale's Visitation. From Canon Raines. 8 pp.

Card. Allen's Defence of Sir William Stanley's Surrender of Deventer. Edited by Thomas Heywood, F.S.A. (25)

Newcome's Autobiography. Edited by Canon Parkinson. Vol. I. pp. i.-xxv. and 1-184 (26.) Vol. II. pp. 185-390 (27)

The Jacobite Trials of 1694 in Manchester. Edited by William Beamont. (28.) [See also 61.]

The Stanley Papers. Part I. the Earls of Derby and the poets of the sixteenth and seventeenth centuries. By Thomas Heywood, F.S.A. (29)
  Part II. The Derby Household Book, 1586-1590. Edited by Canon Raines (31)
  Part III., Vol. I. Papers, &c., of James, seventh Earl of Derby (66.) Part III., Vol. II. (67.) Part III., Vol. III. (70)

Penwortham Priory Documents. Edited by W. A. Hulton (30)

John Byrom's Journal and Literary Remains. Edited by Canon Parkinson. Vol. I. Part I. pp. 1-320 (32.) Vol. I. Part II. pp. 321-639 (34.) Vol. II. Part I. pp. 1-326, and two Indexes (40.) Vol. II. Part II. pp. 327-654 (44)

Lancashire and Cheshire Wills and Inventories. Edited by Rev. G. J. Piccope, M.A. Part I. (33.) Part II. (51.) Part III. (54)

The Shuttleworths; House and Farm Accounts of Gawthorpe Hall. Edited by John Harland, F.S.A. Part I. pp. 1-232 (35.) Part II. pp. 233-472 (41.) Part III. pp. 473-776 (43.) Part IV. pp. 777-1171 (46)

Chetham Miscellanies, Vol. II. Edited by William Langton (37)
  Rights and Jurisdiction of the County Palatine, &c. Edited by J. B. Yates, F.A.S., &c., 37 pp.
  The Scottish Field, a poem of Flodden, 28 pp. Edited by John Robson.
  Examynatyon towcheynge Cokeye More, *temp.* Henry VIII., 30 pp. Communicated by Canon Raines.
  A History of the Ancient Chapel of Denton. By the Rev. John Booker, M.A., 148 pp.
  A Letter from John Bradshawe of Gray's Inn to Sir Peter Legh of Lyme. Edited by W. Langton.

Turton and Gorton Church Libraries. Edited by Gilbert J. French (38)

The Farington Papers. Edited by Miss ffarington (39)

A History of the Ancient Chapels of Didsbury and Chorlton. By Rev. John Booker, M.A. (42)

Memoir and Selections from Poems, &c., of Rev. Thomas Wilson of Clitheroe. By Canon Raines (45)

A History of the Ancient Chapel of Birch. By Rev. John Booker, M.A. (47)

Catalogue of Popery Tracts, temp. circa James II. Edited by Thomas Jones, B.A. Part I. (48.) Part II. (64.)

Lancashire Lieutenancy Papers, under the Tudors and Stuarts. By John Harland, F.S.A. Part I. pp. i.-cxx and 1-96 (49.) Part II. pp. 97-333 (50)

Collectanea Anglo-Poetica. By Rev. Thomas Corser, M.A., &c. Part I. pp. 1-208 (52.) Part II. pp. 209-456 (55.) Part III. pp. i.-x., 1-282 (71.) Part IV. pp. vi., 283-542 (77.) Part V. pp. xi., 250 (91.) Part VI. pp. xi., 251-471 (100.) Part VII. pp. viii., 208 (101.) Part VIII. pp. viii, 209-430 (102.) Part IX. pp. ix., 208 (106.) Part X. pp. 209-342 (108.) Part XI. pp. xii., 343-440 ; Contents 19 ; General Index 37 (111)

Mamecestre. Edited by John Harland, F.S.A. Vol. I. pp. 1-207. (53.) Vol. II. pp. 209-431 (56.) Vol. III. p. 433-627 (58)

Chetham Miscellanies, Vol. III. Edited by William Langton (57)
> On the South Lancashire Dialect, with Biographical Notices of John Collier (*Tim Bobbin.*) By Thos. Heywood, F.S.A., 84 pp.
> Rentale de Cokersand for the year 1501. Edited by Canon Raines. xviii. 46 pp.
> The Names of all the Gentlemen of the best Callinge wthin the Countye of Lancastre, whereof choyse ya to be made of a c'ten number to lend vnto her Matye moneye vpon privie seals in Janvarye 1588. From a MS. in the possession of Canon Raines. 9 pp.
> Some Instruction given by William Booth Esquire to his stewards John Carington and William Rowcrofte, upon the purchase of Warrington by Sir George Booth Baronet and William Booth his Son, A.D. MDCXVIII. Communicated by William Beamont. 8 pp.
> Letter from Sir John Seton, Manchester ye 25 M'ch, 1643. Edited by Thomas Heywood, F.S.A. 15 pp.
> The Names of eight hundred inhabitants of Manchester who took the oath of allegiance to Charles II. in April 1679. Communicated by John Harland, F.S.A. 8 pp.
> The Pole Booke of Manchester, May ye 22d 1690. Edited by William Langton. 43 pp.

History of Lancashire Chantries. Edited by Canon Raines. Vol. I. pp. i.-xxxix., and 1-168 (59.) Vol. II. (60)

Abbot's Journal ; also Account of the Tryalls in Manchester in 1694. Edited by Right Rev. Alexander Goss, D.D. (61)

Discourse of the Warr in Lancashire. Edited by Wm. Beamont (62)

Manchester Court Leet Records, Sixteenth Century. Edited by John Harland. (63.) Continuation of the same, 1586-1602 (65)

Manchester Collectanea. By John Harland. Vol. I. (68.) Vol. II. (72)

Manchester School : Admission Register. Edited by Rev. J. F. Smith, M.A. Vol. I. 1730-1755 (69.) Vol. II. 1776-1807 (73) Vol. III., Part I. pp. vi., 176 (93.) Vol. III., Part II. pp. 177-348 ; Index 19 (94)

Three Lancashire Documents. Edited by John Harland, F.S.A. (74), viz.—
> The Great De Lacy Inquisition, 1311.
> Survey of 1320-46.
> Custom Roll and Rental of the Manor of Ashton-under-Lyne, 1421.

Lancashire Funeral Certificates. Edited by Thomas William King, F.S.A., and Canon Raines (75)

Robert Heywood's Observations and Instructions, Divine and Morall, circa 1630. Edited by James Crossley (76)

Tracts written in the Controversy respecting the Legitimacy of Amicia, daughter of Hugh Cyveliok, Earl of Chester, A.D. 1673-1679. Edited by William Beamont. Part I. pp. xcv., 94 (78.) Part II. pp. 95-322 (79.) Part III. pp. 323-550 (80)

The Visitation of the County Palatine of Lancaster, made in the year 1567, by William Flower, Norroy king of arms. Edited by Canon Raines. xvi. 141 pp. (81)

The Visitation of the County Palatine of Lancaster, made in the year 1613, by Richard St. George, Norroy king of arms. Edited by Canon Raines. xx. 142 pp. (82)

The Visitation of the County Palatine of Lancaster, made in the year 1664-5, by Sir William Dugdale, Knt., Norroy king of arms. Edited by Canon Raines. Part I. pp. xiv., 104 (84.) Part II. pp. 105-224 (85.) Part III. pp. 225-344 ; Index 17 (88)

Annals of the Lords of Warrington for the first five centuries after the Conquest. Edited by William Beamont. Part I. pp. xxvi., 262 (86.) Part II. pp. 263-523 ; Index 11 (87)

The Dr. Farmer Chetham MS., temp. Elizabeth, James I. and Charles I. Edited by Rev. Alexander B. Grosart. Part I. pp. xvi. 120. (89.) Part II. pp. 121-225 (90)

The History of the Parish of Kirkham. By Henry Fishwick, F.R.H.S. vii. 208 pp. ; Appendix 3 ; Index 18 (92)

Abstracts of Inquisitions post mortem, made by Christopher Townley and Roger Dodsworth. Edited by William Langton. viii, 160 pp. ; Index 16 (95.) Vol. II. pp. vii. 188 ; Index 17 (99)

Contributions towards a History of the Ancient Parish of Prestbury, in Cheshire. By Frank Renaud, M.D. viii. 238 pp. ; Index 6 (97)

The Visitation of Lancashire and a Part of Cheshire, made in 1533, by special commission of Thomas Benalt, Clarencieux. Edited by William Langton. xviii. 104 pp. (98.) Part II. pp. x. 105-233 ; Index 27 (110)

The History of the Parish of Garstang. By Col. Henry Fishwick, F.S.A. Part I. pp. vii. 140 (104.) Part II. pp. 141-277 ; Appendix 2 ; Index 20 (105)

Inventories of Goods in the Churches and Chapels of Lancashire, taken in the year 1552. Edited by John Eglington Bailey, F.S.A. Part I., Salford Hundred, pp. ii. 54. (107.) Part II. [in the press.] (113)

Correspondence of Nathan Walworth and Peter Seddon, of Outwood, and other Documents relating to the building of Ringley Chapel. Edited by John Samuel Fletcher. xxix. 89 pp. ; Appendix 15 ; Index 4 (109)

Two "Compoti" of the Lancashire and Cheshire Manors of Henry de Lacy, Earl of Lincoln. xxiv. and xxxiii. Edward I. Transcribed and Translated by Rev. P. A. Lyons, B.A. xxviii. 192 pp. ; Index 8 (112)

Of the first thirty volumes of this series a General Index was published (not numbered amongst the series) in 1863.

General Index to volumes 31 to 114 (excluding Corser's Collectanea Anglo-Poetica). Edited by W. E. A. Axon. (In the press.)

THE RECORD SOCIETY.

This society was founded in 1878, and has for its object the transcribing and publishing of original documents relating to the Counties of Lancaster and Chester. The members of the first Council were *James Crossley, Esq., F.S.A.* (President), *William Beamont; Esq.* (Vice-President), R. C. Christie, M.A. (Vice-President), James Croston, Esq., F.S.A. (Vice-President), Lieut.-Col. Fishwick, F.S.A. (Vice-President), *George Little, Q.C.* (Vice-President), W. Alexander, Abram, *Col. J. L. Chester, LL.D.,* G. E. Cokayne, M.A., F.S.A., Henry H. Howorth, F.S.A., Thomas Hughes, F.S.A., J. Paul Rylands, F.S.A. (Hon. Treasurer), J. P. Earwaker, M.A., F.S.A. (Hon. Sec.). Of these gentlemen, those in italics have either died or retired from the Council, and on the death of Mr. Crossley, in 1883, the Worshipful Chancellor Christie was chosen the President ; and on the list of the Council for the year 1886-7 there are in addition to the nine original members remaining, the Hon. and Rev. G. T. O. Bridgeman (Vice-President), Sir H. Fox Bristowe, Q.C. (Vice-President), J. Eglington Bailey, F.S.A., and the Rev. J. H. Stanning, M.A. The following are the publications of the society (comprised in thirteen volumes), which have already appeared :—

₊ Among the APPENDICES to the original edition were two collections of imperfect abstracts of the Oliverian Survey of Church Lands in 1650, and of Dr. Ducarel's Repertory of the Endowment of Vicarages 1779, from the MSS. in the Lambeth Library. The complete text of the Lancashire and Cheshire Church Surveys, 1649-1655, edited for the Record Society by Colonel Fishwick, and the fuller extracts given by Canon Raines in his edition of the *Notitia Cestriensis,* and now embodied, for the most part, in the parish histories of the present work, do away with the special value of these, and they are not reprinted.

APPENDIX IX.

POPULATION OF LANCASHIRE, ITS PARISHES, TOWNSHIPS, &c.,

In 1801, 1811, 1821, 1831, 1841, 1851, 1861, 1871, and 1881.

The nine official censuses of the population of the United Kingdom in the above years furnish the data for ascertaining the increase or otherwise in the numbers of the people in eight decennial periods, the first five of which compose the first half of the nineteenth century. In this place our attention must chiefly be confined within the limits of the county palatine of Lancaster. Perhaps one of the most remarkable features in the official returns for the half century is the great increase in the population of Lancashire, both absolutely *per se*, and comparatively as regards the other most populous counties of England. The population of the entire county in 1801 was 673,486 persons (322,722 males and 350,764 females). The population in 1881 had risen to 3,454,441 persons (1,669,864 males and 1,784,577 females), being an increase in the eighty years of 2,780,955 persons (1,347,142 males and 1,433,813 females). In other words, the population of Lancashire increased in the first eighty years of the present century nearly *four hundred and thirteen per cent.* In eighty years it had increased its numbers more than fivefold. Compare this vast increase with the two next populous counties, Middlesex (small in area, but including so large a portion of the metropolis) and Yorkshire (the largest and one of the most thickly-peopled counties), and what are the results? In 1801, Middlesex had a population of 818,129; Yorkshire of 859,133; Lancashire had then a smaller population than either by 150,000 to 180,000. In 1881 the population of Middlesex was 2,920,485, and that of Yorkshire 2,886,564; so that in actual numbers, within its borders, Lancashire exceeded Middlesex in 1881 by 533,956 persons, or contained a population more than 18 per cent. in excess of that of the metropolitan county. Lancashire had a larger population than Yorkshire in 1881 by 567,877, though Yorkshire has more than thrice the area of Lancashire (Yorkshire, 3,829,286; Lancashire, 1,219,220 statute acres). In other words, while the population of Middlesex increased in the eighty years 256 per cent, and that of Yorkshire 235 per cent, that of Lancashire increased 413 per cent. The statistics of the cotton trade and manufacture show that this vast increase is mainly if not wholly due to the rapid growth and progress of this great staple industry. The population of the county of Lancaster in the seven periods named is returned as follows in the official censuses :—

	1801.	1811.	1821.	1831.	1841.	1851.	1861.	1871.	1881.
Persons	673,486	828,499	1,052,948	1,336,854	1,667,054	2,031,236	2,429,440	2,849,259	3,454,441
Males..	322,722	394,194	512,524	650,389	814,847	991,090	1,173,424	1,372,664	1,669,864
Females.	350,764	434,305	540,424	686,465	852,207	1,040,146	1,256,016	1,476,595	1,784,577

INCREASE IN THE INTERVALS OF CENSUS.

	1801 to 1811.	1811 to 1821.	1821 to 1831.	1831 to 1841.	1841 to 1851.	1851 to 1861.	1861 to 1871.	1871 to 1881.
Persons	155,013	224,449	283,906	330,200	364,182	398,204	419,819	605,182
Males	71,472	118,330	137,865	164,458	176,243	182,334	199,240	297,200
Females	83,541	106,119	146,041	165,742	187,939	215,870	220,579	307,982

RATES OF INCREASE (PER CENT) DECENNIAL PERIODS 1801-1881.

22	27	27	24	22	20	17	21

The following table exhibits the area, houses, and number of persons of each sex in the county in each of its six hundreds, and in its Parliamentary and municipal boroughs, on the night of the 8th of April, 1881 :—

COUNTY OF LANCASTER, April 8, 1881.

Area.	Houses.			Population.		
Statute Acres.	Inhabited.	Un-inhabited.	Building.	Persons.	Males.	Females.
1,219,220	655,307	68,929	5,697	3,454,441	1,669,864	1,784,577

PARLIAMENTARY DIVISIONS, EXCLUSIVE OF PARLIAMENTARY BOROUGHS.

	Area in Acres.	Houses.			Population.		
		Inhabited.	Uninhabited.	Building.	Persons.	Males.	Females.
North Lancashire	536,209	49,657	3,776	418	273,389	137,365	136,024
North-East Lancashire	159,571	48,553	4,173	637	238,355	114,550	123,805
South-East Lancashire	187,929	105,688	13,769	896	534,435	254,483	279,952
South-West Lancashire	250,263	86,785	9,762	1,326	482,436	235,592	246,844

PARLIAMENTARY BOROUGHS.

	Area in Acres.	Houses.			Population.		
		Inhabited.	Uninhabited.	Building.	Persons.	Males.	Females.
Preston (Northern Division)	2,820	18,905	1,805	182	93,720	42,986	50,734
Blackburn (North-Eastern Division)...	4,065	19,412	1,562	245	100,620	47,483	53,137
Burnley	3,981	12,530	657	93	63,638	30,837	32,801
Clitheroe	16,032	2,955	172	49	14,472	6,967	7,505
[1] Ashton-under-Lyne, part of (South Eastern Division)	2,145	8,943	724	74	43,424	20,399	23,025
Bolton (South-Eastern Division...	2,362	21,060	1,624	64	105,965	50,236	55,629
Bury „ ...	3,652	10,107	548	92	50,178	23,799	26,379
Manchester City „ ...	6,359	77,529	8,809	234	393,585	189,005	204,580
Oldham „ ...	12,310	31,019	2,644	247	152,513	73,292	79,221
Rochdale „ ...	4,172	15,016	1,781	14	68,866	31,985	36,881
Salford „ ...	5,170	34,206	4,493	217	176,235	84,610	91,625
[1] Stalybridge, part of „	349	1,343	195	11	6,401	3,089	3,312
[1] Stockport, part of „ ...	480	3,158	356	14	14,550	6,699	7,851
Liverpool City, South-Western Division	5,210	92,307	10,294	816	552,508	271,996	280,512
[1] Warrington, part of (South-Western Division)	2,887	7,376	482	23	40,957	20,883	20,074
Wigan	2,188	8,767	1,303	45	48,194	23,508	24,686
Total	1,208,154	655,807	68,929	5,697	3,454,441	1,669,864	1,784,577

Under the Poor-Law Registration Acts, the county has been formed into a number of clusters or groups of adjacent parishes and townships, called Registration Districts, numbered consecutively 453 to 482. Of these districts the following table exhibits the area in statute acres, and the population (males and females) in the years 1871 and 1881 :—

AREA AND POPULATION OF REGISTRATION DISTRICTS IN 1871 AND 1881.

No.	Districts.	Area in Statute Acres.	Population.					
			Persons.		Males.		Females.	
			1871.	1881.	1871.	1881.	1871.	1881.
453	Liverpool	2,470	238,411	210,164	116,777	104,290	121,634	105,874
454	Toxteth Park	3,598	85,842	117,028	40,817	55,341	45,025	61,687
455	West Derby	97,479	257,083	359,273	122,195	174,164	134,888	185,108
456	Prescot	55,592	92,551	117,960	47,161	60,932	45,390	67,028
457	Ormskirk	90,662	59,310	83,212	27,794	38,380	31,516	44,832
458	Wigan	48,398	111,874	139,918	56,331	70,460	55,543	69,458
459	Warrington	31,168	54,394	70,218	27,797	36,084	26,597	34,134
460	Leigh	24,356	41,924	56,318	20,340	27,655	21,584	28,663
461	Bolton	46,426	158,408	192,405	75,841	91,985	82,567	100,420
462	Bury	33,527	109,155	129,608	52,111	61,645	57,044	67,963
463	Barton-upon-Irwell	24,555	51,571	72,815	23,968	33,973	27,603	38,842
464	Chorlton	11,697	211,384	258,226	100,278	122,027	111,106	136,199
465	Salford	6,040	128,890	181,526	61,291	87,199	67,671	94,327
466	Manchester	1,646	173,985	148,794	83,426	72,005	90,562	76,789
467	Prestwich	11,348	77,968	121,287	36,956	58,321	41,012	62,966
468	Ashton-under-Lyne	38,563	130,626	154,526	61,271	73,205	69,355	81,321
469	Oldham	17,104	126,982	168,461	61,414	81,008	65,568	87,453
470	Rochdale	34,822	109,858	121,912	52,249	57,305	57,609	64,607
471	Haslingden	26,712	79,955	95,293	38,252	45,461	41,704	49,829
472	Burnley	63,672	87,809	118,334	42,716	57,319	45,093	61,015
473	Clitheroe	119,226	21,081	23,502	10,544	11,831	10,537	11,671
474	Blackburn	45,855	143,810	175,954	68,379	83,617	75,431	92,337
475	Chorley	54,456	43,004	47,730	20,880	23,044	22,124	24,686
476	Preston	67,539	115,846	129,160	54,327	60,325	61,519	68,885
477	Fylde	59,032	30,626	40,910	14,401	19,318	16,225	21,592
478	Garstang	61,115	12,186	12,375	6,320	6,374	5,866	6,001
479	Lancaster	62,498	32,661	40,838	16,051	20,262	16,610	20,576
480	Lunesdale	75,734	6,978	7,132	3,546	3,568	3,432	3,564
481	Ulverston	141,124	36,172	43,681	18,401	22,229	17,771	21,452
482	Barrow-in-Furness	16,967	18,911	47,259	10,902	25,575	8,009	21,684

The whole of these areas either include water or relate to parishes to which a portion of the tidal water or foreshore of contiguous rivers or creeks has been allotted, though not included within the boundaries thereof by the Ordnance Survey Department.

[1] These Parliamentary boroughs are situated partly in Cheshire. Their entire areas and populations are as follows—Ashton-under-Lyne: area 2,149, population 43,480. Stalybridge: area 2,214, population 39,671. Stockport: area 2,200, population 59,553. Warrington: area 3,783, population 45,254.

The aggregate rateable value on the 25th March, 1886, was, for county assessment, £18,623,910 ; for police assessment, £8,783,444. Received for the year, by county rate (2½d.), £167,980 ; by police rate (2·6471d.), £96,880. Total receipts, £439,777 ; total expenditure, £434,222. Amount of loans outstanding March 25th, 1886, £699,699.

What may be called the vital statistics of the county in its various poor-law unions are furnished by the following official return of the aggregate number of marriages, births, and deaths registered in each of the superintendent registrars' districts in Lancashire[1] in the ten years 1871-80, the excess of registered births over deaths, and the increase or decrease of population in the interval of the censuses of 1871 and 1881 :—

No.	Parish or Union.	Population 1871.	Population 1881.	Registered in the Ten Years 1871-1880. Marriages.	Births.	Deaths.	Excess of Registered Births over Deaths. 1871-80.	Increase or Decrease of Population between the Censuses of 1871 & 1881. Increase.	Decrease.
453	Liverpool	238,411	210,164	33,468	78,670	75,291	3,379		28,247
454	Toxteth Park	85,842	117,028 }	31,055	157,200	95,651	61,549	{ 31,186	
455	West Derby	257,083	359,273 }					{ 102,190[2]	
456	Prescot	92,551	117,960	7,601	44,529	24,126	20,403	25,409	
457	Ormskirk	59,310	83,212	5,136	23,866	14,690	9,176	23,902	
458	Wigan	111,871	139,918	10,917	57,623	32,445	25,178	28,044	
459	Warrington	54,394	70,218	5,044	25,614	13,841	11,773	15,824	
460	Leigh	41,924	56,318	4,107	20,144	11,618	8,526	14,394	
461	Bolton	158,408	192,405	15,202	68,755	42,687	26,068	33,997	
462	Bury	109,155	129,608	10,599	43,432	28,074	15,358	20,453	
463	Barton-upon-Irwell	51,571	72,815	4,500	21,895	13,056	8,839	21,244	
464	Chorlton	211,384	258,226	15,713	89,245	55,473	33,772	46,842	
465	Salford	128,890	181,526	12,820	65,798	42,909	22,889	52,636	
466	Manchester	173,988	148,794 }	37,316	102,867	79,433	23,434	{	25,194
467	Prestwich	77,968	121,787 }					{ 43,819	
468	Ashton-under-Lyne	130,616	154,526	12,716	53,929	35,954	17,975	43,900	
469	Oldham	126,982	168,461	12,274	55,653	37,077	18,576	41,479	
470	Rochdale	109,878	121,912	9,844	46,510	27,174	13,336	12,054	
471	Haslingden	79,956	95,293	8,067	32,071	19,385	12,686	15,337	
472	Burnley	87,809	118,334	9,336	39,271	24,115	15,156	30,525	
473	Clitheroe	21,081	23,502	1,712	7,192	4,511	2,681	2,421	
474	Blackburn	143,810	175,954	13,730	62,836	40,427	22,409	32,144	
475	Chorley	43,004	47,730	3,530	17,100	10,262	6,838	4,726	
476	Preston	115,846	129,160	10,789	46,384	34,358	12,026	13,314	
477	Fylde	30,626	40,910	2,845	12,102	7,602	4,500	10,284	
478	Garstang	12,186	12,375	858	3,855	2,192	1,663	189	
479	Lancaster	32,661	40,838	2,971	11,979	8,369	3,610	8,177	
480	Lunesdale	6,978	7,132	284	2,042	1,266	776	154	
481	Ulverston	36,172	43,681 }	6,014	31,398	15,176	16,222[4]	{ 7,509	
482	Barrow-in-Furness	18,911	47,259 }					{ 28,348	

The foregoing tables represent the aggregate population of certain populous areas and places. The following table exhibits the number of inhabited houses, the families or separate occupiers, and the population of every civil parish or township in Lancashire, enumerated in the official census in 1881, with the poor law unions in which they are respectively situated :—

INHABITED HOUSES, FAMILIES OR SEPARATE OCCUPIERS, AND POPULATION OF THE CIVIL PARISHES OR TOWNSHIPS.

(By "civil parish or township" is meant a place in which a poor rate is separately levied. In cases where an ancient parish consists of two or more civil parishes, they are indented under the name of the ancient parish. The figures in the last column are the reference numbers of the registration district.)

Civil Parish or Township.	Inhabited Houses.	Families or Separate Occupiers.	Population.	Poor Law Union in which situate.
Aldingham	210	212	1,152	Ulverston, 481.
Altcar	87	96	550	Ormskirk, 457.
Angerton	4	4	32	Ulverston, 481.
Ashton-in-Makerfield ancient parish—				
Ashton-in-Makerfield	1,730	2,128	9,824	Wigan, 458.
Haydock	1,002	1,058	5,863	Warrington, 459.
Ashton-under-Lyne	15,418	16,108	75,310	Ashton-under-Lyne, 468.
Aughton	628	657	3,145	Ormskirk, 457.

[1] By a Parliamentary return issued in 1867, it appears that in Lancashire the average annual rate of mortality per 1,000 living was, in 1841, 50·28 ; in 1851, 60·26 ; in 1855, 26·8 ; in 1865, 28·3. It further appears that, in this county, the proportional numbers of men and women to 100 marriages that signed the marriage register with marks were as follow : In 1855—men 33·2, women 59·2 ; in 1865—men 24·4, women 46·1.

[2] The civil parish of Toxteth formed part of the West Derby District until 1st January, 1881. The marriages, births, deaths, and excess of births over deaths in the two districts of West Derby and Toxteth Park are shown together.

[3] The Union and District of Prestwich formed part of Manchester District until 1st October, 1874. The marriages, births, deaths, and excess of births over deaths registered in the two unions and districts of Manchester and Prestwich are here shown together.

[4] The District of Barrow-in-Furness (consisting of the civil parish of Barrow-in-Furness, as extended by the Barrow-in-Furness Corporation Act 1875) formed part of the district of Ulverston prior to July, 1876. The marriages, births, deaths, and excess of births over deaths registered in the two districts of Ulverston and Barrow-in-Furness are here shown together.

INHABITED HOUSES, &c.—*continued*.

Civil Parish or Township.	Inhabited Houses.	Families or Separate Occupiers.	Population.	Poor Law Union in which situate.
Bispham ancient parish—				
Bispham-with-Norbreck	133	134	714	} Fylde, 477.
Layton-with-Warbreck	2,645	2,714	12,711	
Blackburn ancient parish—				
Balderston	107	107	487	
Billington	285	294	1,410	
Blackburn	17,673	18,449	91,958	} Blackburn, 474.
Clayton-in-le-Dale	62	69	295	
Cuerdale	9	9	58	Preston, 476.
Darwen, Lower	920	928	4,531	
Darwen, Over	5,557	5,847	27,626	
Dinckley	22	25	123	
Eccleshill	146	155	716	
Harwood, Great	1,237	1,383	6,287	
Harwood, Little	137	139	715	
Livesey	1,176	1,301	6,065	} Blackburn, 474.
Mellor	243	243	1,096	
Osbaldeston	40	46	154	
Pleasington	89	99	459	
Ramsgreave	54	54	240	
Rishton	720	752	4,055	
Salesbury	50	67	184	
Samlesbury	158	166	752	Preston, 476.
Tockholes	107	108	484	Blackburn, 474.
Walton-in-le-Dale	1,840	1,992	9,286	Preston, 476.
Wilpshire	53	58	280	} Blackburn, 474.
Witton	901	979	4,356	
Bolton-le-Moors ancient parish—				
Anglezarke	21	21	99	Chorley, 475.
Blackrod	766	774	4,234	Wigan, 458.
Bolton, Great	8,919	10,113	45,694	
Bolton, Little	9,007	9,361	44,452	
Bradshaw	186	155	755	
Breightmet	316	316	1,525	
Edgeworth	341	358	1,862	
Entwisle	68	69	341	
Harwood	397	408	1,811	} Bolton, 461.
Lever, Darcy	430	441	1,994	
Lever, Little	857	900	4,413	
Longworth	22	23	106	
Lostock	149	166	782	
Quarlton	51	51	271	
Rivington	69	70	330	Chorley, 475.
Sharples	769	784	3,710	
Tonge-with-Haulgh	1,806	1,496	6,731	} Bolton, 461.
Turton	1,158	1,228	5,653	
Bolton-le-Sands ancient parish—				
Bolton-le-Sands	176	182	785	Lancaster, 479.
Kellet, Nether	57	59	279	
Kellet, Over	94	100	494	} Lunesdale, 480.
Llyne-with-Hest	66	66	301	Lancaster, 479.
Brindle	237	256	1,173	Chorley, 475.
Burton-in-Kendal ancient parish, *part of* [1]—				
Dalton	19	19	123	Kendal, 579.
Bury ancient parish—				
Bury	8,071	8,613	39,288	Bury, 462.
Coupe-Lench, Newhallhey, and Hall Carr	775	808	3,695	Haslingden, 471.
Elton	2,262	2,513	11,947	
Heap	3,837	3,972	17,686	} Bury, 462.
Musbury	221	236	1,010	} Haslingden, 471.
Tottington Higher End	790	825	3,926	
Tottington Lower End	3,336	3,421	16,428	} Bury, 462.
Walmersley-cum-Shuttleworth	1,140	1,150	5,519	
Cartmel ancient parish—				
Allithwaite, Lower	204	219	975	
Allithwaite, Upper	162	165	713	
Broughton, East	208	254	1,251	
Cartmel Fell	59	59	293	} Ulverston, 481.
Holker, Lower	233	233	1,093	
Holker, Upper	169	178	849	
Staveley	79	79	426	

[1] Burton-in-Kendal ancient parish is mostly in Westmorland. The entire parish contains 2,158 persons.

INHABITED HOUSES, &c.—*continued.*

Civil Parish or Township.	Inhabited Houses.	Families or Separate Occupiers.	Population.	Poor Law Union in which situate.
Childwall ancient parish—				
Allerton ...	145	145	830	⎫
Childwall	27	31	187	⎬ West Derby, 455.
Garston	1,750	1,898	10,271	⎭
Hale	120	120	571	⎫
Halewood	335	372	1,857	⎬ Prescot, 456.
Speke	96	96	513	⎭
Wavertree	2,050	2,225	11,097	West Derby, 455.
Woolton, Little	197	225	1,159	⎫ Prescot, 456
Woolton, Much	907	1,020	4,541	⎭
Chipping ancient parish—				
Chipping	200	220	987	⎫ Clitheroe, 473.
Thornley-with-Wheatley	74	79	349	⎭
Chorley	3,812	3,363	19,178	Chorley, 475.
Claughton	17	19	100	Lunesdale, 480.
Clitheroe Castle	1	1	16	Clitheroe, 473.
Cockerham ancient parish—				
Cockerham	123	127	761	⎫ Lancaster, 479.
Ellel	353	360	1,787	⎭
Forton	131	131	595	Garstang, 478.
Thurnham, *part of* [1]	29	29	124	Lancaster, 479.
Cockersand Abbey	4	4	36	Lancaster, 479.
Colton	341	358	1,783	Ulverston, 481.
Croft, with Southworth	214	216	1,032	Warrington, 459.
Croston ancient parish—				
Bispham	50	54	280	Ormskirk, 457.
Bretherton	147	154	707	⎫
Croston	372	372	1,791	⎬ Chorley, 475.
Mawdesley	179	186	928	⎭
Ulnes-Walton	78	83	386	
Croxteth Park	7	7	39	West Derby, 455.
Dalton-in-Furness ancient parish—				
Barrow-in-Furness	6,789	8,580	47,259	Barrow-in-Furness, 482.
Dalton-in-Furness	2,383	2,535	13,339	Ulverston, 481.
Deane ancient parish—				
Farnworth	3,943	4,209	20,708	⎫
Halliwell	2,528	2,652	12,551	
Heaton	268	276	1,461	
Horwich	828	862	3,761	
Hulton, Little	1,131	1,230	5,711	⎬ Bolton, 461.
Hulton Middle	411	429	2,051	
Hulton, Over	183	186	984	
Kearsley	1,431	1,500	7,253	
Rumworth	939	963	4,952	
West Houghton	1,828	2,011	9,197	⎭
Derby, West	18,869	21,696	101,162	West Derby, 455.
Eccles ancient parish—				
Barton-upon-Irwell	5,292	5,628	25,994	⎫ Barton-upon-Irwell, 463
Clifton	492	506	2,578	⎭
Pendlebury	1,525	1,589	8,162	⎫ Salford, 465.
Pendleton	7,991	8,186	40,216	⎭
Worsley	4,029	4,151	21,207	Barton-upon-Irwell, 463.
Eccleston ancient parish—				
Eccleston	179	185	900	⎫ Chorley, 475.
Heskin	76	76	382	⎭
Parbold	97	98	529	⎫ Wigan, 458.
Wrightington	310	333	1,520	⎭
Flixton ancient parish—				
Flixton	377	385	1,776	⎫ Barton-upon-Irwell, 463.
Urmston	456	481	2,212	⎭
Garstang ancient parish—				
Barnacre, with Bonds	176	178	912	⎫
Bilsborrow	38	58	197	
Cabus	31	33	178	
Catterall	127	131	612	
Claughton	112	114	548	
Cleveley	8	8	51	
Garstang	175	182	783	⎬ Garstang, 478.
Holleth	7	8	50	
Kirkland	66	67	314	
Nateby	64	64	393	
Pilling	272	274	1,020	
Winmarleigh	61	62	351	
Wyresdale, Nether	113	117	606	⎭

[1] Thurnham is partly in the ancient parish of Lancaster. The entire township contains 721 persons.

INHABITED HOUSES, &c.—*continued.*

Civil Parish or Township.	Inhabited Houses.	Families or Separate Occupiers.	Population.	Poor Law Union in which situate.
Golborne..	891	954	4,502	Leigh, 460.
Halsall ancient parish—				
Downholland	136	136	748	⎫
Halsall	224	227	1,368	⎪
Lydiate	200	209	1,071	⎬ Ormskirk, 457.
Maghull	267	270	1,429	⎪
Melling	153	163	802	⎭
Halton	134	140	731	Lunesdale, 480.
Hawkshead ancient parish—				
Claife	110	110	547	⎫
Hawkshead, with Monk Coniston & Skelwith	242	250	1,205	⎬ Ulverston, 481.
Satterthwaite	75	83	452	⎭
Hesketh-with-Becconsall	176	178	863	Ormskirk, 457.
Heysham	134	135	632	Lancaster, 479.
Hoole ancient parish—				
Hoole, Little	82	83	440	⎫ Preston, 476.
Hoole, Much	119	122	581	⎭
Huyton ancient parish—				
Huyton-with-Roby	693	830	4,060	⎫
Knowsley	259	260	1,248	⎬ Prescot, 456.
Tarbock	110	119	629	⎭
Kirkby Ireleth ancient parish—				
Broughton, West	231	235	1171	⎫
Dunnerdale and Seathwaite....................	55	55	299	⎬ Ulverston, 481.
Kirkby Ireleth	343	343	1722	⎭
Kirkham ancient parish—				
Bryning-with-Kellamergh	19	19	114	⎫
Clifton-with-Salwick	72	84	418	⎬ Fylde, 477.
Eccleston, Little with Larbreck	39	40	197	⎭
Freckleton	260	262	1134	Preston, 476.
Goosnargh-with-Newsham	239	248	1197	Preston, 476.
Greenalgh-with-Thistleton	77	78	380	Fylde, 477.
Hambleton	83	88	389	Garstang, 478.
Kirkham	730	777	3840	⎫
Medlar-with-Wesham	188	202	1035	⎪
Newton-with-Scales	55	56	267	⎪
Ribby-with-Wrea	78	78	392	⎪
Singleton, Great and Little.....................	66	66	357	⎬ Fylde, 477.
Treales, Roseacre, and Wharles	105	105	560	⎪
Warton	90	90	408	⎪
Weeton-with-Preese	81	82	425	⎪
Westby-with-Plumpton	100	100	534	⎭
Whittingham..	123	151	2158	Preston, 476.
Lancaster ancient parish—				
Aldcliffe	14	14	94	⎫ Lancaster, 479.
Ashton-with-Stodday	40	41	207	⎭
Bleasdale	47	47	410	Garstang, 478.
Bulk	18	18	117	Lancaster, 479.
Caton-with-Littledale	233	234	1085	Lunesdale, 480.
Fulwood	330	370	3725	Preston, 476.
Gressingham	32	36	152	Lunesdale, 480.
Heaton-with-Oxcliffe	18	18	136	⎫
Lancaster	3621	3896	20,663	⎬ Lancaster, 479.
Middleton	27	27	157	⎭
Myerscough	74	75	384	Garstang, 478.
Overton	62	73	325	⎫ Lancaster, 479.
Poulton	861	886	3931	⎭
Preesall-with-Hackinsall	174	176	848	Garstang, 478.
Quernmore..	102	104	585	Lunesdale, 480.
Scotforth	347	359	2,263	⎫ Lancaster, 479.
Skerton	523	545	2,838	⎭
Stalmine-with-Stainall.....	96	99	501	Garstang, 478.
Thurnham, *part of* [1]	101	114	597	⎫ Lancaster, 479.
Wyersdale, Over...................................	85	87	513	⎭
Leigh ancient parish—				
Astley...	510	561	2,669	⎫
Atherton...	2,377	2,453	12,602	⎪
Bedford	1,551	1,677	7,246	⎬ Leigh, 460.
Pennington..	1,324	1,453	6,640	⎪
Tyldesley-with-Shackerley	1,934	2,077	9,954	⎪
West Leigh...	1,468	1,707	7,848	⎭

[1] Thurnham is partly in the ancient parish of Cockerham. The entire township contains 721 persons.

INHABITED HOUSES, &c.—*continued.*

Civil Parish or Township.	Inhabited Houses.	Families or Separate Occupiers.	Population.	Poor Law Union in which situate.
Leyland ancient parish—				
Clayton-le-Wood	124	141	582	}
Cuerden	108	122	573	
Euxton	242	251	1,147	
Heapey	81	91	369	
Hoghton	194	210	871	} Chorley, 475.
Leyland	1,047	1,087	4,961	
Wheelton	305	319	1,570	
Whittle-le-Woods	435	449	1,937	
Withnell	398	416	2,106	}
Liverpool	31,634	44,718	210,164	Liverpool, 453.
Lowton	496	551	2,357	Leigh, 460.
Lytham	971	1,014	5,268	Fylde, 477.
Manchester ancient parish—				
Ardwick	6,334	6,920	31,197	Chorlton, 464.
Beswick	1,603	1,621	7,957	
Blackley	1,281	1,347	6,075	} Prestwich, 467.
Bradford	3,205	3,383	16,121	
Broughton	6,156	6,654	31,534	Salford, 465.
Burnage	163	166	848	Chorlton, 464.
Cheetham	4,511	4,894	25,721	Prestwich, 467.
Chorlton-upon-Medlock	10,935	12,546	55,598	} Chorlton, 464.
Chorlton-with-Hardy	454	467	2,332	
Crumpsall	974	1,008	8,154	Prestwich, 467.
Denton	1,534	1,562	7,660	Ashton-under-Lyne, 468.
Didsbury	931	983	4,601	Chorlton, 464.
Droylsden	2,348	2,459	11,254	Ashton-under-Lyne, 468.
Failsworth	1,625	1,777	7,912	Prestwich, 467.
Gorton	6,635	7,149	33,096	Chorlton, 464.
Harpurhey	990	1,057	4,810	Prestwich, 467.
Haughton	1,029	1,061	5,051	Ashton-uuder-Lyne, 468.
Heaton Norris	4,165	4,574	20,347	Stockport, 443.
Hulme	14,235	15,813	72,147	} Chorlton, 464.
Levenshulme	712	741	3,557	
Manchester	29,446	32,095	148,794	Manchester, 466.
Moss Side	3,407	3,773	18,184	Chorlton, 464.
Moston	685	776	3,466	} Prestwich, 467.
Newton	6,261	6,758	31,240	
Openshaw	3,349	3,552	16,153	Chorlton, 464.
Reddish	1,109	1,181	5,557	Stockport, 443.
Rusholme	1,709	1,875	9,227	Chorlton, 464.
Salford	19,476	22,212	101,584	Salford, 465.
Stretford	3,697	4,013	19,018	Barton-upon-Irwell, 463.
Withington	1,663	1,736	11,286	Chorlton, 464.
Melling ancient parish—				
Arkholme-with-Cawood	56	68	297	}
Farleton	14	14	122	
Hornby	74	75	358	
Melling-with-Drayton	36	38	167	} Lunesdale, 480.
Roeburndale	21	22	112	
Wennington	29	29	127	
Wray-with-Bolton	136	157	626	}
Middleton ancient parish—				
Ainsworth	359	375	1,729	}
Ashworth	33	33	142	} Bury, 462,
Birtle-cum-Bamford	347	369	2,265	
Hopwood	923	976	4,440	}
Lever, Great	679	684	3,673	Bolton, 461.
Middleton	2,253	2,342	10,346	Oldham, 469.
Pilsworth	146	158	758	Bury, 462.
Thornham	385	397	1,860	Oldham, 469.
Mitton ancient paish, *part of* [1]—				
Aighton, Bailey, and Chaigley	237	352	1,663	Clitheroe, 473.
Newchurch Kenyon ancient parish—				
Culcheth	445	480	2,267	} Leigh, 460.
Kenyon	46	54	233	
Newton-in-Makerfield	1,926	2,027	10,580	Warrington, 459.
North Meols ancient parish—				
Birkdale	1,557	1,745	8,705	} Ormskirk, 457.
North Meols	6,171	7,299	33,763	

[1] The ancient parish of Mitton is mostly in the West Riding of Yorkshire. The entire parish contains 3,656 persons.

INHABITED HOUSES, &c.—continued.

Civil Parish or Township	Inhabited Houses.	Families or Separate Occupiers	Population.	Poor Law Union in which situate.
Orm-kirk ancient parish—				
Bickerstaffe..	389	414	2,269	
Burscough	458	484	2,290	
Lathom	806	852	4,161	Ormskirk, 457.
Orm-kirk....	1,255	1,380	6,651	
Scarisbrick	414	429	2,232	
Skelmersdale...	1,012	1,290	5,707	
Pennington	307	311	1,698	Ulverston, 481.
Penwortham ancient parish—				
Farington	376	413	2,017	
Howick	16	16	62	
Hutton	79	79	389	Preston, 476.
Longton	284	259	1,443	
Penwortham	315	322	1,642	
Poulton-le-Fylde ancient parish—				
Carleton	77	79	377	
Hardhorn-with-Newton	77	79	420	
Marton	471	473	2,303	Fylde, 477.
Poulton-le-Fylde	285	286	1,225	
Thornton	1,351	1,427	7,589	
Prescot ancient parish—				
Bold......	159	161	880	Prescot, 456.
Cronton	85	95	468	
Cuerdley	32	37	227	Warrington, 459.
Ditton	252	252	1,412	
Eccleston	3,217	3,532	18,026	Prescot, 456.
Parr..	1,934	2,166	11,278	
Penketh	224	253	1,239	Warrington, 459.
Prescot	1,069	1,117	5,346	
Rainford	671	784	3,745	Prescot, 456.
Rainhill	436	461	2,219	
Sankey, Great	110	123	630	Warrington, 459.
Sutton	2,108	2,259	12,695	
Whiston	416	464	2,705	Prescot, 456
Widnes	4,362	4,639	24,935	
Windle	3,600	3,784	19,473	
Preston ancient parish—				
Barton	64	64	363	
Broughton	120	121	590	
Eleston	8	9	43	
Fishwick...	416	434	2,142	
Grim-argh-with-Brockholes	56	58	369	Preston. 476.
Haighton	42	42	215	
Lea, Ashton, Ingol and Cottam	571	582	2,913	
Preston	18,489	20,896	91,578	
Ribbleton	117	118	575	
Prestwich ancient parish—				
Alkrington	78	83	380	
Chadderton	3,492	3,701	16,899	Oldham, 469.
Crompton	1,992	2,038	8,797	
Heaton, Great	78	78	376	
Heaton, Little	175	175	828	Prestwich, 467.
Oldham	22,555	23,889	111,343	Oldham, 469
Pilkington	2,641	2,693	13,144	Bury, 462.
Prestwich	1,458	1,606	8,627	Prestwich, 467.
Royton	2,255	2,519	10,582	Oldham, 469.
Tonge	1,519	1,630	7,354	
Radcliffe	3,295	3,582	16,267	Bury, 462.
Ribchester ancient parish—				
Alston	326	337	1,589	
Dilworth..	428	453	2,116	
Dutton	52	52	259	Preston. 476.
Hothersall	27	27	132	
Ribchester	259	265	1,282	
Rochdale ancient parish, part of [1]—				
Blatchinworth-with-Calderbrook	1,636	1,650	7,891	
Butterworth	1,869	2,000	8,411	Rochdale, 470.
Castleton	7,681	7,850	35,272	
Spotland	8,456	8,608	40,140	
Todmorden and Walsden	2,026	2,070	9,237	Todmorden, 493.
Wardleworth	4,363	4,425	19,711	Rochdale, 470.
Wuerdle and Wardle	2,147	2,212	10,187	

[1] The ancient parish of Rochdale is partly in the West Riding of Yorkshire. The entire parish contains 153,448 persons.

INHABITED HOUSES, &c.—*continued.*

Civil Parish or Township	Inhabited Houses	Families or Separate Occupiers	Population	Poor Law Union in which situate
Rufford	149	175	905	Ormskirk, 157.
St. Michael-on-Wyre ancient parish.—				
Eccleston, Great	139	144	628	Garstang, 478.
Elswick	55	55	242	Fylde, 477.
Inskip with Sowerby	105	105	542	
Rawcliffe, Out	141	141	815	Garstang, 478.
Rawcliffe, Upper, with Tarnacre	116	117	618	
Woodplumpton	272	284	1,239	Preston, 476.
Sefton ancient parish—				
Aintree	51	51	277	
Crosby, Great	1,595	1,792	9,373	
Crosby, Little	73	85	553	
Ince-Blundell	90	94	516	
Litherland	1,226	1,318	7,204	West Derby, 455.
Lunt	19	20	104	
Netherton	66	70	386	
Orrell and Ford......................................	81	81	637	
Sefton...	66	70	382	
Thornton	54	63	275	
Southworth with Croft (*see* Croft with Southworth).				
Standish ancient parish—				
Adlington	643	652	3,258	
Anderton	59	59	317	
Charnock Heath......................................	165	175	916	Chorley, 475.
Charnock Richard	127	132	685	
Coppull	324	357	1,826	
Duxbury	58	61	323	
Shevington...	305	347	1,570	Wigan, 458.
Standish-with-Langtree	765	861	4,261	
Welsh Whittle	19	19	115	Chorley, 475.
Worthington	47	54	255	Wigan, 458.
Tarleton	381	388	1,900	Ormskirk, 157.
Tatham	109	109	534	Lunesdale, 480.
Thornton-in-Lonsdale ancient parish, *part of* [1]				
Ireby	15	15	78	
Toxteth Park..	20,677	24,624	117,028	Toxteth Park, 454.
Tunstal ancient parish—				
Burrow-with-Burrow	43	43	214	
Cantsfield	18	18	104	Lunesdale, 480.
Leck	54	55	271	
Tunstal	20	21	104	
Ulverston ancient parish—				
Blawith	32	32	158	
Church Coniston	193	210	965	
Egton-with-Newland...............................	216	216	998	
Lowick	73	73	376	
Mansriggs	10	10	64	Ulverston, 481.
Osmotherley	81	85	474	
Subberthwaite	28	28	149	
Torver..	42	43	202	
Ulverston	1,957	2,036	10,008	
Urswick	251	258	1,287	
Walton-on-the-Hill ancient parish—				
Bootle-cum-Linacre	1,309	5,286	27,371	West Derby, 455.
Everton	19,133	23,278	109,812	
Fazakerley	95	95	533	
Formby	756	816	3,908	Ormskirk, 157.
Kirkby	264	265	1,401	West Derby, 455.
Kirkdale	9,793	11,405	58,145	
Simonswood	73	81	465	Ormskirk, 457.
Walton-on-the-Hill	3,061	3,231	18,715	West Derby, 455.
Warrington ancient parish—				
Burtonwood	224	231	1,268	
Poulton-with-Fernhead	118	149	742	
Rixton-with-Glazebrook	173	173	881	Warrington, 459.
Warrington	7,676	7,802	40,957	
Woolston-with-Martinscroft	103	105	501	

[1] The ancient parish of Thornton-in-Lonsdale is mostly in the West Riding of Yorkshire. The entire parish contains 1,024 persons.

INHABITED HOUSES, &c.—*continued.*

Civil Parish or Township.	Inhabited Houses.	Families or Separate Occupiers.	Population.	Poor Law Union in which situate.
Warton ancient parish—				
Borwick	42	46	246	Lunesdale, 480.
Carnforth	367	369	1,879	
Priest-Hutton	44	46	213	
Silverdale	102	109	489	Lancaster, 479.
Warton-with-Lindeth	284	304	1,471	
Yealand-Conyers	58	59	309	
Yealand-Redmayne	40	42	210	
Whalley ancient parish, *part of—* [1]				
Accrington	6,397	6,730	31,435	Haslingden, 471.
Altham	75	76	395	
Barley-with-Wheatley-Booth	89	91	314	Burnley, 472.
Barrowford..............................	836	842	3,842	
Booths, Higher	1,280	1,317	6,239	
Booths, Lower	1,209	1,275	6,196	Haslingden, 471.
Bowland, Little	18	19	106	Clitheroe, 473.
Briercliffe-with-Extwisle	252	254	1,147	Burnley, 472.
Burnley	5,572	6,123	28,744	
Chatburn	155	158	771	Clitheroe, 473.
Church	991	1,038	4,850	Blackburn, 474.
Clayton-le-Moors	1,313	1,405	6,695	
Clitheroe..................................	2,034	2,158	10,176	Clitheroe, 473.
Cliviger	421	424	1,952	Burnley, 472.
Colne	2,207	2,234	10,313	
Downham	64	64	272	Clitheroe, 473.
Dunnockshaw	44	45	212	
Foulridge	193	197	890	
Goldshaw Booth	77	80	355	Burnley, 472.
Habergham Eaves...	6,985	7,608	35,033	
Hapton	398	471	2,155	
Haslingden	2,892	3,048	14,298	Haslingden, 471.
Henheads	45	45	233	
Heyhouses	22	23	77	
Higham-with-West Close Booth	167	172	751	Burnley, 472.
Huncoat	184	188	930	
Ightenhill Park	41	45	205	
Leagram	18	18	100	Clitheroe, 473.
Marsden, Great and Little	3,351	3,503	16,725	Burnley, 472.
Mearley	6	6	30	
Mitton, Henthorn, and Colcoats	13	16	73	Clitheroe, 473.
Newchurch-with-Bacup	5,896	6,385	28,261	Haslingden, 471.
Old Laund Booth	83	83	332	Burnley, 472.
Oswaldtwistle..............................	2,470	2,540	12,206	Blackburn, 474.
Padiham	1,784	1,969	8,346	Burnley, 472.
Pendleton	301	317	1,312	Clitheroe, 473.
Reed	194	206	909	
Reedley Hallows, Felley Close, and New Laund Booth	122	123	667	Burnley, 472.
Roughlee Booth..............................	96	96	323	
Simonstone	89	90	421	
Trawden	476	515	2,164	
Twiston	30	36	128	Clitheroe, 473.
Whalley	194	202	895	
Wheatley Carr Booth	9	9	39	Burnley, 472.
Wiswall	138	168	737	Clitheroe, 473.
Worsthorne-with-Hurstwood	224	226	1,093	Burnley, 472.
Worston	19	19	62	Clitheroe, 473.
Yate and Pickup Bank	143	147	682	Blackburn, 474.
Whittington	76	76	346	Lunesdale, 480.
Wigan ancient parish—				
Abram	438	591	2,638	
Aspull	1,481	1,589	8,113	
Billinge Chapel End	388	402	1,935	
Billinge Higher End	284	288	1,402	
Dalton	90	94	494	
Haigh	218	224	1,186	
Hindley	2,687	3,062	14,715	Wigan, 458.
Ince-in-Makerfield........	2,926	3,327	16,007	
Orrell	843	920	4,299	
Pemberton	2,518	2,801	13,762	
Upholland	861	934	4,435	
Wigan......................	8,767	10,142	48,194	
Winstanley................................	107	115	545	

[1] The ancient parish of Whalley extends into the West Riding of Yorkshire. The entire parish contains 244,895 persons.

INHABITED HOUSES, &c.—continued.

Civil Parish or Township.	Inhabited Houses.	Families or Separate Occupiers.	Population	Poor Law Union in which situate.
Winwick ancient parish—				
Houghton, Middleton and Arbury	41	48	242	} Warrington, 459.
Winwick-with-Hulme	86	94	487	
Total........................	655,307	725,246	3,454,441	

VALUATION OF PROPERTY FOR ASSESSING THE COUNTY RATE.[1]

In order to form a basis or standard on which to assess the county rate it has been the practice to make a valuation of the yearly value of the property in every parish, township, and place, throughout the county, at irregular periods. One such valuation was made in the year 1829, and its results are given in the first edition of this work (1836), in tables preceding the history of each of the six hundreds. Of course that valuation is now useless, both because of the great increase in the extent and the value of property and because also of the different principle now applied to obtain the basis or standard required. Another valuation was made in 1854, and still more recent ones in 1866, 1872, 1877, and 1884, and we propose to place these later valuations in juxtaposition, for convenience of comparison, and also to annex to these the population according to the censuses of 1851, 1861, 1871, and 1881, and the area of acreage of each township or place, according to the Ordnance Survey, in statute acres. Before giving the tables, however, for the several hundreds, it is necessary briefly to explain the principle on which the valuation in each case has been arrived at.

An Act, entitled "An Act to consolidate and amend the Statutes relating to the Assessment and Collection of County Rates in England and Wales," was passed in 15 and 16 Vict. (1852), under the powers and authority of which the justices of the county of Lancaster, at their annual General Session of the Peace at Preston, on the 28th December, 1882, appointed a committee of twenty-two magistrates, to be—

"A Committee for the purpose of preparing a Basis or Standard for fair and equal County Rates, such Basis or Standard to be founded and prepared rateably and equally, according to the full and fair Annual Value of the Property, Messuages, Lands, Tenements, and Hereditaments, rateable to the relief of the Poor in every Parish, Township, Borough, or Place, whether Parochial or Extra-Parochial—that is to say, according to the net Annual Value of any Property, as the same is or may be required by Law to be estimated for the purpose of assessing the Rates for the relief of the Poor."

The committee accordingly prepared a basis or standard, which was laid before the Court of Annual General Session of the Peace at Preston on the 27th December 1883 ; and the usual notices being given in the newspapers that such basis or standard would be taken into consideration at the following Court of Annual Session, it was then (April 3rd, 1884) considered, allowed, and confirmed.

The principle of rating adopted by the committee was the following :—

"For the purpose of estimating the net annual value of the property in each parish, township, or place, the committee first ascertained the gross estimated value thereof, and from such gross value made the following deductions :—

"1. From the value of all lands, tithes, canals, navigations, docks, watercourses, reservoirs, quarries, delphs, and brickyards, one-twelfth part. And

"2. From the value of all buildings (except farm buildings), mines, railways, and gasworks, one-sixth part.

In the following tables, the full heading of column 2 is, "Basis or Standard for County Rates, being the Value as allowed in the year 1854, after making Deductions ;" and the full heading of columns 3 to 6 inclusive "Basis or Standard for County Rates, being the Value as allowed after making Deductions" in the several years named. It will be seen that we have abbreviated these headings.

LONSDALE HUNDRED.

NORTH OF THE SANDS.

Township.	Basis, etc. 1854.	Basis, etc. 1866.	Basis, etc. 1872.	Basis, etc. 1877.	Basis, etc. 1884.	Population in 1851.	1861.	1871.	1881.	Area in Statute Acres.
	£	£	£	£	£	Persons.	Persons.	Persons.	Persons.	Acres.
Aldingham	7,695	8,640	8,914	10,066	10,126	968	1,011	1,061	1,152	4,812
Allithwaite, Lower......	4,641	6,366	7,850	8,350	10,600	888	933	1,009	975	3,211
Allithwaite, Upper......	2,640	2,829	3,826	4,340	5,018	746	729	776	713	2,682
Angerton	455	551	722	686	1,014	32	31	36	32	2,195
Barrow-in-Furness......	...	...	75,652	168,714	241,046	...	...	18,584	47,259	10,967
Blawith	1,011	1,069	1,116	1,454	1,464	229	193	146	158	2,995
Broughton East..	3,572	6,408	7,980	10,082	12,802	470	534	1,007	1,251	3,425
Broughton West	5,389	7,098	7,736	8,906	10,064	1,297	1,183	1,085	1,171	7,298
Cartmel Fell	2,734	3,072	3,150	3,498	3,638	351	308	297	293	4,958
Claife	3,021	3,859	4,184	5,004	5,322	540	540	563	517	4,579
Church Coniston	1,938	3,427	5,086	3,546	3,622	1,287	1,324	1,106	965	7,424
Colton	8,471	10,560	11,810	12,818	13,470	2,008	1,794	1,860	1,783	14,322
Dalton-in-Furness	19,447	68,128	32,246	107,964	160,470	4,683	9,152	9,310	13,339	7,223
Dunnerdale and Seath- waite	1,804	2,158	2,158	2,364	2,496	321	289	291	299	10,258
Egton with Newland...	4,681	5,696	6,500	7,806	8,692	1,222	1,231	1,148	998	3,661
Hawkshead, Monk Co- niston, and Skelwith.	5,686	7,063	7,986	9,282	9,924	1,271	1,144	1,085	1,205	10,429
Holker, Lower	4,096	5,444	5,900	7,146	9,012	1,225	1,160	1,115	1,093	2,387
Holker, Upper	5,360	6,816	7,558	8,432	9,294	1,134	1,035	850	849	7,140
Kirkby Ireleth	8,287	9,058	9,982	10,762	11,524	1,728	1,666	1,763	1,722	9,702
Lowick	1,934	2,261	2,276	2,428	2,588	411	468	468	376	2,261

[1] From information obligingly furnished by Henry Alison, Esq., County Treasurer, Preston.—C.

rst volume of "The History of the County Palatine and

of Lancaster," is completed with the present part (XIV).

me cloth cases, gilt, for binding the volume are now ready.

2s. 6d.   Kindly order as soon as possible, either direct from

blisher, or through your bookseller.

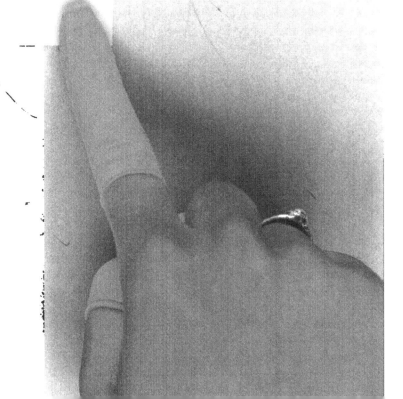

LONSDALE HUNDRED—North of the Sands—*continued.*

Township.	Basis, etc. 1854.	Basis, etc. 1866.	Basis, etc. 1872.	Basis, etc. 1877.	Basis, etc. 1884.	Population in 1851.	1861.	1871.	1881.	Area in Statute Acres.
	£	£	£	£	£	Persons.	Persons.	Persons.	Persons.	Acres.
Mansriggs	646	764	784	832	876	64	69	73	64	569
Osmotherley	1,867	2,806	2,854	3,752	4,118	325	419	405	474	1,929
Pennington	2,739	6,188	7,022	18,292	41,218	489	879	1,112	1,698	2,845
Satterthwaite...........	2,497	2,785	2,848	3,318	3,406	472	397	394	452	7,322
Staveley	2,919	3,365	3,712	4,132	4,130	399	409	438	426	4,199
Subberthwaite	682	856	996	988	1,032	150	152	146	149	1,-87
Torver..................	998	1,384	1,562	1,450	1,500	193	194	209	202	3,816
Ulverston	16,845	23,770	26,874	38,124	47,124	6,742	7,414	7,607	10,008	3,120
Urswick	5,486	6,797	7,550	11,800	10,900	891	1,080	1,144	1,287	4,043
Total North of Sands..	127,996	209,218	264,834	475,836	646,490	30,557	35,738	55,083	90,940	151,009

SOUTH OF THE SANDS.

Township.	Basis, etc. 1854.	Basis, etc. 1866.	Basis, etc. 1872.	Basis, etc. 1877.	Basis, etc. 1884.	Population in 1851.	1861.	1871.	1881.	Area in Statute Acres.
	£	£	£	£	£	Persons.	Persons.	Persons.	Persons.	Acres.
Aldcliffe	1,141	1,325	1,460	1,718	1,732	85	74	68	94	1,016
Arkholme with Cawood	2,997	3,643	4,250	4,670	5,266	330	331	360	297	3,016
Ashton with Stodday..	2,120	2,519	2,742	3,182	3,264	173	184	191	207	1,949
Bolton-le-Sands	4,543	6,471	6,756	7,296	8,762	686	692	753	785	1,580
Borwick	1,487	1,638	2,078	2,194	2,542	199	194	209	246	846
Bulk	2,423	2,661	3,370	3,492	4,524	124	109	116	117	1,158
Burrow with Burrow...	2,578	2,882	3,570	3,974	4,152	228	225	236	214	2,426
Cantsfield	1,626	1,763	2,150	2,144	2,380	155	116	108	104	1,222
Carnforth	2,484	4,824	7,746	10,760	18,542	294	393	1,091	1,879	1,459
Caton	5,735	7,036	7,538	8,810	9,592	1,434	1,160	1,059	1,085	8,396
Claughton	1,339	1,851	2,114	2,392	2,730	106	94	85	100	1,581
Cockerham	6,344	7,264	8,740	9,634	9,678	774	778	808	761	5,562
Cockersand Abbey ...	400	482	524	524	522	42	33	26	36	346
Dalton....................	1,664	1,981	2,116	2,466	2,430	100	129	120	123	2,167
Ellel	8,327	12,620	13,608	15,722	18,578	1,484	1,968	1,615	1,787	5,814
Farleton ..	1,223	1,359	1,418	1,522	2,220	75	75	49	122	1,051
Gressingham	2,026	2,182	2,280	2,676	3,034	187	158	134	152	2,015
Halton	4,831	5,287	6,050	6,680	7,338	718	670	615	731	3,914
Heaton with Oxcliffe...	2,328	2,668	2,758	3,526	3,876	174	165	169	136	2,036
Heysham	3,112	3,862	4,466	4,954	5,742	593	567	628	632	1,774
Hornby	2,331	3,229	3,378	3,518	3,954	874	317	323	358	1,961
Ireby	923	1,070	1,226	1,228	1,370	111	113	103	78	1,141
Nether Kellet	2,493	2,621	2,718	2,952	3,268	319	284	275	279	2,082
Over Kellet	3,410	4,047	4,276	4,852	5,306	488	425	423	494	3,210
Lancaster	35,988	40,698	47,430	59,880	85,126	14,604	14,487	17,245	20,663	1,494
Leck	2,203	2,550	2,724	3,300	3,620	285	324	229	271	4,636
Melling with Wreaton..	1,358	1,809	2,142	2,326	2,716	197	169	182	167	1,062
Middleton	1,501	1,799	1,880	2,150	2,050	185	182	184	157	1,200
Overton	1,784	2,081	2,348	2,460	2,470	334	305	296	325	1,837
Poulton, Bare, and Torrisholme	5,422	10,370	14,558	19,652	29,134	1,301	2,236	3,005	3,931	1,725
Priest Hutton	1,432	1,780	2,134	2,288	2,514	234	218	185	213	1,085
Quernmore	4,862	6,226	6,862	7,606	8,568	579	563	555	585	6,789
Roeburndale	1,948	2,483	2,524	2,906	2,924	206	144	130	112	8,841
Scotforth	5,860	8,106	9,404	11,366	14,392	693	955	1,139	2,263	2,880
Silverdale	1,076	1,657	2,266	2,852	5,400	240	294	343	489	1,168
Skerton	5,393	7,199	8,178	8,456	13,064	1,586	1,556	1,817	2,838	1,316
Slyne with Hest	2,937	4,218	4,678	5,140	6,090	309	312	307	301	1,143
Tatham	5,074	5,978	6,418	6,938	9,082	654	588	586	534	8,547
Thurnham	2,197	2,944	3,884	4,066	4,126	706	717	618	721	2,095
Tunstall	1,419	1,714	2,012	2,226	2,252	146	138	105	104	1,076
Warton with Lindeth.	3,583	5,732	8,706	9,902	14,100	600	581	1,035	1,471	2,824
Wennington	1,183	1,263	1,554	1,696	1,844	189	180	168	127	980
Whittington	4,784	5,341	5,948	6,796	6,632	414	421	460	346	4,416
Wray with Botton ...	3,557	4,491	4,674	5,032	5,546	833	797	584	626	6,526
Wyresdale, Over	4,094	4,822	5,274	6,482	6,894	680	524	500	513	17,319
Yealand Conyers	2,478	2,917	3,396	3,818	4,418	306	272	300	309	1,582
Yealand Redmayne	2,258	2,984	3,242	3,570	4,108	226	209	227	210	2,136
Total of South Sands..	170.280	214,447	249,568	291,794	367,572	34,760	35,426	39,759	48,093	140,399
Total of North Sands..	127,996	209,218	264,834	475,836	646,490	30,557	35,738	55,083	90,940	151,009
Total of Lonsdale Hundred	298,276	423,665	514,402	767,630	1,014,062	65,317	71,164	94,842	139,033	291,408[1]

[1] is total is less than the return for the census by 1,082 acres, the extent of reclaimed land in Lonsdale North not yet apportioned to any township.

AMOUNDERNESS HUNDRED.

Township.	Basis, etc. 1854.	Basis, etc. 1866.	Basis, etc. 1872.	Basis, etc. 1877.	Basis, etc. 1884.	Population in				Area in Statute Acres.
						1851.	1861.	1871.	1881.	
	£	£	£	£	£	Persons.	Persons.	Persons.	Persons.	Acres.
Alston	3,351	4,746	5,382	6,946	7,784	807	1,098	1,337	1,589	2,040
Barnacre with Bonds...	5,692	8,120	9,150	11,090	14,738	875	907	922	912	4,495
Barton	3 336	5,191	5,570	6,554	6,736	370	343	338	368	2,707
Bilsborrow	1,770	2,031	2,262	2,794	3,194	152	176	185	197	852
Bispham with Norbreck	2,665	3,840	4,376	4,914	4,570	293	437	547	714	1,644
Bleasdale	1,905	2,744	2,954	3,812	3,608	295	372	376	410	7,298
Broughton	6,196	7,407	7,980	9,412	9,414	685	709	601	590	2,367
Bryning with Kellamergh	1,617	1,665	1,742	1,920	1,894	126	116	115	114	1,061
Cabus	1,863	2,493	2,690	2,864	3,172	238	209	171	178	1,383
Carleton	3,789	4,022	4,362	5,078	5,820	400	363	433	377	2,012
Catterall	3,065	3,718	4,110	4,814	4,722	1,036	867	672	612	1,742
Claughton	4,575	6,077	6,542	8,072	8,800	641	608	526	548	3,786
Cleveley	1,286	2,170	2,506	2,914	3,694	73	62	65	51	620
Clifton with Salwick...	5,487	5,914	5,880	7,424	8,656	471	447	447	418	3,489
Eccleston, Great	2,589	3,220	3,280	3,548	4,002	631	641	565	628	1,469
Eccleston, Little, with Larbreck	1,625	1,862	2,044	2,084	2,220	215	209	192	197	1,280
Elston	1,005	941	932	1,148	1,242	54	53	53	43	962
Elswick	1,555	1,841	1,758	2,018	2,374	307	290	254	242	1,087
Fishwick	5,028	7,103	7,424	8,448	9,422	1,005	1,884	1,912	2,142	693
Forton	2,271	2,541	3,044	3,094	3,376	582	574	549	595	1,279
Freckleton	3,792	4,294	5,306	5,642	6,506	968	879	930	1,134	2,417
Fulwood	5,971	7,970	10,512	14,840	18,894	1,748	2,313	3,079	3,725	2,117
Garstang	2,439	2,450	2,744	2,858	3,154	839	714	687	783	503
Goosnargh with Newsham	8,865	10,535	11,084	12,264	13,450	1,453	1,307	1,258	1,197	8,673
Greenhalgh with Thistleton	2,880	3,279	3,352	3,736	4,482	362	383	365	380	1,897
Grimsargh with Brockholes	3,108	3,638	3,892	4,150	...	360	301	357	369	1,950
Municipal	...	...	...	...	410	...	...	...	...	...
Rural	...	...	...	...	4,346	...	...	...	...	...
					4,756					
Haighton	1,388	1,600	1,650	1,884	2,162	198	222	219	215	1,078
Hambleton	1,982	2,590	2,984	3,114	3,534	346	366	351	389	1,553
Hardhorn with Newton	4,385	5,197	5,442	7,312	8,496	386	386	436	420	2,651
Holleth	362	454	502	540	576	28	30	35	50	358
Hothersall	886	1,383	1,602	1,822	1,922	152	159	120	132	1,039
Inskip with Sowerby..	3,422	3,888	4,182	4,610	5,012	680	663	593	542	2,979
Kirkham	5,737	6,879	7,688	8,684	11,076	2,799	3,380	3,593	3,840	857
Kirkland	1,905	1 996	1,998	2,236	2,514	429	388	336	314	974
Layton with Warbreck	13,095	31,776	53,750	72,420	122,352	2,564	3,907	7,092	12,711	2,359
Lea, Ashton, Ingol, and Cottam	8,361	10,240	12,672	15,820	...	743	911	2,081	2,913	3,488
Municipal	...	...	...	...	9,676	...	...	...	...	...
Rural	...	...	...	...	12,018	...	...	...	...	...
					21,694					
Lytham	13,359	18,504	21,490	25,660	36,404	2,698	3,194	3,904	5,268	5,310
Marton	6,339	8,526	9,712	10,694	...	1,650	1,691	1,982	2,303	4,707
Municipal	...	...	...	...	5,680	...	...	...	...	...
Rural	...	...	...	...	8,696	...	...	...	...	...
					14,376					
Medlar with Wesham...	3,245	5,230	5,378	7,542	9,002	170	563	860	1,035	1,966
Myerscough	4,181	5,322	5,866	6,560	7,248	459	426	418	384	2,7C7
Nateby	2,327	2,742	2,870	3,190	3,936	325	385	435	393	2,087
Newton with Scales ...	2,832	2,794	3,344	3,678	3,594	299	286	292	267	1,523
Pilling	6,033	7,441	8,462	9,318	10,514	1,281	1,388	1,572	1,620	6,060
Poulton in le Fylde ...	4,011	4,221	4,902	6,060	7,670	1,120	1,141	1,161	1,225	914
Preesall with Hackinsall	4,510	5,335	6,070	6,218	6,992	823	812	837	848	3,393
Preston	168,770	201,637	216,360	268,556	318,844	68,537	81,101	83,515	91,578	2,127
Rawcliffe, Out	4,605	5,789	6,706	7,356	7,930	791	771	832	815	4,593
Rawcliffe, Upper, with Tarnacre	4.128	4,873	5,502	5,948	6,958	697	682	700	618	3,839
Ribbleton	1,675	2,105	2,360	2,770	...	189	175	247	575	744
Municipal	...	...	...	...	2,708	...	...	...	...	...
Rural	...	..	...	...	1,100	...	...	...	...	...
					3,808					

AMOUNDERNESS HUNDRED—*continued.*

Township.	Basis, etc. 1854.	Basis, etc. 1866.	Basis, etc. 1872.	Basis, etc. 1877.	Basis, etc. 1884.	Population in				Area in Statute Acres.
						1851.	1861.	1871.	1881.	
	£	£	£	£	£	Persons.	Persons.	Persons.	Persons.	Acres.
Ribby with Wrea	2,549	2,878	2,930	3,058	3,374	406	444	466	392	1,387
Singleton, Great and Little	3,302	4,402	4,500	5,136	5,494	293	338	317	357	2,923
Stalmine with Stainall.	2,884	3,548	4,062	4,496	5,218	508	471	521	501	2,583
Thornton	13,762	21,144	22,122	27,570	46,484	4,134	5,084	5,203	7,589	6,387
Treales, Roseacre, and Wharles	5,285	6,076	6,110	7,870	8,668	696	632	625	560	4,100
Warton	2,638	2,897	3,160	3,280	3,526	473	446	444	408	2,540
Weeton with Preese ...	3,803	4,598	4,982	6,650	7,072	465	465	433	425	2,973
Westby with Plumpton	5,866	6,604	6,844	8,520	9,754	707	601	535	534	3,598
Whittingham	4,028	4,722	5,204	5,618	6,286	677	583	664	2,158	3,192
Winmarleigh	2,216	2,541	2,626	3,014	3,406	262	246	289	381	2,342
Woodplumpton	8,905	10,266	11,726	12,462	18,366	1,574	1,462	1,290	1,239	4,971
Wyresdale, Nether ...	4,271	5,229	5,908	6,414	7,014	704	667	549	606	4,215
Total of Amounderness Hundred	414,272	525,239	592,544	718,318	896,956	113,243	130,728	139,883	162,118	158,295

BLACKBURN HUNDRED.

Township.	Basis, etc. 1854.	Basis, etc. 1866.	Basis, etc. 1872.	Basis, etc. 1877.	Basis, etc. 1884.	Population in				Area in Statute Acres.
						1851.	1861.	1871.	1881.	
	£	£	£	£	£	Persons.	Persons.	Persons.	Persons.	Acres.
Accrington	28,395	61,773	68,890	96,656	115,178	10,374	17,688	21,788	31,435	3,425
Aighton, Bailey, and Chaigley	5,978	6,590	6,960	8,110	9,460	1,613	1,500	1,524	1,663	6,300
Altham	2,123	2,785	3,410	4,304	4,504	426	410	401	395	1,440
Balderston	2,301	2,582	2,800	3,128	3,562	660	532	475	487	1,808
Barley with Wheatley Booth	1,816	2,316	2,236	2,216	2,462	542	485	354	314	2,625
Barrowford Booth	5,556	8,673	11,030	11,282	14,200	2,875	2,880	3,110	3,842	2,355
Billington	4,047	5,225	6,102	7,830	8,680	882	1,038	1,204	1,410	3,139
Blackburn	101,470	180,641	244,932	290,600	361,374	46,536	63,126	76,339	91,958	3,681
Bowland with Leagrim	2,912	3,213	3,408	5,418	5,324	240	234	236	206	4,664
Briercliffe with Extwistle	3,856	5,240	7,822	7,440	9,160	1,612	1,332	1,263	1,147	4,227
Burnley	40,621	57,841	66,334	82,480	...	14,706	19,971	21,501	28,744	1,996
Municipal	...	...	...	...	103,738					
Rural	...	...	...	...	6,486					
					110,224					
Chatburn	1,812	2,340	2,554	3,230	3,958	503	521	584	771	894
Chipping	4,907	5,377	5,668	7,596	7,978	1,134	1,074	1,113	987	5,634
Church	7,165	15,350	15,818	16,464	21,790	2,035	4,753	4,450	4,850	528
Clayton-in-le-Dale......	1,797	1,928	1,942	3,080	3,546	471	375	275	295	1,715
Clayton-in-le-Moors ...	8,485	14,568	17,316	18,414	20,974	3,392	4,682	5,390	6,695	1,059
Clitheroe	17,107	21,326	23,948	29,722	36,548	7,244 {	6,990	8,208	10,176	2,375
Clitheroe Castle........	46	71	72	100	114 }		10	9	16	6
Cliviger	7,752	12,780	14,888	17,766	17,848	1,441	1,770	1,674	1,952	6,819
Colne	17,156	19,814	27,518	30,602	38,614	8,987	7,906	8,633	10,313	4,635
Coupe Lench, Newhallhey, and Hall Carr..	5,083	10,867	11,026	13,504	13,984	2,154	2,851	3,638	3,695	1,499
Cuerdale........	985	1,077	1,100	1,158	1,208	80	56	60	58	684
Darwen, Lower	8,203	11,126	17,232	21,580	...	3,521	3,301	3,876	4,531	2,667
Blackburn	...	...	...	...	17,768					
Over Darwen ...	...	...	...	...	8,518					
					26,286					
Darwen, Over............	20,143	44,215	62,916	82,714	109,978	11,702	16,492	21,278	27,626	5,134
Dilworth..................	2,664	4,325	5,532	6,774	7,880	833	959	1,730	2,116	1,248
Dinckley..................	606	605	742	898	1,268	151	120	119	123	608
Downham	2,079	2,066	2,226	2,426	2,492	362	292	282	272	2,300
Dunnockshaw	361	680	798	870	910	86	167	186	212	389
Dutton	1,597	1,760	2,058	2,296	2,500	446	312	257	259	1,899
Eccleshill	1,634	2,463	2,840	3,926	...	598	543	633	716	797
Municipal	...	...	...	...	630					
Rural	...	...	...	...	3,186					
					3,816					
Foulridge	4,172	5,438	5,688	6,314	7,020	1,233	988	827	890	2,455
Goldshaw Booth	1,720	2,606	2,682	2,914	2,824	620	406	358	355	2,334

BLACKBURN HUNDRED—*continued.*

Township.	Basis, etc. 1854.	Basis, etc. 1866.	Basis, etc. 1872.	Basis, etc. 1877.	Basis, etc. 1884.	Population in				Area in Statute Acres.
						1851.	1861.	1871.	1881.	
	£	£	£	£	£	Persons.	Persons.	Persons.	Persons.	Acres.
Habergham Eaves	33,840	64,000	84,168	103,670	...	12,549	18,013	23,423	35,033	4,217
Municipal	...	...	...	...	96,882	...	...	...	...	
Rural	...	...	...	...	37,910	...	...	...	...	...
					134,792					
Hapton	4,186	9,108	10,244	12,344	16,818	550	1,003	1,586	2,155	4,008
Harwood, Great........	5,374	11,008	14,248	18,084	24,060	2,548	4,070	4,907	6,287	2,863
Harwood, Little........	1,930	2,316	2,558	4,542	6,004	316	270	311	715	895
Haslingden..............	18,102	31,203	36,258	48,360	56,086	9,030	10,109	12,000	14,298	4,342
Henheads	721	826	846	1,118	1,720	160	211	201	233	317
Heyhouses..............	384	430	502	574	566	147	128	84	77	322
Higham with West-Close-Booth	2,029	2,752	3,128	3,514	3,850	839	759	791	751	1,584
Higher Booths	10,439	17,497	20,260	24,482	24,910	3,827	5,131	5,667	6,239	4,412
Huncoat	1,975	3,354	3,762	4,258	5,580	598	839	854	930	990
Ightenhill Park........	1,678	2,205	4,570	1,562	5,522	176	161	149	205	760
Livesey	6,903	15,344	20,110	28,746	...	2,649	3,581	4,035	6,065	2,036
Muncipal.........	...	...	...	...	18,292	...	...	...	...	...
Rural	...	...	...	..	13,796	...	...	...	...	...
					32,088					
Lower Booths	8,408	14,500	15,118	22,442	24,684	3,778	4,655	5,114	6,196	1,600
Marsden	13,466	24,907	32,100	39,766	62,906	6,068	7,342	10,284	16,725	4,689
Mearley	860	1,030	1,026	1,226	1,228	47	47	48	30	1,509
Mellor	3,454	3,734	3,976	4,154	5,376	1,668	1,398	1,178	1,096	1,744
Mitton, Henthorn, and Colcoates..............	839	982	998	1,438	1,344	74	62	55	73	873
Musbury.....	2,552	3,567	4,150	5,168	5,988	1,228	997	1,130	1,010	1,714
Newchurch, Deadwen Clough, Bacup, and Wolfenden	35,891	67,560	79,468	94,296	...	16,915	24,413	26,823	28,261	5,858
Municipal.........	...	...	...	...	50,802	...	...	...	...	...
Rural	...	...	...	...	42,802	...	...	...	...	...
					93,644					
Old Laund Booth	751	901	908	962	1,156	447	423	296	332	431
Osbaldeston	1,126	1,197	1,348	1,544	1,626	250	238	224	154	1,084
Oswaldtwistle	17,138	29,234	32,750	39,162	48,398	7,654	7,701	10,283	12,206	4,883
Padiham..................	10,048	17,980	19,842	23,836	29,434	4,509	5,911	6,914	8,346	1,953
Pendleton	3,772	4,582	4,688	5,510	5,786	1,308	1,446	1,229	1,312	2,826
Pleasington	2,930	3,688	3,910	6,496	5,978	428	422	336	459	1,701
Ramsgreave	1,233	1,347	1,424	1,772	1,948	438	320	263	240	776
Read	2,547	3,687	3,736	5,060	5,156	449	531	634	909	1,548
Reedley Hallows, Filley Close, and New Laund Booth...	2,939	8,329	5,970	6,500	7,524	374	423	588	667	1,446
Ribchester	3,087	3,435	4,148	4,532	4,964	1,650	1,357	1,329	1,282	2,211
Rishton	4,893	8,217	10,700	19,002	23,332	800	1,198	2,577	4,055	2,982
Roughlee Booth.........	1,678	1,825	1,858	1,878	2,162	719	424	372	323	1,141
Salesbury	1,217	1,338	1,478	1,742	1,920	388	331	212	184	1,215
Samlesbury	5,822	6,260	6,484	7,044	8,916	1,435	1,215	810	752	4,379
Simonstone.............	1,128	1,532	1,822	2,158	2,816	365	325	366	421	1,026
Thornley with Wheatley	2,441	3,039	3,050	3,840	3,892	491	409	428	349	3,221
Tockholes	2,299	2,938	3,214	3,202	3,500	939	820	646	484	1,988
Trawden	5,181	7,762	7,504	7,842	9,082	2,601	2,087	2,129	2,164	6,808
Twiston	798	837	822	982	950	161	141	134	128	865
Walton-in-le-Dale	18,024	26,506	30,986	44,262	49,398	6,855	7,383	8,187	9,286	4,683
Whalley	3,334	4,193	4,714	5,556	6,462	945	806	747	895	1,603
Wheatley Carr Booth...	278	340	358	368	390	40	46	36	39	254
Wilpshire	878	1,288	1,458	2,636	3,584	237	228	230	280	1,002
Wiswall	2,461	2,675	2,700	3,412	4,096	747	465	419	737	1,693
Witton	2,503	7,034	8,970	9,724	...	1,367	3,292	3,803	4,356	700
Muncipal.........	...	...	...	...	10,136	...	...	...	...	...
Rural	...	...	...	...	2,268	...	...	...	...	...
					12,404					
Worsthorne withHurstwood ......:..........	2,129	3,696	5,976	8,190	8,276	909	865	996	1,093	3,510
Worston	1,013	1,113	1,132	1,210	1,278	89	84	71	62	1,088
Yate and Pickup Bank	1,664	1,776	1,544	2,278	2,444	1,208	1,111	766	682	850
Total of Blackburn Hundred..............	574,608	950,663	1,159,472	1,432,206	1,739,702	228,329	286,955	335,440	417,085	183,649

LEYLAND HUNDRED.

Township.	Basis, etc. 1854.	Basis, etc. 1866.	Basis, etc. 1872.	Basis, etc. 1877.	Basis, etc. 1884.	Population in				Area in Statute Acres.
						1851.	1861.	1871.	1881.	
	£	£	£	£	£	Persons.	Persons.	Persons.	Persons.	Acres.
Adlington	3,890	5,797	6,924	8,026	9,324	1,090	1,975	2,666	3,258	1,064
Anderton	1,830	2,448	2,974	6,046	6,398	284	243	262	317	1,229
Bispham	1,643	1,682	1,692	1,866	1,908	270	277	284	280	926
Bretherton	3,871	4,539	4,756	4,944	5,584	818	775	683	707	2,437
Brindle	5,503	6,298	7,268	8,388	9,782	1,310	1,501	1,339	1,173	3,104
Charnock Richard	4,743	4,784	5,166	5,736	6,996	872	899	750	685	1,946
Chorley	31,171	43,004	50,032	54,622	60,110	12,684	15,013	16,864	19,478	3,614
Clayton-in-le-Woods	2,910	3,159	3,338	3,438	3,446	747	705	607	582	1,431
Coppull	5,677	5,407	8,040	9,390	14,398	1,107	1,230	1,484	1,826	2,280
Croston	5,087	6,823	7,340	8,350	10,498	1,500	1,790	1,518	1,791	2,361
Cuerden	2,778	3,130	3,610	3,800	3,896	521	666	647	573	808
Duxbury	2,509	2,476	2,624	2,624	2,736	324	341	325	323	1,012
Eccleston	4,142	4,795	5,070	5,232	5,196	671	965	953	900	2 090
Euxton	7,826	8,446	9,664	10,270	12,072	1,631	1,491	1,182	1,147	2,934
Farington	7,923	8,611	10,574	16,610	17,270	1,932	1,791	1,797	2,017	1,860
Heapey	1,895	1,888	2,314	3,090	4,796	495	396	290	369	1,464
Heath Charnock	3,622	4,830	5,316	6,888	7,332	799	772	1,034	916	1,598
Hesketh with Becconsall	2,307	4,439	5,122	5,370	6,030	692	804	799	863	4,736
Heskin	1,882	2,046	2,186	2,394	2,708	358	439	336	382	1,242
Hoghton	4,750	4,549	5,300	6,794	8,778	1,373	1,201	906	871	2,224
Hoole, Little	1,553	2,531	2,662	2,754	3,266	202	424	453	440	1,223
Hoole, Much	2,661	2,970	3,094	3,360	3,528	775	708	644	581	1,776
Howick	1,034	1,163	1,242	1,502	1,698	116	93	80	62	754
Hutton	3,473	3,777	3,866	4,242	5,216	500	461	395	389	2,745
Leyland	11,797	14,448	17,582	21,282	27,556	3,617	3,755	3,839	4,961	3,726
Longton	5 418	6,623	7,094	7,916	9,308	1,687	1,637	1,455	1,443	3,650
Mawdsley	5,068	5,263	5,760	6,258	6,904	887	912	886	928	2,950
Parbold	2,383	3,093	4,186	4,588	5,258	473	474	477	529	1,150
Penwortham	7,528	8,028	9,680	12,128	13,656	1,487	1,506	1,578	1,642	2,270
Rufford	4,734	6,455	6,552	7,046	8,182	861	865	819	905	3,120
Shevington	4,690	7,694	7,100	5,556	6,570	1,147	1,615	1,924	1,570	1,728
Standish with Langtree	10,178	17,348	19,890	20,250	22,880	2,655	3,054	3,698	4,261	3,265
Tarleton	6,844	8,838	8,796	9,434	10,208	1,945	1,987	1,917	1,900	5,553
Ulnes Walton	3,602	4,151	4,494	4,866	6,276	556	488	414	386	2,106
Welch Whittle	892	1,822	1,654	1,796	1,180	140	148	111	115	596
Wheelton	3,012	4,384	4,866	5,752	6,428	1,041	1,260	1,471	1,570	1,696
Whittle-in-le-Woods	4,894	5,492	5,614	5,680	6,628	2,310	2,151	1,805	1,937	1,355
Withnell	5,010	6,227	8,030	10,044	11,446	1,975	2,059	1,966	2,106	3,628
Worthington	1,877	2,390	2,916	4,160	5,964	176	133	188	255	659
Wrightington	6,431	6,949	7,848	8,622	9,556	1,613	1,618	1,525	1,520	3,916
Total of Leyland Hundred	199,038	248,795	282,236	321,114	370,946	53,641	58,622	60,311	65,958	88,244

SALFORD HUNDRED.

Township.	Basis, etc. 1854.	Basis, etc. 1866.	Basis, etc. 1872.	Basis, etc. 1877.	Basis, etc. 1884.	Population in				Area in Statute Acres.
						1851.	1861.	1871.	1881.	
	£	£	£	£	£	Persons.	Persons.	Persons.	Persons.	Acres.
Ainsworth	5,419	5,691	6,576	7,932	8,794	1,781	1,803	1,854	1,729	1,309
Alkrington	1,569	1,904	2,400	2,478	2,754	373	423	388	380	798
Anlezarke	997	1,665	2,326	6,248	6,516	179	134	195	99	2,793
Ardwick	49,898	69,171	83,034	116,984	128,928	15,777	21,757	28,066	31,197	509
Ashton-under-Lyne	150,370	...	...	...	...	56,959	66,801	64,558	75,310	9,486
Municipal	...	127,400	113,264	124,354	152,164	...	...	...	...	...
Stalybridge	...	...	23,526	25,902	34,800	...	...	...	...	...
Rural	...	78,627	91,262	111,174	129,674	...	...	...	...	...
		206,027	228,052	261,430	316,638	...				
Ashworth	1,230	1,605	1,658	1,724	1,544	277	233	174	142	1,021
Aspull	10,265	14 556	21,804	27,670	26,672	3,278	4,290	6,387	8,113	1,905
Barton-upon-Irwell	42,319	55,310	75,636	108,454	129,268	12,687	14,216	18,915	25,994	10,621
Beswick	1,928	3,000	6,580	14,890	20,728	404	881	2,506	7,957	96
Birtle-cum-Bamford	6,287	6,888	8,618	9,104	...	1,850	2,350	2,148	2,265	1,429
Heywood	...	...	...	...	408	...	...	...	...	...
Bury	...	...	...	...	1,774	...	...	...	...	...
Rural	...	...	...	...	6,304	...	...	...	...	...
					8,486					

SALFORD HUNDRED—*continued.*

Township.	Basis, etc. 1854.	Basis, etc. 1866.	Basis, etc. 1872.	Basis, etc. 1877.	Basis, etc. 1884.	Population in				Area in Statute Acres.
						1851.	1861.	1871.	1881.	
	£	£	£	£	£	Persons.	Persons.	Persons.	Persons.	Acres.
Blackrod	8,442	13,812	12,550	21,468	20,560	2,509	2,911	3,800	4,234	2,388
Blackley	8,231	10,685	14,018	18,134	21,680	3,503	4,112	5,173	6,075	1,840
Blatchinworth and Calderbrook	12,245	18,416	26,032	32,000	35,080	3,895	4,860	6,692	7,891	4,781
Bolton, Great	93,352	118,356	152,964	184,174	204,148	39,923	43,435	45,313	45,694	826
Bolton, Little	49,688	...	...	...	...	20,468	25,891	36,698	44,452	1,779
Municipal	...	79,014	108,898	132,226	148,778	...	...	...	...	...
Rural	...	5,704	7,932	11,500	12,772	...	...	...	...	...
	84,718	116,830	143,726	161,550						
Bradford	5,094	10,320	20,048	33,418	45,584	1,572	3,523	7,168	16,121	288
Bradshaw	3,749	4,407	4,364	5,348	5,730	853	792	870	755	1,156
Breightmet	4,302	5,850	6,356	7,354	6,254	1,540	1,562	1,500	1,525	873
Broughton	52,202	70,551	99,064	138,968	158,896	7,126	9,885	14,961	31,534	1,426
Burnage	2,984	3,791	4,352	4,592	6,110	563	624	706	848	666
Bury	73,099	92,446	116,814	136,970	167,360	25,484	30,397	32,611	39,283	2,330
Butterworth	20,281	32,006	...	...	...	5,786	6,704·	7,923	8,411	7,766
Municipal	...	...	2,478	2,892	3,122	...	...	...	...	...
Rural	...	...	36,280	43,248	47,200	...	...	...	...	...
		38,758	46,140	50,322						
Castleton	57,201	...	...	...	...	17,400	23,771	31,344	35,272	3,812
Heywood	...	...	...	...	7,100	...	...	...	...	...
Rochdale	...	48,244	92,800	125,078	130,200	...	...	...	..	...
Rural	...	41,839	21,422	37,454	23,082	...	...	...	...	...
	90,083	114,222	162,532	160,382						
Chadderton	18,739	33,463	51,402	75,378	90,936	6,188	7,486	12,203	16,899	3,082
Cheetham	58,981	75,470	96,684	113,190	137,920	11,175	17,446	21,617	25,721	919
Chorlton-upon-Medlock	143,151	162,952	202,528	256,388	266,848	35,558	44,795	50,281	55,598	646
Chorlton-cum-Hardy	4,241	6,193	10,710	13,004	18,596	761	739	1,466	2,332	1,280
Clifton	10,170	14,982	17,562	30,984	28,920	1,647	2,140	2,366	2,578	1,194
Crompton	16,063	22,985	26,608	37,112	49,348	6,375	7,032	7,3(2	9,797	2,864
Crumpsall	13,848	19,895	24,842	26,404	40,018	3,151	4,285	5,342	8,154	733
Denton	7,568	11,351	16,358	21,724	28,564	3,146	3,335	5,117	7,660	1,706
Didsbury	9,780	13,552	20,614	28,830	42,952	1,449	1,829	3,064	4,601	1,553
Droylsden	16,902	24,903	28,744	33,760	44,644	6,280	8,798	8,973	11,254	1,621
Edgeworth	3,513	4,189	5,084	5,876	6,186	1,230	1,350	1,675	1,862	2,925
Elton	22,360	32,056	41,474	46,312	...	6,778	8,172	9,591	11,947	2,553
Municipal	...	...	...	...	40,832	...	...	...	...	...
Rural	...	...	...	...	14,716	...	...	..	...	...
				55,548						
Entwistle	1,921	2,715	3,882	4,074	5,832	486	422	339	341	1,668
Failsworth	10,527	16,967	18,536	30,548	38,496	4,433	5,113	5,685	7,912	1,073
Farnworth	17,403	29,965	42,446	59,022	67,836	6,389	8,720	13,550	20,708	1,502
Flixton	5,797	6,476	7,234	8,524	12,754	1,334	1,302	1,512	1,776	1,564
Gorton	17,132	41,485	66,884	91,516	110,380	4,476	9,897	21,616	33,096	1,484
Halliwell	14,924	24,406	34,890	43,516	...	3,959	5,953	8,706	12,551	2,480
Municipal	...	...	...	...	36,214	...	...	...	...	...
Rural	...	...	...	...	14,662	...	...	...	...	...
					50,876					
Harpurhey	2,274	3,452	6,606	11,130	17,296	458	827	1,571	4,810	193
Harwood	3,410	4,788	5,098	5,656	4,970	2,057	2,055	1,976	1,811	1,240
Haughton	5,636	10,830	12,042	15,558	16,434	3,042	3,871	4,276	5,051	887
Heap	42,808	53,646	65,826	72,676	...	16,048	17,353	17,252	17,686	2,938
Bury	...	...	...	...	8,342	...	...	...	...	...
Heywood	...	...	...	...	72,180	...	...	..	...	...
Rural	...	...	...	...	2,930	...	...	...	...	...
					83,452					
Heaton	4,912	8,909	11,542	17,686	19,762	826	955	1,126	1,461	1,744
Heaton, Great	2,286	2,458	2,510	2,702	3,190	150	159	191	376	875
Heaton, Little	1,558	2,246	2,486	2,694	3,292	800	838	786	828	532
Heaton Norris	47,202	...	...	...	...	15,697	16,333	16,481	20,347	2,116
Municipal	...	40,337	44,520	59,774	60,484	...	...	...	...	...
Rural	...	13,050	21,440	33,636	41,016	..	...	...	...	...
		53,387	65,960	93,410	101,500					

SALFORD HUNDRED—*continued.*

Township.	Basis, etc. 1854.	Basis, etc. 1866.	Basis, etc. 1872.	Basis, etc, 1877.	Basis, etc. 1884.	Population in				Area in Statute Acres
						1851.	1861.	1871.	1881.	
	£	£	£	£	£	Persons.	Persons.	Persons.	Persons.	Acres.
Hopwood..............	8,326	16,342	21,446	28,164	...	1,575	2,281	3,655	4,440	2,126
Municipal	...	...	...	...	19,760	...	...	...	...	...
Rural	...	...	...	...	9,622	...	...	...	...	...
					29,382					
Horwich	11,799	14,027	14,706	16,148	15,990	3,952	3,471	3,671	3,761	3,254
Hulme..............	145,023	180,073	199,622	233,766	252,034	53,482	68,433	74,731	72,147	477
Hulton, Little	8,110	13,862	18,752	25,790	26,598	3,184	3,390	4,805	5,714	1,707
Hulton, Middle	4,420	4,594	5,230	8,582	8,464	888	790	911	2,051	1,517
Hulton, Over	3,899	5,205	6,508	8,696	9,112	452	447	574	984	1,316
Kearsley	13,732	20,031	22,020	29,256	29,150	4,236	5,003	5,830	7,253	997
Levenshulme	7,342	9,364	13,668	18,458	22,102	1,902	2,095	2,742	3,557	606
Lever, Darcy	5,654	6,018	7,678	9,872	10,210	2,091	2,071	2,048	1,994	499
Lever, Great	6,373	10,958	17,140	26,904	30,894	719	722	1,428	3,673	867
Lever, Little	10,553	15,690	18,130	21,354	16,092	3,511	3,890	4,204	4,413	807
Longworth	962	1,722	1,772	2,360	1,924	152	154	113	106	1,654
Lostock	3,688	4,718	7,010	7,236	8,592	620	580	670	782	1,520
Manchester..............	730,346	882,998	1,177,820	1,499,854	1,579,552	186,986	185,410	173,988	148,794	1,646
Middleton	18,434	21,814	22,938	27,756	34,568	8,717	9,876	9,472	10,346	1,930
Moss Side	12,396	21,691	38,388	68,766	102,744	943	2,695	5,403	18,184	421
Moston	6,446	7,975	12,134	15,224	19,108	904	1,199	1,663	3,466	1,297
Newton	36,518	43,259	62,892	83,502	117,170	10,801	14,907	19,446	31,240	1,585
Oldham	119,669	214,242	265,622	374,860	480,060	52,820	72,333	82,629	111,343	4,730
Openshaw............	14,011	28,532	45,580	62,846	83,608	3,759	8,623	11, 08	16,153	579
Pendlebury.............	13,252	22,572	28,068	42,326	33,776	2,750	3,548	5,163	8,162	1,031
Pendleton	58,334	84,497	110,608	151,186	192,420	14,224	20,900	25,489	40,246	2,254
Pilkington	34,070	44,255	53,250	61,702	74,522	12,863	12,303	11,949	13,144	5,469
Pilsworth	4,150	4,650	5,354	7,178	..	373	343	386	758	1,483
Heywood.........	...	...	...	...	4,806	...	...	...	...	...
Bury	...	...	...	...	64	...	...	...	...	...
Rural	...	...	...	...	4,666	...	...	...	...	...
					9,536					
Prestwich	13,883	22,557	31,382	34,396	43,706	4,096	5,288	6,820	8,627	1.917
Quarlton	1,181	1,390	1,362	1,406	1,518	361	253	264	271	798
Radcliffe	24,508	36,158	47,194	61,172	...	6,293	8,838	11,446	16,267	2,533
Municipal	...	...	...	...	926	...	...	...	...	...
Rural	...	...	...	...	80,146	...	...	...	...	...
					81,072					
Reddish	8,354	8,304	15,566	27,802	30,578	1,218	1,363	2,329	5,557	1,541
Rivington	2,106	3,451	4,258	12,152	12,094	412	369	531	330	2,768
Royton	17,632	19,263	25,674	36,896	47,008	6,974	7,493	7,794	10,582	1,372
Rumworth	4,883	7,511	...	...	...	1,386	1,861	3,226	4,952	1,244
Municipal	...	...	7,616	9,892	10,918	...	...	...	...	...
Rural	...	...	5,254	6,538	6,860	...	...	...	...	...
			12,870	16,430	17,778					
Rusholme	25,817	33,906	40,010	50,004	63,110	3,679	5,380	5,910	9,227	974
Salford	159,328	189,587	246,674	332,326	382,904	63,423	71,002	83,277	101,584	1,329
Sharples.........	11,076	13,236	15,222	19,352	20,902	3,904	3,294	3,315	3,710	3,999
Spotland	75,645	...	...	...	...	28,476	30,378	35,611	40,140	14,174
Bacup	...	...	...	...	39,140	...	...	...	...	...
Rochdale.........	...	22,917	47,486	52,772	54,432	...	...	...	...	...
Rural	...	79,867	82,132	109,142	66,084	...	...	...	...	...
		102,784	129,618	161,914	159,656					
Stretford.............	28,669	49,960	66,212	99,600	121,942	4,998	8,757	11,945	19,018	3,255
Thornham	5,346	6,950	9,016	10,710	10,490	1,510	2,027	2,079	1,860	1,936
Todmorden and Walsden	25,719	34,067	37,774	43,554	40,442	7,699	9,146	9,333	9,237	7,007
Tonge	6,529	11,760	13,274	19,182	24,234	3,831	4,606	5,115	7,254	392
Tonge with Haulgh ...	8,721	...	...	...	...	2,826	3,539	4,050	6,731	1,099
Municipal	...	6,962	11,022	13,008	16,304	...	...	...	...	...
Rural	...	6,280	8,070	11,186	14,790	...	...	...	...	...
		13,242	19,092	24.194	31,094					
Tottington Higher End	12,466	15,785	16,560	22,286	24,366	2,958	3,726	3,595	3,926	3,545
Tottington Lower End	26,894	33,277	44,852	53,664	...	10,691	11,764	12,531	16,428	5,271
Municipal	...	...	...	..	6,576	...	...	...	...	...
Rural	...	...	...	...	55,548	...	...	..	...	...
					62,124					

SALFORD HUNDRED—*continued.*

Township.	Basis, etc. 1854.	Basis, etc 1866.	Basis, etc. 1872.	Basis, etc. 1877.	Basis, etc. 1884.	Population in				Area in Statute Acres.
						1851.	1861.	1871.	1881.	
	£	£	£	£	£	Persons.	Persons.	Persons.	Persons.	Acres.
Turton....................	11,209	15,012	19,444	21,488	27,462	4,158	4,513	4,942	5,653	4,614
Urmston	3,871	4,172	6,236	9,526	15,954	730	748	996	2,242	993
Walmersley-cum- Shuttleworth	16,856	20,684	26,490	29,410	...	4,802	5,298	5,558	5,519	5,065
Municipal	...	...	...	...	564	...	...	...	...	...
Rural	...	...	...	...	33,998	...	...	...	...	...
					34,562					
Wardleworth	41,399	52,337	63,878	77,834	75,174	14,103	17,840	19,300	19,711	766
Westhoughton	12,026	18,811	26,092	33,224	42,904	4,547	5,156	6,609	9,197	4,341
Withington	12,027	23,404	43,078	73,124	88,060	1,492	2,712	6,291	11,286	2,502
Worsley	31,684	37,239	50,404	71,760	83,700	10,189	11,875	15,837	21,207	6,928
Wuerdale and Wardle..	19,769	...	...	...	...	7,255	8,201	8,988	10,487	3,523
Municipal	...	515	10,086	11,452	13,488	...	...	...	...	...
Rural	...	23,369	18,960	23,248	22,708	...	...	...	...	...
		23,884	29,046	34,700	36,196					
Total of Salford Hundred........	3,049,263	4,082,799	5,269,222	6,848,754	7,807,172	937,589	1,112,951	1,273,779	1,546,152	224,928

WEST DERBY HUNDRED.

Township.	Basis, etc. 1854.	Basis, etc. 1866.	Basis, etc. 1872.	Basis, etc. 1877.	Basis, etc. 1884.	Population in				Area in Statute Acres.
						1851.	1861.	1871.	1881.	
	£	£	£	£	£	Persons.	Persons.	Persons.	Persons.	Acres.
Abram.........	4,990	6,624	8,576	14,692	24,748	968	911	1,065	2,638	1,982
Aintree	3,212	3,829	4,016	5,204	6,380	312	300	278	277	850
Allerton	6,267	9,539	13,754	17,746	22,192	482	559	717	830	1,586
Altcar	5,600	5,868	5,930	6,826	7,166	501	540	570	550	4,083
Ashton-in-Makerfield..	16,822	32,393	43,488	50,964	58.384	5,679	6,566	7.463	9,824	6,250
Astley	7,325	8,594	9,400	12,788	12,656	2,237	2,109	2,030	2,669	2,685
Atherton	13,070	22,490	30,972	37,768	46,976	4,655	5,907	7,531	12,602	2,426
Aughton	11,854	15,271	18,682	21,918	26,940	1,655	1,870	2,597	3,145	4,610
Bedford	12,008	15,929	17,184	19,816	25,618	5,384	6,558	6,610	7,246	2,826
Bickerstaffe..............	9,785	11,725	12,068	15,970	18,520	1,667	1,637	1,910	2,269	6,444
Billinge Chapel End ...	3,445	5,091	4,212	4,538	4,292	1,777	2,015	1,961	1,935	1,161
Billinge Higher End ...	3,438	3,903	3,940	3,570	4,164	900	1,051	1,267	1,402	1,571
Birkdale	2,678	11,909	21,288	30,728	50,918	625	1,286	3,375	8,705	2,215
Bold	7,636	9,647	11,444	12,946	16,778	773	798	921	880	4,483
Bootle-cum-Linacre ...	18,538	45,254	68,660	103,770	278,692	4,106	6,414	16,247	27,374	1,404
Burscough	11,032	13,219	13,170	15,608	19,200	2,480	2,461	2,202	2.290	4,960
Burtonwood	8,499	10,507	13,030	13,638	15,658	831	990	1,112	1,268	4,193
Childwall	2,899	3,800	4,034	4,110	4,328	166	174	197	187	1,729
Cronton	2,305	2,393	2,936	3,350	4,430	439	412	429	468	1,143
Crosby, Great..........	12,700	28,832	44,568	50,936	70,490	2,403	3,794	6,362	9,373	2,168
Crosby, Little..........	3,489	4,500	4,564	5,434	5,828	407	418	432	553	1,811
Croxteth Park	1,698	1,614	1,500	2,098	2,096	41	46	31	39	959
Cuerdley...	2,426	3,329	4,058	5,396	6,460	193	192	187	227	1,723
Culcheth	9,430	12,254	13,142	15,404	16,234	2,395	2,214	2,266	2,267	5,369
Dalton	3,203	3,329	3,548	3,764	3.472	462	453	497	494	2,104
Ditton	3,787	5,082	7,550	8,352	13,338	584	764	1,139	1,412	1,938
Downholland	4,867	5,470	5,686	6,044	6,138	756	748	757	748	3,473
Eccleston	21,356	28,627	35,736	43,888	...	8,509	11,640	13,832	18,026	3,569
Municipal	...	...	...	...	35,756	...	...	...	...	...
Rural	...	...	...	...	24,424	...	...	...	...	...
					60,180					
Everton	81,000	208,047	266,604	280,020	329,520	25,883	54,848	90,937	109,812	693
Fazackerley	5,052	5,852	6,754	8,604	9,088	427	407	454	533	1,709
Formby	6,489	9,073	10,898	14,160	23,060	1,594	1,780	2,016	3,908	6,619
Garston	21,537	36,300	49,246	64,318	73.108	2,756	4,720	7,840	10,271	1,625
Golborne...............	5,397	11,403	16,016	21,684	23.420	1,910	2,776	3,688	4,502	1,679
Haigh	7,094	8,102	13,932	17,756	15,556	1,220	1,171	1,201	1,186	2,135
Hale..........	3,453	3,714	3,900	4,022	4,536	629	648	665	571	2,612
Halewood	6,617	9,748	13,846	20,264	27,820	1,146	1,205	1,790	1,857	3,988
Halsall.................	8,599	10,504	10,988	11,472	12,454	1,194	1,204	1,336	1,368	6,995
Haydock	8,804	11,983	16,156	20,786	20,358	1,994	3,615	5,286	5,863	2,409

WEST DERBY HUNDRED—*continued.*

Township.	Basis, etc. 1854.	Basis, etc. 1866.	Basis, etc. 1872.	Basis, etc. 1877.	Basis, etc. 1884.	Population in				Area in Statute Acres.
						1851.	1861.	1871.	1881.	
	£	£	£	£	£	Persons.	Persons.	Persons.	Persons.	Acres.
Hindley	16,000	25,271	32,572	50,952	55,664	7,023	8,477	10,627	14,715	2,611
Houghton, Middleton, and Arbury	1,614	2,019	2,092	2,278	2,258	238	253	252	242	853
Huyton with Roby	14,968	23,179	33,300	37,468	45,000	1,785	2,079	3,184	4,060	3,054
Ince Blundell	4,771	5,660	5,604	6,360	6,532	561	572	540	516	2,316
Ince-in-Makerfield	20,701	48,070	35,700	50,904	64,760	3,670	8,266	11,989	16,007	2,320
Kenyon	4,587	5,779	6,542	9,672	8,726	293	274	234	233	1,685
Kirkby	7,114	9,502	10,000	12,154	13,206	1,460	1,415	1,397	1,401	4,175
Kirkdale	31,505	155,648	180,984	251,600	368,554	9,893	16,135	32,978	58,145	926
Knowsley	9,364	9,826	10,234	13,612	13,746	1,486	1,349	1,283	1,248	5,058
Lathom	18,406	21,821	24,100	27,844	34,896	3,291	3,385	3,659	4,161	8,694
Litherland	12,491	23,661	30,552	34,550	54,672	2,252	3,632	4,884	7,204	1,205
Liverpool	1,040,400	1,520,391	1,883,526	1,921,416	2,046,024	258,236	269,742	238,411	210,164	2,470
Lowton	5,611	7,165	7,628	8,572	9,574	2,140	2,384	2,144	2,357	1,830
Lunt	1,126	1,152	1,200	1,264	1,208	75	78	103	104	477
Lydiate	5,171	6,133	6,594	6,876	7,414	842	848	848	1,071	1.995
Maghull	7,430	8,555	9,982	11,520	13,726	1,056	1,144	1,284	1,429	2,098
Melling	5,160	5,809	6,372	6,990	7,896	662	728	771	802	2,118
Netherton	2,632	3,400	3,416	3,708	3,942	258	286	350	386	1,126
Newton-in-Makerfield	14,848	28,424	34,308	40,666	52,254	3,719	5,909	8,244	10,580	3,103
North Meols	27,605	81,302	...	...	...	8,694	14,661	22,274	33,763	8,467
Municipal	...	...	91,870	168,172	219,343	...	...	...	...	...
Rural	...	...	12,582	7,156	10,854	...	...	...	...	...
			104,452	175,328	230,202					
Ormskirk	10,308	12,338	13,284	15,456	20,664	6,183	6,426	6,127	6,651	578
Orrell	4,793	5,486	7,290	10,022	10,816	2,762	2,932	3,561	4,299	1,618
Orrell and Ford	2,344	2,800	3,256	3,506	5,020	279	358	414	637	727
Parr	10,628	19,342	22,756	27,636	31,660	4,875	8,253	9,281	11,278	1,633
Pemberton	13,339	22,557	27,908	41,242	47,028	5,252	6,870	10,374	13,762	2,894
Penketh	2,789	4,054	5,344	6,092	8,122	679	784	1,042	1,239	1,059
Pennington	9,676	13,666	15,528	19,284	25,888	4,573	5,015	5,423	6,640	1,483
Poulton with Fearnhead	3,732	4,234	4,306	4,882	5,722	708	672	687	742	1,320
Prescot	9,092	9,050	9,502	10,966	12,916	6,393	5,136	5,077	5,546	270
Rainford	8,622	12,123	16,546	19,908	24,622	2,333	2,784	3,336	3,745	5,872
Rainhill	7,682	10,826	14,698	14,814	15,054	1,522	2,130	2,308	2,219	1,640
Rixton with Glazebrook	3,471	4,402	4,276	6,684	7,652	796	752	739	881	2,988
Sankey, Great	3,655	5,658	5,472	7,060	8,590	527	563	630	630	1,923
Scarisbrick	12,128	15,367	16,500	18,834	22,030	2,109	2,112	2,143	2,232	8,397
Sefton	2,763	3,209	3,280	3,584	4,118	433	430	390	382	1,234
Simonswood	2,976	3,537	3,652	6,504	7,246	470	461	451	465	2,645
Skelmersdale	3,366	7,477	12,332	27,444	36,184	760	1,028	3,171	5,707	1,941
Southworth with Croft	3,743	4,715	5,006	5,050	5,246	1,097	1,094	1,033	1,032	1,884
Speke	4,837	5,750	7,652	9,372	14,064	534	571	509	513	3,734
Sutton	26,667	49,213	74,172	98,902	97,178	5,288	9,223	10,905	12,695	3,725
Thornton	2,041	2,264	2,314	2,434	2,552	298	291	294	275	774
Torbock	3,799	4,142	4,286	5,194	6,542	681	626	647	629	2,413
Toxteth Park	18,592	...	...	...	...	61,334	69,284	85,842	117,028	3,598
Municipal	...	266,800	318,968	372,426	453,850	...	...	...	...	...
Rural	...	30,650	43,502	60,854	123,716	...	...	...	...	...
		297,450	362,470	433,280	577,566					
Tyldesley with Shackerley	14,152	17,875	28,296	43,326	48,132	5,397	6,029	6,408	9,954	2,490
Upholland	12,147	14,423	16,924	22,078	20,406	3,359	3,463	4,158	4,435	4,685
Walton on the Hill	18,487	22,881	30,988	46,284	124,620	2,469	3,598	6,459	18,715	1,944
Warrington	52,390	...	...	...	...	20,800	24,050	29,894	40,957	2,887
Municipal	...	60,779	89,318	106,248	139,024	...	..	...	...	...
Rural	...	6,847	6,936	10,102	16,808	...	...	...	...	...
		67,626	96,254	116,350	155,832					
Wavertree	27,782	45,798	66,170	73,648	94,266	4,011	5,392	7,810	11,097	1,838
West Derby	144,190	...	...	...	...	32,973	52,694	77,969	101,162	6,203
Municipal	...	136,179	172,114	201,918	240,126	...	...	...	...	...
Rural	...	109,476	158,104	171,434	212,044	...	...	...	...	...
		245,655	330,218	373,352	452,170	...				
Westleigh	8,728	17,191	24,918	29,120	34,288	3,750	4,434	5,590	7,848	1,883
Whiston	8,658	9,547	12,168	20,302	20,884	1,825	1,727	2,058	2,705	1,783
Widnes	11,195	30,564	56,736	91,692	121,234	3,217	6,905	14,359	24,935	3,339

WEST DERBY HUNDRED—*continued.*

Township.	Basis, etc. 1854.	Basis, etc. 1866.	Basis, etc. 1872.	Basis, etc. 1877.	Basis, etc. 1884.	Population in 1851.	1861.	1871.	1881.	Area in Statute Acres.
	£	£	£	£	£	Persons.	Persons.	Persons.	Persons.	Acres.
Wigan	63,894	84,847	97,396	123,964	163,592	31,941	37,658	39,110	48,194	2,188
Windle	24,042	43,324	56,190	65,716	...	9,870	12,229	15,016	19,473	3,150
Municipal	...	...	...	...	81,550	..	...	...	...	...
Rural	...	...	...	...	9,400	...	...	...	...	..
					90,950					
Winstanley................	4,592	6,206	6,856	8,244	7,606	675	633	602	545	1,859
Winwick with Hulme..	5,337	7,241	9,456	10,388	10,362	469	451	456	487	1,440
Woolston with Martinscroft	2,774	2,936	3,598	4,066	4,620	516	496	501	504	1,566
Woolton, Little	6,333	8,715	11,890	15,588	15,830	1,016	1,062	1,128	1,159	1,388
Woolton, Much	11,222	15,802	19,602	22,814	22,350	3,669	3,586	4,684	4,541	795
Total of West Derby Hundred	2,374,199	3,798,806	4,734,124	5,539,168	6,795,072	633,117	769,020	915,240	1,124,095	260,548

SUMMARY.

Hundred.	Basis, etc. 1854.	Basis, etc. 1866.	Basis, etc. 1872.	Basis, etc. 1877.	Basis, etc. 1884.	Population in 1851.	1861.	1871.	1881.	Area in Statute Acres.
	£	£	£	£	£	Persons.	Persons.	Persons.	Persons.	Acres.
Lonsdale	298,276	423,665	514,402	767,630	1,010,772	65,317	71,164	94,842	139,033	291,408
Amounderness ...	414,272	525,239	592,544	718,018	896,956	113,243	130,728	139,883	162,118	158,295
Blackburn	574,608	950,663	1,159,472	1,432,206	1,738,740	228,329	286,955	335,440	417,085	183,649
Leyland	199,038	248,795	282,236	321,114	370,946	53,641	58,622	60,311	65,958	88,244
Salford	3,049,263	4,082,799	5,269,222	6,848,754	7,791,862	937,589	1,112,951	1,273,779	1,546,152	224,928
West Derby	2,374,199	3,798,806	4,734,124	5,539,168	6,789,222	633,117	769,020	915,240	1,124,095	260,548
Grand Total of County ...	6,909,656	10,029,967	12,552,000	15,626,890	18,598,498	2,031,236	2,429,440	2,819,495	3,454,441	1,207,072

Signed, by order of the Committee,

C. R. JACSON, *Chairman.*

Allowed and confirmed by the Court of Annual General Session of the Peace held by adjournment at Preston, in and for the County Palatine of Lancaster, on Thursday, the Third day of April, in the forty-seventh year of the reign of Queen Victoria, and in the year of our Lord one thousand eight hundred and eighty-four, pursuant to the Statute.

Le Gendre N. Starkie (Colonel),
Chairman.

Two or three Tables present useful summaries :—

No. 1.—TABLE SHOWING THE VALUATION OF THE VARIOUS POOR-LAW UNIONS IN THE COUNTY (1884).

Union.	Total.	Union.	Total.
*Ashton-under-Lyne	£406,280	Manchester (Township)	£1,579,552
Barton-upon-Irwell	392,538	Oldham	739,398
Barrow-in-Furness	241,046	Ormskirk	570,982
Blackburn	733,936	Prescot	659,112
Bolton	831,828	Preston	568,588
Burnley	503,796	Prestwich	508,188
Bury	616,382	Rochdale	516,810
Chorley	259,058	Salford	767,996
Chorlton	1,185,472	*Stockport	132,078
*Clitheroe	90,910	*Todmorden	40,442
Fylde, The..	333,864	Toxteth Park	577,566
Garstang	123,312	Ulverston	405,444
Haslingden	360,560	*Warrington	303,134
*Kendal	2,430	West Derby	1,932,582
Lancaster	268,806	Wigan	577,948
Leigh	251,512		
Liverpool (Township)	2,046,024	Total...........£18,623,910	
Lunesdale	96,336		

* Part in other Counties.

No. 2.—VALUATION OF CITIES AND BOROUGHS HAVING COURTS OF QUARTER SESSIONS.

Hundred.	City or Borough.	Comprising the Township of	Valuation of the Township.	Valuation of City or Borough.
			£	£
Salford	Bolton	Great Bolton	204,148	
		Little Bolton (part of)	148,778	
		Halliwell (part of)............	36,214	416,362
		Rumworth do.	10,918	
		Tonge-with-Haulgh (part of)	16,304	
West Derby	Liverpool	Liverpool	2,046,024	
		Everton	329,520	
		Kirkdale	368,554	3,438,074
		Toxteth Park (part of)	453,850	
		West Derby do.	240,126	
Salford	Manchester	Manchester	1,579,552	
		Ardwick	128,928	
		Beswick	20,728	2,386,010
		Chorlton-upon-Medlock	266,848	
		Cheetham	137,920	
		Hulme	252,034	
West Derby	Wigan	Wigan........ ..,.............	....	163,592
			Total.........	6,404,038

No. 3.—VALUATION OF BOROUGHS NOT HAVING GRANTS OF QUARTER SESSIONS, HAVING THEIR OWN POLICE, AND NOT LIABLE TO BE RATED FOR COUNTY CONSTABULARY PURPOSES.

Hundred.	Borough.	Comprising the Township of	Valuation of Township.	Valuation of Borough.
			£	£
Blackburn	Accrington	Accrington	......	115,178
Salford	Ashton-under-Lyne	Ashton-under-Lyne (part of).	......	152,164
Salford	Stalybridge	Do. do. ..	......	34,800
Lonsdale	Barrow-in-Furness	Barrow-in-Furness......... ..	......	241,046
Blackburn	Blackburn	Blackburn	361,374	
		Little Harwood	6,004	
		Lower Darwen (part of) .. .	17,768	413,574
		Livesey (part of)	18,292	
		Witton do.	10,136	
Lonsdale	Lancaster	Lancaster	......	85,126
Salford	Oldham	Oldham	......	480,060
Amounderness	Preston	Fishwick	9,422	
		Grimsargh-with-Brockholes (part of)	410	
		Lea, Ashton, Ingol, and Cottam (part of)	9,676	341,060
		Preston	318,844	
		Ribbleton (part of)	2,708	
Salford	Rochdale	Butterworth do.	3,122	
		Castleton do.	130,200	
		Spotland do.	54,432	276,416
		Wardleworth	75,174	
		Wuerdale and Wardle (part of)	13,488	
Salford	Salford	Broughton	158,896	
		Pendleton	192,420	734,220
		Salford	382,902	
Salford	Stockport	Heaton Norris (part of)	......	60,484
West Derby	Southport	North Meols do.	......	219,348
West Derby	Warrington	Warrington do.	......	139,024
			Total	£3,292,500

Valuation of Boroughs as above having their own Police £3,292,500

Valuation of Boroughs having separate Courts of Quarter Sessions 6,404,038

9,696,538

Valuation of part of County rateable for County Constabulary 8,927,372

Total Valuation of the County £18,623,910

No. 4.—THE FOLLOWING TOWNSHIPS ARE NOT LIABLE TO CONTRIBUTE TOWARDS THE REPAIRS OF BRIDGES.

Hundred.	Township.	Valuation of Township.	Total exempt in Hundred.
		£	£
Lonsdale	¹ Lancaster	85,126	85,126
Amounderness	Preston	318,844	318,844
Blackburn	{ Clitheroe	36,548	} 36,662
	{ Clitheroe Castle	114	
West Derby	{ Altcar	7,166	} 17,528
	{ Winwick-with-Hulme	10,362	
			158,160
West Derby	{ Liverpool	2,046,024	} 2,209,616
	{ Wigan	163,592	

Valuation of County ex Boroughs having separate Quarter Sessions £12,219,872
    Deduct—Townships exempt from contributing as above... 458,160

Valuation upon which Rates are levied for County and Hundred Bridges £11,761,712
Valuation of Boroughs having separate Quarter Sessions £6,404,038
    Deduct—Liverpool and Wigan Townships exempt 2,209,616

Valuation for Orders upon Boroughs having separate Quarter Sessions 4,194,422

Total Valuation of County contributing towards the repair of County and Hundred Bridges £15,956,134

The following Table shows the amounts of various rates laid for different purposes, as County and Hundred Bridges, Houses of Correction, salary of Chairman of Quarter Sessions, and payments for the County Constabulary force. In each column we have omitted the shillings and pence, as immaterial to the substantial result :—

No. 5.—VALUATION OF THE WHOLE OF THE COUNTY IN HUNDREDS, INCLUDING BOROUGHS HAVING GRANTS OR QUARTER SESSIONS. THE AMOUNTS STATED IN THE HEADS OF THE COLUMNS INDICATE THE AMOUNT OF A RATE AT SO MUCH IN THE POUND ON THE BASIS OR STANDARD.

Hundred.	Annual Value. 1884.	Rate of a penny.	7-8ths of a penny.	Three far-things.	5-8ths of a penny.	Half-penny.	3-8ths of a penny.	Far-thing.	3-16ths of a penny.	1-8th of a penny.	1-12th of a penny.	1-16th of a penny.	1-24th of a penny.	1-32nd of a penny.
	£	£	£	£	£	£	£	£	£	£	£	£	£	£
Lonsdale	1,014,062	4,225	3,697	3,168	2,640	2,112	1,584	1,056	792	528	352	264	176	132
Amounderness	896,956	3,737	3,270	2,802	2,335	1,868	1,401	934	700	467	311	233	155	116
Blackburn	1,739,702	7,248	6,342	5,436	4,530	3,624	2,718	1,812	1,359	906	604	453	302	226
Leyland	370,946	1,545	1,352	1,159	966	772	579	386	289	193	128	96	64	48
Salford	7,807,172	32,529	28,463	24,397	20,331	16,264	12,198	8,132	6,099	4,066	2,710	2,033	1,355	1,016
West Derby	6,795,072	28,312	24,773	21,234	17,695	14,156	10,617	7,078	5,308	3,539	2,359	1,769	1,179	884
Total	18,623,910	77,599	67,899	58,199	48,499	38,799	29,099	19,399	14,549	9,699	6,466	4,849	3,233	2,424

No. 6.—OMITTING BOROUGHS HAVING GRANTS OF QUARTER SESSIONS. FOR THE COUNTY TREASURER, FOR GENERAL PURPOSES, FOR COUNTY LUNATIC ASYLUMS, AND FOR MAIN ROADS.

Hundred.	Annual Value. 1884.	Rate of a penny.	7-8ths of a penny.	Three far-things.	5-8ths of a penny.	Half-penny.	3-8ths of a penny.	Far-thing.	3-16ths of a penny.	1-8th of a penny.	1-12th of a penny.	1-16th of a penny.	1-24th of a penny.	1-32nd of a penny.
	£	£	£	£	£	£	£	£	£	£	£	£	£	£
Lonsdale	1,014,062	4,225	3,697	3,168	2,640	2,112	1,584	1,056	792	528	352	264	176	132
Amounderness	896,956	3,737	3,270	2,802	2,335	1,868	1,401	934	700	467	311	233	155	116
Blackburn	1,739,702	7,248	6,342	5,436	4,530	3,624	2,718	1,812	1,359	906	604	453	302	226
Leyland	370,946	1,545	1,352	1,159	966	772	579	386	289	193	128	96	64	48
Salford	5,004,800	20,853	18,246	15,640	13,083	10,426	7,820	5,213	3,910	2,606	1,737	1,303	868	651
West Derby	3,193,406	13,305	11,642	9,979	8,316	6,652	4,989	3,326	2,494	1,663	1,108	831	554	415
Total	12,219,872	50,916	44,551	38,187	31,822	25,458	19,093	12,729	9,546	6,364	4,243	3,182	2,121	1,591

·₀· The omission of the shillings and pence in the several Hundreds causes an apparent inaccuracy in the total.

¹ Contributes to the cost of Caton (Lune) Bridge.

URBAN SANITARY AUTHORITIES.

(The initials M.B. stand for Municipal Borough, L.B. Local Board, and I.C. Improvement Commissioners.)

Authorities.	Character of Authority.	Population, 1881.	Rateable Value, 1881.	Authorities.	Character of Authority.	Population, 1881.	Rateable Value, 1881.
			£				£
Abram	L.B.	2,638	25,000	Littleborough	L.B.	10,405	36,381
Accrington	M.B.	31,435	113,820	Little Crosby	L.B.	583	6,076
Adlington	L.B.	3,258	9,708	Little Hulton	L.B.	5,724	24,2̃3
Allerton	L.B.	830	19,000	Little Lever	L.B·	4,413	15,340
Ashton-in-Makerfield	L.B.	9,825	57,547	Little Woolton	L.B.	1,159	16,140
Ashton-under-Lyne	M.B.	37,027	139,960	Liverpool	M.B.	552,508	3,168,559
Aspull	L.B.	8,111	24,814	Lytham	I.C.	5,616	28,391
Astley Bridge	L.B.	5,613	26,013	Manchester	M.B.	341,414	2,411,509
Atherton	L.B.	12,602	48,083	Middleton	M.B.	18,952	55,141
Audenshaw	L.B.	5,930	32,838	Milnrow	L.B.	7,021	34,340
Bacup	M.B.	25,034	81,010	Mossley	M.B.	13,382	55,043
Barrow-in-Furness	M.B.	47,100	220,860	Moss Side	L.B.	18,129	101,768
Barton, Eccles, Winton, and				Much Woolton	L.B.	4,712	21,248
Monton	L.B.	21,785	99,154	Nelson	L.B.	10,381	44,838
Billinge	L.B.	3,882	18,661	Newton Heath	L.B.	30,000	100,450
Birkdale	L.B.	8,706	51,826	Norden	L.B.	4,044	16,355
Blackburn	M.B.	104,012	383,097	Oldham	M.B.	111,343	564,026
Blackpool	M.B.	14,229	148,190	Openshaw	L.B.	16,153	80,883
Blackrod	L.B.	4,234	19,337	Ormskirk	L.B.	6,651	19,673
Bolton	M.B.	105,414	400,811	Orrell	L.B.	4,299	11,058
Bootle-cum-Linacre	M.B.	27,374	404,888	Oswaldtwisle	L.B.	12,206	43,635
Brierfield	L.B.	4,088	13,015	Over Darwen	M.B.	31,833	103,602
Burnley	M.B.	58,751	213,630	Padiham and Hapton	L.B.	8,983	29,752
Bury	M.B.	52,213	219,308	Pemberton	L.B.	13,763	49,974
Castleton	L.B.	4,017	25,524	Poulton, &c.	L.B.	3,931	29,903
Chadderton	L.B.	16,897	81,500	Prescot	L.B.	6,418	18,676
Childwall	L.B.	207	4,012	Preston	M.B.	96,537	325,973
Chorley	M.B.	19,478	61,652	Prestwich	L.B.	8,627	40,500
Church	L.B.	4,850	19,015	Radcliffe	L.B.	16,267	75,233
Clayton-le-Moors	L.B.	6,694	20,418	Rainford	L.B.	3,745	22,715
Clitheroe	M.B.	10,176	32,522	Ramsbottom	L.B.	18,000	84,334
Colne and Marsden	L.B.	11,970	45,303	Rawtenstall	L.B.	29,226	106,384
Crompton	L.B.	9,797	42,842	Reddish	L.B.	5,557	29,707
Croston	L.B.	1,791	10,189	Rishton	L.B.	4,056	21,730
Crumpsall	L.B.	8,151	38,722	Rochdale	M.B.	68,866	252,186
Dalton-in-Furness	L.B.	13,339	94,208	Royton	L.B.	11,433	44,000
Denton and Haughton	L.B.	12,711	40,367	St. Ann's-on-the-Sea	L.B.	1,179	11,085
Droylsden	L.B.	8,687	30,000	St. Helens	M.B.	61,830	247,483
Failsworth	L.B.	7,907	34,043	Salford	M.B.	176,235	755,847
Farnworth	L.B.	20,708	63,632	Skelmersdale	L.B.	5,707	31,340
Fleetwood	I.C.	8,000	32,254	Southport	M.B.	32,206	221,000
Fulwood	L.B.	3,725	16,383	Standish-with-Langtree	L.B.	4,261	22,065
Garston	L.B.	10,131	85,557	Stretford	L.B.	19,025	122,437
Gorton	L.B.	33,091	102,613	Swinton and Pendlebury	L.B.	18,108	70,000
Grange	L.B.	1,150	3,172	Todmorden	L.B.	23,861	76,582
Great Crosby	L.B.	5,100	35,562	Toxteth Park	L.B,	10,371	128,758
Great Harwood	L.B.	6,287	23,405	Trawden	L.B.	2,164	9,589
Haslingden	L.B.	16,291	63,778	Turton	L.B.	5,653	24,610
Haydock	L.B.	5,863	19,302	Tyldesley, &c.	L.B.	9,953	46,738
Heaton Norris	L.B.	5,797	36,353	Ulverston	L.B.	10,008	43,703
Heywood	M.B.	22,979	96,234	Upholland	L.B.	4,435	23,595
Hindley	L.B.	14,715	57,270	Walton-le-Dale	L.B.	9,286	31,651
Horwich	L.B.	3,761	15,642	Walton-on-the-Hill	L.B.	18,772	174,652
Hurst	L.B.	6,382	20,420	Warrington	M.B.	41,452	140,703
Huyton-with-Roby	L.B.	4,060	30,089	Waterloo-with-Seaforth	L.B.	9,107	86,941
Ince-in-Makerfield	L.B.	16,009	63,476	Wavertree	L.B.	11,157	101,542
Kearsley	L.B.	7,241	23,880	West Derby	L.B.	33,614	212,048
Kirkham	L.B.	3,840	10,716	Westhoughton	L.B.	9,197	36,865
Lancaster	M.B.	20,663	92,000	Whitefield	L.B.	9,516	40,242
Lathom	L.B.	4,161	31,950	Whitworth	L.B.	12,000	49,603
Lees	L.B.	3,511	12,056	Widnes	L.B.	24,919	28,828
Leigh	L.B.	21,733	83,863	Wigan	M.B.	48,194	66,445
Levenshulme	L.B.	4,360	19,073	Withington	L.B.	17,108	42,461
Leyland	L.B.	4,961	27,822	Wuerdle and Wardle	L.B.	4,631	21,259
Litherland	L.B.	2,486	13,920				

POOR LAW (AND RURAL SANITARY) AUTHORITIES.

Unions and Authorities.	Area Acres.	Population (1881).	Rateable Value (1886).	Unions and Authorities.	Area Acres.	Population (1881).	Rateable Value (1886).
			£				£
Ashton-under-Lyne (P.L.A.)	3,8579	154,501	594.186	Leigh (R.S.A.)	13,247	12,027	67,200
Ashton-under-Lyne (R.S.A.)	24,928	12,910	72,093	Liverpool†	2,470	207,132	2,086,555
Barrow-in-Furness†	16,937	47,276	221,602	Lunesdale	75,734	7,132	86,380
Barton-upon-Ir ell	24,552	72,811	403,744	Manchester†	1,577	148,799	1,502,766
Blackburn (P.L.A.)	45,855	175,948	673,804	Oldham	16,230	168,459	590,336
Blackburn (R.S.A.)	...	8,102	60,025	Ormskirk	87,884	83,179	560,182
Bolton	46,413	192,413	779.036	Prescot	53,140	117,938	634,816
Burnley (P.L.A.)	63,674	118,391	529,202	Preston (P.L.A.)	67,539	129,147	549,997
Burnley (R.S.A.)	47,012	26,011	151,652	Preston (R.S.A.)	49,219	15,907	143,270
Bury	33,527	129,608	572,969	Prestwich	11,346	121,269	480,793
Chorley (P.L.A.)	54,426	47,726	234,723	Rochdale*	34,822	121,910	468,557
Chorley (R.S.A.)	43,663	18,244	145,147	Salford*	6,040	181,525	783,908
Chorlton*	11,697	258,206	1,170,706	Todmorden	84,994	35,526	141,887
Clitheroe	119,226	23,493	155,803	Toxteth Park†	3,598	116,729	543,272
Fylde	59,032	40,663	355,664	Ulverston	126,568	19,184	176,842
Garstang	60,199	12,375	122,999	Warrington	31,071	70,222	309,054
Haslingden	26,712	95,293	352,347	West Derby (P.L.A.)	35,909	358,073	2,168,358
Lancaster	60,038	40,769	296,698	West Derby (R.S.A.)	18,597	13,597	56,386
Leigh (P.L.A.)	24,352	56,315	245,481	Wigan	48,396	139,867	567,953

COUNTY POLICE DIVISIONS.
For Petty Sessional Purposes.

Police Divisions.	Petty Sessions held at	Days of Holding Petty Sessions.
N. Lonsdale	Ulverston (also Barrow)	Every Thursday (11 o'clock).
"	Cartmel	First Tuesday.
"	Hawkshead	Alternate Mondays.
S. Lonsdale	Hornby	Once a month.
"	Lancaster	Every Saturday.
Garstang	Garstang	Alternate Thursdays.
"	Preston	Every Saturday.
Kirkham	Kirkham, Fleetwood, and Blackpool	Court House at each place every alternate Monday.
L. Blackburn	Blackburn	Every Wednesday.
"	Haslingden	Alternate Mondays.
"	Over arwen	Every Thursday.
"	Walton-le-Dale	Alternate Fridays.
"	Clitheroe	Every fourth Tuesday.
Church	Church	Every Thursday.
"	Blackburn	Every Wednesday.
"	Clitheroe (County)	Once a month.
"	Clitheroe (Borough)	Once a month.
H. Blackburn	Burnley (Borough)	Every Wednesday.
"	Burnley (County)	Alternate Mondays.
Rossendale	Bacup	Every Wednesday.
"	Rawtenstall	Alternate Thursdays.
"	Haslingden	Alternate Mondays.
Leyland Hundred	Chorley and Croston	Chorley, every Tuesday ; Croston, every 2nd Wednesday.
Leyland	Leyland	Every 2nd Monday.
Bolton	County Police Station, Bolton	Mondays and Thursdays, every week.
Bury	Bury (County)	} Mondays and Thursdays, every week.
"	Bury (Borough)	
"	Heywood (Borough)	Wednesdays.
Rochdale	Rochdale	Every Wednesday.
"	Middleton	Alternate Thursdays.
"	Todmorden	Alternate Thursdays.
"	Royton	Every Wednesday.
Ashton-under-Lyne	Ashton-under-Lyne	Mondays, Wednesdays, and Saturdays.
Manchester	Manchester, Worsley, Heaton Norris, and Gorton	} Manchester, daily ; Worsley, alternate Fridays ; Gorton, every Wednesday ; Heaton Norris, alternate Mondays.
West Derby and Bootle	Liverpool	Liverpool, every Monday, Wednesday, and Saturday.
Bootle (County)	Liverpool	Every Monday, Wednesday, and Saturday.
Bootle (Borough)	Bootle (Borough)	Daily.
Ormskirk	Ormskirk	First Friday.
"	Southport	1st and 3rd Thursdays.
Prescot	Prescot, Widnes, and Woolton	{ Prescot, 1st and 3rd Tuesdays ; Widnes, every Wednesday ; and Woolton, 1st and 3rd Fridays.
St. Helens	St. Helens	Monday, fortnightly.
Warrington	Leigh	Every Monday.
"	Warrington and Newton-le-Willows	{ Warrington, 1st and 3rd Wednesdays ; Newton-le-Willows, 2nd and last Saturdays.
Wigan	Wigan	Every Monday and Friday.

* Poor-Law Unions.   † Poor-Law Parishes only—not Rural Sanitary Authorities.

COUNTY MAGISTRATES AND DEPUTY LIEUTENANTS.

The following List of Magistrates on the Commission of the Peace for the County Palatine of Lancaster is compiled from the Official List, obligingly furnished by Frederic Campbell Hulton, Esq., Clerk of the Peace for the County. It has been corrected so as to represent the state of the Commission in October 1887. Marked thus * are Deputy Lieutenants and Magistrates, the others are Magistrates only.

LONSDALE HUNDRED.

Ainslie, Aymer, Esq., Hall-Garth, Kellet, Carnforth. October 14, 1872.

Ainslie, Montague Mordaunt, Esq., Hawkshead, and 59A, Davies Street, Berkeley Square, London, W. January 4, 1847.

Ainslie, William George, Esq., M.P., Ulverston. May 14, 1874.

Ainsworth, David, Esq., The Flosh, Whitehaven. May 22, 1879.

*Ainsworth, David, Esq. (Lieut.-Colonel), Broughton Hall, Grange, Cartmel. October 20, 1869.

Archibald, Charles William, Esq., Rusland Hall, Ulverston. August 22, 1883.

Askew, Henry William, Esq., Burswood Park, Walton-on-Thames. December 31, 1855.

Atkinson-Grimshaw, Richard, clerk, Torquay. February 14, 1859.

Baines, Lazarus Threlfall, Bawtrey Hall, Yorkshire. October 18, 1875.

Baldwin, William John Atkinson, Esq. (Colonel), Dalton-in-Furness, and The Albany, London, W. February 19, 1868.

Barratt, James William Henry, Esq., Holywath, Coniston, Ambleside. May 18, 1887.

Barton, Edward, Esq., Warton Grange, Carnforth. October 18, 1886.

Beck, William Alcock, Esq. (Major), Hawkshead, Ambleside. April 4, 1859.

Bent, Baldwin Harry, Esq., Stowe Hill, Bury St. Edmunds, Suffolk. January 5, 1857.

Bird, Charles Henry, Esq., Crookey, Garstang. January 15, 1867.

Blades, Charles, Esq., Moor Platt, Caton, Lancaster. June 27, 1887.

*Bolden, William Bolden, Esq., Hyning, Carnforth. April 4, 1836.

Bowman, Thomas, Esq., Roger Ground, Hawkshead. December 31, 1849.

Brancker, John Houghton, Esq., The Crow Trees, Melling, near Carnforth. August 12, 1885.

Bridson, Joseph Ridgway, Esq., Bryerswood, Windermere. April 20, 1870.

Brogden, Alexander, Esq., London. June 27, 1864.

Cavendish, Lord Edward, M.P., Holker Hall, Cartmel. October 18, 1875.

Clarke, John Edward Henry, Esq., Hollen Oak, Haverthwaite, Ulverston. April 3, 1878.

Cook, Henry, Esq., Salthouse Villa, Barrow-in-Furness. January 1, 1883.

Cowper, James Canham, Esq., Keenground, Hawkshead, Ambleside. April 7, 1879.

Cragg, William Smith, Esq., Arkholme, Kirkby Lonsdale. April 5, 1869.

Cranke, John, Esq., Ulverston. July 12, 1878.

*Cross, Right Hon. Viscount, G.C.B., Eccleriggs, Broughton-in-Furness. April 17, 1860.

Dawson, Edward Bousfield, Esq., Aldcliffe Hall, Lancaster. October 18, 1875.

*Devonshire, The Most Noble the Duke of, K.G., Holker Hall, Cartmel. January 4, 1836.

Dickson, Arthur Benson, Esq., Abbotts Reading, Haverthwaite, Ulverston. December 30, 1872.

Edmondson, Thomas Grassyard, Esq., Grassyard Hall, Caton, Lancaster. February 7, 1867.

*Fell, John, Esq., Dane Ghyll, Furness Abbey, Barrow-in-Furness. July 16, 1861.

Fell, Samuel Gregson, Esq., Walton House, Llangollen. April 5, 1857.

*Fenwick, Thomas Fenwick, Esq., Burrow, Kirkby Lonsdale. April 8, 1878.

Fitzgerald, Sir Gerald Dalton, Bart., 42, Grosvenor Place, London, S.W. October 19, 1868.

*Ford, William, Esq., Ellel Hall, Lancaster. June 30, 1851.

Gale, Henry Richmond Hoghton, Esq., Bardsea Hall, Ulverston. January 5, 1857.

Garnett, Charles Henry, Esq., Wyreside, Lancaster. June 29, 1874.

*Garnett, Henry, Esq., Wyreside, Lancaster. April 3, 1854.

Garnett, Robert, Esq., Leyfield, Kirkby Lonsdale, Carnforth. February 22, 1882.

*Garnett, William, Esq., Quernmore Park, Lancaster. November 23, 1874.

Gillow, Richard Charles, Esq., Lancaster, July 1, 1878.

Gillow, Richard Thomas, Esq., Leighton Hall, Carnforth. April 4, 1853.

Grafton, Frederick William, Esq., Heysham Hall, Lancaster. August 27, 1871.

Greene, Dawson Cornelius, Esq. (Lieut.-Colonel), Whittington Hall, Kirkby Lonsdale, Carnforth. July 1, 1867.

Greene, Henry Dawson, Esq., Whittington Hall, Kirkby Lonsdale. October 28, 1884.

Greg, Albert, Esq., Escowbeck, Caton, Lancaster. April 2, 1877.

Gregson, Bryan Padgett, Esq., Caton, Lancaster. June 28, 1875.

Harker, John, Esq., M.D., Hazel Grove, near Carnforth. October 20, 1886.

Hargreaves, William, Esq., 66, Cambridge Terrace, Hyde Park, London. October 19, 1842.

Harris, Samuel James, Esq., Halton Park, Lancaster. June 27, 1887.

Harrison, Wordsworth, Esq., The Lund, Ulverston. April 7, 1879.

*Hartington, Right Hon. the Marquis of, M.P., Holker Hall, Cartmel. December 30, 1860.

Hibbert, Henry, Esq., Broughton Grove, Grange-over-Sands. January 5, 1881.

Hibbert, Percy John, Esq., Plumtree Hall, Milnethorpe. April 6, 1885.

*Hibbert, Right Hon. John Tomlinson, Hampsfield, Grange-over-Sands, July 9, 1855.

Hibbert, Thomas Johnson, Esq., Broughton Grove, Cartmel. June 27, 1870.

Higgin, William Housman, Esq., Q.C., Springfield, Lancaster. August 23, 1869.

*Hornby, Edmund Geoffrey Stanley, Esq., Dalton Hall, Burton, Westmorland. June 29, 1863.

Johnson, Christopher, Esq., Lancaster. January 2, 1882.

Kennedy, James Douglass, Esq. (Captain), Scarthwaite, Lancaster. October 20, 1875.

Kennedy, Matthew, Esq., Low Nook, Ambleside. January 11, 1869.

Lane, William, Esq., Walker Ground, Hawkshead. March 1, 1887.

Leeming, Richard, Esq., Greaves House, Lancaster. January 2, 1882.

Le Fleming, Stanley Hughes, Esq., Rydal Hall, Ambleside. April 7, 1884.

Lister, Edward, Esq., c/o A. M. Martin, Esq., 22, Kidbrook Grove, Blackheath, London. July 4, 1883.

Little, James William, Esq., Armadale, Barrow-in-Furness. April 5, 1880.

*Marshall, John Rowlandson, Esq., Hollington House, Hollington, Hastings. November 28, 1850.

Marshall, Victor Alexander Ernest, Esq., Waterhead House, Coniston, Ambleside. October 14, 1878.

*Marton, George Blucher Heneage, Esq. (Lieut.-Colonel), Capernwray Hall, Carnforth. June 29, 1863.

Midgley, James Herbert, Esq., Berners Close, Grange-over-Sands. June 28, 1886.

North, Bordrigge North, Esq., Newton, Kirkby Lonsdale. October 18, 1886.

North North, Esq., Newton Cottage, Kirkby Lonsdale. August 18, 1865.

Paley, Temple Chevallier, Esq., Cartmel, Carnforth. January 10, 1881.

Park, William, Esq., West Mount, Barrow-in-Furness. January 1, 1883.

Petch, William, Esq., Cavendish Park, Barrow-in-Furness. January 1, 1883.

Preston, George Theophilus Robert, Esq., Ellel Grange, Lancaster. October 18, 1869.
Preston, Right Hon. Lord Stanley of, G.C.B., Witherslack Hall, Grange, and 5, Portland Place, London, W. January 20, 1866.
*Ramsden, Sir James, Knight, Furness Abbey, Lancashire. August 24, 1864.
Rawlinson, Robert, Esq., 4, Lansdowne Villas, Cheltenham. May 23, 1872.
Redmayne, Giles, Esq., Brathay Hall, Ambleside. May 23, 1872.
Ridehalgh, George John Miller, Esq. (Lieut.-Colonel), Fell Foot, Newby Bridge, Ulverston. January 6, 1869.
*Rigge, Henry Fletcher, Esq., Wood Broughton, Grange. June 29, 1868.
Royds, Charles Twemlow, Clerk, Heysham, Lancaster. October 19, 1868.
Royds, Francis Twemlow, Clerk, Heysham Rectory, Lancaster. January 4, 1886.
Saunders, Charles Morley, Esq., Wennington Hall, Lancaster. May 28, 1877.
Schneider, Henry William, Esq., Belsfield, Windermere. July 14, 1874.
Sharp, Edward, Esq., Linden Hall, Carnforth. January 4, 1886.
Smith, Josiah Timmis, Esq., Rhine Hill, Stratford-on-Avon. December 30, 1872.

Starkie, John Piers Chamberlain, Esq., Ashton Hall, Lancaster. February 22, 1865.
Storey, Sir Thomas, Knight, Lancaster. April 7, 1873.
Strongitharm, Augustus Horace, Esq., Priorslea, Barrow-in-Furness. January 1, 1883.
Sunderland, John William, Esq., Swarthdale, Ulverston. October 18, 1875.
Wadham, Edward, Esq., Millwood, Dalton-in-Furness. January 4, 1869.
Waithman, Joseph, Esq., Chudleigh, Devonshire. January 17, 1865.
Waithman, Robert William, Esq., Moyne Park, Ballyglunin, Co. Galway. April 5, 1852.
Welch, Henry Edward Parker, Esq., Leck Hall, Kirkby Lonsdale. June 27, 1887.
Welch, Henry Thomas, Esq., Leck Hall, Kirkby Lonsdale. January 2, 1860.
Westray, Robinson, Esq., Barrow-in-Furness. February 26, 1880.
Whalley, Joseph Lawson, Esq. (Lieut.-Colonel), 2, Queen Street, Lancaster. May 22, 1879.
Whitle, Robert, Esq. (Lieut.-Colonel), Cheltenham. January 6, 1864.
Williamson, James, Esq., M.P., Ryelands, Lancaster. January 3, 1881.
Wilson, Thomas Newby, Esq., The Landing, Ulverston. November 23, 1874.

AMOUNDERNESS HUNDRED.

Anderton, Wilfrid Francis, Esq., Haighton Hall, Preston. August 23, 1870.
Beaumont, Thomas Richard, Esq., Preston. January 8, 1869.
Bickerstaff, Robert, Esq. (Lieut.-Colonel), Swillbrook, Preston. October 16, 1872.
Birley, Edmund, Esq., Clifton Hall, Preston. July 3, 1850.
Birley, Hutton, Esq., Kirkham. February 17, 1875.
*Birley, William, Esq., The Larches, Preston. January 5, 1859.
Booth, John Billington, Esq., Overleigh House, Preston. October 20, 1869.
Bowdler, William Henry, Esq., The Square, Kirkham. July 30, 1877.
*Brockholes, William Joseph Fitzherbert, Esq., Claughton Hall, Garstang. January 5th, 1876.
Chadwick, Frank, Esq., Burholme, Whitewell, Clitheroe. January 15, 1867.
Chapman, William, Esq., Wyre Bank, Garstang. January 7, 1880.
Cocker, William Henry, Esq., Blackpool. February 17, 1875.
Coventry, His Honour Judge Millis, 1, Temple Gardens, London, E.C. August 10, 1887.
Cunliffe, Ellis, Esq. (Major), Lytham. January 4, 1860.
Dunderdale, Robert, Esq., Poulton-le-Fylde. October 20, 1869.
Fair, Thomas, Esq., Westwood, Lytham. February 17, 1875.
*Fazackerley-Westby, Jocelyn Tate, Esq., Mowbreck Hall, Kirkham. December 1, 1862.
Fish, James, Esq., Dean Street, South Shore, Blackpool. June 8, 1886.
German, James, Esq. (Major), Vine Court, Sevenoaks, Kent. June 28, 1853.
Hall, Henry, Esq., 8, Scarisbrick Street, Southport. May 18, 1882.
Hammond, Joseph Hutchinson, Esq., M.D., Winckley Square, Preston. November 30, 1877.

Handley, Richard, Esq., 9, Carlton Terrace, Blackpool. May 20, 1885.
Hermon, Sidney Albert, Esq., Newnham House, Lytham. May 20th, 1885.
Hornby, Hugh Phipps, Esq., St. Michael's, Garstang. October 19, 1881.
Irvin, David, Esq., Preston. October 20, 1869.
Jackson, Jonathan, Esq., Vale House, Garstang. February 18, 1876.
*Jacson, Charles Roger, Esq., Barton Hall, Preston October 17, 1849.
Lowndes, Edward Chaddock, Esq., Castle Combe, Chippenham, Wilts. July 3, 1867.
Mucklow, Edward, Esq., Grange. June 28, 1869.
Oliverson, Richard, Esq., 37, Gloucester Square, Hyde Park, London, W. January 2, 1861.
Park, William Philip, Esq., Osborne House, Fulwood, Preston. February 17, 1875.
Pedder, Richard, Esq., Finsthwaite, Ulverston. October 13, 1866.
Pedder, Wilson, clerk, The Vicarage, Churchtown, Garstang. January 7, 1869.
Porter, William, Esq., 12, Upper Queen's Terrace, Fleetwood. May 20, 1885.
Satterthwaite, John, Esq., 14, Bushell Place, Preston. July 1, 1885.
Simpson, Albert, Esq., Elmhurst, Garstang. May 18, 1870.
Smith, Robert, Esq., Dilworth House, Longridge. June 30, 1886.
Stott, Samuel, Esq., Woodfield, Lytham. May 20, 1885.
Williams, Robert Hankinson, Esq., M.D., Great Eccleston, Garstang. January 15, 1867.

BLACKBURN HUNDRED.

Aitken, Thomas, Esq., Holmes, Bacup. October 20, 1869.
Appleby, Arthur, Esq., Enfield, Accrington. January 4, 1882.
Armitstead, James Fisher, Esq., Cobwall House, Blackburn. May 27, 1869.
Ashton, Ralph Shorrock, Esq., Woodlands, Over Darwen. July 4, 1855.
*Aspinall, Ralph John, Esq., Standen Hall, Clitheroe. April 7, 1875.
*Assheton, Ralph, Esq., Downham, Clitheroe. May 18, 1854.
Barlow, James, Esq., Croft House, Accrington. August 22, 1883.
Birkbeck, John, Esq., Giggleswick, Settle. October 20, 1847.
Birtwistle, William, Esq., Great Harwood, near Accrington. May 27, 1870.
Bolton, Henry Hargreaves, Esq., Heightside, Newchurch-in-Rossendale. October 26, 1885.

Briggs, Henry, Esq., M.D., Bank Parade, Burnley. February 22, 1882.
Briggs, James, Esq., Newfield, near Blackburn. May 27, 1869.
*Brooks, Thomas, Esq., Sunnyside, Rawtenstall. July 4, 1855.
Brooks, William, Esq., Sunnyside House, Rawtenstall. January 2, 1884.
Butler-Bowdon, John Erdeswick, Esq. (Colonel), Pleasington Hall, Blackburn. August 3, 1872.
Calvert, Richard, Esq., Walton-le-Dale, Preston. January 7 1874.
*Coddington, William, Esq., M.P., Wycollar, near Blackburn. February 25, 1867.
Dewhurst, Robert, Esq., Little Moor House, Clitheroe. April 6, 1859.
Dimmock, James, Esq., Over Darwen. July 3, 1872.

Dugdale, Adam, Esq., Griffin Lodge, Blackburn. July 1, 1874.

Dugdale, James, Esq., Ivy Bank, Burnley. April 10, 1867.

Dugdale, Joseph, Esq., Claremont, Blackburn. December 1, 1884.

Dugdale, William, Esq., Symonstone Hall, Padiham. May 19, 1874.

Eccles, James, Esq., 15, Durham Villas, Phillimore Gardens, Kensington, London, W. June 29, 1870.

Eccles, John, Esq., Farington House, near Preston. April 4, 1883.

Eccles, Richard, Esq., Lower Darwen, Blackburn. January 7. 1852.

Eccles, Thomas Mitchell, Esq., Crosshill, Blackburn. January 7, 1884.

Ecroyd, Edward, Esq., Edgend, Burnley. October 17, 1881.

Ecroyd, William Farrer, Esq., Spring House, near Burnley. October 17, 1866.

Every-Halstead, Charles Edward, Esq., Rowley, near Burnley. August 22, 1883.

*Feilden, Montague Joseph, Esq. (Major), Island of Hern, near Guernsey, April 5, 1838.

Feilden, Randle Joseph, Esq. (General), M.P., Witton Park, Blackburn. February 18, 1876.

Feilden, Sir William Leyland, Bart., Strada House, Scarborough. January 5, 1859.

Fish, John, Esq., 40, Park Avenue, Southport. October 20, 1869.

Flowerdew, Richard John, Esq., Walton Hall, Preston. April 6, 1870.

Folds, James, Esq., Brunshaw, Burnley. April 10, 1867.

Fort, Richard, Esq., Read Hall, Whalley. April 7, 1880.

Garnett, James, Esq., Waddow Hall, Clitheroe. April 7, 1880.

Garnett, William, Esq., Clitheroe. February 26, 1870.

Gatty, Frederick Albert, Esq., Accrington. July 3, 1872.

Greenway, Charles, Clerk, Darwen Bank, Over Darwen. February 19, 1868.

Greenwood, John, Esq., Tarleton House, Burnley. October 16, 1878.

Grimshaw, John Smalley, Esq., Woodside House, Huncoat, Accrington. August 29, 1873.

Handsley, Robert, Esq., Reedley Lodge, Burnley. October 19, 1885.

Hardman, Henry Hoyle, Esq., Horncliffe House, Rawtenstall. April 10, 1867.

Hargreaves, John, Esq. (Lieut.-Colonel), Broad Oak, Accrington. April 8, 1868.

Harrison, Henry, Esq., Stanley, Blackburn. June 30, 1880.

Hartley, Henry Waddington, Esq., Fence Gate, Burnley. October 15, 1879.

Harrison, Jonathan Atkinson, Esq., M.D., Hazlewood, Haslingden. November 26, 1884.

Heyworth, Eli, Esq., Springfield, Blackburn. June 30, 1880.

Hindle, James, Esq., Sabden, near Whalley. February 26, 1870.

Hodges, John Fowden, Esq., Bolney Court, Henley-on-Thames. April 5, 1838.

*Holden, Henry, Esq. (Lieut.-Colonel), Reedley House, Burnley. November 30, 1848.

*Hopwood, John Turner, Esq., Hetton Hall, Rutlandshire. October 20, 1858.

Hornby, William Henry, Esq., M.P., Brookhouse, Blackburn. August 22, 1879.

Howorth, John, Esq., Park View, Burnley. April 6, 1882.

Howorth, John, Esq., Woodlands, Bolton-by-Bowland, Clitheroe. July 5, 1852.

Huntington, Charles Philip, Esq., Astley Bank, Darwen. January 14, 1879.

Huntingdon, William Balle, Esq., Woodlands, Darwen. April 20, 1886.

*Hutchinson, Robert Hopwood, Esq., Highfield, near Blackburn, February 25, 1867.

Ingham, His Honour Judge Theophilus Hastings, Marton House, Skipton. February 26, 1847.

Irving, William, Esq., M.D., Park Gate, Blackburn. December 1, 1884.

Jackson, Robert Raynsford, Esq. (Colonel), Ashurst, West Hill, Sydenham, S.E. April 9, 1851.

Johnston, James, Esq., Alum Scar, Pleasington, near Blackburn. May 27, 1869.

Kay-Shuttleworth, Right Hon. Sir Ughtred James, Bart., M.P., Gawthorpe Hall, Burnley. October 20, 1869.

Kerr, James, Esq., Dunkenhalgh, Accrington. November 3, 1885.

Lightfoot, John Emanuel, Esq., Quarry Hill, Accrington January 7, 1874.

Longworth, Solomon, Esq., Whalley. April 7, 1880.

Mason, Thomas, Esq., Alkincoats, Colne. October 19, 1885.

Munn, Robert Whitaker, Esq., Heath Hill, Stacksteads, near Manchester. August 1, 1878.

Openshaw, Frederick, Esq., Hothersall Hall, Ribchester, near Preston. April 6, 1887.

Parker, Edward, Esq., Browsholme Hall, Clitheroe. August 29 1873.

Peel, William, Esq., Knowlmere Manor, Clitheroe. October 20, 1875.

*Pilkington, James, Esq., Blackburn. February 26, 1847.

*Petre, Henry, Esq., Dunkenhalgh, Accrington. April 6, 1859.

Potter, John Gerald, Esq., Ernsdale, Over Darwen. April 7, 1852.

Ranken, William Bayne, Esq., Hoddlesden, Over Darwen. October 13, 1866.

Riley, John, Esq., Hapton House, Hapton, near Accrington. August 22, 1883.

Rushton, James, Esq., Forest House, Newchurch-in-Rossendale. June 29, 1874.

Shaw, Henry, Esq., Highfield, Blackburn. May 27, 1869.

Shaw, Thomas, Esq., The Gables, Colne. April 11, 1887.

Shorrock, Eccles, Esq., Low Hill House, Lower Darwen. July 4, 1855.

Simpson, William Walmsley, Esq., Winkley, Whalley. August 22, 1883.

Smith, George Ashworth, Esq., Westbourne, Helmshore. November 26, 1884.

Smith, Thomas Thornber, Esq., Hill End, near Burnley. April 11, 1887.

Smith, William, Esq., Springhill, Accrington. June 30, 1886.

Snape, William, Esq., Lynwood, Darwen. February 21, 1877.

*Starkie, Le Gendre Nicholas, Esq. (Lieut.-Colonel), Huntroyd, Padiham. October 18, 1865.

Swale, Hogarth John, Clerk, Ingfield, Settle. July 4, 1855.

Tattersall, William, Esq., Quarry Bank, Blackburn. April 7 1886.

Taylor, James, Clerk, Bamber Bridge, Preston. October 21, 1868.

Tipping, William, Esq., Brasted Park, Sevenoaks, Kent. November 28, 1850.

Thompson, John, Esq., Beardwood Cliffe, Blackburn. December 1, 1884.

Thompson, Richard, Esq., Bramley Meade, Whalley. February 17, 1886.

Thursby, John Ormerod Scarlett, Esq., Ormerod House, near Burnley, August 22, 1883.

Thursby, Sir John Hardy, Bart. (Lieut.-Colonel), Ormerod House, Burnley, and Holmhurst, Christchurch. October 19, 1853.

Thwaites, Daniel, Esq., Blackburn. May 20, 1852.

Thwaites, John, Esq., Troy, Blackburn. May 27, 1858.

Townsend, Richard, Esq., Bent Gate, near Haslingden. May 23, 1872.

Trappes, Charles James Byrnand, Esq., Nidd Lodge, Higher Broughton, Manchester. January 15, 1867.

Trappes, Thomas Byrnand, Esq. (Major), Clayton Hall, Accrington. December 1, 1862.

Tunstill, Robert, Esq., Briarfield House, near Burnley. February 24, 1881.

Tunstill, William, Esq., Reedyford House, Burnley. May 24, 1869.

Walmsley, George, Esq., Paddock House, Church, Accrington, October 18, 1854.

Warburton, John, Esq., Greenfield, Haslingden. November 26, 1884

Weld, John, Esq., Leagrim Hall, Preston. July 4, 1860.

Whittaker, John, Esq., Lostock Hall, Preston. April 4, 1883.

Whitaker, John, Esq., Winsley Hall, near Shrewsbury. July 4, 1855.

Whitaker, Thomas, Esq., Beech Lodge, Haslingden, via Manchester. February 26, 1872.

Whittaker, Thomas, Esq., Prospect Hill, Walton-le-Dale, Preston. October 21, 1868.

*Whitaker, Thomas Hordern, Esq., The Holme, Burnley January 10, 1842.

*Worsley-Taylor, Henry Wilson, Esq., Moreton Hall, Whalley. January 4, 1882.

Wraith, Lawrence Hargreaves, Esq., Newfield, near Blackburn. January 9, 1879.

LEYLAND HUNDRED.

Baldwin, Thomas Rigbye, Clerk, Leyland. July 4, 1855.

Birley, Frederick Hornby, Esq., 13, Hyde Road, Ardwick, Manchester. May 24, 1880.

Blundell, John, Esq., Boodle's, St. James's Street, London, S.W. January 17, 1860.

Boulton, Alfred Ramsden, Esq., Harrock Hall, Wigan. December 2, 1868.

Bretherton, Norris, Esq., Moss House, Farington. June 30, 1886.

Bretherton, William, Esq., Runshaw Hall, Chorley. September 29, 1866.

Cooper, John, Esq., The Oaks, Preston. October 20, 1852.

Crosse, Thomas Richard, Esq. (Lieut.-Colonel), Shaw Hill, Chorley. August 19, 1880.

Davies, Benjamin, Esq., Adlington Hall, Chorley. November 1, 1877.

De Trafford, Sigismund Cathcart, Esq., Croston Hall, Preston. April 9, 1879.

*Eckersley, Nathaniel, Esq., M.P., Standish Hall, Wigan. January 2, 1850.

Fermor-Hesketh, Sir Thomas George, Baronet, Rufford Hall, Ormskirk. April 9, 1873.

Goggin, James Frederick, Clerk, Rufford, Ormskirk. October 31, 1868.

Hare, Theodore Julius, Esq., Crooke Hall, Chorley. May 23, 1878.

Jackson, Edward, Esq., Rye Bank, Wheelton, Chorley. April 6, 1885.

Marriage, David, Esq., Burgh Hall, Chorley. April 6, 1885.

Park, John, Esq., Ollerton Hall, Chorley. January 5, 1859.

Pedder, Charles Denison (Colonel), Kilbourne Hall, Derby. August 29, 1878.

Rawcliffe, Henry, Esq., Gillibrand Hall, Chorley. October 18, 1882.

*Rawstorne, Lawrence, Esq., Hutton Hall, Preston. November 28, 1866.

Shackleton, Richard, Esq., Withnell Hall, Chorley. October 20, 1880.

Silvester, Frederick, Esq. (Lieut.-Colonel), North Hall, Standish, Wigan. May 7, 1874.

Smethurst, Augustus William, Esq., Rookwood, Chorley. July 1, 1857.

Sparling, John, Clerk, Hillington Hall, Lynn, Norfolk. October 17, 1855.

Stanning, John, Esq., Broadfield, Leyland. October 15, 1884.

Stonor, Charles Joseph, Esq., Anderton Hall, Chorley. October 6, 1866.

Thom, John, Esq., Lark Hill, Chorley. May 24, 1869.

Thom, Robert Wilson, Esq. (Lieut.-Colonel), Birkacre, Chorley. May 26, 1884.

*Townley-Parker, Thomas Townley, Esq., Cuerden Hall, Preston, and Lytham. November 3, 1847.

Whitehead, James, Esq., Brindle Lodge, Preston. July 2, 1879.

Wood, Christopher William, Esq., Brinscall Hall, Chorley. April 8, 1885.

SALFORD HUNDRED.

Agnew, William, Esq., Summer Hill, Pendleton, Manchester, and 11, Great Stanhope Street, Hyde Park, London. August 3, 1869.

Ainsworth, Walton, Esq., Rivington, Chorley. October 15, 1883.

Ainsworth, Richard Henry, Esq., Smithills Hall, Bolton. April 10, 1867.

Aitken, Thomas, Esq., Manchester Road, Bury. April 11, 1887.

Andrew, Charles, Esq., Compstall, Stockport. May 24, 1869.

Andrew, Eli, Esq., The Ridge, Chapel-en-le-Frith, Derbyshire. September 25, 1866.

Andrew, Frank, Esq., 32, Chester Square, Ashton-under-Lyne. June 8, 1886.

Andrew, George, Esq., Apsley House, Mossley, Manchester. February 27, 1865.

Armitage, Benjamin, Esq., Chomlea, Pendleton, Manchester. August 3, 1869.

Armitage, Benjamin, Esq., Sorrel Bank, Eccles Old Road, Pendleton. August 24, 1886.

Armitage, Samuel Fletcher, Esq., Peel Hall, Little Hulton. October 20, 1884.

Armitage, Vernon Kirk, Esq., Swinton Park, Manchester. May 21, 1882.

Arrowsmith, Peter Rothwell, Esq., 28, Exchange Alley, Liverpool. December 10, 1855.

Ashton, John Howarth, Esq. (Major), County Police Court, Strangeways, Manchester. July 8, 1867.

Ashton, Thomas, Esq., Ford Bank, Didsbury, Manchester. May 24, 1852.

Ashton, Thomas Gair, Esq., 36, Charlotte Street, Manchester. February 27, 1882.

Ashworth, Charles Egerton, Esq., Droylsden, Manchester. January 11, 1869.

Ashworth, Edmund, Esq., Egerton Hall, Bolton. August 22, 1883.

Ashworth, Edmund, Esq., Rivercourt Lodge, Upper Mall, Hammersmith, London, W. February 3, 1869.

Ashworth, Edward, Esq., Staghills, Waterfoot, Manchester. May 24, 1869.

Ashworth, George Binns, Esq., Birtenshaw House, Bolton. October 26, 1874.

Barlow, Samuel, Esq., Stakehill House, Chadderton, Manchester. October 25, 1869.

*Barnes, Thomas, Esq., Farnworth, Bolton. August 27, 1849.

Barnes, Alfred, Esq., Farnworth, Manchester. December 30, 1861.

Bates, Ralph, Esq., Acres Bank, Stalybridge. April 15, 1867.

Bayley, William, Esq., Stamford Lodge, Stalybridge. January 10, 1859.

Bazley, Charles Henry, Esq., West Bank, Kersal, Manchester. July 5, 1869.

Bealey, Adam Crompton, Esq., The Manor House, Bury. February 21, 1887.

Bealey, Richard, Esq., The Close, Radcliffe, Manchester. February 25, 1856.

Becker, John Leigh, Esq., Springbank, Ashley Road, Altrincham, Cheshire. May 22, 1867.

Bentley, John, Esq., Haughton Hall, Denton. July 9, 1883.

Blackburne, Henry Clegg, Esq., The Acres, Middleton. October 20, 1884.

Bridgford, Robert, Esq., C.B. (Colonel), Hilton House, Prestwich, Manchester. August 8, 1881.

Bridson, Thomas Ridgway, Esq., Bolton. January 26, 1867.

Brierley, James, Esq., Westhill, Rochdale. October 22, 1866.

Brierley, John, Esq., The Clough, Whitefield, Manchester. February 21, 1887.

Brierley, Joseph, Esq., Castleton, Rochdale. November 23, 1866.

Briggs, Arthur Lemuel, Esq., Thornleigh, Bolton. March 22, 1883.

Briggs, William, Esq., Halifax, January 11, 1841.

Bright, Jacob, Esq., M.P., Alderley Edge, Manchester. February 9, 1858.

Bright, John Albert, Esq., Rose Hill, Rochdale. June 1, 1885.

Bright, Thomas, Esq., Greenbank, Rochdale. October 23, 1865.

Broadhurst, Henry Tootal, Esq., Woodhill, Prestwich, Manchester. January 13, 1869.

*Brooks, Sir William Cunliffe, Bart., M.P., Barlow Hall, Manchester. November 1, 1870.

Buckley, Abel, Esq., M.P., Moss Lodge, Ashton-under-Lyne. October 23, 1865.

Buckley, James Frederick, Esq., The Nook, Greenfie'd, Saddleworth. April 15, 1867.

*Buckley, Nathaniel, Esq., Ryecroft, Ashton-under-Lyne. August 26, 1861.

Butterworth, Alfred, Esq., Werneth, Oldham. April 13, 1885.

Butterworth, James, Esq., Rake Bank, Rochdale. February 28, 1859.

Chadwick, John, Esq., Buile Hill, Eccles Old Road, Manchester. October 25, 1869.

*Chadwick, John, Esq., Woodville, Reddish, Stockport. January 10, 1853.

Chadwick, James, Esq., High Bank, Prestwich, Manchester. January 11, 1869.

Chapman, Edward, Esq., Hill End, Mottram-in-Longdendale. April 10, 1871.

Cheetham, John Frederick, Esq., Stalybridge. October 24, 1870.

Cheetham, Joshua Milne, Esq., Singleton House, Higher Broughton, Manchester. May 24, 1869.

Christy, Richard, Esq., Walngate, Sussex. July 4, 1864.

Christie, Richard Copley, Esq., Glenwood, New Egham, Staines. October 31, 1878.

Clegg, Harry, Esq., Plas Llanfair, Llanfair P.G. Anglesey. July 7, 1884.

Clegg, James Wild, Esq., Mumps House, Oldham. August 17, 1885.

Cooke, William Walker, Esq., Denton, near Manchester. August 7, 1877.

Cooper, John, Esq., Holly Bank, Royton. October 6, 1887.

Coward, Edward, Esq., Heaton House, Heaton Mersey, Manchester. October 26, 1885.

Craven, Thomas, Esq., Merlewood, Chorlton-cum-Hardy, Manchester. August 24, 1886.

Crompton, Abram, Esq., High Crompton, Shaw, Oldham. January 11, 1886.

Crompton, Joshua, Esq., High Crompton, Oldham. January 11, 1869.

Cross, Edward, Esq., Bradford House, Great Lever, Bolton. April 9, 1883.

Cross, Herbert Shepherd, Esq., M.P., Mortfield, Bolton. October 26, 1874.

Crossley, Daniel Jones, Esq., Fallingroyd, Hebden Bridge. June 1, 1885.

Crowther, Frank Gemmill, Esq., Beaumonds, Rochdale. August 28, 1882.

Darbishire, George Stanley, Esq., Wyndham Club, London. August 8, 1881.

Dearden, James Griffith, Esq., Rochdale Manor, Rochdale. October 22, 1866.

Dickins, Albert Lungley, Esq., Park Lane, Higher Broughton, Manchester. October 13, 1884.

Dickins, Thomas, Esq., Edgemoor House, Higher Broughton, Manchester. July 5, 1858.

*Egerton, Hon. Algernon Fulke, M.P., Worsley Old Hall, Manchester. January 24, 1861.

Ellesmere, The Right Hon. the Earl of, Worsley, Manchester. October 23, 1871.

Fair, Jacob Wilson, Esq., Haighlands, Wigan. October 15, 1884.

*Fairbairn, Sir Thomas, Bart., Brambridge House, Winchester. May 23, 1853.

Fenton, James, Esq., Hazlehurst, Bamford, Rochdale. April 15, 1867.

Fenton, Joseph, Esq., Bashall Lodge, Clitheroe. Jan. 3, 1853.

*Fenton, William, Esq., Churchdale, Ashford, Bakewell, Derbyshire. February 28, 1848.

Fielden, John, Esq., Dobroyd, Todmorden. February 27, 1865.

Fielden, Samuel, Esq., Centre Vale, Todmorden. January 7, 1878.

Flattely, Daniel Irvine, Esq., Newton Villa, Longsight, Manchester. February 26, 1880.

Fowler, Robinson, Esq., Manchester. August 28, 1865.

Galloway, John, Esq., junior, The Cottage, Old Trafford, Manchester. November 26, 1884.

Garnett, Jeremiah, Esq., The Grange, near Bolton. April 5, 1886.

Garnett, Stewart, Esq., Pendleton, Manchester. October 6, 1887.

*Gray, William, Esq. (Colonel), Farley Hall, Reading. December 10, 1855.

Greaves, Hilton, Esq., Derker Hall, Oldham. August 18, 1876.

Greenwood, John, Esq., Glen View, Todmorden. May 23, 1887.

Greg, Arthur, Esq., Eagley, near Bolton. February 26, 1880.

Hadwen, Joseph, Esq., Fairfield, Manchester. April 11, 1870.

*Hardcastle, Edward, Esq., M.P., Headlands, Prestwich, Manchester. April 13, 1874.

Hardcastle, Thomas, Esq., Bradshaw Hall, Bolton-le-Moors. July 6, 1885.

Hargreaves, John, Esq., Greensnook House, Bacup. October 21, 1885.

Hargreaves, William, Esq., Moss Bank, Bolton. April 10, 1867.

Harrison, Thomas, Esq., West Hill, Stalybridge. January 10, 1853.

Harter, James Collier, Esq., Manchester. May 23, 1859.

Hartley, William, Esq., Simpson Hill House, Heywood. April 8, 1878.

Hartley, William, Esq., The Orchard, Heywood. May 22, 1882.

Harvey, James, Esq., The Whinns, Alderley Edge, Manchester. May 24, 1869.

Heap, James, Esq., Cliffe House, New Hey, Rochdale. August 27, 1872.

Heape, Benjamin, Esq., Northwood, Prestwich, near Manchester. July 7, 1879.

Heape, Robert Taylor, Esq., Highfield, Rochdale. August 7, 1858.

Heginbottom, Thomas, Esq., Stamford House, Ashton-under-Lyne. August 28, 1882.

Henderson, Charles Paton, Esq., junior, County Police Court, Strangeways, Manchester. October 17, 1881.

Herford, Edward, Esq., Westbank, near Macclesfield. May 30, 1870.

Heron, Sir Joseph, Knight, Rookswood, Broughton Park, Manchester. May 26, 1873.

Heywood, Arthur Henry, Esq., Elleray, Windermere. December 3, 1860.

Heywood, Edward Stanley, Esq., Light Oaks, Manchester. April 13, 1874.

Heywood, Harvey, Esq., Spring Vale, Middleton. October 13, 1884.

*Heywood, James, Esq., 26, Kensington Palace Gardens, London, W. October 22, 1838.

*Heywood, Oliver, Esq., Claremont, Pendleton, Manchester. July 7, 1851.

*Hibbert, Right Hon. John Tomlinson, Hampsfield, Grange-over-Sands. July 9, 1863.

*Hick, John, Esq., Mytton Hall, Whalley. June 30, 1858.

Higgin, William Housman, Esq., Q.C., Winter's Buildings, 82, St. Ann Street, Manchester. August 23, 1869.

Hinchcliffe, George, Esq., Stoodley Lodge, Todmorden. July 14, 1864.

Hinmers, William, Esq., Lancaster Road, Eccles, Manchester. January 9, 1865.

Holt, James Maden, Esq., Balham House, Balham Hill, London, S.W. April 5, 1858.

Houldsworth, Sir William Henry, Bart., M.P., Norbury Booths Hall, Knutsford. February 24, 1884.

Hoyle, Edward, Esq., Moorlands, Bacup. April 8, 1867.

*Hulton, William Wilbraham Blethyn, Esq., Hulton Park, Bolton. October 15, 1873.

Hurst, Richard, Esq., Springhill, Rochdale. October 24, 1864.

*Hutchinson, John, Esq. (Lieut.-Colonel), Bury. August 25, 1858.

Hutton, His Honour Judge Crompton, County Court Office, Bolton. April 5, 1875.

Hutton, James Frederick, Esq., Victoria Park, Manchester. August 23, 1880.

Ingham, John Arthur, Esq., The Shaw, Todmorden. October 23, 1882.

Isherwood, Thomas, Esq., Springfield House, Heywood. January 2, 1884.

Jordan, His Honour Judge Thomas Hudson, Prestwich Park, Prestwich, Manchester. November 28th, 1883.

Joule, Benjamin St. John Baptist, Esq., Wardle Road, Sale, Cheshire. October 22, 1866.

Kay, Edward Greenwood, Esq., Mill House, Whitworth, Rochdale. October 23, 1865.

Kay, Richard, Esq., Chamber House, Heywood. February 27, 1865.

Kearsley, Edward Sanderson, Esq. (Major), No. 6, Pembroke Villas, Richmond Green, Surrey, S.W. February 19, 1868.

Kennedy, John Lawson, Esq., Ardwick House, Manchester. July 3, 1854.

Kenworthy, Benjamin Mellor Esq., Ashton-under-Lyne. July 4, 1864.

Kenyon, James, Esq., Walshaw Hall, near Bury. November 17, 1877.

Kershaw, James, Esq., Delamere Place, Ashton-under-Lyne. February 2, 1867.

Knowles, Andrew, Esq., Swinton Old Hall, Pendlebury, Manchester. December 1, 1884.

Knowles, John, Esq., Westwood, Pendlebury, Manchester. August 29, 1882.

Knowles, Samuel, Esq., Stormer Hill, Tottington, near Bury. July 5, 1875.

Lancashire, Josiah Henry, Esq., Deeplish Hill, Rochdale. June 1, 1885.

Lancashire, Oswald Philip, Esq., Butts House, Leigh, Manchester. May 18, 1887.

Law, Alfred, Esq., Honresfeld, Littleborough.   June 1, 1885.

Leach, Abraham, Esq., Waterhead, Oldham.   October 25, 1869.

Leake, Robert, Esq., M.P., The Dales, Whitefield, Bury, and 34, Hill Street, Berkeley Square, London, W.   February 28, 1881.

Lee, Henry, Esq., Sedgley Park, Manchester.   May 24, 1869.

Lees, Edward Brown, Esq., Kelbarrow, Grasmere, Westmorland.   April 15, 1867.

Lees, Eli, Esq., M.P., Werneth Park, Oldham.   July 5, 1869.

Lees, John Arthur, Esq., Alkrington Mount, Middleton.   October 15, 1884.

Lees, Joseph, Esq., Werneth Grange, Oldham.   October 6, 1887.

Lees, Joseph Crompton, Esq., Clarkesfield, Lees, Oldham.   August 17, 1885.

Leigh, Henry, Esq., Moorfield, Swinton, Manchester.   April 13, 1874.

Leresche, John Henry Proctor, Esq., 60, King Street, Manchester.   January 11, 1886.

Littlewood, John Stothert, Esq., Healey Hall, Rochdale.   July 8, 1878.

Lord, George, Esq., Heathlands, Prestwich, Manchester.   October 24, 1881.

*Loyd, Edward, Esq. (Lieut.-Colonel), Lillesden, near Hawkhurst, Kent.   April 20, 1841.

*Maclure, John William, Esq., M.P., The Home, Whalley Range, Manchester.   January 11, 1864.

Maden, Henry, Esq., Rockcliffe House, Bacup.   May 24, 1869.

Mantell, Sir John Iles, Knight, Manchester.   October 25, 1869.

Mart, Joseph Foveaux, Esq., Crescent, Salford, Manchester.   October 29, 1867.

Mason, Rupert, Esq., Audenshaw Hall, Fairfield, Manchester.   June 28, 1886.

Mayall, John, Esq., Rock Bank, Mossley, Ashton-under-Lyne.   February 20, 1884.

Mayson, John Schofield, Esq., Hawthorn Lea, Langham Road, Bowdon, Cheshire.   July 4, 1864.

Mellor, George, Esq., Holly Bank, Ashton-under-Lyne.   May 31, 1858.

Mellor, John Edward, Esq., Mottram Road, Stalybridge.   August 16, 1886.

Mellor, John James, Esq., The Woodlands, Whitefield, Manchester.   April 10, 1867.

Mellor, Jonathan, Esq., Polefield, Prestwich, Manchester.   July 4, 1859.

Mellor, Robert, Esq., Higher House, Royton, near Oldham.   August 17, 1885.

Mellor, Thomas, Esq., Firs Hall, Failsworth.   October 25, 1881.

Mellor, Thomas Walton, Esq., Ashton-under-Lyne.   March 2, 1863.

Micholls, Edward, Esq., The Limes, Victoria Park, Manchester.   October 26, 1885.

Milne, Alfred, Esq., Manchester.   July 15, 1862.

Milne-Redhead, Richard, Esq., Springfield, Seedley, Manchester.   September 15, 1866.

Molesworth, George Mill Frederick, Esq., Town House, Rochdale.   October 24, 1853.

Mosley, Joseph, Esq., Cringle Hall, Levenshulme, Manchester.   October 26, 1885.

Neild, Jonathan, Esq., Dunster, Rochdale.   January 10, 1859.

Openshaw, John Hamilton, Esq., Stand House, Whitefield, Manchester.   February 21, 1887.

Ormerod, Abraham, Esq., Ridgefoot House, Todmorden.   July 7, 1856.

Ormerod, James, Esq., Halliwell Lodge, Bolton.   July 25, 1875.

Ormrod, James Cross, Esq., East Bank, Halliwell, Bolton.   March 22, 1883.

Peacock, Richard, Esq., M.P., Gorton Hall, Manchester.   October 22, 1866.

*Pender, John, Esq., Arlington Street, London, W.   April 13, 1863.

Petrie, James, Esq., Rylands, Birkdale, Southport.   February 3, 1869.

*Philips, Robert Needham, Esq., The Park, Manchester.   April 20, 1841.

Pilkington, Edward, Esq., Clifton House, Clifton, Manchester.   October 22, 1883.

*Platt, Samuel Radcliffe, Esq., Werneth Park, Oldham.   January 16, 1873.

Pochin, Henry Davies, Esq., Barn Elms, Barnes, Surrey, S.W.   April 11, 1870.

Porritt, James, Esq., Stubbins Vale House, Ramsbottom, near Manchester.   November 17, 1877.

*Potter, Thomas Bayley, Esq., M.P., 31, Courtfield Gardens, South Kensington, London, S.W.   July 7, 1851.

*Radcliffe, Joshua, Esq., Balderstone Hall, Rochdale.   October 17, 1866.

*Radcliffe, Joshua Walmsley, Esq., Werneth Park, Oldham.   January 16, 1883.

Reyner, Arthur Edward, Esq., Thornfield Hall, Ashton-under-Lyne.   April 11, 1881.

Reyner, Joseph Buckley, Esq., Thornfield Hall, Ashton-under-Lyne.   May 24, 1869.

Riley, John, Esq., Oldham.   November 26, 1863.

Robinson, James Salkeld, Esq., Roach Bank, Rochdale.   August 28, 1882.

Ross, Colin George, Esq., Swinton Park, Manchester.   November 26, 1884.

Rothwell, Richard Rainshaw, Esq., Sharples Hall, Bolton.   February 2, 1867.

Rowland, John, Esq., Thorncliffe, Royton, Oldham.   April 15, 1867.

*Rowley, Alexander Butler, Esq., Hurst, Ashton-under-Lyne.   May 28, 1866.

Rowley, Walter Thomas, Esq., The Grange, Hurst, Ashton-under-Lyne.   April 11, 1881.

*Royds, Albert Hudson, Esq., Falinge Lawn, Rochdale.   January 3, 1853.

*Royds, Clement Molyneux, Esq., Greenhill, Rochdale.   September 29, 1866.

Royds, Edmund Albert Nuttall, Esq., Brownhill, Rochdale.   November 28, 1873.

Royle, Peter, Esq., M.D., Vernon Lodge, Brooklands, Manchester.   July 4, 1864.

Rushton, Thomas Henry, Esq., Halliwell Hall, Bolton.   April 20, 1886.

Russell, His Honour Judge John Archibald, Q.C., 2, Harcourt Buildings, Temple, London.   November 11, 1870.

Rylands, John, Esq., Longford Hall, Stretford, Manchester.   May 24, 1869.

Schofield, Christopher James, Esq., Whalley Villa, Whalley Range, Manchester.   January, 8, 1883.

Scholfield, James Henry, Esq., North View, Whitworth, Rochdale.   February 27, 1882.

Schwabe, Frederick Salis, Esq., Rhodes House, Middleton, Manchester.   December 6, 1880.

Seville, Thomas, Esq., Blythe House, Southport.   October 25, 1869.

Sidebottom, Alfred Kershaw, Esq., Whitegates, Mottram, Cheshire.   October 22, 1866.

Slater, William, Esq., Holmes, Sharples, Bolton.   June 1, 1885.

Smith, David, Esq., Birch View, Brighton Grove, Rusholme, Manchester.   April 15, 1878.

Smith, Fereday, Esq., Bridgewater Offices, Manchester.   July 5, 1858.

Smithson, Thomas, Esq., Facit, Rochdale.   February 27, 1882.

Summers, James Wooley, Esq., Thomson Cross, Stalybridge.   August 25, 1884.

Sutcliffe, Gamaliel, Esq., Stoneshay Gate, Heptonstall.   May 23, 1887.

Sutcliffe, James Smith, Esq., Beach House, Bacup.   January 4, 1869.

Sutcliffe, John Crossley, Esq., Lee, Hebden Bridge.   May 27, 1850.

Sutcliffe, Thomas, Clerk, 24, York Road, Birkdale, Southport.   July 4, 1864.

Sykes, Edmund Howard, Esq., Edgeley, Stockport.   April 15, 1867.

Taylor, Herbert Coupland, Esq., Todmorden Hall, Todmorden.   June 1, 1885.

Taylor, John, Esq., Brookdale, Newton Heath, Manchester.   October 22, 1866.

Topp, Alfred, Esq., Farnworth, Bolton.   July 6, 1870.

Tweedale, John, Esq., Beightons, Rochdale.   October 23, 1865.

Tweedale, Robert Leach, Esq., Beightons, Rochdale.   October 23, 1865.

Underdown, Robert George, Esq., Northleigh, Seymour Grove, Old Trafford, Manchester.   November 26, 1884.

Walker, Charles, Esq., 17, The Grove, Boltons, South Kensington, London, S.W.   May 22, 1882.

Walker, John Scholes, Esq., Limefield, Bury.   January 10, 1876.

*Walker, Oliver Ormerod, Esq., Chesham, Bury, Lancashire.   April 8, 1863.

Walker, Richard, Esq., Belle Vue, Bury, Lancashire. October 22, 1877.
Walker, William Ormerod, Esq., Summerfield, Bury, Lancashire. April 7, 1875.
Walmsley, Edward, Esq., Heaton Norris, Stockport. July 8, 1861.
Wardley, James, Esq., 69, Nelson Street, Oxford Road, Manchester. May 27, 1869.
Watkin, Sir Edward William, Bart., M.P., Rosehill, Northenden, Manchester. October 24, 1864.
West, Henry Wyndham, Esq., Q.C., Temple, London, E.C. January 9, 1871.
Whitaker, Charles, Esq., Royelands, Rochdale. June 1, 1885.
Whitehead, Francis Frederick, Esq., Beech Hill, Saddleworth. April 15, 1867.
Whitehead, Henry, Esq., Haslam Hey, Elton, Bury. February 21, 1887.
Whitehead, John, Esq., Penwortham Priory, Preston. April 7, 1875.
Whitehead, John Blakey, Esq., Rawtenstall, Manchester. April 8, 1863.
Whitehead, Thomas Hoyle, Esq., Holly Mount, Rawtenstall. August 1, 1878.
Whittaker, John, Esq., Mount Sion House, Radcliffe, near Manchester. November 1, 1881.
Whittaker, Robert, Esq., Birch House, Lees, Oldham. June 3, 1879.
Whittam, William Barton, Esq., Birch House, Farnworth. April 15, 1867.

Whitworth, Benjamin, Esq., Manchester. May 22, 1862.
Willans, Thomas Benjamin, Esq., Rochdale. August 19, 1872.
Wilson, Sir Matthew, Bart., Eshton Hall, Skipton. July 16, 1827.
Withington, George Richard, Esq. (Captain), Pyrland Hall, Taunton. August 25, 1858.
Wood, John, Esq., Arden, Stockport. September 15, 1866.
Wood, George William Rayner, Esq., Singleton Lodge, Manchester. April 8, 1878.
Wood, Richard, Esq., Plumpton, Heywood, Manchester. April 8, 1878.
Wood, Thomas Broadbent, Esq., Middleton, Manchester. February 22, 1869.
Worrall, James, Esq., Whalley Range, Manchester. April 11, 1864.
Worrall, James, Esq., junior, Woodlands, Whalley Range, Manchester. October 19, 1885.
Worrall, Joseph Hardman, Esq., 8, Rochdale Road, Bacup. August 1, 1878.
Wright, Edward Abbott, Esq., Castle Park, Frodsham, Cheshire. July 5, 1852.
Wrigley, Edward Wright, Esq., Thorneycroft, Werneth, Oldham. August 17, 1885.
Wrigley, Edwin Grundy, Esq., Howick House, Preston. October 22, 1872.
Wrigley, Frederick, Esq., Broadoaks, Bury. February 21, 1887.
Wrigley, James, Esq., Holbeck, Windermere. October 18, 1869.
Wrigley Oswald Osmond, Esq., Bridge Hall, Bury. May 22, 1882.

WEST DERBY HUNDRED.

Armitage, Ziba, Esq., Heathfield, Grappenhall, near Warrington. January 16, 1883.
Barrett, William Scott, Esq., 41, Oldhall Street, Liverpool. August 25, 1884.
Barron, George Bretherton, Esq., M.D., Summerseat, Southport. September 3, 1877.
Barry, Charles, Esq., Highfield, Lathom, Ormskirk. January 4, 1886.
*Bates, Sir Edward, Bart., Bellfield, West Derby, Liverpool; and Gyrn Castle, Flintshire. October 30, 1866.
Bidwill, Peter Silvester, Esq. (Lieut.-Colonel), Bella Vista, Sandy Cove, Kingstown. May 18, 1870.
Bingham, John, Esq., Elmhurst, Wavertree, near Liverpool. April 22, 1884.
Blackburne, John Ireland, Esq. (Colonel), Hale, Warrington. April 17, 1860.
Bleckly, Henry, Esq., Westwood, Altrincham. April 8, 1867.
Blinkhorn, William, Esq., Sutton Grange, St. Helens. April 18, 1876.
*Blundell, Nicholas, Esq. (Colonel), Crosby Hall, Liverpool. April 17, 1855.
Bouth, Frederick William Delamere, Esq., Woodfield, Leigh, Manchester. November 29, 1873.
Brancker, William Hill, Esq., Bispham Hall, Wigan. December 3, 1849.
Bright, Heywood, Esq., Sandheys, West Derby, Liverpool. January 17, 1882.
Brock, John, Esq., Wellfield, Farnworth, Widnes. April 19, 1881.
*Brocklebank, Ralph, Esq., Childwall Hall, Liverpool. November 2, 1858.
*Brocklebank, Sir Thomas, Bart., Springwood, Allerton, Liverpool. July 15, 1856.
Brocklebank, Thomas, Esq., The Hollies, Woolton, near Liverpool. August 23, 1887.
Bromilow, David, Esq., Bitteswell Hall, Lutterworth, Leicestershire. April 23, 1850.
Brown, Alexander Hargreaves, Esq., M.P. (Lieut.-Colonel), Richmond Hill, Liverpool. January 18, 1870.
Burrell, John Stamp, Esq., 53, Huskisson Street, Falkner Square, Liverpool. October 18, 1858.
Burrows, Abraham, Esq., Green Hall, Atherton, Manchester. January 18, 1881.
Burton, Edward, Esq., Eaves Hall, near Clitheroe. April 15, 1867.
Burton, Frederick, Esq., Hopefield, Pendleton, Manchester. April 11, 1887.
Castellain, Alfred, Esq., Aigburth, Liverpool. April 23, 1867.

Chamberlain, George, Esq., Helensholme, Birkdale, Southport. April 20, 1870.
*Chambers, John Hickinbotham, Esq. (Lieut.-Colonel), Cobham, Surrey. May 27, 1858.
Collier, His Honour Judge John Francis, Liverpool. July 14, 1874.
Comber, Thomas, Esq., 13, Exchange Buildings, Liverpool. April 4, 1877.
Crawford and Balcarres, the Right Hon. the Earl of, Haigh Hall, Wigan. February 22, 1871.
Crosfield, John, Esq., Walton Lea, near Warrington. October 28, 1884.
Daglish, Robert Shaw, Esq., Orrell Lodge, Wigan. April 19, 1887.
Deacon, Henry Wade, Esq., Appleton House, Widnes. March 1, 1887.
Dent, William Dent, Esq., Oxford Road, Bootle. January 14, 1879.
*Derby, Right Hon. the Earl of, K.G., Knowsley, Prescot. November 1, 1854.
Earle, Arthur, Esq., Childwall Lodge, Wavertree, Liverpool. February 23, 1882.
Earle, Frederick William, Esq., Edenhurst, Huyton, Liverpool. July 13, 1858.
*Earle, Sir Thomas, Bart., Allerton Tower, Woolton, Liverpool. April 17, 1887.
Eccles, Alexander, Esq., Oakhill, Roby, near Liverpool. March 2, 1886.
Eckersley, Charles, Esq., Fullwell, Tyldesley. July 3, 1882.
Eckersley, James, Esq., Adlington, Chorley, April 19, 1887.
Eckersley, James Carlton, Esq., Standish Hall, Wigan. July 11, 1882.
*Edwards-Moss, John Edward, Esq., 17, Roland Gardens, Queen's Gate, London, S.W. July 11, 1882.
Edwards-Moss, Sir Thomas, Baronet, Otterspool, Liverpool. January 2, 1852.
Evans, George Henry, Esq., Avenue House, Leigh, Lancashire. April 7, 1884.
Evans, Joseph, Esq., Haydock Grange, near St. Helens. January 14, 1868.
Evans, William Lees, Esq., Fazackerley House, Prescot. January 15, 1867.
Fenton, James, Esq., Langley Cottage, Maidencoombe, Torquay. April 5, 1858.
Fernie, William James, Esq., Moss Lane, Aintree. July 14, 1863.
ffarington, Richard Atherton, Esq., Mariebonne, Wigan. February 27, 1882.
Fletcher, Alfred, Esq., Allerton, Liverpool. January 20, 1874.

Fletcher, Ralph, Esq., Atherton, Manchester. January 1, 1879.

Formby, Richard, junior, Esq , Shorrock's Hill, Formby Point, Liverpool. February 21, 1878.

Forwood, Sir William Bower, Knight, Ramleh, Blundell Sands, Liverpool. January 17. 1882.

Gair, Henry Wainwright, Esq., Smithdown Road, Wavertree, Liverpool. February 17, 1886.

Gamble, David, Esq. (Lieut.-Colonel), St. Helens. July 11, 1865.

Gamble, Josiah Christopher Esq., Cowley Hill, St. Helens. February 22, 1882.

*Gaskell, Henry Lomax, Esq., Kidderton Hall, Woodstock, Oxon. October 30, 1849.

Gaskell, Holbrook, Esq., Woolton Wood, Liverpool. January 6, 1851.

Gaskell, Holbrook, junior, Esq., Clayton Lodge, Aigburth, Liverpool. April 19, 1881.

Gaskell, Josiah, Esq., Burgrave Lodge, Ashton-in-Makerfield. October 22, 1883.

*Gibbon, Edward, Esq., Gateacre, Liverpool. October 28, 1856.

Gibson, William, Esq., Greenbank House, Birkdale, Southport. April 6, 1887.

Gillespie, Thomas John, Esq., Park House, Newton-le-Willows, December 5, 1881.

Gilmour, Hamilton Boswell, Esq., Uunderlea, Aigburth, Liverpool July 11, 1865.

Gladstone, Arthur Robertson, Esq., Court Hey, Broad Green, Liverpool. October 31, 1871.

Gooch, William Frederick, Esq., Mount Villa, Wargrave, Newton-le-Willows. January 20, 1885.

Gossage, Frederick Herbert, Esq., Camphill, Woolton, Liverpool. October 29, 1878.

Graves, William Samuel, Esq., Dowsefield, Woolton, Liverpool. November 2, 1886.

Greenall, Edward, Esq., Grappenhall, Warrington. August 25, 1858.

Greenall, Sir Gilbert, Bart., M.P., Walton Hall, Warrington. January 12, 1843.

Greenall, James Fenton, Esq. (Lieut.-Colonel), Grappenhall Lodge, Warrington. April 23, 1867.

Guest, Richard, Esq., Etherstone Hall, Leigh, Manchester. April 6, 1859.

Gunning, Sir George William, Bart., Horton House, Northampton. April 8, 1856.

Gunston, Thomas Bernard, Esq., Halshead House, Prescot. April 20, 1869.

Hamilton, Charles Edward, Esq. (Lieut.-Colonel), Newton-le-Willows. January 5, 1876.

Hartley, Joseph, Esq., Leigh, Lancashire. February 27, 1882.

Hayes, Thomas Travers, Esq., Fairfield, Leigh, Lancashire. April 7, 1884.

Heald, William Norris, Esq., Parr's Wood, Didsbury, Manchester. September 15, 1866.

Hewlett, Alfred, Esq., The Grange, Wigan. August 17, 1874.

Hewlett, William Henry, Esq., Strickland House, Standish, Wigan. April 19, 1887.

*Holt, Robert Durning, Esq., Sefton Park, Liverpool. July 12, 1870.

Holt, William Durning, Esq., Whin Moor, Sandfield Park, Liverpool. April 21, 1863.

*Hornby, Thomas Dyson, Esq., Olive Mount, Wavertree, Liverpool. April 5, 1865.

Hornby, William Windham, Esq. (Rear-Admiral), 6, Roland Houses, South Kensington, London, W. November 2, 1858.

*Horsfall, George Henry, Esq., Liverpool. July 13, 1858.

Houghton, Robert, Esq., Lowton House, Lowton, Newton-le-Willows. January 7, 1874.

Ismay, Thomas Henry, Esq., Beach Lawn, Waterloo, Liverpool. April 23, 1878.

Jary, Robert Herbert Heath, Esq. (Major), Bitteswell Hall, Lutterworth, Leicestershire. September 15, 1866.

Johnson-Ferguson, Jabez Edward, Esq., Kenyon Hall, near Manchester. January 16, 1883.

Johnson, John, Esq., Bank House, Runcorn. October 31, 1854.

Kellett, William, Esq., Portland Bank, Southport. April 19, 1887.

Kershaw, John Atherton, clerk, Ormskirk. May 18, 1848.

Laird, William, Esq., 23, Castle Street, Liverpool. November 2, 1858.

Lamb, William James, Esq., Eskdale, Birkdale. November 1, 1877.

*Langton, Charles, Esq., Barkhill, Aigburth, Liverpool. July 13, 1869.

Lathom, Right Hon. the Earl of, Lathom House, Ormskirk. October 29, 1861.

Lee, Thomas, Esq., Alder House, Atherton. October 13, 1873.

Leigh, Roger, Esq., Barham Court, Maidstone. February 17, 1869.

Lightbound, Thomas, Esq., Rosehill, Lydiate, Ormskirk. April 19, 1870.

Lindsay, Honourable Colin, Haigh Hall, Wigan. January 3, 1884.

Longton, Edward John, Esq., M.D., The Priory, Southport. October 18, 1886.

Macrea, George Gordon, Esq., The Uplands, West Derby, Liverpool. August 19, 1875.

Marsh, John, Esq., Rann Lea, Rainhill. June 29, 1870.

Marshall, Thomas, Esq., The Larches, Wigan. April 19, 1870.

Marson, James, Esq., Hill Cliffe, Appleton, near Warrington. January 16, 1883.

Mayhew, Horace, Esq., Bank House, Wigan. January 10, 1876.

McCorquodale, Alexander Cowan, Esq., The Willows, Newton-le-Willows. December 4, 1882.

*McCorquodale, George, Esq. (Colonel), Newton-le-Willows. February 29, 1859.

McMicking, Gilbert, Esq., 55, Prince's Gate, London, S.W. April 19, 1870.

Mercer, John, Esq., Alston Hall, Preston. May 27, 1869.

Morris, John Grant, Esq., Allerton Priory, Liverpool. July 12, 1859.

Moss, Gilbert Winter, Esq., The Beach, Aigburth, Liverpool. April 19, 1859.

Musgrove, Edgar, Esq., 57, York Road, Birkdale, Southport. January 19, 1864.

Muspratt, Edmund Knowles, Esq., Seaforth Hall, Liverpool. October 20, 1880.

Nicholson, Richard, Esq., Whinfield, Southport. January 9, 1879.

Parker, Samuel Sandbach, Esq., The Cottage, Aigburth, Liverpool. January 20, 1885.

Pennington, Richard, Esq, junior, Muncaster Hall, Rainford, St. Helens. July 1, 1867.

Perkins, Hugh, Esq., Fulwood Park, Liverpool. January 20, 1880.

Pickford, Henry Davis, Esq., Harrock Hill, near Ormskirk. August 23, 1887.

Pilkington, Charles, Esq., The Grove, Huyton, Liverpool. December 4, 1882.

Pilkington, George, Esq., Stoneleigh, Woolton, near Liverpool. October 16, 1878.

Pilkington, George Augustus, Esq., M.D., Belle Vue, Lord Street West, Southport. October 25, 1880.

Pilkington, Richard, Esq., Rainford Hall, St. Helens. April 18, 1876.

Pilkington, Thomas, Esq., Knowsley Cottage, Prescot. October 21, 1868.

Pilkington, William, Esq., Roby Hall, Liverpool. April 19, 1859.

Pilkington, William Windle, Esq. (Major), Cowley Hill, St. Helens. April 20, 1869.

Pownall, John, Esq., Tyn-y-Bryn, Bettws-y-Coed, North Wales. February 18, 1874.

Powys, Honourable Leopold William Henry, Bewsey Old Hall, Warrington. April 21, 1868.

*Prescott, John Esq., Dalton, near Wigan. October 31, 1860.

Raffles, Thomas Stamford, Esq., Liverpool. July 17, 1860.

*Rathbone, William, Esq., M.P., Greenbank, Liverpool. July 14, 1868.

Rigby, Samuel, Esq., Fern Bank, Liverpool Road, Chester. July 13, 1869.

Rylands, John, Esq., Thelwall Grange, near Warrington. August 5, 1861.

*Sandbach, William Robertson, Esq., 10, Prince's Gate, Hyde Park, London, S.W. July 17, 1855.

Smethurst, Arthur Clough, Esq., Charnock House, Chorley. October 20, 1869.

Smith, James Barkeley, Esq., Barkeley House, Seaforth, Liverpool April 23, 1878.

Stanton, Henry, Esq., Warrington. January 12, 1843.

Steble, Richard Fell, Esq. (Lieut.-Colonel), Ransdale Bank, Scarborough. October 13, 1873.

St. George, Howard, clerk, Billinge Parsonage, Wigan. May 27, 1858.

Stubs, Peter, Esq., Statham Lodge, Warrington. April 23, 1867.

Swire, Samuel, Esq., Crown House, Southport. September 3, 1877.

*Sullivan, Sir Edward, Bart., Ravenhead, St. Helens. November 1, 1864.

Symonds, Charles Price, Esq., Ormskirk. October 30, 1866.

Taylor, James, Esq., Rendcomb Park, Cirencester. December 19, 1864.

Taylor, Richard, Esq., Woodfield, Wigan. January 10, 1876.

Taylor, Thomas, Esq., Aston Rowant, Tetsworth, January 10, 1848.

Thompson, Henry Yates, Esq , 26a, Bryanston Square, London, W. October 30, 1866.

*Thompson, Samuel Henry, Esq., Thingwall Hall, Liverpool. June 13, 1848.

Thompson, His Honour Judge Thomas Perronet Edward, Dudlow Grange, Wavertree, Liverpool. July 14, 1874.

Timmis, Thomas Sutton, Esq., Cleveley, Allerton, Liverpool. January 20, 1885.

Tinsley, James, Esq , Stockton Lodge, near Warrington. April 22, 1884.

Tobin, James Aspinall, Esq., Liverpool. July 13, 1858.

Tomlinson, Ralph, Esq., Cintra, Lathom, Ormskirk. April 6, 1881.

Trimble, Robert, Esq. (Lieut.-Colonel), Cuckoo Lane, Little Woolton, Liverpool. July 13, 1869.

Twyford, Edward Penrose, Esq., M.D., St. Helens, Lancashire. April 19, 1870.

Walker, Robert Seddon, Esq., 16, Parkfield Road, Prince's Park, Liverpool. February 19, 1868.

Walmesley, Humphrey Jeffrey, Esq., Westwood House, Wigan. July 27, 1878.

Wannop, William, clerk, Burscough, Ormskirk. April, 5, 1858.

Welsby, Richard Coupland, Esq., Swanpool House, Aughton, Ormskirk. January 4, 1886.

Welsby, William, E-q. (Colonel), The Grange, Southport. January 9, 1879.

Wetherall, George Nugent Ross, Esq., Astley Hall, Manchester. December 6, 1886.

Whitley, William, Esq., 5, New Square, Lincoln's Inn, London. September 15, 1866.

Willis, Henry Rodolph DeAnyers, Esq., Halsnead, Prescot. October 31, 1871.

Withington, Thomas Ellames, Esq. (Captain), Culcheth Hall, Warrington. July 30, 1857.

Wood, John Coates, Esq., Beaconsfield, Derby Street, Ormskirk. January 19, 1886.

Wood, Robert Philip, Esq., Bank House, Maghull, Liverpool. June 29, 1870.

Woodcock, Henry, Esq., Bolnore, Haywards Heath, Sussex. April 5, 1865.

Woodcock, Herbert Spencer, Esq., The Elms, Wigan. August 17, 1874.

Wright, Caleb, Esq., M.P., Lower Oak, Tyldesley, Manchester. April 20, 1869.

Wright, William, Esq., Sunnyside, Balcombe, near Hayward's Heath, Sussex. July 5, 1857.

Wrigley, John, Esq., Brockholme, Formby. April 7, 1884.

Young, Edward, Esq., Lyons, East Cliff, Bournemouth. February, 19, 1868.

PUBLIC OFFICERS FOR THE COUNTY PALATINE.

High Sheriff (1887-8)—Sir John Hardy Thursby, Bart., Ormerod House, Burnley.

Lord Lieutenant—The Right Hon. the Earl of Sefton, Croxteth, Liverpool.

Constable of Lancaster Castle—The Right Hon. Lord Winmarleigh, Winmarleigh, Garstang.

Chancellor of the Duchy—The Right Hon. Lord John Manners, Waterloo Bridge, London, W.C.

Clerk of the Council and Registrar of the Duchy—J. G. D. Engleheart, Esq., Waterloo Bridge, London, W.C.

Under Sheriff—T. F. Artindale, gentleman, Burnley.

Acting Under Sheriffs and Clerks to the Lieutenancy—Messrs. Wilson, Deacon, Wright and Wilsons, Preston.

Registrar of the Chancery—Alexander Pearce, gentleman.

Seal Keeper and Clerk of Assize and Associate—Thomas Moss Shuttleworth, gentleman, Preston.

Clerk of the Peace—Frederic Campbell Hulton, gentleman, Preston.

Deputy Clerks of the Peace—Thomas Wilson, gentleman, Highwood, Walton-le-Dale, and Samuel Campbell Hulton Sadler gentleman, Southport.

County Treasurer—Henry Alison, Esq., Preston.

Chief Constable—Lieut.-Col. Moorsom, Preston.

Assistant Chief Constable—Capt. Charles Villiers Ibbetson, Preston.

County Auditor—Mr. H. W. Johnston, Preston.

County Lunatic Asylum (*Lancaster*)—D. M. Cassidy, Esq., M.D., D.Sc., Superintendent.

Law Clerk to Visitors—William Thomas Sharp, gentleman, Lancaster.

Clerk and Steward—Mr. Peter Dutton, Lancaster.

County Lunatic Asylum (*Prestwich*)—Henry Rooke Ley, Esq., Superintendent.

Law Clerk to Visitors—Henry Thomas Crofton, gentleman, Manchester.

Treasurer and Clerk—Mr. Robert Coates, Prestwich.

County Lunatic Asylum (*Rainhill*)—T. L. Rogers, Esq., M.D., Rainhill, Superintendent.

Law Clerk to Visitors—W. Swift, gentleman, Liverpool.

Clerk and Steward—Mr. R. C. Lewis, Rainhill.

County Lunatic Asylum (*Whittingham*)—John A. Wallis, Esq., M.D., Whittingham, Preston, Superintendent.

Law Clerk to Visitors—F. C. Hulton, gentleman, Preston.

Clerk and Steward—Mr. T. Dilworth, Whittingham.

Chief Warder of Her Majesty's Prison (*Lancaster*)—Mr. W. R. Shenton.

Keepers of Her Majesty's Prisons—*Preston*, Mr. John Haverfield. *Manchester (Strangeways)*, Major Preston. *Kirkdale*, Major Knox.

Coroners—Mr. H. J. Robinson, Blackburn ; Mr. F. Price, 8, St. James's Square, Manchester ; Mr. F. N. Molesworth, Rochdale ; Mr. J. Broughton Edge, St. James's Square, Manchester ; Mr. Samuel Brighouse, Ormskirk ; Dr. Gilbertson, Preston ; Mr. Lawrence Holden, Lancaster.

Mr. John Poole, Coroner for the Liberty and Manor of Furness, Ulverston ; Mr. William Ashcroft, Coroner for the Manor of Walton-le-Dale ; Mr. F. Smith, Coroner for the Manor of Prescot ; Mr. J. R. Buckton, Coroner for the Manor of Hale.

County Analysts—James Campbell Brown, Esq., D.Sc , 27, Abercromby Square, Liverpool ; Walter C. Williams, Esq., B.Sc. School of Medicine, Dover Street, Liverpool (Assistant Analyst).

BRIDGEMASTERS AND SURVEYORS.

Lonsdale Hundred (North)—Mr. Philip Hartley, Ulverston.

Lonsdale Hundred (South)—Mr. Edward Graham Paley, Lancaster.

Amounderness Hundred—Mr. William Radford, No. 1, Princess Street, Manchester.

Blackburn Hundred—Mr. William Radford, Manchester.

Leyland Hundred—Mr. William Radford, Manchester.

Salford Hundred—Mr. William Radford, Manchester.

West Derby Hundred—Mr. George Holme, Westminster Chambers, 1, Crosshall Street, Liverpool.

Ditto County Bridges—Mr. William Radford, Manchester.

SCHOOL BOARDS.

Boards.	Unions of	Population (1881).	No. of Members.	Boards.	Unions of	Population (1881).	No. of Members.
Ashton-under-Lyne	Municipal borough	37,040	9	*Hambleton	Garstang	389	5
Bacup	,,	25,034	9	Heaton	Bolton	1,461	5
Barrow-in-Furness	,,	47,100	11	*Kirkby Ireleth (U. D.)	Ulverston	1,754	5
Blackburn	,,	104,014	13	*Newchurch-in-Rossendale	Haslingden	3,228	9
Bolton	,,	105,414	13	*Pleasington	Blackburn	459	5
Bootle-cum-Linacre	,,	27,374	9	*Poulton	Lancaster	3,931	5
Burnley	,,	58,882	9	Prescot	Prescot	5,546	7
Liverpool	,,	552,425	15	Royton	Oldham	10,582	9
Manchester	,,	373,585	15	*Shevington	Wigan	1,570	5
Oldham	,,	111,343	13	*Skelmersdale	Ormskirk	5,707	7
Rochdale	,,	68,865	11	Southworth-with-Croft	Warrington	1,045	5
Salford	,,	176,235	15	*Thornton-with-Fleetwood	The Fylde	7,589	7
Wigan	,,	48,194	11	†Tottington Higher End	Haslingden	3,926	5
*Barrowford (U. D.)	Burnley	3,952	7	*Ulnes Walton	Chorley	386	5
*Birkdale	Ormskirk	8,705	7	*Ulverston and Mansriggs (U. D.)	Ulverston	10,072	7
*Burtonwood	Warrington	1,268	5	*Walmersley-cum-Shuttle-			
*Crumpsall	Prestwich	8,154	7	worth (ex municipal)	Bury	5,390	7
*Dalton-in-Furness	Ulverston	13,309	7	Walton-on-the-Hill	West Derby	18,715	11
*Edgeworth (U. D.)	Bolton	2,474	5	*Westhoughton and Lostock			
*Egton-with-Newland	Ulverston	998	5	(U. D.)	Bolton	9,997	7
*Forton (U. D.)	Garstang	696	7	*Widnes	Prescot	24,935	11
*Great Sankey	Warrington	360	5				

* Boards formed compulsorily under sec. 10 or 40 of the Education Act.   *† Board formed under sec. 12 of the Education Act.*

` THE COUNTY COURTS.

On the 1st January, 1868, the statute passed on the 20th of August, 1867, to amend the Acts relating to the jurisdiction of the County Courts came into force, materially diminishing the business in the Common Law Courts. A plaint may now be entered in the County Court within the district of which the defendant or one of the defendants shall dwell or carry on his business at the time of bringing the action or suit, or it may be entered by leave of the Judge or Registrar in the County Court within the district in which the defendant or one of the defendants dwelt or carried on business at any time within six months next before the time of action or suit brought, or with the like leave in the County Court in the district of which the cause of action or suit wholly or in part arose. In actions for goods, &c., the plaintiff may issue a summons, and if the defendant shall not file notice of his intention to defend, judgment may be entered up. Proceedings commenced in a metropolitan County Court, the same are to be continued therein if the defendant resides in the district of one of such courts. No action is to be maintainable in any court for beer, &c., consumed on the premises. Costs are not to be recoverable in the superior courts where less than £20 in contract or £10 in tort is recovered, and the Act authorising the trial of issues before the Sheriff, where the sum sought to be recovered does not exceed £20, is repealed. In actions commenced in the superior courts, where the sum does not exceed £50, the Judge may remit the same to a County Court, and proceedings in equity in the Court of Chancery, which might have been commenced in the County Courts, may be remitted to them, and matters to £500 for specific performance, &c., to be dealt with in a similar manner. Actions for malicious prosecution, assault, false imprisonment, seduction, &c., in the superior courts, to be remitted to the County Courts; and in eject-ments, or where the property does not exceed £20 a-year, are to be heard in the County Courts. There are provisions as to costs, &c., and Registrars may act as high bailiffs. In equity proceedings, where the trust money or stock does not exceed £500, to be transferred to the County Courts, and invested in Post-Office Savings Banks. No action or suit is to be commenced in any hundred or inferior court, and persons holding office affected to be entitled to compensation. A high bailiff may now interplead.

END OF THE FIRST VOLUME.

JOHN HEYWOOD, Excelsior Steam Printing and Bookbinding Works, Hulme Hall Road, Manchester.